Hornbook Series and Basic Legal Texts
Nutshell Series

and

Black Letter Series

of

WEST PUBLISHING COMPANY
P.O. Box 64526
St. Paul, Minnesota 55164–0526

Accounting

Faris' Accounting and Law in a Nutshell, 377 pages, 1984. Softcover. (Text)

Administrative Law

Gellhorn and Levin's Administrative Law and Process in a Nutshell, Third Edition, 479 pages, 1990. Softcover. (Text)

Admiralty

Maraist's Admiralty in a Nutshell, Second Edition, 379 pages, 1988. Softcover. (Text)

Schoenbaum's Hornbook on Admiralty and Maritime Law, Student Edition, 692 pages, 1987 with 1989 pocket part. (Text)

Agency—Partnership

Reuschlein and Gregory's Hornbook on the Law of Agency and Partnership, Second Edition, 683 pages, 1990. (Text)

Steffen's Agency-Partnership in a Nutshell, 364 pages, 1977. Softcover. (Text)

American Indian Law

Canby's American Indian Law in a Nutshell, Second Edition, 336 pages, 1988. Softcover. (Text)

Antitrust—see also Regulated Industries, Trade Regulation

Gellhorn's Antitrust Law and Economics in a Nutshell, Third Edition, 472 pages, 1986. Softcover. (Text)

Hovenkamp's Black Letter on Antitrust, 323 pages, 1986. Softcover. (Review)

Hovenkamp's Hornbook on Economics and Federal Antitrust Law, Student Edition, 414 pages, 1985. (Text)

Sullivan's Hornbook of the Law of Antitrust, 886 pages, 1977. (Text)

Appellate Advocacy—see Trial and Appellate Advocacy

Art Law

Duboff's Art Law in a Nutshell, 335 pages, 1984. Softcover. (Text)

Banking Law

Banking Law: Selected Statutes and Regulations. Softcover. 263 pages, 1991.

Lovett's Banking and Financial Institutions Law in a Nutshell, Second Edition, 464 pages, 1988. Softcover. (Text)

Civil Procedure—see also Federal Jurisdiction and Procedure

Clermont's Black Letter on Civil Procedure, Second Edition, 332 pages,

---

List current as of June, 1991

Civil Procedure—Cont'd

1988. Softcover. (Review)

Friedenthal, Kane and Miller's Hornbook on Civil Procedure, 876 pages, 1985. (Text)

Kane's Civil Procedure in a Nutshell, Third Edition, 303 pages, 1991. Softcover. (Text)

Koffler and Reppy's Hornbook on Common Law Pleading, 663 pages, 1969. (Text)

Siegel's Hornbook on New York Practice, Second Edition, Student Edition, 1068 pages, 1991. Softcover. (Text)

Commercial Law

Bailey and Hagedorn's Secured Transactions in a Nutshell, Third Edition, 390 pages, 1988. Softcover. (Text)

Henson's Hornbook on Secured Transactions Under the U.C.C., Second Edition, 504 pages, 1979, with 1979 pocket part. (Text)

Nickles' Black Letter on Commercial Paper, 450 pages, 1988. Softcover. (Review)

Speidel's Black Letter on Sales and Sales Financing, 363 pages, 1984. Softcover. (Review)

Stockton's Sales in a Nutshell, Second Edition, 370 pages, 1981. Softcover. (Text)

Stone's Uniform Commercial Code in a Nutshell, Third Edition, 580 pages, 1989. Softcover. (Text)

Weber and Speidel's Commercial Paper in a Nutshell, Third Edition, 404 pages, 1982. Softcover. (Text)

White and Summers' Hornbook on the Uniform Commercial Code, Third Edition, Student Edition, 1386 pages, 1988. (Text)

Community Property

Mennell and Boykoff's Community Property in a Nutshell, Second Edition, 432 pages, 1988. Softcover. (Text)

Comparative Law

Glendon, Gordon and Osakwe's Comparative Legal Traditions in a Nutshell. 402 pages, 1982. Softcover. (Text)

Conflict of Laws

Hay's Black Letter on Conflict of Laws, 330 pages, 1989. Softcover. (Review)

Scoles and Hay's Hornbook on Conflict of Laws, Student Edition, approximately 1100 pages, November 1991 Pub. (Text)

Siegel's Conflicts in a Nutshell, 470 pages, 1982. Softcover. (Text)

Constitutional Law—Civil Rights

Barron and Dienes' Black Letter on Constitutional Law, Third Edition, 440 pages, 1991. Softcover. (Review)

Barron and Dienes' Constitutional Law in a Nutshell, Second Edition, 483 pages, 1991. Softcover. (Text)

Engdahl's Constitutional Federalism in a Nutshell, Second Edition, 411 pages, 1987. Softcover. (Text)

Marks and Cooper's State Constitutional Law in a Nutshell, 329 pages, 1988. Softcover. (Text)

Nowak and Rotunda's Hornbook on Constitutional Law, Fourth Edition, approximately 1275 pages, August, 1991 Pub. (Text)

Vieira's Constitutional Civil Rights in a Nutshell, Second Edition, 322 pages, 1990. Softcover. (Text)

Williams' Constitutional Analysis in a Nutshell, 388 pages, 1979. Softcover. (Text)

Consumer Law—see also Commercial Law

Epstein and Nickles' Consumer Law in a Nutshell, Second Edition, 418 pages, 1981. Softcover. (Text)

Contracts

CALAMARI AND PERILLO'S BLACK LETTER ON CONTRACTS, Second Edition, 462 pages, 1990. Softcover. (Review)

CALAMARI AND PERILLO'S HORNBOOK ON CONTRACTS, Third Edition, 1049 pages, 1987. (Text)

CORBIN'S TEXT ON CONTRACTS, One Volume Student Edition, 1224 pages, 1952. (Text)

FRIEDMAN'S CONTRACT REMEDIES IN A NUTSHELL, 323 pages, 1981. Softcover. (Text)

KEYES' GOVERNMENT CONTRACTS IN A NUTSHELL, Second Edition, 557 pages, 1990. Softcover. (Text)

SCHABER AND ROHWER'S CONTRACTS IN A NUTSHELL, Third Edition, 457 pages, 1990. Softcover. (Text)

Copyright—see Patent and Copyright Law

Corporations

HAMILTON'S BLACK LETTER ON CORPORATIONS, Second Edition, 513 pages, 1986. Softcover. (Review)

HAMILTON'S THE LAW OF CORPORATIONS IN A NUTSHELL, Third Edition, 518 pages, 1991. Softcover. (Text)

HENN AND ALEXANDER'S HORNBOOK ON LAWS OF CORPORATIONS, Third Edition, Student Edition, 1371 pages, 1983, with 1986 pocket part. (Text)

Corrections

KRANTZ' THE LAW OF CORRECTIONS AND PRISONERS' RIGHTS IN A NUTSHELL, Third Edition, 407 pages, 1988. Softcover. (Text)

Creditors' Rights

EPSTEIN'S DEBTOR-CREDITOR LAW IN A NUTSHELL, Fourth Edition, 401 pages, 1991. Softcover. (Text)

NICKLES AND EPSTEIN'S BLACK LETTER ON CREDITORS' RIGHTS AND BANKRUPTCY, 576 pages, 1989. (Review)

Criminal Law and Criminal Procedure—see also Corrections, Juvenile Justice

ISRAEL AND LaFAVE'S CRIMINAL PROCEDURE—CONSTITUTIONAL LIMITATIONS IN A NUTSHELL, Fourth Edition, 461 pages, 1988. Softcover. (Text)

LaFAVE AND ISRAEL'S HORNBOOK ON CRIMINAL PROCEDURE, Second Edition, Student Edition, approximately 1200 pages, December, 1991 Pub. (Text)

LaFAVE AND SCOTT'S HORNBOOK ON CRIMINAL LAW, Second Edition, 918 pages, 1986. (Text)

LOEWY'S CRIMINAL LAW IN A NUTSHELL, Second Edition, 321 pages, 1987. Softcover. (Text)

LOW'S BLACK LETTER ON CRIMINAL LAW, Revised First Edition, 443 pages, 1990. Softcover. (Review)

Domestic Relations

CLARK'S HORNBOOK ON DOMESTIC RELATIONS, Second Edition, Student Edition, 1050 pages, 1988. (Text)

KRAUSE'S BLACK LETTER ON FAMILY LAW, 314 pages, 1988. Softcover. (Review)

KRAUSE'S FAMILY LAW IN A NUTSHELL, Second Edition, 444 pages, 1986. Softcover. (Text)

MALLOY'S LAW AND ECONOMICS: A COMPARATIVE APPROACH TO THEORY AND PRACTICE, 166 pages, 1990. Softcover. (Text)

Education Law

ALEXANDER AND ALEXANDER'S THE LAW OF SCHOOLS, STUDENTS AND TEACHERS IN A NUTSHELL, 409 pages, 1984. Softcover. (Text)

Employment Discrimination—see also Gender Discrimination

PLAYER'S FEDERAL LAW OF EMPLOYMENT DISCRIMINATION IN A NUTSHELL, Second Edition, 402 pages, 1981. Softcover. (Text)

PLAYER'S HORNBOOK ON EMPLOYMENT DISCRIMINATION LAW, Student Edition,

Employment Discrimination—Cont'd
708 pages, 1988. (Text)

Energy and Natural Resources Law—see also Oil and Gas

Environmental Law—see also Energy and Natural Resources Law; Sea, Law of

FINDLEY AND FARBER'S ENVIRONMENTAL LAW IN A NUTSHELL, Second Edition, 367 pages, 1988. Softcover. (Text)

RODGERS' HORNBOOK ON ENVIRONMENTAL LAW, 956 pages, 1977, with 1984 pocket part. (Text)

Equity—see Remedies

Estate Planning—see also Trusts and Estates; Taxation—Estate and Gift

LYNN'S AN INTRODUCTION TO ESTATE PLANNING IN A NUTSHELL, Third Edition, 370 pages, 1983. Softcover. (Text)

Evidence

BROUN AND BLAKEY'S BLACK LETTER ON EVIDENCE, 269 pages, 1984. Softcover. (Review)

GRAHAM'S FEDERAL RULES OF EVIDENCE IN A NUTSHELL, Second Edition, 473 pages, 1987. Softcover. (Text)

LILLY'S AN INTRODUCTION TO THE LAW OF EVIDENCE, Second Edition, 585 pages, 1987. (Text)

MCCORMICK'S HORNBOOK ON EVIDENCE, Fourth Edition, Student Edition, approximately 1200 pages, January 1992 Pub. (Text)

ROTHSTEIN'S EVIDENCE IN A NUTSHELL: STATE AND FEDERAL RULES, Second Edition, 514 pages, 1981. Softcover. (Text)

Federal Jurisdiction and Procedure

CURRIE'S FEDERAL JURISDICTION IN A NUTSHELL, Third Edition, 242 pages, 1990. Softcover. (Text)

REDISH'S BLACK LETTER ON FEDERAL JURISDICTION, Second Edition, 234 pages, 1991. Softcover. (Review)

WRIGHT'S HORNBOOK ON FEDERAL COURTS, Fourth Edition, Student Edition, 870 pages, 1983. (Text)

First Amendment

Future Interests—see Trusts and Estates

Gender Discrimination—see also Employment Discrimination

THOMAS' SEX DISCRIMINATION IN A NUTSHELL, Second Edition, approximately 400 pages, 1991. Softcover. (Text)

Health Law—see Medicine, Law and

Human Rights—see International Law

Immigration Law

WEISSBRODT'S IMMIGRATION LAW AND PROCEDURE IN A NUTSHELL, Second Edition, 438 pages, 1989, Softcover. (Text)

Indian Law—see American Indian Law

Insurance Law

DOBBYN'S INSURANCE LAW IN A NUTSHELL, Second Edition, 316 pages, 1989. Softcover. (Text)

KEETON AND WIDISS' INSURANCE LAW, Student Edition, 1359 pages, 1988. (Text)

International Law—see also Sea, Law of

BUERGENTHAL'S INTERNATIONAL HUMAN RIGHTS IN A NUTSHELL, 283 pages, 1988. Softcover. (Text)

BUERGENTHAL AND MAIER'S PUBLIC INTERNATIONAL LAW IN A NUTSHELL, Second Edition, 275 pages, 1990. Softcover. (Text)

FOLSOM, GORDON AND SPANOGLE'S INTERNATIONAL BUSINESS TRANSACTIONS IN A NUTSHELL, Third Edition, 509 pages, 1988. Softcover. (Text)

Interviewing and Counseling

SHAFFER AND ELKINS' LEGAL INTERVIEWING AND COUNSELING IN A NUTSHELL, Second Edition, 487 pages, 1987. Soft-

Interviewing and Counseling—Cont'd
cover. (Text)

Introduction to Law—see Legal Method and Legal System

Introduction to Law Study
HEGLAND'S INTRODUCTION TO THE STUDY AND PRACTICE OF LAW IN A NUTSHELL, 418 pages, 1983. Softcover. (Text)

KINYON'S INTRODUCTION TO LAW STUDY AND LAW EXAMINATIONS IN A NUTSHELL, 389 pages, 1971. Softcover. (Text)

Judicial Process—see Legal Method and Legal System

Juvenile Justice
FOX'S JUVENILE COURTS IN A NUTSHELL, Third Edition, 291 pages, 1984. Softcover. (Text)

Labor and Employment Law—see also Employment Discrimination, Workers' Compensation
LESLIE'S LABOR LAW IN A NUTSHELL, Second Edition, 397 pages, 1986. Softcover. (Text)

NOLAN'S LABOR ARBITRATION LAW AND PRACTICE IN A NUTSHELL, 358 pages, 1979. Softcover. (Text)

Land Finance—Property Security—see Real Estate Transactions

Land Use
HAGMAN AND JUERGENSMEYER'S HORNBOOK ON URBAN PLANNING AND LAND DEVELOPMENT CONTROL LAW, Second Edition, Student Edition, 680 pages, 1986. (Text)

WRIGHT AND WRIGHT'S LAND USE IN A NUTSHELL, Second Edition, 356 pages, 1985. Softcover. (Text)

Legal Method and Legal System—see also Legal Research, Legal Writing
KEMPIN'S HISTORICAL INTRODUCTION TO ANGLO-AMERICAN LAW IN A NUTSHELL, Third Edition, 323 pages, 1990. Softcover. (Text)

REYNOLDS' JUDICIAL PROCESS IN A NUTSHELL, Second Edition, approximately 310 pages, 1991. Softcover. (Text)

Legal Research
COHEN'S LEGAL RESEARCH IN A NUTSHELL, Fourth Edition, 452 pages, 1985. Softcover. (Text)

COHEN, BERRING AND OLSON'S HOW TO FIND THE LAW, Ninth Edition, 716 pages, 1989. (Text)

Legal Writing and Drafting
SQUIRES AND ROMBAUER'S LEGAL WRITING IN A NUTSHELL, 294 pages, 1982. Softcover. (Text)

Legislation—see also Legal Writing and Drafting
DAVIES' LEGISLATIVE LAW AND PROCESS IN A NUTSHELL, Second Edition, 346 pages, 1986. Softcover. (Text)

Local Government
MCCARTHY'S LOCAL GOVERNMENT LAW IN A NUTSHELL, Third Edition, 435 pages, 1990. Softcover. (Text)

REYNOLDS' HORNBOOK ON LOCAL GOVERNMENT LAW, 860 pages, 1982, with 1990 pocket part. (Text)

Mass Communication Law
ZUCKMAN, GAYNES, CARTER AND DEE'S MASS COMMUNICATIONS LAW IN A NUTSHELL, Third Edition, 538 pages, 1988. Softcover. (Text)

Medicine, Law and
HALL AND ELLMAN'S HEALTH CARE LAW AND ETHICS IN A NUTSHELL, 401 pages, 1990. Softcover (Text)

JARVIS, CLOSEN, HERMANN AND LEONARD'S AIDS LAW IN A NUTSHELL, 349 pages, 1991. Softcover. (Text)

KING'S THE LAW OF MEDICAL MALPRACTICE IN A NUTSHELL, Second Edition, 342 pages, 1986. Softcover. (Text)

Military Law
SHANOR AND TERRELL'S MILITARY LAW IN A NUTSHELL, 378 pages, 1980. Softcover. (Text)

Mortgages—see Real Estate Transactions

Natural Resources Law—see Energy and Natural Resources Law, Environmental Law

Office Practice—see also Computers and Law, Interviewing and Counseling, Negotiation

HEGLAND'S TRIAL AND PRACTICE SKILLS IN A NUTSHELL, 346 pages, 1978. Softcover (Text)

Oil and Gas—see also Energy and Natural Resources Law

HEMINGWAY'S HORNBOOK ON THE LAW OF OIL AND GAS, Third Edition, Student Edition, approximately 700 pages, Aug., 1991 Pub. (Text)

LOWE'S OIL AND GAS LAW IN A NUTSHELL, Second Edition, 465 pages, 1988. Softcover. (Text)

Partnership—see Agency—Partnership

Patent and Copyright Law

MILLER AND DAVIS' INTELLECTUAL PROPERTY—PATENTS, TRADEMARKS AND COPYRIGHT IN A NUTSHELL, Second Edition, 437 pages, 1990. Softcover. (Text)

Products Liability

PHILLIPS' PRODUCTS LIABILITY IN A NUTSHELL, Third Edition, 307 pages, 1988. Softcover. (Text)

Professional Responsibility

ARONSON AND WECKSTEIN'S PROFESSIONAL RESPONSIBILITY IN A NUTSHELL, Second Edition, approximately 500 pages, 1991. Softcover. (Text)

ROTUNDA'S BLACK LETTER ON PROFESSIONAL RESPONSIBILITY, Second Edition, 414 pages, 1988. Softcover. (Review)

WOLFRAM'S HORNBOOK ON MODERN LEGAL ETHICS, Student Edition, 1120 pages, 1986. (Text)

Property—see also Real Estate Transactions, Land Use, Trusts and Estates

BERNHARDT'S BLACK LETTER ON PROPERTY, Second Edition, approximately 375 pages, 1991. Softcover. (Review)

BERNHARDT'S REAL PROPERTY IN A NUTSHELL, Second Edition, 448 pages, 1981. Softcover. (Text)

BURKE'S PERSONAL PROPERTY IN A NUTSHELL, 322 pages, 1983. Softcover. (Text)

CUNNINGHAM, STOEBUCK AND WHITMAN'S HORNBOOK ON THE LAW OF PROPERTY, Student Edition, 916 pages, 1984, with 1987 pocket part. (Text)

HILL'S LANDLORD AND TENANT LAW IN A NUTSHELL, Second Edition, 311 pages, 1986. Softcover. (Text)

Real Estate Transactions

BRUCE'S REAL ESTATE FINANCE IN A NUTSHELL, Third Edition, approximately 270 pages, 1991. Softcover. (Text)

NELSON AND WHITMAN'S BLACK LETTER ON LAND TRANSACTIONS AND FINANCE, Second Edition, 466 pages, 1988. Softcover. (Review)

NELSON AND WHITMAN'S HORNBOOK ON REAL ESTATE FINANCE LAW, Second Edition, 941 pages, 1985 with 1989 pocket part. (Text)

Regulated Industries—see also Mass Communication Law, Banking Law

GELLHORN AND PIERCE'S REGULATED INDUSTRIES IN A NUTSHELL, Second Edition, 389 pages, 1987. Softcover. (Text)

Remedies

DOBBS' HORNBOOK ON REMEDIES, 1067 pages, 1973. (Text)

DOBBYN'S INJUNCTIONS IN A NUTSHELL, 264 pages, 1974. Softcover. (Text)

FRIEDMAN'S CONTRACT REMEDIES IN A NUTSHELL, 323 pages, 1981. Softcover. (Text)

Remedies—Cont'd

O'Connell's Remedies in a Nutshell, Second Edition, 320 pages, 1985. Softcover. (Text)

Sea, Law of

Sohn and Gustafson's The Law of the Sea in a Nutshell, 264 pages, 1984. Softcover. (Text)

Securities Regulation

Hazen's Hornbook on the Law of Securities Regulation, Second Edition, Student Edition, 1082 pages, 1990. (Text)

Ratner's Securities Regulation in a Nutshell, Third Edition, 316 pages, 1988. Softcover. (Text)

Securities Regulation, Selected Statutes, Rules, and Forms. Softcover. 1331 pages, 1991.

Sports Law

Schubert, Smith and Trentadue's Sports Law, 395 pages, 1986. (Text)

Tax Practice and Procedure

Morgan's Tax Procedure and Tax Fraud in a Nutshell, 400 pages, 1990. Softcover. (Text)

Taxation—Corporate

Schwarz and Lathrope's Black Letter on Corporate and Partnership Taxation, Approximately 500 pages, September, 1991 Pub. Softcover. (Review)

Weidenbruch and Burke's Federal Income Taxation of Corporations and Stockholders in a Nutshell, Third Edition, 309 pages, 1989. Softcover. (Text)

Taxation—Estate & Gift—see also Estate Planning, Trusts and Estates

McNulty's Federal Estate and Gift Taxation in a Nutshell, Fourth Edition, 496 pages, 1989. Softcover. (Text)

Taxation—Individual

Hudson and Lind's Black Letter on Federal Income Taxation, Third Edition, 406 pages, 1990. Softcover. (Review)

McNulty's Federal Income Taxation of Individuals in a Nutshell, Fourth Edition, 503 pages, 1988. Softcover. (Text)

Posin's Hornbook on Federal Income Taxation, Student Edition, 491 pages, 1983, with 1989 pocket part. (Text)

Rose and Chommie's Hornbook on Federal Income Taxation, Third Edition, 923 pages, 1988, with 1989 pocket part. (Text)

Taxation—International

Doernberg's International Taxation in a Nutshell, 325 pages, 1989. Softcover. (Text)

Bishop and Brooks' Federal Partnership Taxation: A Guide to the Leading Cases, Statutes, and Regulations, 545 pages, 1990. Softcover. (Text)

Schwarz and Lathrope's Black Letter on Corporate and Partnership Taxation, Approximately 500 pages, September, 1991 Pub. Softcover. (Review)

Taxation—State & Local

Gelfand and Salsich's State and Local Taxation and Finance in a Nutshell, 309 pages, 1986. Softcover. (Text)

Torts—see also Products Liability

Kionka's Black Letter on Torts, 339 pages, 1988. Softcover. (Review)

Kionka's Torts in a Nutshell: Injuries to Persons and Property, 434 pages, 1977. Softcover. (Text)

Malone's Torts in a Nutshell: Injuries to Family, Social and Trade Relations, 358 pages, 1979. Softcover. (Text)

Prosser and Keeton's Hornbook on Torts, Fifth Edition, Student Edition, 1286 pages, 1984 with 1988 pocket part. (Text)

Trade Regulation—see also Antitrust, Regulated Industries

McManis' Unfair Trade Practices in a Nutshell, Second Edition, 464 pages, 1988. Softcover. (Text)

Schechter's Black Letter on Unfair Trade Practices, 272 pages, 1986. Softcover. (Review)

Trial and Appellate Advocacy—see also Civil Procedure

Bergman's Trial Advocacy in a Nutshell, Second Edition, 354 pages, 1989. Softcover. (Text)

Goldberg's The First Trial (Where Do I Sit? What Do I Say?) in a Nutshell, 396 pages, 1982. Softcover. (Text)

Hegland's Trial and Practice Skills in a Nutshell, 346 pages, 1978. Softcover. (Text)

Hornstein's Appellate Advocacy in a Nutshell, 325 pages, 1984. Softcover. (Text)

Jeans' Handbook on Trial Advocacy, Student Edition, 473 pages, 1975. Softcover. (Text)

Trusts and Estates

Atkinson's Hornbook on Wills, Second Edition, 975 pages, 1953. (Text)

Averill's Uniform Probate Code in a Nutshell, Second Edition, 454 pages, 1987. Softcover. (Text)

Bogert's Hornbook on Trusts, Sixth Edition, Student Edition, 794 pages, 1987. (Text)

McGovern, Kurtz and Rein's Hornbook on Wills, Trusts and Estates–Including Taxation and Future Interests, 996 pages, 1988. (Text)

Mennell's Wills and Trusts in a Nutshell, 392 pages, 1979. Softcover. (Text)

Simes' Hornbook on Future Interests, Second Edition, 355 pages, 1966. (Text)

Turano and Radigan's Hornbook on New York Estate Administration, 676 pages, 1986. (Text)

Waggoner's Future Interests in a Nutshell, 361 pages, 1981. Softcover. (Text)

Water Law—see also Environmental Law

Getches' Water Law in a Nutshell, Second Edition, 459 pages, 1990. Softcover. (Text)

Wills—see Trusts and Estates

Workers' Compensation

Hood, Hardy and Lewis' Workers' Compensation and Employee Protection Laws in a Nutshell, Second Edition, 361 pages, 1990. Softcover. (Text)

WEST'S LAW SCHOOL ADVISORY BOARD

CURTIS J. BERGER
Professor of Law, Columbia University

JESSE H. CHOPER
Dean and Professor of Law,
University of California, Berkeley

DAVID P. CURRIE
Professor of Law, University of Chicago

YALE KAMISAR
Professor of Law, University of Michigan

MARY KAY KANE
Professor of Law, University of California,
Hastings College of the Law

WAYNE R. LaFAVE
Professor of Law, University of Illinois

RICHARD C. MAXWELL
Professor of Law, Duke University

ARTHUR R. MILLER
Professor of Law, Harvard University

GRANT S. NELSON
Professor of Law, University of California, Los Angeles

ROBERT A. STEIN
Dean and Professor of Law, University of Minnesota

JAMES J. WHITE
Professor of Law, University of Michigan

CHARLES ALAN WRIGHT
Professor of Law, University of Texas

*

HANDBOOK
ON
ENVIRONMENTAL LAW

WILLIAM H. RODGERS, JR.

Professor of Law

Georgetown University Law Center

HORNBOOK SERIES

ST. PAUL, MINN.
WEST PUBLISHING CO.
1977

COPYRIGHT © 1977
By
WEST PUBLISHING CO.
All rights reserved

Library of Congress Catalog Card Number: 77–70558

ISBN No. 0–314–33231–6

Hornbook Series and the key symbol appearing on the front cover are registered trademarks of West Publishing Co. Registered in U.S. Patent and Trademark Office.

Rodgers Environmental Law HB
6th Reprint—1991

To Janet

*

PREFACE

This text is aimed primarily at the student of environmental law. The subject now appears in the law school curriculum in the form of staple upper level courses in land use planning, environmental, energy, and resources law, specialized seminars in law, science, and technology, and as important segments of many basic courses—torts, administrative law, legislation, and property, to mention the prominent examples. Confessing that the student is the principal intended beneficiary carries with it an admission that the law as stated here is not bereft of critical or editorial comment. Yet, I admit to an inability to accept the distinction that holds that the student is somebody who needs reasons without authority while the practitioner is somebody who needs rules without explanation. This text attempts to express what the law is, and often a view of what ought to be, upon the understanding that all who grapple with the subject need to consider reflectively how our legal system has met the demands of environmental quality.

Anyone but vaguely familiar with the topic will recognize the sheer impossibility of restating definitively a body of law that is subject to flux and change at a pace that would astonish our intellectual predecessors who drifted comfortably on the currents of the common law. Administrative lawmaking, in particular, has added a complexity and a lack of permanence that has changed dramatically the study and understanding of today's law students. There may be value, nonetheless, in attempting to describe this rapidly moving target at a fixed point in time. Our cutoff date, which is only an approximate one, is January 1, 1977, so that this text reflects the major developments through the 94th Congress. More important is the recognition that the topic of environmental law is influenced strongly by legal principles that are not subject to summary overruling in tomorrow's Federal Register. It is hoped that these doctrines are captured and expressed in the pages following; the book attempts to do this without pretensions of comprehensiveness. The errors of omission remaining must await correction by other writers or by future editions of this text.

At several points in the text I have sought to confess possible bias by disclosing an involvement, usually as an attorney, in cases cited as authority. These cases include

—Rodgers v. FTC, 492 F.2d 228 (9th Cir. 1973) cert. denied 419 U.S. 883 (1974).

PREFACE

- —United States v. Washington, 520 F.2d 676, 5 ELR 20552 (9th Cir. 1975), cert. denied 423 U.S. 1086 (1976).
- —In re Virginia Elec. & Power Co., 7 AEC 1183 (1974), aff'd NRCI=75/11, 10 (1975), aff'd sub nom. North Anna Environmental Coalition v. Nuclear Regulatory Comm'n, —— U.S. App.D.C. ——, 533 F.2d 655 (1976).
- —Lombardo v. Handler, 397 F.Supp. 792 (D.D.C.1975), aff'd per curiam —— U.S.App.D.C. ——, 543 F.2d 1043 (1976).
- —EDF v. Montrose Chemical Corp., Civil No. 70-2389ALS (M.D. Cal. Oct. 22, 1970).
- —In re Virginia Elec. & Power Co., LBP 75-54, 2 NRC 498 (1975), modified ALAB 324, 3 NRC 347, modified NRCI=76/11, 480 (1976), petition for review pending VEPCO v. Nuclear Regulatory Comm'n, Civil No. 76-2275 (4th Cir. Nov. 12, 1976).
- —Dep't of Game v. Puyallup Tribe, Inc., 86 Wash.2d 664, 548 P.2d 1058, cert. granted —— U.S. —— (1976).
- —Regenstein v. Anderson, Civil No. 2193-73 (D.D.C. Dec. 18, 1973).
- —In re NPDES for Blue Plains Sewage Treatment Plant, EPA Permit No. DC 0021199, Doc. No. DC-AH-0001.
- —In re Proposed Regulations for Labeling and Advertising Requirements for Detergents, FTC Dkt. No. 215-32.

I also have participated, as an attorney or witness, in state administrative proceedings addressing proposed restrictions on persistent pesticides (Washington) and air pollution from copper smelters (Washington, Montana, Arizona, and New Mexico). Naturally enough, since I usually lose before the courts and agencies, I have reargued many of the issues in these pages.

In preparing the manuscript I have had the able assistance of Mrs. Leslie B. Allred, for which I am grateful. For many years I also have received guidance and aid from the library staffs at the University of Washington and at Georgetown University. My thanks are extended to Marion Gallagher at the University of Washington, and to Harry Boyles and his successor, Harry Martin, at the Georgetown University Law Center, as well as their staffs.

While the book was in progress, I have taught courses in environmental and resources law, and have benefitted greatly from the thoughts and efforts of my students at Georgetown. Those whose contributions are not otherwise noted in the footnotes include Jack Schenendorf, Andy Wolf, Margaret Tessier, Chris Lipaj, Richard

PREFACE

Tinney, Jerry Schrepple, Richard Forschler, Jim Dougherty, William Sierks, Henry Fellows, Carlos Recio, Linda McCauley, Robert Gray, and John Aisenbrey. Special thanks are in order for David Prensky, my chief editor and friend, who influenced in no small way the final version of the manuscript.

WILLIAM H. RODGERS, JR.

Washington, D. C.
May, 1977

*

SUMMARY OF CONTENTS

Chapter		Page
I.	Introduction to Environmental Law	1
II.	Common Law and the Variations	100
III.	Air Pollution	208
IV.	Water Pollution	354
V.	Noise Pollution	551
VI.	Solid Waste/Resource Recovery	619
VII.	National Environmental Policy Act	697
VIII.	Pesticides and Toxic Substances	835
Table of Cases		909
Index		929

*

TABLE OF CONTENTS

CHAPTER I. INTRODUCTION TO ENVIRONMENTAL LAW

Sec.		Page
1.1	Definitions and Postulates	1
1.2	Interdisciplinary Demands	5
1.3	Technology Assessment	10
1.4	The Legal Context	14
1.5	Scope of Judicial Review	16
1.6	Standing	23
1.7	Sovereign Immunity: Generally	30
1.8	Sovereign Immunity: Federal Tort Claims Act	34
	a. Discretionary Function Exemption	34
	b. Requirement of Negligent or Wrongful Act	37
	c. Misrepresentation Exemption	38
1.9	The Techniques of Deference: Exhaustion, Primary Jurisdiction and Ripeness	39
	a. Exhaustion	40
	b. Primary Jurisdiction	43
	c. Ripeness, Finality, and Mootness	46
1.10	Freedom of Information Act	49
	a. Intra-agency Memoranda	52
	b. Investigatory Files	56
	c. Trade Secrets	58
	d. National Security	61
	e. Medical Files and Personal Privacy	62
	f. The Specific Statutory Exemptions	63
1.11	Advisory Committee Act	64
1.12	National Academy of Sciences	72
1.13	Citizen Suits	75
	a. General Effect	76
	b. Grounds for Relief	79
	c. Remedies	83
	d. Other Citizen Suit Enforcement Provisions	87
1.14	Population Control	89
	a. Contraception	94
	b. Abortion	95
	c. Sterilization	97

TABLE OF CONTENTS

CHAPTER II. COMMON LAW AND THE VARIATIONS

Sec.		Page
2.1	Continuity of Principles: Nuisance Law	100
2.2	Public Nuisance	102
2.3	Private Nuisance	107
2.4	Nuisance: Extent of the Hurt	112
2.5	Nuisance: Utility of the Offending Activity	116
2.6	Nuisance: Control by the Best Technology	121
2.7	Nuisance: Place of the Hurt	129
2.8	Nuisance: Who Was There First	132
2.9	Nuisance: The Defenses	134
2.10	Nuisance: The Effect of Statutes	136
2.11	Nuisance: The Remedy	143
2.12	Federal Common Law of Nuisance	150
2.13	Trespass	154
2.14	Strict Liability for Abnormally Dangerous Activities	158
2.15	Riparian Rights; Prior Appropriation	163
	a. Riparian Rights	163
	b. Prior Appropriation	168
2.16	Public Trust Doctrine	170
	a. Scope of the Doctrine	171
	b. Procedural Functions	177
	c. Substantive Limits	180
	d. Legislative and Constitutional Modifications	182
2.17	Land Development Controls	186
	a. Growth Controls	187
	b. Special Purpose Land Use Regulation	196
	c. Generalized Planning Efforts	201
	d. The Taking Issue	203

CHAPTER III. AIR POLLUTION

3.1	Background	208
3.2	The Clean Air Act: A Summary	214
3.3	Designating Regions; Issuing Criteria and Control Techniques Documents	221
3.4	National Ambient Air Quality Standards	224
3.5	The Implementation Plans: Procedure	230
3.6	The Implementation Plans: Ameliorating Features	238
3.7	Implementation Plans: General Requirements	248
	a. Monitoring	248
	b. Pre-construction Review	250
	c. Intergovernmental Cooperation	252
	d. State Agency Requirements	253
	e. Revision Authority	254

TABLE OF CONTENTS

Sec.		Page
3.8	Implementation Plans: Emission Limitations	254
3.9	Economic and Technical Defenses	259
	a. Promulgation of the National Standards	259
	b. Adoption of the State Implementation Plans	260
	c. EPA Approval or Disapproval of State Plans	261
	d. Appellate Review of the Administrator's Action	263
	e. State and Federal Variance Proceedings	264
	f. Collateral Attack by Injunction	265
	g. Defensively in Enforcement Proceedings	265
	h. Contempt Proceedings	267
3.10	New Source Performance Standards	267
3.11	Hazardous Air Pollutant Emission Standards	276
3.12	Prevention of Significant Deterioration	279
3.13	Mobile Sources: Generally	287
3.14	Mobile Sources: Motor Vehicle Emission Standards	294
3.15	Mobile Sources: In-Use Vehicles	301
	a. Warranties	301
	b. Anti-tampering Provisions	304
	c. Certification and Recalls	305
3.16	Mobile Sources: Transportation Control Plans	310
	a. Reducing Emissions from In-use Vehicles	315
	(i) Mandatory Inspection and Maintenance	315
	(ii) Mandatory Retrofit	316
	(iii) Service Station Vapor Controls	317
	b. Reducing Total Vehicle Miles of Travel	317
	(i) Bus and Carpool Priority Treatment	317
	(ii) Transit Improvement	318
	(iii) Carpooling	318
	(iv) Employer Transit Incentive	318
	(v) Management of Parking Supply	319
	(vi) Gas Rationing	320
	(vii) Bicycle Lanes	321
	(viii) Vehicle Free Zone	321
	(ix) Selected Vehicle Use Prohibitions	322
	c. Judicial Review of the Transportation Plans	322
3.17	Indirect Sources	325
3.18	Registration and Regulation of Fuel Additives	330
3.19	Enforcement	336
	a. Miscellaneous Powers	336
	b. Administrative Orders	343
	c. State Enforcement	347
	d. Federal Facilities	352

TABLE OF CONTENTS

CHAPTER IV. WATER POLLUTION

Sec.		Page
4.1	Background	354
4.2	Federal Water Pollution Control Act: A Summary	361
4.3	Coverage: Groundwater	368
4.4	Coverage: Nonpoint Sources	375
	a. Definition of Point Sources	375
	b. The Study and Planning Provisions	377
	c. Related Federal and State Law	379
	(i) Construction	380
	(ii) Mining	381
	(iii) Silvicultural	383
	(iv) Agricultural	384
4.5	Rivers and Harbors Appropriation Act of 1899	387
	a. The Meaning of Refuse	388
	b. The Navigable Waters Requirement	390
	c. The Sewage Exception	392
	d. Culpability	393
	e. Remedies	395
	f. Contemporaneous Significance	397
4.6	Disposal of Dredged and Fill Material	399
	a. Dredged or Fill Material	400
	b. Navigable Waters	401
	c. Remedies	403
	d. Criteria for Site Selection and Permit Issuance	405
	e. Activities of the Corps of Engineers	407
	f. Related Federal and State Laws	408
4.7	Disposal of Sewage Sludge	409
4.8	Water Quality Standards	415
4.9	Planning Provisions: Generally	424
	a. Basin Planning	426
	b. State Planning	428
	c. Areawide Planning	432
	d. Facility Planning	435
4.10	Planning: Facilities and Construction Grants	435
	a. Overview of Title II	436
	b. Mechanics of Facility Planning and Construction	440
	c. Substantive Requirements for Federally Funded Facilities	445
	d. Planning of Multi-purpose Federal Projects	448
4.11	Effluent Standards: National Pollutant Discharge Elimination System Generally	451

TABLE OF CONTENTS

Sec.		Page
4.12	Effluent Standards: Industrial Sources	462
4.13	Effluent Standards: Municipal Sources	470
4.14	Effluent Standards: Pretreatment	477
4.15	Effluent Standards: Toxic Pollutants	481
4.16	Ocean Dumping	488
	a. Coverage	488
	b. Issuance of Permits and Selection of Sites	490
	c. Overlap Between the Act and FWPCA	496
	d. Enforcement	498
4.17	Oil Pollution: Prohibitions, Penalties and Cleanup	499
	a. Prohibitions	499
	b. Penalties	501
	c. Cleanup	505
	d. Other Hazardous Substances	506
4.18	Oil Pollution: Regulation	507
	a. Section 311(j) Regulations	507
	b. Other Regulatory Statutes	509
	c. Offshore Drilling	513
	d. International Regulation	515
	e. State Regulation	515
4.19	Oil Pollution: Compensation	517
	a. Federal Law	518
	b. State Law	522
	c. International Law and Voluntary Agreements	523
4.20	Thermal Pollution	524
	a. Effects and Control Options	525
	b. Common Law and Other Miscellaneous Legal Controls	527
	c. Federal Water Pollution Control Act	531
	d. Section 316	532
4.21	Enforcement	534
	a. Miscellaneous Powers	534
	b. Municipal Treatment Works and Federal Facilities	541
	c. State Enforcement Powers	545

CHAPTER V. NOISE POLLUTION

5.1	Background	551
5.2	The Noise Control Act: A Summary	553
5.3	Nontransportation Sources: Common Law	558
5.4	Nontransportation Sources: Regulation	563
	a. State Regulation	564
	b. Federal Regulation	568
	c. Municipal Regulation	573
5.5	Transportation Sources (Aircraft): Common Law	575

TABLE OF CONTENTS

Sec.		Page
5.6	Transportation Sources (Railroads, Motor Vehicles): Common Law	581
5.7	Transportation Sources (Aircraft): Regulation	583
	a. Source Regulation	584
	(i) New Sources	587
	(ii) Existing Sources	589
	b. Operations Regulation	591
	(i) Federal Law	591
	(ii) Local Law	594
	c. Land Use	598
	(i) Federal Law	598
	(ii) Local Law	600
5.8	Transportation Sources (Railroads, Motor Vehicles): Regulation	601
	a. Planning Controls	602
	b. Operational and Source Controls	604
5.9	Transportation Sources: National Environmental Policy Act	611
5.10	Occupational Noise Exposure	615

CHAPTER VI. SOLID WASTE/RESOURCE RECOVERY

6.1	Background	619
6.2	Common Law	623
6.3	Solid Waste Disposal Act: A Summary	627
	a. The Early Years	627
	b. The 1970 Legislation	629
	c. Resource Conservation and Recovery Act of 1976	635
6.4	Federal Guidelines: Disposal and Resource Recovery	637
	a. Disposal and Collection Guidelines	640
	b. Resource Recovery	643
6.5	Indirect Federal Role	645
	a. Ad Hoc Regulation	645
	b. Other Incidental Influences on Resource Use Decisions	646
6.6	Energy Conservation	653
	a. Automotive Fuel Economy	654
	b. Consumer Products Other Than Automobiles	658
	c. Industrial Energy Conservation	660
	d. State and Federal Energy Conservation Programs	662
6.7	The State Role	664
	a. Residential and Commercial Solid Waste	665
	b. Resource Recovery	671
6.8	The Local Role	673
	a. Nuisance Law and Zoning Ordinances	675
	b. Conventional Regulations	675
	c. Innovations in Source Reduction and Resource Recovery	678

TABLE OF CONTENTS

Sec.		Page
6.9	Special Problems	678
	a. Junked Automobiles	679
	b. Other Bulk Consumer Goods	683
	c. Nonreturnable Beverage Containers	684
	d. Miscellaneous Consumer Products	688
6.10	Hazardous Wastes	689
	a. Present Practice	689
	b. 1976 Amendments	694

CHAPTER VII. NATIONAL ENVIRONMENTAL POLICY ACT

Sec.		Page
7.1	Introduction	697
7.2	The Implementing Institutions	704
	a. Council on Environmental Quality	705
	b. Environmental Protection Agency	708
	c. The Other Agencies	712
	d. The Congress	713
7.3	Review of Agency Decision-Making: General Procedure	716
7.4	Review of Agency Decision-Making: Environmental Impact Statement Procedures	725
7.5	Review of Agency Decision-Making: Substance	738
	a. Good Faith Test	739
	b. Miscellaneous Standards of Section 101	741
	c. The Balancing Test	744
	(i) Cost-Benefit Analysis	745
	(ii) Maximum Mitigation	747
7.6	The Recurring Issues: Whether	750
	a. Major Actions and Significant Effects	751
	b. The Federal Requirement	761
	c. Exceptions	764
7.7	The Recurring Issues: When	767
	a. Proposals for Action	767
	b. Delayed Federal Involvement	774
7.8	The Recurring Issues: Who	777
	a. Delegation	778
	b. The Multiple Agency Problem	783
7.9	The Recurring Issues: What	785
	a. Programmatic Impact Statements	785
	b. Segmentation	787
	c. Alternatives	792
7.10	The Recurring Issues: Remedies	798

TABLE OF CONTENTS

Sec.		Page
7.11	State Environmental Policy Acts	809
	a. Applicability	811
	b. Responsibility for Preparation	816
	c. Content	817
	d. Procedures and Implementing Institutions	818
	e. Substantive Consequences	821
7.12	National Environmental Policy Act: Complementary Federal Law	822
	a. Procedural Protection	823
	b. Substantive Obligations	828

CHAPTER VIII. PESTICIDES AND TOXIC SUBSTANCES

8.1	Background	835
8.2	Common Law	841
8.3	Federal Environmental Pesticide Control Act: Background and Summary	846
	a. Early Enactments	846
	b. Federal Environmental Pesticide Control Act of 1972	849
	c. The 1975 Amendments	853
	d. Miscellaneous Provisions of Federal Law	856
8.4	Registration: Generally	857
8.5	Registration: Classification, Misbranding and Labeling	863
	a. Classification	863
	b. Labeling and Misbranding	868
8.6	Registration: Exceptions	871
	a. Experimental Uses	871
	b. Emergency Uses	874
	c. Special Local Needs	876
	d. Miscellaneous Exemptions	878
8.7	Cancellation; Suspension	879
8.8	Tolerances	888
8.9	Enforcement	893
8.10	Toxic Substances	898
	a. New Chemical Substances	899
	b. Existing Chemical Substances	901
	c. Miscellaneous Requirements	906

Table of Cases 909

Index 929

HANDBOOK
ON
ENVIRONMENTAL LAW

ENVIRONMENTAL LAW

Chapter I

INTRODUCTION TO ENVIRONMENTAL LAW

§ 1.1 Definitions and Postulates

Discovering a workable definition of environmental law is a little bit like the search for truth: the closer you get the more elusive it becomes. One influential writer describes the environment as "the house created on earth for living things."[1] Ecology is thus "the science of planetary housekeeping."[2] Building on these definitions, environmental law can be defined as the law of planetary housekeeping. It is concerned with protecting the planet and its people from activities that upset the earth and its life-sustaining capacities.

A corollary of this definition is that man himself is the most notorious upsetter of life on earth. His interventions in the environment, often well intentioned, have led to unanticipated and dangerous effects. Pogo is not too far wrong when he says, "We have met the enemy and he is us." While this is disturbing, it is also optimistic: what man has done wrong man can set straight. Environmental law does not pretend to repeal the wind and the rain and the laws of ecology. It is aimed at man and seeks to control his activities.

Environmental law is not concerned solely with the natural environment—the physical condition of the land, air, water. It embraces also the human environment—the health, social and other man-made conditions affecting a human being's place on earth. The National Environmental Policy Act of 1969 ties its requirements for the preparation of impact statements to "major Federal actions significantly affecting the quality of the *human environment*."[3] Urban environmental ills, Judge Feinberg has written, include "noise, traffic, overburdened mass transportation systems, crime, congestion and even availability of drugs."[4] Environmental law thus focuses upon people from the perspective of their external surroundings, both natural and

---

1. B. Commoner, The Closing Circle 32 (1972). "'The environment'," Professor David Currie points out, "is not a modest concept; it embraces . . . 'the universe and all that surrounds it.'" D. P. Currie, Cases and Materials on Pollution, preface (1975), quoting comedian Peter Cook.

2. Ibid.

3. Section 102(2)(C), 42 U.S.C.A. § 4332(2)(C) (emphasis added).

4. Hanly v. Mitchell (I), 460 F.2d 640, 647, 2 ELR 20216, 20220 (2d Cir. 1972), cert. denied 409 U.S. 990.

artificial. It goes without saying that these surroundings are important: "Our physical nature, our mental health, our culture and institutions, our opportunities for challenge and fulfillment, our very survival—all of these are directly related and affected by the environment in which we life." [5]

Pollution has been defined as a resource out of place. This definition conveys at least three ideas helpful to the study of the law of planetary housekeeping. The first is that a pollution problem isn't necessarily solved by putting it somewhere else. The nineteenth century water pollution case of Fletcher v. Bealey [6] was a suit by a pulp manufacturer fearful of water pollution by vat waste from an upstream alkali plant. The dispute arose because the wastes at issue were ameliorated only temporarily by earlier litigation between the same parties which resulted in a court order requiring the dumping of vat waste on a landfill. With the passage of time, the vat waste threatened to pollute the river by seepage and runoff, and the deferment came due. Similarly, the British Alkali Act of 1863 prompted effective control of hydrochloric gases from alkali works.[7] The gases were reduced to hydrochloric acid, which in turn was dumped into the water. An air pollution problem was traded for a water pollution problem; the resource was still out of place, until uses could be found for the acid.

Modern examples of postponing, relocating and aggravating pollution problems by shifting a resource from one place to another are legion. State water pollution agencies generally made their appearance in the 1950's, whereas the air pollution regulatory regimes did not arrive until the 1960's. Water pollution controllers understandably were anxious to do something about sulfite waste liquor from pulp mills, a documented threat to marine life. One way to get the waste liquor out of the water was to require the companies to burn it, which was a commendable solution if you were obliged only to protect water quality without regard to air quality. Another example: one day in 1970 citizens of Los Angeles awoke to read in the newspaper that large quantities of fish from Santa Monica Bay had been seized by Food and Drug Administration officials because of contamination by DDT in excess of tolerance levels. The DDT was traced to the Hyperion treatment plant of the Los Angeles Sewer District Authority and from there to the Montrose Chemical Corporation plant in Torrence, California, the sole manufacturer of DDT in the United States. A lawsuit was filed and settled.[8] The DDT wastes, formerly

---

5. Council on Environmental Quality, First Ann.Rep. vi (1970).

6. 28 Ch.D. 688 (High Court of Justice, Chancery Division, 1885).

7. See Squires, Clean Power from Coal, 169 Science 821 (1970).

8. Environmental Defense Fund, Inc. v. Montrose Chem. Corp. (S.D.Cal., complaint dismissed June 14, 1971), reported in BNA, 2 Environment Rep.—Current Developments 181 (1971).

discharged into the Los Angeles sewer system, were now trucked to a landfill. The pollution problem, of course, did not disappear; it was contained, postponed, moved to another place.

Modern society puts resources out of place in fiendishly complex variations. The chemicals DDT and polychlorinated biphenyls (PCB's), to mention but two examples, are toxic substances distributed in biological organisms throughout the planet. The United States Department of Defense literally searched worldwide to find a disposal site for nerve gas wastes;[9] a proper place could not be found, only a place of least resistance. At Hanford, Washington, tanks with a life expectancy of a few decades hold radioactive wastes capable of retaining their toxicity for centuries. The pollution problem does not disappear by putting it elsewhere or assigning the consequences to future generations.

The definition of pollution as a resource out of place connotes waste as well as mismanagement. It is a fact that pollution control measures are not necessarily costly and unproductive but can be valuable savers of resources. This was the experience in 1970 for several pulp producer-defendants named in mercury pollution lawsuits, who discovered savings by severely cutting losses on a costly and coincidentally toxic chemical.[10] Dow Chemical Company management predicts that pollution control efforts at the company's plants throughout the world ultimately will prove to be moneymaking operations.[11] Waste oil from automobile crankcases is a valuable resource for the re-refining industry. Newspapers discarded in suburbia are the forest of the future for pulp producers. It is generally accepted dogma that energy savings are realized by the recycling of used materials.[12] Avoiding pollution often means saving resources.

A third idea inherent in the definition of pollution as a resource out of place is that people will use resources and their value is measured by reference to human needs. The Wilderness Act of 1964, indeed, lists "conservation" as a "use."[13] Environmental cases often are viewed as contests between the despoilers and the preservers, the users and the conservers. They are better seen as disputes between

---

9. Rodgers, Nerve Gas to the Northwest and Beyond, 1 Environmental Letters 111 (1971).

10. See Hearings on Mercury Pollution and the Enforcement of the Refuse Act of 1899, Before the Subcomm. on Conservation and Natural Resources of the House Comm. on Government Operations, 92d Cong., 1st Sess. (1971).

11. Address by Chester E. Otis, Manager, Environmental Affairs, Dow Chemical Co., EPA-Industry Meeting on International Pollution Control Activities, Washington, D. C., June 13, 1973.

12. Council on Environmental Quality, Fourth Ann.Rep. 204 (1973); ch. 6 below.

13. Pub.L. No. 88–577, § 4(b), 78 Stat. 893, 16 U.S.C.A. § 1133(b); see Minnesota Public Research Group v. Butz, 358 F.Supp. 584, 596, 3 ELR 20457, 20461 (D.Minn.1973), aff'd 498 F.2d 1314, 4 ELR 20700 (8th Cir. 1974).

different types of users. This "competing user" view is observed clearly in the case law, as where a limited resource (for example, a run of salmon) is shared among different user groups (for example, Indian and non-Indian commercial and sport fishermen).[14] The concept of competing users becomes blurred in another case where one interest would fell the forest and sell the trees while another would call the forest "wilderness" and use it as a place to go or as a place to know where one could go.

Different uses spring from different motivations. And different uses have diverse consequences upon the resources. All the contestants, nonetheless, can be considered users.

A concluding thought regarding the definition of pollution is that it does not necessarily presuppose a responsible or culpable cause, Pogo to the contrary notwithstanding. While people are often the immediate culprit, sometimes they are not. Resources may be put out of place by a blizzard induced by natural meteorological forces as well as by the misfiring of a weather modification program. Sulfur dioxide is emitted naturally as swamp gas as well as from fossil fuel fired steam electric plants. The Smoky Mountains got their name from a natural pollution—tarpenes emitted by the many conifers growing on the slopes. It is said that all the air pollution produced by man on earth falls short of the amount of particulates and gases produced by just three volcanic eruptions.[15]

Recitations of naturally induced pollution often precede arguments that controlling people-caused pollution therefore would be futile or unproductive. This explains perhaps why the Coordinating Research Council (an amalgam of auto and oil interests engaged in joint research under the auspices of the Environmental Protection Agency) took a special interest in natural sources of carbon monoxide.[16] It of course misses the point to argue that since nature is a part of the problem we should ignore the human part of the problem. As we shall see, people are very much responsible for worldwide environmental degradation and must be very much a part of the solution if there is to be one.

14. United States v. Washington, 520 F.2d 676, 5 ELR 20552 (9th Cir. 1975), cert. denied, 423 U.S. 1086 (1976).

15. Reported in Industry Week, Aug. 17, 1970, at 27.

16. On October 26, 1973, EPA formally severed its ties with the Coordinating Research Council as a consequence of growing concern within the agency that the relationship was affecting adversely EPA's "appearance of objectivity." 119 Cong.Rec. 3900–01 (1973), see id. at 28681–85 (remarks of Sen. Muskie); J. Esposito, Vanishing Air 186–87 (1970). See also E. Robinson & R. Robbin, Gaseous Atmospheric Pollutants from Urban and Natural Sources, in Global Effects of Environmental Pollution 50 (S. F. Singer ed. 1970); National Air Pollution Control Administration, Air Quality Criteria for Carbon Monoxide (1970).

§ 1.2 Interdisciplinary Demands

The student of environmental law should be alert to where his study fits in the body of knowledge generally and the corpus of the law particularly. A challenging and rewarding aspect of the study and practice of environmental law is the necessity for coming to grips with other disciplines essential to understanding the technological forces at issue. The lawyer traditionally is the generalist, the expert in the process who brings the pieces together. Especially is this so in environmental cases where the pieces are often complex, and where causes, effects and remedies disregard traditional disciplinary and administrative compartments. Illustrative is the pesticide case which may combine the expertise of the wildlife biologist, the entomologist (that branch of zoology dealing with insects), the toxicologist (who is concerned with the effects of poisons), public health, agricultural and silvicultural administrators. The factual questions can present an "enormous problem in biogeochemistry" tracing or predicting the "entire process" of transport and transformation of a chemical, from its initial release into the environment to its ultimate degradation or sequestration.[1]

The air pollution case may bring together the epidemiologist (investigator of the causes of epidemics), the botanist, the atmospheric chemist and the meteorologist (to advise us what happens when the pollutant leaves the stack), the economist, and the chemical engineer (to advise on equipment to be placed in the stack to minimize effects). More than a dozen disciplines and subdisciplines were brought to bear on the question of dating the most recent movement of a fault zone discovered in the reactor excavations of a nuclear power plant.[2] Examples: structural geology (the study of the structure of rocks), stratigraphy (that branch of geology dealing with the formation, composition and sequence of stratified rocks as part of the earth's crust), paleontology (the science dealing with past geological ages), geomorphology (the study of land surfaces) and seismology (the science of earthquakes). A recent study on stripmining drew upon a body of knowledge comprised of "geology, climatology, geochemistry, hydrology, microbiology, together with information about mining and reclamation practices, government regulation and details of specific topographies, mineral seams, vegetation and soils."[3] A well known case challenging the Reserve Mining Company's discharge

---

1. Nisbet, Banning DDT: An Ill-Planned Biogeochemical Experiment, Technology Review, Dec. 1974, p. 10; see Gelpe & Tarlock, The Uses of Scientific Information in Environmental Decisionmaking, 48 S.Cal.L.Rev. 371 (1974).

2. U. S. Atomic Energy Commission, In re Virginia Elec. & Power Co. (North Anna Nuclear Power Station, Units 1, 2, 3 and 4), Dkt.Nos. CPPR-77, -78 (Show Cause), Tr. 1174-78 (Testimony of Dr. John Gibbons, Apr. 1974).

3. National Academy of Sciences, Rehabilitation Potential of Western Coal Lands xvi (1974).

of taconite and asbestos into Lake Superior required testimony from over 200 expert witnesses.[4] The Environmental Defense Fund has convened a panel of more than twenty experts from different disciplines to combat environmental abuses of off-road vehicles on public lands.

The student of environmental law confronts many examples of scientific insights and terminology from various disciplines influencing the direction of the law. One prominent illustration is that a stream polluted with sewage in time can cleanse itself and recover, re-establishing necessary levels of dissolved oxygen and other constituents of high quality water.[5] This biological principle supported a major legal premise of the Water Quality Act of 1965, which was that waste carrying capacities of watercourses should be used and exploited.[6] Ground-level concentrations of air pollutants can be reduced by dispersion at high altitudes; this meteorological reality prompted a tall stack air pollution control strategy which prevailed for the better part of a century and is presently popular in many quarters.[7]

The economists' notion of technological externalities—costs passed on from a polluting firm to the community at large—looms large in the understanding of the justifications for a particular legal decision.[8] Put simply, pollution imposes costs but so does its avoidance. From an economic perspective, the problem is "to allocate rights and liabilities in such a way as to minimize the sum of the costs of smoke damage and of avoiding smoke damage."[9] Many economists urge the taxing of effluent discharges to reflect the costs of off-site disposal. While the levy or discharge fee approach largely has been rejected in the United States in favor of regulatory regimes typified by the federal Clean Air Act and the Water Pollution Control

---

4. United States v. Reserve Mining Co., 380 F.Supp. 11, 4 ELR 20573 (D.C. Minn.1974), stayed 498 F.2d 1073, 4 ELR 20598 (8th Cir.), rev'd in part 514 F.2d 492, 5 ELR 20596 (8th Cir. 1975).

5. See Bartsch, Biological Aspects of Stream Pollution, 20 Sewage Works J. 292–95 (1948).

6. See § 4.1 below.

7. U. S. Dep't. of HEW, Tall Stacks, Various Atmospheric Phenomena and Related Aspects (1969); Rodgers, Tacoma's Tall Stack, The Nation, May 11, 1970; see § 3.8 below.

8. Davis & Kamien, Externalities and the Quality of Air and Water, in Economics of Air & Water Pollution 13–19 (W. Walker ed. 1969); Coase, The Problem of Social Cost, 3 J.Law & Econ. 1 (1960), Calabresi & Melamed, Property Rules, Liability Rules, and Inalienability: One View of the Cathedral, 85 Harv.L.Rev. 1089 (1972); Michelman, Pollution as a Tort: A Non-Accidental Perspective on Calabresi's Costs, 80 Yale L.J. 647 (1971).

9. R. A. Posner, Economic Analysis of Law 24 (1972); see Krier, Book Review, 122 U.Pa.L.Rev. 1664, 1685–93 (1974) (containing a thoughtful discussion of economic issues of environmental law raised in the Posner book). See also Kneese, Man and His Habitat: Problems of Water Pollution, 21 Bull.Atom.Scientists 2–8 (1965).

Act, economic thinking is treated respectfully in the leading teaching materials on environmental law.[10]

The extension of environmental law into other disciplinary domains is nowhere better illustrated than by the explicit directive in section 102(2)(A) of the National Environmental Policy Act. This obliges all agencies of the Federal Government to "utilize a systematic, interdisciplinary approach which will insure the integrated use of the natural and social sciences and the environmental design arts in planning and in decisionmaking along with economic and technical considerations." [11] Numerous reorganization proposals, typified by the emergence of the Environmental Protection Agency at the federal level,[12] reaffirm also the universal understanding that the law regarding the nation's physical condition cannot live in isolated compartments of government bureaucracy.

Students and practitioners of environmental law often are called upon to resort to analytical techniques refined by other disciplines. Perhaps best known is a cost-benefit analysis which attempts to put the discipline of the marketplace into the government investment and regulatory decisions. Another illustration is the economists' input-output analysis showing generally what each industry in the economy buys from and sells to one another and to final users (consumers and governments).[13] This technique would be helpful to an understanding of the employment effects of adopting certain environmental measures such as a ban on non-returnable beverage containers or petroleum allocation for one reason or another.

Another analytical technique likely to prove useful to lawyers is the total energy concept advanced by various authorities.[14] This theoretical construct scrutinizes a recommended course of conduct in light of the total energy requirements of the policy proposed and alternatives to it. The concept raises such fundamental questions as whether nuclear energy generated at a facility is worth the investment of energy made throughout the system needed to produce it (fuel enrichment, fuel transportation, etc.); or whether oil shale is an attractive energy source compared to the energy costs associated with finding, producing, upgrading and delivering it; or whether a

---

10. E. g., E. H. Hanks, A. D. Tarlock & J. L. Hanks, Environmental Law & Policy: Cases and Materials ch. 5 (1974).

11. 42 U.S.C.A. § 4332(2)(A); see §§ 7.3, 7.4 below.

12. Reorganization Plan No. 3 of 1970, 35 Fed.Reg. 15623, 84 Stat. 2086 (Dec. 2, 1970).

13. See Kutscher & Brown, Industrial Use of Petroleum: Effect on Employment, Monthly Labor Review, March, 1974, at 3.

14. Gilliland, Energy Analysis and Public Policy, 189 Science 1051 (1975); see Section 5 of the Non-Nuclear Energy Research and Development Act of 1974, Pub.L. No. 93–577, § 5(a)(5), 88 Stat. 1880, 42 U.S.C.A. § 5904(a)(5) (the potential for production of net energy by the proposed technology at the stage of commercial application shall be analyzed and considered in evaluating proposals for funding).

source of air pollution should be compelled to install an electrostatic precipitator to control emissions in light of the resources put out of place by the manufacture, transport and operation of the pollution control system itself.

A systems analysis technique, widely used today, is another example of the interdisciplinary approach to environmental studies. It grew out of a variety of mathematical techniques, employed with some effectiveness during World War II, to compare alternative deployments of military personnel and resources.[15] After the War, these concepts gained wider currency and use, not only in the military but also in business and government. The technique involves "peering further into the future, including a greatly expanded number of variables, examining a wider range of possible action, and taking higher-level alternatives into account." [16]

The central theme of such analysis "is a constant awareness of the complexity and inter-relatedness of causes, effects, objectives and policy options." [17] Thus, a systems approach to auto-caused air pollution focuses not only upon the vehicle but upon other modifiable events in the chain—for example, individual use preferences (locations of homes and jobs, driving and maintenance patterns) or traffic management (vehicular flow, parking availability, gasoline pricing). It is sufficient for present purposes to acknowledge that while a systems approach elevates understanding and conveys a somewhat fuller sense of options, so does it extend the range of legal and political conflict. If economic sacrifices and dramatic changes of habit are called for somewhere along the system that produces urban air pollution, it is understandable that people and corporations prefer that sacrifices be made elsewhere. Different constituencies bear the brunt of reform if reductions in carbon monoxide or hydrocarbons are realized by tightening emission standards on new vehicles as opposed to requiring pollution control retrofit of pre-1968 vehicles or by insisting that close-in commuters ride bicycles to work. Expansion of the policy options by systems analysis brings a dilution of responsibility familiar to the law. It goes without saying that the perspective of the lawsuit, designed to resolve disputes between individual parties, only occasionally comprehends the range of remedial options throughout a system.

The major variables of an environmental system may be represented in a formula called a model. Modeling is a relatively common management technique used in environmental decision-making (particularly as regards air and water quality). It is a simulation de-

---

15. L. L. Jaffe & L. T. Tribe, Environmental Protection 272 (1971) [hereinafter cited as Jaffe & Tribe].

16. R. McKean, Efficiency in Government Through Systems Analysis 7 (1958); Watt, The Nature of Systems Analysis, in Systems Analysis in Ecology (K. Watt ed. 1966).

17. Jaffe & Tribe at 272.

signed to aid prediction by identifying how a change in one parameter will affect other parameters. For example, an air quality model "provides a link between alterations in emission levels due to source control strategies and the changes in airborne pollutant concentration levels that can be expected to result" from the controls. A complete model involves consideration of "source emission patterns, chemical transformations, atmospheric transport, and removal processes, all in terms of time and location." The model "may be mathematical in nature, consisting of a series of related equations describing physical and chemical processes, or it may be physical in nature, consisting of a laboratory simulation involving a wind or water tunnel, or a chemical reactor." [18] In litigation, the inquiry is likely to focus on the validity of the assumptions used in a particular model.[19]

Yet another interdisciplinary tool of potential use to environmental decision-makers is the so-called Quality of Life concept.[20] The idea grows out of widespread dissatisfaction with various indicators of progress, notably the gross national product (GNP), and looks toward a better system of reporting the net effect of an aggregate life experience. The concept is often encountered as "a slogan—a call to think bigger." [21] Clearly a generally acceptable index of welfare is unachievable. And, "as the parts which make up the quality of life become greater in number, the term becomes less scientific and more moral and political." [22]

Nonetheless, attempts have been made to develop "hard" statistical evidence of experiences like health and crime and to identify and measure, through survey studies, the qualities of life that concern people. Most of us would be able to compile a list of the variables thought important in our human and natural environments. These listings, without attempting to aggregate the factors, are commonly called social indicators. They can be useful in describing the state of the environment and changes taking place as a result of governmental or private actions. Without more, social indicators obviously present difficulties in interpreting the overall quality of life when there are divergent trends among variables selected: as, for example, when the improvement in the water quality indicator is accompanied by an increase of unemployment resulting from a shutdown of a pollution generating factory.[23]

18. National Academy of Sciences, National Academy of Engineering, Report by the Coordinating Comm. on Air Quality Studies, in Sen. Comm. on Public Works, Air Quality and Automobile Emission Control, Doc.No. 24, 93d Cong., 2d Sess., pt. 1, at 91 (Comm.Print 1974).

19. Texas v. EPA, 499 F.2d 289, 4 ELR 20744 (5th Cir. 1974).

20. See Environmental Protection Agency, The Quality of Life Concept: A Potential New Look for Decision Makers (1973).

21. Id. at II–192 (Norman C. Dalker, The Quality of Life).

22. Inhaber, Environmental Quality: Outline for a National Index for Canada, 186 Science 798 (1974).

23. Supra note 20, at II–114 (Y. P. Jorn, Data Requirements for a Quality Growth Policy).

Quality of life indices go a step further by attempting to attach objective (preferably numerical) measurements to such factors as air, water and land quality.[24] To be anticipated are future efforts to construct objective quality-of-life indices or, short of that, models to study the interrelationships and trade-offs among socioeconomic-ecological variables [25] (such as the use of the input-output techniques previously mentioned). The National Environmental Policy Act encourages this trend by requiring federal agencies to "identify and develop methods and procedures . . . which will insure that presently unquantified environmental amenities and values may be given appropriate consideration in decisionmaking along with economic and technical considerations." [26]

The law student and lawyer might have a tendency to shun the Quality of Life concept and similar theories as incomprehensible or scorn them as unworkable. A wiser attitude is to recognize their limited legitimate purpose (to inform the decision-maker) and evaluate them accordingly. In a day when the public opinion poll is the lifeblood of the political system it hardly makes sense to suggest that opinions on and measurements of quality of life are meaningless in the process of environmental law-making.

§ 1.3 Technology Assessment

One multidisciplinary analytical technique meaning many things to many people is the concept of technology assessment. As the name implies, it anticipates nothing less than a comprehensive sizing-up of the social, environmental, and human effects of a technological innovation.[1] Technology assessment offers a new and valuable perspective and has produced useful information for decision-makers. It has not proven to be a disciplined regulator of technology.

The proverb "look before you leap," however hackneyed, has a basis in human experience. The problem today is that the visibility is poorer and the leaps farther and faster than ever before. The potency of the technological forces on the loose is well-known: forests can be leveled, mountains moved, rivers diverted, weather repealed; we can produce industrial chemicals, radioactive isotopes, agents of warfare capable of putting the future of life on the planet in doubt; and we can "experiment, God-like, with genetic materials and life

---

24. Inhaber, supra note 22; see Indicators of Environmental Quality (W. A. Thomas ed. 1972). The Council on Environmental Quality defines environmental indices as "data aggregated to provide a picture of some aspect of environmental quality." First Ann.Rep. 236 (1970).

25. Supra note 20, at II–115.

26. 42 U.S.C.A. § 4332(2)(B); see § 7.3 below.

1. See Subcomm. on Computer Services of the Senate Comm. on Rules and Administration, Technology Assessment for the Congress, 92d Cong., 2d Sess. 8 (Comm. Print 1972).

itself."[2] Emmanuel Mesthene of the Harvard University Program in Science and Technology says simply: "[W]e have now, or know how to acquire, the technical capability to do very nearly everything we want."[3]

The ultimate power to do anything suggests two responses: the first is to predict what happens if we do it; the second is to decide whether we want to do it, to control by law the direction and pace of technological change. Technology assessment has helped us learn but not decide.

The movement owes much to former Representative Emilio Q. Daddario, Chairman of the House Subcommittee on Science, Research and Development, which, in the late 1960's held a series of hearings and commissioned studies focussing upon planning failures in anticipating technological fallout from programs such as the SST and the introduction of DDT.[4] The term "technology assessment" as it is understood today was coined first in a 1966 report of the Daddario Subcommittee,[5] which warned against the "traditional assumption" that technological bugs could be worked out on a "leisurely shakedown cruise"[6] and recommended an "early warning"[7] system to evaluate technology for the benefit of Congress.

An eventual result of this activity was the Technology Assessment Act of 1972,[8] which created the Office of Technology Assessment (OTA) as an independent advisor to the Congress, with Mr. Daddario becoming its first director. The Act declares, "[I]t is essential that, to the fullest extent possible, the consequences of technological applications be anticipated, understood, and considered in determination of public policy on existing and emerging national problems."[9] The "basic function" of OTA is to provide Congress with "early indications of the probable beneficial and adverse impacts"[10] of the applications of technology, including their "physical, biological, economic, social and political effects."[11] OTA is instructed to:[12]

2. Speth, The Federal Role in Technology Assessment and Control, in Environmental Law Institute, Federal Environmental Law 420 (E. L. Dolgin & T. G. P. Guilbert eds. 1974).

3. Quoted in id. at 425 n. 10.

4. E. g., House Comm. on Science and Astronautics, Technical Information for Congress, H.R.Doc.No.137, 91st Cong., 1st Sess. (1969); National Academy of Engineering, A Study of Technology Assessment and Choice (1969).

5. House Comm. on Science and Astronautics, Inquiries, Legislation, Policy Studies Re: Science and Technology—Second Progress Report of the Subcommittee on Science, Research and Development, 89th Cong., 2d Sess. (Comm.Print 1966).

6. Id. at 24.

7. Id. at 27.

8. Pub.L. No. 92–484, 86 Stat. 797, 2 U.S.C.A. § 471 et seq.

9. Section 2(b), id. § 471(b).

10. Section 3(c), id. § 472(c).

11. Section 2(d)(1), id. § 471(d)(1).

12. Section 3(c), id. § 471(c).

(1) identify existing or probable impacts of technology or technological programs;

(2) where possible, ascertain cause-and-effect relationships;

(3) identify alternative technological methods of implementing specific programs;

(4) identify alternative programs for achieving requisite goals;

(5) make estimates and comparisons of the impacts of alternative methods and programs;

(6) present findings of completed analyses to the appropriate legislative authorities;

(7) identify areas where additional research or data collection is required to provide adequate support for the assessments and estimates described in paragraph (1) through (5) above; . . . .

With this legislation Congress brought into being a roving technological assessor with an open-ended license to study problems from a variety of disciplinary points of view. The Office is at work on such subjects [13] as technological issues affecting the nation's food supply; present and future utilization of the oil and gas resources of the United States Outer Continental Shelf; the development of an energy information system for congressional committees; urban mass transit systems, with emphasis on automatic train control technology; the technical and economic feasibility of using solar energy to generate electricity for small communities; the capabilities of current technology to determine whether drug products with the same physical and chemical composition produce comparable therapeutic effects. Time will tell whether the study of problems by OTA principally through the use of contracts with outside consultants will clarify significantly future technological choices. Ultimately it may be necessary to confront the questions of whether clarifying options is a precursor of technological controls and, if so, imposed by whom and toward what ends.

Technology assessment as an information-getter has received ad hoc endorsement from other directions as well. Executive agencies have carried out a number of broad assessments of proposed technological applications, typified by the well known 1971 National Academy of Sciences study, *Jamaica Bay and Kennedy Airport*.[14] Indeed, the National Academy of Sciences has been in the business of technology assessment for many years. At present, the Academy should

---

13. Office of Technology Assessment, First Ann.Rep. 24 (1974); OTA Press Release, OTA Announces Assessment of "On Site" Solar-Electric Systems, July 3, 1974; OTA Drug Bioequivalence Study Panel Report, Drug Bioequivalence, July, 1974 (the first OTA assessment to be delivered to Congress); see Comment, The Office of Technology Assessment Says ERDA's National Energy Plan Slights Energy Conservation, 6 ELR 10017 (1976).

14. Discussed in V. Coates, Technology and Public Policy (1972).

be regarded as a government advisor on technological questions of far greater stature and influence than the foundling Office of Technology Assessment.[15]

Federal legislation regularly directs technological change to proceed with caution and only after careful study. Illustrative are Section 122 of the Rivers and Harbors Authorization Act of 1971 and Section 136 of the Federal-Aid Highway Act of 1970, both of which require the administrative decision-maker to prepare and use

> guidelines designed to assure that possible adverse economic, social and environmental effects relating to any proposed project . . . have been fully considered in developing such project, and that the final decisions on the project are made in the best overall public interest.[16]

Clearly the dominant legal contributor to technology assessment in recent years has been the National Environmental Policy Act's requirement that an impact statement accompany each proposal for "major Federal action significantly affecting the quality of the human environment."[17] The leading case of Scientists' Institute for Public Information v. AEC[18] held that the AEC was obliged to prepare an environmental impact statement for its research and development program aimed at commercializing the Liquid Metal Fast Breeder Reactor. The court reasoned, quite persuasively, that the allocation of today's research money dictates the application of tomorrow's technology. To the extent that NEPA reaches back into the early planning or research stages of federal programs,[19] it obviously performs a technology assessment function.

A perceptive synthesis of the technology assessment movement by J. G. Speth[20] criticizes Congress' inability to move the concept beyond the information-producing stage to the level of regulating and guiding technology. He proposes an independent Technology Assessment Agency which should be given "explicit standards for determining what subjects should be assessed, when the assessments occur and what they should contain."[21] Speth recognizes, however, that heightened public awareness, political reforms and political action are part of any technological evaluation process. It seems unlikely that an administrative agency, neatly and decisively, can assume a dominant decision-making role on the future of technologies. The fate of the Liquid Metal Fast Breeder Reactor, like that of the SST, will be debated in many forums, the most important of which is the Congress itself.

15. § 1.12 below.

16. Pub.L. No. 91–611, § 122, 84 Stat. 1823 (rivers and harbors); Pub.L. No. 91–605, § 136(b), 84 Stat. 1734, 23 U.S.C.A. § 109(h) (highways).

17. 42 U.S.C.A. § 4332(2)(C).

18. 156 U.S.App.D.C. 395, 481 F.2d 1079, 3 ELR 20525 (1973).

19. See § 7.7 below.

20. Note 2, supra.

21. Id. at 457.

Technology assessment furnishes a point of view somewhat broader than that of environmental protection, focussing not only on the pathological effects on ecology of technologies but more broadly on the impact of technology on man. Professor Tribe observes: "To the extent it succeeds in exposing the roots not only of the much discussed ecological crisis but also of other human perturbations flowing in part or in whole from ill-conceived patterns of technological development, technology assessment is more fundamental and more comprehensive than environmental management, and promises deeper understanding of appropriate long-range strategies. Moreover, it is at least possible that defining the natural environment as the primary object of social protection would misallocate human energies and priorities by ignoring vital interests and values that occasionally conflict with fully optimizing environmental quality." [22] This writer agrees that there is occasionally an anti-people tendency in the ecology movement.[23] To the extent that technology assessment puts people in the center of the universe (takes an anthropocentric perspective), it offers a welcome point of view. On the other hand, as with a systems analysis that spins out causes and effects *ad infinitum*, a concept of technology assessment that definitively attempts to record or predict admitted imponderables suffers from a want of resolving power. A society that experiences nightly miscalculations in weather forecasting is entitled to skepticism about the reliability of ever more complex prophetic missions. There is a certain paralysis and a perpetual need for more study that attends the broader themes of systems analysis and technology assessment. A narrower perspective that leads to action is more in keeping with the lawyer's tradition. That is one of the strengths of the National Environmental Policy Act.[24]

§ 1.4 The Legal Context

Environmental law does not live in isolation from other legal specialties any more than it does from other non-legal disciplines. It is concerned with civil liabilities and borrows heavily from tort and property law. Like other bodies of law, it functions within constitutional limits, a few of them of particular significance (such as deciding when a restriction on the use of private property is a compensable taking).[1] It can involve the interpretation of contracts,[2] enforcement of the criminal law, an understanding of trust responsibilities,[3]

---

22. Legal Frameworks for the Assessment and Control of Technology, 9 Minerva 243, 245–46 (1971), quoted in L. L. Jaffe & L. T. Tribe, Environmental Protection 95 (1971).

23. See § 2.17 below (discussing exclusionary zoning).

24. See ch. 7 below.

1. See Soper, The Constitutional Framework of Environmental Law, in Environmental Law Institute, Federal Environmental Law 20 (E. L. Dolgin & T. G. P. Guilbert eds. 1974); § 2.17 below.

2. New Windsor v. Rowan, 3 ELR 20204 (S.D.N.Y.1973); Sierra Club v. Hardin, 325 F.Supp. 99, 1 ELR 20161 (D.C.Alas.1971).

3. § 2.16 below.

the complexities of tax law. It influences industrial conduct and thus raises issues of antitrust law.[4] It deals with the intricacies of legislation; indeed the evolution of the Rivers and Harbors Appropriation Act of 1899 [5] is a classic case study in public law.

Above all, the problem "of the restoration and maintenance of a livable environment is, to a large extent, the problem of the control of administrative agencies by the courts." [6] Environmental cases have contributed significantly to the development of principles of administrative law in three major areas to be discussed in the text: (1) scope of judicial review of administrative decision-making; [7] (2) standing; [8] and (3) sovereign immunity.[9] Many other specialized administrative law principles have been applied and refined in environmental cases, including the doctrines of exhaustion of administrative remedies,[10] primary jurisdiction,[11] and ripeness.[12] Of considerable importance have been the environmental and technology cases assuring citizen access to the agencies and the disclosure of information under the Freedom of Information Act [13] and the Advisory Committee Act.[14] These developments will be discussed here with the understanding that a more complete analysis is presented better in a text on administrative law.

Understandably, the lawyering that produces so many important doctrinal advances in the administrative law field engages other day to day intricacies of the administrative process. Environmental lawyers draft rules, comment on somebody else's draft rules, attend meetings where administrative rules and policies are discussed. Formal proceedings with environmental consequences are legion.

4. American Bar Ass'n, Section of Antitrust Law, Report of the Committee on Antitrust Aspects of Environmental Law (1975).

5. 30 Stat. 1151 (1899); see J. L. Mashaw & R. A. Merrill, Introduction to the American Public Law System: Cases and Materials ch. 1 (1975).

6. Sive, Some Thoughts of an Environmental Lawyer in the Wilderness of Administrative Law, 70 Colum.L.Rev. 612, 615 (1970); see Jaffe, The Administrative Agency and Environmental Control, 20 Buffalo L. Rev. 231 (1970); Anderson, Some Perspectives on Environmental Decision-Making in the Administrative Process, 4 ELR 50123 (1974).

7. See § 1.5 below.

8. See § 1.6 below.

9. See §§ 1.7, 1.8 below.

10. Izaak Walton League v. St. Clair, 497 F.2d 849, 4 ELR 20556 (8th Cir. 1974); see § 1.9 below.

11. See § 1.9 below; cf. Parker v. United States, 309 F.Supp. 593, 1 ELR 20522 (D.C.Colo.1970), aff'd 448 F.2d 793, 1 ELR 20489 (10th Cir. 1971), cert. denied 405 U.S. 989 (1972).

12. Environmental Defense Fund, Inc. v. Hardin, 138 U.S.App.D.C. 391, 398, 428 F.2d 1093, 1100, 1 ELR 20050, 20053 (1970) ("At some point administrative delay amounts to a refusal to act, with sufficient finality and ripeness to permit judicial review"); see § 1.9 below.

13. See § 1.10 below.

14. See § 1.11 below.

The permits, licenses, and approvals which are the grist of air and water pollution control and major land development projects are litigated daily before scores of federal, state and municipal authorities. Many federal agencies at one time or another will entertain adjudicatory proceedings with important environmental aspects: examples are the Environmental Protection Agency (a pesticide revocation proceeding), the Nuclear Regulatory Commission (a construction license hearing for a nuclear reactor), the Federal Power Commission (a relicensing proceeding on a hydroelectric project), the Corps of Engineers (a hearing on a permit to dredge and fill).

The practice of environmental law also involves day to day lobbying of administrative decision-makers. The halls of the Federal Power Commission and the Federal Energy Administration are alive with legal representatives of the energy industries with a watchful eye for the new ruling or potential ruling that might affect a client. In some parts of the country, notably Washington, D. C., industry lawyers will find their counterparts in various representatives of public groups. It is a fact, for example, that staff lawyers for the Natural Resources Defense Council and the Environmental Defense Fund have influenced federal environmental policy, not only in court but before the agencies as well.

Legislative modifications of principles of administrative law contribute to environmental protection. Best known and most important is the National Environmental Policy Act and its progeny at the state and local level.[15] Also noteworthy is the Michigan Environmental Protection Act of 1970 [16] and its progeny. Professor Joseph Sax, principal draftsman of the Michigan Act, has criticized the performance of administrative agencies on environmental matters,[17] and his creation is responsive to that criticism. The Michigan Act limits agency authority by relaxing standing requirements, allowing a wide-ranging judicial review of polluting activity and clarifying the parties' burdens of proof.

§ 1.5 Scope of Judicial Review

The preferred status of environmental concerns is well established. They involve fundamental interests of life and health which "have always had a special claim to judicial protection." [1] To protect these interests from administrative arbitrariness, "it is necessary, but not sufficient, to insist on strict judicial scrutiny of administrative actions. For judicial review alone can correct only the most egre-

---

15. Ch. 7 below.

16. § 2.16 below.

17. Defending the Environment (1971).

1. Environmental Defense Fund, Inc. v. Ruckelshaus, 142 U.S.App.D.C. 74, 87, 439 F.2d 584, 597, 1 ELR 20059, 20064 (1971); accord, Certified Color Mfrs. Ass'n v. Matthews, —— U.S. App.D.C. ——, ——, 543 F.2d 284, 296, 6 ELR 20629, 20637 (1976); Maryland-National Capital Park & Planning Comm'n v. Postal Serv., 159 U.S.App. D.C. 158, 487 F.2d 1029 (1973).

gious abuses. Judicial review must operate to ensure that the administrative process itself will confine and control the exercise of discretion. Courts should require administrative officers to articulate the standards and principles that govern their discretionary decisions in as much detail as possible. Rules and regulations should be freely formulated by administrators, and revised when necessary. Discretionary decisions should more often be supported with findings of fact and reasoned opinions. When administrators provide a framework for principled decision-making, the result will be to diminish the importance of judicial review by enhancing the integrity of the administrative process, and to improve the quality of judicial review in those cases where judicial review is sought." [2]

The Administrative Procedure Act [3] (APA) itself draws several lines of immediate significance: some agency action is "committed to agency discretion by law" and entirely unreviewable in the court; [4] at the other extreme, courts are empowered to set aside agency action in violation of procedures required by law [5] or contrary to statutory command.[6] The courts' power to review legal questions *de novo* is to be contrasted with their more limited authority to review agency factual determinations (under the familiar substantial evidence test [7] for agency actions subject to formal hearing requirements and the arbitrary and capricious test for most other actions [8]). The distinction between the law reviewable *de novo* and the facts reviewable under more limited standards is a treacherous one, and has engaged the attention of a long line of distinguished judges and scholars.[9]

It is sufficient for present purposes to point out that the allocation of functions between agencies and courts on the basis of the fact-law distinction is influenced importantly by the very practical factor of "the comparative qualification of the court and of the agency on the particular question." [10] Judges in environmental cases often resist the suggestion that "expertise" is a curtain automatically drawn at the end of the administrative performance to cut off judi-

2. Environmental Defense Fund, Inc. v. Ruckelshaus, 142 U.S.App.D.C. at 88, 439 F.2d at 595, 1 ELR at 20064–65. Compare Sax, The (Unhappy) Truth About NEPA, 26 Okla.L.Rev. 239, 248 (1973) (describing the paragraph quoted in text as "a dubious example of wishful thinking").

3. 5 U.S.C.A. § 706.

4. Id. § 701(a)(2); Citizens to Preserve Overton Park, Inc. v. Volpe, 401 U.S. 402, 411, 91 S.Ct. 814, 820–21, 28 L.Ed.2d 136, 150 (1971).

5. 5 U.S.C.A. § 706(2)(D).

6. Id. § 706(2)(C).

7. Id. § 706(2)(E).

8. Id. § 706(2)(A).

9. See authorities cited in Sive, Some Thoughts of an Environmental Lawyer in the Wilderness of Administrative Law, 70 Colum.L.Rev. 612, 620 n. 30 (1970); National Labor Relations Bd. v. Marcus Trucking Co., 286 F.2d 583 (2d Cir. 1961) (Friendly, J.).

10. Davis, Administrative Law § 30.07, at 556 (3d ed. 1972).

cial review.[11] The fact-law distinction and its consequences for the scope of review nonetheless continues to bedevil the courts and makes hazardous any firm predictions.[12]

The Supreme Court in Citizens to Preserve Overton Park, Inc. v. Volpe [13] made clear that courts reviewing agency actions affecting environmental values must be aggressive overseers. At issue was the action of the Secretary of Transportation allowing the expenditure of federal funds to build Interstate Highway I–40 through Overton Park, a 342-acre city park located near the center of Memphis, Tennessee. The relevant statutes [14] forbid the Secretary from authorizing the use of federal funds to finance the construction of highways through public parks if a "feasible and prudent" alternative route exists. If no alternative is available, the statutes permit him to approve the construction only if there has been "all possible planning to minimize harm" to the park.

Reaffirming the earlier holding in Abbott Laboratories v. Gardner,[15] the Court in *Overton Park* gave an extremely narrow reading to the APA exception precluding judicial review where "agency action is committed to agency discretion by law." [16] Unreviewable administrative action is said to occur only where there is no "law to apply," [17] which means for practical purposes that the issue is almost non-existent. Turning next to the standard of review, the Court saw the question initially as defining the scope of the Secretary's authority. In this case, the statutory reference to a "feasible" alternative was read to allow construction through the park only if the Secretary finds "that as a matter of sound engineering it would not be feasible to build the highway along any other route." [18] The reference to a "prudent" alternative, contrary to the argument that this invites a wide-ranging discretionary inquiry by the administra-

---

11. Comm. for Nuclear Responsibility, Inc. v. Seaborg, 149 U.S.App.D.C. 380, 385, 463 F.2d 783, 788 (D.C. Cir. 1971) (per curiam), aff'd 404 U.S. 917; Leventhal, Environmental Decisionmaking and the Role of the Courts, 122 U.Pa.L.Rev. 509, 515 (1974).

12. See, e. g., Hanly v. Kleindienst (II), 471 F.2d 823, 2 ELR 20717 (2d Cir. 1972), cert. denied 412 U.S. 908 (1973) (discussing the scope of review of the NEPA threshold question of whether an action is one "significantly affecting the quality of the human environment").

13. 401 U.S. 402, 91 S.Ct. 814, 28 L. Ed.2d 136 (1971); see Pitts v. Camp, 411 U.S. 138, 93 S.Ct. 1241, 36 L.Ed. 2d 106 (1973).

14. Section 4(f) of the Department of Transportation Act of 1966, as amended, 82 Stat. 824, 49 U.S.C.A. § 1653(f); Section 18(a) of the Federal-Aid Highway Act of 1968, 82 Stat. 823, 23 U.S.C.A. § 138; see Gray, Section 4(f) of the Department of Transportation Act, 32 Md.L.Rev. 327 (1973).

15. 387 U.S. 136, 87 S.Ct. 1507, 18 L. Ed.2d 681 (1967).

16. 5 U.S.C.A. § 701(a)(2).

17. 401 U.S. at 411, 91 S.Ct. at 821, 28 L.Ed.2d at 150, quoting S.Rep.No. 752, 79th Cong., 1st Sess. 26 (1945).

18. 401 U.S. at 412, 91 S.Ct. at 821, 28 L.Ed.2d at 150.

tor, was read to allow approval of parkland construction only if "alternative routes present unique problems." [19] The Court thus drew strict legal lines allowing parkland to be used as a highway only if another route was physically out of the question or uniquely unacceptable on other grounds (economics, safety, and so on). The important point is that the judicial definition of the administrator's powers imposes a significant measure of substantive control over the result because judgments transgressing these boundaries are unlawful,[20] and ought to be reviewable *de novo* in the courts.

The determination that the statute should be read as meaning that the agency has acted within the limits of its assigned authority is the beginning not the end of the inquiry. Most challenges to administrative decisions in the environmental arena involve agency action admittedly within the legislative charter but alleged nonetheless to be unfair, incomplete or otherwise unjustified. Judicial second-guessing of the facts under these circumstances, the APA advises, typically requires a finding that the actual choice by the administrator was "arbitrary, capricious, an abuse of discretion, or otherwise not in accordance with law." [21] *Overton Park* goes further to make clear that, in reviewing actions within the scope of an administrator's discretion, the court "must consider whether the decision was based on a consideration of the relevant factors and whether there has been a clear error of judgment." [22] In a much quoted phrase, we are told that while the inquiry into the facts is to be "searching and careful, the ultimate standard of review is a narrow one. The Court is not empowered to substitute its judgment for that of the agency." [23] Elsewhere *Overton Park* emphasizes that the reviewing court must engage in a "substantial inquiry" and "a thorough, probing, in-depth review." [24]

The "substantial inquiry" or hard look doctrine of *Overton Park* is a tenet of modern administrative law and a catechism of environmental law. It means that courts will accept nothing less than fairly conceived, fully explained, and rationally based administrative discretionary judgments. Judge Harold Leventhal, a respected analyst of the administrative process, says the courts must take a hard look to assure that agencies (1) abide by fair and reasonable procedures, (2) give good faith consideration to matters assigned to them, and (3)

---

19. 401 U.S. at 414, 91 S.Ct. at 822, 28 L.Ed.2d at 151.

20. See Note, Citizens to Preserve Overton Park, Inc. v. Volpe: Environmental Law and the Scope of Judicial Review, 24 Stan.L.Rev. 1117 (1972).

21. 5 U.S.C.A. § 706(2)(A).

22. 401 U.S. at 417, 91 S.Ct. at 823–24, 28 L.Ed.2d at 153, citing L. Jaffe, Judicial Control of Administrative Action 182 (1965).

23. 401 U.S. at 416, 91 S.Ct. at 824, 28 L.Ed.2d at 153.

24. 401 U.S. at 416, 91 S.Ct. at 823, 28 L.Ed.2d at 153.

produce results that are defensible in reason.[25] The metamorphosis in judicial attitude from the days of the cursory glance to the hard look has been gradual, and indeed sometimes lines of authority appear to be mutually oblivious.[26] In the environmental field, however, there is a clear benchmark in the pre-*Overton Park* decision of the Second Circuit in Scenic Hudson Preservation Conference v. FPC (I),[27] involving Consolidated Edison's efforts to construct a pumped storage hydroelectric project in an area of unique beauty on the Hudson River. The issues in *Scenic Hudson* were squarely within the scope of the administrator's authority to determine whether the prospective project would be "best adapted to a comprehensive plan for improving or developing a waterway" for various uses, "including recreational purposes."[28] The court held the Commission failed to inquire into and consider all relevant facts and alternatives (including the use of gas turbines and inter-connections)[29] and measures to minimize adverse effects (including the burying of transmission lines and the installation of devices to protect fish life).[30] The hard look turned up an unduly limited perspective and a procedural smugness where the staff and the Commission sat by passively, refusing to develop on the record important facts on alternatives and mitigation clearly within their competence to produce.

In recent years, courts (often under the explicit guise of the hard look doctrine) have insisted upon procedural fairness from administrators: sometimes a right to a hearing, possibly with opportunity for cross-examination;[31] disqualification of biased decision-makers;[32]

25. Leventhal, supra note 11, at 511. This article builds on several of Judge Leventhal's opinions in the field of administrative law, including the well known Greater Boston Television Corp. v. Federal Communications Comm'n, 143 U.S.App.D.C. 383, 444 F.2d 841 (1970), cert. denied 401 U.S. 950 (1972).

26. Compare Citizens to Preserve Overton Park, Inc. v. Volpe, 401 U.S. 402, 91 S.Ct. 814, 28 L.Ed.2d 136 (1971) with National Labor Relations Bd. v. Hearst Publications, Inc., 322 U.S. 111, 64 S.Ct. 851, 88 L.Ed. 1170 (1944) (upholding NLRB interpretation of "employees" within the meaning of the National Labor Relations Act; the approach has been reaffirmed many times but contrasts strikingly with that of *Overton Park*).

27. 354 F.2d 608, 1 ELR 20292 (2d Cir. 1965), cert. denied 384 U.S. 941 (1966), aff'd after remand 453 F.2d 463, 1 ELR 20496 (2d Cir. 1971) (explicitly rejecting a more stringent standard of review for environmental cases), cert. denied 407 U.S. 926 (1972) (Douglas, J., dissenting); see A. Talbot, Power Along the Hudson: The Storm King Case and the Birth of Environmentalism (1972); Note, Of Birds, Bees, and the FPC, 77 Yale L.J. 117 (1967).

28. Section 10(a) of the Federal Power Act, 16 U.S.C.A. § 803(a).

29. 354 F.2d at 618, 621, 1 ELR at 20296, 20297–98.

30. 354 F.2d at 623, 1 ELR at 20298.

31. International Harvester Co. v. Ruckelshaus, 155 U.S.App.D.C. 411, 426–27, 478 F.2d 615, 630–31, 3 ELR 20133, 20137–38 (1973); Appalachian Power Co. v. Environmental Protection Agency, 477 F.2d 495, 503, 3 ELR 20310, 20313 (4th Cir. 1973).

32. See Greene County Planning Bd. v. Federal Power Comm'n (I), 455 F.2d 412, 2 ELR 20017 (2d Cir. 1972),

Sec. 1.5   SCOPE OF JUDICIAL REVIEW   21

production of the entire record (expert views and opinions, technological data, upon which the administrator acted);[33] provision of an opportunity to supplement the record, through pre-trial discovery devices or direct testimony from officials who participated in the decision.[34] A burden may be imposed upon the agency to justify the reliability of its methodology,[35] to produce all supporting documentation necessary to an understanding of what the agency did,[36] to explain fully the benefits expected from the administrative action,[37] and to come forward with relevant evidence on alternatives[38] (including the alternative of taking no action). None of these procedural protections is more important than the gradual shifting of the burden to the agency staff to address fully all issues raised, come forward with relevant documentation from its files, and produce witnesses with knowledge on pertinent subjects.

Courts are equally diligent to require agencies to consider fairly matters assigned to them and to rationalize their actions. The administrator cannot base his decision on factors deemed irrelevant under the legislation, as where economics are heeded in the setting of standards supposedly controlled by health and safety considerations alone,[39] or where politics influences the decision that "there is no feasible and prudent alternative" to the sacrifice of parkland to a highway.[40] Linking an administrative decision to political pressures

cert. denied 409 U.S. 849; cf. Environmental Defense Fund, Inc. v. Corps of Engineers (Tennessee-Tombigbee), 492 F.2d 1123, 1129, 4 ELR 20329, 20331 (5th Cir. 1974); Environmental Defense Fund, Inc. v. Corps of Engineers (Gillham Dam), 470 F.2d 289, 295, 2 ELR 20740, 20742 (8th Cir. 1974).

33. Appalachian Power Co. v. Environmental Protection Agency, 477 F.2d 495, 507–08, 3 ELR 20310, 20315 (4th Cir. 1973).

34. Citizens to Preserve Overton Park, Inc. v. Volpe, 401 U.S. 402, 91 S.Ct. 814, 28 L.Ed.2d 136 (1972). A twenty-five day trial ensued following remand in *Overton Park*. See id., 335 F.Supp. 873, 2 ELR 20061 (W.D.Tenn.1972), rev'd 494 F.2d 1212, 4 ELR 20327 (6th Cir. 1974). This thorough inquiry has been described aptly as an example of "the hard look doctrine in spades." Leventhal, supra note 11, at 514.

35. Int'l Harvester Co. v. Ruckelshaus, 155 U.S.App.D.C. 411, 438, 478 F.2d 615, 642, 3 ELR 20133, 20144–45 (1973).

36. Texas v. Environmental Protection Agency, 499 F.2d 289, 307–08 & nn. 30–31, 4 ELR 20744, 20752 & nn. 30–31 (5th Cir. 1974); see Portland Cement Ass'n v. Ruckelshaus (I), 158 U.S.App.D.C. 308, 325, 486 F.2d 375, 392, 3 ELR 20642, 20650–51 (1973), cert. denied 417 U.S. 921 (1974).

37. Environmental Defense Fund, Inc. v. Environmental Protection Agency, 150 U.S.App.D.C. 348, 359, 465 F.2d 528, 539, 2 ELR 20228, 20234 (1972).

38. Scenic Hudson Preservation Conference v. Federal Power Comm'n (I), 354 F.2d 608, 1 ELR 20292 (2d Cir. 1965), cert. denied 384 U.S. 941 (1966). See also Udall v. Federal Power Comm'n, 387 U.S. 428, 87 S.Ct. 1712, 18 L.Ed.2d 869 (1967).

39. Waterford v. Water Pollution Control Bd., 5 N.Y.2d 171, 182 N.Y.S.2d 789, 156 N.E.2d 427 (1959).

40. D. C. Federation of Civic Associations v. Volpe, 148 U.S.App.D.C. 207, 459 F.2d 1231, 1 ELR 20572 (1971), cert. denied 405 U.S. 1030 (1972) (involving the proposed Three Sisters Bridge across the Potomac River).

uncalled for by the statute would appear to be a potentially fertile ground for invalidating administrative action.

The standard of articulation required of the agencies is an exacting premise of the hard look doctrine. The APA itself requires a "concise general statement" of the "basis and purpose" of agency rules.[41] But the courts have not hesitated to go further, the best known example being Kennecott v. EPA,[42] which remanded a challenge to the secondary ambient air quality standard for sulfur oxides (60 micrograms per cubic meter—annual arithmetic mean) to the administrator "to supply an implementing statement that will enlighten the court as to the basis on which he reached the 60 standard from the material in the Criteria."[43] (The so-called "Kennecott statements" soon became a regular feature of EPA decision-making.)

An agency may be required to respond to responsible criticism of its methodology and to disclose information that becomes available even after the issuance of a rule or the taking of action.[44] A unilateral remand-for-explanation may not suffice: "when the question is one which the Agency may never have fully confronted and which may deserve further input both from Agency and outside sources, only a remand for further hearings and an extended record seems adequate."[45] The agency burden has been likened to a private party's "burden of refutation or explanation,"[46] which expresses nicely the continuing obligation of the bureaucracy to justify and explain its actions. While the standard of review is said to be a static and a narrow one, the standard of rationalization is ever more demanding; the connection between better explanations and better results is obvious. Judicial review thus is said to rest upon the premise that courts and agencies "together constitute a partnership in furtherance of the public interest, and are 'collaborative instrumentalities of justice.'"[47]

41. 5 U.S.C.A. § 553(c).

42. 149 U.S.App.D.C. 231, 462 F.2d 846, 2 ELR 20116 (1972).

43. 149 U.S.App.D.C. at 235, 462 F.2d at 850, 2 ELR at 20119; see Natural Resources Defense Council v. Environmental Protection Agency, 478 F.2d 875, 881–82, 3 ELR 20375, 20377 (1st Cir. 1973).

44. Portland Cement Ass'n v. Ruckelshaus (I), 158 U.S.App.D.C. 308, 325–26, 486 F.2d 375, 392–93, 3 ELR 20642, 20650–52 (1973), cert. denied 417 U.S. 921 (1974).

45. South Terminal Corp. v. Environmental Protection Agency, 504 F.2d 646, 665, 4 ELR 20768, 20774 (1st Cir. 1974).

46. Portland Cement Ass'n v. Ruckelshaus (I), 158 U.S.App.D.C. 308, 326, 486 F.2d 375, 393, 3 ELR 20642, 20651 (1973), cert. denied 417 U.S. 921 (1974); see United States v. Allegheny-Ludlum Steel Corp., 406 U.S. 742, 750, 92 S.Ct. 1941, 1946, 32 L.Ed.2d 453, 460 (1972) (stating that the "soundness of the reasoning" of the agency is inquired into to ascertain only that the conclusions are "rationally supported").

47. Greater Boston Television Corp. v. Federal Communications Comm'n, 143 U.S.App.D.C. 383, 393–94, 444 F.2d 841, 851–52 (1970), cert. denied 406 U.S. 950 (1972).

This discussion of judicial review has purposely avoided consideration of the National Environmental Policy Act (NEPA), which, if anything, has elevated the hard look to a penetrating autopsy of agency actions affecting the environment.[48] It is important to recognize that the standards of procedural fairness and rational results raised to new heights by NEPA were born and still flourish elsewhere. The hard look at agency actions impacting the environment proceeds independently of NEPA.[49]

§ 1.6 Standing

In the space of a few years the question of standing in environmental litigation has shifted from a significant doctrinal barrier to a nettlesome technicality. Standing still may lead to headaches but not the migraines and skull fractures of a few short years ago.

A discussion of the modern law of standing can begin with the Supreme Court's 1970 decision in Association of Data Processing Service Organizations v. Camp,[1] which affirmed a two-pronged test: (1) "injury in fact, economic or otherwise," and (2) "whether the interest sought to be protected by this complainant is arguably within the zone of interests to be protected or regulated by the statute or constitutional guarantee in question."[2] A case can be made that the second part of the test has atrophied substantially,[3] so that all that remains is an inquiry into whether in fact there has been injury.

The great majority of standing cases in recent years explore the farther reaches of the types of hurts that must be shown to satisfy the injury-in-fact requirements. An unsuccessful effort to abolish the problem for all organizations with a reputation for environmental concern was the Sierra Club's suit challenging various administrative actions approving the location of a $35 million ski complex in the Mineral King Valley of the Sierra Nevada Mountains of California, adjacent to Sequoia National Park. In what was intended to be a test case on the subject of standing, the Sierra Club alleged simply:

> Membership of the club is approximately 78,000 nationally, with approximately 27,000 members residing in the San Francisco Bay area. For many years the Sierra Club by its activities and conduct has exhibited a special interest in the conservation and the sound maintenance of the national parks, game refuges, and

---

48. See §§ 7.3, 7.4 below.

49. See, e. g., § 2.16 below (discussing the public trust doctrine).

1. 397 U.S. 150, 90 S.Ct. 827, 25 L.Ed. 2d 185 (1970).

2. 397 U.S. at 154, 90 S.Ct. at 830, 25 L.Ed.2d at 188. The injury in fact test has its origins in the case and controversy requirements of the U.S. Const., art. III.

3. See 3 K. C. Davis, Administrative Law Treatise §§ 22.00–.03 (1970 Supp.); Davis, The Liberalized Law of Standing, 37 U.Chi.L.Rev. 450 (1970); Stewart, The Reformation of American Administrative Law, 88 Harv.L.Rev. 1667, 1723–47 (1975).

forests of the country, regularly serving as a responsible representative of persons similarly interested. One of the principal purposes of the Sierra Club is to protect and conserve the natural resources of the Sierra Nevada Mountains. Its interests would be vitally affected by the acts hereinafter described and would be aggrieved [sic] by those acts of the defendants . . . .

The language used in the Mineral King complaint was borrowed from the 1965 decision in Scenic Hudson Preservation Conference v. FPC (I),[4] which upheld the standing to sue under the judicial review provisions of the Federal Power Act of an unincorporated association consisting of a number of conservationist organizations. That court would accord standing to those who "by their activities and conduct" have exhibited "a special interest" in "the aesthetic, conservational, and recreational aspects of power development."[5] Affirmation of this simple equation of caring equals standing was not to be quickly realized.

The Supreme Court ruled in Mineral King that the complaint was defective because the Sierra Club "failed to allege that it or its members would be affected in any of their activities or pastimes by the . . . development. Nowhere in the pleadings or affidavits did the Club state that its members use Mineral King for any purpose, much less that they use it in any way that would be significantly affected by the proposed actions of the respondents."[6] A "special interest" in a problem or a value preference that a dispute be resolved a certain way was not sufficient to support standing. An actual "use" adversely affected was required.

The immediate consequence of the *Sierra Club* decision in most cases was to require the addition of individuals as plaintiffs, and the inclusion of allegations that they had used the affected resources and were injured in fact by defendants' conduct. Otherwise, litigation

---

4. 354 F.2d 608, 1 ELR 20292 (2d Cir. 1965), cert. denied 384 U.S. 941 (1966).

5. 354 F.2d at 615, 1 ELR at 20293, citing Dep't of Game v. Federal Power Comm'n, 207 F.2d 391 (9th Cir. 1953), cert. denied 347 U.S. 936 (1954).

6. Sierra Club v. Morton, 405 U.S. 727, 735, 92 S.Ct. 1361, 1366, 31 L.Ed. 2d 636, 643 (1972). Standing is a favored topic among commentators. See, e. g., Albert, Standing to Challenge Administrative Action: An Inadequate Surrogate for Claim for Relief, 83 Yale L.J. 425 (1974); Baude, Sierra Club v. Morton: Standing Trees In a Thicket of Justiciability, 48 Ind.L. J. 197 (1973); Berger, Standing to Sue in Public Actions: Is It a Constitutional Requirement?, 78 Yale L.J. 816 (1969); Jaffe, The Citizen as Litigant in Public Actions: The Non-Hohfeldian or Ideological Plaintiff, 116 U. Pa.L.Rev. 1033 (1968); Sax, Standing to Sue: A Critical Review of the Mineral King Decision, 13 Nat.Res.J. 76 (1973); Scott, Standing in the Supreme Court: A Functional Analysis, 86 Harv.L.Rev. 645 (1973). A well known but not particularly influential essay is that of Christopher D. Stone, Should Trees Have Standing? Toward Legal Rights for Natural Objects (1974) (reprint of an article originally appearing in 45 So.Calif.L.Rev. 450 (1972)).

proceeded as before. (One national conservation group with a successful litigation record, the Natural Resources Defense Council, was caught short by the *Sierra Club* decision because it did not have a regular membership; the response: NRDC successfully solicited members, explaining that a nationwide constituency was important to ensure its standing.) The Sierra Club was soon in business again in the Mineral King case by simply adding a few allegations that certain members used, hiked in, and enjoyed the wilderness areas threatened by the ski development, and that their pleasures would be compromised by the proposed complex.[7] Other examples of relatively easy satisfaction of the injury-in-fact test are lawsuits challenging a pesticide spray program [8] and air pollution from a fossil fuel power plant [9] where potential injury could be demonstrated; and developments affecting a beach,[10] water resource,[11] or urban environment [12] in a way demonstrably compromising the complaining parties' current use and enjoyment.

In one respect, Sierra Club v. Morton was a healthy development: the inclusion of actual users as plaintiffs might add a perspective and a point of view that deserves a voice. Litigation where users are parties might yield subtle differences in tactics from the lawsuit that is solely the inspiration and responsibility of a professional environmental group based in Washington, D. C.; the Environmental Defense Fund might have something to learn from the citizen user. But, admitting that, it is quite another thing to say that EDF and its members are not sufficiently interested to sue without joining a user, or that they can only sue by joining a local front man; or worse, that no one can sue in resource disputes where "users" cannot be found.[13]

One fortuitous technique for extending standing to apparent non-users is to premise an injury-in-fact on a denial of access to information required to be produced by law, notably the National Environmental Policy Act or the Freedom of Information Act. Scientists'

7. Sierra Club v. Morton, 348 F.Supp. 219, 2 ELR 20576 (1972).

8. Environmental Defense Fund, Inc. v. Environmental Protection Agency, 150 U.S.App.D.C. 348, 465 F.2d 528, 2 ELR 20228 (1972).

9. Citizens for Clean Air, Inc. v. Corps of Engineers, 349 F.Supp. 969, 2 ELR 20650 (S.D.N.Y.1972).

10. E. g., Rucker v. Willis, 484 F.2d 158, 3 ELR 20912 (4th Cir. 1973).

11. E. g., Sierra Club v. Froehlke (Wallisville-Trinity River), 359 F.Supp. 1289, 3 ELR 20248 (S.D.Tex.1973),

rev'd 499 F.2d 982, 4 ELR 20731 (5th Cir. 1974).

12. E. g., Hanly v. Mitchell (I), 460 F.2d 640, 2 ELR 20216 (2d Cir. 1972), cert. denied 409 U.S. 990.

13. Sax, supra note 6, at 85; see Conservation Council of North Carolina v. Costanzo (I), 505 F.2d 498, 502, 5 ELR 20028, 20029 (4th Cir. 1974) (per curiam) (remanding to allow plaintiffs an opportunity to demonstrate "a prior non-permissive use" of certain privately held lands). Compare the discussion of "users" in § 1.1 above.

Institute for Public Information v. AEC [14] suggests that organizational harm to a group in the business of informing the public about a project in a NEPA case suffices to sustain standing,[15] although the decision rests more narrowly on the ground that organizational members (like anybody else in the country) could be injured in fact by the plutonium releases from future breeder reactors. An injury to the right to know and to communicate that knowledge to others obviates the necessity for addressing the aesthetic, economic, or conservational interests of the traditional user.

For a time, it appeared that the injury equals user test was sufficiently loose to pose no serious obstacle to environmental litigants. A few post-Sierra Club v. Morton cases found no standing despite clear allegations of injury,[16] a few others found no injury had been alleged.[17] But, for the most part, the courts were content to accept general allegations of injury from parties obviously interested in the outcome.[18] Typical of this attitude is the decision in Sierra Club v. Mason,[19] involving a challenge to the Corps of Engineers' dredging of New Haven Harbor. Plaintiffs alleged generally that they lived and

---

14. 156 U.S.App.D.C. 395, 481 F.2d 1079, 3 ELR 20525 (1973).

15. 156 U.S.App.D.C. at 402–03 n. 29, 481 F.2d at 1086–87 n. 29, 3 ELR at 20528–29 n. 29; Davis v. Coleman, 521 F.2d 661, 671, 5 ELR 20633, 20635 (9th Cir. 1975); Natural Resources Defense Council, Inc. v. Security & Exch. Comm'n, 389 F.Supp. 689, 696–98, 5 ELR 20074, 20076–77 (D.C.D.C. 1974).

16. E. g., Higginbotham v. Barrett, 473 F.2d 745, 3 ELR 20151 (5th Cir. 1973); People for Environmental Progress v. Leisz, 373 F.Supp. 589, 4 ELR 20706 (C.D.Cal.1974).

17. E. g., Natural Resources Defense Council, Inc. v. Environmental Protection Agency, 507 F.2d 905, 5 ELR 20032 (9th Cir. 1974); Natural Resources Defense Council, Inc. v. Environmental Protection Agency, 481 F.2d 116, 3 ELR 20579 (10th Cir. 1973); Johnson v. Morton, 456 F.2d 68, 2 ELR 20076 (5th Cir. 1972); Massachusetts Air Pollution & Noise Abatement Comm. v. Brinegar, —— F.Supp. ——, 6 ELR 20214 (D.C.Mass. 1975); Delaware River Port Authority v. Tiemann, 403 F.Supp. 1117 (D.C. N.J.1975). Compare Citizens for Food & Progress, Inc. v. Musgrove, 397 F. Supp. 397, 399, 5 ELR 20676, 20678 (N.D.Ga.1975) (no injury) with Beaucatcher Mtn. Defense Ass'n v. Coleman, —— F.Supp. ——, ——, 6 ELR 20198 (W.D.N.C.1975) (injury).

18. E. g., Harlem Valley Transp. Ass'n v. Stafford, 360 F.Supp. 1057, 3 ELR 20639 (S.D.N.Y.1973) (stressing the litigation record of the Natural Resources Defense Council); Davis v. Coleman, 521 F.2d 661, 671, 5 ELR 20633, 20635 (9th Cir. 1975) ("The procedural injury implicit in agency failure to prepare an EIS—the creation of a risk that serious environmental impacts will be overlooked—is itself a sufficient 'injury in fact' to support standing, provided this injury is alleged by a plaintiff having a sufficient geographical nexus to the site of the challenged project that he may be expected to suffer whatever environmental consequences the project may have"); Fort Story—Its Future? v. Schlesinger, 7 ERC 1141 (E.D.Va.1974) ("substantially every citizen living in a reasonable proximity to the anticipated project may maintain an action").

19. 351 F.Supp. 419, 2 ELR 20694 (D. C.Conn.1972), injunction dissolved, 365 F.Supp. 47, 4 ELR 20186 (D.C. Conn.1973); see Montgomery Environmental Coalition v. Fri, 366 F. Supp. 261, 4 ELR 20182 (D.C.D.C. 1973).

worked in the New Haven area and were concerned about adverse effects of the project; precise "uses" and threatened injuries to those "uses" were not spelled out. The court found such allegations unnecessary:

> To oblige him [the plaintiff] to allege more than a generalized, non-frivolous threat to the environment in which he lives, works or plays might, in some cases, require him to state what has not yet been determined but what may be detailed in the environmental impact statement he wants prepared.[20]

The relaxation of the injury-in-fact requirements was encouraged by the 1973 Supreme Court decision in United States v. SCRAP(I).[21] Plaintiffs were an incorporated group of law students intent on challenging under NEPA an Interstate Commerce Commission order approving a 2.5% surcharge on freight shipments on the ground that the surcharge perpetuated a discrimination between recycled and virgin materials and thus encouraged excessive consumption of natural resources. A complaint, amended in light of Sierra Club v. Morton, alleged that SCRAP's

> members use the forests, streams, mountains and other resources in the Washington area for camping, hiking, fishing and sightseeing, and . . . this use is disturbed by the adverse environmental impact caused by nonuse of recyclable goods.

Mr. Justice Stewart, joined by three other Justices, held the pleading sufficient, noting (not seriously, it seemed), "Of course, pleadings must be something more than an ingenious academic exercise in the conceivable."[22] *SCRAP* quite clearly is a case where the alleged adverse effects are nationwide and where plaintiffs were in no better position than anybody else to demonstrate injury. It is difficult to conceive how a member of SCRAP would have been able to prove that his hiking pleasures were diminished by the challenged action by as much as the addition of a single beer can to the landscape.

The suggestion that the Supreme Court was expanding its actual user concept to include all protected persons genuinely concerned received a rude setback in the 5–4 decision in Warth v. Seldin.[23] The Court denied standing to various groups and non-resident individuals challenging certain Penfield, New York zoning practices which allegedly excluded persons of low and moderate income. The majority opinion, authored by Mr. Justice Powell, held "that a plaintiff who seeks to challenge exclusionary zoning practices must allege specific, concrete facts demonstrating that the challenged practices harm *him*,

---

20. 351 F.Supp. at 424, 2 ELR at 20695.

21. 412 U.S. 669, 93 S.Ct. 2405, 37 L.Ed.2d 254 (1973).

22. 412 U.S. at 689, 93 S.Ct. at 2416, 37 L.Ed.2d at 270.

23. 422 U.S. 490, 95 S.Ct. 2197, 45 L.Ed.2d 343 (1975). Compare § 2.17 below (discussing exclusionary zoning).

and that he personally would benefit in a tangible way from the courts' intervention." [24] Found insufficient were claims by non-resident minority individuals that the town's zoning policies barred them from securing housing in Penfield; by taxpayers of nearby Rochester that they were paying higher taxes to support public housing forced upon them by the exclusionary practices of Penfield; by a group with members resident in Penfield claiming they were deprived of the benefits of living in a racially and ethnically integrated community; and by a home building association claiming lost profits for its members because of an inability to construct low and moderate income housing in Penfield. While Warth v. Seldin can be explained away as an instance of insufficient pleading or of disqualification under the zone of interest test,[25] it reaffirms (albeit by a sharply divided court) that the standing doctrine requires the party plaintiff to show a concrete injury in fact to personal interests by reason of the conduct challenged. Warth v. Seldin encourages preliminary jousting [26] over an issue that was deservedly and unmistakably in retreat.

A perceptive essay by Professor Joseph Sax demolishes the notion that persons "injured in fact" by activities affecting natural resources are confined to actual users.[27] Fortunately, the concept of a "user" is an elastic one which can be stretched to protect against injuries to environmental values recently recognized.[28] In Sierra Club v. Morton,[29] Mr. Justice Blackmun noted that Mr. Justice Douglas' dissenting opinion made "only one addition to the customary criteria (the existence of a genuine dispute; the assurance of adversariness; and a conviction that the party whose standing is challenged will adequately represent the interests he asserts), that is, that the litigant be one who speaks knowingly for the environmental values he asserts." Senator Philip Hart, Chairman of the Senate Subcommittee on the Environment, in 1973 introduced an environmental citizen suit bill that would have granted standing to "any person or persons who are adversely affected or aggrieved by the action or activity which is the subject of the suit and who speak knowingly for the environmental values asserted in such suit." [30]

---

24. 422 U.S. at 508, 95 S.Ct. at 2210, 45 L.Ed.2d at 358. (emphasis in original) (footnote omitted).

25. Notes 32–35, infra.

26. It is easy enough to challenge standing allegations and launch a probe aimed at disproving them. E. g., Conservation Council of North Carolina v. Costanzo (II), 398 F.Supp. 653, 657, 5 ELR 20666, 20668 (E.D. N.C.1975), aff'd 528 F.2d 250, 6 ELR 20116 (4th Cir.) Discovery contests over standing are discouraging to litigators anxious to reach the merits.

27. Sax, supra note 6, at 82–85. The same could be said for the view that the only persons "injured in fact" by exclusionary zoning practices are property holders within a community denied an opportunity to build low-cost housing.

28. See C. Stone, supra note 6; § 1.1 above (discussing "users").

29. 405 U.S. at 759, 92 S.Ct. at 1377, 31 L.Ed.2d at 656 (dissenting).

30. S. 1104, 93d Cong., 1st Sess. (1973).

Present prospects for generic legislation expanding the concept of standing generally are virtually nil. But the Congress at the same time enacts a wide range of laws protecting environmental values; these laws presuppose injury to the citizens on whose behalf they are enacted.[31] If a suit otherwise reflects the usual attributions of adversariness, the inquiry into standing seems destined to begin and end with the question of whether the plaintiff truly cares, which is not too far different from saying he must speak knowingly for the environmental values asserted. That is what is just below the surface of an "injury in fact."

There remains only to consider the destiny of the second part of *Data Processing's* standing test: "whether the interest sought to be protected by the complainant is arguably within the zone of interests to be protected or regulated by the statute or constitutional guarantee in question." Professor Davis interprets this to mean: "*A person whose legitimate interest is injured in fact should have standing unless congressional intent is discernible that the interest he asserts is not to be protected.*"[32] In environmental cases, the zone of interests requirement has been read to allow a suit by small farmers to enjoin a Bureau of Reclamation Project for non-compliance with the single owner acreage limit requirements (restricting the holdings of project beneficiaries to 160 acres)[33] but preclude NEPA actions by developers[34] and competitors[35] motivated by economic not environmental concerns.

In recent years, Congress has expanded the zone of environmental interests protected by statute. That legislation can be read also as expanding the interests of citizens which should be protected against injury. The combination should allow a suit by a plaintiff claiming "no status other than that of an interested citizen for whose

---

31. Citizen suit statutes have been read as dispensing with the need for "injury in fact" standing allegations. § 1.13 below.

32. K. C. Davis, supra note 3, at § 22.00–5, at 726; see Colligan v. Activities Club of New York, Ltd., 442 F.2d 686 (2d Cir. 1971), cert. denied 404 U.S. 1004.

33. Bowker v. Morton, 4 ELR 20255 (N.D.Cal.1973).

34. Zlotnick v. Redev. Land Agency, 2 ELR 20235 (D.C.D.C.1972), aff'd 161 U.S.App.D.C. 238, 494 F.2d 1157 (1974).

35. Gifford-Hill & Co. v. Federal Trade Comm'n, 173 U.S.App.D.C. 135, 138, 523 F.2d 730, 733, 6 ELR 20019, 20020 (1975) (per curiam); Clinton Community Hospital Corp. v. Southern Maryland Medical Center, 374 F.Supp. 450, 4 ELR 20670 (D.C.Md.1974), aff'd per curiam 510 F.2d 1037, 5 ELR 20180 (4th Cir. 1975); Port of Astoria v. Hodel, 5 ELR 20657 (D.C.Or.1975); cf. Rhode Island Comm. on Energy v. General Serv. Admin., 397 F.Supp. 41, 5 ELR 20685 (D.R.I.1975) (abutting landowners who are not unsuccessful bidders not within zone of interests protected by the Federal Property and Administrative Services Act of 1949). But see National Helium Corp. v. Morton, 455 F.2d 650, 1 ELR 20578, (10th Cir. 1971), cert. denied 416 U.S. 993 (1974); Crosley Bldg. Corp. v. Sampson, —— F.Supp. ——, 5 ELR 20711 (D.C.D.C.1975); Duke City Lumber Co. v. Butz, 382 F.Supp. 362, 5 ELR 20080 (D.C.D.C. 1974); Chemical Leaman Tank Lines v. United States, 376 F.Supp. 508 (D.C.Del.1973).

benefit the Congress has enacted protective legislation." The plaintiff "would allege that the injury to him is a reduction in the natural heritage of resources that Congress seeks to protect for a variety of reasons, only one of which is immediate physical use and occupation —a national natural resource bank account of which he, along with every other citizen, is a legitimate account holder." [36]

§ 1.7 Sovereign Immunity: Generally

The antiquated doctrine of sovereign immunity, which has befuddled courts and commentators for several centuries, is not likely to be resolved in this text on environmental law.[1] Because the doctrine makes frequent appearances in environmental cases, it, nonetheless, deserves mention here.

Interpreting the well known decision in Larson v. Domestic Foreign Commerce Corp.,[2] the Supreme Court in Dugan v. Rank[3] invoked sovereign immunity to bar a suit by water rights claimants along the San Joaquin River, below Friant Dam, California, against several parties, including officials of the United States Bureau of Reclamation. The action sought and won in the court below a decree enjoining federal authorities from impounding and diverting water at the dam to the detriment of the full natural flow of the river. Compliance was impossible without forcing the abandonment of parts of the Central Valley Reclamation Project, which had been authorized and funded by the Congress. Reasoning that the decree would interfere with " 'public administration' " and " 'expend itself on the public treasury,' "[4] the Supreme Court invoked sovereign immunity to bar the suit against the United States or its officers.

Dugan v. Rank records two exceptions to the doctrine of sovereign immunity: " '(1) action by officers beyond their statutory powers, and (2) even though within the scope of their authority, the powers themselves or the manner in which they are exercised are constitutionally void.' "[5] The claim by the water users was said not to be within the exceptions because the disappearance of their water rights was a taking authorized by the Congress; the only remedy available was an action for damages "rather than a stoppage of the government project."

---

36. Sax, supra note 6, at 84 (footnote omitted).

1. See 3 K. C. Davis, Administrative Law Treaties, ch. 27 (Supp.1970); Jacobs, The Eleventh Amendment and Sovereign Immunity (1972).

2. 337 U.S. 682, 69 S.Ct. 1457, 93 L.Ed. 1628 (1949).

3. 372 U.S. 609, 83 S.Ct. 999, 10 L.Ed. 2d 15 (1963).

4. 372 U.S. at 621, 83 S.Ct. at 1006, 10 L.Ed.2d at 23, quoting Land v. Dollar, 330 U.S. 731, 738, 67 S.Ct. 1009, 1012, 91 L.Ed. 1209, 1216 (1947).

5. 372 U.S. at 621–22, 83 S.Ct. at 1007, 10 L.Ed.2d at 25, quoting Malone v. Bowdoin, 369 U.S. 643, 647, 82 S.Ct. 980, 983, 8 L.Ed.2d 168, 171 (1962).

Sec. 1.7 SOVEREIGN IMMUNITY: GENERALLY

Dugan v. Rank and its progeny, according to an authority in the field of water law, has "come to mean that officials of the United States can seize water from a person dependent upon its use for his livelihood and business, in violation of state law or in violation of federal law."[6] The problem is that confusion in the case law has made it difficult to tell where sovereign immunity ends and violations of law begin.

Nonetheless, sovereign immunity is clearly on the retreat, mostly for the reason that courts are gaining confidence in applying the "violation of law" exception of Dugan v. Rank. Indeed, the practice of environmental law in no small part specializes in stopping the government in its tracks. Many courts give short shrift to *Dugan* and frequently will enjoin construction projects for noncompliance with the National Environmental Policy Act.[7] The Environmental Defense Fund, in particular, has an active water law litigation program, with complaints typically alleging a wide range of legal violations. Dugan v. Rank presents no problem,[8] which means apparently that sovereign immunity shields the United States from suits in equity by water users but not by environmentalists.

Officials exceeding their statutory authority have been stripped of their sovereign immunity defenses in a wide variety of situations: planning of a highway project,[9] non-enforcement of water pollution laws,[10] operation of an airport,[11] pollution of a river by the dumping of dredgings,[12] impoundment of funds destined for water pollution control purposes,[13] the flaring of natural gas in a cavity created by a nuclear detonation.[14] The best rationale for the cases is "that [sec-

6. F. Trelease, Federal-State Relations, in Water Law, National Water Commission Legal Study No. 5, at 215 (1971).

7. E. g., Minnesota Environmental Control Citizens Ass'n v. Atomic Energy Comm'n, 3 ELR 20034 (D.Minn.1972); see § 7.10 below.

8. See, e. g., Environmental Defense Fund, Inc. v. Corps of Engineers, 325 F.Supp. 728, 1 ELR 20130, 20132 (E.D.Ark.1971); Environmental Defense Fund, Inc. v. Froehlke, 473 F.2d 346, 3 ELR 20001 (8th Cir. 1972).

9. Ward v. Ackroyd, 344 F.Supp. 1202, 2 ELR 20405 (D.C.Md.1972) (holding that state officials waive immunity under the Eleventh Amendment by applying for and accepting federal aid highway funds).

10. Kalur v. Resor, 335 F.Supp. 1, 1 ELR 20637 (D.C.D.C.1971).

11. Nestle v. Santa Monica, 6 Cal. 3d 920, 101 Cal.Rptr. 568, 496 P.2d 480 (1972).

12. Sioux Valley Empire Elec. Ass'n, Inc. v. Butz, 367 F.Supp. 686 (D.C.S.D.1973); cf. Morash & Sons, Inc. v. Commonwealth, 363 Mass. 612, 296 N.E.2d 461 (1973) (rejecting sovereign immunity defense in an action to enjoin state from storing rock salt on its property so as to pollute plaintiffs' water supply).

13. New York v. Train, 161 U.S.App.D.C. 114, 494 F.2d 1033, 4 ELR 20188 (1974), aff'd 420 U.S. 35, 95 S.Ct. 839, 43 L.Ed.2d 1 (1975).

14. Crowther v. Seaborg, 312 F.Supp. 1205 (D.C.Colo.1970); see Gage v. Commonwealth Edison Co., 356 F.Supp. 80, 3 ELR 20068 (N.D.Ill.1972).

tion] 10(a) of the Administrative Procedure Act . . . means what it says. A person suffering legal wrong because of agency action within the meaning of a relevant statute, is entitled to judicial review thereof. It would not be a difficult feat of construction to interpret this language as constituting a limited consent to sue." [15]

Many (but by no means all) of the sovereign immunity cases can be explained as instances where the matters involved were "committed to agency discretion" under the APA. This might protect, for example, the conduct of the Bureau of Reclamation attacked in *Dugan*, the decision of the Secretary of the Interior to destroy animals in a national park without a state permit,[16] or the judgment of the Administrator of the FAA to allow the introduction of noisy stretch jets into Washington National Airport.[17] Fitting snugly under the "committed to discretion" rationale are the decisions in McQueary v. Laird,[18] where the Court refused to enjoin the storage of chemical and biological warfare agents at the Rocky Mountain Arsenal in Colorado, finding no enforceable mandates in the Military Storage Act; and Sierra Club v. Hickel,[19] where *Larson* was invoked to justify a refusal to look behind a completed exchange of lands between the Secretary of Interior and two public utilities.

It would be a disservice, however, to suggest that sovereign immunity always can be avoided by the simple expedients of alleging conduct in excess of lawful authority and finding enough "law to apply" to steer clear of the narrow "committed to agency discretion" exception.[20] Despite the strongest repudiation of the doctrine by eminent authorities,[21] it surfaces just often enough to encourage its con-

---

15. Cramton, Nonstatutory Review of Federal Administrative Action: The Need for Statutory Reform of Sovereign Immunity, Subject Matter Jurisdiction and Parties Defendant, 68 Mich.L.Rev. 387, 417–18 n. 143 (1970). See Scanwell Labs, Inc. v. Shaffer, 137 U.S.App.D.C. 371, 424 F.2d 859 (1970). But see Washington v. Udall, 417 F.2d 1310 (9th Cir. 1969). Congress ended the debate with Pub.L.No.94–574, 90 Stat. 2721 (1976), amending 5 U.S.C.A. § 702, expressly waiving sovereign immunity under the APA.

16. New Mexico State Game Comm'n v. Udall, 410 F.2d 1197, 3 ELR 20450 (10th Cir. 1969), cert. denied 396 U.S. 961.

17. Virginians for Dulles v. Volpe, 344 F.Supp. 573, 2 ELR 20360 (E.D. Va.1972), rev'd 541 F.2d 442, 6 ELR 20581 (4th Cir. 1976).

18. 449 F.2d 608, 1 ELR 20607 (10th Cir. 1971).

19. 467 F.2d 1048, 2 ELR 20586 (6th Cir. 1972), cert. denied 411 U.S. 920 (1973); cf. San Juan County v. Russell, 340 F.Supp. 1306 (D.C.Utah 1971), aff'd per curiam 458 F.2d 515 (10th Cir. 1972); see Large, Is Anybody Listening? The Problem of Access in Environmental Litigation, 1972 Wis.L.Rev. 62, 66–71 (1972).

20. See Citizens to Preserve Overton Park, Inc. v. Volpe, 401 U.S. 402, 91 S.Ct. 814, 28 L.Ed.2d 136 (1971); § 1.5 above.

21. E. g., K. C. Davis, supra note 1, §§ 25.18, 27.00; Byse, Proposed Reforms in Federal "Nonstatutory" Judicial Review: Sovereign Immunity, Indispensable Parties, Mandamus, 75 Harv.L.Rev. 1479, 1482–88 (1962); Cramton, Nonstatutory Review of

Sec. 1.7   SOVEREIGN IMMUNITY: GENERALLY

tinued invocation by government lawyers with nothing better to argue. It would be difficult to conceive of a clearer directive than Section 3 of the Colorado River Storage Act, which provides that "no dam or reservoir constructed under the authorization of this Act shall be within any national park or monument." [22] Particularly inappropriate was the invocation of Dugan v. Rank as support for protecting the Commissioner of the Bureau of Reclamation and the Secretary of the Interior from an action challenging official decisions allowing the waters of Lake Powell impounded behind Glen Canyon Dam to encroach into the Rainbow Bridge National Monument.[23]

Several other cases resurrect the sovereign immunity defense where it is said the relief sought would work an "intolerable burden" on government functions.[24] These cases may be correct in result for the reason that the form of equitable relief is always discretionary and the presence of a government as a party may affect the remedy.[25] But it helps analysis not at all to suggest that some gross illegalities are excusable because the "king can do no wrong" and is thus immune from suit. Despite violations of law, a court may refuse to enjoin the construction of a dam nearly completed,[26] but some relief may be appropriate, sovereign immunity to the contrary notwithstanding. Professor Jaffe maintains that the doctrine of sovereign immunity "has never had, and does not have today, much impact on the judicial control of administrative illegality." [27] But this doctrinal plague of sovereign immunity occasionally strikes. The doctrine should never serve to shield administrative wrongdoing from judicial review. The administrator may be right on the merits or free to err within appropriate

---

Federal Administrative Action: The Need for Statutory Reform of Sovereign Immunity, Subject Matter Jurisdiction, and Parties Defendant, 68 Mich.L.Rev. 389, 428–36, 468–70 (1970); Davis, Sovereign Immunity Must Go, 22 Ad.L.Rev. 383 (1970); Mikva, Sovereign Immunity: In a Democracy the Emperor Has No Clothes, 1966 U.Ill.L.F. 828, 846–48 (1966); Power, New Wealth and New Harms—The Case for Broadened Governmental Liability, 23 Rutgers L.Rev. 449 (1969); Scalia, Sovereign Immunity and Nonstatutory Review of Federal Administrative Action: Some Conclusions from the Public Lands Cases, 68 Mich.L.Rev. 867 (1970). See generally Hearings on Sovereign Immunity, Before the Subcomm. on Administrative Practice and Procedure of the Senate Comm. on the Judiciary, 91st Cong., 2d Sess. (1970).

22. 43 U.S.C.A. § 620.

23. Friends of the Earth v. Armstrong, 485 F.2d 1 (10th Cir. 1973), cert. denied 414 U.S. 1171 (1974). Equally ill-founded is the holding of the decision that the prohibition against flooding a national monument had been repealed by implication.

24. Schlafly v. Volpe, 495 F.2d 273, 279 (7th Cir. 1974); Ass'n of Northwest Steelheaders v. Corps of Engineers, 485 F.2d 67, 70, 3 ELR 20807 (9th Cir. 1973) (per curiam); Washington v. Udall, 417 F.2d 1310 (9th Cir. 1969).

25. See Rule 65, Fed.R.Civ.P. (excusing the United States from posting bond when an injunction is sought).

26. See § 7.10 below.

27. Judicial Control of Administrative Action 197 (1965).

limits of his discretion. But the king can do no wrong only where he has acted lawfully.

Despite the fact that environmental lawsuits usually seek equitable relief, often against administrative agencies, suits for money damages are not unheard of. It is here that the doctrine of sovereign immunity is clouded by state and federal tort claims acts.

§ 1.8 Sovereign Immunity: Federal Tort Claims Act

The Federal Tort Claims Act makes the United States liable under the local law of the place of the tort for the negligent or wrongful acts or omissions of federal employees within the scope of their employment "in the same manner and to the same extent as a private individual under like circumstances."[1] The Act contains a laundry list of exceptions,[2] a few of them (such as the exception for the activities of the Tennessee Valley Authority) of special pertinence in environmental cases. Generally, the significance of the Act in the environmental arena mirrors experience elsewhere. The exceptions proving most troublesome, in descending order of importance, are those involving (1) the "discretionary function or duty" of any federal agency or employee, (2) conduct not deemed to be a "negligent or wrongful act or omission," and (3) the tort of "misrepresentation."

a. *Discretionary Function Exemption*

The leading case of Dalehite v. United States[3] draws distinctions between the planning level and the operational level in exempting the government from liability for negligence in adopting a plan for exporting fertilizer, controlling its manufacture, handling and shipping of the product and failing to supervise the shipboard loading.[4] A number of "planning level" judgments in the environmental field have been exempted from liability for negligence: changing the course of the Missouri River;[5] postponing the hunting season to protect migratory fowl;[6] conducting tests of nuclear explosions;[7] predicting the

---

1. 28 U.S.C.A. § 1346(b).

2. Other exemptions extend to claims arising from the activities of a federal land bank, those arising in a foreign country, or caused by the imposition of a quarantine, among others. Id. § 2680.

3. 346 U.S. 15, 73 S.Ct. 956, 97 L.Ed. 1427 (1953); see Reynolds, The Discretionary Function Exception of the Federal Tort Claims Act, 57 Geo. L.J. 81 (1968).

4. Prosser, Law of Torts 973 (4th ed. 1971).

5. Coates v. United States, 181 F.2d 816 (8th Cir. 1950); see Boston Edison Co. v. Great Lakes Dredge & Dock Co., 423 F.2d 891 (1st Cir. 1970).

6. Sickman v. United States, 184 F.2d 616 (7th Cir. 1950), cert. denied 341 U.S. 939.

7. Bartholomae Corp. v. United States, 135 F.Supp. 651 (S.D.Cal.1955); Bulloch v. United States, 133 F.Supp. 885 (D.C.Utah 1955).

Sec. 1.8 SOVEREIGN IMMUNITY: CLAIMS ACT

course of a hurricane;[8] choosing a herbicide to control vegetation on government controlled land;[9] locating and operating a cannon-testing ground;[10] selecting and approving sites for the deposit of dredge spoils;[11] issuing a permit to construct a power plant;[12] issuing grazing permits;[13] and drawing down water from a flood control reservoir.[14] Many of these so-called planning level or "discretionary" cases have involved errors of design specifications in public works projects.[15]

A well known decision in the Ninth Circuit summarizes the types of distinctions encouraged by *Dalehite*: "[D]iscretionary to undertake fire-fighting, lighthouse, rescue, or wrecked-ship marking services, but not discretionary to conduct such operations negligently; discretionary to admit a patient to an army hospital, but not discretionary to treat the patient in a negligent manner; discretionary to establish a post office at a particular location, but not to negligently fail to establish handrails; discretionary to establish control towers at airports and to undertake air traffic separation, but not to conduct the same negligently; discretionary to reactivate an airbase, but not to construct a drainage and disposal system thereon in a negligent fashion; and discretionary for the Civil Aeronautics Authority to conduct a survey in low flying, twin-engine airplane, but not for pilots thereof to fly negligently."[16] By most accounts, the *Dalehite* immunity for "discretionary" decisions is too sweeping and is often invoked to protect government blunders of the worst order and at the lowest levels.

A leading opinion interpreting California law takes an approach different from *Dalehite*: "Courts and commentators have . . . centered their attention on an assurance of judicial abstention in areas in which the responsibility for *basic policy decisions* has been committed to coordinate branches of government."[17] Professor Davis praises this emphasis on whether immunity is needed to protect

---

8. Bartie v. United States, 216 F.Supp. 10 (W.D.La.1963), aff'd 326 F.2d 754 (5th Cir. 1964), cert. denied 379 U.S. 852.

9. Harris v. United States, 205 F.2d 765 (10th Cir. 1953).

10. Barroll v. United States, 135 F.Supp. 441 (D.C.Md.1955).

11. Dolphin Gardens, Inc. v. United States, 243 F.Supp. 824 (D.C.Conn. 1965).

12. Hooper v. United States, 331 F.Supp. 1056 (D.C.Conn.1971).

13. Powell v. United States, 23 F.2d 851 (9th Cir. 1955).

14. Spillway Marina, Inc. v. United States, 445 F.2d 876 (8th Cir. 1971).

15. United States v. Morrell, 331 F.2d 498 (10th Cir. 1964); United States v. Ure, 225 F.2d 709 (9th Cir. 1955) (lining of an irrigation canal); Thomas v. United States, 81 F.Supp. 881 (W.D.Mo.1949) (installation of a revetment).

16. United Air Lines, Inc. v. Wiener, 335 F.2d 379, 393 (9th Cir. 1964), cert. dismissed 379 U.S. 951.

17. Johnson v. State, 69 Cal.2d 782, 793, 73 Cal.Rptr. 240, 248, 447 P.2d 352, 360 (1968) (emphasis in original).

high policy-making functions as opposed to asking, by rote as it were, whether the conduct attacked could be fairly described as "discretionary" or at the planning level.[18] The case law is gradually shrinking the discretionary exception to protect only policy-making decisions. In recent years, the exception has been rejected in situations quite clearly involving the exercise of some "discretion" by agency employees: controlling discharges from a sewage disposal plant;[19] conducting airport operations;[20] registering a viral vaccine to control polio;[21] planning, constructing and maintaining a sewer line;[22] closing garbage dumps in Yellowstone National Park as part of the Park Service's grizzly bear management program;[23] revoking a license;[24] designing and constructing a drainage ditch;[25] designating a pesticide spray zone and supervising the operation;[26] selecting the time and manner of test firing a rocket.[27]

Despite this modest movement to contain the discretionary exception in recent years, it is clear that the field of tort claims has not fully comprehended the radical extension of judicial review of administrative action occasioned by the hard look doctrine.[28] The principal justification for exempting discretionary decisions of the government from tort liability is that courts are reluctant or incompetent to sit in judgment on the reasonableness or wisdom of executive action,[29] particularly regulatory judgments. But this dogma is not unshakeable; interestingly, discretionary matters exempted from review under the Administrative Procedure Act are sparse while discretionary matters exempted from tort liability remain abundant. Some of the best known examples of "discretionary" activity protected from liability under the Tort Claims Act today would be subject to demanding review under the National Environmental Policy Act and the APA: changing the course of a river; adopting measures to pro-

18. 3 K. C. Davis, Administrative Law Treatise § 25.08 (Supp.1970).

19. State v. Bowling Green, 3 ELR 20159 (Ohio Ct.App.1972), aff'd 38 Ohio St.2d 281, 313 N.E.2d 409, 4 ELR 20730 (1974).

20. Nestle v. Santa Monica, 6 Cal.3d 920, 101 Cal.Rptr. 568, 496 P.2d 480, 2 ELR 20417 (1972).

21. Griffin v. United States, 351 F. Supp. 10 (E.D.Pa.1972), aff'd 500 F. 2d 1059 (3d Cir. 1974).

22. Fagliarone v. North Bergen, 78 N.J.Super. 154, 188 A.2d 43 (1963). Compare Kent v. Hamilton Township, 82 N.J.Super. 113, 196 A.2d 798 (1964).

23. Martin v. United States, 392 F. Supp. 243 (C.D.Cal.1975), rev'd 546 F. 2d 1355 (9th Cir. 1976).

24. Hendry v. United States, 418 F.2d 774 (2d Cir. 1969).

25. Seaboard Coast Line R.R. v. United States, 473 F.2d 714 (5th Cir. 1973).

26. Motors Ins. Corp. v. Aviation Specialties, Inc., 304 F.Supp. 973 (D.C. Mich.1969).

27. Pigott v. United States, 451 F.2d 574 (5th Cir. 1971).

28. See § 1.5 above.

29. James, The Federal Tort Claims Act and the 'Discretionary Function' Exception: The Sluggish Retreat of an Ancient Immunity, 10 U.Fla.L.Rev. 184 (1957).

tect migratory fowl; conducting a nuclear test; carrying out a grazing permit program; disposing of dredge spoils.[30]

It is of course a different matter to sue for specific relief than for money damages. Review under NEPA has concentrated on procedural matters to the exclusion of second-guessing agency decisions on the merits.[31] At the same time, a case can be made that an injunction before-the-fact represents a greater intrusion into the affairs of government than a money judgment after-the-fact.[32] If the government can be stopped in its tracks for failing to consider environmental effects before it builds a dam, it is not immediately apparent why tort liability should not ensue for fish killed as a result of miscalculations in designing or locating the dam. In a society where distinctions between governmental and private decision-making become ever more obscure, justifications for radical differences in liabilities become ever more labored.

Tort immunity is stoutly defended as necessary to protect political blunders in high places—the premature lifting of price controls, unwise imposition of tariffs, pollution standards too tightly written. But the fact is that in these standardless areas liability would be unlikely even in the absence of the discretionary exemption. The problem today is not too little protection of agency discretion but too much of it. Congress is under continuing pressure to provide indemnification for many adversely affected by discretionary decisions—even those that are soundly based.[33] Section 15 of the Federal Environmental Pesticide Control Act of 1972,[34] to mention but one example, calls for indemnity payments to persons suffering losses by reason of the suspension or cancellation of a registered pesticide. The courts can assist a general legislative reconsideration of the subject by narrowing the "discretionary" exception to protect only high policy decisions.

b. *Requirement of Negligent or Wrongful Act*

Not only has the Supreme Court unnecessarily expanded the "discretionary function" exception,[35] it has limited theories of liabili-

30. See cases cited in notes 5–7, 11 and 13, supra; § 7.6 below.

31. See §§ 7.3–.5 below.

32. See Dugan v. Rank, 372 U.S. 609, 626, 83 S.Ct. 999, 1009, 10 L.Ed.2d 15, 27 (1963) ("In an appropriate proceeding there would be a determination of not only the extent of such a servitude but the value thereof based upon the differences between the value of respondents' property before and after the taking. Rather than a stoppage of the government project, this is the avenue of redress open to respondents").

33. E. g., Hearings on Cyclamates (H.R. 13366), Before the Ad Hoc Subcomm. of the House Comm. on the Judiciary, 92nd Cong., 2d Sess. (1972); Senate Comm. on Agriculture and Forestry, Poultry Indemnity Payments, S.Rep. No.772, 93d Cong., 2d Sess. (1974) (proposing compensation for those affected by seizures of pesticide-contaminated poultry products).

34. 7 U.S.C.A. § 136m; see § 8.2 below (discussing liability for damages caused by pesticides).

35. For somewhat more generous readings of the "discretionary" exception

ty under the Act. The issue is whether the congressional waiver of liability for conduct deemed "negligent or wrongful" embraces strict liability as distinguished from fault-oriented negligence. In the 1972 decision of Laird v. Nelms,[36] the Supreme Court answered the question in the negative, disallowing a claim for property damage allegedly resulting from a sonic boom caused by United States military airplanes flying over North Carolina on a training mission. Technically, the Laird v. Nelms decision is weak, invoking as *stare decisis* the twenty-year-old, much criticized opinion in *Dalehite*. The decision probably also misreads the congressional aim of the Tort Claims Act although the legislative materials are not unequivocal.[37]

Practically, Laird v. Nelms is absurd: it freezes federal tort law into fault-oriented moulds of negligence that fall far short of the full agenda of liabilities in each and every state. It eschews broad classes of liability without fault, both the traditional (trespass, liability for abnormally dangerous activities) and the new (strict products liability). Environmental claims (as for example, damages for sonic boom) are especially dependent upon strict liability theories [38] and thus are peculiarly hard hit by Laird v. Nelms. It is difficult enough to sue the government without starting with a two or three theory handicap justified neither by policy nor legislative mandate.

c. *Misrepresentation Exemption*

A third important qualifier on the federal government's waiver of tort liability applies to instances of "misrepresentation." [39] The Supreme Court, once again, has gotten maximum mileage out of this exception by refusing to limit it to cases of intentional deceit and allowing the government to avoid liability for negligent misrepresentations of its agents.[40] This interpretation leads inevitably to broad arguments that "would exempt from tort liability any operational malfunction by the government that involved communications in any form." [41] Thus, a "misrepresentation" was found and immunity ap-

than that of *Dalehite*, see Rayonier, Inc. v. United States, 352 U.S. 315, 77 S.Ct. 374, 1 L.Ed.2d 354 (1957); Indian Towing Co. v. United States, 350 U.S. 61, 76 S.Ct. 122, 100 L.Ed. 48 (1955).

36. 406 U.S. 797, 92 S.Ct. 1899, 32 L.Ed. 2d 499 (1972); see Peck, Laird v. Nelms: A Call for Review and Revision of the Federal Tort Claims Act, 48 Wash.L.Rev. 391 (1973).

37. Jacoby, Absolute Liability Under the Federal Tort Claims Act, 24 Fed. Bar J. 139 (1964); Peck, Absolute Liability and the Federal Tort Claims Act, 9 Stan.L.Rev. 433 (1957).

38. See § 2.14 below.

39. 28 U.S.C.A. § 2680(h), as amended, Pub.L.No.93–253, § 2, 88 Stat. 50 (1974). The 1974 amendments, not addressing the misrepresentation exception, waive immunity for various intentional tort claims arising out of the activities of investigative or law enforcement officers.

40. United States v. Neustadt, 366 U.S. 696, 81 S.Ct. 1294, 6 L.Ed.2d 614 (1961) (disallowing a claim based on the negligent overstatement of fair market value by an FHA appraiser).

41. Ingham v. Eastern Air Lines, Inc., 373 F.2d 227, 238 (2d Cir. 1967) (im-

plied where a government doctor erroneously notified the plaintiff that his hogs were afflicted with cholera, prompting him to inject the animals with live vaccine, which led to the death of several of them.[42]

In its most outrageous applications, the "misrepresentation" exception protects the government from regulatory mistakes leading to the condemnation of products. An example is Mizokami v. United States,[43] where plaintiff's spinach was seized for contamination with the pesticide heptachlor. It was later admitted that the original tests were in error and that the spinach was uncontaminated. The "misrepresentation" barred liability. Plaintiffs eventually went to Congress and secured a private law authorizing the Court of Claims to determine the losses, which were adjudged to be $301,974.33. How much wiser it would have been to have allowed the suit in the first place under the Act.

Congress never has made clear why relief should be denied to citizens who suffer losses as a result of fraud or deceit by government agents. It should abolish the misrepresentation exemption for the same reasons it waived immunity for police abuses in 1974.[44] Short of that, the Supreme Court should limit the exemption to cases of intentional misrepresentation; Congress, quite clearly, already has waived immunity for negligence.

§ 1.9 The Techniques of Deference: Exhaustion, Primary Jurisdiction, and Ripeness

As a specialized body of administrative law, environmental law implicates longstanding doctrines of accommodation between the courts and agencies.[1] These go by many names and cover disputed territory—exhaustion and primary jurisdiction, mootness and justiciability, ripeness and finality. They serve a variety of functions but the bottom line, as the practitioner is well aware, is that they can defeat a lawsuit, either through outright dismissal or indefinite postponement. In some respects, environmental issues are unique, although these special qualities pull in different ways on the question of how much deference is owed by the courts to the agencies. At issue often are fundamental questions of health and safety, which may encourage judges to be less scrupulous in avoiding a trampling of ad-

---

posing liability because claim involved principally operational negligence); see DeLange v. United States, 372 F.2d 134 (9th Cir. 1967).

42. Rey v. United States, 484 F.2d 45 (5th Cir. 1973).

43. 188 Ct.Cl. 736, 414 F.2d 1375 (1969); see Anglo-American & Overseas Corp. v. United States, 242 F.2d 236 (2d Cir. 1957).

44. Note 39, supra.

1. The leading analyses include A. Bickel, The Least Dangerous Branch (1963) (discussing techniques of decision avoidance of the U. S. Supreme Court); 3 K. C. Davis, Administrative Law Treatise chs. 19–21 (1958); L. Jaffe, Judicial Control of Administrative Action chs. 4, 10–11 (1965).

ministrative toes. This concern for public health has played a role in sharpening the scrutiny of administrative action in the normal course of judicial review.[2] Environmental causes often are represented by parties of limited means, require speedy action, and challenge the conduct of agencies that are influenced by special interests, smitten by political winds, or paralyzed by mediocrity. These are reasons for judicial intervention. Environmental causes also are likely to involve complex technological and scientific questions, affect society in profound ways, and require a uniform and broad-based approach. These are reasons for judicial abstention. The reconciliation of the roles of the courts and the agencies will be considered here under the headings of (1) exhaustion of administrative remedies, (2) primary jurisdiction, and (3) ripeness, finality, and mootness.

a. *Exhaustion*

Exhaustion of administrative remedies "emerges as a defense to judicial review of an administrative action not as yet deemed complete."[3] It applies "where a claim is cognizable in the first instance by an administrative agency alone; judicial interference is withheld until the administrative process has run its course."[4] The idea is to give the administrative agency the first chance to dispose of the dispute. Primary jurisdiction, on the other hand, "applies where a claim is originally cognizable in the courts, and comes into play whenever enforcement of the claim requires the resolution of issues, which, under a regulatory scheme, have been placed within the special competence of an administrative body; in such a case the judicial process is suspended pending referral of such issues to the administrative body for its view."[5]

Exhaustion of administrative remedies is applied with considerable flexibility,[6] and in certain state courts it is highly disfavored.[7] The leading United States Supreme Court decision in McKart v. United States[8] articulates a number of factors that must be weighed by judges in deciding whether an applicant should be told to go elsewhere: the degree of injury to the plaintiff; the necessity for protecting the integrity of the agency functions; the likelihood that judicial review would be enhanced by the application of agency expertise or the accumulation of a record; and the improvement of judicial efficiency by avoiding intervention and giving the agency the first chance to set the matter straight. Similarly, there is considerable

2. § 1.5 above.

3. Jaffe, Primary Jurisdiction, 77 Harv. L.Rev. 1037 (1964).

4. United States v. Western Pac. R.R., 352 U.S. 59, 63, 77 S.Ct. 161, 165, 1 L. Ed.2d 126, 132 (1956) (Harlan, J.).

5. Ibid.

6. E. g., McKart v. United States, 395 U.S. 185, 89 S.Ct. 1657, 23 L.Ed.2d 194 (1969).

7. A leading case is Nolan v. Fitzpatrick, 9 N.J. 477, 89 A.2d 13 (1952).

8. 395 U.S. 185, 89 S.Ct. 1657, 23 L.Ed. 2d 194 (1969).

room for maneuver in most generic statements of the exhaustion doctrine;[9] it is shot through with exceptions for occasions when the agency is acting without jurisdiction, in a way that threatens national security, in clear violation of constitutional rights, and so on. The key factors, in this author's opinion, are whether the plaintiff will be disadvantaged seriously by being sent elsewhere and, if so, whether that inconvenience is justified by an improvement in the prospects for effective judicial review. Common occasions for relaxing the exhaustion requirements are those where the administrative remedy is inadequate or hypothetical and those where the principal questions are legal and not in need of factual or technical elaboration.

In environmental cases, courts strive to apply the factors cited as relevant in *McKart*, and they generally achieve the desired flexibility in result. Thus, the exhaustion defense has been rejected in air and water pollution enforcement cases where no administrative proceedings were pending and none were contemplated,[10] in a noise case where the administrative remedy before the Federal Aviation Administration was hypothetical at best,[11] in NEPA cases where claims of failure to comment on draft impact statements were raised as a complete bar to an attack on statement adequacy,[12] and in a Freedom of Information Act case where the principal issue was one of law and the administrative remedy newly contrived.[13] These and related exhaustion of remedy cases [14] stress the viability of the available ad-

---

9. E. g., Layton & Fine, The Draft and Exhaustion of Administrative Remedies, 56 Geo.L.J. 315, 322–31 (1967); see K. C. Davis, supra, note 1, § 20.03, at 69.

10. State ex rel. Spannaus v. United States Steel Corp., — Minn. —, 240 N.W.2d 316, 6 ELR 20433 (1976) (exhaustion and primary jurisdiction case; no administrative proceedings at state level; refusal to defer to federal NPDES permit proceeding); State v. Dairyland Power Coop., 52 Wis.2d 45, 187 N.W.2d 878, 1 ELR 20325 (1971) (exhaustion and primary jurisdiction case).

11. Illinois ex rel. Scott v. Butterfield, 396 F.Supp. 632, 5 ELR 20587 (N.D. Ill.1975).

12. Natural Resources Defense Council, Inc. v. Tennessee Valley Authority, 367 F.Supp. 128, 3 ELR 20725 (E.D. Tenn.1973), aff'd per curiam 502 F.2d 852, 4 ELR 20737 (6th Cir. 1974); see Ecology Center of Louisiana, Inc. v. Coleman, 515 F.2d 860, 5 ELR 20488 (5th Cir. 1975) (failure to comment or participate in a hearing in a highway NEPA case; court remands for application of *McKart* factors to determine whether the exhaustion defense should be allowed). These cases, as *McKart*, raise the exhaustion argument in its harshest setting because the consequence is outright preclusion not merely deferral of plaintiffs' claims.

13. Diapulse Corp. v. Food & Drug Administration, 500 F.2d 75 (2d Cir. 1974).

14. E. g., Natural Resources Defense Council, Inc. v. Train, 166 U.S.App.D. C. 312, 323, 510 F.2d 692, 703, 5 ELR 20046, 20051 (1974) ("the court may promptly proceed to the merits of the action when it is confident or becomes confident that agency recourse is futile, as where the agency's position is firm"); Harlem Valley Transp. Ass'n v. Stafford, 360 F.Supp. 1057, 1064, 3 ELR 20639, 20641 (S.D.N.Y.1973), aff'd 500 F.2d 328, 4 ELR 20638 (2d Cir. 1974) (ripeness argument; the administrative order is "complete, likely to wreak irreparable injury if wrong, and effectively reviewable only now rather than later") (footnote omitted).

ministrative remedy and the ease of an immediate judicial disposition. On the other hand, the exhaustion defense has been raised successfully in a case challenging the compatibility of mining with the mandates of the Wilderness Act,[15] an action to enjoin operation of twenty nuclear power plants raising technical questions about the adequacy of safety systems,[16] and an attack on various aspects of the largest timber sale ever conducted by the U.S. Forest Service.[17] These and other cases sustaining the exhaustion defense do so on the assumption that plaintiffs are being consigned to real and viable remedies and that permitting the administrative process to run its course will be of material assistance to any subsequent judicial review.

For the most part, plaintiffs with environmental claims dread the exhaustion defense for it can lead to an extended purgatory in the administrative process with prospects for success dismal and demands on time and resources substantial.[18] There is a tendency among practitioners to view any remedy before an unfriendly agency as an exercise in futility, and, therefore, to jump the gun on judicial review wherever possible. While the courts of course are wholly unsympathetic to claims of agency bias in their broadest form, they recognize the futility argument. Thus, a plaintiff will not be diverted to administrative procedures that are plainly inadequate [19] or unavailable as a matter of right.[20] And plaintiffs should not be forced to try their luck with procedures that are recently concocted, largely informal, superfluous, or petty. Indeed, there would be adequate justifica-

15. Izaak Walton League v. St. Clair, 497 F.2d 849, 852–53, 4 ELR 20556, 20558 (8th Cir. 1974) ("the factual questions regarding the effect of mining activity upon the wilderness, and whether a permit should issue with restrictions that would be adequate to protect the wilderness quality of the [Boundary Waters Canoe Area] are those types of questions peculiarly within the competence of the Forest Service, and statutorily delegated to it by the Wilderness Act").

16. Nader v. Ray, 363 F.Supp. 946, 953, 3 ELR 20801 (D.C.D.C.1973) (stating that the reasons for exhaustion apply with "special force" where "specialized and complex problems" of nuclear safety are involved); cf. Nader v. Nuclear Regulatory Comm'n, 168 U.S. App.D.C. 255, 513 F.2d 1045, 5 ELR 20342 (1975) (failure to participate in an administrative rulemaking forecloses a later collateral attack) (alternative holding); Gage v. Atomic Energy Comm'n, 156 U.S.App.D.C. 231, 479 F. 2d 1214, 3 ELR 20479 (1973) (same).

17. Sierra Club v. Hardin, 325 F.Supp. 99, 115–16, 1 ELR 20161, 20167–68, (D. C.Alas.1971), remanded 3 ELR 20292 (9th Cir. 1973) (barring NEPA claims raised by plaintiffs).

18. Attorneys for pesticide industries presumably feel this way about the Environmental Protection Agency, which may explain why pesticide disputes account for so much of the leading case law on ripeness. See § 8.7 below.

19. E. g., American Fed'n of Gov't Employees v. Acree, 155 U.S.App.D.C. 20, 475 F.2d 1289 (1973); Elmo Div. of Drive-X Co. v. Dixon, 121 U.S.App.D. C. 113, 348 F.2d 342 (1965); Illinois ex rel. Scott v. Butterfield, 396 F.Supp. 632, 5 ELR 20587 (N.D.Ill.1975).

20. Rosado v. Wyman, 397 U.S. 397, 90 S.Ct. 1207, 25 L.Ed.2d 442 (1970). But see Ricci v. Chicago Mercantile Exch., 409 U.S. 289, 93 S.Ct. 573, 34 L.Ed.2d 525 (1973).

tion for the courts to cock a skeptical eye towards exhaustion claims from agencies with established reputations for treating intervenors as invaders from Mars. A remedy that must be exhausted should be taken seriously by the agency that offers it if it is to be given credence by the courts that enforce it.

Questions of law, with rare exceptions, should not be deferred under an exhaustion rationale. There is invariably a sacrifice in convenience to require a party to go back to the agency, and there is no point in demanding it if the court can resolve the issue. There is no policy to be served by a superfluous gathering of facts or an accumulation of legal opinions from non-authoritative sources. The exception would be in a case where the legal question is tied closely to the expertise of the agency so that securing an administrative opinion might be an enlightening exercise.

b. *Primary Jurisdiction*

Primary jurisdiction defenses normally arise in nuisance cases or other enforcement efforts under generic statutory provisions. Courts are extremely reluctant to find nuisance remedies impliedly repealed by administrative mechanisms,[21] which means, among other things, that primary jurisdiction arguments, even if successful, almost never lead to dismissal but only to a stay of consideration by the court. Justifications for the doctrine of primary jurisdiction resemble those for exhaustion—the court sees a need to secure the views of an agency before making its own judgment; the legislature has assigned a body with technical expertise to resolve disputed issues of fact; a respect for the autonomy of the executive branch and enhancement of judicial efficiency suggests a backing away. Like the exhaustion defense primary jurisdiction is the bane of practitioners whose path to the courthouse is blocked by a formidable, often unfriendly, administrative swamp.[22]

The indicia of a primary jurisdiction decision are easy enough to identify but difficult to isolate as dispositive. Mr. Justice Harlan, explaining the refusal of the U.S. Supreme Court to exercise its original jurisdiction in a mercury pollution case, provides a classic justification: "[T]his case is an extraordinarily complex one both because of the novel scientific issues of fact inherent in it and the multiplicity of governmental agencies already involved. Its successful resolution

---

21. E. g., Ohio River Sand Co. v. Commonwealth, 467 S.W.2d 347 (Ky.1971); State v. Dairyland Power Coop., 52 Wis.2d 45, 187 N.W.2d 878, 1 ELR 20325 (1971). Compare § 2.10 below.

22. Schwartz, Primary Administrative Jurisdiction and the Exhaustion of Litigants, 41 Geo.L.J. 495 (1953); Note, The Doctrine of Primary Jurisdiction: A Reexamination of Its Purpose and Practicability, 48 Geo.L.J. 563 (1960). See Note, Primary Jurisdiction in Environmental Cases: Suggested Guidelines for Limiting Referral, 48 Ind.L.J. 676 (1973); Casenote, Environmental Law: Primary Jurisdiction—Role of Courts and Administrative Agencies, 1972 Wis.L.Rev. 934.

would require primarily skills of fact-finding, conciliation, detailed coordination with—and perhaps not infrequent deference to—other adjudicatory bodies, and close supervision of the technical performance of local industries." [23] Yet, complexity alone repeatedly is held to be an insufficient justification for the courts to decline the exercise of jurisdiction clearly bestowed.[24] It is pertinent to a primary jurisdiction deferral that the agency exercise "a broad, continuing administrative relationship to the subject matter;" [25] yet, courts have deferred in situations where the agency has lost track entirely of the administrative proceeding.[26] It is relevant to ask whether deferral will dispose entirely of the controversy; [27] yet, deferrals are ordered where an administrative decision hardly could be dispositive.[28]

The environmental case law is not always reconcilable: the primary jurisdiction defense is rejected in air pollution cases where the facts are not seriously contested,[29] where the agency itself is in court seeking relief,[30] where the chief issue is a question of law concerning the appropriateness of the remedy,[31] and where ongoing negotiations cannot obscure clear violations of law.[32] It is rejected in water pollution cases where the agency is fully disposed to accept the judicial forum.[33] The defense is accepted in air pollution cases where the court sees a need for administrative fact-finding or expert judgment,[34] where the subject matter is dominated thoroughly by an

23. Ohio v. Wyandotte Chem. Corp., 401 U.S. 493, 504–05, 91 S.Ct. 1005, 1013, 28 L.Ed.2d 256, 266 (1971) (while primary jurisdiction is not mentioned by name the rationale is manifest).

24. E. g., Friends of the Earth v. Carey, 535 F.2d 165, 173, 6 ELR 20488, 20492 (2d Cir. 1976) (courts may not refuse citizen enforcement of an approved air pollution implementation plan on ground that the task of supervision would be "unduly burdensome" and the problems involved " 'highly technical' "); United States v. Rohm & Haas Co., 500 F.2d 167, 175, 4 ELR 20738, 20741 (5th Cir. 1974).

25. W. Gellborn & C. Byse, Administrative Law 302 (6th ed. 1974).

26. United States v. Moretti, Inc. (I), 478 F.2d 418 (5th Cir. 1973).

27. W. Gellhorn & C. Byse, supra note 25, at 299.

28. Schofield v. Material Transit, Inc., 42 Del.Chan. 144, 206 A.2d 100 (1960) (deferring on air pollution nuisance claim; retaining jurisdiction on claims alleging noise and vibration damage). Indeed, it is clear that "a litigant whose complaint is referred to the agency having primary jurisdiction must ordinarily be prepared to exhaust not only available administrative remedies but also any statutory procedures for judicial review before he can attempt to revive his suit." J. L. Mashaw & R. A. Merrill, Introduction to the American Public Law System 1043 (1975).

29. Houston Compressed Steel Corp v. State, 456 S.W.2d 768 (Tex.Civ.App. 1970).

30. State ex rel. Spannaus v. United States Steel Corp., —— Minn. ——, 240 N.W.2d 316, 6 ELR 20433 (1976).

31. State v. Dairyland Power Coop., 52 Wis.2d 45, 187 N.W.2d 878, 1 ELR 20325 (1971).

32. Friends of the Earth v. Carey, 535 F.2d 165, 6 ELR 20488 (2d Cir. 1976).

33. United States v. Rohm & Haas Co., 500 F.2d 167, 4 ELR 20738 (5th Cir. 1974).

34. State v. Arizona Pub. Serv. Co., 85 N.M. 165, 510 P.2d 98, 3 ELR 20496 (1973); Schofield v. Material Transit,

administrative presence,[35] and where the agency is actively considering the problem.[36] It is accepted in water pollution cases where the administrative process offers expertise of longstanding,[37] where the agency might validate a course of conduct the court would be inclined to outlaw,[38] and where an administrative disposition of the dispute is likely to be forthcoming.[39] The key factors appear to be an active and continuing involvement by the administrative agency and a strong likelihood that the agency decision will dispose of the controversy.

As with exhaustion arguments, the defense of primary jurisdiction should not be lightly invoked to frustrate environmental claims. The legislature, after all, has given the courts the power to decide, and, though it also has vested an agency with a piece of the action, it very rarely goes so far as to supersede the general authority of the courts.[40] There are few topics of environmental law that are not touched in some way by an administrative presence, and broad applications of primary jurisdiction can carve out a sizeable chunk of jurisdiction in important areas—federal[41] and state[42] nuisance law, public trust law,[43] or litigation under the Rivers and Harbors Act.[44] While retention of jurisdiction by the court gives a litigant a chance to allege he is being abused by the administrative process, the fact is that a stay of indeterminate length is but a step short of outright dismissal.[45] Also, primary jurisdiction applies most comfortably in

Inc., 42 Del.Chan. 144, 206 A.2d 100 (1960).

35. Chicago v. General Motors Corp., 332 F.Supp. 285, 1 ELR 20408 (N.D. Ill.1971), aff'd 467 F.2d 1262, 2 ELR 20636 (7th Cir. 1972) (dismissing products liability claim for auto-caused air pollution).

36. State v. Arizona Pub. Serv. Co., 85 N.M. 165, 510 P.2d 98, 3 ELR 20496 (1973); cf. Buckeye Power, Inc. v. Environmental Protection Agency (II), 525 F.2d 80, 84, 5 ELR 20701, 20702 (6th Cir. 1975) (refusing to review aspects of Ohio's implementation plan on ripeness grounds; processes of adjustment "are presently proceeding exactly as, and where this statute contemplated, and [because] no final resolution as to them has been arrived at, this case is not presently ripe for judicial review").

37. Potomac River Ass'n, Inc. v. Lundeberg Maryland Seamanship School, Inc., 5 ELR 20388 (D.C.Md.1975); see Ellison v. Rayonier, Inc., 156 F.Supp. 214 (W.D.Wash.1957).

38. United States v. Joseph G. Moretti, Inc. (I), 478 F.2d 418, 3 ELR 20414 (5th Cir. 1973).

39. White Lake Improvement Ass'n v. Whitehall, 22 Mich.App. 262, 177 N.W. 2d 473 (1970).

40. A rare example, later overruled legislatively, is T.I.M.E., Inc. v. United States, 359 U.S. 464, 79 S.Ct. 904, 3 L.Ed.2d 952 (1959).

41. § 2.12 below.

42. §§ 2.1–.11 below.

43. § 2.16 below; see Sax & Conner, Michigan's Environmental Protection Act of 1970: A Progress Report, 70 Mich.L.Rev. 1004, 1019–27 (1972) (discussing continued viability of primary jurisdiction doctrine in cases brought under Michigan's statutory variation on the public trust doctrine).

44. § 4.5 below.

45. Note 28, supra.

the setting of a regulated industry where agency supervision is constant, detailed and comprehensive; this analogue applies imperfectly to some types of pollution control oversight, which may be sporadic, superficial, and piecemeal. The courts should surrender their jurisdiction on environmental cases only upon strong suggestions from the legislature that they ought to, firm indications that the agency is capable of, and interested in, disposing of the dispute and clear assurances that plaintiff is being sent to a competent forum that will resolve his claims, not on a wild goose chase.

c. *Ripeness, Finality, and Mootness*

The doctrines of ripeness and finality "are designed to prevent premature judicial intervention in the administrative process, before the administrative action has been fully considered, and before the legal dispute has been brought into focus." [46] The "basic rationale" is to bar the courts "from entangling themselves in abstract disagreements over administrative policies" and "to protect the agencies from judicial interference until an administrative decision has been formalized and its effects felt in a concrete way by the challenging parties." [47] As with the exhaustion and primary jurisdiction doctrines, there is considerable room for discretion in invoking ripeness or lack of finality as a reason for withholding a decision on the issues presented. The courts ask, as they do in exhaustion and primary jurisdiction cases, how badly plaintiffs will be hurt by deferring a decision and how confidently a judgment can be made on the state of the record presented.

In environmental cases, arguments that the issue has been taken to court too soon are accepted where interlocutory review was sought of the initial decision of an FPC administrative law judge,[48] where evidence was excluded from an adjudicatory hearing,[49] where an or-

---

46. Environmental Defense Fund, Inc. v. Hardin, 138 U.S.App.D.C. 391, 396, 428 F.2d 1093, 1098, 1 ELR 20050, 20052 (1970) (footnote omitted); see Poe v. Ullman, 367 U.S. 497, 528, 81 S.Ct. 1752, 1769, 6 L.Ed.2d 989, 1010 (1961) (Harlan, J. dissenting) (a finding of lack of ripeness rests properly "in the fact that the need for some further procedure, some further contingency of application or interpretation, whether judicial, administrative or executive, . . . served to make remote the issue which was sought to be presented to the Court"); Davis v. Ichord, 143 U.S.App.D.C. 183, 196, 442 F.2d 1207, 1220 (1970) (the test of ripeness is whether "the controversy is so sharpened by a specific factual context as to permit a sure-footed judicial appraisal of the pertinent factors") (Leventhal, J.); Natural Resources Defense Council, Inc. v. Nuclear Regulatory Comm'n, 539 F.2d 824, 836–37, 6 ELR 20513, 20518 (2d Cir. 1976) ("the appropriate inquiry to determine finality is whether the process of administrative decision making has reached a stage where judicial review will not be disruptive of the agency process and whether legal consequences will flow from the action taken").

47. Abbott Laboratories v. Gardner, 387 U.S. 136, 148–49, 87 S.Ct. 1507, 1515, 18 L.Ed.2d 681, 691 (1967).

48. Sherry v. Algonquin Gas Transmission Co., 3 ELR 20227 (D.Mass.1972).

49. Thermal Ecology Must Be Preserved v. Atomic Energy Comm'n, 139 U.S. App.D.C. 366, 368, 433 F.2d 524, 526 (1970).

der was entered narrowing the scope of the proceeding,[50] where the Commission deferred ruling on a motion requiring the staff to revise and recirculate a draft impact statement prior to further hearings,[51] and where the Administrator of EPA issued an order of cancellation, which is the forerunner of an extensive administrative inquiry into the justification for pesticide registrations.[52] On the other hand, review of arguably non-final orders decisive in effect is allowed where the agency denied requested directives requiring the staff to prepare an impact statement prior to hearing and to pay expenses and fees to be incurred,[53] demurred to a complaint charging antitrust violations in connection with an anti-litter initiative campaign,[54] ruled that an EIS need not be prepared prior to an ICC abandonment hearing,[55] and issued a pesticide suspension order that had an immediate drastic effect on sales.[56]

In addition to cases seeking to challenge interlocutory rulings at the agency level, the ripeness doctrine is unfurled in a number of other contexts where judicial review arguably is stymied by the hypothetical issues presented. Claims of ripeness were rejected in a NEPA action challenging contract approvals for an aluminum plant

---

50. Ecology Action v. Atomic Energy Comm'n, 492 F.2d 988, 4 ELR 20289 (2d Cir. 1974) (Friendly, J.) (an important ruling whose rationale could preclude interlocutory review of several types of administrative decisions including, for example, rulings of the EPA General Counsel defining the scope of NPDES permit proceedings, § 4.11 below).

51. Greene County Planning Bd. v. Federal Power Comm'n (II), 490 F.2d 256, 259–60, 4 ELR 20080, 20082 (2d Cir. 1973) (Mansfield, J., dissenting) ("The FPC first defers, then transfers, all in an attempt to thwart review and to insulate the hearing process from the data that this Court had earlier ordered that it make available for scrutiny at the hearing. . . . Where an agency's use of procedural cat-and-mouse games in an effort to avoid a final order amounts to a sham, and its conduct, if successful, would thwart our explicit mandate, I believe that its action is sufficiently 'final' to permit review").

52. Pax Co. v. United States (arsenic trioxide), 454 F.2d 93, 97, 2 ELR 20087, 20088 (10th Cir. 1972) ("Inasmuch as the completion of the administrative cycle in the present case could result in Pax suffering no harm whatsoever, the reasons for refusing to short circuit the administrative process are the more compelling"); Dow Chem. Co. v. Ruckelshaus (2, 4, 5–T II), 477 F.2d 1317, 3 ELR 20343 (8th Cir. 1973).

53. Greene County Planning Bd. v. Federal Power Comm'n (I), 455 F.2d 412, 2 ELR 20017 (2d Cir. 1972), cert. denied 409 U.S. 849.

54. Rodgers v. Federal Trade Comm'n, 492 F.2d 228 (9th Cir. 1973) (per curiam) (the author was plaintiff and an attorney of record in the case).

55. Harlem Valley Transp. Ass'n v. Stafford, 360 F.Supp. 1057, 1063–64, 3 ELR 20639, 20641 (S.D.N.Y.1973), aff'd 500 F.2d 328, 4 ELR 20638 (2d Cir. 1974) (Frankel, J.) (following *Greene County*) ("The orders in each instance are complete, likely to wreak irreparable injury if wrong, and effectively reviewable only now rather than later") (footnote omitted).

56. Environmental Defense Fund, Inc. v. Ruckelshaus (DDT II), 142 U.S.App. D.C. 74, 80, 439 F.2d 584, 590, 1 ELR 20059, 20061 (1971) (dictum). Contra, Nor-Am Agricultural Prods., Inc. v. Hardin (mercury compounds), 435 F.2d 1151, 1 ELR 20032 (7th Cir. 1970) (en banc) (reasoning that administrative autonomy is necessary to protect health and safety).

whose construction depended upon approvals not yet in hand,[57] but were accepted in a NEPA action challenging imminent approvals of certain subsidiary facilities of the Alaska pipeline where the application process was incomplete.[58] The pipeline case, to be sure, was decided on other grounds, raised questions of immense public importance calling for judicial caution, and arrived in the appellate courts with evidentiary gaps casting doubt upon a confident disposition. Ripeness claims have been heeded in attempts to challenge a proposed rule that would affect sulfur oxide emissions from a copper smelter,[59] preliminary revisions of an implementation plan still under active consideration,[60] a reallocation of public trust properties where no land was yet exchanged,[61] a rule authorizing FDA inspectors to examine certain processes raising legal questions but causing no particular damage until enforced in a concrete setting,[62] and the issuance of a compliance order where pre-enforcement review was thought to interfere with summary administrative powers to protect public health.[63]

Needless to say, the twin tests for ripeness of appropriateness for judicial review and assessment of hardship on the parties do not yield firm predictions. Early review can be helpful to the parties but harmful to the courts. A decision on the merits should be forthcoming if the court can proceed to judgment with confidence. The confidence factor increases if the issues are more legal than factual, if the way to decision is unlikely to become less obstructed by satisfaction of certain contingencies, or if the ruling approaches decisiveness on important issues at stake in the administrative process.

Mootness, like the doctrines of standing and ripeness, is rooted in constitutional considerations of "case and controversy." It is applied occasionally in environmental cases where the controversy has evaporated altogether.[64] Yet it is inapplicable in certain conflicts "capable

---

57. Port of Astoria v. Hodel, 5 ELR 20657 (D.C.Or.1975).

58. Wilderness Soc'y v. Morton, 156 U.S.App.D.C. 121, 479 F.2d 842, 3 ELR 20085 (1973) (en banc), cert. denied 411 U.S. 917.

59. Anaconda Co. v. Ruckelshaus, 482 F.2d 1301, 3 ELR 20719 (10th Cir. 1973).

60. Buckeye Power, Inc. v. Environmental Protection Agency (II), 525 F.2d 80, 5 ELR 20701 (6th Cir. 1975).

61. New Jersey Sports & Exposition Authority v. McCrane, 61 N.J. 1, 30–31, 292 A.2d 545, 560 (1972).

62. Toilet Goods Ass'n v. Gardner, 387 U.S. 158, 87 S.Ct. 1520, 18 L.Ed.2d 697 (1967).

63. Getty Oil Co. (Eastern Operations), Inc. v. Ruckelshaus, 467 F.2d 349, 2 ELR 20683 (3d Cir. 1972). Compare Vining, Direct Judicial Review and the Doctrine of Ripeness in Administrative Law, 69 Mich.L.Rev. 1443, 1493–95 (1971) (reading *Abbott Laboratories* as supporting a presumption of pre-enforcement judicial review).

64. E. g., Massachusetts Air Pollution & Noise Abatement Comm. v. Brinegar, — F.Supp. —, 6 ELR 20214 (D.C.Mass.1975) (NEPA challenge to demonstration flights of Concorde where flights were completed with no reasonable expectation of recurrence); Potomac River Ass'n, Inc. v. Lundeberg Maryland Seamanship School, Inc., 5 ELR 20388 (D.C.Md.1975) (all work under contested Corps of Engineers permits had been completed and the permits had expired; primary jurisdiction applied to some claims).

of repetition yet evading review." [65] This might include, for example, this year's pesticide spray program,[66] regulatory action affecting a salmon run that recurs annually,[67] or an aggravated form of trespass that might happen again. A recent review of Supreme Court decisions makes clear that mootness claims can be defeated by a demonstration of different types of harm: "a continuing harm to the plaintiff; the likelihood of future recurrence of past harm, either to the plaintiff personally or the group he represents; and the probability that similar cases arising in the future will evade judicial review." [68]

§ 1.10 Freedom of Information Act

The public's need for information is "especially great" in the fields of science and technology, "for the growth of specialized scientific knowledge threatens to outstrip our collective ability to control its effects on our lives." [1] The need for information and the reluctance of governmental agencies to disclose it have made the Freedom of Information Act [2] (FOIA) an indispensable tool of environmental practice. Information requests, successful and unsuccessful, have sought reports and data across the gamut of environmental concerns: estimates of natural gas reserves; health hazards in industrial plants; deficiencies in meat inspections; improper handling of pesticides; lead additives in gasoline; excessive radiation levels in homes; accidents in National Parks; faulty maintenance of water levels at hydroelectric projects for the protection of game fish; air pollution from copper smelters; adverse effects of detergents on water quality; and risks associated with the siting of nuclear reactors.

The Freedom of Information Act is a valuable supplement to, and sometimes an improvement on, agency discovery procedures in adjudicatory hearings. The Act of course can be invoked independently of any pending or threatened proceeding. Any request that "reasonably describes" the records sought and is made in accordance

---

65. Southern Pac. Terminal Co. v. Interstate Commerce Comm'n, 219 U.S. 498, 515, 31 S.Ct. 279, 283, 55 L.Ed. 310, 316 (1911); Roe v. Wade, 410 U.S. 113, 125, 93 S.Ct. 705, 713, 35 L.Ed.2d 147, 161 (1973).

66. Challenges to spraying programs often involve a rush to the courthouse before the action proceeds. E. g, Save America's Vital Environment, Inc. v. Butz, 2 ELR 20563 (M.D.Ga. 1972) (mirex); Lee v. Resor, 2 ELR 20665 (M.D.Fla.1972) (2, 4–D); Audubon Soc'y of Rhode Island v. Hayes, 2 ELR 20509 (R.I.Super.Ct.1972) (sevin). If the action is completed, it very well may present a situation "capable of repetition, yet evading review."

67. This issue is raised in United States v. Washington, Civil Nos. 76–1112, 76–1186 (9th Cir.). The author is an attorney of record in the case.

68. Note, The Mootness Doctrine in the Supreme Court, 88 Harv.L.Rev. 373 (1974).

1. Soucie v. David, 145 U.S.App.D.C. 144, 157, 448 F.2d 1067, 1080, 1 ELR 20147, 20152 (1971).

2. Pub.L. No. 89–554, 80 Stat. 383 (1966), 5 U.S.C.A. § 552, as amended Pub.L. No. 93–502, 88 Stat. 1561 (1974).

with agency rules (which may include a fee for search and duplication) must be "promptly" complied with.[3] Anecdotes about unanswered queries, exorbitant fees, prolonged delays are part of the history of the Freedom of Information Act.[4] The 1974 amendments, however, significantly relieve these procedural obstacles by relaxing the standard of specificity for a request (from "identifiable records" to those only "reasonably" described); [5] by requiring a determination within ten days after the receipt of a request, except in unusual circumstances; [6] by limiting fees to "reasonable standard charges for document search and duplication" and discouraging them altogether for minor requests, those from indigents, and requests for information "primarily benefiting the general public;" [7] and by providing for judicially imposed sanctions against agency employees responsible for withholding records "without reasonable basis in law." [8] The 1974 amendments further encourage judicial review of agency denials of information by imposing the burden of justifying nondisclosure on the agency; [9] by inviting the court to examine disputed documents *in camera;* [10] by requiring the production of any "reasonably segregable portion" of a record despite the deletion of exempt portions; [11] by requiring the government to file a responsive pleading within 30 (as distinguished from the usual 60) days; [12] by giving docket priority to information complaints; [13] and by authorizing the court to assess against the United States "reasonable attorney fees and other litigation costs reasonably incurred in any case . . . in which the complainant has substantially prevailed." [14]

The utility of the Freedom of Information Act is illustrated by those agency adjudicatory proceedings where discovery substantially is abbreviated (e. g., a Nuclear Regulatory Commission hearing on the licensing of a nuclear reactor [15]) or denied altogether (e. g., an Environmental Protection Agency hearing on the issuance of a waste discharge permit [16]). In such proceedings, the Freedom of Information Act serves as a reasonably effective discovery tool. To mention

---

3. 5 U.S.C.A. § 552(a)(3).

4. See, e. g., Hearings on the Availability of Information to Congress, Before the Subcomm. on Foreign Operations and Government Information of the House Comm. on Government Operations, 93d Cong., 1st Sess. (1973); House Comm. on Government Operations, Administration of the Freedom of Information Act, H.R.Rep. No. 1419, 92d Cong., 2d Sess. (1972).

5. 5 U.S.C.A. § 552(a)(3).

6. Id. § 552(a)(6)(A).

7. Id. § 552(a)(4)(A).

8. Id. § 552(a)(4)(F).

9. Id. § 552(a)(4)(B).

10. Ibid.

11. Id. § 552(b).

12. Id. § 552(a)(4)(C).

13. Id. § 552(a)(4)(D).

14. Id. § 552(a)(4)(E).

15. 10 CFR § 50.58.

16. 40 CFR § 125.36(i).

but one example, the Act was used to gain access to documents from the files of the United States Geological Survey (USGS) that were prepared in the course of the agency's review, in its capacity as a consultant to the Atomic Energy Commission, of geological faults uncovered in the reactor excavations of Virginia Electric & Power Company's (Vepco's) North Anna Nuclear Power Station, located approximately 80 miles south of Washington, D.C. Although USGS was not a party to the proceedings (and thus immune from most discovery), the documents were reached under the Freedom of Information Act. Among the documents disclosed was a letter by a geologist summarizing his observations on the site as follows: "In general, I think [Vepco] has a pretty good story. Nevertheless, I would keep my fingers crossed and would not want to live near the North Anna Plant." [17] Of such disclosure is environmental controversy made.

It is unnecessary to rehearse here the extensive treatment given the Act in the law reviews and case law.[18] A discussion of the environmentally related cases sufficiently highlights why and how FOIA plays such a pivotal legal role in the fields of science and technology. The operative premise of the legislation is that all agency records ought to be disclosed except where specifically protected under nine exemptions,[19] which are at the heart of the Act. The exemptions relieve the agencies from disclosing matters that are:

(1) (A) specifically authorized under criteria established by an Executive order to be kept secret in the interest of national defense or foreign policy and (B) are in fact properly classified pursuant to such Executive order;

(2) related solely to the internal personnel rules and practices of an agency;

(3) specifically exempted from disclosure by statute . . . ;

17. Exhibit NX–39, In re Virginia Elec. and Power Co. (North Anna Power Station, Units 1, 2, 3, 4), Constr. Permits No. CPPR–77, –78 (Show Cause) (1974). The court of appeals was unimpressed. North Anna Environmental Coalition v. Nuclear Regulatory Comm'n, 174 U.S.App.D.C. 428, 533 F.2d 655 (1976). See also Rhode Island Comm. on Energy v. General Serv. Admin., 397 F.Supp. 41, 5 ELR 20685 (D.R.I.1975) (well documented NEPA case prepared largely on basis of FOIA disclosures).

18. For a comprehensive bibliography and summary of cases prior to January 1, 1974, see Senate Subcomm. on Administrative Practice and Procedures of the Comm. on the Judiciary, Freedom of Information Act Source Book: Legislative Materials, Cases, Articles, S.Doc.No.82, 93d Cong., 2d Sess. (1974). A later compendium of cases appears in 121 Cong.Rec. S16610 (daily ed. Sept. 24, 1975). See generally, Davis, The Information Act: A Preliminary Analysis, 34 U.Chi.L. Rev. 761 (1967); Kramer & Weinberg, Freedom of Information Act, 63 Geo. L.J. 49 (1974); Tuoni, NEPA and the Freedom of Information Act: A Prospect for Disclosure, 4 Environmental Affairs 179 (1975); Project, Government Information and the Rights of Citizens, 73 U.Mich.L.Rev. 971, 1022–163 (1975); Note, FOIA Amendments of 1974: An Analysis, 26 Syr.L.Rev. 951 (1975); Note, Developments Under the Freedom of Information Act—1975, 1976 Duke L.J. 366 (1976).

19. 5 U.S.C.A. § 552(b).

(4) trade secrets and commercial or financial information obtained from a person and privileged or confidential;

(5) inter-agency or intra-agency memorandums or letters which would not be available by law to a party other than an agency in litigation with the agency;

(6) personnel and medical files and similar files the disclosure of which would constitute a clearly unwarranted invasion of personal privacy;

(7) investigatory files compiled for law enforcement purposes [subject to several qualifications];

(8) contained in or related to examination, operating, or condition reports prepared by, on behalf of, or for the use of, an agency responsible for the regulation or supervision of financial institutions; or

(9) geological and geophysical information and data, including maps, concerning wells.

Of the nine exemptions, those proving to be the most important in environmental litigation involve: (1) intra-agency memoranda; (2) investigatory files; (3) trade secrets; (4) national security; (5) medical files; and (6) specific statutory exemptions.

a. *Intra-agency Memoranda*

The rationale of exemption 5 is that for public policy reasons the law should encourage "the free and uninhibited exchange and communications of opinions, ideas and points of view among government personnel."[20] The primary concern of the exemption is to protect the confidentiality of the decision-making process. Here, as elsewhere, the law is decidedly schizophrenic; for while the purpose of exemption 5 quite clearly is to allow the administrative decision-maker to deliberate in confidence with his advisors, the hard look doctrine of judicial review intrudes upon this confidentiality and probes the hows and whys of the decision, even to the extent of allowing an interested outsider to take the deposition of the Secretary of the Department of Transportation.[21] The exemption 5 case law draws several important lines attempting to reconcile these discordant themes.

The Supreme Court, interpreting the language that allows non-disclosure of intra-agency memoranda only insofar as they "would not be available by law to a party . . . in litigation with the

---

20. Verrazzano Trading Corp. v. United States, 349 F.Supp. 1401, 1406 (U.S. Customs Ct.1972); see Note, The Freedom of Information Act and the Exemption for Intra-Agency Memoranda, 86 Harv.L.Rev. 1047 (1973).

21. Citizens to Preserve Overton Park v. Volpe, 401 U.S. 402, 91 S.Ct. 814, 28 L.Ed.2d 136, 1 ELR 20110 (1971); see Nathanson, Probing the Mind of the Administrator: Hearing Variations and Standards of Judicial Review under the Administrative Procedures Act and other Federal Statutes, 75 Colum.L.Rev. 721 (1975); § 1.5 above.

agency," has made it clear that exemption 5 carries over the privileges well established in the context of civil discovery.[22] The attorney's work-product privilege "clearly applies" to memoranda prepared in contemplation of litigation strategy,[23] and equally clearly does not apply to opinions explaining why litigation will not be undertaken. The latter documents are final decisions and the "working law," which the public is entitled to know.[24] This distinction is important and correct, as clear as is the difference between a prehearing strategy session and an agency rule of law. Opinions of the general counsel obviously can be an important source of administrative law.

The meaning of an "agency" is one issue that arises in distinguishing between mere advice within the decision-making process and a final decision. The Act, defining an agency principally as an "authority of the United States," is not decisive.[25] In Soucie v. David,[26] the court concluded that the now defunct Office of Science and Technology (OST) was an "agency" under the FOIA because it was an administrative unit with substantial independent authority in the exercise of specific functions. The court required disclosure of an OST report evaluating the supersonic transport aircraft (the SST) program, rejecting an exemption 5 claim that the document was a privileged intra-agency communication between the OST and the President. Going the other way is International Paper Co. v. Federal Power Commission,[27] which refused to treat the staff of the Commission as a separate entity for the purpose of defeating an exemption 5 claim. Obviously, staff recommendations, like counsel opinions, range in function from preliminary advice to final decisions.

Exemption 5 has been "authoritatively construed" as distinguishing between "materials reflecting deliberative or policymaking processes on the one hand, and purely factual investigative matters on the other."[28] Claims of meddling in the agencies' inner councils thus can

22. National Labor Relations Bd. v. Sears, Roebuck & Co., 421 U.S. 132, 95 S.Ct. 1504, 44 L.Ed.2d 29 (1975). See also Vaughn v. Rosen, 173 U.S.App. D.C. 187, 523 F.2d 1136 (1975); Schwartz v. Internal Revenue Serv., 167 U.S.App.D.C. 301, 511 F.2d 1303 (1975); Mead Data Control, Inc. v. Dep't of Air Force, 402 F.Supp. 460 (D.C.D.C.1975).

23. 421 U.S. at 154, 95 S.Ct. at 1518, 44 L.Ed.2d at 49.

24. E. g., Environmental Protection Agency, 1 Collection of Legal Opinions: December 1971–December 1973.

25. 5 U.S.C.A. § 551(e); see Lombardo v. Handler, 397 F.Supp. 792 (D.D.C. 1975), aff'd per curiam — U.S.App. D.C. —, 543 F.2d 1043 (1976) (discussed in § 1.12 below).

26. 145 U.S.App.D.C. 144, 448 F.2d 1067 (1971).

27. 438 F.2d 1349 (2d Cir. 1971), cert. denied 404 U.S. 827; see Bagge, The Federal Power Commission and Freedom of Information Act, 23 Ad.L.Rev. 153 (1971).

28. Ethyl Corp. v. Environmental Protection Agency, 478 F.2d 47, 49, 3 ELR 20428 (4th Cir. 1973); see Renegotiation Bd. v. Grumman Aircraft Engineering Corp., 421 U.S. 168, 189–90, 95 S.Ct. 1491, 1503, 44 L.Ed.2d 57, 74 (1975); Environmental Protec-

be avoided by confining inquiries to factual matters; boilerplate requests under the Act typically bristle with references to "factual" information. The search for facts may reveal medical and scientific data considered by the agency in proposing regulations,[29] or even accident[30] and investigation[31] reports, some of which contain certain conclusions or opinions by the investigator. Test data, field observations, interview records, and question and answer correspondence all should be readily available in response to properly worded requests.

Some staff factual analyses and discussions that are intimately a part of the decision-making process, nonetheless, may be kept confidential. That is the apparent rationale of Renegotiation Board v. Grumman Aircraft Engineering Corp.,[32] where the Court approved the nondisclosure of staff draft decisions whose full reasoning never was adopted by the Board. The same justification is evident also in Montrose Chemical Corp. v. Train,[33] where a DDT manufacturer sought staff-prepared summaries of the factual evidence adduced in the 9200 page transcript developed during the EPA hearings to cancel DDT registrations. One of the documents at issue was entitled "Analysis of Risks Attributed to DDT," and the other was entitled "Summary and Analysis of Evidence of Benefits." Both summaries principally were factual and thus arguably discoverable under exemption 5. They also were part of the decision-making process which exemption 5 is designed to protect. The court struck the balance in favor of non-disclosure, concluding that the summaries of the factual material in the public record reflected a deliberative process, which exemption 5 is intended to shelter.

Confined to the narrow situation of record summaries of complex administrative cases, *Montrose Chemical* is not clearly wrong. Montrose sought not only facts but how the staff evaluated the facts and how the Administrator reached his decision. While it is difficult to foresee any serious encroachment on the agency's decision-making process by these disclosures, the manufacturer was denied access only to a convenient summary of factual material that was otherwise

tion Agency v. Mink, 410 U.S. 73, 89, 93 S.Ct. 827, 837, 35 L.Ed.2d 119, 133, 3 ELR 20057, 20060 (1973). See also United States v. J. B. Williams Co., 402 F.Supp. 796 (S.D.N.Y.1975) (holding that exemption 5 does protect predecisional memoranda but does not apply to post decisional memoranda that merely explain decision); Sierra Club v. Morton, 395 F.Supp. 1187, 5 ELR 20383 (D.D.C.1975) (holding that exemption 5 does not apply to annual budget request for the National Wildlife Refuge System); Conservation Foundation v. Dep't of Interior, 2 ELR 20356 (D.C.D.C.1972) (holding that exemption 5 does not apply to National Outdoor Recreation Plan).

29. Ethyl Corp. v. Environmental Protection Agency, supra note 28.

30. Moore-McCormack Lines, Inc. v. I.T.O. Corp., 508 F.2d 945 (4th Cir. 1974).

31. Machin v. Zuckert, 144 U.S.App. D.C. 335, 316 F.2d 336 (1963), cert. denied 375 U.S. 896 (still authoritative although it preceded passage of the Act).

32. 421 U.S. 168, 95 S.Ct. 1491, 44 L.Ed.2d 57 (1975).

33. 160 U.S.App.D.C. 270, 491 F.2d 63, 4 ELR 20160 (1974).

available. Inveterate seekers of information are not likely to discount the utility of syntheses, indices and summaries of voluminous records and therefore would quarrel with the court's solicitous protection of the decision-making process. Mild disagreement would become strong dissent, however, if the rationale of *Montrose* is invoked to prevent the disclosure of facts not otherwise available on the ground that the form or content of the presentation would reveal unduly the process of decision-making. Decisions based on secret evidence surely are no more defensible than decisions based on secret law.

It would seem that as one moves farther from the point of decision and down the chain of command the law might be less solicitous of protecting opinions and advice intertwined with factual observations. One court has held, however, that hand written notes of Atomic Energy Commission staff members are exempt, both as intra-agency memoranda and because personal notations are not "agency" records.[34] As a general proposition, the decision is wrong. Memos and notes containing opinions that are written at the field level ought to be available. A notation by one staff member to another that he is "getting the feeling of a 'run-around'" or "believes that we ought to stop fooling around with these guys" might be construed as a factual conclusion that the applicant's data is insufficient or as a policy recommendation advocating intensification of the investigation. Either interpretation warrants disclosure.

Techniques for sorting out the privileged from the public information vary. In EPA v. Mink,[35] Mr. Justice White wrote that the public's access to internal memoranda is governed by "the same flexible, commonsense approach that has long governed private parties' discovery of such documents involved in litigation with Government agencies." This approach "continues to extend to the discovery of purely factual material appearing in those documents in a form that is severable without compromising the private remainder of the documents."[36] Typically, the process involves an *in camera* inspection by the court, unless the agency resisting disclosure demonstrates that the documents are purely advisory and contain no separable factual information. The lower federal courts have imposed strict procedural obligations on agencies opposing disclosure, such as discouraging the *en masse* submission of allegedly privileged documents and requiring "a relatively detailed analysis in manageable segments" and

---

34. Porter County Chapter of Izaak Walton League, Inc. v. Atomic Energy Comm'n, 380 F.Supp. 630, 5 ELR 20274 (N.D.Ind.1974); see Note, The National Environmental Policy Act, The Freedom of Information Act and the Atomic Energy Commission: The Need for Environmental Information, 47 Ind.L.J. 755 (1972).

35. 410 U.S. 73, 91, 93 S.Ct. 827, 838, 35 L.Ed.2d 119, 134 (1973).

36. 410 U.S. at 91, 93 S.Ct. at 838, 35 L.Ed.2d at 134.

a "particularized and specific justification" for exemptions.[37] Following judicial review, agency documents often are ordered produced with pages, paragraphs, and even words missing.

While Congress has no immediate inclination to abolish the intra-agency communication exemption, the justifications for it continue to erode. Secrecy in the deliberative process is under attack by the hard look doctrine. In addition, the Advisory Committee Act effectively exposes a consequential aspect of government decision-making.[38] Finally, various "government in the sunshine" proposals would force disclosure of additional important aspects of the decision-making process.[39]

b. *Investigatory Files*

Government investigations conducted for enforcement purposes can be extremely significant to private parties. The settlement of litigation without disclosures can offend the right to know. The smog conspiracy case is a well known example.[40] But disclosures also can compromise investigative techniques and the rights of private parties. Prior to the 1974 amendments, courts actively sought to prevent damaging publication of investigative files. Thus, it was decided that a file could be "compiled for law enforcement purposes" even though an adjudication was not "imminent or even likely, either at the time the material was amassed or at the time disclosure [was] sought." [41] Exemption 7 was applied to prevent disclosure of material relating to the assassination of President Kennedy long after the possibility of a prosecution; [42] of a report on the My Lai incident that formed the basis for prosecutions that, with but one exception, had been

---

37. Ash Grove Cement Co. v. Federal Trade Comm'n, 167 U.S.App.D.C. 249, 511 F.2d 815 (1975); Cuneo v. Schlesinger, 157 U.S.App.D.C. 368, 484 F.2d 1086 (1973), cert. denied 415 U.S. 977 (1974); Vaughn v. Rosen, 157 U.S.App.D.C. 340, 484 F.2d 820 (1971), cert. denied 415 U.S. 977 (1974). Comment, Vaughn v. Rosen, Toward True Freedom of Information, 122 U.Pa.L.Rev. 731 (1974).

38. See § 1.11 below.

39. See Government in the Sunshine Act, Pub.L. No. 94-409, 90 Stat. 1241, 5 U.S.C.A. §§ 552b, 557. See generally Comm. on Government Operations, Government in the Sunshine Act, S.Rep.No.354, 94th Cong., 1st Sess. (1975); Comm. on Rules and Administration, Government in the Sunshine Act, S.Rep.No.381, 94th Cong., 1st Sess. (1975); Hearings on S.260, Before the Subcomm. on Reorganization, Research, and International Organizations of the Senate Comm. on Government Operations, 93d Cong., 2d Sess. (1974).

40. In re Multidist. Vehicle Air Pollution, 481 F.2d 122 (9th Cir. 1973).

41. Center for Nat'l Policy Review on Race and Urban Issues v. Weinberger, 163 U.S.App.D.C. 368, 371, 502 F.2d 370, 373 (1974) (upholding non-disclosure of 22 "open and active" files involving HEW review of public school segregation and discrimination practices). See also Note, Amendment of the Seventh Exemption Under FOIA, 16 Wm. & Mary L.Rev. 697 (1975).

42. Weisberg v. Dep't of Justice, 160 U.S.App.D.C. 71, 489 F.2d 1195 (1973) (en banc), cert. denied 416 U.S. 993 (1974).

concluded;[43] and of material amassed in connection with a civil enforcement proceeding that was only "conceivable."[44]

An important distinction drawn in the case law is that between "information acquired essentially as a matter of routine," which is usually subject to disclosure, and information collected where the agency inquiry focuses "with special intensity upon a particular party," which brings exemption 7 into play.[45] The exemption is not necessarily established "by the mere fact that one of the purposes of opening a file is investigative, or that sanctions hover as a possibility somewhere down the road, or that some material in some file may at some point be used for some law enforcement purpose."[46] Instead, courts are governed by "good sense and the essential heft of the case."[47] As with exemption 5 for intra-agency communications, the government must come forward with hard specifics, rather than loose generalities, to protect its investigative files. The same rules on disclosing segregable material should apply.

Congressional dissatisfaction with broad readings of exemption 7 led to an amendment in 1974.[48] The law now exempts "investigatory records compiled for law enforcement purposes, but only to the extent that the production of such records would (A) interfere with enforcement proceedings, (B) deprive a person of a right to a fair trial or an impartial adjudication, (C) constitute an unwarranted invasion of personal privacy, (D) disclose the identity of a confidential source and, in the case of a record compiled by a criminal law enforcement authority in the course of a criminal investigation, or by an agency conducting a lawful national security intelligence investigation, confidential information furnished only by the confidential source, (E) disclose investigative techniques and procedures, or (F) endanger the life or physical safety of law enforcement personnel."[49]

Exemption 7 narrows substantially the protection of government investigative files. It calls for a closely focused inquiry into whether a disclosure in fact will compromise a pending case, injure a potential defendant, or reveal unusual enforcement techniques.[50] Information

---

43. Aspin v. Dep't of Defense, 160 U.S.App.D.C. 231, 491 F.2d 24 (1973).

44. Ditlow v. Brinegar, 161 U.S.App.D.C. 154, 494 F.2d 1073 (1974) (per curiam), cert. denied 419 U.S. 974; see Exxon Corp. v. Federal Trade Comm'n, 384 F.Supp. 755 (D.C.D.C. 1974) (upholding non-disclosure of a report on the petroleum industry).

45. Center for Nat'l Policy Review on Race and Urban Issues v. Weinberger, 163 U.S.App.D.C. 368, 371–72, 502 F.2d 370, 373–74 (1974).

46. 163 U.S.App.D.C. at 373, 502 F.2d at 375.

47. Ibid.

48. Comm. of Conference, Freedom of Information Act Amendments, H.R.Rep.No.1380, 93d Cong., 2d Sess. 12 (1974) [hereinafter cited as Conference Report].

49. Section 2(b), amending 5 U.S.C.A. § 552(b)(7).

50. See Frankel v. Securities & Exch. Comm'n, 460 F.2d 813, 817 (2d Cir.

gathered in connection with a typical civil enforcement proceeding encountered in environmental cases eventually should see the light of day. Disclosure also cannot interfere with cases formally concluded or those assigned to an indefinite administrative limbo. Indeed, there is little reason to believe that publicly conducted enforcement deliberations are incompatible with the rights of parties in many situations.[51] Thus, the justifications offered for continued confidentiality after an enforcement file has been closed are unwarranted in many environmental cases: corporations are not entitled to protection on personal privacy grounds, and in the unusual situation where an informer is involved, much of the file can be disclosed without compromising his identity. The protection of "investigative techniques and procedures" is aimed only at highly confidential investigative strategies and not at staff manuals, instructions, or "routine techniques and procedures already well known to the public such as ballistics tests, fingerprinting and other scientific tests or commonly known techniques." [52]

An enforcement proceeding that results in a consent decree, a modest fine, or a no-action decision often is a sore spot with outsiders who expect more. Especially is this true where the enforcer's reasons, and particularly his evidence, are not disclosed. Requiring a legitimate law enforcement objective to justify nondisclosure should improve the quality—and certainly the accountability—of discretionary justice by the prosecutor. Disclosure is a mild form of public review of prosecutorial discretion.

c. *Trade Secrets*

The 1974 amendments made no changes to the exemption for "trade secrets and commercial or financial information obtained from a person and privileged or confidential." The use of the trade secrets exemption often has raised hackles in environmental circles not known to be sensitive to problems of commercial espionage.[53] In-

---

1972), cert. denied 409 U.S. 889. The 1974 amendments should not be read as repudiating interpretations such as Wellford v. Hardin, 444 F.2d 21 (4th Cir. 1971) (rejecting privacy objections to the release of warning letters sent to meat and poultry producers). The addition of a privacy factor to exemption 7 should be read only as precluding the disclosure of intimate details about individuals. Compare note 78, infra. But see J. L. Mashaw & R. A. Merrill, Introduction to the American Public Law System 651 (1975).

51. Cf. Nebraska Press Ass'n v. Stuart, 427 U.S. 539, 554, 96 S.Ct. 2791, 2800, 49 L.Ed.2d 683, 701 (1976) (pre-trial gag order). See also Ditlow v. Brinegar, 161 U.S.App.D.C. 154, 494 F.2d 1073 (1974) (requiring disclosure of correspondence between the National Highway Traffic Safety Administration and auto manufacturers); §§ 3.19, 4.21 below (air and water pollution enforcement).

52. Conference Report at 12.

53. See Hearings on the Federal Insecticide, Fungicide and Rodenticide Act Extension, Before the House Comm. on Agriculture, H.R.Doc.No.0, 94th Cong., 1st Sess. 387–93 (1975) (statement of Dr. Jack D. Early, Vice President, National Agricultural Chemicals Ass'n). See also Natural

dustrial processes, protected as trade secrets, are often very public polluters. The common practice in the past of hiding effluent or emission data behind the trade secrets screen is repudiated expressly in the Clean Air Amendments of 1970 [54] and the Federal Water Pollution Control Act Amendments of 1972,[55] both of which declare emissions data to be public information. Of all the abuses prompting this legislative response, none is better known than the trade secrets barrier successfully erected to postpone for six years a proposed Department of Interior inventory of industrial water wastes.[56]

The major issue in the case law interpreting the trade secrets exemption is whether it protects three classes of material (i. e.,—(1) trade secrets; (2) commercial or financial information; and (3) privileged or confidential information) or only two (i. e., (1) trade secrets and (2) commercial or financial information which is privileged or confidential). The first interpretation, for reasons that are obvious, creates a "cavernous" [57] loophole for any material in agency files perceived as "confidential." It is rejected by the balance of academic and judicial opinion.[58]

A leading case interpreting exemption 4 is National Parks & Conservation Ass'n v. Morton,[59] where a conservation group attempted to gain access to agency records that included audits of concessionaires operating within national parks. The court explained that commercial and financial matter is "confidential" for purposes of the exemption if disclosure is likely to have either of the following effects: "(1) [to] impair the Government's ability to obtain necessary information in the future; or (2) [to] cause substantial harm to the competitive position of the person from whom it was obtained." [60]

Resources Defense Council v. Environmental Protection Agency, 478 F.2d 875, 893, 3 ELR 20375, 20382 (1st Cir. 1973) (holding that EPA erred in approving the Massachusetts air pollution implementation plan, which, among other things, allowed certain emission reports to be held confidential as trade secrets).

54. Pub.L. No. 91–604, § 114(c), 84 Stat. 1688 (1970), 42 U.S.C.A. § 1857c–9(c).

55. Pub.L. No. 92–500, § 308(b)(2), 86 Stat. 858 (1972), 33 U.S.C.A. § 1318 (b)(2).

56. For details, see D. Zwick, Water Wasteland 243–52 (1971).

57. Katz, The Games Bureaucrats Play: Hide and Seek Under the Freedom of Information Act, 48 Tex.L.Rev. 1261, 1263 (1970).

58. See id. at 1261–70; Brockway v. Dep't of Air Force, 518 F.2d 1184 (8th Cir. 1975); Rabbitt v. Dep't of the Air Force, 383 F.Supp. 1065 (S.D. N.Y.1974). But see Koch, The Freedom of Information Act: Suggestions for Making Information Available to the Public, 32 Md.L.Rev. 189, 216 (1972).

59. 162 U.S.App.D.C. 223, 498 F.2d 765, 4 ELR 20385 (1974), subsequent appeal — U.S.App.D.C. —, 547 F.2d 673 (1976).

60. 162 U.S.App.D.C. at 228, 498 F.2d at 770, 4 ELR at 20387; see Sterling Drug, Inc. v. Federal Trade Comm'n, 146 U.S.App.D.C. 237, 248, 450 F.2d 698, 709 (1971), quoting S.Rep.No.813, 89th Cong., 2d Sess. 9 (1964) (stating the test of disclosure to be whether the information sought is of the type "which would customarily not be released to the public by the person from whom it was obtained"). See

Quite clearly, the Government's ability to obtain information in the future is not impaired by disclosing documentation it requires; but disclosure very well might discourage future contributions from volunteers whose confidences are breached.[61] Nevertheless, the courts do not allow agencies to dictate the terms of disclosure, by automatically honoring their promises of confidentiality.[62] Instead, there must be an independent judicial determination that the material is commercial and financial in nature and that it is confidential.

Whether the disclosure of commercial information jeopardizes a competitive position requires a case by case inquiry. The court in *National Parks & Conservation Ass'n* remanded for such a determination despite conceding the plausibility of the argument that national park concessionaires were monopolists with no competitive interest to protect. A finding of competitive injury may be sustained more easily where information is sought, not by a public interest group, but by a competitor.[63]

Exemption 4's protection of "trade secrets" involves an inquiry into one of the law's murkier regions.[64] A "trade secret", for purposes of the Freedom of Information Act, "may consist of any formula, pattern, device or compilation of information which is used in one's business, and which gives him an opportunity to obtain an advantage over competitors who do not know or use it." [65] The courts have read this exemption narrowly by insisting that the government carry its burden of demonstrating that the information withheld is commercially valuable.[66] EPA regulations implementing the Freedom of Information Act impose the burden of establishing "trade secret" protection on the party opposing disclosure.[67]

also Charles River Park A, Inc., v. Dep't of Housing & Urban Dev., 171 U.S.App.D.C. 286, 519 F.2d 935 (1975); Continental Oil Co. v. Federal Power Comm'n, 519 F.2d 31 (5th Cir. 1975).

61. See Tobacco Inst. v. Federal Trade Comm'n, Civ.No. 3035–67 (D.C.D.C. April 11, 1968) (refusing to disclose questionnaires submitted in confidence to the government by persons and organizations interested in the subject of smoking and health). The holding is an improper application of exemption 4 since the material was not commercial or financial. It also probably is not justified under exemption 6, which protects personal privacy.

62. See, e. g., Petkas v. Staats, 163 U.S.App.D.C. 327, 501 F.2d 887 (1974); Save the Dolphins v. Dep't of Commerce, 404 F.Supp. 407 (N.D.Cal.1975).

63. Compare McCoy v. Weinberger, 386 F.Supp. 504 (W.D.Ky.1974) (refusing to disclose to a competitor an unaudited cost report of a nursing home) with Hughes Aircraft Co. v. Schlesinger, 384 F.Supp. 292 (C.D.Cal. 1974) (requiring disclosure of the Hughes Aircraft Affirmative Action Plan). See also National Parks & Conservation Ass'n v. Kleppe, —— U. S.App.D.C. ——, 547 F.2d 673 (1976).

64. See Note, Developments in the Law —Competitive Torts, 77 Harv.L.Rev. 888, 947–59 (1964).

65. Restatement of Torts § 757, Comment b (1939).

66. Washington Research Project, Inc. v. Dep't of Health, Educ. & Welfare, 164 U.S.App.D.C. 169, 175–76 n. 6, 504 F.2d 238, 244–45 n. 6 (1974), cert. denied 421 U.S. 963 (1975) (holding that a noncommercial scientist's research design is not a trade secret or item of commercial information).

67. 40 CFR § 11.5.

Sec. 1.10 FREEDOM OF INFORMATION ACT

The House Report accompanying the Freedom of Information Act affirms broadly that a "citizen must be able to confide in its government." [68] Fortunately, this sentiment is repudiated by the basic thrust and dominant purposes of the Act, particularly as applied to corporations, which have no personal right of privacy.[69] Instead, the presumption ought to be that communications between a corporation and the government are the public's business. Cautious corporate counsel long ago recognized that submitting information to the government is tantamount to making it public—by leak, application of the Act, mistake or otherwise.

d. *National Security*

EPA v. Mink [70] arose out of an effort by Congresswoman Patsy Mink and several others to gain access to a number of documents prepared by an "Under Secretaries Committee" on the proposed underground nuclear test known as "Cannikin," which eventually was conducted at Amchitka Island, Alaska. Six of the documents were described in an affidavit as having been classified "Top Secret" or "secret" pursuant to Executive Order 10501.[71] The issue concerning these documents was whether the mere assertion of the secret classification is sufficient to trigger the exemption, or alternatively, whether an *in camera* inspection by the court is permissible to sift out the "non-secret components." Reading the exemption both literally and narrowly, Mr. Justice White concluded that the Court's inquiry was confined to a determination of whether the "secret" stamp had been invoked by the Executive. If the classification had been invoked, the documents were "specifically required by Executive order to be kept secret in the interest of the national defense or foreign policy."

The holding in *Mink* was a serious blow to the utility of the Freedom of Information Act. Mr. Justice Brennan, concurring and dissenting in part, pointed out that Executive Order 10501, which was promulgated years before passage of the Act, simply delegated the right to classify to agency heads who, in turn, could adopt blanket classifications without reference to the content of a particular document.[72] The result was a surrender of a good deal of information to executive ukase.

---

68. House Comm. on Gov't Operations, Clarifying & Protecting the Right of the Public to Information, H.R.Rep.No. 1497, 89th Cong., 2d Sess. 10 (1966).

69. Robertson v. Dep't of Defense, 402 F.Supp. 1342, 1348 (D.C.D.C.1975). See also Note, In Camera Inspections Under the FOIA, 41 U.Chi.L.Rev. 557 (1974).

70. 410 U.S. 73, 93 S.Ct. 827, 35 L. Ed.2d 119 (1973).

71. 18 Fed.Reg. 7049 (1953), 3 CFR 280 (1970), superseded by Exec.Order No. 11652, 37 Fed.Reg. 5209 (1972).

72. 410 U.S. at 97, 93 S.Ct. at 840–41, 35 L.Ed.2d at 137–38.

Congress moved quickly to repair the damage done by EPA v. Mink by enacting the 1974 amendments, which exempt documents "(A) specifically authorized under criteria established by an Executive order to be kept secret in the interest of national defense or foreign policy and (B) are in fact properly classified pursuant to such Executive order."[73] The Conference Report expressed an intention to "override" EPA v. Mink;[74] this objective was realized by requiring an *in camera* inspection of the documents at issue and a judicial determination of the propriety of the documents' classification.[75]

The power to classify is the power to define the understanding of others. It is a power best put in perpetual jeopardy by requiring the declassification of material after the national security exigencies are past, by threatening or actually imposing sanctions for errors of judgment, and by subjecting executive decisions to external judicial review. Since reasonable men might differ about the national security implications of, for example, research into the use of marine mammals as weapons systems, or the encouragement of blizzards in the enemy's homeland, most would agree the classifier's judgment should not be blindly accepted.

e. *Medical Files and Personal Privacy*

Exemption 6 exempts from disclosure "personnel and medical files and similar files the disclosure of which would constitute a clearly unwarranted invasion of personal privacy." As with the trade secrets exemption, the rationale for this provision is based on powerful policy considerations. At the same time, an overly broad reading of the protection of privacy policy could nullify a substantial part of the Act since many disclosures arguably embarrass someone (perhaps the author or recipient of a document or persons mentioned in it). Accordingly, it is wholly out of line to conclude, as some have, that any material deemed "confidential" should be protected on privacy grounds under exemption 4,[76] or that a staff member's privacy is entitled to protection under exemption 5.[77]

Exemption 6 goes quite far enough to prevent "a clearly unwarranted invasion of personal privacy," such as the medical or personnel files specifically mentioned. It has been read only as precluding

---

73. Section 2(a), amending 5 U.S.C.A. § 552(b)(1).

74. Conference Report at 12.

75. 5 U.S.C.A. § 552(a)(4)(B); see Comment, Judicial Review of Classified Documents: Amendments to the Freedom of Information Act, 12 Harv.J. Legis. 415 (1975).

76. Koch, The Freedom of Information Act: Suggestions for Making Information Available to the Public, 32 Md.L.Rev. 189, 217 (1972).

77. Porter County Chapter of the Izaak Walton League, Inc. v. Atomic Energy Comm'n, 380 F.Supp. 630 (N.D.Ind.1974).

disclosure of "intimate details" of a "highly personal nature."[78] Thus, an interested party was allowed to gain access to monitoring data compiled by the EPA on the radiation levels in certain homes in Vail, Colorado, which had been exposed to uranium mining tailings.[79] Privacy often can be protected by excision of certain references and other limited editing, which the Act prefers to blanket nondisclosures.

f. *The Specific Statutory Exemptions*

Non-disclosure of matters "specifically exempted from disclosure by statute" is narrowly limited by judicial construction and legislative action. The courts have rejected decisively attempts to base "specific" exemptions on vague statutory directives to protect broad categories of information.[80] The exemption "require[s] that the statutes in question either clearly identify some classes of documents to be kept confidential or, at the very least, prescribe specific standards by which an administrative agency can determine the propriety of disclosure."[81] A backing away from this proposition by the Supreme Court in 1975[82] was abruptly put to rest by the Congress the following year.[83]

It was never in doubt that access to information is indispensable to attorneys practicing environmental law. Thus, the Freedom of Information Act by now is a close friend of many practitioners. But another important statute—the federal Advisory Committee Act—is a virtual stranger to all but a few.

---

78. Robles v. Environmental Protection Agency, 484 F.2d 843, 845, 3 ELR 20796 (4th Cir. 1973), citing Note, Invasion of Privacy and the Freedom of Information Act: Getman v. N.L.R.B., 40 Geo.Wash.L.Rev. 527, 532 (1972); see Rose v. Dep't of the Air Force, 495 F.2d 261 (2d Cir. 1974).

79. Robles v. Environmental Protection Agency, supra note 78.

80. Sears, Roebuck & Co. v. General Serv. Administration, 166 U.S.App. D.C. 194, 509 F.2d 527 (1974) (rejecting suggestion that 18 U.S.C.A. § 1905 is a "specific" exemption); Stretch v. Weinberger, 495 F.2d 639 (3d Cir. 1974); M. A. Schapiro & Co. v. Securities & Exch. Comm'n, 339 F.Supp. 467 (D.D.C.1972).

81. Cutler v. Civil Aeronautics Bd., 375 F.Supp. 722, 724 (D.C.D.C.1974) (requiring the C.A.B. to disclose certain contingency plans for cutback of airline services to conserve fuel during the 1973 oil embargo).

82. Federal Aviation Administration v. Robertson, 422 U.S. 255, 265, 95 S.Ct. 2140, 2147, 45 L.Ed.2d 164, 173 (1975) (holding that the term "specific" as used in exemption 3 does not mean that the exemption only applies to documents specified by the subject statute).

83. Pub.L. No. 94–405, § 5 (1976), amending 5 U.S.C.A. § 552(b)(3) to read:

(3) specifically exempted from disclosure by statute (other than section 552b of this title), provided that such statute (A) requires that the matters be withheld from the public in such a manner as to leave no discretion on the issue, or (B) establishes particular criteria for withholding or refers to particular types of matters to be withheld

. . . .

See S.Rep. No. 1178, 94th Cong., 2d Sess. (1976).

§ 1.11 Advisory Committee Act

A potentially valuable instructor for practitioners and students of environmental law is the Federal Advisory Committee Act of 1972.[1] During 1970 and 1971, congressional hearings were held documenting the confusion of policies among federal agencies overseeing hundreds of advisory committees, many of them dealing with natural resources, environmental, health and safety measures.[2] First were the procedural disclosures—little was known about the number of committees, who sat on them, or what they did. They often met in secret, excluded unfriendly faces, and charged exorbitant fees for their minutes, if they kept any at all.

More important were revelations that advisory committees more than occasionally acted as important policy makers. Working from within an agency, they can shape regulations, influence research, veto new drugs, or approve sites for nuclear reactors. This is true not only of the better known committees—the Nuclear Regulatory Commission's Advisory Committee on Reactor Safeguards, the Department of Interior's National Petroleum Council, the Department of Commerce's National Industrial Pollution Control Council [3]—but also of the lesser known committees, such as the Department of Interior's Joint Task Force on Eutrophication, which played an early role in government decision-making on phosphates in detergents; the National Air Pollution Control Administration's primary nonferrous smelting industry liaison committee, which had a hand in shaping government research on the industry's air pollution problems; and the Technical Advisory Committee to the Office of Pipeline Safety, which made its contribution by revising a questionnaire designed to probe such pertinent topics as the depth and age of natural gas pipelines in the ground.

The range and scope of issues considered by advisory committees is amply illustrated by simply listing the committees advising a single federal agency (the Environmental Protection Agency) identified in the March 1973 First Annual Report on Federal Advisory

---

1. Pub.L. No. 92–463, 86 Stat. 770 (1972), 5 U.S.C.A. app. I, as amended Pub.L. No. 94–409, 90 Stat. 1247 (1976). This section draws upon several published works by the author on the subject. See W. Rodgers, Corporate Country: A State Shaped to Suit Technology (1973); Rodgers, The National Industrial Pollution Control Council: Advise or Collude?, 13 B.C.Ind. & Com.L.Rev. 719 (1972); Rodgers, The Persistent Problem of the Persistent Pesticides: A Lesson in Environmental Law, 70 Colum.L. Rev. 567 (1970); Rodgers, The Back-Room Arm Twisters, The Nation, June 8, 1974, at 722.

2. See Hearings on Advisory Committees (S. 3067), Before the Subcomm. on Intergovernment Relations of the Senate Comm. on Government Operations, 91st Cong., 2d Sess. (1970).

3. For further details, see Rodgers, The National Industrial Pollution Control Council: Advise or Collude?, 13 B.C. Ind. & Com.L.Rev. 719 (1972). See also Steck, Private Influences on Environmental Policy: Case of the National Industrial Pollution Control Council, 5 Environmental L. 241 (1975).

Committees:[4] Advisory Committee on the Revision and Application of Drinking Water Standards, Aldrin/Dieldrin Advisory Committee, Air Pollution Chemistry and Physics Advisory Committee, Air Pollution Research Grants Advisory Committee, Coal Desulfurization Advisory Committee, Coal Preparation Industrial Advisory Committee, Effluent Standards and Water Quality Information Advisory Committee, Engineering and Urban Health Sciences Study Section, Environmental Radiation Exposure Advisory Committee, Grain and Feed Industrial Advisory Committee, Hazardous Materials Advisory Committee, Meteorology Advisory Committee, Mirex Advisory Committee, National Air Pollution Control Techniques Advisory Committee, National Air Pollution Manpower Development Advisory Committee, National Air Quality Criteria Advisory Committee, Paint and Varnish Advisory Committee, Petrochemical Industry Advisory Committee, Phosphate Industry Liaison Committee, President's Advisory Committee on Environmental Merit Awards Program, President's Air Quality Advisory Board, Primary Aluminum Industry Liaison Committee, Soap and Detergent Industrial Advisory Committee, Technical Advisory Group for Municipal Waste Water Systems, and Water Pollution Control Advisory Board. While not all of these committees influence policy, many of them do in important and subtle ways.

The Advisory Committee Act contains two basic legislative strategies for the taming and supervision of advisory committees. It imposes loose management controls on their creation, membership and jurisdiction and strict procedural requirements on how they conduct business. On the management side, Congress found it necessary to stress that "the function of advisory committees should be advisory only and that all matters under their consideration should be determined, in accordance with law, by the official, agency or officer involved."[5] Each standing committee of the Congress is directed to reassess advisory committees under its jurisdiction with a view towards possible abolition or merger. Congressional committees authorizing advisory committees in the future are obliged to include in the authorizing bill "a clearly defined purpose" for the advisory group, a requirement that the "membership of the advisory committee . . . be fairly balanced in terms of the points of view represented," and a provision "to assure that the advice and recommendations of the advisory committee will not be influenced inappropriately by the appointing authority or by any special interest."[6] The President is ordered to "make an annual report to the Congress on the activities, status, and changes in the composition of advisory commit-

---

4. Section 6(c).

5. Section 2(b)(6).

6. Section 5(b). It is doubtful that these directives, addressing the future conduct of standing committees of the Congress, are subject to judicial review.

tees in existence during the preceding calendar year." [7] Each agency head is directed to designate an Advisory Committee Management Officer and to adopt "uniform administrative guidelines and management controls for advisory committees established by that agency." [8] The Office of Management and Budget is given authority to review advisory committee activities of the agencies and to prescribe "administrative guidelines and management controls" for the committees.[9] The OMB guidelines now extant add some administrative gloss to the Act.[10]

The procedural strictures on the activities of advisory committees are considerable. Meetings or other actions shall not be undertaken prior to the preparation and filing of a charter with various authorities (including the head of the agency to whom the committee reports and standing congressional committees having legislative jurisdiction). The charter must describe the committee's objectives, scope of activity, and other details of its operation.[11] The Act requires, subject to certain exceptions, that each committee give "timely notice" of its meetings in the Federal Register,[12] open its deliberations to the public,[13] allow interested persons to attend and make statements,[14] make available at cost transcripts of meetings,[15] and arrange for "detailed minutes" of each meeting containing a record of people in attendance, an "accurate description of matters discussed and conclusions reached," and copies "of all reports received, issued or approved by the advisory committee." [16] Subject to the exemptions of the Freedom of Information Act, the Advisory Committee Act assures public access to "the records, reports, transcripts, minutes, appendixes, working papers, drafts, studies, agenda, or other documents which were made available to or prepared for or by each advisory committee." [17] It is apparent that the Act declares war on the intimacy of the advisory committee process; the instruments of attack are full disclosure, open debate and accountability.

7. Section 6(c). These reports—the third one was published in March of 1975—are important contributions to the literature on advisory committees although they consist of little more than a catalogue of existing committees.

8. Section 8.

9. Sections 7(b), (c).

10. OMB Circ. No. A–63 (rev. Mar. 27, 1974), Transmittal Memorandum, Nos. 1 and 2, July 19, 1974, reproduced as App. C to the President's Third Ann. Rep. on Federal Advisory Committees (1975). The current OMB guidelines supersede the joint OMB-Department of Justice Memorandum on Implementation of the Federal Advisory Committee Act, 38 Fed.Reg. 2306 (1973), which in many particulars was a more detailed and spirited implementation of the congressional purposes expressed in the Act.

11. Section 9(c).

12. Section 10(a)(2).

13. Section 10(a)(1).

14. Section 10(a)(3).

15. Section 11.

16. Section 10(c).

17. Section 10(b).

A wide range of problems has arisen in determining when the Act applies. An "advisory committee" is defined broadly to include any committee "established or utilized" by the President or by one or more agencies "in the interest of obtaining advice or recommendations".[18] This definition has been criticized as "not a model of draftsmanship,"[19] and it leaves room for considerable judicial maneuvering through the shoals of the legislative history. Although the trend of the case law is not yet clear, the federal district courts have been chary of broad readings that would upset traditional patterns of the government's advisory apparatus. Thus, it has been held that a committee is not "established" by statute unless it is specifically named and defined in the legislation to which it owes its existence.[20] Nor is it "utilized" unless an agency assumes a regular, ministerial responsibility for its activities.[21]

Three potentially sweeping exceptions to the Act involve (1) sub-groups, (2) ad hoc groups, and (3) private contractors. The sub-group problem arises when attempts are made to limit coverage of the Act to full committee meetings at high policy making levels (for example, the often ceremonial meetings of the National Petroleum Council), while the day to day business of disseminating advice takes place in subcommittees or panels of one kind or another. The Act makes clear that an "advisory committee" includes "any subcommittee or other subgroup."[22] The inquiry thus should focus on the activities of each particular group and its points of contact with the government. If an agency "utilizes" a committee for informational purposes (that is, supervises its activity or relies heavily on its advice), then the Act should apply.

18. Section 3(2) reads in full as follows:

The term "advisory committee" means any committee, board, commission, council, conference, panel, task force, or other similar group, or any subcommittee or other subgroup thereof (hereafter in this paragraph referred to as "committee"), which is—

(A) established by statute or reorganization plan, or

(B) established or utilized by the President, or

(C) established or utilized by one or more agencies,

in the interest of obtaining advice or recommendations for the President or one or more agencies or officers of the Federal Government, except that such term excludes (i) the Advisory Commission on Intergovernmental Relations, (ii) the Commission on Goverment Procurement, and (iii) any committee which is composed wholly of full-time officers or employees of the Federal Government.

19. Nader v. Baroody, 396 F.Supp. 1231, 1232 (D.D.C.1975).

20. Lombardo v. Handler, 397 F.Supp. 792, 796 (D.D.C.1975), aff'd —— U.S. App.D.C. ——, 543, F.2d 1043 (1976).

21. 397 F.Supp. at 797–800; Nader v. Baroody, 396 F.Supp. 1231 (D.C.D.C. 1975). But see Food Chem. News, Inc. v. Davis, 378 F.Supp. 1048 (D.C. D.C.1974) (applying the statute to an informal advisory group proposing amendments to regulations).

22. Section 3(2).

Still more important is the treatment of an ad hoc single purpose group that is not formally established by an agency but convenes to give advice on the policy issues of the moment. Coverage of these groups would bring about an airing of government decision-making on an unprecedented scale. The reason is that informal contacts on regulatory matters within the agencies are routine to the point of being everyday occurrences: environmental groups meet with officials of the Federal Energy Administration to urge a reconsideration of proposed regulations on the posting of the octane content of gasoline; industry groups meet with officials of the Federal Trade Commission to state their views on labeling requirements for phosphates in detergents, or they meet with the Food and Drug Administration to discuss issues such as lead in toothpaste and asbestos in talc; officials of the International Ass'n of Fish and Game Commissioners meet with employees of the Department of Interior to discuss regulatory matters of mutual interest regarding the control of predators or the listing of the grizzly bear as an endangered species. Whether and when these ad hoc meetings of congenial spirits are the meetings of "advisory committees" is probably the most important issue of interpretation posed by the Advisory Committee Act. One reasoned district court decision has exempted periodic meetings between high officials of the executive branch and major business and other private groups.[23] Although the court was moved by a desire to protect the confidentiality of the President's executive communications (he participated personally in some of the meetings), there is strong language in the opinion construing the Act as not applying to "all amorphous, ad hoc group meetings" nor to meetings that are "unstructured, informal and not conducted for the purpose of obtaining advice on specific subjects indicated in advance."[24] Other decisions have read the Act more generously to impose the public meeting requirements on arguably ad hoc groups convened to urge specific regulatory action.[25]

23. Nader v. Baroody, 396 F.Supp. 1231, 1232 (D.C.D.C.1975) ("In some fifteen separate meetings at the White House, representatives of the housing construction and residential financing industries, senior citizens, life insurance industry, agriculture and livestock industries, electric utilities, printing industry, professional service firms, food processing firms, women business leaders, National Council of Churches, home economists in business, grocery manufacturers, youth and technology, and insurance have met"). See also Consumers Union v. Dep't of Health, Educ. & Welfare, 409 F.Supp. 473 (D.C.D.C.1976) (exempting ad hoc meetings between departmental personnel and organization representing cosmetics industry). But see Center for Auto Safety v. Tieman, 414 F.Supp. 215 (D.C.D.C.1976) (holding that meeting between representatives of the Department of Transportation and organization representing state highway and transportation departments must be open to public).

24. 396 F.Supp. at 1233, 1234–35.

25. Food Chem. News, Inc. v. Davis, 378 F.Supp. 1048 (D.C.D.C.1974); Aviation Consumer Action Project v. Washburn, Civ. No. 1838–73 (D.D.C. Sept. 6, 1974), reprinted in 120 Cong. Rec. E6604 (daily ed. Oct. 17, 1974).

Clearly the Act should not be defeated by the simple expedient of an agency refusing to acknowledge formally its committees that meet periodically to discuss predetermined matters. A strong case can be made that the legislation was designed to force disclosure of the agenda and deliberations whenever agency officials meet with an outside group "in the interest of obtaining advice or recommendations" on important matters. There is a wide range of activity falling between monthly meetings with a small group of trade association executives to discuss pending or planned regulatory initiatives and a one-time-only meeting with visiting boy scouts to talk about insignificant matters. Courts should read the Advisory Committee Act as favoring disclosure whenever outside groups meet with agency personnel to discuss matters of consequence. (The public meeting and disclosure requirements can be imposed even though longer range management controls do not apply.[26])

Another important district court opinion, on its reading of the legislative history, has concluded that the Act does not apply to persons or organizations having contractual relationships with federal agencies.[27] This contractual relationship exemption, like those for subgroups or ad hoc committees, cuts a wide swath in coverage; its immediate effect, quite likely, is to exclude from coverage hundreds of advisory committees of the National Academy of Sciences whose relationship with the federal agencies invariably is contractual in nature. The mere existence of a contract, however, should not automatically lift the requirements of the Advisory Committee Act from meetings between an agency and its consultants.[28] The question remains whether the group consulted is "established or utilized" by an agency "in the interest of obtaining advice or recommendations." The Act unquestionably should apply when the agency controls its contractor or contractors' committees as it does its own. It also might very well apply if an agency defers substantially to the work of the committees of its contractors without actually controlling their day to day operations.[29] But the question of coverage under the Act turns upon the degree of control and direct supervision associated with the word "utilized" and not at all upon whether a "contract" exists between the agency and a committee.

While the courts have been reluctant to extend the reach of the Advisory Committee Act beyond formally designated committees, they also have read narrowly the disclosure exemptions incorporated by reference to the Freedom of Information Act. A perusal of the

26. Food Chem. News, Inc. v. Davis, supra note 25.

27. Lombardo v. Handler, 397 F.Supp. 792, 802 (D.C.D.C.1975), aff'd — U.S. App.D.C. —, 543 F.2d 1043 (1976).

28. See 397 F.Supp. at 800 n. 22.

29. OMB Circular A–63, Dec. 6, 1973, § 1310.31(b)(3) (draft), never finally adopted, made it clear that "when in fact an agency is using a committee of an association for advice, the Act applies, even though the association serves as a conduit between the agency and the committee."

Federal Register reveals a parade of committee meetings closed by invoking one or another of the exemptions: the Commission on American Shipbuilding is closed for national security reasons; the Department of Interior's General Technical Advisory Committee invokes the trade secret doctrine to bar the public from a discussion of coal gasification research projects; committees advising the Commissioner of Food and Drugs on the safety and effectiveness of drugs are closed ostensibly to protect the integrity of the agency's investigatory files and its intra-agency communications. In the advisory committee context, the courts are even more skeptical of non-disclosures than they are in response to routine Freedom of Information Act requests. The principal reason is that the information sought to be withheld in an advisory committee case already has been disclosed to select members of the public convened as the committee. Some of the questions are obvious: how credible are trade secret claims when the information already is being shared with committee members who may be involved in the same business? How serious is the threat of general disclosure of agency investigative techniques when a partial disclosure readily is made to committee members? Does not the sharing of information with committee members raise an inference that full public disclosure will not compromise the national security?

The exemption 5 protection of intra-agency communications may disappear entirely within the context of advisory committees. Three district courts already have so indicated.[30] The rationale for abolishing exemption 5 as a justification for closing advisory committee meetings is that once an agency shares information with nongovernmental advisors it waives its claims of confidentiality. Any desire that the agency has to bring outsiders into its confidential decision-making processes is overridden by the basic purpose of the Advisory Committee Act to force the disclosure of private operation of government levers. The Act, after all, twice emphasizes that the committee function is to give advice and not decide.[31] Elimination or the drastic narrowing of exemption 5 would bring about substantial revelations of the work of many advisory committees—the Nuclear Regulatory

---

30. Aviation Consumer Action Project v. Washburn, Civ. No. 1838–73 (D.D.C. Sept. 6, 1974) (Bryant, J.) ("Exemption Five . . . cannot be invoked by defendants or their agents or employees as to documents which have been voluntarily disclosed by the agency to members of an advisory committee who are not full-time officers or employees of the Federal Government"); Nader v. Dunlop, Civ. No. 769–73 (D.D.C. Nov. 9, 1973) (Green, J.) ("This Court, too, finds the express congressional intent to provide public access to Advisory Committee meetings irreconcilable in this case with the defendants' expansive reading of the . . . exemption"); Gates v. Schlesinger, Civ. No. 1864–73 (D.D.C. Oct. 10, 1973) (Robinson, J.) ("In the circumstances of this case, the court finds exemption 5 inapplicable by its terms and irreconcilable by result with the very purpose of the Federal Advisory Committee Act").

31. Section 2(a)(6), 9(b).

Sec. 1.11   **ADVISORY COMMITTEE ACT**   71

Commission's Advisory Committee on Reactor Safeguards is one prominent example among many.

Compliance with the Advisory Committee Act is spotty:[32] the "detailed minutes" may be lessons in brevity; the "timely" notice sometimes issues after the meeting is held; the "fairly balanced" membership often has a decided tilt. Inaccessible meeting sites are much in demand; government advisors have been known to meet in the executive suites of an oil company, at a local restaurant, or on the chairman's yacht. Agency determinations closing a meeting need not be made public and are likely to be uninstructive in any case. The Freedom of Information Act exemptions are invoked zealously, often in great breadth and with little or no explanation.

Experience over time will increase sentiment for amending the Act. The most likely topics for legislative clarification include the ad hoc committee problem and the elimination of exemption 5 protection for intra-agency communications disclosed to committees, if the courts alone do not bring about that result. The addition of sanctions against agency employees for refusing to comply is predictable, just as they were added to the Freedom of Information Act by the 1974 amendments. The eventual imposition of a verbatim minutes requirement for the deliberations of major advisory committees also is not unlikely. Executive Order 11007, signed by President Kennedy in 1962, was a predecessor of the 1972 Advisory Committee Act and called for the keeping of verbatim minutes of all industry advisory committees. Many advisory committees today voluntarily prepare verbatim transcripts—among others, the Department of Transportation's Advisory Committee on Mass Transportation, the National Petroleum Council, EPA's Advisory Committee on the Revision and Application of Drinking Water Standards, the Department of Interior's National Advisory Board for Wild Free-Roaming Horses and Burros.

This section concludes where it began—with an admonition to recognize and explore the advisory committee apparatus as a source of information on issues of science and technology. A concluding illustration of the importance of committees is offered: the Environmental Protection Agency's Hazardous Materials Advisory Committee (HMAC) grew out of an ad hoc committee convened in 1969 by then HEW Secretary Robert Finch as a direct consequence of the DDT conflict to study pesticides and their relationship to human health.[33]

---

32. See Oversight Hearings on Advisory Committee Act, Before the Subcomm. on Budgeting, Management, and Expenditures of the Senate Comm. on Government Operations, 93d Cong., 1st Sess. (1973–74). See also Perritt & Wilkinson, Open Advisory Committee and the Political Process: The Federal Advisory Committee Act After Two Years, 63 Geo. L.J. 725 (1975); Stein, FOIA & FACA: Freedom of Information in the "Fifth Branch"?, 27 Ad.L.Rev. 31 (1975); Note, Federal Advisory Committee Act: A Key to Washington's Back Door, 20 S.D.L.Rev. 380 (1975).

33. Dep't of HEW, Report of the Secretary's Commission on Pesticides and Their Relationship to Environmental

The group includes academicians, industrialists and citizens, and, in the intervening years, has addressed a wide variety of environmental and public health issues. A partial listing of the Committee's evaluations from its First Annual Report [34] is as follows:

> —the environmental impact of the compounds hexachlorobenzene and hexachlorobutadiene;
>
> —the carcinogenicity of ethylene thiourea;
>
> —the dangers of freon propellants which are widely used in aerosols;
>
> —EPA's cadmium study;
>
> —nitrates and nitrites;
>
> —the extent and significance of phthalates and plasticizers in the environment;
>
> —EPA's draft proposal "Guidelines for Evaluating the Safety of Pesticidal Chemicals";
>
> —EPA's Office of Water Program's proposed "Designation of Hazardous Substances";
>
> —a proposed approach to the ranking of relative hazards of toxic materials;
>
> —the environmental hazards of flame retardant chemicals,[35] which include such agents as arsenic, fluorine, and lead.

It goes without saying that these reports disclose a wide policy-making or at least policy-influencing role for HMAC. Advisory Committees should not be overlooked. They are potential lawmakers of consequence.

§ 1.12 National Academy of Sciences

One government advisor of extraordinary influence is the National Academy of Sciences.[1] Incorporated by Act of Congress in 1863 and charged with investigating and reporting on subjects

---

Health (1969) (Mrak Commission Report). See also Rodgers, The Persistent Problem of the Persistent Pesticides: A Lesson in Environmental Law, 70 Colum.L.Rev. 567 (1970) (commenting on the Mrak Commission recommendations).

34. July 1971–July 1972, at 2–5.

35. Mentioned as a possible topic of further study in the minutes of the Hazardous Materials Advisory Committee (HMAC), Jan. 22, 1973.

1. The leading text on the work of the Academy is P. Boffey, The Brain Bank of America (1975). The leading journalistic discussions are D. S. Greenberg's three-part series in 156 Science 222, 360, 498 (1967); Claude E. Barfield's two-part series in 3 National J. 101, 220 (1970); and John Walsh's two-part series in 160 Science 242, 353 (1971).

Sec. 1.12 NATIONAL ACADEMY OF SCIENCES

"whenever called upon by any department of the Government",[2] the Academy today is a preeminent government advisor on questions of science, technology and the environment. Its work is carried out largely through hundreds of advisory committees of volunteers from all segments of the scientific community.[3] Typically, the scope of work and questions to be answered by a particular study are defined by contract negotiations between the sponsoring agency and the Academy.

Virtually every citizen is affected daily by the recommendations of Academy committees.[4] Our houses may be built in accordance with minimum property standards based, in part, on Academy advice to the Federal Housing Administration. Medicine prescribed by our doctors is available because an Academy task force told the Food and Drug Administration it was apt to be effective. The air we breathe and the water we drink is influenced by Academy recommendations to the Environmental Protection Agency. The food we eat contains chemicals whose safety is approved by some Academy committees and whose nutrients are recommended by other Academy committees.

The Academy's advisory influence is far-reaching. In recent years,[5] to mention but prime examples, it has analyzed the problem of housing people from different racial and social groups in the same neighborhood; advised the Navy on long-range technical problems affecting mine and undersea warfare; recommended against a plan to expand runways at Kennedy airport in New York for environmental reasons; predicted the likely ecological impact of a new sea-level Panama Canal; studied the genetic vulnerability of food crops to various diseases; analyzed the design and construction of highways; assessed the hazards of enzyme-containing detergents; evaluated the grizzly bear management program of the National Park Service in Yellowstone National Park; assessed the environmental and health hazards of lead, a number of pesticides, radiation, fluorides and other pollutants; advised the Atomic Energy Commission on the disposal of radioactive wastes; and studied the long-range effects of stripmining coal in the western United States. In 1972, a typical year, the Academy issued approximately 280 advisory reports plus another 100 or so brief letter reports that were submitted to government agencies but generally not made public.

Many Academy reports prove important to the resolution of technical or environmental controversies, a few are of seminal significance. The Academy's influential report on *The Growth of World*

---

2. Act of Mar. 3, 1863, ch. 111, § 3, 12 Stat. 806, 36 U.S.C.A. § 253.

3. Boffey, supra note 1, at 11–12.

4. Id. at 3–5. The text paraphrases the Boffey text.

5. Some of the examples are taken from the Boffey text.

Population made credible the warning that "other than the search for lasting peace, no problem is more urgent" [6] than the high rate of population growth. Academy reports played roles of varying significance [7] in the controversies over the SST, the use of herbicides in Vietnam, the problems of atmospheric lead, the use of the food dye known as Red No. 2, and even the consequences of nuclear warfare.[8]

The Academy is rapidly becoming a familiar fixture in legislation calling for studies on technological and environmental questions. The Academy President's annual report for 1975 [9] lists ten bills pending that would involve the Academy in studies on, among other things, the entire government structure for research and development, the civilian power functions of the Nuclear Regulatory Commission, the status of technology for surface and open pit mining for minerals other than coal, surface mining of coal in Alaska, standards for "residues" in meat and other products, and the threat to the ozone layer of the stratosphere from homogenated compounds in commercial use.

Occasionally, the Congress gives Academy findings the imprimatur of a legal determination. The best known but by no means only example [10] is section 202(c)(1) of the Clean Air Act of 1970 [11] which ordered the Administrator of EPA to enter into arrangements with the Academy to conduct "a comprehensive study and investigation of the technological feasibility of meeting the emissions standards" prescribed under the Act. The Administrator's decision on suspension of the automobile emission standards was tied to a finding, among other criteria, that "the National Academy of Sciences has not indicated that technology, processes or other alternatives are available to meet such standards." [12]

Similarly, Academy reports turn up regularly in administrative and judicial proceedings involving environmental issues. The Environmental Defense Fund cited an academy report as supporting evidence in its 1971 suit to put a halt to the use of the pesticide mirex in

---

6. NAS, The Growth of World Population 2 (1963).

7. Reported in Boffey, supra note 1, at 113–244.

8. Boffey, Nuclear War: Federation Disputes Academy on How Bad Effects Would Be, 190 Science 248 (1975).

9. April 22, 1975, at 21–22.

10. Others include: Federal Environmental Pesticide Control Act of 1972, Pub.L.No.92–516, § 2(d), 86 Stat. 984, 7 U.S.C.A. § 136d(d); Marine Mammal Protection Act of 1972, Pub.L.No. 92–522, §§ 201, 203, 88 Stat. 1043, 1044, 16 U.S.C.A. §§ 1401, 1403; Safe Drinking Water Act of 1974, Pub.L.No.93–523, § 2(a), 88 Stat. 1662, 42 U.S.C.A. § 300g–1(e)(1).

11. 42 U.S.C.A. § 1857f–1(c)(1).

12. Id. § 1857f–1(b)(5)(C); see International Harvester Co. v. Ruckelshaus, 155 U.S.App.D.C. 411, 429–31, 478 F.2d 615, 633–35, 3 ELR 20133, 20139–41 (1973).

the fire ant campaign in several southern states.[13] An academy report on the status of stack gas control technology for sulfur oxides was used defensively by several companies resisting more stringent controls for copper smelters in various western states.[14] All of the authors of an academy report on asbestos appeared as either witnesses or advisors in the Reserve Mining litigation; the conclusions of the report became important source material in the lawsuit.[15] The judicial decisions on challenges to the EPA regulations restricting the lead content of gasoline for health purposes dwell heavily on the Academy's work.[16]

For the student and practitioner, the challenge becomes one of discovering the work of the Academy and applying it where useful. Presently being litigated is the question of whether the Academy is an "agency" and its committees "advisory committees" for purposes of the Freedom of Information Act and Advisory Committee Act.[17] Regardless of how this question is answered by the courts as a general matter, it is still possible that the facts surrounding a particular advisory arrangement might indicate that an academy committee is "utilized" by an agency and therefore subject to the Advisory Committee Act.[18] Academy-watching can be a fruitful exercise.

§ 1.13 Citizen Suits

In recent years Congress has acted repeatedly to give citizens an enforcement role under the environmental laws.[1] While these citizen

---

13. Boffey, supra note 1, at 211–14.

14. Kennecott Copper Corp. v. Train, 526 F.2d 1149, 1152–53 n. 16, 6 ELR 20102, 20103 n. 16 (9th Cir. 1975); see Air Quality & Stationary Source Emission Control, Report by the Commission of Engineering, Natural Research Council, prepared for Senate Comm. on Public Works, S.Doc. No.4, 94th Cong., 1st Sess. (1975).

15. See Hills, Cross-Examination of Expert Witnesses in Pollution Cases, in American Law Institute/American Bar Ass'n, Study Materials on Environmental Law-V 227, 244–47 (1975) (illustrating use of the Academy study to impeach a witness' testimony).

16. Ethyl Corp. v. Environmental Protection Agency, — U.S.App.D.C. —, —, — F.2d —, —, 5 ELR 20096, 20105, vacated pending rehearing en banc, 5 ELR 20450 (1975), rev'd en banc — U.S.App.D.C. —, —, 541 F.2d 1, 45, 6 ELR 20267, 20291–92, cert. denied — U.S. — (1976); see NAS Comm. on Biologic Effects of Atmospheric Pollutants, Airborne Lead in Perspective (1972).

17. Lombardo v. Handler, 397 F.Supp. 792 (D.C.D.C.), aff'd per curiam — U.S.App.D.C. —, 543 F.2d 1043 (1976). (The author is an attorney of record in the proceeding).

18. See letter from Robert G. Dixon, Jr., Assistant Attorney General, Dep't of Justice, to Peter B. Hutt, Assistant General Counsel, Dep't of HEW, Nov. 27, 1973, filed in Brief for Appellants, Joint App. at 118, Lombardo v. Handler, Civil No. 75-1959 (D.C.Cir., filed Nov. 10, 1975).

1. 15 U.S.C.A. § 2619 (Toxic Substances Control Act); 16 U.S.C.A. § 1540(g) (Endangered Species Act of 1973); 33 U.S.C.A. § 1413(g) (Marine Protection, Research, and Sanctuaries Act of 1972); id. § 1365 (Federal Water Pollution Control Act Amendments of 1972); id. § 1515 (Deepwater Port Act of 1974); 42 U.S.C.A. § 300j–8 (Safe Drinking Water Act); id. § 1857h–2 (Clean Air Amendments of 1970);

suit provisions are drawn cautiously, they represent a substantial qualification of two of the more durable dogmas of public law. The first is that prosecution and enforcement is solely the business of public officials and the perpetrator. The second, a corollary of the first, is that regulatory and enforcement priorities are left to the administrator with little or no interference from outsiders, particularly the courts. While Congress by no means has discarded the notion of public control of public prosecutions, the routine fashioning of citizen suit provisions recognizes that compliance with environmental laws is the business of an alert community as well as of trained specialists. Several hypotheses justify citizen enforcement:[2] it is less costly; the private enforcer is in a better position to weigh costs and benefits of a particular initiative; total resources devoted to enforcement are augmented; and competition from the private sector sharpens the response of public officials. Congress' embracing a citizen role in enforcement also presumably discounts considerations that might justify keeping the public on the sidelines:[3] uneven enforcement and discrimination; undermining a consistent enforcement policy; loss of control by public decision-makers; and collusive suits to protect polluters. To a certain extent the proliferation of citizen suit provisions is a vote for chaos and against confidential disposition, which turns upside down pollution enforcement preferences of the past.[4] This section addresses (1) the general effect of the citizen suit statutes, (2) the grounds for relief, (3) the remedies including counsel fees, and (4) the other citizen enforcement provisions.

a. *General Effect*

Section 304 of the Clean Air Amendments of 1970,[5] which was the first and became the prototype for federal citizen suit legislation, states that "any person" may commence a civil action on his own behalf against "any person," including the United States and any other governmental instrumentality or agency to the extent permitted by the Eleventh Amendment to the Constitution. A "person" is defined in the Clean Air Act to include, among others, individuals, corporations, states, and municipalities.[6] The immediate consequence is to open the federal courts to citizen suits without regard to diversity of citizenship or jurisdictional amount. A second consequence, perhaps more important than the first, is that the citizen suit provisions should be read as doing away with the necessity for the normal "inju-

---

id. § 4911 (Noise Control Act of 1972); id. § 6305 (Energy Policy and Conservation Act); id. § 6972 (Resource Conservation and Recovery Act of 1976). See also 15 U.S.C.A. § 2073 (Consumer Product Safety Act).

2. J. L. Mashaw & R. M. Merrill, Introduction to the American Public Law System 892 (1975).

3. Ibid.

4. Compare §§ 3.19, 4.20 below.

5. 42 U.S.C.A. § 1857h–2(a).

6. Id. § 1857h(e).

ry in fact" standing allegations.[7] The reason for this is that Congress has determined that "any person" has sufficient interest to sue to protect a universal resource such as clean air.[8] While the Supreme Court has indicated that standing rests ultimately on the "case and controversy" requirements of the Constitution,[9] the congressional extensions allowing suits by "any person" should not run into constitutional difficulty where private attorneys general are enforcing pollution laws.[10] In Section 505(g) of the Federal Water Pollution Control Act Congress chose to retain minimal standing requirements by defining "a citizen" who is eligible as a plaintiff as "a person or persons having an interest which is or may be adversely affected." [11]

In addition to relaxing jurisdictional and standing requirements, Congress erected procedural barriers to citizen litigation. The most important of these is a 60-day notice requirement. The Clean Air Act, which is typical, forbids commencement of an action "prior to 60 days after the plaintiff has given notice of the violation (i) to the Administrator, (ii) to the State in which the violation occurs, and (iii) to any alleged violator of the standard, limitation, or order." [12] The notice provisions are intended to afford the agency an opportunity to do the job, not to frustrate citizen actions with procedural trickery,[13] and should be construed "flexibly and realistically" to advance this essential purpose.[14] While a few citizen suits have foundered on the notice requirements,[15] most courts have balked at strict

---

7. § 1.5 above; cf. Illinois v. Rosing, —— F.Supp. ——, 5 ELR 20717 (N.D. Ill.1975) (FWPCA citizen suit provision is *pro tanto* a waiver of sovereign immunity).

8. Metropolitan Washington Coalition for Clean Air v. District of Columbia, 167 U.S.App.D.C. 243, 248 n. 26, 511 F.2d 809, 814 n. 26, 5 ELR 20335, 20337 n. 26 (1975) (per curiam). The traditional "injury in fact" and "zone of interest" tests are based upon a reading of the Administrative Procedure Act. § 1.5 above.

9. Warth v. Seldin, 422 U.S. 490, 498–502, 95 S.Ct. 2197, 2205, 45 L.Ed.2d 343, 348–49 (1975); Snel, Standing Revisited: Are There New Barriers to Prosecution of Environmental Suits by Private Membership Organizations?, 14 Land & Natural Res. Div. J. 25 (1976).

10. Section 17(a) of the Deepwater Port Act of 1974, 33 U.S.C.A. § 1515(a), limits citizen suits to occasions where a "case or controversy" is present. This invites the dismissal of collusive suits involving no genuine dispute. Other citizen suit provisions would be read the same way.

11. 33 U.S.C.A. § 1365(g); see Natural Resources Defense Council, Inc. v. Train, 166 U.S.App.D.C. 312, 320–21 nn.47–48, 510 F.2d 692, 700–01 nn. 47–48, 5 ELR 20046, 20050 nn.47–48 (1974).

12. 42 U.S.C.A. § 1857h–2(b)(1)(A).

13. Natural Resources Defense Council, Inc. v. Callaway, 524 F.2d 79, 84 n.4, 5 ELR 20640, 20642 n.4 (2d Cir. 1975); see Comm. on Public Works, National Air Quality Standards Act of 1970, S. Rep.No.1196, 91st Cong., 2d Sess. 37 (1970) [hereinafter cited as Senate Report].

14. Friends of the Earth v. Carey, 535 F.2d 165, 175, 6 ELR 20488, 20493 (2d Cir. 1976).

15. Smoke Rise, Inc. v. Washington Suburban Sanitary Comm'n, 4 ELR 20427 (D.Md.1974); Illinois v. Rosing, —— F.Supp. ——, 5 ELR 20717 (N.D.

readings. Thus, statutory notice has been satisfied by the mere service of the initial complaint,[16] by letters not specifically denominated as a notice of suit,[17] by notice not conforming exactly to administrative regulations,[18] and by notice to the primary state officials but not all agencies involved.[19] By statute, Congress ordinarily chooses to dispense with extended notice requirements where urgent action is called for.[20]

Despite the ease with which notice obstacles may be cleared, they nonetheless pose an unusual precondition to a lawsuit. One theory that dispenses with notice requirements altogether, which has been accepted by two courts of appeals,[21] is that the citizen suit provisions of the environmental laws do not provide the exclusive bases of jurisdiction. Congress routinely includes a savings clause in citizen suit formulations (reserving rights of action under other provisions of law).[22] Thus, jurisdiction can be grounded alternatively on a general federal question basis or perhaps under the Administrative Procedure Act. Under these circumstances, the citizen suit provisions of the Federal Water Pollution Control Act, which retain the traditional test of standing, may be said to "add little to the jurisdiction of federal courts as a practical matter. That may come to depend on whether the Supreme Court sustains the view . . . that the Administrative Procedure Act is a grant of jurisdiction. It may come to depend on the number of instances in which actions cannot satisfy the jurisdictional amount provision of 28 U.S.C. § 1331." [23]

Another typical precondition bars a citizen suit "if the Administrator or State has commenced and is diligently prosecuting a civil

---

Ill.1975); see Massachusetts v. United States Veterans Administration, 541 F.2d 119, 6 ELR 20666 (1st Cir. 1976).

16. Riverside v. Ruckelshaus, 3 ELR 20043 (C.D.Cal.1972).

17. National Wildlife Federation v. Coleman, 400 F.Supp. 705, 5 ELR 20566 (S.D.Miss.1975), rev'd on other grounds 529 F.2d 359, 6 ELR 20344 (5th Cir. 1976).

18. Montgomery Environmental Coalition v. Fri, 366 F.Supp. 261, 4 ELR 20182 (D.C.D.C.1973) (notice was served prior to promulgation of the regulations).

19. Friends of the Earth v. Carey, 535 F.2d 165, 6 ELR 20488 (2d Cir. 1976).

20. E. g., 42 U.S.C.A. § 1857h–2(b) (for violation of a hazardous air pollutant emission standard); ibid (for violation of a federal enforcement order).

21. Natural Resources Defense Council, Inc. v. Train, 166 U.S.App.D.C. 312, 510 F.2d 692, 5 ELR 20046 (1975); Conservation Soc'y of Southern Vermont, Inc. v. Secretary of Transp. (I), 508 F.2d 927, 938–39 & n.62, 5 ELR 20068, 20074 & n.62 (2d Cir. 1974), vacated on other grounds 423 U.S. 809 (1975). Contra, Highland Park v. Train, 519 F.2d 681, 5 ELR 20408 (7th Cir. 1975).

22. Compare Nat'l R. R. Passenger Corp. v. Nat'l Ass'n of R. R. Passengers, 414 U.S. 453, 94 S.Ct. 690, 38 L.Ed.2d 646 (1974) (an example of a restrictive remedy created by Congress).

23. Natural Resources Defense Council, Inc. v. Train, 166 U.S.App.D.C. 312, 322, 510 F.2d 692, 702, 5 ELR 20046, 20050–51 (1974) (footnotes omitted); see Califano v. Sanders, —— U.S. ——, 97 S.Ct. 980, 51 L.Ed.2d 192 (1977).

action in a court of the United States or a State to require compliance with the standard, limitation, or order, but in any such action in a Court of the United States any person may intervene as a matter of right." [24] This provision is meant to be a time-saver and duplication-avoider. It is open to potential abuse because officialdom may attempt to foreclose a serious citizen suit by a narrowly conceived compromise action. The requirement that the publicly initiated action be prosecuted "diligently" offers scant protection in fact, although the possibility of an allegation of lack of diligence opens up interesting discovery and proof issues. The opportunity to intervene as of right provides a more meaningful protection to protest a settlement thought to be ill-conceived.[25] Most important of all, as the U.S. Court of Appeals for the District of Columbia has pointed out,[26] private actions ambitious in scope are not preempted by public actions more narrowly drawn. The idea is to avoid a duplication of enforcement effort not a restriction of citizen suits by litigation of lesser breadth. *A fortiori* is it true that citizen suits should not be stayed or dismissed on the theory that the Administrator is attempting to negotiate a settlement [27] or prefers to sit on the sidelines.[28]

b. *Grounds for Relief*

Congress, in making way for citizen suits, did not "fling the courts' door wide open." Relief is confined to "clear-cut violations by polluters or defaults by the Administrator . . . ." [29] Under the Clean Air Act a citizen may sue any person alleged to be in violation of an "emission standard or limitation" or an "order" issued by the Administrator or the State with respect to such a standard or limitation.[30] The other statutes, with more or less precision, invite suits to correct violations of specific standards.[31] Insofar as the Ad-

24. 42 U.S.C.A. § 1857h–2(b)(1)(B).

25. See Ohio ex rel. Brown v. Callaway, 497 F.2d 1235, 4 ELR 20492 (6th Cir. 1974) (allowing intervention as of right under FWPCA). Conversely, the government may intervene as of right in citizen suits to protect its view of a proper outcome. E. g., 42 U.S.C.A. § 1857h–2(c)(2).

26. Montgomery Environmental Coalition v. Washington Suburban Sanitary Comm'n, Civil No. 75–1389 (D.C.Cir. 1976).

27. Friends of the Earth v. Carey, 535 F.2d 165, 6 ELR 20488 (2d Cir. 1976).

28. Metropolitan Washington Coalition for Clean Air v. District of Columbia, 167 U.S.App.D.C. 243, 248–49, 511 F. 2d 809, 814–15, 5 ELR 20335, 20337 (1975) (per curiam) ("the Administrator has the right to intervene in the suit, but he is not required to be a participant in such litigation and his absence does not render the action infirm").

29. Natural Resources Defense Council, Inc. v. Train, 166 U.S.App.D.C. 312, 320, 510 F.2d 692, 700, 5 ELR 20046, 20050 (1974).

30. 42 U.S.C.A. § 1857h–2(a)(1).

31. 15 U.S.C.A. § 2619(a)(1) (Toxic Substances Control Act) (any "violation of this Act or any rule promulgated . . . or order issued . . . to restrain such violation"); 16 U.S.C.A. § 1540(g)(1)(A) (Endangered Species Act of 1973) ("any provision of this Act or regulation issued under the authority thereof");

ministrator is concerned, the Clean Air Act permits a citizen suit only "where there is alleged a failure of the Administrator to perform any act or duty under this chapter which is not discretionary . . . ."[32] Confining citizen suit relief to nondiscretionary activities of the enforcing authority also is the norm,[33] although there are some departures from it.[34]

The courts must define the meaning of standard, limitation, order, or other requirement that may be enforced by a citizen suit. Enforceable are the specific limitations of an implementation plan under the Clean Air Act, including the strategies of reducing business district parking, banning selectively taxicab cruising, imposing tolls on bridge traffic, and establishing requirements for night-time freight movement.[35] Not enforceable is a commitment to stabilize transit fares not included as an "express strategy of the plan."[36] Enforceable are standards relied upon in the issuance of an ocean dumping permit [37] and an obligation to shut down an incinerator made part of an implementation plan,[38] but not a restriction on the construction of

33 U.S.C.A. § 1415(g)(1) (Marine Protection, Research, and Sanctuaries Act of 1972) ("any prohibition, limitation, criterion or permit established or issued by or under this subchapter"); id. § 1365(a)(1) (Federal Water Pollution Control Act Amendments of 1972) ("an effluent standard or limitation" or "an order"); id. § 1515(a)(I) (Deepwater Port Act of 1974) ("any provision of this Act or any condition of a license issued pursuant to this Act"); 42 U.S.C.A. § 300j–8(a)(1) (Safe Drinking Water Act) ("any requirement prescribed by or under this title"); id. § 4911(a)(1) (Noise Control Act of 1972) ("any noise control requirement"); id. § 6305(a)(1) (Energy Policy and Conservation Act) ("any provision . . . or rule under this part"); id. § 6972(a)(1) (Resource Conservation and Recovery Act of 1976) ("any permit, standard, regulation, condition, requirement, or order").

32. 42 U.S.C.A. § 1857h–2(a)(2).

33. 15 U.S.C.A. § 2619(a)(2) (Toxic Substances Control Act) ("any act or duty under this Act which is not discretionary"); 33 U.S.C.A. § 1365(a)(2) (Federal Water Pollution Control Act Amendments of 1972) ("any act or duty which is not discretionary"); id. § 1515(a)(2) (Deepwater Port Act of 1974) ("any act or duty . . . which is not discretionary"); 42 U.S.C.A. § 300j–8(a)(2) (Safe Drinking Water Act) ("any act or duty . . . which is not discretionary); id. § 4911(a)(2)(A), (B) (Noise Control Act of 1972) ("any act or duty . . . which is not discretionary"); id. § 6305(a)(2) (Energy Policy and Conservation Act) ("any act or duty . . . which is not discretionary"); id. § 6972(a)(2) (Resource Conservation and Recovery Act of 1976) ("any act or duty under this Act which is not discretionary").

34. E. g., 16 U.S.C.A. § 1540(g)(1)(B) (Endangered Species Act of 1973) (authorizing an action against the Secretary of Interior to compel application of prohibitions against the taking of resident endangered species or threatened species). Authorization to sue to correct violations of "any provision" of the Endangered Species Act, id. § 1540(g)(1)(A), appears without qualification as to discretionary activities.

35. Friends of the Earth v. Carey, 535 F.2d 165, 6 ELR 20488 (2d Cir. 1976).

36. 535 F.2d at 176, 6 ELR at 20494.

37. Natural Resources Defense Council, Inc. v. Callaway, 524 F.2d 79, 83–84, 5 ELR 20640, 20642 (2d Cir. 1975).

38. Metropolitan Washington Coalition for Clean Air v. District of Columbia, 167 U.S.App.D.C. 243, 511 F.2d 809, 5 ELR 20335 (1975) (per curiam); cf.

Sec. 1.13 CITIZEN SUITS

a shopping center omitted from the plan [39] and not an obligation withdrawn by revision.[40] A violation of water quality standards will support a citizen suit to enforce "an effluent standard or limitation," [41] but a violation of air quality standards will not justify a citizen suit to enforce "an emission standard or limitation." [42] Other issues have arisen over types of violations that may be corrected by citizen suit.[43] If a principle is detectable, it is that Congress is aiming at reasonable specificity in the directives enforceable by citizen suits. Even on the basis of this limited rationale,[44] it makes little sense to exempt from citizen suit enforcement, whether by legislative or judicial policy choice, an unassailable legal obligation such as the ambient air quality standards.

Sorting out the non-discretionary obligations of the Administrator that may be enforced by citizens is another task of uncertain scope.[45] Historically, the availability of the writ of mandamus to compel performance of an official duty has turned upon a similarly frustrating distinction between ministerial and discretionary actions.[46] A close look at the cases describes the inquiry more accurately as whether "the administrator exceeded the *permissible scope* of his discretion." [47] The close scrutiny doctrine of judicial review under the Administrative Procedure Act comes down at the same point by examining the statutory limits of the Administrator's discretion.[48] Predictably, non-discretionary activity for purposes of statutory citizen suits will come to include instances where the Administrator transgresses the bounds of his discretion and not only the extraordinary cases where he has no discretion at all.

Bleiler v. Wellesley, 2 ELR 20067 (Mass.Super.Ct.1971) (state citizen suit provision) (enforcing restrictions on the operations of an incinerator).

39. Plan for Arcadia, Inc. v. Anita Associates, 501 F.2d 390, 4 ELR 20689 (9th Cir. 1974).

40. Metropolitan Washington Coalition for Clean Air v. District of Columbia, 167 U.S.App.D.C. 243, 247, 511 F.2d 809, 813, 5 ELR 20335, 20336 (1975) (per curiam).

41. Montgomery Environmental Coalition v. Fri, 366 F.Supp. 261, 4 ELR 20181 (D.C.D.C.1973). But cf. Stream Pollution Control Bd. v. United States Steel Corp., 512 F.2d 1036, 5 ELR 20261 (7th Cir. 1975) (denying intervention as of right under FWPCA because common law nuisance action is not a suit to enforce a "standard, limitation or order").

42. Thompson v. Chicago, 5 ELR 20283 (N.D.Ill.1975).

43. E. g., Weltner v. Producers Pipeline Co., —— F.Supp. ——, 6 ELR 20068 [Dig.] (D.C.Kan.1975) (oil is not "a pollutant" for purposes of citizen suits under FWPCA).

44. State citizen suit provisions often permit enforcement of a wider range of obligations. § 2.16 below.

45. Compare §§ 1.5 (discussing scope of review), 1.8 (discussing Federal Tort Claims Act) above.

46. W. Gellhorn & C. Byse, Administrative Law 150–60 (6th Ed. 1974).

47. Note, Mandamus in Administrative Actions: Current Approaches, 1973 Duke L.J. 207, 211 (1973) (emphasis in original).

48. § 1.5 above.

It belabors the obvious to observe that statutory assignments of administrative discretion range from the bewilderingly vague to the tight and specific.[49] It is evident also that non-discretionary mandates enforceable by citizen suit are likely to be found at the tight end of the spectrum where directives are mandatory in tone. One of the most important of these is Section 7 of the Endangered Species Act, which has been read for purposes of a citizen suit as imposing on federal agencies "the mandatory duty to insure that their actions will not either (i) jeopardize the existence of an endangered species, or (ii) destroy or modify critical habitat of an endangered species." [50] A widely used legislative technique in federal environmental law is to incorporate mandatory deadlines for implementing statutory policies. These are routinely enforced in citizen suits. Thus, relief has been ordered for a failure to meet statutory timetables for the publication of a report and proposed regulations under the Noise Control Act,[51] for the preparation of an implementation plan under the Clean Air Act following disapproval of a state plan,[52] and for the publication of effluent limitation guidelines and a number of other reports under the Federal Water Pollution Control Act.[53] Non-discretionary is the Administrator's duty to allot all funds appropriated by Congress for the construction of sewage treatment plants,[54] to list lead as a criteria pollutant under the Clean Air Act,[55] to adopt a definition of "navigable waters" consistent with the terms of the Federal Water Pollution Control Act,[56] to implement a policy of no-significant deterioration under the Clean Air Act,[57] and to decide whether nuclear waste materials are "pollutants" under the Federal Water Pollution Control Act.[58] Discretionary is the Administrator's duty to bring an emergency action under the Federal Water Pollution Control Act,[59] to list hy-

49. See § 7.12 below (discussing numerous statutory mandates in federal environmental law).

50. National Wildlife Federation v. Coleman, 529 F.2d 359, 371, 6 ELR 20344, 20349 (5th Cir. 1976); § 7.12 below.

51. PROD, Inc. v. Train, —— F.Supp. ——, 6 ELR 20341 (D.D.C.1976).

52. Riverside v. Ruckelshaus, 3 ELR 20043 (C.D.Cal.1972).

53. Natural Resources Defense Council, Inc. v. Train, 166 U.S.App.D.C. 312, 510 F.2d 692, 5 ELR 20046 (1974); Natural Resources Defense Council, Inc. v. Fri, 3 ELR 20587 (D.C.D.C. 1973) (by stipulation).

54. City of New York v. Train, 358 F.Supp. 669 (D.C.D.C.1973), aff'd 161 U.S.App.D.C. 114, 494 F.2d 1033, 4 ELR 20188 (1974), aff'd 420 U.S. 35, 95 S.Ct. 839, 43 L.Ed.2d 1 (1975).

55. Natural Resources Defense Council, Inc. v. Train, 411 F.Supp. 864, 6 ELR 20366 (S.D.N.Y.1976).

56. Natural Resources Defense Council, Inc. v. Callaway, 392 F.Supp. 685, 5 ELR 20285 (D.C.D.C.1975).

57. Sierra Club v. Ruckelshaus, 344 F.Supp. 253, 2 ELR 20262 (D.D.C. 1972), aff'd per curiam 2 ELR 20656 (D.C.Cir. 1972), aff'd by an equally divided court 412 U.S. 541, 93 S.Ct. 2770, 37 L.Ed.2d 140 (1973).

58. Train v. Colorado Public Interest Research Group, 426 U.S. 1, 96 S.Ct. 1938, 48 L.Ed.2d 434 (1976).

59. Comm. for Consideration of Jones Fall Sewage System v. Train, 375 F. Supp. 1148 (D.C.Md.1974), aff'd en banc 539 F.2d 1006, 6 ELR 20703 (4th Cir. 1976).

drochloric acid and silicon dioxide as hazardous air pollutants and to establish emission standards for them,[60] to revise standards of performance for new coal-fired power plants,[61] and to determine that an action is environmentally "unsatisfactory" for purposes of Section 309 of the Clean Air Act.[62] The best barometer of action that is "not discretionary" is the statutory framework delimiting the administrator's authority.

c. *Remedies*

Section 304(a) of the Clean Air Act states that the district courts "shall have jurisdiction, without regard to the amount in controversy or the citizenship of the parties, to enforce . . . an emission standard or limitation, or . . . an order, or to order the Administrator to perform an act or duty, as the case may be."[63] The other citizen suit provisions generally follow this pattern,[64] except that a water pollution violation may give rise to a civil penalty,[65] and

---

60. Thompson v. Chicago, 5 ELR 20283 (N.D.Ill.1975).

61. Oljato Chapter of the Navajo Tribe v. Train, 169 U.S.App.D.C. 195, 515 F.2d 654, 5 ELR 20481 (1975).

62. Sierra Club v. Morton, 379 F.Supp. 1254 (D.C.Colo.1974).

63. 16 U.S.C.A. § 1857h–2(a).

64. 15 U.S.C.A. § 2619(a) (Toxic Substances Control Act) ("The district courts of the United States shall have jurisdiction over suits brought under this section without regard to the amount in controversy or the citizenship of the parties"); 16 U.S.C.A. § 1540(g)(1) (Endangered Species Act) ("the district courts shall have jurisdiction, without regard to the amount in controversy or the citizenship of the parties, to enforce any . . . provision or regulation, as the case may be"); 33 U.S.C.A. § 1415(g)(1) (Marine Protection, Research, and Sanctuaries Act) ("the district courts shall have jurisdiction, without regard to the amount in controversy or the citizenship of the parties, to enforce [any] prohibition, limitation, criterion or permit, as the case may be"); id. § 1515(a) (Deepwater Port Act) ("the district court shall have jurisdiction, without regard to the amount in controversy or the citizenship of the parties, to enforce any provision of this Act or any condition of a license issued pursuant to this Act, or to order the Secretary to perform [an] act or duty, as the case may be"); 42 U.S.C.A. § 300j–8(a) (Safe Drinking Water Act) ("the district courts shall have jurisdiction, without regard to the amount in controversy or the citizenship of the parties, to enforce . . . any requirement prescribed by or under this title or to order the Administrator to perform an act or duty . . . , as the case may be"); id. § 6305(a) (Energy Policy and Conservation Act) ("The United States district courts shall have jurisdiction, without regard to the amount in controversy or the citizenship of the parties, to enforce such provision or rule, as the case may be"); id. § 6972(a) (Resource Conservation and Recovery Act) ("the district court shall have jurisdiction, without regard to the amount in controversy or the citizenship of the parties, to enforce such regulation or order, or to order the Administrator to perform such act or duty as the case may be").

65. 33 U.S.C.A. § 1365(a) (the "district courts shall have jurisdiction, without regard to the amount in controversy or the citizenship of the parties, to enforce . . . an effluent standard or limitation, or . . . an order, or to order the Administrator to perform [an] act or duty, as the case may be, and to apply any appropriate civil penalties . . . ").

noise control violations may be corrected only by injunction.[66] The power to enforce standards and issue orders includes a general equitable authority to direct action compatible with those goals.[67] Thus, a court might develop a schedule of compliance for an offending source, appoint a Special Master to oversee compliance, and impose monitoring and reporting obligations. The Administrator may be ordered to promulgate guidelines and reports in accordance with a prescribed timetable.[68] The Settlement Agreement resulting from a citizen suit challenging Environmental Protection Agency regulation of toxic water pollutants commits the agency to a substantial and detailed regulatory program.[69]

An important question, as yet unresolved, is whether monetary damages may be recovered in a citizen suit. With the possible exception of the Noise Control Act, which appears by its terms to foreclose such a claim,[70] the general invitation "to enforce" a standard or limitation can be read as permitting an assessment of money damages where appropriate. Neither legislative history [71] nor the precedents [72] are particularly enlightening. If Congress chooses to leave the question unresolved, the answer must be found in the general purposes of citizen suits. The aim of commissioning citizens in the clean-up effort appears to be advanced decisively by allowing them to recover actual damages inflicted by the offender. A similar argument might justify even the imposition of punitive damages in an appropriate case. There is ample precedent for the fashioning of civil remedies under a wide variety of regulatory statutes.[73] That the issue

---

66. 42 U.S.C.A. § 4911(a) ("The district courts . . . shall have jurisdiction, without regard to the amount in controversy, to restrain [a] person from violating [a] noise control requirement or to order [the] Administrator to perform [an] act or duty, as the case may be").

67. Compare §§ 2.11 (nuisance remedies), 3.19 (air pollution remedies), 4.20 (water pollution remedies), 7.10 (NEPA remedies) below. The discretion may be exercised also in favor of withholding relief. Conservation Soc'y of Southern Vermont v. Secretary of Transp. (I), 508 F.2d 927, 935, 5 ELR 20068, 20073–74 (2d Cir. 1974), vacated on other grounds 423 U.S. 809 (1975).

68. Natural Resources Defense Council, Inc. v. Train, 166 U.S.App.D.C. 312, 510 F.2d 692, 5 ELR 20046 (1974); Natural Resources Defense Council, Inc. v. Fri, 3 ELR 20587 (D.C.D.C. 1973) (by stipulation).

69. Natural Resources Defense Council, Inc. v. Train, 6 ELR 20588 (D.C. D.C.1976) (Final Order and Decree).

70. Note 66, supra.

71. The possibility of a recovery of money damages is mentioned only in the context that section 304 specifically preserves any rights or remedies that may exist under other law. Senate Report, supra note 13, at 38. See also Comm. of Conference, Clean Air Amendments of 1970, H.R.Rep.No. 1783, 91st Cong., 2d Sess. 56 (1970).

72. Delaware Citizens for Clean Air, Inc. v. Stauffer Chem. Co., 367 F. Supp. 1040, 1047–48, 4 ELR 20129, 20132 (D.C.Del.1973) (assuming without deciding that private claims for damages may be pursued under the citizen suit provisions of the Clean Air Act).

73. E. g., J. I. Case Co. v. Borak, 377 U.S. 426, 84 S.Ct. 1555, 12 L.Ed.2d

is slow to develop in the context of federal environmental citizen suits is difficult to understand, unless the answer is found in the general reluctance of the bar to abandon established forums and theories in favor of a test case of uncertain promise.

An issue of considerable practical consequence is who pays the bill for environmental litigation. It is an unfortunate but inescapable fact of life that the energy of the legal system is responsive largely to financial incentives. In 1975, much to the chagrin of many practicing lawyers who handle environmental cases, the Supreme Court held that an award of attorneys fees in private litigation is dependent upon express congressional sanction.[74] The citizen suit measures meet that objection; Section 304(d) of the Clean Air Act is illustrative: "The court, in issuing any final order in any action brought pursuant to subsection (a) of this section, may award costs of litigation (including reasonable attorney and expert witness fees) to any party, whenever the court determines such award is appropriate . . . ."[75] This means that citizen suit litigation may be handled on a contingency basis, although the path to recovery is strewn with obstacles.

It is important to note that litigation costs may be awarded "to any party." This includes federal and state agencies, although there may be an Eleventh Amendment barrier as to the latter.[76] It means that plaintiffs may be assessed with litigation costs, although one attempt by the government to invoke this theory has been rejected summarily for lack of a showing of "bad faith."[77] Unless plaintiffs are protected from awards of litigation costs for all but extreme instances of bad faith and frivolous assertion, the ends of the citizen suit measures will be served poorly. It takes but a small risk of potential liability for attorneys' fees to dry up all but the open and shut litigation. With recovery of their own costs a serious speculative venture for many financially strapped plaintiffs, the spectre of paying for a well heeled defense would deter all but the foolhardy or the

---

423 (1964); Gomez v. Florida State Employment Serv., 417 F.2d 569 (5th Cir. 1969); § 4.5 below (discussing the implication of private damage remedies from the Rivers and Harbors Act of 1899).

74. Alyeska Pipeline Serv. Co. v. Wilderness Soc'y, 421 U.S. 240, 95 S.Ct. 1612, 44 L.Ed.2d 141 (1975).

75. 42 U.S.C.A. § 1857h–2(d); see 15 U.S.C.A. §§ 2618(d), 2619(c)(2), 2620(b)(4)(C) (Toxic Substances Control Act); 42 U.S.C.A. § 6305(d) (Energy Policy and Conservation Act); id. § 6972(e) (Resource Conservation and Recovery Act).

76. Comment, Federal Powers and the Eleventh Amendment: Attorneys' Fees in Private Suits Against the State, 63 Cal.L.Rev. 1167 (1975). The question was not addressed in Alyeska. 421 U.S. at 269–70 n. 44, 95 S.Ct. at 1627–28 n. 44, 44 L.Ed.2d at 160 n. 44.

77. PROD, Inc. v. Train, —— F.Supp. ——, ——, 6 ELR 20341, 20343 (D.C. D.C.1976) (refusing government request for reimbursement for services of counsel in preparing a defense to a notice of deposition which was later vacated).

eternally optimistic. Litigation costs also may be assessed against prevailing private parties, although it surely stretches the concepts of fairness to require the winner to foot the bill for the costs of the loser.[78] The courts may come around eventually to adopting per se rules precluding the assessment of litigation costs against private party winners and against private parties championing the protection of public resources.

Any fee awarded "should represent the reasonable value of the services rendered, taking into account all the surrounding circumstances, including, but not limited to, the time and labor required on the case, the benefit to the public, the skill demanded by the novelty or complexity of the issues, and the incentive factor."[79] The bad faith of the defendant is relevant both because a churlish, hard-nosed defense makes pursuit of the case that much more difficult, and because a cost award should serve a deterrence function. It has been suggested that the "reasonable value" of a fee award can ignore the prevailing low rates for public interest litigation,[80] although it can be argued that public litigation is satisfying and enjoyable work that remains attractive at less than first-class levels of pay. The courts certainly have not restricted citizen suit attorneys to starvation wages.[81] Time and labor expended must be "documented meticulously" at the risk of a substantial reduction in the size of an award.[82] The benefit to the public is difficult to assess, although the courts have found a public service in a suit that only modestly speeds up the preparation of regulatory proposals.[83] Assessing public benefit is that much more difficult where the express aims of the litigation are partially or wholly unfulfilled or where success is measured by subtle shifts in position or "voluntary" adjustments preempting plaintiffs' objections.

---

78. See Sierra Club v. Lynn, 502 F.2d 43, 66, 4 ELR 20844, 20853–54 (5th Cir. 1974), cert. denied 421 U.S. 994 (1975) (plaintiff was partially successful). The courts point out that government parties who can spread the costs are in a different position.

79. Wilderness Soc'y v. Morton, 161 U.S.App.D.C. 446, 456, 495 F.2d 1026, 1036, 4 ELR 20279, 20284 (1974) (en banc), rev'd on other grounds sub nom. Alyeska Pipeline Serv. Co. v. Wilderness Soc'y, 421 U.S. 240, 95 S.Ct. 1612, 44 L.Ed.2d 141 (1975).

80. 161 U.S.App.D.C. at 457, 495 F.2d at 1037, 4 ELR at 20284.

81. PROD, Inc. v. Train, —— F.Supp. ——, 6 ELR 20341 (D.D.C.1976) (awarding fee at hourly rates of $30, $35, and $40) (rates requested were cut in half on ground that no bad faith was shown and the issues were relatively simple); Natural Resources Defense Council, Inc. v. Fri, 5 ELR 20173 (D.D.C.1974) (awarding fee at hourly rates of $30 and $40).

82. Natural Resources Defense Council, Inc. v. Fri, supra note 81 (hours discounted by a factor of 45 per cent).

83. PROD, Inc. v. Train, —— F.Supp. ——, 6 ELR 20341 (D.C.D.C.1976) (draft of proposed regulation accelerated three or four weeks as a result of the lawsuit); Natural Resources Defense Council, Inc. v. Fri, 5 ELR 20173 (D.C.D.C.1974). Compare Citizens Ass'n of Georgetown v. Washington, 175 U.S.App.D.C. 356, 535 F.2d 1318, 6 ELR 20524 (1976) (per curiam) (disallowing award of attorneys' fees on claim not within citizen suit jurisdiction).

What plaintiffs may characterize as a "healthy airing of the issues" defendants can describe as "frivolous delaying tactics." In the end, only the good sense of federal judges can distinguish the worthy from the silly causes, and the solid from the slippery performances. There may be substantial public benefit from a crisp, clear loss in the courts pointing up the need for legislation; and there may be little public benefit from a total victory on a minor point of order. The complexity of the issues and the skill displayed also are subjects especially suited to resolution by the trial judge. An award can make a distinction between a lawsuit raising obvious issues, or issues that were conceived in other forums, and one that is distinguished for its originality.

On the question of incentives, a court should inquire into whether a fee plays a positive role in the bringing of future actions or the motivation for the one at bar. Ordinarily, the answer is in the affirmative. But some citizen suits raise issues that invariably would be litigated by others, either government or private parties, and if procedural advantages are earned by professions of service without pay,[84] then service without pay may be fully appropriate. The litigation costs award plays an incentive function, and payments should not be made in disregard of this factor.

d. *Other Citizen Suit Enforcement Provisions*

Both the Clean Air Act[85] and the Federal Water Pollution Control Act[86] as well as other environmental statutes[87] provide for direct judicial review in the courts of appeals of many actions of the Administrator. Under the Clean Air Act, for example, the Administrator's actions in promulgating an ambient air quality standard or standard of performance are reviewable directly in a court of appeals under section 307, while his failures to act are reviewable only in a district court under section 304. The dichotomy between action and inaction is imperfect, however, and there very well may be instances of concurrent jurisdiction in the district and circuit courts.[88] There are

---

84. Wilderness Soc'y v. Morton, 161 U.S.App.D.C. 446, 464, 495 F.2d 1026, 1044, 4 ELR 20279, 20287 (1974) (Wilkey, J., dissenting), rev'd on other grounds 421 U.S. 240, 95 S.Ct. 1612, 44 L.Ed.2d 141 (1975).

85. 42 U.S.C.A. § 1857h–5.

86. 33 U.S.C.A. § 1369.

87. E. g., 15 U.S.C.A. § 2618 (Toxic Substances Control Act); 42 U.S.C.A. § 300j–7 (Safe Drinking Water Act); id. § 4915 (Noise Control Act); id. § 6976(a) (Resource Conservation and Recovery Act).

88. Oljato Chapter of the Navajo Tribe v. Train, 169 U.S.App.D.C. 195, 202–03 n. 9, 515 F.2d 654, 661–62 n. 9, 5 ELR 20481, 20484 n. 9 (1975) (While challenges under sections 304 and 307 appear to involve separate issues "overlap is conceivable, for instance, where the Administrator acts but in the view of the challengers, does not act far enough. If nondiscretionary duties are involved, the challenge might fairly be said to lie under § 304 and § 307"). The courts are divided over whether counsel fees are recoverable in a section 307 suit. Compare Natural Resources Defense Council, v. EPA, 529 F.2d 755, 6 ELR 20777

examples under both the air [89] and water [90] pollution acts of plaintiffs' selecting the wrong forum to settle a quarrel with the Administrator. The appropriate circumstances for direct appellate review require a close look at the pertinent statutes. It is useful to keep in mind that the topic of citizen suits is not exhausted without considering fully review mechanisms working in tandem with the formally denominated citizen suit provisions.

Considered below [91] are state legislative modifications of the public trust doctrine, which generally go beyond federal citizen suit provisions in both substantive and procedural specifics. The federal preference for allowing citizen suits to correct only clear-cut violations of pre-existing standards is deemed insufficiently ambitious by several of the state citizen suit provisions. Missing from the federal measures also are provisions on burden of persuasion and the narrowing of certain doctrines of administrative deference commonly found in the state provisions.

Another type of citizen suit takes the form of citizen intervention and other participation in administrative agency proceedings affecting the environment. Citizen involvement is now the expected norm in several types of proceedings before agencies, such as the Federal Power Commission, the Environmental Protection Agency, and the Nuclear Regulatory Commission. One generic issue that has emerged is whether federal administrative agencies will provide financial support (through expert witness and attorney fees) for citizen interventions.[92] Regardless of how the question of financial incentives is ultimately resolved, the administrative citizen suit is a functioning reality. Indeed, so long as citizen suits in the courts are tied closely to what has happened earlier in the administrative process, it is a fair prediction that law of considerable consequence will be fashioned within the agencies. To mention but one example among

(5th Cir. 1976) (denying recovery) with Natural Resources Defense Council, Inc. v. EPA, 484 F.2d 1331, 3 ELR 20803 (1st Cir. 1973) (allowing it).

89. Oljato Chapter of the Navajo Tribe v. Train, supra note 88 (affirming a dismissal of an action challenging the Administrator's refusal to revise previously promulgated standards of performance for new coal-fired power plants for want of jurisdiction under section 304).

90. Cf. § 4.11 below (discussing confusion over review of effluent limitations in the courts of appeals and guidelines in the district courts).

91. § 2.16.

92. Note, Federal Agency Assistance to Impecunious Intervenors, 88 Harv.L. Rev. 1815 (1975); Comment, Agency Funding of Indigent Public Interest Intervenors in Administrative Proceedings, 6 ELR 10052 (1976); Hearings on Public Participation in Federal Agency Proceedings, S. 2715, Before the Subcomm. on Administrative Practice and Procedure of the Senate Comm. on the Judiciary, 94th Cong., 2d Sess. (1976); see 15 U.S. C.A. § 2605(c)(4)(A) (Toxic Substances Control Act). See also 41 Fed.Reg. 50829 (1976) (announcing termination of proposed rulemaking concerning the provision of financial assistance to participants in Nuclear Regulatory Commission proceedings pending congressional action).

many, one of the largest civil penalties in the enforcement history of the Nuclear Regulatory Commission was imposed in a proceeding initiated by a citizens group.[93] The principle established is one of strict liability for the accuracy of information contained in filings required for the licensing of nuclear power plants, and the remedy fashioned also breaks new ground.[94] It is noteworthy also that the *Scenic Hudson* case, acknowledged generally as marking the opening of a new era of modern environmental law, began as a routine move to expand the scope of a glacial administrative proceeding, and it was a spectacularly unsuccessful move at that.[95]

§ 1.14 Population Control

Many analysts of environmental problems see the issues clustering around two broad strategies: a population policy and a technology policy. In greatly simplified terms, those stressing the population issue view efforts to control the adverse effects of technologies as being little more than a holding action pending stabilization of the world's population.[1] If population growth is not brought under control, production increases cannot keep pace with the consequence that at some undetermined point (a generation or so in the future) the world will suffer a catastrophic drop in numbers and wealth, despite our best efforts to restrain further growth.[2] The only long term

---

93. In Re Virginia Elec. & Power Co., LBP 75-54, 2 NRC 498 (1975) ($60,000), modified ALAB 324, 3 NRC 347 (1976) ($17,500), further modified NRCI 76/11,480 (1976) ($32,500), petition for review pending VEPCO v. Nuclear Regulatory Comm'n, Civil No. 76-2275 (4th Cir.). The author is an attorney of record in the proceeding.

94. Ibid. (The order conditioned the permits of the applicant upon issuance of a statement by the chief executive officer expressing a commitment to discharge its regulatory responsibilities, preparation of management evaluation and analysis of its current organizational structure to implement the statement of policy, and preparation of an analysis and report on its contract policy to assure that contractors are committed to their compliance responsibilities. Also, a strong recommendation was made that the civil penalty imposed be paid out of net profit and not be considered an operating expense chargeable to the ratepayers. The staff was requested to evaluate the licensee's performance in depth to determine whether more extensive monitoring was required. Several of these conditions were eliminated in the course of administrative appeals).

95. Scenic Hudson Preservation Conference v. Federal Power Comm'n (I), 354 F.2d 608, 1 ELR 20292 (2d Cir. 1965), cert. denied 384 U.S. 941 (1966).

1. P. Ehrlich, The Population Bomb (1968); Ehrlich & Holdren, Impact of Population Growth, 171 Science 1212 (1971). For a debate on the different strategies, compare Ehrlich & Holdren, Review: The Closing Circle, 14 Environment 24 (1972) with Commoner, Review: The Closing Circle, id. at 25. On the futility of controlling the breeding of mankind by appeals to the conscience, see Hardin, The Tragedy of the Commons, 162 Science 1243 (1968).

2. D. H. Meadows, D. L. Meadows, J. Randers & W. W. Behrens, The Limits to Growth (1972). But see Models of Doom (H. S. D. Cole, C. Freeman, M. Jahoda & K. L. R. Davitt eds. 1973); M. Mesarovic & E. Pestel, Mankind at the Turning Point (1974).

remedy therefore is to bring population growth under control (however these limits are defined)—voluntarily if possible, but by compulsion if necessary. Others, although not discounting population growth entirely, place the principal onus for environmental degradation on technological foolishness.[3] Their remedy is not so decisive as ceilings on population size but is stiff enough—for the United States alone the elimination of $600 billion worth of ecologically faulty capital equipment.[4]

Needless to say, it has been no contest between the population and technology strategies in how the law has responded to environmental ills; for centuries, environmental problems have been dealt with solely in terms of restricting how a technology operates or, more likely, where it operates. The population growth origins of conflicts occasioned by production and commerce and technological expansion were beyond the perspective of the law. The few pages here devoted to a brief statement of the law of population control contrast sharply with the hundreds of pages in this text discussing the laws governing the use and abuses of technology. The space allocation fairly reflects legal priorities as they exist. It also may reflect, in similar disproportion, society's shortsightedness about the roots of the problem.

The law of population control can be defined as embracing those measures aimed at restricting the size and growth of a society's population to relieve demands upon available resources. Since the number of people on the planet influences dramatically its condition, the law of population control is a crucial (many would say the most important) variable of the law of planetary housekeeping.

Population control should be distinguished from population distribution. In a sense, any measures that slow growth, limit access to facilities or cut down on the builder's options are population distribution measures to the advantage of those who got there first. Boca Raton, Florida[5] or Petaluma, California[6] quite clearly influence where people live and work by imposing ceilings on the number of building units the cities can accommodate. They are controlling population by distributing the people elsewhere. The same result follows if Los Angeles keeps out people in the interests of achieving a livable quotient of air quality or if Oregon discourages tourism to protect its beaches.

No-growth and no-people measures are population control measures only from the point of view of those inside the exclusive circle.

3. B. Commoner, The Closing Circle (1971).

4. Id. at 284–85.

5. See The Use of Land: A Citizens' Policy Guide to Urban Growth 39 (A Task Force Report sponsored by the Rockefeller Brothers Fund) (1973); § 2.17 below.

6. See Constr. Indust. Ass'n of Sonoma County v. Petaluma, 375 F.Supp. 574, 4 ELR 20454 (N.D.Cal.1974), rev'd 522 F.2d 897, 5 ELR 20519 (9th Cir. 1975), cert. denied 424 U.S. 934 (1976).

The no-growth barriers can be drawn tightly to protect a local, regional, or even a national population. The United States immigration policy for many years reflected a determination to keep "inferior races" elsewhere on the planet implemented through country-of-origin quotas.[7] These quotas were dropped in the Immigration Act of 1965 in favor of hemispheric quotas and priorities based on family reunification, asylum for refugees, and needed skills and professions.[8] But the 1965 Act hardly amounted to an open invitation "for the wretched refuse of the Old World's teeming shores to enter our golden door," [9] leaving intact, among other things, the old selection standards, elsewhere described as "the most inclusive list of human frailties to be found anywhere in the English language." [10] Immigration policies hold down the domestic effects of population growth occurring elsewhere. They are no more a response to the problem of worldwide population stabilization than the slow-growth ordinance of Petaluma, California [11] is an answer to population control within the United States.

A valuable essay by Ward E. V. Elliott puts population and the law in historical perspective:

> Federal laws bearing on population control differ from most other federal environmental laws in that they were conceived, interpreted, and enforced almost wholly without reference to any goal of population control or environmental protection. More than most areas of law, even of environmental law, population control is an undeveloped field, more important for what it might be than for what it is or has been.[12]

The United States began to learn about its population problem by looking elsewhere. Many of our experiments have taken place abroad or, if at home, upon the poor and ill-informed. Throughout the 1960's increasing attention was given to the inclusion of family planning as an aim of the foreign assistance program. "In 1966 Congress amended the Foreign Assistance Act and the Food for Peace Act to permit the use of U.S.-owned foreign currencies for family planning programs and population-activities. In 1967 it earmarked for population programs a portion of the foreign aid funds appropriated for fiscal 1968, a practice which it has continued since in amounts increasing from $35 million for fiscal 1968 to $125 million for fiscal 1973." [13] The foreign aid programs must be run by the host country

---

7. Elliott, Federal Law and Population Control, in Environmental Law Institute, Federal Environmental Law 1518, 1542 (E. L. Dolgin & T. G. P. Guilbert eds. 1974) [hereinafter cited as Elliott]. This section is heavily indebted to the work of Professor Elliott.

8. 79 Stat. 911 (1965), 8 U.S.C.A. §§ 1151–53.

9. Elliott at 1543.

10. Ibid., quoting Fairchild, Immigration 399 (1930).

11. § 2.17 below.

12. Elliott at 1523.

13. Id. at 1563–64 (footnotes omitted).

and on a voluntary basis. They are generally not credited with more than marginal success.

At home, legal measures to control population growth and numbers have been similarly unspectacular. A government's policy choices on population control are limited. It can be for it, against it, or remain neutral. If favorably disposed, a government's choices also are limited: it can be content with voluntarism, rely upon persuasion or institute coercion. Generally governments and laws in the United States today are neutral on the subject of birth control and, where favorably disposed, are content with voluntarism. The situation contrasts starkly with the circumstances, now solidly in the past, when the law sought voluntary compliance with effluent or emission limitations upon industrial enterprises. Controlling the timing and number of offspring of human beings to be sure raises policy issues of a different dimension than controlling the timing and quantity of effluent from a chemical plant.

Domestic statutes on birth control fall into three categories: (1) the Comstock laws originating in the 1870's, (2) sundry health services laws of the 1930's and 1960's, and (3) the Family Planning Services and Population Research Act of 1970. A fourth important policy landmark is the publication in 1972 of the final report of the Commission on Population Growth and the American Future.[14]

The original Comstock laws [15] closed the United States mails to obscene literature and articles, including contraceptives and devices for unlawful abortion. Anthony Comstock was a fundamentalist Protestant bent on curbing obscenity, which included birth control by its common connection with sex and "obscene and immoral rubber articles." [16] The federal act of 1873 inspired the passage of obscenity laws in every state but New Mexico; more than half of these specifically prohibited giving contraceptive information and selling contraceptives, although there were some exemptions. Changing mores gradually undermined enforcement of the anti-contraception laws. Comstockery was given a severe setback in 1965 by the United States Supreme Court in Griswold v. Connecticut.[17] The decision held that a constitutional right of privacy protected married persons from Connecticut's Comstock laws which forbade the use of contraceptives and the aiding of others in the use of contraceptives. The federal Comstock laws also were narrowed progressively by judicial decisions [18]

---

14. Population and the American Future (1972) [hereinafter cited as the Commission Report].

15. 17 Stat. 599 (1873), 19 U.S.C.A. § 1305, as amended to exempt contraceptives, Pub.L. No. 91–662, § 1, 84 Stat. 1973 (1971); see Silverstein, From Comstockery Through Population Control, 6 N.C.Cent.L.J. 8 (1974).

16. Quoted in Elliott at 1566.

17. 381 U.S. 479, 85 S.Ct. 1678, 14 L.Ed.2d 510 (1965).

18. Cases cited in Elliott at 1566 n. 168.

prior to their drastic modification by Congress in 1971.[19] The fall of the Comstock laws was a bellwether in the legal curriculum of population control.

A second collection of laws reflect a growing tendency to offer family planning information and, perhaps inevitably, even to persuade citizens to pursue family planning. Elliott summarizes the developments:

> Public health assistance funds under the Social Security Act of 1935 had been used surreptitiously on a small scale by health and welfare agencies since the late 1930's, particularly in the South. In 1964, under the Economic Opportunity Act of 1964 authorization for "special programs and assistance," the Office of Economic Opportunity (OEO) granted $8,000 for a family planning program in Corpus Christi, Texas, the first open birth control aid provided by any federal agency . . . . In 1966, along with the two bills authorizing family planning aid abroad, Congress passed the Comprehensive Health Planning and Services Act (Partnership for Health), authorizing grants for special health problems, including birth control, to public and private nonprofit organizations.[20]

The Social Security Amendments of 1972 made mandatory an obligation to inform all recipients of Aid to Families with Dependent Children of the availability of family planning services and to make available services to all eligible persons desiring them.[21]

A third federal legislative landmark was the Family Planning Services and Population Research Act of 1970, which gives affirmative authority and additional funds for federal assistance to family planning.[22] The Act establishes an Office of Population Affairs in the Department of Health, Education, and Welfare to coordinate and assist family planning programs and education. The duties of the Office are confined to making family planning services available, not encouraging their use. No funds are to be used where abortion is to be a method of family planning. Conditioning eligibility under other programs upon the acceptance of family planning is a form of coercion expressly prohibited.[23]

The work of the U. S. Commission on Population Growth and the American Future is better known for what was said than the response it inspired. But the Commission's principal recommen-

---

19. Act of Jan. 8, 1971, Pub.L. No. 91–662, 84 Stat. 1973, 18 U.S.C.A. §§ 1461–62.

20. Elliott at 1567.

21. Pub.L. No. 92–603, § 299E(c), 86 Stat. 1462, amending 42 U.S.C.A. § 602(a)(15)(A).

22. Pub.L. No. 91–572, 84 Stat. 1504, 42 U.S.C.A. §§ 300–300a–6; see Office of Population Affairs, A Five-Year Plan for Family Planning Services and Population Research, Fourth Progress Report to the U. S. Congress, May 1975.

23. 42 U.S.C.A. §§ 300a–6, 300a–8.

dations [24] eventually may reappear as policies expressed by law: most controversial was the recommendation of a relaxation of abortion laws "with the admonition that abortion should not be considered a primary means of fertility control"; the Commission urged that "all administrative restrictions on access to voluntary contraceptive sterilization be eliminated so that the decision be made solely by physician and patient." Several predictable recommendations were made on the subjects of population education, improved population statistics and research, a stronger Office of Population Affairs in HEW and other institutional changes, including planning for a stabilized population. "By one means or another," the Commission pointed out, "an average of zero growth over the long term—a stabilized population—must and inevitably will be reestablished."[25]

Recent case law, much of it constitutional, has radically affected birth control practices in three broad categories: (1) contraception, (2) abortion, and (3) sterilization. It is important to emphasize in this context that there is evidence for the view that as many as one-sixth of all births in the United States are unwanted.[26] Perfecting birth control simply to avoid unwanted births thus might take us substantially down the road toward population stabilization. The legal controversy has focused principally upon the removal of obstacles to the individual's exercise of free choice on matters of birth control and family planning.

a. *Contraception*

Voluntarism is now the law regarding access to contraceptives. It was probably the practice before and after the two leading Supreme Court decisions, which are important more for the principle than the consequences. Griswold v. Connecticut, in striking down laws discouraging use of contraceptives, strongly affirmed a "zone of privacy . . . surrounding the marriage relationship" protected from state interference by constitutional considerations.[27] There exists a "marital right to bear children and raise a family" free from state laws either forbidding the use of birth control devices or, according to a crucial dictum, requiring family limitation.

What was good for the married became good for the unmarried in Eisenstadt v. Baird,[28] invalidating a Massachusetts law that forbade the distribution of contraceptives without a license and barred even licensed physicians and pharmacists from distributing contraceptives to unmarried persons. Mr. Justice Brennan's majority opinion thought it dubious under *Griswold* that any prohibition on contracep-

24. See Commission Report, supra note 14, at 141–47.

25. Id. at 16.

26. See id. at 97–98.

27. 381 U.S. at 485–86, 85 S.Ct. at 1682, 14 L.Ed.2d at 515–16.

28. 405 U.S. 438, 92 S.Ct. 1029, 31 L.Ed.2d 349 (1972).

tion was constitutionally permissible, but that in any event "the rights must be the same for the unmarried and married alike." [29] *Griswold* and *Eisenstadt* together cast serious doubts on any legislative or administrative efforts to curtail the inoffensive dissemination of information on birth control (including contraception, abortion, and sterilization).[30]

Interestingly, the only Justice mentioning population policy in the two cases was Mr. Justice White in *Griswold* who noted simply that Connecticut had no policy of promoting population expansion.[31] But he, like the others, focused on the conflict between the claims of individual choice and those of state power not on the pros and cons of birth control. The contraception cases strongly affirm freedom of choice, but this is a freedom to have children as well as to refrain. It is a freedom to reduce the 15% of unwanted births and a freedom against state efforts to compel a reduction of the remaining 85%.

Mr. Justice Goldberg did not go so far in *Griswold* as to shut the door on the constitutionality of compulsory measures of birth control. He did describe a limitation on family size as a "totalitarian" interference with the right of privacy supportable only on a showing of "compelling state interest." [32] Given the urgency of the claims generally attending discussions of population control, it is not unreasonable to suggest that if some forms of compulsory birth control enactments eventually reach the Supreme Court, they will not be prejudiced hopelessly by the *Griswold* and *Eisenstadt* cases.[33]

b. *Abortion*

Abortion raises all the problems of the contraception laws plus the additional enormous perplexities of the health of the mother and the life of the fetus. Common law, effective in most of the states until the Civil War, prohibited abortion only after the quickening of the fetus (first signs of movement), which normally takes place between the 16th and 18th week of pregnancy. After the Civil War most of the states modified the common law rule to ban all abortion except when necessary to save the mother's life. By 1966 all 50 states and the District of Columbia had prohibited abortion by statute. A gradual and partial relaxation of the bans came with the adoption by many

29. 405 U.S. at 453, 92 S.Ct. at 1038, 31 L.Ed.2d at 362.

30. See Atlanta Coop. News Project v. Postal Service, 350 F.Supp. 234 (N.D.Ga.1972) (invalidating on First Amendment grounds the Postal Service's refusal to accept for mailing information on how and where abortions could be obtained); Bigelow v. Virginia, 421 U.S. 809, 95 S.Ct. 2222, 44 L.Ed.2d 600 (1974); Messerman, Abortion Counselling: Shall Women Be Permitted to Know?, 23 Case W. Res.L.Rev. 810 (1972).

31. 381 U.S. at 505, 85 S.Ct. at 1693, 14 L.Ed.2d at 527 (concurring).

32. 381 U.S. at 497, 85 S.Ct. at 1688, 14 L.Ed.2d at 522 (concurring).

33. See Note, Legal Analysis and Population Control: The Problem of Coercion, 84 Harv.L.Rev. 1856, 1890–93 (1971).

states of the American Law Institute's Model Penal Code Section 230.3, permitting abortion where specified medical authorities agree that birth would endanger the mother's health, or where the child would be born seriously deformed, or is the product of rape or incest. By the early 1970's a perceptible movement was underway in the state legislatures to liberalize the law of abortion by reverting to rules similar to those extant at common law.

In 1973 the Supreme Court forged ahead of state and federal legislatures by striking down a Texas abortion statute of the pre-Model Penal Code variety and a Georgia statute along the lines of the Code.[34] Although the Court in Roe v. Wade disclaimed an attempt to resolve "the difficult question of when life begins,"[35] the legislative-type lines that it drew certainly depend upon the stage of development of the fetus: during the first trimester (prior to quickening) the state has no interest that justifies overriding the decision of the mother, in consultation with her physician, to terminate the pregnancy;[36] during the second trimester (after quickening but before viability of the fetus), when the risks to the mother from an abortion may exceed those of normal childbirth, the state can intervene with reasonable regulations to protect maternal health; only after viability (usually after 28 weeks of pregnancy) can the state, to vindicate the interest in potential life, go so far as to forbid abortion except when it is necessary to preserve the life and health of the mother.

Roe v. Wade certainly takes a large step toward validating abortion as an alternative birth control choice among those wishing to resort to it. The Supreme Court was not moved substantially by the birth control potential of abortions, however, saying only "population growth, pollution, poverty and racial overtones tend to complicate and not to simplify the problem"[37] (thought to be difficult enough on religious, moral and philosophical grounds). It remains to be seen whether abortions will affect the birthrate significantly and thus gain recognition as a serious birth control alternative.[38]

---

34. Roe v. Wade, 410 U.S. 113, 93 S.Ct. 705, 35 L.Ed.2d 147 (1973); Doe v. Bolton, 410 U.S. 179, 93 S.Ct. 739, 35 L.Ed.2d 201 (1973). The commentary on the decisions is extensive. E. g., Bryn, An American Tragedy: The Supreme Court on Abortion, 41 Fordham L.Rev. 807 (1973); Ely, The Wages of Crying Wolf: A Comment on Roe v. Wade, 82 Yale L.J. 920 (1973); Wellington, Common Law Rules and Constitutional Double Standards: Some Notes on Adjudication, 83 Yale L.J. 221 (1973).

35. 410 U.S. at 159, 93 S.Ct. at 730, 35 L.Ed.2d at 181.

36. The state can regulate abortions in the first trimester for health purposes. See 410 U.S. at 163, 93 S.Ct. at 732, 35 L.Ed.2d at 182. See also Planned Parenthood of Central Missouri v. Danforth, 428 U.S. 52, 96 S.Ct. 2831, 49 L.Ed.2d 788 (1976) (holding that state constitutionally may not require spousal consent and may not impose a blanket parental consent provision for minors as a condition for an abortion).

37. 410 U.S. at 116, 93 S.Ct. at 708–09, 35 L.Ed.2d at 156.

38. See Elliott at 1535–36, 1574–75 n. 207 (discussing the importance of

c. *Sterilization*

Voluntary sterilization, on the other hand, is an established practice thought to be an increasingly significant restraining force on the birth rate in the United States. A 1970 study of fertility [39] reported that almost three million married people under the age of 45 had undergone voluntary sterilization for contraceptive reasons, accounting for 16 per cent of couples able to bear children but not intending to have any more. Only Utah [40] still forbids voluntary sterilization, although in several other jurisdictions physicians are in doubt about possible penalties if sterilization operations are performed. The situation was clarified somewhat by the holding in Hathaway v. Worcester City Hospital,[41] which struck down on equal protection grounds a hospital's policy against use of its facilities for sterilization operations when other medically indistinguishable surgical procedures were allowed. It is doubtful that similar hospital rules—such as those requiring a certain number of chidren prior to the operation—can survive.

The issue of free choice has come to the fore on sterilization, just as it has on abortion. A sharp debate has arisen over the concentration of family planning efforts of the Department of HEW on low-income groups and individuals.[42] Sudden governmental attention to the breeding capacities of the poor and the black can be seen as hostile or beneficent, depending upon the motivation. Wholly apart from this question of motives is the further question of whether the socially or economically depressed are subjected to subtle pressures through the welfare process or otherwise to submit to sterilization. In Relf v. Weinberger,[43] Judge Gesell ordered the United States to stop paying for the sterilization of children and mentally incompetent persons, invalidating HEW regulations authorizing the operations as inconsistent with the Public Health Act [44] and the Social Security Act.[45] The court also ordered modifications of consent forms to reflect prominently the advice required to be given to prospective patients prior to sterilization that no federal benefits may be denied because of a refusal to be sterilized. The decision does as much as the law can do to assure that consent is voluntary.[46]

abortion for population control in various countries and predictions of the impact in the United States).

39. Commission Report, supra note 14, at 164.

40. Utah Code Ann. §§ 64-10-1 to -12; cf. N.C.Gen.Stat. § 90-271 (requiring spousal consent to a contraceptive sterilization).

41. 475 F.2d 701 (1st Cir. 1973).

42. Compare Blake, Population Policy for Americans: Is the Government Being Misled?, 164 Science 522 (1969), and Schultz, Federal Population Policy: A Decade of Change, 15 Vill.L. Rev. 788 (1970) with Harkavy, Jaffe & Wishik, Family Planning and Public Policy: Who Is Misleading Whom, 165 Science 367 (1969).

43. 372 F.Supp. 1196 (D.D.C.1974).

44. 42 U.S.C.A. § 300 et seq.

45. Id. § 602(a)(15).

46. Not quite. In 1975, Congress made it a criminal offense to coerce

Difficult issues of consent were raised in the 1973 damage suit, filed by attorneys with the Southern Poverty Law Center, against the federally-funded family planning clinic in Montgomery, Alabama, over the sterilization of two young girls, aged 12 and 14. The girls, both black and one apparently retarded, were sterilized after HEW guidelines prohibited the continued use of depo-provera, an experimental "three month injection" birth control drug which the clinic had been administering to the girls at the mother's request. The litigation is likely to turn on factual questions as to who consented to what upon what understanding. It raises a potpourri of questions: "what constitutes informed consent for minors, illiterates, and retarded people, parental versus minors' rights, rights of [a] nonresident father, racial discrimination, eugenic factors, use of experimental drugs, and procedures for supervising and funding federally sponsored programs."[47] The immediate HEW response was to impose an age ceiling for those seeking federally assisted sterilizations.[48]

Incompetents who cannot consent present the legal issue of compulsory sterilization. About half the states have laws requiring compulsory eugenic sterilization, intended to restrict the transmission of insanity, feeble-mindedness, or habitual criminality to future generations.[49] One of these laws was upheld in the 1927 Supreme Court decision in Buck v. Bell[50] where Mr. Justice Holmes coined the famous phrase: "Three generations of imbeciles are enough."[51] (The evidence of imbecility as regards at least two of the three generations, by the way, was less than compelling.) Skinner v. Oklahoma[52] imposed equal protection limitations on *Buck* by striking down an Oklahoma statute authorizing the sterilization of offenders committing "felonies involving moral turpitude" while exempting certain white-collar crimes. A statement of the "rule of law" regarding compulsory sterilization hardly can be definitive: a compulsory sterilization law might be sustained if a state establishes a scientific basis for assuming that traits such as imbecility are hereditary, if there is a compelling state interest in excising those traits from the population, if the application of law is procedurally circumspect, and if the law avoids irrational distinctions between groups similarly situated. Governments that have exercised the power to take life in many ways are not likely to be disabled from preventing the future birth of one certain to be a homicidal maniac. On the other hand, conceding

any person to undergo an abortion or sterilization procedure by threatening loss of program benefits. 42 U.S.C.A. § 300a–8.

47. Elliott at 1577.

48. Zero Population Growth, Nat'l Rep., Aug. 1973, at 8; see 42 CFR § 50.202; 45 CFR § 205.35.

49. See Greenawalt, Criminal Law and Population Control, 24 Vand.L.Rev. 465, 487–89 (1971).

50. 274 U.S. 200, 47 S.Ct. 584, 71 L.Ed. 1000 (1927).

51. 274 U.S. at 207, 47 S.Ct. at 585, 71 L.Ed. at 1002.

52. 316 U.S. 535, 62 S.Ct. 1110, 86 L.Ed. 1655 (1942).

the power to so manipulate the gene pool understandably raises the spectre of genocide and the use of sterilization to cause "races or types which are inimical to the dominant group to wither and disappear." [53] A legal claim to priority in breeding rights is not easily established.

Compulsory sterilization of misfits is never likely to become a major force in birth control. In 1952 it was estimated that no more than 52,000 people had been sterilized under these statutes.[54] The scientific premise which allows the unfailing prediction of the consequences of future births is waivering.[55] Compulsion in birth control, if it becomes an option forced upon us, is more likely and fruitfully to be applied broadly to the population, than selectively against genetic discards. The courts are likely to insist upon that course.

53. 316 U.S. at 541, 62 S.Ct. at 1113, 86 L.Ed. at 1660 (Douglas, J.).

54. H. F. Pilpel & T. Zavin, Your Marriage and the Law 205 (1952).

55. Rabin, Population Control Through Financial Incentives, 23 Hastings L.J. 1353, 1360 (1972); see Elliott at 1576–79.

Chapter II

COMMON LAW AND THE VARIATIONS

§ 2.1 Continuity of Principles: Nuisance Law

Environmental law as it is known today is an amalgam of common law and statutory principles. The impact of technology on man contributed in no small way to doctrinal developments in nuisance,[1] trespass,[2] negligence,[3] and strict liability for abnormally dangerous activities.[4] The dominant water law theories[5] and the public trust doctrine[6] influence uses of the staple resources—water and land. A host of non-common law doctrines, such as a taking by eminent domain, play an important role today.[7]

The deepest doctrinal roots of modern environmental law are found in principles of nuisance. The infinite variety of wrongs covered by this amorphous theory is well known to any student of the law, but deserves emphasis here. There is simply no common law doctrine that approaches nuisance in comprehensiveness or detail as a regulator of land use and of technological abuse. Nuisance actions have involved pollution of all physical media—air, water, land—by a wide variety of means. Singled out for treatment in this text are pollution problems occasioned by noisy activities,[8] the disposal of solid wastes[9] and the use of pesticides.[10] Nuisance actions have challenged virtually every major industrial and municipal activity which is today the subject of comprehensive environmental regulation—the operation of land fills, incinerators, sewage treatment facilities, activities at chemical plants, aluminum, lead and copper smelters, oil refineries, pulp mills, rendering plants, quarries and mines, textile mills and a host of other manufacturing activities. Nuisance litigation has influenced energy policy at all stages—fuel exploration, transportation, siting of facilities, fuel combustion, waste disposal and reclamation. Nuisance theory and case law is the common law backbone of modern environmental and energy law.

1. See §§ 2.2–.12 below.
2. See § 2.13 below.
3. See § 2.14 below.
4. See ibid.
5. See § 2.15 below.
6. See § 2.16 below; Sax, The Public Trust Doctrine In Natural Resource Law: Effective Judicial Intervention, 68 Mich.L.Rev. 471 (1970).
7. See §§ 2.17, 5.5 below; Walla Walla v. Conkey, 6 Wn.App. 6, 492 P.2d 589, 2 ELR 20172 (1971) (treating pollution of waters by municipality's discharge of inadequately treated wastes as an unconstitutional taking).
8. See § 5.5 below.
9. See § 6.2 below.
10. See § 8.2 below.

From nuisance cases alone, "[o]ne could easily write an informative account of the development of the Industrial Revolution." [11] Many of the cases are on the "troubled frontier" [12] between the old and new occupations: riverside dwellers and textile mills, which demanded canals and water power; textile mills and smoky blast furnaces; farmers and hydraulic mines. Today, conflicts are equally representative: airports and residents; power plants and foresters; oil transporters and fishermen. Nuisance litigation can result from controversies over the siting of an oil refinery, the disposal of sewage sludge, an expansion of a landfill, run-off from a construction site, or, indeed, the siting of a half-way house.

It is also useful to keep in mind that in broad outline substantive legal principles governing the correction of environmental insults have not changed materially for centuries. Private nuisance law long has forbidden substantial and unreasonable intrusions upon the use and enjoyment of another's property. The law is experienced in dealing with the culprit who wishes to dispose of sulfuric acid in your backyard. Although today it is customary to attach numbers to the types of invasions deemed "substantial and unreasonable", expressed as air or water quality standards, the principles of the action remain fundamentally unchanged.

One of the first nuisance cases, reported by Fitz Herbert in the sixteenth century, involved city officials who permitted swine to run loose distributing their dung in the alleys and lanes resulting in the air being so "corrupted and infected" that a "dreadful terror" afflicted the masters and scholars residing there.[13] Upon a complaint a writ was issued directing that the streets and lanes be cleansed and "for the future kept clean from dung and dunghills." The threat of contempt apparently sufficed to overcome any claims that technology was unavailable to restrain healthy swine; that the problem could be met by increasing the height of the stack on the piggery; or that odors were without a remedy absent a scientifically reliable technique for measuring the offense. A disagreeable stench, recognizable by anyone with a functioning nose, was thought to justify resort to the best techniques available to sweeten the air.

That the principles of the sixteenth century survive in large measure today is nowhere better illustrated than by one of the first decisions under the revolutionary Michigan Environmental Protection Act of 1970.[14] The problem, this time, was offensive odors from a hog finishing barn. The standard, once again, was whether the odors were controlled by the best techniques available, although it can be presumed that the technological challenges today are no less imposing

11. Z. Chaffee & E. D. Re, Cases & Materials on Equity 795–96 (4th ed. 1958).

12. Id. at 796.

13. Discussed in id. at 794.

14. Mich.Comp.Laws Ann. § 691.1201 (201) et seq.; § 2.16 below.

than they were in the sixteenth century. The principal discernible difference between precedents four centuries apart was in result. The Michigan court explained, "Although it would probably be accepted as fact by most humans that the odor of swine and other animal wastes are disagreeable, it should be recognized that they are what might be termed 'natural' odors in an agricultural area as distinguished from man created odors of a disagreeable nature. Further, that if the animal wastes are handled and disposed of in accordance with good farming practice then such odors as may enter the atmosphere could well be considered the result of normal farm operations and not a nuisance." [15] The key to the law of nuisance is found not in the statement of principles but in their application.

§ 2.2 Public Nuisance

Nuisance is a word derived from the French word for harm. A public nuisance can be defined as an unreasonable interference with a right common to the general public.[1] A private nuisance is a substantial and unreasonable interference with the use and enjoyment of land.[2] Despite the historically accurate insistence that public and private nuisances have "little or nothing in common," [3] the differences are fast disappearing. The only practical ones are that a public official can sue to restrain a public nuisance and that the defenses of prescriptive rights, estoppel, laches and the like are unavailable if the conduct involved is a public nuisance.[4] Public nuisances also are not confined to protecting interests in land. But the two concepts are quite alike when consideration is given to the ultimate question of whether a particular activity interferes unreasonably with protected rights. Conduct may constitute a public and private nuisance simultaneously, and both doctrines are often discussed without distinction in the case law.[5]

---

15. Crandall v. Biergans, 2 ELR 20238, 20239 (Mich.Cir.Ct.1972); see Sax & Conner, Michigan's Environmental Protection Act of 1970, 70 Mich.L.Rev. 1004, 1037 (1972).

1. Restatement, Second, Torts § 821B (Tent. Draft No. 16, 1970) reads as follows:

(1) A public nuisance is an unreasonable interference with a right common to the general public.

(2) Circumstances which may sustain a holding that an interference with a public right is unreasonable include the following:

(a) whether the conduct involves a substantial interference with the public health, the public safety, the public peace, the public comfort or the public convenience, or

(b) whether the conduct is proscribed by a statute, ordinance or administrative regulation, or

(c) whether the conduct is of a continuing nature or has produced a permanent or long-lasting effect and to the actor's knowledge, has a substantial detrimental effect upon the public right.

2. See id. § 821D.

3. Id. at 6.

4. Id. at 35; § 2.9 below.

5. State v. Galaxy Chem. Co., 1 ERC 1660 (Md.Cir.Ct.1970); Capurro v.

As recently as 1969, it was accepted dogma on the floor of the American Law Institute that a public nuisance is a "criminal interference with a right common to all members of the public" resulting in liability "only to those who have suffered harm of a kind different from that suffered by other members of the public exercising the public right."[6] Of the three important aspects of this definition (a criminal interference, impact upon common rights of the public, a "different" kind of injury as a prerequisite to suit), the only one surviving in the current Restatement definition of a public nuisance is that rights common to the general public be affected.

The requirement that a public nuisance interfere with a "right common to the general public" has "seldom arisen" in litigation[7] according to Dean Prosser. The reason is that any activity that substantially interferes with the private interests of a large number of individuals is likely to interfere with public rights as well, be they rights to clean air, clean water or a quiet environment.[8] Moreover, any interference with the rights of a small group of people[9] inevitably would still be actionable as a private nuisance, albeit not as a public nuisance in a suit by public officials.

The association of a public nuisance with the criminal law is a correct reading of history[10] but somewhat misleading today. The

---

Galaxy Chem. Co., 2 ELR 20386 (Md. Cir.Ct.1972) (chemical plant emissions enjoinable as a public nuisance also constitute a private nuisance to persons suffering a diminution of property values); Commonwealth v. United States Steel Corp., 1972 Equity No. 1550 (Pa.Ct.C.P. Allegheny County 1972).

6. The quotations come from the Restatement, Second, Torts §§ 821B, 821C originally submitted to and approved at the annual meeting of the American Law Institute in 1969. The substantial revisions that followed are detailed in Wade, Environmental Protection, The Common Law of Nuisance and the Restatement of Torts, 8 The Forum 165 (1972); see Bryson & Macbeth, Public Nuisance, the Restatement (2d) of Torts, and Environmental Law, 2 Ecol.L.Q. 241 (1972).

7. W. L. Prosser, Law of Torts 586 (4th ed. 1971).

8. See Fort Smith v. Western Hide & Fur Co., 153 Ark. 99, 239 S.W. 724 (1922) (odors from furs stored in city); Mount Pleasant v. Van Tassell, 7 Misc. 2d 643, 166 N.Y.S.2d 458 (1957), aff'd

6 A.D.2d 880, 177 N.Y.S.2d 1010 (odors, rats, and flies from piggery); Baltzeger v. Carolina Midland Ry., 54 S.C. 242, 32 S.E. 358 (1899) (public health affected by malarial waters); Dworkin v. Lakeview, 327 S.W.2d 351 (Tex.Civ.App.1959) (odors, noise, and dust). In a small number of states, such as New York and Oklahoma, statutes define a public nuisance to include interference with any "considerable number of persons." N.Y. Penal Law § 240.45 (McKinney); Okla.Stat.Ann. tit. 50, § 2. Under these statutes it is unnecessary to conduct even a formal search for a right "common to the general public."

9. Soap Corp. v. Reynolds, 178 F.2d 503 (5th Cir. 1949) (odors from soap factory affecting neighboring residences); Biggs v. Griffith, 231 S.W.2d 875 (Mo.Ct.App.1950) (public address system affecting nearby landowners); Hartung v. County of Milwaukee, 2 Wis.2d 269, 86 N.W.2d 475 (1957) (quarry).

10. Prosser, Private Action for Public Nuisance, 52 Va.L.Rev. 997 (1966).

fact of the matter is we are unlikely if ever to see another conviction for the common law crime of public nuisance (and still more unlikely to see it sustained on appeal against constitutional attack). Condemning conduct as a "public nuisance" is hardly more informative than condemning it as a "crime". The Model Penal Code reduces public nuisance to several specific offenses under the general heading of offenses against public order and decency.[11] Thus, public nuisance as a crime currently is exclusively a creature of statute, and the statutory definitions are not necessarily tied to historical understandings of the meaning of a public nuisance.

The power to abate, not indict, is the crux of the offense.[12] That we are dealing fundamentally with a civil remedy, albeit one to be pursued usually by the officers of the state, means that the coincidental condemnation of the same conduct under the criminal law should be viewed as simply one factor to be considered in deciding whether civil relief should be available. That is exactly what the Restatement accomplishes by identifying as an ingredient of the reasonableness of the interference with the public right "whether the conduct is proscribed by a statute, ordinance or administrative regulation." [13]

Virtually every state has a sizable list of statutes branding as public nuisances a wide range of activities. A search of the laws in a given jurisdiction may provide both comic filler [14] and surprisingly useful material: the lawsuit challenging environmental fall-out from the local dump, sewage treatment plant or rock concert is obviously aided if a statute proscribes the challenged conduct.[15]

Another relic of the public nuisance doctrine comparable to its association with the criminal law is the requirement that a private party must suffer from a "different" kind of injury than the public at large in order to maintain a public nuisance action. The reasons for the rules ostensibly are to protect defendants from a multiplicity of actions, to discourage trivial lawsuits, and to prevent interference

---

11. Model Penal Code §§ 250.2 (disorderly conduct), 250.5 (public drunkenness), 250.7 (obstructing public passages), 250.8 (disrupting public gatherings) (Proposed Official Draft 1962).

12. Dean Wade reports that it never was "necessary that the defendant be subject to criminal prosecution." Restatement, Second, Torts § 14 (Tent. Draft No. 16, 1970). Suits for abatement or damages by private individuals suffering specialized injury have been permissible for centuries, and municipalities immune from criminal prosecution may be liable for maintaining a public nuisance.

13. Id. § 821D.

14. Prosser mentions activities ranging from the keeping of a bawdy house to black currant plants to mosquito breeding waters. Supra note 7, at 586.

15. See § 2.10 below; Heck v. Beryllium Corp., 424 Pa. 140, 226 A.2d 87 (1967); cf. Wyandotte Transp. Co. v. United States, 389 U.S. 191, 88 S.Ct. 379, 19 L.Ed.2d 407 (1967); J. I. Case Co. v. Borak, 377 U.S. 426, 84 S.Ct. 1555, 12 L.Ed.2d 423 (1964); see, e. g., Wisconsin Student Ass'n v. Regents of the University of Wisconsin, 318 F.Supp. 591 (W.D.Wis.1970).

Sec. 2.2 PUBLIC NUISANCE 105

with the discretion of public authorities.[16] There is no question that the "different" injury requirement was an historical prerequisite to a private lawsuit on public nuisance grounds.[17] It has been applied with absurd results to deny relief, for the reason that no injury different in kind from that of the public was shown, to a worker afflicted by fumes, dust and smoke from a nearby factory;[18] a large livestock owner aggrieved by an interference with public grazing rights;[19] a frequent user of public waters polluted by defendant.[20] A debate has raged over whether a difference in kind is often in reality only one in degree, with no less a luminary than Dean Prosser shifting to the "difference in kind" school after a careful study of the reported cases.[21]

The Restatement, Second, Torts § 821C(1) retains the requirement by affirming, "In order to recover damages in an individual action for a public nuisance, one must have suffered harm of a kind different from that suffered by other members of the public exercising the right common to the general public which was the subject of interference." Subsection 821C(2) adds a substantial qualifier, however, by declaring, "In order to enjoin or abate the public nuisance, one must . . . have standing to sue as a representative of the general public, as a member of a class in a class action, or as a citizen in a citizen's action."[22] For actions in equity, then, the Restatement banishes the old "different" injury test, requiring nothing more than that the normal standing criteria be met.[23] This is a proper and efficient solution to the problem because the purpose of a showing of a special kind of injury to private suitors in public nuisance actions is virtually indistinguishable from the functions of the law of standing. Both seek to assure concrete disputes, adversariness and public control over public litigation. The "different" injury test properly

---

16. Prosser, supra note 10, at 1007; Jaffe, Standing to Sue in Conservation Suits, in Law and the Environment 123, 131 (Baldwin & Page eds. 1970).

17. Prosser, supra note 10; see, e. g., Whitehead v. Jessup, 53 F. 707 (2d Cir. 1893); Bouquet v. Hackensack Water Co., 90 N.J.L. 203, 101 A. 379 (Ct.Err. & App.1917).

18. Page v. Niagara Chem. Div., 68 So. 2d 382 (Fla.1953).

19. Anthony Wilkinson Live Stock Co. v. McIlquam, 14 Wyo. 209, 83 P. 364 (1905).

20. Gibbons v. Hoffman, 203 Misc. 26, 115 N.Y.S.2d 632 (Sup.Ct.1952); International Shoe Co. v. Heatwole, 126 W.Va. 888, 30 S.E.2d 537 (1944).

21. See Restatement, Second, Torts § 27 (Tent. Draft No. 16, 1970). The disputants would have done better to have heeded the recommendations of Smith, Private Right for Obstruction to Public Right of Passage, 15 Colum. L.Rev. 1, 149 (1915), that anyone who suffers actual harm of any kind can sue to correct a public nuisance.

22. Restatement, Second, Torts, supra note 21, § 821C(2)(c). Standing also is accorded to those who
   (a) have the right to recover damages, as indicated in subsection (1), or
   (b) have authority as a public official or public agency to represent in such matters the state or a political subdivision,
   . . . .

23. See § 1.6 above.

should be read as an historical procedural appendage in a context where the "private attorney general" was unique and usual. Where procedural reform has swept the reasons for the rule aside the requirement also should fall.

Having seemingly conceded as much in Section 821C(2) of the Restatement, Second, one wonders why the limitation remains in Section 821C(1), virtually as a separate substantive element of a public nuisance claim seeking money damages. The only consolation is that the cases in the post-Sierra Club v. Morton [24] era are little disposed to accord significance to the "different" injury test.[25] Any person injured in fact should be able to sue for equitable relief or money damages. When he sues for money damages the public nuisance as to him will be called a private nuisance.[26] There is no longer room in the law for the proposition that a person injured by the conduct of another can be denied money damages because others similarly situated also are hurt while public authorities sit idly by.

Stripped of their criminal and "different" injury requirements, public nuisances in the environmental field can cover a wide range [27] of urban and rural environmental ills: interferences with the public health, as by the operation of a power plant or the keeping of a hogpen or diseased animals or a malarial pond; with the public safety, as

24. 405 U.S. 727, 92 S.Ct. 1361, 31 L.Ed.2d 636 (1972).

25. See Rothstein, Private Actions for Public Nuisance: The Standing Problem, 76 W.Va.L.Rev. 453 (1974). See also Ozark Poultry Prods., Inc. v. Garman, 251 Ark. 389, 472 S.W.2d 714, 2 ELR 20016 (Ark.Sup.Ct.1971) (pre-Sierra Club v. Morton) (rejecting argument that a rendering plant was a public nuisance abatable only at the behest of public officials because it inflicted the same damage on all homeowners); Capurro v. Galaxy Chem. Co., 2 ELR 20386 (Md. Cir.Ct.1972); cf. Paepcke v. Public Building Comm'n, 46 Ill.2d 330, 263 N.E.2d 11, 1 ELR 20172 (1970) (rejecting special damage requirement in taxpayers' suit claiming violation of public trust doctrine). Unfortunate holdovers include Hardy Salt Co. v. Southern Pacific Transp. Co., 501 F.2d 1156 (10th Cir. 1974) and Oppen v. Aetna Ins. Co., 485 F.2d 252, 3 ELR 20808 (9th Cir. 1973) (invoking "special injury" requirement to deny recovery to private pleasure boat owners seeking damages for loss of navigation rights occasioned by the 1969 Santa Barbara oil spill).

26. See Columbia River Fishermen's Protective Union v. St. Helens, 160 Or. 654, 87 P.2d 195 (1939) (finding a different injury in kind to support public nuisance suit for water pollution damage suffered by commercial fishermen).

27. Examples and citations from the older cases can be found in W. L. Prosser, supra note 7, at 583–85. The more recent authorities include Atlanta Processing Co. v. Brown, 227 Ga. 203, 179 S.E.2d 752, 2 ELR 20114 (1971) (rejecting void for vagueness constitutional claims in a public nuisance action against animal byproduct processor); People v. Mack, 19 Cal.App.3d 1040, 97 Cal.Rptr. 448, 2 ELR 20026 (1971) (requiring abatement of booms, fences, low bridges, wires, and cables obstructing a navigable river); State v. Arizona Pub. Serv. Co., 2 ELR 20011 (N.M.Dist.Ct. 1972), rev'd 85 N.M. 165, 510 P.2d 98, 3 ELR 20496 (1973) (action against coal-burning electric generating plants); Commonwealth v. Barnes & Tucker Co., 455 Pa. 392, 319 A.2d 871, 4 ELR 20545 (1974) (discharge of acid drainage from an inactive coal mine held to be a public nuisance).

by the storage of explosives or the transportation of hazardous wastes; with the public peace, as by a rock festival or other loud and disturbing noises; with the public comfort, as by causing bad odors, smoke, dust or vibrations; or with the public convenience, as by obstructing a highway or a navigable stream.

§ 2.3 Private Nuisance

A private nuisance is a substantial and unreasonable interference with the use and enjoyment of an interest in land.[1] That interference may be intentional, or it may be the result of negligent or reckless conduct or of activity which is abnormally dangerous.[2] The emphasis with rare exceptions [3] is not on what is going on in the head of the actor but rather upon the consequences of his act. The typical situation in a pollution case involves a defendant who fully understands what he is doing, i. e., operating some type of establishment offensive or harmful to his neighbors. The legal issue becomes whether a particular intrusion is sufficiently noxious to give rise to a finding of nuisance.

It is important to emphasize that liability for a nuisance (private and public as well) must be premised upon substantial harm.[4] This requirement, although not imposing,[5] avoids condemning under the law of nuisance a wide variety of mildly annoying intrusions upon one's neighbor. One important leg of the substantiality test is that the degree of injury be objectively measured, and thus relief may be denied to the peculiarly vulnerable.[6] Another important indicator of

---

1. The language in text tracks closely to the explanation of Dean John Wade, current Reporter of the Restatement, Second, Torts, in Environmental Protection, The Common Law of Nuisance and the Restatement of Torts, 8 Forum 165, 170 (1972); see Hashim, Private Nuisance Law: Protection of the Individual's Environmental Rights, 8 Suffolk L.Rev. 1162 (1974).

2. Restatement, Second, Torts § 822, at 22 (Tent. Draft No. 17, 1971) reads as follows:

   One is subject to liability for a private nuisance if, but only if, his conduct is a legal cause of an invasion of another's interest in the private use and enjoyment of land, and the invasion is either

   (a) intentional and unreasonable, or

   (b) unintentional and otherwise actionable under the principles controlling liability for negligent or reckless conduct, or for abnormally dangerous conditions or activities.

3. The spite fence case is an unusual example where defendant inflicts harm with pleasure and actually desires to bring about the hurt. E. g., Burke v. Smith, 69 Mich. 380, 37 N.W. 838 (1888) (a leading case); see Sundowner, Inc. v. King, 95 Idaho 367, 509 P.2d 785 (1973).

4. Restatement, Second, Torts § 821F at 58 (Tent. Draft No. 15, 1969) reads: There is liability for a nuisance only to those to whom it causes substantial harm, of a kind which would be suffered by a normal person in the community, or by property in a normal condition and used for a normal purpose.

5. See § 2.4 below.

6. See ibid.

substantial harm is whether the actor's conduct is continuous and persistent or inflicts long-lasting effects.[7]

While private nuisance law generally is confined to protecting rights in land, "any interest sufficient to be dignified as a property right will support the action." [8] This includes the holders of leases, easements and the like. The interest protected in the "use and enjoyment" of this property is to be understood generously as encompassing all those pleasures, comforts and enjoyments normally associated with occupancy. Not only is the actual value and physical integrity of the land protected but the occupant himself is protected from substantial annoyance, physical discomfort or injury or a threat of it that intrudes upon his satisfaction of residing in a particular place.

The property origins of the theory have not been a serious bar to recovery. Almost invariably, activity challenged as a nuisance involves a continuous irritant to others. The relationship that brings plaintiffs into proximity with potential nuisances is usually of property origins: the most likely plaintiff is the resident tenant or homeowner. It is not inconceivable that conduct that would be a nuisance were it to afflict a homeowner also weighs heavily on people lacking the magic property connection—for example, a student in a school or a worker in a factory. In these latter cases, the theory of the lawsuit would be negligence or strict liability, or as a party aggrieved by a public nuisance,[9] and the possibilities of recovery would be virtually coextensive with those under a private nuisance theory.

In both private and public nuisance litigation liability can be imposed in situations where the actor is generally acknowledged to be free from fault. The most explicit acknowledgement of this fact is the recognition that liability for a nuisance can be imposed for activity otherwise actionable under principles controlling liability for abnormally dangerous activities.[10] There is also a strong body of case law effectively giving defendants the power of eminent domain by requiring them to pay plaintiffs permanent damages even though the offending activity is suitably located and controlled with the best available technology.[11] These defendants cannot in any conventional use

---

7. See ibid.

8. W. L. Prosser, Law of Torts 593 (4th ed. 1971).

9. Page v. Niagara Chem. Div., 68 So. 2d 382 (Fla.1953) (negligence).

10. Restatement, Second, Torts § 822, at 22 (Tent. Draft No. 17, 1971).

11. See Richards v. Washington Terminal R. R., 233 U.S. 546, 557, 34 S.Ct. 654, 658, 58 L.Ed. 1088, 1093 (1914) (on the hypothesis that "the damage is not preventable by the employment at reasonable expense of devices such as have been suggested"); Healey v. Citizens' Gas & Elec. Co., 199 Iowa 82, 201 N.W. 118 (1924); Simmons v. Paterson, 60 N.J.Eq. 385, 45 A. 995 (1900); Boomer v. Atlantic Cement Co., 26 N.Y.2d 219, 309 N.Y.S.2d 312, 257 N.E.2d 870 (1970); Susquehanna Fertilizer Co. v. Malone, 73 Md. 268, 276, 20 A. 900 (1890) (holding defendant for substantial harm; "And this, too, without regard to the locality which such business is carried on; and this, too, although the business may be a lawful business, and one useful to the public, and although the

Sec. 2.3   PRIVATE NUISANCE   109

of the term be said to be at fault. The point is simply that "it may be just to require an actor who has commandeered another's property for his own purposes to pay for what he has taken, no matter how faultless and socially useful his conduct has been." [12]

After considerable debate, the American Law Institute has come around to this view. In 1970, a motion was made and passed on the floor of the Institute directing the Reporter to include somewhere in the blackletter the following statement:

> Even though one's conduct is reasonable in the sense that its social utility outweighs the harms and risks it causes, he is subject to liability for damages, but not to an injunction, for a private nuisance, if the resulting interference with another's use and enjoyment of land is greater than it is reasonable to require the other to bear under the circumstances without compensation.[13]

The reporter read two ideas into this instruction: [14] (1) activity may be very useful in general so that it should not be abated and yet be required to "pay its own way" (that is, compensate for the damage caused), and (2) damage to the injured party may be so substantial that payment should be made regardless of the utility of the conduct. These thoughts were incorporated into the Restatement as substantial modifications of the requirement that an intentional nuisance must be "intentional and unreasonable".[15] This aim is accomplished by defining "unreasonable" in two separate sections of the Restatement to include conduct that is not unreasonable at all but should give rise to liability for damage inflicted.[16] Section 826(b) declares that "an intentional invasion of another's interest in the use and enjoyment of land is unreasonable . . . if . . . the harm caused by

---

best and most approved appliances and methods may be used in the conduct and management of the business."); Louisville & Nashville Terminal Co. v. Lellyett, 114 Tenn. 368, 85 S.W. 881 (1905) (plaintiff's property was invaded by smoke, soot, dust and noise from defendant's nearby terminal yard and roundhouse; jury charge upheld stating it would be no defense "to prove that the yards [were] at a suitable locality, or that the business is a lawful business and one useful to the public, or that the best and most approved appliances and methods are used in the conduct and management of the business."); Bartel v. Ridgefield Lumber Co., 131 Wash. 183, 189, 229 Pac. 306, 308 (1924) (requiring a suitably located lumber mill using "the best and most approved appliances and methods" to pay for damages inflicted on plaintiff's nearby farm).

12. James, Memorandum on the Element of Fault in Private Nuisance, in Restatement, Second, Torts App. A., at 131, 156 n. 43 (Tent. Draft No. 16, 1970).

13. 47 ALI Proceedings 312, 323–25 (1970).

14. Wade, supra note 1, at 170.

15. Restatement, Second, Torts § 822, at 22 (Tent. Draft No. 17, 1971).

16. This is candidly recognized in the comments: "It may be reasonable to continue an important activity if payment is made for the harm it is causing, but unreasonable to continue it without paying." Id. at 66 (Tent. Draft No. 16, 1970).

the conduct is substantial and the financial burden of compensating for this and other harms does not render infeasible the continuation of the conduct." [17] Section 829A, intended to be a specific application of the § 826 rule, declares that "an intentional invasion of another's interest in the use and enjoyment of land is unreasonable and the actor is subject to liability if the harm resulting from the invasion is substantial and greater than the other shall be required to bear without compensation." [18]

The result of these revisions has been a well deserved victory for forces in the American Law Institute led by Fleming James and Robert Keeton, who were determined to assure that nuisance law in the future was capable of combatting pollution problems. Although the Restatement affirms that deliberate conduct resulting in harm to others must be "intentional and unreasonable" as a condition of liability, this condition will be met, in Fleming James' words, "even where the condition or conduct causing [the invasion] is socially useful, is maintained and conducted with all due care and in a suitable and convenient location, if the harm caused is reasonably great." [19] The nuances of fault are not necessarily the nuances of nuisance. The Restatement reformulation only can expand the reach of a doctrine whose present horizons already are vast.[20]

Nuisance, it has been said, "is a good word to beg a question with." [21] A description of the process of decision-making confirms this suspicion: the authorities advise us that what is involved is a "weighing process" [22] where the actor's conduct will be condemned as unreasonable if "the gravity of the harm outweighs the utility of the actor's conduct." [23] The gravity of the harm is its seriousness from an objective, legal viewpoint; the utility of the conduct is its meritoriousness from the same standpoint.[24] This process is said to be indistinguishable for private and public nuisances; indeed, a famous

---

17. Id. at 3 (Tent. Draft No. 18, 1972). Subsection (a) makes the invasion unreasonable if "the gravity of the harm outweighs the utility of the actor's conduct." See § 2.11 (discussing balancing in connection with remedies).

18. Restatement, Second, Torts 4 (Tent. Draft No. 18, 1972).

19. James, supra note 12, at 140.

20. See W. L. Prosser, supra note 18, at 590–93. Nuisance law has been called "the great grab bag, the dust bin of the law." Awad v. McColgan, 357 Mich. 386, 389, 98 N.W.2d 571, 573 (1959).

21. Awad v. McColgan, 357 Mich. at 390, 98 N.W.2d at 573, quoting Thayer, Public Wrong and Private Action, 27 Harv.L.Rev. 317, 326 (1914).

22. 1 F. Harper & F. James, The Law of Torts § 1.24, at 73 (1956).

23. Restatement, Second, Torts, § 826 (a), at 3 (Tent. Draft No. 18, 1972).

24. See id. at 34–35 (Tent. Draft No. 17, 1971). Note that one operating an industrial establishment employing 5,000 people might regard his activity as highly meritorious despite its pollution, whereas the legal merit of the conduct might be greatly reduced by the fact that he was not using the best technology to prevent pollution.

public nuisance case found candlemaking in a town quite reasonable because "Le utility del chose excusera le noisomeness del stink." [25]

The weighing or balancing process in a nuisance case, like many other similar legal exercises,[26] involves an evaluation of incommensurables. The criteria of decision-making are called "factors" by the Restatement, and are actually nothing more than a listing, not even an exhaustive listing, of the indicators of decision-making. In the language of the Restatement, factors illuminating the gravity of the harm include the extent and character of the injury, the social value of the use invaded, its suitability to the locality and the burden of avoiding the harm imposed on the person harmed.[27] The utility of the conduct is influenced by its social value, its suitability to the locality and the impracticality of avoiding the invasion.[28]

For present purposes, these factors will be slightly rearranged and discussed under the following headings: (1) extent of the hurt (§ 2.4); (2) value of defendant's enterprise (§ 2.5); (3) state of the art in controlling the hurt (§ 2.6); (4) place of the hurt (§ 2.7); (5) who was there first (§ 2.8); (6) effect of statutes (§ 2.9); and (7) the importance of the remedy (§ 2.10). In the case law, sometimes one, sometimes several of the indicators emerge as decisive.[29] In the discussion that follows the reader should keep in mind that the law of

---

25. Quoted in J. Stephen, A General View of the Criminal Law of England 106 (1890).

26. See § 7.5 below (discussing the balancing process under the National Environmental Policy Act).

27. Restatement, Second, Torts § 827, at 36 (Tent. Draft No. 17, 1971) lists five factors under gravity of harm:

In determining the gravity of the harm from an intentional invasion of another's interest in the use and enjoyment of land, the following factors are important:

(a) the extent of the harm involved;

(b) the character of the harm involved;

(c) the social value which the law attaches to the type of use or enjoyment invaded;

(d) the suitability of the particular use or enjoyment invaded to the character of the locality;

(e) the burden on the person harmed of avoiding the harm.

28. Section 828 lists under utility of conduct two factors:

(a) the social value which the law attaches to the primary purpose of the conduct;

(b) suitability of the conduct to the character of the locality.

Id. at 41. Other factors are identified in separate sections—id. § 829 (Tent. Draft No. 18, 1972) (conduct malicious or indecent); id. § 829A (conduct resulting in substantial harm greater than the other reasonably should be required to bear without compensation); id. § 820 (Tent. Draft No. 16, 1970) (invasion avoidable); id. § 831 (conduct unsuited to locality).

29. E. g., Georgia v. Tennessee Copper Co., 237 U.S. 678, 35 S.Ct. 752, 59 L.Ed. 1173 (1916) (avoidable injury); Reserve Mining Co. v. United States, 514 F.2d 492, 5 ELR 20596 (8th Cir. 1975) (risk of substantial harm); Spur Indust., Inc. v. Del E. Webb Dev. Co., 108 Ariz. 178, 494 P.2d 700, 2 ELR 20390 (1972) (en banc) (incompatible land use); Vowinckel v. N. Clark & Sons, 216 Cal. 156, 13 P.2d 733 (1932).

nuisance virtually defies synthesis,[30] that cases can be found to support virtually any proposition, and that often courts treat as synonymous the discretion they exercise regarding the propriety of equitable relief and the discretion they assume in determining whether a nuisance exists.

§ 2.4 Nuisance: Extent of the Hurt

Not surprisingly, courts in nuisance cases deem it pertinent to delve into the extent and character of the hurt inflicted upon the plaintiff. The law does not concern itself with "trifles", and therefore a "real and appreciable"[1] invasion of the plaintiff's interests must be established before he can succeed. Thus, the "wafted odors of sauces and stews,"[2] an occasional whiff of smoke, the temporary muddying of a well, a modest intrusion by roots and branches, activity slightly depreciating the value of plaintiff's land, the maintenance of an unsightly but otherwise harmless establishment generally will not rise to the level of a nuisance.[3] On the other hand, the substantiality test is not particularly demanding and can be satisfied easily by proving physical damage to tangible property[4] and *a fortiori* actual harm to human health.

The standard for determining whether a hurt is substantial, moreover, is objectively judged by reference to the senses of a "normal person in the community."[5] If this person would perceive the interference in question as offensive, annoying or intolerable, then the interference would be substantial. The idiosyncracies of the hypersensitive plaintiff are supposed to be discounted. The rule has been invoked, however, to deny relief not only to individuals of extreme personal tastes and aesthetic sensitivity but also to those who are physically vulnerable—with a heart condition, bronchitis, or susceptible to convulsions brought about by loud noises.[6]

30. Some of the better attempts have been F. Harper & F. James, supra note 22, §§ 1.23–.29; VI–American Law of Property §§ 28.22–.35 (Casner ed. 1954); W. L. Prosser, supra note 8, ch. 15; see D. Mandelker, The Zoning Dilemma (1971) (for a useful discussion of the relationship between nuisance and zoning law).

1. Restatement, Second, Torts, at 59, comment c. (Tent. Draft No. 15, 1969).

2. Reported in the Wash. Post, Dec. 29, 1974, p. 2, col. 1.

3. Illustrative cases are found in Restatement, Second, Torts, supra note 1, at 63–64.

4. Jost v. Dairyland Power Coop., 45 Wis.2d 164, 172 N.W.2d 647 (1970) (ruling as a matter of law that $395 worth of damage to an alfalfa crop was "substantial"); see Whalen v. Union Bag & Paper Co., 208 N.Y. 1, 101 N.E. 805 (1913) (damages to farm from pulp mill of $100 per year).

5. Restatement, Second, Torts, supra note 1, at 58. The same rule holds where the injury results to abnormally susceptible property. E. g., Belmar Drive-In Theater Co. v. Illinois State Toll Highway Comm'n, 34 Ill.2d 544, 216 N.E.2d 788 (1966) (drive-in theater injured by light intrusions); Lynn Open Air Theater v. Sea Crest Cadillac-Pontiac, Inc., 294 N.E.2d 473 (Mass.Ct.App.1973) (same).

6. Illustrative cases, many at the turn of the century, are found in Restate-

Sec. 2.4   EXTENT OF THE HURT

In creating an objective victim in both mental and physical particulars, the development of nuisance law lags behind tort principles generally and environmental law advances specifically. The reasonable and objective man of tort law traditionally becomes quite subjective when the physical characteristics of the actor or the victim are considered.[7] That is the justification for the dogma that you take your victim as you find him.[8] A basic premise of the Clean Air Act of 1970, to mention a current illustration, is to establish ambient air standards adequate to protect the old, the infirm, those afflicted with cardiac, asthmatic or bronchitis conditions [9]—the same vulnerabilities nuisance law professes to disregard under an objective standard. The perpetrator of the invasion of another's property, moreover, is treated quite subjectively with great solicitation accorded peculiarities of process, cost and operations.[10] It is doubtful that the rigorously objective standard applied to the victim by the Restatement will long endure,[11] at least where physical injury is inflicted. Indeed, it would be theoretically possible under the Restatement test to commit a homicide by directing maddening noise at a peculiarly susceptible neighbor and at the same time avoid civil liability for maintaining a nuisance.

Application of an objective standard is necessary but difficult where the alleged nuisance is solely aesthetic, a concept that is peculiarly subjective.[12] The well known dicta of Parkersberg Builders Material Co. v. Barrack [13] is that:

> evolutional concepts respecting the right and duty of society to protect itself from undesirable and disagreeable conditions are not of necessity confined to municipal zoning ordinances. There is a growing belief that that which is offensive to the view, an eyesore, a landscape-blight, may attain such significance as to warrant equitable interposition.

On the other hand, other cases show a marked reluctance to accord relief even from economic losses arising mostly from aesthetic displeasure.[14] Courts in nuisance cases, no less than legislatures act-

---

ment, Second, Torts, supra note 1, at 64.

7. Id. § 283C.

8. E. g., Vosbury v. Putney, 80 Wis. 523, 50 N.W. 403 (1891).

9. See § 3.4 below.

10. See § 2.5 below.

11. Kutner v. Delaware Tool Steel Corp., 209 F.Supp. 326 (D.C.Del.1962), can be read as applying a subjective standard to deny relief to a used car dealer aggrieved by noise from an adjoining tool manufacturing plant.

12. Needless to say, an aesthetic injury often involves more. Today's interference with a view may be tomorrow's interference with solar energy.

13. 118 W.Va. 608, 611–12, 191 S.E. 368, 370–71 (1937).

14. E. g., Bostick v. Smoot Sand & Gravel Corp., 154 F.Supp. 744 (D.C. Md.1957) (denying relief to a land developer whose high cost homes along

ing within the police power,[15] no doubt can and should enforce aesthetic values. But an objective standard is properly applied to make sure that one person's annoyance is not actionable unless it reflects a community's values. Hurting others is accomplished in other ways with greater efficiency than by simply being ugly.

Protecting people from eyesores is not thought to be as important as protecting them from sore eyes. As was said in Board of Commissioners v. Elm Grove Mining Co.,[16] "public health comes first. Even in as useful and important industry as the mining of coal, an incidental consequence, such as here involved, cannot be justified or permitted unqualifiedly, if the health of the public is impaired thereby." It was a health threat created by arsenic emissions that prompted the court in American Smelting & Refining Co. v. Godfrey[17] to order a copper smelter to install bag houses so that the discharges could be "fully arrested." And it was a health threat from asbestos contamination of drinking water supplies that prompted the courts to consider establishing a rule of absolute abatement, even where the only alternative is a plant shutdown with widespread economic dislocation.[18]

A line of nuisance cases illustrating the importance of the extent of the hurt are those where no injury as yet has been consummated, but relief is granted nonetheless against the threat of injury. Obviously, in most cases involving nothing more than a fear that something will go wrong anticipatory relief is denied.[19] But if the threat

the Potomac were reduced in value when views were blighted by a dredging company's cranes, shovels and barges); Fontainebleau Hotel Corp. v. Forty-Five Twenty-Five, Inc., 114 So. 2d 357 (Fla.App.1959) (nearby hotel cast shadow on the beach); People ex rel. Hoogasian v. Sears, Roebuck & Co., 52 Ill.2d 301, 287 N.E.2d 677 (1972) (television reception distorted by world's tallest building); cf. Commonwealth v. National Gettysburg Battlefield Tower, Inc., 454 Pa. 193, 311 A.2d 588 (1973) (denying injunctive relief against maintenance of an unsightly observation tower under Pennsylvania constitutional provision reserving to the People "a right to clean air, pure water, and to the preservation of the natural, scenic, historic and aesthetic values of the environment"); Flowers v. Northampton Bucks County Municipal Authority, 2 ELR 20313 (Pa.Ct.C.P.1972) (psychic objections and depreciation of property values insufficient grounds for relief against construction of water storage tanks). See also Noel, Unaesthetic Sights As Nuisances, 25 Cornell L.Q. 1 (1939).

15. See Berman v. Parker, 348 U.S. 26, 33, 75 S.Ct. 98, 102–03, 99 L.Ed. 27, 38 (1954). Unsightly billboards and junkyards were one of the first concerns of federal legislation. Highway Beautification Act, 23 U.S.C.A. § 131.

16. 122 W.Va. 442, 451, 9 S.E.2d 813, 817 (1940).

17. 158 F. 225, 234 (8th Cir. 1907).

18. United States v. Reserve Mining Co., 380 F.Supp. 11, 4 ELR 20573 (D. C.Minn.), injunction stayed, 498 F.2d 1073, 4 ELR 20598 (8th Cir.), stay denied, 419 U.S. 802 (1974), modified and remanded, 514 F.2d 492, 5 ELR 20596 (8th Cir. 1975), further proceedings, 408 F.2d 1212, 6 ELR 20481 (D.Minn.1976).

19. E. g., Fletcher v. Bealey, 28 Ch.D. 688 (1885) (fear of future water pollution); Commerce Oil Ref. Corp. v. Miner, 281 F.2d 465, 474 (1st Cir. 1960) (no anticipatory injunction unless a nuisance is " 'practically certain to result' "); Green v. Castle Concrete Co., 181 Colo. 309, 509 P.2d 588, 4

is a severe one likely to produce extensive property damage or physical injury, as from the storage of explosives or incendiary materials, relief may be forthcoming.[20] So, too, if the proposed action would produce demonstrably clashing land uses.[21] A major difficulty with modern pollution cases is that they deal not so much with provable injuries but with risks and thus the question of the degree of injury is complicated both by actual uncertainties and burden of proof preferences.[22]

One factor of importance to an evaluation of the extent of injury is whether the actor's conduct is of a continuing nature or has produced permanent or long-lasting effects.[23] Thus, nuisance law may excuse a single failure of pollution control facilities,[24] an isolated invasion by drifting pesticides,[25] a one-time only overflow of a sewer outlet,[26] or a debris-burning incident lasting only a few days.[27] Courts and commentators in the past have gone so far as to say that recurrence over time is a necessary prerequisite of a nuisance deter-

ELR 20365 (1973) (refusing to enjoin quarrying activity); McQuail v. Shell Oil Co., 40 Del.Ch. 410, 183 A.2d 581 (1962) (refusing to enjoin a proposed oil refinery); Stephens v. Bacon Park Commissioners, 212 Ga. 426, 93 S.E. 2d 351 (1956). Note that representations that there will be no pollution later may strengthen the case for an injunction if the predictions prove to be wrong. Smith v. Staso Milling Co., 18 F.2d 736 (2d Cir. 1927).

20. E. g., Cumberland Torpedo Co. v. Gaines, 201 Ky. 88, 255 S.W. 1046 (1923) (explosives); Richardson v. Murphy, 198 Or. 640, 259 P.2d 116 (1953) (inflammable buildings and materials).

21. Isley v. Little, 217 Ga. 586, 124 S.E.2d 80 (1962) (drag strip reasonably certain to be a nuisance to nearby residents); Strong v. Winn-Dixie Stores, Inc., 235 S.C. 552, 555, 112 S.E.2d 646 (1960) (proposed supermarket would inevitably be a nuisance in a "residential neighborhood unique for its beauty and historic value").

22. See, e. g., Ethyl Corp. v. Environmental Protection Agency (II), 165 U. S.App.D.C. 282, 506 F.2d 1321, 6 ELR 20267, cert. denied, — U.S. — (1976) (leaded gasoline); Reserve Mining Co. v. United States, 514 F.2d 492, 5 ELR 20596 (8th Cir. 1975) (asbestos); Environmental Defense Fund, Inc. v. Environmental Protection Agency, 150 U.S.App.D.C. 348, 465 F.

2d 528, 2 ELR 20228 (1972) (aldrin-dieldrin); Environmental Defense Fund, Inc. v. Ruckelshaus (II), 142 U. S.App.D.C. 74, 439 F.2d 584, 1 ELR 20059 (1971) (DDT). See also Meyers, An Introduction to Environmental Thought: Some Sources and Some Criticisms, 50 Ind.L.J. 426 (1975); Tarlock, A Comment on Meyers' Introduction to Environmental Thought, 50 Ind.L.J. 454 (1975).

23. Restatement, Second, Torts § 821B (c), at 3 (Tent. Draft No. 17, 1971) lists as a factor conducive to a determination about whether an interference with a public right is unreasonable "the circumstance that the conduct is of a continuing nature or has produced a permanent or long-lasting effect, that its detrimental effect upon the public right is substantial, and that the actor knows and has reason to know of that effect."

24. But see E. Rauh & Sons Fertilizer Co. v. Shreffler, 139 F.2d 38 (6th Cir. 1943) (finding nuisance).

25. See S. A. Gerrard Co. v. Fricker, 42 Ariz. 503, 27 P.2d 678 (1943) (plaintiff recovers on negligence theory).

26. But see Ambrosini v. Alisal Sanitary Dist., 154 Cal.App.2d 720, 317 P.2d 33 (1957) (holding city liable).

27. But see Yates v. Missouri Pac. R.R., 168 Ark. 170, 269 S.W. 353 (1925) (plaintiff recovers).

mination. This is usually the case with a nuisance and almost always the case of a nuisance subject to an injunction. But nuisance law is applied also in a narrow category of cases where substantial harm is inflicted by a single incident of brief duration.[28] These single invasion cases are more likely to be analyzed under a trespass theory.[29]

The cases recognize but fail to articulate a distinction between social nuisances and technological nuisances. The leading case of Nicholson v. Connecticut Half-Way House, Inc.,[30] involved a lawsuit by residential property owners objecting to a half-way house for former convicts proposed for location in their neighborhood. The injury claimed was a diminution of property values and a fear that residents of the half-way house would commit criminal acts in the neighborhood. The court denied an injunction, characterizing plaintiffs' concern "as a speculative and intangible fear." Plaintiffs "have neither alleged nor offered evidence to prove any specific acts or pattern of behavior which would cause them harm so as to warrant the drastic injunctive relief." [31]

One wonders whether the result would or should be different if plaintiffs produced social scientific data suggesting a recidivism rate among half-way house residents that might be reflected in the crime rate of the surrounding neighborhood. Perhaps the explanation is that physical effects from a particular technology can be measured or predicted with greater certainty than social effects from a half-way house.[32] Or perhaps the law should recognize explicitly a greater tolerance level for social action affecting the rights of others than for technological actions. *Nicholson* rejects a reduction in property value based upon subjective revulsion as justifying relief from a nuisance. Other cases follow a similar approach.[33] It is appropriate to insist upon strong and objective showings of harm lest the concept of nuisance be exploited unfairly as a technique of social exclusion.[34]

§ 2.5 Nuisance: Utility of the Offending Activity

Liability theories based on fault require an evaluation of the utility of the offender's conduct and alternatives for avoiding harm avail-

---

28. See Restatement, Second, Torts, supra note 1, at 62 (giving example of an explosion shaking plaintiff's building to pieces and a five-minute pesticide spraying incident ruining plaintiffs' crops).

29. § 2.13 below.

30. 153 Conn. 507, 218 A.2d 383 (1966).

31. 153 Conn. at 511, 218 A.2d at 386.

32. The subtleties in identifying threshold levels or synergistic effects or the pertinence of studies on animals to human health tend to discount the suggestion that physical effects are proven more easily than social effects.

33. McCaw v. Harrison, 259 S.W.2d 457 (Ky.1953); White v. Bernhart, 41 Idaho 665, 241 P. 367 (1925). Contra, Everett v. Paschall, 61 Wash. 47, 111 P. 879 (1910).

34. Compare § 2.17 below.

Sec. 2.5 UTILITY OF OFFENDING ACTIVITY 117

able to him. The clearest case for liability is where defendant's action offers little or no socially redeeming value and is easily avoided. He foresees that his conduct will cause harm, and foresees it with pleasure. Under traditional nuisance principles, liability follows if the actor is "inspired solely by hostility and a desire to cause harm to the other."[1] The typical case is where defendant constructs a spite fence with the objective of depriving his neighbor of a view, light or rays of the sun.[2]

Purposeful retaliation is the exception not the rule. Defendants' objectives in pollution cases invariably are to produce useful products, often with processes representing an investment of millions of dollars and employing hundreds of workers. These are the cases where the imperatives of modern technology strongly test the viability of nuisance law. They are discussed variously and often under the headings of "balance of equities," "balance of hardships," "balance of injuries," "balance of conveniences."[3]

It would seem indispensable to a "balance of equities" to identify clearly (and quantify if possible) the factors to be included on both sides of the scale. In private nuisance cases, this is rarely done. On the plaintiffs' side, consideration surely must be given to the injury inflicted on the complaining parties and any class represented.[4] The great unanswered question is whether consideration also should be given to all the hurts and risks inflicted upon people not before the court. The answer presumably turns upon one's view of the judicial process: is it simply a vehicle for resolving disputes between named parties or does it serve also to settle broader social questions raised by parties legitimately before the court? The nuisance tradition favors the narrower view [5] but that tradition is at war with current trends, perhaps best expressed by the evolution of the standing doctrine.[6]

On the defendants' side, the same questions must be answered about what goes onto the scale: costs only to the enterprise before

---

1. Restatement of Torts § 829 (1939). The same tort under another name holds that one who does an unreasonable act for the purpose of causing harm to another will be held liable for that harm. Restatement, Torts § 870 (1939).

2. See Hutcherson v. Alexander, 264 Cal.App.2d 126, 70 Cal.Rptr. 366 (1968); cf. Cook County v. Lloyd A. Fry Roofing Co., 59 Ill.2d 131, 319 N.E.2d 472 (1974) (weighing bad faith in discounting pleas of economic hardship and technological infeasibility).

3. See Morris & Keeton, Balancing the Equities, 18 Tex.L.Rev. 412 (1940); Annot., 40 A.L.R.3d 601 (1971).

4. On defining a class for purposes of litigation in the federal courts, see Zahn v. International Paper Co., 414 U.S. 291, 94 S.Ct. 505, 38 L.Ed.2d 511 (1973). In a public nuisance action, the state as plaintiff presumably can put into the balance all evidence of injuries or threatened injuries.

5. Boomer v. Atlantic Cement Co., 26 N.Y.2d 219, 309 N.Y.S.2d 312, 257 N.E.2d 870 (1970).

6. § 1.6 above.

the court or costs also that may be inflicted upon others?[7] Most confusing about the cases, however, is that the "balancing" process can occur not once but twice and mean two different things: many cases weigh the value of defendant's business enterprise against the harm inflicted, but this balancing process even when tipped in favor of defendant may lead to the conclusion either that no nuisance exists[8] or that, if it does, relief is to be confined to a money judgment.[9] An example of the latter is the famous case of Richard's Appeal,[10] which legitimatized the status of Pittsburgh as the "Smoky City."[11]

For many years, a debate has ensued over the propriety of "balancing" in nuisance cases, with the advocates often neglecting to make clear the purpose of the balancing. The rhetoric of the opposing schools of thought pits those opposed to extortion, on the one hand, and private confiscation on the other.[12] Balancing met with favor in the leading case of Madison v. Ducktown Sulfur, Copper & Iron Co.,[13] where the court said: "In order to protect by injunction several small tracts of land, aggregating in value less than $1,000, we are asked to destroy other property worth nearly $2,000,000, and wreck two great mining and manufacturing enterprises . . . . The result would be practically a confiscation of the property of the defendants for the benefit of complainants—an appropriation without compensation." The opposing view is expressed in Hulbert v. California Portland Cement Co.,[14] granting an injunction over the objections of the greater hardship pleas by the defendant: "If the smaller interest

---

7. *Boomer,* interestingly, gave consideration to the 300 workers employed at the plant who were not parties. 26 N.Y.2d at 225, 309 N.Y.S.2d at 316, 257 N.E.2d at 873.

8. E. g., Waschak v. Moffat, 379 Pa. 441, 109 A.2d 310 (1954); Pennsylvania Coal Co. v. Sanderson, 113 Pa. 126, 6 A. 453 (1886); Powell v. Superior Portland Cement, Inc., 15 Wash. 2d 14, 129 P.2d 536 (1942).

9. Riter v. Keokuk Electro-Metals Co., 248 Iowa 710, 82 N.W.2d 151 (1957) (large factory furnishing work in the community); Storey v. Central Hide & Rendering Co., 148 Tex. 509, 226 S.W.2d 615 (1950); Koseris v. J. R. Simplot Co., 82 Idaho 263, 352 P.2d 235 (1960); Fargason v. Economy Furniture, Inc., 356 S.W.2d 212 (Tex. Civ.App.1962); see Monroe Carp Pond Co. v. River Raisin Paper Co., 240 Mich. 279, 215 N.W. 325 (1927) (use of a stream unreasonable but an injunction refused because defendant's investment was fifteen million dollars while plaintiff's damages were ten thousand dollars).

10. 57 Pa. 105 (1868).

11. See id. at 111–12 ("Whatever injury may have, or shall result to, [plaintiff's] property from the defendant's works, . . . is such only as is incident to a lawful business conducted in an ordinary way, and by no unusual means").

12. See D. B. Dobbs, Remedies 357–62 (1973).

13. 113 Tenn. 331, 366–67, 83 S.W. 658, 666–67 (1904) (awarding damages but not an injunction).

14. 161 Cal. 239, 251, 118 P. 928, 933 (1911), quoting Woodruff v. North Bloomfield Gravel Mining Co., 18 F. 753, 807 (9th Cir. 1884); see Bemmerly v. Lake County, 55 Cal.App.2d 829, 132 P.2d 249 (1942); Hark v. Mountain Fork Lumber Co., 127 W.Va. 586, 34 S.E.2d 348 (1945).

Sec. 2.5   UTILITY OF OFFENDING ACTIVITY   119

must yield to the larger, all small property rights, and all small and less important enterprises, industries or pursuits would sooner or later be absorbed by the large, more powerful, few . . . . ."

The dispute should be resolved by reference to the purpose of the balancing. In the first place, the value of defendant's enterprise should be entirely disregarded on the substantive question of whether a nuisance exists.[15] To condemn intentional conduct as a nuisance a "substantial" and "unreasonable" injury must be established. Surely anybody whose property or person is hurt by a polluter should not have the "substantiality" of his injury measured by the size of the offender's bankroll. Damaged gladiolas or emphysema by anybody's hand are still damaged gladiolas or emphysema. Once reasonableness is divorced from notions of fault, which is accomplished by the case law reflected in the Restatement, surely the infliction of substantial injury on the plaintiff does not become "reasonable" if the defendant manages to surpass a certain litmus of the gargantuan. On the contrary, big defendants who carry insurance and who can pass along costs and afford controls, are among the least likely candidates for licenses to trample little plaintiffs.[16]

If a substantial and unreasonable injury has been inflicted on the plaintiff, the question of the remedy remains. The value of defendant's activities is demonstrably significant in this regard. It is here, and here alone, that balancing principles come into play.[17] Suffice it

---

15. Recent cases are consistent with this proposition. See, e. g., Guttinger v. Calaveros Cement Co., 105 Cal.App.2d 383, 233 P.2d 914 (1951); Alonso v. Hills, 95 Cal.App.2d 778, 214 P.2d 50 (1950); Schlotfelt v. Vinton Farmers' Supply Co., 252 Iowa 1102, 109 N.W.2d 695 (1961); Weaver v. Yoder, 89 Ohio L.Abs. 402, 184 N.E.2d 622 (C. P. of Tuscarawas County 1961); Crushed Stone Co. v. Moore, 369 P.2d 811 (Okl.1972); Smith v. Pittston Co., 203 Va. 711, 127 S.E.2d 79 (1962); Jost v. Dairyland Power Coop., 45 Wis.2d 164, 172 N.W.2d 647 (1969). See also Meriwether Sand & Gravel Co. v. State, 181 Ark. 216, 26 S.W.2d 57 (1930); Hulbert v. California Portland Cement Co., 161 Cal. 239, 118 P. 928 (1911); Wente v. Commonwealth Fuel Co., 232 Ill. 526, 83 N.E. 1049 (1908); Brede v. Minnesota Crushed Stone Co., 143 Minn. 374, 173 N.W. 805 (1919); Hennessey v. Carmony, 50 N.J.Eq. 616, 25 A. 374 (1892); Sullivan v. Jones & Laughlin Steel Co., 208 Pa. 540, 57 A. 1065 (1905). See generally Note, Nuisance Abatement: Use of the Comparative Injury Doctrine, 1971 Urban L.Ann. 206; Note, Torts—Comparative Injury Doctrine of Nuisance, 49 N.C.L.Rev. 402 (1971); Current Development, Enjoining Private Nuisances: Consideration of the Public Interest, 43 U.Colo.L. Rev. 225 (1971).

16. Even in traditional nuisance terms, perhaps costs to a defendant that can be passed along are to be accorded different treatment than costs that must be absorbed by the offending enterprise. Cf. Portland Cement Ass'n v. Ruckelshaus, 158 U.S.App.D.C. 308, 486 F.2d 375, 3 ELR 20642 (1973), cert. denied 417 U.S. 921 (1974) (holding Administrator adequately had taken into account "costs" in promulgating stationary source air pollution standards for new cement plants in a study concluding that costs of control equipment could be passed on with no substantial competitive effects).

17. The spite fence and related cases are inconsistent with this recommended approach because they include a consideration of the near total lack of value of defendant's conduct in the determination of whether a nuisance exists. Notes 1, 2, supra. These cases, however, actually are cases

to say that there are a wide range of options between the extremes of a shut-down and the mere award of a money judgment.[18]

The no-balancing remedy cases are every bit as wrong as those insisting on balancing to determine whether a nuisance exists. It is a fast fading tradition that insists that an injunction must issue once a nuisance is established and a money judgment remedy is shown to be inadequate.[19] Even the leading case of the no-balancing school, Whalen v. Union Bag & Paper Co.,[20] represents a departure from the doctrine. *Whalen* is repeatedly mis-cited for the proposition that a pulp mill representing an investment of over a million dollars was shut down to prevent pollution of a small stream. The decree actually gave defendants one year to come up with alternatives to a shutdown,[21] and subsequent compromises extended the life of the plant. *Whalen* was overruled explicitly by the case of Boomer v. Atlantic Cement Co.[22] which granted an injunction against operation of a cement plant subject to being vacated "upon payment by defendant of such amounts of permanent damage" as the lower court should determine on remand.

In one sense, the gradual rise to ascendancy of the balancing doctrine for remedy purposes is compelled by the nature of modern environmental problems. There are both technological and legal imperatives associated with enterprises that are years in incubation, representing millions of dollars of investment, that are deeply implicated in the economic and political fabric of society.[23] A no-balancing principle of remedies is far more demanding as applied to today's nuclear reactor, oil refinery, jet aircraft, or giant feedlot than to yesterday's brick kiln or pigpen.[24] The same considerations that call for balancing in the remedy context call for its abolition in the liability context: the economic power of the oil refinery that allows it to resist the shut-down sought by adjoining property holders also affords it an opportunity to absorb or pass along the costs of compensation.

where the remedy and the definition of the hurt are coextensive. An injunction always issues if defendant's spiteful conduct causes sufficient injury. They could be analyzed precisely as recommended above.

18. § 2.11 below.

19. See Annot., 61 A.L.R. 924 (1929).

20. 208 N.Y. 1, 101 N.E. 805 (1913), modifying 145 App.Div. 1, 129 N.Y.S. 391 (1911).

21. See 145 App.Div. at 3–4, 129 N.Y.S. at 393 (Betts, J., dissenting). It is interesting to note that Union Bag & Paper Co., reorganized and renamed the Union Bag-Camp Paper Corp., eventually moved to Savannah, Georgia, where its operations were unencumbered by New York's *Whalen* doctrine, and where it came to be the largest industrial polluter on the Savannah River. J. Fallows, The Water Lords 10, 191 (1971).

22. 26 N.Y.2d 219, 224–25, 309 N.Y.S. 2d 312, 315, 257 N.E.2d 870, 872–73 (1970).

23. These themes are developed by the author in Corporate Country (Rodale Press, 1973). See also Bunner, Nuisance Law and the Industrial Revolution, 3 J. Legal Studies 403 (1974).

24. See North Anna Environmental Coalition v. Nuclear Regulatory Comm'n, — U.S.App.D.C. —, 533 F.2d 655 (1976).

It should be noted that the balancing process in the context of the remedy involves more than a simple cost-benefit analysis allowing the defendant to avoid abatement whenever the total costs appear to the court to exceed the total damages caused by the pollution (both to the plaintiffs and all others).[25] One important reason for this is that the factors involved in the balancing process of a nuisance determination (extent and place of the hurt, who was there first, the effect of legislation, and so on) also may carry weight on the question of the appropriateness of the remedy. A superb recent example is the case of Harrison v. Indiana Auto Shredders Co.[26] where the court evaluated several factors (compliance with zoning and pollution laws, character of the neighborhood, technological and operational efforts to control, lack of an imminent hazard to health) and concluded that injunctive relief was inappropriate to correct air and noise pollution from an auto shredding plant. Considered in the balance was not only the economic contribution of the enterprise ("payroll, taxes, investment of profits") but also the fact that the company was making "a direct contribution toward improving the environment and conserving its natural resources by the recycling of abandoned automobiles."[27]

§ 2.6 Nuisance: Control by the Best Technology

It is true that nuisance law has served for many centuries as a common law of zoning. But its land use powers have not overshadowed its powers as a mechanism of technological control.

Requiring the defendant to shut down and move elsewhere always has been an extreme remedy. If the injury to neighbors can be relieved by technological innovation instead of relocation, innovation is preferred. Even the classic case of Campbell v. Seaman,[1] which affirmed an injunction against operation of a brick kiln emitting sulfur oxides to the detriment of nearby ornamental trees, accepted the inevitability of a shutdown only upon a record showing the technical and economic unfeasibility of the defendant reverting from an anthracite coal process to a cleaner wood process.

Case law in this century involving a single type of industrial operation—copper and lead smelting—illustrates the constant pressure exerted by courts seeking better processes and improved technologies. The remedy in the 1907 case of American Smelting & Refining Co. v. Godfrey[2] was not to close down the smelter but to decree the installation of bag houses as an arsenic control measure and to impose limitations upon the sulfur content of ore as a means of reducing sulfur

---

25. See § 2.11 below.

26. 528 F.2d 1107, 6 ELR 20179 (7th Cir. 1975) (also reversing and remanding as regards monetary and punitive damages).

27. 528 F.2d at 1121, 6 ELR at 20185.

1. 63 N.Y. 568 (1876).

2. 158 F. 225 (8th Cir. 1907).

oxide emissions. Similarly, emissions control were anticipated in the 1912 decree ordering the Selby, California lead smelter to cease creating a public nuisance with "noxious and injurious gases and smoke." [3] Around the same time a consent decree between the United States and the Anaconda Company ordered the copper smelter at Anaconda, Montana to stop pollution with the "most scientific control processes then practically available." [4] In 1915 the Supreme Court ordered yet another copper smelter to limit sulfur emissions to twenty tons a day during the summer months [5] (some smelters today have emissions in excess of 60 tons an hour), which prompted a technological breakthrough in the form of the lead chamber process for producing sulfuric acid from smelter stack emissions.[6] More recent authority continues the pressure for technological and process change.[7]

Often the nuisance can be remedied by changes in process, timing or location falling short of "state of the art" technological advances. Thus an airport may be prohibited from authorizing low level flights over plaintiff's residence but free to construct additional runways or acquire extended acreage; [8] a poultry feed plant may be required to adjust its processes to reduce foul odors and loud noises; [9] a city may be obliged to burn garbage in lesser quantities to minimize odors and smoke; [10] hours at a truck terminal may be readjusted; [11] a different fuel required; [12] nighttime operations restricted where noise is involved; [13] or nighttime operations required where a pesticide application is involved; [14] activities in the vicinity

3. People v. Selby Smelting & Lead Co., 163 Cal. 84, 124 P. 692, 1135 (1912).

4. The decree is reprinted in the Report of the Anaconda Smelter Smoke Commission Covering the Period May 1, 1911 to October 1, 1920, at 13–15.

5. Georgia v. Tennessee Copper Co., 206 U.S. 230, 27 S.Ct. 618, 51 L.Ed. 1038 (1907), 237 U.S. 474, 35 S.Ct. 631, 59 L.Ed. 1054 (1915) (motion to enter a final decree), 237 U.S. 678, 35 S.Ct. 752, 59 L.Ed. 1173 (1915) (decree), modified 240 U.S. 650, 36 S.Ct. 465, 60 L.Ed. 846 (1916).

6. See Rodgers, "Tacoma's Tall Stack", The Nation, May 11, 1970, p. 553.

7. For a history of the recent evolution of the smelter sulfur control regulations, see W. Rodgers, Corporate Country ch. 3 (Rodale Press, 1973).

8. Vanderslice v. Shawn, 26 Del.Ch. 225, 27 A.2d 87 (1942); see § 5.7 below.

9. Kosich v. Poultrymen's Serv. Corp., 136 N.J.Eq. 571, 43 A.2d 15 (1945).

10. Smith v. Ann Arbor, 303 Mich. 476, 6 N.W.2d 752 (1942); see § 6.2 below.

11. Firth v. Scherzberg, 366 Pa. 443, 77 A.2d 443 (1951).

12. McCarty v. Natural Carbonic Gas Co., 189 N.Y. 40, 81 N.E. 549 (1907) (use of soft coal enjoined); See Sam Warren & Sons Stone Co. v. Grueser, 307 Ky. 98, 209 S.W.2d 817 (1948) (stopping use of diesel power as a means of reducing noise).

13. Hansen v. Independent School Dist. No. 1, 61 Idaho 109, 98 P.2d 959 (1940); Green v. Smith, 231 Ark. 94, 328 S.W.2d 357 (1959) (noise from catching and loading chickens at nighttime; case remanded for finding as to whether night loading necessitated by industry practice or standards).

14. See § 8.2 below.

of plaintiff may be forbidden; [15] some but not all of defendants' kilns abated.[16]

But where juggling of the process will not suffice, "state of the art" controls may be required. This is true even in the older cases where a greater tolerance of technological damage might be expected. Thus, in 1931, pollution from 50 coke ovens of the Donner-Hanna Coke Plant at Buffalo, New York was held to be only a "petty annoyance" to the neighbors and a form of activity that was "indispensable to progress." [17] Twenty-five years and 200 ovens later the company was still immune from an injunction but the rationale had become that the plant contained properly operated "modern" control equipment, and the emissions were therefore "unavoidable." [18]

Many courts use injunctive relief to compel defendants to control emissions consistently with the "state of the art" or the "best technology." [19] Other courts invoke the "state of the art" test to deny injunctive relief if defendants are using the most modern anti-pollution control methods available.[20] Still others grant injunctions ordering shutdowns on the grounds that "state of the art" controls or improved operations hold no further promise of relief.[21] Yet others

15. Kellerhals v. Kallenberger, 251 Iowa 974, 103 N.W.2d 691 (1960) (corn grinding forbidden within 150 feet of plaintiff's residence).

16. Vowinckel v. N. Clark & Sons, 216 Cal. 156, 13 P.2d 733 (1932).

17. Bove v. Donner-Hanna Coke Corp., 142 Misc. 329, 254 N.Y.S. 403 (Sup. Ct.1931), aff'd 236 App.Div. 37, 258 N.Y.S. 229 (1932).

18. Buffalo v. Savage, 1 Misc.2d 337, 342, 148 N.Y.S.2d 191, 196 (Sup.Ct.), aff'd mem., 309 N.Y. 941, 132 N.E.2d 313 (1955).

19. E. g., Renken v. Harvey Aluminum, Inc., 226 F.Supp. 169 (D.C.Or. 1963) (requiring control unless defendant could show it was prohibitively expensive); DeBlois v. Bowers, 44 F.2d 621, 623 (D.C.Mass.1930) (air pollution) ("The question whether the defendants have done everything reasonably practicable to avoid the cause of the offense is important. Reasonable care must be used to prevent annoyance . . ."); cf. Texas E. Transmission Corp. v. Wildlife Preserves, Inc., 48 N.J. 261, 225 A.2d 130 (1966), appeal after remand, 49 N.J. 403, 230 A.2d 505 (1967); Stevens v. Rockport Granite Co., 216 Mass. 486, 104 N.E. 371 (1914) (general injunction against nuisance; the expectation was that control devices could prevent noise from reaching plaintiff); Bicknell v. Boston, 5 ELR 20712 (Mass.Super.Ct.1975) (enforcing administrative abatement order against operation of an incinerator upon proof that disposal alternatives were available).

20. E. g., Koseris v. J. R. Simplot Co., 82 Idaho 263, 352 P.2d 235 (1960); People v. Peterson, 31 Misc.2d 738, 226 N.Y.S.2d 1004 (Erie County Ct. 1961); Hall v. Budde, 293 Ky. 436, 169 S.W.2d 33 (1943) (hog farm); cf. Harrisonville v. W. S. Dickey Clay Mfg. Co., 289 U.S. 334, 53 S.Ct. 602, 77 L.Ed. 1208 (1933) (denying injunctive relief against stream pollution by a city where sewage treatment facilities would be prohibitively expensive); Olson v. Arctic Enterprises, Inc., 349 F.Supp. 761 (D.M.D.1972) (finding for defendant in products liability case where best technology used); Folmar v. Elliott Coal Mining Co., 441 Pa. 592, 272 A.2d 910, 1 ELR 20182 (1971) (finding injury insubstantial in trespass air pollution case where no showing was made that control was technologically and economically feasible).

21. Associated Contractors Stone Co. v. Pewee Valley Sanitarium & Hos-

award damages (and effectively give defendants the power of eminent domain) for nuisances occurring notwithstanding utilization of "state of the art" control technology.[22]

Terms such as "state of the art" or "best technology" are not used with consistent meanings in the case law. At a minimum the "best technology" test is invoked to impose upon the defendant an obligation to control its effluent in accordance with the best practices currently in operation in a given industry.[23] The term also can be used to require resort to a control technology known and available in the laboratories and design rooms but not yet generally applied in practice.[24] This second and more stringent interpretation is in accord with that line of negligence case law holding that conformity with an industry-wide custom is not necessarily a complete answer to a charge of lack of due care. The reason for this is that "a whole calling may have unduly lagged in the adoption of new and available devices."[25] A third and yet more stringent variation of the "best technology" test places the burden upon the defendant to demonstrate that he has exhausted both technological opportunities then in use and those still in the laboratory but potentially useful.[26]

---

pital, 376 S.W.2d 316 (Ky.1964) (closing down rock quarry upon defendant's admission that less offensive operations were impossible); cf. Gelsumino v. E. W. Bliss Co., 10 Ill.App. 3d 604, 295 N.E.2d 110 (1973) (rejecting "state of the art" defense in products liability case).

22. See cases cited in § 2.3 n. 11 above.

23. E. g., Hannum v. Gruber, 346 Pa. 417, 31 A.2d 99 (1943); Ebur v. Alloy Metal Wire Co., 304 Pa. 177, 155 A. 280 (1931).

24. Cf. Portland Cement Ass'n v. Ruckelshaus, 158 U.S.App.D.C. 308, 486 F.2d 375, 3 ELR 20642 (1973), cert. denied 417 U.S. 921 (1974) (interpreting new source performance standards of Clean Air Act § 306, 42 U.S.C.A. § 1857C–6(a)(1)); § 3.10 below. The Senate gave this explanation of an earlier (and stronger) draft of the provision:

> As used in this section, the term 'available control technology' is intended to mean that the [Administrator] should examine the degree of emission control that has been or can be achieved through the application [of] technology which is available or normally can be made available. This does not mean that the technology must be in actual, routine use somewhere. It does mean that the technology must be available at a cost and at a time which the [Administrator] determines to be reasonable.

Senate Comm. on Public Works, National Air Quality Standards Act of 1970, S.Rep. No. 1196, 91st Cong., 2d Sess. 16 (1970); see §§ 3.19, 4.20 below.

25. The T. J. Hooper, 60 F.2d 737, 740 (2d Cir. 1932) (Hand, J.); see Marsh Wood Prods. Co. v. Babcock & Wilcox Co., 207 Wis. 209, 219, 240 N.W. 392, 396 (1932) (negligence alleged in failing to test boiler for soundness by microscopic examination) ("The fact that it was not the practice of [boiler] tube manufacturers generally to use these tests, and that such an examination is not incorporated in the specifications of the American Society of Mechanical Engineers, or required or provided for in the Wisconsin Boiler Code, is certainly strong evidence against the position taken by Professors McCaffery and McKay [the metallurgical experts who had urged a microscopic examination]; but it does not dispose of their evidence as a matter of law").

26. Cf. Noel v. United Aircraft Corp., 219 F.Supp. 556 (D.C.Del.1963), aff'd

A fourth, and most extreme, standard requires defendants to control their pollutants regardless of the state of the art. Defendants, if given time, still can develop technological answers to the problems. Failing that, they must shut down or move. It is not beyond the power of a court, as part of its equitable authority, to administer a continuing experimental or research effort to develop a solution.[27] Obviously a legislature has a wider range of options. To mention but two examples, the Clean Air Act of 1970 decrees a level of performance for auto emission controls that generally is recognized as forcing the state of the art under a threat of going out of business.[28] Legislators seeking to inspire electrical utilities to greater research and development heights have debated a number of elaborate administrative solutions to reverse what is viewed as a stubborn preference for technological stagnation.[29] Threats of a shutdown are but one extreme possibility among many.

The dominant thrust of the case law is to require exhaustion of the possibilities of operational or technological controls before treating the issues as needing a land use accommodation (leading almost always to a shutdown by the defendant or the exercise of private eminent domain by him through the payment of permanent damages to plaintiff).[30] The assignment of burdens can be decisive.[31] Despite

---

342 F.2d 232 (3d Cir. 1965) (negligence case) (liability premised upon a failure to equip a propeller system manufactured by defendant with "every safety device which reasonable engineering minds could have devised," 219 F.Supp. at 573; defendant failed to introduce evidence of any attempt on its part to launch "an accelerated program to produce acceptable alternative safety devices" where "engineers, technicians, and sufficient funds were made available and the program put in charge of a responsible head with directions to push the program vigorously," id. at 572). On rehearing, the Court of Appeals backed away from the broadest interpretations of the district court's decision. 342 F.2d at 241. See also Society of the Plastics Indus., Inc., v. Occupational Safety & Health Administration, 509 F.2d 1301, 1309, 5 ELR 20157, 20161 (2d Cir. 1975) (interpreting Occupational Safety and Health Act) (the Secretary "may raise standards which require improvements in existing technologies or which require the development of new technology, and he is not limited to issuing standards based solely on devices already fully developed").

27. Georgia v. Tennessee Copper Co., 206 U.S. 230, 27 S.Ct. 618, 51 L.Ed. 1038 (1907), 237 U.S. 474, 35 S.Ct. 631, 59 L.Ed. 1054 (1915) (motion to enter a final decree), 237 U.S. 678, 35 S.Ct. 752, 59 L.Ed. 1173 (1915) (decree), modified 240 U.S. 650, 36 S. Ct. 465, 60 L.Ed. 846 (1916).

28. International Harvester Co. v. Ruckelshaus, 155 U.S.App.D.C. 411, 478 F.2d 615, 3 ELR 20133 (1973).

29. E. g., Hearings on Energy Research and Development: II (S. 357), Before the Senate Comm. on Commerce, S. Doc. No. 22, 93d Cong., 1st Sess. (1973); Hearings on Energy Research and Development Policy Act (S. 1283), Before the Senate Comm. on Interior & Insular Affairs, S. Doc. No. 13, 93d Cong., 1st Sess. (1973); Hearings on Energy Waste and Energy Efficiency in Industrial and Commercial Activities, Before the Senate Comm. on Commerce, S. Doc. No. 102, 93d Cong., 2d Sess. (1974).

30. Compare § 2.11 below (discussing Spur Indus., Inc. v. Del E. Webb Dev. Co., 108 Ariz. 178, 494 P.2d 700, 2 ELR 20390 (1972) (en banc) (where defendant was required to move but at plaintiff's expense).

31. See A. Reitze, Environment Law 5–23 (2d ed. North American Inter-

occasional language in the cases indicating that plaintiff has the burden of establishing the technological feasibility of controls,[32] the law should be to the contrary. Plaintiff of course must show that a substantial injury has been inflicted upon his use and enjoyment of property.[33] He might even be required to come forward with some evidence on the possibilities of control. With that accomplished, however, the burden should shift to the defendant to demonstrate that operational and technological control opportunities are exhausted, and therefore the intrusion must be viewed as "reasonable." [34] Plaintiff can strengthen his case by presenting evidence on control options. But it is properly the defendant, as keeper of the state of the art, who should be obliged to come forward with evidence that his operations conform to the state of the art.

In many nuisance cases, courts are forced to make a judgment about whether research and development or other innovation can be expected to relieve the problem in the foreseeable future. The court in Boomer v. Atlantic Cement Co. opted for a land use approach giving defendant the power of eminent domain upon the assumption that the amelioration of air pollution depends upon "technical research" in great depth: "It is likely to require massive public expenditure and to demand more than any local community can accomplish and to depend on regional and interstate controls." [35] Dissenting Judge Jasen was considerably more sanguine, believing that the defendant could find a way to control the dust in 18 months. Another case reflecting the research and development factor is Fletcher v. Bealey, where the

national, 1971) (reporting that virtually all air pollution, with the possible exception of emissions from coke ovens, can be controlled by existing technology).

32. Hannum v. Gruber, 346 Pa. 417, 425–26, 31 A.2d 99, 103 (1943) (defendant dye works shifted from soft coal to anthracite, raised the height of its stack and installed other pollution control devices; "Plaintiffs have not shown anything left undone by defendants which should have been done"; case nonetheless was remanded with directions to take further testimony and require a report by outside consultants "to determine whether defendants have done all that can reasonably be demanded of them to reduce the annoyance complained of"); see Vile v. Pennsylvania R. R., 246 Pa. 35, 91 A. 1049 (1914) (air pollution) (evidence of control alternatives offered by plaintiffs adequate when given by expert and based on "actual experiments" at a phosphate plant).

33. Burden questions also may arise on questions of proof of injury.

34. E. g., Renken v. Harvey Aluminum, Inc., 226 F.Supp. 169 (D.C.Or.1963); see Herring v. H. W. Walker Co., 409 Pa. 126, 185 A.2d 565 (1962) (once nuisance is shown, defendant has burden of showing it has done all it could; remand to give defendant opportunity to explore alternatives); Webb v. Rye, 108 N.H. 147, 230 A.2d 223 (1967) (remand to trial court to consider possibility of attaching an after-burner or other device to eliminate smoke or odors from a municipal incinerator); cf. Cullum v. Topps-Stillman's, Inc., 1 Mich.App. 92, 134 N.W.2d 349 (1965) (defendant given time to cure nuisance; court suggests some areas for experiment); Grzelka v. Chevrolet Motor Car Co., 286 Mich. 141, 281 N.W. 568 (1938) (defendant not required to employ means of unknown or doubtful efficacy).

35. 26 N.Y.2d 219, 223, 309 N.Y.S.2d 312, 314, 257 N.E.2d 870, 871 (1970).

court refused injunctive relief against pollution threatened by "vat waste" partly for the reason that "in ten years' time it is highly probable that science (which is now at work on the subject) may have discovered the means for rendering this green liquid innocuous." [36]

One wonders whether judicial restraint assures instead that science is unlikely to come up with the answer. Scientists and engineers, after all, may not have an innate interest in studying how to control cement emissions or render green liquid vat waste innocuous. Scientific inquiry, particularly applied scientific inquiry, has a way of responding to felt concerns and social and economic pressures. A court's finding that there is likely to be an adequate remedy at science is one less reason for there ever to be an adequate remedy at science.[37]

One line of cases illustrating the tendency of the courts to require exhaustion of the technological options are those distinguishing between permanent sources of damage and temporary sources of damage.[38] The chief practical difference[39] between a "permanent" nuisance and a "temporary" one is the measure of money damages: recovery of diminished market value is allowed for a permanent nuisance (effectively giving defendant the power of eminent domain), whereas a temporary nuisance is remedied only by a judgment for depreciation in use value plus any special damages. The difference is illustrated by Idaho Gold Dredging Co. v. Payette Lumber Co.[40] where defendant's use of grease on timber chutes polluted a stream so that the gold in it would not amalgamate and thus could not be mined by plaintiff. If the damage had been halted upon cessation of defendant's use of the grease, the nuisance would have been temporary and plaintiff's damages would have been confined to a recovery for reduced property values and special damages. But the pollution continued despite cessation of use of the grease; the nuisance was thus permanent, and permanent diminution of value was selected as the measure of damages.

A nuisance or trespass is usually not regarded as permanent unless it is physically permanent or likely to continue indefinitely.[41] The test of physical permanence, repeatedly applied, is whether a change in process or control technology could avoid the nuisance. If process change or technological options are available, the nuisance is viewed as temporary for purposes of money damages, and an injunc-

---

36. 28 Ch.D. 688, 700 (1885).

37. See notes 26, 30, supra.

38. See D. B. Dobbs, Remedies § 5.4 (1973) for complete discussion of this and related issues.

39. There are others, including the application of the statute of limitations. Id. at 336–37.

40. 52 Idaho 766, 22 P.2d 147 (1933).

41. D. B. Dobbs, supra note 38, at 336.

tion typically will be granted ordering changes in the operation.[42] On the other hand, "if the operation is being carried out in the best manner possible and it still causes a nuisance, no change for the better is predictable, and in such cases the nuisance is permanent in the physical sense." [43] If the court goes on to conclude that a nuisance is permanent in a legal sense,[44] what it is saying is that as a matter of policy defendant ought to be permitted to continue the nuisance upon a single payment of damages. Not surprisingly, defendants who create permanent nuisances often are municipalities or large industrial enterprises who otherwise have statutory powers of condemnation. Acknowledging their authority to create permanent nuisances and buy off the injured with a lump sum reaffirms this power through the common law.

There is another option for treating nuisances that persists notwithstanding state of the art controls—require them to shut down.[45] Claims of private confiscation, on the one hand, and extortion on the other [46] thus are fairly descriptive of the choices that must be made between grossly incompatible land uses. The rules requiring exhaustion of technological and operational options narrow the range of the either/or choices that must be made if coexistence between neighbors is impossible.

42. Ibid n. 24 includes the following cases: Harrisonville v. W. S. Dickey Clay Mfg. Co., 289 U.S. 334, 53 S.Ct. 602, 77 L.Ed. 1208 (1933) (sewage plant with primary treatment not a permanent nuisance because it was possible to resort to secondary treatment); Phoenix v. Johnson, 51 Ariz. 115, 75 P.2d 30 (1938) (odors from sewage plant due to negligent maintenance not permanent); Ryan v. Emmetsburg, 232 Iowa 600, 4 N.W.2d 435 (1942) (sewer odors not permanent because they could be abated by scientific advance); Aldworth v. Lynn, 153 Mass. 53, 26 N.E. 229 (1891) (percolation from a pond not permanent because it was technologically controllable); Flanigan v. Springfield, 360 S.W.2d 700 (Mo.1962) (odors from a sewage plant not permanent because it was scientifically feasible and practicable to abate them); Shearing v. Rochester, 51 Misc.2d 436, 273 N.Y.S.2d 464 (1966) (trash-burning not permanent because it was remediable by discontinuing it; this case can be viewed as either a process change or shutdown case); Frey v. Queen City Paper Co., 79 Ohio App. 64, 66 N.E.2d 252 (1946) (power plant releasing smoke with high ash content not permanent because abatable); Oklahoma City v. West, 155 Okl. 63, 7 P.2d 888 (1931) (sewer discharge not permanent if it can be abated "by the expenditure of money and labor"); Norfolk & W. Ry. v. Allen, 118 Va. 428, 87 S.E. 558 (1915) (pumping water from stream above plaintiff's mill not permanent because it was remediable by discontinuing it; this case can be viewed as either a process change or shutdown case).

43. D. B. Dobbs, supra note 38, at 339, n. 25, citing Northern Indiana Pub. Serv. Co. v. Vesey, 210 Ind. 338, 200 N.E. 620 (1936) (nuisance permanent upon a finding that manner of operation could not be effectively changed); Robertson v. Cincinnati, N. O. & Tex. Pac. Ry., 207 Tenn. 272, 339 S.W.2d 6 (1960) (railroad switch yards with noise and light incident to operation could not be changed); Cheskov v. Port of Seattle, 55 Wash.2d 416, 348 P.2d 673 (1960) (airport operations could not be changed).

44. See D. B. Dobbs, supra note 38, at 337–38.

45. Note 21, supra.

46. See § 2.5 above.

§ 2.7 Nuisance: Place of the Hurt

A nuisance, it has been long established, may consist of the right thing in the wrong place—"like a pig in the parlor instead of the barnyard." [1] This is true although the enterprise attacked is otherwise useful and operated in accordance with the best pollution control technology. The Restatement (First) of Torts gives an example: a slaughterhouse and packing plant located in a suburban district, albeit with "all the practical devices which are available" for the elimination of offensive smells, sights and sounds.[2]

One ancient and fuzzy legal line suggesting the importance of the place of the activity is the distinction between a nuisance per se and a nuisance in fact.[3] A nuisance per se is defined as an activity, occupation or structure which constitutes a nuisance anywhere regardless of how it is operated. Obviously, there are not many of these social or technological outlaws: the cases usually involve houses of prostitution, gambling establishments, illegal stills or the like. A nuisance in fact, on the other hand, is an activity, operation or structure which constitutes a nuisance only because of its location, surroundings or manner of operation. This covers just about everything since all the legal activities of man have their place somewhere, even, to be sure, the disposal of excessive supplies of nerve gas.[4]

Being the right thing in the right place is not necessarily a complete answer to a charge of nuisance. There is authority for the proposition that control by the best technology and a suitable location may not be a complete answer in a nuisance case. An illustrative case is Bartel v. Ridgefield Lumber Co.,[5] where defendant's lumber mill was located in the manufacturing district of a saw mill town in timber country. Smoke, sawdust and half-burned embers damaged plaintiff's nearby farm. The court affirmed a denial of an injunction but reversed as to damages, saying:

> Where a trade or business is carried on in such [a] manner as to materially interfere with the reasonable and comfortable enjoyment by another of his property or which occasions material injury to the property itself, a wrong is done for which an action for damages will lie, without regard to the legality where such business is carried on and notwithstanding the business be en-

---

1. Euclid v. Ambler Realty Co., 272 U.S. 365, 388, 47 S.Ct. 114, 118, 71 L.Ed. 303, 311 (1926) (Sutherland, J.).

2. Restatement of Torts § 831, at 263, illustration 1 (1939); see Baltimore & Potomac R. R. v. Fifth Baptist Church, 108 U.S. 317, 2 S.Ct. 719, 27 L.Ed. 739 (1883), discussed and distinguished in Richards v. Washington Terminal Co., 233 U.S. 546, 555–58, 34 S.Ct. 654, 657–58, 58 L.Ed. 1088, 1092–93 (1914); Evans v. Moffat, 192 Pa.Super. 204, 160 A.2d 465 (1960).

3. See generally D. B. Hagman, Urban Planning and Land Development Control Law § 158 (1971); VI–A American Law of Property § 28.27 (A. J. Casner ed. 1974).

4. Rodgers, Nerve Gas to the Northwest, 1 Environmental Letters (1971).

5. 131 Wash. 183, 229 P. 306 (1924).

tirely lawful, and notwithstanding the best and most approved appliances and methods may be used in the construction and maintenance of the business.[6]

On the other hand, the character of the community is an important factor in determining the "reasonableness" of activities with spillover effects. Expectations on either side reflect this understanding. People who live in business or manufacturing districts, in Mellor's often quoted words, must not "[s]tand upon extreme rights and bring actions in respect of every matter of annoyances."[7] Nor can smelters and rendering plants reside inconspicuously in suburban neighborhoods without expectations of making amends. The idea is fundamental to all notions of zoning or land use control.

The common law of nuisance is used by the courts consciously and conspicuously to accomplish land use functions. On occasions nuisance law is virtually equated with a common law of zoning.[8] Consistently with this approach, nonconforming uses have been rooted out of rural or residential areas by nuisance law—piggeries, petroleum storage facilities, dance pavilions, undertaking establishments, riding academies, automobile raceways,[9] feedgrinding and fertilizer sales businesses,[10] rock quarries,[11] and auto businesses.[12] Similarly, citizens, left without remedies, are effectively ousted from business districts, unless they can learn to live with the telltale signs of breweries, rendering plants, gas stations,[13] ice houses,[14] grain mills,[15] metal fabricating facilities,[16] oil refineries,[17] and auto manufacturing

6. 131 Wash. at 189, 229 P. at 308; see Clifton Iron Co. v. Dye, 87 Ala. 486, 6 So. 192 (1888); Koseris v. J. R. Simplot Co., 82 Idaho 263, 352 P.2d 235 (1960); Demarest v. Hardham, 34 N.J.Eq. 469, 472–73 (1881); Bohan v. Post Jervis Gas Light Co., 122 N.Y. 18, 25 N.E. 246 (1890).

7. From instructions to the jury, in Tipping v. St. Helen's Smelting Co., 4 B. & S. 608, 610–11, 122 Eng.Rep. 588, 599 (Q.B.1863) (Mellor, J.).

8. For an excellent summary by a leading scholar, see Mandelker, The Role of Law in the Planning Process, 30 Law & Contemp. Problems 26 (1965); Parkersburg Builders Material Co. v. Barrack, 118 W.Va. 608, 611–12, 191 S.E. 368, 370–71 (1937). See also D. Mandelker, The Zoning Dilemma (1971).

9. See examples in American Law of Property, supra note 3, §§ 28.26, at 76–77 nn. 6, 9, 28.27, at 78–79 n. 13.

10. Schlotfelt v. Vinton Farmer's Supply Co., 252 Iowa 1102, 109 N.W.2d 695 (1961).

11. Shaw v. Salt Lake County, 119 Utah 50, 224 P.2d 1037 (1950).

12. Dale v. Bryant, 75 Ohio L.Abs. 401, 141 N.E.2d 504 (Ct.App.1957).

13. See Beuscher & Morrison, Judicial Zoning Through Recent Nuisance Cases, 1955 Wis.L.Rev. 440, 451–52. See also id. at 443 (noting a "definite increase in judicial sensitivity to the 'character of the neighborhood' ").

14. Haber v. Paramount Ice Corp., 239 App.Div. 324, 267 N.Y.S. 349 (1933) (2d Dep't), aff'd 264 N.Y. 98, 190 N.E. 163.

15. McCarty v. Macy & Co., 167 Cal. App.2d 164, 334 P.2d 156 (1959).

16. Riter v. Keokuk Electro-Metals Co., 248 Iowa 710, 82 N.W.2d 151 (1957).

17. Daigle v. Continental Oil Co., 277 F.Supp. 875 (D.D.C.1967) (applying Louisiana law).

plants.[18] In these cases the courts, depending upon the strength of the proof, may draw careful lines akin to the most meticulous work of a zoning administrator; or they may express only in general terms the different land use considerations prevailing in, say, rural areas as opposed to close-in fringe areas or older, closely settled areas.[19] Plainly, development trends, present and future, are useful in varying degrees to a decision of whether a particular activity is being conducted in the wrong place.[20]

Consideration of the character of the neighborhood as an element of nuisance decision-making obviously cannot ignore the nearly universal impact of zoning or other land-use legislation. Generally, both non-conformity and conformity evidence is relevant and admissible but not necessarily decisive.[21] A statute might eliminate the issue, as has been done in Michigan which decrees that "[b]uildings erected . . . or uses carried on in violation of any provision of local ordinances or regulations . . . are hereby declared to be a nuisance per se."[22] Absent decisive legislative direction, the courts do and should consider administrative judgments to be an important, albeit not decisive, ingredient in defining the character of a neighborhood.[23] There is an obvious difference between carefully crafted and generally respected zones of activity in a community and a planner's dream. Courts can defer to a considered judgment and a reasoned order without pledging unqualified allegiance to the shaded area on somebody's map.

Notwithstanding the importance of the place of the activity to determination of nuisance, the manner of operation cannot be neglected. Not only may a nuisance be the right thing in the wrong place, it may be the wrong thing in the right place. This is simply another way of affirming the dual land use and technological control objectives of nuisance law.[24]

18. Roy v. Chevrolet Motor Car Co., 262 Mich. 663, 247 N.W. 774 (1933).

19. Beuscher & Morrison, supra, note 13, passim.

20. See Oak Haven Trailer Court, Inc. v. Western Wayne County Conservation Ass'n, 3 Mich.App. 83, 141 N.W.2d 645 (1966) (holding that a gun club was not a nuisance, relying in part upon a prediction that the swampy nature of the property would forbid future development).

21. Perrin's Appeal, 305 Pa. 42, 156 A. 305 (1931); Dawson v. Laubersweiler, 241 Iowa 650, 43 N.W.2d 726 (1950); Rockenback v. Apostle, 330 Mich. 338, 47 N.W.2d 636 (1951). It has been held to be reversible error to exclude evidence of zoning laws. See Walker v. Delaware Trust Co., 314 Pa. 257, 171 A. 458 (1934). But see Ellis v. Blanchard, 45 So.2d 100 (La.App. 1950).

22. Mich.Comp.Laws Ann. § 125.587.

23. See D. G. Hagman, supra note 3, § 162; Harrison v. Indiana Auto Shredders Co., 528 F.2d 1107, 6 ELR 20179 (7th Cir. 1975).

24. See § 2.11 below.

§ 2.8 Nuisance: Who Was There First

The priority in time of conflicting uses is pertinent to the question of whether a nuisance is proven. The issue arises typically as a defense to a nuisance claim on the theory that plaintiff has "come to the nuisance".[1] The Restatement (Second) of Torts states the rule as follows:[2]

> The fact that plaintiff has acquired or improved his land after a nuisance interfering with it has come into existence is not itself sufficient to bar his action, but is a factor to be considered in determining whether the nuisance is actionable.

It is sound economics to treat the new owner of property afflicted by his neighbor's pollution differently from the owner who was there before the pollution commenced. The reason for this is that the new owner who "comes to the nuisance" generally pays less for the property since the value of his purchase is reduced accordingly by the invading noise, odors or pollution. This person gets a "windfall" to the extent he can restore his land to its original unpolluted state by application of the law of nuisance. There is also a hint in the case law that an equity court should not be sympathetic to one who effectively buys a claim with a purpose of blackmailing somebody else;[3] or to another who subsequently uses his property in a vulnerable way so that avoidance of harm to it only can be accomplished by a prohibitive expense on the part of his neighbor.[4] In many cases, the defense of coming to the nuisance shades imperceptibly into the issue of the character of the neighborhood, as where plaintiff is a new arrival in a former residential area where industrial plants are beginning to appear.[5]

On the other hand, if "windfalls" are to be avoided, it is unsound policy to reward defendants who successfully drive off their neighbors, forcing them to sell at depressed prices. Allowing the defense of "coming to the nuisance" to be raised against the new property owner gives the defendant a prescriptive right or an easement in the adjoining lands when typically he has paid for nothing and simply ap-

---

1. Annot., Coming to a Nuisance, 42 ALR3d 344 (1972).

2. § 840D, at 123 (Tent. Draft No. 16, 1969); See Vowinckel v. N. Clark & Sons, 216 Cal. 156, 13 P.2d 733 (1932) (defendant there first but expanded operations after plaintiff arrived).

3. Edwards v. Allouez Mining Co., 38 Mich. 46, 31 Am.Rep. 301 (1878).

4. East St. John Shingle Co. v. Portland, 195 Or. 505, 246 P.2d 554 (1952). But see § 2.9 n.1 below (rejecting assumption of risk defense in nuisance cases).

5. Restatement, Second, Torts, supra note 2, § 840D, at 124–25, illustration 3 and supporting cases; York v. Stallings, 217 Or. 13, 341 P.2d 529 (1959) (plaintiff built home 500 feet from railroad track which foreshadowed future commercial development); Steele v. Queen City Broadcasting Co., 54 Wash.2d 402, 341 P.2d 499 (1959) (granting damages but denying injunction against erection of a television tower on adjoining property, partly on the ground that two nearby towers had blighted the neighborhood).

propriated another's property for his own purposes. As explained in Campbell v. Seaman,[6] "One cannot erect a nuisance upon his land adjoining vacant lands owned by another and thus measurably control the uses to which his neighbor's land may be in the future subjected." Upon this and similar reasoning a large number of cases reject the "coming to the nuisance" defense both in actions for damages and for injunctions.[7]

Thus, the question of who was there first may introduce a few factors of significance in the balancing process of nuisance assessment. It is a fact that the rule poses "no serious problem"[8] to the maintenance of a suit. More often than not, priority in time is but a factor to be considered in fashioning a remedy to accommodate conflicting land uses litigated under a nuisance theory.[9]

Priority of use may be relevant not only to classic nuisance litigation but also to the decision of whether a taking has occurred in connection with regulatory endeavors accomplishing nuisance abatement results. In Hadacheck v. Sebastion,[10] for example, the Supreme Court rejected taking claims while sustaining an ordinance forbidding the use of brick kilns in a residential neighborhood. No compensation was required although the complainant's brick manufacturing operation was reduced drastically in value and although the brick maker was there first. It has been suggested that "the noise, smoke, and fumes emitted by the brick manufacturing operation corresponded fairly closely to the traditional kind of activity subject to abatement under common law theories of nuisance; thus to refuse to allow the concept of property to embrace the right to carry out such activities need not be viewed as doing violence to legitimate expectations about the rights that accompany property ownership."[11] The result might have been different if complainant had established both a clear priority of use and exhausted technological and operational opportunities to minimize the land use conflict. The nuisance abatement theory in the context of a taking claim "then is a means of determining those types of cases in which an owner's expectations concerning the use of his land can be said to be unjustified, requiring him to take the risk that such uses will be subsequently restricted. Under this approach one avoids the objection that property has been redefined in new directions that could not have been anticipated."[12]

6. 63 N.Y. 568, 584 (1876).

7. See cases cited in Restatement, Second, Torts, supra note 2, at 125.

8. Note, Private Remedies for Water Pollution, 70 Colum.L.Rev. 734, 744 (1970).

9. See § 2.11 below.

10. 239 U.S. 394, 36 S.Ct. 143, 60 L.Ed. 348 (1915); see § 2.17 below (discussing the taking issue).

11. Soper, The Constitutional Framework of Environmental Law, in Environmental Law Institute, Federal Environmental Law 20, 65–66 (E. L. Dolgin & T.G.P. Guilbert eds. 1974).

12. Id. at 66 (footnote omitted), citing Michelman, Property Utility, and Fairness: Comments on the Ethical Foundations of "Just Compensation" Law, 80 Harv.L.Rev. 1165, 1242–45 (1967).

§ 2.9 Nuisance: The Defenses

The defense of coming to the nuisance is certainly not synonymous with a contributory negligence plea and is doomed to failure if invoked in an attempt to bar plaintiffs on the ground that they voluntarily subjected themselves to unreasonable risks.[1] The reason for this is that in a vast majority of cases nuisance is premised upon intentional conduct by the defendant. Contributory negligence is not a defense to an intentional tort, as was convincingly demonstrated by the leading case of Steinmetz v. Kelley,[2] where defendant unsuccessfully sought to justify an assault and battery in a saloon on the ground that plaintiff unwisely failed to depart when requested to do so.

In the narrow category of cases where nuisance is based upon truly negligent conduct (that is, an offensive condition develops on defendant's land without his actual knowledge), the Restatement (Second) of Torts preserves the defense of contributory negligence.[3] An example given is where water accumulates on A's property as a result of his negligence and inflicts damage on the property of B who reasonably could have taken steps to avoid the damage.[4] The most that can be said for this defense is that it would be unlikely to arise, even if it could be reconciled with the general rule that a party cannot be contributorily negligent in maintaining his own property.[5]

Only slightly more promising are the defenses of prescriptive rights, estoppel, laches or the statute of limitations. Occasionally they are successful,[6] but they fail almost always if the complainant happens to be suing to vindicate a public nuisance. Estoppel requires more than passive acquiescence, such as actual consent or positive encouragement. It is said to consist of three elements, each of them difficult to prove in an environmental case: (1) a misleading com-

---

1. See Williams v. Blue Bird Laundry Co., 85 Cal.App. 388, 259 P. 484 (1927) (assumption of risk no defense to a nuisance case); Greater Westchester Homeowners' Ass'n v. City of Los Angeles, 6 ELR [Dig.] 20051 (Super. Ct.L.A.County 1975) (same); Washington Monthly, Dec. 1974, at 17, reporting a suit by South Charleston, West Virginia residents claiming injury from chlorine gas released from an FMC Corporation bleach plant. The defense was contributory negligence based on the reasoning that plaintiffs voluntarily moved their homes into an area where chemical plants operate. Compare § 2.11 below (referring to the "avoidable consequences" doctrine).

2. 72 Ind. 442 (1880).

3. § 840B, at 113 (Tent. Draft No. 16, 1969).

4. Id. at 114, illustration 2.

5. Leroy Fibre Co. v. Chicago, Minn. & St. Paul R. R., 232 U.S. 340, 34 S.Ct. 415, 58 L.Ed. 631 (1914).

6. E. g., Crawford v. Magnolia Petroleum Co., 62 S.W.2d 264 (Tex.Civ. App.1933) (plaintiff sold land to defendant for use as a carbon black plant); Consumers' Light and Power Co. v. Holland, 118 Okl. 132, 247 P. 50 (1926) (two-year statute of limitations); W. G. Duncan Coal Co. v. Jones, 254 S.W.2d 720 (Ky.1953) (prescriptive right established where stream was polluted by acid mine drainage); see VI–A American Law of Property § 28.32 (A. J. Casner ed. 1974).

munication by the actor, either by words or silence; (2) reliance upon that communication by another; (3) material harm to that other person if the actor is later permitted to assert a claim inconsistent with his earlier conduct.[7] Manifestly, defendants who help themselves to their neighbors' resources or use adjoining properties as disposal sites are unlikely to prevail by asserting that the parties encroached upon are equitably estopped from asserting their claims.

A prescriptive right to maintain a private nuisance, if recognized at all,[8] requires an open interference under claim of right with the knowledge and acquiescence of the injured continuously for a period comparable to the statute of limitations for recovering possession of real property.[9] An assertion of prescriptive rights is thus dependent upon proving a knowing acquiescence in conduct no thinking person would abide if he knew about it. It is also dependent upon an extremely technical requirement that the annoyance the plaintiff was said to acquiesce in must continue with unabated intensity for an extended period of time. A change in the degree of the effluent alone is likely to be sufficient to break the continuity requirement.

Laches, of course, is a creature of equity and does not hold great doctrinal promise for those who claim they should be allowed to take another's property without compensation. In blackletter specifics, laches requires only a showing of unreasonable delay in asserting a claim and prejudice occasioned to the defendant by reason of the delay.[10] It is thus a commonly raised defense because many defendants can show they now have more at stake than they would have had if the suit had been brought earlier. The defense is disfavored on various grounds that rights of significance to the public should not be lost through the neglect of individuals, that persons suing large enterprises should not be expected to adhere to firm timetables and that those responsible for annoyances to others should not be encouraged to make an issue of the victim's conduct.[11] Because the laches defense is peculiarly dependent upon the discretion of the court and the facts of the case, generalities about it are unreliable. Laches will be raised routinely as a defense so long as the courts occasionally accept it.

7. D. B. Dobbs, Remedies § 2.3, at 42 (1973).

8. It is not in New Jersey. Benton v. Kernan, 127 N.J.Eq. 434, 13 A.2d 825 (1940). Nor in Pennsylvania. Commonwealth v. Barnes & Tucker Co., 455 Pa. 392, 319 A.2d 871, 4 ELR 20545 (1974) (also rejecting defenses of estoppel, laches and waiver).

9. See Curry v. Farmers Livestock Market, 343 S.W.2d 134 (Ky.1961); Cook Industries, Inc. v. Carlson, 334 F.Supp. 809, 2 ELR 20548 (N.D.Miss. 1971).

10. D. B. Dobbs, supra note 7, at 43, citing Lake Developing Enterprises v. Kojetinsky, 410 S.W.2d 361 (Mo.App. 1966).

11. See § 7.10 below discussing the defense of laches in cases under the National Environmental Policy Act. See also Bortz Coal Co. v. Air Pollution Commission, 2 Pa.Comm. 441, 452, 279 A.2d 388, 395, 1 ELR 20393, 20395 (1971) ("There is no prescriptive right to cause injury to another, and this basic premise has existed every day of the operation of these coke ovens").

Distinct doctrinal defenses in nuisance cases are insignificant. The all important justifications of technological infeasibility or economic hardship are subsumed in the basic tort of whether there has been a substantial and unreasonable interference with the use and enjoyment of another's property. Other generic defenses, such as an absence of cause in fact,[12] primary jurisdiction or exhaustion of administrative remedies,[13] are far more likely to succeed than the unrepentant assertions that the nuisance should be excused or forgiven. With this much said, it is important to remember the point made clear in the discussion of remedies:[14] the richness of fact situations raised in the nuisance context makes imperfect the strongly held assumption that polluters as a group are better cost avoiders and ought to be obliged to pay the bill without regard to fault.[15] Indeed, it is often difficult to distinguish between polluter and victim, as where the smoke from plaintiff's chimneys backed up into his own house when defendant changed the status quo by raising the height of the wall of the adjoining property.[16] This mutuality of pollution problems, expressed in the balancing test of nuisance law, means the conduct and circumstances of both parties is potentially at issue.

§ 2.10 Nuisance: The Effect of Statutes

Statutory modifications of the common law of nuisance are legion. In the first place, the legislature often undertakes to define nuisances, moving the line either way within the broad limits of the police power.[1] An example of a generic statute expanding the reach of nuisance law would be a zoning ordinance declaring nonconforming uses to be nuisances per se.[2] Courts invariably defer to the legislative judgment that certain conduct creates sufficient harm to justify condemnation as nuisance.[3]

---

12. See Michie v. Great Lakes Steel, 2 ELR 20001 (E.D.Mich.1971), aff'd 495 F.2d 213, 4 ELR 20324 (6th Cir. 1974) (all defendants contributing to air pollution are jointly liable); Chicago v. Commonwealth Edison Co., 24 Ill.App.2d 624, 321 N.E.2d 412 (1974) (no causation in sulfur oxide air pollution case).

13. § 1.9 above.

14. § 2.11 below.

15. Katz, The Function of Tort Liability in Technology Assessment, 38 U.Cin.L.Rev. 587, 606–22 (1969); see Michelman, Pollution As a Tort: A Non-Accidental Perspective on Calabresi's Costs, 80 Yale L.J. 647 (1971).

16. Bryant v. Lefever, 4 C.P.D. 172 (1878–79), discussed in the classic essay by Coase, The Problem of Social Cost, 3 J.Law & Econ. 1 (1960).

1. Commonwealth v. Parks, 155 Mass. 531, 532, 30 N.E. 174 (1892) (Holmes, J.). Compare § 6.7 below (state laws on disposal of solid waste often simply incorporate bans against maintaining nuisances).

2. See Farmington v. Scott, 374 Mich. 536, 132 N.W.2d 607 (1965) (holding a zoning ordinance precluding a swimming pool supply business in a residential zone to be reasonable and upholding an injunction based on another ordinance condemning nonconforming uses as nuisances per se).

3. See Bakersfield v. Miller, 64 Cal.2d 93, 48 Cal.Rptr. 889, 410 P.2d 393 (1966), cert. denied 384 U.S. 988; cf.

Sec. 2.10   THE EFFECT OF STATUTES

Of greater practical importance than legislative expansions of nuisance law are legislative limitations upon it. An illustration of a generic limitation is a statute declaring that conduct "done or maintained under the express authority of a statute" is exempt from judicial condemnation as a nuisance.[4] Here, too, the constitutional strictures on the reach of the police power are minimal. The Supreme Court has made clear that "while the legislature may legalize what otherwise would be a public nuisance, it may not confer immunity from action for a private nuisance of such a character as to amount in effect to a taking of private property for public use."[5] But the principles that require compensation for direct confiscations do not foreclose wide variations in police power adjustments among conflicting property uses.[6] Generally, a legislature does not take B's property by sanctioning the release of, say, one part per million of sulfur dioxide from A's smokestack onto B's land although a court might be moved in a nuisance case to restrict releases to .5 ppm. Nor would the legislature be taking A's property by requiring a reduction to .25 ppm although a court might be satisfied with a less expensive control effort.

The far-reaching potential significance of legislatively sanctioned modifications of nuisance law is easily illustrated: are sulfur oxide emissions damaging to health and property immune from correction by injunction if the source is operating under a compliance schedule established by state law pursuant to the format of the federal Clean Air Act?[7] Is acid mine drainage damaging to marine life immune from suit if the discharges are administratively sanctioned under state law?[8] Does a nuisance suit for excessive noise founder on the de-

Escondido v. Desert Outdoor Advertising Co., 8 Cal.3d 785, 106 Cal.Rptr. 172, 505 P.2d 1012, 3 ELR 20293 (1973), cert. denied 414 U.S. 828 (specific legislative acts concerning nuisances, regulating the placement of signs and billboards along freeways, excuses compliance with general zoning laws).

4. West's Ann.Cal.Civ.Code § 3482; Rev.Code Wash.Ann. § 7.48.160. In Pennsylvania, the Supreme Court held that the state's Air Pollution Control Act effectively preempted the common law of public nuisance as applied to burning coal refuse piles. Commonwealth v. Glen Alden Corp., 418 Pa. 57, 210 A.2d 256 (1965). The legislature acted quickly to reinstate nuisance law as applied to air pollution sources. See Brookhaven v. American Rendering Inc., 434 Pa. 290, 251 A.2d 626 (1969).

5. Richards v. Washington Terminal Co., 233 U.S. 546, 553, 34 S.Ct. 654, 657, 58 L.Ed. 1088, 1091 (1914); see Urie v. Franconia Paper Corp., 107 N.H. 131, 218 A.2d 360 (1966).

6. F. Bosselman, D. Collies & J. Banta, The Taking Issue (1973); § 2.17 below.

7. Cf. State ex rel. Norvell v. Arizona Pub. Serv. Co., 85 N.M. 165, 510 P.2d 98 (1973) (reading state law as vesting an administrative agency with primary jurisdiction to consider air pollution from a coal-fired power plant challenged as a public nuisance). Contra, State v. Dairyland Power Co-op., 52 Wis.2d 45, 187 N.W.2d 878, 1 ELR 20325 (1971) (same question discussed under rubric of exhaustion of administrative remedies).

8. See People v. New Penn Mines, Inc., 212 Cal.App.2d 667, 28 Cal.Rptr. 337 (1963) (holding that attorney general's power to sue for public nuisance was preempted by establishment of administrative apparatus to deal with

fense that the offending aircraft satisfy FAA certification requirements and the local port authority's operational controls? [9] The broad question is under what circumstances can yesterday's common law nuisance become today's respectable business. Legislation establishing administrative remedies often is used defensively—to validate and legitimate conduct that might under judicial scrutiny at common law be said to interfere unreasonably with the use and enjoyment of another's property.

The doctrinal issues raised by the concept of legalized nuisance are expressed variously—primary jurisdiction, exhaustion of administrative remedies, preemption.[10] Ultimately the question involves nothing more than determining what the words of the legislation mean when they assign standard-setting responsibilities to an administrative agency or prescribe how or where a particular polluting enterprise can be operated. While generalities are dangerous and always subject to the specifics of the legislation, it can be said that the courts are reluctant to embrace the concept of legalized nuisance. The assigned reasons are a combination of canards and sound rules of interpretation—legislative modifications of the common law are strictly construed, repeal by implication is disfavored,[11] statutory delegations to administrative authorities generally should be read to supplement not supplant existing remedies.[12] A fundamental institutional reason is that courts are not inclined to relinquish sweeping powers to correct technological and land use abuses unless legislatures unmistakably dictate the terms of surrender. Thus, issues of legalized nuisance for the most part involve a close reading of statutes. The preference is for a narrow construction: many courts hold that either the location of the nuisance or the methods employed were not intended to be authorized,[13] or that while a public nuisance was legalized

water pollution); cf. White v. Long, 12 Ohio App.2d 136, 231 N.E.2d 337 (1967) (state approval of a discharge influences court to invoke de minimis rule in private suit for injunction).

9. E. g., Swetland v. Curtiss Airports Corp., 55 F.2d 201 (6th Cir. 1932); United States v. New Haven, 447 F.2d 972 (2d Cir. 1971); Atkinson v. Dallas, 353 S.W.2d 275 (Tex.Civ.App.1961), cert. denied 370 U.S. 939 (1962); Hanover v. Morristown, 118 N.J.Super. 136, 286 A.2d 728 (Ch.1972), aff'd 121 N.J.Super. 536, 298 A.2d 89.

10. Notes 7–9, supra; Annot., Right to Maintain Action to Enjoin Public Nuisance as Affected by Existence of Pollution Control Agency, 60 ALR3d 665 (1974); see § 1.9 above.

11. Pottock v. Continental Can Co., 42 Del.Ch. 296, 210 A.2d 295 (1965); State v. Dairyland Power Coop., 52 Wis.2d 45, 187 N.W.2d 878, 1 ELR 20325 (1971).

12. United States v. United States Steel Corp., 356 F.Supp. 556, 3 ELR 20204 (S.D.Ill.1973); Shumaker v. New York & Pennsylvania Co., 367 Pa. 40, 79 A.2d 439 (1951).

13. Tuebner v. California St. R. R., 66 Cal. 171, 4 P. 1162 (1884) (location and methods); Squaw Island Freight Terminal Co. v. Buffalo, 273 N.Y. 119, 7 N.E.2d 10 (1937) (methods); Cogswell v. New York, N. H. & N. R. R., 103 N.Y. 10, 8 N.E. 537 (1886) (location); Board of Commissioners of Lake County v. Mentor Lagoons, Inc., 6 Ohio Misc. 126, 216 N.E.2d 643 (1965); Kennedy v. Moog, 48 Misc.2d 107, 264 N.Y.S.2d 606 (1965), aff'd in part 26 A.D.2d 768, 271 N.Y.S.2d 928 1966), aff'd 21 N.Y.2d 966, 290 N.Y.S.

Sec. 2.10 THE EFFECT OF STATUTES

a private nuisance was not.[14] There is a similar tendency to treat warily assertions that nuisance remedies have been preempted [15] or that administrative authorities must be heard from [16] before the nuisance claims are litigated.

A distinction must be drawn between legislation authorizing conduct in a certain place (i. e., zoning laws) and legislation authorizing conduct in a certain manner (i. e., pollution control laws). With regard to private nuisance,[17] the "vast weight" [18] of authority is that zoning laws are not complete defenses in nuisance actions.[19] The rationale is that just because a business is lawful for one purpose does not necessarily mean it is lawful for another purpose. This reasoning is quite correct in light of the dual land use and technological control objectives of nuisance law. Zoning laws tell us something about the propriety of the place but nothing about the propriety of the operations.

The case law respects this difference. Even in states giving legislative exemptions from nuisance law for conduct authorized by zoning laws,[20] courts have insisted upon improved technological controls, either as a matter of statutory interpretation [21] or judicial gloss.[22]

2d 193, 237 N.E.2d 356 (1968); Messer v. Dickinson, 71 N.D. 568, 3 N.W.2d 241 (1942) (methods); Choctaw, O. & G. R. R. v. Drew, 37 Okla. 396, 130 P. 1149 (1913) (location); Townsend v. Norfolk Ry. & Light Co., 105 Va. 22, 52 S.E. 970 (1906) (location).

14. Green v. Castle Concrete Co., 181 Colo. 309, 509 P.2d 588, 4 ELR 20365 (1973) (dictum); see text accompanying note 5, supra.

15. People v. Los Angeles, 160 Cal. App.2d 494, 325 P.2d 639 (1958); J. D. Jewell, Inc. v. Hancock, 226 Ga. 480, 175 S.E.2d 847 (1970); State v. Huntington, 67 Misc.2d 875, 325 N.Y. S.2d 674 (1971), aff'd 37 A.D.2d 858, 326 N.Y.S.2d 981.

16. § 1.9 above; see State v. Huntington, supra note 15; State v. Dairyland Power Coop., 52 Wis.2d 45, 187 N.W.2d 878, 1 ELR 20325 (1971); Pottock v. Continental Can Co., 42 Del.Ch. 296, 210 A.2d 295 (1965); State ex rel. Shevin v. Tampa Elec. Co., 291 So.2d 45 (Fla.App.1974).

17. In the area of public nuisances, once a state authorizes certain activity later attacks are difficult. Note, Nuisance and Legislative Authorization, 52 Colum.L.Rev. 781, 782 (1952). This preclusion generally but not always extends to private persons suing to prevent a public nuisance. Id. at 784, discussing the cases.

18. Note, The Effect of Zoning Ordinances on the Law of Nuisance, 54 Mich.L.Rev. 266, 270 (1955).

19. Williams v. Bluebird Laundry Co., 85 Cal.App. 388, 259 P. 484 (1927) (legislatively overruled in 1935 by Cal.Code Civ.Proc. § 731(a)); Scallet v. Stock, 363 Mo. 721, 253 S.W.2d 143 (1952); Tortorella v. H. Traiser & Co., 284 Mass. 497, 188 N.E. 254 (1933) (dictum); Ellis v. Blanchard, 45 So.2d 100 (La.App.1950); Soukoup v. Republic Steel Corp., 78 Ohio App. 87, 66 N.E.2d 334 (1946); Bruskland v. Oak Theatre, 42 Wash.2d 346, 254 P. 2d 1035 (1953); Kosich v. Poultrymen's Serv. Corp., 136 N.J.Eq. 571, 43 A.2d 15 (1945); cf. Transcontinental Gas Pipe Line Corp. v. Gault, 198 F.2d 196 (4th Cir. 1952) (natural gas compressor station "booster plant," constructed with approval of Federal Power Commission, a noisy nuisance as operated).

20. Cal.Civ.Code § 348a; Rev.Code Wash.Ann. § 7.48.160.

21. Gelfand v. O'Haver, 33 Cal.2d 218, 200 P.2d 790 (1948) (enjoined the operation of a music studio in a residence on the ground of lack of soundproofing).

22. Bruskland v. Oak Theatre, Inc., 42 Wash.2d 346, 254 P.2d 1035 (1953).

The same is true in those jurisdictions embracing the minority rule giving presumptive validity to activity being carried out consistently with local zoning ordinances.[23] Being the right thing in the right place does not tell us the business is being operated the right way.[24]

Another important distinction is whether the legislative authorization can be read as addressing both the remedies of injunction and money damages. Courts thus may construe the claimed authorization as precluding only suits for an injunction not damages,[25] and of course in many cases plaintiffs seek only monetary relief.[26] Once again, the fact that a person is conducting his business in a proper place defined by legislative or administrative action is no answer to the question of whether he ought to pay for damages inflicted while conducting his business there. This rationale is sufficiently broad to allow damage suits for public nuisances now legislatively sanctioned.[27]

The difference between the technological and land use control functions of nuisance law are observed clearly where the legislative authorization extends only to the manner of operation as opposed to the place of operation. No one could argue seriously that the securing of a waste discharge permit satisfies also zoning obligations under the law. A recognition that the questions are separate and distinct has prompted a number of legislative proposals for combining the issues in a single determination by a single authority. The best known are the various "one-stop" mechanisms for the licensing of electric generating plants.[28]

---

23. Robinson Brick Co. v. Luthi, 115 Colo. 106, 169 P.2d 171 (1946); Jedneak v. Minnesota General Elec. Co., 212 Minn. 226, 4 N.W.2d 326 (1942) (refusing to enjoin powerplant operated in an industrial zone but inflicting injury on neighboring landowners); Patterson v. Peabody Coal Co., 3 Ill.App.2d 311, 122 N.E.2d 48 (1954) (refusing to enjoin coal washer and dryer operated in an area zoned for industry but causing injury to plaintiff); Bove v. Donner-Hanna Coke Corp., 236 App.Div. 37, 258 N.Y.S. 229 (1932) (refusing to enjoin an around-the-clock coke oven located in an industrial zone despite substantial injury to a private landowner).

24. See, e. g., Urie v. Franconia Paper Co., 107 N.H. 131, 218 A.2d 360 (1966) (paper mill on industrial watercourse); Kozesnik v. Montgomery, 24 N.J. 154, 131 A.2d 1 (1957) (dictum) (area zoned for rock quarry); cf. Commerce Oil Ref. Corp. v. Miner, 170 F.Supp. 396 (D.R.I.1959) (enjoining construction of an oil refinery; allowing a collateral attack on a zoning ordinance permitting it).

25. E. I. DuPont de Nemours v. Dodson, 49 Okl. 58, 150 P. 1085 (1915); Kuntz v. Werner Flying Serv., 257 Wis. 405, 410, 43 N.W.2d 476 (1950); cf. Squaw Island Freight Terminal Co. v. Buffalo, 273 N.Y. 119, 7 N.E.2d 10 (1937); Bohnsack v. McDonald, 26 Misc. 493, 56 N.Y. 347 (Sup.Ct.1899).

26. E. g., § 2.17 below; Richards v. Washington Terminal Co., 233 U.S. 546, 34 S.Ct. 654, 58 L.Ed. 1088 (1913).

27. Note, supra note 17, at 785–86.

28. E. g., Rodgers, Siting Power Plants in Washington State, 47 Wash.L.Rev. 9 (1971); Best, Recent State Initiatives on Power Plant Siting: A Report and Comment, 5 Nat.Res.L. 668 (1972); Bronstein, State Regulation

Sec. 2.10 THE EFFECT OF STATUTES

The treatment of legislative or administrative standards of operation depends, in the last analysis, upon what the statute says. Non-conformity evidence is almost always decisive. The violation of a permit or effluent standard generally is per se evidence of unreasonable operation for purposes of nuisance law.[29] Conformity evidence, on the other hand, may require a closer analysis. It may be accepted as strong evidence of what is reasonable for purposes of nuisance law.[30] Or, as is more likely, it may be read as meaning that defendant has complied only with the statutory or administrative minimum. There is a reluctance, in both air[31] and water[32] pollution cases, to accept evidence of compliance with an administrative discharge permit as answering fully an inquiry under nuisance law. This is explained in a comment to the Restatement (Second) of Torts:[33]

> Legislation prohibiting some but not other conduct is not ordinarily construed as authorizing the latter. In the case of negligence as a matter of law, the standard defined by a legislative enactment is normally a minimum standard, applicable to the ordinary situations contemplated by the legislation. Thus, travelling at less than the speed limit may still be negligence if traffic conditions indicate that a lesser speed is required. . . . The same general principle applies to public nuisance. Consideration may appropriately be given, however, to the fact that acts were taken in reliance upon legislation, as when expensive screening processes were installed, to reduce the level of pollution to a legislative maximum.

Thus, administrative performance standards may be read as a ceiling below which traditional concepts of nuisance apply. While it is relevant that defendant has moved part way towards obviating the nuisance pursuant to an administrative mandate, so too is it significant if

---

of Power Plant Siting, 3 Environmental L. 273 (1973).

29. See, e. g., Reserve Mining Co. v. United States, 514 F.2d 492, 524, 5 ELR 20596, 20609 (8th Cir. 1974); Heck v. Beryllium Corp., 424 Pa. 140, 226 A.2d 87 (1967) (defendant has a duty to adhere to minimum emission standard for beryllium set by the Atomic Energy Commission); Maitland v. Twin City Aviation Corp., 254 Wis. 541, 37 N.W.2d 74 (1949) (court upholds an injunction enjoining the flying of aircraft below 500 feet during mink-whelping season, noting that the decree ordered nothing more than what was required under aviation regulations); cf. State v. Alexander Bros., Inc., 43 Ohio App.2d 154, 334 N.E.2d 492, 5 ELR 20030 (1974) (strip-mining in violation of state licensing requirements justifies injunctive relief without reference to normal equitable requirements).

30. E. g., Olympia Oyster Co. v. Rayonier, Inc., 229 F.Supp. 855 (W.D. Wash.1964).

31. Venuto v. Owens-Corning Fiberglas Corp., 22 Cal.App.3d 116, 99 Cal. Rptr. 350 (1971); cf. Hubbard-Hall Chem. Co. v. Silverman, 340 F.2d 402 (1st Cir. 1965); Rayborn v. Smiley, 253 So.2d 664, 2 ELR 20084 (La.App. 1971) (compliance by rendering plant with state and federal health requirements no defense to private nuisance action).

32. People v. Reedley, 66 Cal.App. 409, 226 P. 408 (1924).

33. § 821B, at 6 (Tent. Draft No. 18, 1972).

plaintiffs continue to suffer after some control efforts are undertaken or in the interim while they are being undertaken.

Wholly apart from the impact of statutes on nuisance principles is the question of whether the legislation itself creates a separate claim for relief. This issue is self-explanatory if the legislature has acted explicitly. Often, however, the issue is whether a cause of action is created by implication. The courts must parse the language of the statute and the legislative materials to determine whether the purpose of the act warrants creation of judicial remedies.[34] In creating a judicial remedy for a breach of the Federal Safety Appliance Act,[35] for example, the Supreme Court has stated that "[a] disregard of the command of a statute is a wrongful act, and where it results in damage to one of the class for whose especial benefit the statute was enacted, the right to recover damages from the party in default is implied." [36]

Under this rationale an employee should be able to recover damages from an employer who fails to adhere to legislated safety standards. A close case is presented by legislatively created water quality standards which can be viewed either as general measures of environmental quality or specific directives for the benefit of water users damaged by violations.[37] An example of legislation held not to have created a civil damage remedy by implication is Section 101(c) of the National Environmental Policy Act,[38] which reads, "[t]he Congress recognizes that each person should enjoy a healthful environment and that each person has a responsibility to contribute to the preservation and enhancement of the environment." The reasoning that finds no remedy here by implication is that the language is only precatory at best and that the legislative history discloses rejection of a similar provision that would have vested the federal courts with jurisdiction to enforce any rights created.[39] It is difficult to quarrel with the conclusion.

34. See J. I. Case Co. v. Borak, 377 U.S. 426, 84 S.Ct. 1555, 12 L.Ed.2d 423 (1964); Wyandotte Transp. Co. v. United States, 389 U.S. 191, 88 S.Ct. 379, 19 L.Ed.2d 407 (1967); Texas & N. O. R. R. v. Brotherhood of Ry. & S. S. Clerks, 281 U.S. 548, 568–69, 50 S.Ct. 427, 433, 74 L.Ed. 1034, 1045–46 (1930); Fitzgerald v. Pan American World Airways, 229 F.2d 499 (2d Cir. 1956) (Civil Aeronautics Act of 1938); Note, Implying Civil Remedies from Federal Regulatory Statutes, 77 Harv. L.Rev. 285 (1963); cf. United States v. Republic Steel Corp., 362 U.S. 482, 80 S.Ct. 884, 4 L.Ed.2d 903 (1960) (deriving an injunctive remedy by implication from the Rivers and Harbors Act of 1899).

35. 45 U.S.C.A. §§ 1–16.

36. Texas & Pac. Ry. v. Rigsby, 241 U.S. 33, 39, 36 S.Ct. 482, 484, 60 L.Ed. 874, 877 (1916).

37. Note, Water Quality Standards in Private Nuisance Actions, 79 Yale L.J. 102 (1969). Compare § 4.5 below (discussing the implication of private remedies under the Rivers and Harbors Act).

38. 42 U.S.C.A. § 4331(c).

39. See Comm. of Conference, National Environmental Policy Act of 1969, H.R.Rep. No. 765, 91st Cong., 1st Sess. 8 (1969); § 7.5 below.

§ 2.11 Nuisance: The Remedy

The student and practitioner of environmental law must be conversant with the wide range of equitable remedies used today as a matter of course in complex litigation. The choice for the court is by no means a choice between no relief or money damages or perhaps an injunction ordering a cessation of the offending activity. Remedial opportunities are confined only by the imagination of counsel and the practicalities of the situation. Often, they fall into four broad categories: (1) damages, (2) land use accommodations, (3) technological accommodations, (4) operational controls.

The damages remedy obviously is aimed at making whole the plaintiff's losses by a money judgment. The land use remedy recognizes a fundamental incompatibility of the conflicting uses and anticipates that one or the other of the parties should relocate; typically, defendant either is forced to shut down or buy out the plaintiff. The technological remedy rejects a land use adjustment in favor of an approach normally requiring defendant to install the best control technology and operate it to the maximum efficiency. It is, in a sense, a technological alternative to a land use decision. The fourth remedy, that of operational controls, interferes least with defendant's enterprise. It usually requires no costly capital investments in technological solutions. It requires only that the actor conduct his enterprise with more skill or care or in a different manner or at a different time to minimize the harm.

That environmental cases are steeped in the equitable tradition of the imaginative remedy is nowhere better demonstrated than by Learned Hand's splendid decision in the case of Smith v. Staso Milling Co.,[1] where the owner of a summer residence was beseiged by water, air and noise pollution from defendants' crushing mill. Each aspect of the nuisance was remedied differently: as to the water pollution the "injury [was] so substantial and the wrong deliberate"[2] (affecting plaintiff's drinking water despite many assurances to the contrary) that defendant was flatly required to avoid further injury to plaintiff (whether by technological controls, buying him out or moving elsewhere); as to the air pollution defendant was required only to operate the best known arresters at maximum efficiency (and thus was spared a shutdown); as to the noise defendant was required only to halt blasting at night while plaintiff's house was occupied so as to avoid unreasonably jarring the building. Damages also were awarded. The case combines the four dominant remedial approaches of environmental cases (damages, land use accommodations between the parties, technological and operational controls).

Two other leading cases illustrating the interplay of available remedies are Boomer v. Atlantic Cement Co.[3] and Spur Industries Inc.

---

1. 18 F.2d 736 (2d Cir. 1927).

2. 18 F.2d at 738.

3. 26 N.Y.2d 219, 309 N.Y.S.2d 312, 257 N.E.2d 870 (1970).

v. Del E. Webb Development Co.[4] In *Boomer* a cement plant representing an investment of $45 million inflicted damages from dirt, smoke and vibration upon neighboring landowners. The New York Court of Appeals, determined to avoid shutting down the offending plant, granted an injunction conditioned on the payment of permanent damages to plaintiffs to compensate them for their total economic loss, present and future, caused by defendant's operations (the trial court had fixed permanent damages at $185,000). The result, of course, as Judge Jason in dissent recognized,[5] is to give the defendant the power to condemn adjoining properties. It was the plaintiff, not the defendant, who was required to move or otherwise make a land use accommodation. Judge Jason would have given the defendant 18 months to come up with a technological answer to abatement before forbidding continuing discharge (presumably by a shutdown if technological accommodations were unavailable).

Spur Industries was a suit by a land developer whose lot sales in Sun City, Arizona were being adversely affected by odors and flies from a nearby cattle feedlot. Technological or operational options apparently were out of the question as the "admittedly good feedlot management and good housekeeping practices"[6] of defendant were incapable of eliminating odor and flies associated with the production of over 1 million pounds of wet manure per day. The situation was one where considerations of who was there first and the character of the neighborhood favored the defendant. With plaintiff having come to the nuisance (or more accurately having brought others to the nuisance), the court struck the following land use accommodation: the feedlot could be permanently enjoined, but the developer was required to indemnify the feedlot operator a reasonable amount for the cost of moving or shutting down. The result is the reciprocal of *Boomer:* plaintiff, not the defendant, is given the power of condemnation.[7]

The rules on damages are quite straightforward. If the nuisance (whether air, water or noise pollution) is permanent, the measure of damages is the depreciation in the market value of the realty by reason of the nuisance.[8] This is the measure of damages for a

---

4. 108 Ariz. 178, 494 P.2d 700 (1972) (en banc).

5. 26 N.Y.2d at 231, 309 N.Y.S.2d at 321, 257 N.E.2d at 876.

6. 108 Ariz. at 183, 494 P.2d at 205.

7. See Calabresi & Melamed, Property Rules, Liability Rules and Inalienability: One View of the Cathedral, 85 Harv.L.Rev. 1089, 1102–24 (1972); Michelman, Pollution As a Tort: A Non-Accidental Perspective on Calabresi's Costs, 80 Yale L.J. 647 (1971). On the reciprocal nature of pollution problems, see Coase, The Problem of Social Costs, 3 J. Law & Econ. 1 (1960), especially id. at 11–15 (discussing Bryant v. Lefever, 4 C.P.D. 172 (1878–79), where defendant's increase in the height of his house caused plaintiff's chimneys to smoke whenever he lighted fires).

8. Spaulding v. Cameron, 38 Cal.2d 265, 239 P.2d 625 (1952); Robertson v. Cincinnati, New Orleans & Tex. Pac. Ry.,

Sec. 2.11   **THE REMEDY**   145

condemnation. Some courts, apparently on the theory that the "condemnation" is not complete until the tortfeasor pays the depreciation, allow plaintiff to recover not only for diminution in his land value by reason of the nuisance, but also for special damages, such as loss of crops, which he suffered before trial.[9] In addition to damages for the taking of the property, recovery may be had for consequential damages to the possessor resulting from the invasion, such as injuries to his own health [10] or loss of services of his family.[11] It is clear, however, that plaintiffs cannot secure both a damages judgment for reduced market value due to permanent injury to property and an injunction abating the cause of the depreciation.[12]

Where the nuisance is not permanent and abatement can be accomplished, the "plaintiff usually recovers the depreciation in the rental or use value of his property during the period in which the nuisance exists, plus any special damages." [13] Professor Dodd explains [14] the refinements of the rules:

> Discomfort or inconvenience in the use of property is, of course, relevant both to establish special damage and as evidence bearing on the loss of rental or use value. Damages for temporary nuisances are not necessarily limited to depreciated rental values or use values, however. Where the nuisance is the kind that does more or less tangible harm to the premises, the cost of repair or restoration may be the appropriate measure of damages, just as

---

207 Tenn. 272, 339 S.W.2d 6 (1960) (Chattanooga choo-choo noise); see D. B. Dobbs, Remedies 332–33 (1973); Comment, Nuisance Damages as an Alternative to Compensation for Land Use Restrictions in Eminent Domain, 47 Calif.L.Rev. 998 (1974). See also § 2.6 above (discussing permanent and temporary nuisances).

9. Lassiter v. Norfolk & Carolina R.R., 126 N.C. 509, 36 S.E. 48 (1900).

10. Vann v. Bowie Sewerage Co., 127 Tex. 97, 90 S.W.2d 561 (1936); O'Connor v. Aluminum Ore Co., 224 Ill.App. 613 (1922); Millett v. Minnesota Crushed Stone Co., 145 Minn. 475, 177 N.W. 641 (1920); Dixon v. New York Trap Rock Corp., 293 N.Y. 509, 58 N.E.2d 517 (1944), motion denied 294 N.Y. 654, 60 N.E.2d 385 (1945); Evansville v. Rhinehart, 142 Ind.App. 164, 233 N.E.2d 495 (1968).

11. United States Smelting Co. v. Sisam, 191 F. 293 (8th Cir. 1911); Towaliga Falls Power Co. v. Sims, 6 Ga.App. 749, 65 S.E. 844 (1909); Millett v. Minnesota Crushed Stone Co., 145 Minn. 475, 177 N.W. 641 (1920).

12. Spaulding v. Cameron, 38 Cal.2d 265, 239 P.2d 625 (1952) (Traynor, J.); cf. Shearing v. Rochester, 51 Misc.2d 436, 273 N.Y.S.2d 464 (Sup.Ct.1966) (permanent injunction against trash-burning, but damages confined to 6 cents because of lack of proof of diminished rental value to time of trial).

13. D. B. Dobbs, supra note 8, at 333; see California Orange Co. v. Riverside Portland Cement Co., 50 Cal.App. 522, 195 P. 694 (1920) (damages measured by loss of crop); Ledbetter Bros., Inc. v. Holcomb, 108 Ga.App. 282, 132 S.E.2d 805 (1963); Bates v. Quality Ready-Mix Co., 261 Iowa 696, 154 N.W.2d 852 (1968); Love Petroleum Co. v. Jones, 205 So.2d 274 (Miss.1967). See also Harrisonville v. W. S. Dickey Clay Mfg. Co., 289 U.S. 334, 53 S.Ct. 602, 77 L.Ed. 1208 (1933) (Brandeis, J.); United States v. Fixico, 115 F.2d 389 (10th Cir. 1940).

14. See Superior Constr. Co. v. Elmo, 204 Md. 1, 102 A.2d 739 (1954) (mud slide; damages include restoration cost and loss of use).

it is the appropriate measure where similar harm is done in trespass cases.

Most important is the fact that recovery for depreciated property can be supplemented by compensation for annoyance, discomfort and inconvenience.[15] This means that plaintiffs routinely attempt to prove the irritation and frustration occasioned by the interference with their abode even though the losses are not easily susceptible of expression in dollars. Thus compensation has been allowed for annoyance occasioned by dust [16] and other air pollutants,[17] sewage fumes,[18] and the dumping of solid wastes on plaintiff's property.[19] Damages to health, such as costs of hospitalization, are recoverable *a fortiori*.[20] An award may be supplemented substantially by punitive damages.[21]

Because of the historical association of nuisance law with the rights of the landowner, there is a small problem created when the nuisance inflicts injury or illness on a member of the landowner's family rather than on the landowner himself. This is circumvented in different ways but decisively in the case law: one solution is to allow the owner to recover only for his discomfort, with the recognition that it is increased to the extent his family suffers;[22] another is

---

15. Theoretically, these damages "might result in overpayment, since the depreciation in the rental value is itself a result of the discomfort or potential discomfort of the occupant." D. B. Dobbs, supra note 8, at 334 & n. 15. See Kentucky West Virginia Gas Co. v. Lafferty, 174 F.2d 848 (6th Cir. 1949) (interpreting Kentucky law as abandoning earlier rule against allowing recovery for both personal discomfort and loss of rental value). But cf. Price v. Dickson, 317 S.W.2d 156 (Ky.1958) (discomfort an element in determining diminution of land use value). Compare Nitram Chem. v. Parker, 200 So.2d 220 (Fla.App.1967) (allowing recovery for damages to property based on a subjective measure of loss to plaintiff); Adams Constr. Co. v. Bentley, 335 S.W.2d 912 (Ky.1960) (same).

16. Riblet v. Spokane-Portland Cement Co., 45 Wash.2d 346, 274 P.2d 574 (1954).

17. Northern Indiana Pub. Serv. Co. v. Vesey, 210 Ind. 338, 200 N.E. 620 (1936) (owner of greenhouse sued gas company; judgment allowed for past, present and future damage); Capurro v. Galaxy Chem. Co., 2 ELR 20386 (Md.Cir.Ct. Caroline County 1972).

18. Oxford v. Spears, 228 Miss. 433, 87 So.2d 914 (1956). But see McKee v. Akron, 176 Ohio S.Ct. 282, 199 N.E. 2d 592 (1964) (municipality not liable for alleged nuisance arising from operation of sewage treatment plant).

19. Herzog v. Grosso, 41 Cal.2d 219, 259 P.2d 429 (1953).

20. United States Smelting Co. v. Sisam, 191 F.2d 293 (8th Cir. 1911); Birmingham Water Works Co. v. Martini, 2 Ala.App. 652, 56 So. 830 (1911); Thrasher v. Atlanta, 178 Ga. 514, 173 S.E. 817 (1934); Evansville v. Rinehart, 142 Ind.App. 164, 233 N. E.2d 495 (1968); Gorman v. Sabo, 210 Md. 155, 122 A.2d 475 (1956); Capurro v. Galaxy Chem. Co., 2 ELR 20386 (Md.Cir.Ct. Caroline County 1972); Louisville & N. Terminal Co. v. Lellyett, 144 Tenn. 368, 85 S.W. 881 (1905); see D. B. Dobbs, supra note 8, at 543–44.

21. E. g., Lemler v. Nevada Cement Co., 2 ELR 20176 (Nev.Dist.Ct. Lyon County, 1971) (assessing 1.8 million dollars as exemplary damages) (for operation of a cement plant without a filtration system).

22. Millett v. Minnesota Crushed Stone Co., 145 Minn. 475, 177 N.W. 641 (1920).

Sec. 2.11 THE REMEDY

to allow the head of the household to recover for his spouse's separate illness;[23] yet another is to devise a rule that an occupant or possessor who is not a legal interest owner can recover if he has suffered special damages;[24] still another is to circumvent the property ownership rule of private nuisance law entirely by basing recovery on either negligence[25] or on the theory that anyone who suffers special damage from a public nuisance can recover.[26] It is only a question of method or theory, not result, as to whether family members can recover.

Special damages recoverable in nuisance cases include direct damage to property, even though rental or use value is unaffected. This includes crop losses,[27] injury to cattle and decreases in milk production,[28] damage to domestic animals, plants, clothes on the line and paint on the house.[29] The usual rules of proximate cause apply, which traditionally has meant that prospective pecuniary advantages, such as anticipated profit or improved earning capacity, are considered uncompensable items of damage on grounds of remoteness.[30] But there is considerable authority the other way,[31] even to the extent of allowing recovery for lost profits by showing simply a steady decline of gross receipts.[32] Owners of hotels and riparians owning fishing and swimming facilities located on polluted waters can recover their economic losses.[33] The same is true of commercial fishermen[34] whose interests appear indistinguishable from charter boat operators, motel

23. See Gormon v. Sabo, 210 Md. 155, 122 A.2d 475 (1956).

24. Kentucky West Virginia Gas Co. v. Lafferty, 174 F.2d 848 (6th Cir. 1949) (applying shorter personal injury statute to the personal discomfort and illness claims).

25. Page v. Niagara Chem. Div., 68 So.2d 382 (Fla.1953).

26. Hampton v. North Carolina Pulp Co., 223 N.C. 535, 27 S.E.2d 538 (1943).

27. United Verde Copper Co. v. Ralston, 46 F.2d 1 (9th Cir. 1931); California Orange Co. v. Riverside Portland Cement Co., 50 Cal.App. 522, 195 P. 694 (1920); Vautier v. Atlantic Ref. Co., 231 Pa. 8, 79 A. 814 (1911); cf. Northern Indiana Pub. Serv. Co. v. Vesey, 210 Ind. 338, 200 N.E. 630 (1936) (damage to greenhouse plants).

28. Fairview Farms, Inc. v. Reynolds Metals Co., 176 F.Supp. 178 (D.C.Or. 1959).

29. E. g., Griffin v. Northridge, 67 Cal. App.2d 69, 153 P.2d 800 (1944) (flowers); Wheat v. Freeman Coal Mining Corp., 23 Ill.App.3d 14, 319 N.E.2d 290 (1974) (clothing and exterior of house blackened by coal dust); Pettengill v. Turo, 159 Me. 350, 193 A.2d 367 (1963) (ornamental trees); Berg v. Reaction Motors Div., Theokol Chem. Corp., 37 N.J. 396, 181 A.2d 487 (1962) (structural damage to residence).

30. See Hi Hat Elkhorn Coal Co. v. Inland Steel Co., 370 F.2d 117 (6th Cir. 1966) (defendant dumping of sludge prevented plaintiff from mining coal; loss of profits held to be speculative and non-compensable).

31. D. B. Dobbs, supra note 8, at 345.

32. Schatz v. Abbott Laboratories, Inc., 51 Ill.2d 143, 281 N.E.2d 323, 2 ELR 20251 (1972) (air pollution damage to movie theatre business; damages for lost profits allowed despite no evidence of prior profits).

33. Union Oil Co. v. Oppen, 501 F.2d 558, 4 ELR 20618 (9th Cir. 1974).

34. Ibid.

owners and beach concessionaires with an economic stake in the integrity of public waters.

In addition to recovering what he has lost through depreciation or special damages as a result of the nuisance, plaintiff can recover reasonable costs to defend himself from further invasion. This would include costs of soundproofing, defensive landscaping and the like.[35] Usually it is the defendant who is required to modify his operations or process to alleviate the nuisance. But occasionally, plaintiff will act defensively, then sue for the cost of the improvements. A good example is Stratford Theater, Inc. v. Town of Stratford,[36] where a sewer line backed up and overflowed into plaintiff's theatre. Plaintiff hired a contractor to install lateral sewer lines and, the charges being reasonable, was allowed to recover them from defendant. A failure to take reasonable defensive measures, in extreme situations, might bar recovery for some damages under a theory of "avoidable consequences." [37]

Once a court settles upon the desirability of equitable relief, the range of remedies is virtually unlimited: "balancing the equities" can be accomplished entirely within the gamut of established practice. Routinely, the courts combine technological and operational limitations.[38] Where construction activities are involved, remedies range from simple injunctions to elaborate restoration requirements.[39] The

---

35. See Schatz v. Abbott Laboratories Inc., 51 Ill.2d 143, 281 N.E.2d 323, 2 ELR 20251 (1972) (assuming that expenditures for air conditioning and insulation were reasonable).

36. 140 Conn. 422, 101 A.2d 279 (1953); See Piedmont Cotton Mills, Inc. v. General Warehouse No. Two, Inc., 222 Ga. 164, 149 S.E.2d 72 (1966) (floodwater diverted by defendant and concentrated by plaintiff); Nally & Gibson v. Mulholland, 399 S.W.2d 293 (Ky.1966) (same result achieved when court considered costs of new water supply replacing a pond polluted by the nuisance to be a "factor" for consideration in determining diminution in use value); Annot., 41 ALR2d 1064 (1955).

37. See Arminius Chem. Co. v. Landrum, 113 Va. 7, 19–20, 73 S.E. 459, 465 (1912).

38. See, e. g., §§ 2.13, 5.3, 6.2, 8.2 below. Interesting and imaginative decrees can be found in New Jersey v. City of New York, 283 U.S. 473, 51 S.Ct. 519, 75 L.Ed. 1176 (1931), 296 U.S. 259, 56 S.Ct. 188, 80 L.Ed. 214 (1935) (fouling of beaches by city's ocean dumping of garbage and refuse); Wisconsin v. Illinois, 278 U.S. 367, 49 S.Ct. 163, 73 L.Ed. 426 (1929), 281 U.S. 179, 50 S.Ct. 266, 74 L.Ed. 799 (1930), 289 U.S. 395, 710, 53 S.Ct. 671, 788, 77 L.Ed. 1283, 1465 (1933) (diversion of water from Lake Michigan to dilute and carry away Chicago sewage; the decree resulted ultimately in the construction of a treatment works); see Activated Sludge, Inc. v. Sanitary District of Chicago, 64 F.Supp. 25 (N.D.Ill.1946); Nebraska v. Wyoming, 325 U.S. 589, 65 S.Ct. 1332, 89 L.Ed. 1815 (1945), 325 U.S. 665, 66 S.Ct. 1, 89 L.Ed. 1857 (allocation of waters of North Platte River among three states; injunction against improper diversions for irrigation); Lakeland Property Owners Ass'n v. Northfield, 2 ELR 20331 (Mich.Cir.Ct.1972) (operation of sewage treatment plant).

39. See, e. g., People v. Mack, 2 ELR 20026 (Cal.Ct.App.1971) (an order to remove bridges, fences and other obstructions blocking navigable waters); cf. §§ 4.5 (Rivers and Harbors Act), 7.10 (National Environmental Policy Act) below.

Sec. 2.11 THE REMEDY 149

decrees in but two cases involving air pollution by copper smelters illustrate an extraordinary agenda of opportunities:[40] defendant may be required to reduce production, install emission control devices, limit the sulfur content of its ore, restrict the lead time of its curtailment practices, report systematically on ores processed, emissions released, byproducts captured, keep complete weather records (on wind, humidity, temperature and pressure), give "free and full access" to books, records, and premises by a court appointed expert, pay for the experts or medical committees, provide medical examinations to persons who are or may be affected by emissions, establish a fund for those injured by fumes.

Court-appointed experts and masters often are relied upon to help formulate relief in complex environmental cases, such as those involving the control of air,[41] water[42] or noise[43] pollution. Experimentation may be required[44] and other pressures imposed[45] to im-

40. The provisions mentioned are found in the stipulations and decrees of Georgia v. Tennessee Copper Co., 206 U.S. 230, 27 S.Ct. 618, 51 L.Ed. 1038 (1907), 237 U.S. 474, 35 S.Ct. 631, 59 L.Ed. 1054 (1915) (motion to enter final decree) 237 U.S. 678, 35 S.Ct. 752, 59 L.Ed. 1173 (1915) (entry of final decree), modified 240 U.S. 650, 36 S.Ct. 465, 60 L.Ed. 846 (1916); El Paso v. American Smelting & Ref. Co., No. 70–1701 (Tex.Dist.Ct. El Paso County, May 11, 1972) (Judgment and Order of Injunction).

41. E. g., Georgia v. Tennessee Copper Co., supra note 40; Martin Bldg. Co. v. Imperial Laundry Co., 220 Ala. 90, 124 So. 82 (1929). Court-appointed experts in resource allocation cases are the rule rather than the exception. E. g., Hidalgo County Water Improvement Dist. v. Cameron County Water Control & Improvement Dist., 250 S.W.2d 941 (Tex.Civ.App.1952), discussed in Development in the Law—Injunctions, 78 Harv.L.Rev. 994, 1067–69 (1965) (water); United States v. Washington, 520 F.2d 676, 5 ELR 20552 (9th Cir.), cert. denied 423 U.S. 1086 (1975) (fishing).

42. E. g., New Jersey v. City of New York, 283 U.S. 473, 51 S.Ct. 519, 75 L.Ed. 1176 (1931); Wisconsin v. Illinois, 278 U.S. 367, 49 S.Ct. 163, 73 L.Ed. 426 (1929); Wilmont Homes v. Weiler, 42 Del.Ch. 8, 202 A.2d 576 (1964) (periodic flooding) (defendant required to install a drainage system in accordance with a detailed engineering plan; if work was not commenced within 30 days, a contractor could be employed to make the installation at the expense of defendant); cf. Arizona v. California, 373 U.S. 546, 83 S.Ct. 1468, 10 L.Ed.2d 542 (1963).

43. Godard v. Babson–Dow Mfg. Co., 313 Mass. 280, 47 N.E.2d 203, 145 A.L.R. 603 (1943) (vibration).

44. Cf. Arizona Copper Co. v. Gillespie, 230 U.S. 46, 55, 33 S.Ct. 1004, 1006, 57 L.Ed. 1384, 1388 (1912) (downstream irrigator injured by upstream tailing wastes from copper mining and reduction operation; injunction granted against discharge of tailings into water; trial court directed to retain jurisdiction to permit reasonable experiments to be made to ascertain the probability of successfully erecting and maintaining settling basins to effectually dispose of the tailings and slimes without detriment); Noel v. United Aircraft Corp., 219 F.Supp. 556, 573 (D.C.Del.1963), aff'd 342 F.2d 232 (3rd Cir. 1965) (negligence case) (finding negligence for failure to equip a propeller system with "every safety device which reasonable engineering minds could have devised"; district court points to a failure by defendant to "launch an accelerated program to produce acceptable alternative safety devices" in which "engineers, technicians, and sufficient funds were made available and the program put in charge of a responsible head with directions to push the program vigorously").

45. Cook Indus. Inc. v. Carlson, 334 F.Supp. 809, 2 ELR 20549 (N.D.Miss.

prove technological or operational capabilities of control. As explained in the comments of the Restatement of Torts,[46] "In the prevention or reduction of industrial nuisance and stream pollution, much can often be accomplished by an order requiring experiments to be conducted in the defendant's plant under neutral scientific supervision. To the chemist and engineer, there are few smoke, gas or refuse nuisances which cannot be diminished or eliminated through the application of modern technical skill. Such experiments should be undertaken before an injunction against nuisance or stream pollution is denied on ground of relative hardship or of countervailing public interest." On this reasoning, courts have referred cases to experts to determine whether the pollution can be abated[47] and have granted relief on the expert's advice that control was technologically feasible.[48]

§ 2.12 Federal Common Law of Nuisance

In 1972, the Supreme Court in Illinois v. Milwaukee held that the general federal question jurisdiction supported claims of interstate water pollution of Lake Michigan asserted by the State of Illinois against several municipalities in Wisconsin.[1] This new federal common law of interstate pollution raises several problems, theoretical and practical.

In the first place, it is generally understood that "the federal courts may make substantive law only in effectuation of a policy derived from the Constitution or from a valid act of Congress."[2] The source of the federal common law of interstate pollution is not at all clear. The remedy of abatement sought by Illinois was not provided for by any federal legislation but the Court did go out of its way to review the statutes at hand, which suggests it was implying the remedy from acts of Congress.[3] Other language in the opinion indicates the doctrine is constitutional in origin—for example, the Court re-

---

1971) (defendant directed to "make an adequate engineering study and take all proper steps to abate" nuisance); Ratzlaff v. Franz Foods, 250 Ark. 1003, 468 S.W.2d 239 (1971), 38 Mo.L. Rev. 161 (1973).

46. § 941, comment e (1939).

47. Martin Bldg. Co. v. Imperial Laundry Co., 220 Ala. 90, 124 So. 82 (1929) (whether a smoke nuisance could be remedied by installation of a stoker or other approved device).

48. Godard v. Babson Dow Mfg. Co., 313 Mass. 280, 47 N.E.2d 303 (1943) (vibration nuisance could be remedied by the installation of certain types of individual motors) (for subsequent contempt proceedings, see 319 Mass. 345, 65 N.E.2d 555 (1946)).

1. Illinois v. Milwaukee, 406 U.S. 91, 92 S.Ct. 1385, 31 L.Ed.2d 712 (1972).

2. Hill, The Erie Doctrine in Bankruptcy, 66 Harv.L.Rev. 1013, 1050 (1953).

3. Cf. Wyandotte Transp. Co. v. United States, 389 U.S. 191, 88 S.Ct. 379, 19 L.Ed.2d 407 (1967) (implying reimbursement remedy in favor of the United States from Rivers and Harbors Appropriation Act of 1899); Neches Canal Co. v. Miller & Vidor Lumber Co., 24 F.2d 763 (5th Cir. 1928) (implying a private right of action for violation of Section 9 of the 1899 Act, 33 U.S.C.A. § 401).

Sec. 2.12   FEDERAL COMMON LAW OF NUISANCE

lied heavily upon interstate air pollution [4] and water allocation cases [5] where the complaining party was a state capable of invoking the original jurisdiction of the Supreme Court.[6] It is likely the law-making powers of federal courts in interstate cases rest upon both constitutional and statutory foundations: federal judicial competence in suits by states to correct out-of-state nuisances can be derived from the state non-resident jurisdictional grant in the Constitution; [7] similarly, federal environmental statutes leave many gaps that can be filled by judge-made law.

Illinois v. Milwaukee raises a host of questions: [8] may a private citizen sue under the federal common law? Must interstate pollution be involved? Does the federal common law include additional remedies only for the violation of standards set under a federal statute? Or does it extend also to remedies against private polluters who violate the purposes of statutes, such as interstate non-resident disputes over non-degradation, even where administrative implementation is anticipated? Does the federal common law work a modification of the primary jurisdiction doctrine? Does it authorize abatement of pollution that is not prohibited either by the terms or the policies of federal statutes? Is it limited in scope to the traditional reach of the common law of nuisance? Does it preempt state nuisance law that otherwise might apply? Will it prompt a modification of the Supreme Court's traditional reluctance to invoke its original jurisdiction?

It will take several years to answer these questions although the case law is beginning to appear. A district court has held that a private citizen cannot invoke the doctrine since the authority relied upon in Illinois v. Milwaukee involved exclusively state plaintiffs and stressed the necessity of maintaining a remedy for the sovereigns who had joined the Union.[9] At the same time the federal district courts, with but a single exception,[10] have allowed the United States to in-

---

4. Georgia v. Tennessee Copper Co., 206 U.S. 230, 27 S.Ct. 618, 51 L.Ed. 1038 (1907). The Supreme Court also relied upon Texas v. Pankey, 441 F.2d 236, 1 ELR 20089 (10th Cir. 1971).

5. E. g., Kansas v. Colorado, 206 U.S. 46, 27 S.Ct. 655, 51 L.Ed. 956 (1907); Nebraska v. Wyoming, 325 U.S. 589, 65 S.Ct. 1332, 89 L.Ed. 1815 (1945). Meyers, The Colorado River, 19 Stan. L.Rev. 1 (1966).

6. Cf. Missouri v. Illinois, 200 U.S. 496, 519–20, 26 S.Ct. 268, 269, 50 L.Ed. 572, 578 (1906) (Holmes, J.) (discussing Supreme Court's law-making powers under grant of original jurisdiction).

7. U.S.Const. art. III, § 2.

8. Many of them raised in D. P. Currie, Cases and Materials on Pollution 508–09 (1975).

9. Comm. for Consideration of Jones Falls Sewage System v. Train, 375 F. Supp. 1148 (1974), aff'd en banc — F.2d —, 6 ELR 20703 (4th Cir. 1976). The holding in Illinois v. Milwaukee can be explained as a narrow attempt to provide a forum to states seeking to correct an out-of-state nuisance. The federal courts seemingly were closed to these claims by the decision in Ohio v. Wyandotte Chem. Corp., 401 U.S. 493, 91 S.Ct. 1005, 28 L.Ed. 2d 256 (1971).

10. United States v. Lindsay, 357 F. Supp. 784 (E.D.N.Y.1973) (dictum).

voke the federal common law in actions to abate pollution.[11] These cases stress [12] the statutory origins of the rights implied in Illinois v. Milwaukee although one court of appeals has gone further to treat as open the question of whether "the federal common law of public nuisance extends to all of our navigable waters, and perhaps to all tributaries of interstate waters" [13] regardless of a statutory basis.

The federal common law clearly does not extend to a local air pollution claim without interstate effects.[14] It probably does extend to the fashioning of additional remedies for the violation of established federal standards, which has been a common practice in the federal courts under many statutory schemes.[15] It might very well bring about a modification of the primary jurisdiction doctrine, under which the court suspends decision on a case properly before it pending consideration by a specialized administrative body. Indeed, Mr. Justice Douglas was hard put [16] in Illinois v. Milwaukee to distinguish Ohio v. Wyandotte Chemicals Corp.,[17] a conventional primary jurisdiction case where the Supreme Court declined to allow the filing of an original jurisdiction complaint raising complex factual questions regarding mercury pollution of Lake Erie.[18] The recognition of a federal common law encourages federal courts to question the propriety of deferring decisions on cases properly before them for no reason other than that the legislature has given some concurrent responsibilities to an administrative agency.

The scope of the rights recognized in Illinois v. Milwaukee is uncertain, partly because of their obscure origin. If federal judge-made law is dependent upon statutes, it would be patently improper for the

11. United States v. Stoeco Homes, Inc., 359 F.Supp. 672, 3 ELR 20722 (D.N.J.1973); United States v. United States Steel Corp., 356 F.Supp. 556, 3 ELR 20204 (N.D.Ill.1973); United States v. Ira S. Bushey & Sons, Inc., 346 F.Supp. 145, 2 ELR 20557 (D.C.Vt. 1972).

12. See for example, the discussion by Judge Oakes in United States v. Ira S. Bushey & Sons, Inc., supra note 11.

13. Stream Pollution Control Bd. v. United States Steel Corp., 512 F.2d 1036, 5 ELR 20261 (7th Cir. 1975) (Stevens, J.).

14. See Reserve Mining Co. v. United States, 514 F.2d 492, 520, 5 ELR 20596, 20607 (8th Cir. 1975) ("Federal nuisance law contemplates, at a minimum, interstate pollution of air and water"); Byram River v. Port Chester, 4 ELR 20816 (D.C.Conn.1974), following transfer, 394 F.Supp. 618, 5 ELR 20440 (S.D.N.Y.1975).

15. Note 2, supra. Perhaps the best known case is J. I. Case Co. v. Borak, 377 U.S. 426, 84 S.Ct. 1555, 12 L.Ed. 2d 423 (1964).

16. See 406 U.S. at 102 n. 3, 92 S.Ct. at 1392 n. 3, 31 L.Ed.2d at 723 n. 3.

17. 401 U.S. 493, 91 S.Ct. 1005, 28 L.Ed.2d 256 (1971); see Woods & Reed, The Supreme Court and Interstate Environmental Quality: Some Notes on the Wyandotte Case, 12 Ariz.L.Rev. 691 (1971).

18. The aspect of the decision in *Wyandotte* indicating that the federal courts are without jurisdiction to entertain interstate nuisance suits initiated by state plaintiffs (401 U.S. at 498 n. 3, 91 S.Ct. at 1009–10 n. 3, 28 L.Ed.2d at 263 n. 3) is overruled by Illinois v. Milwaukee. Compare § 1.9 above (discussing primary jurisdiction).

Sec. 2.12 FEDERAL COMMON LAW OF NUISANCE

courts to fashion remedies supportable neither by the letter nor by the policies of the legislation said to be the source of the law. Nice questions arise in any event about whether federal interstate pollution law is coextensive with state nuisance law. The question very well may be academic for the reason that relief under federal or state law is peculiarly a matter of equitable discretion—with the courts evaluating such issues as the capabilities of control technology and degree of injury, particularly at the remedy phase. There is a tantalizing statement in Illinois v. Milwaukee that a state with high water quality standards may insist that its strict standards be honored, and that it not be compelled to subjugate itself to the more degrading standards of a neighbor.[19] This suggestion that the federal common law demands cleaner water is counterbalanced by language in other cases suggesting it may be satisfied with water that is dirtier.[20]

A federal common law of interstate pollution may be a mixed blessing to environmentalists.[21] One problem is pre-emption: whether state remedies can coexist with rules of federal common law. If the federal judge-made law owes its existence to statutes, the question will be answered by determining what Congress meant when it enacted the law. Presumably if Congress neglects to spell out the full reach of federal remedies, it usually will not at the same time make clear that state remedies must be displaced. A constitutionally derived federal environmental right, on the other hand, may preempt all state law in the narrow domain in which it functions.[22] This suggests two general answers to the pre-emption question: yes, in suits by states against out-of-state nuisances; no, in all other cases until Congress says otherwise.

It is clear that Illinois v. Milwaukee does not modify the Supreme Court's traditional reluctance to become an arbiter of environmental claims under its original jurisdiction. This longstanding view was reaffirmed recently in Washington v. General Motors Corp.,[23] where the Court denied a motion for leave to file a complaint by eighteen states against four auto manufacturers and their trade associations charging a conspiracy to retard development of air pollution control technology. The Supreme Court stated that "[a]s a matter of law as well as prac-

---

19. 406 U.S. at 107, 92 S.Ct. at 1395, 31 L.Ed.2d at 726.

20. Missouri v. Illinois, 200 U.S. 496, 521, 26 S.Ct. 268, 270, 50 L.Ed. 572, 579 (1907) ("it does not follow that every matter which would warrant a resort to equity by one citizen against another in the same jurisdiction equally would warrant an interference by this court with the action of a state").

21. For a strong statement opposing the doctrine, see Note, Federal Common Law and Interstate Pollution, 85 Harv.L.Rev. 1439 (1972). Contrast Comment, Federal Common Law and the Environment: Illinois v. Milwaukee, 2 ELR 10168 (1972).

22. Hinderlider v. LaPlata & Cherry Creek Ditch Co., 304 U.S. 92, 58 S.Ct. 803, 82 L.Ed. 1202 (1938); Hill, Constitutional Remedies, 69 Colum.L.Rev. 1109, 1143–46 (1969).

23. 406 U.S. 109, 92 S.Ct. 1396, 31 L.Ed.2d 727 (1972).

tical necessity corrective remedies for air pollution . . . necessarily must be considered in the context of localized situations."[24] The Court in Illinois v. Milwaukee protected its docket again by declining to assume jurisdiction over the controversy, remitting the parties to a district court.

Federal common law of course must give way to federal statutes. The immediate reach of Illinois v. Milwaukee was narrowed by the Federal Water Pollution Control Act Amendments of 1972.[25] Application of the federal common law in the future requires the courts to be alert to whether Congress has made a clear choice in confining the range of available remedies.

§ 2.13 Trespass

Trespass is a theory closely related to nuisance and occasionally invoked in environmental cases. The distinction between the two originally was the difference between the old action of trespass and the action on the case: if there was a direct and immediate physical invasion of plaintiff's property, as by casting stones or water on it, it was a trespass; if the invasion was indirect, as by the seepage of water, it was a nuisance.[1]

Today, with the abandonment of the old procedural forms, the line between trespass and nuisance has become "wavering and uncertain."[2] The basic distinction is that trespass can be defined as any intentional invasion of the plaintiff's interest in the exclusive possession of property, whereas a nuisance requires a substantial and unreasonable interference with his use and enjoyment of it. That is to say, in trespass cases defendant's conduct typically results in an encroachment by "something" upon plaintiff's exclusive rights of possession.

The first and most important proposition about trespass and nuisance principles is that they are largely coextensive. Both concepts

---

24. 406 U.S. at 116, 92 S.Ct. at 1399, 31 L.Ed.2d at 732. Compare Vermont v. New York, 406 U.S. 186, 92 S.Ct. 1603, 31 L.Ed.2d 785 (1972), special master appointed, 408 U.S. 917 (accepting jurisdiction in a suit by Vermont for abatement of papermill sludge on the bottom of Lake Champlain charging derelictions by New York as land-owner and in controlling the papermill). The different results in Washington v. General Motors Corp. and Vermont v. New York, which were decided on the same day, are explicable because under the relevant statute (28 U.S.C.A. § 1251) suits by one state against another are within the original and exclusive jurisdiction of the Supreme Court. See also Idaho v. Oregon, — U.S. —, 97 S.Ct. 544, 48 L.Ed.2d 201 (1976) (per curiam).

25. Pub.L. No. 92–500, 86 Stat. 816 (1972), 33 U.S.C.A. § 1251 et seq.

1. The distinction is recognized in such cases as Pan American Petroleum Co. v. Byars, 228 Ala. 372, 153 So. 616 (1934). An excellent discussion of the historical evolution of the law of trespass is found in 1 F. Harper & F. James, The Law of Torts 4–16 (1956).

2. W. L. Prosser, Law of Torts 594 (4th ed. 1971); O'Connell, Streamlining Appellate Procedures, 56 Am.Jud. Soc'y J. 234, 238 (1973).

Sec. 2.13　TRESPASS

are often discussed in the same cases without differentiation between the elements of recovery.[3] Plainly, many types of conduct interfere simultaneously with plaintiff's interests in exclusive possession and use and enjoyment of his property: the blasting nuisance making his home insufferable may be a trespass when it throws rocks into his garden;[4] the flooding of his land, which is a trespass, may deprive him of all use and enjoyment;[5] an invasion of his land by pesticides simultaneously interferes with exclusive possession and compromises his use and enjoyment.[6]

It is also true that in the environmental arena both nuisance and trespass cases typically involve intentional conduct by the defendant who knows that his activities are substantially certain to result in an invasion of plaintiff's interests.[7] The principal difference in theories is that the tort of trespass is complete upon a tangible invasion of plaintiff's property, however slight, whereas a nuisance requires proof that the interference with use and enjoyment is "substantial and unreasonable." This burden of proof advantage in a trespass case is accompanied by a slight remedial advantage as well. Upon proof of a technical trespass plaintiff always is entitled to nominal damages.[8] It is possible also that a plaintiff could get injunctive relief against a technical trespass—for example, the deposit of particles of an air pollutant on his property causing no known adverse effects. The protection of the integrity of his possessory interests might justify the injunction even without proof of the substan-

---

3. E. g., Hall v. DeWeld Mica Corp., 244 N.C. 182, 93 S.E.2d 56 (1956) (emissions from mica mining and separating plant); Sheppard Envelope Co. v. Arcade Malleable Iron Co., 335 Mass. 180, 138 N.E.2d 777 (1956); see Folmar v. Elliott Coal Mining Co., 441 Pa. 592, 272 A.2d 910, 1 ELR 20182 (1971) (air pollution from coal-cleaning plant considered a trespass and analyzed as a nuisance).

4. Compare Beecher v. Dull, 294 Pa. 17, 143 A. 498 (1928) (nuisance) and Green v. T. A. Shoemaker & Co., 111 Md. 69, 73 A. 688 (1909) (nuisance) with Asheville Constr. Co. v. Southern R. R., 19 F.2d 32 (4th Cir. 1927) (trespass) and Mulchanock v. Whitehall Cement Mfg. Co., 253 Pa. 262, 98 A. 554 (1916) (trespass) and Hakkila v. Old Colony Broken Stone Co., 264 Mass. 447, 162 N.E. 895 (1928) (both).

5. Compare Lawson v. Price, 45 Md. 123 (1876) (trespass) and Groover v. Hightower, 59 Ga.App. 491, 1 S.E.2d 446 (1939) (trespass) with Rindge v. Sargent, 64 N.H. 294, 9 A. 723 (1886) (nuisance); Mueller v. Fruen, 36 Minn. 273, 30 N.W. 886 (1886) (both); Irvine v. Oelwein, 170 Iowa 653, 150 N.W. 674 (1914) (both).

6. Cf. Loe v. Lenhardt, 227 Or. 242, 362 P.2d 312 (1961) (trespass actionable only if liability established for negligence or abnormally dangerous activities).

7. An invasion of the exclusive possession of land, no less than an interference with the use and enjoyment of it, historically could be premised upon negligent or abnormally dangerous activity in addition to intentional conduct. Now, the first two types of invasions are governed, respectively, by general principles of negligence and liability for abnormally dangerous activities, "leaving only [conduct intended to cause an intrusion] as constituting the modern tort of 'trespass' upon land." 1 Harper & James, supra note 1, at 11–12.

8. E. g., Lee v. Stewart, 218 N.C. 287, 10 S.E.2d 804 (1940); Price v. Osborne, 24 Tenn.App. 525, 147 S.W.2d 412 (1940); Schumpert v. Moore, 24 Tenn.App. 695, 149 S.W.2d 471 (1941).

tial injury necessary to establish a nuisance. Of course absent proof of injury, or at least a reasonable suspicion of it, courts are unlikely to invoke their equitable powers to require expensive control efforts.

While the strict liability origins of trespass encourage courts to eschew a balancing test in name,[9] there is authority for denying injunctive relief if defendant has exhausted his technological opportunities for control.[10] If adopted generally, this principle would result substantially in a coalescence of nuisance and trespass law. Acknowledging technological or economic justifications for trespassory invasions does away with the historically harsh treatment of conduct interfering with another's possessory interests.

Just as there may be proof advantages in a trespass theory, there may be disadvantages also. Potential problems lurk in the ancient requirements that a trespassory invasion be "direct or immediate" and that an "object" or "something tangible" be deposited upon plaintiff's land. Some courts hold that if an intervening force, such as wind or water, carries the pollutants onto the plaintiff's land, then the entry is not "direct."[11] Others define "object" as requiring something larger or more substantial than smoke, dust, gas, or fumes.[12]

Both of these concepts are nonsensical barriers, although the courts are slow to admit it. The requirement that the invasion be "direct" is a holdover from the forms of action, and is repudiated by contemporary science of causation. Atmospheric or hydrologic systems assure that pollutants deposited in one place will end up somewhere else, with no less assurance of causation than the blaster who watches the debris rise from his property and settle on his neighbor's land. Trespassory consequences today may be no less "direct" even if the mechanism of delivery is viewed as more complex.

The insistence that a trespass involve an invasion by a "thing" or "object" was repudiated in the well known (but not particularly influential) case of Martin v. Reynolds Metals Co.,[13] which held that gaseous and particulate fluorides from an aluminum smelter constituted a trespass for purposes of the statute of limitations:

> [L]iability on the theory of trespass has been recognized where the harm was produced by the vibration of the soil or by the

---

9. See Fairview Farms, Inc. v. Reynolds Metals Co., 176 F.Supp. 178 (D. C.Or.1959); 1 F. Grad, Environmental Law 2–37 to –45 (1973).

10. Arvidson v. Reynolds Metals Co., 125 F.Supp. 481 (W.D.Wash.1954), aff'd 236 F.2d 224 (9th Cir. 1956), cert. denied 352 U.S. 968 (1957) (involving same plant as *Fairview Farms, Inc.*, supra, note 9); see Folmar v. Elliott Coal Mining Co., 441 Pa. 592, 272 A.2d 910, 1 ELR 20182 (1971).

11. Murphy, Environmental Law: New Legal Concepts in the Antipollution Fight, 36 Mo.L.Rev. 78, 84–85 (1971).

12. Ibid; see Ryan v. Emmetsburg, 232 Iowa 600, 4 N.W.2d 435 (1942) (gas); Casenote, 39 Tex.L.Rev. 244, 245 (1960) ("the overwhelming majority of courts have held that invasions by dust, soot and cinders, ashes and sawdust, noxious odors and fumes, and gases, if actionable at all, constitute a nuisance").

13. 221 Or. 86, 92, 342 P.2d 790, 793 (1959).

concussion of the air which, of course, is nothing more than the movement of molecules one against the other.

. . .

The view recognizing a trespassory invasion where there is no 'thing' which can be seen with the naked eye undoubtedly runs counter to the definition of trespass expressed in some quarters. [Citing the Restatement (First), Torts and Prosser]. It is quite possible that in an earlier day when science had not yet peered into the molecular and atomic world of small particles, the courts could not fit an invasion through unseen physical instrumentalities into the requirement that a trespass can result only from a *direct* invasion. But in this atomic age even the uneducated know the great and awful force contained in the atom and what it can do to a man's property if it is released. In fact, the now famous equation $E=MC^2$ has taught us that mass and energy are equivalents and that our concept of 'things' must be reframed. If these observations on science in relation to the law of trespass should appear theoretical and unreal in the abstract, they become very practical and real to the possessor of land when the unseen force cracks the foundation of his house. The force is just as real if it is chemical in nature and must be awakened by the intervention of another agency before it does harm.

Martin is quite right in hastening the demise of the "direct" and "tangible" limitations on the law of trespass. But any disappearance of these limits on the doctrine is likely to be accompanied by modifications of its strict liability advantages also. While parts per billion of fluorides or rays of light or magnetic invasions may work a trespass as effectively as flying rocks, it would seem that relief (particularly injunctive relief) should not follow without further inquiry into the limits of technology and prevailing land use patterns.

With regard to remedies, the trespass and nuisance cases are quite alike. *Martin* points up an important difference because the statutes of limitation for nuisances are generally shorter than those for trespasses.[14] The measure of damages for a permanent trespass, like a nuisance, is depreciation of market value.[15] Special damages have included awards for injury to dairy cows and loss of milk production,[16] harm to gladiolas, the expense of moving the business,[17] depreciated property values,[18] and other unspecified property damage.[19]

14. See Jurgensmeyer, Control of Air Pollution Through Assertion of Private Rights, 1967 Duke L.J. 1126.

15. Fairview Farms, Inc. v. Reynolds Metal Co., 176 F.Supp. 178 (1959).

16. Fairview Farms, Inc. v. Reynolds Metal Co., supra note 15.

17. Reynolds Metals Co. v. Lampert, 316 F.2d 272 (9th Cir. 1963).

18. McElwain v. Georgia-Pacific Corp., 245 Or. 247, 421 P.2d 957 (1966). For a discussion of special rules of damages in trespass cases where raw materials have been severed from the freehold, see Crofoot Lumber, Inc. v. Ford, 191 Cal.App.2d 238, 12 Cal. Rptr. 639 (1961) (logging carried out by trespasser).

19. Davis v. Georgia-Pacific Corp., 251 Or. 239, 445 P.2d 481 (1968).

Punitive damages are awarded for not doing "everything reasonably possible to eliminate or minimize the damage to adjoining properties." [20] Injunctions are governed by the same considerations as in nuisance cases: one decree in the Oregon aluminum plant litigation gave defendant a year to install adequate emission controls upon penalty of a shutdown.[21]

§ 2.14 Strict Liability for Abnormally Dangerous Activities

Another conscript in the doctrinal ranks of environmental conflict is the theory of strict liability for abnormally dangerous conditions and activities. The doctrine is simple and effective, requiring only proof that the condition or activity qualifies as "abnormally dangerous" and was the cause in fact of plaintiff's harm. Like the duty question in negligence law, the issue of whether conduct is "abnormally dangerous" for purposes of strict liability is a question of law for the court.

The seminal decision of Rylands v. Fletcher [1] is well known to every law student and deserves but a brief statement. Defendants, mill owners in coal mining country, constructed a reservoir upon their land. The water burst through the filled-up shaft of an abandoned coal mine and flowed along connecting passages into the adjoining mines of the plaintiff causing damage. Defendants had no knowledge of the latent defect in their soil and were thus free from fault. The case at the time was inappropriate for resolution as a trespass because the flooding was not direct and immediate; nor as a nuisance, as the term was then understood, since defendant's conduct was not offensive to the senses and the damage was non-recurring.

Liability was imposed on other grounds. Justice Blackburn, in the Exchequer Chamber, saw the issue in terms of the need to control the excesses of dangerous technologies: "We think that the true rule of law is that the person who for his own purposes brings on his land and collects and keeps there anything likely to do mischief if it escapes, must keep it at his peril, and if he does not do so, is prima facie answerable for all the damage which is the natural consequence of its escape." [2] In the House of Lords, Lord Cairns saw the dispute as a land use conflict, condemning defendant's reservoir as a "non-natural use" of the land as distinguished from activity "for which it might in the ordinary course of the enjoyment of land be used." [3]

---

20. McElwain v. Georgia-Pacific Corp., 245 Or. 247, 252, 421 P.2d 957, 960 (1966); see Davis v. Georgia-Pacific Corp., 251 Or. 239, 445 P.2d 481 (1968).

21. Renken v. Harvey Aluminum, Inc., 226 F.Supp. 169 (D.C.Or.1963).

1. Fletcher v. Rylands, 3 H. & C. 774, 159 Eng.Rep. 737 (1865), rev'd L.R. 1 Ex. 265 (1866), aff'd L.R. 3 H.L. 330 (1868).

2. L.R. 1 Ex. 279–80.

3. L.R. 3 H.L. at 338.

Sec. 2.14 ABNORMALLY DANGEROUS ACTIVITIES

Over the years, the opinions of Blackburn and Cairns and the concepts of the degree of danger and the place it occurs have been given equal prominence. These generalities serve to distinguish the concept not at all from nuisance law, which stresses the extent of the hurt and the location of the offense. Dean Prosser insists that the English cases affirm that strict liability is confined to things or activities that are "extraordinary," "exceptional," or "abnormal" and does not apply to the "usual and normal." [4] But "non-natural uses," according to the cases collected in the Prosser hornbook,[5] include many common activities which are simply high in risk: water collected in large quantities in hydraulic power mains; gas stored in quantity; and high-powered electricity transmitted under the streets. Indeed, it is said that "the storage in quantity of explosives or inflammable liquids, or blasting, or the accumulation of sewage, or the emission of creosote fumes, or pile driving which sets up excessive vibration, all have the same element of the unusual, excessive and bizarre, and have been considered 'non-natural' uses, leading to strict liability when they result in harm to another." [6] Another synthesizing principle might be that these are common commercial activities causing damage to others.

American cases follow the English pattern, with emphasis being placed on the risks created and the location of the activity. They include "water collected in quantity in a dangerous place, or allowed to percolate; explosives or inflammable liquids stored in quantity in the midst of a city; blasting; pile driving; crop dusting; the fumigation of part of a building with cyanide gas; drilling oil wells or operating refineries in thickly settled communities; an excavation letting in the sea; factories emitting smoke, dust or noxious gases in the midst of a town . . . ." [7]

Conditions and activities exempted from the reach of Rylands v. Fletcher generally are less likely to clash with prevailing land use patterns. They include: [8] a dam in the natural bed of a stream; agricultural spray in a farmhouse; coal mining operations regarded as usual and normal; and vibrations and other damage from ordinary building, earth moving, and railroad tunnel construction activities. An authority oft-mentioned is Turner v. Big Lake Oil Co.,[9] which refused to impose strict liability for the escape of salt water from ponds constructed and used by defendants in the operation of oil wells. The rationale of the court was that oil is big business in Texas, and "the

---

4. Law of Torts 506 (4th ed. 1971), quoting several cases.

5. The cases and descriptions are collected in id. at 506–07.

6. Id. at 507 (footnotes omitted).

7. Id. at 509–10 (footnotes omitted); see McLane v. Northwest Natural Gas Co., 255 Or. 324, 467 P.2d 635 (1970) (holding the surface storage of pressurized petroleum liquid gas to be abnormally dangerous activity).

8. Id. at 510–11, citing numerous cases (footnotes omitted).

9. 128 Tex. 155, 96 S.W.2d 221 (1936).

construction of basins or ponds to hold this saltwater is a necessary part of the oil business." [10]

While Texas may be zoned for oil, Delaware is zoned for chemicals. Fritz v. E. I. DuPont de Nemours & Co.,[11] declined to hold DuPont strictly liable to a railroad employee injured by chlorine fumes escaping from a chemical plant. While the court did not explicitly state that chemical manufacturing was protected by special rules of liability in Delaware, it did say:

> [I]t was not unlawful for DuPont to have on its premises chlorine gas, nor was its presence there unusual, and it cannot be said that the mere possession of chlorine gas by DuPont without more was dangerous per se in the light of recognized industrial use.[12]

Elsewhere, courts are not at all reluctant to impose strict liability for damage caused by the release of toxic chemicals.[13] The location of the activity may be decisive.

Not to be overlooked is that while many American jurisdictions may have rejected Rylands v. Fletcher by name, the same results are achieved under nuisance principles. A nuisance may be premised upon unintentional conduct otherwise actionable under principles controlling liability for abnormally dangerous activities or conditions. By this doctrinal route liability is imposed for "water collected in quantity in the wrong place or allowed to percolate; . . . oil wells or abnormal mining operations; the accumulation of sewage; concussion or vibration from a rock crusher; and in addition such things as smoke, dust, bad odors, noxious gases and the like from industrial enterprises . . . ." [14] The decision reflected in the Restatement (Second) of Torts to impose liability without fault in many circumstances of nuisance [15] hastens the coalescence of the two historical doctrines.

The Restatement of Torts stresses strict liability rules in terms strongly suggesting nuisance law. Section 520 of Tentative Draft No. 10 of the Restatement (Second) lists the factors to be considered in determining whether an activity is abnormally dangerous:

> (a) Whether the activity involves a high degree of risk of some harm to the person, land or chattels of others;
>
> (b) Whether the gravity of harm which may result from it is likely to be great;

---

10. 128 Tex. at 170, 96 S.W.2d at 226; see Bianchini v. Humble Pipe Line Co., 480 F.2d 251, 3 ELR 20385 (5th Cir. 1973) (applying Louisiana law) (refusing to impose strict liability for oil damage to oysters caused by non-negligent rupturing of pipeline).

11. 6 Terry (Del.) 427, 75 A.2d 256 (1950).

12. 6 Terry (Del.) at 437, 75 A.2d at 261.

13. Note 7, supra.

14. W. L. Prosser, supra note 4, at 512–13.

15. See § 2.3 below.

Sec. 2.14 ABNORMALLY DANGEROUS ACTIVITIES

(c) Whether the risk cannot be eliminated by the exercise of reasonable care;

(d) Whether the activity is not a matter of common usage;

(e) Whether the activity is inappropriate to the place where it is carried on; and

(f) The value of the activity to the community.

Clauses (a) to (e), Professor Katz points out,[16] "renew, amplify and refine the notions put forward by [Justice] Blackburn and Lord Cairns in an era of simpler technology, in a narrower context, and in a rougher form. Clause (f), however, introduces a different note, reminiscent of the balance of considerations in nuisance doctrine and the cost-benefit analyses of technology assessment."

None of the clauses, of course, offers any particularly useful resolving power. Read together, the message for the decision-maker is simply to decide whether it should dispense with an inquiry into fault for some types of high risk activity generally difficult to control. The most severe limitation on the Restatement's list is that for activity "not a matter of common usage." The sentiment behind the limitation is to prevent strict liability from carrying the day in areas of commonplace but still deadly activity, notably the driving of automobiles.[17]

The "common usage" limitation is of doubtful utility. The reference to a "non-natural use" in Rylands v. Fletcher was invoked to condemn conduct that in itself was not particularly unusual (namely, building a reservoir) but rather was being conducted in the wrong place. Second, it overstates the cases considerably to synthesize them as representing "the unusual, excessive or bizarre", unless air pollution, backed-up sewage, and construction activity is to be consigned to the outer reaches of abnormal. Third, the "common usage" limitation on liability is discriminatory by throwing the strict liability book at the little fellows who handle society's dirty work (like crop dusting, fumigating, and the disposal of hazardous wastes), while forgiving the bigger offenders who distribute their toxic substances in pursuit of occupations commonly undertaken.[18]

For these reasons, it is believed that courts should free themselves from the doctrinal straitjacket confining the potential of Rylands v. Fletcher to the bizarre or outlandish. The question in those cases is whether strict liability should be imposed upon particular high risk enterprises. That question should be answered by reference to such factors as who is better able to insure against the risk, allocate the costs, and reduce or warn against the dangers.[19] Justice

---

16. The Function of Tort Liability in Technology Assessment, 38 U.Cin.L. Rev. 587, 644 (1969).

17. Restatement, Torts § 520, comment e (1939).

18. Compare Fritz v. E. I. DuPont de Nemours & Co., 6 Terry (Del.) 427, 75 A.2d 256 (1950).

19. E. g., Calabresi, Some Thoughts on Risk Distribution and the Law of

Blackburn had the right idea when he suggested that operating a technology that gets out of hand usually is reason enough for imposing liability.

Recent case law generally has adhered to the unambitious contours prescribed for it in the Restatement. One reason for this is that extensions that might have been sought in the name of Rylands v. Fletcher have been rationalized as products liability cases under Section 402A of the Restatement, Second, Torts.[20] Typical of the modern *Rylands*-vintage cases is Spano v. Perini,[21] allowing recovery for damage suffered from blasting without proof of negligence and without proof of an actual physical invasion necessary to sustain a trespass. The reasoning of Chief Judge Fuld was, quite simply, that a person engaged in dangerous activity should bear its costs.

Strict liability for abnormally dangerous activities is of continuing significance in environmental litigation. Obviously, toxic pollutants and hazardous substances designated under the Federal Water Pollution Control Act[22] and hazardous air pollutants listed under the Clean Air Act[23] may be the product of activity that could be considered abnormally dangerous. The same can be said for other high risk activities not explicitly condemned by an administrative agency. Even if the "common usage" limitation is retained, strict liability could be imposed against the sources of rare and toxic pollutants (such as arsenic), albeit not against the common sources of sulfur dioxide. All editions and drafts of the Restatement have regarded the operation of the SST as an abnormally dangerous activity resulting in strict liability for ground injuries to persons or properties caused by sonic booms.[24] A case can be made that damages caused by oil spills, including the Santa Barbara mishap, should be compensated on a strict liability basis.[25]

Torts, 70 Yale L.J. 499 (1961); Michelman, Pollution as a Tort: A Non-Accidental Perspective on Calabresi's Costs, 80 Yale L.J. 647 (1971).

20. E. g., Chicago v. General Motors Corp., 467 F.2d 1262, 2 ELR 20636 (7th Cir. 1972); Hall v. E. I. DuPont de Nemours & Co., 345 F.Supp. 353 (E.D.N.Y.1972); Diamond v. General Motors Corp., 20 Cal.App.3d 374, 97 Cal.Rptr. 639, 2 ELR 20046 (1971). See also Carter, Michigan's PBB Incident: Chemical Mix-Up Leads to Disaster, 192 Science 240 (1976) (reporting the settlement of 335 claims for a total of $22.5 million growing out of massive damage to the Michigan farm economy by the mixing of a fire retardant into livestock feed).

21. 25 N.Y.2d 11, 302 N.Y.S.2d 527, 250 N.E.2d 31 (1969).

22. Sections 307, 311, 33 U.S.C.A. §§ 1317, 1321; see § 4.15 below; State v. Jersey Central Power & Light Co., 69 N.J. 102, 351 A.2d 337 (1976); Cities Service Co. v. State, 312 So.2d 799 (Fla.Dist.Ct.App.1975).

23. Section 112, 42 U.S.C.A. § 1857c–7; see § 3.11 below.

24. Restatement, Second, Torts § 520A & comments a–d (Tent. Draft No. 10, 1964); see United States v. Gravelle, 407 F.2d 964 (10th Cir. 1969).

25. Katz, supra note 16, at 645–55; see Union Oil Co. v. Oppen, 501 F.2d 558, 563 n. 3 (9th Cir. 1974) (leaving question open); Green v. General Petroleum Corp., 205 Cal. 328, 330, 270 P. 952, 953 (1928) (imposing strict liability "for injuries to [the plaintiffs'] property occasioned by the 'blowing-out' of an oil-well during drilling operations by defendant");

Obviously, legislation can resolve questions of strict liability quite decisively. The Price-Anderson Act both limits liability and imposes strict liability up to those limits for nuclear catastrophes.[26] Strict liability for damage from oil pollution has been imposed by several states in recent years.[27] The same is true of certain types of damages inflicted by pesticides.[28] Any venture into the field obviously deserves a review of statutory and administrative materials.

§ 2.15 Riparian Rights; Prior Appropriation

This is not the place nor the author for definitive utterances on water law.[1] A few of its prominent interfaces with what is known as environmental law nonetheless deserve mention.

Prevalent in the United States are two general doctrines for allocating rights among water users—the common law of riparian rights and the mostly statutory doctrine of prior appropriation. Although there is some overlap, the law of riparian rights holds sway in the eastern states where water supply historically was no problem, while the doctrine of prior appropriation is followed in the western states (e. g., Alaska, Arizona, Colorado, Idaho, Nevada, New Mexico, Utah, and Wyoming), which are traditionally afflicted by scarcity.

a. *Riparian Rights*

The law of riparian rights is concerned primarily with the rights of riparian proprietors with respect to the use of water in watercourses and lakes; in many respects, it is a wet version of the law of nuisance. A "watercourse" is to be understood as a stream of water and its channel, both of natural origin, where the water flows constantly or recurrently on the surface of the earth in a reasonably definite course.[2] A "lake" comprehends a reasonably permanent body of water substantially at rest in a depression of the surface of the earth.[3] A "riparian proprietor" includes a person in possession of

---

cf. United States v. General Motors Corp., 403 F.Supp. 1151 (D.Conn.1975).

26. Pub.L. No. 85–256, § 4, 71 Stat. 576 (1957), 42 U.S.C.A. § 2210, as amended ($500,000,000 maximum aggregate liability for single incident).

27. The Florida statute was sustained in Askew v. American Waterways Operators, 411 U.S. 325, 93 S.Ct. 1590, 36 L.Ed.2d 280 (1973); see Florida Oil Spill Prevention and Pollution Control Act, Fla.Stat.Ann. § 376.011 et seq.; § 4.19 below. See also Lansco v. Dep't of Environmental Protection, 138 N.J.Super. 275, 350 A. 2d 520 (1975) (holding insurer liable for clean-up costs arising out of an oil spill).

28. E. g., 7 U.S.C.A. §§ 135(b), (n), (t) (bees); id. § 450 (dairy products); id. § 1444a(d) (cotton).

1. The well known authorities include C. J. Meyers & A. D. Tarlock, Water Resource Management: A Casebook in Law and Public Policy (1971), J. Sax, Water Law, Planning and Policy (1968); F. J. Trelease, Water Law: Resource Use and Environmental Protection (2d ed. 1974); Davis, Theories of Water Pollution Litigation, 1971 Wis.L.Rev. 738. The leading text is Waters & Water Rights (R. E. Clark ed. 1967).

2. Restatement of Torts § 841 (1939).

3. Id. § 842.

riparian land or who owns an estate in it.[4] "Riparian land" is a parcel of land which includes a part of the bed of a watercourse or lake or which borders upon a public watercourse or lake.[5]

The common law of riparian rights is further subdivided into two fundamentally different theories. There is, in the first place, the natural flow theory adopted by the English courts and some American jurisdictions. This is a "rather absolutist concept," which holds that all riparian owners "are entitled to have the stream flow past their land as it was wont to do in the state of nature."[6] The second category is the reasonable use theory under which each riparian proprietor is protected only from unreasonable uses which cause harm to his own reasonable use of the water. There is obviously greater latitude under the reasonable use theory to promote the use and development of water resources.

The Restatement (Second) of Torts, under the guidance of water authority Frank J. Trelease, reflects a fundamental decision to divorce water pollution cases[7] from the common law of riparian rights. This is accomplished by declaring that the pollution of water which creates a nuisance to another is not the exercise of a riparian right.[8] The consequence is that water pollution disputes between riparian owners are to be analyzed not under a theory of riparian rights but under the familiar doctrines of nuisance, trespass, or strict liability for abnormally dangerous activities. An example would be a coal company owning land riparian to a stream withdrawing water, using it, and returning it to the stream in a polluted condition.[9] To the extent the use of the water deprives a downstream riparian owner of his supply, it is a riparian rights case; but to the extent it pollutes the water, the activity is not a riparian use and will be analyzed under a theory of nuisance or strict liability. The distinction is that

---

4. Id. § 844.

5. Id. § 843.

6. J. Sax, supra note 1. Absolutism has received a revival in recent times with the discovery of the flat prohibitions of the Rivers and Harbors Act of 1899 and the no discharge goal of the Federal Water Pollution Control Act Amendments of 1972. See §§ 4.5, 4.11 below.

7. For this purpose water pollution is to be understood as meaning the impregnation of waters with refuse or noxious substances. Restatement of Torts § 832, comment (1939).

8. Restatement, Second, Torts § 849 (Tent.Draft No. 17, 1971) reads:

(1) An interference with the use of water caused by an act or conduct which is not itself a use of water but which affects its quality or quantity in some other manner may subject the actor to liability if the act or conduct

(a) constitutes a nuisance

(b) constitutes a trespass, or

(c) is negligent, reckless or abnormally dangerous with respect to use.

(2) The pollution of water by a riparian proprietor which creates a nuisance by causing harm to another person's interest in land or water is not the exercise of a riparian right.

9. Id. at 63, illustration 2.

between a water quality and water quantity controversy, although more than occasionally they are one and the same.[10]

There is much to be said for the Restatement's analysis.[11] In the first place, the western states, which give no recognition to riparian uses, often treat pollution as a nuisance.[12] Moreover, while in riparian jurisdictions pollution may be treated under a riparian theory,[13] so too has it been analyzed regularly as a nuisance.[14] At least one leading riparian law jurisdiction, Wisconsin, consistently treats all pollution cases as nuisance cases.[15] Sometimes a court uses both theories to support the result.[16] Kansas has invented a new tort, "pollution," which is indistinguishable from nuisance.[17]

Certainly in the vast majority of cases the same set of facts yield the same result whether analyzed under a riparian rights or a nuisance theory. The riparian rights pollution cases discuss the familiar nuisance considerations of who was there first, the state of the art, and the degree of injury.[18] They also tend to blur the dif-

10. Many pollution control techniques are consumptive—for example, evaporation by a senior irrigation appropriator in order to reduce salinity. See D. K. Hartley & V. S. Price, Problems of Agricultural Users In Implementing P.L. 92–500 (1975) (prepared for the National Commission on Water Quality). Similarly, water uses are often consumptive and polluting.

11. This paragraph in text and accompanying footnotes adheres closely to the discussion in Restatement, Second, Torts 67–68 (Tent.Draft No. 17, 1971).

12. Wilmore v. Chaino Mines, Inc., 96 Colo. 319, 44 P.2d 1024 (1934); Northpoint Irrigation Co. v. Utah & Salt Lake Canal Co., 16 Utah 246, 52 P. 168 (1898). Note, however, that prior appropriation right jurisdictions have special rules for pollution. See 13 R. E. Clark, supra note 1, at 212 et seq.; Game & Fish Comm'n v. Farmer's Irrigation Co., 162 Colo. 301, 426 P.2d 562 (1967).

13. See Davis, supra note 1.

14. Nolan v. New Britain, 69 Conn. 668, 38 A. 703 (1867); Hodges v. Pine-Product Co., 135 Ga. 134, 68 S.E. 1107 (1910); West Muncie Strawboard Co. v. Slack, 164 Ind. 21, 72 N.E. 879 (1904); Newton v. Grundy Center, 246 Iowa 916, 70 N.W.2d 162 (1955); Livezey v. Bel Air, 174 Md. 568, 199 A. 838 (1938); Weeks-Thorn Paper Co. v. Glenside Woolen Mills, 64 Misc. 305, 118 N.Y.S. 1027 (Sup.Ct.), aff'd 204 N.Y. 536, 97 N.E. 1118 (1909); Pennsylvania R. R. v. Sagamore Coal Co., 281 Pa. 233, 126 A. 386 (1924); Shoffner v. Sutherland, 111 Va. 298, 68 S.E. 996 (1910); American Cyanamid Co. v. Sparto, 267 F.2d 425 (5th Cir. 1959); Indianapolis Water Co. v. American Strawboard Co., 53 F. 970 (D.Ind.1893).

15. Thomas v. Clear Lake, 270 Wis. 630, 72 N.W.2d 541 (1955); Tiede v. Schneidt, 105 Wis. 470, 81 N.W. 826 (1900); Middlestadt v. Waupaca Starch & Potato Co., 93 Wis. 1, 66 N.W. 713 (1896).

16. Kennebunk, Kennebunkport and Wells Water Dist. v. Maine Turnpike Authority, 147 Me. 149, 84 A.2d 433 (1951).

17. Atkinson v. Herington Cattle Co., 200 Kan. 298, 436 P.2d 816 (1968); Rusch v. Phillips Petroleum Co., 163 Kan. 11, 180 P.2d 270 (1947).

18. E. g., Sandusky Portland Cement Co. v. Dixon Pure Ice Co., 221 F. 200, 204 (7th Cir. 1915) (court grants injunction although noting that "to restrain defendant from emptying its heated water into Rock river will result in great hardship and expense"); Westville v. Whitney Home Bldrs., 40 N.J.Super. 62, 84, 122 A.2d 233, 244 (1956) (refusing injunction on com-

ferences between the natural flow and reasonable use theories so natural flow language may appear in a decision elsewhere reflecting reasonable use qualifications.[19] In all these cases it can fairly be said that what is unreasonable for purposes of nuisance law is unreasonable for purposes of the law of riparian rights.

But there are some respects in which a riparian rights theory affords greater leverage against a polluter than the law of nuisance: those jurisdictions taking seriously their natural flow preferences, for example, can invoke the doctrine to approve relief where there has been virtually no damage. The natural flow cases make clear that the riparian's right to the stream in its natural purity is not dependent on whether the downstream plaintiff is making use of the stream's water [20] or whether defendant is diverting enough water to affect adversely plaintiff's use.[21] Under a nuisance theory these injuries probably would be deemed insubstantial.

In addition, the degree of control suggested by the natural flow theory is essentially "clean water in, clean water out." [22] Reference to the state of the art and the costs of control thus are not as pronounced as they would be under a nuisance theory. The natural flow theory also may lift the burden of proving technological feasibility of controls from those claiming injury or the possibility of injury. While the natural flow theory is said to be in retreat,[23] there is certainly a touch of absolutism left in a nation that sets as a legislative goal for 1985 the elimination of the discharge of all pollutants into the water.[24] The natural flow theory represents absolutism in the common law of water pollution control.

Apart from water pollution, the law of riparian rights retains considerable significance in other water use and allocation disputes. The Restatement (Second) of Torts comes down on the side of a rule subjecting a riparian proprietor to liability "for making an unreasonable use of the water of a watercourse or lake which causes harm to another riparian proprietor's reasonable use of water or to his land." [25] Factors pertinent to the decision on reasonableness include the purpose of the respective uses, the suitability of the uses to the water-

bined grounds that defendant's sewage treatment plant was high in efficiency and injury to plaintiffs was only psychological). See text accompanying notes 27–34, infra.

19. R. E. Clark, supra note 1, § 211.1 (B), at 56 n. 39.

20. Mann v. Willey, 64 N.Y.S. 589 (App.Div.1900), aff'd 168 N.Y. 664, 61 N.E. 1131 (1901); cf. § 2.13 above (discussing the law of trespass).

21. Anaheim Union Water Co. v. Fuller, 150 Cal. 327, 88 P. 978 (1907) (enjoining diversion by upstream nonriparians).

22. Cf. §§ 3.11, 4.15 below (discussing no discharge policies regarding hazardous air and water pollutants).

23. F. Trelease, Cases and Materials on Water Law: Resource Use and Environmental Protection 269 (1974).

24. Federal Water Pollution Control Act Amendments of 1972, § 101(a), 33 U.S.C.A. § 1251(a).

25. § 850A (Tent.Draft No. 17, 1971).

course or lake, the economic and social value of the competing uses, the practicability of avoiding the harm by adjusting methods or quantity of uses of the respective proprietors, the protection of existing capital investments in land, and the burden of requiring the user causing harm to bear the loss.[26] This language of use accommodation and technological adjustment strongly echoes the law of nuisance.

Because riparian law treats the right to use water as an interest in real property, it reflects the same remedial compromises observed in the land use nuisance cases (damages, land use accommodations such as shutdowns, technological and operational adjustments). There is a similar emphasis on the extent of the hurt, and a tendency to deny relief where damages are insubstantial[27] or grant it readily where the loss is heavy,[28] particularly if wilfully done. Courts in riparian cases will inquire into who was there first[29] and the character of the uses on the watercourse.[30] They look closely at the state

26. Id. § 850.

27. Bollinger v. Henry, 375 S.W.2d 161 (Mo.1964) (refusing injunction because damages to plaintiff not substantial); Restatement, Second, Torts 114 (Tent. Draft No. 17, 1971) (discussing several cases upholding the reasonableness of uses not inflicting substantial economic harm on plaintiffs.) Contra, note 20, supra (applying the natural flow theory).

28. Collens v. New Canaan Water Co., 155 Conn. 477, 234 A.3d 825 (1967); Bauerle v. Board of County Road Commissioners, 388 Mich. 520, 201 N.W.2d 799, 3 ELR 20081 (1972).

29. Strobel v. Kerr Salt Co., 164 N.Y. 303, 321, 58 N.E. 142, 147 (1900) ("It is also material, sometimes, to ascertain which party first erected his works and began to appropriate the water"); see Restatement, Second, Torts 115–17, comment (Tent.Draft No. 17, 1971) (discussing several cases stressing significance of priority of use).

30. Thompson v. Enz, 385 Mich. 103, 106, 188 N.W.2d 579, 580 (1971) (emphasizing that defendants got approval from all governmental agencies and "proceeded to invest so much in th[e] project [a lakesite housing development involving construction of canals] prior to commencement of this declaratory action . . . as to render it inequitable now to forbid completion"); Botton v. State, 69 Wash.2d 751, 420 P.2d 352 (1966) (unreasonable use for one riparian owner, the state, to authorize uses by the public interfering with rights of other riparian owners); Bach v. Sarich, 74 Wash.2d 575, 579, 445 P.2d 648, 651 (1968) (apartment building extending 180 feet into a 19-acre lake held not a riparian use (much less a reasonable one) since it was not "intimately associated with the water"). See Johnson & Morry, Filling and Building on Small Lakes—Time for Judicial and Legislative Controls, 45 Wash.L.Rev. 27 (1970). The Restatement, Second, Torts § 855 (Tent.Draft No. 17, 1971) takes the position that the reasonableness of a use of water by a riparian proprietor is not affected by the classification of the use as riparian or non-riparian (that is, whether or not the use is made on or in connection with the riparian land). There is law to the contrary, much of it within the natural flow jurisdictions. See, e. g., Stratton v. Mt. Hermon Boys' School, 216 Mass. 83, 103 N.E. 87 (1913) (holding that a diversion out of the watershed is per se unreasonable). The principal argument for abolishing the riparian use limitation is that growth and development is unduly restricted by it. See Ziegler, Water Use Under Common Law Doctrines, in Water Resources and the Law 49, 70–72 (1958). An environmental argument in rebuttal is that indulging a presumption that water should be used close to its source is a reliable hedge against over-exploitation and waste.

of the art to prevent wasting the resource [31] and to determine whether technological or operational modifications might accommodate better the rights of the parties.[32] They are inclined to require large defendants to pay for damages inflicted even if a balancing of the equities does not justify injunctive relief.[33] And they must be alert, no less than in nuisance cases, to the impact of legislation or administrative regulation upon the rights at issue.[34] To mention but one example, an industry discharging its wastes into a municipal sewer system in violation of regulations may be liable per se to riparians ultimately injured by the effluent.[35]

b. *Prior Appropriation*

Turning to the prior appropriation jurisdictions, the general rule is that one who first appropriates water and puts it to beneficial use acquires a vested right to continued diversion and use of that water against all claimants junior to him in point of time; "first in time, first in right" is the shorthand formula. This doctrine for a long time has posed two substantial barriers to conservation or preservation values. The first is that some uses for "mere personal pleasure" were held unreasonable unlike those made for commerce and profit.[36] This concept now has been rather thoroughly exploded so that the notion of a "beneficial use" for which an appropriation can be made generally is understood to embrace aesthetic, recreational, preservational, and pollution control purposes.[37]

31. Warner Valley Stock Co. v. Lynch, 215 Or. 523, 336 P.2d 884 (1959) (forbidding wasteful and inefficient method of diversion); cf. Colorado Spring v. Bender, 148 Colo. 458, 366 P.2d 552 (1961) (suggesting that diversion of underground aquifer by senior appropriator must be more efficient albeit not beyond his economic reach).

32. Rancho Santa Margarita v. Vail, 11 Cal.2d 501, 558–59, 81 P.2d 533, 562 (1938) ("in considering whether an injunction should be granted . . ., it is the duty of the trial court to ascertain whether there is a physical solution of the problem that will avoid waste" and protect the rights of the parties).

33. Furrer v. Talent Irrigation Dist., 466 P.2d 605, 613 (Or.1970) ("the courts have established the principle that if the plaintiff's land is harmed by the conduct of the defendant, the latter cannot escape compensating the plaintiff for the harm simply by showing that the defendant's use had a greater social value than the plaintiff's").

34. See Beuscher, Appropriation Water Law Elements in Riparian Doctrine States, 10 Buffalo L.Rev. 448 (1961). The Restatement, Second, Torts § 857 (3) (Tent.Draft No. 17, 1971) states that a non-riparian exercising a right to use public or private water created by governmental authority, permit, or license is not subject to liability for the use of a watercourse or lake which will interfere with or prevent the initiation of a new use of the water by a riparian proprietor.

35. Springer v. Joseph Schlitz Brewing Co., 510 F.2d 468 (4th Cir. 1975); cf. Ratzlaff v. Franz Foods, 250 Ark. 1003, 468 S.W.2d 239 (1971), 38 Mo. L.Rev. 161 (1973) (nuisance theory).

36. Restatement, Second, Torts, § 95 (Tent.Draft No. 17, 1971).

37. Wash.Rev.Code Ann. § 90.54.020 (1): "use of water for domestic, stock watering, industrial, commercial, ag-

Sec. 2.15   RIPARIAN RIGHTS   169

The second barrier, which is more serious, requires an actual diversion of the water in order to effectuate a valid appropriation. Thus, even assuming the use of water for fish propagation purposes is a "beneficial use," the "appropriation" requirement might not be fulfilled unless the water is diverted to a fish hatchery for the benefit of artificial stock instead of being maintained in the natural stream to protect the native stock.[38] There has been an administrative decision holding that no impedance of flow or diversion is necessary for an appropriation to be completed,[39] and some limited legislative activity.[40] It remains to be seen whether the prior appropriation jurisdictions can be persuaded to abandon the assumption that the only legally protected uses of water are those repudiating the laws of nature.

The diversion requirement illustrates the bias built into the appropriation system in favor of development and consumption, even wasteful consumption (because future claims are based on past withdrawals).[41] The biases of riparian rights law, of course, are the other way: the doctrine has been used "to claim the right to stop others

ricultural, irrigation, hydroelectric power production, mining, fish and wildlife maintenance and enhancement, recreational, and thermal power production purposes, and preservation of environmental and aesthetic values, and all other uses compatible with the enjoyment of the public waters of the state, are declared to be beneficial." Pertinent cases and statutes are discussed in Hutchins, Selected Problems in the Law of Water Rights in the West 314–16 (1942).

38. State ex rel. Reynolds v. Miranda, 83 N.M. 443, 493 P.2d 409 (1972); see Colorado River Water Conservation Dist. v. Rocky Mountain Power Co., 158 Colo. 331, 406 P.2d 798 (1965). The Colorado legislature in 1973 overruled *Colorado River Water Conservation District* by amending Colo.Rev. Stat. § 148–21–3(6). This provision formerly defined an appropriation as "the diversion of a certain portion of the waters of the state and the application of the same to a beneficial use." The section now reads: "Appropriation means the application of a certain portion of the waters of the State to a beneficial use." Professor Trelease acknowledges that other portions of the Colorado statute show that the new law is designed to permit the use of the appropriation technique to preserve and enhance recreational and environmental values but questions "whether an appropriation without a diversion is a suitable vehicle for this purpose." Supra note 23, at 42. To this author it seems eminently suitable.

39. In re Donald E. Bevan v. State, Wash. Dep't of Ecology, Pollution Control Hearings Bd. No. 48 (1972) (allowing a faculty member of the College of Fisheries to appropriate without diversion to accomplish his research objectives which involved introducing fish not native to the creek for spawning purposes).

40. In 1973 Colorado broadened the statutory definition of "beneficial use" to include appropriations by the state of such minimum flows between specific points on natural streams and lakes "as are required to preserve the natural environment to a reasonable degree." Colo.Rev.Stat. § 148–121–3 (7). The law is implemented by granting the Colorado Conservation Board the power to appropriate the minimum flow. See also Richie, Some Reflections on Environmental Considerations in Water Rights Administration, 2 Ecology L.Q. 695 (1972).

41. For an economic analysis of both the prior appropriation and riparian rights systems, see Gaffney, Economic Aspects of Water Resource Policy, 28 Am.J.Econ. & Sociology 131 (1969).

from developing water which the riparian was not using." [42] Indeed, the natural flow theory is radically anti-developmental in outlook; it puts in issue literally every use that might adversely affect downstream quantity and quality. The riparian rights doctrine, by gravitating towards the reasonable use theory, has moved to accommodate development. The question remains whether prior appropriation theories will bend to the needs of the environment. There is certainly scant justification for waste in a land of scarcity (i. e., the western states).

Professors Meyers and Tarlock explain [43] that most of the western prior appropriation pollution cases have been conflicts between junior upstream miners and senior downstream farmers. The rule is that "while a proper use of the stream for mining purposes necessarily contaminates it to some extent, such contamination or deterioration of the quality of the water cannot be carried to such a degree as to inflict substantial injury upon another user of the waters of [the] stream." [44] Although there is some language affirming that a prior appropriator "is entitled to have the water . . . in its natural state of purity," [45] in fact as between a senior appropriator and a junior appropriator who pollutes the stream, "the standard seems to be one of reasonable use." [46] This is the standard of nuisance law.

Where the senior appropriator pollutes to the detriment of the junior appropriator, there is said to be no remedy, on the rationale that the senior could have destroyed the junior in any event by taking all the water. There is a suggestion in one case [47] that the senior has the duty to preserve the quality of the water if he can do so at slight expense and convenience. These wasteful aspects of prior appropriation law must be corrected, if at all, by other private remedies (such as nuisance law) or by public regulation.

There is a common bond between the common law of land use and water use. There is no reason for the doctrines of nuisance and riparian rights to coexist, mutually oblivious of the policies that influence both.

§ 2.16 Public Trust Doctrine

The public trust doctrine is a collection of common law principles [1] serving a function for the states comparable to what the close

42. Id. at 137.

43. Selected Legal and Economic Aspects of Environmental Protection 82 (1971).

44. Ravndal v. Northfolk Placers, 60 Idaho 338, 91 P.2d 368, 371 (1939).

45. Wright v. Best, 19 Cal.2d 368, 378, 121 P.2d 702, 709 (1942).

46. C. Meyers & D. Tarlock, supra note 43, at 82.

47. Suffolk Gold Co. v. San Miguel Consol. Mining Co., 9 Colo.App. 407, 48 P. 828 (1897), appeal dismissed 24 Colo. 468, 52 P. 1027 (1898).

1. Constitutional and statutory provisions have played an important role, historically and contemporaneously.

scrutiny doctrine [2] and the National Environmental Policy Act [3] have meant for federal judicial review of agency actions affecting the environment. There are differences, of course, but the striking similarities in function between these state and federal legal theories that are radically remote in origin offer a strong synthesis of contemporary environmental law. This section (1) outlines the scope of the public trust doctrine, then emphasizes its (2) procedural and (3) substantive functions, and some of the more important (4) legislative and constitutional modifications. Any attempt at a shorthand statement of the principles of public trust must come with a disclaimer: the constitutional and legislative variations among the states approach the infinite, and many states fulfill some of the identical policy functions under different doctrinal rubrics—prescriptive rights,[4] custom,[5] dedication [6] or other property theory.[7]

a. *Scope of the Doctrine*

Public trust law recognizes that some types of natural resources are held in trust by government for the benefit of the public.[8] These

See text accompanying notes 89–127, infra.

2. § 1.5 above.

3. Ch. 7 below.

4. E. g., Daytona Beach v. Tona-Rama, Inc., 271 So.2d 765 (Fla.Ct.App.1972), vacated 294 So.2d 73 (Fla.1974) (public had acquired a prescriptive easement in beach property on which defendant desired to construct an observation tower).

5. Daytona Beach v. Tona-Rama, Inc., 271 So.2d 765 (Fla.Ct.App.1972), vacated 294 So.2d 73 (Fla.1974) (alternative holding); State ex rel. Thorton v. Hay, 254 Or. 584, 462 P.2d 671 (1969).

6. Gion v. Santa Cruz, 2 Cal.3d 29, 84 Cal.Rptr. 162, 465 P.2d 50 (1970); Gewirtz v. Long Beach, 69 Misc.2d 763, 330 N.Y.S.2d 495, 2 ELR 20523 (Sup.Ct.1972), aff'd 45 A.D.2d 841, 358 N.Y.S.2d 957 (1974); Seaway Co. v. Attorney General, 375 S.W.2d 923 (Tex.Civ.App.1964); see Berger, Nice Guys Finish Last, 8 Calif.W.L.Rev. 75 (1971).

7. E. g., Southern Idaho Fish & Game Ass'n v. Picabo Livestock Co., 2 ELR 20472 (Idaho Dist.Ct.1972) (landowner cannot prevent members of the public from using a fishing stream) (interpreting a patent subject to certain vested rights).

8. 1 Waters & Water Rights §§ 36.3, 36.4 (Clark ed. 1967); Sax, The Public Trust Doctrine in Natural Resource Law: Effective Judicial Intervention, 68 Mich.L.Rev. 471 (1970) (the leading analysis). See also Cohen, The Constitution, the Public Trust Doctrine, and the Environment, 1970 Utah L. Rev. 388 (1970); Jaffee, The Public Trust Doctrine Is Alive and Kicking in New Jersey Tidalwaters: Neptune City v. Avon-by-the-Sea—A Case of Happy Atavism? 14 Nat.Res.J. 309 (1974); Nanda & Ris, The Public Trust Doctrine: A Viable Approach to International Environmental Protection, 5 Ecology L.Q. 291 (1976); Olson, The Public Trust Doctrine: Procedural and Substantive Limitations on the Governmental Reallocation of Natural Resources in Michigan, 1975 Detroit Coll.L.Rev. 161 (1975); Yannacone, Agricultural Lands, Fertile Soils, Popular Sovereignty, the Trust Doctrine, Environmental Impact Assessment and the Natural Law, 51 N.Dak. L.Rev. 616 (1975); Comment, The Mississippi Public Trust Doctrine: Public and Private Rights in the Coastal Zone, 46 Miss.L.J. 84 (1975); Comment, California Beach Access: The Mexican Law and the Public Trust, 2 Ecology L.Q. 571 (1972); Comment, The Pennsylvania Public Trust Doctrine: Its Use as a Re-

resources are protected by the trust against unfair dealing and dissipation, which is classical trust language suggesting the necessity for procedural correctness and substantive care. Where a resource is held available for the free use of the general public, Professor Sax has written, "a court will look with considerable skepticism upon any governmental conduct which is calculated either to reallocate the resource to more restrictive uses or to subject public uses to the self-interest of private parties." [9] The public trust doctrine demands fair procedures, decisions that are justified, and results that are consistent with protection and perpetuation of the resource. The recurring questions call for an identification of the resources impressed with the trust and the public uses encumbering them. That is to say, the first steps in analysis require an understanding of what public resources are committed perpetually to what public uses.

Historically, the public trust doctrine applies to the area "below the low water mark on the margin of the sea and the great lakes, the waters over those lands, and the waters within rivers and streams of any consequence." [10] It extends to the "foreshore," which is the land lying between the ordinary high water and low water marks over which the tide ebbs and flows.[11] The foreshore should be understood as including not only the shore and bed of the sea but also that of bays, estuaries, navigable rivers, channels, and creeks.[12] Resources protected by the public trust include parklands,[13] small inland lakes,[14]

straint on Government, 13 Duquesne L.Rev. 551 (1975); Comment, "Public Trust" as a Constitutional Provision in Montana, 33 Mont.L.Rev. 175 (1972); Note, California's Tidelands Trust for Modifiable Public Purposes, 6 Loyola L.A.L.Rev. 485 (1973); Note State Citizen Rights Respecting Greatwater Resource Allocation: From Rome to New Jersey, 25 Rutgers L.Rev. 571 (1971); Note, The Public Trust Doctrine in Tidal Areas: A Sometimes Submerged Traditional Doctrine, 79 Yale L.J. 762 (1970) (containing a useful historical summary); Casenote, Expanding the Definition of Public Trust Uses, 51 N.C.L. Rev. 316 (1972).

9. Sax, supra note 8, at 490. Compare the dimensions of the close scrutiny doctrine of judicial review (§ 1.5 above) and the basic purposes of the National Environmental Policy Act (§ 7.1 below).

10. Sax, supra note 8, at 556.

11. Note, The Public Trust in Tidal Areas: A Sometimes Submerged Traditional Doctrine, 79 Yale L.J. 762 n. 1 (1970); see County of Hawaii v. Sotomura, 517 P.2d 57 (Hawaii 1973) (land held in trust fixed by vegetation line which may be modified by wave action).

12. See George, The Public Trust Doctrine: Historical Origins and Present Scope, at 2 (unpublished paper, completed for seminar in environmental law, Georgetown U. Law Center, May 1975).

13. E. g., Gould v. Greylock Reservation Comm'n, 350 Mass. 410, 215 N.E. 2d 114 (1966); Stephenson v. Monroe, 43 A.D.2d 897, 351 N.Y.S.2d 232, 4 ELR 20364 (1974) (per curiam); see Young v. Public Bldg. Comm'n, 5 Ill.App.3d 892, 284 N.E.2d 485 (1972) (pointing out that the public trust in parks, recreational areas and historical sites is statutory in origin).

14. But see Pigorsh v. Fahner, 386 Mich. 508, 194 N.W.2d 343, 2 ELR 20279 (1972) (navigable lake comprising 70 acres; court allows private

marshland,[15] and wildlife,[16] but not non-navigable subterranean groundwaters.[17] The scope of the trust is extended by statute in Michigan authorizing legal actions "for the protection of the air, water and other natural resources and the public trust therein from pollution, impairment or destruction," [18] and by constitutional amendment in Pennsylvania declaring the Commonwealth a trustee of the public natural resources and recognizing the people's right "to clean air, pure water, and to the preservation of the natural, scenic, historic and aesthetic values of the environment." [19]

It has been said that state and federal governments serve as "public guardian[s] of those valuable natural resources which are not capable of self-regeneration and for which substitutes can not be made by man." [20] Perhaps trust protection requires identification of a resource whose natural and primary uses are public in nature and for which there is a public need.[21] It takes no great inferential leap to conclude that public trust protection ought to be extended to all air, water, and land resources, the preservation of which is important to society.[22] Yet, an accurate description of where the courts have gone confines the public trust doctrine to navigable waters, the foreshore and the parklands. For the most part, public nuisance [23] is the inland version of the public trust doctrine although, not surprisingly, history records public trust theory being applied in the

owner to exclude public from lake access).

15. Freeborn v. Bryson, 297 Minn. 218, 210 N.W.2d 290, 4 ELR 20215 (1973) (interpreting Minnesota Environmental Rights Act) (marshland and open water ponds part of a larger slough continuing for several miles to a lake).

16. Geer v. Connecticut, 161 U.S. 519, 16 S.Ct. 660, 40 L.Ed. 793 (1896); Dep't of Environmental Protection v. Jersey Central Power & Light Co., 133 N.J.Super. 375, 336 A.2d 750, 5 ELR 20370 (1975), rev'd on other grounds 69 N.J. 102, 351 A.2d 337 6 ELR 20352 (1976); State v. Bowling Green, 38 Ohio St.2d 281, 313 N.E.2d 409, 4 ELR 20730 (1974); Etling, Who Owns the Wildlife? 3 Environmental L. 23 (1973).

17. Eau Claire v. Dep't of Natural Resources, 2 ELR 20512 (Wis.Cir.Ct. 1972).

18. Mich.Comp.Laws Ann. § 691–1202 (1).

19. Pa.Const. art. 1, § 27.

20. Cohen, supra note 8, at 388.

21. Cf. Bonelli v. Arizona, 414 U.S. 313, 94 S.Ct. 517, 38 L.Ed.2d 526 (1974) (holding that lands resurfacing as a result of a federal channelization project were owned not by the state but by the riparian holder).

22. Sax, supra note 8, at 556–57 (the protection applied in conventional trust cases "would be equally applicable and equally appropriate in controversies involving air pollution, the dissemination of pesticides, the location of right of way for utilities, and strip mining or wetland filling on private lands in a state where governmental permits are required").

23. § 2.2 above.

classical nuisance context,[24] nuisance theory being applied in the classical public trust context,[25] and both theories being applied together.[26]

The public uses for which the trust is administered, like the public resources to which it extends, are loosely and flexibly defined. The foundations of contemporary public trust law generally are ascribed to Illinois Central R. R. v. Illinois,[27] where Mr. Justice Field wrote that the state holds title to the lands under the navigable waters of Lake Michigan, and this title is "held in trust for the people of the state that they may enjoy the navigation of the waters, carry on commerce over them, and have liberty of fishing therein, freed from the obstruction or interference of private parties." [28] This triumvirate of public rights (in navigation, commerce, and fishing) is by no means static and includes rights to use and enjoy the public water for a wide variety of recreational purposes. "[I]n this latter half of the twentieth century," Justice Hall has written for the New Jersey Supreme Court, it is not difficult to find that "the public rights in tidal lands are not limited to the ancient prerogatives of navigation and fishing, but extend as well to recreational uses, including bathing, swimming and other shore activities." [29] The Supreme Court of California, too, has gone out of its way to observe that in "administering the trust the state is not burdened with an outmoded classification favoring one mode of utilization over another . . . . There is a growing public recognition that one of the most important public uses of the tidelands—a use encompassed within the tidelands trust—is the pre-

---

24. E. g., Stephenson v. Monroe, 43 A.D.2d 897, 351 N.Y.S.2d 232, 4 ELR 20364 (1974) (establishment of sanitary landfill in a public park); State v. Bowling Green, 38 Ohio St. 2d 281, 313 N.E.2d 409, 4 ELR 20730 (1974) (fish kill occasioned by operation of a sewage treatment plant); see Sax & Conner, Michigan's Environmental Protection Act of 1970: A Progress Report, 70 Mich.L.Rev. 1002, 1027–30, 1035–41 (1972) (describing cases brought under the Michigan statute that could have been adjudicated as common law nuisance cases).

25. E. g., Potomac River Ass'n, Inc. v. Lundeberg Maryland Seamanship School, Inc., 5 ELR 20388 (D.C.Md. 1975) (suit for damages for harm to oyster beds caused by dredge and fill operations conducted under a Corps of Engineers permit; defendant liable in nuisance only for damages caused by activities outside the scope of the Corps permit).

26. E. g., Maryland Dep't of Natural Resources v. Amerada Hess Corp., 350 F.Supp. 1060, 2 ELR 20606 (D.C. Md.1972) (suit for damages from oil spill allowed under public trust theory but disallowed under public nuisance theory solely because of non-recurring nature of the incident); Obrecht v. National Gypsum Co., 361 Mich. 399, 105 N.W.2d 143 (1960) (transfer of portions of the bed of Lake Huron to a private company for construction of a loading dock attacked on public trust grounds; erection of loading dock itself attacked as a public nuisance); Grosse Isle v. Dunbar & Sullivan Dredging Co., 15 Mich.App. 556, 167 N.W.2d 311 (1969) (dredging activities attacked by private parties on nuisance and zoning grounds, and by the state on public trust grounds).

27. 146 U.S. 387, 13 S.Ct. 110, 36 L.Ed. 1918 (1892).

28. 146 U.S. at 452, 13 S.Ct. at 118, 36 L.Ed. at 1042.

29. Neptune City v. Avon-by-the-Sea, 61 N.J. 296, 309, 294 A.2d 47, 54, 2 ELR 20519, 20522 (1972).

servation of those lands in their natural state, so that they may serve as ecological units for scientific study, for open space, and as environments which provide food and habitat for birds and marine life, and which favorably affect the scenery and climate of the area." [30] It does not measurably advance the analysis to discover that public trust lands must be administered flexibly to protect a growing agenda of uses (some of them conflicting). Nor is there significant resolving power in the general formulations of the scope of the public trust obligation, although they are worth repeating before we look more closely at what a circumspect administration of the trust entails. Thus, it is said that administration of trust lands must avoid a substantial impairment of the public uses,[31] involves a balancing process between competing uses,[32] and requires a judgment about whether a reallocation of uses is reasonable [33] or whether the transaction challenged was for a proper trust purpose.[34] A violation of the public trust rests upon a finding of an unreasonable interference with the use and enjoyment of trust rights, while nuisance law also protects against the unreasonable interference with the use and enjoyment of certain property rights. Needless to say, the key to the understanding of public trust law, as with nuisance law,[35] is not an acquaintance with the formulae of decision-making but rather with its indicators and how they are aligned in particular cases.

Before turning to the decision-making obligations imposed by the trust, it deserves emphasis that trust issues arise in various contexts. Commonly, they are invoked to challenge a governmental action, as in the granting of an easement for construction of a coal unloading facility and power plant water pipes on a lakeshore,[36] a grant of bottom lands for the erection of a private navigational fa-

30. Marks v. Whitney, 6 Cal.3d 251, 259–30, 98 Cal.Rptr. 790, 796, 491 P. 2d 374, 380, 2 ELR 20049, 20050 (1971); see Just v. Marinette County, 56 Wis.2d 7, 18, 201 N.W.2d 761, 768 (1972).

31. Illinois Central R. R. v. Illinois, 146 U.S. 387, 452–53, 13 S.Ct. 110, 118, 36 L.Ed. 1018, 1042 (1892); In re Trempealeau Drainage Dist. Merwin v. Houghton, 146 Wis. 398, 410, 131 N.W. 838, 842 (1911) ("substantial infringement").

32. State v. Public Serv. Comm'n, 275 Wis. 112, 118, 81 N.W.2d 71, 73 (1957) (stating five rules enumerating implementation of the public trust doctrine, quoted in full, note 68, infra) (the fifth standard is whether "the disappointment of those members of the public who may desire to boat, fish or swim in the area is negligible when compared with the greater convenience to be afforded those members of the public who use the city park").

33. E. g., Nanda & Ris, supra note 8, at 304 ("the ultimate test of alienability [of trust lands] is one of reasonableness").

34. Stephenson v. Monroe, 43 A.D. 2d 897, 351 N.Y.S.2d 232, 4 ELR 20364 (1974) (disposal of refuse in a park inconsistent with park purposes).

35. §§ 2.1–.11 above.

36. Superior Pub. Rights, Inc. v. Dep't Natural Resources, 6 ELR [Dig.] 20435 (Mich.Cir.Ct. Ingham County 1976) (sustained).

cility,[37] or the issuance of permits to prospect for oil and gas on state tidal lands.[38] Public trust issues may be invoked defensively, as where a private citizen resists a condemnation action on the ground that the taking would impair beneficial uses in the trust properties;[39] or defends against a trespass,[40] quiet title[41] or injunction action[42] with a claimed superior public use; or opposes regulation by asserting an uninhibited public use.[43] The public trust doctrine may be invoked offensively by one private party against another, as in a suit to enforce a public right to a beach access route[44] or to restrain a dissipation of trust properties.[45] It may be invoked offensively by the government, as in a suit for damages to trust property[46] or to protect trust uses from encroachment by other government entities[47] or by private parties.[48] Perhaps most important, legislative powers to refine, qualify, and enhance the trust may be protected against taking

37. Milwaukee v. State, 193 Wis. 423, 214 N.W. 820 (1927) (sustained).

38. Boone v. Kingsbury, 206 Cal. 148, 273 P. 797 (1929) (sustained).

39. Eyde v. State, 393 Mich. 453, 225 N.W.2d 1 (1975) (arising under Michigan Environmental Protection Act); Texas Eastern Transmission Corp. v. Wildlife Preserves, Inc., 48 N.J. 261, 225 A.2d 130 (1966) (requiring a trial on whether alternative routes existed); cf. Freeborn v. Bryson, 297 Minn. 218, 210 N.W.2d 290, 4 ELR 20215 (1973) (arising under Minnesota Environmental Rights Act).

40. Forestier v. Johnson, 164 Cal. 24, 127 P. 156 (1912).

41. Diamond Match Co. v. Savercool, 218 Cal. 665, 24 P. 783 (1933); cf. International Paper Co. v. State Highway Dep't, 271 So.2d 395 (Miss.1972), cert. denied 414 U.S. 827 (1973) (quiet title action initiated against state).

42. Bohn v. Albertson, 107 Cal.App.2d 738, 238 P.2d 128 (1951).

43. Chain O'Lakes Protective Ass'n v. Moses, 53 Wis.2d 579, 193 N.W.2d 708, 2 ELR 20110 (1972) (permit not required for diversion of water); Menzer v. Elkhart Lake, 51 Wis.2d 70, 186 N.W.2d 290 (1971) (reject public trust defense to noise controls implemented by prohibiting use of power boats); Neptune City v. Avon-by-the-Sea, 61 N.J. 296, 294 A.2d 47, 2 ELR 20519 (1972) (invalidating fee against nonresident beach users as discriminatory).

44. Dietz v. King, 3 Cal.3d 29, 84 Cal. Rptr. 162, 465 P.2d 50 (1970).

45. Sierra Club v. Dep't of Interior, 376 F.Supp. 90, 4 ELR 20444 (N.D.Cal. 1974), further proceedings 398 F. Supp. 284, 5 ELR 20514 (N.D.Cal. 1975) (Redwood National Park).

46. Maryland Dep't of Natural Resources v. Amerada Hess Corp., 350 F.Supp. 1060, 2 ELR 20606 (D.Md. 1972).

47. E. g., State v. Bowling Green, 38 Ohio St.2d 281, 313 N.E.2d 409, 4 ELR 20730 (1934) (damage claim for a fish kill); Milwaukee v. State, 193 Wis. 423, 214 N.W. 820 (1927) (attorney general challenging city's land exchange with steel company); People ex rel. San Francisco Bay Conservation & Dev. Comm'n v. Emeryville, 69 Cal.2d 533, 72 Cal.Rptr. 790, 446 P.2d 790 (1968) (statutory interpretation).

48. See State v. Jackson, 376 S.W.2d 341 (Tex.1964) (holding that the Fish and Game Commission is without authority to prohibit certain types of seine nets) (question of statutory interpretation). If it is accepted that the state has no common law powers to prevent over-exploitation of a resource, which is doubtful, the legislature manifestly can (and usually does) supply those powers.

Sec. 2.16   PUBLIC TRUST DOCTRINE

claims to the extent the resources regulated already are impressed with public easements.[49]

b. *Procedural Functions*

At the threshold, the procedural importance of the public trust doctrine is reflected in concepts of standing. Individual plaintiffs, as members of the general public, are entitled to object to a reallocation of public uses,[50] although occasionally the special injury requirement that hampers prosecution of public nuisances[51] also closes the door on judicial scrutiny of claimed invasions of the public trust.[52] In reviewing claimed encroachments upon public uses, courts take a hard look to determine that the trustee has acted "with diligence, fairness and faithfulness" to protect public interests in the resource.[53] Thus, the courts may require the preparation of findings,[54] the holding of hearings,[55] and the exploration of alternatives[56] to assure that the impact on the reallocation of uses is considered fully. Compliance with these procedural forms, coupled with evidence that the adverse effect has been minimized, satisfy the requirements of judicial review.[57] Simi-

---

49. See Just v. Marinette County, 56 Wis.2d 7, 201 N.W.2d 761, 3 ELR 20167 (1972). Compare § 2.17 below (discussing the taking issue). The public trust doctrine also limits legislative power by forbidding alienation of certain trust properties. The origins of this limitation are presumably constitutional and very well may be found in doctrines of delegation. See text accompanying note 67, infra. The point deserves further analysis.

50. E. g., Marks v. Whitney, 6 Cal.3d 251, 98 Cal.Rptr. 790, 491 P.2d 374, 2 ELR 20049 (1971). Compare § 1.6 above (on standing generally).

51. § 2.2 above.

52. E. g., Kerpelman v. Board of Pub. Works, 261 Md. 436, 276 A.2d 56 (1971) (no standing to challenge validity of sale of state owned tidelands to private parties); Rogers v. Park & Planning Comm'n, 253 Md. 687, 253 A.2d 713 (1969) (no standing to enjoin road construction in public park); Texas Oyster Growers Ass'n v. Odom, 385 S.W.2d 899 (Tex. Civ.App.1965) (action barred by sovereign immunity, lack of standing, and nonreviewability of discretionary administrative decision). Contra, Paepcke v. Public Bldg. Comm'n, 46 Ill.2d 330, 341, 263 N.E.2d 11, 18, 1 ELR 20172, 20175 (1970) (rejecting special injury requirement as a test of standing in public trust cases).

53. 1 V. Yannacone, B. Cohen & S. Davison, Environmental Rights and Remedies § 2:1, at 14 (1972).

54. Obrecht v. National Gypsum Co., 361 Mich. 399, 105 N.W.2d 143 (1960) (trust lands cannot be alienated for private use in the absence of findings that the transfer will improve trust holdings and that the disposition may be made without detriment to the lands and waters remaining); cf. Ray v. Mason County Drain Comm'n, 393 Mich. 294, 224 N.W.2d 883, 5 ELR 20176 (1975) (requiring detailed findings of fact under Michigan Environmental Protection Act).

55. See New Jersey Sports & Exposition Authority v. McCrane, 61 N.J. 1, 292 A.2d 545, 3 ELR 20597 (1972).

56. See Texas Eastern Transmission Corp. v. Wildlife Preserves Inc., 48 N.J. 261, 225 A.2d 130 (1966); cf. Cleveland Elec. Illuminating Co. v. Scapell, 4 ELR 20375 (Ohio C.P. Cuyahoga County 1974) (action for condemnation of a transmission line easement; court suggests undergrounding within the boundaries of a park).

57. See, e. g., In re Environmental Hearings on the Proposed Sports Complex in the Hackensack Meadowlands, 62 N.J. 248, 300 A.2d 337 (1973) (per curiam); Payne v. Kassab, 11 Pa. Comm. 14, 29–30, 312 A.2d 86, 94

larly, a combination of careless procedures and questionable results will bring judicial intervention—as where an administrative recommendation for a drainage proposal is accompanied by a cavalier finding that "public rights of trapping, hunting, fishing and navigation will, by no means, be wholly destroyed." [58]

That the decision-maker consider carefully the effects of the reallocation of the public resource is illustrated by the rule that only a direct and explicit legislative narrowing of resource uses will be honored. The legislature should express "not merely the public will for the new use," the Supreme Judicial Court of Massachusetts has explained, but also "its willingness to surrender or forego the existing use." [59] The rule may be expressed as a presumption in favor of continuing public uses to be overcome only upon a showing of necessity.[60] Thus, absent strong evidence that the encroachment is deemed justifiable, courts will not imply lightly that lawmakers have sanctioned the dumping of solid waste in a public park,[61] the exchange of valuable wetlands for state highway purposes,[62] the transformation of major segments of a public park into a privately managed ski resort,[63] or the sacrifice of a wildlife preserve to a public utility pipeline.[64] On the other hand, where the legislature has considered carefully the consequences of a change in use and has ordered the modification with care and qualifications, courts are unlikely to find any invasion of the public trust, as where the use of state wetlands is approved for a sports

(1973), aff'd —— Pa. ——, 361 A.2d 263 (1976) (public hearings, adequate record and findings; also a "reasonable effort to reduce the environmental incursion to a minimum").

58. In re Crawford County Levee & Drainage Dist. No. 1, 182 Wis. 404, 406, 196 N.W. 874, 875 (1924) (a substantial destruction suffices to justify judicial intervention).

59. Robbins v. Dep't of Public Works, 355 Mass. 328, 331, 244 N.E.2d 577, 580 (1969); see People v. California Fish Co., 166 Cal. 576, 138 P. 79 (1913); State v. Ashmore, 236 Ga. 401, 224 S.E.2d 334, 6 ELR 20438 (1976).

60. Gould v. Greylock Reservation Comm'n, 350 Mass. 410, 215 N.W.2d 114 (1966); see 1 V. Yannacone, B. Cohen & S. Davison, supra note 53, at 14:

> Plaintiffs bringing suit under the Trust Doctrine will have the benefits of presumptions in favor of the protection of trust resources. Classical trust law regarding the continuance of the trust and the prohibition against invasion of corpus, can be asserted. The duty of the trustee to preserve the resource and protect it against loss, dissipation or diminution and to act with diligence, fairness and faithfulness in doing so, is well established in trust law. The presumptions result in shifting the burden to the despoiler of the environment to come forward with the evidence to prove the *necessity* for damaging the trust corpus.

(footnote omitted) (emphasis in original).

61. Stephenson v. Monroe, 43 A.D.2d 897, 351 N.Y.S.2d 232, 4 ELR 20364 (1974).

62. Robbins v. Dep't of Pub. Works, 355 Mass. 328, 244 N.E.2d 577 (1969).

63. Gould v. Greylock Reservation Comm'n, 350 Mass. 410, 215 N.E.2d 144 (1966).

64. Texas Eastern Transmission Corp. v. Wildlife Preserves, Inc., 48 N.J. 261, 225 A.2d 130 (1966).

stadium and race track,[65] or parkland is reallocated for the use of school facilities.[66]

Perhaps the strongest source of the procedural demands for administering trust properties is found in notions of delegation. While constitutional in its origins, the major objections of excessive delegations of law-making powers to private or administrative bodies are procedural—an absence of standards means a consequent lack of notice of what the rules are; administration without rules is likely to be erratic, unpredictable, and discriminatory; and people are deprived of opportunities to participate in the development of rules affecting their lives.[67] There is a great deal of this sentiment in the law of public trust, which insists not only that trust properties be devoted to public purposes but also that public bodies control the use.[68] A circumspect and faithful administration of the trust requires that control remain in public hands. Alarums are that much more urgent where the divestiture of control is tainted by suggestions of fraud or profiteering at the expense of the public. Thus, use reallocations of trust properties giving private parties a strong say in administration are accorded a rough reception in the courts, as where the entire waterfront of the city of Chicago is handed over lock, stock, and barrel to a rail-

---

65. New Jersey Sports & Exposition Authority v. McCrane, 61 N.J. 1, 292 A.2d 545, 3 ELR 20597 (1972) (by implication); cf. Boone v. Kingsbury, 206 Cal. 148, 273 P. 797, cert. denied 280 U.S. 517 (1929) (approving the leasing of tidelands for oil development).

66. Paepcke v. Public Bldg. Comm'n, 46 Ill.2d 330, 263 N.E.2d 11, 1 ELR 20172 (1970).

67. See Amalgamated Meat Cutters v. Connolly, 337 F.Supp. 737 (D.D.C. 1971) (three-judge court) (sustaining delegation); Bayside Timber Co. v. Board of Supervisors of San Mateo County, 20 Cal.App.3d 1, 97 Cal.Rptr. 431 (1971) (invalidating delegations of authority over logging operations to private interests). Compare § 1.11 above (discussing delegation problems arising from the use of advisory committees).

68. The most complete shorthand expression of the standards governing decisions affecting trust properties is found in State v. Public Serv. Comm'n, 275 Wis. 112, 118, 81 N.W.2d 71, 73–74 (1958). In concluding that the use of filled lake bed for park improvements (including a parking area and other changes) did not violate the obligations of the trust, the court attached importance to these facts:

1. Public bodies will control use of the area.

2. The area will be devoted to public purposes and open to the public.

3. The diminution of lake area will be very small when compared to the whole of Lake Wingra.

4. No one of the public uses of the lake as a lake will be destroyed or greatly impaired.

5. The disappointment of those members of the public who may desire to boat, fish, or swim in the area to be filled is negligible when compared with the greater convenience to be offered those members of the public who use the city park.

These factors were endorsed specifically by the Illinois Supreme Court in Paepcke v. Public Bldg. Comm'n, 46 Ill.2d 330, 263 N.E.2d 11, 1 ELR 20172 (1970).

road;[69] where undeveloped parklands are transferred through a long term lease under nominal guidelines to private interests intent upon developing a ski resort;[70] where tidelands are exchanged so as to leave two-thirds of the immediate bay area in private hands;[71] or where part of the bed of Lake Huron is transferred to a private company for purposes of constructing a loading dock.[72] On the other hand, the placement of management powers in private hands, even by outright alienation of public properties, may be upheld if the transfer makes sense from the overall perspective of enhancing the public uses. Thus, a grant of bottom lands to a steel company has been upheld where the transfer was consistent with the city's general plans for harbor development,[73] and exchanges are approved where they settle a genuine boundary dispute.[74]

c. *Substantive Limits*

While the procedural demands of the close scrutiny doctrine of judicial review [75] are much in evidence in public trust cases, the crucial limits are substantive. The test of unreasonable interference suggests the analogue of nuisance law, and the cases confirm the influence. One of the dominant themes of nuisance law is that adverse effects must be controlled to the limits of technological capability.[76] This means, depending on the context, that maximum efforts are required to minimize harm, and that management practices must strive for performance levels most compatible with protecting the environment. This standard of maximum mitigation is made explicit by the courts in Pennsylvania, which have developed a test for protecting the trust that asks whether there was a "reasonable effort to reduce the environmental incursion to a minimum." [77] A similar standard is endorsed implicitly by courts who require an examination of the least damaging alternatives to actions that impair

---

69. Illinois Central R. R. v. Illinois, 146 U.S. 387, 13 S.Ct. 110, 36 L.Ed. 1018 (1892).

70. Gould v. Greylock Reservation Comm'n, 350 Mass. 410, 215 N.E.2d 114 (1966).

71. Orange v. Heim, 30 Cal.App.3d 694, 106 Cal.Rptr. 825 (1973) (interpreting constitutional provisions).

72. Obrecht v. National Gypsum Co., 361 Mich. 399, 105 N.W.2d 143 (1960).

73. Milwaukee v. State, 193 Wis. 423, 214 N.W. 820 (1927).

74. Long Beach v. Mansell, 3 Cal.2d 462, 91 Cal.Rptr. 23, 476 P.2d 423 (1970).

75. § 1.5 above.

76. § 2.6 above.

77. Payne v. Kassab, 11 Pa.Comm. 14, 35–36, 312 A.2d 86, 97 (1973), aff'd —— Pa. ——, 361 A.2d 263 (1976) (upholding a decision to widen city streets that would encroach slightly on a river common); see Bucks County Bd. of Commissioners v. Public Util. Comm'n, 11 Pa.Comm. 487, 313 A.2d 185 (1973) (upholding an order of the Public Utility Commission granting approval to transport petroleum products by pipeline to be used for electrical generation).

Sec. 2.16 PUBLIC TRUST DOCTRINE

trust uses,[78] or a showing of mitigation implemented concurrently with the change in uses.[79] The maximum mitigation or best technology principle thus finds expression in the public trust arena.

Beneficiaries of the public trust are resource users, and one also would expect principles of use allocation to emerge from the case law. Perhaps the most basic of these is the equal opportunity to use and enjoy. The much touted decision in Neptune City v. Avon-by-the-Sea,[80] invalidating beach user fees that discriminated against nonresidents, wrote this principle firmly into the fabric of public trust law.

Another substantive doctrine discernible in the generalities of the public trust is that of nondegradation or, as expressed in a less dogmatic form, no significant deterioration.[81] The notion is that there are public rights in public resources, and, whatever else happens, these rights should not be eroded, traded away, or cheapened. The concept is strongly conservationist, giving preference to existing use patterns. Although the trustee is not held to impossible standards and is given leeway to manage in the overall public interest,[82] there is no dearth of decisions, many of them quite recent, that only can be called uncompromising in their protection of the trust. Thus, there are instances of application of a per se rule against conveyances of trust properties to a private party;[83] findings of impairment of the trust where it is diminished in size or the uses adversely affected to any degree;[84] or insistence "that the uses which are made of the property must be in some sense related to the natural uses peculiar to that resource."[85] While these purest expressions of non-degradation are not the prevailing rule everywhere,[86] it appears that the con-

---

78. Texas Eastern Transmission Corp. v. Wildlife Preserves, Inc., 48 N.J. 261, 225 A.2d 130 (1966).

79. See In re Environmental Hearings on the Proposed Sports Complex in the Hackensack Meadowlands, 62 N.J. 248, 300 A.2d 337 (1973) (per curiam).

80. 61 N.J. 296, 294 A.2d 47, 2 ELR 20519 (1972); cf. Dep't of Game v. Puyallup Tribe, 414 U.S. 44, 94 S.Ct. 330, 38 L.Ed.2d 254 (1973) (enforcing principle of non-discrimination in allocation contest between Indian and non-Indian steelhead fishermen).

81. Cf. § 3.12 below (discussing no significant deterioration under the Clean Air Act).

82. See, e. g., Paepcke v. Public Bldg. Comm'n, 46 Ill.2d 330, 263 N.E.2d 11, 1 ELR 20172 (1970).

83. International Paper Co. v. State Highway Dep't, 271 So.2d 395 (Miss. 1972), cert. denied 414 U.S. 827 (1973).

84. E. g., Grosse Isle v. Dunbar & Sullivan Dredging Co., 15 Mich.App. 556, 167 N.W.2d 311 (1969) (impairment of use) (burden on defendant to show a lack of substantial invasion); Nedtweg v. Wallace, 237 Mich. 14, 208 N.W. 51 (1926) (McDonald, J., dissenting) (diminution in size) (99 year lease of 3,000 acres of lake bed upon finding that land unsuitable for any other beneficial public use).

85. Sax, supra note 8, at 477; cf. § 2.15 above, n. 30 (discussing status of riparian rights rule that a reasonable use must be water related).

86. Sax, supra note 8, passim.

census as regards the public trust is at least a stiff insistence on protection. Public uses must be preserved; limited encroachments that are tolerated must be justified as an enhancement of what remains. It is not enough that the invasion be conducted with care and damage kept to a minimum. The encroachment must be justified by necessity [87] and perhaps only upon the proffer of an adequate substitute.[88] If there is no substitute for an irreplaceable resource, the invasion is unacceptable. The pattern that emerges comes very close to a doctrine that can be described as no significant deterioration of public rights in public resources.

d. *Legislative and Constitutional Modifications*

Resources subject to the trust are often a topic of constitutional and legislative action. Several of the states in which public trust law is well established, including California [89] and Wisconsin,[90] have had longstanding constitutional commitments to the protection of public resources. Other states recently adopting environmental bills of rights in their constitutions, such as Pennsylvania,[91] are likely to experience an expansion in the reach of public trust protections and a revival of enforcement. The newer constitutional provisions vary widely in content, ranging from declarations of the right to a decent environment to statements of a commitment to maintain, preserve, and improve the environment.[92] While the case law is not developed fully, state constitutional provisions have been invoked in a variety of contexts with various degrees of success—water pollution caused by acid mine drainage,[93] a reservoir construction project in a river alleged to be environmentally unique,[94] a utility district's decision to forego water reclamation in favor of purchase from a federal project,[95] the

---

87. E. g., Gould v. Greylock Reservation Comm'n, 350 Mass. 410, 215 N.E. 2d 114 (1966); see Mich.Comp.Laws Ann. § 486.252C.

88. Cf. United States v. Certain Property in the Borough of Manhattan, 403 F.2d 800 (2d Cir. 1968) (discussing substitute facility doctrine under the law of condemnation).

89. Cal.Const. art. XV, §§ 2–3.

90. Wis.Const. art. IX, § 1.

91. Art. I, § 27.

92. See Frye, Environmental Provisions in State Constitutions, 5 ELR 50028 (1975).

93. Commonwealth v. Barnes & Tucker Co., 455 Pa. 392, 319 A.2d 871, 4 ELR 20545 (1974) (citing Pa.Const. art. I, § 27 in course of discussion leading to conclusion that discharge of acid mine drainage constituted a public nuisance).

94. Scattering Fork Drainage Dist. v. Ogilvie, 19 Ill.App.3d 386, 311 N.E.2d 203 (1973) (rejecting allegation that the Embarass River was environmentally unique on grounds of failure of proof).

95. Environmental Defense Fund, Inc. v. East Bay Municipal Util. Dist. No. 1, 52 Cal.App.3d 828, 125 Cal.Rptr. 601 (1975) (interpreting Cal.Const. art. XIV, § 3, which states that the "right to use water . . . shall not extend to the waste or unreasonable use or unreasonable method of use or unreasonable method of diversion of water").

inefficient and wasteful transmission of water by a cattle ranch,[96] a ban on the importation of fish under a certain size as a conservation measure,[97] a regulatory prohibition against commercial fishing for striped bass,[98] a ban against the operation of seaplanes on 700 bodies of water within the New York forest preserve,[99] the filling of submerged lands adjacent to lakefront property,[1] a condemnation proceeding to aid the construction of a nuclear power plant,[2] and even the erection of an unsightly sign in an industrial area.[3]

Considerable attention is directed to the question of whether state constitutional provisions are self-executing in the sense they create substantive rights directly enforceable in court. The early return on this issue appears to be no in Pennsylvania [4] and perhaps in Illinois.[5] The interstitial and supplementary role of constitutional

96. Erickson v. Queen Valley Ranch Co., 22 Cal.App.3d 578, 99 Cal.Rptr. 446 (1971) (interpreting Cal.Const. art. XIV, § 3).

97. Salasnek Fisheries, Inc. v. Cashner, 9 Ohio App.2d 233, 224 N.E.2d 162 (1967) (citing Ohio Const. art. 2, § 36, which is a general police power measure).

98. Opinion to the Senate, 87 R.I. 37, 137 A.2d 525 (1958) (interpreting R.I. Const. art. 1, § 27, which provides that "the people shall continue to enjoy and freely exercise all the right of fishery, and the privileges of the shore, to which they have been heretofore entitled under the charter and usages of this state").

99. In re Helms v. Diamond, 76 Misc.2d 253, 349 N.Y.S.2d 917 (Sup.Ct. Schenectady County 1973) (declining to enter a preliminary injunction against enforcement partly in reliance upon N.Y.Const. art. 14, § 1, which states that "the lands of the state, now owned or hereafter acquired, constituting the forest preserve as now fixed by law, shall be forever kept as wild forest lands"). See Ass'n for the Protection of the Adirondacks v. MacDonald, 253 N.Y. 234, 170 N.E. 905 (1930).

1. People ex rel. Director of Conservation v. Babcock, 38 Mich.App. 336, 196 N.W.2d 489 (1972) (injunction affirmed) (applying Mich.Const. art. 4, § 52, which states that "the conservation and development of the natural resources of the State are hereby declared to be of paramount public concern in the interest of the health, safety, and general welfare of the people").

2. Seadade Indus., Inc. v. Florida Power & Light Co., 245 So.2d 209, 1 ELR 20214 (Fla.1971) (interpreting Fla. Const. art. II § 7, which declares that the protection of natural resources shall be the policy of the state).

3. State v. Diamond Motors, Inc., 50 Hawaii 33, 429 P.2d 825 (1967) (interpreting Hawaii Const. art. VIII, § 5, which provides that the state has the power "to conserve and develop its natural beauty, objects and places of historic or cultural interest, sightliness and physical good order," and grants the state the authority to regulate private property in order to effect those purposes).

4. Commonwealth v. National Gettysburg Battlefield Tower, Inc., 454 Pa. 193, 311 A.2d 588, 3 ELR 20876 (1973). The court was split sharply in the Gettysburg battlefield case and the issue has been treated as still open by some courts of the state. See authorities collected in Frye, supra note 92, at 50032 n. 50.

5. See Scattering Fork Drainage Dist. v. Ogilvie, 19 Ill.App.3d 386, 311 N.E.2d 203 (1974) (dictum). But see Pana v. Crowe, 13 Ill.App.3d 90, 299 N.E.2d 770 (1973) (holding Ill.Const. art. 11 is too general in terms to override a state anti-injunction statute). See also Michigan State Highway Comm'n v. Vanderkloot, 392 Mich. 159, 220 N.W.2d 416, 4 ELR 20694 (1974) (dividing 3–3 on the issue).

provisions is likely to be of greater long run significance—such as establishing claims of standing, reinforcing allegations of nuisance, and making clear that protection of the public trust extends beyond the beaches to the mountains, the prairies, and other unique and fragile resources. The potentialities of the public trust are enormous and need only be awakened not discarded nor superseded.

Statutes in many jurisdictions address the management of public trust resources, usually on the side of strengthening the terms of the trust. Even in Florida, which still sanctions the disposition of tidelands to private parties, the sales are hedged by strong procedural protections.[6] Several states have enacted measures to protect wetlands,[7] and they generally survive constitutional attack.[8] The creation of executive mechanisms to administer trust properties simultaneously enhances judicial review and circumscribes it. Judicial review is enhanced by assuring the preparation of an administrative record and an orderly approach to the issues; it is narrowed by imposing an administrative apparatus between the litigants and the courts.

Perhaps the best known legislative variation of the public trust theme is the Michigan Environmental Protection Act of 1970,[9] which has inspired similar efforts in seven other states.[10] The Michigan Act,

6. Fla.Stat. § 253.12; see F. Maloney, S. Plager & F. Baldwin, Water Law and Administration: The Florida Experience ch. 12 (1968).

7. E. g., California, Coastal Zone Conservation Act, 18 Cal.Pub.Res.Code § 27000 et seq., as amended; Delaware, Delaware Coastal Zone Act, 7 Del. Code Ann. § 7001 et seq. and Delaware Wetlands Law of 1973, 7 Del. Code Ann. § 6601 et seq.; Maine, Wetlands Protection Act, 12 Me.Rev. Stat.Ann. §§ 4751–58 and Mandatory Shoreline Zone and Subdivision Control Act, Me.Rev.Stat.Ann. §§ 4811–14; Mississippi, Coastal Wetlands Protection Act, Miss.Code Ann. § 49–27–1 et seq.; New Jersey, Coastal Area Facility Review Act, N.J.S.A. § 13.19–1 et seq. and New Jersey Wetlands Act of 1970, N.J.S.A. § 13:19A–1 et seq.; Rhode Island, Coastal Resource Management Council Act, Gen.Laws R.I. § 46–23–1 et seq.; Washington, Seashore Conservation Area Act, Rev.Code Wash.Ann. §§ 43.51.650–.690 and Coastal Water Protection Act, Rev.Code Wash.Ann. §§ 90.48.370–.410.

8. E. g., Rykar Indust. Corp. v. Gill, 4 ELR 20226 (Conn.Super.Ct.1973) (rejecting taking and police power arguments); Sibson v. State, 115 N.H. 124, 336 A.2d 239, 5 ELR 20300 (1975) (rejecting taking argument); J. M. Mills, Inc. v. Murphy, —— R.I. ——, 352 A.2d 661, 6 ELR 20455 (1976) (rejecting delegation, equal protection and taking arguments); see Binder, Taking Versus Reasonable Regulation: A Reappraisal in Light of Regional Planning and Wetlands, 45 U.Fla.L.Rev. 1 (1972).

9. Mich.Comp.Laws Ann. §§ 691–1201 to –1207. For reports on case law developed under the Act, see Sax & Conner, Michigan's Environmental Protection Act of 1970: A Progress Report, 70 Mich.L.Rev. 1003 (1972); Sax & Dimento, Environmental Citizen Suits: Three Years Experience Under the Michigan Environmental Protection Act, 4 Ecology L.Q. 1 (1974).

10. Conn.Gen.Stat.Ann. §§ 22a–14 to –20; Fla.Stat.Ann. § 403.412; Ind. Code §§ 13–6–1–1 to –6–6–6; Mass. Gen.Laws Ann. ch. 214, § 7A; Minn. Stat.Ann. §§ 116B.01–.13; N.J.Stat. Ann. §§ 2A:35A–1 to –14; S.D.Comp. Laws Ann. §§ 21–10A–1 to –15. For commentaries, see Hatch, Massachusetts and Michigan: Two States with

in pertinent part, gives standing to any person or political subdivision of the state to bring an action "for the protection of the air, water and other natural resources and the public trust therein from pollution, impairment or destruction." [11] The plaintiff has the burden of making "a prima facie showing" that the conduct of the defendant "has, or is likely to pollute, impair or destroy the air, water or other natural resources or the public trust therein . . . ." [12] The burden then shifts to the defendant to rebut the prima facie showing "by the submission of evidence to the contrary," or, by way of affirmative defense, "that there is no feasible and prudent alternative to defendant's conduct and that such conduct is consistent with the promotion of the public health, safety and welfare in light of the state's paramount concern for the protection of its natural resources from pollution, impairment or destruction." [13] The court is empowered to require of a plaintiff a cash bond not to exceed $500 [14] and is authorized to fashion equitable relief (but not to assess money damages) to protect public trust rights.[15] Also included are provisions that lessen the deference of the courts to administrative proceedings by narrowing the doctrines of primary jurisdiction and exhaustion of administrative remedies [16] and by expanding the scope of judicial review of administrative anti-pollution standards.[17]

Other states offer variations of the Michigan themes. Massachusetts requires, as a precondition of an environmental suit, that the damage caused or about to be caused by the defendant constitutes "a violation of a statute . . . or regulation the major purpose of which is to prevent or minimize damage to the environment." [18] Massachusetts also defines "damage to the environment" in considerable detail.[19] Minnesota protects "natural resources," [20] and Connecticut insists on proof of "unreasonable pollution, impairment or destruc-

an Answer, 6 Lincoln L.Rev. 119 (1970); Johnson, The Environmental Protection Act of 1971, 46 Conn.B.J. 422 (1972); McGregor, Private Enforcement of Environmental Law: An Analysis of the Massachusetts Citizen Suit Statute, 1 Env.Aff. 606 (1971); Note, The Minnesota Environmental Rights Act, 56 Minn.L.Rev. 575 (1972).

11. Mich.Comp.Laws Ann. § 691–1202 (1).

12. Id. § 691–1203.

13. Ibid.

14. Id. § 691–1202a.

15. Id. § 691–1204(i).

16. Id. § 691–1204(2), (3), (4). Compare § 1.9 above.

17. Mich.Comp.Laws Ann. § 691–1202 (2).

18. Mass.Gen.Laws Ann. ch. 21, § 7A; see Boston v. Massachusetts Port Authority, 364 Mass. 639, 308 N.E.2d 488 (1974) (allegations of a procedural failure to obtain prior approval of parking garage plans are adequate under the Act but the proof established no violation). Compare § 1.13 above (discussing federal citizen suit statutes).

19. Mass.Gen.Laws Ann. ch. 21, § 7A.

20. Minn.Stat.Ann. § 116B–02(4) ("Natural resources shall include, but not be limited to, all mineral, animal, botanical, air, water, land, timber, soil, quietude, recreational and historical resources. Scenic and esthetic resources shall also be considered natural resources when owned by a government unit or agency").

tion."[21] There are other differences as to the definition of the prima facie case, reviewability of administrative action, and scope of procedural and substantive protections.[22]

The Michigan Act and its progeny tighten both procedural and substantive constraints associated with public trust law. The grant of standing and directives for closer judicial review of agency actions affecting natural resources are familiar themes of modern environmental law.[23] The clarification of the burdens of proof is an important procedural advance that will make easier the task of judicial review. In Ray v. Mason County Drain Comm'n,[24] the Michigan Supreme Court made clear that the trial courts must develop detailed findings to facilitate the hard look at agency action the Act requires. In language reminiscent of obligations that have evolved under the National Environmental Policy Act,[25] the court observed that "the defendant may find it necessary to bring forward field studies, actual tests, and analyses which support his contention that the environment has not or will not be polluted, impaired or destroyed by his conduct. Such proofs become necessary when the impact upon the environment resulting from a defendant's conduct cannot be ascertained with any degree of reasonable certainty absent empirical studies or tests. For example, in this case one of defendant's witnesses, a conservation engineer, conceded that without a detailed study of the configurations in the area he could not say how the wetlands were dependent upon the water table and whether they were subject to drying up if the water table were lowered [by a channelization program]."[26] While couched in a procedural obligation of a burden to study before proceeding, this language has substantive connotations too: if risks cannot be put to rest, justification for action may be lacking. The Michigan Act reinforces also the demands of necessity that must precede an invasion of the trust (no "feasible and prudent alternative"[27]), and thus adds fiber to the principle of no significant deterioration of public uses in trust resources.

§ 2.17 Land Development Controls

Historically, the chief legal limitations on land use judgments were found in the private law of nuisance and restrictive covenants.[1]

21. Conn.Gen.Stat.Ann. § 22a–16.

22. See Comment, Three Recent Cases: State Environmental Protection Acts Revisited, 1975 Detroit Coll.L.Rev. 265.

23. §§ 1.5–.7 above.

24. 393 Mich. 294, 224 N.W.2d 883, 5 ELR 20173 (1975). An authoritative interpretation of the Minnesota Act is found in Freeborn v. Bryson, 297 Minn. 218, 210 N.W.2d 290, 4 ELR 20215 (1973).

25. § 7.9 below.

26. 393 Mich. at 311–12, 224 N.W.2d at 891, 5 ELR at 20179 (footnote omitted).

27. Compare Citizens to Preserve Overton Park v. Volpe, 401 U.S. 402, 91 S.Ct. 814, 28 L.Ed.2d 136 (1975); §§ 7.12 below, 1.5 above.

1. §§ 2.1–.11 above; D. G. Hagman, Urban Planning and Land Develop-

The twentieth century brought classic zoning and the checkerboarding of communities into residential, commercial and industrial categories.[2] Any developer today, whether of an aluminum plant,[3] trailer court,[4] or hundreds of endeavors in between, must contend not only with established nuisance principles but more likely with a variety of zoning and planning requirements. Land development law is a principal determinant of whether the project proceeds and, if so, subject to what limitations. The topic of land use planning usually is a separate entry in the law school curriculum, and has spawned a body of significant scholarship.[5] The writers have dealt, among others, with two fundamental societal clashes raising environmental issues—housing opportunities for minorities and the poor, and constitutional prohibitions against the taking of private property without just compensation. They often arise in the same context. Recognizing that these complex issues resist a thorough restatement, the present effort addresses (1) growth controls, (2) special purpose land use regulation, (3) generalized planning endeavors, and (4) the taking issue.

a. *Growth Controls*

The familiar law of zoning [6] is today, and always has been, exclusionary in the sense that certain types of uses are barred from certain areas. Manifestly, physical environmental factors represent a major element in decisions reflected by a zoning judgment. Certain types of development simply should not proceed in the face of natural limitations imposed by water supply, soil or climate conditions, threats of flood or earthquake.[7] A zoning exclusion may be prompted, however, not only by an assessment of physical limitations but also by the fact that people may resist neighborhood change for a variety of other reasons—social preferences, an insistence upon traditional ways, or just plain orneriness. Thus, environmental protection may represent an indispensable goal, a ruse justifying social exclusion, or some combination of the two. The tension be-

ment Control Law ch. 13 (1971) [hereinafter cited as Hagman].

2. See Futrell, The Hidden Crisis in Georgia Land Use, 10 Ga.L.Rev. 53, 69–71 (1975).

3. Smith v. Skagit County, 453 P.2d 832, 75 Wash.2d 715 (1969).

4. Rodo Land, Inc. v. Bd. of County Commissioners, 517 P.2d 873 (Colo. Ct.App.1974).

5. E. g., J. Beuscher & R. Wright, Cases and Materials on Land Use (1969); Future Land Use, Energy, Environmental and Legal Constraints (R. W. Burchell & D. Listokin eds. 1975); G. Lefcoe, Cases and Materials on Land Development Law (2d ed. 1974); D. R. Mandelker, Managing Our Urban Environment (2d ed. 1971, Supp. 1974); Hagman, supra note 1; D. G. Hagman, Cases and Materials on Public Planning and Control of Urban and Land Development (1973).

6. See generally Hagman, supra note 1, ch. 5; R. Babcock, The Zoning Game (1966); S. Toll, Zoned America (1969).

7. § 2.4 above.

tween the law as physical protector and as social discriminator is reflected in the National Environmental Policy Act [8] and its state counterparts,[9] which require consideration of social impact along with physical effects. The exclusionary function of zoning is an issue of enduring significance, and it is one where the choice of the right side requires more than a knee-jerk judgment.

Not surprisingly, environmental factors, both physical and social, have come to the forefront of reported cases growing out of the administration of the zoning laws. Thus, the tentative approval of a proposed subdivision is remanded for another look at drainage and erosion problems,[10] an approval of an aluminum plant in a rural, idyllic setting is condemned as spot zoning (where a small area is specially zoned for an inconsistent use),[11] a zoning amendment is set aside where it would lead to a shopping center in a residential district,[12] an application to expand a nonconforming use is turned down where it would aggravate a use conflict between a dairy business and neighboring homeowners,[13] a subdivider is given approval to go ahead only upon the condition that he dedicate certain property for environmental enhancement purposes.[14] Virtually every step that a local government may take in administering zoning and subdivision laws may find environmental issues dispositive.[15]

8. §§ 7.1–.10 below.

9. § 7.11 below.

10. Hamlin v. Matarazzo, 120 N.J. Super. 164, 293 A.2d 450 (1972).

11. Smith v. Skagit County, 453 P.2d 832, 75 Wash.2d 715 (1969).

12. Cresskill v. Dumont, 28 N.J.Super. 26, 100 A.2d 182 (1953) (applying the standard test of whether the amendment would alter the character of the neighborhood).

13. Carter v. Harper, 182 Wis. 148, 196 N.W. 451 (1923).

14. E. g., Associated Home Builders v. Walnut Creek, 4 Cal.3d 633, 94 Cal. Rptr. 630, 484 P.2d 606 (1971) (upholding dedication requirement for park or recreation purposes); Prudential Trust Co. v. Laramie, 492 P.2d 971 (Wyo.1972); cf. Mayor & Council of Rockville v. Brookeville Turnpike Constr. Co., 246 Md. 117, 228 A.2d 263 (1966) (upholding dedication requirement as condition of annexation). But see Bd. of Supervisors v. Rowe, 216 Va. 128, 216 S.E.2d 199 (1975), 10 U.Rich.L.Rev. 440 (1976) (invalidating ordinance imposing dedication obligations).

15. E. g., Stone v. Maitland, 446 F.2d 83, 3 ELR 20443 (5th Cir. 1971) (denial of a variance request from a city ordinance prohibition against construction of gasoline stations not a taking); Biderman v. Morton, 497 F.2d 1141, 4 ELR 20487 (2d Cir. 1974) (issuance of construction permits and granting of zoning variance; no federal basis for jurisdiction to restrain municipalities from approving what is alleged to be overdevelopment of Fire Island); Citizens Ass'n of Georgetown, Inc. v. Zoning Comm'n, 477 F.2d 402, 3 ELR 20127 (D.C.Cir. 1973) (revocation of emergency amendment to zoning regulations preserving status quo pending further study; zoning commission directed to file a statement of reasons); Walsh v. Spadaccia, 73 Misc.2d 866, 343 N.Y.S.2d 45, 3 ELR 20419 (Sup.Ct.1973) (site approval for construction of apartment units on a lake; approval by the town invalidated on the ground of likely pollution of the lake by eutrophication); see Peters, Durham, New Hampshire: A Victory for Home Rule, 5 Ecol.L.Q. 53 (1975) (state legislative vote reaffirming home rule led to abandonment of plans for an oil refinery without an actual request for a zoning variance).

Sec. 2.17　　LAND DEVELOPMENT CONTROLS　　189

The erratic or ad hoc environmental assessment that appears in administration of the zoning laws becomes more systematic in states adopting environmental policy acts (SEPA's).[16] Already it is clear that the SEPA's may have perhaps their greatest impact on local land use planning and zoning decisions. The leading California case of Friends of Mammoth v. Board of Supervisors of Mono County [17] sent repercussions through the building industry in that state by requiring the preparation of an environmental impact report in connection with the issuance of a permit to construct a condominium in an undeveloped rural area. Rapidly accumulating case law has required impact statements on a variety of other local government land use actions—issuance of a grading permit,[18] a city annexation,[19] the adoption of an amendment to a zoning ordinance,[20] the issuance of a conditional use permit,[21] the renewal of a building permit,[22] the approval of a preliminary subdivision plat,[23] and the sanctioning of a housing subdivision.[24]

The linkage between explosive and uncontrolled growth and losses in the quality of life is documented thoroughly,[25] and known to many by personal experience. Concern for the protection of people, from both technological encroachments and other people, is found in Supreme Court opinions beginning with Village of Euclid v. Ambler Realty Co.,[26] upholding a zoning law against a taking claim, where the Court invoked the spectre of a parade of parasitic apartment houses invading residential areas and becoming nuisances.[27] The use

---

16.　§ 7.11 below.

17.　8 Cal.3d 247, 104 Cal.Rptr. 761, 502 P.2d 1049, 2 ELR 20673 (1972).

18.　Juanita Bay Valley Community Ass'n v. Kirkland, 9 Wash.App. 59, 510 P.2d 1140 (1973).

19.　Bozung v. Local Agency Formation Comm'n, 13 Cal.3d 263, 118 Cal. Rptr. 249, 529 P.2d 1017, 4 ELR 20338 (1974).

20.　People v. Kern County, 39 Cal.App. 3d 830, 115 Cal.Rptr. 67 (1974).

21.　Concerned Citizens of Palm Desert, Inc. v. Riverside County Bd. of Supervisors, 38 Cal.App.3d 272, 113 Cal. Rptr. 338 (1974).

22.　Eastlake Community Council v. Roanoke Associates, 82 Wash.2d 475, 513 P.2d 36, 3 ELR 20867 (1973).

23.　Loveless v. Yantis, 82 Wash.2d 754, 513 P.2d 1023 (1973).

24.　Montana Wilderness Ass'n v. Bd. of Health & Environmental Sciences, 6 ELR 20043 (Mont.Dist.Ct.1975).

25.　See, e. g., F. Bosselman & D. Callies, The Quiet Revolution in Land Use Control (1971); R. Dasmann, The Destruction of California (1965); Environment: A New Focus of Land-Use Planning (D. M. McAllister ed. 1973); The Use of Land: A Citizens Policy Guide to Urban Growth (W. K. Reilly ed. 1973); Carter, Dade County: The Politics of Managing Urban Growth, 192 Science 982 (1976); Hoben, The Cost of Sprawl, in 6 HUD Challenge 24 (1975). See also J. Jacobs, The Death and Life of Great American Cities (1961); L. Mumford, The Highway and the City (1956).

26.　272 U.S. 365, 47 S.Ct. 114, 71 L.Ed.2d 303 (1926).

27.　272 U.S. at 394–95, 47 S.Ct. at 120–21, 71 L.Ed. at 313–14:
　　[V]ery often the apartment house is a mere parasite, constructed in

of the police power to protect people from offensive technological and residential invasions is defined broadly in Berman v. Parker,[28] sustaining a comprehensive plan for the redevelopment of an area of the District of Columbia, and more recently in the much mooted case of Belle Terre v. Boraas,[29] sustaining an ordinance prohibiting more than two unmarried people from living together within the village. Mr. Justice Douglas defined the problem: "The regimes of boarding houses, fraternity houses, and the like present urban problems. More people occupy a given space; more cars rather continuously pass by; more cars are parked; noise travels with crowds." And the scope of the power to search for a solution: "A quiet place where yards are wide, people few, and motor vehicles restricted are legitimate guidelines in a land use project addressed to family needs. This goal is a permissible one . . . . The police power is not confined to the elimination of filth, stench and unhealthy places. It is ample to lay out zones where family values, youth values, and the blessings of quiet seclusion, and clean air make the area a sanctuary for people."[30] A recent endorsement of this limited scope of judicial review reflected by a conventional police power analysis appears in Construction Industry

order to take advantage of the open spaces and attractive surroundings created by the residential character of the district. Moreover, the coming of one apartment house is followed by others, interfering by their height and bulk with the free circulation of air and monopolizing the rays of the sun which otherwise would fall upon the smaller homes, and bringing, as their necessary accompaniments, the disturbing noises incident to increased traffic and business, and the occupation, by means of moving and parked automobiles, of larger portions of the streets, thus detracting from their safety and depriving children of the privilege of quiet and open spaces for play, enjoyed by those in more favored localities, —until, finally, the residential character of the neighborhood and its desirability as a place of detached residences are utterly destroyed. Under these circumstances, apartment houses, which in a different environment would be not only entirely unobjectionable but highly desirable, come very near to being nuisances.

28. 348 U.S. 26, 33, 75 S.Ct. 98, 102–03, 99 L.Ed. 27, 38 (1954) ("It is within the power of the legislature to determine that the community should be beautiful as well as healthy, spacious as well as clean, well-balanced as well as carefully patrolled") (once the public purpose is established, the means for executing the project are for Congress to determine).

29. 416 U.S. 1, 94 S.Ct. 1536, 39 L.Ed. 2d 797 (1974).

30. 416 U.S. at 10, 94 S.Ct. at 1541, 39 L.Ed.2d at 804. Mr. Justice Marshall, dissenting on the ground that the ordinance unreasonably burdened First Amendment associational rights, also read broadly the legitimate reach of the zoning power: "[L]ocal zoning authorities may properly act in furtherance of the objectives asserted to be served by the ordinance at issue here: restricting uncontrolled growth, solving traffic problems, keeping rental costs at a reasonable level, and making the community attractive to families. The police power which provides the justification for zoning is not narrowly confined. And, it is appropriate that we afford zoning authorities considerable latitude in choosing the means by which to implement such purposes." 416 U.S. at 13–14, 94 S.Ct. at 1543, 39 L.Ed.2d at 807, citing *Berman.*

Ass'n v. Petaluma,[31] which upheld a five-year municipal housing and zoning plan imposing a 500 unit ceiling on housing projects of five or more units. Judge Choy, conceding an exclusionary purpose and effect, wrote: "We must determine further whether the *exclusion* bears any rational relationship to a *legitimate state interest* . . . . If . . . a legitimate state interest is furthered by the zoning regulation, we must defer to the legislative act."[32] He concluded: "[T]he concept of the public welfare is sufficiently broad to uphold Petaluma's desire to preserve its small town character, its open spaces and low density of population, and to grow at an orderly and deliberate pace."[33] Thus, the validity of the Petaluma plan is tested by the same undemanding standard of lunacy that would be applied, let us say, to a law forbidding an optician from fitting old glasses into new frames without a prescription.[34]

The sweep of the preceding paragraph, however, is qualified substantially by a recognition that the law protects housing opportunities for minorities and for the poor. Zoning restrictions on growth take many forms, both classical (low density requirements such as height limits, lot size minimums, bans on multi-family dwellings) and the innovative (phased zoning tempo and sequence controls of which the Petaluma and Ramapo[35] plans are best known). The subject of exclusionary zoning has come to mean the use of these growth restriction techniques with the purpose or effect of walling out racial minorities and poor people, who are often one and the same.[36] Of

31. 522 F.2d 897, 5 ELR 20519 (9th Cir. 1975), cert. denied 424 U.S. 934 (1976) (rejecting constitutional right to travel, substantive due process and burden on commerce claims).

32. 522 F.2d at 906, 5 ELR at 20522 (emphasis in original).

33. 522 F.2d at 909, 5 ELR at 20523 (footnote omitted).

34. Williamson v. Lee Optical Co., 348 U.S. 483, 75 S.Ct. 461, 99 L.Ed. 563 (1955).

35. Golden v. Planning Bd. of the Town of Ramapo, 30 N.Y.2d 359, 334 N.Y.S.2d 138, 285 N.E.2d 291 (1972) (sustaining plan as consistent with zoning enabling legislation). The land in the town subject to the ordinance "is designated for residential use, but permission to subdivide the land for this purpose is withheld unless the landowner can show the availability to the parcel of adequate public services. The landowner can provide the services himself, or he can wait for the town, which, pursuant to its capital budget program, provides for the extension and improvement of public services over an 18-year period." Note, Phased Zoning: Regulation of the Tempo and Sequence of Land Development, 26 Stan.L.Rev. 585, 588–89 (1974) (footnotes omitted).

36. Construction Indus. Ass'n v. Petaluma, 522 F.2d 897, 905 n. 10, 5 ELR 20519, 20522 n. 10 (9th Cir. 1975), cert. denied 424 U.S. 934 (1976); see R. Babcock & F. Bosselman, Exclusionary Zoning: Land Use Regulation and Housing in the 1970's (1973); M. H. Danielson, The Politics of Exclusion (1976); Williams & Norman, Exclusionary Land Use Controls: The Case of Northeastern New Jersey, 22 Syra. L.Rev. 475 (1971); Roberts, Demise of Property Law, 57 Cornell L.Rev. 1 (1971); Sager, Tight Little Islands: Exclusionary Zoning, Equal Protection and the Indigent, 21 Stan.L.Rev. 767 (1969); Note, Exclusionary Zoning and Equal Protection, 84 Harv.L.Rev. 1645 (1971).

course, growth restrictions may be enforced by means other than the zoning laws—a sewer hookup ban is a prime example [37]—and they may be used with similar uneven effects. A growth restriction measure with racially discriminatory consequences, according to hornbook law, is inherently suspect and it survives only upon a showing of a compelling justification,[38] not mere rationality.

Growth restriction measures, most prominently zoning, have been widely attacked in state and federal courts in recent years on a variety of theories: federal right of travel, due process, taking and equal protection grounds, inconsistency with state zoning and enabling laws and sundry constitutional provisions. The cases usually involve disputes over the purpose and effect of a particular growth restriction measure. If a racially or economically discriminatory purpose or effect is shown, the justification invariably is couched in the language of environmental protection. The easiest cases, and the ones swiftly dealt with, are those where sewer or other facilities are made available for some projects but not for a minority project.[39] Often the issues arise in the context of a particular housing project, as by a hasty rezoning to exclude or an obstinate refusal to rezone to include. Under these circumstances proof of racial discrimination is likely to be easier, and the courts will look with skepticism upon a suddenly discovered pressing need for parkland, newly emergent sewerage and flooding problems, instantaneous overcrowding, and other contrived environmental ills.[40] The Pennsylvania Supreme Court has brushed aside as "patently ridiculous" the claim that two- or three-acre minimum sized lots were necessary to protect the character of the neighborhood and to prevent a build-up of sewerage problems.[41]

37. E. g., Rivkin, Growth Control Via Sewer Moratoria, 33 Urban Land 10 (1974); § 4.21 below (discussing sewer moratorium as a water pollution enforcement device); see Cutler, Legal and Illegal Methods of Controlling Community Growth, 1961 Wis.L.Rev. 370.

38. E. g., United Farmworkers of Florida Housing Project, Inc. v. Delray Beach, 493 F.2d 799, 4 ELR 20497 (5th Cir. 1974); United States v. Black Jack, 508 F.2d 1179 (8th Cir. 1974); Metropolitan Housing Corp v. Arlington Heights, 517 F.2d 409 (7th Cir.), rev'd on other grounds — U.S. —, 97 S.Ct. 555, 50 L.Ed.2d 450 (1976).

39. E. g., United Farmworkers of Florida Housing Project, Inc. v. Delray Beach, 493 F.2d 799, 4 ELR 20497 (5th Cir. 1974).

40. E. g., Kennedy Park Homes Ass'n v. Lackawanna, 436 F.2d 108 (2d Cir. 1970), cert. denied 401 U.S. 1010 (1971); Dailey v. Lawton, 425 F.2d 1037 (10th Cir. 1970); Crow v. Brown, 332 F.Supp. 382 (N.D.Ga.1971), aff'd per curiam 457 F.2d 788 (5th Cir. 1972).

41. Appeal of Kit-Mar Builders, Inc., 439 Pa. 466, 476, 268 A.2d 765, 769 (1970); see, e. g., Southern Burlington County NAACP v. Mt. Laurel, 67 N.J. 151, 336 A.2d 713, cert. denied 423 U.S. 808 (1975) (exclusively zoned for single family detached dwellings and multi-family dwellings designed for middle and upper income people) (rejecting justification of inadequate water and sewer facilities); Oakwood at Madison, Inc. v. Madison, 117 N.J. Super. 11, 283 A.2d 353, 2 ELR 20670 (1971) (one to two acre minimum lot size and severe restrictions on multi-family units) (rejecting justification of prevention of development in flood plain zone); Appeal of Girsh, 437 Pa. 237, 263 A.2d 395 (1970) (prohibition

There is also a strong insistence in the case law that municipalities, while given latitude to plan their growth, must provide for the housing needs of their residents. This is perhaps said best by Judge Browning in Southern Alameda Spanish Speaking Organization (SASSO) v. Union City: [42]

> Surely, if the environmental benefits of land use planning are to be enjoyed by a city and the quality of life of its residents is accordingly to be improved, the poor cannot be excluded from enjoyment of the benefits. Given the recognized importance of equal opportunities in housing, it may well be, as a matter of law, that it is the responsibility of a city and its planning officials to see that the city's plan as initiated or as it develops accommodates the needs of its low-income families, who usually—if not always—are members of minority groups.

That dictum soon was put to work by the New Jersey Supreme Court in Southern Burlington County NAACP v. Mt. Laurel,[43] which, as a matter of state constitutional law, developed and enforced a municipal obligation to accept a fair share of regional growth including the provision of housing opportunities for low and moderate income people. Even under *Mt. Laurel*, however, genuine environmental factors may justify freezes on growth if they are reasonably necessary to protect the public values at stake.[44]

Despite the wide divergence between the language of *Belle Terre* and *Mt. Laurel,* factors emerge from the decisions that tend to narrow the gap in evaluating the legitimacy of growth restriction measures. Important in *Petaluma* was the fact that the plan made provision for the housing needs of low income groups and stopped short of an unwaivering population freeze. Motive may be important.[45] Greater

---

of apartment houses) (rejecting justification of strained municipal services and rural roads and protection of character of community); National Land & Inv. Co. v. Kohn, 419 Pa. 504, 215 A.2d 597 (1965) (4 acre minimum lot size) (rejecting justification of sewage needs, water pollution, inadequacy of roads and necessary fire protection, and preservation of historic sites and open spaces); Fairfax County Bd. of Supervisors v. Carper, 200 Va. 653, 107 S.E.2d 390 (1959) (rezoning to 2 acre lot minimum) (rejecting justification of water and sewer problems, fire protection, and inadequate school facilities); Kavanewsky v. Zoning Bd. of Appeals, 160 Conn. 397, 279 A.2d 567 (1971) (increase in minimum lot sizes from 1 to 2 acres) (rejecting justification of desire to maintain rural character and keep out undesirable businesses).

42. 424 F.2d 291, 295–96 (9th Cir. 1970).

43. 67 N.J. 151, 336 A.2d 713, cert. denied 423 U.S. 808 (1975); see, e. g., Ackerman, The Mount Laurel Decision: Expanding the Boundaries of Zoning Reform, 1976 U.Ill.L.F. 1.

44. 67 N.J. at 187, 336 A.2d at 731 ("to have a valid effect, the danger and impact must be substantial and very real (the construction of every building or the improvement of every plot has some environmental impact) —not simply a make weight to support exclusionary housing measures or preclude growth—and the regulation adopted must be only that reasonably necessary for public protection of a vital interest").

45. E. g., Yick Wo v. Hopkins, 118 U.S. 356, 6 S.Ct. 1064, 30 L.Ed. 220

leeway may be accorded where a community desiring to retain its rural character is outside natural growth corridors [46] or where the need for housing on a regional basis is less than urgent.[47] It may be relevant that the developer challenging a restriction is moved more by a desire to make a fast buck than to assure quality development,[48] that the lines of restriction are drawn carefully as to location and size,[49] that the area protected is uniquely beautiful or vulnerable,[50] that the lines drawn do not appear to serve purely private interests [51] or local concerns at the expense of the region.[52] Of overriding importance is that a community should be given time to decide and to plan its future. Moratoria of various types, some of potentially extended duration, are sustained on this rationale.[53] The fact that the

(1886) (despite the firm dogma that motive is irrelevant in assessing the constitutionality of legislation); cf. Arlington Heights v. Metropolitan Housing Corp., — U.S. —, 97 S.Ct. 555, 50 L.Ed.2d 450 (1976) (equal protection challenge).

46. Steel Hill Dev., Inc. v. Sanbornton, 469 F.2d 956, 3 ELR 20018 (1st Cir. 1972) (upholding 3 to 6 acre lot restrictions); see Oakwood at Madison, Inc. v. Madison, 117 N.J.Super. 11, 20, 283 A.2d 353, 358, 2 ELR 20670, 20672 (1971) ("[A] municipality must not ignore housing needs, that is, its fair proportion of the obligation to meet the housing needs of its own population and of the region. . . . The general welfare does not stop at each municipal boundary").

47. Steel Hill Dev., Inc. v. Sanbornton, note 46 supra; cf. Ybarra v. Los Altos Hills, 503 F.2d 250, 4 ELR 20743 (9th Cir. 1974) (one acre minimum; one primary dwelling unit per acre) (applying the rational relationship test; rejecting the compelling interest standard because plaintiffs failed to show unavailability of other low cost housing in Santa Clara County and thus wealth was not a suspect classification).

48. See Steel Hill Dev., Inc. v. Sanbornton, 469 F.2d 956, 3 ELR 20018 (1st Cir. 1972).

49. E. g., County Commissioners v. Miles, 246 Md. 355, 228 A.2d 450 (1967) (upholding 5 acre minimum lot size; but area affected comprised only 6.7 per cent of the county, involved an especially beautiful country estate section of a river, and was done pursuant to a long-range plan); Golden v. Planning Bd. of the Town of Ramapo, 30 N.Y.2d 359, 380, 334 N.Y.S.2d 138, 153, 285 N.E.2d 291, 303 (1971) ("We may assume, therefore, that the present amendments are the product of foresighted planning calculated to promote the welfare of the township").

50. Confederation de la Raza Unida v. Morgan Hill, 324 F.Supp. 895 (N.D. Cal.1971) (charming mountainous area of a city); County Commissioners v. Miles, 246 Md. 355, 228 A.2d 450 (1967) (beautiful country estate section of a river).

51. Note, Phased Zoning: Regulation of the Tempo and Sequence of Land Development, 26 Stan.L.Rev. 585, 591 & n. 24 (1974) (pointing out that zoning must serve a public interest under enabling statutes); see Fagin, Regulating the Timing of Urban Development, 20 L. & Contemp.Prob. 298 (1955).

52. See Oakwood at Madison, Inc. v. Madison, 117 N.J.Super., 11, 30, 383 A.2d 353, 358, 2 ELR 20670, 20672 (1971) ("The general welfare cannot stop at each municipal boundary"); Bosselman, Can the Town of Ramapo Pass a Law to Bind the Rights of the Whole World?, 1 Fla.St.U.L.Rev. 234 (1973).

53. E. g., Cappture Realty Corp. v. Bd. of Adjustment, 126 N.J.Super. 200, 313 A.2d 624 (1973) (upholding zoning prohibition against all new development in a flood prone area pending construction of flood control works); Meadowland Regional Dev. Agency v. Hackensack Meadowlands Dev. Comm'n, 119 N.J.Super. 572, 293 A.2d 192 (App.Div.), cert. denied 62 N.J.

restrictions in *Ramapo* were temporary (albeit over an 18-year period) also was an important part of the justification there upheld.[54] So read, the commitment is not one to irrevocable exclusion but to planned receptivity, and one based on preserving the quality of life, minimizing adverse effects of growth and channeling it in the direction of overall community benefit. Judge Coffin, rejecting a substantive due process argument aimed at 3- and 6-acre lot restrictions that effectively kept a recreational development out of a tiny rural town, stresses the need for time to decide as a reason for overlooking the "crude manner" in which the town devised its slow-growth policy:[55]

> We are disturbed by the admission here that there was never any professional or scientific study made as to why six, rather than four or eight, acres was reasonable to protect the values cherished by the people of Sanbornton. On reviewing the record, we have serious worries whether the basic motivation of the town meeting was not simply to keep outsiders, provided they wished to come in quantity, out of the town. We cannot think that an expansion of population, even a very substantial one, seasonal or permanent, is by itself a legitimate basis for permissible objection. Were we to adjudicate this as a restriction for all time, and were the evidence of pressure from land-deprived and land-seeking outsiders more real, we might well come to a different conclusion. Where there is natural population growth it has to go somewhere, unwelcome as it may be, and in that case we do not think it should be channeled by the happenstance of what town gets its veto in first. But, at this time of uncertainty as to the right balance between ecological and population pressures, we cannot help but feel that the town's ordinance, which severely restricts development, may properly stand for the present as a legitimate stop-gap measure.

72, 299 A.2d 69 (1972) (upholding an ordinance freezing construction in 10,000 acres pending adoption of a comprehensive plan for redevelopment); Westwood Forest Estates v. South Nyack, 23 N.Y.2d 424, 428–29, 297 N.Y.S.2d 129, 132–33, 244 N.E.2d 700, 702–03 (1969); State v. Snohomish County, 79 Wash.2d 619, 488 P.2d 511 (1971) (approving rural use zone classification for five years as a "holding zone" that might help prevent haphazard commercial developments). Of course moratoria can be attacked both as conceived and as administered. Compare Ogo Associates v. Torrance, 37 Cal.App.3d 830, 112 Cal.Rptr. 761 (1974) (allowing proof of racial and economic discrimination in the enactment of a construction moratorium) with Belle Harbor Realty Corp. v. Kerr, 43 A.D. 2d 727, 350 N.Y.S.2d 698 (1973) (requiring issuance of a building permit; denial was based on ground that sewer facilities were inadequate but there were no comprehensive plans to improve the system).

54. See Note, Phased Zoning: Regulation of the Tempo and Sequence of Land Development, 26 Stan.L.Rev. 585, 612–16 (1974) (reciting reasons why phased zoning is more likely to survive attack than low-density zoning); Note, Time Control on Land Use: Prophylactic Law for Planners, 57 Cornell L.Rev. 827 (1972).

55. Steel Hill Dev., Inc. v. Sanbornton, 469 F.2d 956, 962, 3 ELR 20018, 20020 (1st Cir. 1972).

> In effect, the town has bought time for its citizens not unlike the action taken in referendum by the City of Boulder, Colorado to restrict growth on an emergency basis . . . .

The moratorium must be spent wisely on developing a plan defensible in reason. Judge Coffin observed: [56]

> Hopefully, Sanbornton has begun or soon will begin to plan with more precision for the future, taking advantage of numerous federal or state grants for which it might qualify. Additionally, the New Hampshire legislature, to the extent it expects small towns like Sanbornton to cope with environmental problems posed by private developments, might adopt legislation similar to the federal National Environmental Policy Act . . . ., and thereby require developers to submit detailed environmental statements, if such power does not already reside within the town's arsenal of laws. Thus, while we affirm the district court's determination at the present time, we recognize that this is a very special case which cannot be read as evidencing a general approval of six-acre zoning, and that this requirement may well not indefinitely stand without more homework by the concerned parties.

It is tempting while evaluating the validity of growth restriction measures to become enmeshed in the contrasts between the hands-off approach of *Belle Terre* or the strict scrutiny approach of *Mt. Laurel*, or to view the debate as turning decisively on whether the right to decent housing, apart from racial discrimination, is declared fundamental, to be abridged only upon a showing of a compelling justification.[57] It is useful to recognize, however, that courts in other contexts on environmental questions are demanding reasoned decision-making, results that are justified, and restrictions that are carefully drawn.[58] That the case law on growth controls points this way also suggests that environmental justifications must be firmly based. There is precedent, after all, for requiring a strict showing of conservational necessity where the overall public sacrifice hits hardest on those least able to bear it.[59]

b. *Special Purpose Land Use Regulation*

It is rapidly becoming dogma that land use planning should transcend local boundaries, accommodate ecological unities, look beyond

---

56. 469 F.2d at 962, 3 ELR at 20021.

57. See Lindsey v. Normet, 405 U.S. 56, 74, 92 S.Ct. 862, 874, 31 L.Ed.2d 36, 50 (1972).

58. §§ 1.5 above (close scrutiny doctrine of judicial review), 2.16 above (public trust doctrine), 7.4 below (National Environmental Policy Act), 7.11 below (state environmental policy acts).

59. United States v. Washington, 520 F.2d 676, 5 ELR 20552 (9th Cir.), cert. denied 423 U.S. 1086 (1975) (requiring a strict showing of conservational necessity to justify the closing of off-reservation Indian fishing).

Sec. 2.17 LAND DEVELOPMENT CONTROLS

the case at hand, steer development into desired channels, and protect resources of regional significance.[60] Unfortunately, the legislative process rarely moves comprehensively, preferring instead the ad hoc, or one-time-only solution. Land development controls of this type are legion; three examples are discussed here—recreational developments in Vermont, oil refineries in Maine and power plants in Washington State. All three represent different regulatory treatments of certain types of large-scale development. They are discussed with the recognition that what the law says and how it works may be two different questions.

Recreational or second-home developments have created consumer and environmental ills of no small moment, as the literature [61] and the case law [62] attest. It can cause no small environmental or social shock to drop a major development into a typically rural area, ill prepared to deal with it. Vermont responded to this problem by creating a Land Use and Development Act with both regulatory and planning functions.[63] The regulatory provisions, which have come to predominate,[64] involve the establishment of a statewide environmental board and district environmental commissions. The commissions are empowered to issue permits [65] (appellate authority rests in the board [66]) as a precondition to commencing construction of a "subdivision" or "development" as defined in the Act.[67] Procedural provisions are set forth—for the content of an application, notice, hearing,

---

60. E. g., I. McHarg, Design With Nature (1969); The Nature Conservacy, The Preservation of Natural Diversity: A Survey and Recommendations (1975); Senate Comm. on Interior & Insular Affairs, National Land Use Policy: Background Papers on Past and Pending Legislation and the Roles of the Executive Branch, Congress and the States in Land Use Policy and Planning, 92d Cong., 2d Sess. (1972); Haskell, Land Use and the Environment: Public Policy Issues, 6 Environment Rep.—Monograph No. 20 (1975); Intergovernmental Relations in Land Use Planning, in Council of State Governments, Land: State Alternatives for Planning and Management 15 (1975).

61. E. g., CEQ, Fifth Ann.Rep. 21–26 (1974); R. Fellmeth, Politics of Land 181–205 (1973); M. Paulson, The Great Land Hustle (1972); The Use of Land, supra note 25, at 269–93.

62. E. g., Flint Ridge Dev. Co. v. Scenic Rivers Ass'n, 426 U.S. 776, 96 S.Ct. 2430, 49 L.Ed.2d 205 (1976); Steel Hill Dev., Inc. v. Sanbornton, 469 F.2d 956, 3 ELR 20018 (1st Cir. 1972); In re Spring Valley Dev., 300 A.2d 736 (Me.1973); cf. Friends of Mammoth v. Board of Supervisors of Mono County, 8 Cal.3d 247, 104 Cal. Rptr. 761, 502 P.2d 1049, 2 ELR 20673 (1972).

63. 10 Vt.Stat.Ann. § 6001 et seq.

64. See F. Bosselman & D. Callies, supra note 25, at 54–107; P. Myers, So Goes Vermont (1974).

65. 10 Vt.Stat.Ann. § 6086; see id. § 6081(a) ("No person shall sell or offer for sale any interest in any subdivision located in this state, or commence construction on a subdivision or development, or commence development without a permit . . .").

66. Id. § 6089.

67. Id. §§ 6001(3), (19). The definition of development exempts certain significant activities, including construction for farming, logging or forestry purposes below 2500 feet elevation or electric generation or transmission facilities.

burden of proof, disposition and appeal.[68] Issuance of a permit is dependent upon satisfying a stiff set of environmental criteria covering the spectrum (air and water pollution, waste disposal, water and energy conservation, protection of streams, soils and wildlife habitat, impact on growth).[69] Strong substantive standards, familiar to environmental law,[70] include the tests of best technology,[71] maximum mitigation[72] and non-degradation[73] with respect to various features of a planned development. In its single-case particulars, the Act is a particularly strong effort.

The Vermont legislation also has planning features with a potential for supplementing the case-by-case mechanism with a comprehensive framework. The environmental board is directed to adopt a capability and development plan designed to guide economic development in the state consistently with environmental aims.[74] The capability and development plan in turn is to serve as a basis for the board adopting a statewide land use plan, consisting of a map and statement of present and prospective uses "which determine in broad categories the proper use of the lands in the state whether for forestry, recreation, agriculture or urban purposes, the plans to be further implemented at the local level by authorized land use controls such as subdivision regulations and zoning."[75] The land use plan serves as a basis for regulatory (i. e., the issuance of permits) and non-regulatory decision-making. The non-regulatory approaches "may include public acquisition of land and easements, resource payments to private landowners permitting public use of their lands, and taxation of land . . . ."[76] But for the somewhat narrow perspective of a relevant "development," the Vermont act offers an example of a single purpose planning endeavor that blossomed into a legislative charter which can be administered as an effective, comprehensive planning tool.

68. Id. §§ 6083–85, 6087–89.

69. Id. § 6086.

70. Compare §§ 2.6 (nuisance), 2.16 (public trust) above; §§ 7.5, 7.11 (federal and state environmental policy acts) below.

71. 10 Vt.Stat.Ann. § 6086(a)(1)(C) (must demonstrate that applicant's design "has considered water conservation, incorporates multiple use or recycling where technically and economically practical, utilizes the best available technology for such applications, and provides for continued efficient operation of these systems"); id. § 6086(a)(9)(F) (planning and design of subdivision or development must "reflect the principles of energy conservation and incorporate the best available technology for efficient use or recovery of energy").

72. Id. § 6086(a)(8)(A)(ii) (requiring utilization of "all feasible and reasonable means of preventing or lessening the destruction, or imperilment" of wildlife habitat).

73. Id. § 6086(a)(9)(C) (must demonstrate that the subdivision or development "will not significantly reduce the potential [of forest or of secondary agricultural soils] for commercial forestry, including but not limited to specialized forest uses such as maple production or Christmas tree production . . . .").

74. Id. § 6042.

75. Id. § 6043.

76. Ibid.

Maine offers an example of a legislative effort going beyond the immediate source of inspiration (oil terminal facilities) but falling short of the planning potential realized by Vermont. The Maine Site Location Act [77] singles out any development which "may substantially affect the environment." [78] An Environmental Improvement Commission is established to approve or disapprove proposed developments, and impose "terms and conditions as are appropriate and reasonable." [79] Environmental criteria are established for project approval, although the statute uses only loose generalities.[80] Provisions are made for notice to the Commission of proposed developments, hearings and the enforcement of orders.[81] If construction is undertaken without notifying the Commission, an order may issue requiring the builder "to restore the area affected . . . to its condition prior thereto as near as may be to the satisfaction of the Commission." [82] The Maine law goes only so far as to permit a site-by-site consideration of major developments. It lacks entirely any system of comprehensive planning to influence developmental decisions before they are put in issue by specific proposals.

Washington State offers another example of a statewide land development control that lacks any significant planning element and, moreover, addresses but a single type of facility. The United States Supreme Court has made it clear that the Federal Power Commission's licensing authority over hydroelectric projects does not reach fossil-fuel fired thermal electric generating plants.[83] Congress seems little disposed to legislate on the subject,[84] which means as a practical matter that the states retain most of the significant powers of approval.[85]

77. Maine Rev.Stat.Ann. §§ 481–88.

78. Id. § 482(a); see In re Spring Valley Dev., 300 A.2d 736 (Me.1973) (applying Act to a recreational development) (rejecting a variety of constitutional objections).

79. Maine Rev.Stat.Ann. § 483.

80. Id. § 484 (conditioning project approval upon a Commission finding, among others, that the developer "has made adequate provision for fitting the development harmoniously into the existing natural environment and that the development will not adversely affect existing uses, scenic character, or natural resources in the municipality or in neighboring municipalities").

81. Id. §§ 483–86.

82. Id. § 485.

83. Chemehuevi Tribe v. Federal Power Comm'n, 420 U.S. 395, 95 S.Ct. 1066, 43 L.Ed.2d 278 (1975).

84. Hearings have been held for several years but there has been no strong push for enactment. See, e. g., Hearings on Land Resource Planning Assistance Act (S. 619) and the Energy Facilities Planning and Development Act (S. 984), Before the Subcomm. on the Environment and Land Resources of the Senate Comm. on Interior & Insular Affairs, 94th Cong., 1st Sess. (1975); Hearings on Power Plant Siting and Environmental Protection, Before the Subcomm. on Communications and Power of the House Comm. on Interstate and Foreign Commerce, H.R.Doc. No. 32, 92d Cong., 1st Sess. (1971).

85. Of course the Federal Power Commission licenses hydroelectric projects and the Nuclear Regulatory Commission licenses nuclear plants. Even as to these, the states retain significant powers.

State legislation on the subject has appeared in various forms,[86] with Washington's effort being one of the first and most innovative. The Washington State Thermal Power Plant Siting Act [87] establishes a Thermal Power Plant Site Evaluation Council, made up for the most part of representatives of state agencies having regulatory responsibilities over the location and operation of power plants. The Council is given general rulemaking powers and is authorized to receive applications for site locations, conduct hearings, and prepare written reports to the Governor, who personally approves or rejects the application for site certification. By regulation, an applicant must submit evidence demonstrating compliance with health, air and water quality standards and other environmental criteria. The utilities' *sine qua non* in the process leading to passage of the Act was a "one stop" service, which is responsive to the delays and added costs attributable to involvement in the licensing exercise of literally dozens of regulatory agencies, sometimes working at cross-purposes.[88] The "one stop" took the form of a declaration that the siting act "shall govern and control" [89] in the event of conflict with other provisions of state law, and later was invoked in an unsuccessful attempt by the utilities to justify a Council override of established environmental requirements of state law. The *quid pro quo* for environmental lobbyists was an insistence that the "one stop" be "a full, fair stop, with the public interest fully protected and environmental precautions strictly prescribed." [90] The "fair stop" takes the form of public adjudicatory hearings on certification applications, disclosure obligations, the appointment of a "counsel for the environment" to "represent the public and its interest in protecting the quality of the environment for the duration of the certification proceedings," [91] and provisions for

---

86. See, e. g., Best, Recent State Initiatives on Power Planting Siting: A Report and Comment, 5 Nat.Res. L. 668 (1972); Bronstein, State Regulation of Power Plant Siting, 3 Env. Law. 273 (1973); Case & Schoenbrad, Electricity or the Environment: A Study of Pubic Regulation Without Public Control, 61 Cal.L.Rev. 961 (1973); Ross, Power and the Environment: A Statutory Approach to Electrical Facility Siting, 47 Wash.L. Rev. 35 (1971); Van Vaalen, Industrial Siting Legislation: The Wyoming Industrial Development Information and Siting Act—Advance or Retreat? 11 Land & Water L.Rev. 27 (1976); Willrich, The Energy-Environment Conflict: Siting Electrical Power Facilities, 58 Va.L.Rev. 257 (1972); Note, State Regulation of Power Plant Siting, 47 Ind.L.J. 742 (1972).

87. Wash.Rev.Code §§ 80.50.010–.900; see Rodgers, Siting Power Plants in Washington State, 47 Wash.L.Rev. 9 (1971); Leed, The Citizen Role in Thermal Power Plant Siting, in Washington State University, Thermal Power Conference Proceedings 21 (1975).

88. Luce, Power for Tomorrow: The Siting Dilemma, 25 Record of the Association of the Bar of the City of New York 13, 19 (1970) ("taking as an example our proposed oil and gas fired units at the Astoria plant, we will need three approvals from Federal agencies, four from New York State agencies and at least twenty from New York City agencies, the exact number depending on the final design of the plant").

89. Wash.Rev.Code § 80.50.110(1).

90. Rodgers, supra note 87, at 25–26.

91. Wash.Rev.Code § 80.50.080.

an "independent consultant" who is hired by the Council with funds collected from the applicant to study the environmental consequences of the proposal.[92]

While the Washington act has some innovative features (notably, the counsel for the environment and the independent consultant), it is an awkward device for resolving individual applications. The Governor has the last word, tight time constraints abbreviate the possibilities of study (the Council must report to the Governor within twelve months of receiving an application; the Governor must decide within 60 days).[93] As a planning device, the Washington act is an utter failure. The Council sits only "to rule upon proposals advanced by the utilities, according to their timetable and within their order of priorities. Making long-range judgments about suitable alternative sites is a process still controlled, in the Pacific Northwest, by the power companies operating through the Joint Power Planning Council under the auspices of the Bonneville Power Administration."[94]

c. *Generalized Planning Efforts*

Broad planning endeavors affecting land use take a variety of forms. The Vermont Land Use Development Act, discussed above,[95] is an effort providing most of the tools necessary to plan for and cope with significant developments. Local growth control undertakings, such as the Ramapo plan, can be sophisticated and detailed, although they perforce reflect the insularity of their local government sponsors. Environmental policy acts can serve as planning mechanisms, although their use in this regard has been limited and their strength found mostly in the individualized treatment of specific projects.[96] Comprehensive regional planning may yet appear under the Federal Water Pollution Control Act although early signs have not been auspicious.[97]

Some regional or critical area planning efforts have been lauded in the literature. The work of the San Francisco Bay Conservation and Development Commission is one.[98] High hopes are held for the several coastal zone management regimes that are proceeding now with sponsorship provided by the federal Coastal Zone Management

---

92. Id. § 80.50.070. This provision institutionalizes the objective scientific inquiry so often lost in an adversary context. It protects the consultant and the applicant from the suspicion of collusion by "sanitizing" the funding for research through the medium of the Council.

93. By amendment in 1974, the Council, upon request of an applicant, is authorized to study a potential site prior to the receipt of an application. Id. § 80.50.175. This study is to serve as a substitute for an environmental impact statement.

94. Rodgers, supra note 87, at 32 (footnote omitted).

95. See text accompanying notes 60–76 supra.

96. §§ 7.9, 7.11 below.

97. § 4.9 below.

98. See F. Bosselman & D. Callies, supra note 25, at 108–35.

Act of 1972.[99] The "wave of the future in state land use planning efforts"[1] is said to be represented by Florida's Environmental Land and Water Management Act of 1972,[2] which is based upon the American Law Institute's Model Land Development Code[3] and is consistent with principles represented by proposed federal land use legislation which has come close to enactment.[4] The Florida act gives the state planning agency the power to prepare and recommend guidelines to determine whether a particular project is a "development of regional impact."[5] A "development of regional impact" means "any development which, because of its character, magnitude, or location, would have a substantial effect upon the health, safety, or welfare of citizens of more than one county."[6] These large-scale developments are accorded special study and must meet prescribed environmental criteria during the course of an administrative review process that may include an appeal to the Florida Land and Water Adjudicatory Commission.[7] Statewide authorities also are empowered to designate "areas of critical state concern" that may be within a single county. An area of "critical state concern" falls into one of three categories:[8] (1) "an area containing, or having a significant impact upon, environmental, historical, natural, or archeological resources of regional or statewide significance;" (2) "an area significantly affected by, or having a significant effect upon, an existing or proposed major public facility or other area of major public investment;" or (3) "a proposed area of major development potential, which may include a proposed site of a new community, designated in a state land development plan." A designation must be justified by findings and "recommend specific principles for guiding the development of the area."[9] It is supposed to lead to the enactment and administration of detailed land development regulations for the area by local authorities in the first instance but subject to state review.

The "critical area" format thus approves a state presence only in important cases. It singles out the "critical" areas and subjects

---

99. Pub.L. No. 92–583, 86 Stat. 1280, 16 U.S.C.A. §§ 1451–64, as amended Pub.L. No. 94–370, 90 Stat. 1013 (1976).

1. Futrell, supra note 2, at 82.

2. Fla.Stat.Ann. ch. 380; see P. Myers, Slow Start in Paradise (1974); Finnell, Saving Paradise: The Florida Environmental Land and Water Management Act of 1972, 1973 Urb.L.Ann. 103; Comment, Area of Critical State Concern: Its Potential for Effective Regulation, 26 U.Fla.L.Rev. 858 (1974). Oregon is another state with comprehensive land-use legislation. Ore.Rev.Stat. § 197.010 et seq.; see Comment, Oregon's New State Land Use Planning Act—Two Views, 54 Ore.L.Rev. 203 (1975). Hawaii is a third. Hawaii Rev.Stat. tit. 11, §§ 205–2 to –37; see F. Bosselman & D. Callies, supra note 25, at 5–53.

3. Now the ALI Model Land Dev. Code (Apr.1975 draft).

4. See 120 Cong.Rec. H5019, H5042 (daily ed., June 11, 1974) (house bill defeated by a vote of 211–204; a bill has twice passed the Senate).

5. Fla.Stat.Ann. § 380.06(2).

6. Id. § 308.06(1).

7. Id. §§ 380.06, 380.07.

8. Id. § 308.05(2)(a)–(c).

9. Id. § 380.05(1)(a).

them to special regulation not unlike, let us say, the separate regimes operative in the Hackensack Meadowlands, San Francisco Bay, the environs of Lake Tahoe and the Adirondack Park.[10] Proponents of these approaches view them as a means for overcoming the chief deficiencies of local planning (controlling growth, protecting vital regional resources, accepting and coping with major development)[11] without embracing statewide zoning. Opponents fear a threat to government power at local levels and further constraints on the freedom to develop. It goes without saying that the suggestion of a state power to preclude locally sanctioned development, or to compel the acceptance of a development locally opposed, is an issue not summarily resolved.

d. *The Taking Issue*

No regime of land development control can proceed with any seriousness without confronting the provision of the Fifth Amendment (or its state constitutional counterparts) that "private property" shall not "be taken for public use without just compensation." The taking issue is one of the motifs of environmental law and arises in every conceivable context where opportunities to maximize the economic value of land are constrained by society's desire to further resource preservation and other quality of life goals. Taking claims, to mention but a few examples, have come forth by the drove in the context of regulations affecting billboards,[12] stripmining,[13] clearcutting,[14]

10. See F. Bosselman & D. Callies, supra note 25, at 108–35, 291–98.

11. See Senate Comm. on Interior & Insular Affairs, National Land Use Policy: Background Papers on Past and Pending Legislation and the Roles of the Executive Branch, Congress, and the States in Land Use Policy and Planning, 92d Cong., 2d Sess. 11 (Comm. Print 1972).

12. E. g., Escondido v. Desert Outdoor Advertising, Inc., 8 Cal.3d 785, 106 Cal.Rptr. 172, 505 P.2d 1012, 3 ELR 20293, cert. denied 414 U.S. 828 (1973) (no taking); Dep't of Pub. Works v. Adco Advertisers, 35 Cal. App.3d 507, 110 Cal.Rptr. 849, 4 ELR 20469 (1973) (same); Grant v. Baltimore, 212 Md. 301, 129 A.2d 363 (1957) (same); John Donnelly & Sons, Inc. v. Outdoor Advertising Bd., ——Mass. ——, 339 N.E.2d 709, 6 ELR 20123 (1975) (same); State Thruway Authority v. Ashley Motor Court, Inc., 10 N.Y.2d 151, 218 N.Y.S.2d 640, 176 N.E.2d 566 (1961) (same). But see Santa Barbara v. Modern Neon Sign Co., 189 Cal.App.2d 188, 11 Cal. Rptr. 57 (1961) (aesthetics alone invalid justification); Eskind v. Vero Beach, 159 So.2d 209 (Fla.1973) (same). See generally Hagman, supra note 1, at 139–44. See also Lamm & Yasinow, The Highway Beautification Act of 1965: A Case Study in Legislative Frustration, 46 Denver L.J. 437 (1969).

13. E. g., Pennsylvania Coal Co. v. Mahon, 260 U.S. 393, 43 S.Ct. 158, 67 L.Ed. 322 (1922) (taking); Midland Elec. Coal Co. v. Knox County, 1 Ill. 2d 200, 115 N.E.2d 275 (1953) (same); Potomac Sand & Gravel Co. v. Governor, 266 Md. 358, 293 A.2d 241, cert. denied 409 U.S. 1040 (1922) (no taking); see Goldblatt v. Hempstead, 369 U.S. 590, 82 S.Ct. 987, 8 L.Ed.2d 130 (1962) (same); Bureau of Mines v. George's Creek Coal & Land Co., 272 Md. 143, 321 A.2d 748, 4 ELR 20822 (1974) (remanding for determination of whether stripmining ban was confiscatory); see Binder, A Novel Approach to Reasonable Regulation of Strip Mining, 34 U.Pitt.L. Rev. 339, 357–70 (1973).

14. Cf. State v. Dexter, 32 Wash.2d 551, 202 P.2d 906, aff'd per curiam

historic preservation,[15] zoning of the coastal region,[16] swamplands [17] and flood plains,[18] low-density phased zoning,[19] construction moratoria,[20] and pest control.[21] Despite a formidable accumulation of scholarship,[22] and thousands of judicial opinions, the line between a noncompensable regulation and a compensable taking remains uncertain. The four principal theories for testing taking claims, summarized cogently by Professor Soper,[23] are familiar to most students of the law: the most obvious is the case of outright physical appropri-

338 U.S. 863 (1949) (rejecting taking claim against a statute requiring those engaged in commercial logging to make provision for reforestation).

15. Maher v. New Orleans, 516 F.2d 1051, 5 ELR 20524 (5th Cir. 1975) (no taking); Penn Central Transp. Co. v. City of New York, 50 App.Div. 2d 166, 377 N.Y.S.2d 20, 6 ELR 20251 (1975) (same).

16. E. g., Candlestick Properties, Inc. v. San Francisco Bay Conservation & Dev. Comm'n, 11 Cal.App.3d 557, 89 Cal.Rptr. 897, 3 ELR 20446 (1970) (no taking); Bartlett v. Zoning Comm'n, 161 Conn. 24, 282 A.2d 907, 1 ELR 20177 (1971) (taking); Brecciaroli v. Commissioner of Environmental Protection, — Conn. —, 362 A.2d 948, 5 ELR 20319 (1975) (no taking) (distinguishing *Bartlett*); State v. Johnson, 265 A.2d 711 (Me.1970) (taking); MacGibbon v. Board of Appeals (III), — Mass. —, 340 N.E.2d 487, 6 ELR 20444 (1976) (taking) (by implication); Sibson v. State, 115 N.H. 124, 336 A.2d 239, 5 ELR 20300 (1975) (no taking); J. M. Mills, Inc. v. Murphy, — R.I. —, 352 A.2d 661, 6 ELR 20455 (1976) (no taking); Just v. Marinette County, 56 Wis.2d 7, 201 N.W.2d 761, 3 ELR 20167 (1972) (no taking); see Binder, Taking Versus Reasonable Regulation: A Reappraisal in Light of Regional Planning and Wetlands, 25 U.Fla.L.Rev. 1 (1972).

17. E. g., Morris County Land Improvement Co. v. Parsippany-Troy Hills, 40 N.J. 539, 193 A.2d 232 (1963) (taking).

18. E. g., Turner v. Del Morte, 24 Cal. App.3d 311, 101 Cal.Rptr. 93 (1972) (no taking); Dooley v. Town Plan & Zoning Comm'n, 151 Conn. 304, 197 A.2d 770 (1964) (taking); Turnpike Realty Co. v. Dedham, 362 Mass. 221, 284 N.E.2d 891, 3 ELR 20221 (1972), cert. denied 409 U.S. 1108 (1973) (no taking); see Plater, The Takings Issue in a Natural Setting: Floodlines and the Police Power, 52 Tex.L.Rev. 201 (1974).

19. Steel Hill Dev., Inc. v. Sanbornton, 469 F.2d 956, 3 ELR 20018 (1st Cir. 1972); Golden v. Planning Bd., of the Town of Ramapo, 30 N.Y.2d 359, 334 N.Y.S.2d 138, 285 N.E.2d 291 (1971); see cases cited in note 41, supra.

20. See cases cited in note 53, supra.

21. Cf. Miller v. Schoene, 276 U.S. 272, 48 S.Ct. 246, 72 L.Ed. 568 (1928) (statute required destruction of red cedar trees infected by cedar rust to protect nearby apple orchards; no taking).

22. E. g., F. Bosselman, D. Callies & J. Banta, The Taking Issue (1973); Costonis, "Fair" Compensation and the Accommodation Power: Antidotes for the Taking Impasse in Land Use Controversies, 75 Colum.L.Rev. 1021 (1975); Dunham, Griggs v. Allegheny County in Perspective: Thirty Years of Supreme Court Expropriation Law, 1962 Sup.Ct.Rev. 63; Michelman, Property, Utility, and Fairness: Comments on the Ethical Foundations of "Just Compensation" Law, 80 Harv. L.Rev. 1165 (1967); Sax, Takings and the Police Power, 74 Yale L.J. 36 (1964); Sax, Takings, Private Property and Public Rights, 81 Yale L.J. 149 (1971); Van Alstyne, Taking or Damaging by Police Power: The Search for Inverse Condemnation Criteria, 42 S.Cal.L.Rev. 1 (1970).

23. The Constitutional Framework of Environmental Law, in Environmental Law Institute, Federal Environmental Law 20, 50–71 (E. L. Dolgin & T. G. P. Guilbert eds. 1974).

ation, by trespass or otherwise.[24] The second theory, which emerges from the law of nuisance,[25] is that compensation is not required when regulatory restrictions are imposed on property uses that might be abated in any event as a nuisance.[26] A third theory, suggested also by nuisance law,[27] calls for a balancing process, resolving the question of compensation by reference to the extent of the hurt suffered by the property owner compared to the public benefit derived from the action taken. Fourth, and perhaps best known, is the theory that ties compensability to the loss of value suffered by the landowner. "One fact for consideration" in determining the limits of the police power, Mr. Justice Holmes wrote in the famous case of Pennsylvania Coal Co. v. Mahon, "is the extent of the diminution. When it reaches a certain magnitude, in most if not all cases there must be an exercise of eminent domain and compensation to sustain the action." [28]

The direction of the case law in recent time suggests that the constraints of taking principles do not impair severely environmental protection endeavors, even where there has been a substantial diminution of value. The nuisance theory, which of course allows for an uncompensated shutdown,[29] justifies the curtailment of land use practices entailing adverse effects of pollution or threatening the health or safety of nearby property owners or public resources. *Ramapo*,[30] *Sanbornton* [31] and other cases [32] espouse a go-slow approach on environmental questions that defers the taking claim because of the need for careful study and deliberate implementation. "The basis for this theory," Professor Soper points out, "is the new awareness that natural systems are interrelated in complex ways that often make it extremely difficult to predict the full range of consequences likely to follow from changes in any part of the system. The literature of the past ten years is replete with examples of adverse effects caused by changes in land use that were recognized only after the fact. Swamps were drained and aquatic production was reduced. Houses were built on steep slopes and landslides occurred. Flood plains were

---

24. See Pumpelly v. Green Bay Co., 80 U.S. (13 Wall.) 166, 20 L.Ed. 557 (1871) (taking where plaintiff's land flooded under state law authorizing construction of dams for flood control purposes).

25. §§ 2.1–.11 above.

26. See Hadacheck v. Sebastion, 239 U.S. 394, 36 S.Ct. 143, 60 L.Ed. 348 (1915) (no taking) (plaintiff's property drastically reduced in value by city ordinance forbidding use of brick kiln in residential neighborhoods) (plaintiff was there first).

27. § 2.4 (discussing the balancing test) above.

28. 260 U.S. 393, 413, 43 S.Ct. 158, 159, 67 L.Ed. 322, 325 (1922).

29. § 2.11 above.

30. Golden v. Planning Bd. of the Town of Ramapo, 30 N.Y.2d 359, 334 N.Y.S.2d 138, 285 N.E.2d 291 (1972).

31. Steel Hill Dev., Inc. v. Sanbornton, 469 F.2d 956, 3 ELR 20018 (1st Cir. 1972).

32. E. g., Candlestick Properties, Inc. v. San Francisco Bay Conservation & Dev. Comm'n, 11 Cal.App.3d 557, 89 Cal.Rptr. 897, 3 ELR 446 (1970).

occupied and aquifers were depleted. Examples such as these provide pressure in some cases to place what might be called a legislative moratorium over alteration in certain critical ecological systems pending a fuller understanding of the potential consequences of such alterations." [33]

The case of Just v. Marinette County,[34] sustaining a local shoreland zoning ordinance against claims of confiscation, modifies in another way the diminution of value standard. The court points out the conservation purposes of the ordinance:[35] "In the instant case we have a restriction on the use of a citizen's property, not to secure a benefit for the public, but to prevent a harm from the change in the natural character of the citizens' property. . . . What makes this case different from most condemnation or police power zoning cases is the interrelationship of the wetlands, the swamps and the natural environment of the shorelands to the purity of the water and to such natural resources as navigation, fishing, and scenic beauty." The court adverts to the public interest in certain natural resources:[36] "The shoreland zoning ordinance preserves nature, the environment, and natural resources as they were created and to which the people have a present right. The ordinance does not create or improve the public condition but only preserves nature from the despoilage and harm resulting from the unrestricted activities of humans." The source of the public rights in certain natural resources is of course the law of public trust.[37] It holds that regardless of the incidents of formal title certain resources are held in trust subject to use restrictions consistent with that trust. Maintaining the integrity of irreplaceable natural resources is one of those trust obligations. Thus taking claims may fail under *Just* if the property affected by the restriction is impressed with the public trust.

Professor Soper points out how well-considered legislation can affect the vote on confiscation claims.[38] The nuisance, moratorium or public trust theories are not to be read as *carte blanche* approvals to do away with the landowner's economic values willy-nilly: "By providing procedures to adjust regulations on a case-by-case basis, and by carefully tailoring restrictions to keep them as closely commensurate as possible to the problem that justifies the restrictions in the first place, the burden on property owners can be reduced and the potential constitutional obstacle more easily surmounted."[39] If there is a consistent theme of contemporary environmental law, it is that

---

33. Supra note 123, at 68–69.

34. 56 Wis.2d 7, 201 N.W.2d 761, 3 ELR 20167 (1972).

35. 56 Wis.2d at 16–17, 201 N.W.2d at 767–68, 3 ELR at 20168.

36. 56 Wis.2d at 23–24, 201 N.W.2d at 771, 3 ELR at 20170 (footnote omitted).

37. § 2.16 above.

38. Supra note 123, at 70–71.

39. Id. at 71.

government actions affecting natural resources will be given close scrutiny, regardless of whether these actions are taken in the name of conservation or development.[40]

[40] § 1.5 above (close scrutiny doctrine of judicial review); § 2.16 above (public trust doctrine); § 7.4 below (National Environmental Policy Act); § 7.11 below (state environmental policy acts).

Chapter III

AIR POLLUTION

§ 3.1 Background

The modern law of air pollution still is governed largely by the Clean Air Amendments of 1970,[1] despite some erosion occasioned by recent discovery of the energy problem. Any seminal legislative effort is the product of many converging influences, and the Clean Air Act is no exception. A few of the dominant contributors deserve emphasis.

First, the experience of hundreds of years of attempting to control air pollution by the application of nuisance and other common law doctrines was not swept aside. Thus, Congress' general expression in the 1970 amendments to disavow an intention to preempt state and local regulation (section 116), except in limited circumstances, is an important policy pronouncement. The amendments build on the common law superstructure; they do not repudiate it. Throughout the Act are found policy expressions with derivations deep in the common law: the "best technology" principle is invoked to control emissions from new sources (section 111); hazardous air pollutants are subject to strict control at the source (section 112); regulation anticipates the full range of emission limitations, operational and land use controls well known to students of nuisance law (section 110); the administrative remedies of extending control efforts over time (section 110) and requiring the production of reports, monitoring and emissions data (section 114) are techniques often used by courts in common law cases.

A second dominant influence in the genealogy of the Clean Air Amendments of 1970 was the federal regulatory experience in the field of water pollution. Terms, concepts, procedures borrowed from one field are applied to the other, as intermittent legislative activity gradually strengthened the federal presence in both fields. Perhaps the best example of this cross-fertilization (or, in some cases, cross-contamination) is the crucial "no significant deterioration" policy which is premised upon the general language of the findings and purposes clause of the 1970 Amendments (section 101)[2] but must be understood against the background of a dispute that had been raging un-

---

1. Pub.L. No. 91–604, 84 Stat. 1676, 42 U.S.C.A. § 1857 et seq., as amended.

2. The key language is the congressional expression of purpose in section 101(b)(1), 42 U.S.C.A. § 1857(b)(1), "to protect and enhance the quality of the Nation's air resources so as to promote the public health and welfare and the productive capacity of its population." See § 3.12 below.

der the Federal Water Pollution Control Act of 1965.[3] There are other examples: the reliance, albeit limited, upon ambient air quality standards as a regulatory technique (sections 108, 109), was influenced by the ritual of the water quality standards which dominated the rationale of the 1965 water pollution legislation; the ideas of state implementation plans (section 110) and enforcement by the elaborate conference procedure (section 115) had their origins in the water pollution experience.

A third, and obvious, influential contributor to the contents of the Clean Air Amendments of 1970 was the federal air pollution legislation of earlier times. In many respects, the 1970 amendments represented an abrupt and radical departure from the established regulatory path. Prominent in this regard is the demonstrable preference for emission standards on stationary sources (sections 110, 111, 112), the vesting of powers to review and rewrite state implementation plans in a federal authority, the Administrator of EPA (section 110), and the grant of direct federal enforcement powers (sections 113, 303 [dealing with emergency powers]). In other respects, the 1970 amendments simply carried over legislative relics of the past, perpetuating them in the statutes at large but not in the dynamics of the law-making process. On this list is found the air quality control regions (section 107), largely functionless shells carried over from the Air Quality Act of 1967,[4] and the conference abatement procedures (section 115), borrowed also from earlier air pollution statutes which in turn followed the pattern established in the water pollution field.

Because an understanding of today's enactments is so much a product of their history a more complete outline of federal air pollution legislation would be appropriate. The story begins with the Air Pollution Control Act of 1955,[5] which defined the federal role as being confined largely to research. The Act authorized the Secretary of Health, Education and Welfare to recommend, support and undertake research programs for air pollution control. It declared that air pollution control responsibility rested primarily with the states, a sentiment repeated with a diminishing ring of authority through three major revisions up to and including the Clean Air Amendments of 1970.[6] And it authorized the Surgeon General to conduct investigations into specific or local pollution problems upon request of any state or local government.

3. Pub.L. No. 89–234, 79 Stat. 903. For a discussion of the genesis of the no significant deterioration policy, see T. Jorling, The Federal Law of Air Pollution Control, in Environmental Law Institute, Federal Environmental Law 1058, 1078–82 (E. L. Dolgin & T. G. P. Guilbert eds. 1974).

4. Pub.L. No. 90–148, 81 Stat. 485.

5. Pub.L. No. 84–145, 69 Stat. 322.

6. Section 101(a)(3), 42 U.S.C.A. § 1857(a)(3), states "that the prevention and control of air pollution at its source is the primary responsibility of States and local governments."

Federal regulation got a foothold with the passage of the Clean Air Act in 1963.[7] The Act declared that its purposes, programs and procedures aimed "to achieve the prevention and control of air pollution," [8] although the scope and extent of the perceived air pollution problem were nowhere spelled out. Federal investigations of specific pollution problems no longer were dependent upon a state or local government request, mandated by the 1955 Act, but were tied instead to an equally narrow jurisdictional determination that the pollution affect another state in addition to the state of the source.[9] Federal abatement was legally conceivable, though barely so, because it was dependent both upon activity in one state with effects in another and a request from a governor for federal intervention or an independent determination by the Secretary of HEW that the pollution source endangered "health or welfare" in the other state.[10] Actual abatement turned also upon the completion of bizarre conference procedures where federal, state, and local officials convened for meetings and discussions with representatives of various pollution sources.[11] Only a court could order abatement, and then only after giving "due consideration to the practicability of complying with such standards as may be applicable and to the physical and economic feasibility of securing abatement of any pollution proved . . . ." [12] That directive, if anything, was a more narrow charter, and more generous to the polluting source, than the standards of discretion traditionally applied by equity courts considering abatement of common law nuisances.

The 1963 Act expanded the research and technical assistance program initiated in 1955 and provided for grants to state and local agencies to aid them in developing or improving their control programs. The Act also provided for the establishment of air quality criteria by the Department of HEW. Then, and now, criteria were to reflect scientific knowledge of the effects of various pollution concentrations.[13] They were designed to be a statement of cause and effect, not a rule of law, to be acted upon by the states only if they were so inspired.

Congress' first attempt at a comprehensive regulatory scheme for air pollution was the Air Quality Act of 1967.[14] The Act present-

---

7. Pub.L. No. 88–206, 77 Stat. 392, as amended.

8. Id. § 1.

9. Id. § 5(c)(1)(c).

10. Id. § 5(f).

11. Id. § 5. Compare § 3.19 below (discussing enforcement).

12. Pub.L. No. 88–206, § 5(g).

13. Id. § 3(c)(2), (3); see Comm. on Public Works, Clean Air Act, S.Rep. No. 638, 88th Cong., 1st Sess. 6–7 (1963).

14. Pub.L. No. 90–148, 81 Stat. 485, as amended [hereinafter cited as 1967 Act]. Pertinent authorities on the 1967 Act include Edelman, Air Pollution Abatement Procedures Under the Clean Air Act, 10 Ariz.L.Rev. 30 (1968); Martin & Symington, A Guide to the Air Quality Act of 1967, 33

ed a consistent and coherent, but hardly a credible, regulatory scheme. The first four steps were clearly prescribed: (1) establishment of atmospheric areas and air quality control regions; (2) issuance of "air quality criteria" and "control techniques" reports; (3) adoption of ambient air standards by the states within the air quality regions; (4) development of plans, also by the states, to implement the ambient air standards.[15]

The 1967 Act first required HEW to define the broad "atmospheric areas" of the nation.[16] An atmospheric area is a segment of the country where climate, meteorology and topography—factors influencing concentrations of air pollution—are generally homogeneous. These imaginary lines soon were drawn by the National Air Pollution Control Administration (now the Air Pollution Control Office of EPA) and are recognized today. There are eight atmospheric areas covering the contiguous, forty-eight states, plus two others for Alaska and Hawaii.

A second aspect of step one required the Department to designate "air quality control regions." [17] A region can be defined as a group of communities that should be treated as a unit for purposes of setting and implementing air quality standards. This administrative designation is guided by both the scientific factors used to define atmospheric areas (meteorological and topographical considerations) but also political factors and the concentration of air pollution sources.[18] In June of 1968, NAPCA named 32 of the largest and most severely polluted urban communities in the country as the initial air quality control regions.

There are today in existence 247 "air quality control regions" drawn on maps prepared by EPA. Most of the regions came into being pursuant to the authority of the 1967 Air Quality Act, although some of the more recent areas were designated in accordance with directives of the Clean Air Amendments of 1970.[19] The notion of the air quality control region is scientifically sensible; it confirms the

Law & Contemp. Prob. 239 (1968); O'Fallon, Deficiencies in the Air Quality Act of 1967, in id. at 275; Reitze, The Role of the "Region" in Air Pollution Control, 20 Case W.Res. L.Rev. 809 (1969). Carefully edited materials for use in law school are found in J. E. Krier, Environmental Law and Policy 300–30 (1971).

15. Two nicely contrasting views of the 1967 procedures are found in Middleton, Summary of the Air Quality Act of 1967, 10 Ariz.L.Rev. 25 (1968) (Dr. John G. Middleton formerly was Administrator of the National Air Pollution Control Administration) and J. Esposito, Vanishing Air 155–58 (1970) (John Esposito was one of the chief critics of the work of NAPCA from an environmental perspective).

16. 1967 Act § 107(a)(1).

17. Id. § 107(a)(2).

18. The designation of air quality control regions was "based on jurisdictional boundaries, urban-industrial concentrations, and other factors including atmospheric areas necessary to provide adequate implementation of air quality standards." Ibid.

19. Id. § 107(c).

obvious to suggest that regional air pollution problems are unresponsive to political boundaries, and dependent instead upon meteorological and topographical factors, traffic patterns, and the like. It is equally clear that drawing lines on a map to represent an "air quality control region"—for example, the New York-New Jersey-Connecticut Metropolitan Areas or the Metropolitan Boston Intrastate Region—hardly advances the objective of reducing air pollution within that region. The regions are fictitious entities without political powers.[20] Governmental controls, if needed, must come from existing federal, state or local jurisdictions. That the Air Quality Act of 1967 did not rework the federal system into the mould of the meteorologist of course does not alone make the legislation a geopolitical or legal failure.

Step two under the 1967 Act required HEW to develop and issue "criteria of air quality" and reports on "pollution control techniques" for single agents and combinations of agents.[21] As indicated, the criteria documents were provided for first in the 1963 Act, and were designed to be a comprehensive statement of cause and effect for the pollutants discussed.[22] Similarly, the "control techniques" documents were supposed to represent a definitive expression on the state of the art—the best technology, its costs, possible changes in fuel use or industrial processes.[23]

Step three under the 1967 Act was for the states to adopt ambient air standards within the air quality control regions. These standards were to be "consistent with" the criteria and control techniques reports.[24] An ambient air standard, simply stated, is a legal expression of the permissible amounts of pollutants allowed in the atmosphere generally. Typically, it is expressed in terms of time (hourly, 30 days, yearly) and permissible quantity (in either parts per million or micrograms per cubic meter of air or both). Ambient air standards are a measure of community performance not individual performance. Thus, state X might decide that the annual ambient air standard for sulfur oxides within a particular air quality control region is .02 parts per million. Without more, it is obvious that such a standard barely qualifies as a legal expression, as that term is generally

20. Reitze, supra note 14.

21. 1967 Act §§ 107(b), (c).

22. National Air Pollution Control Administration, Guidelines for the Development of Air Quality Standards and Implementation Plans, May 1969, at 3 reads:
Air quality criteria documents summarize available information on the relationship between exposures to air pollution and their effects on man and his environment, including injury to health, damage to materials and vegetation, reduction of visibility, economic losses and so on.

23. Id. at 4 states that control techniques documents are reports that provide information on the availability and applicability of techniques for the prevention and control of air pollutants and their sources and on the cost and effectiveness of such techniques.

24. 1967 Act § 108(c)(1).

understood. Nothing of consequence follows from the year-end announcement of whether all sulfur oxide sources in a region combined to "violate" the ambient air standard. As a general expression of community values or goals, the ambient air standard ranks with an official statement of desire to reduce the regional annual inflation rate to less than 10 per cent or the unemployment rate under 6 per cent. It is acceptable as a general policy aim, meaningless as a legal mechanism for achieving that aim.

Step four under the 1967 Act was the crucial step that would transform the ambient air standards into meaningful directives for individual sources. The air "cannot be fined, imprisoned, sued, treated or restored by human beings."[25] The 1967 Act anticipated that the states individually would prepare implementation plans setting emission standards (maximum amounts of allowable releases of particular pollutants) for individual sources together with timetables for compliance. After designation of the regions and publication of the criteria and control documents (for which there was no timetable in the law), the 1967 Act assumed that fifteen months would be consumed by the process of setting the ambient air standards and developing the implementation plans.[26] The Clean Air Amendments of 1970 arrived while the states were engaged in various aspects of standard-setting and plan-preparation under the Air Quality Act.

Steps 5 and 6 under the 1967 Act (federal review and enforcement) scarcely had been unlimbered before the 1970 changes. The federal government was given authority to review state ambient air standards for consistency with the criteria and control techniques documents and to review the state implementation plans for consistency with the standards.[27] One unanswered question was whether the federal government was empowered to develop an implementation and enforcement plan if the state plan was found inadequate.[28] Congress answered that question in the affirmative by the 1970 amendments.

The sixth and final step under the 1967 Act dealt with enforcement, and obviously there was not much of that since most energies were expended developing the plans which were to be enforced. The interminable conference procedures were carried over from the 1963 Act. During the first five years of experience (1963–68) the conference procedures were invoked in nine interstate areas, covering parts of 13 states and the District of Columbia.[29] Overall, the conferences provided little, if any, improvement in air quality. They afforded the factual grist for more than one doctoral thesis and newspaper expose.

25. J. Esposito, supra note 15, at 156.

26. 1967 Act § 108(c)(1).

27. Id. § 107(c)(1).

28. See Martin & Symington, supra note 14, at 260–61.

29. Edelman, supra note 14, at 30–36; see Note, Air Pollution in the Marietta-Parkersburg Area: A Case History, 32 Ohio St.L.J. 58 (1971).

A single case survived the gauntlet of the conference procedures and made it to the courts.[30] That was the case of the Bishop Processing Company, which operated a rendering and animal reduction plant near Bishop, Maryland, subject to the jurisdictional accident that odors from the plant wafted across state lines to pollute the air of nearby Selbyville, Delaware. Back in 1956, upon complaint of six citizens, Bishop Processing was abated as a private nuisance and permanently enjoined from releasing "noxious and offensive gases and odors."[31] There followed a two-decade tour through judicial and administrative processes, much of it serving as a test case for the conference abatement procedures of the 1963 and 1967 Acts.[32] Bishop Processing and its environmental problems easily survived the test and serve today as a suitable epitaph for the Air Quality Act of 1967 and its predecessors.

§ 3.2 The Clean Air Act: A Summary

The Clean Air Act currently represents a comprehensive programmatic and regulatory system on the subject of air pollution. To begin with, the Act, as amended through 1970, is subdivided into three titles. Title I covers generally the subject of stationary sources of air pollution. Title II deals with control of emissions from mobile sources, notably automobiles, trucks and aircraft. Title III embraces various administrative and judicial review provisions. Viewed somewhat differently, the Act can be subdivided on a functional basis: it has a programmatic element (furnishing technical and financial assistance, establishing research programs, and the like), and a regulatory element (covering the creation of standards, adoption of implementation plans, enforcement and so on).

Before focusing closely on the key provisions on stationary sources in this chapter, it may be helpful to summarize the sections generally. Title I begins with a broad statement of findings and purposes (Section 101), which we now know have been read to support a policy of nondegradation.[1] Section 102 authorizes the Administrator of EPA to encourage cooperative activities (including the development of uniform laws) among states and local governments for the preven-

---

30. For an amusing and wholly convincing account, see J. Esposito, supra note 15, at 114–18.

31. Bishop Processing Co. v. Davis, 213 Md. 465, 475, 132 A.2d 445, 450 (1956), quoting with approval the decree issued by the lower court.

32. See Bishop Processing Co. v. Gardner, 275 F.Supp. 780 (D.Md.1967). For the litigation affecting curtailment of operations, see United States v. Bishop Processing Co., 287 F.Supp. 624 (D.Md.1968), aff'd 423 F.2d 469 (4th Cir.), cert. denied 398 U.S. 904 (1970). In an order of July 14, 1971, the company was found in contempt but was afforded an opportunity to purge itself by controlling air pollution during vegetable oil processing operations. United States v. Bishop Processing Co., Civil No. 19274/76 (D. Md.).

1. § 3.12 below (no significant deterioration).

tion and control of air pollution. Section 103 directs the Administrator to establish a national research and development program for the prevention and control of air pollution. Part of this program includes an obligation to "render technical services and provide financial assistance to air pollution control agencies and other appropriate public or private agencies, institutions, and organizations, and individuals . . ." (section 103(2)). This provision should be interpreted to mean that the Administrator, in an appropriate case, could authorize or direct federal technical experts to appear as witnesses supporting the position of private parties in state or local administrative proceedings. The Administrator also is authorized to conduct epidemiological studies on the effects of air pollutants as well as clinical and laboratory investigations into the carcinogenic (cancer-causing), mutagenic (mutation-causing) and teratogenic (malformity-causing) effects of air pollutants. Both short-term and long-term research by EPA obviously influences the evolution of public policy on air pollution issues.

Section 104 instructs the Administrator to give "special emphasis to research and development into new and improved methods, having industrywide application, for the prevention and control of air pollution resulting from the combustion of fuels." This extends to the laboratory and pilot plant testing of processes, up to and including the construction and operation of demonstration plants. Some EPA research programs were transferred to the Federal Energy Administration by the Energy Reorganization Act of 1974 [2] creating the new agency.

Section 105 establishes grant programs under which the Administrator is authorized to support, in varying percentage amounts, the costs of planning and operating the programs of air pollution control agencies. The term "air pollution control agency" is defined in the Act to include various state, interstate, city, county or other local government authority charged with enforcing ordinances and laws relating to the prevention and control of air pollution.[3] The federal grant programs [4] are important to the survival of many state and local air pollution control efforts. Grant conditions require the production of some information on air pollution control,[5] and leverage afforded by the federal money is not to be disregarded in considering relationships between EPA and local officials.

Section 106 contains special provisions for federal support of interstate air quality agencies or commissions. Section 102(c) gives the consent of Congress to two or more states to negotiate compacts

2. Pub.L. No. 93–438, § 104(g), 88 Stat. 1237, adding 42 U.S.C.A. § 5814(g) (development of alternative automotive power systems).

3. Section 302(b), 42 U.S.C.A. § 1857h(b).

4. 40 CFR §§ 35.501–.538(2).

5. Id. § 35.530(c).

to advance cooperative air pollution control efforts. Interstate air pollution control agreements and compacts have been created from time to time.[6] Writers have urged that the ideal compact for the control of air pollution would establish an administrative body with broad monitoring, standard-setting and enforcement powers.[7] The prognosis for this type of jurisdictional renovation is weak to the point of disappearance.[8] While air pollution problems may overwhelm the limitations of traditional political boundaries, it will take more than air pollution to spark a revolution in urban government.

The heart of the federal stationary source air pollution control program is found in the 1970 Amendments in sections 107 (air quality control regions), 108 (air quality criteria and control techniques), 109 (ambient air quality standards), 110 (implementation plans), 111 (standards of performance for new stationary sources), 112 (national emission standards for hazardous air pollutants), 113 (federal enforcement) and 114 (inspections, monitoring and entry). Section 119 (authorizing certain suspensions and extensions of deadlines for qualifying power plants) was added by the Energy Supply and Environmental Coordination Act of 1974. These provisions will be addressed separately elsewhere in this chapter.

Section 115 retains the old conference procedure for abatement in certain cases (such as international pollution problems). A conference may not be called with respect to an air pollutant for which (at the time the conference is called) a national primary or secondary ambient air quality standard is in effect under section 109.[9] The procedure was retained primarily as a vehicle for bringing the then-pending conferences to a conclusion. Not a single post-1970 air pollution conference has been convened under section 115; this sorry procedure is a fading memory.

The creation of a complex system of public regulation often affects preexisting remedies in subtle ways. Section 116 of the Act carefully restricts federal powers of preemption. Outright preemption is accomplished only under sections 209 (emission standards for new motor vehicles), 211(c)(4) (controls or prohibitions respecting use of a fuel or fuel additive) and 233 (emission standards for any aircraft or aircraft engine). With these exceptions, section 116 declares that "nothing in this Act shall preclude or deny the right of any State or political subdivision thereof to adopt or enforce (1) any

---

6. See Note, Interstate Agreements for Air Pollution Control, 1968 Wash. U.L.Q. 205, 270–78; cf. 1 F.Grad, Environmental Law: Pollution Control § 304, at 3–193 to –201 (1975) (summarizing interstate compacts on water pollution).

7. Note, A Model Interstate Compact for the Control of Air Pollution, 4 Harv.J.Legis. 369, 370 (1967).

8. See Green, State Control of Interstate Air Pollution, 33 Law & Contemp.Prob. 315, 323–24 (1968); J. Krier, Environmental Law and Policy 311–20 (1971).

9. Section 115(b)(4), 42 U.S.C.A. § 1857 d(b)(4). Compare § 3.19 below (on enforcement).

standard or limitation respecting emissions of air pollutants or (2) any requirement respecting control or abatement of air pollution." The only qualification fixes federal standards as a floor, not a ceiling, so that "if an emission standard or limitation is in effect under an applicable implementation plan or under Section 111 (new source standards) or 112 (hazardous air pollutant standards), such State or political subdivision may not adopt or enforce any emission standard or limitation which is less stringent than the standard or limitation under such plan or section."

The act of federalizing the standard-setting process generally exerts pressure for the uniform treatment of common sources of air pollution throughout the nation. (One reason for this is that most of the expertise is concentrated at the national level). Section 116 arrests this tendency by allowing maximum state and local authority to require greater efforts from polluting sources than are required by federal standards. This situation obtains not only in the easy cases where federal emission standards are not at all inconsistent with state or local abatement measures involving, let us say, additional reporting or land use controls. But it obtains in the hard cases as well because states and localities specifically are authorized to improve upon emission standards set pursuant to federal law and thus demand a more substantial technological commitment from an individual source. Section 116 should be read as simply establishing a federal floor on performance standards.[10] A separate question is whether state or local authorities can muster technical expertise and persuasive rationales to justify stricter standards when those imposed under federal authority purport to protect fully property and health values.

In addition to preserving remedies under local law, the Act establishes a citizen suit provision (section 304) that rapidly has become a prototype for federal environmental statutes.[11] It authorizes a civil action against any person (including a government entity) who is alleged to be in violation of "(A) an emission standard or limitation under this Act or (B) an order issued by the Administrator or a State with respect to such a standard or limitation." It also authorizes a suit against the Administrator "where there is alleged a failure of the Administrator to perform any act or duty under this Act which is not discretionary with the Administrator." Costs of litigation (including reasonable attorney and expert witness fees) may be awarded.[12]

The Act reflects recent congressional preferences for including advisory committees in the decision-making process of regulatory sta-

---

10. See § 2.11 above.

11. § 1.13 above.

12. Section 304(d), 42 U.S.C.A. § 1857 h–2(d); see § 1.13 above.

tutes.[13] Section 202(b)(5)(D) [14] effectively gives a committee of the National Academy of Sciences a voice in the decision to suspend the auto emission standards. Section 117 establishes the President's Air Quality Advisory Board (with members appointed by the President) and vests it with authority to consult with the Administrator on policy matters. Section 117(f) makes clear that the Administrator "shall, to the maximum extent practicable within the time provided, consult with appropriate advisory committees, independent experts, and Federal departments and agencies" prior to taking certain actions regarding issuance of criteria documents, new source performance or hazardous emission standards, and motor vehicle emission standards. Similarly, section 108(b)(1) obliges the Administrator to issue information on air pollution control techniques only "after consultation with appropriate advisory committees" and federal departments and agencies. Although this language on prior consultation is not ironclad, there is authority for the proposition that a legislative directive to do something where "practicable" means something more than doing it if you feel so disposed.[15]

Affirmation of the significance of the advisory process is repeated elsewhere in the Act: under section 103(a)(4) the Administrator is obliged to "establish technical advisory committees composed of recognized experts in various aspects of air pollution to assist in the examination and evaluation of research progress and proposals and to avoid duplication of research." Under section 108(b)(2) he is invited to establish "a standing consulting committee for each air pollutant" to assist in the development of information on pollution control techniques. Under section 117(d) he is directed to establish advisory committees to obtain assistance in the development and implementation of air quality criteria, recommended control techniques, standards and research and development. Committee members "shall include, but not be limited to, persons who are knowledgeable concerning air quality from the standpoint of health, welfare, economics or technology." A notable absentee from the Clean Air Act advisory committee provisions is a prohibition against use of advisors who may have a conflict of interest, akin to that found in the Federal Water Pollution Control Act Amendments of 1972.[16]

Title II contains several key sections on mobile sources to be discussed elsewhere in this chapter: [17] establishment of motor vehicle emission (section 202) and fuel (section 211) standards, prohibited

---

13. See § 1.11 above.

14. Redesignated § 202(b)(5)(C) by the Energy Supply and Environmental Coordination Act of 1974, § 5(d), Pub.L. No. 93–319, 88 Stat. 246; see § 1.12 above (discussing the National Academy of Sciences).

15. Cf. Calvert Cliffs' Coord. Comm. v. Atomic Energy Comm'n, 146 U.S.App. D.C. 33, 52, 449 F.2d 1109, 1128, 1 ELR 20346, 20356, cert. denied 404 U.S. 942 (1972).

16. Section 304(h)(2)(D), 33 U.S.C.A. § 1314(h)(2)(D).

17. §§ 3.13–.18 below.

acts (section 203), compliance testing and certification (section 206), and compliance by vehicles in use (section 207). A study provision on the practicability of establishing fuel economy improvement standards was added by the Energy Supply and Environmental Coordination Act of 1974,[18] and this study in turn [19] led to legislation establishing standards the following year.

Some of the provisions of Title III deserve mention. Section 303 authorizes the Administrator, under prescribed conditions, to take direct action in the federal district courts if he finds that an air pollution source or sources "is presenting an imminent and substantial endangerment to the health of persons."[20] Section 304, previously mentioned, prescribes the conditions for citizen suits. Section 306 forbids, with several severe qualifications, federal agencies from contracting with persons convicted of an offense under section 113(c)(1). Section 307 addresses general provisions relating to judicial or administrative proceedings, including enforcement of subpoenas and petitions for review in the Courts of Appeals. The controversial subject of the mandatory licensing of patents is covered in section 308.

Section 309 is an extraordinary measure giving the Administrator a roving commission to review and comment in writing on the environmental impact of various activities to be taken by other federal departments and agencies. This provision making EPA a general environmental busybody and gossip is best viewed as a supplement to procedures under the National Environmental Policy Act, and therefore will be discussed in Chapter Seven.[21] Suffice it to note for the present that the rich potentiality of section 309 scarcely has been tapped. Promise unfulfilled describes several of the other innovative provisions of the 1970 Amendments, including the mandatory patent licensing provisions[22] and procurement disqualification for convicted offenders.[23] A provision that is a model of imaginative draftsmanship and a virtual administrative dead letter is Section 212 of the Act, which establishes the Low-Emission Vehicle Certification Board to put the government's buying power on the side of clean motor vehicles. It is a splendid idea which has not worked.[24]

18. Pub.L. No. 93–319, § 10, 88 Stat. 261, 42 U.S.C.A. § 1857f–6f. Other study provisions in the 1974 Act deal with the health effects of sulfur oxide emissions, energy conservation, various transportation control features of the implementation plans, and other topics.

19. See § 6.6 below (discussing the Energy Policy and Conservation Act of 1975).

20. 42 U.S.C.A. § 1857h–1; see § 3.19 below.

21. § 7.2 below.

22. See Schwartz, Mandatory Patent Licensing of Air Pollution Control Technology, 57 Va.L.Rev. 719 (1971).

23. Section 306(a), 42 U.S.C.A. § 1857 h–4(a).

24. See Comptroller General, Potential for Using Electric Vehicles on Federal Installations (1976). Compare § 5.2 below (mentioning provisions for establishing a Low-Noise-Emission Product Advisory Committee under the Noise Control Act).

Important provisions for the practitioner and student are found in Section 312 of the Act, which requires the Administrator, among other things, to make "a detailed estimate of the cost of carrying out the provisions of this [Act]." These economic cost studies are updated annually. They address costs of control for individual industries and thus are documents of potential significance in various legal proceedings.[25]

Section 313 of the Act requires an annual report from the Administrator on "measures taken toward implementing the purpose and intent of this [Act] . . .." The reports are sufficient to establish at least a mild acquaintance with regulatory action in the preceding year. The reason for this is that Congress took the trouble to specify in section 313 ten subjects to be addressed in the annual reports: (1) progress and problems associated with automotive exhaust emissions; (2) development of air quality criteria and recommended emission control requirements; (3) status of enforcement actions; (4) status of state ambient air standards setting, including plans for implementation and enforcement; (5) extent of development and expansion of air pollution monitoring systems; (6) progress and problems relating to development of new and improved control techniques; (7) development of instrumentation to monitor emissions and air quality; (8) standards set or under consideration relating to emission standards for moving sources; (9) status of state, interstate, and local pollution control programs; and (10) reports and recommendations made by the President's Air Quality Advisory Board.

In 1976, Congress' first major overhaul of the 1970 amendments came within an eyelash of passage.[26] Most of the changes under discussion represent an incremental evolution of the 1970 legislation, largely consistent with developing case law, and can be expected to

---

25. Needless to say, struggles over polluting technologies have a way of generating technical and economic analyses, inside and outside of the government. Illustrative of this process is the dozen studies, one macroeconomic (determining the impact of air and water pollution abatement costs on general economic variables such as growth, inflation, unemployment, interest rates), eleven microeconomic (analyzing the effect of pollution abatement costs on sales, prices, profits, plant closings and employment in individual industries) completed in 1972 under contract with the Council on Environmental Quality, the Environmental Protection Agency, and the Department of Commerce. See The Economic Impact of Pollution Control: A Summary of Recent Studies (1972). These studies were an important ingredient in the continuing legal debate over the extent of controls required for eleven affected industries—automobiles, baking, cement manufacturing, electric power generating, fruit and vegetable canning and freezing, iron foundries, leather tanning, nonferrous metals smelting and refining (aluminum, copper, lead, zinc), petroleum refineries, pulp and paper mills, and steel making.

26. See, e. g., Comm. on Public Works, Clean Air Amendments of 1976, S. Rep. No. 717, 94th Cong., 2d Sess. (1976); Comm. on Interstate and Foreign Commerce, Clean Air Act Amendments of 1976, H.R.Rep. No. 1175, 94th Cong., 2d Sess. (1976).

emerge with finality in the none too distant future. Compliance date extensions for both stationary and mobile sources are virtually certain to be enacted, along with tighter requirements for improved technologies. The emphasis as to stationary sources is likely to be on continuous emission reduction systems,[27] and as to mobile sources on the development of a clean car,[28] although the latter assignment at times looks like a search for the holy grail. Congress shows strong signs of accepting the principle of no significant deterioration,[29] with qualifications, and of discouraging the more hotly contested features of transportation controls [30] and the regulation of indirect sources.[31] A rewriting of the provisions on new source performance standards is expected,[32] and a repudiation of the Supreme Court decision protecting federal facilities from state permit requirements.[33] There is considerable room for improvement in the enforcement provisions of the 1970 amendments,[34] some of which probably will be corrected, along with improvements in emission controls on in-use vehicles.[35] The familiar pattern of mandating studies is likely to reappear in future amendments—an expansion of the role of the National Academy of Sciences in overseeing auto emission standards,[36] special investigations of the health effects of sulfates and compounds threatening the ozone layer, perhaps the creation of a National Commission on Air Quality, based on experience in the field of water pollution,[37] to recommend future legislative adjustments.

§ 3.3 Designating Regions; Issuing Criteria and Control Techniques Documents

Under the Clean Air Act a stationary source means any building, structure, facility or installation which emits or may emit any air pollutant.[1] The term "installation" should be construed generously to mean any identifiable geographical area which is a source of air pollutants. This would include, for example, a field that is burned over to remove stubble or a parking garage.[2] A mobile source, not defined in the Act, is a moving source of air pollutants—notably, any ve-

27. § 3.8 below.

28. §§ 3.13, 3.14 below.

29. § 3.12 below.

30. § 3.16 below.

31. § 3.17 below.

32. § 3.10 below.

33. § 3.19 below.

34. Ibid.

35. § 3.15 below.

36. § 3.14 below.

37. § 4.1 below.

1. Section 111(a)(3), 42 U.S.C.A. § 1857 c–6(a)(3). This definition appears separately in the section providing for standards of performance for new stationary sources and thus should be viewed as addressing a narrower problem than that of all stationary sources.

2. See § 3.17 below (discussing indirect sources).

hicle used for transportation. An air pollutant means any air pollution agents or combination of agents.[3]

The process for setting and enforcing ambient air standards is easily understood. It involves (1) designation of air quality control regions, (2) issuance of air quality criteria and information on air pollution control techniques for major pollutants, (3) establishment of national ambient air quality standards for major pollutants, (4) preparation of implementation plans by the states, (5) review and revision of those plans by the Administrator, and (6) enforcement of the plans. These procedures resemble those established under the Air Quality Act of 1967, except for a strengthening of the federal role in several respects. The federal government today has a great deal to say about the actual emission standards prescribed for individual stationary and mobile sources.

Section 107 was designed to bring about an "early completion" [4] of the process of designating air quality control regions. This was accomplished by retaining previously designated regions, authorizing the Administrator, within ninety days, to designate new interstate or intrastate regions, and declaring portions of a state not previously designated to be regions unto themselves, subject to further subdivision. The Congress' aim was to impart into the process of designation those factors bearing on effective implementation of air-quality standards, such as meteorology, topography and urban-industrial concentrations.[5] Of course, while the designation of regions was to be sensitive to the scientific vagaries of pollution control, the primary responsibility for assuring air quality within political boundaries is that of the states.[6] Divorcing the regions from any and all responsibility for standards-setting, enforcement or planning is the principal reason for concluding that their function is little more than ceremonial.[7] The states are free, indeed are encouraged, to fashion their implementation plan strategies in response to the varying demands of different air quality control regions. This is done occasionally, but the fact remains that implementation plans that are state-conceived, state-drafted and state-enforced are not regional plans.

---

3. Section 302(g), 42 U.S.C.A. § 1857 h(g).

4. Comm. on Public Works, National Air Quality Standards Act of 1970, S.Rep. No. 1196, 91st Cong., 2d Sess. 7 (1970) [hereinafter cited as Senate Report].

5. Id. at 8.

6. Section 107(a), 42 U.S.C.A. § 1857 c–2(a), is quite clear:
   Each state shall have the primary responsibility for assuring air quality within the entire geographic area comprising such State by submitting an implementation plan for such State which will specify the manner in which national primary and secondary ambient air quality standards will be achieved and maintained within each air quality control region in such state.

7. See J. Krier, Environmental Law and Policy 315 (1971).

Sec. 3.3   **DESIGNATING REGIONS**   223

The second step, issuance of the air quality criteria and control techniques information for ubiquitous pollutants, also is a carry-over from the earlier versions of the Act. There is no doubt that the criteria and control techniques documents, respectively, are conceived as being basic inquiries into cause and effect and state of the art. According to section 108(a)(2), air quality criteria for an air pollutant "shall accurately reflect the latest scientific knowledge useful in indicating the kind and extent of all identifiable effects on public health or welfare which may be expected from the presence of such pollutant in the ambient air, in varying quantities." [8] Public health in this context means the health of any group of the population, including sensitive or vulnerable groups.[9] Public welfare "includes, but is not limited to, effects on soils, water, crops, vegetation, manmade materials, animals, wildlife, weather, visibility, and climate, damage to and deterioration of property, and hazards to transportation, as well as effects on economic values and on personal comfort and well-being." [10] The Act states specifically that the criteria, "to the extent practicable," shall include information on "variable factors (including atmospheric conditions)" which may alter the effects of a pollutant on public health or welfare, on the synergistic effects (interaction) of different air pollutants and on "any known or anticipated adverse effects on welfare." [11] The explicit requirement that the criteria documents address anticipated effects on welfare obviously should not be read as encouraging neglect of anticipated effects on health.

Information on air pollution control techniques, according to section 108(b)(1), "shall include data relating to the technology and costs of emission control. Such information shall include such data as are available on attainable technology and alternative methods of prevention and control of air pollution. Such information shall also include data on alternative fuels, processes, and operating methods which will result in elimination [or] significant reduction of emissions." [12] This information obviously is addressed to technological alternatives and control options which have been the grist of air pollution controversies for the better part of a century. It goes without saying that control techniques documents, once published, are not intended to freeze the state of the art.[13]

Obviously, the criteria and control techniques documents are important to students and practitioners confronting cause-in-fact or state of the art questions regarding a particular industry. The documents are potentially admissible as evidence in administrative or ju-

---

8. 42 U.S.C.A. § 1857c–3(a)(2).

9. Senate Report, supra note 4, at 9.

10. Section 302(h), 42 U.S.C.A. § 1857h(h).

11. Section 108(a)(2), 42 U.S.C.A. § 1857c–3(a)(2).

12. 42 U.S.C.A. § 1857c–3(b)(1).

13. Senate Report, supra note 4, at 9.

dicial proceedings;[14] they are explicitly identified as source material in the Administrator's determination in establishing national primary and secondary ambient air quality standards under Section 109 of the Act;[15] they are regularly cited, quoted, denounced, and invoked in various administrative forums on air pollution questions. It cannot be said, however, that the criteria and control techniques documents have influenced greatly the decisions of the courts.[16] The probable reasons are that the documents represent only summaries of the conclusions of others, are soon outdated, sometimes wrong, and are based upon hypotheses that often do not apply to a single source faced with control obligations.[17]

§ 3.4 National Ambient Air Quality Standards

After designation of the air quality control regions and issuance of the criteria and control techniques documents, step three of the Clean Air Act procedure calls for the Administrator to establish primary and secondary national ambient air quality standards for each criteria pollutant. A criteria pollutant is one for which a criteria document issues. It is identified pursuant to section 108(a)(1)[1] of the Act, which reads: "For the purpose of establishing national primary and secondary ambient air quality standards," the Administrator shall publish within thirty days, and thereafter revise, a list which includes each air pollutant:

(A) which in his judgment has an adverse on public health and welfare;

(B) the presence of which in the ambient air results from numerous or diverse mobile or stationary sources; and

(C) for which air quality criteria had not been issued before the date of enactment of the Clean Air Amendments of 1970, but for which he plans to issue air quality criteria under this section.

---

14. See Chicago v. Commonwealth Edison Co., 24 Ill.App.3d 624, 321 N.E.2d 412 (1974); Miller & Borchers, Private Lawsuits and Air Pollution Control, 56 A.B.A.J. 465 (1970).

15. It was argued but not resolved in Kennecott Copper Corp. v. EPA, 149 U.S.App.D.C. 231, 462 F.2d 846, 2 ELR 20116 (1972), that EPA's national secondary ambient air standard for sulfur oxides was not properly "based" on the criteria document in accordance with Section 109 of the Act.

16. E. g., Chicago v. Commonwealth Edison Co., 24 Ill.App.2d 624, 321 N.E. 2d 412 (1974); see Allyn v. United States, 461 F.2d 810, 818, 2 ELR 20473, 20477 (Ct.Cl.1972) (David, J., concurring in part, dissenting in part) (expressing concern at the failure of the court to consider ambient air standards for CO in rejecting hazardous pay claim by quarantine inspectors working near automobiles).

17. See D. P. Currie, Cases & Materials on Pollution 205–08 (1975).

1. 42 U.S.C.A. § 1857c–3(a)(1).

Section 108(a)(2)[2] directs the Administrator to issue air quality criteria for any air pollutant within twelve months of its listing. These criteria pollutants are special cases: they are ubiquitous and injurious, the cream of the dirty crop, typified by sulfur oxides and carbon monoxide.

The stated purpose of section 108 is to "require acceleration of the issuance of air quality criteria and information on control techniques as an integral part"[3] of the system of ambient air quality standards and implementation plans. The actual effect is to accelerate nothing since the time limitations on issuance of air quality criteria and control techniques documents do not come into play until the Administrator exercises his discretion to list a pollutant as a ubiquitous evil and the intended subject of air quality criteria. Neglecting to list tolls the obligation to produce criteria and control techniques documents. At the time of the passage of the 1970 amendments, air quality criteria already had been issued for five major pollutants (sulfur oxides, particulates, carbon monoxide, hydrocarbons and photochemical oxidants.) Other pollutants of broad national impact identified by the Senate Subcommittee on Air and Water Pollution in its report accompanying the bill that ultimately become the 1970 amendments were fluorides, nitrogen oxides, polynuclear organic matter, lead and odors.[4] Of these five candidates, a single one (nitrogen oxides) since has been listed by the Administrator on his own volition as a criteria pollutant,[5] and one other (lead) has been listed by compulsion as a result of a citizen suit.[6]

Once listed, the standards for criteria pollutants are established in accordance with a fixed timetable. National primary ambient air quality standards "shall be ambient air quality standards the attainment and maintenance of which in the judgment of the Administrator, based on [the] criteria and allowing an adequate margin of safety are requisite to protect the public health."[7] It is clear from the legislative history that the public whose health is to be protected includes "particularly sensitive citizens such as bronchial asthmatics and emphysematics who in the normal course of daily activity are exposed to the ambient environment."[8] An ambient air quality stand-

2. Id. § 1857c–3(a)(2).

3. Comm. on Public Works, National Air Quality Act of 1970, S.Rep. No. 1196, 91st Cong., 2d Sess. 7 (1970) [hereinafter cited as Senate Report].

4. Id. at 9.

5. See 36 Fed.Reg. 22385 (1971), adding 40 CFR pt. 401.

6. Natural Resources Defense Council, Inc. v. Train, 411 F.Supp. 864, 6 ELR 20366 (S.D.N.Y.1976), aff'd 545 F.2d 320, 7 ELR 20004 (2d Cir.) (indicating a listing is required once the Administrator determines a pollutant from numerous sources causes adverse effects but leaving open the question of whether a claim of impossibility might excuse the obligation to establish standards).

7. Section 109(b)(1), 42 U.S.C.A. § 1857 c–4(b)(1).

8. Senate Report, supra note 3, at 10. The Report thus makes allowance

ard, therefore "should be the maximum permissible ambient air level of an air pollution agent or class of such agents (related to a period of time) which will protect the health of any group of the population."[9] The standards thus are tied to a medical judgment about how low the level of ambient pollutants must be to prevent injury to people, either directly or by aggravation of preexisting diseases.[10]

The "adequate margin of safety" referred to in the Act was included to protect against potential health hazards not yet identified by research.[11] Presumably the language would justify a health-related standard based upon ambiguous or incomplete data.[12] This legislative technique is imaginative and sound: it is one way to confront the perpetual problem of assigning the burden of proof in cases of uncertain, marginal, and potentially serious technological risks. The Clean Air Act allows the administrative prohibition of certain activities without actual proof of health hazards to an identifiable group, so long as the prohibition can be defended as a scientifically supportable margin of safety.

The national secondary ambient air quality standards prescribed under the Act "shall specify a level of air quality the attainment and maintenance of which in the judgment of the Administrator, based on [the] criteria, is requisite to protect the public welfare from any known or anticipated adverse effects."[13] As indicated above,[14] the public welfare that must be protected "includes, but is not limited to,

for vulnerable groups but does not discard an objective standard entirely in favor of a subjective one:
> In requiring that national ambient air quality standards be established at a level necessary to protect the health of persons the Committee recognizes that such standards will not necessarily provide for the quality of air required to protect those individuals who are otherwise dependent on a controlled internal environment such as patients in intensive care units or new-born infants in nurseries. However, the Committee emphasizes that included among those persons whose health should be protected by the ambient standard are particularly sensitive citizens such as bronchial asthmatics and emphysematics who in the normal course of daily activity are exposed to the ambient environment. In establishing an ambient standard necessary to protect the health of those persons, reference should be made to a representative sample of persons comprising the sensitive group rather than to a single person in such a group.

9. Id. at 10.

10. See D. P. Currie, Cases & Materials on Pollution 208–19 (1975) (raising several interesting questions regarding the establishment of ambient pollution standards).

11. Senate Report, supra note 3, at 10.

12. See Jorling, The Federal Law of Air Pollution Control, in Environmental Law Institute, Federal Environmental Law 1058, 1083 (E. L. Dolgin & T. G. P. Guilbert eds. 1974); cf. Kennecott Copper Corp. v. EPA, 149 U.S.App.D.C. 231, 234 n. 13, 462 F.2d 846, 849 n. 13, 2 ELR 20116, 20118 n. 13 (1972) (raising but not resolving question of whether and how much the agency under the statute was allowed a "margin of error" in setting a secondary standard at a level below documented effects).

13. Section 109(b)(2), 42 U.S.C.A. § 1857c–4(b)(2).

14. § 3.3.

effects on soils, water, crops, vegetation, man-made materials, animals, wildlife, weather, visibility, and climate, damage to and deterioration of property, and hazards to transportation, as well as effects on economic values and on personal comfort and well-being." [15] The reference to "economic values" should be read as authorizing protection from effects of economic significance not otherwise mentioned (such as offenses to aesthetic values) rather than indicating that economically significant effects are the only ones that count.[16] The standards are dictated by the needs of the people and things that can be hurt not the laws of economics. Protecting public welfare from both "known or *anticipated* adverse effects" affords the environment a margin of safety in the standards, albeit not one as expansive as that extended the protection of public health. The primary and secondary standards, together, are conceived as establishing a minimally acceptable level of ambient air quality protecting man and his environment from all known effects and some that, although not known, are legitimate subjects of concern.[17]

The notion of fixing national ambient air quality standards for major pollutants is not easily defensible, and has some aspects of the absurd. Part of the problem is due to the concept of ambient air standards themselves, which are lofty measures of excellence bereft of meaning short of specific directives about who should do what to achieve high quality air for the benefit of all. It also taxes credulity to suggest that a single standard of air quality can be expressed and achieved alike in the skies from Pittsburgh to Albuquerque. Nor should the administrative difficulties be overlooked: will a single national standard reflect a compromise of competing views instead of

---

15. Section 302(h), 42 U.S.C.A. § 1857h.

16. Compare the interpretation advanced by EPA in refusing to make more stringent the three-hour secondary sulfur standard (38 Fed.Reg. 25678, 25680 (1973)):
   The revised criteria document presents the results of studies which indicate that visible injury to some types of vegetation (minor leaf spotting) can result from short-term concentrations of SO_2 which do not exceed the current standards . . . . The Administrator has given careful consideration to the question of whether this degree of injury can be responsibly defined as an adverse effect within the meaning of the Clean Air Act. . . .
   In his judgment, standards developed solely to protect against minor visible injury are not necessarily requisite to protect the public welfare from adverse effects.

The statute, however, contains nothing suggesting that "adverse" effects must be grave or serious or those worth preventing. See D. P. Currie, supra note 10, at 209.

17. Senate Report, supra note 3, at 10 puts it this way:
   National air quality standards are authorized because the Committee has recognized that protection of health is a national priority, but the Committee also recognizes that man's natural and man-made environment must be preserved and protected. Therefore, the bill provides for the setting of national ambient air quality goals at levels necessary to protect public health and welfare from any known or anticipated adverse effects of air pollution—including effects on soils, water, vegetation, man-made materials, animals, wildlife, visibility, climate, and economic values.

the highest learning on the subject? Will use of a national standard as a basic premise for technological change (*i. e.*, sulfur oxide controls) prove unfeasible in light of continually accumulating knowledge on the subject of health and environmental effects and the need to experiment with controls? More important are the economic questions: [18] Why should a national standard ignore individual economies of the affected parties that received such close scrutiny at common law? Or regional efficiencies? Even if national standards are justified on some basis (need to avoid parochialism, interstate conflict, manipulation by the special interest), why should the standards be uniform instead of variable?

With all this said, national ambient air quality standards can be defended. The alternative of the states establishing and enforcing their own ambient air quality standards was tried and found wanting under the Air Quality Act of 1967. If the need for a federal presence is conceded, surely no better performance standard can be found than that emissions do not hurt people or the environment. And if freedom from human or environmental harm is embraced as an objective, regional variations must be minimal or non-existent because scientific measures of effects are not likely to fluctuate greatly depending upon the place of the hurt.[19] There is, to be sure, a certain leveling and compromising effect of federal standards, but this problem is minimized in the Act by preserving the autonomy of states and local governments to improve upon them if they wish. Claims of economic insanity of national standards are answered by pointing out that the standards setting-enforcement system invites economic and technical arguments on half a dozen occasions.[20] Setting the standards solely by reference to effects does not disavow economically efficient means of achieving them.

In accordance with the timing prescribed by section 108, the Administrator published proposed national ambient air standards for six criteria pollutants (sulfur oxides, particulates, carbon monoxide, photochemical oxidants, hydrocarbons and nitrogen oxides) on January 30, 1971.[21] Final rules were promulgated on April 30, 1971.[22] It was generally recognized that EPA's sulfur oxides standards were more lenient than those in force in many parts of the country which included hourly standards, and in some cases five minute and even

---

18. See Krier, The Irrational National Air-Quality Standards: Macro- and Micro-Mistakes, 22 U.C.L.A.L.Rev. 323, 327 (1974).

19. Some variation is conceivable given synergistic effects among pollutants. That is, sulfur oxide effects may depend in part on the extent of particulates in the ambient air. See HEW, Air Quality Criteria for Sulfur Oxides 153–62 (1969).

20. See § 3.9 below; cf. South Terminal Corp. v. EPA, 504 F.2d 646, 675, 4 ELR 20768, 20780 (1st Cir. 1974) ("minimum public health requirements are often, perhaps usually, set without consideration of other economic impact").

21. 36 Fed.Reg. 1502 (1971).

22. See note 22 on page 229.

Sec. 3.4 AMBIENT AIR QUALITY STANDARDS

three minute standards. The legal integrity (if not the practical persuasiveness) of these state and local regulations of course is preserved by the no-preemption provisions of section 116. Whether for this or some other reasons, no legal challenges to the standards were launched by those claiming them to be too lax. The basic premises of the national clean-up effort were in place.

The only attack on the federal ambient air quality standards came from the other direction, and focused upon the annual secondary standard for sulfur oxides of 60 micrograms per cubic meter. The litigation in Kennecott Copper Corp. v. EPA [23] added a footnote to the hard look doctrine [24] by requiring an agency explanation of the reasoning process (anticipated effects? margin of error? or otherwise?) by which the standard was derived. The immediate consequence of the decision was a withdrawal of the annual and 24-hourly

---

22. 36 Fed.Reg. 22384 (1971), 40 CFR pt. 50. The national ambient air standards are:

Federal Standard

Substance	Primary	Secondary
SO_2	80 microgm/m^3 [0.03 p.p.m.] annual arithmetic mean 365 microgm/m^3 [0.14 p.p.m.] maximum in 24 hours	*60 microgm/m^3 [0.02 p.p.m.] annual arithmetic mean *260 microgm/m^3 [0.1 p.p.m.] maximum in 24 hours 1,300 microgm/m^3 [0.5 p.p.m.] maximum in 3 hours
Particulates	75 microgm/m^3 annual geometric mean 260 microgm/m^3 maximum in 24 hours	60 microgm/m^3 annual geometric mean 150 microgm/m^3 maximum in 24 hours
CO	10 milligm/m^3 [9 p.p.m.] maximum in 8 hours 40 milligm/m^3 [35 p.p.m.] maximum in 1 hour	10 milligm/m^3 [9 p.p.m.] maximum in 8 hours 40 milligm/m^3 [35 p.p.m.] maximum in 1 hour
Photochemical	160 microgm/m^3 [0.08 p.p.m.] maximum in 1 hour	160 microgm/m^3 [0.08 p.p.m.] maximum in 1 hour
HC (corrected for methane)	160 microgm/m^3 [0.24 p.p.m.] maximum in 3 hours, 6 a.m.–9 a.m.	160 microgm/m^3 [0.24 p.p.m.] maximum in 3 hours, 6 a.m.–9 a.m.
NO_2	100 microgm/m^3 [0.05 p.p.m.] annual arithmetic mean	100 microgm/m^3 [0.05 p.p.m.] annual arithmetic mean

Maximum concentrations are not to be exceeded more than once per year. P.p.m. means parts per million.

* The secondary standard for SO_2 was relaxed in 1973 by withdrawal of the annual and 24-hourly measurements. Note 25, infra.

23. 149 U.S.App.D.C. 231, 462 F.2d 846, 3 ELR 20116 (1973).   24. § 1.5 above.

secondary standards for sulfur oxides.[25] Its longer-range impact has been to enforce the obligations of reasoned decision-making within the agency, which as a practical matter has led to the preparation of so-called *Kennecott* statements to accompany various regulatory initiatives.

Consistently with their dignity as national health standards, the ambient air quality standards remain a subject of continuing debate. There has been pressure to tighten the primary sulfur oxide standards and to promulgate separate standards for suspended particulate sulfates (produced as a result of atmospheric chemical reactions of sulfur dioxide).[26] On the other hand, there is reputable authority for the proposition that the carbon monoxide standards may be more stringent than necessary.[27] Future revisions may be expected. It is fair to state, however, that the Environmental Protection Agency is more than a little reluctant to expand the list of criteria pollutants. The reason for this is that a listing and the setting of standards is but a prelude to an enormous administrative undertaking aimed toward eventual compliance.

§ 3.5 The Implementation Plans: Procedure

After establishment of the national ambient air quality standards, the directives for meeting them are prescribed by the state implementation plans developed under Section 110 of the Act.[1] It may be helpful at the outset to stress what the implementation plans are not: they are not comprehensive plans for controlling all pollutants from all sources within a state. They are, instead, plans which provide "for implementation, maintenance and enforcement"[2] of national primary and secondary ambient air quality standards within each air quality region (or portions of an air quality region) in a given state. Thus a state implementation plan, like the federal standards it is designed to satisfy, is aimed at the big problems of the criteria

---

25. 38 Fed.Reg. 25678 (1973), 40 CFR § 50.5. The original Kennecott statement is found in 37 Fed.Reg. 9577 (1972). The proposed changes in the sulfur oxide standards appear in 38 Fed.Reg. 11355 (1973).

26. For a summary of recent data on the health effects of major air pollutants, see Senate Comm. on Public Works, Summary of Proceedings, National Academy of Sciences Conference on Health Effects of Air Pollution, Oct. 3–5, 1973, S.Doc. No. 13, 93d Cong., 1st Sess. (Comm. Print 1973); Hearings on Energy and Environmental Standards, Before the Subcomm. on Energy of the House Comm. on Science and Technology, H.R.Doc. No. 45, 93d Cong., 1st & 2d Sess. 460–502 (1973) (testimony of Dr. John Finklea, Director, National Environmental Research Center, EPA).

27. See National Academy of Sciences Coordinating Comm. on Air Quality Studies, Report on Air Quality and Automobile Emission Control, Prepared for the Senate Comm. on Public Works, 93d Cong., 2d Sess. 117 (Comm. Print 1974).

1. 42 U.S.C.A. § 1857c–5.

2. Section 110(a), 42 U.S.C.A. § 1857c–5(a).

pollutants, such as sulfur oxides and carbon monoxide. Many sources and pollutants (and ergo many legal problems) are not addressed in the plans. Thus, a stationary source of air pollution can be subject to regulation under the implementation plans for some of its emissions (say, sulfur dioxide) while for others (say, odors) may be subject to no regulation at all apart from the common law.

At the same time it is inaccurate to say that implementation plans address only the six pollutants which are the subject of national ambient air quality standards. The reason for this is that three of the six (hydrocarbons, particulates and photochemical oxidants) are generic, including more than one chemical element or compound. Particulates, for example, include any particulate detected by applicable test procedures,[3] which means any particle ranging in size from 100 to 0.1 microns and in chemical content from lead to flour to just about anything else. The thought occurring to the layman, that a sensible regulatory scheme might draw distinctions between the chemical constituents as well as the size of particulates, has been raised by experts as well,[4] albeit not extensively by the regulators.

Before looking closely at the development of the plans, some general observations are in order. The plan is conceived to be the "principal component"[5] of control efforts for pollution agents singled out by the national standards. Section 110 sets forth eight general requirements for a legally sufficient plan.[6] It is supposed to assign specific emission limitations to individual sources and establsh timetables for compliance by those sources; set up procedures to review new sources; establish systems to monitor air quality; and provide for enforcement. Section 110 requires a detailed demonstration that the state has the necessary laws and administrative capacity to assure that the standards are met by the combined efforts of individual source owners. A citizen should be able to pick up a plan, read it, and understand that if company X meets the obligations and timetables there prescribed it will have done its share to assure that health and environmental damage from the criteria air pollutants will be an unfortunate memory of the past within that air quality region and state. This is not a fairy tale. It is the conception and purpose of the law.

The 1970 amendments, unlike the 1967 Act, steer a determined course towards meeting the standards. This is accomplished by prescribing national deadlines for overall compliance and, within the framework of those deadlines, tight timetables for state preparation of the plans and EPA review of them to assure compliance with

3. Set forth in 40 CFR pt. 50, app. B.

4. Ad Hoc Panel on Abatement of Emissions from Stationary Sources, National Research Council, National Academy of Engineering, Abatement of Particulate Emissions from Stationary Sources (1972).

5. Comm. on Public Works, National Air Quality Standards Act of 1970, S.Rep.No.1196, 91st Cong., 2d Sess. 12 (1970) [hereinafter cited as Senate Report].

6. Section 110(a)(2) is quoted in full in note 8, infra.

the Act. Section 110(a)(1)[7] gives each state nine months after promulgation or revision of a national ambient air standard to develop a plan providing for "implementation, maintenance and enforcement" of the standard within the air quality control regions within its borders. For the six criteria pollutant standards promulgated on April 30, 1971, the submission date for implementation plans thus was January 31, 1972. The Act goes on to obligate the Administrator, within four months after the date required for submission, to "approve or disapprove" the plan or portions of it.[8] In the case of a plan imple-

---

7. 42 U.S.C.A. § 1857c–5(a)(1) reads in full as follows:

Each State shall, after reasonable notice and public hearings, adopt and submit to the Administrator, within nine months after the promulgation of a national primary ambient air quality standard (or any revision thereof) under section 109 for any air pollutant, a plan which provides for implementation, maintenance, and enforcement of such primary standard in each air quality control region (or portion thereof) within such State. In addition, such State shall adopt and submit to the Administrator (either as a part of a plan submitted under the preceding sentence or separately) within nine months after the promulgation of a national ambient air quality secondary standard (or revision thereof), a plan which provides for implementation, maintenance, and enforcement of such secondary standard in each air quality control region (or portion thereof) within such State. Unless a separate public hearing is provided, each State shall consider its plan implementing such secondary standard at the hearing required by the first sentence of this paragraph.

8. Section 110(a)(2), 42 U.S.C.A. § 1857c–5(a)(2), reads in full as follows:

The Administrator shall, within four months after the date required for submission of a plan under paragraph (1), approve or disapprove such plan or each portion thereof. The Administrator shall approve such plan, or any portion thereof, if he determines that it was adopted after reasonable notice and hearing and that—

(A)(i) in the case of a plan implementing a national primary ambient air quality standard, it provides for the attainment of such primary standard as expeditiously as practicable but (subject to subsection (e)) in no case later than three years from the date of approval of such plan (or any revision thereof to take account of a revised primary standard); and (ii) in the case of a plan implementing a national secondary ambient air quality standard, it specifies a reasonable time at which such secondary standard will be attained;

(B) it includes emission limitations, schedules, and timetables for compliance with such limitations, and such other measures as may be necessary to insure attainment and maintenance of such primary or secondary standard, including, but not limited to, land-use and transportation controls;

(C) it includes provision for establishment and operation of appropriate devices, methods, systems, and procedures necessary to (i) monitor, compile, and analyze data on ambient air quality and, (ii) upon request, make such data available to the Administrator;

(D) it includes a procedure, meeting the requirements of paragraph (4), for review (prior to construction or modification) of the location of new sources to which a standard of performance will apply;

(E) it contains adequate provisions for intergovernmental cooperation, including measures necessary to insure that emissions of air pollutants from sources located in any air quality control region will not interfere with the attainment or maintenance of such primary or secondary standard in any portion of such region outside of such State or in any other air quality control region;

Sec. 3.5 IMPLEMENTATION PLANS: PROCEDURE

menting a national primary ambient air quality standard approval is mandatory if the Administrator determines that it was adopted after reasonable notice and hearing and it "provides for the attainment of the primary standard as expeditiously as practicable but . . . in no case later than three years from the date of approval." [9] (The concept of "practicability" allows for the stretching out of compliance dates within the three year maximum if technology is unavailable or the economics prohibitive.) [10] For secondary standards, plans must be approved if they specify a "reasonable time" at which the standards are to be attained. A lapse of time is "reasonable" if there is a step by step plan for compliance over time with firm prospects of satisfying the standards.[11]

Each adoption or revision of a state plan must be preceded by "reasonable notice and public hearings." [12] The Clean Air Act extends no right to an adjudicatory hearing,[13] and most states treat prepara-

(F) it provides (i) necessary assurances that the State will have adequate personnel, funding, and authority to carry out such implementation plan, (ii) requirements for installation of equipment by owners or operators of stationary sources to monitor emissions from such sources, (iii) for periodic reports on the nature and amounts of such emissions; (iv) that such reports shall be correlated by the State agency with any emission limitations or standards established pursuant to this Act, which reports shall be available at reasonable times for public inspection; and (v) for authority comparable to that in section 303, and adequate contingency plans to implement such authority;

(G) it provides, to the extent necessary and practicable, for periodic inspection and testing of motor vehicles to enforce compliance with applicable emission standards; and

(H) it provides for revision, after public hearings, of such plan (i) from time to time as may be necessary to take account of revisions of such national primary or secondary ambient air quality standard or the availability of improved or more expeditious methods of achieving such primary or secondary standard; or (ii) whenever the Administrator finds on the basis of information available to him that the plan is substantially inadequate to achieve the national ambient air quality primary or secondary standard which it implements.

9. The quotation in text omits the reference to section 110(e), 42 U.S.C.A. § 1857c–5(e), under which a governor of a state can request an extension of the time for compliance with the primary standards.

10. See Train v. Natural Resources Defense Council, Inc., 421 U.S. 60, 97 & n. 30, 95 S.Ct. 1470, 1490 & n. 30, 43 L.Ed.2d 731, 756 & n. 30 (1975) (reserving decision on whether a loosely written Georgia variance provision satisfies the practicability standard).

11. The legislative history indicates that "progress in this direction would be made as rapidly as possible." Senate Report, supra note 5, at 11. At least, this should require a "constant effort" to attain compliance. Jorling, The Federal Law of Air Pollution Control, in Environmental Law Institute, Federal Environmental Law 1058, 1087 (E. L. Dolgin & T. G. P. Guilbert eds. 1974).

12. Sections 110(a)(1), (3)(A), 42 U.S. C.A. §§ 1857c–5(a)(1), (3)(A).

13. Appalachian Power v. EPA, 477 F. 2d 495, 3 ELR 20310 (4th Cir. 1973); Duquesne Light Co. v. EPA, 481 F.2d 1, 3 ELR 20483 (3d Cir. 1973); cf. United States v. Allegheny Ludlum Steel Corp., 406 U.S. 742, 92 S.Ct. 1941, 32 L.Ed.2d 453 (1972) (making

tion of the plans as involving legislative-type decisions where affected parties may appear and present statements but not participate further through cross-examination and submission of questions, unless a particular need is shown.[14] The Administrator of EPA, in reviewing state plans, generally acts as an appellate tribunal.[15] A debate has arisen over whether the EPA decision on the adequacy of a state plan should be characterized as informal rulemaking for purposes of the Administrative Procedure Act, thus requiring publication of notice and a limited participation by interested persons through submission of views and sometimes oral presentation.[16] The cases are developing a consensus[17] that EPA should afford limited participation and submission of views for the reason that a full record and a reasoned decision is a necessary prerequisite to effective judicial review. A legislative-type hearing before the Administrator is required if the state holds no public hearing at all,[18] or an inadequate one,[19] in connection with the development of the plan. It is settled that EPA's decision on the adequacy of a state plan requires neither the preparation of an environmental impact statement[20] nor a hearing conducted with trial-type procedures.[21]

The principal reason for restricting procedural rights before the Administrator is that he must act quickly under the statutory scheme: he has only four months to approve or disapprove a submitted plan;[22]

clear that formal adjudicatory hearings are dependent upon legislative language requiring hearings "on the record").

14. Appalachian Power v. EPA, supra note 13; cf. International Harvester Co. v. Ruckelshaus, 155 U.S.App.D.C. 411, 427, 478 F.2d 615, 631, 3 ELR 20133, 20138 (1973).

15. See Union Elec. Co. v. EPA, 427 U.S. 246, 96 S.Ct. 2518, 49 L.Ed.2d 474 (1976).

16. Compare Indiana & Michigan Elec. Co. v. EPA, 509 F.2d 839, 5 ELR 20191 (7th Cir. 1975) with Buckeye Power v. EPA (I), 481 F.2d 162, 3 ELR 20634 (6th Cir. 1973).

17. Granite Steel v. EPA, 501 F.2d 925, 4 ELR 20810 (7th Cir. 1974); Appalachian Power Co. v. EPA, 477 F.2d 495, 3 ELR 20310 (4th Cir. 1973); Anaconda v. Ruckelshaus, 482 F.2d 1301, 3 ELR 20719 (10th Cir. 1973); Buckeye Power v. EPA (I), supra note 16.

18. Section 110(c)(1), 42 U.S.C.A. § 1857c–5(c)(1).

19. Duquesne Light Co. v. EPA, 481 F.2d 1, 3 ELR 20483 (3d Cir. 1973).

20. Energy Supply and Environmental Coordination Act of 1974, § 7(c)(1), Pub.L. No. 93–319, 88 Stat. 246, adding 15 U.S.C.A. § 793(c)(1) (specifying that no action taken under the Clean Air Act shall be deemed a major federal action significantly affecting the quality of the human environment within the meaning of the National Environmental Policy Act). The courts independently had reached the same conclusion. E. g., Duquesne Light Co. v. EPA, supra note 19; Appalachian Power Co. v. EPA, 477 F.2d 495, 3 ELR 20310 (4th Cir. 1973); Portland Cement Ass'n v. Ruckelshaus (I), 158 U.S.App.D.C. 308, 486 F.2d 375, 3 ELR 20642 (1973), cert. denied 417 U.S. 921 (1974); see § 7.6 below.

21. E. g., Anaconda v. Ruckelshaus, 482 F.2d 1301, 3 ELR 20719 (10th Cir. 1973); Indiana & Michigan Elec. Co. v. EPA, 509 F.2d 839, 5 ELR 20191 (7th Cir. 1975).

22. Section 110(a)(2), 42 U.S.C.A. § 1857c–5(a)(2).

within six months after the date required for submission, he must promulgate regulations setting forth portions of an implementation plan found not to be in accordance with the requirements of the Act.[23] The Administrator's duty to disapprove non-conforming plans and replace them with regulations that will meet the standards is enforceable in the courts.[24]

Administrative decisions leading to the adoption of the plans are many and complex.[25] EPA's Office of Air Quality Planning and Standards has published a series of documents comprising Guidelines for Air Quality Maintenance Planning and Analysis. The purpose of the series is to provide state and local agencies with information and guidance in the preparation of air quality maintenance plans. An air quality maintenance plan is an administrative creation for maintaining compliance with the standards during critical regions over a twenty-year period.[26] An air quality maintenance plan is responsive to yet another administrative creation, an air quality maintenance area, which is an area having the potential of exceeding the national standards within the next twenty years.[27] These areas are singled out for special management precautions, including an analysis of projected growth and the development and preparation of a control strategy to accommodate it.[28] A listing of the first twelve published documents in the *Guidelines* series suggests the range of issues confronted by management efforts to maintain the standards: Designation of Air Quality Maintenance Areas, Plan Preparation, Control Strategies, Land Use and Transportation Considerations, Case Studies in Plan Development, Overview of Air Quality Maintenance Area Analysis, Projecting County Emissions, Computer-Assisted Area Source Emissions Gridding Procedure, Evaluating Indirect Sources, Reviewing New Stationary Sources, Air Quality Monitoring and Data Analysis, Applying Atmospheric Simulation Models to Air Quality Maintenance Areas.

---

23. Section 110(c)(1), 42 U.S.C.A. § 1857c–5(c)(1).

24. Natural Resources Defense Council, Inc. v. EPA, 154 U.S.App.D.C. 384, 475 F.2d 968, 3 ELR 20155 (1973) (invalidating wholesale EPA two-year extensions for all states where transportation control measures were necessary to permit attainment of the primary standards); Riverside v. Ruckelshaus, 3 ELR 20043 (C.D.Cal. 1972) (requiring EPA Administrator to publish proposed regulations sufficient to assure compliance with the primary standards).

25. 40 CFR pt. 50 (Guidelines for the Preparation, Adoption and Submittal of Implementation Plans).

26. 40 CFR § 51.42. The Administrator may modify a plan to extend to a shorter period but not less than 10 years. Id. §§ 51.42, 51.63. See also 39 Fed.Reg. 46612–13 (1974) (discussing relationship between air quality maintenance plans and the no significant deterioration regulations).

27. 40 CFR § 51.12(e); see 40 Fed.Reg. 18726 (1975) (final approval of designation of air quality maintenance areas within twenty-one states and territories).

28. 40 CFR § 51.12(g).

The classification system and the use of modeling are illustrations of administrative techniques for developing the implementation plans which have been subjected to close judicial review under the hard look doctrine. The classification system, like the identification of air quality maintenance areas, is another creature of administration having no explicit basis in the Act.[29] It is a management tool used to differentiate areas of relatively impure air where improvement of air quality is required (Priority I) from areas of relative purity where the present air quality only need be maintained (Priority II). Priority III regions are those where no significant air quality problems are anticipated.[30] EPA uses its priority system to justify administrative obligations of different types. Thus, air quality data for carbon monoxide and photochemical oxidants need not be made part of an implementation plan for Priority III regions,[31] while the opposite is true for Priority I regions.[32]

One aspect of the classification system [33] affecting the Metropolitan Providence Interstate Air Quality Control Region was challenged successfully in the courts on the ground that it presumed "what must, in some places, be fiction: that, if a region lacks a city of over 200,000, its air is relatively pure in the absence of measured data to the contrary." [34] EPA essentially conceded that its scheme might classify as Priority III the polluted air in an area of high population not having any cities with a population greater than 200,000, but defended the choice on the ground that initial control strategies (which in this case would involve regulation of automobile use) might as well be concentrated in large cities having a centralized government and thus greater capacity for control. The court conceded that this might be "the only feasible approach" but ruled that the Clean Air contemplated achieving national standards within the allowable time everywhere.[35] The case was remanded for a further justification of the Priority III classification and an explanation of whether measured data might require a different classification.

29. For a full description, see 40 CFR § 51.3. See also Hearings on Implementation of Transportation Controls, Before the Subcomm. on Air and Water Pollution of the Senate Comm. on Public Works, 93d Cong., 1st Sess. 421–36 (1973).

30. 39 Fed.Reg. 42510 (1974), 40 CFR § 51.21 (Prevention of Significant Air Quality Deterioration).

31. 40 CFR § 51.14(d)(3).

32. Id. § 51.14(a)(1).

33. At issue was Id. § 51.3(b)(2), which reads:
In the absence of measured data to the contrary, classification with respect to carbon monoxide, photochemical oxidants, and nitrogen dioxide will be based on the following estimate of the relationship between these pollutants and population: Any region containing an area whose 1970 'urban place' population, as defined in the U. S. Bureau of Census, exceeds 200,000 will be classified Priority I. All other regions will be classified Priority III.

34. Natural Resources Defense Council, Inc. v. EPA, 478 F.2d 875, 880, 3 ELR 20375, 20376 (1st Cir. 1973).

35. 478 F.2d at 881, 3 ELR at 20376.

Sec. 3.5 IMPLEMENTATION PLANS: PROCEDURE 237

An air quality model, mentioned in chapter one,[36] is a simulation scheme by which the emission of pollutants can be related to atmospheric concentrations nearby.[37] A complete model involves consideration of source emission patterns, chemical transformations, atmospheric transport, removal processes working in the atmosphere, all in terms of time and location. To describe modeling is to describe its critical role in evaluating state implementation plans. It is by application of somebody's model that yields the answer to the ultimate question of whether the emission limitations proposed for sulfur oxide sources A–Z in a particular air quality control region will suffice to produce acceptable air quality. The model is the middleman between emission and air quality standards, the interpreter that translates the language of one set of standards into the requirements of the other. Change a few assumptions of the model and stiffer emission limitations are required, modify a few additional assumptions and the standards can be relaxed throughout the system. It goes without saying that modeling assumptions, no less than simple priority classifications, must pass muster on the basis of reasoned explanations demanded by contemporary notions of judicial review.[38]

Under the scheme of the Act, the deadline for meeting the primary standards under most of the plans was May 31, 1975. (The plans originally were due on January 31, 1972; four months were allowed for EPA review, and three years for compliance.) The deadline was not met in many air quality control regions. The task of revising and enforcing the implementation plans continues. Among the major deficiencies [39] have been provisions regarding the maintenance of ambient air quality, transportation controls [40] and regulation of complex sources.[41] Discussed elsewhere are the substantive requirements of the implementation plans,[42] including the critical compo-

---

36. § 1.2 above.

37. For a good, short discussion of modeling see National Academy of Sciences, Coordinating Comm. on Air Quality Studies Report on Relationship of Emissions to Ambient Air Quality, Prepared for the Senate Comm. on Public Works, 93d Cong., 2d Sess. 91–128 (Comm. Print 1974).

38. See Texas v. EPA, 499 F.2d 289, 298–99, 4 ELR 20744, 20747–48 (5th Cir. 1974) (sustaining EPA decision rejecting a Texas model, and upholding EPA's "straight rollback" model which assumes that reductions in oxidant pollutants will be proportional to reductions in reactive hydrocarbon emissions) ("Necessity, which has mothered the EPA's invention of this model, also protects it from a judicial insistence on greater reliability").

39. For a compliance tabulation, see 3 ELR 10031 (1973). Summaries of litigation concerning the plans are reported in id. at 10022, 10090, 10133. As of July 1976, 45 state implementation plans were deemed inadequate to provide for attainment and maintenance of the standards. Beginning in July 1976, EPA commenced publishing in the Federal Register a series of detailed critiques of state plan deficiencies. See 6 ELR 1018 (1976).

40. § 3.16 below.

41. § 3.17 below.

42. § 3.7 below.

nents of economic and technological feasibility [43] and emissions limitations.[44] Next addressed is an important procedural decision of the Supreme Court that affects the substance of the plans in important ways.

§ 3.6 The Implementation Plans: Ameliorating Features

The Clean Air Act is a potpourri of postponements, revisions, extensions and suspensions. The term variance does not appear in the Act, although the four terms that are used can be characterized as variances because they offer relief to individual sources from the cleanup obligations of the Act. The reach of all four ameliorating features is reasonably well settled.

In 1975, the Supreme Court decision in Train v. Natural Resources Defense Council, Inc.,[1] answered in the negative the question of whether the states would be held closely to the original commitments of the implementation plans. At issue was the validity of the inclusion in the Georgia plan of a sweeping variance procedure authorizing relaxation of standards for single or multiple sources "because of special circumstances which would render strict compliance unreasonable, unduly burdensome or impractical."[2] The Court approved the variance procedure, holding it could be applied to excuse any source whose continued emissions would not compromise the basic statutory aim of achieving and maintaining the national ambient air standards.

The decision in *Train* reflects a reading of the statute that encourages a liberal granting of variances by state authorities. The Court was presented with three possible interpretations: the Fifth Circuit below, reading literally the postponement provisions of section 110(f),[3] held that relief from "any requirement of an applicable implementation plan" could be extended only upon compliance with the stringent provisions of section 110(f).[4] The First Circuit,[5] followed by the Second[6] and the Eighth[7] Circuits, approved the granting of variances prior to the three-year date for mandatory attainment of primary standards (the pre-attainment period) but disapproved them thereafter (the post-attainment period). The reasoning was

---

43. § 3.9 below.

44. § 3.8 below.

1. 421 U.S. 60, 95 S.Ct. 1470, 43 L.Ed.2d 731 (1975).

2. Ga.Code Ann. § 88–912 is quoted in full in Train v. Natural Resources Defense Council, Inc., 421 U.S. at 69–70 n.6, 95 S.Ct. at 1477 n.6, 43 L.Ed.2d at 740 n.6.

3. 42 U.S.C.A. § 1857c–5(f).

4. Natural Resources Defense Council, Inc. v. EPA, 489 F.2d 390, 4 ELR 20204 (5th Cir. 1974).

5. Natural Resources Defense Council, Inc. v. EPA, 478 F.2d 875, 3 ELR 20375 (1st Cir. 1973).

6. Natural Resources Defense Council, Inc. v. EPA, 494 F.2d 519, 523, 4 ELR 20345, 20346 (2d Cir. 1974).

7. Natural Resources Defense Council, Inc. v. EPA, 483 F.2d 690, 693–94, 3 ELR 20821, 20822–23 (8th Cir. 1973).

that implicit in the Act could be found a congressional judgment to allow the states "greater flexibility" during the pre-attainment period. The Environmental Protection Agency, supported in result but not in reasoning by the Ninth Circuit,[8] read an authority to grant variances into section 110(a)(3), which states that the Administrator "shall approve any revision of an implementation plan applicable to an air quality control region if he determines that it meets the requirements of [the law] and has been adopted by the State after reasonable notice and public hearings."[9]

In sustaining the agency view that the revision authority of section 110(a)(3) sanctions any and all variances short of those condoning a violation of the national standards, the Supreme Court reasoned that the eight conditions of section 110(a)(2) provided the sole criteria against which the state plans are to be measured. The Court wrote: "The Act gives the Agency no authority to question the wisdom of a State's choices of emission limitations if they are part of a plan which satisfies the standards of § 110(a)(2), and the Agency may devise and promulgate a specific plan of its own only if a state fails to submit an implementation plan which satisfies those standards. . . . Thus, so long as the ultimate effect of a State's choice of emission limitations is compliance with the national standards for ambient air, the State is at liberty to adopt whatever mix of emission limitations it deems best suited to its particular situation."[10] The Court read the pertinent legislative history as supporting the view that the postponement provisions of section 110(f) offer "a safety valve by which may be accorded, under certain carefully specified circumstances, exceptions to the national standards themselves."[11] It found no purpose to make postponement "the exclusive mechanism for any ameliorative modification of a plan, no matter how minor."[12] It detected "normal usage" support for its distinction between minor revisions consistent with the standards and major postponements contradicting the standards: "to 'postpone' is to defer, whereas to 'revise' is to remake or amend. In the implementation plan context, normal usage would suggest that a postponement is a deferral of the effective date of a requirement which remains a part of the applicable plan, whereas a revision is a change in the plan itself which deletes or modifies the requirement."[13]

---

8. Natural Resources Defense Council, Inc. v. EPA, 507 F.2d 905, 913, 5 ELR 20032, 20035 (9th Cir. 1974).

9. 42 U.S.C.A. § 1857c–5(a)(3), redesignated section 110(a)(3)(A) by Energy Supply and Environmental Coordination Act of 1974, § 4(a), Pub. L. No. 93–319, 88 Stat. 246.

10. 421 U.S. at 79, 95 S.Ct. at 1482, 43 L.Ed.2d at 746.

11. 421 U.S. at 81, 95 S.Ct. at 1482, 43 L.Ed.2d at 747.

12. 421 U.S. at 83, 95 S.Ct. at 1484, 43 L.Ed.2d at 748.

13. 421 U.S. at 89, 95 S.Ct. at 1486–87, 43 L.Ed.2d at 751–752. The Fifth Circuit was moved by a different plain meaning:

> A revision is a change in a generally applicable requirement; a post-

The law in the wake of *Train* is clear in two respects: first, the Court has sanctioned a broad category of variances, called "revisions", where individual sources or categories of sources can escape from the strictures of the implementation plans so long as they can demonstrate no incompatibility with achievement and maintenance of the national ambient air standards. Effectively, the Court created two categories of variances: minor variances (or revisions) are those that do not jeopardize compliance with the national standards. These minor variances, like revisions generally, can be granted only after notice and at least a legislative-type hearing at the state or federal level. Major variances (or postponements) do jeopardize compliance with the standards and can be granted only pursuant to section 110(f).

It also is clear after *Train* that section 110(f), previously described by courts of appeals as "strict" [14] and "no remedy at all," [15] will be confined to the realm of the extraordinary. By its terms, the provision [16] authorizes the Administrator to grant "for not more than one year" upon application of a Governor a postponement of an implementation plan directive to a stationary source only after finding good faith efforts to comply, technological impossibility, maximum reduction in health hazards by resort to operational controls, and that continued operation is "essential to national security or to the public health or welfare." This allows a one year reprieve from a shutdown and then only upon the strongest of showings after a trial-type

ponement or variance [is a] change in the application of a requirement to a particular party. The distinction between the two is familiar and clear.

Natural Resources Defense Council, Inc. v. EPA, 489 F.2d 390, 401, 4 ELR 20204, 20208 (5th Cir. 1974).

14. 489 F.2d at 399, 4 ELR 20207.

15. Buckeye Power v. EPA (I), 481 F.2d 162, 169, 3 ELR 20634, 20636 (6th Cir. 1973).

16. 42 U.S.C.A. § 1857c–5(f) reads in part:

(1) Prior to the date on which any stationary source or class of moving sources is required to comply with any requirement of an applicable implementation plan the Governor of the State to which such plan applies may apply to the Administrator to postpone the applicability of such requirement to such source (or class) for not more than one year. If the Administrator determines that—

(A) good faith efforts have been made to comply with such requirement before such date,

(B) such source (or class) is unable to comply with such requirement because the necessary technology or other alternative methods of control are not available or have not been available for a sufficient period of time,

(C) any available alternative operating procedures and interim control measures have reduced the impact of such source on public health, and

(D) the continued operation of such source is essential to national security or to the public health or welfare, then the Administrator shall grant a postponement of such requirement.

(2) Any determination under paragraph (1) shall (i) be made on the record after notice to interested persons and opportunity for hearing, (ii) be based upon a fair evaluation of the entire record at such hearings, and (iii) include a statement setting forth in detail the findings and conclusions upon which the determination is based.

hearing before the Administrator. It is a statutory version of New York's old *Whalen* [17] case, which for many years stood for the proposition that balancing has no place in nuisance litigation. Few source owners would be attracted to the section 110(f) procedure because it promises cleanup or shutdown not further delay at the end of the year. The Supreme Court reads the provision sensibly as a "safety valve" allowing a tightly controlled temporary release from the national standards themselves. Section 110(f) affirms, however, the ironclad aspects of the national standards: they are to be met, even at the penalty of severe economic dislocation.

The Court in *Train* was faced with bad choices: applying section 110(f) to every minor modification of the original plan suggests a literalism too determined even for a Congress fed up with the perpetual postponements of the 1967 Act. On the other hand, the 1970 amendments meant to establish "a rigorous time sequence" [18] that includes the imposition of non-negotiable commitments. As the Fifth Circuit observed, "the plan of the statute was to secure ambitious commitments at the planning stage, and then, by making it difficult to depart from those commitments, to assure that departures would be made only in cases of real need." [19] By striking the balance in favor of flexibility, the Court shortened the odds on the standards being met and maintained although it could do little else given the language of the statute and particularly the position of EPA. The principal objection to the minor-major variance distinction is an administrative one: it calls for a difficult judgment about whether emissions from a single source prevent a plan for all sources from assuring a predetermined ambient air quality. This decision can be factually perplexing,[20] unanswerable as a matter of meteorology,[21] potentially discrim-

17. Whalen v. Union Bag Paper Co., 208 N.Y. 1, 101 N.E. 805 (1913).

18. Comm. on Public Works, National Air Quality Standards Act of 1970, S.Rep. No. 1196, 91st Cong., 2d Sess. 12 (1970) [hereinafter cited as Senate Report].

19. Natural Resources Defense Council, Inc. v. EPA, 489 F.2d 390, 403, 4 ELR 20204, 20209 (5th Cir. 1974).

20. In the words of the First Circuit: To allow a polluter to raise and perhaps litigate [the issue of whether a variance would prevent maintenance of a national standard] is to invite protracted delay. The factual question could have endless refinements: is it the individual variance-seeker or others whose pollution is preventing maintenance of the standards?

Natural Resources Defense Council, Inc. v. EPA, 478 F.2d 875, 886, 3 ELR 20375, 20379 (1st Cir. 1973).

21. See Stumph & Duprey, Trends in Air Pollution Control Regulations, in Hearings on Air Pollution, Before the Subcomm. on Air and Water Pollution of the Senate Comm. on Public Works, 91st Cong., 2d Sess. 396, 397 (1970):

Most emission control standards adopted in recent years by state and local agencies have been based on maximum application of modern control technology rather than atmospheric dispersion. Some reasons for this tendency include: . .

6. Realization that emissions from multiple sources are practically untraceable after discharge into a common air envelope.

inatory because it allots the air on a first-come, first-served basis and administratively haphazard because it encourages a piecemeal modification of plans by forums not looking at the whole picture. With all this said, the Supreme Court in *Train* certainly could not repudiate on grounds of unworkability a scheme advanced and endorsed by the agency charged by Congress with enforcing the Act.

The Supreme Court's decision in *Train* correctly insists that the validity of the implementation plans must be measured against the eight standards of section 110(a)(2). Since the language and purpose of section 110(a)(2) call for plans that achieve and maintain the standards, it is difficult to discover a prohibition there against approval of state plans allowing adjustments not threatening ultimate compliance. Despite the difficulties in making the decision, surely there is such a thing as a truly minor variance envisaged by *Train*. It is nonetheless likely that many minor variances will be difficult to obtain and of doubtful value: they certainly cannot be granted in any region presently in violation of standards since the revision by definition would prolong non-compliance; the variance-seeker has the burden—a heavy one—of proving a modification of its schedule would not compromise the goals of the plan; and success in a state variance proceeding does not protect a source from enforcement actions unless and until EPA approves the revision.[22]

The decision in *Train* wisely eschews reliance on the language in section 110(a)(2) calling for attainment of a primary standard "as expeditiously as practicable but . . . in no case later than three years from the date of approval." The First Circuit invoked the language to support its conclusion that state deferral mechanisms in the pre-attainment period were permissible.[23] The Ninth Circuit, in a virtual *tour de force*, went a step further to extend "this rationale . . . to the time after national standards are to be achieved."[24] Not explained was how a flat legislative directive to use "practicable" means to achieve compliance by a date certain could be read to excuse compliance by the date certain so long as "practicable" means are used thereafter.

The difficulty with using the "expeditiously as practicable" language to justify state variances during either the pre- or post-attainment period is that the language was included in the Act to tighten not relax the pressure for compliance. The original Senate bill included a flat three-year deadline for attaining the national standards,[25] but the Conference Committee changed the language to provide for

22. Delaware Citizens for Clean Air, Inc. v. Stauffer, 367 F.Supp. 1040, 4 ELR 20129 (D.Del.1973).

23. Natural Resources Defense Council, Inc. v. EPA, 478 F.2d 875, 887, 3 ELR 20375, 20379 (1st Cir. 1973).

24. Natural Resources Defense Council, Inc. v. EPA, 507 F.2d 905, 913, 5 ELR 20032, 20035 (9th Cir. 1974).

25. S. 4358, § 111(a)(2), in Senate Report, supra note 18, at 86.

attainment "as expeditiously as practicable but in no case later than three years" from the date of the plan's approval. This change must be read as further restricting a state's discretion (exercised through its variance laws) to allow sources to linger on the way to meeting the national standards. The phrase "as expeditiously as practicable" can be read only as requiring a state to impose maximum available controls on all sources at the earliest possible date. Any variance *a fortiori* delays attainment of the standards beyond the date previously considered the earliest one practicable.

The Supreme Court in *Train* found authority for minor variances not in the "expeditiously as practicable" language but in the general structure of section 110(a)(2) and EPA's power to approve plan revisions. The Supreme Court characterized as "specious" an argument that a "revision" [26] was a word of art in the Act applying only to general plan changes to accelerate abatement or to accommodate the plans to other major policy shifts. The argument is by no means specious [27] but is nonetheless wrong for the reason that the Act is very much in need of a general procedure to accommodate an assortment of plan modifications or corrections not compromising basic legislative aims.[28]

The *Train* decision sets the contours of two ameliorating features of the Act: (1) major variances or section 110(f) postponements; (2) minor variances or section 110(a)(3) revisions. The Act also explicitly anticipates plan revisions in four additional circumstances: (1) if the Administrator promulgates new ambient air quality standards; (2) if improved or more expeditious methods of controlling pollution become available, allowing the state to achieve existing standards sooner;[29] (3) if the Administrator finds on the basis of new evidence, contrary to his earlier judgment in approving the plan, that it is now "substantially inadequate" to achieve the national standards within the state's chosen deadlines;[30] or (4) if the Administrator finds that the state's plan can be revised to conserve oil at fuel-burning stationary sources without interfering with the attainment and maintenance of any national ambient air quality standards.[31]

---

26. 421 U.S. at 98, 95 S.Ct. at 1490, 43 L.Ed.2d at 756.

27. Section 110(a)(2)(H), 42 U.S.C.A. § 1857c–5(a)(2)(H), requires a revision authority in state plans to accommodate events such as the revision of a national ambient air quality standard. It is not wholly implausible to read the provision as allowing revisions only in the circumstances specified and none other.

28. See Detroit Edison Co. v. EPA, 496 F.2d 244, 4 ELR 20388 (6th Cir. 1974)

(holding that an EPA "clarification" of the Michigan Implementation Plan actually was a "revision" triggering the informal rulemaking requirements).

29. Section 110(a)(2)(H)(i), 42 U.S.C.A. § 1857c–5(a)(2)(H)(i).

30. Section 110(a)(2)(H)(ii), 42 U.S.C.A. § 1857c–5(a)(2)(H)(ii).

31. Section 110(a)(3)(B), 42 U.S.C.A. § 1857c–5(a)(3)(B).

The fuel-savings revision subsection was added by the Energy Supply and Environmental Coordination Act of 1974.[32] It directs EPA to review each state plan with an eye towards recommending revisions that might conserve oil without jeopardizing attainment of the standards. The subsection amounts to a legislative confirmation of EPA's administratively conceived Clean Fuels Policy, under which the agency encouraged states to delay implementation of the secondary standards so that available clean fuels could be concentrated where needed to protect the public health.[33] EPA was concerned about environmental "overkill" arising principally from low sulfur restrictions (usually applied indiscriminately on an areawide or statewide basis) that would produce air of a higher quality than that demanded by the federal standards. Needless to say, "environmental overkill" as a conspicuous concern of national policy arrived with the oil embargo of 1973–74.

Along with the postponements and revisions must be considered the extensions and suspensions. The Act initially provides for two types of extensions. Under one the "Administrator may, whenever he determines necessary, extend the period for submission of any plan or portion [of a plan] which implements a national secondary ambient air quality standard for a period not to exceed eighteen months from the date otherwise required for submission of [the] plan."[34] Extension of a deadline for the primary standards is less easily achieved. Section 110(e)(1) reads, in part: "Upon application of a Governor of a State at the time of submission of any plan implementing a national ambient air quality standard, the Administrator may . . . extend the three-year period . . . for not more than two years for an air quality control region . . . ."[35] But an extension is strictly conditioned upon a determination by the Administrator that (1) one or more emission sources are unable to comply "because the necessary technology or other alternatives are not available or will not be available soon enough to permit compliance" within the three-year period; and (2) the State has exhausted "reasonably available alternative means of attaining such primary standard and has justifiably concluded" that attainment is impossible. Moreover, extensions are allowable only if "interim measures" are imposed upon the sources where technology is a barrier to meeting the standards.[36] Thus, extensions under section 110(e), like extensions under the common law of nuisance, are tied closely to proof of technological

---

32. Pub.L. No. 93–319, § 4, 88 Stat. 256.

33. See Hearings on Energy Emergency Legislation, Before the Senate Comm. on Interior and Insular Affairs, 93d Cong., 1st Sess. 67–76 (1973) (testimony of Russel E. Train, Administrator, EPA).

34. Section 110(b), 42 U.S.C.A. § 1857c–5(b).

35. 42 U.S.C.A. §§ 1857c–5(e)(1)(A), (B).

36. Id. § 1857c–5(e)(2)(B).

impossibility and conditioned strictly by requiring resort to available controls.

A practical barrier to section 110(e) extensions is that they require foresight by governors who are obliged to make the request "at the time of submission of any plan implementing a national ambient air quality standard." That time initially was January 31, 1972, and the date slipped by before the enormity of the task became apparent.[37] That the section 110(e) requirements are not easily circumvented is indicated by the fact that when the Administrator initially announced approvals and disapprovals of state implementation plans on May 31, 1972, he granted wholesale two-year extensions to all states where transportation control measures were necessary to permit attainment of the primary standards.[38] The rationale for the extension was simply that administrative difficulty made it impossible for EPA to develop supportable plans for noncomplying states within the time prescribed under section 110(c). Recognizing the "best of faith" on the part of the Administrator,[39] the U. S. Court of Appeals for the District of Columbia nonetheless ordered him to rescind the extensions, require the submission of fully complying plans from the states, and condition future extensions upon compliance with § 110(e). The position of the plaintiff, found persuasive by the court, was that while fully workable plans for all states might not be feasible within the time allotted, a formal tour through section 110(e) might produce ideas for "interim measures of control" that could prove beneficial.

The oil embargo of 1973–74 left a legislative legacy in the form of the Energy Supply and Environmental Coordination Act of 1974 [40] (ESECA), which authorizes temporary suspensions and longer extensions of implementation plan deadlines applicable to some power plants. A purpose of the Act is to lessen United States dependence on foreign oil imports. Its method is to require, where feasible, the conversion to the use of coal of gas-and-oil-burning electrical utilities. The Administrator of the Federal Energy Administration is given

---

37. Hearings on Clean Air Act Oversight, Before the Subcomm. on Public Health and Environment of the House Comm. on Interstate and Foreign Commerce, 93d Cong., 1st Sess., pt. 2, 953, 955 (1973) (statement of Samuel A. Bleicher, Deputy Director, Regulation and Enforcement, Ohio Environmental Protection Agency) (explaining how the fortuitous invalidation of the Ohio implementation plan on procedural grounds required a resubmission at which time the Ohio governor could seek a two year extension under section 110(e) not sought under the earlier plan; the Ohio plan was invalidated in Buckeye Power v. EPA (I), 481 F.2d 162, 3 ELR 20634 (6th Cir. 1973)).

38. 37 Fed.Reg. 10842, 10844–45 (1972).

39. Natural Resources Defense Council, Inc. v. EPA, 154 U.S.App.D.C. 384, 386, 475 F.2d 968, 970, 3 ELR 20155 (1973).

40. Pub.L. No. 93–319, 88 Stat. 246; see Ayres, Enforcement of Air Pollution Controls on Stationary Sources Under the Clean Air Amendments of 1970, 4 Ecology L.Q. 441 (1975); Meltz The ESECA Coal Conversion Program: Saving Oil the Hard Way, 5 ELR 50146 (1974); Pederson, Coal Conversion and Air Pollution: What the Energy Supply and Environmental Coordination Act of 1974 Provides, 4 ELR 50101 (1974).

broad authority to prohibit any powerplant from burning natural gas and petroleum products as its primary energy source and to require certain powerplants to be designed and constructed so as to be able to accommodate coal as a fuel.[41] FEA orders are not effective without the approval of the EPA Administrator, who is given similar broad authority to assure compliance with clean air goals and modify them in limited respects to accommodate fuel shifts from clean oil to dirty coal.[42]

The first of two ameliorative features in the 1974 amendments is a grant of authority to EPA to suspend temporarily (until no later than June 30, 1975) any stationary source fuel or emission limitation applicable to plants in three categories:[43] (1) those unable to comply solely because of fuel unavailability; (2) those prohibited from using petroleum products or natural gas by reason of an FEA order; (3) those beginning conversion to the use of coal in the six-month period September 15, 1973 to March 15, 1974. A temporary suspension is conditioned upon EPA finding the source is able to comply with all primary standard conditions and meet any "interim standard" conditions the Administrator chooses to impose.[44] Although temporary suspensions were obtainable without certain health-protection precautions required of longer extensions, they added little to the authority of states to grant "minor" variances not threatening the standards, a power widely exercised during the oil embargo in 1973 and 1974 before validation of the practice by the 1975 *Train* decision.[45]

The second plan modification feature of the 1974 amendments is a power in EPA to grant a "compliance date extension" until January 1, 1979 relieving qualifying sources from the application of air pollution requirements discouraging the burning of coal (whether or not they are included in the applicable implementation plan).[46] The only sources qualifying are those affected by FEA orders requiring a shift to coal and those which "began conversion" to coal between the September 15, 1973–March 15, 1974 dates.[47] The conditions for securing

---

41. Pub.L. No. 93–319, § 2, 15 U.S.C.A. § 792.

42. Id. § 3, adding Clean Air Act § 119, 42 U.S.C.A. § 1857c–10.

43. Section 119(b)(1)(A), 42 U.S.C.A. § 1857c–10(b)(1)(A).

44. Sections 119(b)(1)(A), (b)(3), 42 U.S.C.A. §§ 1857c–10(b)(1)(A), (b)(3).

45. See Pederson, supra note 40, at 50107–08.

46. Section 119(c)(1), 42 U.S.C.A. § 1857c–10(c)(1).

47. The statute further defines "began conversion" as meaning:
action by the source during the period beginning on September 15, 1973, and ending on March 15, 1974 (such as entering into a contract binding on such source for obtaining coal, or equipment or facilities to burn coal; expending substantial sums to permit such source to burn coal; or applying for an air pollution variance to enable such source to burn coal) which the Administrator finds evidences a decision (made prior to March 15, 1974) to convert to burning coal as a result of the unavailability of an adequate supply of fuels required for

an extension are more demanding than those for temporary postponements: the Administrator must find that an extension is necessary to accommodate coal burning, that during the period of the extension all primary standards will be met and, further, that the plant not be located in an air quality region where the primary standard is being violated. This latter requirement is known as the "regional limitation." It is an ingenious legislative device that disqualifies for an extension any plant in high risk areas, and does not permit proof that an extension would fail to aggravate the situation.[48] To this regional disqualifier is a further requirement that an extension be coupled with an EPA-prepared plan for compliance. The plan must call for controls at least to the degree required in the original implementation plan [49] and ultimately must result in "continuous emission reduction systems . . . to burn coal, and to achieve the degree of emission reduction required."[50] The significance of this is that it rules out operational controls as a long run objective and insists upon technological modifications (notably the installation of scrubbers) or reliable sources of clean fuels.[51] Procedures are available allowing the Administrator to revoke or modify a suspension or compliance date extension for non-compliance with various conditions or if the burning of coal is thought to create a "significant risk" to public health.[52] The "significant risk" provision has a rich legislative history and was intended to reach health hazards associated with sulfates which are not addressed in the national standards but are created by atmospheric reactions of sulfur dioxide.[53]

    compliance with the applicable implementation plan, and a good faith effort to expeditiously carry out such decision.

Ibid.

48. Section 119(c)(2)(D), 42 U.S.C.A. § 1857c–10(c)(2)(D).

49. Section 119(c)(2)(C), 42 U.S.C.A. § 1857c–10(c)(2)(C).

50. Section 119(c)(2)(B), 42 U.S.C.A. § 1857c–10(c)(2)(B).

51. See § 3.8 below.

52. Section 119(c)(3)(B)(iii), 42 U.S.C.A. § 1857c–10(c)(3)(B)(iii), calls for corrective action if the Administrator finds:
    the burning of coal by such source will result in an increase of emissions of any air pollutant for which national ambient air quality standards have not been promulgated (or an air pollutant which is transformed in the atmosphere into an air pollutant for which such a standard has not been promulgated), and that such increase may cause (or materially contribute to) a significant risk to public health.
. . .

53. The lengthy legislative history on ESECA is collected in Pederson, supra, note 40, at 50102 n.5 (citing six committee reports). Confirmation of the application of the "significant risk" provision to the sulfates problem is found in Comm. of Conference, Energy Supply and Environmental Coordination Act of 1974, H.R.Rep. No. 1085, 93d Cong., 2d Sess. 35 (1974).

§ 3.7 Implementation Plans: General Requirements

Section 110(a)(2)[1] addresses eight topics that must be addressed in the state implementation plans: (1) attaining the standards within the time prescribed; (2) inclusion of emission limitations and other controls; (3) monitoring; (4) pre-construction review of new sources; (5) intergovernmental cooperation; (6) administrative requirements for state agencies; (7) inspection and testing of motor vehicles; (8) a revision authority. Several of the more important requirements are discussed separately.[2] This section addresses the obligations for monitoring, pre-construction review, intergovernmental cooperation, state agency requirements and the revision authority.

a. *Monitoring*

The monitoring provisions of the state implementation plans for stationary sources[3] work three significant changes in prior practice: compulsory monitoring by the source, disclosure of emissions data which traditionally was treated as a trade secret, and correlation of that data with the standards which effectively requires public performance reports on individual sources. Not surprisingly, many traditional state restrictions reshaped slightly for inclusion in the implementation plans have fared poorly in the courts. Among the provisions struck down have been portions of the Massachusetts plan calling for periodic reports on emissions from stationary sources at the request of the authorities instead of as a matter of course;[4] and other plans allowing emission reports to be held confidential as trade secrets.[5] Informal[6] or even formal[7] interpretations of state law by state authorities requiring disclosure of emission information have not per-

---

1. 42 U.S.C.A. § 1857c–5(a)(2).

2. See §§ 3.8 (emission limitations); 3.9 (economic and technological); 3.16 (transportation controls); 3.17 (indirect source regulations) below.

3. Section 110(a)(2)(C), 42 U.S.C.A. § 1857c–5(a)(2)(C), calls for the establishment of systems to monitor and analyze data on ambient air quality. Section 110(a)(2)(F), 42 U.S.C.A. § 1857c–5(a)(2)(F), states that a plan must provide:

   . . . (ii) requirements for installation of equipment by owners or operators of stationary sources to monitor emissions from such sources, (iii) for periodic reports on the nature and amounts of such emissions; (iv) that such reports shall be correlated by the State agency with any emission limitations or standards established pursuant to this Act, which reports shall be available at reasonable times for public inspection; . . .

4. Natural Resources Defense Council, Inc. v. EPA, 478 F.2d 875, 892, 3 ELR 20375, 20382 (1st Cir. 1973).

5. Ibid. The Administrator disapproved the New Jersey and Vermont plans because of state "confidentiality" statutes similar to those of Massachusetts. See 37 Fed.Reg. 10880, 10899 (1972). The Fifth Circuit cites fourteen other state provisions that have been invalidated by EPA. Natural Resources Defense Council, Inc. v. EPA, 489 F.2d 390, 398 n. 25, 4 ELR 20204, 20206 n. 25 (5th Cir. 1974).

6. 489 F.2d at 398, 4 ELR at 20206.

7. Natural Resources Defense Council, Inc. v. EPA, 494 F.2d 519, 522–23, 4 ELR 20345–46 (2d Cir. 1974) (letters from the Attorney General of the state of New York).

suaded the courts to refrain from invalidating provisions susceptible to readings that might deter disclosures.[8] The courts stress the association between disclosures of emissions data and the citizen suit provisions, acknowledging that citizen enforcement is dependent upon "access to any and all information they will need in prosecuting enforcement suits or in deciding whether to bring them."[9]

Hard questions regarding access to emissions and other data on operations are yet to be answered. EPA interpretations of the disclosure provisions require only that the state plan demonstrate an authority to compel self-reporting of emissions and the public disclosure of what is reported.[10] Does the Act give the Administrator authority to require verification of the accuracy of emissions reports through unannounced inspections or otherwise? Or to require that monitoring equipment be installed in prescribed ways to assure the accuracy of data reported? Or to require continuous monitoring or reporting by an independent party to prevent biased self-reporting? The Act certainly grants this authority as part of the Administrator's section 114[11] powers of inspection, monitoring and entry. Arguably, he could require as conditions of an adequate state implementation plan the powers he has undeniably to develop a replacement for a disapproved plan.[12] Section 114, in any event, gives the Administrator broad authority to prescribe monitoring equipment and reports[13] and to exercise a right of entry to copy records, sample emissions and inspect monitoring equipment.[14] (The statutory obligation to con-

8. But cf. Natural Resources Defense Council, Inc. v. EPA, 507 F.2d 905, 5 ELR 20037 (9th Cir. 1974) (upholding Arizona provision stating, in part: "No provision of this section shall be construed to prohibit the appropriate governmental agency from publishing quantitative and qualitative statistics pursuant to the emission of pollutants").

9. Natural Resources Defense Council, Inc. v. EPA, 489 F.2d 390, 397, 4 ELR 20204, 20206 (5th Cir. 1974). Compare §§ 1.13 above (citizen suits), 3.19 below (enforcement).

10. 40 CFR §§ 51.10(e), 51.11(a)(b); see id. § 51.19 (source surveillance).

11. 42 U.S.C.A. § 1857c–9.

12. Under section 110(a)(2)(F), 42 U.S.C.A. § 1857c–5(a)(2)(F), a state plan must contain "requirements" for installation of monitoring equipment, for periodic reports on emissions and for public access to the reports. Any requirements for unannounced inspections or third-party reporting would have to be accommodated by this language.

13. Section 114(a)(1), 42 U.S.C.A. § 1857c–9(a)(1), states that the Administrator may require "the owner or operator of any emission source to (A) establish and maintain such records, (B) make such reports, (C) install, use and maintain such monitoring equipment or methods, (D) sample such emissions (in accordance with such methods, at such locations, at such intervals, and in such manner as the Administrator shall prescribe), and (E) provide such other information as he may reasonably require; . . . ." See § 3.19 below (discussing section 114).

14. Section 114(a)(2), 42 U.S.C.A. § 1857c–9(a)(2) states that:

The Administrator or his authorized representative, upon presentation of his credentials—

(A) shall have a right of entry to, upon, or through any premises in which an emission source is

fine inspection and sampling to "reasonable times" should not preclude unannounced visits during normal working hours.) Section 114 draws one distinct line: all emissions data to which the Administrator has access must be disclosed whereas all other data may be entitled to trade secret protection upon a "satisfactory showing" to the Administrator.[15]

b. *Pre-construction Review*

A state implementation plan must include a procedure "for review (prior to construction or modification) of the location of new sources to which a standard of performance will apply." [16] By its terms, this calls for authority to prevent construction or modification of any new source "subject to the new source performance standards" at any location the state determines "will prevent the attainment or maintenance of the standards" in a given region. The procedure also must assure that "prior to commencing construction or modification of any source," the owner or operator submit to the state "such information as may be necessary" to permit it to make the decision.[17] Basically, what is required is that new sources under the Clean Air Act be subjected to a regulatory regime before-the-fact theoretically not unlike the licensing procedure applicable for many years to, let us say, nuclear reactors. The principal differences are that the skeletal requirements of the Clean Air Act for pre-construction review affirm only that the procedure assure an informed judgment on the siting of the facility. The state is left with considerable leeway with regard to its preferences for hearings, specifying the information required, and so on.

EPA requires much more than pre-construction review of major new sources subject to the new source performance standards. A satisfactory implementation plan must enable a state or local agency to determine whether the construction or modification of any facility or structure "will result in violations of applicable portions of the control strategy or will interfere with attainment or maintenance of a national standard either directly because of emissions from it, or indirectly because of emissions resulting from mobile source activities associated with it." [18] This brings a wide range of activities under pre-construction review procedures. It necessarily anticipates a pow-

located or in which any records required to be maintained under paragraph (1) of this section are located, and

(B) may at reasonable times have access to and copy any records, inspect any monitoring equipment or method required under paragraph (1), and sample any emissions which the owner or operator of such source is required to sample under paragraph (1).

15. Section 114(c), 42 U.S.C.A. § 1857 c–9(c).

16. Section 110(a)(2)(D), 42 U.S.C.A. § 1857c–5(a)(2)(D).

17. Section 110(a)(4), 42 U.S.C.A. § 1857c–5(a)(4).

18. 40 CFR § 51.18.

er within a local or state agency to veto or require modifications of proposed new construction with air pollution possibilities. EPA undoubtedly can require the plans to include this authority as a necessary adjunct of its power to assure attainment and maintenance of the standards. The state's discretion to prescribe procedures for implementation of pre-construction review is limited only by a directive to provide "opportunity for public comment prior to a pre-construction review decision." [19]

Litigation has contributed little to clarifying the content of pre-construction review. It is clear that a state's plan does not merit approval unless it ensures that new sources will not inhibit the attainment or maintenance of the federal standards.[20] It is not clear whether an approvable state permit system explicitly must mention location or land-use considerations,[21] although certainly it should if the directive to achieve the standards is taken seriously. Nor have the courts [22] been exorcised particularly over the precision with which the state provisions clearly express what is understood to be the law, namely, that the new source gets no permit unless it complies with a state's control strategy.[23]

In November 1976 the Environmental Protection Agency proposed a "tradeoff" policy applicable under its pre-construction review regulations.[23a] The policy, as proposed, reflects an administrative judgment that the Clean Air Act "allows a major new or expanded source to locate in an area that exceeds a national ambient air quality standard . . . [provided] that the new source's emissions will be controlled to the greatest degree possible; that more than equivalent offsetting emission reductions ('emission offsets') will be obtained from existing sources; and that there will be progress toward achievement of the NAAQS."[23b] The proposed policy would permit new source emission increases to be traded off against old source emission reductions regardless of source ownership although proposed reductions used for credit purposes must be made federally enforceable by revision of the state implementation plan. The tradeoff policy obviously is responsive to the stark reality that the Act anticipates attain-

---

19. Id. § 51.18(h)(1), (2).

20. Natural Resources Defense Council, Inc. v. EPA, 483 F.2d 690, 694, 3 ELR 20821, 20823 (8th Cir. 1973); Natural Resources Defense Council, Inc. v. EPA, 507 F.2d 905, 918, 5 ELR 20032, 20037 (9th Cir. 1974).

21. The Eighth Circuit insists that "it is logical to assume that a rational permit system would inherently require consideration of the location of pollution sources", Natural Resources Defense Council, Inc. v. EPA, 483 F. 2d at 694, 3 ELR at 20823, while holding that the Iowa Plan was explicit on the question. Compare § 3.12 below (no significant deterioration).

22. Natural Resources Defense Council, Inc. v. EPA, 478 F.2d 875, 888, 3 ELR 20375, 20380 (1st Cir. 1973).

23. 40 CFR § 51.18(d).

23a. See 41 Fed.Reg. 55525 (1976) (Interpretive Ruling for Implementation of the Requirements of 40 CFR 51.18).

23b. Id. at 55528 (footnote omitted).

ment and maintenance of the primary standards within a fixed period of time. A flat curtailment on significant new sources within noncomplying regions is the remedy strongly suggested. Allowing an old source to trade off its own or somebody else's contribution to a regional violation in return for the privilege of continuing the offense in another form seems a curious way to insure and maintain compliance. While several of EPA's imaginative readings have met with success in the courts, the tradeoff policy is a test of faith unlikely to succeed without legislative approval.

Apart from the serious problem of new sources in noncomplying regions, the major battleground over pre-construction review procedures in the future should be within the states defining those procedures. The Clean Air Act instigated the process, the details will be developed elsewhere. This is one of those several instances where the practice coincides with the Act's expressed purpose that the prevention and control of air pollution at its source is the primary responsibility of states and local governments.[24]

c. *Intergovernmental Cooperation*

The EPA implementation of the intergovernmental cooperation provision [25] requires simply that each plan provide assurances that the state agency having primary responsibility for implementing the standards in any region "promptly transmit" to other state agencies information on factors such as construction of new industrial plants which may affect significantly air quality in any adjoining region.[26] The courts have rejected the contention that the statutory phrase "intergovernmental cooperation" anticipates binding enforcement agreements.[27] A simple exchange of information, like that called for by the regulation, suffices to satisfy the statutory language. The Second Circuit points out that Congress' consent in 1970 to the negotiation of compacts and direction to the Administrator to encourage these agreements [28] suggests they are not mandated by the "intergovernmental cooperation" touchstone.[29] It is difficult to quarrel with the conclusion.

---

24. Section 101(a)(3), 42 U.S.C.A. § 1857(a)(3).

25. Section 110(a)(2)(E), 42 U.S.C.A. § 1857c–5(a)(2)(E), states that a plan must contain "adequate provisions for intergovernmental cooperation, including measures necesary to ensure that emissions of air pollutants from sources located in any air quality control region will not interfere with the attainment or maintenance of such primary or secondary standard in any portion of such region outside of such state or in any other air quality control region; . . . ."

26. 40 CFR § 51.21(c).

27. Natural Resources Defense Council, Inc. v. EPA, 483 F.2d 690, 3 ELR 20821 (8th Cir. 1973); Natural Resources Defense Council, Inc. v. EPA, 494 F.2d 519, 4 ELR 20345 (2d Cir. 1974).

28. Sections 102(a), (c), 42 U.S.C.A. §§ 1857a(a), (c).

29. Natural Resources Defense Council, Inc. v. EPA, 494 F.2d 519, 526, 4 ELR 20345, 20348 (2d Cir. 1974).

A more interesting issue is the obvious substantive requirement that a state implementation plan not create problems for air quality control regions in other states. A state plan must contain "measures necessary to ensure" that local pollutants will not "interfere" with attainment of the standards elsewhere. This obliges the Administrator to put a halt to control strategies that take advantage of prevailing winds to put the problem in somebody else's backyard. This probably requires controls at the source and excludes dispersion techniques. An aggrieved state conceivably could sue successfully an offending sister state or source under the common law of interstate pollution [30] and the Administrator under the citizen suit provisions for approving an inadequate plan.

d. *State Agency Requirements*

An approvable implementation plan must provide "necessary assurances that the State will have adequate personnel, funding and authority to carry out such implementation plan." [31] The EPA regulation implementing this provision requires only that the states come forward with a "description" of their resources, current and anticipated, to carry out the plan.[32] Providing assurances, according to the dictionary understanding, would be to make a showing that inspires confidence that the state has the necessary wherewithal to carry out the plan. And, "at first glance, a description does not seem to inspire confidence or provide certainty that the state will have adequate personnel, funding and authority to carry out its plan." [33] Yet the courts have been disinclined to require specific pledges or affirmations from, let us say, the governor that there will be a continuing commitment to carry out the plan. The determination of what assurances are "necessary" is left to the discretion of the Administrator,[34] and he has adduced enough evidence to make that judgment when he simply requires a state to inventory its resources. If a state is candid enough to acknowledge a marked discrepancy between resources and needs—in effect refuses to provide the "necessary assurances" under the statute—a court will not accept a blind affirmation by the Administrator that what is reported to be deficient actually is satisfactory.[35] The hard look doctrine takes hold at least to forbid the Administrator from confirming what the state denies. A court can do little else; the "necessary assurances" Congress sought are to be found in its own and the state legislatures' appropriations processes.

30. See § 2.12 above.

31. Section 110(a)(2)(F)(i), 42 U.S.C.A. § 1857c–5(a)(2)(F)(i).

32. 40 CFR § 51.20.

33. Natural Resources Defense Council, Inc. v. EPA, 478 F.2d 875, 883, 3 ELR 20375, 20377 (1st Cir. 1973).

34. 478 F.2d at 884, 3 ELR at 20381; Natural Resources Defense Council, Inc. v. EPA, 494 F.2d 519, 527, 4 ELR 20345, 20348 (2d Cir. 1974).

35. Natural Resources Defense Council, Inc. v. EPA, 494 F.2d at 527, 4 ELR at 20348.

e. *Revision Authority*

An acceptable implementation plan must provide "for revision, after public hearings" to take into account revisions of the national ambient air quality standards, improvements in methods of achieving the standards, or a later finding by EPA that the state plan "is substantially inadequate" to achieve the standards.[36] This requires that the plan "expressly provide"[37] for revision after public hearings "on occasions and under the circumstances described in the federal statute." It is not enough that a state agency responsible for implementing the plan have general powers to revise the rules. Congress wanted the powers of revision expressed in the plan, and that is that. The Supreme Court in Train v. Natural Resources Defense Council[38] made clear that the specification of revision powers in the plan does not preclude resort to revisions for other purposes consistently with the Act.[39]

§ 3.8 Implementation Plans: Emission Limitations

According to the deceptively simple guidance of the Clean Air Act, a state implementation plan must be approved if "it includes emission limitations, schedules and timetables for compliance with such limitations, and such other measures as may be necessary to insure attainment and maintenance of such primary or secondary standard, including, but not limited to, land-use and transportation controls."[1] An emission limitation is an inclusive term referring to any type of control to reduce emissions into the air, including partial or total shutdown orders on a permanent basis or restrictions of the sulfur content of fuel.[2] An emission limitation commonly is an emission standard, which can be defined as a directive setting specific quantitative limits

---

36. Section 110(a)(2)(H), 42 U.S.C.A. § 1857c–5(a)(2)(H), states that a plan must provide "for revision after public hearings, of such plan (i) from time to time as may be necessary to take account of revisions of such national primary or secondary ambient air quality standard or the availability of improved or more expeditious methods of achieving such primary or secondary standard; or (ii) whenever the Administrator finds on the basis of information available to him that the plan is substantially inadequate to achieve the national ambient air quality primary or secondary standard which it implements." See 40 CFR § 51.6.

37. Natural Resources Defense Council, Inc. v. EPA, 478 F.2d 875, 883, 3 ELR 20375, 20377 (1st Cir. 1973).

38. 421 U.S. 60, 95 S.Ct. 1470, 43 L.Ed. 2d 731 (1975).

39. § 3.6 above.

1. Section 110(a)(2)(B), 42 U.S.C.A. § 1857c–5(a)(2)(B).

2. Natural Resources Defense Council, Inc. v. EPA, 489 F.2d 390, 394 n. 2, 4 ELR 20204 n. 2 (5th Cir. 1974). Train v. Natural Resources Defense Council, Inc., 421 U.S. 60, 78, 95 S.Ct. 1470, 1481, 43 L.Ed.2d 731, 745 (1975), describes emission limitations as "regulations of the composition of substances emitted into the ambient air." This has been construed as requiring one or more systems which control the "kinds and amounts" of air contaminant emissions, that is, scrubbers and not intermittent controls. Big Rivers Elec. Corp. v. EPA, 523 F.2d 16, 5 ELR 20532 (6th Cir. 1975).

on amounts of pollutants individual sources can release into the air.[3] A "schedule" within the meaning of the Clean Air Act is a description over time of construction or other plant modifications necessary to bring a source into compliance. A "timetable for compliance" is a description of the occasions when emission reductions are to be achieved by a given source. In administrative parlance, a "compliance schedule" means the dates by which a source must comply with specific limitations contained in an implementation plan representing increments of progress towards ultimate compliance.[4]

A crucial concept not mentioned in the Act is a "control strategy." This means a "combination of measures designated to achieve the aggregate reduction of emissions necessary for attainment and maintenance of a national standard. . . . "[5] The Act makes clear that a control strategy appearing in an implementation plan should include a mix of "emission limitations" and "other measures" necessary to meet the standards "including, but not limited to, land-use and transportation controls." Discussed elsewhere are land-use controls, represented by the no significant deterioration policy,[6] and the transportation controls.[7] The statutory reference to "other measures" should be read generously to embrace any conceivable effluent tax, operational or land-use accommodations.[8] Among these are the "dispersion enhancement techniques" which seek to alleviate pollutants in the ambient air, not through emission controls, but by increasing dispersion throughout the atmosphere. Prominent among the dispersion enhancement techniques are the use of gas heaters and tall stacks to boost emissions to higher altitudes where greater dispersion can be achieved, and intermittent or supplementary controls. These techniques may involve staggering the hours of operation at major sources of pollution to exploit meteorological conditions favorable to dispersion and cutting back on production when the weather turns bad.[9] Intermittent controls can be very sophisticated, involving continuous weather prediction, the use of computers and constant shifts in production among many plants in a power generating network.[10] Dispersion enhancement techniques are praised by sup-

3. 421 U.S. at 78, 95 S.Ct. at 1481, 43 L.Ed.2d at 745.

4. 40 CFR § 51.1(p), (q).

5. 40 CFR § 51.1(n).

6. See § 3.12 below.

7. See § 3.16 below.

8. See § 2.11 above (discussing nuisance remedies). Compare § 1.2 above (discussing systems analysis).

9. See Natural Resources Defense Council, Inc. v. EPA, 489 F.2d 390, 394 n. 2, 4 ELR 20204 n. 2 (5th Cir. 1974). Arguably, a temporary curtailment could be considered an "emission limitation" under the Act. A better reading would respect the historical differences between emission limitations as decisive fixes at the source, milder adjustments in operations and land use accommodations.

10. See, e. g., Hearings on Energy and Environmental Standards, Before the Subcomm. on Energy of the House Comm. on Science and Technology, H.R.Doc.No.45, 93d Cong., 1st & 2d Sess. 289–446 (1973) (the TVA system).

porters as a closed-loop system and condemned by opponents as the rhythm method of pollution control.

Emission limitations and dispersion enhancement techniques are in certain ways mutually exclusive and represent fundamentally conflicting strategies of pollution control. The choice between the two points up a conflict between operational controls and source controls recurring across the environmental spectrum: jet noise can be alleviated by improved traffic controls or redesign of the engines; oil pollution by careful release of oily ballast (called the load-on-top procedure) or by redesign of the vessels (with double bottoms or segregated ballast); pesticides pollution by careful use or by redesigned products specific in effect; litter by laws encouraging tidy people or by redesigned containers suitable for reuse. Source controls are usually more effective and more expensive. They are preferred most often by the victim but not the polluter.

The debate over operational and source controls is especially acute in the air pollution arena, particularly regarding major sources of sulfur oxides such as copper smelters and coal-burning power plants. The electrical utilities regularly extol the virtues of dispersion enhancement techniques [11] while EPA urges the installation of stack gas cleaning scrubber technology.[12] Dispersion enhancement is said, on the one hand, to be far less expensive, sufficiently reliable, and proven. It is said, on the other, to be unproven, unenforceable, a threat to job security and a potential aggravator of health hazards.[13]

Section 110(a)(2)(B) on its face authorizes state implementation plans to include both "emission limitations" and "other measures" (such as dispersion enhancement techniques) that are "necessary" to achieve the standards. The important question is whether federal law in any way controls the mix of measures a state may invoke to meet the standards. The Fifth Circuit has read section 110(a)(2)(B) as permitting dispersion enhancement only as a last resort when "necessary" to meet the standards. Thus, Georgia's tall stack strat-

11. See, e. g., ibid; Hearings on Clean Air Act Oversight, Before the Subcomm. on Environmental Pollution of the Senate Comm. on Public Works, S.Doc.No.H–42, 93d Cong., 2d Sess. 23, 35 (1974). See also J. Esposito, Vanishing Air 104 (1970).

12. Environmental Protection Agency, National Strategy for Control of Sulfur Oxides from Electric Power Plants (1974).

13. A collection of pertinent documents on the pros and cons of dispersion enhancement techniques were inserted by Sen. Muskie in 119 Cong.Rec. 19183–205 (1973). The author's views on the copper smelting industry's closed-loop control system, which calls for curtailing production during adverse weather conditions, are recorded previously:

[it] is a cosmetic strategy for keeping smelting technology intact, a reason for putting men out of work, an excuse for avoiding emission controls, another pitch for a tall stack. It is a lawyer's paradise of uncertainties in meteorological prediction, instrument calibration, reading of ambient data and sorting out of sulfur dioxide sources.

Corporate Country 79 (1973); see Rodgers, Tacoma's Tall Stack, The Nation, May 11, 1970, at 553.

egy may be included in a state plan "only (1) if it is demonstrated that emission limitation regulations included in the plan are sufficient standing alone, without the dispersion strategy, to attain the standards; or (2) if it is demonstrated that emission limitation sufficient to meet the standard is unachievable or infeasible, and that the state has adopted regulations which will attain the maximum degree of emission limitation achievable." [14] Although the question is a difficult one, this policy of maximum feasible emission limitations is accommodated by the language and structure of the Act and its legislative history. The placement of the word "necessary" suggests that other measures are to be imposed on a "needs only" basis after exhaustion of emission limitation opportunities. This is roughly consistent with the common law of nuisance which sought to exhaust technological opportunities for control before turning to land use accommodations.[15] Moreover, the regulatory structure is tied throughout to emission limitations, with prime examples being the new source performance standards,[16] the section 111(d) plans to control existing sources of non-criteria pollutants [17] and the citizen suit provisions.[18] The argument as to the latter is that confining citizen suits to preventing violations of "an emission standard or limitation" would make very little sense if substantial portions of the state control strategies involved techniques difficult to characterize as an "emission standard or limitation." [19] There is also in the legislative history considerable evidence that emission limits and compliance schedules were viewed as the chief means for forcing action to meet the standards.[20] Control at the source thus is accorded a preference by a running commentary throughout the text and supporting legislative materials.

The Supreme Court decision in *Train* contains language hinting at a discretion in the states to achieve compliance by any means seen fit.[21] Any decision on the meaning of the legislation also will be af-

14. National Resources Defense Council, Inc. v. EPA, 489 F.2d 390, 410, 4 ELR 20204, 20213 (5th Cir. 1974) (emphasis in original); cf. South Terminal Corp. v. EPA, 504 F.2d 646, 4 ELR 20768 (1st Cir. 1974) (freeze on parking spaces can be imposed if needed to meet the national standards). Compare note 26, infra.

15. See §§ 2.6, 2.11 above.

16. Section 111, 42 U.S.C.A. § 1857c–6.

17. 42 U.S.C.A. § 1857c–6(d).

18. Section 304, 42 U.S.C.A. § 1857h–2.

19. See § 3.4 above.

20. E. g., Comm. on Public Works, National Air Quality Standards Act of 1970, S.Rep.No.1196, 91st Cong., 2d Sess. 12 (1970):

The Committee bill would establish tools as potential parts of an implementation plan and would require that emission requirements be established by each state for sources of air pollution agents or combination of such agents in such region and that these emission requirements be monitored and enforceable.

In addition to direct emission controls, other potential parts of an implementation plan include land use and air and surface transportation controls . . . .

21. Train v. Natural Resources Defense Council, Inc., 421 U.S. 60, 79, 95 S. Ct. 1470, 1482, 43 L.Ed.2d 731, 746 (1975) ("Thus, so long as the ultimate

fected greatly by how EPA reads it. But the Act certainly decrees reliable and permanent controls to "insure" the standards are maintained once met. Emission limitations typically afford that guarantee of reliability and permanence. Intermittent or supplementary controls are consigned to a role that is truly supplementary, given their history of lack of success,[22] and their high dependence upon an unusual concurrence of widespread monitoring, astute prediction and operator goodwill.

The emissions limitation or "something else" debate occasionally will succumb to explicit legislation. The ultimate decision on a general requirement for scrubbers on coal-burning power plants, for example, is so important that it is likely to be addressed on more than one occasion by the Congress. The Energy Supply and Environmental Coordination Act of 1974 "contains an explicit (though lukewarm) endorsement of 'scrubbers' despite the intense campaign that has been waged against them by the power industry." [23] This takes the form of conditioning a compliance date extension for a coal-burning plant upon a commitment to "continuous emission reduction systems" to meet the sulfur standards.[24] The purpose, quite clearly, is to rule out intermittent or supplementary controls as a means of achieving final compliance with the implementation plan requirements.[25] Two inferences are possible although neither one is appropriate: one is that a congressionally articulated policy of disavowal of supplementary control systems should be read retroactively into the general language of section 110(a)(2)(B). The other is that Congress' invention in 1974 of language describing "continuous emission reduction systems" should be read to mean that no connotations of permanency or durability can be found in the 1970 term "emission limitations." Whether the 1970 Act accords a preference to fixes at the source should be resolved independently of the 1974 amendments.

The accumulating precedents gradually are putting to rest the notion that tall stacks and other dispersion enhancement techniques

effect of a State's choice of *emission limitations* is in compliance with the national standards for ambient air, the State is at liberty to adopt whatever mix of *emission* limitations it deems best suited to its particular situation") (emphasis added).

22. U. S. Dep't HEW, Tall Stacks, Various Atmospheric Phenomena, and Related Aspects, May, 1969, at 12 ("whereas stack heights have increased by a factor of about 4, emission rates have increased by a factor of approximately 6. Thus, a good share of the benefits of increased stack height are offset by the release of more contaminants from the stack").

23. Pederson, Coal Conversion and Air Pollution: What the Energy Supply and Environmental Coordination Act of 1974 Provides, 4 ELR 50101 (1974).

24. Sections 119(c)(2)(B), (C), 42 U.S. C.A. §§ 1457c–10(c)(2)(B), (C).

25. Comm. of Conference, Energy Supply and Environmental Coordination Act of 1974, H.R.Rep.No.93–1085, 93rd Cong., 2d Sess. 36–38 (1974).

are acceptable substitutes for controls at the source.[26] Unfortunately, EPA's inability to resolve decisively the issue has resulted in a *de facto* reliance upon tall stacks to achieve controls in many parts of the country.[27] The rhythm method, to be sure, is better than nothing but it is born of desperation and succeeds by chance.

§ 3.9 Economic and Technical Defenses

The owner of any source subject to regulation under the Clean Air Act deserves an answer to two basic questions: (1) what forums are available to state my views? (2) what issues can be raised before those forums? Invariably, two major defenses of a polluting source are that the controls proposed are economically unjustifiable or technologically unfeasible. The ultimate question thus is whether a particular forum affords opportunities to assert economic and technical objections.

The elaborate system of forums and remedies appearing from the inception of the national ambient air quality standards to their ultimate enforcement include the following: (1) adoption of the standards; (2) adoption of the state implementation plan; (3) EPA approval or disapproval of a state plan; (4) appellate review of the Administrator's action regarding a plan; (5) state or federal variance proceedings; (6) collateral injunctive actions in the courts; (7) state or federal enforcement proceedings; (8) contempt proceedings for violation of an enforcement order. This legal system is every bit as elaborate as the ecological system it is designed to protect. As with any system, an evaluation of the efficacy of a particular remedy depends upon the relief available elsewhere. A few generalizations can be offered, nonetheless, on the basis of the Act, the case law and some inferential leaps of considerable distance.

a. *Promulgation of the National Standards*

One difficulty in determining whether and when economic and technical defenses may be raised is that statements on the subject often are made without distinguishing between different forums serving different purposes. This is true, for example, of much of the legislative history suggesting that sources meet the standards or shut down.[1] A closer look confirms that statements insisting economics and technology are never material or always material are equally dogmatic and equally wrong.

---

26. Natural Resources Defense Council, Inc. v. EPA, 489 F.2d 390, 4 ELR 20204 (5th Cir. 1974), rev'd on other grounds, 421 U.S. 60, 95 S.Ct. 1470, 43 L.Ed.2d 731 (1975); Big Rivers Elec. Corp. v. EPA, 523 F.2d 16, 5 ELR 20532 (6th Cir. 1975); Kennecott Copper Corp. v. Train, 526 F.2d 1149, 6 ELR 20102 (9th Cir. 1975).

27. See Natural Resources Defense Council, Inc. v. EPA, 529 F.2d 755, 6 ELR 20413 (5th Cir. 1976) (upholding in contempt proceeding EPA decision giving "credit" for dispersive effect of certain tall stacks initiated prior to court disapproval).

1. See text accompanying notes 13–17 infra.

One forum where economics and technology are manifestly immaterial is the setting of the national ambient air quality standards. These are dictated solely by reference to estimates of effects and without regard to the economics or technology of control.[2] Neither the "adequate margin of safety" language of the primary standards nor the "adverse effects" language of the secondary standards invites economic or technical balancing.[3] "Minimum public health requirements are often, perhaps usually," Judge Campbell has written, "set without consideration of other economic impact."[4] The challenge may be imposing, particularly since it assumes a scientific capability of setting a no-effects level,[5] but is presently required by the Clean Air Act. While there is room for judgment in setting the standards, it is improper to ask whether the goal is worthwhile or whether it can be achieved.

b. *Adoption of the State Implementation Plans*

While economics and technology are disregarded when the standards are set, "it is at the implementation stage that a state will consider these things. In devising their control strategy, the States will determine who can do what, how much it is going to cost, if we should require sixty percent reduction for this industry and forty percent for this one or vice versa, and when these things will be applied."[6] This prescription is eminently sensible. The eight general requirements of the implementation plans confine discretion in a few specifics (such as by requiring emissions limitations, the disclosure of emissions data, and maintaining the standards). Beyond that, the states are free to develop cost-effective and technology sensitive control strategies. For that matter, insofar as the Clean Air Act is concerned, they are free to develop cost-insensitive and technologically perverse plans. They are free to adjust and vary controls among individual and classes of sources. They can draw lines on the basis of employment effects, impact on tax revenues, economics and technology. The Supreme Court has made clear that under section 110(a)(2), EPA "is *required* to approve a state plan which provides for the timely attainment and subsequent maintenance of ambient air standards, and which also satisfies that section's other general requirements. The

---

2. See § 3.4 above.

3. See ibid.

4. South Terminal Corp. v. EPA, 504 F.2d 646, 675, 4 ELR 20768, 20780 (1st Cir. 1974).

5. Recent studies indicate there is no threshold level for sulfur oxides below which adverse health effects disappear. See Environmental Protection Agency, National Strategy for Control of Sulfur Oxides from Electric Power Plants 2 (1974). This state of affairs has been long recognized as regards certain toxics. See Dep't of HEW, Report of the Secretary's Commission on Pesticides and Their Relationship to Environmental Health (1969) (The Mrak Commission Report).

6. Baum, The Federal Program for Air Quality, 5 Nat.Res.L. 165, 169 (1972); see Union Elec. Co. v. EPA, 427 U.S. 246, 96 S.Ct. 2518, 49 L.Ed.2d 474 (1976).

Sec. 3.9   ECONOMIC AND TECHNICAL DEFENSES   261

Act gives the Agency no authority to question the wisdom of a state's choices of emission limitations if they are part of a plan which satisfies the standards of [section] 110(a)(2), and the Agency may devise and promulgate a specific plan of its own only if a State fails to submit an implementation plan which satisfies those standards." [7]

c. *EPA Approval or Disapproval of State Plans*

Until the Supreme Court resolved the issue in Union Electric Co. v. Environmental Protection Agency,[8] the circuits were split sharply over whether EPA was obliged under the Act to disapprove aspects of a state plan found to be economically or technologically unfeasible.[9] The problem was compounded by the fact that the agency disavowed this authority while engaging simultaneously in a review that plainly probed economic and technical aspects of the state plans.[10] The question must be answered ultimately by reference to the general requirements of the implementation plans in section 110(a)(2), which contains precious little to justify an EPA economic and technical veto power. The only language supportive in the slightest are the requirements that a state plan achieve a primary standard "as expeditiously as practicable" within three years and a secondary standard "within a reasonable time." This suggests EPA could invalidate a technologically unfeasible state plan provision that called for meeting the primary standards too soon to be "practicable" or for meeting the secondary standards with "unreasonable" haste.[11] But the same language clearly precludes EPA from invalidating portions of a state plan as technologically unfeasible if it is part of a strategy

7. Train v. Natural Resource Defense Council, Inc., 421 U.S. 60, 79, 95 S.Ct. 1470, 1482, 43 L.Ed.2d 731, 746 (1975).

8. 427 U.S. 246, 96 S.Ct. 2518, 49 L.Ed. 2d 474 (1976).

9. Compare Indiana & Michigan Elec. Co. v. EPA, 509 F.2d 839, 5 ELR 20191 (7th Cir. 1975) (EPA has no power to review on economic and technical grounds) and Union Elec. Co. v. EPA, 515 F.2d 206 (8th Cir. 1975) (same) with St. Joe Minerals Corp. v. EPA, 508 F.2d 743, 5 ELR 20188 (3d Cir. 1975) (EPA required to disapprove parts of a plan that are economically and technically unfeasible) and Appalachian Power Co. v. EPA, 477 F.2d 495, 3 ELR 20310 (4th Cir. 1973) and Buckeye Power v. EPA (II), 525 F.2d 80, 5 ELR 20701 (6th Cir. 1975) (affirming the power but withholding its exercise on grounds of ripeness) and Duquesne Light Co. v. EPA (II), 522 F.2d 1186, 5 ELR 20539 (3d Cir. 1975); see Bleicher, Economic and Technical Feasibility in Clean Air Act Enforcement Against Stationary Sources, 89 Harv.L.Rev. 316 (1976).

10. See Oversight Hearings on the Clean Air Act, Before the Subcomm. on Air and Water Pollution of the Senate Comm. on Public Works, 92d Cong., 2d Sess. 230, 236, 256 (1972) (describing EPA plan review process), cited as justifying EPA and subsequent judicial review of economic and technical factors in St. Joe Minerals Corp. v. EPA, 508 F.2d at 749, 5 ELR at 20190; Appalachian Power Co. v. EPA, 477 F.2d at 506, 3 ELR at 20311–12.

11. See St. Joe Minerals Corp. v. EPA, 508 F.2d 743, 748, 5 ELR 20188, 20190 (3d Cir. 1975); Natural Resources Defense Council, Inc. v. EPA, 507 F.2d 905, 913, 5 ELR 20032, 20035 (9th Cir. 1974). But see 42 U.S.C.A. § 1857d–1 (preserving state power to enforce more stringent emission standards).

Rodgers Environmental Law HB—10

to meet or maintain the health-based standards after the three-year compliance period.[12] A source always can shut down to meet the national standards, and the Act clearly anticipates the possibility.

There is strong evidence in the legislative history that considerations of health were to take precedence over economic or technological factors. The Senate Public Works Committee determined, quite explicitly, "that existing sources of pollutants either should meet the standard of the law or be closed down."[13] This view was well known at common law,[14] clearly prevailed in conference,[15] was expressed in the floor debates,[16] has been confirmed retroactively by a key legislator,[17] recognized by courts of contrasting temperament,[18] and survived later amendments inspired by the energy crisis. The Supreme Court in *Union Electric* was quite correct in concluding that the Administrator of EPA is not authorized by the Clean Air Act to invoke economic or technical justifications to rewrite a state implementation plan.

There is an important difference between the evaluation of an implementation plan generally and the application of that plan to a specific source, however. Quite clearly, when the state undertakes to develop a plan economic and technical factors predominate. Why should source A be required to close down to meet the national standards when the same result can be achieved by enforcing modest controls against source B? Consistently with this view, economic and technical arguments were in the forefront during initial development of the state plans. This flexibility can be found in section 110(a)(2) of the Act which calls for meeting the primary standards "as expeditiously as practicable" and the secondary standards "within a reasonable time."

12. Indiana & Michigan Elec. Co. v. EPA, 509 F.2d 839, 844, 5 ELR 20191, 20193 (7th Cir. 1975).

13. Comm. on Public Works, National Air Quality Standards Act of 1970, S.Rep. No. 1196, 91st Cong., 2d Sess. 2–3 (1970) [hereinafter cited as Senate Report].

14. See § 2.11 above.

15. See Natural Resources Defense Council, Inc. v. EPA, 507 F.2d 905, 914 n. 14, 5 ELR 20032, 20035 n. 13 (9th Cir. 1974).

16. E. g., 116 Cong.Rec. 32918 (1970) ("it might as well be said that the philosophy of the bill abandons the old assumption of requiring the use of only whatever technology is already proven and at hand and of permitting pollution to continue when it is not economically feasible to control it") (Sen. Cooper); id. at 42381 ("Predictions of technological impossibility or infeasibility were not considered sufficient reasons to avoid tough standards and deadlines, and thus to compromise the public health") (Sen. Muskie).

17. See Hearings on Implementation of the Clean Air Act Amendments of 1970, Before the Subcomm. on Air and Water Pollution of the Senate Comm. on Public Works, S.Doc. No. H–10, 92d Cong., 2d Sess. 18–19, 21, 24 (1972) (Sen. Eagleton).

18. Compare Natural Resources Defense Council, Inc. v. EPA, 489 F.2d 390, 402, 4 ELR 20204, 20208–09 (5th Cir. 1974) with Natural Resources Defense Council, Inc. v. EPA, 507 F.2d 905, 914 n. 14, 5 ELR 20032, 20035 n. 13 (9th Cir. 1974).

But the economic and technical factors take on a different hue when raised in the context of an individual source complaining about emission standards applicable to it, either through a variance proceeding or by piecemeal review of a portion of the plan. There is no problem if a source argues that economics or the state of the art justify an extension of compliance schedules necessary to meet secondary standards or in other circumstances where the primary standards are not in jeopardy. But that is not true where cost and technical factors are invoked to seek relief from a compliance schedule of consequence to the maintenance of primary standards. In such a case the decision-maker (usually a state authority passing on an application for a variance) should decide whether the degree of control called for is necessary to achieve the primary standards. If it is, it should turn a deaf ear on arguments pertaining to cost and state of the art. The law anticipates compliance within the prescribed time or a shutdown.

It is simply bad law to require the Administrator to disapprove all portions of state implementation plans calling for "technologically unfeasible" controls. Some "technologically unfeasible" controls are needed to achieve primary standards. The remedy in such an event is a rapid and spectacular improvement of technological capabilities or a shutdown. There is no basis in the Act or its legislative history allowing the Administrator to disapprove "technologically unfeasible" plans.

d. *Appellate Review of the Administrator's Action*

Section 307(b) [19] makes the United States Court of Appeals for the District of Columbia the exclusive forum for reviewing action of the Administrator in promulgating any national primary or secondary ambient air standard, any hazardous pollutant or new source performance emission standard, and certain other standards. A petition for review of the Administrator's action in approving or promulgating (but not disapproving [20]) any implementation plan or in extending compliance dates for coal-burning sources (section 119) are reviewable in the United States Court of Appeals for the "appropriate circuit." The "appropriate circuit" is any circuit containing a portion of the air quality control region affected.[21] Petitions must be filed within thirty days of the approval or promulgation of a plan.

Obviously the courts of appeals' disposition to review economic and technical aspects of the implementation plans turns upon a judg-

---

19. 42 U.S.C.A. § 1857h–5(b); see Dayton Power & Light Co. v. EPA, 520 F.2d 703, 5 ELR 20415 (6th Cir. 1975) (holding that attacks on EPA no significant deterioration regulations can be heard only in the D.C. Circuit).

20. Utah Int'l, Inc. v. EPA, 478 F.2d 126, 127, 3 ELR 20407, 20408 (10th Cir. 1973).

21. Senate Report, supra note 13, at 40.

ment about whether the Administrator is empowered to do so.[22] The decision in *Union Electric* has made clear that under the traditional standards of review, according to Citizens to Preserve Overton Park v. Volpe,[23] the Administrator has no authority to disapprove state implementation plans on economic and technical grounds. Of course after the Administrator acts, the hard look doctrine [24] emerges with a vengeance to provide one of the strongest unifying bonds between judicial review of disparate federal environmental statutes. Thus, under the Clean Air Act judicial review is said to rest on the premise that agency and court "together constitute a 'partnership' in furtherance of the public interest, and are 'collaborative instrumentalities of justice.' The court is in a real sense part of the total administrative process." [25] This view has several connotations: EPA is held to a strict standard of articulating the basis of its decisions,[26] is subject to unusual orders controlling its discretion,[27] may be directed to supply additional information to the court,[28] and to certify a full and complete "record of expert views and opinions, the technological data and other relevant material, including the state hearings, on which the Administrator himself acted." [29] The standard of review is severe and close, and the Administrator will be confined by the Act as the courts read it. The courts have read it as precluding state plan disapproval for economic and technical reasons.

e. *State and Federal Variance Proceedings*

Train v. Natural Resources Defense Council, Inc.,[30] approves state and federal variances or revisions for economic and technical reasons so long as they do not jeopardize compliance with the standards. When an adjustment of the standards is required, the stringent postponement provisions of section 110(f) apply.[31] This one year-only reprieve is an explicit application of the clean-up or shut down philosophy heard so often in the legislative history.[32]

22. See cases collected in note 9, supra; Union Elec. Co. v. EPA, 515 F.2d 206 (8th Cir. 1975) aff'd 427 U.S. 246, 96 S.Ct. 2518, 49 L.Ed.2d 474 (1976).

23. 401 U.S. 402, 91 S.Ct. 814, 28 L.Ed. 2d 136 (1971).

24. See § 1.5 above.

25. Kennecott Copper Corp. v. EPA, 149 U.S.App.D.C. 231, 233–34, 462 F.2d 846, 848–49, 2 ELR 20116, 20118 (1972). quoting Greater Boston Television Corp. v. FCC, 143 U.S.App.D.C. 383, 393–94, 444 F.2d 841, 851–52 (1971), cert. denied 403 U.S. 923.

26. Kennecott Copper Corp. v. EPA, supra note 25.

27. Duquesne Light Co. v. EPA (I), 481 F.2d 1, 3 ELR 20483 (3d Cir. 1973).

28. Natural Resources Defense Council, Inc. v. EPA, 478 F.2d 875, 881, 3 ELR 20374, 20376 (1st Cir. 1973); Texas v. EPA, 499 F.2d 289, 4 ELR 20744 (5th Cir. 1974).

29. Appalachian Power Co. v. EPA, 477 F.2d 495, 507, 3 ELR 20310, 20315 (4th Cir. 1973).

30. 421 U.S. 60, 95 S.Ct. 1470, 43 L. Ed.2d 731 (1975).

31. § 3.6 above; see Union Elec. Co. v. EPA 427 U.S. 246, 96 S.Ct. 2518, 2530, 49 L.Ed.2d 474, 489 (1976).

32. See text accompanying notes 13–17 supra.

Sec. 3.9 ECONOMIC AND TECHNICAL DEFENSES

f. *Collateral Attack by Injunction*

Shortcircuiting administrative processes by actions for injunctions in the courts never has been a favored procedure.[33] Experience under the Clean Air Act is consistent with this wisdom. Congress specifically provided in section 307 for review of an approval of an implementation plan, among other matters, only in the Courts of Appeals. The courts thus have rejected attempts to enjoin EPA approval of an implementation plan,[34] promulgation of a substitute plan,[35] or enforcement of notices of violation.[36] The rationale for non-interference is a familiar one:

> To allow review by way of injunction in the case at bar could only serve to cause delay and to take the case up in a district court removed from the scene is not appropriate either, for it could conceivably encourage forum shopping and the thwarting of procedures which Congress has carefully adopted. It follows then that where, as here, Congress has specifically designated a forum for judicial review of administrative action and does so in unmistakable terms except under extra-ordinary conditions, that forum is exclusive.[37]

g. *Defensively in Enforcement Proceedings*

Delaying economic and technical challenges to an implementation plan until enforcement is sought is risky. It is well settled that the range of defenses is restricted for those who choose to violate the rules instead of seeking relief before-the-fact.[38] Section 307(b)(2) of the Act [39] embraces this concept by stating that any action of the Administrator subject to review in the ordinary course in the courts of appeals "shall not be subject to judicial review in civil or criminal proceedings for enforcement." The longstanding split of authority over whether economic and technical objections were reviewable directly in the courts of appeals [40] presented a trap for the unwary: failure to raise objections directly could result in later foreclosure. Until the scope of direct review was clarified, practitioners could be expected to seek relief at the first opportunity in the courts of appeals.

---

33. See Myers v. Bethlehem Shipbuilding Corp., 303 U.S. 41, 58 S.Ct. 459, 82 L.Ed. 638 (1938).

34. Arizona Pub. Serv. Co. v. Fri, 3 ELR 20894 (D.Ariz.1973).

35. Anaconda v. Ruckelshaus, 482 F.2d 1301, 3 ELR 20719 (10th Cir. 1973); see Granite Steel Co. v. EPA, 501 F.2d 925, 4 ELR 20810 (7th Cir. 1974).

36. Getty Oil Co. (Eastern Operations) v. Ruckelshaus, 467 F.2d 349, 2 ELR 20683 (3d Cir. 1972), cert. denied 409 U.S. 1125; West Penn Power Co. v. Train, 522 F.2d 302, 5 ELR 20557 (3d Cir. 1975).

37. Anaconda Co. v. Ruckelshaus, 482 F.2d 1301, 1304–05, 3 ELR 20719, 20720–21 (10th Cir. 1973).

38. Walker v. Birmingham, 388 U.S. 307, 87 S.Ct. 1824, 18 L.Ed.2d 1210 (1967); see § 3.19 below (discussing conflicting treatment of the issue under state law).

39. 42 U.S.C.A. § 1857h–5(b)(2).

40. Note 9, supra.

The structure of the Act, now clear after the Supreme Court's decisions in *Train* and *Union Electric*, disallows direct economic and technical attacks on the legislative-type judgments of the implementation plans but permits them in individual source trial-type hearings in variance or enforcement proceedings.[41]

The federal enforcement provisions under section 113,[42] particularly as administered by EPA, strongly support the variance analogy.[43] The usual result of this negotiating session is the issuance of an enforcement order, which shall "specify a time for compliance which the Administrator determines is reasonable, taking into account the seriousness of the violation and any good faith efforts to comply with applicable requirements." [44] This language can be read as according a broad discretion in EPA to extend implementation plan requirements by enforcement orders so long as the substantive requirements or standards themselves are not jeopardized.[45]

A case study on the dangers of preclusion in enforcement proceedings is represented by the *Getty Oil* dilemma.[46] In *Getty*, the Administrator approved and adopted a portion of the Delaware plan requiring the company to furnish an associated power station with low sulfur fuel. Getty neglected to petition the appropriate Circuit Court for review of the Administrator's decision within the thirty days prescribed by section 307, choosing instead to launch a double-barreled attack in state forums—first, by seeking a variance from a state administrative agency and, while an appeal was pending from an adverse decision there, by bringing a successful action in the courts to stay enforcement by the state of the objectionable features of the Delaware plan. The federal EPA, however, not being a party to the state injunction proceeding, was free to initiate an enforcement action against Getty. Getty's federal suit to enjoin enforcement failed. The Third Circuit observed that Getty's appeal was "a paradigm of confession and avoidance" and an attempted "end run" around the

---

41. See Indiana & Michigan Elec. Co. v. EPA, 509 F.2d 839, 5 ELR 20191 (7th Cir. 1975); Buckeye Power v. EPA (I), 481 F.2d 162, 173, 3 ELR 20634, 20638 (6th Cir. 1973) (dictum) (stating that economic and technical defenses can be asserted as defenses in enforcement proceedings if no adequate hearing afforded during original approval of the plan); West Penn Power Co. v. Train, 522 F.2d 302, 5 ELR 20557 (3d Cir. 1975) (same). See also Union Elec. Co. v. EPA, 427 U.S. 246, 266, 96 S.Ct. 2518, 2519–20, 49 L.Ed.2d 474, 488–89 (1976) (dictum) (indicating that defense may be available "where consideration of such claims will not substantially interfere with the primary congressional purpose of prompt attainment of the national air quality standards," such as during the development of the original implementation plan, under the extension and postponement provisions, and in enforcement proceedings).

42. 42 U.S.C.A. § 1857c–8.

43. See § 3.19 below.

44. Section 113(a)(4), 42 U.S.C.A. § 1857c–8(a)(4).

45. See § 3.19 below.

46. Getty Oil Co. (Eastern Operations) v. Ruckelshaus, 467 F.2d 349, 2 ELR 20693 (3d Cir. 1972), cert. denied 409 U.S. 1125.

Act.[47] Getty's dilemma was that although it had succeeded in having the state temporarily repudiate its own sulfur regulations, in the meantime they had become frozen for enforcement purposes by the federal government prior to the exhaustion of state remedies. Getty "was presented with the choice of either compliance or breach, until such time as its application for a variance is favorably considered."[48] One court has sought to relieve the problem by requiring EPA either to refrain from pursuing enforcement action prior to completion of the state proceedings or to hold its own legislative-type hearing on the company's claims of unfeasibility.[49] A better solution is to recognize the federal enforcement proceeding as the appropriate forum for claims of economic and technical impossibility.[50]

h. *Contempt Proceedings*

The defense of technological impossibility has been allowed in civil contempt proceedings to enforce air pollution requirements.[51] Culpability requirements normally apply in contempt proceedings so the result is not surprising. This defense will not be widely recognized for the reasons that a hearing on economics and technology earlier in the process should foreclose consideration of the issues in a contempt proceeding, that the defense of "impossibility" is difficult to sustain, and that it always is possible to meet the standards by shutting down.

§ 3.10 New Source Performance Standards

The "best technology" principle for controlling emissions so well known at common law is applied to new sources of air pollution under Section 111 of the Act.[1] A "new source" means "any stationary source, the construction or modification of which is commenced after the publication of regulations (or, if earlier, proposed regulations) prescribing a standard of performance under this section which will be applicable to such source."[2] A stationary source means "any building, structure, facility, or installation which emits or may emit any air pollutant."[3] Because the legal existence of a new source under section 111 is dependent upon a regulatory initiative by the Administra-

---

47. 467 F.2d at 358, 359, 2 ELR at 20686, 20687.

48. 467 F.2d at 358, 2 ELR at 20686.

49. Duquesne Light Co. v. EPA (I), 481 F.2d 1, 3 ELR 20483 (3d Cir. 1973).

50. See § 3.19 below.

51. Dep't of Environmental Resources v. Pennsylvania Power Co., 461 Pa. 675, 337 A.2d 823 (1975). The possibility also is suggested by dicta in Buckeye Power v. EPA (I), 481 F.2d 162, 176, 3 ELR 20634, 20638 (6th Cir. 1973) and Indiana & Michigan Elec. Co. v. EPA, 509 F.2d 839, 847, 5 ELR 20191, 20195 (7th Cir. 1975).

1. 42 U.S.C.A. § 1857c-6.

2. Section 111(a)(2), 42 U.S.C.A. § 1857 c-6(a)(2); see 40 CFR §§ 60.2(h), (i).

3. Section 111(a)(3), 42 U.S.C.A. § 1857 c-6(a)(3); see 40 CFR § 60.2(b). Compare § 3.3 above (discussing field burnings as within the definition of stationary source).

268   AIR POLLUTION   Ch. 3

tor, there are a host of new sources, as the term is commonly understood, that have come into being since the passage of the 1970 amendments, untouched by federal performance standards.

The Senate Committee on Public Works listed nineteen categories of stationary sources the administration advised probably would be subject to the provisions of section 111.[4] On December 23, 1971,[5] EPA promulgated new source performance standards for five categories (fossil fuel-fired steam generators, incinerators, portland cement plants, nitric and sulfuric acid plants), and on March 8, 1974,[6] issued standards for seven additional categories (asphalt concrete plants, petroleum refineries, storage vessels for petroleum liquids, secondary lead smelters, secondary brass and bronze ingot production plants, iron and steel plants, and sewage treatment plants). As of September 1, 1976, standards have been promulgated for a total of 24 new source categories.[7] The list will continue to grow, spawning the inevitable petitions to review in the Court of Appeals for the District of Columbia.[8]

A "standard of performance" which the Administrator issues for a new source under the Act means [9]

---

4. Comm. on Public Works, National Air Quality Standards Act of 1970, S.Rep. No. 1196, 91st Cong., 2d Sess. 15 (1970) [hereinafter cited as Senate Report]. They include:
    Cement manufacturing;
    Coal cleaning operations;
    Coke byproduct manufacturing;
    Cotton ginning;
    Ferroalloy plants;
    Grain milling and handling operations;
    Gray iron foundries;
    Iron and steel operations;
    Municipal incinerators;
    Nitric acid manufacturing;
    Nonferrous metallurgical operations (e. g. aluminum reduction, copper, lead, and zinc smelting);
    Petroleum refining;
    Phosphate manufacturing;
    Phosphoric acid manufacturing;
    Pulp and paper mill operations;
    Rendering plants (animal matter);
    Sulfuric acid manufacturing;
    Soap and detergent manufacturing;
    Steam electric power plants.

5. 35 Fed.Reg. 24876 (1970), 40 CFR §§ 60.40–.85 (subpts. D–H).

6. 39 Fed.Reg. 9308 (1974), 40 CFR §§ 60.90–.154 (subpts. I–O).

7. The other new source categories for which standards have been promulgated are: primary copper smelters, 41 Fed.Reg. 2332 (1976), adding 40 CFR § 60.160; primary zinc smelters, id., adding 40 CFR § 60.170; primary lead smelters, id., adding 40 CFR § 60.180; primary aluminum reduction plants, 41 Fed.Reg. 3826 (1976), adding 40 CFR § 60.190; phosphate fertilizer industry: wet process phosphoric acid plants, 40 Fed.Reg. 33152 (1975), adding 40 CFR § 60.200; phosphate fertilizer industry: superphosphoric acid plants, id., adding 40 CFR § 60.210; phosphate fertilizer industry: diamonium phosphate plants, id., adding 40 CFR § 60.-220; phosphate fertilizer industry: triple superphosphate plants, id., adding 40 CFR § 60.230; phosphate fertilizer industry: triple superphosphate storage facilities, id., adding 40 CFR § 60.240; coal preparation plants, 41 Fed.Reg. 2332 (1976), adding 40 CFR § 50.250; ferroalloy production facilities, 41 Fed.Reg. 18498 (1976), adding 40 CFR § 60.260; steel plants: electricarc furnaces, 40 Fed.Reg. 43850 (1975), adding 40 CFR § 60.270.

8. Section 307(b), 42 U.S.C.A. § 1857 h–5(b).

9. Section 111(a)(1), 42 U.S.C.A. § 1857 c–6(a)(1). The Administrator must maintain a list of stationary sources which "may contribute significantly

Sec. 3.10 NEW SOURCE PERFORMANCE STANDARDS

a standard for emissions of air pollutants which reflects the degree of emission limitation achievable through the application of the best system of emission reduction which (taking into account the cost of achieving such reduction) the Administrator determines has been adequately demonstrated.

Two issues are apparent on the face of this legislation: the extent to which cost is taken into account, and the extent to which a process "adequately demonstrated" must be shown to have been in actual operation. Another question is whether the standards of performance will be applied to older sources undergoing substantial modifications. These issues of cost, a demonstrated technology and modified sources have proven extremely important to the evaluation of section 111.

The leading opinion on section 111 is Judge Leventhal's powerful effort in Portland Cement Ass'n v. Ruckelshaus,[10] which favored the regulator with generous interpretations of the feasibility and cost requirements but favored the regulated by invoking the hard look doctrine to look behind the reasoning of the new source performance standards. Judge Leventhal read the "best technology" provisions as providing leverage for improvement:

> We begin by rejecting the suggestion of the cement manufacturers that the Act's requirement that emission limitations be 'adequately demonstrated' necessarily implies that any cement plant now in existence be able to meet the proposed standards. Section 111 looks toward what may fairly be projected for the regulated future, rather than the state of the art at present, since it is addressed to the standards for new plants . . . . .[11]

The court found the standard "analogous" to the one pertaining to auto emissions,[12] and observed, "The Administrator may make a projection based on existing technology, though that projection is subject to the restraints of reasonableness and cannot be based on 'crystal ball' inquiry."[13] The fact that the standards prescribed will take effect immediately narrows the "latitude of projection" but the standards anticipate a prediction not a dry application of what has been.[14]

---

to air pollution which causes or contributes to the endangerment of public health or welfare." Id. § 1857c–6(b)(1)(A). The "significant contributor" designation triggers timing requirements on the publication of standards. Id. § 1857c–6(b)(1)(B).

10. 158 U.S.App.D.C. 308, 486 F.2d 375, 3 ELR 20642 (1973), on remand 168 U.S.App.D.C. 248, 513 F.2d 506, 5 ELR 20341 (1975).

11. 158 U.S.App.D.C. at 324, 486 F.2d at 391, 3 ELR at 20650.

12. See § 3.14 below.

13. 158 U.S.App.D.C. at 324, 486 F.2d at 391, 3 ELR at 20650, citing International Harvester Co. v. Ruckelshaus, 155 U.S.App.D.C. 411, 425, 478 F.2d 615, 629, 3 ELR 20133, 20137 (1973).

14. Essex Chem. Corp. v. Ruckelshaus, 158 U.S.App.D.C. 360, 366, 486 F.2d 427, 433, 3 ELR 20732, 20735 (1974), cert. denied 416 U.S. 969. ("An adequately demonstrated system is one which is shown to be reasonably re-

This is a bold interpretation of the "adequately demonstrated" requirement. Linking the new source performance standards to the motor vehicle emission standards is to associate the concept with "drastic medicine" [15] designed to "force the state of the art." [16] Moreover, a case could have been made that the Conference Committee's rejection of a stiffer version of the new source performance standards developed by the Senate Committee on Public Works [17] should be construed as indicating a desire to go slowly—or at least to make clear that industry not be stampeded into control commitments based upon unproven technologies.[18]

Judge Leventhal was equally emphatic that the reference to the "taking into account the cost of achieving such reduction" in section 111 is not to be read as requiring a quantified cost-benefit analysis, showing the benefit to ambient air concentrations measured against the cost of control devices:

> However desirable in the abstract, such a requirement would conflict with the specific time restraints imposed on the Administrator. The difficulty, if not impossibility, of quantifying the benefit to ambient air concentrations, further militates against the imposition of such an imperative on the agency. Such studies should be considered by the Administrator, if adduced in comments, but we do not inject them as a necessary condition of the action.[19]

There is no question after *Portland Cement* that the Administrator must consider such matters as the impact of the new source standards on the amount of total facility investment required to be devoted to pollution control, whether costs of control can be passed on to product users, product quality and its general availability at reasonable costs, availability of the product in certain areas, and whether widely adopted control practices or production processes will be rendered obsolete. But there is a great deal of difference between a standard of judicial review simply requiring the Administrator to consider

---

liable, reasonably efficient, and which can reasonably be expected to serve the interest of pollution control without becoming exorbitantly costly in an economic or environmental way").

15. 166 Cong.Rec. 32904 (1970) (Sen. Muskie) (speaking of the auto standards).

16. Id. at 33120 (newspaper report of statement of Sen. Eagleton introduced into the record by Sen. Muskie).

17. The Senate would have required that the standards reflect
the greatest degree of emission control which the Secretary determines to be achievable through application of the latest available control technology, processes, operating methods, or other alternatives.
Senate Report, supra note 4, at 90.

18. The Report of the Conference is silent on the language finally adopted in section 111. See Comm. of Conference, Clean Air Amendments of 1970, H.R.Rep. No. 1783, 91st Cong., 2d Sess. 9, 45 (1970) [hereinafter cited as Conference Report].

19. 158 U.S.App.D.C. at 316, 486 F.2d at 387, 3 ELR at 20648 (footnote omitted).

Sec. 3.10 NEW SOURCE PERFORMANCE STANDARDS

economic costs in a reasoned way, which is the present standard,[20] and requiring him to apply economic factors correctly within a particular frame of reference such as a cost-benefit analysis.

No court or administrative authority yet has addressed the potential conflict between the requirement that the Administrator consider economic feasibility in establishing new source emission standards but disregard it in requiring that the primary standards protecting health be met. The problem can and should be resolved by insisting that new sources not become health hazards; the consideration that must be given economics under section 111 need not be read as contradicting the disqualification of economics insofar as health standards are concerned. New sources have total freedom to choose the safest sites and use the best controls. New sources need not shut down to meet the standards; they must never commence operations in places where health and the air quality standards protecting it are put in jeopardy.

Not only must the system be adequately demonstrated and cost justified, it must reflect the degree of emission limitation "achievable" through application of the best system available. An "achievable standard" is one "which is within the realm of the adequately demonstrated system's efficiency and which, while not at a level that is purely theoretical or experimental, need not necessarily be routinely achieved within the industry prior to its adoption."[21] The concept has been applied to uphold a standard for some sulfuric acid plants (4.0 pounds of SO_2 per ton of sulfuric acid produced) not being met by others in the industry.[22]

It has been held that when the Administrator makes his "best system" and "achievable limitation" determination he must take into account counter-productive environmental effects.[23] As Judge Leventhal aptly observed in *Portland Cement*,[24] "[w]e cannot imagine that Congress intended that 'best' could apply to a system which did more damage to water than it prevented to air." Section 111 standards may be issued without compliance with the procedures of the National Environmental Policy Act for the reason that the decision requires the "functional equivalent" of a NEPA statement.[25] The require-

---

20. Portland Cement Ass'n v. Ruckelshaus, 158 U.S.App.D.C. 308, 486 F.2d 375, 3 ELR 20642 (1973), cert. denied 417 U.S. 921 (1974); Essex Chem. Corp. v. Ruckelshaus, 159 U.S.App.D.C. 360, 486 F.2d 427, 3 ELR 20732 (1973), cert. denied 416 U.S. 969 (1974); National Asphalt Pavement Ass'n v. Train, — U.S.App.D.C. —, 539 F.2d 775 (1976).

21. Essex Chem. Corp. v. Ruckelshaus, 158 U.S.App.D.C. at 366–67, 486 F.2d at 433–34, 3 ELR at 20735 (1973).

22. 158 U.S.App.D.C. at 370, 486 F.2d at 437, 3 ELR at 20736.

23. 158 U.S.App.D.C. at 366, 486 F.2d at 433, 3 ELR at 20735.

24. 158 U.S.App.D.C. at 319 n. 42, 486 F.2d at 386 n. 42, 3 ELR at 20647 n. 42.

25. 158 U.S.App.D.C. at 317, 486 F.2d at 384, 3 ELR at 20646.

ment of functional equivalency has been applied rigorously,[26] not as a technique of lip-service avoidance, so it is accurate to acknowledge that the rationale of a section 111 standard must address generally the range of alternatives addressed by NEPA. This remains true despite Congress' decision in 1974 to exempt generally from NEPA actions taken under the Clean Air Act.[27]

While interpreting section 111 to give the Administrator considerable leeway to require industry to stretch its technological capabilities, the courts also have required the agency to dot the "i's" and cross the "t's" on the reasons offered in defense of its standards. This literacy test for the Administrator is fully in the mainstream of contemporary judicial review of administrative action.[28] Generally, section 111 standards are based on information and data derived from (1) inspections and stack tests of existing facilities; (2) consultations with operators, designers, and state and local control officials; and (3) review of available literature. The Administrator must be careful that his tests represent the real world, and his consultations and literature reviews provide instruction. Courts [29] view skeptically tests on plants operating at less than full capacity, conducted contrary to established procedures, or based on questionable or undisclosed methodology, conclusions resting upon ambiguous sampling data or published literature without indication of specifics, contradicting "basic chemistry," [30] or ignoring thoughtful criticism, literature findings on emissions controls containing no data indicating the percentage capacity of the plants tested, discussions with plant designers, operators and officials unrecorded in the record, or acknowledgments without explanation that the solution recommended might produce a pollution problem of a different kind. When all is said and done, however, the agency's conclusions will be sustained if based on reasoned decision-making.[31]

One extremely important question has never been litigated. New sources, it must be remembered, include stationary sources constructed

26. Essex Chem. Corp. v. Ruckelshaus, 158 U.S.App.D.C. 360, 372, 486 F.2d 427, 439, 3 ELR 20732, 20738 (1973), cert. denied 416 U.S. 969 (1974) (requiring Administrator to consider alternative of no control for some recycle sulfuric acid plants and to consider problem of sludge byproduct from lime slurry scrubbing systems in coal-fired steam generators).

27. Energy Supply and Environmental Coordination Act of 1974, § 7(c), Pub. L. No. 93–319, 88 Stat. 246, 15 U.S. C.A. § 793(c).

28. See § 1.5 above.

29. Portland Cement Ass'n v. Ruckelshaus, 158 U.S.App.D.C. 308, 486 F.2d 375, 3 ELR 206542 (1973), cert. denied 417 U.S. 921 (1974); Essex Chem. Corp. v. Ruckelshaus, 158 U.S.App. D.C. 308, 486 F.2d 375, 3 ELR 20642, cert. denied 417 U.S. 921 (1974); Essex Chem. Corp. v. Ruckelshaus, 158 U.S. App.D.C. 360, 486 F.2d 427, 3 ELR 20732 (1973), cert. denied 416 U.S. 969 (1974).

30. Portland Cement Ass'n v. Ruckelshaus, 158 U.S.App.D.C. at 331, 486 F.2d at 398, 3 ELR at 20654.

31. Portland Cement Ass'n v. Train, 168 U.S.App.D.C. 248, 513 F.2d 506, 5 ELR 20341 (1975), cert. denied 423 U.S. 1025; National Asphalt Pavement Ass'n v. Train, —— U.S.App.D.C. ——, 539 F.2d 775 (1976).

Sec. 3.10 NEW SOURCE PERFORMANCE STANDARDS

or modified after standards of performance have been prescribed.[32] The Act defines the term "modification" to mean "any physical change in, or change in the method of operation of, a stationary source which increases the amount of any air pollutant emitted by such source or which results in the emission of any air pollutant not previously emitted."[33] The purpose, quite clearly, is to assure that new source performance standards are applied to installations modifying operations to increase or change the mix of its pollutants. This is a common occurrence for a number of reasons, not the least of which is that a company might prefer to expand production at an established facility rather than run the gauntlet of regulation and possible community hostility to a new plant. EPA has experienced difficulty in implementing the "modified" source requirements. Initially, it defined "modification" to exempt several categories clearly covered by the Act.[34] Then, it invented a new category of "reconstruction" which "is intended to apply where an existing facility's components are replaced to such an extent that it is technologically and economically feasible for the reconstructed facility to comply with the applicable standards of performance."[35] A recent regulation declares no "modification" of an existing facility is deemed to occur despite physical and operational changes increasing emissions if other facilities are closed to avoid an overall increase in the total emission rate at a source.[36] This "bubble concept" thus allows the trading off of emission increases from one facility with emission reductions from another. It is of questionable validity under the statutory definition of "modification" and the general purpose of section 111, which is to require maximum performance from newly constructed facilities.[37]

The difficulties with modified, reconstructed or changed facilities demonstrate that section 111 speaks mainly to the atypical situa-

---

32. Section 111(a)(2), 42 U.S.C.A. § 1857c–6(a)(2).

33. Section 111(a)(4), 42 U.S.C.A. § 1857c–6(a)(4).

34. 40 CFR § 60.2(h) defines "modification" to excuse increases in production not in excess of the operating design capacity of the affected facility, any increases in the hours of operation, and uses of alternative fuels or raw materials if prior to the date of an effective standard the facility was designed to accommodate this alternative use. The definition is revised in 40 Fed.Reg. 58416, 58418 (1975).

35. 40 Fed.Reg. 58416, 58417 (1975), adding 40 CFR §§ 60.14 (modification), and 60.15 (reconstruction).

36. 40 CFR § 60.14(d), as added 40 Fed.Reg. 58416, 58419 (1975).

37. A "modification" is a physical or operational change at a stationary source "which increases the amount of any air pollutant emitted by such source." A "modification" still increases the amount of an air pollutant from a source even though offsetting reductions are accomplished for other reasons. Surely section 111 does not mean to tolerate a horrendously controlled new facility because of a fortuity that has led to the coincidental shutdown of 90 per cent of the other capacity at a given source. Nor does it appear that the statutory definition of "modification" means to invite control by bargaining, which is at the heart of the "bubble concept." Compare § 3.7 above (discussing the tradeoff policy for new sources in noncomplying regions).

tion. The rules are clear when a new source covered by the performance standards is constructed at a new site. But the source and the site often are partly new, partly old, and peripherally covered by the Act. It is accepted dogma that problems of retroactivity and interference with established business patterns are minimized when regulation hits hard at new construction and future conduct. Difficulties in distinguishing the new from the old and the future from the past provide unexpected complications.

Procedures leading up to a determination that a new source complies with federal emission standards under section 111 are clear in some respects but wholly ambiguous in others.[38] An owner or operator of a new source can secure an advisory opinion on whether actions intended to be taken constitute "construction," "re-construction" or "modification" for purposes of the Act.[39] He can request EPA to review plans for construction and provide technical advice.[40] He must comply with certain notification, record keeping, and performance test requirements (including affording the Administrator an opportunity to have an observer present).[41] The regulations are utterly silent on how the Administrator decides, what form his decision takes and what conditions he may attach to it.[42] No provision is made for a hearing or participation by interested persons. It may be that the judgment on new source performance standards someday will be subjected to adjudicatory hearing procedures like those governing application for waste discharge permits under the Federal Water Pollution Control Act. The decisions can be equally important.

A standard of performance for a new source is an "emission limitation" enforceable by citizen suit.[43] Relief can be obtained if the Administrator or a state authorizes the construction of a new source without an adequate showing that the standards will be met.[44] Elimination of a pre-construction review procedure in the 1970 conference [45] in no way can be read as precluding pre-construction review; the standards must be met, and it is only a question of timing whether a decision on non-compliance can be made before or after the fact. An attack upon the new source standards themselves must be pur-

38. The Senate bill would have established a pre-construction certification procedure for new sources but the requirement was dropped in Conference. Compare Senate Report, supra note 4, at 91–93 with Conference Report, supra note 18, at 46.

39. 40 CFR § 60.5.

40. Id. § 60.6.

41. Id. §§ 60.7, 60.8.

42. It is possible for the Administrator to delegate to the states his authority to implement the new source performance standards (except as to new sources owned or operated by the United States). Section 111(c)(1), 42 U.S.C.A. § 1857c–6(c)(1).

43. Contra Sierra Club v. Drain, 5 ELR 20435 (D.C.Neb.1975).

44. Sierra Club v. Drain, supra note 43.

45. Compare Senate Report, supra note 4, at 17 with Conference Report supra note 18, at 46–47.

sued by petitioning the Administrator and seeking review of an adverse decision in the United States Court of Appeals for the District of Columbia.[46]

Section 111(d) of the Act [47] establishes a procedure to regulate existing sources that might otherwise fall through the cracks of the regulatory scheme.[48] (Of course falling through the cracks of federal regulation might mean tougher treatment at the hands of states or localities under common law principles.) The provision directs the Administrator to prescribe regulations under which each state would develop a plan (comparable to a section 110 implementation plan) establishing emission standards for any pollutants (except for criteria or hazardous pollutants) from existing sources covered by new source performance standards. The idea was that "since standards of performance governing new sources are comprehensive, regulating the emissions of all pollutants from such sources,"[49] the Administrator needed the power to fill in the gaps for pollutants covered by new source standards but not by the criteria or hazardous emission standards. The Administrator can—and did—derail this authority by limiting his new source rulemakings to pollutants covered by the ambient standards. Falling through the cracks have been chlorine gas, hydrogen chloride, chromium, manganese and many other pollutants.

Section 111(d) points up the flexibility EPA has to choose among the criteria, hazardous, non-deterioration and new source performance standards regulatory techniques. Indeed, in the case of fluoride emissions from aluminum reduction plants this flexibility led to paralysis as the agency, torn between the alternatives, exercised none of them.[50] Trespass and nuisance law under the circumstances is not

---

46. Olijato Chapter of the Navajo Tribe v. Train, 169 U.S.App.D.C. 195, 202, 515 F.2d 654, 661, 5 ELR 20481, 20484 (1975) (challenging new source performance standards for coal-burning steam electric power plants as being too lax because they can be met by burning low-sulfur coal with no controls).

47. 42 U.S.C.A. § 1857c–6(d).

48. The Senate bill, S.4358, 91st Cong., 2d Sess. (1970), included a section 114 authorizing direct federal controls over selected agents. Senate Report, supra note 4, at 93–95. It was rewritten in conference to become section 111(d). See Jorling, The Federal Law of Air Pollution Control, in Federal Environmental Law Institute, Federal Environmental Law 1058, 1106–07 & n.226 (E. L. Dolgin & T. G. P. Guilbert eds. 1974). Candidates for regulation under the original section 114 (and now under 111(d)) include arsenic, chlorine gas, hydrogen chloride, copper, maganese, nickel, vanadium, zinc, barium, boron, chromium, selenium, pesticides, radioactive substances. See Senate Report, supra note 4, at 7:
> Available information indicates that these pollution agents are generally emitted from the stationary sources that would be subject to performance standards.

49. Jorling, supra note 48, at 1106 (emphasis in original).

50. George, The Aluminum Industry as a Source of Fluorides: The Proposed New Source Emission Standards (unpublished paper submitted for course in environmental law, Georgetown U. Law Center, Jan. 1974). But see 41 Fed.Reg. 3826 (1975), adding 40 CFR § 60.192 (imposing new source standards for fluoride emissions from primary aluminum reduction plants).

to be forgotten, a point confirmed by the seventeen year struggle of Paul and Verla Martin to protect their 1500 acre cattle ranch from an aluminum plant in Troutdale, Oregon.[51]

§ 3.11 Hazardous Air Pollutant Emission Standards

A second basis for federal emission standards (in addition to the new source performance standards under section 111) is found in section 112,[1] which gives the Administrator authority to impose emission standards on both new and existing sources of hazardous air pollutants.

The hazardous emission standard provisions parallel the new source requirements in certain particulars: the Administrator must first list a hazardous air pollutant,[2] and then embark on a standard-setting process that includes a non-adjudicatory public hearing.[3] After the effective date of a regulation, existing sources are given an automatic reprieve of ninety days,[4] and may get a waiver from the Administrator "of up to two years" if he finds "that such period is necessary for the installation of controls and that steps will be taken during the period of the waiver to assure that the health of persons will be protected from imminent endangerment."[5] Construction and modification of new sources [6] of hazardous pollutants, unlike new sources under section 111, explicitly is subject to pre-construction review and administrative veto "unless the Administrator finds that such source if properly operated will not cause emissions in violation of such standard." [7] Both new and existing sources may win an unusual presidential exemption "of not more than two years", subject to extensions, "if he finds that the technology to implement such standards is not available and the operation of such source is required for reasons of national security." [8]

The Act defines a "hazardous air pollutant" as an "air pollutant to which no ambient air quality standard is applicable and which in

---

51. Mr. Martin died and his widow eventually sold out to the Reynolds Aluminum Co. See P. Keeton & R. F. Keeton, Cases and Materials on Torts 377 (1971) (quoting a newspaper account).

1. 42 U.S.C.A. § 1857c–7.

2. Section 112(b)(1)(A), 42 U.S.C.A. § 1857c–7(b)(1)(A).

3. Section 112(b)(1)(B), 42 U.S.C.A. § 1857c–7(b)(1)(B).

4. Section 112(c)(1)(B)(i), 42 U.S.C.A. § 1857c–7(c)(1)(B)(i).

5. Section 112(c)(1)(B)(ii), 42 U.S.C.A. § 1857c–7(c)(1)(B)(ii).

6. The term "new source" is defined for purposes of section 112 to mean "a stationary source the construction or modification of which is commenced after the Administrator proposes regulations under this section establishing an emission standard which will be applicable to such source." Section 112(a)(2), 42 U.S.C.A. § 1857c–7(a)(2).

7. Section 112(c)(1)(A), 42 U.S.C.A. § 1857c–7(c)(1)(A).

8. Section 112(c)(2), 42 U.S.C.A. § 1857c–7(c)(2).

Sec. 3.11 HAZARDOUS EMISSION STANDARDS

the judgment of the Administrator may cause, or contribute to, an increase in mortality or an increase in serious irreversible, or incapacitating reversible, illness."[9] This is a broad definition extending to many air pollutants with prospects for killing and disabling people, and indeed might include the criteria pollutants were not they specifically exempted. But the legislative history discloses an intention to reach only a "limited number of pollutants," under section 112,[10] with asbestos, cadmium, mercury, and beryllium specifically mentioned. The Administrator has accepted the invitation to construe the provisions narrowly. Initially listed under the terms of the Act were three hazardous air pollutants (beryllium, mercury and asbestos). Emission standards for these pollutants were proposed December of 1971,[11] but not finally promulgated until May of 1973 [12] under court order.[13] At the end of 1975 vinyl chloride was added to the list.[14] Efforts to persuade the Administrator to exercise his "hazardous air pollutant" powers against numerous other candidates, including arsenic and lead, have proven unavailing.

Under the Act, the Administrator "shall establish any [emission] standard at the level which in his judgment provides an ample margin of safety to protect the public health from such hazardous air pollutants." As in setting national ambient air quality standards,[15] the administrative judgment on an emission standard for a hazardous pollutant should be dictated solely by public health considerations without regard to the costs or feasibility of control. Quite clearly, the standard might require no releases (zero emissions) although "a total prohibition on emissions is a step that ought to be taken only where a danger to health . . . exists."[16] The authority to compel a shutdown or total curtailment when health hazards exist of course is well understood at common law.

The occasion for existing sources to argue economics and technology is in a waiver request to the Administrator.[17] Exhaustion of that two year reprieve leaves only the possibility of a presidential exemption which can be forthcoming upon a finding of technological im-

---

9. Section 112(a)(1), 42 U.S.C.A. § 1857c–7(a)(1).

10. Comm. on Public Works, National Air Quality Standards Act of 1970, S. Rep. No. 1196, 91st Cong., 2d Sess. 20 (1970) [hereinafter cited as Senate Report]. This narrow interpretation however, was based upon a general understanding that S.4358 required a "prohibition of emissions" of pollutants designated "hazardous." Id. at 94–95. Elimination of a presumptive zero emission standard in section 112 thus might justify its application to a broader range of pollutants.

11. 36 Fed.Reg. 24877 (1971).

12. 38 Fed.Reg. 8826 (1973), 40 CFR pt. 61.

13. Environmental Defense Fund, Inc. v. Ruckelshaus, 3 ELR 20173 (D.D.C. 1973).

14. 40 Fed.Reg. 59477 (1975).

15. See § 3.5 above.

16. Senate Report, supra note 10, at 19.

17. See text accompanying note 5 supra.

possibility of control and a national security need for continued operation.[18]

The regulations on hazardous air pollutants add a great deal to the statute: "modification" is defined,[19] as under section 111, to exempt sources not previously producing at designed capacity. Procedures are established for applications for approval of construction or modification of new sources,[20] for waiver requests for existing sources,[21] as well as for decision-making on waivers.[22] A source operating under a waiver, interestingly, also can secure a waiver of emission tests,[23] which seems to make no sense at all unless the Administrator needs no emission data "to assure that the health of persons will be protected from imminent endangerment" during the period of the waiver.

Regulations[24] under section 112 are conventional in content and potentially useful in private litigation: visible emissions from asbestos mills or manufacturing facilities are prohibited unless the owner or operator elects to use fabric filter air cleaning collection devices; the surfacing of roadways with asbestos tailings is, with a single exception, prohibited; demolition operations of buildings insulated or fireproofed with friable (easily crumbled) asbestos material must be preceded by notice to the Administrator and a number of operational precautions (such as wetting) to reduce the air pollution hazard. This is a far-reaching regulation, and one that is widely violated, given the fact there are thirty thousand demolition operations conducted each year in the United States.[25]

Beryllium emissions from stationary sources (extraction plants, ceramic plants, foundries, incinerators, and propellant plants)[26] are subjected either to an emission standard of 10 grams of beryllium over a 24-hour period, or at the option of the owner or operator, an ambient air standard of .01 grams per cubic meter in the vicinity of the source averaged over a thirty day period.[27] Stack stampling[28] or air sampling[29] is called for depending upon the option exercised. There is a serious legal question whether the ambient air standard option offered to sources of beryllium can be reconciled with section 112, which speaks of "emission standards" once in the section heading

18. See text accompanying note 8 supra.

19. 40 CFR § 61.02(j).

20. Id. § 61.07.

21. Id. § 61.10.

22. Id. § 61.11.

23. Id. § 61.13.

24. Examples are taken from id. §§ 61.22, 61.23.

25. See G. W. Fishbein, Occupational Health & Safety Newsletter, Oct. 22, 1974, at 8.

26. A "propellant plant" means any facility engaged in the mixing, casting or machining of propellant. See 40 CFR § 61.31(k).

27. Id. § 61.32.

28. Id. § 61.33.

29. Id. § 61.34.

and another dozen or so occasions in the text. The difference between emission standards and ambient air standards is well understood, and Congress obviously was inclined to control hazardous pollutants at the source not subject to the vagaries of air sampling, wind direction and meteorological prediction associated with the enforcement of ambient air standards.

The mercury emission standards [30] are prescribed only for certain mercury sources (those processing mercury ore to recover mercury and those using mercury chlor-alkili cells to produce chlorine gas and alkili metal hydroxide). Although section 112, unlike section 111, does not invite the Administrator to distinguish among classes, types and sizes within categories of sources, the omission should not be read as significant. It makes technical sense for the Administrator to treat differently discrete types of sources of the same hazardous pollutant, and there is nothing in the legislative history indicating a stubborn intention to insist upon the foolish. The basic emission standard for stationary sources of mercury is set at no more than 2300 grams (around five pounds) per 24-hour period.[31] This is no small amount of a highly toxic substance, and it may well be that mercury sources will be among those upon which a state or locality will seek to impose more stringent standards.

§ 3.12 Prevention of Significant Deterioration

No single aspect of the air quality laws has generated more controversy than the nondegradation issue, more accurately described as the "no significant deterioration" issue. The textual basis for the conflict is thin to the point of disappearance. Congress expressed as a purpose of the Clean Air Amendments of 1970, in language that could offend no one, a low intensity bromide: "to protect and enhance the quality of the Nation's air resources so as to promote the public health and welfare and the productive capacity of its population." [1] From this small seed sprang a legal jungle involving such im-

---

30. Id. §§ 61.50–.53.

31. Id. § 61.52.

1. Section 101(b)(1), 42 U.S.C.A. § 1857(b)(1). For a discussion of the no significant deterioration issue, see Jorling, The Federal Law of Air Pollution Control, in Environmental Law Institute, Federal Environmental Law 1058, 1077–82 (E. L. Dolgin & T. G. P. Guilbert eds. 1974). The evolution of the issue is set forth in Sierra Club v. EPA, —— U.S.App.D.C. ——, 540 F.2d 1114, 6 ELR 20669 (1976). See also Mandelker & Rothschild, The Role of Land-Use Controls in Combating Air Pollution Under the Clean Air Act of 1970, 3 Ecology L.Q. 235 (1973); Comment, Clean Air Act and Significant Deterioration of Air Quality: The Continuing Controversy, 5 Environmental Affairs 145 (1974); Comment, Non-Degradation and Pollution Control Alternatives Under the Clean Air Act of 1970, 9 Land & Water L. Rev. 507 (1974); Comment, Nondegradation Controversy: How Clean Will Our "Clean Air" Be?, 1974 U. Ill.L.F. 314; Comment, Review of EPA's Significant Deterioration Issues: An Example of the Difficulties of the Agency-Court Partnership in Environmental Law, 61 Va.L.Rev. 1115 (1975); Brown & Lipaj, Implications of a Prevention of Significant Deter-

penetrable questions as whether federal law prohibits all local development that threatens to degrade air quality.

The legislative appreciation of the issue is more substantial than the textual reference. The debate in recent times goes back to 1967 when Secretary of the Interior Stewart Udall construed his authority under the Federal Water Pollution Control Act of 1965 [2] to require disapproval of any state water quality standard implementation plan unless it assured non-degradation of high quality water. This policy was articulated and approved by administration spokesmen at the hearings preceding passage of the Clean Air Amendments of 1970, upon the understanding that the law should not condone "backsliding" in areas blessed by air quality above the national standards.[3] The key Senate Report contains an endorsement of an undefined non-deterioration policy.[4] Thus, the legislative history must be read as endorsing vaguely a view that state plans should not allow good air to go bad.

The Administrator of the Environmental Protection Agency demonstrated no more inclination than the Congress to define insignificant deterioration and, indeed, waffled badly along the way. The Administrator embraced the concept when he promulgated the National Primary and Secondary Ambient Air Quality Standards [5] but qualified it when he promulgated the Requirements for Preparation, Adoption and Submittal of Implementation Plans.[6] How the administrative left hand was moved to restrain the administrative right hand

ioration Policy on State Growth Management (unpublished paper presented to APCA Conference, Portland, Oregon, June 29, 1976).

2. Section 1(a), 33 U.S.C.A. § 1151, originally enacted in Pub.L. No. 89–234, 79 Stat. 903 (1965) ("The purpose of this Act is to enhance the quality and value of our water resources and to establish a national policy for the prevention, control and abatement of water pollution").

3. Hearings on Air Pollution, Before the Subcomm. on Air and Water Pollution of the Senate Comm. on Public Works, 91st Cong., 2d Sess. 132–33, 143 (1970); see Hearings on Air Pollution and Solid Waste Recycling, Before the Subcomm. on Public Health and Welfare of the House Comm. on Interstate and Foreign Commerce, H.R.Doc. No. 49, 91st Cong., 2d Sess. 281 (1970).

4. Comm. on Public Works, National Air Quality Standards Act of 1970, S. Rep. No. 1196, 91st Cong., 2d Sess. 2 (1970) ("In areas where current air pollution levels are already equal to or better than the air quality goals, the Secretary shall not approve any implementation plan which does not provide, to the maximum extent practicable, for the continued maintenance of such ambient air quality").

5. 36 Fed.Reg. 22384 (Nov. 25, 1971), adding 40 CFR § 50.2(c), reads: "The promulgation of national primary and secondary ambient air quality standards shall not be considered in any manner to allow significant deterioration of existing air quality in any portion of any state."

6. 36 Fed.Reg. 22398 (Nov. 25, 1971), adding 40 CFR § 51.12(b), reads: "In any region where measured or estimated ambient levels of a pollutant are below the levels specified by an applicable secondary standard, the plan shall set forth a control strategy which shall be adequate to prevent such pollution levels from exceeding such secondary standard."

Sec. 3.12 PREVENTION OF DETERIORATION

is an interesting vignette.[7] The end result, in any event, was that the state plans were thought to be acceptable even when they allowed for deterioration to the secondary standards.

The courts then entered the fray, and proceeded to revive the "no significant deterioration" principle although they did no better than the Administrator and the Congress in defining it. A suit by the Sierra Club produced a brief memorandum opinion in the district court and an order enjoining the Administrator from approving portions of state implementation plans allowing air pollution to rise to the level of the secondary standards.[8] Affirmed per curiam by the Court of Appeals[9] and then by an equally divided Supreme Court,[10] the district court's brief discussion became, for an extended period, the last word.

In July of 1973 the Administrator proposed[11] four quite different plans for defining no significant deterioration of air quality: (1) a nationwide standard (called an Air Quality Increment Plan) allowing a certain amount of pollution above an established base line (e. g., 15 micrograms per cubic meter for sulfur dioxide on an annual average); (2) an Emission Limitation Plan under which a total sum of maximum allowable emissions would be calculated for each air quality control region and assigned on a first come, first served basis to new sources; (3) a Local Definition Plan allowing the judgment on how much pollution was "significant" to be made on a case by case basis by the states; (4) an Area Classification Plan requiring a state to classify its land area into one of two zones having assigned deterioration increments—Zone I allowing only minimal pollution and Zone II permitting greater increments to accommodate normal growth.

Each of the four plans required, as a minimum, application of the "best available control technology" to specified categories of new sources. They would have required a pre-construction review of sixteen major stationary source categories to determine whether there would be a violation. The proposed regulations specified that control systems adequate to comply with new source performance standards under Section 111 of the Act[12] generally would suffice to fulfill the best available control technology requirements of the no significant

---

7. The story is told, in part, in the Hearings on Implementation of the Clean Air Amendments, Before the Subcomm. on Air and Water Pollution of the Senate Comm. on Public Works, S.Doc. No. H–31, 92d Cong., 2d Sess. 12–13, 246 (1972); see Note, Clean Air Act Amendments of 1970: A Congressional Cosmetic, 61 Geo. L.J. 153, 172–79 (1972).

8. Sierra Club v. Ruckelshaus, 344 F. Supp. 253 (D.C.D.C.1972). On November 9, 1972 the Administrator disapproved all state implementation plans to the extent they failed to provide for the prevention of significant deterioration of air quality. 37 Fed. Reg. 23836.

9. 2 ELR 20656 (1972).

10. 412 U.S. 541, 93 S.Ct. 2770, 37 L. Ed.2d 140 (1973).

11. 38 Fed.Reg. 18986 (July 16, 1973).

12. See § 3.10 above.

deterioration proposals. But this rule of equivalency had one significant exception—for sulfur dioxide emissions from fossil fuel-fired steam electric plants. The new source performance standards were set at a level requiring use of a control system on plants burning high sulfur coal but not low sulfur coal. The no significant deterioration proposals, according to EPA, required "that a case-by-case analysis of fossil fuel-fired electric plants be conducted to determine if emissions can and should be further reduced." [13] The suggestion, if nothing else, demonstrates how the "best technology" for purposes of non-deterioration can be better than the "best technology" for purposes of new sources.

In the wake of the EPA proposals, a national debate ensued over the no significant deterioration policy.[14] Discussion addressed basic principles: Should the Clean Air Act be read to impose a national no-growth or slow-growth policy? Or a detailed land-use policy? If no-growth or slow-growth is sometimes desirable, should it require the weighing of a number of factors in addition to air quality? How can a non-degradation policy which effectively freezes growth patterns be reconciled with the constitutional right to travel?[15] Or with authority indicating that growth restrictions must be justified in light of resource and facility availability (e. g., water or sewage capacity)?[16] Does a policy of non-degradation provide a respectable cover for exclusionary zoning? How can increments of pollution be deemed "significant" when they do not rise to the level of measurable effects represented by the secondary standards? How can they be deemed "significant" if the costs of avoiding deterioration exceed even hypothetical benefits? Why should additional technological or land use limits be imposed beyond the best technology requirements of the new source performance standards? Why should pollution be controlled only to the extent it doesn't change basic aspects of our socioeconomic system? Why focus upon the "protect and enhance" language of the Act to the exclusion of the "productive capacity" language of the same clause?

The debate addressed also problems of implementation: Can the policy legally be limited to but two of the criteria pollutants (sulfur dioxide and particulates)? Why excuse such major potential new sources of air pollution as highways, large shopping centers and

---

13. 38 Fed.Reg. at 18986.

14. EPA held hearings on its proposals in several cities. The issue has been continuously alive in the Congress. See generally Hearings on Nondegradation Policy of the Clean Air Act, Before the Subcomm. on Air and Water Pollution of the Senate Comm. on Public Works, S.Doc. No. H–16, 93d Cong., 1st Sess. (1973).

15. See § 2.17 above; cf. Construction Industry Ass'n of Sonoma County v. Petaluma, 375 F.Supp. 574, 4 ELR 20454 (N.D.Cal.1974), rev'd 522 F.2d 897, 5 ELR 20519 (9th Cir. 1975), cert. denied 424 U.S. 934 (1976).

16. See, e. g., § 2.17 above; Golden v. Planning Bd. of the Town of Ramapo, 30 N.Y.2d 359, 334 N.Y.S.2d 138, 285 N.E.2d 291, 2 ELR 20296 (1972).

Sec. 3.12 PREVENTION OF DETERIORATION 283

new towns? Is a separate treatment of fossil-fuel fired power plants justified? How can an allowance of pollution several times above pre-existing levels be deemed "insignificant" on the fortuitous ground that the secondary standards are not yet exceeded? Can economic and social factors properly be considered in deciding whether a particular increment of pollution is "significant"? What baselines are used? What regions covered? Who decides?

In August of 1974 the Administrator reproposed [17] and in December adopted [18] no significant deterioration regulations based on a modified version of the original Area Classification Plan proposal. The plan has four basic features: (1) zoning [19] of land areas in a state by reference to air quality, initially by the Administrator; (2) pre-construction review of new sources to ascertain compatibility with zoning requirements; (3) re-zoning by state or local officials to reflect changing growth patterns; (4) review of the re-zoning decisions by the Administrator. More specifically, air quality zoning involves the classification of much of the land area in a given state (for example, on the basis of several large counties) by limiting levels of new pollution. Class I is an area where practically any change in air quality would be considered "significant" and thus inappropriate. Class II covers areas where deterioration normally accompanying moderate well-controlled growth would be considered insignificant. In Class III areas pollution up to the level of the national standards is deemed insignificant. Permissible pollution increments are defined solely by reference to particulates and sulfur dioxide,[20] not the four auto-caused criteria pollutants. All areas are designated Class II as of the effective date of the regulation.[21]

---

17. 39 Fed.Reg. 30999 (Aug. 27, 1974).

18. Id. at 42510 (Dec. 5, 1974), amending 40 CFR §§ 52.01, 52.21.

19. The EPA strongly shuns the "zoning" characterization in favor of "classification." While the regulations obviously lack most of the constraints associated with comprehensive zoning, they do guide land use decisions to the point of prohibition.

20. The area designations adopted allow the following increases in pollutant concentrations over baseline concentrations:

Pollutant	Class I (micrograms/cubic meter)	Class II (micrograms/cubic meter)
Particulate matter		
Annual geometric mean	5	10
24-hour maximum	10	30
Sulfur dioxide		
Annual arithmetic mean	2	15
24-hour maximum	5	100
3-hour maximum	25	700

40 CFR § 52.21(c)(2).

21. Id. § 52.21(c)(3).

Procedurally and administratively, "the significant deterioration review is virtually identical to existing new source review procedures included in the implementation plan and, in fact, application could probably be made on the same forms." [22] The idea is to single out major categories of polluters [23] and require them to demonstrate at the preconstruction stage that their emissions, in combination with those from other sources, will not result in a violation of the air quality increments allowed in a given area.[24] Because the new source performance standards do not yet reach all the major categories, a general "best available control technology" requirement is imposed, preferably in terms of a specific emission standard applicable to a given source.[25] A definition of "modification" is provided [26] to excuse application of the no significant deterioration requirements to sources that are not starting anew but simply adjusting some of their old operations. The consequence is to permit deterioration (at least for purposes of the no significant deterioration policy) by new fuel policies albeit not by new construction. The basic regulatory premise forbids any owner or operator from "commencing construction or modification" of a source after June 1, 1975 until receiving an administrative go-ahead.[27] Provisions are included requiring an applicant to come forward with information necessary to support a judgment as to compliance [28] and allowing public comment (but not a public hear-

22. 39 Fed.Reg. 42510, 42512 (Dec. 5, 1974).

23. The 18 categories of stationary sources subject to no significant deterioration preconstruction review are: fossil-fuel steam electric plants (more than 100 million BTU per hour heat input); coal cleaning plants; kraft pulp mills; portland cement plants; primary zinc smelters; iron and steel mills; primary aluminum ore reduction plants; primary copper smelters; municipal incinerators (capable of charing more than 250 tons of refuse per day); sulfuric acid plants; petroleum refineries; lime plants; phosphate rock processing plants; by-product coke oven batteries; sulfur recovery plants; carbon black plants (furnace process); primary lead smelters; fuel conversion plants. 40 CFR § 51.11(d)(1)(i)–(xviii). Criteria for adding new sources to the list were adopted in 40 Fed.Reg. 42011 (Sept. 10, 1975), amending 40 CFR § 52.21(d)(2)(i), and a nineteenth source category (ferroalloy production facilities) was added, id., adding 40 CFR § 52.21(d)(1)(xix).

24. 40 CFR § 51.21(d)(2)(i); see id. § 52.01(f).

25. Id. § 52.21(d)(2)(ii). If a precise emission standard is found by the Administrator to be "infeasible," he "may instead prescribe a design or equipment standard requiring the application of best available control technology." A design or equipment standard of course is a directive requiring the installation of named control equipment of a specific design.

26. Id. § 52.01(d).

27. Id. § 52.21(d)(2); see id. § 52.21(d)(1). An owner has commenced construction when he "has undertaken a continuous program of construction or expansion" or has contracted to do so. Id. § 52.21(b)(9). Administration of this clause presents the same problems of momentum well known in the construction of nuclear facilities, where the plant is committed substantially prior to the administrative decision. See Gage v. Commonwealth Edison Co., 356 F.Supp. 80, 3 ELR 20068 (N.D.Ill.1972). Compare 10 CFR § 50.10(c). See also § 7.7 below (discussing the timing issue under the National Environmental Policy Act).

28. Id. § 52.21(d)(3).

ing).[29] Time limits are imposed on the administrative decision-making process,[30] which are a boon to source supporters worried about administrative foot-dragging and a bane to source opponents worried about superficial decisions based on incomplete information.

Rezoning (or reclassification) judgments are inherent to a working land use plan. A state may submit to the Administrator a proposal to redesignate an area subject to several conditions.[31] One of these is that "at least one public hearing [must be] held in or near the area affected."[32] The hearings are non-adjudicatory in nature unless the state prefers otherwise. Any proposed redesignation must be based on a record giving consideration to "(1) growth anticipated in the area, (2) the social, environmental, and economic effects of such redesignation upon the area being proposed for redesignation and upon other areas and States, and (3) any impacts of such proposed redesignation upon regional or national interests."[33]

The next step in the procedure will be for the Administrator to approve or disapprove the redesignation (subject to the procedures that have evolved for approving state plans). Approval normally will be forthcoming unless there has been non-compliance with procedural requirements or the state "arbitrarily and capriciously" disregards growth patterns, regional impact, or social, environmental or economic effects within the area proposed for redesignation.[34] The "arbitrary and capricious" test is a false promise of limited review for the reason that effects are not to be judged by reference to any standards. The important message is that the Administrator retains broad discretion to unfurl the federal presence whenever a particular redesignation strikes him the wrong way—undoubtedly a *cause celebre* where a state proposes to downgrade a Class I pristine area to accommodate an oil refinery or to upgrade a Class II or III urban area to keep out an oil refinery.

The classification system promises to make sense out of nondegradation despite several problems. The exclusion of major auto-caused criteria pollutants (CO, NOx, HC) is indefensible in principle, particularly if the gap is not filled by enforcement of the indirect source standards.[35] As a practical matter, however, confining nondegradation principles to the pollutants sulfur oxides and total suspended particulates means that the policy falls mostly on industrial siting decisions and not on the more volatile community phased-growth measures. Class III areas allowing pollution to the limit of the stand-

29. Id. § 52.21(e).

30. Ibid.

31. Id. § 52.21(c)(3).

32. Id. § 52.51(c)(3)(ii)(a).

33. Id. § 52.21(c)(3)(iii)(d).

34. Id. § 52.21(c)(3)(vi)(a).

35. See § 3.17 below. The regulations including the decision to exclude auto-caused pollution were sustained in all particulars by Sierra Club v. EPA, —— U.S.App.D.C. ——, 540 F.2d 1114, 6 ELR 20669 (1976).

ards also are difficult to defend as "insignificant" pollution sanctuaries. It is a sensible idea to limit the regulations to major new sources and to require them to demonstrate they will not be causes in fact of violations. The contributions of minor sources, not themselves subject to regulation, must be taken into account by the larger sources. Ideally, the no significant deterioration regulations provide purely a land use function, reducing siting options for sources with pollution loads threatening permissible increments. The concept is breached by introduction of the "best available control technology" concept although the need to repair deficiencies in the concept of the new source performance standards is well recognized. The ultimate effect is to impose that ageless twofold demand on major new sources—pick a suitable site and install appropriate controls. To the extent the federal government may have been too lenient in prescribing new source performance standards, a new source might choose to improve upon the "best technology" because, in so doing, it can extend its siting options and expansion opportunities. Theoretically, a zero release new source has unlimited land use options (up to and including a wilderness area), at least insofar as the Clean Air Act is concerned.

Courts have been reluctant to enforce the no significant deterioration principle during its formative years. Claims have been dismissed on grounds of primary jurisdiction,[36] because the doctrine was unenforceable against individual sources [37] and because it did not impose an "emission limitation" enforceable by citizen suit.[38] In recent times, courts have been more receptive to non-degradation arguments [39] although no court has gone so far as to invalidate a site for the reason that air quality would be deteriorated significantly. In the future, judicial relief should be granted against new sources threatening to prevent maintenance of the "significant" increments no less certainly than against new sources threatening to prevent maintenance of the national standards.

Assuring the perpetuation of clean air sanctuaries is a worthy national goal. Some exceptional environments ought to be preserved,

---

36. New Mexico Citizens for Clean Air & Water v. Train, 6 ERC 2061 (D.N. M.1974) (by implication).

37. See Plan for Arcadia, Inc. v. Anita Associates, 379 F.Supp. 311 (C.D. Cal.1975), aff'd 501 F.2d 390, 4 ELR 20689 (9th Cir.), cert. denied 419 U.S. 1034 (1974) (holding that where there are no emission standards for an indirect source, construction may not be enjoined because facility would cause deterioration of ambient air quality); Wuillamey v. Werblin, 364 F.Supp. 237, 3 ELR 20899 (D.C.N.J. 1973) (same).

38. New Mexico Citizens for Clean Air & Water v. Train, 6 ERC 2061 (D.C. N.M.1974); Citizens Ass'n of Georgetown v. Washington, 370 F.Supp. 1101, 4 ELR 20292 (D.C.D.C.1974).

39. E. g., Sierra Club v. Drain, 5 ELR 20435 (D.C.Neb.1975). See also National Asphalt Pavement Ass'n v. Train, — U.S.App.D.C. —, —, 539 F.2d 775, 783 (1976); Sierra Club v. EPA, — U.S.App.D.C. —, 540 F.2d 1114, 6 ELR 20669 (1976) (upholding the prevention of significant deterioration regulations).

if the notion of setting aside parks and wilderness areas has merit, which obviously it does. Disallowing significant deterioration is a hedge aganst health effects not yet known and a convenient administrative barometer of progress that reads simply: "the problem will not get worse." The slow-growth potentialities of no significant deterioration also are overrated because it is true that virtually all stationary sources of industrial air pollution are technologically controllable.[40] The chief objection to a non-degradation policy—that growth should be determined by a mix of factors of which air quality is but one—is not met by abandoning attempts to implement the air quality dimension. Requiring before-the-fact proof of conformity with general air quality objectives puts us just about where we want to be: maintaining air quality is a principle deserving vindication but it is not a principle so revered as to dictate industrial siting opportunities.[41]

§ 3.13 Mobile Sources: Generally

Regulatory options for controlling air pollution from mobile sources are not unlike the options for stationary sources: the technology can be controlled at the source (through emission standards or the regulation of fuel or fuel additives); operational controls can be enforced (through transportation control plans); or the equivalent of a shutdown can be decreed (through programs designed to hasten the abandonment of a dominant technology, the internal combustion engine). These systems of control are mutually interdependent, so that if the choice is made to relax emission standards tighter restrictions on usage must be imposed if given air quality objectives are to be met. All the options are provided for in the Clean Air Act, amended substantially by the Clean Air Amendments of 1970.

Several historical strands converge to produce today's regulatory regime to control air pollution from the automobile, the dominant mobile source.[1] It is redundant to dwell on the significance of the automobile to American society—it sustains the economy, dictates land-use patterns, provides freedom for the population while exacting enormous costs.[2] An authoritative legal expression of the automobile's

---

40. See National Academy of Sciences, Air Quality and Stationary Source Emissions, Prepared for the Senate Comm. on Public Works, S.Doc. No. 4, 94th Cong., 1st Sess. 385–484, 808–909 (1975); Control of Sulfur Oxides, Report of the Administrator of the Environmental Protection Agency to the Congress of the United States, S.Doc. No. 59, 94th Cong., 1st Sess. 17–33 (1975).

41. Compare § 2.17 above (discussing single-purpose industrial siting legislation).

1. For an important study see Columbia University Legislative Drafting Research Fund, The Automobile and the Regulation of Its Impact on the Environment (1974) [hereinafter cited as Columbia University Automobile Study].

2. See, e. g., Speech of Robert L. Sansom, Assistant Administrator for Air and Water Programs, EPA, The Automobile as a Social Machine, Jan. 10, 1973.

dominance is the federal Highway Trust Fund,³ which for the past two decades has diverted billions of dollars into a roadbuilding program that has frozen patterns of transportation, perpetuated trends in suburban living and in the process aggravated urban air pollution. The Trust Fund has been slightly scarred in recent years on the floor of the Congress,⁴ but its survival shows clearly America's ambivalence towards the automobile. The Federal Aid Highway Act of 1970 ⁵ continued the Trust Fund while simultaneously the Clean Air Amendments of 1970 began to question the premises upon which it was based.

The 1970 amendments recognize that voluntary efforts by auto manufacturers are not about to solve the air pollution problem. The law-making proceeded contemporaneously with prosecution of the smog conspiracy case. In 1969 the federal government had brought an action against the Automobile Manufacturers Association and its members, charging a conspiracy to frustrate the introduction of pollution control technology. The lawsuit ended in a consent decree, negotiated by the new administration, which forbade the defendants from joint research, publicity and politicking on matters of emissions control.⁶ Since then, a number of states have pursued the litigation seeking to saddle the manufacturers with costs of retrofitting current vehicles to make up for the deterioration of air quality attributable to the conspiracy. This litigation thus far is an unfulfilled alternative ⁷ to various restrictions imposed upon individual drivers under the transportation control plans.

3. Federal Aid Highway Act of 1958, Pub.L. No. 85–767, 72 Stat. 921, 23 U.S.C.A. § 101 et seq., as amended; see Mashaw, The Legal Structure of Frustration: Alternative Strategies for Public Choice Concerning Federally Aided Highway Construction, 122 U. Pa.L.Rev. 1 (1973).

4. See 23 U.S.C.A. § 142, as added, Pub. L. No. 91–605, § 111(a), 84 Stat. 1719 (1970), as amended, Pub.L. No. 93–87, § 121(a), 87 Stat. 259 (1973) (authorizing the use of a portion of the Trust Fund for improving mass transportation systems, including the purchase of buses and renovation of fixed rail facilities and rolling stock). See also Opinion of the Justices, —— Mass. ——, 352 N.E.2d 197, 6 ELR 20730 (1976) (authorizing diversion of state highway trust fund monies for construction of bicycle lanes).

5. Pub.L. No. 91–605, 84 Stat. 1714.

6. United States v. Automobile Mfrs. Ass'n, 1969 Trade Cas. ¶ 72907 (C.D. Cal.1969); see United States v. Automobile Mfrs. Ass'n, 307 F.Supp. 617 (C.D.Cal.1969), appeal dismissed sub nom., City of New York v. United States, 397 U.S. 248 (1970) (denying intervention to parties seeking to contest the consent decree); 117 Cong. Rec. 15626–37 (1971) (an internal Justice Department document recommending criminal prosecutions in the "smog conspiracy" case).

7. Washington v. General Motors Corp., 406 U.S. 109, 92 S.Ct. 1396, 31 L.Ed.2d 727 (1972) (denying leave to file complaint under the Court's original jurisdiction); In re Multidist. Vehicle Air Pollution, 481 F.2d 122 9th Cir.), cert. denied sub nom., Morgan v. Automobile Mfrs. Ass'n, 414 U.S. 1045 (1973) (holding the states lacked standing to seek damages, but not injunctive relief, under the antitrust laws); id., 367 F.Supp. 1298 (C.D.Cal.1973) (on remand), aff'd 538 F.2d 231 (9th Cir. 1976) (holding antitrust laws afforded no basis for equitable relief sought by plaintiffs).

Another antitrust issue of longer standing is the relationship of the automobile manufacturers to other transportation technologies, notably passenger buses. A recent study for the Senate Subcommittee on Antitrust and Monopoly "focuses on three powerful automobile companies which eliminated competition among themselves, secured control over rival bus and rail industries, and then maximized profits by substituting cars and trucks for trains, streetcars, subways and buses."[8] The tangled history of trust-busting on matters of urban transportation[9] suggests that auto-caused air pollution in the cities is not to be swept away coincidentally as a result of structural attacks on the dominant transportation industries.

The mobile source provisions of the Clean Air Act, no less than its stationary source provisions, are shaped by earlier experience. Motor vehicle exhaust emissions have received the continuous attention of Congress ever since the passage of the Air Pollution Act of 1955[10] (although the vehicle was not mentioned in the language or reports on the Act). The 1955 Act authorized the Surgeon General, in cooperation with state and local agencies and "with the industries involved," to conduct limited investigations of air pollution problems. In 1956, the Special Subcommittee on Traffic Safety of the House Interstate and Foreign Commerce Committee studied the motor vehicle exhaust problem, with members visiting manufacturing plants to examine research progress. The problem was officially noticed in the Motor Vehicle Exhaust Study Act of 1960, which gave the Surgeon General two years to produce a report and recommendations on, among other things, "the amounts and kinds of such substances which, from the standpoint of human health, are safe for motor vehicles to discharge into the atmosphere under the various conditions under which such vehicles may operate."[11] In the 1963 Clean Air Act the federal government encouraged the cooperation within the industry it was to condemn a few years later under the antitrust laws. The Act directed the Secretary of HEW to appoint a technical committee with membership from "automotive vehicle, exhaust control device, and fuel manufacturers," and to encourage continued efforts

---

8. Snell, American Ground Transportation: A Proposal for Restructuring the Automobile, Truck, Bus and Rail Industries, Subcomm. on Antitrust and Monopoly of the Senate Comm. on the Judiciary, 93d Cong., 2d Sess. 1 (Comm. Print 1974).

9. E. g., United States v. National City Lines, 186 F.2d 526 (7th Cir. 1951).

10. Pub.L. No. 84–159, 69 Stat. 322. In 1950 Dr. Arlie Haagen-Smit, a California biochemist who later served on the California Air Resources Board, discovered the photochemical effect where unburned hydrocarbons from automobiles, under appropriate meteorological conditions, can combine with nitrous oxides from motor vehicles under the influence of sunlight to form photochemical smog, a serious air pollutant.

11. Pub.L. No. 86–493, § 1, 74 Stat. 1625. An excellent summary of the early history and 1970 amendments is found in Anestis, Automotive Air Pollution and the Clean Air Amendments of 1970, in L. L. Jaffe & L. H. Tribe, Environmental Protection 243–72 (1971).

by the affected industries "to develop devices and fuels to prevent pollutants from being discharged from the exhaust of automotive vehicles." [12] The technical advisory committee, of course, remains widely popular [13] although the practice in the field of auto emissions was curtailed in 1973 when EPA responded to heavy criticism by severing its support for a joint industry-government group that had been the focus of the agency's research efforts.[14]

In 1965, the Motor Vehicle Air Pollution Control Act [15] initiated a process of regulation from which there was no turning back. The Secretary was authorized to continue his research programs and extend them to cover the problem of sulfur emissions produced by the combustion of sulfur-containing fuels, which was to emerge a decade later as a major blight on the catalytic converter technology. For the first time, the Secretary was given authority to prescribe emission standards for any pollutant from any class of new vehicles, provided he gave "appropriate consideration to technological feasibility and economic costs." The Act prohibited the manufacture or sale of non-conforming vehicles, or the rendering inoperative of any pollution control device prior to sale to the ultimate purchaser. Violations could be enjoined and fines up to $1,000 imposed for each offense. Used vehicles and vehicles intended for export were not subject to regulation.

The much-criticized voluntary certification provisions got their start in the 1965 Act. It allowed any manufacturer to submit to the Secretary for testing "any new motor vehicle or new motor vehicle engine" to determine compliance. If the vehicle or engine conformed to the regulations, the Secretary was obliged to issue a certificate of conformity, and any vehicle or engine sold by the manufacturer "which is in all material respects substantially the same construction as the test vehicle or engine" for which a certificate issued was deemed to be in conformity with the regulations. The 1965 Amendments also imposed recordkeeping obligations on the manufacturers associated with the standard-setting process but included a clause, popular in legislation then and now, protecting from public disclosure information containing trade secrets.

The following years brought the Clean Air Amendments of 1966,[16] making limited technical changes, and the Air Quality Act of 1967,[17] Title II of which was named the National Emission Standards Act. Here are found the first provisions dealing with the registration (but

12. Pub.L. No. 88–206, § 6, 77 Stat. 392.

13. See § 1.11 above.

14. See 119 Cong.Rec. 39600–01 (1973) (letter from Russell E. Train, Administrator, EPA to M. K. McLeod, Coordinating Research Council, Oct. 26, 1973). See also id. at 28681–85 (remarks and documents submitted by Sen. Muskie concerning EPA's relationship with the CRC).

15. Pub.L. No. 89–272, 79 Stat. 922.

16. Pub.L. No. 89–675, 80 Stat. 954.

17. Pub.L. No. 90–148, 81 Stat. 485.

not the regulation) of fuel additives. Limited pre-emption regarding emissions standards was prescribed, with a provision allowing the Secretary, after notice and public hearing, to waive pre-emption for a state which had adopted standards for the control of emissions on new vehicles prior to March 30, 1966. The only state so qualifying was California. The provision has been continued in later versions of the Act, allowing California to function as a laboratory for standards not applied nationally until some time thereafter.

The first federal emission standards, pertaining to crankcase and tailpipe emissions (hydrocarbons and carbon monoxide) from gasoline-powered vehicles, were promulgated in 1966, to become effective with the 1968 model year.[18] Identical standards were applied to all 1966 model cars sold in California. Standards for 1970 were further tightened, but by this time the legislative process had taken over.

Following passage of the 1967 Act, increasing attention was given to the auto emissions problem. Oversight hearings were continued and other congressional committees entered the picture with hearings focusing on alternatives to the internal combustion engine.[19] By this

---

18. 31 Fed.Reg. 5170 (1966). The following chart marks the evolution of the federal automobile emission standards:

	HC [a]	CO	NOx
Uncontrolled (pre-1968)[b]	8.7 g/mile	87.0 g/mile	4.4 g/mile
1968–69 federal standards [c]	6.2	51.0	NS
1970–71 federal standards [d]	4.1	34.0	NS
1972 federal standards [e]	3.0	28.0	NS
1973–74 federal standards [f]	NC	NC	3.1
1975 [g] and 1976 [h]			
federal standards (49 states)	1.5	15.0	NC
California standards	0.9	9.0	2.0
1977 federal standards [i]	1.5	15.0	2.0
1978 federal standards [j]	0.41	3.4	0.4

[a] All values based on 1975 testing procedures. See 37 Fed.Reg. 24250 (1972). See also Columbia Automobile Study, supra note 1, at ch. 4.
[b] Ibid.
[c] 31 Fed.Reg. 5170 (1966).
[d] 33 Fed.Reg. 8304 (1968).
[e] 35 Fed.Reg. 17288 (1970).
[f] 40 CFR §§ 85.073–1, 85.074–1.
[g] Id. § 85.075–1.
[h] Pub.L. No. 93–319, § 5(a), 88 Stat. 258 (1974), amending 42 U.S.C.A. § 1857f–1(b)(1)(A); 40 CFR § 85.076–1.
[i] Pub.L. No. 93–319, § 5(b), 88 Stat. 258 (1974), amending 42 U.S.C.A. § 1857f–1(b)(1)(B)(NOx); 40 CFR § 86.077–1 (HC and CO).
[j] Pub.L. No. 93–319, § 5(b), 88 Stat. 258 (1974), amending 42 U.S.C.A. § 1857f–1(b)(1)(B); 40 CFR § 86.078–8.
NS—no standard
NC—no change

---

19. See Hearings on Automobile Steam Engine and Other External Combustion Engines, Before the Senate Comm. on Commerce and the Subcomm. on Air & Water Pollution of the Senate Comm. on Public Works, 90th Cong., 1st Sess. (1969). On alternatives to the internal combustion engine, see R. Ayres & F. McKenna, Alternatives to the Internal Combus-

time, the automobile generally was recognized as the greatest single contributor to total national air pollution.[20] The major pollutants from motor vehicle exhausts—carbon monoxide, hydrocarbons, oxides of nitrogen, lead compounds—were acknowledged hazards to health and property. Today, four of the six major criteria pollutants—CO, HC, NOx, photochemical oxidants—are mostly caused by the passenger auto.

Against this background, Congress in 1970 began to consider ways to strengthen the Act. It was, by then, fashionable to talk of outlawing the internal combustion engine altogether. Notwithstanding this, the bill that emerged from the House Committee on Interstate and Foreign Commerce in June of 1970 contained an altogether conventional package of reforms:[21] prototype testing was made mandatory instead of voluntary; manufacturers were required to warrant that each new motor vehicle or engine have emission control systems substantially of the same construction as the prototypes tested (although a performance warranty was not required); the Secretary was given a year to report to the Congress on the results of research into low cost instrumentation techniques for measuring pollutants from automobiles; he was authorized to set standards respecting any emission product from a fuel or fuel additive which "will endanger the public health or welfare;" and he was empowered, "giving appropriate consideration to technological feasibility and economic costs," to prescribe standards for any class of aircraft or aircraft engines. The bill was passed by the House on June 10.[22]

Meanwhile, Senator Muskie's Subcommittee on Air and Water Pollution was working in executive session on a bill that would depart abruptly from the approaches then under discussion. Credit (or blame) for the change in the thinking is generally assigned to a report by four staff members of the National Air Pollution Control Administration (NAPCA), then within HEW, published in mid-June 1970. Entitled "Federal Motor Vehicle Emission Goals for Carbon Monoxide, Hydrocarbons, and Nitrogen Oxides, Based on Desired Air Quality Levels" and commonly known as the Barth Report,[23] it concluded that to achieve ambient air quality levels which would provide "minimum safety margin considerations" for the protection of public health, reductions from uncontrolled levels of carbon monoxide, hydrocarbons, and nitrogen oxides by 92.7, 99 and 93.6 percent, re-

tion Engine (1972); Columbia University Automobile Study, supra note 1, at 8–124 n. 78 (collecting authorities).

20. A summarizing report, quite current for the times, was that of the Morse Panel, The Automobile and Air Pollution: A Program For Progress, Report of the Panel on Electrically Powered Motor Vehicles to the U. S. Department of Commerce, Oct. 1967.

21. Comm. on Interstate and Foreign Commerce, Clean Air Act Amendments of 1970, H.R.Rep.No.1146, 91st Cong., 2d Sess. (1970).

22. 116 Cong.Rec. 19200–44 (1970).

23. The authors were D. Barth, J. Romanowsky, E. Schuck and N. Cernansky.

Sec. 3.13 MOBILE SOURCES: GENERALLY

spectively, would have to be realized by 1980. The Senate Subcommittee generally accepted the desired percentage reductions in emissions but concluded that the "earliest possible date" [24] for compliance would be 1975, basing its judgment on estimates that by then NAPCA's advanced power systems research and development program would produce two second-generation prototypes capable of meeting the goals and that several unconventional engines (including the steam (rankine) engine, sterling and hybrid turbine) also could meet similar limits. Thus, the Senate Bill reported out in 1970 contained a provision setting an emission standard for the model year 1975 requiring a 90 per cent reduction from allowable emissions for 1970 model years,[25] and this ultimately was adopted by the Congress. This legislatively mandated giant step toward a clean car became the central premise of the 1970 Amendments.

Congress' move in the 1970 Amendments of course was a product of many forces: inadequate past performances, recognition of a problem out of control, the desire to initiate a dramatic solution, and the understanding that mistakes could be repaired by later amendment. Legislation whose time has come seems obvious and inevitable in retrospect only. It was not hyperbole for Senator Baker to state at the time on the floor of the Senate, "This may be the biggest industrial judgment" made in the United States "in this century." [26]

The mobile source provisions of the Act establish a comprehensive regulatory scheme: section 202 [27] reaffirms the Administrator's authority to prescribe emission standards applicable to any air pollutant from any class of new motor vehicles or new motor vehicle engines. This power to control what comes out of the exhaust has its counterpart in section 211,[28] which gives the Administrator the power to regulate the fuels and fuel additives going into the vehicle. Section 206 [29] specifies the compliance testing and certification procedures designed to assure compliance with emission standards; section 208 [30] deals with the keeping of records necessary to determine compliance. The control of vehicles in use is governed by section 207,[31] which extends to the ultimate purchaser of the vehicle a design warranty and, under certain circumstances, a performance warranty for the useful life of the vehicle (5 years or 50,000 miles, whichever first occurs). If a determination is made that a substantial number of vehicles in use do not conform to the regulations, a recall may be or-

---

24. Comm. on Public Works, National Air Quality Standards Act of 1970, S.Rep.No.1196, 91st Cong., 2d Sess. 26 (1970).

25. Id. at 101–03 (S. 4358, § 202).

26. 116 Cong.Rec. 33085 (1970).

27. 42 U.S.CA. § 1857f–1; § 3.14 below.

28. 42 U.S.C.A. § 1857–6c; § 3.18 below.

29. 42 U.S.C.A. § 1857f–5; §§ 3.14, 3.15 below.

30. 42 U.S.C.A. § 1857f–6.

31. Id. § 1857f–5a; § 3.15 below.

dered. Even more important to the regulation of vehicles in use is section 110(a)(2)(B) of the Act,[32] which makes clear that transportation controls play a role in state implementation plans designed to meet federal ambient air quality standards.

Other provisions of Title II deal with prohibited acts (section 203);[33] section 204[34] vests the federal district courts with jurisdiction to enjoin various violations of section 203; section 205[35] authorizes a civil penalty of not more than $10,000 for certain violations of section 203, and specifies that certain violations constitute a separate offense with regard to each motor vehicle. The recognition that new technologies may be called for is acknowledged not only by the stringency of the standards but also by section 212,[36] establishing a Low Emission Vehicle Certification Board with powers to certify vehicles that would be favored for purposes of government procurement. The remaining provisions deal with aircraft emission standards (sections 231–34),[37] preemption (section 209)[38] and state grant programs (section 210).[39] A new section 213, calling for a fuel economy improvement study, was added by the Energy Supply and Environmental Coordination Act of 1974.[40] The study soon was completed[41] and led in turn to major regulatory initiatives on fuel economy in the Energy Policy and Conservation Act of 1975.[42]

§ 3.14 Mobile Sources: Motor Vehicle Emission Standards

While controversy has attended the regulation of emissions from aircraft,[1] motorcycles,[2] trucks[3] and buses, the treatment of pollutants from the private automobile offers the critical test for the 1970 amendments. Section 202(a)(1) of the Act[4] directs the Adminis-

32. 42 U.S.C.A. § 1857c–5(a)(2)(B).

33. Id. § 1857f–2; § 3.16 below.

34. 42 U.S.C.A. § 1857f–3.

35. Id. § 1857f–4.

36. Id. § 1857f–6e.

37. Id. § 1857f–9 to –12.

38. Id. § 1857f–6a.

39. Id. § 1857f–6b.

40. Pub.L. No. 93–319, § 10, 88 Stat. 246, 42 U.S.C.A. § 1857f–6f.

41. Dep't of Transportation & Environmental Protection Agency, Potential for Motor Vehicle Fuel Economy Improvement (1975); see Comm. on Interstate and Foreign Commerce, Energy Policy and Conservation Act of 1975, H.R.Rep. No. 340, 94th Cong., 1st Sess. 87–95 (1975).

42. Pub.L. No. 94–163, 89 Stat. 871; see § 6.6 below.

1. 40 CFR pt. 87; see Kaplow, A Report on Jet Pollution (1972) (a report of the Aviation Consumer Action Project).

2. 42 Fed.Reg. 1122 (1977), adding 40 CFR §§ 86.401–78 to .544–78; see Twomey, Control of Motorcycle Emissions, Jan. 1974 (unpublished paper, completed for a course in environmental law, Georgetown U. Law Center).

3. 40 CFR §§ 85.701–.74–39, 86.777–1 to .977–15 (subpts. H–J).

4. 42 U.S.C.A. § 1857f–1(a)(1); see Report to the EPA Administrator, Auto Emission Control: The Technical Status and Outlook as of December 1974,

Sec. 3.14   VEHICLE EMISSION STANDARDS

trator to prescribe emission standards "applicable to the emission of any air pollutant from any class or classes of new motor vehicles or new motor vehicle engines, which in his judgment causes or contributes to, or is likely to cause or to contribute to, air pollution which endangers the public health or welfare." The term motor vehicle means any self-propelled vehicle designed for transporting persons or property on a street or highway.[5] It includes trucks, buses and motorcycles, but not vessels or locomotives which were included in the Senate bill [6] but ultimately dropped, and not aircraft which are regulated elsewhere in the Act.[7] The terms "new motor vehicle" and "new motor vehicle engine" mean a vehicle or engine the title to which has never been transferred to an ultimate purchaser.[8] The elimination of the language from predecessor provisions requiring the Administrator to give "appropriate consideration to technological feasibility and economic costs" in setting standards quite clearly means he is not supposed to consider these factors. The standards "should be a function of the degree of control required, not the degree of technology available today." [9] The degree of control required is that necessary to protect the public health or welfare, as those terms are used in the Act.

The standards prescribed must be applicable to vehicles and engines for their "useful life," [10] which means in the case of light duty passenger vehicles a period of use of five years or fifty thousand miles, whichever first occurs.[11] The Administrator has read this provision, incorrectly it appears, to allow replacement of a critical component part—the catalyst—at the expense of the vehicle owner once during the useful life of the vehicle.[12] To be sure, the statutory warranty assuring that a vehicle conforms to the applicable regulations for "its useful life" may be conditioned on "reasonable and necessary" maintenance by the owner.[13] But Congress surely did not mean the "useful life" durability requirement could be bypassed by the simple expedient of consigning to maintenance the principal investment needed to assure a "useful life." The emission standards are to take ef-

Senate Comm. on Public Works, S. Doc.No.3, 94th Cong., 1st Sess. (Comm. Print 1975).

5. Section 214(2), 42 U.S.C.A. § 1857f–7(2).

6. Comm. on Public Works, National Air Quality Standards Act of 1970, S.Rep.No.1196, 91st Cong., 2d Sess. 23, 101 (1970) [hereinafter cited as Senate Report].

7. 42 U.S.C.A §§ 1857f–9 to –12.

8. Section 214(3), 42 U.S.C.A. § 1857f–7(3).

9. Senate Report, supra note 6, at 24.

10. Section 202(a)(1), 42 U.S.C.A. § 1857f–1(a)(1).

11. Section 202(d), 42 U.S.C.A. § 1857f–1(d).

12. In re Applications for Suspension of 1975 Motor Vehicle Exhaust Emission Standards, Decision of the Environmental Protection Agency Administrator, May 12, 1972, at 12 [hereinafter cited as Decision of Administrator on 1975 Standards].

13. Sections 207(a)(1), (d), 42 U.S.C.A. §§ 1857f–5a(a)(1), (d).

fect "after such period as the Administrator finds necessary to permit the development and application of the requisite technology, giving appropriate consideration to the cost of compliance." [14] Thus, the technical and economic factors banished in developing the standards are imported into the equation in determining time for compliance.

Congress' dramatic intervention in 1970 in the auto emissions controversy took the form of requiring for the 1975 model year a 90 per cent reduction from the maximum level hydrocarbon and carbon monoxide emissions allowable under the standards "applicable to light duty vehicles and engines manufactured in model year 1970." [15] For nitrogen oxides, Congress required for the 1976 model year a 90 per cent reduction "from the average of emissions of oxides of nitrogen actually measured from light duty vehicles manufactured during model year 1971 which are not subject to any Federal or State emission standard for oxides of nitrogen." [16] The term "light duty vehicles" touched by the 90 per cent reduction requirements should be equated with passenger cars.[17] It includes multi-purpose passenger vehicles [18] but not light weight trucks.[19] In 1974, Congress extended the statutory deadlines for two years.[20]

This "drastic medicine," [21] designed to force the state of the art, was relieved only to the extent Congress provided, in Senator Baker's words, "a 'realistic escape hatch': the manufacturers could petition the Administrator of the EPA for a one-year suspension of the 1975 [now 1977] requirements, and Congress took the precaution of directing the National Academy of Sciences to undertake an ongoing study of the feasibility of compliance with the emission standards. The 'escape hatch' provision addressed itself to the possibility that the NAS study or other evidence might indicate that the standards would be unachievable despite all good faith efforts at compliance." [22] The "escape hatch" is found in Section 202(b)(5)(C) of the Act,[23] which di-

14. Section 202(a)(2), 42 U.S.C.A. § 1857f–1(a)(2).

15. Section 202(b)(1)(A), 42 U.S.C.A. § 1857f–1(b)(1)(A).

16. Section 202(b)(1)(B), 42 U.S.C.A. § 1857f–1(b)(1)(B). Anestis, Automotive Air Pollution and the Clean Air Amendments of 1970, in L. L. Jaffe & L. H. Tribe, Environmental Protection 243, 254–55 n. 98 (1971), notes an interesting problem of interpretation raised by General Motors' voluntary decision to include NO_x controls on 1971 cars even though they were "not subject to any Federal or State emission standard for oxides of nitrogen."

17. International Harvester Co. v. Ruckelshaus, 155 U.S.App.D.C. 411, 435, 478 F.2d 615, 639, 3 ELR 20133, 20142–43 (1973).

18. Ibid.

19. Ibid.

20. Energy Supply and Environmental Coordination Act of 1974, § 5(a), Pub. L. No. 93–319, 88 Stat. 258, amending 42 U.S.C.A. § 1857f–1(a)(1)(A).

21. 116 Cong.Rec. 32904 (1970) (Sen. Muskie).

22. International Harvester Co. v. Ruckelshaus, 115 U.S.App.D.C. at 419, 478 F.2d at 623, 3 ELR at 20134.

23. 42 U.S.C.A. § 1857f–1(b)(5)(C), formerly section 202(b)(5)(D), 42 U.S. C.A. § 1857f–1(b)(5)(D), redesignated

rects the Administrator to grant a one-year suspension of the standards, after a public hearing:

> only if he determines that (i) such suspension is essential to the public interest or the public health and welfare of the United States, (ii) all good faith efforts have been made to meet the standards established by this subsection, (iii) the applicant has established that effective control technology, processes, operating methods, or other alternatives are not available or have not been available for a sufficient period of time to achieve compliance prior to the effective date of such standards, and (iv) the study and investigation of the National Academy of Sciences conducted pursuant to subsection (c) of this section and other information available to him has not indicated that such technology, processes, or other alternatives are available to meet such standards.

Before discussing the suspension provisions, a few general observations about the auto emission standards are in order. First, the Act invites discretion in fixing the baseline and measuring deviations from it. Requiring at least a 90 per cent reduction in emissions is not much of a standard until the law answers the question 90 per cent of what. For CO and HC, the legal baseline is "at least" 90 per cent of the emissions "allowable under the standards under this section applicable to light duty vehicles and engines manufactured in model year 1970." The Administrator read this as meaning not the emissions "allowable under the standards" but the emissions actually produced by the 1970 certified vehicles,[24] which were considerably higher. This puts a premium on rewarding gross noncompliance in 1970. Somewhat more defensible is the Administrator's change of the test procedures (to include a hot start) which also had the effect of relaxing actual emissions standards.[25] A judicial challenge claiming the agency's combined judgments on the baseline and testing procedures effectively raised the 1975 standards for hydrocarbons several-fold, however, failed on the ground the Administrator acted within his assigned discretion.[26] The message for the student, applicable to all pollutants and all standards, is that the content of the standards cannot be divorced from the methodology by which compliance is adjudged.

Another important discretionary judgment is whether the 90 per cent reduction in emissions must be achieved by each vehicle coming off the assembly line or only by averaging emissions from all vehicles

---

by Energy Supply and Environmental Coordination Act of 1974, § 5(d), Pub. L. No. 93–319, 88 Stat. 258.

24. 36 Fed.Reg. 3529 (1971).

25. Columbia University Legislative Drafting Research Fund, The Automobile and the Regulation of Its Impact on the Environment 8–27, 8–128 nn. 117, 121 (1974) [hereinafter cited as Columbia University Automobile Study].

26. Natural Resources Defense Council, Inc. v. Ruckelshaus, 359 F.Supp. 1028, 3 ELR 20787 (D.D.C.1973).

in a given class. The concept of "averaging", which is important to many pollution issues,[27] can be defined as a means of measuring compliance by the average of representative samples rather than by each constituent sample. An averaging concept permits a finding of compliance despite deviations from the norm by individual samples (here automobiles). EPA's position on averaging is unclear.[28] The statute implicitly supports it since the standards are made applicable to the plural class or classes of new motor vehicles. Going the other way, and probably decisive, are the warranty provisions and other parts of the Act [29] clearly anticipating compliance by individual motor vehicles. In light of evidence of major gaps in performance between vehicles tested for compliance and certification and those coming off the assembly line,[30] it is difficult to defend a testing procedure dependent upon "averaging," whether applied to certification or assembly line vehicles.[31]

The hearing held in connection with a suspension decision is a curious affair where speakers address a panel of agency decisionmakers and "cross-examination" is conducted by submitting written questions to the presiding officer who decides whether to direct them to the speaker. In International Harvester Co. v. Ruckelshaus [32] the Court of Appeals for the District of Columbia held that this interrogatory-on-the-spot procedure satisfies the manufacturers' rights of due process, subject to the proviso that a right of cross-examination might extend "on critical points where the general procedure proved inadequate to probe 'soft' and sensitive subjects and witnesses." [33] *International Harvester* is widely cited as authoritative on the conduct of non-adjudicatory hearings prevalent in environmental law.

Fair hearing procedures are part of the hard look doctrine [34] applied to the mobile source regulations by *International Harvester* no less rigorously than to the stationary source regulations by *Port-*

27. See § 4.11 below (discussing grab and composite samples for purposes of water pollution control).

28. Jorling, The Federal Law of Air Pollution Control, in Environmental Law Institute, Federal Environmental Law 1058, 1118–19 (E. L. Dolgin & T. G. P. Guilbert eds. 1974).

29. Section 110(a)(2)(G), 42 U.S.C.A. § 1857c–5(a)(2)(G), requires a state implementation plan to provide "to the extent necessary and practicable, for periodic inspection and testing of motor vehicles to enforce compliance with applicable emission standards."

30. See 41 Fed.Reg. 31475 (1976). See also id. at 31483, adding 40 CFR §§ 86.601–.613 (selective enforcement auditing procedures for assembly line vehicles).

31. See Columbia University Automobile Study, supra note 25, at 6–39 to –40 (explaining the manufacturers' expectation that all prototypes will meet the standards but that a "substantial fraction" of production vehicles will not).

32. 115 U.S.App.D.C. 411, 478 F.2d 615, 3 ELR 20133 (1973).

33. 115 U.S.App.D.C. at 427, 478 F.2d at 631, 3 ELR at 20138.

34. See § 1.5 above.

land Cement Ass'n.[35] A series of decisions by the Administrator [36] and the *International Harvester* opinion have clarified greatly the grounds for suspension and the detail of justification required. Although a suspension may be granted only if the Administrator determines that all four criteria of section 202(b)(5)(C) are satisfied, the safety valve may not be held "too rigidly" because it is an integral part of the scheme that includes tough standards.[37] Together, the suspension criteria afford the Administrator broad discretion to decide whether suspension for a year makes sense. The first criterion invites a decision on whether suspension is "essential to the public interest or the public health or welfare." Consideration of the "public interest" or the "public health and welfare" surely invites evaluation of ecological and health costs of continued pollution, economic costs to the industry, impact on consumer buying and driving patterns, effects on fuel economy, interferences with driveability, increased vehicle costs, boomerang health effects of a new technology. An Administrator considering the "public interest" and the "public health and welfare" cannot be blind to the consequences of his actions.

The requirement that "good faith efforts" be made to meet the standards calls for a level of expenditures consistent with the challenge and a coherent program aimed at timely compliance.[38] Retaliatory action taken against a supplier for unfavorable testimony at a public hearing theoretically suffices to establish bad faith although the Administrator has balked at such a finding "in the absence of a very high degree of certainty" that the acts of a manufacturer require it.[39] A company need not spend more money than is necessary to meet the standards so that even a "significant decline" in the emission testing of vehicles will not support a finding of bad faith if the standards are met.[40] The devastating impact of a finding of bad faith for all practical purposes assures the extinction of the provision.

---

35. See § 3.10 above.

36. Decision of Administrator on 1975 Standards, supra note 12; In re Applications for Suspension of 1975 Motor Vehicle Exhaust Emission Standards, Decision of the Administrator on Remand from the United States Court of Appeals for the District of Columbia Circuit, Apr. 11, 1973 [hereinafter cited as Decision of Administrator on Remand]; In re Applications for Suspension of 1976 Motor Vehicle Exhaust Emission Standards, Decision of the Administrator, June 30, 1973; In re Applications for Suspension of 1977 Motor Vehicle Exhaust Emission Standards, Decision of the Administrator, Mar. 5, 1975 [hereinafter cited as Decision of Administrator on 1977 Standards]; see Hearings on Decision of the Administrator of the Environmental Protection Agency Regarding Suspension of the 1975 Auto Emission Standards, Before the Senate Subcomm. on Air & Water Pollution, 93rd Cong., 1st Sess. (1973) [hereinafter cited as Hearings on Suspension of 1975 Standards].

37. 115 U.S.App.D.C. at 437, 478 F.2d at 641, 3 ELR at 20144.

38. Decision of Administrator on Remand, supra note 36, at 38–42.

39. Id. at 41.

40. Decision of Administrator on 1977 Standards, supra note 36, at 58–59.

The suspension criterion regarding the availability of effective control technology has received the greatest attention. A technology can be "available" even though it is not "in being" at the time of the application.[41] Projections of technological advances, on the other hand, cannot be loosely made because of "lead time needed for production."[42] Leverage for stretching the state of the art is provided by the requirement that the manufacturer establish by a preponderance of the evidence that effective control technology is unavailable. At the same time, the hard look doctrine imposes upon the agency an obligation to come forward with "a reasoned presentation of the reliability of a prediction and methodology that is relied upon to overcome a conclusion, of lack of available technology, supported prima facie by the only actual and observed data available, the manufacturers' testing."[43] Requiring the manufacturer to come forward with available data and the agency to explain what it means is a useful tool of judicial review of technological predictions.

A control technology is "effective" and "available" if the basic demand for new passenger vehicles can be met even though the controls "might occasion fewer models and a more limited choice of engine types."[44] An "effective" control technology is not one "that did more harm to public health in one aspect than it prevented in another."[45] The potential health risks of sulfates and sulfuric acid emissions from catalyst equipped cars was the reason for the Administrator's decision in 1975 suspending the 1977 standards.

One of the more interesting features of the suspension clause is that giving the National Academy of Sciences a say on whether technology is available to meet the standards. This provision, consistently with the Academy's role as a unique government advisor,[46] "makes the NAS conclusion a necessary but not sufficient condition of suspension."[47] The Administrator is obliged to engage the Academy "to conduct a comprehensive study and investigation of the technological feasibility of meeting the emissions standards,"[48] and on one occasion when he was disposed to discontinue the Academy studies he was persuaded to change his mind by timely congressional intervention.[49]

---

41. International Harvester Co. v. Ruckelshaus, 115 U.S.App.D.C. at 424, 478 F.2d at 628, 3 ELR at 20137.

42. 115 U.S.App.D.C. at 425, 478 F.2d at 628, 3 ELR at 20137 (footnote omitted).

43. 115 U.S.App.D.C. at 444, 478 F.2d at 648, 3 ELR at 20148.

44. 115 U.S.App.D.C. at 436, 478 F.2d at 640, 3 ELR at 20144.

45. Decision of Administrator on 1977 Standards, supra note 36, at 12.

46. See § 1.12 above.

47. International Harvester Co. v. Ruckelshaus, 155 U.S.App.D.C. at 445, 478 F.2d at 649, 3 ELR at 20148.

48. Section 202(c)(1), 42 U.S.C.A. § 1857f–1(c)(1).

49. Letter from Representative Paul Rogers, Chairman of the Subcomm. on Public Health and Environment of the House Comm. on Interstate and Foreign Commerce to Robert Fri, Acting EPA Administrator, May 21, 1973.

The Administrator also is obliged to furnish the Academy information it deems necessary for conducting its study,[50] and Academy personnel are given access to subpoenaed material held confidential from the public under the provisions of 18 U.S.C.A. § 1905.[51] The Academy, in turn, must submit semiannual reports on the progress of its work to the Administrator and the Congress.[52] In all, the Academy submitted five reports pursuant to the Act,[53] and published independently a number of other reports by panels and sub-panels of its Committee on Motor Vehicle Emissions.[54] The most significant legal consequence of the NAS publications is that their presumed authority compels a careful consideration by the Administrator and permits him to depart from those conclusions only on grounds persuasively reasoned.

§ 3.15 Mobile Sources: In-Use Vehicles

The federal auto emission control program obviously is designed to accomplish more than that a few prototype vehicles successfully navigate the Federal Certification Test Procedure.[1] Congress was aware in 1970 that more than half the cars tested on the road failed to meet emission standards.[2] The amendments meant to assure that each new vehicle coming off the assembly line meets the standards for its "useful life" of five years or fifty thousand miles.[3] Several of the problems of controlling in-use vehicles (inspection and maintenance, retrofit of old cars) are dealt with in the transportation control plans.[4] The key features of the statutory scheme for maintaining quality of emission control systems in individual vehicles are the warranty, anti-tampering, certification and recall provisions.

a. *Warranties*

Attemped enforcement of automobile warranties has spawned its own literature of frustration. Experience under the Clean Air Act

50. Section 202(c)(4), 42 U.S.C.A. § 1857f–1(c)(4).

51. Section 307(a)(1), 42 U.S.C.A. § 1857h–5(a)(1).

52. Section 202(c)(3), 42 U.S.C.A. § 1857f–1(c)(3).

53. The fifth in the series was transmitted on November 27, 1974.

54. E. g., Report to the Panel on Alternate Power Sources for Low-Emission Automobiles, Apr. 1973; Consultant Report to CMVE, Emissions and Fuel-Economy Test Methods and Procedures, Sept. 1974; Report of the Emission Control Systems Panel to CMVE, Automotive Spark Ignition Engine Emission Control Systems to Meet the Requirements of the 1970 Clean Air Amendments, May 1973; Report of the Catalyst Panel to CMVE, Evaluation of Catalysts as Automotive Exhaust Treatment Devices, Mar. 1973 (rev.); Report by the Panel on Manufacturing and Producibility to CMVE, Manufacturability and Costs of Proposed Low-Emission Automotive Engine Systems, Jan. 1973.

1. 40 CFR pt. 85.

2. Comm. on Public Works, National Air Quality Standards Act of 1970, S.Rep. No. 1196, 91st Cong., 2d Sess. 29–30 (1970).

3. Sections 202(a)(1), (d), 42 U.S.C.A. §§ 1857f–1(a)(1), (d).

4. See § 3.16 below.

has not impaired this legend. The Act creates two warranties, one of design, the other of performance. The design or production warranty requires the manufacturer to warrant to the purchaser that the vehicle is "designed, built, and equipped so as to conform at the time of sale with applicable regulations" and that it is "free from defects in materials and workmanship which cause the vehicle to fail to conform with applicable regulations for its useful life." [5] This provision thoroughly explodes any notion that individual vehicles need not conform so long as an "acceptable" average is maintained.[6] Also the substantive guarantee may not be as weak as it is generally thought to be: it is, first of all, not explicitly conditioned upon the owner abiding by instructions on maintenance. Even if this obligation is assumed, a promise of a vehicle "designed, built and equipped" to meet the standards at time of sale seems to require a car that complies. The phrase "defects in materials and workmanship" also suggests warranty liability attaches simply if the system does not work as expected.[7] The argument the other way, of course, is that "defects in materials and workmanship" is a phrase used in its ordinary sense and thus condemns not well-made systems that fail to meet the standards but poorly made systems that fail to meet the standards.

The serious difficulties with the design warranty are practical. There is, in the first place, the usual agenda of burdens in warranty enforcement (the cost of the product is comparatively small, certainly not more and usually considerably less than $200, many people don't know their rights, inconvenience is incurred in getting the car repaired). Add to this the fact that warranty enforcement at the time of sale requires an effective end-of-assembly-line test which has not been developed,[8] and enforcement thereafter requires an effective

---

5. Section 207(a), 42 U.S.C.A. § 1857f–5(a).

6. See § 3.14 above.

7. Cf. Cronin v. J. B. E. Olson Corp., 8 Cal.3d 121, 104 Cal.Rptr. 433, 401 P.2d 1153 (1972).

8. See Columbia University Legislative Drafting Research Fund, The Automobile and the Regulation of Its Impact on the Environment 6–38 to –47 (1974) [hereinafter cited as Columbia University Automobile Study]; Comptroller General, Report to the Congress, Cleaner Engines for Cleaner Air: Progress and Problems in Reducing Air Pollution from Automobiles 26–29 (1972). Compare note 26, infra. Congress also was aware in 1970 that an effective in-use vehicle test was unavailable. The House saw it as a justification for not adopting a performance warranty: "Because of the present unavailability of adequate, low cost testing devices to test automobile emissions while vehicles are in actual use, the committee decided that a performance warranty would be inappropriate at this time." Comm. on Interstate and Foreign Commerce, Clean Air Amendments of 1970, H.R.Rep. No. 1146, 91st Cong., 2d Sess. 12 (1970). The performance warranty of section 207(b) ultimately was made dependent upon development of a satisfactory test but the design warranty of section 207(a) was to take effect within 60 days. This raises a question of how, in the absence of an emissions test, a purchaser is to show that a vehicle "fails to conform with applicable emissions control regulations." EPA suggests "the only possible answer" is that the defect "must affect the conformity of the vehicle to emissions-related design specifications." This means the warranty

and cheap in-use test which does not exist. Enforcement of any warranty provision, moreover, is dependent upon motivating the beneficiary. This means that the warranty provisions are tied closely to a vehicle emissions inspection program with a penalty component for drivers of nonconforming vehicles. Any in-use vehicle inspection and maintenance program is likely to be politically objectionable, administratively onerous and of limited utility.[9] In fact, inspection and maintenance is not widely practiced. A driver immune from liability for noncompliance is thus a lukewarm candidate for citizen enforcer.

Section 207(b) [10] creates a performance warranty that the emission control system will perform throughout its "useful life" subject to several conditions. The first and decisive one (since it has never been met) is that the Administrator must determine that "there are available testing methods and procedures" to ascertain individual vehicle compliance, that these procedures are in accordance with "good engineering practice" and that they are "reasonably capable of being correlated" with the federal test for certification. A section 207(b) warranty also requires the manufacturer to bear the cost of a nonconformity only if the vehicle is maintained and operated in accordance with instructions and the nonconformity results in the ultimate purchaser having to bear a penalty. The maintenance obligation makes many warranty issues a subject of debate even if the requirement stops somewhere short of replacing a principal component at the expense of the vehicle owner.[11] The penalty condition, independently of the testing requirement, means that warranties will remain in limbo unless and until a serious inspection and maintenance effort is pursued.

One commentator notes that the "apparent intent" of section 207(b) "is to make the manufacturer responsible for the repair of any vehicle, properly operated and maintained, which fails to pass an

---

should cover defects in those parts and elements of design required to be described in the application for a certificate of conformity. EPA Legal Opinion on Section 207 of the Clean Air Act and Related Provisions, Sept. 20, 1973, in 1 EPA, Collection of Legal Opinions December 1970–December 1973, 182, 188.

9. Columbia University Automobile Study, supra note 8, at 6–26. ("the uncertainties in evaluating the emissions reduction achievable through inspection/maintenance programs are readily apparent. The above evaluation suggests that 6–12 percent reductions in HC emissions and 6–10 percent reductions in CO are reasonable expectations for inspection/maintenance programs a few years after implementation"); see id. at 9–25 to –33.

10. 42 U.S.C.A. § 1857f–5(b).

11. See § 3.14 above (discussing EPA's position on catalyst replacement). Section 207(c), 42 U.S.C.A. § 1857f–5(c), requires the manufacturer to furnish with each new motor vehicle or engine written instructions for "maintenance and use" of the vehicle "as may be reasonable and necessary to assure the proper functioning of emission control devices and systems." If EPA finds maintenance instructions to be deficient, the agency may seek judicial relief to compel compliance. Section 203(a)(4)(B), 42 U.S.C.A. § 1857f–2(a)(4)(B).

in-use inspection and thereby subjects the vehicle owner to a penalty." [12] The inadequacies of testing procedures, ambiguities of the reasonable maintenance requirements, and doubts about benefits of in-use vehicle inspection combine to frustrate the aim of the warranty provisions. If in-use inspection is ever taken seriously, some serious legislative reconsideration of the warranty provisions is in order. One idea would be to make the manufacturers strictly liable for any penalties imposed and give them rights to observe or participate in the tests of individual vehicles that could lead to their liability. Another idea would be to extend the statutory "useful life" warranty beyond half the actual life of the vehicle. In practice, the problem of noncompliance among in-use vehicles and nonenforcement of quality controls places greater pressure upon the transportation control plans to achieve air quality aims.

b. *Anti-tampering Provisions*

Nonconforming individual vehicles and rapid deterioration in-use are not the only quality assurance problems. Conscious alterations and other tampering in hopes of improving fuel economy and performance are distressingly common practices.[13] The technological answer to this problem would be to make emissions control systems defeat-proof [14] or, better yet, emission free vehicles that are inherently defeat-proof.

The actual answer has been a clumsy limitation on the operators' practices which has failed to solve anti-tampering while creating potential restrictions on competition. Section 203(a)(3) [15] makes it unlawful (and subject to a civil penalty) (1) for "any person to remove or render inoperative" any control device "prior to its sale and delivery to the ultimate consumer" or (2) for "any manufacturer or dealer knowingly to remove or render inoperative any . . . device . . . after . . . sale and delivery to the ultimate purchaser." Although a case can be made that this prohibition extends to an individual prompting a dealer to commit a violation,[16] the fact is the anti-tampering ban does not apply to individuals working alone or

---

12. Columbia University Automobile Study, supra note 8, at 6–38; see 41 Fed.Reg. 50566 (1976) (Advanced Notice of Proposed Rulemaking Regarding Emission Control Warranty).

13. See Wash.Post. Feb. 28, 1974, at B1, col. 1 (reporting on an incomplete EPA survey of 1800 late model vehicles in the District of Columbia, finding disconnection of exhaust controls on 13 percent of the cars and possible tampering short of disconnection in a further 35 percent).

14. Some 1973 model year autos incorporated design features that "defeated" the emission control system (by automatically shutting down or bypassing it) at certain engine temperature ranges or when the engine was being taxed by optional items, such as air conditioners. EPA considers these devices to be illegal. EPA Advisory Circular No. 24, 37 Fed.Reg. 28775 (1972).

15. 42 U.S.C.A. § 1857f–2(a)(3).

16. EPA Legal Opinion on Tampering Violations Under § 203(a)(3) of the Clean Air Act, Aug. 10, 1973, in 1 EPA, Collection of Legal Opinions December 1970–December 1973, 209.

even to independent garages and service stations. If the logic of punishing the abuser of the thing be accepted, which is debatable,[17] the prohibition against tampering should extend across-the-board.

The anti-tampering provisions permit an argument by manufacturers that the warranties may be conditioned upon constraining dealers to the use of original parts for emission-related equipment. This type of tie-in arrangement is not only grossly anti-competitive but also not necessarily a contributor to clean air since it forbids experimentation with parts and equipment representing improvements on the original. EPA has sought to allay uncertainty among new vehicle dealers and automotive aftermarket parts manufacturers by circulating a stated policy on anti-tampering.[18] This makes clear that use of nonoriginal equipment as a replacement part or add-on system is permissible if the dealer has a "reasonable basis" for knowing it will not adversely affect emissions performance. A "reasonable basis" exists if the dealer reasonably believes the replacement part is designed to perform the same function as that of the part replaced or if a representation to that effect is made in writing by the part manufacturer. The problem of reconciling the competitive needs of the aftermarket parts industry with quality assurance of emission control systems promises to endure. Ultimately it may lead to further regulation of the aftermarket parts industry, either by some form of certification of categories of parts, or warranting of emission-related parts.

c. *Certification and Recalls*

The basic premise of the auto emissions program calls for testing of new motor vehicles or engines and EPA issuance of a certificate of conformity for "not in excess of one year" [19] upon a finding that the vehicles or engines tested conform to the emission standards of section 202.[20] Each manufacturer must pass certification tests for each of its various engine families. For the 1974 model year, for example, the following engine families were tested: American Motors (4), Chrysler (5), Ford (17), General Motors (14), Toyota (5), Volkswagen (2), and so on.[21] The testing procedure is described as follows:[22]

> [A]utomobile manufacturers are required to submit applications for certificates of conformity containing data gathered during

---

17. Compare § 6.9 below (discussing whether litter is a people problem or a technological problem).

18. Office of Enforcement and General Counsel, Mobile Source Enforcement Memorandum No. 1A, Interim Tampering Enforcement Policy, June 25, 1974.

19. Interestingly, a certificate extending "not in excess of one year" under the statute remains effective throughout a model year longer than 365 days. EPA Legal Opinion on Duration of Certificate of Conformity, June 16, 1972, in 1 EPA, Collection of Legal Opinions December 1970–December 1973, 191.

20. See sections 206(a)(1), (2), 42 U.S.C.A. §§ 1857f–5(a)(1), (2).

21. Columbia University Automobile Study, supra note 8, at 7–2.

22. Id. at 4–7 to –12, 4–15.

both phases of a two-part test program, before mass production of any given model year vehicle commences. The first phase of the test program provides data on the durability of the emission control system over extended mileage. A fleet of prototype vehicles (only a few in each engine family) are driven 50,000 miles, following a specified speed-time schedule. Emissions are measured every 4,000 miles, and a deterioration factor (the average emissions at 50,000 miles/the average emission at 4,000 miles) is determined from a straight line fit to the measured emissions data. The second phase of testing provides data on exhaust emissions which show the performance of the control equipment after the engine has been broken in, but before substantial mileage has been accumulated. These data are known as 4,000 mile emission data. They are measured on a few vehicles in each manufacturer's engine families.

If all vehicles in an engine family conform to the regulations, a certificate of conformity issues.

The certificate of conformity is an authorization approving the manufacture and sale of new motor vehicles "which conform, in all material respects, to the design specifications that applied to those vehicles described in the application for certification and which are produced" during the model year.[23] Sales of vehicles not covered by a certificate of conformity are prohibited [24] and the certificate may be revoked if "the Administrator determines that all or part of the vehicles or engines so covered do not conform with the regulations with respect to which the certificate of conformity was issued." [25] The critical administrative judgment that has been made—one not necessarily dictated by the Act—[26] is that production vehicles not meeting

---

23. 40 CFR §§ 85.074–30, 85.075–30.

24. See section 203(a)(1), 42 U.S.C.A. § 1857f–2(a)(1).

25. Section 206(b)(2)(A)(i), 42 U.S.C.A. § 1857f–5(b)(2)(A)(i).

26. Section 206(b) of the Motor Vehicle Air Pollution Control Act of 1965, Pub.L. No. 89–272, 79 Stat. 994, read as follows:
   Any new motor vehicle or any motor vehicle engine sold by such manufacturer which is in all material respects substantially the same construction as the test vehicle or engine for which a certificate has been issued . . ., shall for the purposes of this Act be deemed to be in conformity with the regulations issued under section 202 of this title.

Section 203(a)(1) of the 1965 Act, 79 Stat. 994, forbade the sale of a vehicle not in conformity with emission standard regulations. It could be argued that the elimination of section 206(b) and the modifications of section 203(a)(1) to require only that vehicles be certified rather than meet the standards in the 1970 amendments reflects a congressional judgment that all vehicles covered by a certificate should meet the standards. See Comm. of Conference, Clean Air Amendments of 1970, H.R.Rep. No. 1783, 91st Cong., 2d Sess. 50–51 (1970) ("The Administrator may test (or prescribe tests to be performed by the manufacturer) all or a sample of vehicles or engines on the assembly line to determine whether such vehicles or engines actually conform with applicable emission standards. If the Administrator determines that such vehicles or engines do not con-

the standards conform to the certificate so long as they are of the same general design of the prototype tested. This conclusion rests on the assumption that "the purpose of the certification program was to give the manufacturer *assurance* that its production cars would conform to legal requirements . . . [even though the construction] of a production car differed from that of a prototype for reasons not practically within the control of the manufacturer, such as the differences in production processes between necessarily hand-built certification prototypes and mass-produced production cars."[27] Another purpose of the certification program, one would suppose, is to approve the sale of vehicles in a production line only after an adequate showing that the cars will meet emission requirements.

As with a typical regulatory license, a certificate of compliance may be hard to get, qualified when issued or revoked after issuance. A test failure may result in additional testing or a formal hearing.[28] A certificate of conformity may be withheld or denied (or suspended or revoked if it already has been issued) for false or incomplete information in the application, the submission of inaccurate test data circumventing the intention of the Act, or denying any EPA enforcement officer the right of entry and inspection for various purposes.[29] (The Act vests broad rights in EPA to inspect records, files, and facilities of the manufacturers and to enter any plant for the purpose of conducting tests of vehicles or engines).[30] Various conditions, including a consent to inspections, are written into the certificates.[31] Obviously, because a certificate denial or revocation, no less than a license revocation for, let us say, a $200 million nuclear power plant, has astronomical economic implications, the civil penalty provisions are inherently more credible as a sanction.[32]

Since certificates of conformity are not put in jeopardy by the routine sale of nonconforming vehicles, quality assurance is heavily dependent upon the in-use controls of the warranties, anti-tampering bans and recalls. The recall provisions, like the strictures on warranties, and anti-tampering, are neither strict nor strictly applied. If

form, he may suspend or revoke [certificates] in whole or in part"). This position is rejected in EPA Legal Opinion on Section 207 of the Clean Air Act and Related Provisions, Sept. 20, 1973, in 1 EPA, Collection of Legal Opinions December 1970–December 1973, 182, 184.

27. EPA Legal Opinion on Section 207 of the Clean Air Act and Related Provisions, supra note 26, at 184 (emphasis in original).

28. 40 CFR §§ 85.074–30(b)(3), 85.005.

29. 40 CFR § 85.074–30(c)(1).

30. Section 206(c), 42 U.S.C.A. § 1857f–5(c). On July 28, 1976, EPA adopted a selective enforcement audit of cars and light duty trucks coming off the assembly line. 41 Fed.Reg. 31471, adding 40 CFR pt. 86. The regulations provide that no more than 10 percent of the vehicles tested may fail any one of the three emission standards adjusted for deterioration. 40 CFR § 86.610.

31. 40 CFR § 85.074–30(a)(2).

32. Section 205, 42 U.S.C.A. § 1857f–4.

the Administrator determines that "a substantial number" of any class of vehicles, "although properly maintained and used", do not conform to the emission regulations, he is obliged to require the manufacturer at its own expense to submit a plan for correcting the nonconformities.[33] This plan anticipates conventional recall campaigns (with the owner receiving notice to take his car into his dealer for repairs) which have not been wholly successful in the past.[34] To remedy this problem, it has been recommended that the Act be amended to impose on owners of recalled vehicles an obligation to present them for repair and to require the manufacturer to provide a free loaner car and otherwise defray expenses to the owner.[35] Once again, any technical regulatory control of mass behavior confronts enormous compliance obstacles.

One commentator has urged that the threshold determination of a "substantial" number of nonconforming vehicles should be read "to impose a reasonable man test on the likelihood that the cause of the malfunction in those vehicles found actually not in compliance would indicate that other vehicles in a production class are not in compliance."[36] The purpose of the determination of "substantial" numbers is not "to defeat recall, but rather to avoid *de minimis* recall."[37] The limited use of the recall provisions,[38] however, indicates they are reserved for instances of gross noncompliance. Indeed, if the certification provisions are read as being incapable of intercepting nonconforming vehicles coming off the assembly line, it would make little sense administratively to recall the violators that were not stopped at the plant gates initially. Inflexible certification and ineffective recall does not add up to quality assurance of in-use emission control systems.

Other enforcement features of the mobile source provisions are meant to deter the sale of nonconforming vehicles. Various provi-

---

33. Section 207(c), 42 U.S.C.A. § 1857f–5a(c).

34. See Nader, Dodge & Hotchkiss, What To Do With Your Bad Car (1971).

35. Columbia University Automobile Study, supra note 8, at 8–88.

36. Jorling, The Federal Law of Air Pollution Control, in Environmental Law Institute, Federal Environmental Law 1058, 1122 (E. L. Dolgin & T. G. P. Guilbert eds. 1974).

37. Ibid.

38. Between November 1972 and December 1974, approximately 1.5 million vehicles were recalled for corrections of defects in pollution control systems. EPA Enforcement—Two Years of Progress 18 (1975). Of the 50 recall campaigns during that period, only 4 were ordered by EPA. Ibid. The first, and largest, EPA-ordered recall involved 826,000 Chrysler vehicles which were violating the emission standards for NOx. EPA, Progress in the Prevention and Control of Air Pollution in 1974, 55–56 (1975). Between December 1974 and December 1975, approximately 186,000 vehicles were recalled voluntarily by the manufacturers. EPA Enforcement—A Progress Report 25 (1976).

sions of the Act [39] and regulations [40] require manufacturers to maintain and submit information necessary to determine compliance. The key prohibitions address the sale or importation of a vehicle not covered by a certificate of conformity, refusing to make reports or permit access by EPA inspectors, and noncompliance with recall and maintenance instruction obligations. Some violations are punishable by a civil penalty not to exceed $10,000, and some of these (including sale of a vehicle not covered by a certificate) constitute a separate offense with respect to each vehicle.[41]

A precedent setting enforcement action concluded in March of 1973 when the Ford Motor Company pleaded nolo contendere to a 350 count criminal indictment and signed a civil consent decree in actions filed by the United States in the Eastern District of Michigan.[42] The gravamen of the charges was that four of Ford's applications for certificates of conformity omitted to provide the records of numerous instances of maintenance performed on the fuel systems or engines of several prototype test vehicles. The civil judgment called for, among other things, the preparation of "written procedures governing the conduct of [the] emissions certification activities designed better to assure compliance with the reporting requirements of the Regulations." Combined civil and criminal penalties amounted to seven million dollars. Certificates ultimately issued after proper testing was completed.[43] Another recent enforcement action was initiated against American Motors Corporation by the California Air Resources Board for, among other things, submission of inaccurate test data. The remedy there sought also combined a substantial monetary penalty with assurances that the emission control effort would be taken seriously.[44] Raiding the offender's pocketbook and rewriting

---

39. Sections 208(a), 203(a)(2), 113(c)(2), 42 U.S.C.A. §§ 1857f–6(a), 1857f–2(a)(2), 1857c–8(c)(2).

40. E. g., 40 CFR § 85.006.

41. 42 U.S.C.A. § 1857f–4.

42. United States v. Ford Motor Co., Doc. No. 396–59 (E.D.Mich. Feb. 13, 1973).

43. The Ford matter is detailed in a series of EPA Press Releases: Ford Requests Withdrawal of Applications for Certification of 1973 Models, May 18, 1972; EPA, Ford Meet on Certification Problems, May 26, 1972; Ruckelshaus Announces Requirements for Limited Certification of 1973 Ford Cars, June 2, 1972; Ford May Export Uncertified Cars to Canada, Aug. 8, 1972; Ford Receives Limited Certificates of Conformity, Aug. 20, 1972; EPA Refers Investigation of Ford to Justice, Sept. 20, 1972; EPA Finds Ford 200 Cubic Inch Engine Not Eligible for Certification, Sept. 26, 1972.

44. Letter from William H. Lewis, Executive Officer, California Air Resources Board to Fred Stewart, Vice President, Vehicle Environmental and Safety Regulations, AMC, Jan. 5, 1976 (suggesting waiver of 75 per cent of total fine of $4,279,200 if the company promptly paid 25 per cent and committed the remainder to an emissions control and fuel economy program approved by the ARB Executive Officer); see Wash. Post, Nov. 11, 1976, at A12, col. 3 (reporting settlement between AMC and the California Air Resources Board requiring the payment of $1.1 million by AMC over a 5 year period).

his compliance procedures are among the more useful pollution control enforcement techniques.[45]

§ 3.16 Mobile Sources: Transportation Control Plans

Obviously, the amount of pollutants from motor vehicles is influenced not only by emission standards but by the degree and extent of vehicle usage. Indeed, emission standards might be superfluous if individuals are forbidden from driving in certain places at certain times. Control at the source or control of the use or location of the source are remedial options with roots deep in the common law.

The legal authority for what has become known as the transportation control plans is Section 110(a)(2)(B) of the Act, which says that a state implementation plan must include emission limitations, schedules and timetables for compliance "and such other measures as may be necessary to insure attainment and maintenance of [the] primary and secondary standard[s], including, but not limited to, land-use and transportation controls."[1] The Senate Committee on Public Works was aware that "transportation controls" might require the retroactive application of emission control devices on used vehicles, new transportation programs and systems, traffic control regulations and other steps to insure "that moving sources will be located and operated so as not to interfere with the implementation, maintenance and enforcement of any applicable air quality standard or goal."[2] The "moving sources" subject to control under the plans include not only motor vehicles and aircraft subject to emissions standards under the Act, but also trains, barges and ships not covered by emission standards.[3] It was understood that residential, employment and transportation patterns might be "subject to modification" to achieve clean air objectives.[4] Nonetheless, it is fair to say also that Congress in 1970 did not fully appreciate the far-reaching and potentially disruptive implications of the transportation control plans: the emphasis in the debates was on cracking down on the manufacturers and controlling pollution at the source, rather than on revising the driving habits of the average motorist.

A transportation control measure is any measure directed toward reducing emissions of air pollutants from transportation sources.[5]

---

45. §§ 1.13 above (citizen suits); 3.19 below (air pollution enforcement).

1. 42 U.S.C.A. § 1857c–5(a)(2)(B).

2. Comm. on Public Works, National Air Quality Standards Act of 1970, S.Rep. No. 1196, 91st Cong., 2d Sess. 11 (1970) [hereinafter cited as Senate Report].

3. 116 Cong.Rec. 42392 (1970) (Sen. Muskie); see Texas v. EPA, 499 F.2d 289, 316–17, 4 ELR 20745, 20757 (5th Cir. 1974).

4. Ibid. Senate Report, supra note 1, at 1 states: "[A]s much as seventy-five percent of the traffic may have to be restricted in certain large metropolitan areas if health standards are to be achieved within the time required by this bill."

5. 40 CFR § 51.1(r); see 36 Fed.Reg. 15486 (1971).

Sec. 3.16 TRANSPORTATION CONTROL PLANS

The statutory phrase authorizes a wide variety of options reasonably related to influencing the public to opt for a less polluting means of transit,[6] including reducing vehicle use, changing traffic flow patterns, decreasing emissions from individual motor vehicles, or altering existing transportation preferences. Transportation controls thus embrace measures both restricting usage of and reducing emissions from in-use vehicles (retrofit of used cars, inspection and maintenance programs), and accordingly blur the distinction between emission controls as something the manufacturer worries about at the plant and transportation controls as something the vehicle owner worries about on the road.

The phrase "land use" authorizes a variety of controls normally subsumed under zoning and planning devices.[7] This includes in some circumstances off-street parking regulations forbidding private landowners from using their land for parking and a preconstruction permit system for large sources.[8] The land-use components of the implementation plans are equally important justifications for the transportation and indirect source control[9] strategies.

Transportation control measures require difficult judgments about effects on air quality, driver response to various restrictions, the economic impact of competing measures. The Administrator's ignorance on the subject prompted him to give the states an extra year to prepare the transportation control portions of their implementation plans and to extend for two years the statutory deadline for attaining air quality standards for transportation-related pollutants (CO, NOx, HC and photochemical oxidants).[10] This was contrary to the implementation plan submission and compliance date deadlines, and the U. S. Court of Appeals for the District of Columbia so held,[11] ordering the Administrator to rescind the extensions and put in motion the arduous process of developing transportation plans where needed to meet the standards. After the original submission to EPA of the implementation plans early in 1972, it was determined that

6. South Terminal Corp. v. EPA, 504 F.2d 646, 668, 4 ELR 20768, 20776 (1st Cir. 1974).

7. 504 F.2d at 668–69, 4 ELR at 20776.

8. Ibid. In 1974, Congress took steps to circumscribe EPA power as regards management of parking supply. See text accompanying notes 49–61 infra.

9. See § 3.17 below.

10. 37 Fed.Reg. 10845 (May 31, 1974): The Administrator has determined that the lead-time necessary for development, adoption, and implementation of transportation control measures generally precludes their application . . . soon enough to permit attainment of the primary standards within the time period prescribed by the Act. . . . Accordingly, it is the Administrator's judgment that 2-year extensions are justified in cases where transportation control measures will be necessary.

11. Natural Resources Defense Council, Inc. v. EPA, 154 U.S.App.D.C. 384, 475 F.2d 698, 3 ELR 20155 (1973); see Riverside v. Ruckelshaus, 3 ELR 20043 (C.D.Cal.1972) (ordering similar relief for the Metropolitan Los Angeles Intrastate Air Quality Control Region).

the photochemical oxidant air quality standard was exceeded in 54 air quality control regions and the carbon monoxide standard in 29.[12] Combined, air quality in 66 control regions, representing roughly 60 per cent of the nation's population, exceeded one or both of the standards. Further estimates disclosed the emission standards for new cars would reduce the number of problem regions to 27. These regions,[13] representing major metropolitan areas, are the places where the transportation control campaigns have been waged.

12. See J. Horowitz & S. Kuhotz, Transportation Controls to Reduce Automobile Use and Improve Air Quality in Cities: The Need, the Options and Effects on Urban Activity, Environmental Protection Agency, Nov. 1974, at 1 [hereinafter cited as EPA Transportation Controls Report]. This report was prepared pursuant to Section 4(b)(2)(A) of the Energy Supply and Environmental Coordination Act of 1974, Pub.L. No. 93–319, 88 Stat. 245. Another source is Holmes, Horowitz, Reid & Stolpmar, The Clean Air and Transportation Controls: An EPA White Paper, Aug. 1973 [hereinafter cited as EPA White Paper].

13. EPA Transportation Controls Report, supra note 12, at 7. Table 5 reads:

1971–1972 Air Quality Levels in Regions Projected to Exceed Primary Ambient Air Quality Standards in 1975

**Carbon Monoxide—
8 Hour Average (ppm)**

10–15

Indianapolis
Minneapolis-St. Paul

16–20

San Diego
San Francisco
San Joaquin
National Capital
Seattle
Spokane
Chicago

21–24

Sacramento
Baltimore
Boston
Springfield
Portland
Pittsburgh
Salt Lake City

25–35

Fairbanks
Phoenix-Tucson
Denver
Philadelphia

36–42

Los Angeles
New York City

**Oxidant—
1 Hour Average (ppm)**

.10–.15

Phoenix-Tucson
Philadelphia
Pittsburgh
Dallas-Ft. Worth
San Antonio
Indianapolis
Rochester
Cincinnati
Portland
Seattle
Springfield

.16–.20

Denver
National Capital
New York City

.21–.30

Sacramento
San Joaquin
Baltimore
Boston

.31–.40

San Diego
San Francisco
Houston-Galveston

Greater than .40

Los Angeles

In compliance with the court order, EPA moved [14] to require several states to submit transportation plans and land-use control strategies by April 15, 1973, assuring compliance with the standards by the May 31, 1975 deadlines. The plans were late to arrive and usually were found to be inadequate when they did, which meant that EPA was obliged to promulgate plans for states not having their own.[15] At the time of submission virtually all the state governors requested two-year extensions under section 110(e) on the ground that "the necessary technology or other alternatives are not available or will not be available soon enough to permit compliance" by 1975. These extensions were granted by the Administrator, subject to the general condition that implementation of all "reasonably available" interim measures be undertaken as expeditiously as practicable.[16] A transportation control measure is not "reasonably available" if it is too costly, viewed in terms of "the period of time during which the reductions provided are needed to meet the national standard." [17]

Before turning to the specifics of the plans a few general comments are appropriate. The first is that land use and transportation control plans are a second choice to be adopted only "as may be necessary" to supplement emission limitations to meet the standards.[18] Transportation plans, like intermittent stack gas controls,[19] are last resorts not preferred policies. The second is that the transportation controls are still not enough since informed predictions indicate that

14. 38 Fed.Reg. 6290 (Mar. 8, 1973) (advance notice of proposed rulemaking); 38 Fed.Reg. 15834 (June 18, 1973), amending 40 CFR §§ 51.11, 51.18 (final guidelines); 38 Fed.Reg. 7323 (Mar. 20, 1974).

15. See, e. g., 38 Fed.Reg. 31388 (Nov. 13, 1973) (promulgating a transportation control plan for the New Jersey portions of the New Jersey-New York-Connecticut Interstate and Metropolitan Philadelphia Interstate Air Quality Control Regions). The New York City plan was the first state-developed plan approved in its entirety. For the view that the New York City plan is a "fiasco," rather than a model, see Hearings on Implementation of Transportation Controls, Before the Subcomm. on Environmental Pollution of the Senate Comm. on Public Works, 93d Cong., 2d Sess. pt. 3, at 426 (1974) (statement of David G. Hawkins, Natural Resources Defense Council) [hereinafter cited as Hearings on Transportation Controls].

16. The requirement of "reasonable" interim measures of control is statutory. Section 110(e)(2), 42 U.S.C.A. § 1857c–5(e)(2). A table showing compliance date and percentage of CO and HC reduction needed in each city to meet the standards is found in EPA Transportation Controls Report, supra note 12, at 25 (Table 14).

17. Texas v. EPA, 499 F.2d 289, 315, 4 ELR 20744, 20756 (5th Cir. 1974).

18. Texas v. EPA, supra note 17, at 311, 4 ELR at 20756; South Terminal Corp. v. EPA, 504 F.2d 646, 674, 4 ELR 20768, 20780 (1st Cir. 1974) ("Assuming EPA prevails in establishing the need for the controls, it is immaterial that they do not fall equally upon every operator"). Compare District of Columbia v. Train, 172 U.S.App.D.C. 311, 521 F.2d 971, 6 ELR 20007 (1975), cert. granted 426 U.S. 904 (1976) (requiring cost-benefit analysis for a bicycle lane requirement).

19. See § 3.8 above.

at least ten heavily polluted regions are unlikely to meet the transportation-related standards by 1977 without the implementation of "extreme traffic restraint measures" creating "severe economic and social disruption" [20] (e. g., gas rationing, outright travel bans). This state of despair will be accommodated only by amendment to the Act.[21] The third point is that prescriptions about what areas are required to submit transportation control plans may change as new air quality data readings bring new candidates to the forefront.[22] Fourth, discussion of the wide-ranging alternatives of the plans does not mean that the same or similar measures cannot be adopted or enforced for a variety of reasons (air pollution control, revenue raising, energy saving) by states and locales themselves independently of the Clean Air Act. Despite heavy criticism, the transportation control features of the Clean Air Act awakened ideas that slumbered too long.

The transportation plans evolved through the process of proposals, counter-proposals, public hearings, negotiation between federal, state and local officials, and ultimate ukase which has been the pattern of the implementation plans. Probably no single issue has tested the limits of cooperation between jurisdictions more,[23] and that is understandable because so much is at stake. EPA relies [24] upon the following priorities, in ascending order of severity, to develop transportation control measures for inclusion in the plans: (1) additional stationary source control; (2) inspection and maintenance programs; (3) measures to reduce vehicle miles traveled; (4) retrofitting used cars; and (5) limiting gasoline supplies. The criteria for selection include enforceability or effectiveness, the quality of existing or proposed transit service in impacted areas, potential economic and social disruption.[25] Judging from the rhetoric, some locales view the plans as economically and socially disruptive experiments producing few benefits by oppressive means.

Now extant are transportation control plans in 29 metropolitan areas (the New York City and Philadelphia Air Quality Control Regions contain two metropolitan areas).[26] The strategies for reducing motor vehicle emissions under the transportation control plans fall into four general categories: (1) reducing emissions from in-use vehicles (improved inspection and maintenance, retrofitting of older

20. EPA Transportation Controls Report, supra note 12, at 2.

21. See id. at 69, app. C. (Proposed Clean Air Act Amendment for Transportation Control Plans).

22. See id. at 26.

23. For a sample of the sentiments aroused, see Hearings on Transportation Controls, supra note 15, pt. 1, at 135 (Martin J. Kenneally, Assistant Air Pollution Control Officer, County of Riverside) (describing EPA officials as "very obnoxious to work with," "noncooperative," "very mandatory in their ways").

24. EPA Transportation Controls Report, supra note 12, at 30.

25. Id. at 2.

26. 40 CFR pt. 52.

vehicles); (2) improving present and future traffic flows (better traffic management, pre-construction review of major facilities attracting traffic); (3) building up alternatives to the low-occupancy passenger car (more buses, exclusive bus lanes, computer carpool matching, bikeways); (4) discouraging use of the passenger vehicle (parking surcharges, prohibitions against on-street parking, gas rationing). Strategy (1) is aimed at a better emission performance by the cars on the road; strategies (2), (3) and (4) are designed to take cars off the road and reduce total vehicle miles of travel. Understandably, cities grappling with transportation control strategies tend to opt for the alternatives least disruptive to their citizens' lives—more buses instead of prohibitions against parking garages, more vehicle inspections instead of retrofit, more carpooling instead of bikeways, more "Meter Maids" to enforce on-street parking restrictions than parking bans, surcharges or gas rationing.

Nonetheless, transportation control plans have spawned a number of significant legal measures. The following are the more notable.

a. *Reducing Emissions from In-use Vehicles*
   i. *Mandatory Inspection and Maintenance*

Subjecting in-use vehicles to mandatory inspection and maintenance is given a high priority by EPA but remains a subject of debate. An inspection and maintenance program can be defined as a program to reduce emissions from in-use vehicles through identifying vehicles that need emission control related maintenance and requiring that it be performed.[27] These programs spark predictable antagonisms between the control-at-the-source and control-of-the-operator schools. The individual vehicle owner asks why the law comes down so hard on him after tolerating a substantial output of non-conforming vehicles in the manufacturing process.

Any inspection and maintenance program involves substantial costs in setting up and maintaining inspection facilities, repairing vehicles that fail inspections and enforcing quality performance in the service industry. Obviously, policing the service industry is a challenge that dwarfs the problem of policing the manufacturers. A partial listing of the requirements for the City of Chicago plan suggest the cost and administrative difficulties involved: the plan must include "provisions ensuring that failed vehicles receive within thirty days the maintenance necessary to achieve compliance with the inspection standards. These shall, at a minimum impose sanctions against individual owners and repair facilities, require retest of failed vehicles following maintenance, require plans for the establishment of a certification program to ensure that repair facilities performing the required maintenance have the necessary equipment, parts, and knowledgeable operators to perform the tests satisfactorily,

---

27. Id. § 52.731(a)(1) (State of Illinois Air Pollution Implementation Plan).

. . . ." [28] Air quality benefits of inspection and maintenance programs are said to be modest: "6 to 12 percent reduction in HC emissions, and 6 to 10 percent reductions in CO are reasonable expectations for such programs after a few years of implementation." [29] The equities of a mandatory inspection and maintenance program, it goes without saying, are influenced importantly by the weakness of the warranty provisions and the extent of the vehicle owner's maintenance obligation.[30]

ii. *Mandatory Retrofit*

Requiring an individual to install a pollution control device in an older vehicle, like the mandatory inspection and maintenance program, brings forth complaints that the regulator is concentrating on the wrong part of the system that includes all means of controlling automotive emissions. The antitrust action by several states against the manufacturers in the wake of the smog conspiracy case [31] represents an attempt to shift from the consumers to the auto makers the costs of a retrofit program, which are substantial.[32] The principal retrofit regulations [33] for individually owned passenger vehicles include the catalyst converter system, costing $55 to $200, the air bleed to intake manifold system, costing $20 to $60, and the vacuum spark advance disconnect system, costing $200.

A retrofit strategy conceived by any administrator involves a number of serious issues, not the least of which is whether clean air benefits can be achieved more cheaply by other means. Retrofit programs are manifestly regressive, saddling low income, old car owners with significant control costs. There is a further question

---

28. Id. § 52.731(d)(3); see EPA White Paper, supra note 12.

29. Columbia University Legislative Drafting Research Fund, The Automobile and the Regulation of Its Impact on the Environment 9–27 (1974) [hereinafter cited as Columbia University Automobile Study]. But, so too, are the benefits of the new car emission controls—10 to 14 per cent anticipated average reduction per year. Id. at 9–29.

30. § 3.15 above.

31. § 3.13 n. 6 above.

32. Press Briefing of Acting EPA Administrator Robert Fri, July 27, 1973, at 45–46 (estimating overall costs of transportation control strategies to be somewhere in the "low billions"; costs of the retrofit program in the Los Angeles area alone are estimated to be one billion dollars). Columbia University Automobile Study, supra note 29, at 9–31, uses a nationwide cost figure of $1.5 billion for retrofitting 20 million vehicles in areas where it has been proposed.

33. E. g., 40 CFR § 52.244 (requiring catalyst retrofit for several California air quality control regions); id. § 52.-2039 (requiring an air bleed to intake manifold retrofit in the Allegheny County portion of the Southwest Pennsylvania Intrastate AQCR and the Pennsylvania portion of the Metropolitan Philadelphia Interstate AQCR); id. § 52.2447 (requiring a vacuum spark advance disconnect retrofit for the Virginia portion of the National Capital Interstate AQCR); id. § 52.2444 (requiring an air fuel control retrofit for medium duty vehicles in the Virginia portion of the National Capital Interstate AQCR). See also Pennsylvania v. EPA, 500 F.2d 246, 5 ELR 20618 (3d Cir. 1974) (sustaining air-bleed retrofit requirement in the Philadelphia plan).

about the wisdom of pressing a potentially futile policy to the point of putting the man on the street in jail. Finally is the question of effectiveness of a retrofit strategy, which is impressive at the outset but diminishes over the time necessary to get the job done. "Retrofit may appear an attractive concept on paper", according to a leading study on the subject, "but the details do not stand up to careful analysis." [34]

iii. Service Station Vapor Controls

The transportation control plans often include control of hydrocarbon vapors from service stations [35] on the theory that the regulation of emissions from in-use vehicles extends to and includes the services that make the vehicle go. The average service station sells approximately 25,000 gallons of gasoline per month "and in the process is estimated to emit nearly 400 pounds of hydrocarbon vapor." [36] These vapor losses are due principally to tank truck unloading and the fueling of individual vehicles; there is a potential for reducing these emissions by 90 per cent.[37] Consequently, the regulations appearing are aimed at these sources.[38] They require generally modification of dispensing nozzles.

b. Reducing Total Vehicle Miles of Travel [39]

i. Bus and Carpool Priority Treatment

This policy is accomplished by allocating highway facilities preferentially for the use of buses and carpools for the purpose of increasing their speed. Preventing cheaters among carpoolers is a difficult enforcement problem. One inventive commuter using the Golden Gate Bridge carpool priority lane went to the trouble of acquiring two mannequins, dressing them in coats and ties and inviting them aboard as carpoolers. The regulations generally call for the establishment

---

34. See Columbia University Automobile Study, supra note 29, at 6–84. Id. at 6–47 to –84 contains a thorough discussion of retrofit strategies. The study concludes:

    A legal requirement to retrofit some 20 million vehicles in the 29 air pollution control regions that require transportation controls in their implementation plan would be both unwise and unrealistic. Because such programs are unlikely to be completed before 1979, the effectiveness is marginal in relation to the cost.
    Id. at 9–30.

35. E. g., 40 CFR § 52.1144 (Boston Intrastate Region). Portions of the regulation were challenged but not resolved in South Terminal Corp. v. EPA, 504 F.2d 646, 4 ELR 20768 (1st Cir. 1974).

36. EPA Transportation Controls Report supra note 12, at 10.

37. R. K. Burr & P. A. Boys, Systems and Costs to Control Hydrocarbon Emissions from Stationary Sources, Environmental Protection Agency, Aug. 1973.

38. See 39 Fed.Reg. 21049 (June 18, 1974) (calling for comment on the feasibility of the requirements).

39. These provisions are summarized in EPA Transportation Controls Report, supra note 12, at 26–29.

of the system subject to limited requirements for enforcement, prominent markings, hours of operation.[40]

ii. *Transit Improvement*

The success of any measure to lure or force people out of their cars is dependent upon the attractiveness of alternatives. Means of improving transit service "include fleet expansions, route restructuring and bus priority treatment," [41] and these measures are being pursued under the transportation control plans.[42] Obviously, public transit decisions implicate a wide range of issues of local and federal law (including the Urban Mass Transportation Assistance grant programs).[43] Their inclusion as part of the state implementation plans creates another legal leverage point.

iii. *Carpooling*

Many transportation control plans "include measures that provide computerized carpool matching programs and preferential carpool treatment programs." [44] The matching programs "provide for the formation of carpools, and the preferential treatment programs provide incentives such as free parking to encourage carpools." [45]

iv. *Employer Transit Incentive*

These regulations require employers with large parking facilities to submit a plan which encourages the use of carpools and mass transit, "while at the same time discourag[ing] the use of single-passenger automobiles for work-related commuting." [46] The plan, for the Boston Intrastate Region, for example, requires employers of 50 or more people to prepare a plan reducing the number of available employee parking spaces by 25 per cent.[47] The plan must include provisions for assistance to employees "for any necessary adjustment from single occupancy automobile transportation to carpooling or mass transit usage that may result from implementation of this section. By way of example and not limitation, the procedure may include such measures as computerized carpooling, minibus service from place of employment to mass transit parking lots, or a payroll deduction plan

---

40. E. g., 40 CFR §§ 52.261 (San Francisco Bay Area Region), 52.263 (Los Angeles Region), 52.1108 (Metropolitan Baltimore Intrastate AQCR).

41. EPA Transportation Controls Report, supra note 12, at 20.

42. E. g., 40 CFR § 52.2493 (cities of Seattle and Spokane).

43. See 40 Fed.Reg. 42976 (Sept. 17, 1975), 23 CFR §§ 450.100–.122 (requiring as a condition of receiving mass transit grants proposals to curb auto use).

44. EPA Transportation Controls Report, supra note 12, at 26; see, e. g., 40 CFR § 52.1104 (Metropolitan Baltimore Intrastate AQCR).

45. EPA Transportation Controls Report, supra note 12, at 26.

46. Ibid; see 40 CFR § 52.1590 (New Jersey portions of the New Jersey-New York-Connecticut and Metropolitan Philadelphia Interstate AQCR's).

47. 40 CFR §§ 52.1135(h), (i).

Sec. 3.16 TRANSPORTATION CONTROL PLANS

for commuter transit passes." [48] The rationale of these regulations is to encourage employers to give some thought to overcoming the commuting (and ergo the air pollution) woes of their employees. Some positive consequences have resulted through the use of company-purchased vans, carpooling, charter buses.

v. *Management of Parking Supply*

Control over parking influences the use of vehicles in many ways. On-street parking controls have been around for years but are now appearing regularly in transportation control plans as a means of discouraging commuter car travel into downtown areas. A second type of parking regulation, novel in concept, treats parking managers as stationary sources of pollutants. The term "management of parking supply" includes any requirement that a new facility with a given number of parking spaces receive a permit or other prior approval, issuance of which is conditioned upon air quality considerations.[49] Indeed, "management of parking supply" may be considered as including all policies for controlling automobile use through changes in the supply, price and design of parking spaces.[50] As proposed,[51] the parking management supply regulations effective in nineteen regions would require preconstruction approval of all new or modified facilities with associated parking of 250 or more spaces. Where applicable, the parking management supply regulations are considered to be in lieu of the indirect source requirements [52] so that single sources can avoid duplicate filings.[53] The parking management supply regulations are more demanding than the indirect source requirements in that they require a showing that "there is a clear economic or social need for the facility." [54] Acting pursuant to authority in the Energy Supply and Environmental Coordination Act of 1974,[55] the Administrator suspended indefinitely the effective date of any regulations for the management of parking supply.[56] Even without a permit requirement, a large parking facility likely to attract enough traffic to vio-

---

48. Id. § 52.1135(i)(3).

49. Energy Supply and Environmental Coordination Act of 1974, § 4(b), Pub. L. 93–319, 88 Stat. 256, adding 42 U.S.C.A. § 1857c–5(c)(2)(D)(ii).

50. See Zaelke & Russell, Energy Conservation Through Automobile Parking Management, Environmental Law Institute Energy Conservation Project, Rep. No. 6 (1976).

51. 39 Fed.Reg. 30440 (Aug. 22, 1974).

52. § 3.17 below.

53. 39 Fed.Reg. 25291 (July 9, 1974).

54. 40 CFR § 52.251(e)(1) (applicable to several regions in California). The provision states that no approval to construct or modify a facility shall be granted in the absence of an administrative determination that there is a clear economic or social need for the facility, and that it will be so designed and located as to minimize any adverse impact on air quality; or
. . . .

55. Pub.L. No. 93–319, § 4(b), 88 Stat. 256, adding 42 U.S.C.A. § 1857c–5(c)(2)(C).

56. 40 Fed.Reg. 2586 (Jan. 13, 1975) (pending amendment); id. at 29713 (July 14, 1975) (suspended indefinitely pending congressional action).

late the standards might be vulnerable under the citizen suit provisions violating not an "emission standard" but a "limitation." [57]

A third type of parking regulation is the parking surcharge which is a tax, fee or other charge on parking spaces or other area used for the temporary storage of motor vehicles.[58] The idea is to discourage individual automobile usage (as well as to raise money for mass transit or other purposes). The National Capital Region portion of the District of Columbia plan, for example, did away with free parking for federal employees and required the imposition of rates comparable to the going commercial rate.[59] A hefty surcharge of up to several hundred dollars per year for every government employee living in the Washington, D. C. area not only provided a parking disincentive but also sparked a political incentive to work a change in the law. Congress responded quickly to the cries of outrage about the parking surcharges from various parts of the country,[60] and in the 1974 ESECA voided parking surcharges previously required and forbade them in the future unless adopted and submitted by a state as part of its implementation plan.[61]

vi. *Gas Rationing*

Denying drivers gasoline is an efficient way to cut down on driving. It is also a radical intervention in the economy and one that

57. See, e. g., Wuillamey v. Werblin, 364 F.Supp. 237, 3 ELR 20899 (D.C.N.J.1973) (finding proof insufficient that proposed sports complex will cause violation of federal ambient air quality standards; court refuses to enforce a proposed management of parking supply regulation); Movement Against Destruction v. Volpe, 361 F.Supp. 1360, 1401, 3 ELR 20667, 20683 (D.C.Md.1973), aff'd per curiam 500 F.2d 29, 4 ELR 20278 (4th Cir. 1974) (proof does not establish that highway will produce future violations of CO standards raised in suit under 23 U.S.C.A. § 109(h), (j)); Citizens Ass'n of Georgetown v. Washington, 370 F.Supp. 1101, 4 ELR 20292 (D.C. D.C.1974) (denying motion for preliminary injunction to prevent completion of two buildings alleged to threaten violation of air quality standards; court to allow proof that construction will result in violation of standards in 1977 but expresses reluctance to act when indirect source review procedures do not apply retroactively by their terms); Citizens for Clean Air v. Corps of Engineers, 349 F.Supp. 696, 705, 2 ELR 20650, 20654 (S.D.N.Y.1972) (allegations that power plant would violate ambient air quality sufficient to establish standing to challenge permit issued by Corps of Engineers).

58. Energy Supply and Environmental Coordination Act of 1974, § 4(b), Pub.L.No. 93–319, 88 Stat. 256, adding 42 U.S.C.A. § 1857c–5(c)(2)(D)(i).

59. 39 Fed.Reg. 33702, 40 CFR § 52.-486a.

60. 119 Cong.Rec. 41127 (1973) ("high-handed arrogance," "tyranny of the bureaucracy") (Rep.Hudnut).

61. Pub.L No. 93–319, § 4(b), 88 Stat. 256, adding 42 U.S.C.A. § 1857c–5(c)(2)(B); see 39 Fed.Reg. 1848 (Jan. 15, 1974) (EPA withdrawal of parking surcharge regulations). A further expression of Congress' dissatisfaction with how the transportation plans came into being was the insistence in ESECA that no requirement relating to management of parking supply or preferential bus-carpool lanes could be imposed without a public hearing on appropriate notice within the affected area (an obligation, coincidentally, already extant under Section 110). Pub.L. No. 93–319, § 4(b), adding 42 U.S.C.A. § 1857c–5(c)(2)(E).

will arrive, if at all, not under the banner of clean air but under the threat of interdiction of oil supplies. EPA originally proposed two types of gas rationing regulations in the transportation plans: one would have become effective in 1974 or 1975 and would have placed a lid on gasoline sales at 1973 levels (an airborne sewer moratorium). The other would become effective on May 31, 1977, deadline day, to reduce an area's gasoline supply to the extent necessary to achieve the standards. This amounts to a national moratorium on activity in the interests of clean air. The latter provision still resides in several plans [62] although no one expects a national shut-down order to materialize.[63] After its brief venture into the rationing business, EPA has lost its zeal for such draconian measures. It is not unfair to suggest that Congress speak explicitly on so profound and divisive an idea.

vii. *Bicycle Lanes*

A contemporary United States' bicycle boom coincided with the needs of the Clean Air Act. The bicycle alternative was one of few widely praised at public hearings on the transportation plans. Separate bikeways are appearing, but not nearly fast enough to meet the demand. A bikeway is a bicycle route providing for a restrictive right-of-way of adequate dimensions to accommodate the exclusive use of bicycles.[64] The policy challenge, as anyone knows who has given it a try, is that the bike rider runs the risks of being killed outright on the highway, of suffocating from the fumes, and of having his bike purloined once he arrives. The solution is to provide "segregated bikeways and adequate support facilities." [65] Possible sources of the money needed are the federal and state highway trust funds which are being breached for the benefit of bicycles at a somewhat faster rate than for the benefit of mass transit. Bikeways are one of the happy, albeit less effective, ways of reducing auto emissions.

viii. *Vehicle Free Zone*

Vehicle free zones are areas in a city (typically ten blocks or less) set aside for pedestrians.[66] They appear as conditions to control local carbon monoxide problems in the implementation plans of Springfield, Mass., the Camden-Trenton area of New Jersey, and Salt Lake City, Utah.[67] Traffic is banned from portions of the central

---

62. E. g., 40 CFR § 52.1592 (New Jersey portions of the New Jersey-New York-Connecticut and Metropolitan Philadelphia Interstate AQCR's).

63. EPA Transportation Controls Report, supra note 12 at 28; see Affidavit of Russell E. Train, Administrator, EPA, filed in Brown v. EPA, 521 F.2d 827, 5 ELR 20546 (9th Cir. 1975), cert. granted 426 U.S. 904 (1976) (predicting that gasoline rationing will not be implemented).

64. E. g., 40 CFR § 51.2340 (Provo, Utah).

65. EPA Transportation Controls Report, supra note 12, at 29.

66. Id. at 28.

67. 40 CFR §§ 52.1153 (Springfield), 42.1591 (Trenton), 52.2342 (Salt Lake City).

districts of over one hundred cities in Europe and Japan, with resultant reductions in five to ten hour concentrations of CO of 50 per cent to 80 per cent being reported.[68] The notion of downtown malls to revive central business districts is under consideration in scores of cities for reasons of economics and aesthetics far transcending air pollution considerations.[69] Indeed, vehicle free zones often meet with success in reducing pollution and increasing retail sales. The currency of the idea is another example of the transportation control plans being a magnet for larger land-use initiatives.

ix. *Selected Vehicle Use Prohibitions*

During hearings on the plans EPA floated the suggestion of dividing the vehicle population into five categories; cars in each category would be required to display a different colored decal and would be forbidden from making an appearance on one day of the working week. The proposals reached not only central city driving, but nearby expressways (i. e., Route 128 in Boston). The recommendations were dropped on grounds of unfairness, unenforceability,[70] and substantial opposition by affected interests.

A similar policy is reflected in proposals to ban high polluting trucks from downtown areas during certain periods. Objections were raised on predictable grounds of economic disruption and discrimination. EPA did go so far as to promulgate a heavy-duty truck delivery ban during morning hours for parts of northern New Jersey.[71] The grounds for objection were that similar emission reductions from gas-powered trucks could be achieved by a carburetor retrofit modification.[72] The experience confirms the adage that technological solutions suddenly become attractive when the cruder land use option of the shutdown looms as an alternative.

c. *Judicial Review of Transportation Plans*

Questions surrounding the transportation plans are deeply divisive by definition: the impact on people and businesses is great, the benefits to be realized speculative, established habits are put in jeopardy. The plans in many ways are excellent proving grounds for conflicting values.

In the courts, the viability of the transportation plans turns largely upon the answer to a single question: whether the states may be ordered by EPA to implement and enforce various aspects of the strategies, upon threat of penalties for failing to do so.[73] Courts upholding

---

68. EPA White Paper, supra note 12, at 25.

69. See, e. g., California Mall Act, Cal. St. & Hwy.Code §§ 156–57.4.

70. EPA Transportation Controls Report, supra note 12, at 29.

71. 40 CFR § 51.1586.

72. EPA Transportation Controls Report, supra note 12, at 29.

73. 40 CFR § 52.23, the generic enforcement provision challenged in sev-

Sec. 3.16 TRANSPORTATION CONTROL PLANS

the authority stress the unworkability of federal enforcement of the details of the plans,[74] while those withholding it emphasize the revolutionary aspects of a federal administrative agency controlling a state's political process in important ways.[75] The controversy is likely to be resolved by Congress directly or by a Supreme Court holding that the enforcement provisions of section 113 [76] authorize no penalties against a state, thus forcing Congress to confront the issue one way or another.

Otherwise, consistently with the hard look doctrine,[77] the courts define EPA powers generously while examining closely the procedures followed and rationales advanced. Thus, the courts have found authority for some of the plans' more obnoxious features, including a retrofit requirement for pre-1968 vehicles that would "fall heavily on the poor," [78] and a freeze on parking spaces in some areas.[79] Constitutional claims of taking without compensation have been summarily rejected.[80] While it might be arbitrary and capricious for the agency "to reject obviously less burdensome but equally effective controls in favor of more expensive or onerous ones," the Act does not require EPA "to engage in exhaustive cost benefit studies or to initiate elaborate planning exercises." [81]

---

eral major attacks on the implementation plans, reads:

Failure to comply with any provisions of this part [dealing with transportation control plans] shall render the person or Governmental entity so failing to comply in violation of a requirement of an applicable implementation plan and subject to enforcement action under Section 113 of the Clean Air Act. With regard to compliance schedules, a person or Governmental entity will be considered to have failed to comply with the requirements of this part if it fails to timely submit any required compliance schedule, if the compliance schedule when submitted does not contain each of the elements it is required to contain, or if the person or Governmental entity fails to comply with such schedule.

74. Pennsylvania v. EPA, 500 F.2d 246, 5 ELR 20618 (3d Cir. 1974).

75. Maryland v. EPA, 530 F.2d 215, 5 ELR 20651 (4th Cir. 1975), cert. granted 426 U.S. 904 (1976); Brown v. EPA, 521 F.2d 827, 5 ELR 20546 (9th Cir. 1975), cert. granted 426 U.S. 904 (1976); District of Columbia v. Train, 172 U.S.App.D.C. 311, 521 F.2d 971, 6 ELR 20007 (1975), cert. granted 426 U.S. 904 (1976).

76. 42 U.S.C.A. § 1857c–8.

77. § 1.5 above.

78. Pennsylvania v. EPA, 500 F.2d 246, 253, 5 ELR 20618, 20621 (3d Cir. 1974) (footnote omitted); see District of Columbia v. Train, 172 U.S.App.D.C. 311, 521 F.2d 971, 6 ELR 20007 (1975), cert. granted 426 U.S. 904 (1976).

79. South Terminal Corp. v. EPA, 504 F.2d 646, 4 ELR 20768 (1st Cir. 1974).

80. 504 F.2d at 681–82, 4 ELR at 20783–84.

81. 504 F.2d at 676, 4 ELR at 20780. But see District of Columbia v. Train, 172 U.S.App.D.C. 311, 354, 521 F.2d 971, 997, 6 ELR 20007, 20018 (1975), cert. granted 426 U.S. 904 (1976). Unlike the situation where the Administrator refuses to exercise economic and technical oversight of a state-developed plan, see § 3.9 above, the transportation plans largely have been developed by the Administrator himself who must exercise reasoned economic and technical judgments as would the state in developing a plan initially.

At the same time, the courts have looked sharply at the tracks of the agency, demanding reasoned decisions and fair procedures. Remands are in order where a requirement is based upon an unsubstantiated demonstration of need,[82] inadequate monitoring data,[83] questionable methods of sampling,[84] computations unresponsive to tenable objections,[85] judgments insensitive to cost considerations [86] or directives framed in standardless generalities.[87] The courts police closely notice, publication, and hearing requirements,[88] the extent to which the technical roots of decision-making are fully exposed,[89] and each and every technical step in the decision-making process.[90] One court directed the Administrator to include in the plan a provision requiring periodic reconsideration of goals and progress in light of current data.[91] Another assumed a supervisory role sufficiently rigorous to include pre- and post-argument conferences.[92] And a third directed the Administrator to respond by affidavit to its specific concerns.[93]

Two concluding thoughts about the transportation control plans are appropriate. The first is that the uncertainties of feasibility, costs and benefits of various measures may not be resolved definitively in the abstract by administrative solomons. The area is peculiarly susceptible to experimentation, the *ad hoc* solution, the pilot study. That is another way of saying the state and local laboratories of the federal system are ideally suited to test the taxes, bans, incentives and other ideas pushed to the fore by the Clean Air Act. The issue, although partly one of power, is also one of will and imagination to test new ideas for modifying ingrained habits.

82. 504 F.2d at 671, 4 ELR at 20777; see District of Columbia v. Train, 172 U.S.App.D.C. 311, 521 F.2d 971, 6 ELR 20007 (1975), cert. granted 426 U.S. 904 (1976) (bicycle regulations).

83. 504 F.2d at 665, 4 ELR at 20774; see Pennsylvania v. EPA, 500 F.2d 246, 5 ELR 20618 (3d Cir. 1974).

84. 504 F.2d at 665, 4 ELR at 20774.

85. Texas v. EPA, 449 F.2d 289, 308–10, 4 ELR 20744, 20752–53 (5th Cir. 1974).

86. 499 F.2d at 315, 4 ELR at 20756–57 (requiring vapor recovery during vehicle refueling); Maryland v. EPA, 530 F.2d 215, 224, 5 ELR 20651, 20654 (4th Cir. 1975), cert. granted 426 U.S. 904 (1976) (same).

87. South Terminal Corp. v. EPA, 504 F.2d 646, 670, 4 ELR 20768, 20777 (1st Cir. 1974); Maryland v. EPA, 530 F.2d at 221, 5 ELR at 20651 (invalidating provision calling for employers mass transit plans).

88. Maryland v. EPA, 530 F.2d at 221–22, 5 ELR at 20653–54 (obliging EPA to comply with notice and publication rulemaking requirements of the APA); South Terminal Corp. v. EPA, supra note 87.

89. Texas v. EPA, 499 F.2d 289, 305–08, 4 ELR 20744, 20751–52 (5th Cir. 1974).

90. Ibid.

91. South Terminal Corp. v. EPA, 504 F.2d 646, 666–67, 4 ELR 20768, 20775 (1st Cir. 1974).

92. Texas v. EPA, 499 F.2d 289, 4 ELR 20744 (5th Cir. 1974).

93. Brown v. EPA, 521 F.2d 827, 5 ELR 20546 (9th Cir. 1975), cert. granted 426 U.S. 904 (1976).

The second thought flows from the first and is that the transportation control plans are not only important to air quality but are an ingredient also of urban transportation planning generally. The predominance of the automobile, the dogma has it, has produced air pollution to be sure—and traffic congestion, declining public transportation facilities, excessive noise and energy consumption, multibillion dollar losses in life and property, and hundreds of thousands of people uprooted and dispossessed by highway construction programs. That the problems are connected require no better illustrations than gasoline rationing, advanced first as an air pollution control measure but pursued as an energy conservation measure; or lower speed limits, proposed as an energy conservation measure and praised as a safety measure; or downtown parking bans, suggested as a way to control air pollution and defended as a means of reviving commercial and cultural life in urban areas.

Inevitably, environmental values typified by the transportation control plans of the Clean Air Act are recognized formally in the law of transportation decision-making. Air pollution effects (including possible violation of features of the transportation control plans) are among those required to be considered under the National Environmental Policy Act in connection with highway development proposals.[94] The Department of Transportation has initiated a program to support carpool demonstration projects, pursuant to the Emergency Highway Energy Conservation Act.[95] Mass transit capital grant applications under the Urban Mass Transportation Assistance Act[96] are now reviewed for consistency with applicable transportation control plans[97] and are conditioned upon local efforts to curb auto use.[98] Section 109(j) of the Federal Aid Highway Act[99] requires the Secretary of Transportation, after consultation with the Administrator of EPA, to assure that highways constructed in the federal-aid system are consistent with the state implementation plans. This legal activity adds to the prestige of the rationale for the transportation control strategies if not their specifics.

§ 3.17 Indirect Sources

One significant aspect of EPA's reluctant venture into transportation and land use controls is the review of indirect sources. An indirect source is a facility or installation which may attract mobile source activity resulting in emissions of an air pollutant for which

---

94. § 7.9 below.

95. Pub.L. No. 93–643, § 120(b), 88 Stat. 2289 (1974), 23 U.S.C.A. § 101 note.

96. Pub.L. No. 88–365, 78 Stat. 302 (1964), 49 U.S.C.A. §§ 1601–11, as amended.

97. EPA Transportation Controls Report, supra note 12, at 46.

98. 40 Fed.Reg. 42976 (1975), adding 23 CFR §§ 450.100–.122.

99. Pub.L. No. 91–605, § 136(b), 84 Stat. 1734 (1970), 23 U.S.C.A. § 109(j); see 23 CFR pt. 770.

there is a national standard (notably, cars producing carbon monoxide).[1] Indirect sources include:[2]

> highways and roads;
> parking facilities;
> retail, commercial, and industrial facilities;
> recreation, amusement, sports and entertainment facilities;
> airports;
> office and government buildings;
> education facilities.

Pre-construction review of indirect sources is a land-use function of considerable importance to local governments.

Consideration of any indirect source controls [3] should proceed against the background of three related land-use progeny of the air pollution laws: (1) air quality maintenance areas; (2) no significant deterioration; and (3) the transportation control plans.

As mentioned elsewhere [4] EPA regulations require states to identify areas which, due to current air quality and projected growth rates, have the potential for exceeding national ambient air quality standards in the next twenty years.[5] These areas are called Air Quality Maintenance Areas and require special management precautions, such as the development of a control strategy to accommodate expected growth.[6] Maintenance portions of the state plans are incomplete until this is accomplished. The power to review indirect sources (and perforce turn them away) is an important, perhaps the most important, element in a comprehensive strategy for air quality maintenance.

Indirect source review with the aim of maintaining air quality for all practical purposes represents the no-significant deterioration policy for auto-caused pollutants. EPA consistently has excluded these pollutants (CO, HC, NOx, photochemical oxidants) from its various efforts to implement the no-significant deterioration policy. If, as appears to be the case,[7] indirect source review disapproval is tied to a prediction that auto traffic at a new facility will cause or aggravate a violation of the standards, then the policy allows pollution to the level of existing standards. Whatever can be said for it, such a policy cannot be described as resulting in no significant deterioration.

1. 40 CFR § 52.22(b)(i). The focus is on CO, and not the other automotive pollutants, because CO levels are most easily attributed to a specific indirect source. See note 15, supra.

2. Id. § 52.22(b)(i)(a)–(h).

3. For an EPA opinion that the regulation of indirect sources is required under the Clean Air Act, see Opinion on Complex Sources, March 26, 1973, in 1 EPA, Collection of Legal Opinions December 1970–December 1973, 212.

4. See § 3.5 above.

5. 38 Fed.Reg. 15834 (June 18, 1973), 40 CFR § 51.12.

6. Id. § 51.12(g).

7. Id. §§ 52.22(b)(4)(i), (5)(i), (6)(i).

Sec. 3.17 INDIRECT SOURCES

A third important perspective of the indirect source controls is their relationship to the transportation controls generally. Both sprang from the same court decision,[8] and both are designed to enlist considerations of traffic movement and reduction of vehicle miles traveled to supplement emission controls in an attempt to meet the standards. Their common origins are confirmed by the administrative decision to treat compliance with the parking management supply regulations as satisfying the indirect source requirements.[9] Both parking management and indirect source approvals may be conditioned upon measures to minimize vehicle miles traveled. For shopping centers, for example, this might mean efforts to serve the center by bus or Dial-A-Ride system; payment of one-half the round trip fare by center merchants with proof of purchase; measures to encourage carpooling, walking and biking, or the use of mass transit.[10]

On-again, off-again consideration of EPA indirect source regulations that would mandate pre-construction review has involved more than a few trips to the Federal Register.[11] The concept, of course, is no different in principle than the one that has prompted before-the-fact review of everything from nuclear reactors to new herbicides in an attempt to minimize potential adverse effects. Objections to the concept track the familiar grounds of added costs, discouraged initiative, unnecessary red tape, impossibility of predicting the unknowable, piecemeal planning that are raised against many pre-operation review procedures.

Assuming the EPA mandatory proposals eventually take effect, the size of a project subject to review depends upon whether it is inside or outside a Standard Metropolitan Statistical Area (a creature of the U. S. Office of Management and Budget having a population of 50,000 or more). Inside SMSA's, a proposed parking facility having an associated parking area of 1000 cars or more (500 for a proposed modified parking facility) is subject to the regulations; outside an SMSA the operative numbers are 2000 and 1000. Thus, the key

---

8. Natural Resources Defense Council, Inc. v. EPA, 154 U.S.App.D.C. 384, 475 F.2d 968, 3 ELR 20155 (1973) (per curiam). One paragraph of the order also required the Administrator to "review the maintenance provisions of all state implementation plans presently approved." 154 U.S.App. D.C. at 388, 475 F.2d at 972, 3 ELR at 20156. The response eventually resulted in development of the air quality maintenance areas and plans.

9. See § 3.16 above.

10. See Gordian Associates, Inc., A Briefing Paper on the Indirect Source Review and Parking Supply Management Regulations, Mar. 12, 1975, at 17.

11. Six to be exact, as of this writing. 38 Fed.Reg. 9539 (April 18, 1973); 38 Fed.Reg. 15824 (June 18, 1973); 38 Fed.Reg. 29893 (Oct. 30, 1973); 39 Fed.Reg. 7276 (Feb. 25, 1974); 39 Fed.Reg. 25292 (July 9, 1974). The regulations are codified in 40 CFR § 52.22, suspended until July 1, 1975 by 39 Fed.Reg. 45015 (Dec. 30, 1974), adding 40 CFR § 52.22(b)(16), and suspended indefinitely on June 30, 1975 by 40 Fed.Reg. 28064 (July 3, 1975).

issue on applicability is whether "an 'associated parking area' of the requisite size is to be 'owned and/or operated in conjunction with' a facility." [12] Comparable cutoff points are provided for highways (any new highway section with an anticipated average annual daily traffic volume of 20,000 vehicles or more within ten years of construction, 10,000 for a modified highway), and airports (for new airports, 50,000 or more operations per year by regularly scheduled air carriers or use by 1,600,000 or more passengers per year; same figures as to increases for modifications of existing facilities).

For sources subject to the regulations, construction or modification is conditioned upon prior approval by the Administrator or his delegate. The process is expected to follow the usual norms: [13] the applicant is required to produce a map showing the location of the site and the topography of the area, the location of associated parking areas, points of ingress and egress, and principal adjoining roads and highways; information must be provided on the maximum number of vehicle trips expected to occur, average daily traffic volumes, peaking characteristics, and so on within one-fourth mile of all boundaries of the site; it may be necessary to submit "measured air quality data at the proposed site prior to construction or modification." It is anticipated that for highways and airports certainly, and probably for other indirect sources, the submission of a federal or locally required environmental impact statement might satisfy all data needs.

The administrative standard for compliance is whether the indirect source will cause a violation of the control strategy of a state plan, delay the attainment of the national standards for carbon monoxide by the date specified in the state plan, or cause a violation of the CO standards.[14] This hardly reflects a no significant deterioration policy, dependent as it is upon a judgment of whether the source causes a violation or exacerbates an existing violation. The CO-only standard is used for the reason that the Administrator believes that available analytical techniques cannot connect up ambient air concentrations of photochemical oxidants and nitrogen dioxide to specific indirect sources,[15] although his judgment on the matter has been questioned.

While it would appear that the supermarket or amusement park attracting enough traffic to violate the CO standard is the super-

12. See 39 Fed.Reg. 25293 (July 9, 1974).

13. 40 CFR §§ 52.22(b)(3)(i)–(k).

14. See id. §§ 52.22(b)(4)(i)(a)–(c).

15. See 39 Fed.Reg. 25295 (July 9, 1974); J. Horowitz & S. Kuhotz, Transportation Controls to Reduce Automobile Use and Improve Air Quality in Cities: The Need, the Options and Effects on Urban Activity, Environmental Protection Agency, Nov. 1974, at 32. See also Sierra Club v. EPA, — U.S.App.D.C. —, 540 F.2d 1114, 6 ELR 20669 (1976) (upholding EPA's decision to exclude auto-caused pollutants from no significant deterioration regulations on grounds of difficulty of monitoring and judging effects).

market or amusement park that cannot be built at the chosen location, the Administrator insists that design changes can save most facilities.[16] Thus, if it is predicted that an indirect source will cause a violation, the Administrator "may impose reasonable conditions on an approval related to the air quality aspects of the proposed indirect source so that such source, if constructed or modified in accordance with [the] conditions," [17] could satisfy the law. These include "binding commitments" for roadway improvements, additional mass transit facilities, mass transit incentive programs for employees and patrons and improved traffic flow characteristics.[18] Technical guidelines have been published on how traffic flows can be improved and other measures undertaken to meet the standards.[19] Reduced project size and relocation are possibilities (indeed, the indirect source regulations have been criticized as encouraging smaller projects and greater urban sprawl).

The principal legal issues regarding indirect sources are predictable borderline questions of coverage: the "associated parking area" must be "a separate and discrete localized facility associated with a particular indirect source," [20] not simply the total sum of parking spaces within, let us say, an urban renewal area. Issues will arise over how much site work is permissible prior to approval. These are not answered fully by the regulatory definition of "to commence construction" which means "to engage in a continuous program of construction including site clearance, grading, dredging, or land filling specifically designed for an indirect source in preparation for the fabrication, erection, or installation of the building components of the indirect source." [21]

Policy questions surrounding indirect source regulations will be debated for some time.[22] Costs of compliance are said to be reasons for delay. The problem of catching projects partially completed more than once has pushed up the effective date of the regulations. Air pollution-oriented indirect source review is but a narrowly focused, albeit significant, aspect of more broadly defined objectives of land use control.[23] Indirect source review thus is destined to be a perpetual

16. See 39 Fed.Reg. 7270 (Feb. 25, 1974), for an expression of this view.

17. 40 CFR § 52.22(b)(9).

18. Id. §§ 52.22(b)(9)(i)–(iii).

19. EPA Office of Air Quality Planning and Standards, Guidelines for the Review of the Impact of Indirect Sources on Ambient Air Quality, July 1974.

20. 39 Fed.Reg. 25293 (July 9, 1974).

21. 40 CFR § 52.22(b)(vi).

22. For an early contribution to the debate, see Harbridge House, Inc., Draft Report on the Economic and Land Use Impact of Regulations to Review New Indirect Sources of Air Pollution Prior to Construction, Prepared for the Office of Planning and Evaluation, EPA, Aug. 1974.

23. See Fletcher, The Land Use Implications of the Clean Air Act of 1970 and the Federal Water Pollution Control Act Amendments of 1972, Report of the Library of Congress, Oct. 1974; Mandelker & Rothschild, The Role of Land Use Controls in Combatting Air Pollution Under the Clean Air Act of 1970, 3 Ecology L.Q. 235 (1973).

candidate for absorption into broader programs and the continuing subject of procedural reforms such as the "one stop" idea associated with power plant siting.[24]

Regardless of whether indirect source review becomes a systematic and accepted part of administrative practice to curb air pollution, indirect sources will be subject to review on environmental grounds. Eventual omission of a mandatory federal requirement does not preclude states or localities from enforcing indirect source review obligations.[25] Despite the proof problems, a citizen suit might interdict indirect source construction that might lead to violations of ambient air standards.[26] Other theories run the gamut of zoning [27] and nuisance [28] laws, the National Environmental Policy Act and related state statutes,[29] and some yet to be named. The question is not whether someone will make a judgment about effects before-the-fact but who, when and how.

§ 3.18 Registration and Regulation of Fuel Additives

"We are not concerned with what goes into the tank", Senator Baker said during the debate on the 1970 Amendments, "but with what comes out the tailpipe." [1] Unfortunately, what comes out the tailpipe is a byproduct of what goes into the tank. Regulation reaches not only the tailpipe but also the tank, albeit to a different degree.

EPA has enacted regulations governing the registration of fuel additives.[2] It maintains a list of registered additives.[3] Notifications and limited disclosures (concerning range of concentration, purpose of the additive, toxicity and other effects of emissions resulting from its use, test procedures employed) are required from fuel manufacturers or processors and additive manufacturers.[4] The delivery of fuel for introduction into interstate commerce is conditioned upon compliance with the registration provisions.[5] Registration may be withdrawn for non-compliance.[6] The provisions function as a mild early warning system for the Administrator and

---

24. See § 2.17 above; Rodgers, Siting Power Plants in Washington State, 46 Wash.L.Rev. 8 (1971).

25. See 41 Fed.Reg. 6765 (Feb. 13, 1976) (EPA approval of an amendment to the Connecticut plan incorporating an indirect source review procedure).

26. See Wuillamey v. Werblin, 364 F.Supp. 237 (D.C.N.J.1973) (proposed sports complex) (relief denied).

27. § 2.17 above.

28. See Wuillamey v. Werblin, 364 F. Supp. 237 (D.C.N.J.1973) (dictum).

29. See ch. 7 below.

1. 119 Cong.Rec. 32920 (1970).

2. 40 CFR pt. 79.

3. Id. § 79.16(b).

4. Id. §§ 79.20–21.

5. Id. § 79.4.

6. Id. §§ 79.10–14.

do not approach the rigorous pre-clearance procedures applicable to drugs or pesticides.[7]

EPA could demand more under the registration provisions than it has been inclined to do. The agency is empowered to require the manufacturer of any fuel or fuel additive "to conduct tests to determine potential public health effects of such fuel or additive (including, but not limited to, carcinogenic, teratogenic, or mutagenic effects)."[8] Procedures and protocols for conducting tests can be prescribed.[9] Test results "shall not be considered confidential", a commitment to openness which is eroded by the general trade secret protection provision adopted in the regulations.[10] The major unanswered question is the extent to which the Administrator can delay registering a fuel or fuel additive pending completion of required tests. The answer seems to be for as long as it takes to complete adequate tests (which may be several years) although in so doing the registration provisions would be transformed into a serious, before-the-fact decision-making procedure.

EPA's regulation of fuel additives thus far has been devoted to lead, recording in the process an instructive chapter in the history of law and technology. Under Section 211(c)(1) the Administrator may "control or prohibit the manufacture, introduction into commerce, offering for sale, or sale of any fuel or fuel additive" in two distinct situations: (1) "if any emission products of such fuel or fuel additive will endanger the public health or welfare;"[11] and (2) "if emission products of such fuel or fuel additive will impair to a significant degree the performance of any emission control device or system which is in general use, or which the Administrator finds has been developed to a point where in a reasonable time it would be in general use were such regulation to be promulgated."[12] These judgments are conditioned upon the Administrator considering certain data including, in the case of a prohibition to protect an emission control system, "a cost benefit analysis comparing emission control devices or systems which are or will be in general use and require the proposed control or prohibition with emission control devices or systems which are or will be in general use and do not require the proposed control or prohibition."[13] No fuel or fuel additive may be prohibited in the absence of a finding by the Administrator "that in his judgment such prohibition will not cause the use of any other fuel or fuel additive which will produce emissions

7. See § 8.4 below.

8. Section 211(b)(2)(A), 42 U.S.C.A. § 1857f–6c(b)(2)(A).

9. Section 211(b)(2)(B), 42 U.S.C.A. § 1857f–6c(b)(2)(B).

10. 40 CFR § 79.3.

11. Section 211(c)(1)(A), 42 U.S.C.A. § 1857c–6c(c)(1)(A).

12. Section 211(c)(1)(B), 42 U.S.C.A. § 1857f–6c(c)(1)(B).

13. Section 211(c)(2)(B), 42 U.S.C.A. § 1857f–6c(c)(2)(B).

which will endanger the public health or welfare to the same or greater degree than the use of the fuel or fuel additive proposed to be prohibited." [14] This is an unusual findings requirement, albeit a compelling one, since it asks of the Administrator nothing more than a pledge that the cure will not be worse than the disease.

EPA issued two sets of regulations regulating lead additives: the first required oil producers and large retailers to market at least one grade of lead-free gasoline after July 1, 1974 for the purpose of protecting catalytic converter emission control systems.[15] The second called for a phased reduction of the lead content of all other motor vehicle gasoline, reaching a floor by 1979 of .5 grams of lead per gallon.[16] The latter regulations were aimed at protecting the public health. Litigation that followed resulted in sustaining the regulations protecting the integrity of catalytic converters, to be condemned shortly thereafter as health hazards themselves, but in invalidating (temporarily at least) the regulations protecting the health of inner city children. Consistency never was said to be a virtue of the law.

The catalytic converter regulations require the marking of cars fitted with catalytic converters, forbid retailers from introducing leaded gas into marked cars, and oblige large retailers to offer at least one grade of unleaded fuel. The regulations for the most part were sustained in Amoco Oil Co. v. EPA,[17] an important if conventional application of the hard look doctrine of judicial review.[18] The court read section 211(c)(2)(B) as creating "a rebuttable presumption that the Agency should maintain a *laissez faire* posture with regard to fuel regulation." [19] This could be overcome by particularized findings justifying a program of fuel regulation. The court stopped short of applying the particularized findings requirement to "the many subsequent and detailed regulations" made during the exercise of that power [20] and especially to legislative-type policy decisions.[21] *Amoco Oil* reaffirms the necessity for an agency

---

14. Section 211(c)(2)(C), 42 U.S.C.A. § 1857f–6c(c)(2)(C).

15. 38 Fed.Reg. 1254 (1973), 40 CFR §§ 80.2(g), 80.24, 80.5, 80.22.

16. 38 Fed.Reg. 33741 (1973), 40 CFR § 80.20(a)(1)(ii).

17. 163 U.S.App.D.C. 162, 501 F.2d 722, 4 ELR 20397 (1974).

18. See § 1.5 above.

19. 163 U.S.App.D.C. at 176, 501 F.2d at 736, 4 ELR at 20403 (footnote omitted).

20. 163 U.S.App.D.C. at 176, 501 F.2d at 736, 4 ELR at 20403–04.

21. 163 U.S.App.D.C. at 180–81, 501 F.2d at 740–41, 4 ELR at 20406:

[W]e read Section 211(c)(2)(B) as incorporating the commonsense approach which the courts have developed in applying Section 4(c) of the APA. Where EPA's regulations turn crucially on factual issues, we will demand sufficient attention to these in the statement to allow the fundamental rationality of the regulations to be ascertained. Where, by contrast, the regulations turn on choices of policy, on an assessment of risks, or on predictions dealing with matters on the frontiers of scientific knowledge, we will demand adequate reasons and explanations, but not 'findings'

Sec. 3.18   REGULATION OF FUEL ADDITIVES   333

explaining fully the hows, whys and wherefores of its decision-making,[22] but did not read section 211 as repudiating the normal practice of administrative legislating without trial-type findings of fact. Under this approach, the court deferred to the agency's .05 gram/gallon ceiling definition of "unleaded gasoline", which represented an informed legislative-type policy decision.[23]

EPA's efforts to get the lead out for health purposes had a more tangled history. The decision by a divided court (Wilkey and Tamm, JJ., with Wright, J., dissenting) in Ethyl Corp. v. EPA (I),[24] was that the "will endanger" language of Section 211(c)(1)(A) justified the prohibition of a fuel additive only when it produced an emission actually causing a significant health hazard (including documented harm) to a substantial portion of the general population.[25] The court held also, after a detailed examination of the factual basis for the Administrator's decision, that he had made a clear error of judgment in finding a significant correlation between air and blood lead levels and thus that auto emissions contributed significantly to blood lead levels in adults or children.[26] The original *Ethyl* decision represents an extreme example of the hard look doctrine being applied to permit point by point judicial rebuttal of administrative decision-making.[27] Upon a petition for rehearing, the case was heard *en banc*, and EPA's health-based regulations eventually were upheld by a sharply divided court.[28] The several opinions offer useful exegeses of the procedural and substantive connotations of the hard look or close scrutiny doctrine of judicial review. Judge Wright's majority opinion, for example, suggests that a relaxation of judicial oversight may attend an administrative judgment seeking to protect the public health against obscure and hypothetical risks:[29]

> Where a statute is precautionary in nature, the evidence difficult to come by, uncertain or conflicting because it is on the frontiers of scientific knowledge, the regulations designed to protect the public health, and the decision that of an expert administrator, we will not demand rigorous step-by-step proof of cause and effect. Such proof may be impossible to obtain if the precautionary purpose of the statute is to be served. Of

of the sort familiar to the world of adjudication.

22. 163 U.S.App.D.C. at 179, 501 F.2d at 739, 4 ELR at 20405.

23. 163 U.S.App.D.C. at 182, 501 F.2d at 742, 4 ELR at 20407.

24. 5 ELR 20096, vacated pending rehearing en banc 5 ELR 20450 (D.C. Cir. 1975).

25. 5 ELR at 20099.

26. Id. at 20112.

27. See § 1.5 above.

28. Ethyl Corp. v. EPA (II), — U.S. App.D.C. —, 541 F.2d 1, 6 ELR 20267, cert. denied — U.S. — (1976).

29. — U.S.App.D.C. at —, 541 F.2d at 28, 6 ELR at 20281 (footnote omitted).

course, we are not suggesting that the Administrator has the power to act on hunches or wild guesses. *Amoco* makes it quite clear that his conclusions must be rationally justified.

This should be read not as relaxing the burden of explanation of how a policy judgment is arrived at but as recognizing that imponderables may be dealt with and risks addressed without insisting upon a smoking gun in the suspect's hand.

Ethyl is equally significant for purposes of appreciating legislative allocations of the burdens of uncertainty in technological cases. The Clean Air Act, in four different places, uses slightly different formulations to describe health and environmental hazards which will trigger regulatory initiatives. In ascending order of severity, section 109 [30] authorizes the establishment of national primary ambient air quality standards, at a level "allowing an adequate margin of safety," that are "requisite to protect the public health." Secondary standards must be set at a level "requisite to protect the public welfare from any known or anticipated adverse effects associated with the presence of such air pollutant in the ambient air." Section 202 [31] authorizes the establishment of motor vehicle emission standards for any emission "which in [the Administrator's] judgment causes or contributes to, or is likely to cause or to contribute to, air pollution which endangers the public health or welfare". Section 211(c)(1)(A),[32] at issue in *Ethyl*, allows the control or prohibition of any fuel additive which "will endanger the public health or welfare". Section 112 [33] calls for action against a "hazardous air pollutant" which "in the judgment of the Administrator may cause, or contribute to, an increase in mortality or an increase in serious irreversible, or incapacitating reversible, illness."

The first proposition established by *Ethyl* is the wholly unremarkable one that Congress may draw lines in regulating health risks, resolving doubts on the side of precaution or requiring a dead body count as a precondition of action. It is unarguable that the hazardous emission standards were aimed at higher risk, more toxic or "worse" pollutants than, for example, the ambient air standards. Thus, although there is room for disagreement on specifics, it is quite correct for the court to point out that the Administrator has wide latitude in establishing ambient air standards,[34] somewhat less so in fixing motor vehicle emission standards,[35] and still less in con-

---

30. 42 U.S.C.A. §§ 1857c–4(b)(1), (2).

31. Id. § 1857f–1(a)(1).

32. Id. § 1857f–6c(c)(1)(A).

33. Id. § 1857c–7(a)(1).

34. Ethyl Corp. v. EPA (I), 5 ELR at 20103–04.

35. All three judges agreed that emission standards are justified more easily than fuel prohibitions:
When EPA acts under § 211(c)(1)(A), it is essentially telling manufacturers how to make their fuels, a task Congress felt the agency should enter upon only with trepidation . . . . On the other hand, when the agency acts under

Sec. 3.18 REGULATION OF FUEL ADDITIVES 335

trolling fuel additives or hazardous air pollutants.[36] Congress, if not so in the past, is now well advised to express itself clearly in defining the risks that must be established as a predicate of action.

The immediate issue in *Ethyl* was whether Congress required a dead body count or at least some wounded in action when it made fuel additive regulation dependent upon a finding that it produces emissions that "will endanger" the public health or welfare. The meaning of "endanger," the opinions agreed, is that which causes a hazard constituting no more than danger or peril.[37] The differences arose over Judge Wilkey's view that the danger or peril to be avoided under the statute is synonymous with actual injury:

> There is no distinction possible here between actual and potential, between past and future harm. The Administrator is dealing with a *continuing situation*. If there can be found potential harm from lead in exhaust emissions, the best (and only convincing) proof of such potential harm is what has occurred in the past, from which the Administrator can logically deduce that the same factors will produce the same harm in the future.[38]

Not only does this interpretation read the "will endanger" standard as meaning "will cause damage to", which Congress presumably knew how to say if it wanted to, but also it erects a standard of proof that would be dangerously rigorous in other contexts. Some risks of holocaust associated with nuclear reactors, for example, must be minimized at very great costs although the hypothetical accident never has occurred. A "margin of safety" allowance for standards more strict than the level of recorded damage is a perfectly sensible hedge against bad news yet to come. One can conceive of no poorer application of a smoking gun standard of proof than in the case of ubiquitous environmental pollutants—of which DDT and lead are prime examples. Actual proof of damage at low level concentrations experienced by just about everyone would be a national disaster. As Judge Wright says, section 211 should not be read as requiring "that the Administrator sit idly by as the storm approaches,

---

§ 202, it is only mandating an end product—regulated emissions. The method for achieving the required result is entirely in the hands of the manufacturers.
Id. at 20103. This is clear from the statute which requires consideration of emission controls under section 202 as a condition of fuel or fuel additive control. Section 211(c)(2)(A), 42 U.S.C.A. § 1857f–6c(c)(2)(A).

36. 5 ELR at 20124 (Wright, J., dissenting).

37. Ibid. Compare Reserve Mining Co. v. EPA, 514 F.2d 492, 514–20, 5 ELR 20596, 20605–06 (8th Cir. 1975); Freeman Coal Mining Co. v. Interior Bd. of Mining Operations Appeals, 504 F.2d 741 (7th Cir. 1974) (interpreting the meaning of "imminent danger" in the Federal Coal Mine Health and Safety Act).

38. 5 ELR 20099 (Wilkey, J.) (emphasis in original).

consigned to wait until its damage is felt before taking largely superfluous preventive action." [39]

Once the Administrator is recognized as more than a functionary implementing "foregone conclusions," [40] it must be acknowledged that he exercises some discretion. Within the policy guidelines of the "will endanger" standard, he must act, "in part on 'factual issues,' but largely 'on choices of policy, on an assessment of risks, [and] on predictions dealing with matters on the frontiers of scientific knowledge.'" [41] Courts take hard looks at administrative action but are supposed to stop short of substituting their own views for the agencies'.

§ 3.19 Enforcement

While federal air pollution enforcement authority has matured somewhat from the embarrassing days when a finding of interstate effects was a condition of intervention,[1] enforcement certainly is not the strong suit of the Clean Air Act. Enforcement should be understood as embracing all those means by which dischargers may be compelled to comply. Under the Act, EPA and the ordinary citizen [2] are given modest roles in enforcement, while substantial authority remains in the hands of the states. This section discusses (1) the miscellaneous enforcement powers of EPA, (2) the underrated role of EPA's civil administrative orders, (3) state enforcement powers, and (4) the unique problem of enforcement against federal facilities.

a. *Miscellaneous Powers*

As with most administrative schemes in the environmental arena,[3] the EPA Administrator has authority to require recordkeeping and gain entry pursuant to his enforcement and other powers. Thus, under section 114 the Administrator may require [4] the owner or operator of any emission source to (1) establish or maintain records, (2) make reports, (3) install, use, or maintain monitoring equipment or methods, (4) sample emissions in accordance with methods and at places and intervals prescribed by the Administrator, and (5) supply other information "as he may reasonably

---

39. Id. at 20126 (dissenting).

40. Id. at 20128.

41. Ibid., quoting Amoco Oil Co. v. EPA, 163 U.S.App.D.C. 162, 181, 501 F.2d 722, 741, 4 ELR 20397, 20406 (1974).

1. § 3.1 above.

2. §' 1.13 above.

3. Compare § 8.9 below (discussing enforcement under the pesticide laws).

4. 42 U.S.C.A. § 1857c–9(a)(1). In addition to enforcement, the section 114 powers may be used for a number of other purposes—developing or assisting in the development of an implementation plan or standard of performance for new or hazardous emissions, carrying out the emergency power provisions of section 303 or the suspension powers of section 119.

require . . . ." Authorized employees also are given a right of entry, upon presentation of credentials, into any premises where an emission source or records required to be maintained are located. At reasonable times they may have access to and copy records, inspect monitoring equipment or methods, and sample any emissions the owner is required to control.[5] These are broad powers to make unannounced inspections and secure information potentially of evidential value in an enforcement proceeding. Moreover, the information is made public except to the extent the Administrator is persuaded it is entitled to trade secret protection.[6]

These powers are confined by constitutional considerations but not seriously so. The question of the reasonableness of warrantless searches turns upon "whether frequent, unannounced inspections are essential to effective enforcement of the pollution control scheme."[7] The answer ordinarily is in the affirmative, given the possibilities of rapid-fire curtailments, manipulation of monitoring equipment, and so on.[8] Where a conspicuous plume brings the inspectors, this too would establish probable cause without the normal warrant procedure. The normal difficulties of compulsory self-incrimination raised by the mandatory recordkeeping and sampling requirements are overcome largely by the fact that the privilege extends only to private citizens and not corporations.[9] Even as to individuals, it is stated authoritatively "that routine recordkeeping requirements of the kind imposed in the provisions from the federal air and water pollution control acts . . . are not likely to lead to cognizable Fifth Amendment claims."[10]

Each state may develop and submit to the Administrator a procedure for carrying out the inspection, monitoring, and entry provisions of section 114, and, with limited exceptions, the Administrator is authorized to delegate these powers to the states without diminishing his own authority to enforce the section.[11] Early

---

5. Id. § 1857c–9(a)(2).

6. Id. § 1857c–9(a)(3). The statute makes clear that emissions data may be withheld from the public under no circumstances. E. g., Natural Resource Defense Council, Inc. v. Environmental Protection Agency (Massachusetts), 478 F.2d 875, 3 ELR 20375 (1st Cir. 1973).

7. Soper, The Constitutional Framework of Environmental Law, in Environmental Law Institute, Federal Environmental Law 20, 44 (E. L. Dolgin & T. G. P. Guilbert eds. 1974); see Air Pollution Variance Bd. of Colorado v. Western Alfalfa Corp., 416 U.S. 861, 94 S.Ct. 2114, 40 L.Ed.2d 607 (1974). See also Note, Air Pollution Variance Bd. v. Western Alfalfa: Constitutional Limits on Enforcement of Air Pollution Laws, 5 Environmental L. 147 (1974).

8. See Comment, Camara and See: A Constitutional Problem with Effect on Air Pollution Control, 10 Ariz.L.Rev. 120 (1968).

9. E. g., George Campbell Painting Co. v. Reid, 392 U.S. 286, 88 S.Ct. 1978, 20 L.Ed.2d 1094 (1968).

10. Soper, supra note 7, at 47.

11. 42 U.S.C.A. § 1857c–9(b). Delegation of monitoring and inspection

experience under the Act, however, indicates that delegation has been extensive but "without any criteria as to when the [Administrator] would require owners or operators of emission sources to furnish the specified information."[12] In fact, many potential violations are poorly investigated and thus never reach the enforcement stage. Since access to reliable information on emissions data is indispensable to meaningful enforcement, the day to day implementation of the monitoring and recordkeeping requirements under the implementation plans (section 110) and the enforcement provisions (section 114) is consistently topical.

One popular enforcement technique recently receiving a severe blow in the courts is that of the opacity standard. Opacity can be defined as the degree to which emissions reduce the transmission of light and obscure the view of an object in the background. In its new source performance standards EPA established a 10 per cent opacity standard for particulate matter from Portland cement stationary sources, a similar standard for "acid mist" discharges from sulfuric acid plants, and a 20 per cent opacity standard for particulate matter discharges from coal-fired steam generators. Upon judicial review, all three standards were remanded to the Administrator for a showing that the opacity measurements could be made with reasonable accuracy.[13] Manufacturers in Portland Cement Ass'n v. Ruckelshaus had pointed to various tests conducted in which trained inspectors varied widely in their estimates of the opacity of known plumes. The courts were determined to assure that the EPA standards be objective so that the manufacturer could be assured that his own test results would be duplicated by the agency.[14] The problem, quite clearly, was that the law might be measured by the length of the chancellor's foot or, rather, the degree of his astigmatism.

There is no question that states and locales widely use the opacity standard in their regulations.[15] There is no doubt also that the stand-

powers is not permitted for new sources owned or operated by the United States.

12. Jorling, The Federal Law of Air Pollution Control, in Environmental Law Institute, Federal Environmental Law 1058, 1101 (E. L. Dolgin & T. G. P. Guilbert eds. 1974) (footnote omitted).

13. Portland Cement Ass'n v. Ruckelshaus (I), 158 U.S.App.D.C. 308, 486 F.2d 375, 3 ELR 20642 (1972), cert. denied 417 U.S. 921 (1974); Essex Chem. Corp. v. Ruckelshaus, 158 U.S. App.D.C. 360, 486 F.2d 427, 3 ELR 20372 (1973).

14. Cf. Chrysler Corp. v. Dep't of Transp., 472 F.2d 659, 675 (6th Cir. 1972) (National Traffic and Motor Vehicle Safety Act of 1966).

15. E. g., Alabama, Ala. Air Pollution Control Comm'n, Rules and Regulations § 4.1.1(b) (60% for visible emissions); Arkansas, Ark. Air Pollution Control Code § 2(y) (20% for new equipment used in a manufacturing process); Colorado, Colo. Air Pollution Control Bd., Regulations, Reg. No. 1(A)(1) (20% for visible emissions); District of Columbia, D.C. Health Regs. § 8–2:713 (same); Illinois, Ill. Pollution Control Bd., Rules and Regulations, ch. 2, R 202(a)(1),

ard is a preferred enforcement option for a low budget operation. (There are indications in EPA's Portland cement regulations that the cost of running a test by one proposed method on a single baghouse approaches $10,000 to $15,000 [16]). The problems of distinguishing visually between an opacity violation and water vapor also have been noted in the courts.[17]

If there is a device that can save the opacity standard for enforcement purposes, it will be the Ringelmann Chart. This primitive standby from the dark ages of air pollution enforcement is simply a chart containing blocks of various shades of grey coinciding with particulate emissions of an indicated percentage opacity. A trained inspector can glance at his Ringelmann Chart, compare it with the color of the plume against the sky and offer an informed opinion about whether the emissions violated the opacity standards of the regulations. This procedure has "tremendous shortcomings" from an enforcement perspective.[18] It also is grossly subjective and potentially unfair to offenders although it is by no means impossible to identify a cloud of black smoke against the sky as air pollution even if the finer distinctions are judgmental. Enforcement actions based upon Ringelmann Chart readings have been sustained over objections ranging from procedural due process to inadequacy of proof.[19] The Ringel-

(3) (30% for existing sources and 20% for new sources); Maine, Me. Dep't of Environmental Protection, Implementation Plan for Air Quality Control, ch. 10, § 100.1.1 (40% for visible emissions); Michigan, Mich. Air Pollution Control Comm'n, General Rules, R 336.41 (20% for visible emissions); New York, 6A N.Y.Codes, Rules, and Regs. § 211.3 (same); Oregon, Ore.Adm.Rules, ch. 340, §§ 21–015(1), (2) (40% for existing sources and 20% for new sources); Washington, Wash.Adm.Code § 18–04–040(1) (same); Wisconsin, Wis. Adm. Code § NR 154.11(6) (same).

16. Portland Cement Ass'n v. Ruckelshaus (I), 158 U.S.App.D.C. 308, 334 n. 99, 486 F.2d 375, 401 n. 99, 3 ELR 20642, 20655 n. 99 (1972), cert. denied 417 U.S. 921 (1974).

17. State v. Lloyd A. Fry Roofing Co., 9 Or.App. 189, 495 P.2d 751, 757–58 (1972), rev'd on other grounds 502 P.2d 253 (Ore.), on remand 502 P.2d 1162 (Or.Ct.App.).

18. J. Krier, Environmental Law & Policy 363 n. 1 (1971):
It measures density, not volume. Thus, one can simply build a larger-mouthed stack and avoid violations. The Ringelmann method cannot be used at night, nor during times of high winds, rain or humidity.

See Western Alfalfa v. Air Pollution Variance Bd., 3 ERC 1399, 1401 (Colo. Dist.Ct.1971) (holding that a Ringelmann reading is insufficient evidence to support a finding of emission violations where the emission is mixed with nonpolluting steam and more reliable tests are available); cf. North American Coal Corp. v. Air Pollution Comm'n, 2 Pa.Comm. 469, 279 A.2d 356 (1971) (holding that observations by air pollution engineer without on site reference to Ringelmann Chart are insufficient to support abatement order); Bortz Coal Co. v. Dep't of Environmental Resources, 7 Pa.Comm. 362, 299 A.2d 670 (1973) (upholding finding of violation where evidence supported by evidence from several testing devices, including the Ringelmann Chart, the MSA Smokescope, and the Plebrico Smoke Chart). See also Rankin, Visual Plume Readings—Too Crude for Clean Air Laws, 7 Nat.Res.L. 457 (1974).

19. Air Pollution Variance Bd. v. Western Alfalfa Corp., 416 U.S. 861, 94 S.Ct. 2114, 40 L.Ed.2d 607 (1974);

mann Chart may lack sophistication but it works and is usable. A single test costing $20,000 is a superb monument to the intricacies of modern pollution law but it has as much pertinence to the problems of day to day enforcement as the Rolls Royce does to mass transit.

Two EPA enforcement powers of limited significance are those involving conference procedures and emergencies. The conference procedure is carried over in all of its elaborate grandeur from the early days of the Clean Air Act.[20] Future conferences may be called only with respect to an air pollutant for which there is no national ambient air standard.[21] Conferences initiated prior to the adoption of ambient air standards are unaffected, and these (notably the Selbyville, Delaware-Bishop, Maryland and the Parkersburg, West Virginia-Marietta, Ohio Abatement Conferences) have demonstrated remarkable longevity. While the conference procedure can be expected to wither and die, it can rise again upon the unhappy concurrence of chance events (e. g., a non-criteria pollutant endangering health or welfare, requests by a governor, etc.).

Although it is more a symbolic than a practical power, section 303 [22] gives the Administrator martial law authority to sue in an appropriate United States District Court to restrain any person contributing to an air pollution problem "presenting an imminent and substantial endangerment to the health of persons," provided he finds also "that appropriate State or local authorities have not acted to abate such sources." This power was exercised but once, in the fa-

Northwestern Laundry v. Des Moines, 239 U.S. 486, 36 S.Ct. 206, 60 L.Ed. 396 (1916); State v. Arizona Mines Supply Co., 107 Ariz. 199, 484 P.2d 619, 1 ELR 20286 (1971); People v. Plywood Mfgs., 137 Cal.App.2d 859, 291 P.2d 587 (1955), appeal dismissed per curiam sub nom., Union Oil Co. v. California, 351 U.S. 929 (1956); People v. Int'l Steel Corp., 102 Cal. App.2d 935, 226 P.2d 587 (1951); Miami v. Coral Gables, 233 So.2d 7 (Fla.1970); Bd. of Health v. New York Central R. R., 10 N.J. 294, 90 A.2d 729 (1952); Dep't of Health v. Concrete Specialties, Inc., 112 N.J. Super. 407, 271 A.2d 595 (1970); Penn-Dixie Cement Corp. v. Kingsport, 189 Tenn. 450, 225 S.W.2d 270 (1949); Sittner v. Seattle, 62 Wash.2d 834, 384 P.2d 859 (1963); cf. Portland Cement Ass'n v. Ruckelshaus (I), 158 U.S.App.D.C. 308, 334, 486 F.2d 375, 401, 3 ELR 20642, 20655 (1972), cert. denied 417 U.S. 921 (1974) (suggesting that a 20% opacity standard might be adequate); St. Paul v. Haugbro, 93 Minn. 59, 100 N.W. 470 (1904) (upholding against claims of unconstitutional vagueness a prohibition against a discharge of "dense smoke"). The Ringelmann Chart has many detractors, and deservedly so. See Western Alfalfa v. Air Pollution Variance Bd., 3 ERC 1399 (Colo.Dist. Ct.1971); Henz, The Ringelmann Number as an Irrebutable Presumption of Guilt—An Outdated Concept, 3 Nat.Res.Law 232 (1970); cf. Bortz Coal Co. v. Air Pollution Comm'n, 2 Pa.Comm. 441, 279 A.2d 388 (1971) (visual evidence alone without reference to Ringelmann standards insufficient basis for conviction). See also 1 F. Grad, Environmental Law: Pollution Control § 2.03, at 2–117 (1975) (discussing the scentometer, a device for identifying offensive odors, which works on Ringelmann principles).

20. Section 115, 42 U.S.C.A. § 1857d; see § 3.1 above.

21. 42 U.S.C.A. § 1857d(b)(4).

22. Id. § 1857h–1.

Sec. 3.19 ENFORCEMENT

mous Birmingham, Alabama case in November 1971, and even then the dispute ended in a settlement of sorts.[23] On several other occasions summary action under section 303 was at hand but was ultimately withheld. Obviously the provision gives the Administrator considerable leverage in discussions with state and local officials over appropriate action, so section 303 is a bargaining chip as well as a direct legal tool. The states themselves also must include in their implementation plans an override "authority comparable to that in [section 303], and adequate contingent plans to implement such authority."[24]

The Administrator's enforcement authority[25] ordinarily is dependent upon a finding that a person is in violation of any requirement of an applicable implementation plan or is in violation of section 111(e) (relating to new source performance standards),[26] section 112(c) (relating to standards for hazardous emissions),[27] section 119(g) (relating to energy-related authorities),[28] or section 114 (relating to inspections and reporting requirements). Upon finding a violation the Administrator has three options: (1) he may issue an order requiring compliance; (2) he may bring a civil action; or (3) he may initiate a procedure to assume generally the power to enforce a state plan.

The third option is a hollow gesture amounting to little more than an invitation to the Administrator to chastise publicly a state that has abandoned any semblance of commitment to the implementation plan, and it has never been invoked. In order to implement the procedure the Administrator is required to make a finding "that violations of an applicable implementation plan are so widespread that such violations appear to result from a failure of the state in which the plan applies to enforce the plan effectively."[29] The Administrator must give the state 30 days' notice, and if the failure to enforce continues beyond that date, there follows a "period of Federally assumed enforcement" for so long as the Administrator determines the state is not doing its job. One problem with this scheme is that during the "period of Federally assumed enforcement" the Administrator is authorized to do little more than what he could do otherwise (i. e., issue orders to comply or bring civil actions).[30] Another problem is

---

23. Compare Rendleman, Legal Anatomy of an Air Pollution Emergency, 2 Environmental Affairs 90 (1972) with Walpole, Another Look at the Air Pollution Crisis in Birmingham, 11 Land & Natural Resources Div. J. 109 (U.S.Dep't of Justice 1973).

24. Section 110(a)(2)(F)(v), 42 U.S.C.A. § 1857c–5(a)(2)(F)(v).

25. Section 113, 42 U.S.C.A. § 1857c–8.

26. § 3.10 above.

27. § 3.11 above.

28. § 3.6 above.

29. Section 113(a)(2), 42 U.S.C.A. § 1857c–8(a)(2).

30. Ibid. One difference, and it is an insignificant one, is that during a period of federally assumed enforcement, the Administrator may sue to correct violations of the implementation plans without complying with 30 day notification requirements. Sec-

that EPA has nowhere near the personnel required for this type of takeover operation. Yet another problem with the procedure is that the mere existence of the provisions for federally assumed enforcement supports an argument that EPA lacks power to order states to enact statutes or regulations or to bring enforcement actions to compel them to do so.[31]

The Administrator's second principal enforcement alternative is to bring an action for equitable relief directly in the United States District Court in which the defendant is located or resides or is doing business. This can be done either to enforce an order previously issued or to correct violations of implementation plans or various other provisions of the Act.[32] Basically, the Administrator has a choice either to proceed administratively or jump immediately into the courts. The court has jurisdiction "to restrain such violation and to require compliance," and this should be read as authorizing the use of the full arsenal of equitable remedies. An industry that is affected by an administrative order enforcing an implementation plan, on the other hand, does not have an option like that of the Administrator to challenge EPA orders directly in the district court.[33]

Saying the Administrator can proceed directly to court to correct violations requires a substantial qualification. As in the typical case, the Administrator is obliged to request the Attorney General to appear and represent him in any civil action instituted under the Act.[34] This presents problems of delay, communications difficulties, or even a full-scale debate (leading to a veto) within the Justice Department over whether the case merits prosecution. To relieve the impasse, Congress wrote, in Section 305 of the Act,[35] "[U]nless the Attorney General notifies the Administrator that he will appear in such action, within a reasonable time, attorneys appointed by the Administrator shall appear and represent him." This is an interesting provision but has significance only to the extent that the principals see fit to use it. The Justice Department does not relinquish readily its role as government litigator.

In addition to the provisions for administrative[36] and judicial compliance orders, the Act contains criminal sanctions. They are

tion 113(b)(2), 42 U.S.C.A. § 1857 c–8(b)(2).

31. See District of Columbia v. Train, 172 U.S.App.D.C. 311, 326, 521 F.2d 971, 986, 6 ELR 20007, 20012 (1975), cert. granted 426 U.S. 904 (1976). See also Brown v. Environmental Protection Agency, 521 F.2d 827, 5 ELR 20546, (9th Cir. 1975), cert. granted 426 U.S. 904 (1976) (California implementation plan); Maryland v. Environmental Protection Agency, 530 F.2d 215, 5 ELR 20651 (4th Cir. 1975), cert. granted 426 U.S. 904 (1976).

32. Section 113(b), 42 U.S.C.A. § 1857 c–8(b).

33. Getty Oil Co. v. Ruckelshaus (I), 467 F.2d 349, 2 ELR 20683 (3d Cir. 1972), cert. denied 409 U.S. 1125 (1973).

34. Section 305, 42 U.S.C.A. § 1857h–3.

35. Ibid.

36. Discussed in text accompanying notes 43–65 infra.

potentially draconian, containing high ceilings but no floors, and to that extent they are not particularly useful for day to day enforcement purposes. Knowing violations of implementation plans, compliance orders, hazardous or new source standards, or suspension conditions "shall be punished by a fine of not more than $25,000 per day of violation, or by imprisonment for not more than one year, or both." [37] Additionally, any person who knowingly makes false statements in various filings under the Act or tampers with a monitoring device faces a maximum penalty of a $10,000 fine or six months imprisonment.[38] Tough sanctions for environmental violations are applied rarely, and the Clean Air Act is no exception. Criminal and even civil enforcement actions in the courts are unusual phenomena, and usually are celebrated highly when they occur.[39] No penalty for violating an implementation plan or tampering has approached in severity the $7 million fine imposed on Ford Motor Company for violating the mobile source provisions.[40]

Somewhere between staggering fines or jail sentences and mild directives to comply with what has been ordered previously lies the sum and substance of an administrative enforcement effort, which EPA lacks under the Clean Air Act. Most prominent among the missing remedies is the power to impose fines administratively. This remedy is widely available in other contexts [41] and offers the flexibility not available through the blunderbuss or the wrist slap. Furthermore, limiting the false representation provision to knowing violations writes it off as a little-used penal instrument, instead of a broad charter of full disclosure provided by comparable provisions under other statutory schemes.[42] Since a purpose of the provision is to require truthful statements in required submissions to the agency, Congress drew the line too charily by reaching only the liars and not the derelicts.

b. *Administrative Orders*

Under section 113, upon 30 days notice, the Administrator may issue an order requiring compliance with any applicable implementa-

---

37. 42 U.S.C.A. § 1857c–8(c)(1). Conviction for a knowing violation of an implementation plan (except during a period of federally assumed enforcement) can occur only after 30 days notice by the Administrator that the violation is occurring.

38. Id. § 1857c–8(c)(2)(a).

39. See, e. g., Wall St.J., Sept. 11, 1974, at 10, col. 3 (announcing EPA-U. S. Steel Corp. consent decree resolving an enforcement action pending in a federal district court).

40. § 3.15 above.

41. E. g., §§ 4.17 (oil pollution), 8.9 (pesticides) below.

42. See Initial Decision of the Atomic Safety and Licensing Bd., In re Virginia Elec. & Power Co. (North Anna Power Station, Units 1 & 2), LBP 75–54, 2 NRC 498 (1975), rev'd in part ALAB 324, 3 NRC 347, rev'd in part NRCI 76/11, 480 (1976), petitions for review pending VEPCO v. Nuclear Regulatory Comm'n, Civil No. 76–2275 (4th Cir.) (Atomic Energy Act).

tion plan.[43] A similar administrative order may be issued, without 30 days notice, to correct violations of new source, hazardous emission, and energy-related standards.[44] An administrative order "shall state with reasonable specificity the nature of the violation, [and] specify a time for compliance the Administrator determines is reasonable, taking into account the seriousness of the violation and any good faith efforts to comply with applicable requirements."[45] The power to issue orders is hedged by other procedural requirements.[46] Except in cases involving violations of hazardous emission standards, the person to whom an order is issued must have an opportunity to confer with the Administrator, and copies of the order must be served upon various parties, including the state air pollution control agency and appropriate corporate officers.

EPA has proposed regulations[47] elaborating somewhat on the section 113 enforcement procedures. Under the proposals the public is given notice and an opportunity for comment and to request a legislative-type public hearing (but not an opportunity to participate in the conference between the polluter and the agency).[48] The administrative record upon which the enforcement order is based must be assembled in a single report and made available to the public.[49] The enforcement action itself "shall require final compliance as expeditiously as practicable" with any plan requirement necessary for attainment or maintenance of a primary standard and "within the shortest reasonable time" as to requirements for secondary standards.[50] The enforcement action also "shall result in a timetable for compliance which contains appropriate increments of progress with specific deadlines for achieving the increments" and must "require the source to apply reasonable interim measures to reduce emissions and protect against pollution concentrations in excess of those specified by a primary standard."[51]

The dominant issue of interpretation under section 113 is whether "any person" directed to comply by administrative or court order includes state or municipal governments. This question soon will

---

43. 42 U.S.C.A. § 1857c–8(a)(1).

44. Id. § 1857c–8(a)(3).

45. Id. § 1857c–8(a)(4).

46. Ibid.

47. 40 Fed.Reg. 14874 (Apr. 2, 1975), proposing 40 CFR pt. 65 (Enforcement Authority: State and Federal Enforcement of Implementation Plan Requirements after Statutory Deadlines).

48. Id., proposing 40 CFR § 65.4.

49. Id., proposing 40 CFR §§ 65.5, 65.6.

50. Id., proposing 40 CFR § 65.3(a)(1). The "expeditiously as practicable" and "reasonable" time requirements obviously are borrowed from the section 110(a)(2)(A), 42 U.S.C.A. § 1857c–5(a)(2)(A), requirements for achieving compliance within the deadlines. It is perhaps ironic that the same unhurried pace is to be maintained for achieving compliance after the deadlines.

51. 40 Fed.Reg. 14874 (Apr. 2, 1976), proposing 40 CFR §§ 65.3(a)(2), (3).

Sec. 3.19   ENFORCEMENT   345

be answered by the Supreme Court,[52] thus resolving serious doubts about the enforceability of EPA's transportation control strategies.[53] More important in the long run is whether EPA's enforcement power becomes a variance mechanism excusing widespread non-compliance on economic or technological grounds. Given the fact that federal compliance orders issue only upon a finding of violation of previously established emission standards or compliance schedules, an invitation to the Administrator to negotiate a "reasonable" time for compliance raises the distinct possibility that the enforcement stage can be transformed into a last ditch variance proceeding. On its face, the maximum pressure the Administrator may exert through compliance orders is to repeat directives already extant; he only can give, but not take away.

Discussed above [54] is the important proposition that opportunities for raising economic and technical defenses to control obligations cannot be viewed in isolation. Potential forums range across a continuum from the adoption of the state implementation plan to the defense of contempt proceedings. The Supreme Court's decision in Union Electric Co. v. Environmental Protection Agency [55] recognizes this fully. While holding that the Administrator must disregard claims of economic and technological infeasibility in approving state implementation plans, the Court identified other possible forums for raising these defenses—state consideration of the implementation plan; relief in state agencies or courts, under the extension and postponement provisions of the Act; [56] and, importantly, in federal enforcement proceedings: "Claims of technological or economic infeasibility, the Administrator agrees, are relevant to fashioning an appropriate compliance order under [section] 113(a)(4)." [57]

The variance procedure approved by dicta in *Union Electric* has been implemented by hundreds of administrative orders, constituting a body of law that is one of the best kept secrets of the Clean Air Act. They are negotiated in informal conferences in which public participation is virtually non-existent.[58] The orders that emerge (called unilateral orders or consent decrees where the company denies

52. Environmental Protection Agency v. Brown, cert. granted 426 U.S. 904 (1976); Environmental Protection Agency v. Maryland, cert. granted 426 U.S. 904 (1976); State Air Pollution Control Bd. v. Train, cert. granted 426 U.S. 904 (1976); Train v. District of Columbia, cert. granted 426 U.S. 904 (1976). For the lower court opinions see note 31, supra.

53. § 3.16 above.

54. § 3.9 above.

55. 427 U.S. 246, 96 S.Ct. 2518, 49 L. Ed.2d 474 (1976).

56. 427 U.S. at 267–68, 96 S.Ct. at 2529–30, 49 L.Ed.2d at 488–89.

57. 427 U.S. at 268, 96 S.Ct. at 2530, 49 L.Ed.2d at 489, citing Brief of Environmental Protection Agency.

58. The proposals for public participation (text accompanying notes 48 and 49 supra) differ markedly from the circumstances under which the current crop of enforcement orders were developed.

the violation) are variances in every sense of the word. Typically, they identify a violation of the relevant implementation plan, recite that EPA has taken into account the seriousness of the violations and any good faith efforts to comply, and spell out "reasonable" requirements and schedules to assure compliance with the provisions being violated. The schedules may call for a phased series of actions—solicitation of bids, completion of purchase agreements, initiation and completion of construction, and progress reports at various stages. They may prescribe interim operating conditions (e. g., Boiler 7 will be operated so as not to exceed 80% of its rated capacity; "cold reserve" boilers will be fired only in emergencies). They may anticipate action over a period of many years (e. g., Boiler 7 will be placed on "cold reserve" by June 30, 1980; Boiler 10 will be retired on June 30, 1989). EPA often reserves in the orders powers it has under the Act anyway—to initiate a section 303 emergency abatement action, to require keeping of records, and to provide for the maintenance of monitoring equipment. These administrative orders disclose none of the features one might expect from a proceeding vigorously contested; i. e., independent monitoring, newspaper announcements of the settlement, study or reporting conditions on health and welfare effects of the time extension, findings on the seriousness of the violation and good faith of the offender, indications that civil or criminal penalties still may be initiated for the period of the delay, or perhaps even waivers of liability or the attachment of penalty conditions for prior dilatory tactics.[59] While there is a limit to the types of conditions affixed to "reasonable" time extensions, EPA has not approached those limits, nor has it provoked any challenges to its authority.

It is difficult to reconcile the emergence of a substantial federal variance program with other features of the Act. The ameliorating provisions elsewhere are tough, demanding, and temporary.[60] The compliance deadlines and the legislative history convey an unmistakeable clean-up or shutdown philosophy.[61] There is nothing in the scant legislative history of the enforcement provisions indicating a contradictory intent.[62] Mr. Justice Powell, concurring in *Union Electric,* was moved to comment on the "draconian possibility" of a shutdown of an electrical utility, observing that "Congress adopted this position despite its apparent awareness that in some cases existing sources that cannot meet the standard of the law must be closed down."[63] These

---

59. Compare Citizens Util. Co. v. Pollution Control Bd., 9 Ill.App.3d 158, 165, 289 N.E.2d 642, 647–48 (2d Dist.1972) (holding that the Illinois statute authorizing variances did not provide for the imposition of a monetary penalty). It goes without saying that an administrative order need not be issued at all.

60. § 3.6 above.

61. § 3.9 above.

62. See Comm. on Public Works, National Air Quality Standards Act of 1970, S.Rep. No. 1196, 91st Cong., 2d Sess. 21–23 (1970) [hereinafter cited as 1970 Senate Report].

63. 427 U.S. at 272, 96 S.Ct. at 2531, 49 L.Ed.2d at 490 (Powell, J.) (footnote omitted).

concerns evaporate if the enforcement provisions are construed, as EPA reads them, to authorize open-ended, case by case long term variances.

It is not entirely fair to describe EPA's enforcement extensions as a cruel farce devouring the heart of the Act without consideration. The enforcement orders provide incremental advantages to the government—the source, after all, is propelled down the path towards compliance, which is the Act's ultimate aim. Waivers as to inspection and monitoring might avoid fourth amendment objections later on; other useful conditions can be extracted; and EPA retains control of the situation by avoiding referrals to the Justice Department. But it would be unfair also to characterize enforcement extensions as anything other than variances legitimating evasions of the original implementation plans.

Ultimately, the legal question with regard to a particular variance involves a judgment about whether the time for compliance, read in light of the conditions attached, is "reasonable." There is nothing in the provision that permits a waiver of the substantive standard.[64] Presumably there are cases where the only "reasonable" time for compliance is immediately, as where the past record discloses intransigence, the public health is jeopardized, or where the questions raised have been aired and rejected earlier. Leisurely compliance schedules are tantamount to abandoning the implementation plan and are thus objectionable. A wide variety of conditions would bear directly on whether a time extension is "reasonable." While the Administrator has discretion, his actions on variances are seriously in need of the close scrutiny of judicial review.[65]

c. *State Enforcement*

The primary responsibilities of the states with regard to air pollution is a sentiment with origins in the Air Pollution Control Act of 1955.[66] The Supreme Court has accorded substance to the state role by its recent holdings in Train v. Natural Resources Defense Council, Inc.,[67] approving the grant of minor variances by state authorities that do not jeopardize the national standards, and in Union Electric Co. v. Environmental Protection Agency,[68] sanctioning state

---

64. § 3.9 above; cf. 42 U.S.C.A. § 1857h–5(b)(2) ("action of the Administrator with respect to which review could have been obtained [in the courts of appeal] shall not be subject to judicial review in civil or criminal proceedings for enforcement"); Newcombe, Impossibility: A Viable Defense Under the Clean Air Act? 1 Colum.J.Env.L. 147 (1974).

65. See § 1.5 above. One way in which enforcement orders might be tested is a citizen suit under section 304, 42 U.S.C.A. § 1857h–2, charging a violation of an emission standard. The enforcement order would be raised defensively.

66. § 3.1 above.

67. 421 U.S. 60, 95 S.Ct. 1470, 43 L.Ed. 2d 731 (1975); § 3.6 above.

68. 427 U.S. 246, 96 S.Ct. 2518, 49 L.Ed.2d 474 (1976).

consideration of claims of economic and technological infeasibility that are not open to question when the Administrator approves an implementation plan. EPA accords substantial deference to state enforcement actions,[69] although conflict between jurisdictions is inevitable.[70] In fact, with the significant exception of EPA's issuance of administrative orders, the initiation of most enforcement actions rests in the hands of state and local authorities.

An understanding of enforcement, even more so than other administrative practices, requires a look beneath the surface of formally prescribed powers and reported cases. Many analyses of state air pollution laws have been undertaken,[71] and these usually emphasize

---

69. See 40 Fed.Reg. 14874, 14881–83 (Apr. 2, 1975), proposing 40 CFR §§ 65.8–.10 (addressing coordination of state and federal enforcement of implementation plan requirements after statutory deadlines); cf. 40 Fed.Reg. 22587 (May 23, 1975) (discussing post-attainment date variances under state implementation plans).

70. See In re Grand Jury Proceedings, United States Steel-Clairton Works, 525 F.2d 151, 6 ELR 20205 (3d Cir. 1975).

71. J. Esposito, Vanishing Air 190–233 (1970) (discussing administration and enforcement in New York City, Wash., D. C., and Houston); 1 F. Grad, Environmental Law: Pollution Control § 2.03, at 2–97 to –123 (1975) (containing a useful discussion of state air pollution control laws and enforcement); J. E. Krier, Environmental Law & Policy 353–97 (1971); Bruch, Environmental Pollution Control Laws in Pennsylvania: A Survey and Analysis, 16 Vill.L.Rev. 815 (1971); Currie, Enforcement Under the Illinois Pollution Law, 70 Nw.U.L.Rev. 389 (1975) (a sophisticated, contemporary analysis); Delogu, Legal Aspects of Air Pollution Control and Proposed State Legislation for Such Control, 1969 Wis.L.Rev. 884; Hassett, Enforcement Problems in the Air Quality Field: Some Intergovernmental Structural Aspects, 4 Ecol.L. Q. 63 (1974); Klein, Pollution Control in Illinois—The Formative Years, 22 De Paul L.Rev. 759 (1973); Kovel, A Case for Civil Penalties: Air Pollution Control, 46 J.Urban L. 153 (1969) (reporting on ineffectiveness of criminal enforcement in Boston); Laitos, Institutional Response to an Environmental Crisis: The Failure of State Air Pollution Control, 48 Denver L.J. 519 (1972); Mix, The Misdemeanor Approach to Pollution Control, 10 Ariz.L.Rev. 90 (1968) (reporting on effectiveness of criminal prosecutions in Los Angeles); Norvell & Bell, Air Pollution Control in Texas, 47 Tex.L. Rev. 1086 (1969); Pollack, Legal Boundaries of Air Pollution Control—State and Local Legislative Purpose and Techniques, 33 Law & Contemp. Prob. 331 (1968); Snell, Pollution Control in Illinois: The Role of the Attorney General, 23 De Paul L.Rev. 961 (1974); Walker, Enforcement of Performance Requirements with Injunctive Procedure, 10 Ariz.L.Rev. 81 (1968); Walker, Laws, Regulations and Ordinances in the Air Pollution Field, 13 Nat.Res.Law 74 (1970); Willick & Windle, Rule Enforcement by the Los Angeles County Air Pollution Control District, 3 Ecol.L.A. 507 (1973); Comment, 1970 Clean Air Amendments: Use and Abuse of the State Implementation Plan, 26 Baylor L.Rev. 232 (1974); Note, State Air Pollution Control Legislation, 9 B.C.Ind. & Com.L. Rev. 712 (1968); Comment, Air Pollution Control in Idaho, 10 Idaho L.Rev. 57 (1973); Comment, The Role of the Michigan Attorney General in Consumer and Environmental Protection, 72 Mich.L.Rev. 1030 (1974); Note, On Building Laws for New Mexico's Environment, 4 N.M.L.Rev. 105 (1973); Comment, Local Government and Air Pollution, 33 Ohio St.L.J. 860 (1972); Comment, Oregon's Statutory and Common Law Efforts to Control Air Pollution: An Analysis and Comparison, 50 Ore.L.Rev. 85 (1970). Note, Legal Aspects of Air Pollution Control in Ohio 1971: Critique and Proposal, 40 U.Cin.L.Rev. 54 (1971); Note, Local Regulation of Air Pollution, 1969 Wash.U.L.Q. 232; Note,

enforcement (although the term usually is understood broadly to embrace variances, settlements and permits, not merely coercive measures). The reported cases, while misleading to the extent they represent the tip of the iceberg, are fully in the mainstream of the close scrutiny doctrine of judicial review.[72] Predictably, the case law often deals with delineating the basic powers of administrative agencies to move against one or another type of air pollution, such as emissions from automobiles,[73] fuel additives,[74] or field burning.[75] A common objection, invariably unsuccessful,[76] is that the legislators or administrators engaged in unreasonable classification decisions by moving against some sources of air pollution while ignoring others. Equally unavailing, with rare exception,[77] is the argument that the vesting of enforcement powers in administrative authorities is an impermissible delegation under local law.[78] Many decisions are reminiscent of federal doctrines of judicial review:[79] cases often are remanded to the agency to improve the state of the record,[80] or they are affirmed with

State Regulation of Air Pollution, 1968 Wash.U.L.Q. 249. Analyses and local and state legislative regimes may be dated by substantial changes wrought in the wake of the Clean Air Act.

72. § 1.5 above.

73. Roberts v. State, 45 Mich.App. 252, 206 N.W.2d 466, 3 ELR 20207 (1973) (neither Secretary of State nor State Director of Highways has power to regulate).

74. Environmental Defense Fund, Inc. v. California Air Resources Bd., 30 Cal.App.3d 829, 103 Cal.Rptr. 598, 3 ELR 20511 (1973) (no power to regulate under California law).

75. E. g., Marion County v. Mid-Willamette Valley Air Pollution Authority, 538 P.2d 960 (Or.Ct.App.1975); State v. Hayes, 520 P.2d 465 (Or.Ct. App.1974).

76. E. g., Ballentine v. Nester, 350 Mo. 58, 164 S.W.2d 378 (1942) (different classifications of coal); Wylie Bros. Constr. Co. v. Albuquerque-Bernalillo County Air Quality Control Bd., 80 N.M. 633, 459 P.2d 159 (1969) (regulating stationary sources but not mobile sources); Oriental Blvd. Co. v.. Heller, 27 N.Y.2d 212, 316 N.Y.S.2d 226, 265 N.E.2d 72 (1970), appeal dismissed 401 U.S. 986 (1971); State v. Eubanks, 2 ELR 20245 (N.C.Super.Ct. 1971) (prohibiting "open burning" but not "smoke stack burning").

77. E. g., Kankakee v. New York Central R. R., 387 Ill. 109, 55 N.E.2d 87 (1944) (power to issue abatement order); Southern Illinois Asphalt Co. v. Environmental Protection Agency, 15 Ill.App.3d 66, 303 N.E.2d 606, 3 ELR 20208 (1973) (civil money penalties).

78. E. g., Lloyd A. Fry Roofing Co. v. Dep't of Health Air Pollution Variance Bd., 179 Colo. 223, 499 P.2d 1176, 2 ELR 20514 (1972) (power to grant variances); Waukegan v. Pollution Control Bd., 57 Ill.2d 170, 311 N.E.2d 146, 4 ELR 20450 (1974) (power to impose civil monetary penalties); Bortz Coal Co. v. Air Pollution Comm'n, 2 Pa.Comm., 441, 279 A.2d 388, 1 ELR 20393 (1971) (power to establish standards); Houston Compressed Steel Corp. v. State, 456 S.W.2d 768 (Tex.Civ.App.1970) (same).

79. See § 1.5 below.

80. See Bortz Coal Co. v. Air Pollution Comm'n, 2 Pa.Comm. 441, 279 A.2d 388, 1 ELR 20393 (1971), further proceedings sub nom., Bortz Coal Co. v. Dep't of Environmental Resources, 7 Pa.Comm. 362, 299 A.2d 670 (1973).

a bow to administrative discretion when the decision is adequately justified.[81]

An important component of contemporary judicial review of administrative decision-making is a strict insistence upon procedural niceties, a proposition that often frustrates air pollution enforcement endeavors. Thus, agencies must turn square corners in implementing their enforcement authority.[82] Persons charged with violations have defended successfully on grounds of inadequate notice,[83] discriminatory enforcement,[84] lack of power of the enforcing agency,[85] or failures of proof, either of a technical element [86] or of the underlying substantive offense.[87] As increasingly sophisticated monitoring and measurement techniques are developed, the relative ease of proving a Ringelmann Chart violation [88] will give way to the need to provide expert testimony "to the effect that tests were performed in a scientifically and technically acceptable manner and that the measuring instruments were functioning properly and were accurately calibrated." [89] Some agencies rely for enforcement on tests run on similar equipment under similar conditions.

Many air pollution enforcement schemes create strict liability civil or criminal penalties,[90] which are demonstrably a more effec-

81. E. g., Associated Indust. of Massachusetts v. Fredette, 2 ELR 20013 (Mass.Super.Ct.1972) (upholding decision denying request for one year postponement of regulation of fuel oil sulfur content); United States Steel v. Gary Air Pollution Control Bd., 4 ERC 1273 (Ind.Super.Ct.1972) (upholding discretionary denial of variance).

82. Shahmoon Indust., Inc. v. Dep't of Health, 93 N.J.Super. 272, 225 A.2d 699 (App.Div.1966), cert. denied 49 N.J. 358, 230 A.2d 392 (1967); St. Regis Paper Co. v. State, 237 So.2d 797 (Fla.Ct.App.1970), modified on other grounds 257 So.2d 253 (Fla. 1971).

83. State v. W. N. C. Pallet & Forest Prods. Co., 3 ELR 20799 (N.C.1973) (dismissing criminal indictment charging violation of opacity standards on grounds of vagueness); cf. Dep't of Health v. Roselle, 34 N.J. 331, 169 A.2d 153 (1961) (reversing contempt conviction for violation of vague order).

84. Wylie Bros. Constr. Co. v. Albuquerque-Bernalillo County Air Quality Control Bd., 80 N.M. 633, 459 P.2d 159 (1969) (defense unsuccessful).

85. Chicago Dep't of Environmental Control Appeal Bd. v. U. S. Steel Corp., 48 Ill.2d 575, 272 N.E.2d 46 (1971) (municipal board lacks subpoena power).

86. State v. Pascagoula Veneer Co., 227 So.2d 286 (Miss.1969) (failure to prove absence of a required permit); George E. Hoffman Sons, Inc. v. Pollution Control Bd., 16 Ill.App.3d 325, 306 N.E.2d 330 (1973) (failure to show that tests were representative of discharger's operation).

87. Bortz Coal Co. v. Air Pollution Comm'n, 2 Pa.Comm. 441, 279 A.2d 388, 1 ELR 20393 (1971) (opacity violation).

88. See note 19, supra.

89. 1 F. Grad, Environmental Law: Pollution Control § 2.03, at 2–118.

90. E. g., State v. Arizona Mines Co., 107 Ariz. 199, 484 P.2d 619, 1 ELR 20287 (1971); People v. Tatje, 203 Misc. 949, 121 N.Y.S.2d 147 (City Ct. 1953). A single air pollution case has resulted in jail time for the offender. See Diamond v. Bruleen Minerals, Ltd., 2 ERC 1107 (N.Y.Sup. Ct.1970) (criminal contempt).

tive enforcement tool than remedies tied to elusive definitions of a culpable offender. Civil injunctions run the gamut of equitable relief.[91] Civil monetary penalties are assessed in many jurisdictions and can be useful adjuncts of enforcement, particularly if tied to administrative orders.[92] The administrative order can be an imaginative instrument of compliance in the right hands,[93] or it can be just another way of handing out loosely written variances. Perhaps the most important question raised in judicial enforcement proceedings —one that has divided both courts [94] and legislatures [95]—is whether economic and technical defenses may be raised collaterally in enforcement proceedings. The correct disposition turns upon whether these claims are aired earlier in the standard setting-enforcement process.[96] If pleas of hardship are heard when the standards are set or when variances are sought, there is no need to open the debate again when enforcement follows. The better model gives consideration to economic and technical claims early in the process, if at all,[97] and limits the agenda at the enforcement stage to whether the agency had power to issue the order or standard, whether it was violated, and what the appropriate remedy should be.

Historically, enforcement of air pollution laws at the state and local level has been weak to the point of disappearance. Tolerance policies are crumbling, however, and generalities about enforcement practices are disappearing also. Enforcement is always a dark figure of administrative law, and informed judgments about it require a closer look at the files than is afforded by conventional sources of legal research.

91. Walker, Enforcement of Performance Requirements with Injunctive Procedure, 10 Ariz.L.Rev. 81 (1968); Wayne County Dep't of Health v. Chrysler Corp., 1 ELR 20410 (Mich.Cir.Ct.1971); Comment, Equity and the Ecosystem: Can Injunctions Clear the Air, 68 Mich.L.Rev. 1254 (1970). Compare § 2.11 above (discussing remedies in nuisance cases).

92. See Currie, supra note 71, at 426–33.

93. See id. at 468–73.

94. Compare State v. Owens-Corning Fiberglass Corp., 100 N.J.Super. 366, 242 A.2d 21 (App.Div.1968), aff'd mem. 53 N.J. 248, 250 A.2d 11 (1969) (rejecting defense) and Houston Compressed Steel v. State, 456 S.W.2d 768 (Tex.Civ.App.1970) (disallowing collateral attack) with People v. Cunard White Star, Ltd., 280 N.Y. 413, 21 N.E.2d 489 (1939) (allowing defense) and Commonwealth v. Pennsylvania Power Co., 12 Pa.Comm. 212, 316 A. 2d 212, 5 ERC 1373 (1973), aff'd 6 ERC 1328 (1974) (allowing defense in contempt proceedings).

95. See Environmental Law Institute, Enforcement of Federal and State Water Pollution Controls 203–04 (1975) (prepared for the National Comm'n on Water Quality) (discussing different treatment of this question under state water pollution laws).

96. See § 3.9 above.

97. A policy judgment can be made that economic or technical defenses be disallowed in meeting certain public health objectives. If controls are unavailable or uneconomical, the consequence may be a shutdown. Cf. Reserve Mining Co. v. Environmental Protection Agency, 514 F.2d 492, 5 ELR 20596 (8th Cir. 1975).

d. *Federal Facilities*

Because federal agencies "have been notoriously laggard in abating pollution,"[98] Congress in the 1970 amendments abandoned past practices of exhorting the agencies to cooperate in abating regional air pollution problems. The result was Section 118 of the Clean Air Act, which makes clear that each agency with facilities discharging air pollutants "shall comply with Federal, State, interstate, and local requirements respecting control and abatement of air pollution to the same extent that any person is subject to such requirements."[99] The President may exempt "any emission source" (except new sources and hazardous emission sources for which a separate exemption procedure applies) from compliance with a requirement "if he determines it to be in the paramount interest of the United States to do so . . .." Section 118 makes clear that no exemption "shall be granted due to lack of appropriation unless the President shall have specifically requested such appropriation as part of the budgetary process and the Congress shall have failed to make available such requested appropriation." Any exemption "shall be for a period not in excess of one year, but additional exemptions may be granted for periods of not to exceed one year upon the President's making a new determination." An annual report to the Congress on the exemptions and the reasons for them also is required.

On its face, section 118 suggests that federal facilities are to be constrained by permits, inspected and prosecuted like any other source under the Clean Air Act. In Hancock v. Train,[1] however, the Supreme Court held that while federal installations must comply with state and local substantive standards, they need not secure permits or otherwise yield to state enforcement endeavors. Thus, the states have the power to lay down the law for federal facilities but not to enforce it. The principal concern that prompted the Court to read narrowly the "requirements" with which federal facilities must comply is that the power to authorize by permit is the power to shutdown, and this authority is not lightly to be implied.

The Supreme Court's reluctance to accept in full the congressional waiver of sovereign immunity represented by section 118 is likely to retard the federal cleanup effort. The Tennessee Valley Authority, to mention but one example, long has been a prime proponent of intermittent controls for sulfur oxide emissions from its coal-burning power stations.[2] That is to say, the position of the federal sources on this

---

98. 1970 Senate Report, supra note 62, at 37 (1970).

99. 42 U.S.C.A. § 1857f.

1. 426 U.S. 167, 96 S.Ct. 2006, 48 L. Ed.2d 555 (1976). Compare § 4.21 below (discussing a companion case arising under the Federal Water Pollution Control Act); Comment, Local Control of Pollution from Federal Facilities, 11 San Diego L.Rev. 972 (1974).

2. See Hearings on Energy and Environmental Standards, Before the

important question of methodology affecting compliance does not differ materially from private sources, and neither should the enforcement options.[3] The vacuum created by the ouster of the states from an enforcement role is not likely to be filled by the Environmental Protection Agency, which has a limited appetite for interagency conflict. After Hancock v. Train, the formal system of presidential variances anticipated by section 118 may be replaced by a system of de facto instances of non-compliance for which there is no practical remedy.

Subcomm. on Energy of the House Comm. on Science and Technology, 93d Cong., 1st & 2d Sess. 289–446 (1973) (statement of Aubrey J. Wagner, Chairman, TVA).

3. § 3.8 above.

Chapter IV

WATER POLLUTION

§ 4.1 Background

Water pollution law today begins with an intimidating 90-page Act of Congress, the Federal Water Pollution Control Act Amendments of 1972.[1] Like the Clean Air Act, the water pollution legislation is but a predictable convergence of several historical forces. In many ways a novel and remarkable legislative effort, the Act still is rooted deeply in the past, expressing principles well accepted for generations.

If anything, the common law retains a stronger hold on the Federal Water Pollution Control Act than it does on the Clean Air Act. In the first place, the essential regulatory framework borrows heavily from the common law: variations of the "best technology" principle are a central premise for regulating the effluent from industrial and municipal sources (section 301). Well established are the remedial techniques of effluent limitations (sections 401, 402), control over the disposal of dredged materials and sewage sludge (sections 401, 404), special precautions for toxic substances (section 307) and health hazards (section 504), detailed inspection and monitoring requirements (section 308). The special statutory provisions governing oil and hazardous substance liability (section 311) cannot be divorced from common law strict liability for abnormally dangerous activities.[2] The national policy on thermal discharges (section 316) is informed by the old thermal pollution riparian rights cases.[3] More importantly, the Federal Water Pollution Control Act, like the Clean Air Act, expressly disavows a purpose to preempt state and local authority by federally conceived effluent limitations and standards of performance (section 510), thus preserving maximum autonomy to other jurisdictions, even within areas of admitted federal competence. The 1972 amendments ignore almost totally nonpoint sources of pollution, such as runoff from agricultural and construction sites, leaving exclusively to the common law and state and local regulation what very well may be the biggest part of the problem.[4] Groundwater quality is another major subject left largely to the common law, and implementing state legislation.[5]

The Clean Air Act, no less than the common law, informs and explains the 1972 water pollution amendments. This is quite pre-

1. Pub.L. No. 92–500, 86 Stat. 816, 33 U.S.C.A. §§ 1251–378. Authoritative analyses of the statute include Zener, The Federal Law of Water Pollution Control, in Environmental Law Institute, Federal Environmental Law 682–791 (E. L. Dolgin & T. G. P. Guilbert eds. 1974).

2. See § 2.14 above.

3. See § 4.20 below.

4. See § 4.4 below.

5. See § 4.3 below.

dictable since the same congressional committees (Senate Public Works, House Committees on Public Works and Interstate and Foreign Commerce), and leaders (Sen. Edmund Muskie, Rep. Paul Rogers) were instrumental in both legislative campaigns. The enforcement provisions of the Water Act (section 309) draw extensively on the Clean Air Act. Repeatedly, the programmatic and regulatory features of the water pollution legislation reflect the legislative ideas applied to air pollution two years earlier. Prominent illustrations are the provisions dealing with the publication of criteria documents (section 304), state implementation plans for controlling water quality (section 303(e)), standards of performance for new sources (section 306) and for toxic pollutants (section 307), inspections, monitoring and entry (section 308), the exercise of emergency powers (section 504), citizen suits (section 505), federal procurement (section 508), preemption (section 510), reports to Congress (section 516), and the creation of prestigious advisory committees with important functions under the Act—the Water Pollution Control Advisory Board (section 503) and the Effluent Standards and Water Quality Information Advisory Committee (section 515).

That Congress learned something from two years of experience under the Clean Air Act is indicated by section 315, creating a national study commission to investigate and report on all aspects of achieving or not achieving the water pollution effluent limitations and goals. The result was an ongoing assessment of most important features of the Act by the National Commission on Water Quality, which conducted a review lasting more than two years and costing some seventeen million dollars. The reports of the Commission [6] are destined to influence importantly future legislative and administrative midcourse corrections. Many of the Commission's contractor and staff reports offer useful analyses of territories largely unexplored. Published reports on the Commission's institutional assessment program, for example, address topics such as the permit program, planning, construction grants, public participation and enforcement.[7]

The 1972 Amendments were shaped also by legislative endeavors of earlier times, notably prior versions of the Federal Water Pollution Control Act, which made its first appearance in 1948,[8] and the

---

6. See National Commission on Water Quality, Staff Draft Report, Nov. 1975 [hereinafter cited as National Commission on Water Quality Staff Draft Report].

7. The Commission's contractor and staff reports are listed in id., app. A.

8. Act of June 30, 1948, Pub.L. No. 80–845, ch. 750, 62 Stat. 1155. Leading historical discussions of water pollution regulation include Hines, Nor Any Drop to Drink: Public Regulation of Water Quality, 52 Iowa L. Rev. 186, 432, 799 (1966); Barry, The Evolution of the Enforcement Provisions of the Federal Water Pollution Control Act: A Study of the Difficulty In Developing Effective Legislation, 68 Mich.L.Rev. 1103 (1970); E. Murphy, Water Purity (1961); D. Zwick, Water Wasteland (1971) (Nader Task Force Report on Water Pollution). For an informative case study, see Reitze, Wastes, Water and

Rivers and Harbors Appropriations Act of 1899,[9] commonly known as the Refuse Act. These two statutory roots are schizophrenic in conception, one espousing the water quality standards approach, the other stressing effluent limitations. (A water quality standard is a legal expression of the amount of pollutants allowed in a defined watercourse; an effluent standard describes the amount of pollutants that can be released legally by a specific source). The two concepts co-existed for several decades, mutually oblivious of one another, until Congress struck the balance mostly (but not entirely) in favor of control at the source in the 1972 amendments.

After its initial appearance in 1948, the Federal Water Pollution Control Act was amended five times [10] prior to the major revisions of 1972. Some concepts remained in the legislation throughout—provisions for conducting studies and investigations, encouraging interstate compacts, a reference to state primacy of regulation. Others gradually evolved in the legislative process—the definitions of the waters covered and the reach of federal enforcement powers, to mention but prime examples. Striking a balance between the costs of control and human health needs was a problem from the beginning. The Senate Report [11] accompanying the 1948 Act quoted with cautious approval from an old common law case [12] refusing to close down a source despite admitted damage from water pollution, but then affirmed that the health of the citizens is of "paramount importance." [13] The 1948 Act allowed a court to order relief from water pollution only after "giving due consideration to the practicability and to the physical and economic feasibility of securing abatement of any pollution proved." [14]

In 1965 came the major step of providing for the establishment of water quality standards applicable to interstate waters.[15] Under a procedure not unlike that now governing the preparation of state implementation plans under the Clean Air Act, either the state or, in the

Wishful Thinking: The Battle of Lake Erie, 20 Case W.L.Rev. 5 (1968).

9. 30 Stat. 1151, 33 U.S.C.A. §§ 403, 407, 411. For background, see Rodgers, Industrial Water Pollution and the Refuse Act: A Second Chance for Water Quality, 119 U.Pa.L.Rev. 761 (1971).

10. Water Pollution Control Act Amendments of 1956, Pub.L.No. 84–660, ch. 518, 70 Stat. 498; Federal Water Pollution Control Act Amendments of 1961, Pub.L. No. 87–88, 75 Stat. 204; Water Quality Act of 1965, Pub.L. 89–234, 79 Stat. 903; Clean Water Restoration Act of 1966, Pub. L. No. 89–753, 80 Stat. 1246; Water Quality Improvement Act of 1970, Pub.L. No. 91–224, 84 Stat 91.

11. Comm. on Public Works, Stream Pollution Control, S.Rep. No. 462, 80th Cong., 1st Sess. 4 (1947) [hereinafter cited as 1948 Senate Report].

12. McCarthy v. Bunker Hill & Sullivan Mining Co., 147 F. 981 (9th Cir. 1906).

13. 1948 Senate Report, supra note 11 at 4.

14. Pub.L. No. 80–845, § 2(d)(7), 62 Stat. 1155.

15. See Barry, supra note 8, at 1114–16.

event of state inaction, the Secretary of Interior, could promulgate water quality criteria and a plan for implementation and enforcement. The standards, regardless of who promulgated them, were required to be

> such as to protect the public health or welfare, enhance the quality of water and serve the purposes of [the] Act. In establishing such standards the Secretary, . . ., or the appropriate State authority shall take into consideration their use and value for public water supplies, propagation of fish and wildlife, recreational purposes, and agricultural, industrial, and other legitimate uses.[16]

The mandate of the 1965 Act was implemented by the gradual adoption of water quality standards.[17] By 1972, states had adopted and obtained federal approval for their standards, with a few exceptions.[18] This "zoning" of interstate waters remains a significant legal tool.[19]

While water quality standards evolved slowly under the auspices of the Federal Water Pollution Control Act, effluent standards were the preferred approach under a nineteenth century statute that saw it unnecessary to measure water quality by reference to "agricultural, industrial, and other legitimate uses." Section 13 of the Rivers and Harbors Act, in primitive absolutes, flatly prohibits the discharging from a ship or shore installation into navigable waters of the United States "any refuse matter of any kind or description whatever other than that flowing from streets and sewers and passing therefrom in a liquid state." [20] This section also forbids depositing "material of any kind in any place on the bank of any navigable water . . . where the same shall be liable to be washed into such navigable water . . . whereby navigation shall or may be impeded or obstructed." A proviso states that the Secretary of the Army "may permit the deposit of any material above mentioned in navigable waters, within limits to be defined under conditions to be prescribed by him." Violations are enjoinable,[21] and may be punished criminally.[22]

The revival of the Rivers and Harbors Act is a familiar chapter in the modern law of water pollution.[23] Highly publicized congres-

---

16. Pub.L. No. 89–234, § 5(a), 79 Stat. 907.

17. See Federal Water Pollution Control Administration, Dep't of the Interior, Guidelines for Establishing Water Quality Standards for Interstate Waters, in Hearings on Activities of the Federal Water Pollution Control Administration—Water Quality Standards, Before the Subcomm. on Air and Water Pollution of the House Comm. on Public Works, 90th Cong., 1st Sess., pt. 2, at 659 (1967).

18. A list of federally approved standards is published in 40 CFR pt. 120.

19. See § 4.8 below.

20. 33 U.S.C.A. § 407.

21. United States v. Standard Oil Co., 384 U.S. 224, 86 S.Ct. 1427, 16 L.Ed.2d 492 (1966).

22. 33 U.S.C.A. §§ 406, 411.

23. See § 4.5 below.

sional interest in section 13, inspired in large part by the House Subcommittee on Conservation and Natural Resources,[24] (chaired by Rep. Henry Reuss), led in rapid succession to the conclusions that thousands of industrial sources of water pollution were operating illegally without permits under the 1899 Act and that something should be done about it. In the summer of 1970 the Corps of Engineers announced that industrial discharges into navigable waters would be subject to new regulations pursuant to section 13 permit procedures,[25] a policy decision soon preempted by higher authority. On December 23 President Nixon promulgated an executive order [26] directing the implementation of a permit program to enforce section 13. He declared, "To deal with those who are disregarding our pollution control laws, a swift and comprehensive enforcement mechanism is provided by this authority." [27] Rules published concurrently by the Corps contained a public warning that widespread violations no longer would be protected by an official tolerance policy.[28]

The water quality standards brought into being by the Federal Water Pollution Control Act and the effluent standards fixed by the Refuse Act Permit Program should be recognized as reflecting fundamentally conflicting regulatory philosophies. They offer, in substance, a repetition of the air pollution debate between the advocates of emission standards and the samplers of ambient air.[29] Fundamentally, the competing schools disagree on how much should be spent on control. But, the economic parameters (especially the external ones) being rarely susceptible to reliable measurement, the disagreement of the two schools manifests itself most frequently over legal procedures for deciding whether to forbid the discharge of wastes into the water. Burdens and standards of proof are familiar language in the debate.

24. House Comm. on Gov't Operations, Our Waters and Wetlands: How The Corps of Engineers Can Help Prevent Their Destruction and Pollution, H.R.Rep.No.917, 91st Cong., 2d Sess. (1970).

25. Corps of Engineers Requirements for Permits for Industrial Discharges Into Navigable Waters, U. S. Army Corps of Engineers News Release, Seattle District, Aug. 4, 1970.

26. Exec.Order No. 11574, 3 CFR 188.

27. Statement by the President Upon Signing an Executive Order Providing for the Establishment of a Federal Permit Program to Regulate the Discharge of Waste into the Waters of the United States, 6 Weekly Comp. of Pres. Doc. 1724 (1970).

28. Permits for Discharge or Deposits into Navigable Waters, 35 Fed.Reg. 20005 (1970), revised and adopted, 36 Fed.Reg. 6565–66 (1971), 33 CFR § 209.131(d)(4):

All discharges or deposits to which the Refuse Act is applicable . . . are unlawful unless authorized by an appropriate permit issued under the authority of the Secretary of the Army. The fact that official objection may not have been raised with respect to past or continuing discharges or deposits does not constitute authority to discharge or deposit or to continue to discharge or deposit in the absence of an appropriate permit. Any such discharges or deposits not authorized by an appropriate permit may result in the institution of legal proceedings in appropriate cases for violation of the provisions of the Refuse Act.

29. See § 3.8 above.

The water quality standards [30] view of water pollution has many implications. It assumes a free use of water for waste disposal up to a point of "unreasonableness", however legally defined, and that the enforcement authority has the burden of proving that discharges harm marine resources or deter other water uses.[31] It assumes the government should share heavily in research and development costs for controls deviating from the norm of no control. It insists that enforcement is a particularly local concern because the unique characteristics of the receiving water, the economics of the discharging plant, and even the prevailing political tolerance level, are relevant to decisions to compel treatment or process change. Early versions of the Federal Water Pollution Control Act adhered closely to these premises.[32]

The "no discharge" prohibitions of the Rivers and Harbors Act look the other way. They focus on the source—not the size, flow and uses of the receiving body of water. Pollution dilution is not part of the lexicon. The concept is absolutist. Rationalization about "reasonable" amounts of pollution is not easily reconciled with a statute declaring it a crime to dump "refuse of any kind or description whatever" into navigable waters. While water quality standards appeal to economic and biological reality, effluent standards are more attuned to political necessity.

The 1972 Amendments represent a victory for the absolutists but not necessarily a defeat for the relativists. A compromise was struck, with the effluent standards assuming a dominant role and the water quality standards serving an important interstitial function. The flat prohibition of the Refuse Act explicitly is "restated" [33] in section 301(a) which declares that "the discharge of any pollutant by any person shall be unlawful," except where permitted under various provisions of the Act setting effluent standards.[34] The 1899 Refuse Act is reincarnated also in the controversial affirmation in section 101

---

30. See, e. g., Dunkelberger & Phillipes, Federal State Relationships in the Adoption of Water Quality Standards Under the Federal Water Pollution Control Act, 2 Nat.Res.L. 47 (1969). For a general economic defense of the stream standards approach to regulating water pollution, see Roberts, River Basin Authorities: A National Solution to Water Pollution, 83 Harv.L.Rev. 1527, 1542–44 (1970).

31. See Krier, Environmental Litigation and the Burden of Proof: Some Comments and Suggestions, in Conservation Foundation Conference on Law and the Environment (1969).

32. The Act assumed that waste disposal is a fundamental water use. See Pub.L. No. 89–234, § 5(a), 79 Stat. 907. Enforcement deferred to local control (Pub.L. No. 80–845, § 8(b), 62 Stat. 1159). The federal government accepted responsibility for proving damage from discharges (Pub.L. No. 89–234, § 5(a), 79 Stat. 907) and a large share of the burden of developing industrial pollution control technology (Pub.L. No. 80–845, § 4, 62 Stat. 1158; Pub.L. No. 89–234, § 3, 79 Stat. 905).

33. Comm. on Public Works, Federal Water Pollution Control Act Amendments of 1971, S.Rep.No.414, 92d Cong., 1st Sess. 71 (1971) [hereinafter cited as 1971 Senate Report].

34. 33 U.S.C.A. § 1311(a).

(a) (1) that "it is the national goal that the discharge of pollutants into the navigable waters be eliminated by 1985." [35] The 1972 definition of "pollution" also has an absolutist ring.[36]

At the same time, the water quality standards developed under the Water Quality Act of 1965 are perpetuated by the 1972 Amendments (section 303), which also invites modification of the standards from time to time. Section 302 of the Act authorizes the Administrator to establish "water quality related effluent limitations" in situations where effluent standards applied in the ordinary course would not achieve desired water quality.[37] Section 302 thus departs from the familiar dogma that effluent standards necessarily demand greater control from a source than water quality standards. Its purpose is to aid in achieving a controversial national goal established by the Congress in the 1972 Amendments: swimmable water everywhere by July 1, 1983,[38] however that may be defined. The wedding of the water quality and effluent standards factions under the 1972 Amendments was celebrated officially in Montgomery Environmental Coalition v. Fri,[39] holding that a water quality standard could be treated as an "effluent standard or limitation" under the citizen suit provisions (section 505) of the Act.

The links to the past of the 1972 Amendments by no means undermine the bold and innovative features of this important legislation. The land use planning provisions of the Act (sections 208, 303(e), 201, 209) have the potential for redefining radically state-federal relationships.[40] The Act expresses a commitment to inspire new concepts of waste treatment (sections 105, 107, 108) and forces their use by technology based effluent standards. Costs of achieving but the first level of technological controls are enormous: $10.8 billion for municipalities, $36.6 billion for industry.[41] The program of permits for all point sources (sections 401, 402), even with the precedent of the Refuse Act, is a mammoth administrative undertaking that has generated over 40,000 permits as of June 30, 1975, with an indeterminate number (anywhere from 50,000 to 100,000) of smaller sources yet

35. 33 U.S.C.A. § 1251(a)(1).

36. Section 502(19), 33 U.S.C.A. § 1362 (19), reads:
The term 'pollution' means the man-made or man-induced alteration of the chemical, physical, biological and radiological integrity of water. For the contrasting view that "water is polluted if it is not of sufficiently high quality to be suitable for the uses people wish to make of it," see National Water Commission, Review Draft—Proposed Report, at 4–4 (1972); see id. at 4–1 to –8 endorsing receiving water quality standards over the no discharge approach of the 1972 amendments.

37. 33 U.S.C.A. § 1312; see § 4.8 below.

38. Section 101(a)(2), 33 U.S.C.A. § 1251(a)(2); see 1971 Senate Report, supra note 33, at 46–47.

39. 396 F.Supp. 260, 4 ELR 20182 (D.D. C.1973).

40. See § 4.9 below.

41. See National Commission on Water Quality Staff Draft Report, supra note 6, at I–16, I–19.

to go.[42] The construction grants program is a juggernaut that is compared often to Federal-Aid Highway Act programs. The bold, even visionary, aspects of the Act are summed up by two expressions of policy that contradict every recorded human experience from Gresham's law to the Peter principle: section 101(3) espouses public participation in the administration of the law [43] and raises interesting questions about whether this policy can become more than lip-service.[44] Section 101(f) [45] goes further yet to espouse a policy favoring minimization of paper work and the cutting of red tape. This is a novel concept for a statute condemned for pushing paper work and red tape off the chart to unrecorded new extremes.

§ 4.2 Federal Water Pollution Control Act: A Summary

Like the Clean Air Act, the Federal Water Pollution Control Act is a comprehensive programmatic and regulatory creation. There are five titles: Title I deals with research and demonstration projects. Title II addresses grants for sewage treatment plants. Title III deals with the setting of standards, inspection and enforcement. Title IV covers permits and licenses and sets up the National Pollutant Discharge Elimination System, replacing the Refuse Act Permit Program. Title V contains general provisions dealing with citizen suits, advisory committees, definitions, judicial review and the like.

This section summarizes the key provisions before turning to a closer look at the controls on municipal and industrial water wastes. Section 101 [1] is a declaration of goals and policy and contains the ambitious no-discharge (by 1985) and swimmable water (by July of 1983) goals. Eight important policies are articulated. Citizen participation and discouragement of red tape are two of them.[2] Of utmost importance is the national policy "that the discharge of toxic

---

42. Id. at V-24.

43. 33 U.S.C.A. § 1251(e), reads:
Public participation in the development, revision, and enforcement of any regulation, standard, effluent limitation, plan, or program established by the Administrator or any state under this Act shall be provided for, encouraged, and assisted by the Administrator and the states. The Administrator in cooperation with the states, shall develop and publish regulations specifying minimum guidelines for public participation in such processes.
The regulations have been published and appear in 38 Fed.Reg. 22756 (1973), 40 CFR pt. 105.

44. Zener, supra note 1, at 762–65; National Commission on Water Quality Staff Draft Report, supra note 6, at V-111 to -14.

45. 33 U.S.C.A. § 1251(f) reads:
It is the national policy that to the maximum extent possible the procedures utilized for implementing this Act shall encourage the drastic minimization of paperwork and interagency decision procedures, and the best use of available manpower and funds, so as to prevent needless duplication and unnecessary delays at all levels of government.

1. 33 U.S.C.A. § 1251.

2. Id. §§ 1251(e), (f).

pollutants in toxic amounts" be prohibited.[3] In light of the broad definition of toxic pollutant (those causing death or disease in any organism),[4] this provision adds leverage to many claims attacking individual discharges. The five other stated national policies are central premises of the Act: (1) to provide federal financial assistance to construct publicly owned waste treatment works;[5] (2) to develop and implement areawide waste treatment management planning processes;[6] (3) to initiate a major research and demonstration effort to develop technology necessary to eliminate the discharge of pollutants into the water;[7] (4) to recognize the primary responsibilities of the states to plan the development and use of land and water resources;[8] and (5) to take steps to assure that foreign countries take meaningful action to eliminate pollution of their waters and international waters.[9]

The remainder of Title I is devoted to a variety of research, demonstration and study provisions. Section 103 restates preexisting law by calling for cooperation among states in developing uniform laws and enacting compacts.[10] Section 104 expands the Administrator's research capacities. It authorizes the establishment of a national water quality surveillance system, which has many potential uses (including evidentiary uses in enforcement proceedings),[11] and is now in operation. Section 104 requires studies on a variety of topics: equipment needed to control sewage from small recreational

3. Id. § 1251(a)(3); § 4.15 below.

4. Section 502(13), 42 U.S.C.A. § 1362 (13), reads:
   The term 'toxic pollutant' means those pollutants, or combinations of pollutants, including disease-causing agents, which after discharge and upon exposure, ingestion, inhalation or assimilation into any organism, either directly from the environment or indirectly by ingestion through food chains, will, on the basis of information available to the Administrator, cause death, disease, behavioral abnormalities, cancer, genetic mutations, physiological malfunctions (including malfunctions in reproduction) or physical deformations, in such organisms or their offspring.

5. Section 101(a)(4), 42 U.S.C.A. § 1251(a)(4); see § 4.10 below.

6. Section 101(a)(5), 33 U.S.C.A. § 1251(a)(5); see § 4.10 below.

7. Section 101(a)(6), 33 U.S.C.A. § 1251(a)(6).

8. Section 101(b), 33 U.S.C.A. § 1251(b).

9. Section 101(c), 33 U.S.C.A. § 1251(c).

10. One of the best known interstate efforts is the Delaware River Interstate Compact. See Ackerman, The Uncertain Search for Environmental Policy: Scientific Factfinding and Rational Decisionmaking Along the Delaware River, 120 U.Pa.L.Rev. 419 (1972); Ackerman, The Uncertain Search for Environmental Policy: The Costs and Benefits of Controlling Pollution Along the Delaware River, 121 U.Pa.L.Rev. 1225 (1973). See also 1 F. Grad, Environmental Law: Pollution Control § 3.04, at 3–193 to –201 (1975) (summarizing interstate compacts on water pollution).

11. Brown & Duncan, Legal Aspects of a Federal Water Quality Surveillance System, 68 Mich.L.Rev. 1131 (1970); see § 4.21 below (on enforcement).

vessels,[12] health and welfare effects of pesticides in water,[13] waste oil,[14] pollution in estuarine zones,[15] reductions in water consumption and total flow of sewage,[16] agricultural pollution,[17] and thermal discharges.[18]

Elsewhere, the 1972 Amendments require the Administrator and other agencies to prepare a wide variety of studies and reports of potential legal significance. These include criteria documents on the health and welfare effects of water pollutants,[19] guidelines on nonpoint sources of pollutants (agricultural, silvicultural, mining, construction activities),[20] a study of the water quality of all navigable waters and the waters of the contiguous zone,[21] reports on the eutrophic condition of publicly owned fresh water lakes in each state,[22] a study of alternative methods of financing water pollution costs, including the establishment of a pollution abatement trust fund,[23] and a special investigation of Lake Tahoe.[24] Overshadowing all other study provisions is section 315,[25] creating the National Commission on Water Quality which has emerged as a persistent if friendly ombudsman of performance under the Act.

Authorizations for appropriations for fiscal year 1972[26] continued the study technique of informing Congress by calling upon the Comptroller General to study and review the research, pilot and demonstration programs relating to the prevention and control of water pollution.[27] Other studies funded were aimed at international

---

12. Section 104(j), 33 U.S.C.A. § 1254 (j).

13. Sections 104(l)(1), (2), 33 U.S.C.A. §§ 1254(l)(1), (2).

14. Section 104(m), 33 U.S.C.A. § 1254 (m); see Waste Oil Study, Report of the Administrator of the Environmental Protection Agency to the Congress, House Comm. on Public Works and Transportation, H.R.Doc. No. 12, 93d Cong., 1st Sess. (Comm. Print 1973); § 6.10 below.

15. Section 104(n), 33 U.S.C.A. § 1254 (n).

16. Section 104(o), 33 U.S.C.A. § 1254 (o).

17. Section 104(p), 33 U.S.C.A. § 1254 (p); see § 4.4 below.

18. Section 104(t), 33 U.S.C.A. § 1254 (t); see Effects and Methods of Control of Thermal Discharges, Report of the Administrator of the Environmental Protection Agency to the Congress, Senate Comm. on Public Works, S.Doc. No. 14, 93d Cong., 1st Sess. (Comm. Print 1973); § 4.20 below.

19. Section 304(a)(1), 33 U.S.C.A. § 1314(a)(1); see § 4.8 below.

20. Section 304(e), 33 U.S.C.A. § 1314 (e); see § 4.4 below.

21. Section 305(a), 33 U.S.C.A. § 1315 (a).

22. Section 314, 33 U.S.C.A. § 1324.

23. Section 317, 33 U.S.C.A. § 1327.

24. Section 114, 33 U.S.C.A. § 1264.

25. 33 U.S.C.A. § 1325.

26. Pub.L. No. 92–500, 86 Stat. 896 (1972).

27. Id. § 5; see U. S. Comptroller General, Report to the Congress, Re-

trade effects of water pollution control,[28] the pros and cons of an environmental court,[29] and improving efficiency in fulfilling the Act's objectives.[30]

In several particulars, the Administrator's authority to study and report extends to research and development. He is authorized to conduct pilot project implementation of plans to treat sewage in rural areas where septic tank or community-wide disposal is impractical;[31] and to develop new methods "for the collection and treatment of sewage and other liquid wastes combined with the treatment and disposal of solid wastes."[32] He is given broad leeway to conduct demonstration projects to control pollution in native villages of Alaska,[33] acid mine drainage[34] and the Great Lakes.[35] Section 108(d)[36] calls for the Corps of Engineers "to design and develop a demonstration waste water management program for the rehabilitation and environmental repair of Lake Erie," which is to be "in addition to, and not in lieu of," other studies aimed at eliminating pollution from Lake Erie.[37]

Section 105 broadly authorizes the Administrator to conduct in-house demonstration projects or to make grants for projects aimed at the pollution problems of storm water runoff and joint treatment systems for industrial and municipal wastes, among others. It also authorizes the Administrator to undertake a model river demonstration project "of advanced pollution control and in-stream enhancement techniques."[38] In-stream enhancement techniques include non-treatment alternatives such as in-stream aeration (injecting air into effluent in order to facilitate aerobic action) and low flow augmentation (maintaining stream flow to improve the capacity of the water to assimilate wastes). In-stream enhancement is a sorry substitute for control at the source.

search and Demonstration Programs to Achieve Water Quality Goals: What the Federal Government Needs to Do (1974).

28. Id. § 6; see Dep't of Commerce, Effects of Pollution Abatement on International Trade, House Comm. on Public Works and Transportation, H.R.Doc. No. 13, 93d Cong., 1st Sess. (Comm. Print 1973); Dep't of Commerce, Effects of Pollution Abatement on International Trade—II, House Comm. on Public and Transportation, H.R.Doc. No. 34, 93d Cong., 2d Sess. (Comm. Print 1974).

29. Id. § 9; see Dep't of Justice, Report of the President Acting Through the Attorney General on the Feasibility of Establishing an Environmental Court System (1973).

30. Id. § 11.

31. Section 304(q)(1), 33 U.S.C.A. § 1314(q)(1).

32. Section 304(q)(2), 33 U.S.C.A. § 1314(q)(2).

33. Section 113, 33 U.S.C.A. § 1263.

34. Section 107, 33 U.S.C.A. § 1257.

35. Section 108, 33 U.S.C.A. § 1258.

36. 33 U.S.C.A. § 1258(d).

37. For background on the problem, see Reitze, Wastes, Water and Wishful Thinking: The Battle of Lake Erie, 20 Case Western L.Rev. 5 (1968).

38. Comm. of Conference, Federal Water Pollution Control Act of 1972, H.R.Rep. No. 1465, 92d Cong., 2d Sess. 104 (1972).

Section 115 is a potentially important provision directing the Administrator "to identify the location of in-place pollutants with emphasis on toxic pollutants in harbors and navigable waterways." In-place pollutants are not defined in the Act but include accumulated sludges and wastes deposited in earlier days. The Administrator also is authorized, acting through the Secretary of the Army, "to make contracts for the removal and appropriate disposal of such materials from critical port and harbor cases." This involves the regulator in activities ordinarily engaged in only by the regulated. Unfortunately, the provision has remained a virtual dead letter,[39] with EPA missing the opportunity to develop a litany of precautions deemed suitable for the disposal of toxic wastes.

Title II contains key constituents of the Act's planning and construction grants provisions. Section 201 calls for the planning and management of waste treatment facilities, to the extent practicable, "on an areawide basis" so as to "provide control or treatment of all point and nonpoint sources of pollution, including in place or accumulated pollution sources."[40] Section 201, dealing as it does with facility planning, is the first step in a planning process that includes also regional planning (section 208), state planning (section 303(e)), and basin planning (section 209). Section 208 contains elaborate provisions for encouraging the development and implementation of areawide waste treatment management plans. Its promise has been largely unfulfilled.[41]

Section 202[42] provides for federal grants for sewage treatment works in the amount of 75 percent of the cost of construction. Section 203[43] calls for each grant applicant to submit to the Administrator for his approval plans, specifications, and estimates for each proposed project for the construction of treatment works. Needless to say, the construction grants, planning and permit programs are supposed to function as an integrated whole. Facilities are to be built in accordance with the areawide plans to meet the permit provisions. One of the most serious failings of the Act is the lack of synchronization of the constituent parts, typified by planning bringing up the rear instead of trailblazing at the front.

Section 301[44] articulates the no discharge policy carried over from the Rivers and Harbors Act of 1899 ("the discharge of any pollutant by any person shall be unlawful") and articulates the various formulations of the "best technology" principle to be met on a scheduled basis by industry and municipal sources moving towards the

---

39. See letter to author from Robert C. Turner, Assistant Counsel for Civil Works, Office of the Chief of Engineers, Department of the Army, Feb. 19, 1976. Compare § 4.6 below.

40. Section 201(c), 33 U.S.C.A. § 1281 (c); see § 4.10 below.

41. See § 4.9 below.

42. 33 U.S.C.A. § 1282.

43. Id. § 1283.

44. Id. § 1311.

1983 swimmable water and the 1985 no discharge goals. The no discharge policy is relaxed only for discharges under permits approved by other sections of the Act. The most important of these is section 402 [45] establishing the National Pollutant Discharge Elimination System as a comprehensive regulatory scheme replacing and supplementing the Refuse Act Permit Program. Section 402(b) allows the Administrator, after finding compliance with a number of conditions, to approve individual state programs for administering the permit system. Significant also is section 404 [46] (prescribing permits for the discharge of dredged or fill material), section 302 [47] (permitting the imposition of more stringent effluent limitations where a combination of sources under normal effluent requirements fail to meet water quality standards), section 306 [48] (governing new sources) and section 307 [49] (prescribing effluent standards for toxic pollutants and pretreatment standards for discharges into treatment works). Discharges from approved aquaculture projects also may be permitted under Section 318 of the Act.[50]

Section 303,[51] like section 301, imparts a great deal of history by continuing existing water quality standards and providing for their approval or disapproval by the Administrator and for their modification from time to time. It also requires the states to establish a priority ranking of waters where compliance with effluent standards will not suffice to assure that water quality standards are met. These are called water quality limited segments. Section 304 [52] directs the Administrator to develop and publish water quality criteria on pollutants (comparable to the criteria documents under the Clean Air Act) and guidelines for effluent limitations for controlling pollution from non-point sources and for the pretreatment of pollutants "which he determines are not susceptible to treatment by publicly owned treatment works." [53]

Section 308 [54] deals with inspection, monitoring and entry, section 309 [55] with enforcement. Special notice and hearing provisions regarding international pollution are found in section 310.[56] Federal facilities are addressed by section 313.[57] Three unique problems are

45. Id. § 1342; see §§ 4.11, 4.12 below.

46. 33 U.S.C.A. § 1344; see § 4.6 below.

47. 33 U.S.C.A. § 1312; see § 4.8 below.

48. 33 U.S.C.A. § 1316; see §§ 4.12, 4.13 below.

49. 33 U.S.C.A. § 1317; see §§ 4.14, 4.15 below.

50. 33 U.S.C.A. § 1328.

51. Id. § 1313; see § 4.8 below.

52. 33 U.S.C.A. § 1314.

53. Section 304(f)(1), 33 U.S.C.A. § 1314(f)(1); see § 4.14 below (on pretreatment standards).

54. 33 U.S.C.A. § 1318.

55. Id. § 1319; see § 4.21 below.

56. 33 U.S.C.A. § 1320.

57. Id. § 1323; see § 4.21 below.

dealt with separately in the Act—oil and hazardous substances (section 311),[58] marine sanitation devices (section 312),[59] and thermal discharges (section 316).[60]

Section 401[61] carries over Section 21(b) of the Water Quality Improvement Act of 1970,[62] which requires any applicant for a federal license or permit to conduct activities which may result in water discharges to provide the licensing agency with a certification from the state where the activity is conducted that the discharge "will comply" with "applicable" limitations. The certification requirement can be waived in the event of "sheer inactivity" on a request for certification for more than one year.[63] Section 401 offers a veto power to states with water quality related concerns about licensing activities of the various federal agencies, including the Environmental Protection Agency, Federal Power Commission, Corps of Engineers, and the Nuclear Regulatory Commission. A denial of a certification can stop the project or a certification can issue with conditions, which must be written into the federal license or permit.[64] Section 401 adds muscle to the no-preemption pretensions of section 510.

Section 403 authorizes, in certain circumstances, the issuance of permits for ocean dumping and directs the Administrator to promulgate guidelines for determining the degradation of waters of the territorial seas, the contiguous zone and the oceans. These provisions must be read together with the Marine Protection, Research and Sanctuaries Act of 1972 (the Ocean Dumping Act),[65] which imposes similar and sometimes contradictory legal requirements.[66]

The general provisions of Title V need be catalogued but briefly; section 501 deals with general matters of administration, including the granting of awards "to those industrial organizations and political subdivisions of states which during the preceding year demonstrated an outstanding technological achievement or an innovative process, method, or device in their waste treatment and pollution

---

58. 33 U.S.C.A. § 1321; see § 4.18 below.

59. 33 U.S.C.A. § 1322.

60. Id. § 1320; see § 4.20 below.

61. 33 U.S.C.A. § 1341.

62. Pub.L. No. 91–224, 84 Stat. 108.

63. Comm. on Public Works, Federal Water Pollution Control Act Amendments of 1972, H.R.Rep. No. 911, 92d Cong., 2d Sess. 122 (1972).

64. Section 401(d), 33 U.S.C.A. § 1341(d); see DeRham v. Diamond, 69 Misc.2d 1, 330 N.Y.S.2d 71, 2 ELR 20207 (1972), rev'd 39 A.D.2d 302, 333 N.Y.S.2d 771, 2 ELR 20499, aff'd 32 N.Y.2d 34, 343 N.Y.S.2d 84, 295 N.E.2d 763, 3 ELR 20327 (1973) (involving state judicial review of administrative decision certifying compliance with water quality standards). State vetos of federal projects reverse longstanding policies. See First Iowa Hydro-Elec. Coop. v. Federal Power Comm'n, 328 U.S. 152, 66 S.Ct. 906, 90 L.Ed. 1143 (1946).

65. Pub.L. No. 92–532, 86 Stat. 1052, 33 U.S.C.A. § 1401 et seq.

66. See § 4.16 below.

abatement programs." [67] Section 502 [68] is the definitions section. Section 505 [69] deals with citizen suits. Section 508 [70] brings federal procurement powers to bear on violators of the Act. Other important subjects covered are administrative procedure and judicial review (section 509),[71] preemption (section 510),[72] impact of the Rivers and Harbors Act of 1899 and the National Environmental Policy Act (section 511),[73] and annual reports to Congress (section 516).[74] The reports section is as fully detailed as is the counterpart provision under the Clean Air Act. The documents, though useful, only scratch the surface of this complex piece of legislation.

It is inevitable that the 1972 amendments will be modified further in the future as Congress continues its assessment of national water pollution ills. Proposals failing enactment in the waning days of the 94th Congress [75] suggest the types of changes to be expected in the foreseeable future. Reduction in the reach of federal dredge and fill permit powers, perhaps by delegating authority to the states, is a strong possibility in light of the anguished pleas of the recently regulated.[76] Streamlining of the facility grants mechanism,[77] also by expanding the role of the states, is high on the agenda. A relaxation of the time for compliance by municipal treatment works is probable, if for no other reason than that wholesale violations are the only alternative.[78] With few exceptions, however, the changes under discussion, and particularly those with chances of enactment, disclose little inclination by the Congress to disavow the basic policy choices made in 1972.

§ 4.3 Coverage: Groundwater

In only a few particulars the definitions of "pollution" or "pollutant" serve to circumscribe jurisdiction under the 1972 Amendments. The Act defines "pollution" as "the man-made or man-induced alteration of the chemical, physical, biological, and radiological integrity

---

67. 33 U.S.C.A. § 1361(e)(1).

68. Id. § 1362.

69. Id. § 1365; see § 1.13 above.

70. 33 U.S.C.A. § 1368; see 41 Fed. Reg. 55931, 55932 (1976) (listing the Allied Chemical Corp., Semet-Solvay Div., Ashland, Ky., Del Monte de Puerto Rico, Inc., Mayaguez, P. R., and Star-Kist Caribe, Inc., Mayaguez, P. R.).

71. Id. § 1369.

72. Id. § 1370.

73. Id. § 1371.

74. Id. § 1376.

75. Comm. on Public Works and Transportation, Federal Water Pollution Control Act Amendments of 1976, H.R.Rep. No. 1107, 94th Cong., 2d Sess. (1976); 122 Cong.Rec. H5229–88 (daily ed. June 3, 1976); id. at S15160–89 (daily ed. Sept. 1, 1976).

76. See §§ 4.5, 4.6 below.

77. See § 4.10 below.

78. See § 4.13 below.

Sec. 4.3   GROUNDWATER   369

of the water."[1] It follows that natural water quality is the norm from which any deviation is measured.[2] A "pollutant" upon this understanding embraces every conceivable man-made or man-induced medium capable of effectuating changes in water quality. The statutory definition of "pollutant" is fully consistent with this understanding, with two exceptions created solely to accomplish limited policy objectives. Thus, a "pollutant" means "dredged spoil, solid waste, incinerator residue, sewage, garbage, sewage sludge, munitions, chemical wastes, biological materials, radioactive materials, heat, wrecked or discarded equipment, rock, sand, cellar dirt and industrial, municipal and agricultural waste discharged into water."[3] The use of the verb "discharged" and its association only with point sources should not be read as meaning that statutory "pollutants" come from point sources alone. The statute elsewhere refers expressly to "nonpoint sources of pollutants"[4] and it requires no great inferential leap to conclude that the "pollution" defined to embrace all man-induced alterations of natural water quality comes from point and nonpoint sources alike.[5]

The broad statutory definition of "pollutant" stilled some debates about coverage—including the longstanding discussion of whether waste heat was "refuse" under Section 13 of the Rivers and Harbors Act. The courts have been inclined to resolve doubtful questions in favor of coverage,[6] even to the extent of interpreting the two exceptions as justifying a reluctance to imply "unexpressed exceptions."[7] The exceptions deal with "sewage from vessels", separately addressed under Section 312 of the Act,[8] and with oil and gas injection wells pertinent to the consideration of groundwater pollution.

Groundwater can be defined as water occurring beneath the surface of the land filling the pore spaces of rock material in which it

1. Section 502(19), 33 U.S.C.A. § 1362(19).

2. See Comm. on Public Works, Federal Water Pollution Control Act Amendments of 1971, S.Rep.No.414, 92d Cong., 1st Sess. 115 (1971) [hereinafter cited as Senate Report]:
   Maintenance of [water quality] integrity requires that any changes in the environment resulting in a physical, chemical or biological change in a pristine water body be of a temporary nature, such that by natural processes, within a few hours, days or weeks, the aquatic ecosystem will return to a state functionally identical to the original.

The statutory definition of course is basically hostile to the water quality standards approach. See § 4.1 above.

3. Section 502(6), 33 U.S.C.A. § 1362(6).

4. Section 304(e), 33 U.S.C.A. § 1314(e).

5. See § 4.4 below for definitions of point and nonpoint sources.

6. See Train v. Colorado Pub. Interest Research Group, Inc., 426 U.S. 1, 96 S.Ct. 1938, 48 L.Ed.2d 434 (1976) (exempting radioactive effluents from the FWPCA definition of "pollutant" only upon the basis of persuasive legislative history).

7. See Colorado Pub. Interest Research Group, Inc. v. Train, 507 F.2d 743, 746–47, 5 ELR 20043, 20045 (10th Cir. 1974), rev'd 426 U.S. 1, 96 S.Ct. 1938, 48 L.Ed.2d 434 (1976).

8. 33 U.S.C.A. § 1322.

is found.[9] Its upper limit is called the groundwater table. An aquifer is an underground layer of rock, sand or gravel from which significant quantities of subsurface water can be produced. Groundwater pollution problems are the product of a complex interplay of hydrology (the science of water, its properties and distribution) and the familiar technological and economic components.[10] The subject, before and after the 1972 Amendments, still is governed chiefly by the common law and state regulation. It is inevitable that the ancient maxim, *cujus est solum, ejus est usque ad coelum et ad infernos* (meaning "to whomever the soil belongs he owns also to the sky and to the depths") will be compromised for subsurface rights [11] as it has been for airspace.[12] Priority and allocation groundwater disputes are intense, and are governed for the most part by familiar water law riparian (reasonable use) and prior appropriation rules.[13] The third major water law doctrine, that of federally reserved rights, recently was applied by the Supreme Court in a groundwater context to preserve the water level in Devil's Hole serving as a habitat for the endangered pupfish.[14] Various regulatory and permit schemes, superimposed on the common law, seek to prevent overappropriation and withdrawals in excess of natural recharge. Meanwhile, groundwater

---

9. The author is indebted for materials on ground water to Ballentine, Legal Control of Ground Water Quality (unpublished paper prepared for a course in environmental law, Georgetown U. Law Center, Fall 1974). A leading effort is Corker, Groundwater: Law Management, and Administration (1971) (National Water Commission Study No. 6). See also Comment, Groundwater Pollution in the Western States—Private Remedies and Federal and State Legislation, 8 Land & Water L.Rev. 537 (1973).

10. Studies on groundwater pollution include D. W. Miller, et al., Ground Water Contamination in the Northeast States, Environmental Protection Agency (1974); D. K. Fuhriman & J. R. Barton, Ground Water Pollution in Arizona, California, Nevada and Utah, Environmental Protection Agency (1971); J. F. Karubian, Polluted Ground Water: Estimating the Effects of Man's Activities, Environmental Protection Agency (1974); National Well Water Ass'n, A Study on Present and Future Justification for Control of Ground Water, Environmental Protection Agency (1974). See also EPA Administrator's Decision Statement No. 5, The EPA Policy on Subsurface Emplacement of Fluids by Well Injection, 39 Fed.Reg. 12922 (1974).

11. See Nelson v. C & C Plywood Corp., 154 Mont. 414, 465 P.2d 314 (1970); Atkinson v. Herington Cattle Co., 200 Kan. 298, 436 P.2d 816 (1968); Finley v. Teeter Stone, Inc., 251 Md. 428, 248 A.2d 106 (1968). Compare Peoples Gas Light & Coke Co. v. Buckles, 24 Ill.2d 520, 182 N.E.2d 169 (1962) (denying compensation to a landowner for gas storage in a formation beneath his surface estate) with Comment, Oil and Gas: Liability and Damages for Underground Trespasses, 27 Calif.L.Rev. 192 (1939) (discussing slant drilling for oil across property lines).

12. See § 5.5 below.

13. The common law and statutory overlay is found in the water law case books. E. g., C. J. Meyers & A. D. Tarlock, Water Resource Management ch. IV (1971); J. L. Sax, Water Law: Planning & Policy ch. 5 (1968); F. J. Trelease, Water Law: Resource Use and Environmental Protection ch. 4 (1974). Compare § 2.15 above.

14. Cappaert v. United States, 426 U.S. 128, 96 S.Ct. 2062, 48 L.Ed.2d 523 (1976).

pollution is regulated if at all mostly by the uneven collection of state laws governing nonpoint source pollution. Individual cases are resolved under the traditional common law theories of riparian rights,[15] trespass,[16] negligence,[17] nuisance,[18] and strict liability.[19] Government sponsored threats to groundwater integrity can be reached by the National Environmental Policy Act[20] and its state counterparts.

The 1972 Amendments address groundwater pollution circuitously but at several points. A frontal assault in the form of federally approved standards for groundwaters was proposed but rejected, according to the Senate Report, "because the jurisdiction regarding groundwaters is so complex and varied from State to State."[21] Limited opportunities for legal controls under the 1972 Amendments have arisen, however, pursuant to (1) section 402(b) as a condition of a state's federally approved permit program; (2) sections 201 and 304 (d)(2) as a condition of federally funded treatment works;[22] and (3) sections 208, 303 and 106(e) as a condition of the continuing planning process.[23] EPA explains its modest FWPCA groundwater pollution control strategy as requiring the agency to use its "regulatory powers incidental to its control of surface discharges; establish groundwater criteria for treatment works it funds; and structure its permit and planning regulations and research activities to encourage states in establishing full groundwater protection programs of their own."[24]

15. Nelson v. C & C Plywood Corp., 154 Mont. 414, 465 P.2d 314 (1970).

16. Phillips v. Sun Oil Co., 307 N.Y. 328, 121 N.E.2d 249 (1954); Pan American Petroleum Co. v. Byars, 230 Ala. 178, 153 So. 616 (1934); Railroad Comm'n v. Manziel, 361 S.W.2d 560 (Tex.1962).

17. Texas Co. v. Giddings, 148 S.W. 1142 (Tex.1912) (imposing liability on a res ipsa theory where a water well was polluted by leakage from an oil pipeline); Martinez v. Arkansas Fuel Oil Corp., 274 S.W.2d 160 (Tex.Civ. App.1954) (finding no negligence because of compliance with oil field custom); North Georgia Petroleum Co. v. Lewis, 128 Ga.App. 653, 197 S.E.2d 437 (1973); Augustine v. Hinne, 201 Kan. 710, 443 P.2d 354 (1968); Alliston v. Shell Petroleum Corp., 55 P.2d 396 (Kan.1936) (no cause in fact); Reinhart v. Lancaster Area Refuse Authority, 201 Pa.Super. 614, 193 A.2d 670 (1963).

18. Tidewater Oil Co. v. Jackson, 320 F.2d 157 (10th Cir. 1963) (water injection case resulting in liability; court does not choose between a nuisance or negligence theory); Burr v. Adam Eidemiller, Inc., 386 Pa. 416, 126 A.2d 403 (1956); Hauck v. Tide Water Pipe Line Co., 153 Pa. 366, 26 A. 644 (1893); Watson v. Great Lakes Pipeline Co., 85 S.D. 310, 182 N.W.2d 314 (1970); Anstee v. Monroe Light & Fuel Co., 171 Wis. 291, 177 N.W. 26 (1970).

19. Berry v. Shell Petroleum Co., 140 Kan. 94, 33 P.2d 953 (1934).

20. Sierra Club v. Lynn, 502 F.2d 43, 4 ELR 20844 (5th Cir. 1974), cert. denied 421 U.S. 944 (1975).

21. Senate Report, supra note 2, at 73.

22. See § 4.10 below.

23. See § 4.9 below.

24. Environmental Protection Agency, Water Strategy Paper: A Statement of Policy for Implementing the Requirements of the 1972 Federal Water Pollution Control Act Amendments (2d ed. 1974).

The Senate Committee, recognizing "the essential link between ground and surface waters," thought it important to require each state as a condition of obtaining approval of a permit program to include "affirmative controls over the injection or placement in wells [of] any pollutants that may affect ground water." [25] Thus, section 402(b)(1)(D) states that one condition of the Administrator's approval of a submitted state program is that he determines that adequate authority exists to issue permits to "control the disposal of pollutants into wells." [26] There are at least three severe limitations on this authority, one hydrologic, two of them legal. The hydrologic difficulty is that the deep well disposal addressed in the Act is but a small part of the problem: groundwater contamination is more generally attributed, according to several authorities,[27] to sources such as landfill leachate (the product of water filtering through pollutants), septic tank drainage, highway de-icing salt, fertilizer, pesticide and herbicide use.[28]

The chief legal gap is that the word "pollutant" is defined in section 502(b) to exclude "water, gas or other material which is injected into a well to facilitate production of oil and gas, or water derived in association with oil or gas production and disposed of in a well, if the well used either to facilitate production or for disposal purposes is approved by authority of the State in which the well is located, and if such State determines that such injection or disposal will not result in the degradation of ground or surface water resources." This is no small exception since there are some 60,000 oil-related brine reinjection wells in the United States as opposed to some 300 industrial and municipal injection wells not excepted by the definition.[29] On the other hand, some issues remain because oil and gas injection wells involve "pollutants" subject to regulation by permit if state approval is not forthcoming or, in the more likely case, if a state determination of no degradation is insupportable in fact.[30]

A second legal difficulty with the 1972 well-injection provisions is occasioned by an EPA opinion that, in the absence of an approved state permit program containing authority to regulate well-injections, the federal agency itself is without power to do so.[31] While

25. Senate Report, supra note 2, at 73. There are other environmental problems with deep well disposal not the least of which is increased earthquake activity due to changing pore pressures.

26. 33 U.S.C.A. § 1342(b).

27. See note 10, supra.

28. Compare § 4.4 below on non-point sources.

29. Ballentine, supra note 9, at 18–19.

30. See Comm. on Public Works, Federal Water Pollution Control Act Amendments of 1972, H.R.Rep.No.911, 92d Cong., 2d Sess. 131 (1972) (indicating that the state determination must be "based on sufficient investigation and evidence").

31. Acting Deputy General Counsel, Environmental Protection Agency, Applicability of NPDES to Disposal of Pollutants Into Wells, Opinion No. 590 (1974); see United States v. GAF Corp., 389 F.Supp. 1379, 5 ELR 20581 (S.D.Tex.1975) (holding the injection

Sec. 4.3   **GROUNDWATER**   373

there is considerable support for this view,[32] it is difficult to understand why EPA does not have the authority it can demand of the states under section 402(b), including the power to control the disposal of pollutants into wells. That the Administrator could disapprove a state program for inadequate powers over injection wells but do nothing to correct the situation himself is a bureaucratic tangle to be unraveled only by stretching the Act severely. These difficulties prompted the Congress to address the injection well problem again in the Safe Drinking Water Act of 1974.[33]

Elsewhere under FWPCA, the Administrator can influence groundwater pollution in important ways. Grants for construction of treatment works are conditioned, among other things, upon a demonstration to the Administrator that "alternative waste management techniques have been studied and evaluated." [34] Alternatives to conventional treatment works prominently include land processing of sewage effluent which is circumscribed by groundwater quality considerations.[35] The Administrator's views on the compatibility of land treatment proposals with groundwater quality thus will influence greatly the viability of the land treatment option. One of the components of an approvable areawide waste treatment management plan is "a process to control the disposal of pollutants on land or in subsurface excavations within such area to protect ground and surface water quality." [36] Groundwater monitoring is another element of the planning processes.[37]

Limited federal authority to protect groundwater quality can be found in the Rivers and Harbors Act of 1899, which applies to a variety of reckless disposal practices affecting navigable waters,[38] and the Federal Environmental Pesticide Control Act, which governs

---

of organic chemical wastes into subsurface wells was not the "discharge of a pollutant" under the Act). Regulations governing federally issued permits under the National Pollutant Discharge Elimination System extend to well disposals only if they are "part of a program to meet the proposed terms and conditions" in a permit otherwise required for a discharge into navigable waters. 40 CFR § 125.26. Compare id. § 124.80 (1974) (requiring as a condition of a state approved program broader authority over injection wells). The distinction is an uneasy one.

32. See United States v. GAF Corp., supra note 31.

33. Text accompanying notes 40–45 infra.

34. Section 201(g)(2)(A), 33 U.S.C.A. § 1281(g)(2)(A); see § 4.10 below.

35. Environmental Protection Agency, Evaluation of Land Application Systems, Mar. 1975; see 6 ELR 10063 (1976).

36. Section 208(b)(2)(K), 33 U.S.C.A. § 1288(b)(2)(K); see § 4.9 below.

37. 40 CFR § 131.400; see 39 Fed.Reg. 31500, app. N (1974) (proposing ground water monitoring in proposed regulations implementing section 106(e) which conditions grants for pollution control programs upon the establishment of a monitoring system).

38. See § 4.5 below; United States v. Armco Steel Corp., 333 F.Supp. 1073, 1 ELR 20517 (S.D.Tex.1971).

the storage and disposal of pesticides and pesticide containers.[39] Far more extensive authority is found in the Safe Drinking Water Act of 1974 which mandates federal regulations for state underground injection programs containing "minimum requirements" for preventing underground injection from endangering drinking water sources.[40] Underground injection, formally defined, means the subsurface emplacement of fluids by well injection.[41] The Safe Drinking Water Act was enacted by Congress with full appreciation of the weaknesses of FWPCA and with a purpose of extending federal authority over injection well sources of groundwater pollution.[42] The consequences of effective implementation will be mature state underground injection control programs, developed under federal auspices.[43]

Section 1424(e) of the Safe Drinking Water Act [44] addresses groundwater pollution in one further important particular by allowing the Administrator of EPA, on his own initiative or upon a citizen petition, to identify certain drinking water aquifers the pollution of which "would create a significant hazard to public health." An identification of one of these vulnerable aquifers leads to the interdiction of federal financial assistance for projects that may pollute the aquifer. Section 1424(e) presents a number of interpretive difficulties,[45] and even under the boldest of readings works no revolutionary changes in the prevailing law of underground water pollution.

39. 39 Fed.Reg. 36847 (1974), 40 CFR § 165.

40. 42 U.S.C.A. § 1421(b)(1).

41. Id. § 1421(d)(1).

42. Comm. on Interstate and Foreign Commerce, Safe Drinking Water Act, H.R.Rep.No.1185, 93d Cong., 2d Sess. 4 (1974). See id. at 29:

In requiring EPA to promulgate minimum requirements for effective State programs to prevent underground injection which endangers drinking water sources, the Committee intends to ratify EPA's policy on deep well injection. (See 39 Fed.Reg. 12922–3, April 9, 1974). This policy was first adopted by the Federal Water Quality Administration of the Department of the Interior on October 15, 1970. The policy opposes storage or disposal of contaminants by subsurface injection 'without strict control and clear demonstration that such wastes will not interfere with present or potential use of subsurface water supplies, contaminate interconnected surface waters or otherwise damage the environment.'

43. See 41 Fed.Reg. 36726, 36730 (1976), proposing 40 CFR pts. 35, 146 (grants for state underground water source protection programs; state underground injection control programs).

44. 42 U.S.C.A. § 1424(e).

45. Hemphill, Section 1424(e) of the Safe Drinking Water Act: An Effective Measure Against Groundwater Pollution?, 6 ELR 50121 (1976); Wheatley & Castaneda, Protection of Underground Drinking Water Supplies: The Gonzalez Amendment to the Safe Drinking Water Act, 8 St. Mary's L.J. 40 (1976). The Edwards Underground Reservoir, underlying San Antonio, Texas, was the first groundwater drinking water source designated under the Act. See 40 Fed.Reg. 38292 (1975).

§ 4.4 Coverage: Nonpoint Sources

The peripheral regulation of groundwater quality under the 1972 Amendments is due partially to the uncertain legal status of non-point sources which are major contributors to groundwater pollution.[1] A nonpoint source can be defined as any source of water pollution or pollutants not associated with a discrete conveyance. It includes run-off from fields, forest lands, mining, construction activity and salt water intrusion (the advancing inland of salt water into coastal aquifers because of reductions in fresh water quantity).[2] Non-point sources produce a wide variety of pollutants: sediments, minerals (including acid mine drainage and heavy metals), nutrients, pesticides, organic wastes (including livestock waste and crop debris), waste oils and thermal pollution.[3] Pollutant loads of suspended solids, nutrients and coliform bacteria from non-point sources far exceed those from point sources.[4]

It is an accurate supposition that non-point sources are exempted from the regulatory reach of the 1972 Amendments. Nonetheless, relevant law can be found in (1) the definition of point sources, (2) the study and planning provisions, and (3) related legislation.

a. *Definition of Point Sources*

Under the 1972 Amendments, the term "point source" means "any discernible, confined and discrete conveyance, including but not limited to any pipe, ditch, channel, tunnel, conduit, well, discrete fissure, container, rolling stock, concentrated animal feeding operation, or vessel or other floating craft, from which pollutants are or

---

1. The author is indebted for materials on nonpoint sources to Bach, Non-Point Source Water Pollution Control Under the Federal Water Pollution Control Act Amendments of 1972 (unpublished paper prepared for the Environmental Law Seminar, Georgetown U. Law Center, Spring 1974).

2. Technically, when sea water moves into coastal surface water it encroaches rather than intrudes. Environmental Protection Agency, Identification and Control of Pollution from Salt Water Intrusion 25 (1973) [hereinafter cited as EPA Salt Water Report].

3. An authoritative series of reports prepared by EPA pursuant to Section 304(e) of the Act, 33 U.S.C.A. § 1314 (e), include: EPA Salt Water Report, supra note 2; Environmental Protection Agency, Methods and Practices for Controlling Water Pollution from Agricultural Nonpoint Sources (1973); Environmental Protection Agency, Processes, Procedures and Methods to Control Pollution Resulting from Silvicultural Activities (1973); Environmental Protection Agency, Processes, Procedures and Methods to Control Pollution from Mining Activities (1973); Environmental Protection Agency, Processes, Procedures and Methods to Control Pollution Resulting from all Construction Activity (1973); Environmental Protection Agency, Ground Water Pollution from Subsurface Excavations (1973); Environmental Protection Agency, The Control of Pollution from Hydrographic Modifications, (1973). See also Environmental Protection Agency, Region X, Water Quality Protection Guide—Logging Roads (Draft Report, 1974).

4. National Commission on Water Quality, Staff Draft Report on Water Quality Analysis and Environmental Impact Assessment of Public Law 92–500, Jan. 1976, at IV–29.

may be discharged."[5] This is a broad definition containing at least one activity (concentrated animal feeding operation) traditionally viewed as a non-point source. Moreover, with concentration within a "discrete conveyance" being the litmus test, numerous other non-point sources are included incidentally. To mention a few examples,[6] runoff from an industrial site may be concentrated in a drain prior to discharge; sedimentation, pesticide residues and other pollutants from a farm may be collected in a ditch connected to a waterway; debris from a timber cutting operation may be gathered in a truck before being dumped into a stream. Subjecting nonpoint source pollution to point source requirements is by no means bad policy: concentrating the problem in "discrete conveyance" is a fairly reliable indicia of "controllability" which is the central aim of the legislation.

EPA officials were concerned that the definition of "point source" was so broad the agency "may be forced to establish standards and issue permits for every pipe or ditch through which run-off is discharged into navigable waters, even where monitoring, measurement, and control techniques necessary to make this system of regulation work may not exist."[7] To alleviate this administrative spectre, EPA regulations excluded from the permit requirements a number of difficult to control point sources[8] along with most discharges from agricultural and silvicultural activities without regard to whether they fell within the "point source" definition.[9] This administrative exception to the Act was given short shrift by Judge Flannery,[10] who decided correctly that the permit program covers each "point source" as defined by Congress not only major point sources, easily controlled point sources, or point sources in the traditional sense. The ruling imposes an enormous administrative task (perhaps requiring issuance of as many as 100,000 additional permits). Drawing lines between point and non-point sources and making other classifications is inevitable. The court explained:[11]

> [Plaintiff] does not contend that every farm ditch, water bar, or culvert on a logging road is properly meant to be a point source under the Act. Moreover, [plaintiff] points out that, while all sources which are eventually defined as point sources should be

---

5. Section 502(14), 33 U.S.C.A. § 1362 (14).

6. Some borrowed from Zener, The Federal Law of Water Pollution Control, in Environmental Law Institute, Federal Environmental Law 682, 766–67 (E. L. Dolgin & T. G. P. Guilbert eds. 1974).

7. Id. at 767.

8. See 40 CFR § 125.4(a)(f) (exempting, among others, effluent from properly functioning marine laundries and showers and uncontrolled discharges "composed entirely of storm runoff").

9. Id. § 125.4(j).

10. Natural Resources Defense Council, Inc. v. Train, 396 F.Supp. 1393, 5 ELR 20401 (D.D.C.1975).

11. 396 F.Supp. at 1401–02, 5 ELR at 20405. Compare § 4.13 below (discussing storm sewers).

regulated under an appropriate permit program, the Administrator would have wide latitude to rank categories and sub-categories of point sources of different importance and treat them differently within a permit program. He would also have substantial discretion to use administrative devices, such as area permits, to make EPA's burden manageable. Admittedly, some sources, such as irrigation return flows and storm sewers, might pose special difficulties. Nevertheless, such difficulties must not stand in the way of Congress' mandate that a comprehensive permit program covering all point sources be established.

It is clear that a nonpoint source escaping the broad definition of "point source" is immune from important features of the Act, notably section 402 creating the National Pollutant Discharge Elimination System. That section allows the Administrator to issue a permit for the "discharge of any pollutant." The key policy provision in the Act, section 301, uses identical language to declare unlawful "the discharge of any pollutant by any person" subject to the various permit provisions. The Amendments define "discharge of a pollutant" and "discharge of pollutants" to include "any addition of any pollutant to navigable waters *from any point source.*" [12] Add to this the fact that section 402 permits clearly anticipate "effluent limitations" which apply only to point sources,[13] and one is led to the conclusion that the no-discharge policy and its implementing mechanism, the permit program, are directed only at point sources. Nonpoint sources, if covered at all, would be reached by the Rivers and Harbors Act of 1899,[14] and other federal and state laws.

b. *The Study and Planning Provisions*

There is a textual, albeit exceeding literal,[15] argument that identifiable non-point sources must apply for permits under section 402. More importantly, the Amendments certainly cannot be read as encouraging non-point source pollution even if they do not expressly forbid it under section 301. The goal of "swimmable" water by 1983 presupposes control of both point and non-point sources. Section 101

---

12. Section 502(12), 33 U.S.C.A. § 1362(12) (emphasis added).

13. See Section 502(11), 33 U.S.C.A. § 1362(11).

14. See § 4.5 below.

15. The argument proceeds as follows: the conduct to which section 402 applies—"the discharge of *any* pollutants" (emphasis added) is not defined and can be read as embracing the discharge of all pollutants whether from point or nonpoint sources. This reading is strengthened by the statutory definition of "discharge" which "when used without qualification includes a discharge of a pollutant, and a discharge of pollutants" which are limited to point sources. Section 502(16), 33 U.S.C.A. § 1362(16). Presumably, when used with a qualifier—for example, "the discharge of any pollutant"—a discharge could apply also to non-point sources. Requiring a permit for non-point sources was well enough accepted to be required in some cases under the Rivers & Harbors Act of 1899. See § 4.5 below.

(a)(5) [16] is quite clear that all sources be held accountable albeit under the planning provisions: "It is the national policy that areawide waste treatment management planning processes be developed and implemented to assure adequate control of sources of pollutants in each State."

The planning provisions of the Act [17] address non-point sources in several particulars. To gain approval under the Act, areawide waste treatment management plans must contain processes to identify and control a number of non-point source pollution problems.[18] EPA's decision to de-emphasize section 208 plans [19] perforce de-emphasizes non-point source controls. The *Water Strategy Paper* [20] says that a state's general responsibility "through its 303(e) planning process and 106 reports [21] [is to] develop a profile of its particular [nonpoint source] problems, and prepare an assessment of what it feels to be the most effective mix of available prevention and control techniques for its particular set of [nonpoint source] problems." This is a somewhat milder prescription than the statutory obligation of section 305(b)(1)(E) [22] which requires (beginning on January 1, 1975 and annually thereafter) a water quality report from each state to the Administrator containing, among other things, "a description

---

16. 33 U.S.C.A. § 1251(a)(5).

17. See § 4.9 below.

18. Sections 208(b)(2)(F)–(K), 33 U.S.C.A. §§ 1288(b)(2)(F)–(K), require a plan to include:
    (F) a process to (i) identify, if appropriate, agriculturally and silviculturally related nonpoint sources of pollution, including runoff from manure disposal areas, and from land used for livestock and crop production, and (ii) set forth procedures and methods (including land use requirements) to control to the extent feasible such sources;
    (G) a process to (i) identify, if appropriate, mine-related sources of pollution including new, current, and abandoned surface and underground mine runoff, and (ii) set forth procedures and methods (including land use requirements) to control to the extent feasible such sources;
    (H) a process to (i) identify construction activity related sources of pollution, and (ii) set forth procedures and methods (including land use requirements) to control to the extent feasible such sources;
    (I) a process to (i) identify, if appropriate, salt water intrusion into rivers, lakes and estuaries resulting from reduction of fresh water flow from any cause, including irrigation, obstruction, ground water extraction and diversion, and (ii) set forth procedures and methods to control such intrusion to the extent feasible where such procedures and methods are otherwise a part of the waste treatment management plan;
    (J) a process to control the disposition of all residual waste generated in such area which could affect water quality; and
    (K) a process to control the disposal of pollutants on land or in subsurface excavations within such area to protect ground and surface water quality.

19. EPA's Water Strategy Paper concedes "non-point source activities will not be oriented at first towards aggressive control and enforcement." Rev. ed. Apr. 30, 1973, at 21.

20. Ibid (footnote added).

21. Federal grants for state pollution control programs are conditioned upon compliance with various reporting requirements of section 106, 33 U.S.C.A. § 1256.

22. 33 U.S.C.A. § 1315(b)(1)(E).

of the nature and extent of non-point sources of pollutants, and recommendations as to the programs which must be undertaken to control each category of such sources, including an estimate of the costs of implementing such programs." The continuing planning process for each state which must be approved by the Administrator under section 303(e) [23] should incorporate "all elements of any applicable areawide waste management plans under section 208 [including of course the non-point source provisions]" but this is dependent upon a 208 plan being in existence. The safest conclusion to draw is that the planning provisions address non-point sources in various ways but that little can be expected in the near future in the form of law to be applied and enforced.

c. *Related Federal and State Law*

With non-point sources effectively excluded from the coverage of FWPCA, one looks elsewhere for the important regimes. They are found scattered throughout the federal statutes at large and, more importantly, in the laws of the states. One computer search of pertinent federal legislation [24] identifies numerous federal statutes affecting activities contributing significantly to nonpoint source water pollution—construction (4), mining (4), silvicultural (14), agricultural (4), soil erosion and sedimentation control (8), and flood plain regulation (3).

In the forefront of any analysis of nonpoint source pollution is the role of the federal government as manager of approximately one-third of the U. S. land area constituting the federal lands.[25] The federal government is intimately involved in a wide range of activities including the development of energy sources on federal lands (oil shale, coal, uranium and geothermal sources [26]) as well as a number of other practices (grazing, silvicultural, construction of roads, railroads and airports, siting of landfills) that can lead to water pollution problems. The National Environmental Policy Act applies to most major activities on federal lands sanctioned by the federal government,[27] and nonpoint source water pollution is likely to be a serious subject of analysis.[28] But NEPA is decidedly nonregulatory, which

23. Id. § 1313(e).

24. Environmental Protection Agency, Compilation of Federal, State and Local Laws Controlling Nonpoint Pollutants (1975) [hereinafter cited as Nonpoint Pollutant Study].

25. Public Land Law Review Commission, One Third of the Nation's Land (1970); see Muys, The Federal Lands, in Environmental Law Institute, Federal Environmental Law 492 (E. L. Dolgin & T. G. P. Guilbert eds. 1974).

26. Stoel, Energy, in Environmental Law Institute, Federal Environmental Law 928 (E. L. Dolgin & T. G. P. Guilbert eds. 1974).

27. § 7.6 below. NEPA does not apply to non-discretionary conveyances of title to persons qualifying under the General Mining Act of 1872. United States v. Kosanke Land Corp., 12 IBLA 282, 3 ELR 30017 (Dep't Inter. Bd. of Land App.1973) (en banc).

28. Natural Resources Defense Council, Inc. v. Morton, 388 F.Supp. 829,

means as a practical matter that a large measure of the control of water pollution from activities on federal lands must be found elsewhere in various regulations,[29] permit and lease conditions, and particularly in the enthusiasm with which they are enforced.[30]

i. *Construction*

Construction activities use up more than a million acres a year in the United States, creating in the process significant run-off pollution problems.[31] The prescription for effective controls (avoiding environmentally sensitive areas, trapping sediment on site, stabilizing exposed soil by timely grading and seeding) calls for a detailed supervision unlikely to materialize. The principal federal presence on construction and other non-point source pollution problems is the Rivers and Harbors Act of 1899, whose chief contemporary significance is its use by U. S. Attorneys against gross forms of non-point source water pollution.[32] Federally financed highway and airport projects must proceed in accordance with water pollution criteria although post-approval conduct is neither regulated nor penalized.[33]

Construction activities of every conceivable type are regulated extensively at the state and local level—through subdivision laws, dredge and fill statutes, regulation of dam and road construction, excavation, grading and earthwork.[34] Several states have statutes comparable to that of the State of Washington, which requires the submission of plans and the written approval of the directors of the fisheries and game departments for any construction that will use or change the natural flow or bed of any river or stream in the state.[35] The submission to a department must provide "complete plans and specifications for the proper protection of fish life," and the respective directors must approve "the adequacy of the means outlined for

5 ELR 20327 (D.D.C.1974) (Bureau of Land Management's grazing program).

29. E. g., 7 CFR pt. 622 (Soil Conservation Service) (watershed project); 30 CFR pt. 211, as amended, 41 Fed.Reg. 20252 (May 17, 1976) (Geological Survey) (coalmining operations); 36 CFR pt. 252 (Forest Service) (exploration and mining operations); 43 CFR pt. 23, as amended, 41 Fed.Reg. 20252 (May 17, 1976) (Dep't of Interior) (surface exploration, mining and reclamation); 41 Fed.Reg. 20252 (May 17, 1976), adding 43 CFR pt. 3041 (BLM) (surface management of federal coal leases).

30. Comptroller General, Report on Administration of Regulations for Surface Exploration, Mining and Reclamation of Public and Indian Coal Lands to the House Conservation and Natural Resources Subcommittee, Aug. 10, 1972; Comptroller General, Report on Improvements Needed in Administration of Federal Coal-Leasing Program to the House Conservation and Natural Resources Subcommittee, Mar. 29, 1972.

31. Nonpoint Pollutant Study, supra note 24, at 82.

32. See § 4.5 below.

33. Nonpoint Pollutant Study, supra note 24, at 30–31.

34. Id. at 82–122.

35. Rev.Code Wash.Ann. § 75.20.100. An amendment in 1975 makes allowance for oral approval in certain emergency conditions provided the oral approval is reduced to writing within 30 days.

the protection of fish life" prior to the commencement of construction.[36] Construction without a permit or in violation of the terms of a permit is a gross misdemeanor. Continued work on a project after a conviction subjects it to abatement as a public nuisance.[37]

The Washington statute and comparable laws afford extensive powers over virtually all construction and other activities (i. e., gravel removal, channelization, and so on) affecting the integrity of a stream bed. It goes without saying that the enormity of the charge and the awkwardness of enforcement through the criminal law leaves a considerable gap between the promise of the statute and its performance. In Washington State, for example, construction and similar activities in and around stream beds has led not only to serious nonpoint source pollution problems but to radical changes in stream flows, diminution of fish life productivity and the virtual eradication of many natural stream beds.[38]

ii. *Mining*

Mining is an activity that has polluted thousands of miles of streams in Appalachia with acid drainage [39] and has caused other severe water quality problems.[40] Among the many federal statutes affecting mining activities,[41] the 1973 amendments [42] to Section 28 of the Mineral Leasing Act are perhaps the most noteworthy. The Secretary of Interior is obliged, for any new project that may have "a significant impact on the environment," to require the applicant "to submit a plan of construction, operation, and rehabilitation" in connection with any right-of-way or permit. Governing regulations must include "requirements for restoration, revegetation and curtailment of erosion of the surface of the land," among others.[43]

The regulation of surface mining and water pollution problems associated with it is the subject of legislation in nearly 30 states [44]

36. Ibid.

37. Ibid.

38. See Washington Dep't of Fisheries, A Catalogue of Washington Streams and Salmon Utilization (1975) (2 vols.).

39. Center for Science in the Public Interest, The Stripping of Appalachia 45–56 (1972). See generally H. M. Caudill, Night Comes to the Cumberlands (1962).

40. See, e. g., Hearings on Adverse Effects of Coal Mining on Federal Reservoir Projects, Before the Subcomm. on Conservation and Natural Resources of the House Comm. on Government Operations, 93d Cong., 1st Sess. (1973).

41. See, e. g., Muys, supra note 25, at 523–27; Dempsey, Forest Service Regulations Concerning the Effect of Mining Operations on Surface Resources, 8 Nat.Res.L. 481 (1975); Haggard, Regulation of Mining Law Activities on Federal Lands, 21 Rocky Mt.Min.L.Inst. 349 (1976).

42. Pub.L. No. 93–153, 87 Stat. 576 (1973).

43. 30 U.S.C.A. § 185.

44. Comm. on Interior & Insular Affairs, Surface Mining Control and Reclamation Act of 1975, H.R.Rep. No. 45, 94th Cong., 1st Sess. (1975). Many of the state statutes are the subject of separate analysis. E. g., Cardi, Strip Mining and the 1971 West Vir-

and was defeated at the federal level in 1975 only by a presidential veto.[45] The basic statutory scheme "is the same for all states. A strip mine operator must obtain a license, usually good for one year. In addition, each stripping operation requires a separate permit and the posting of a bond (frequently $2000) and a flexible amount per acre, such as between $100 and $500. The actual amount of the bond will be determined by the appropriate regulatory commission taking into consideration the difficulty of reclamation. If the operator fails to perform the prescribed reclamation steps, such as backfilling, the bond will be forfeited and the permit suspended. In addition, the operator may be liable to the state for the actual cost of reclamation. The revocation of a permit can result in the automatic denial of future permit applications until past violations have been rectified. The agencies may delete areas sought in the permit application. Some statutes provide that permit fees, bond forfeitures and special fees will go into a special fund which will be used to reclaim past stripped lands."[46] The permit-bonding approach usually involves the imposition of a number of procedural and substantive requirements, either as permit conditions or regulations independently imposed—obligations to provide maps, drainage plans, soil and vegetation surveys, test boring results, provisions to restore land to its original contour, segregate top soil, cover acid producing materials, establish vegetation to prevent soil erosion. Some states impose slope limitations on contour mining; others rule out certain areas as unsuitable for strip-mining.[47] The wisdom of outright prohibitions against certain types

ginia Surface Mining and Reclamation Act, 75 W.Va.L.Rev. 319 (1973); Dietrich, Mined Land Reclamation in the Western United States, 16 Rocky Mt.Min.L.Inst. 143 (1971); Gwynn, Mined Land Reclamation in Montana, 7 Nat.Res.L. 27 (1974); Hagen, North Dakota's Surface Mining and Reclamation Law: Will Our Wealth Make Us Poor? 50 N.Dak.L.Rev. 437 (1974); Schneider, Strip Mining in Kentucky, 59 Ky.L.J. 652 (1972); Comment, South Dakota's Coal and the 1971 Surface Mining Land Reclamation Act, 21 S.Dak.L.Rev. 351 (1976); Note, Land Quality: The Regulation of Surface Mining Reclamation in Wyoming, 9 Land & Water L.Rev. 97 (1974); Note, New Surface Mining in Wisconsin, 1973 Wis.L.Rev. 234; Note, Regulation of Open Cut Mining in Wyoming, 5 Land & Water L.Rev. 449 (1970); Note, Regulation of Strip Mining in Alabama, 23 Ala.L.Rev. 420 (1971); Note, Strip Mine Reclamation Regulation, 39 Mo.L.Rev. 429 (1974); see Note, Local Zoning of Strip Mining, 57 Ky.L.J. 738 (1969). For a summary of the state statutes, see National Academy of Sciences, Rehabilitation Potential of Western Coal Lands app. B (1974).

45. See Dunlap, Analysis of the Legislative History of the Surface Mining Control and Reclamation Act of 1975, 21 Rocky Mt.Min.L.Inst. 11 (1976) (authored by an environmental lobbyist who has worked for passage of federal legislation for several years). See also Hearings on the President's Veto of H.R. 25, Before the Subcomm. on Energy and the Environment of the House Comm. on Interior & Insular Affairs, H.R.Doc. No. 23, 94th Cong., 1st Sess. (1975).

46. Binder, A Novel Approach to Reasonable Regulation of Strip Mining, 34 U.Pitt.L.Rev. 339, 351–52 (1973) (footnotes omitted).

47. See generally A. J. Fritsch, The Enforcement of Strip Mining Laws in Three Appalachian States: Kentucky, West Virginia, and Pennsylvania (CSPI, 1975); Surface Mining Conservation and Reclamation Act,

of mining is an issue that has been debated nationally for many years.[48] As with most nonpoint source water pollution, the principal problem is enforcement. Ohio permits a citizen mandamus action to enforce compliance.[49] In Pennsylvania, mine drainage is treated like point source pollution and is brought under coverage of the permit program.[50]

iii. *Silvicultural*

Commercial timber activities, like mining, occur both on privately and publicly owned lands which complicates the legal situation (perhaps 20 per cent of commercial forests are federally owned [51]). Harvesting practices result in soil sedimentation with an inevitable impact on water resources. Clearcutting (removal of substantially all of the trees in an area) generally accelerates erosion and sedimentation. Yarding operations (where trees are collected after being felled) and roadbuilding also have polluting consequences.[52] The legal picture at the federal level involves consideration of the virtually standardless principles of multiple use and sustained yield and the tight specifics of the National Forest Organic Act of 1897, which has been read as an effective prohibition against clearcutting.[53] A key to the legal role of the federal government is the form timber sales contract, used by the Forest Service and the Bureau of Land Manage-

in 33 Council of State Governments, Suggested State Legislation 22 (1974).

48. See, e. g., Hearings on Surface Mining (S. 77), Before the Subcomm. on Minerals, Materials and Fuels of the Senate Comm. on Interior & Insular Affairs, S.Doc. No. 13, 92d Cong., 1st Sess. (1972); Hearings on Regulation of Surface Mining (H.R. 3), Before the Subcomm. on Environment of the House Comm. on Interior & Insular Affairs, H.R.Doc. No. 11, 93d Cong., 1st Sess. (1973); Hearings on Regulation of Surface Mining Operations (S. 425), Before the Senate Comm. on Interior & Insular Affairs, 93d Cong., 1st Sess. (1973); Hearings on Federal Coal Leasing Program, Before the Subcomm. on Minerals, Materials and Fuel of the Senate Comm. on Interior & Insular Affairs, 93d Cong., 2d Sess. (1974); Hearings on Federal Coal Leasing, Before the Subcomm. on Mines & Mining of the House Comm. on Interior & Insular Affairs, H.R.Doc. No. 63, 93d Cong., 2d Sess. (1974). See also Senate Comm. on Interior & Insular Affairs, The Issues Related to Surface Mining, S.Doc. No. 10, 92d Cong., 1st Sess. (Comm. Print 1971); J. Stacks, Stripping: The Surface Mining of America (1972); Beverly, Development and Legislation of Environmental Regulations for Mining, 15 Rocky Mt.Min.L. Inst. 163 (1969); Bosselman, Control of Surface Mining: An Exercise in Creative Federalism, 9 Nat.Res.L. 138 (1969). Compare § 2.17 above (discussing the taking issue).

49. Ohio Rev.Code § 1513.15(B). Compare §§ 1.13 (citizen suits), 2.16 (public trust) above.

50. See Commonwealth v. Barnes & Tucker Co., 455 Pa. 392, 319 A.2d 871, 4 ELR 20545 (1974).

51. Nonpoint Pollutant Study, supra note 24, at 171–73.

52. See Stone, The Impact of Timber Harvest on Soils and Water, in Report of the President's Advisory Panel on Timber and the Environment app. M, at 427–67 (1973).

53. § 7.12 below; see, e. g., Sierra Club v. Dep't of Interior, 398 F.Supp. 284, 5 ELR 20514 (N.D.Cal.1975). The 1897 Act was repealed by the National Forest Management Act of 1976, Pub. L. No. 94–588, § 13, 90 Stat. 2958.

ment, which contains a number of provisions aimed at preventing erosion and protecting water quality and other environmental values.[54]

State regulation of logging practices typically involves an assignment to an administrative authority of the power to prescribe standards for forest practices.[55] The practices regulated, with a view to protecting soil and water resources, include harvesting, road construction, reforestation, the use of chemicals and fertilizers, slash disposal and other activities. It is possible to control certain practices strictly—partially or selectively banning clearcutting,[56] forbidding certain activities in stream beds, requiring buffer zones around water resources. The preference, however, in the tradition of contemporary administrative law, is for few stringent prohibitions and many vaguely worded and unenforceable reminders.[57] Enforcement is frustrated not only by the lack of firm rules and a scarcity of inspectors but in several states by flagrant conflicts of interest within rulemaking authorities,[58] which for the most part have gone out of style with respect to the regulation of point source pollution.[59]

iv. *Agricultural*

Recent agricultural activity in the United States is characterized "by rapid development of modern technology including widespread use of synthetic fertilizers, chemical pesticides, complex irrigation systems and confined animal feeding areas." [60] These practices cause widespread pollution by sediments, pesticides and pathogens. A Soil Conservation Survey study in 1971 estimated that cropland is responsible for 50% of the total sediment contaminating U. S. inland waterways, and half of this reaches the oceans carrying with it a wide range of organic and inorganic contaminants.[61] Federal erosion control efforts go back to the mid-1930's,[62] and provide financial assistance for a wide range of projects—terracing, stripcropping, contouring.[63] The

54. G. O. Robinson, The Forest Service 72–74 (1975).

55. See, e. g., Or.Rev.Stat. §§ 527.610 et seq; Nonpoint Pollutant Study, supra note 24, at 176–97; Comment, Regulation of Private Logging in California, 5 Ecol.L.Q. 139 (1975).

56. See Nev.Rev.Stat. § 528.050.

57. See Comment, supra note 55, at 179–85. See also D. Barney, The Last Stand (1974); Wood, Clearcut: The Deforestation of America (1972); Bassman, 1897 Organic Act: A Historical Perspective, 7 Nat.Res.L. 503 (1974).

58. See Bayside Timber Co. v. Bd. of Supervisors of San Mateo County, 20 Cal.App.3d 1, 97 Cal.Rptr. 431, 1 ELR 20425 (1st Dist. 1971) (invalidating on delegation grounds the assignment of rulemaking powers to interested members of the timber industry). Many state regulatory schemes follow this pattern.

59. E. g., 33 U.S.C.A. § 1314(h)(2)(D) (personnel qualifications for state NPDES authorities).

60. Nonpoint Pollutant Study, supra note 24, at 56.

61. Ibid.

62. See Act of Apr. 27, 1935, 49 Stat. 163, 16 U.S.C.A. § 590a et seq. (establishing the Soil Conservation Service).

63. 7 CFR §§ 701.73(a), 701.71(b); see Nonpoint Pollutant Study, supra note 24, at 44–49.

Rural Development Act of 1972 expanded the scope of eligible projects to include those for the "prevention and abatement of agricultural related pollution."[64] For many years, the Department of Agriculture's Rural Environmental Assistance Program (now the Agricultural Conservation Program) has been a controversial and important contributor to the control of non-point sources of pollution.[65] Noteworthy also is a recent amendment to the Flood Control Act of 1944 allowing expenditures for the prevention of erosion and sediment damages.[66]

At the state level, provisions to combat agricultural pollution take many forms—soil erosion statutes,[67] grazing,[68] pesticide[69] and fertilizer[70] use laws, the creation of districts to combat erosion caused by wind.[71] Many states provide for the establishment of soil conservation districts under various names, and the powers of several of these have been expanded from planning and education to embrace the adoption and enforcement of land use regulations.[72] These regulations "may specify completion of necessary engineering projects, the observance of particular methods of cultivation including contour cultivating, stripseeding and the planting [of] water conserving plants."[73] They may address cropping programs and the protection of lands exposed by grading, filling, clearing, mineral extraction and other activities.[74] Regulations in Wisconsin, for example, may limit the "size of the area to be exposed, the length of time in season during which it may be exposed," and may require "the establishment of temporary waterways, storm drains, temporary debris basins, terraces and other structural and nonstructural methods to control erosion, runoff and sedimentation."[75]

64. Pub.L. No. 92–419, § 606(a), 86 Stat. 676, amending The Soil Conservation and Domestic Allotment Act, 16 U.S.C.A. § 590g(a).

65. Comptroller General, Report to the Congress: Greater Conservation Benefits Could be Attained Under the Rural Environmental Assistance Program (1972).

66. Department of the Army and Related Agencies Appropriation Act § 101, Pub.L. No. 91–566, 84 Stat. 1484 (1972), amending 33 U.S.C.A. § 701f–3.

67. E. g., Michigan Soil Erosion and Sedimentation Control Act of 1972, Mich.Comp.Laws § 282.101 et seq.; North Carolina Sedimentation Pollution Control Act of 1973, Gen.Stat. of N.C. §§ 113A–50 to –66; see Model State Act for Soil Erosion and Sediment Control, in 32 Council of State Governments, Suggested State Legislation 11 (1973).

68. N.D.Cent.Code §§ 36–08–01 to –09.

69. Ch. 8 below.

70. See, e. g., Ala.Code tit. 2, § 337(9a) et seq.; Ariz.Rev.Stat. § 3–371 et seq.; Colo.Rev.Stat. § 6–12–1 et seq.

71. Tex.Rev.Civ.Stat. arts. 165a–2, 165a–3.

72. See Nonpoint Pollutant Study, supra note 24, at 59–61. Compare § 2.17 above (on land development control).

73. Nonpoint Pollutant Study, supra note 24, at 61.

74. Ibid.

75. Wis.Stat.Ann. § 92.09(5)(f).

Other ideas have been advanced to combat nonpoint source agricultural pollution—the use of a state environmental policy act to resist nitrate pollution of well water,[76] and legislatively imposed restrictions on combined totals of nitrogen and phosphorus applied per acre in the form of fertilizer and animal wastes.[77] The intractability of the problems and incompleteness of solutions attest to the singular difficulty of controlling nonpoint source pollution. It resists the decisive technological fix and is dependent upon the cooperative good will of many or an army of enforcers that society will not tolerate.[78] It is beset by many of the features of the tragedy of the commons where temperance is not worth the effort for the individual and where the cumulation of individual choices is environmentally unacceptable.[79]

One final reference on the subject of nonpoint sources of water pollution is that of flood plain regulation and flood control. Soil erosion and flooding "are two phenomena closely intertwined. Flooding may be a direct result of erosion, while conversely, one of the effects of the inundation of any land by flood waters is soil erosion on a large scale."[80] It is also true that many of the traditional structural means of combatting flooding (massive dams, channelization and the like) themselves have created water quality and land use ills, in some cases encouraging a buildup in areas that could not be adequately protected. The Flood Disaster Protection Act of 1973,[81] addressed principally to flood insurance, also calls for the conditioning of federal reconstruction funds to states and localities upon the adoption of adequate "flood plain ordinances."[82] This represents a recognition that sometimes adjustments must be made to the demands of nature in the form of land use accommodation rather than an insistence that nature yield to structural contrivances.

The fact remains that nonpoint sources of water pollution are hard to quantify, hard to identify and hard to control. Their impact is so pervasive that they often provide a substantial argument that controlling point sources is equally futile.[83] The law, if and when it appears, is erratically applied and mostly ineffective.

---

76. Comment, Nitrate Pollution and the California Environmental Quality Act: The Appropriate Solution to a Neglected Problem, 12 Cal.W.L.Rev. 122 (1975); see § 7.11 below (discussing state environmental policy acts).

77. Note, Draft Proposal for Legislation to Control Water Pollution From Agricultural Sources, 59 Cornell L. Rev. 1097 (1974).

78. Compare § 3.8 above (discussing the debate between operational and source controls in the context of air pollution).

79. Hardin, The Tragedy of the Commons, 162 Science 1243 (1968).

80. Nonpoint Pollutant Study, supra note 24, at 51.

81. 42 U.S.C.A. §§ 4001–03.

82. Id. § 4002(b).

83. See D. Zwick, Water Wasteland 92–115 (1971).

§ 4.5 Rivers and Harbors Appropriation Act of 1899

Nonpoint sources of water pollution today are influenced importantly by the humble specifics of a nineteenth century statute [1] that is almost an insult to the sophisticated wastes of modern technology. It has served nonetheless as a remarkably flexible deterrent to water pollution of every conceivable manner, shape and form. Section 13 of the Rivers and Harbors Act of 1899 in primitive absolutes flatly prohibits discharging from a ship or shore installation into navigable waters of the United States or their tributaries "any refuse matter of any kind or description whatever other than that flowing from streets and sewers and passing therefrom in a liquid state." [2] This section also forbids depositing "material of any kind in any place on the bank of any navigable water . . . where the same shall be liable to be washed into such navigable water . . . whereby navigation shall or may be impeded or obstructed." Section 10 of the Act prohibits "the creation of any obstruction not affirmatively authorized by Congress, to the navigable capacity of any of the waters of the United States," except upon approval of the Secretary of the Army.[3]

---

1. 30 Stat. 1151 (1899).

2. 33 U.S.C.A. § 407, reads:

   That it shall not be lawful to throw, discharge, or deposit, or cause, suffer, or procure to be thrown, discharged, or deposited either from or out of any ship, barge, or other floating craft of any kind, or from the shore, wharf, manufacturing establishment, or mill of any kind, any refuse matter of any kind or description whatever other than that flowing from streets and sewers and passing therefrom in a liquid state, into any navigable water of the United States, or into any tributary of any navigable water from which the same shall float or be washed into such navigable water; and it shall not be lawful to deposit, or cause, suffer, or procure to be deposited material of any kind in any place on the bank of any navigable water, or on the bank of any tributary of any navigable water, where the same shall be liable to be washed into such navigable water, either by ordinary or high tides, or by storms or floods, or otherwise, whereby navigation shall or may be impeded or obstructed: Provided, That nothing herein contained shall extend to, apply to, or prohibit the operations in connection with the improvement of navigable waters or construction of public works, considered necessary and proper by the United States officers supervising such improvement or public work: And provided further, That the Secretary of War, whenever in the judgment of the Chief of Engineers anchorage and navigation will not be injured thereby, may permit the deposit of any material above mentioned in navigable waters, within limits to be defined and under conditions to be prescribed by him, provided application is made to him prior to depositing such material; and whenever any permit is so granted the conditions thereof shall be strictly complied with, and any violation thereof shall be unlawful.

3. Id. § 403, reads:

   That the creation of any obstruction not affirmatively authorized by Congress, to the navigable capacity of any of the waters of the United States is hereby prohibited; and it shall not be lawful to build or commence the building of any wharf, pier, dolphin, boom, weir, breakwater, bulkhead, jetty, or other structures in any port, roadstead, haven, harbor, canal, navigable river, or other water of the United States, outside establish-

Section 13 dealing with discharges and section 10 with obstructions often are invoked in the same litigation where construction activity both pollutes the water and interferes with navigation. Section 10 is a powerful instrument of land use control and will be addressed in the section on dredge and fill disposal.[4] Section 13 is basically an anti-pollution statute and is considered here in the context of the 1972 Amendments. The no discharge premise of section 13 is accepted fully by Section 301(a) of the FWPCA, which makes unlawful the discharge "of any pollutant by any person" unless otherwise approved under the Act. Commonly, U. S. Attorneys jointly plead sections 13 and 301 in pollution cases.

Before turning to the question of how the 1899 Act meshes with the 1972 Amendments, it may be useful to sketch the parameters of section 13. To be addressed are (1) the meaning of refuse; (2) the navigable waters requirement; (3) the sewage exception; (4) culpability; (5) remedies, both private and public; (6) contemporaneous significance involving principally nonpoint sources.

a. *The Meaning of Refuse*

Section 13's pivotal prohibition against depositing "any refuse matter of any kind or description whatever" into navigable waters should be read as precluding any man-induced alteration of natural water quality.[5] This is more than a comprehensive ban against all deposits that injure, obstruct or offend. It is an absolutist insistence that natural water quality be used as a baseline of acceptability.[6] While the plain meaning of "any refuse matter of any kind or description whatever" supports a broad anti-pollution potential, the legislative history might have justified confining section 13 to deposits that obstructed navigation.[7] But the evolution of the section[8] has banished limiting interpretations and solidified its stark mandate. The key decision is United States v. Standard Oil Co.,[9] where the Supreme Court refused to limit the word "refuse" to substances lacking

ed harbor lines, or where no harbor lines have been established, except on plans recommended by the Chief of Engineers and authorized by the Secretary of War; and it shall not be lawful to excavate or fill, or in any manner to alter or modify the course, location, condition, or capacity of, any port, roadstead, haven, harbor, canal, lake, harbor of refuge, or inclosure within the limits of any breakwater, or of the channel of any navigable water of the United States, unless the work has been recommended by the Chief of Engineers and authorized by the Secretary of War prior to beginning the same.

4. See § 4.6 below.

5. See Section 502(19), 33 U.S.C.A. § 1362(19) (defining pollution).

6. Compare § 2.15 above (discussing the natural flow theory of riparian rights).

7. See Druly, The Refuse Act of 1899, 2 Env.Rep.—Monograph No. 11, at 2–3 (1972).

8. Explained admirably for classroom purposes in J. L. Mashaw & R. A. Merrill, Introduction to the American Public Law System: Cases and Materials ch. 1 (1975).

9. 384 U.S. 224, 86 S.Ct. 1427, 16 L.Ed.2d 492 (1966).

a predischarge value and sustained a conviction for accidentally discharging valuable aviation gasoline into the St. John's River. "Oil is oil," reasoned Mr. Justice Douglas for the majority, "and whether useable or not by industrial standards it has the same deleterious effect on waterways." [10] That many environmental contaminants could be doing valuable service elsewhere did not prevent their condemnation as "refuse" when deposited in the water. The dissenters would have confined section 13 to deposits of obstructing refuse matter. Otherwise, observed Mr. Justice Harlan with alarm and insight, "dropping anything but pure water into a river would appear to be a federal misdemeanor." [11]

Before and after *Standard Oil*, judicial decisions have swept aside narrow interpretations of section 13: refuse is "refuse" even though it may be non-obstructing,[12] compatible with water quality standards,[13] consisting of substances found naturally in the water [14] or otherwise harmless.[15] Virtually every conceivable form of pollutant has been condemned, at one time or another, under section 13: discharges of heated water,[16] a wide variety of industrial chemicals,[17] oil,[18] peeled bark, leaching and sunken logs,[19] sedimentation from a stream chan-

10. 384 U.S. at 226, 86 S.Ct. at 1428, 16 L.Ed.2d at 494.

11. 384 U.S. at 234, 86 S.Ct. at 1432, 16 L.Ed.2d at 499.

12. E. g., United States v. Pennsylvania Indus. Chem. Corp., 411 U.S. 655, 93 S.Ct. 1804, 36 L.Ed.2d 567 (1973); United States v. Consolidation Coal Co., 354 F.Supp. 173, 3 ELR 20425 (N.D.W.Va.1973).

13. E. g., United States v. Pennsylvania Indus. Chem. Corp., supra note 12; United States v. United States Steel Corp., 482 F.2d 439, 3 ELR 20389 (7th Cir. 1973), cert. denied 414 U.S. 909.

14. United States v. Hercules, 335 F. Supp. 102, 2 ELR 20097 (D.C.Kan. 1971) (ammonia).

15. See United States v. Pennsylvania Indus. Chem. Corp., 329 F.Supp. 1118, 1122, 1 ELR 20364, 20365 (W.D.Pa. 1971), rev'd on other grounds 461 F.2d 468, 2 ELR 20264 (3d Cir. 1972), modified 411 U.S. 655, 93 S.Ct. 1804, 36 L.Ed.2d 567 (1973). But cf. United States v. Kennebec Log Driving Co., 491 F.2d 562, 570, 4 ELR 20047, 20051 (1st Cir. 1973) cert. denied 417 U.S. 910 (1974) (finding that peeled bark and sunken logs are refuse matter within the meaning of section 13 but remanding for a determination "whether there are certain deposits of material into navigable waters so intimately related to the actual conduct of navigation by water that despite the facial applicability of the statute it could not have been within the contemplation of Congress that it apply in such instances"). On remand, see 399 F.Supp. 754 (D.Me. 1975), aff'd 530 F.2d 446 (1st Cir. 1976).

16. Cf. United States v. Florida Power & Light Co., 311 F.Supp. 1391 (S.D.Fla.1971).

17. E. g., United States v. Dexter Corp., 507 F.2d 1038, 5 ELR 20041 (7th Cir. 1974) (phenolic resin); United States v. American Cyanamid Co., 480 F.2d 1132, 3 ELR 20656 (2d Cir. 1973) (titanium dioxide and calcium carbonate).

18. United States v. White Fuel Corp., 498 F.2d 619, 4 ELR 20531 (1st Cir. 1974).

19. United States v. Kennebec Log Driving Co., 491 F.2d 562, 4 ELR 20047 (1st Cir. 1973), cert. denied 417 U.S. 910 (1974).

nelization project,[20] overflowing settling ponds,[21] dumping of fill,[22] storm-washed debris,[23] depositing loose timber on the bank of a river above the high water mark where it might be washed into the stream,[24] the dumping of dredge spoils,[25] erosion,[26] the collapse or "blow out" of dredge spoil dikes,[27] residue from a strip mine operation,[28] the dumping of fuel matter, sludge, black oil, tar,[29] and grain residues.[30] The phrase "refuse matter of any kind or description whatever" is as broad in connotation as the word "pollutant" under the 1972 Amendments and reaches any changes in natural water quality brought about by the activities of man.[31]

b. *The Navigable Waters Requirement*

Section 13 forbids discharges "into any navigable water of the United States, or into any tributary of any navigable water from which the same shall float or be washed into such navigable water . . . ." Although this retains the navigable waters limitation abandoned in the 1972 Amendments,[32] it does not seriously compromise coverage. Navigable waters extend out as far as the three mile limit[33] and in as far as the smallest tributary. The test of navigability is whether the watercourse could be used for commerce, not whether it is used, and this inquiry extends to "the distant past and the extended future."[34] Under this test section 13 has been applied

20. Natural Resources Defense Council, Inc., v. Grant, 355 F.Supp. 280, 3 ELR 20176 (E.D.N.C.1973).

21. United States v. Kentland-Elkhorn Coal Corp., 353 F.Supp. 451, 3 ELR 20453 (E.D.Ky.1973) (refusing preliminary injunction, however).

22. United States v. Lewis, 355 F.Supp. 1132, 3 ELR 20500 (S.D.Ga.1973).

23. Ibid.

24. See 355 F.Supp. at 1137–38 n. 6, 3 ELR at 20502 n. 6.

25. E. g., United States v. Stoeco Homes, 359 F.Supp. 672, 3 ELR 20722 (D.N.J.1973), rev'd on other grounds 498 F.2d 597, 4 ELR 20390 (3d Cir. 1974), cert. denied 420 U.S. 927 (1975).

26. Ibid.

27. Ibid.

28. United States v. Bigan, 170 F.Supp. 219 (W.D.Pa.1959), aff'd 274 F.2d 729 (3d Cir. 1960).

29. Cf. Warner-Quinlan Co. v. United States, 273 F. 503 (3d Cir. 1921) (under the 1888 Act).

30. Maier v. Publicker Commercial Alcohol Co., 62 F.Supp. 161 (E.D.Pa. 1945), aff'd per curiam 154 F.2d 1020 (3d Cir. 1946).

31. Indeed, "refuse matter" is somewhat broader in scope because "pollutant" is defined under FWPCA, for certain policy reasons, to exempt sewage from vessels and material disposed of by deep well injection. 33 U.S.C.A. § 1362(19). Compare § 4.3 above (discussing groundwater pollution).

32. See § 4.6 below.

33. United States v. Rohm & Haas Co., 500 F.2d 167, 176–77, 4 ELR 20738, 20742 (5th Cir. 1974), cert. denied 420 U.S. 962 (1975) (reversing an injunction forbidding the barging of waste material to sea); see 33 CFR § 209.260(k)(1).

34. United States v. Sunset Cove, Inc., 3 ELR 20370, 20372 (D.C.Or.1973), aff'd in part 514 F.2d 1089, 5 ELR 20407 (9th Cir. 1975).

to a meandering river passable at high tide by motorized dories,[35] a nonnavigable tributary of a navigable river,[36] a stream once navigable now obstructed by a dam,[37] a creek sustaining no commerce,[38] a marshland subject to inundation by high tide,[39] a wetlands area having an overall elevation below mean high water illegally filled more than four decades earlier,[40] man-made canals dredged above the mean high tide line (the average reach of both high tides) connected to navigable waters.[41] Considered nonnavigable is a canal in downtown Richmond, Virginia, filled in and abandoned in 1880 and where now is found a parking lot,[42] and man-made canals above the mean high tide line not connected to tidal waters even though they exhibit tidal fluctuation.[43] The line of exclusion, according to the Fifth Circuit, is drawn around landlocked waters not affecting "the course, condition, capacity or location" of navigable waters.[44]

35. United States v. Sunset Cove, Inc., supra note 34.

36. United States v. Consolidated Coal Co., 354 F.Supp. 173, 3 ELR 20425 (N.D.W.Va.1973).

37. United States v. Kentland-Elkhorn Coal Co., 353 F.Supp. 451, 455–56, 3 ELR 20453, 20454 (E.D.Ky.1973); see George v. Beavark, Inc., 402 F.2d 977, 978 (8th Cir. 1968).

38. United States v. Diamond, 512 F.2d 157, 5 ELR 20334 (5th Cir. 1975).

39. United States v. Lewis, 355 F.Supp. 1132, 3 ELR 20500 (S.D.Ga.1973); see United States v. Stoeco Homes, Inc., 498 F.2d 597, 610, 4 ELR 20390, 20396 (3d Cir. 1974), cert. denied 420 U.S. 927 (1975) ("In tidal waters the test, in our view, remains what it was before 1851 the ebb and flow of the tide").

40. United States v. Stoeco Homes, Inc., 359 F.Supp. 672, 676, 3 ELR 20722, 20723 (D.N.J.1973), rev'd on other grounds 498 F.2d 597, 4 ELR 20390 (3d Cir. 1974), cert. denied 420 U.S. 427 (1975).

41. United States v. Sexton Cove Estates, Inc., 526 F.2d 1293, 6 ELR 20216 (5th Cir. 1976); Weiszmann v. District Engineer, 526 F.2d 1302, 6 ELR 20219 (5th Cir. 1976); see § 4.6 & n. 12 below.

42. James River and Kanawha Canal Parks, Inc. v. Richmond Metropolitan Authority, 359 F.Supp. 611, 640, 3 ELR 20557, 20567 (E.D.Va.1973) ("Quite simply, it ceased to exist as a waterway. Unlike the rivers involved in the previously cited cases, the canal did not continue to flow in a 'natural state' which could be improved to make it navigable. It in fact did not flow at all, as the water was drained from it, and the canal filled with dirt. To be made a navigable waterway the canal could not merely be improved, but would have to be entirely reconstructed, including the addition of a most necessary element—water. It does not, therefore, fall within the sort of waterways with which the Supreme Court was concerned in United States v. Appalachian Elec. Power Co. [311 U.S. 377, 61 S.Ct. 291, 85 L.Ed. 243 (1940)] or Economy Light & Power Co. v. United States [256 U.S. 113, 41 S.Ct. 409, 65 L.Ed. 847 (1921)], which continued to exist as rivers but had become obsolete for navigation").

43. United States v. Sexton Cove Estates, Inc., 526 F.2d 1293, 6 ELR 20216 (5th Cir. 1976); Weiszmann v. District Engineer, 526 F.2d 1302, 6 ELR 20219 (5th Cir. 1976).

44. United States v. Sexton Cove Estates, Inc., 526 F.2d at 1297, 6 ELR at 20218; see Power, The Federal Role in Coastal Development, in Environmental Law Institute, Federal Environmental Law 792, 808–13 (E. L. Dolgin & T. G. P. Guilbert eds. 1974).

No serious jurisdictional obstacles are raised by the language in section 13 indicating that discharges into any tributary of any navigable water are covered only if "the same shall float or be washed into such navigable water." The complaining party need not prove that the discharge into a tributary actually reached navigable waters, only that there is a likelihood of it so doing.[45] The Act is thus read as embracing discharges into tributaries with a potential for reaching navigable waters no less than the dumping of material on the bank with a similar potential for reaching navigable waters ("liable to be washed into"[46]).

c. *The Sewage Exception*

Controversy continues over section 13's exception for refuse matter "flowing from streets and sewers and passing therefrom in a liquid state." The Supreme Court's attempt to still the debate in United States v. Republic Steel Corp.,[47] is wholly unsatisfactory. In approving an action by the federal government to enjoin several steel companies from discharging wastes into the Calumet River without Corps of Engineers' permits, the Court read the exception clause as being limited to sewage or other liquids in suspension.[48] The distinction between refuse in suspension and that in solution is supported neither by the language of the Act nor sensible policy: the most toxic industrial pollutants remain in suspension.

In the wake of *Republic Steel,* a satisfactory rationalization of the sewage exception has been slow to materialize. Some courts hold the exception reaches sewage only,[49] while others insist that industrial

---

45. United States v. American Cyanamid Co., 480 F.2d 1132, 3 ELR 20656 (2d Cir. 1973) (involving a discharge of titanium dioxide and calcium carbonate into a tributary of the Hudson River).

46. See note 2, supra.

47. 362 U.S. 482, 80 S.Ct. 884, 4 L.Ed. 2d 903 (1960).

48. 362 U.S. at 490–91, 80 S.Ct. at 489–90, 4 L.Ed.2d at 909–10:
   The materials carried here are 'industrial solids,' as the District Court found. The particles creating the recent obstruction were in suspension, not in solution. Articles in suspension, such as organic matter in sewage, may undergo chemical change. Others settle out. All matter in suspension is not saved by the exception clause in Section 13. Refuse flowing from 'sewers' in a 'liquid state' means to us 'sewage.' . . . The fact that discharges from streets and sewers may contain some articles in suspension that settle out and potentially impair navigability is no reason for us to enlarge the group to include these industrial discharges.

49. United States v. Asbury Park, 340 F.Supp. 555, 2 ELR 20126 (D.C.N.J. 1972) (holding exception inapplicable to ocean dumping of sewage sludge); United States v. Granite State Packing Co., 343 F.Supp. 57, 61 (D.C.N.H. 1972) (holding exception inapplicable to industrial wastes passed through a municipal sewer system without treatment); United States v. Colgate Palmolive Co., 375 F.Supp. 962, 4 ELR 20707 (D.C.Kan.1974) (same); see United States v. United States Steel, 482 F.2d 439, 443–44, 3 ELR 20388, 20389 (7th Cir. 1973), cert. denied 414 U.S. 909 (dictum) (discussing *Republic Steel*).

wastes introduced into a municipal system are exempt even when diverted and released untreated.[50] The issue should be resolved by reference to the purpose of the clause, which, although obscure, seems to be to single out for exemption those wastes approved for introduction into a sewage system by municipal authorities.[51] Under this approach the right question is not whether the discharge is sewage only or whether it is industrial waste dumped into a sewer. It is whether the discharge is introduced into the system with the approval of public authorities and subject to their control.[52]

Even so construed, the sewage exception is extravagant: urban runoff and combined sanitary-storm sewage overflows create grave pollution problems.[53] The municipal permit program under the 1972 Amendments, conceived to fill the gap left by the sewage exception in the 1899 Act, is sorely lagging.[54] Refuse "flowing from streets and sewers and passing therefrom in a liquid state" remains an issue of considerable urgency.

d. *Culpability*

The scope of section 13 is extended greatly by the disposition of courts to dispense with culpability requirements. It is often said that the Refuse Act is a strict liability statute,[55] creating "public welfare offenses."[56] Under this view "the penalty is supposed to attach without regard to the question of wilfullness or intent, and without regard to the question of mistake or innocence."[57] No court has held that liability is dependent upon fault.[58] The defense of due care or compliance with industry custom is rejected out of hand.[59] At the

50. United States v. Dexter Corp., 507 F.2d 1038, 5 ELR 20041 (7th Cir. 1974).

51. United States v. Pennsylvania Indus. Chem. Corp., 461 F.2d 468, 472–73, 2 ELR 20264, 20265–66 (3d Cir. 1972), rev'd on other grounds 411 U.S. 655, 93 S.Ct. 1804, 36 L.Ed.2d 567 (1973); Rodgers, Industrial Water Pollution and the Refuse Act: A Second Chance for Water Quality, 119 U.Pa. L.Rev. 761, 777–78 (1971).

52. Rodgers, supra note 51, at 781.

53. National Commission on Water Quality, Staff Draft Report on Water Quality Analysis and Environmental Impact Assessment of Public Law 92–500, Jan. 1976, at II–10 to –14 [hereinafter cited as Draft Report on Environmental Impact].

54. See § 4.13 below.

55. United States v. United States Steel Corp., 328 F.Supp. 354, 1 ELR 20341 (N.D.Ind.1970), aff'd 482 F.2d 439, 3 ELR 20388 (7th Cir. 1973), cert. denied 414 U.S. 909; United States v. Interlake Steel Corp., 297 F.Supp. 912 (N.D.Ill.1969).

56. United States v. White Fuel Corp., 498 F.2d 619, 622, 4 ELR 20531, 20532 (1st Cir. 1974).

57. Scow No. 36, 144 F. 932, 933 (1st Cir. 1906); see United States v. Ballard Oil Co., 195 F.2d 369 (2d Cir. 1952); cf. Jaycox v. United States, 107 F. 938 (2d Cir. 1901) (arising under 1888 statute which was a predecessor of the 1899 Act).

58. The Supreme Court has reserved decision on the question. United States v. Standard Oil Co., 384 U.S. 224, 230, 86 S.Ct. 1427, 1430, 16 L. Ed.2d 492, 496 (1966).

59. United States v. White Fuel Corp., 498 F.2d 619, 623, 4 ELR 20531, 20533 (1st Cir. 1974), citing Glenn, The

same time, courts speaking in terms of strict or absolute liability often are sufficiently imprecise about what they mean to leave room for limited defenses—certainly that somebody else was a cause in fact of the loss, and possibly that the discharge was precipitated by the acts of third parties, a natural disaster, or otherwise was impossible to prevent.[60]

The absence of the language of culpability (negligently, recklessly, purposely, and so on) in section 13 suggests we are in the presence of a statute that condemns conduct quite without regard to the state of mind of the offender.[61] One who "suffers" a discharge to occur presumably can do so unwittingly.[62] Section 13 should be treated as a strict liability statute in the literal sense, meaning that the offense is complete if the prohibited act occurs (typically suffering the discharge of refuse into navigable waters). This interpretation should create few difficulties in the great majority of cases where the relief sought is civil or, while criminal in name, civil in consequence—the assessment of a fine against a corporation. Due process implications of quite a different order arise where a criminal characterization and a jail sentence are applied to an individual who is the unwitting instrument of a violation.[63]

A common defense raising questions of culpability is that the defendant was misled by public officials regarding the necessity of a permit for discharges under the 1899 Act.[64] The Supreme Court has

Crime of "Pollution": The Role of Federal Water Pollution Criminal Sanctions, 11 Am.Crim.L.Rev. 835 (1973).

60. United States v. White Fuel Corp., 498 F.2d at 624, 4 ELR at 20533 ("One is not expected to take all conceivable measures to erect a fail-safe system which would be impregnable to sabotage, thievery, accidental intrusions, the negligence of third parties, and extreme natural disasters"). A true strict liability statute would impose liability even if the forbidden event occurred because there was no fail-safe system.

61. Section 16, 33 U.S.C.A. § 411, states that "every person and every corporation that shall violate, or that shall knowingly aid, abet, authorize or instigate a violation of the provisions of sections [13, 14 and 15] shall be guilty of a misdemeanor, and on conviction thereof shall be punished by a fine not exceeding $2,500 nor less than $500, or by imprisonment (in the case of a natural person) for not less than thirty days nor more than one year, or by both such fine and imprisonment, in the discretion of the court, one-half of said fine to be paid to the person or persons giving information which shall lead to conviction." This cuts both ways on the culpability issue. There is no language of culpability qualifying "every person . . . shall violate" but there is ("knowingly") qualifying the offense for aiders and abettors. This can be read as meaning that substantive offenders need not act knowingly but the question arises why Congress meant to punish faultless substantive offenders but only culpable aiders and abettors.

62. United States v. White Fuel Corp., 498 F.2d 619, 622, 4 ELR 20531, 20532 (1st Cir. 1974).

63. Lambert v. California, 355 U.S. 225, 78 S.Ct. 240, 2 L.Ed.2d 228 (1957); cf. Commonwealth v. Koczwara, 397 Pa. 575, 155 A.2d 825 (1959) (approving a fine but holding unconstitutional a jail term for a conviction based upon vicarious liability).

64. The defense is best analyzed as involving reliance upon an official

made it clear that permits need not be made available by the administering authority but that if they are, a party is justified in relying upon official advice on whether one is needed.[65] Defendants under sections 10 and 13 often argue unsuccessfully that they were misled by the conduct of public officials (invoking such theories as laches or estoppel).[66] Although the courts are disposed to consider the arguments on the merits, these defenses are limited sharply: the longstanding administrative interpretation that section 13 applies not to pollution but only to discharges obstructing navigation certainly is not the law today,[67] for example, and no one can rely upon a belief that it is. On the other hand, courts are sympathetic to suggestions that while reliance upon official action rarely is a complete defense, it is worthy of consideration in determining the appropriate remedy.[68]

e. *Remedies*

Relief available in section 13 cases is by no means confined to the criminal and libel provisions specifically prescribed for violations.[69] Remedies are implied freely under the Act,[70] and it can be said with confidence that the full panoply of equitable remedies is available to correct section 13 violations.[71] This relief is seen most

---

statement of the law. Model Penal Code § 2.04(3)(b) (Proposed Official Draft 1962). Permits for discharges no longer can be issued under section 13. FWPCA § 402(a)(5), 33 U.S.C.A. § 1342(a)(5).

65. United States v. Pennsylvania Indust. Chem. Corp., 411 U.S. 655, 93 S.Ct. 1804, 36 L.Ed.2d 567 (1973).

66. United States v. Joseph G. Moretti, Inc., 526 F.2d 1306, 6 ELR 20221 (5th Cir. 1976) (rejecting equal protection defense); Weiszmann v. District Engineer, 526 F.2d 1302, 6 ELR 20219 (5th Cir. 1976) (rejecting laches and equitable estoppel defenses); United States v. Sunset Cove, Inc., 3 ELR 20371, 20373–74 (D.Or.1973), aff'd 514 F.2d 1089, 5 ELR 20407 (9th Cir. 1975) (rejecting an estoppel defense); United States v. Stoeco Homes, Inc., 359 F.Supp. 672, 3 ELR 20722 (D.C. N.J.1973), rev'd on other grounds 498 F.2d 597 (2d Cir. 1974), cert. denied 420 U.S. 927 (1975) (rejecting defenses of estoppel, laches, denial of equal protection); United States v. Lewis, 355 F.Supp. 1132, 1141, 3 ELR 20500, 20503 (S.D.Ga.1973) (rejecting defenses of equitable estoppel, laches and discriminatory enforcement); United States v. Hercules, Inc., 335 F.Supp. 102, 2 ELR 20097 (D.C.Kan.1971) (rejecting equal protection defense).

67. E. g., United States v. Pennsylvania Indus. Chem. Corp., 411 U.S. 655, 93 S.Ct. 1804, 36 L.Ed.2d 567 (1973); United States v. Standard Oil Co., 384 U.S. 224, 86 S.Ct. 1427, 16 L.Ed. 2d 492 (1966).

68. United States v. Pennsylvania Indus. Chem. Corp., supra note 67; United States v. Kennebec Log Driving Co., 491 F.2d 562, 571, 4 ELR 20047, 20051 (1st Cir. 1973), cert. denied 417 U.S. 910 (1974); Sierra Club v. Leslie Salt, 412 F.Supp. 1096, 1104, 6 ELR 20363, 20366 (N.D.Cal.1976) ("equitable principles of fairness" forbid the Corps from requiring permits now for the maintenance of dikes that have been in place without objection for 20 to 50 years).

69. Section 16, 33 U.S.C.A. § 410.

70. E. g., Wyandotte Transp. Co. v. United States, 389 U.S. 191, 88 S.Ct. 379, 19 L.Ed.2d 407 (1967) (implying a reimbursement remedy for section 15 violations); United States v. Republic Steel Corp., 362 U.S. 482, 80 S.Ct. 884, 4 L.Ed.2d 903 (1960) (implying an equitable remedy for section 10 violations).

71. United States v. Consolidation Coal Co., 354 F.Supp. 173, 3 ELR 20425 (N.D.W.Va.1973).

often in the dredge and fill cases.[72] Fines for section 13 violations also can be substantial, despite the twenty-five hundred dollar maximum for each offense, because of the relative ease of establishing multiple violations for continuing offences.[73] For violations of Section 301 of FWPCA (now pleaded routinely along with section 13), the maximum civil penalty is $10,000 per day, which clearly conveys a message of deterrence.[74]

A fascinating debate over section 13 violations in recent years involved the interpretation of the statutory clause stating that "in the discretion of the court, one-half of any fine [is] to be paid to the person or persons giving information which shall lead to conviction." [75] Nearly a dozen cases raised the question of whether an informer could bring an action in the nature of *qui tam* (on behalf of the king) to recover his share of the fine prior to the initiation of a criminal prosecution.[76] That question has been answered in the negative, and properly so,[77] with the consequence that the informer reward provisions of the Rivers and Harbors Act become operative only upon a decision to prosecute. Rewards are payable after a conviction to anyone supplying a missing material link in the chain of evidence.[78] Section 13's application to nonpoint sources, responsible for accidental or irregular discharges, is highly dependent upon detection by the vigilant and informed.

Another important question not yet definitively answered is whether a private party injured by violations under the Act can seek civil redress. The statute is silent on the question, but the trend in the cases favors implying civil remedies, from various sections of the statute, to the advantage of injured parties.[79] Surely the congres-

72. See § 4.6 below.

73. See Hearings on the Refuse Act Permit Program, Before the Subcomm. on the Environment of the Senate Comm. on Commerce, S.Doc.No.7, 92d Cong., 1st Sess. 27–30 (1971) (testimony of John Burns, former executive assistant to the U. S. Attorney, Southern District, New York); United States v. Hercules, Inc., 335 F.Supp. 102, 2 ELR 20097 (D.C.Kan.1971) (holding only one offense was consumated by a continuing act of discharge extending over nine days.).

74. 33 U.S.C.A. § 1319(d); see Weiszmann v. District Engineer, 526 F.2d 1302, 6 ELR 20219 (5th Cir. 1976) (upholding $5,000 fine); United States v. Permenter, —— F.Supp. ——, 6 ELR 20049 (D.C.S.C.1975) (imposing $7,500 civil penalty).

75. Section 16, 33 U.S.C.A. § 411.

76. The cases are collected in Connecticut Action Now v. Roberts Plating Co., 457 F.2d 81, 2 ELR 20157 (2d Cir. 1972).

77. See Rodgers, supra note 51, at 787–92.

78. See Comment, Informer Fees Under the Refuse Act: Deciding Who Gets What, 5 Env.L. 241 (1975); see, e. g., Hughes v. Ranger Fuel Corp., Div. of Pittston Co., 467 F.2d 6, 2 ELR 20577 (4th Cir. 1972); Connecticut Action Now, Inc. v. Roberts Plating Co., 457 F.2d 81, 2 ELR 20157 (2d Cir. 1972); United States v. Anaconda Wire & Cable Co., 342 F.Supp. 1116, 2 ELR 20315 (S.D.N.Y.1972); United States v. T/B NMS No. 40, 330 F.Supp. 781 (S.D.Tex.1971); United States v. St. Regis Paper Co., 328 F.Supp. 660, 1 ELR 20309 (D.C.Wis.1971).

79. Cases cited in note 70, supra; Alameda Conservation Ass'n v. Califor-

sional objectives of no discharges and no obstructions are advanced by commissioning the private citizen in an enforcement effort that is destined to lag given the sheer volume of the violations. The Act, after all, in a dictum often cited for guidance, must be read "charitably in light of the purposes to be served." [80] Some people are within the class protected by the legislation. Private actions would advance its purpose and Congress has not clearly disavowed these remedies. It is too late in the day to deny private enforcement of the Refuse Act.

f. *Contemporaneous Significance*

The most important current function of section 13 is its application to nonpoint sources. The provision itself speaks of causing, suffering or procuring discharges or deposits into the water and thus explicitly reaches the draining, leaching and other hydrological cycles peculiar to nonpoint sources. Section 13 also explicitly condemns deposits "on the bank of any tributary of any navigable water" that may be "washed into" the water, which of course is descriptive of nonpoint sources.[81] The 1970 Justice Department prosecutorial guidelines for section 13 encouraged use of the Act to punish or prevent discharges "either accidental or infrequent" and "not of a con-

nia, 437 F.2d 1087, 1 ELR 20897 (9th Cir. 1971); Neches Canal Co. v. Miller & Vidor Co., 24 F.2d 763 (5th Cir. 1928) (implying private right of action for violation of section 9, 33 U.S.C.A. § 1401); Puente de Reynosa v. McAllen, 357 F.2d 43 (5th Cir. 1966); James River & Kanawha Canal Parks, Inc. v. Richmond Metropolitan Authority, 359 F.Supp. 611, 639, 3 ELR 20556, 20566–67 (E.D.Va.1973); Natural Resources Defense Council, Inc. v. Grant, 355 F.Supp. 280, 3 ELR 20176 (E.D.N.C.1973) (allowing enforcement by "a private attorney general" where defendants are represented by the United States Attorney; suggests a different result in a suit between private parties); Lauritzen v. Chesapeake Bay Bridge & Tunnel Dist., 259 F.Supp. 633 (E.D.Va.1966), aff'd on other grounds 404 F.2d 1001 (4th Cir. 1968); Sierra Club v. Morton, 400 F.Supp. 610 (N.D.Cal.1975) (implying private right of action under sections 9 and 10). Contra, Red Star Towing & Transp. Co. v. Dep't of Transp., 423 F.2d 104 (3d Cir. 1970); H. Christiansen & Sons, Inc. v. Duluth, 154 F.2d 205 (8th Cir. 1946); Sierra Club v. Leslie Salt Co. (I), 354 F.Supp. 1099, 4 ELR 1663 (N.D.Cal. 1972); Guthrie v. Alabama By-Products Co., 328 F.Supp. 1140, 1 ELR 20334 (N.D.Ala.1971), aff'd per curiam 456 F.2d 1294, 2 ELR 20151 (5th Cir. 1972), cert. denied, 410 U.S. 946 (1973) (section 13 does not create a federal cause of action in favor of private plaintiffs claiming pollution damage to riparian lands); Longstrean v. Owen McCaffrey's Sons, 95 Conn. 486, 111 A. 788 (1920).

80. United States v. Republic Steel Corp., 362 U.S. 482, 491, 80 S.Ct. 884, 890, 4 L.Ed.2d 903, 910 (1960).

81. The second clause of section 13 addressing deposits on the "bank of any tributary" is by its terms limited to instances where the deposit is "liable to be washed into the water . . . whereby navigation shall or may be impeded or obstructed." The textual argument that nonpoint source deposits are condemned only if they potentially may obstruct navigation is immaterial since the first clause of section 13 extends to nonpoint source discharges without the obstruction to navigation limitation. See United States v. Esso Standard Oil Co., 375 F.2d 621 (3d Cir. 1967); Rodgers, supra note 51, at 779. Compare § 4.4 above (discussing nonpoint source water pollution).

tinuing nature." [82] Nonpoint sources and hazardous substance spills are thus prime candidates for coverage.

Section 402(a)(5) of the 1972 Amendments [83] is quite explicit on the subject of section 13 permits: "No permit for a discharge into the navigable waters shall be issued under Section 13 of the Act of March 3, 1899, after the date of enactment of this title." This means that the National Pollutant Discharge Elimination System and its permit mechanism takes over entirely the short-lived Refuse Act Permit Program administered by the Corps of Engineers.[84] Interestingly, because the scope of the NPDES program (applying only to point sources) is narrower than the scope of the permit authority under the old section 13 (applying also to nonpoint sources) the effect of a flat prohibition against section 13 permits is to outlaw under the Rivers and Harbors Act certain discharges that formerly could be authorized by permit.[85] Permits issued under the Refuse Act Permit Program are treated as permits under the 1972 Act and continue in "force and effect for their term" unless modified.[86] Applications for permits pending at the time of enactment of the 1972 Amendments "shall be deemed" to be applications under the newer Act.[87] Dischargers with pending applications were granted an immunity under both the Rivers and Harbors Act and the 1972 Amendments until December 31, 1974.[88] A savings provision preserved actions then pending, including section 13 suits,[89] and it has been broadly construed to preserve litigation filed before the 1972 Amendments.[90]

The principal impact of the 1972 Amendments on section 13 is to exempt from coverage point sources operating within the terms of their NPDES permits. Still subject to the flat prohibitions of the 1899 Act are (1) nonpoint source discharges; (2) point sources dis-

82. For a discussion of the 1970 guidelines, see Rodgers, supra note 51, at 792–805.

83. 33 U.S.C.A. § 1342(a)(5).

84. For a discussion of the Refuse Act Permit Program, see Rodgers, supra note 51, at 806–19. Compare §§ 4.11–4.13 below (discussing NPDES).

85. Cf. Scenic Hudson Preservation Conference v. Callaway, 370 F.Supp. 162 (S.D.N.Y.1973), aff'd per curiam 499 F.2d 127, 4 ELR 20530 (2d Cir. 1974) (section 10 survives in its entirety except that deposits approved under permit provisions of the 1972 Act can be made without securing also a section 10 permit); see § 4.6 below.

86. Section 402(a)(4), 33 U.S.C.A. § 1342(a)(4). The RAPP program resulted in the issuance of only 21 permits. Draft Report on Environmental Impact, supra note 53, at V–21.

87. Section 402(a)(5), 33 U.S.C.A. § 1342(a)(5).

88. Section 402(k), 33 U.S.C.A. § 1342 (k). In this respect, Congress abandoned the provisions of the Refuse Act Permit Program which provided that the pendency of a permit application would not prevent a suit. See 36 Fed.Reg. 6564 (1971), as amended, id. at 13835.

89. 33 U.S.C.A. § 1251 note.

90. The cases are collected in United States v. Rohm & Haas Co., 500 F.2d 167, 4 ELR 20738 (5th Cir. 1974), cert. denied 420 U.S. 962 (1975) (rejecting argument that administrative relief must precede judicial enforcement action.)

charging without a permit;[91] (3) point sources discharging in violation of the terms of a permit; (4) spills of oil, hazardous materials or other substances (accidental or irregular discharges from a vessel or other point source).[92] Enough of section 13 remains to count it among the more significant water pollution prohibitions today.

§ 4.6 Disposal of Dredged and Fill Material

Acknowledging the "established role"[1] of the U. S. Army Corps of Engineers in the dredging and maintenance of navigable channels and ports, Section 404[2] of the 1972 Amendments ordains a separate permit program for the discharge of dredged or fill material. Those qualifying for section 404 permits are exempted from the NPDES permit system.[3] Some confusing overlap exists between the reach of the Corps-administered section 404 and EPA's ocean dumping permit program.[4] But there is no difficulty reconciling the key features of the Rivers and Harbors Act with section 404: section 13 discharges not approved by a section 404 permit are disallowed.[5] The section 10 permit program, addressing obstructions to navigation and channel alterations, differs from section 404 in coverage but is administered under exactly the same procedures, even to the extent of using the same forms.[6] The principal difference is that section 404 reaches only discharges while section 10 applies to activities modifying channels without regard to whether there has been a discharge.

The scope of section 404 is measured chiefly by (1) the meaning of dredged or fill material; (2) the definition of navigable waters; (3) available remedies and (4) criteria for site selection and permit issuance. Also pertinent are (5) the activities of the Corps of En-

91. This is a sizeable category. Draft Report on Environmental Impact, supra note 53, at V-24 (discussing status of NPDES permit program; "Ahead, however, are an indeterminate number of dischargers (EPA estimates anywhere from 50,000 to 100,000) such as small feedlots, stormwater sewers, irrigation return flows, etc., which presumably will have to be permitted . . . .").

92. This is another substantial category. The propriety of applying section 13 in such circumstances has been acknowledged by the EPA general counsel. See Zener, The Federal Law of Water Pollution Control, in Environmental Law Institute, Federal Environmental Law 682, 786 (E. L. Dolgin & T. G. P. Guilbert eds. 1974).

1. Zener, The Federal Law of Water Pollution Control in Environmental Law Institute, Federal Environmental Law 682, 741 (E. L. Dolgin & T. G. P. Guilbert eds. 1974); see Hoyer, Corps of Engineers Dredge and Fill Jurisdiction: Buttressing a Citadel Under Seige, 26 U.Fla.L.Rev. 19 (1973).

2. 33 U.S.C.A. § 1344.

3. Section 402(a)(1), 33 U.S.C.A. § 1342 (a)(1).

4. See § 4.16 below.

5. See section 402(a)(5), 33 U.S.C.A. § 1342(a)(5).

6. See 40 Fed.Reg. 31320 (July 25, 1975), 33 CFR § 209.120(m). Compare FWPCA § 511(a), 33 U.S.C.A. § 1371(a). See also Scenic Hudson Preservation Conference v. Callaway, 499 F.2d 127, 4 ELR 20530 (2d Cir. 1974) (per curiam) (dumping of fill material requires a section 404 permit but not a duplicate section 10 permit).

gineers itself and (6) related federal and state laws regulating wetland developments.

a. *Dredged or Fill Material*

Dredged material under section 404 means "material that is excavated or dredged from navigable waters." The term "does not include material resulting from normal farming, [silviculture], and ranching activities, such as ploughing, cultivating, seeding, and harvesting, for production of food, fiber, and forest products."[7] Fill material means "any pollutant used to create fill in the traditional sense of replacing an aquatic area with dry land or changing the bottom elevation of a water body for any purpose." It does not include material from normal farming, timber or harvesting operations or material placed for purposes of maintaining recently damaged dikes, dams or break waters.[8] A discharge of dredged material includes both the dumping of material at a disposal site in navigable waters and the runoff or overflow from a contained land or water disposal area.[9] A discharge of filled material includes a wide range of activities: "placement of fill that is necessary to the construction of any structure in a navigable water; the building of any structure or inpoundment requiring rock, sand, dirt or other pollutants for its construction; site-development fills for recreational, industrial, commercial, residential, and other uses; causeways or road fills; dams and dikes; artificial islands, property protection and/or reclamation devices such as riprap, groins, seawalls, breakwalls and bulkheads and fills; beach nourishment; levees; sanitary land fills; fill for structure such as sewage treatment facilities, intake and outfall pipes associated with power plants, and subaqueous utility lines; and artificial reefs."[10]

Although the definition of dredged and fill material stops short of reaching all types of "refuse" under Section 13 of the Rivers and Harbors Act and "obstructions" or "modifications" under section 10, Section 404 of the FWPCA is no incidental measure. Dredging and filling is economically important and environmentally destructive.[11] It is essential to successful commerce, and it contributes substantially

---

7. 33 CFR § 209.120(d)(4).

8. Id. § 209.120(d)(6).

9. Id. § 209.120(d)(5).

10. Id. § 209.120(d)(7).

11. See Environmental Protection Agency, The Control of Pollution from Hydrographic Modification (1973) (discussing principal effects and preventive operational controls); Comment, Comprehensive Wetlands Protection: One Step Closer to Full Implementation of § 404 of the FWPCA, 5 ELR 10099 (1975) (reporting an estimate by the National Wildlife Federation that the United States already has lost 40 percent of its wetland resources, mostly to filling projects). Still authoritative is the work of the Secretary of the Interior, Report on the National Estuarine Pollution Study, Comm. on Public Works, S.Doc.No.58, 91st Cong., 2d Sess. (Comm. Print 1970).

b. *Navigable Waters*

One of the most explosive environmental issues in recent times is the dramatic expansion of Corps jurisdiction which was tied historically to concepts of navigability. This meant that the Corps used to exercise its authority landward only up to the mean high water line (the average of both high tides) and, on the Pacific Coast, the mean higher high water line (the average of the higher of the two high tides).[12] Sections 10 and 13 of the 1899 Act generally are limited to activities affecting navigable waters and their tributaries.[13] Two developments overwhelmed the restrictions inherent in the concept of "navigable waters": first, a broad judicial construction of "navigability" and, second, an explicit legislative decision to drop any test of "navigability" as a measure of federal power under the 1972 Amendments. Thus the meaning of "navigability" progressed from waters actually in use [14] to those which used to be navigable [15] to those which by "reasonable improvements" could be made navigable [16] to nonnavigable tributaries affecting navigable streams.[17] Nonetheless, "the limitation of navigability still worked to impede efforts to forestall the degradation of the aquatic environment. Not only did small feeder streams and tributaries remain exempt from federal jurisdiction but, more importantly, the wetland areas adjoining the waterways did also." [18]

The 1972 Amendments reject the few remaining constraints associated with the concept of navigability. The Act uses, somewhat in-

---

12. More precisely, the mean high water line is the average of both high tides (occurring during each 24.8 hour period) over a period of 19 years. The mean higher high water line is the average of only the higher or two high tides for the same period of time. See Leslie Salt Co. v. Froehlke, 5 ELR 20039 (N.D.Cal.1974) (upholding Corps regulations extending jurisdiction over permits for the disposal of dredged material on the Pacific Coast to the mean higher high water line).

13. Section 10, 33 U.S.C.A. § 403, reaches obstructions "to the navigable capacity of any of the waters of the United States." Section 13, 33 U.S.C.A. § 407, governs discharges "into any navigable water of the United States, or into any tributary of any navigable water from which the same shall float or be washed into such navigable water."

14. The Daniel Ball, 77 U.S. (10 Wall.) 557, 19 L.Ed. 999 (1870).

15. Economy Light & Power Co. v. United States, 256 U.S. 113, 41 S.Ct. 409, 65 L.Ed. 847 (1921); United States v. Holt State Bank, 270 U.S. 49, 46 S.Ct. 197, 70 L.Ed. 465 (1926) (only by canoe).

16. United States v. Appalachian Elec. Power Co., 311 U.S. 377, 408, 61 S.Ct. 291, 299, 85 L.Ed. 243, 253 (1940).

17. Oklahoma ex rel. Phillips v. Guy F. Atkinson Co., 313 U.S. 508, 529, 61 S.Ct. 1050, 1061, 85 L.Ed. 1487, 1502 (1941).

18. United States v. Holland, 373 F.Supp. 665, 670, 4 ELR 20710, 20712, (M.D.Fla.1974), citing United States v. Cannon, 363 F.Supp. 1045 (D.C.Del. 1973).

discriminately, the historical phrases "navigable waters" and "navigable waters of the United States." [19] But the definitions section and the legislative history eliminate the ambiguity. Section 502(7) defines "navigable waters" to mean "the waters of the United States, including the territorial seas," [20] thus strongly suggesting the banishment of the navigability limitation. This suggestion is made explicit at two key points in the legislative history, the first in the Senate Report indicating a desire to escape from the constrictions of the navigability test,[21] the second in the Conference Report expressing a purpose that the term "navigable waters" be given "the broadest possible constitutional interpretation unencumbered by agency determinations which have been made or may be made for administrative purposes." [22] There is other evidence confirming a congressional purpose to stretch the constitutional tolerance to its limits.[23]

Cases interpreting the 1972 Amendments uniformly reject the navigability restrictions.[24] Thus, jurisdiction has been extended to a

19. Sections 311, 312, 502(12), 33 U.S.C. §§ 1321, 1322, 1362(12).

20. 33 U.S.C.A. § 1362(7). Section 502(8), 33 U.S.C.A. § 1362(8), defines "territorial seas" to mean "the belt of the seas measured from the line of ordinary low water along that portion of the coast which is in direct contact with the open sea and the line marking the seaward limit of inland waters, and extending seaward a distance of three miles."

21. The bill submitted to the Senate as S.2770 defined "navigable waters" to mean "navigable waters of the United States, portions thereof, and the tributaries thereof, including the territorial seas and the Great Lakes." The Committee of Public Works' full explanation is as follows:

> The control strategy of the Act extends to navigable waters. The definition of this term means the navigable waters of the United States, portions thereof, and includes the territorial seas and the Great Lakes. Through narrow interpretation of the definition of interstate waters the implementation [of the] 1965 Act was severely limited. Water moves in hydrologic cycles and it is essential that discharge of pollutants be controlled at the source. Therefore, reference to the control requirements must be made to the navigable waters, portions thereof and their tributaries.

Comm. on Public Works, Federal Water Pollution Control Act Amendments of 1971, S.Rep.No.414, 92d Cong., 1st Sess. 77 (1971). The House definition was more restrictive: "The navigable waters of the United States, including the territorial seas," Comm. on Public Works, Federal Water Pollution Control Act Amendments of 1972, H.R.Rep.No.911, 92d Cong., 2d Sess. 53 (1972). The broader views of the Senate prevailed.

22. Comm. of Conference, Federal Water Pollution Control Act Amendments of 1972, S.Rep.No.1236, 92d Cong., 2d Sess. 144 (1972) [hereinafter cited as Conference Report].

23. See, for example, the remarks on the floor of the House by Rep. Dingell, a knowledgeable authority on water pollution but not a conferee. 118 Cong.Rec. 33756–57 (1972) (stating that the term "navigable waters" means "all the waters of the United States" in a geographical sense. It does not mean "navigable waters of the United States in the technical sense as we sometimes see it in some laws").

24. The EPA view seeks "to extend federal jurisdiction to cases in which the connection to interstate commerce is through the use of the water, rather than through the water itself." Zener, supra note 1, at 691.

Sec. 4.6 DISPOSAL OF DREDGED MATERIAL

nonnavigable stream,[25] nonnavigable, man-made mosquito canals,[26] mangrove wetlands [27] and other swampland areas [28] above the mean high water line. The *coup de grace* came in the 1975 decision of Natural Resources Defense Council, Inc. v. Callaway,[29] which invalidated the Corps' definition of navigability limited to the traditional tests under the section 404 dredge and fill provisions. There followed a heated national debate made more intensive by allegations that the court decision necessitated permits for a rancher who wishes to enlarge his stock pond or a farmer who wants to deepen an irrigation ditch or plough a field.[30] Ultimately, after considering more than 4500 comments, the Corps adopted new definitions, of "navigable waters" for purposes of its section 404 authority.[31] With respect to coastal regions, the Corps now claims jurisdiction over not only waters subject to the ebb and flow of the tide but also coastal and freshwater wetlands and swamps that are contiguous to traditional navigable waters.[32] As regards inland waters, section 404 authority extends to intrastate lakes and streams used for certain interstate purposes (such as recreational use by interstate travelers or industrial use by interstate industries).[33] The definitions reconcile acceptably the congressional mandate to exhaust constitutional limits and the common-sense mandate to develop a workable program.

c. *Remedies*

Many a local dredger and filler will be surprised not only by the appearance of federal authority but also the range of available remedies. Despite the relatively narrow prescriptions for relief in the enforcement provisions of FWPCA [34] and in the Rivers and Harbors Act of 1899, courts imply remedies readily [35] and fashion imag-

---

25. United States v. Ashland Oil & Transp. Co., 364 F.Supp. 349, 4 ELR 20185 (W.D.Ky.1973), aff'd 504 F.2d 1317, 4 ELR 20784 (6th Cir. 1974).

26. United States v. Holland, 373 F. Supp. 665, 4 ELR 20711 (M.D.Fla. 1974).

27. Ibid.

28. Leslie Salt Co. v. Froehlke, 5 ELR 20039 (N.D.Cal.1974).

29. 392 F.Supp. 685, 5 ELR 20285 (D.C. D.C.1975), invalidating 33 CFR § 209.-210(d)(1), 39 Fed.Reg. 12119 (Apr. 3, 1974) and 33 CFR § 209.260.

30. The evolution of the Corps' grappling with the navigability test is described in Comment, Comprehensive Wetlands Protection: One Step Closer to Full Implementation of § 404 of the FWPCA, 5 ELR 10099 (1975); Comment, Corps Issues Interim Rules for Discharges of Dredged and Fill Materials, 5 ELR 10143 (1975). A widely publicized permit decision implementing the new policies is reported in Chief of Engineers, Dep't of the Army, Report on Application for Department of the Army Permits to Dredge and Fill at Marco Island, Florida, 6 ELR 30020 (1976); see Comment, Corps Confirms Policy Against "Unnecessary" Development in Wetlands, 6 ELR 10117 (1976).

31. 40 Fed.Reg. 31320 (July 25, 1975), amending 33 CFR pt. 209.

32. 33 CFR §§ 209.120(d)(1), (2).

33. Id. § 209.120(d)(2)(g).

34. See § 4.21 below.

35. See § 4.5 n. 70 above.

inative relief to meet the equities of the situation. Section 12 of the Rivers and Harbors Act authorizes federal district courts to order "removal of any structures or parts of structures erected in violation" of other sections of the Act (including section 10).[36] This has been read as "slackening the customary equitable criteria" otherwise obtaining under Rule 65 of the Federal Rules of Civil Procedure.[37] Whether or not this is true, courts readily impose civil penalties,[38] enjoin continuing discharges,[39] stop further dredging, filling and construction activities,[40] order the removal of obstructions at the cost of defendants,[41] enjoin the sale of land where the fill is located until it is removed,[42] require defendant to pay in damages the equivalent cost of remedying the situation.[43] A violator may be obliged to remove toxic metals accumulated in the vicinity of the outfall area,[44] prepare an engineering plan for the removal and disposal of unlawful fill,[45] refill excavated canals and replant vegetation,[46] otherwise restore the excavation to its natural condition,[47] establish preserve areas within a development,[48] make its premises available for continuing investigations,[49] measure suspended solids at the point of discharge

36. 33 U.S.C.A. § 406.

37. United States v. Stoeco Homes, 359 F.Supp. 672, 679, 3 ELR 20722, 20724 (D.C.N.J.1973), rev'd on other grounds, 498 F.2d 597, 4 ELR 20390 (3d Cir. 1974).

38. E. g., Weiszmann v. District Engineer, 526 F.2d 1302, 6 ELR 20219 (5th Cir. 1976); United States v. Bayou Des Familles Dev. Corp., 5 ELR 20239 (E.D.La.1975) (arising under Section 10 of the Rivers and Harbors Act and Sections 301 and 309(d) of FWPCA).

39. United States v. Consolidation Coal Co., 354 F.Supp. 173, 3 ELR 20425 (N.D.W.Va.1973).

40. E. g., United States v. Diamond, 4 ELR 20510 (S.D.Ga.1974), aff'd 512 F. 2d 157, 5 ELR 20334 (5th Cir. 1975).

41. United States v. Underwood, 344 F.Supp. 486, 2 ELR 20567 (M.D.Fla. 1972).

42. United States v. Joseph G. Moretti, Inc. (I), 331 F.Supp. 151, 1 ELR 20443 (S.D.Fla.1971), aff'd in part 478 F.2d 418, 3 ELR 20414 (5th Cir. 1973).

43. United States v. Perma Paving Co., 332 F.2d 754 (2d Cir. 1964); United States v. Underwood, 344 F.Supp. 486, 2 ELR 20567 (M.D.Fla.1972).

44. United States v. Marathon Battery Co., 2 ELR 20401 (S.D.N.Y.1972) (consent decree) (arising under Section 13 of the Rivers and Harbors Act and Section 1 of the New York Harbor Act, 33 U.S.C.A. § 441).

45. United States v. Marathon Battery Co., supra note 44; United States v. Lewis, 355 F.Supp. 1132, 3 ELR 20500 (S.D.Ga.1973).

46. United States v. Sexton Cove Estates, Inc., 389 F.Supp. 602, 5 ELR 20348 (S.D.Fla.1975).

47. State v. Seaman, 114 N.J.Super. 19 274 A.2d 810, 2 ELR 20273 (1972) (judgment after jury trial) (arising under state law). But see United States v. American Capital Land Corp., 5 ELR 20705 (S.D.Miss.1975) (refusing to require complete restoration).

48. United States v. Holland, 373 F. Supp. 665, 4 ELR 20711 (M.D.Fla. (1974) (finding violations of Section 301 of the 1972 Amendments without applying Sections 10 or 13 of the Rivers and Harbors Act 1899).

49. United States v. Kentland-Elkhorn Coal Corp., 353 F.Supp. 451, 3 ELR 20453 (E.D.Ky.1973) (despite denying a preliminary injunction).

Sec. 4.6   DISPOSAL OF DREDGED MATERIAL   405

of a retention pond,[50] refrain from financing or otherwise carrying out the construction project,[51] cease selling property pending restoration,[52] take steps to legalize the development,[53] seek state approvals for the development of an incineration system designed to eliminate all discharges,[54] operate a solid waste disposal site in accordance with carefully prescribed sanitary landfill conditions,[55] or perhaps do nothing other than prepare an environmental impact statement.[56] Courts balk at imposing restoration costs personally on a corporate officer for violations of his organization,[57] and require a strong factual basis on the feasibility and environmental advisability of a restoration order.[58] But the overall impression afforded by the remedy cases is that the courts will fashion appropriate relief to correct dredge and fill violations.

d. *Criteria for Site Selection and Permit Issuance*

Under section 404 the Corps must specify in each permit an acceptable disposal site for authorized discharges of dredged or fill material.[59] This requires an analysis of both environmental and economic factors. Sites are selected, first, by applying EPA guidelines

---

50. United States v. Holland, 373 F. Supp. 665, 4 ELR 20711 (M.D.Fla. 1974).

51. Natural Resources Defense Council, Inc. v. Grant, 355 F.Supp. 280, 290, 3 ELR 20176, 20180 (E.D.N.C. 1973).

52. United States v. Joseph G. Moretti, Inc. (II), 387 F.Supp. 1404, 5 ELR 20174 (S.D.Fla.1974) (on remand), rev'd 526 F.2d 1306, 6 ELR 20221 (5th Cir. 1976); cf. United States v. Permenter, 6 ELR 20049 (D.S.C.1975).

53. State v. Seaman, 114 N.J.Super. 19, 274 A.2d 810, 2 ELR 20273 (1972).

54. United States v. Armco Steel, 333 F.Supp. 1073, 1 ELR 20517, modified 2 ELR 20438 (S.D.Tex.1971) (arising under section 13).

55. United States v. Michaelian, 2 ELR 20463 (S.D.N.Y.1972) (arising under section 13) (Frankel, J.).

56. Conservation Council of North Carolina v. Costanzo, 398 F.Supp. 653, 5 ELR 20666 (E.D.N.C.1975), aff'd 528 F.2d 250, 6 ELR 20116 (4th Cir.).

57. United States v. Sexton Cove Estates, Inc., 526 F.2d 1293, 6 ELR 20216 (5th Cir. 1976); United States v. Joseph G. Moretti, Inc. (II), 526 F. 2d 1306, 6 ELR 20221 (5th Cir. 1976).

58. United States v. Sexton Cove Estates, Inc., supra note 57; United States v. Joseph G. Moretti, Inc., supra note 57; Weiszmann v. District Engineer, 526 F.2d 1302, 6 ELR 20219 (5th Cir. 1976).

59. Section 404(b), 33 U.S.C.A. § 1344 (b), reads as follows:
    Subject to subsection (c) of this section, each such disposal site shall be specified for each such permit by the Secretary of the Army (1) through the application of guidelines developed by the Administrator, in conjunction with the Secretary of the Army, which guidelines shall be based upon criteria comparable to the criteria applicable to the territorial seas, the contiguous zone, and the ocean under section 403(c), and (2) in any case where such guidelines under clause (1) alone would prohibit the specification of a site, through the application additionally of the economic impact of the site on navigation and anchorage.

comparable to the ocean discharge guidelines.[60] These place a heavy emphasis on identifying effects and disqualifying ecologically sensitive sites. The Corps' District Engineer, after evaluating applications, either allows the discharge subject to conditions to minimize impact, denies the application or requests more information on which to base his decision. Issuance of a permit in contravention of the guidelines can be corrected in the courts under the citizen suit provisions.[61]

Authority is divided on the necessity of the preparation of an environmental impact statement in connection with the issuance of a section 404 permit.[62] The decision should turn on the scope and size of the activity authorized.[63] Another controversial feature of the Corps' section 404 authority, involving the sites themselves and not the individual permits, is the power to consider "the economic impact of the site on navigation and anchorage" even though the site is disqualified under the environmental criteria. This should be read as justifying Corps approval of discharges at a site if environmentally preferable alternatives are prohibitively expensive or pose a serious impediment to navigation.

Counterbalancing the Corps' economic reinstatement of disqualified sites is EPA's power to withdraw vulnerable sites. Under section 404(c) [64] the Administrator is authorized to prohibit the specification of any defined area as a disposal site upon determining that discharges into the area "will have an unacceptable adverse effect on municipal water supplies, shellfish beds and fishery areas (including spawning and breeding areas), wildlife, or recreational areas." EPA's power is hedged by notice, hearing, consultation (with the

---

60. 40 Fed.Reg. 41291 (1975), 40 CFR pt. 230 (interim final guidelines).

61. See Natural Resources Defense Council, Inc. v. Callaway, 524 F.2d 79, 5 ELR 20640 (2d Cir. 1975) (remanding for further proceedings on whether criteria were violated and, if so, whether the site was justified nonetheless for economic reasons).

62. Compare Natural Resources Defense Council, Inc. v. Callaway, supra note 61 (where an EIS was prepared) with Rucker v. Willis, 358 F.Supp. 425, 3 ELR 20585 (E.D.N.C.1973), aff'd 484 F.2d 158, 3 ELR 20912 (4th Cir.) (holding the issuance of a permit is not a "major Federal action"). See also Casenote, 52 N.C.L.Rev. 654 (1974). Environmental impact statements are required routinely for the Corps' own dredging activities. E. g., Wisconsin v. Callaway, 371 F.Supp. 807, 4 ELR 20296 (W.D.Wis.1974); Sierra Club v. Mason, 365 F.Supp. 47, 4 ELR 20186 (D.C.Conn.1973).

63. See Natural Resources Defense Council, Inc. v. Callaway, 524 F.2d 79, 5 ELR 20640 (2d Cir.1975); § 7.6 below. The Conference Report, supra note 22, at 142, contains an uncharacteristically strong endorsement of the economic importance of dredging:

> It is expected that until such time as feasible alternative methods for disposal of dredged or fill material are available, unreasonable restrictions shall not be imposed on dredging activities essential for the maintenance of interstate and foreign commerce. Consistent with the intent of this Act, the conferees expect that the disposal activities of private dredgers and the Corps of Engineers will be treated similarly.

64. 33 U.S.C.A. § 1344(c).

Secretary of the Army) and special findings requirements. Whether for these or other reasons, EPA is disinclined to move against dumping sites.

Apart from the specifics of the section 404 site selection criteria, the Corps' standards for issuing permits are distressingly vague. It was settled before enactment of the 1972 Amendments that the Corps' section 10 authority was supplemented importantly by the National Environmental Policy Act to justify permit denials on environmental grounds.[65] It is said now that a decision to issue a permit involves a "careful weighing" of the benefits that "reasonably may be expected to accrue" against the "reasonably foreseeable detriments." This "balancing process" involves consideration of a number of factors: "conservation, economics, aesthetics, general environmental concerns, historic values, fish and wildlife values, flood-damage prevention, land-use classifications, navigation, recreation, water supply, water quality, and, in general, the needs and welfare of the people. No permit will be granted unless its issuance is found to be in the public interest." [66]

The Corps' balancing process in issuing permits echoes the balancing of the common law nuisance cases [67] and of modern decisions under the National Environmental Policy Act.[68] It is informed by similar considerations: [69] Corps permits should not issue if the project planned clashes sharply with existing land use patterns, lacks justification for invading water resources, ignores less damaging alternatives, interferes seriously with public rights of navigation or threatens areas of special ecological or historical significance. An inability to minimize expected effects by operational or construction alternatives can lead to a permit denial. Opposition from informed governmental authorities, as under NEPA, may lead to project modifications or outright disqualification.

e. *Activities of the Corps of Engineers*

That the Corps occasionally assumes the role of the kettle assailing the teapot is indicated by the agency's own dredging activities comparable to and surpassing those it regulates. Separate regulations govern the Corps' dredging and disposal [70] although they are comparable in substance to the regulations for private parties. Federal projects are governed by the same criteria EPA prescribes for non-

---

65. Zabel v. Tabb, 430 F.2d 199, 1 ELR 20032 (5th Cir. 1970), cert. denied 401 U.S. 910 (1971); Annot., 25 ALR Fed. 706 (1975).

66. 33 CFR § 209.120(f)(1).

67. See § 2.3 above.

68. See § 7.3 below.

69. See 33 CFR §§ 209.120(f)(2), (3) (g).

70. 39 Fed.Reg. 26635 (1974), 33 CFR § 209.145; see Comptroller General, Report to the Congress: Observations on Dredging Activities and Problems (Corps of Engineers) (1972).

federal activities under section 404(b).[71] This includes the Corps' authority to insist on a site for economic reasons and EPA's authority to withdraw it on environmental grounds. The loosely framed "public interest" factors of project approval are thought to apply[72] although they are not expressly articulated in the regulations.

Procedurally, there are differences between public and private dredging activities: Corps projects presumptively are subject to NEPA[73] although negative declarations are not uncommon.[74] The Corps issues no permits to itself or its contractors, despite suggestions that it do so. Instead, a statement of findings is prepared in support of the decision. If a decision is made to dispose of dredged material in navigable or ocean waters, the statement serves as the functional equivalent of a permit since it must include "conditions under which the disposal will be performed."[75] Violations can be corrected in citizen suits by equitable relief alone.

f. *Related Federal and State Laws*

Concurrently with the expansion of federal power over activity affecting wetlands state laws have emerged as an important force. Typically, they impose a regulatory zoning mechanism on a wide range of activities in wetlands and related coastal regions.[76] Reported cases under these statutes, mostly involving issues of taking and the propriety of permit denials under different regulatory regimes, are rapidly accumulating.[77] Many of the state laws anticipated enactment of the Coastal Zone Management Act of 1972,[78] whose principal *raison d'etre* is to provide financial assistance for state coastal plans. Section 307(c)(3) of the Act[79] requires an applicant for a

71. See note 63, supra.

72. See 39 Fed.Reg. at 26635. See also Minnesota v. Callaway, 401 F.Supp. 524, 5 ELR 20703 (D.C.Minn. 1975), rev'd sub nom. Minnesota v. Hoffman, 534 F.2d 1198, 7 ELR 20066 (8th Cir. 1976) (holding that the Corps must comply with state pollution abatement requirements, including obtaining a permit).

73. See cases cited in note 62, supra.

74. See 33 CFR § 209.145(f).

75. Id. § 209.145(f)(1)(vii).

76. See § 2.16 n. 107 above. Compare Ausness, A Survey of State Regulation of Dredge and Fill in Nonnavigable Waters, 7 Land & Water L.Rev. 65 (1973); Corker, Thou Shalt Not Fill Public Waters Without Public Permission—Washington's Lake Chelan Decision, 45 Wash.L.Rev. 65 (1970), analyzing Wilbour v. Gallagher, 77 Wash.2d 306, 462 P.2d 232 (1969) (en banc); Comment, Private Fills in Navigable Waters: A Common Law Approach, 60 Calif.L. Rev. 225 (1972). See also Power, The Federal Role in Coastal Development, in Environmental Law Institute, Federal Environmental Law 792 (E. L. Dolgin & T. G. P. Guilbert eds. 1974).

77. E. g., Potomac Sand & Gravel Co. v. Mandel, 2 ELR 20101 (Md.Cir.Ct. 1972) (sustaining a qualified ban against dredging within one county despite taking claims); see § 2.16 n. 108 above.

78. Pub.L. No. 92–583, 86 Stat. 1280, 16 U.S.C.A. §§ 1451–64, as amended Pub.L. No. 94–370, 90 Stat. 1013 (1976).

79. 16 U.S.C.A. § 1456(c)(3), as amended Pub.L. No. 94–370, § 6, 90 Stat. 1018 (1976).

federal license to conduct activity affecting land or water uses in a state's coastal zone to furnish a certification that the proposed activity will comply with the state's coastal zone management program. Like the comparable veto provisions over federal projects affecting water quality,[80] this gives the states a practical power to nullify Corps-approved dredging and filling activities.[81]

Unlike the NPDES permit program under Section 402 of FWPCA, section 404 does not provide for delegation of the Corps' permitting authority to the states. The Corps does give deference to a state decision issuing a permit although it retains an ultimate environmental veto.[82] Provision also is made for the Corps to enter into agreements with the states to facilitate joint processing of permits.[83] Formal delegation of decision-making is a likely subject of future legislation.

§ 4.7 Disposal of Sewage Sludge

Sewage sludge was a certified national problem long before it was featured on the "60 Minutes" show of the CBS Television Network. But CBS News correspondent Morley Safer captures the essence of the challenge: "There are plenty of names for it, but the only one we can use on television is sludge; and it's more important than you may think, because unless we're careful and make some important decisions soon, we'll all be buried by it. It works this way. We're spending $20-billion cleaning up our filthy waterways, but somewhere along the way, we ignore the problem of what to do with the mess we collected while cleaning up the mess we made. So today there are hundreds, and soon there'll be thousands, of cities and towns across the country with tons and tons of black slimy waste to be disposed of each day. Like the man says: Here comes the sludge."[1] Indeed, of all the difficulties associated with implementing a massive cleanup program for municipal treatment plants, two stand out—the enormous cost and the enormous quantities of sludge.

The sludge that is coming can be defined as the semisolid residuals removed from the wastewater process stream.[2] Sludge is often under-

---

80. Section 401(a)(1), 33 U.S.C.A. § 1341(a)(1); See 40 CFR § 209.120(f)(3).

81. Apparently, the Corps reserves for itself but not its permittees authority to carry out dredging and filling activities in contravention of a state coastal zone management plan. Compare 33 CFR § 209.120(f)(3) (stating that a permit will not issue if a certification required by law is not forthcoming) with id. § 209.145(h)(2) (requiring referral to the Chief of Engineers for decision of any case where disposal of dredged material associated with a federal project would be inconsistent with approved coastal zone management plan).

82. 40 CFR § 230(5).

83. Id. § 209.120(f)(3).

1. 60 Minutes Transcript, vol. VII, No. 10, March 9, 1975, at 11.

2. See Metcalf & Eddy, Inc., Assessment of Technologies and Costs for Publicly Owned Treatment Works

stood to include the scum (grease and oil), grit (sand, gravel and cinders), and screenings (wood, rags and garbage) removed from sewage by wastewater treatment facilities.[3] Sludge varies widely in appearance (brown, black, gray), moisture content (quite dry to 99 per cent water), odor (putrescent to nearly odorless) and treatability. Obviously, sludge carries the same range of toxic substances as the wastewater from which it is derived (heavy metals, chlorinated hydrocarbons, pathogenic bacteria and viruses).[4] Sludge has many names depending on its characteristics and source (excess activated sludge, humus sludge, chemical sludge).[5] Raw primary sludge is usually gray and slimy in appearance, highly offensive in odor, and consists of fine silt and readily settleable organic matter.[6]

Problems of sludge disposal, treatment, transfer and disposition are growing exponentially. The reasons are many although the requirements of the 1972 Amendments increasing the removal of solids from wastewater streams are the most obvious: the volume of sludges produced by municipal treatment plants will increase by approximately 60 per cent between 1975 and 1985 (to some eight million dry tons per year).[7] At many plants this has meant that the disposal of solids becomes a legal, technological and economic problem rivaling that of the treatment of wastewater. Indeed, many municipal plant sites, severely constricted in size, are grossly ill suited for even temporary storage of the byproducts of upgraded water quality treatment. Concurrently with the growth in the volume of sludges have come restrictions on favored techniques of disposal: incineration runs awry of the air pollution laws on nuisance and health hazard grounds;[8] ocean disposal by barging to sea, accounting for the disposition of over 6.5 million wet tons of sludge in 1974,[9] is coming under the con-

Under Public Law 92–500, Apr. 1975, pt. 3, at 11B–1 (Report to the National Commission on Water Quality) [hereinafter cited as Metcalf & Eddy Treatment Works Study].

3. See id. at 11C–1 to –5; United States v. Asbury Park, 340 F.Supp. 555, 559, 2 ELR 20126, 20127 (D.C.N.J.1972): Sludge, generally, is composed of human excretion, household waste from food preparation, laundry waste, commercial waste, dirt, etc. Items such as corn kernels, tomato seeds and phrophylactics, sanitary napkins, pieces of orange peel, sand, shaving brushes, toothbrushes, plastic diaper liners, plastic toys and filter-tip cigarettes are some of the items frequently found in primary sludge.

4. See National Commission on Water Quality, Staff Draft Report on Water Quality Analysis and Environmental Impact Assessment of Public Law 92–500, Jan. 1976, at III–A–6 & A–7 (including a table on typical sludge characteristics and constituents) [hereinafter cited as Draft Report on Environmental Impact].

5. See Metcalf & Eddy Treatment Works Study, supra note 2, pt. 3, at B–2 to –4.

6. See id. at 11B–2.

7. Draft Report on Environmental Impact, supra note 4, at III–A–4 to –6.

8. See, e. g., Metropolitan Coalition for Clean Air v. District of Columbia, 167 U.S.App.D.C. 243, 511 F.2d 809, 5 ELR 20335 (1975); Bicknell v. Boston, 5 ELR 20712 (Mass.Super.Ct.1975).

9. Council on Environmental Quality, Sixth Ann.Rep. 80, table 9 (1975).

straints of the new ocean dumping laws.[10] The better known cases are those involving the dumping of New York City sludge, which is legally in doubt,[11] and the Philadelphia practice, which has resulted in an EPA order phasing out the ocean disposal of sludge.[12]

Presently, the land application of municipal sludges is emerging as the preferred disposal alternative.[13] Treatment, sometimes advanced treatment, is usually undertaken: dewatering, conditioning (to assist in dewatering and disinfection), thickening and stabilization.[14] Sludge stabilization is a generic term describing techniques for reducing public health hazards (principally by eliminating pathogens) and nuisance odors associated with sludge. The stabilization method used most frequently is anaerobic digestion, which involves biological decomposition and the settling out of solids over a period of time (thirty to sixty days).[15] Practices and suggestions for disposing of treated sludges run the gamut—disposition in sanitary landfills or old strip mines, composting (producing humus-like material from the biodegradable (organic) materials in solid waste),[16] sale as a soil conditioner or low-grade fertilizer,[17] numerous other applications for agricultural

10. See § 4.16 below; cf. United States v. Asbury Park, 340 F.Supp. 555, 2 ELR 20126 (D.N.J.1972) (applying Section 13 of the Rivers and Harbors Act to curtail ocean disposal of sewage sludges).

11. In re New York City, Interim Ocean Disposal Permit No. NY 009. See generally Hearings on Marine Protection, Research, and Sanctuaries Act of 1972, Before the Subcomm. on Ocean and Atmosphere of the Senate Comm. on Commerce, S.Doc. No. 32, 94th Cong., 1st Sess. (1975); Joint Hearings on Ocean Dumping Before the Subcomm. on Fisheries and Wildlife Conservation and the Environment and the Subcomm. on Oceanography of the House Comm. on Merchant Marine and Fisheries, H.R. Doc. No. 10, 94th Cong., 1st Sess. (1975); Joint Hearings on Ocean Dumping—Part 2, Before the Subcomm. on Fisheries and Wildlife Conservation and the Environment and the Subcomm. on Oceanography of the House Comm. on Merchant Marine and Fisheries, H.R.Doc. No. 25, 94th Cong., 2d Sess. (1976).

12. See In re City of Philadelphia, Interim Ocean Disposal Permit No. PA 010, Decision of the Administrator, 5 ELR 30003 (Sept. 25, 1975); see Comment, Test Case on Ocean Dumping: Must Philadelphia Move Toward On-Land Disposal of Sewage Sludge? 5 ELR 10144 (1975); Comment, Latent Risks on Ocean Dumping: EPA Administrator Affirms Philadelphia's Phase Out Order, 5 ELR 10213 (1975). See also Maryland v. Train, 415 F.Supp. 116, 6 ELR 20496 (D.C. Md.1976) (Camden, New Jersey, permit).

13. See, e. g., Process Research, Inc., Environmental Impact Assessment of the Piscataway (Md.) Regional Wastewater Facility, June 1975 (draft), at 5–24 to –29. Compare § 6.10 below (discussing hazardous wastes).

14. Environmental Protection Agency, Alternative Waste Management Techniques for Best Practicable Waste Treatment, Oct. 1975, at 27–31.

15. See id. at 27.

16. The literature on composting is vast. It is followed closely in the periodical *Compost Science*, published semi-annually by Rodale Press, Inc.; see Environmental Protection Agency, Recovery and Utilization of Municipal Solid Waste 55–65 (1971).

17. Well known is Milwaukee, Wisconsin's sale of dried sludge called Milorganite. See Metcalf & Eddy Treatment Works Study, supra note 2, pt. 3 at 13–18.

purposes, enhancement of parks and forests and reclamation of damaged terrain (including even the White House lawn [18]).

The escape of the monster sludge as a result of the imposition of water pollution controls is a classic lesson in how ecological problems are connected, as are their solutions.[19] For the most part, sludge derived from control efforts at the source is disposed of by techniques creating in turn nonpoint sources of water pollution beyond the reach of the 1972 Amendments.[20] This brings greater pressure to bear on the states and localities to deal not only with unprecedented volumes of traditional sludges but with new forms of toxic or potentially toxic wastes. Sludges produced by advanced industrial waste treatment, for example, are not only high in volume [21] but occasionally impossible of disposition. This leads to new legislative and practical initiatives for the control of toxic wastes,[22] which may amount to nothing more than carefully segregating them in the hopes that today's waste, as a result of changing economics, will become tomorrow's sought after material.[23]

Federal law addresses the disposition of sludges tangentially in several ways: landfills are potential candidates for application of the Rivers and Harbors Act.[24] EPA's solid waste disposal guidelines reach the disposal of nontoxic sludges on various federally controlled

---

18. See Wash. Post, July 12, 1975, at D2, col. 4. See also League of Women Voters, Municipal Sludge: What Shall We Do With It? 5 (1976) (reporting on the use of composted sludge to enrich soil for the Constitution Gardens in Washington, D. C.). Agricultural uses are restricted severely by the tendency of crops to pick up heavy metals, such as cadmium, from sludge used for fertilizer or other purposes. See 41 Fed.Reg. 22532 (1976) (Municipal Sludge Management Environmental Factors). See also Senate Comm. on Agriculture & Forestry, Conservation of the Land, and the Use of Waste Materials for Man's Benefit, 94th Cong., 1st Sess. 48–69 (Comm. Print. 1975).

19. See § 1.1 above.

20. See §§ 4.3, 4.4 above.

21. See Draft Report on Environmental Impact, supra note 4, at III–A–6 to –25, esp. A–16 (containing a figure on industrial and municipal sludge production rates). Nine industries alone (iron and steel, textiles, canned and preserved fruits and vegetables, inorganic chemicals, organic chemicals, pulp and paper, plastics and synthetics, petroleum refining and metal finishing) generate annually 21.5 million tons of sludges and brines. If these waste residuals were disposed of on land at a concentration of 25 per cent solids (75 per cent water), an area of one hundred square miles, one foot deep, would be required every year. See id. at II–145 to –147. The staff estimates are based on the work of Environmental Quality Systems, Inc., Environmental Impact of the Disposal of Wastewater Residuals, Aug. 1975 (Draft Report to the National Commission on Water Quality) [hereinafter cited as Report on Disposal of Wastewater Residuals].

22. See § 6.10 below.

23. Optimists call indefinite segregation of wastes "storage for reuse." See Draft Report on Environmental Impact, supra note 4, at II–145 to –146.

24. See § 4.5 above.

disposal sites.[25] More importantly, the construction grants program affords EPA considerable leverage for insisting upon proper sludge disposal by all federally funded facilities.[26] The Administrator is instructed specifically to encourage waste treatment management which, among other things, provides for "the ultimate disposal of sludge in a manner that will not result in environmental hazards." [27] An EPA Bulletin on acceptable methods of sludge disposal has been issued to aid regional administrators in the evaluation of grant applications.[28] It addresses the principal problems of application rates, system operation, monitoring and surveillance, protecting ground water and controlling surface water runoff.

Direct federal regulatory control over the disposal of sewage sludge in many ways is less effective than the indirect leverage afforded by the grants program. Section 405 [29] of the FWPCA prohibits, except in accordance with a permit, the disposal of sewage sludge from a municipal treatment works (including the removal of in-place sludge from one location and its deposit at another), if the planned disposal "would result in any pollutant from such sewage sludge entering the navigable waters." EPA has issued no separate regulations for sludge disposal, treating its authority under section 405 as simply one component of the National Pollutant Discharge Elimination System permit program.[30] Also, EPA has made clear that sludge disposal sites and methods are not at issue in an NPDES permit adjudication unless a "nexus" is shown between proposed disposal plans and predicted pollution of the navigable waters.[31] The legal argument the other way, and it is persuasive, is that the hearing on a permit for a municipal plant ought to consider the full spectrum of alternatives including methods and conditions for sludge disposal.[32] Even if the EPA understanding is upheld in the courts, sludge may become an issue at the permit stage in the not altogether unusual situation where accumulations at the site threaten the maintenance of water quality standards.

---

25. See § 6.4 below. Some sites may exclude digested and dewatered sludges from waste treatment facilities, raw sewage sludges and septic tank pumpings. See 40 CFR §§ 240.200–2, 240.201–2.

26. See § 4.10 below.

27. Section 201(d)(4), 33 U.S.C. § 1281(d)(4).

28. EPA, Draft Technical Bulletin, Acceptable Methods for the Utilization or Disposal of Sludges, Nov. 1974.

29. 33 U.S.C.A. § 1345.

30. 40 CFR § 125.3 (reciting Sections 402 and 405 of the Act as authority for the NPDES regulations). The Administrator's authority under section 405 states that any regulations he issues "shall require the application to such disposal of each criterion, factor, procedure, and requirement applicable to a permit issued under section 402 of this title, as the Administrator determines necessary to carry out the objective of this Act." Section 405(b), 33 U.S.C.A. § 1345(b).

31. Environmental Protection Agency, NPDES Decision of the General Counsel No. 33, Oct. 21, 1975, at 1–7.

32. § 4.13 below.

Combined legislative and administrative judgments thus reduce the reach of the federal regulation of sludge disposal: industrial sludge is covered not at all. The disposal of municipal sludges not presenting a demonstrable threat to waters of the United States is unregulated. The disposal of municipal sludges resulting in water pollution can be permitted under section 405 although in the absence of the provision any such discharges would be barred flatly by Section 301 of the FWPCA [33] and Section 13 of the Rivers and Harbors Act.[34] In practice, sludge disposal issues usually are unexplored in the course of an NPDES permit determination. A boilerplate clause appearing in many municipal permits contains an inoffensive constraint that is often the only evidence of a federal legal interest in the sludge disposal practices of municipal plants:

> Collected screenings, slurries, sludges, and other solids shall be disposed of in such a manner as to prevent entry of those wastes (or runoff from the wastes) into navigable waters or their tributaries.[35]

A substantial and expanding state and local legal presence is found on issues of sludge disposal and related problems of the land treatment of wastewater. One recent head count [36] identifies a wide variety of provisions on key criteria such as site restrictions, depths to groundwater and distances to surface water, leachate monitoring and control, required cover, prevention of surface runoff and pretreatment. Pennsylvania,[37] for example, has solid waste regulations allowing the disposal of digested and 80 percent dewatered sludge in landfills upon approval of the Department of Environmental Protection. Overall, "21 states or 34 percent have some form of formal regulations [on the land disposal of sludge]. Of the 35 states with policies regarding sludge disposal, 18 states or 51 percent allow or regulate disposal in landfills, 20 or 57 percent evaluate disposal on an ad hoc or case-by-case basis, [5] or 14 percent require dewatering, Mississippi and Indiana require some form of stabilization, Wisconsin requires digestion, and Idaho [requires] heat treatment . . . ."[38] On the subject of direct land application of wastewater (believed by many to be an environmentally preferable alternate to conventional

---

33. 33 U.S.C.A. § 1311.

34. See § 4.5 above.

35. National Pollutant Discharge Elimination System Permit for Blue Plains Sewage Treatment Plant, Permit No. DC 0021199, Feb. 25, 1974, at 8.

36. 2 Report on Disposal of Wastewater Residuals, supra note 21, at IX–13 to –16; see Draft Report on Environmental Impact, supra note 4, at V–72 (reporting that 21 states have regulations for land disposal of sludge).

37. 25 Pa.Adm.Code § 75.116(b).

38. Memorandum from Mr. Mike Italiano to Mr. Joe G. Moore, Jr., National Commission on Water Quality, Land Application and Alternative Uses and Disposal Methods of Wastewater and Sludge, Oct. 9, 1975, at 1. [hereinafter cited as Land Application Memo].

treatment and discharge [39]), 22 states have formal regulations. Thirty-eight states require a minimum of secondary treatment of the wastewater. Land application is prohibited in the District of Columbia, discouraged in Rhode Island, and not practiced in Iowa, Nebraska and Ohio.[40] The expansion of the legal system to protect against sludge disposal, or sludge avoidance by land treatment, is an inevitable byproduct of the attack upon point source water pollution.

§ 4.8 Water Quality Standards

Section 303 [1] of the 1972 Amendments provides for EPA review, approval and occasional revision of state water quality standards for both interstate and intrastate waters. The 1965 Act called for the adoption of state standards which are now in effect. Technically, a water quality standard consists of water quality criteria, designated uses,[2] and a plan of enforcement. The terms water quality criteria and water quality standards often are used synonymously, and they are in this text. Water quality criteria can be defined as ambient water standards, which are legal expressions of permissible amounts of pollutants allowed in a defined water segment. This formulation typically appears in one or both of two forms: quantitative and descriptive. Examples of quantitative criteria are: not less than 5 parts per million of dissolved oxygen or more than 500 micrograms per liter of dissolved solids or more than 200 fecal coliform per 100 milliliters. Examples of descriptive criteria are: surface waters must be "free from floating debris, scum and other floating materials attributable to municipal, industrial or other discharges or agricultural practices in amounts sufficient to be unsightly or deleterious." [3]

Designated uses are accomplished by assigning segments of water to certain classes and defining the classes by reference to use. Thus, Class A waters must be suitable for recreation,[4] and Class B waters suitable "for the growth and propagation of fish, other aquatic and

---

39. See § 4.10 below (discussing land application techniques and their status under the grants construction program). See also W. Cowlishaw, Update on Muskegon County, Michigan Land Treatment System (1974); D. Zwick, Water Wasteland 381–89 (1970); Environmental Protection Agency, Final Environmental Impact Statement, Upgrading and Expansion of the WSSC Piscataway Wastewater Treatment Facility to 30 MGD AWT, Sept. 1974, at 49–57.

40. Land Application Memo, supra note 38, at 1.

1. 33 U.S.C.A. § 1313.

2. Section 303(c)(2), 33 U.S.C.A. § 1313(c)(2). See 40 CFR § 120.10 specifying state water quality standards adopted and now in effect. This was a statutory requirement under Section 5 of the 1965 Act. Pub.L. No. 89–234, 79 Stat. 908. Compare note 24, infra.

3. An illustrative General Water Quality Criteria, in EPA, Guidelines for Developing or Revising Water Quality Standards Under the Federal Water Pollution Control Act Amendments of 1972, Apr. 1973, at 23 [hereinafter cited as Guidelines].

4. Id. at 21.

semi-aquatic life both marine and freshwater . . .."[5] And, in past days, Class D waters could be used for "transportation of sewage or industrial wastes, or both without nuisance."[6] The enforcement plans under the 1965 Act were typically vague directives to a particular source, such as to install "secondary treatment or its equivalent," with the details of the obligation a subject of barter between state officials and plant engineers.[7]

The process for adoption and revision of the standards is clearly prescribed by section 303. There is an initial period for federal review and adoption,[8] followed by periodic review and modification (at least once each three years after public hearings).[9] As with the Clean Air Act, the Administrator is obliged to promulgate his own standards applicable to interstate or intrastate waters if recommended changes are not adopted by the states.[10] This procedure of federal review and override, on grounds sometimes quite subjective, contributes to ill feelings among state and federal officials which are exacerbated by other features of the Act. Interestingly, the statutory criterion for federal review of state standards outstanding at the time of the 1972 Amendments is whether they "are consistent with the applicable requirements of this Act as in effect immediately prior to the date of enactment of the Federal Water Pollution Control Act Amendments of 1972."[11] This curious reference back means that the standards are evaluated by the uncertain beacon of the 1965 Act.[12] More interesting yet, standards developed in the future are measured against a vague statutory test—they must "protect the public health or welfare, enhance the quality of water and serve the purposes of this Act"—not materially different from the old 1965 standard.[13]

---

5. Ibid.

6. Urie v. Franconia Paper Corp., 107 N.H. 131, 134, 218 A.2d 360, 362 (1966).

7. Zener, The Federal Law of Water Pollution Control, in Environmental Law Institute, Federal Environmental Law 682, 716–17 (E. L. Dolgin & T. G. P. Guilbert eds. 1974), quoting EPA General Counsel John R. Quarles, Jr., Address Before the American Bar Association National Inst., Oct. 26, 1972, in 3 Env.Rep. — Current Developments 794 (1972).

8. Sections 303(a), (b), 33 U.S.C.A. §§ 1313(a), (b).

9. Section 303(c), 33 U.S.C.A. § 1313(c).

10. Sections 313(a)(2), (3), (b), (c), 33 U.S.C.A. §§ 1313(a)(2), (3), (b), (c); see Kentucky ex rel. Hancock v. Train, —— F.Supp. ——, 6 ELR 20689 (E.D.Ky.1976) (upholding EPA disapproval of Kentucky standards).

11. Sections 303(a)(1), (3)(B), 33 U.S.C.A. §§ 1313(a)(1), (3)(B).

12. The 1965 Act required only that standards take into account the "use and value for public water supplies, propagation of fish and wildlife, recreational purposes, and agricultural, industrial and other legitimate uses." Pub.L.No. 89–234, § 5, 79 Stat. 908. The Water Quality Improvement Act of 1970 added an amendment requiring the standards to take into account "use and value for navigation." Pub.L. No. 91–224, § 112, 84 Stat. 114.

13. Section 303(c)(2), 33 U.S.C.A. § 1313(c)(2), reads, in part:
Such standards shall be such as to protect the public health or welfare, enhance the quality of water and serve the purposes of this Act.

There is enough elsewhere in the Act to justify rejection of state standards not calling for high quality water (indeed, swimmable water by 1983), but congressional reiteration of the 1965 standard illustrates again a continuing tension between the water quality and effluent standards approaches.

Under the 1965 Act considerable debate ensued over whether the federal government could condition its approval of state standards for interstate waters upon a secondary treatment and a nondegradation requirement.[14] The first issue is mooted by the 1972 Amendments but the second remains. EPA, to be sure, requires an antidegradation clause in state standards as a condition of approval,[15] but it is not exactly ironclad as formulated in many of the standards.[16] The 1972 Amendments contain roughly comparable language to that yielding the no significant deterioration policy under the Clean Air Act ("restore and maintain" [17] compared to "protect and enhance" [18]), and express other reasons (including the 1985 no discharge and 1983 swimmable water goals) for reading a strong anti-degradation policy into the law of water pollution. This puts in doubt the legal validity of the qualified anti-degradation clauses in the state standards and judicial interpretations of them.[19] One category of sources where a no significant deterioration policy would be important would be new facilities exempt from new source performance standards under section 306 because EPA as yet has imposed no standards.[20]

> Such standards shall be established taking into consideration their use and value for public water supplies, propagation of fish and wildlife, recreational purposes, and agricultural, industrial, and other purposes, and also taking into consideration their use and value for navigation.

14. Zener, supra note 7, at 715–19; J. C. Davies & B. Davies, The Politics of Pollution ch. 7 (1974); Dunkelberger, The Federal Government's Role in Regulating Water Pollution Under the Federal Water Quality Act of 1965, 3 Nat.Res.L. 3 (1970).

15. See Guidelines, supra note 3, at 20 for an illustrative provision; cf. 40 CFR § 130.22 (requiring state planning process to be consistent with pre-existing antidegradation statement in water quality standards).

16. See Guidelines, supra note 3, at 20: These and other waters of the state will not be lowered in quality unless it has been affirmatively demonstrated to the state water pollution control agency that such a change is justified as a result of necessary economic or social development, and will not interfere with or become injurious to any assigned uses made of or presently possible in such waters.

17. Section 101(a), 33 U.S.C.A. § 1251 (a).

18. See § 3.12 above.

19. Reserve Mining Co. v. Minnesota Pollution Control Agency, 1 ELR 20073 (Minn.Dist.Ct. Lake County 1970), rev'd in part on other grounds 200 N.W.2d 142, 3 ELR 20170 (Minn. Dist.Ct. Lake County 1972) (holding with consent of the state that the antidegradation clause did not apply retroactively to sources existing at the time of adoption; facts do not indicate whether discharges increased after adoption of the clause).

20. See § 4.12 below. For a discussion of nondegradation under the water act, see Donley, Moss, Outen & Speth, Land Use Controls Under the Federal Water Pollution Control Act: A Citizens Guide 12–15 (Natural Resources Defense Council, 1975).

Presently, EPA insists that by 1977 all waters be protected by state standards for recreational uses and for the preservation and propagation of desirable species of aquatic biota.[21] Waters of this quality perforce protect agricultural, industrial or navigational uses. Some waters may be classified at a somewhat lower quality if pollution is occurring naturally or if there are technological limitations upon water quality improvement.[22] Obviously, under section 303(c) litigable issues may arise over whether the approval of certain uses and water quality criteria based on these uses "protect the public health or welfare, enhance the quality of water and serve the purposes of this Act." Despite the breadth of this delegation to EPA, technological or economic feasibility of compliance, for example, should be considered irrelevant to whether the standards protect the public health or welfare.[23]

Far more likely to spawn litigation are the standards themselves. The scope and detail of these legal obligations seem not to be fully appreciated by the legal community.[24] The standards, it must be remembered, impose a practical zoning for uses of virtually all waters of the United States. The criteria cover the principal parameters—temperature, heavy metals, radioactive materials, dissolved oxygen, suspended solids, nutrients, among others. Despite the fact that these requirements are widely violated, litigation invoking the standards is exceedingly rare.[25] The explanation probably is the vagueness and inherent unenforceability of many of the standards along with the difficulty of proof in linking up an individual source to an ambient violation.[26] Lack of interest and awareness by the practicing bar cannot be discounted. There is certainly no dearth of theory: the standards

21. Guidelines, supra note 3, at 4. This interpretation is based upon the "restore and maintain" clause of section 101(a). Council on Environmental Quality, Fifth Ann.Rep. 142 (1974).

22. Guidelines, supra note 3, at 4. See 40 Fed.Reg. 29887, 29889 (1975), proposing an amendment to 40 CFR § 131.11(e)(2)(ii) to allow "lower water quality as a result of necessary or justifiable economic or social development."

23. Cf. Waterford v. Water Pollution Control Bd., 5 N.Y.2d 171, 182 N.Y.S. 2d 785, 156 N.E.2d 427 (1958).

24. Definitive references to this diverse, changing, sometimes secret body of law do not exist. One water quality standards summary can be found in Environmental Protection Agency, Quality Criteria for Water (1976) (Pre-publication Copy). See also 7 Environmental Protection Agency, Legal Compilation: Water, Jan. 1973, at 3721; note 2, supra. An important reference is National Technical Advisory Committee, Report to the Secretary of Interior, Apr. 1968, upon which many of the standards are based.

25. Note, Water Quality Standards in Private Nuisance Actions, 79 Yale L.J. 102 (1969), cites not a single example. See United States v. Douglas County, 3 ELR 20727 (D.Nev.1973) (ordering county officials to refrain from issuing building permits until facilities for the treatment and exportation of sewage from Lake Tahoe Basin is accomplished; action necessary to effectuate water quality standards and implementation plan); In re General Elec. Co., 6 ELR 30007 (N.Y.Dep't of Environmental Conservation 1976).

26. See Olympia Oyster Co. v. Rayonier, Inc., 229 F.Supp. 855 (W.D. Wash.1964).

set measures of conduct that should be respected in either nuisance [27] or negligence [28] cases, to mention prime examples.

The awkwardness of ambient standards as a planning, and particularly an enforcement, device is demonstrated amply under the Clean Air Act.[29] Many of the same criticisms apply to the water quality standards, both before and after the 1972 Amendments. The descriptive criteria, in particular, call for both expert testimony and a receptive forum to transform, let us say, a general obligation to maintain "recreational" uses into a specific obligation to reduce loadings of phosphorus or nitrogen from a particular source. The decision requires, among other things, judgments about the degree of algal bloom that interferes with "recreational" uses such as swimming or boating, estimates of loadings from all other point and nonpoint sources, assumptions about degrees of control elsewhere, and predictions of how a water segment will respond to a hoped for change of parameters. Congress' prescription of an interim water quality goal providing for "recreation in and on the water" by July 1, 1983 [30] of course leaves open these complex questions of meaning and implementation. The no discharge goal of 1985, on the other hand, leaves no doubt about what was meant. Its chief failing is that it is considered incredible by most of those charged with implementing the Act, and therefore is a source of derision instead of inspiration.

An important decision under the 1972 Amendments has ruled that a water quality standard is an "effluent standard or limitation" enforceable under the citizen suit provisions of section 505.[31] The rationale, which is quite correct, is that water quality standards promulgated pursuant to the 1965 Act "are to constitute a floor level of quality until the stiffer effluent limitations of the 1972 Act can be implemented." [32] Discharges contributing to a violation of water quality standards thus are actionable in the federal courts as well as those of the states.

Two other features of the water quality standards deserve mention—the assignment of pollution loads to certain segments of water

---

27. See § 2.10 above.

28. Cf. Martin v. Herzog, 228 N.Y. 164, 126 N.E. 814 (1920).

29. § 3.4 above.

30. 33 U.S.C.A. § 1251(a)(2), reads, in part:
   it is the national goal that wherever attainable, an interim goal of water quality which provides for the protection and propagation of fish, shellfish and wildlife and provides for recreation in and on the water be achieved by July 1, 1983; . . . .

Compare id. § 1312(a), quoted in note 57, infra.

31. Montgomery Environmental Coalition v. Fri., 366 F.Supp. 261, 4 ELR 20181 (D.C.D.C.1973). But cf. Bethlehem Steel Corp. v. EPA, 530 F.2d 215, 6 ELR 20597 (2d Cir. 1976) (EPA partial approval of New York State's revised water quality standards is not the promulgation of "any effluent limitation" reviewable directly in the courts of appeal under 33 U.S.C.A. § 1369(b)(1)(E)).

32. 366 F.Supp. at 265, 4 ELR at 20183.

(and to sources discharging there) and the establishment of water quality related effluent limitations. The pollution load assignment provisions are found in section 303(d),[33] which is addressed also in the planning section.[34] The subsection, quite simply, requires planning to assign pollution rights to certain dischargers. It was included in the Act at the insistence of the House conferees and reflects the historical water quality standards assumption that assimilation of wastes is a fit and proper function of a watercourse. In a sense, section 303(d) represents contingent planning by the Congress for the day when the no discharge objective is abandoned in favor of basin level allocations of assimilative capacity.[35] EPA placed great emphasis upon the development of waste load allocations for the reason that the information can be incorporated immediately into the National Pollutant Discharge Elimination System permits for individual sources.[36]

Section 303(d) comes into play if the technology based effluent limitations are deemed too lax to assure compliance with existing water quality standards. It is triggered by each state identifying waters within its boundaries for which the 1977 effluent limitations of section 301(b)(1)[37] ("best practicable" control technology for industries and secondary treatment for existing sewage treatment plants[38]) are not "stringent enough to implement any water quality standard applicable to such waters." These waters so identified are called water quality limited segments.[39] The provision envisages a six-step procedure for tightening controls on individual sources: (1) identification of the problem waters by the state; (2) priority ranking of these waters by the state; (3) the state establishes the "total maximum daily load" of pollutants for those segments, in accordance with the priority ranking, "at a level necessary to implement the applicable water quality standards with seasonal variations and a margin of safety which takes into account any lack of knowledge concerning the relationship between effluent limitations and water quality";[40] (4) the state submits to the Administrator for his approval the waters identified and the loads established;[41] (5) within thirty days the Administrator approves or disapproves the identification and load as-

33. 33 U.S.C.A. § 1313(d).

34. See § 4.9 below.

35. See H. F. Wise, E. H. Haskell, R. E. Einsweiler & J. J. Bosley, Institutional Assessment of the Implementation of the Planning Requirements of the Water Pollution Control Act Amendments of 1972, Aug. 1975, at II–21 (prepared for the National Commission on Water Quality) [hereinafter cited as National Commission on Water Quality Planning Assessment].

36. See id. at III–1 to –5.

37. 33 U.S.C.A. § 1311(b)(1).

38. See §§ 4.12, 4.13 below.

39. Section 303(d)(1)(A), 33 U.S.C.A. § 1313(d)(1)(A); see § 4.9 below.

40. Section 303(d)(1)(C), 33 U.S.C.A. § 1313(d)(1)(C).

41. Section 303(d)(2), 33 U.S.C.A. § 1313(d)(2).

signment;[42] (6) upon approval, the state incorporates the load allocations into its section 303(e) plan [43] or, upon disapproval, the Administrator establishes loads as "he determines necessary to implement the water quality standards" and then the state incorporates them into the 303(e) plan.[44] The plan itself must include both total maximum daily loads and compliance schedules for individual dischargers.[45] The permits reflect the same loads and compliance schedules.

The purpose of the waste load allocation provisions is understandable: compliance with water quality standards accumulated for the most part as dead letters under the 1965 Act is an unmistakable aim of the 1972 Amendments.[46] To the extent this is not accomplished by application of the 1977 best practicable effluent limitations on individual sources, a further increment in effluent controls is required. This increment is expressed in terms of the total maximum daily loads incorporated in the permit. Loadings are expressed commonly in terms of pounds per day of identifiable pollutants (for example, suspended solids or nitrogen). Thus, a sewage treatment plant satisfying the 1977 secondary treatment requirements might have to go further if the discharge nonetheless results in continuing violations of the water quality standards. In a very practical sense, the NPDES permit decisions [47] must ask whether a discharge from a point source will be consistent with the standards and, if not, what "loads" can be assigned to a source consistently with the standards. In an appropriate case, there is room for an argument that pound loadings from a specific source must be zero since all other sources (both point and nonpoint) contribute loadings that will assure continued violation of the standards.[48]

There are obvious pitfalls in this process, some of them due to inevitable difficulties in linking up individual sources to water quality violations. First, the problem is larger than expected: the 1977 technology based effluent standards will fall short of achieving the water quality standards in more than half the 3100 water quality segments identified by the states.[49] These are waters with a single large discharger, several of them, or areas with large nonpoint source contributions. While there has been a tendency to classify segments as water quality limited when in doubt,[50] the fact remains that the

42. Ibid.

43. These plans are discussed in § 4.9 below.

44. Section 303(d)(2), 33 U.S.C.A. § 1313(d)(2).

45. Sections 303(e)(3)(C), (F), 33 U.S.C.A. §§ 1313(e)(3)(C), (F).

46. See section 301(b)(1)(C), 33 U.S.C.A. § 1311(b)(1)(C).

47. See § 4.11 below.

48. This position is urged in NPDES Permit No. VA 0025402 (City of Richmond).

49. EPA, Water Quality Strategy Paper, Mar. 15, 1974, at 17.

50. See National Commission on Water Quality Planning Assessment, supra note 35, at I–12.

water quality standards retain considerable legal significance despite the onset of the effluent requirements in 1972. Second, considerable guesswork is involved in determining amounts of pollutants that can be introduced into a watercourse consistently with water quality objectives. The Act recognizes this,[51] and the Administrator with help from the National Academy of Sciences [52] has published a criteria document under section 304 reflecting current knowledge of the effects of pollutants on human health, fish and wildlife, plants, shorelines, and so on.[53] This is a criteria document in the sense the term is used in the Clean Air Act—a comprehensive exegesis on causes and effects—and is thus helpful in determining what loads are consistent with water quality standards in what waters. A related acknowledgement of the difficulties of linking up appropriate loads to desired water quality is found in the requirement that a determination of maximum loads reflect a "margin of safety which takes into account any lack of knowledge concerning the relationship between effluent limitations and water quality." [54] This must be read as requiring a firm administrative prediction that particular load reductions will yield desired water quality aims.

However uncertain the relationship between overall loadings and ultimate water quality, the link between loadings from an individual plant and overall water quality is that much more tenuous. What this means as a practical matter is that the modeling assumptions yielding the conclusion that point source X should be permitted to generate loads Y and Z are very much in issue in the NPDES permit process. EPA assumes, quite correctly, that it can exercise a veto over load allocations reflected in discharge permits issued by the states.[55] This stresses, once again, the role of section 303(d) as the bridge between the long extant water quality standards and the recently conceived effluent limitations.

The load allocation authority of section 303(d) must be viewed independently of the Administrator's power to establish "water quality related effluent limitations" under section 302.[56] The latter provision authorizes additional controls above and beyond the 1983 "best available technology" limitations, not merely the 1977 "best practicable" limitations addressed in section 303(d). Section 302 controls

---

51. The state's calculation of the total maximum daily load is to be completed only "for those pollutants which the Administrator identifies under section 304(a)(2) as suitable for such calculation." Section 303(d)(1)(C), 33 U.S.C.A. § 1313(d)(1)(C). Only the basic parameters are deemed "suitable" for calculation—suspended solids, dissolved oxygen, nutrients.

52. National Academy of Sciences, Water Quality Criteria (1972).

53. EPA, Water Quality Criteria (1973). See also EPA, Quality Criteria for Water (1976) (Pre-publication Copy).

54. Section 303(d)(1)(C), 33 U.S.C.A. § 1313(d)(1)(C).

55. Zener, supra note 7, at 721; see section 402(d), 33 U.S.C.A. § 1342(d).

56. 33 U.S.C.A. § 1312.

are a possibility if the Administrator determines that discharges "from a point source or group of point sources . . . would interfere with the attainment or maintenance" of the 1983 swimmable/fishable water goals.[57] In such a case the Administrator can establish "effluent limitations (including alternative effluent control strategies)" which "can reasonably be expected to contribute to the attainment or maintenance of such water quality." This last turn of the screw is hedged closely by notice and hearing requirements affording an opportunity to probe economic or social costs of additional limitations.[58] An affected source can defeat the proposals by showing that regardless of the state of the art "there is no reasonable relationship between the economic and social costs and the benefits to be obtained."[59]

Section 302 is a no nonsense prescription for a final showdown. The "effluent limitations" that can be imposed are by definition better than the best (since they are incremental improvements on the 1983 standards which are quite stringent themselves). The "alternative effluent control strategies" that might be imposed only can be described as drastic. The Senate Report points out that "further reduction of the level of effluent entering the affected waters may not be possible through control technology, yet essential to water quality."[60] Thus "alternative effluent control strategies" may include "the transportation of effluents to other less affected waters or the control of in-plant processes."[61] The obvious option, well known at common law, is a shutdown, the threat of which explains the strict technological, social and economic inquiries under section 302. To be sure, the shutdown option is narrowed by the expanding capabilities of control technology and the increasing size of the investments in jeopardy, but it survives distinctly under the 1972 Amendments.

57. Section 101(a)(2), 33 U.S.C.A. § 1251(a)(2), quoted in note 30, supra. The goal is expressed in section 302 (a), 33 U.S.C.A. § 1312(a) as
  that water quality in a specific portion of the navigable waters which shall assure protection of public water supplies, agricultural and industrial uses, and the protection and propagation of a balanced population of shellfish, fish and wildlife, and allow recreational activities in and on the water . . .
For a discussion of the technological and economic aspects of achieving the 1983 goals, see National Commission on Water Quality, Staff Draft Report on Water Quality Analysis and Environmental Impact Assessment of Public Law 92-500, Jan. 1976, at I-27 to -51 [hereinafter cited as Draft Report on Environmental Impact].

58. Section 302(b)(1), 33 U.S.C.A. § 1312(b)(1).

59. Section 302(b)(2), 33 U.S.C.A. § 1312(b)(2).

60. Comm. on Public Works, Federal Water Pollution Control Act Amendments of 1971, S.Doc. No. 414, 92d Cong., 1st Sess. 46 (1971).

61. Id. at 46-47. The transportation of effluent option is not unknown to the law. Chicago's sewage is transported into the Mississippi Basin rather than into Lake Michigan by reversal of the flow of the Chicago River. See Missouri v. Illinois, 180 U.S. 208, 21 S.Ct. 331, 45 L.Ed. 497 (1901).

Section 302 has remained moribund for several years but appears to have a future. There is no reason why a section 302 hearing cannot be combined with an ordinary NPDES proceeding. Nor does it appear that section 302 limitations looking to 1983 and beyond are an improper subject of current NPDES adjudicatory hearings, if, for example, it is likely that current control strategies will foreclose opportunities for meeting the 1983 goals. Section 302 also affords an opportunity for joining several sources in a single proceeding to assign waste load allocations on a record more dependable than that arising haphazardly in disjointed NPDES proceedings on single permits.

The shutdown possibilities anticipated by section 302 might arise in one context without the 302 procedural protections. Many of the state water quality standards call for swimmable and fishable water now not some time in 1983. These existing standards should be met not later than July 1, 1977.[62] A shutdown or other severe restriction could result either directly by enforcement of these standards or indirectly by imposition of a severe section 303(d) load allocation deemed necessary to meet the standards. Either way, the noncomplying source would not have open to it the technological and economic hardship pleas invited by section 302. Of course, the state water quality standards could be relaxed to accommodate the source, either at the initiative of a state or of EPA which reserves unto itself an authority to disapprove "overly stringent" state standards.[63] It would not be the first time the law was written to conform to the needs of the technology instead of the technology being shaped to conform to the needs of the law.

§ 4.9 Planning Provisions: Generally

Planning is a prelude to informed decision-making. A good plan lays out the options, the costs, the tradeoffs. Sound planning can influence future decision-making, both public and private. At the same time, the action tail often wags the planning dog. Future options are narrowed no more decisively than when they are set, figuratively and literally, in concrete. It is from these perspectives that the planning provisions of the 1972 Amendments are to be examined.[1]

---

62. Section 301(b)(1)(C), 33 U.S.C.A. § 1311(b)(1)(C), requires all dischargers to meet the technology-based effluent limitations or "any more stringent limitation, . . . required to implement any applicable water quality standard established pursuant to this Act." Compare note 48, supra.

63. Opinion of the General Counsel, Disapproval of Overly Stringent State Standards, Aug. 2, 1973, in 1 EPA, Collection of Legal Opinions December 1970-December 1973, at 362. Compare text accompanying note 23, supra.

1. Leading sources include Harold F. Wise Consultants, Institutional Assessment of the Implementation of the Planning Requirements of the Water Pollution Control Act Amendments of 1972, Aug. 1975 (prepared for the National Commission on Water Quality) [hereinafter cited as Planning Assessment]; National Commission on Water Quality, Staff Draft Report on Water Quality Analysis and Environmental Impact Assessment of Public

Sec. 4.9 PLANNING PROVISIONS: GENERALLY

The legislation anticipates planning on four levels (1) basin planning (section 209 [2]), (2) state planning (sections 106 [3] and 303(e) [4]), (3) areawide or regional planning (section 208 [5]) and (4) facility planning (sections 201 [6] and 102 [7]). Despite the fragmentation, the planning provisions hang together. First of all, planning is meant to precede action. There is an understandable progression from plan preparation for an area to construction grants, which may support only facilities in conformity with the plan,[8] to discharge permits, which may be issued only to sources constructed in conformity with the plan.[9] Second, in recognition of the fact that the world does not wait for planners, Congress wanted the plans put together in a hurry. Within one year after designation of a regional planning agency under section 208, the organization must have in operation a continuing areawide waste treatment management planning process.[10] A detailed plan must be submitted to the EPA within two years after that.[11] Only 120 days were allowed for submission (and thirty days for EPA approval or disapproval) of the state continuing planning process under section 303(e).

Third, water pollution planning is meant to inform and point the way for actions to be taken later. Areawide plans under section 208 provide a means for regulating nonpoint sources. They define the specifics of the "best practicable waste treatment technology" which is brought into being by the expenditure of construction grants. The section 303(e) state plans identify maximum loads for water quality limited segments which can be applied against individual sources in the permits.[12] They are supposed to single out stretches of water where the 1983 swimmable water goal will not be met, thus pointing the way to section 302 showdowns.[13] Fourth, the planning provisions are to be mutually supportive. The notion of "planning" under the Act embraces everything from long range population growth projec-

---

Law 92–500, Jan. 1976, at V–104 to –110 [hereinafter cited as Draft Report on Environmental Impact]; Donley, Moss, Outen & Speth, Land Use Controls Under the Federal Water Pollution Control Act: A Citizens Guide, 5 ELR 50092 (1975). The author also is indebted for materials on planning to Kenneth T. Kijawa, An Analysis of the Planning Sections of the Federal Water Pollution Control Act Amendments of 1972 (unpublished paper prepared for a course in environmental law, Georgetown U. Law Center, Fall 1973).

2. 33 U.S.C.A. § 1289.

3. Id. § 1256.

4. Id. § 1313(e).

5. Id. § 1288.

6. Id. § 1281.

7. Id. § 1252.

8. Section 208(d), 33 U.S.C.A. § 1288 (d).

9. Section 208(e), 33 U.S.C.A. § 1288(e).

10. Section 208(b), 33 U.S.C.A. § 1288 (b).

11. Ibid.

12. See § 4.8 above.

13. See ibid.

tions to the design details of an advanced waste treatment plant. There is some overlap in the planning provisions, however, and it is elementary to suggest that information collected for one purpose should not be disregarded for another. Like a jigsaw puzzle, a section 208 areawide waste treatment management plan must establish a regulatory program to implement the waste treatment management requirements of section 201(c).[14] That provision, in turn, makes clear that "to the extent practicable, waste treatment management shall be on an areawide basis and provide control or treatment of all point and nonpoint sources of pollution, including in-place or accumulated pollution sources."[15] Thus, section 208 calls for planning and regulation on an areawide basis and section 201 calls for spending construction grants to build facilities capable of accommodating the across-the-board treatment planned for.

Before turning to the specifics of the planning provisions, it should be said that planning is one of the biggest disappointments of the 1972 Amendments. For the most part, the orderly progression from plan to permit is turned upside down: permits issue, construction grants flow, validating facilities before the plans confirm what has happened. The plans themselves are slow to evolve: of the 600 or so section 303(e) state basin (now water quality management) plans that must be prepared, only 50 to 60 percent reached an "intermediate level" of development by the beginning of fiscal year 1976.[16] Progress on the section 208 areawide plans is even less impressive—only 149 areawide planning agencies were operating by the fall of 1975.[17] Thus "for five to six years after the enactment of the Act, construction grant and NPDES activities will have proceeded without the potential benefit of locally developed areawide wastewater strategies. Those plans which will be developed will accommodate existing permits and facility plans rather than influence their form, size and location."[18] By the same token, the plans that have appeared, with a few exceptions, have affected very little the actions taken on construction grants and permit issuance. It remains to be seen whether, after a poor start, planning can be reestablished as a meaningful force in the evolution of water pollution controls.

a. *Basin Planning*

The only type of basin planning mentioned in the Act is not the section 303(e) basin plans, which are now called water quality management plans, but rather the basin plans mentioned in section 209.[19] This section directs the President, acting through the Water Resources

14. See section 208(b)(2)(C)(i), 33 U.S.C.A. § 1288(b)(2)(C)(i).

15. 33 U.S.C.A. § 1281(c).

16. Draft Report on Environmental Impact, supra note 1, at V-108.

17. Id. at V-109.

18. Ibid.

19. 33 U.S.C.A. § 1289.

Sec. 4.9 PLANNING PROVISIONS: GENERALLY 427

Council, to "prepare a Level B plan under the Water Resources Planning Act for all basins in the United States." Priority is assigned to the development of plans in areas with substantial water quality control problems spelled out in the section 208 areawide planning process. All section 209 accomplishes is to authorize a new source of funding for an already existing program.

The Water Resources Planning Act of 1965 [20] is a development oriented statute ("an act to provide for the optimum development of the Nation's natural resources through the coordinated planning of water and related land resources") that establishes the Water Resources Council (Title I),[21] provides for the creation of River Basin Commissions (Title II),[22] and sets up a program of grants to the states "to assist them in developing and participating in the development of comprehensive water and related land resources plans" (Title III).[23] Several river basin commissions have been created to generate plans pursuant to the statutory directive to prepare and submit "a comprehensive, coordinated, joint plan . . . for water and related land resources development in the area, river basin, or group of river basins" for which the commission was established.[24] They tend to be a prodigious potpourri of every development plan of all agencies in a particular region, sometimes based upon extraordinary assumptions.[25] They are, at the same time, rich resource material on a number of topics not excluding environmental quality. They are pertinent, although hardly critical, components of a water pollution control planning effort since they envisage projects affecting in important ways watershed flows and withdrawals.

The section 209 basin plans, whatever their value, and the EPA planning efforts appear destined to proceed along mutually oblivious paths, offending the understanding of the Act that various planning programs should be integrated. EPA made an "initial contact" with the Water Resources Council to "begin coordination" of the planning work, "but no definitive integration of the two efforts has occurred, and no formal agreement signed."[26] EPA regulations implementing the planning provisions require state planning efforts to incorporate

---

20. Pub.L. No. 89–80, 79 Stat. 244, 42 U.S.C.A. § 1962 et seq.

21. 42 U.S.C.A. § 1962a to a–4.

22. Id. § 1962b to b–6.

23. Id. § 1962c to c–1.

24. Id. § 1962b–3(3).

25. See, e. g., State and Federal Comments on Lower Colorado Region Comprehensive Framework Study of Water and Related Land Resources June 1971, ex. A ("The report has been developed around the basic premise that 4.15 million-acre-feet of water will be imported into the Region by 2020. As indicated, there is not an existing source for augmenting the Region's water supply without considering desalted ocean water").

26. Planning Assessment, supra note 1, at III–47, citing letter from James L. Agee, Assistant Administrator, EPA, to Warren D. Fairchild, Director, Water Resources Council, Nov. 5, 1974.

various aspects of an existing Level B basin plan (such as projected withdrawals, designation of scenic streams, and so on)[27] but close integration of the two efforts is unlikely.

b. *State Planning*

EPA grants for state pollution control programs are conditioned, under Section 106(f)(3) of the Act,[28] upon submission of an annual report for the Administrator's approval of "its program for the prevention, reduction and elimination of pollution in accordance with the purposes and provisions of this Act in such form and content as the Administrator may prescribe." An approvable program, according to the Act, requires, among other things, an authority to seek emergency relief in court from water pollution incidents and to monitor "the quality of navigable waters and to the extent practicable, ground waters including biological monitoring." [29]

The potential of these short term, action oriented program plans is largely unmet. The practice, according to reliable authority,[30] is to "parrot" the format supplied by EPA, producing state versions of EPA's annual "Water Quality Strategy Paper." Virginia and California are cited as examples where state program plans are used to accomplish management objectives. There is every reason to desire, but little reason to expect, the program plans to serve as effective barometers of progress where promised commitments are soon measured against actual results.

The statewide planning provisions of section 303(e)[31] were conceived as a low priority mechanism for carrying over the water quality standards into the 1972 Amendments but have been elevated by EPA to a central planning tool. The predecessor of section 303 (entitled "Water Quality Standards and Implementation Plans") was found only in the House bill and was adopted in conference after arguments that the water quality standards in many cases would require tougher controls than the effluent standards.[32] Subsections 303(a)–(c) continue existing water quality standards and set forth procedures for the Administrator to approve or disapprove of them and for their periodic revision.[33] Subsection 303(d) requires the identification of water quality limited segments, a priority ranking and the assignment of pollution loads to these waters.[34]

27. 40 CFR § 130.33(c), as added 40 Fed.Reg. 29883, 29886 (1975).

28. 33 U.S.C.A. § 1256(f)(3).

29. Section 106(e)(2), (1), 33 U.S.C.A. § 1256(e)(2), (1).

30. Draft Report on Environmental Impact, supra note 1, at V–106.

31. 33 U.S.C.A. § 1313(e).

32. Edelman, Legislative Goals and Constraints for Water Quality Planning, speech reprinted in The Potomac, May 10, 1973, at 9, 12 (published by the Interstate Commission on the Potomac River Basin).

33. See § 4.8 above.

34. See ibid.

Sec. 4.9 PLANNING PROVISIONS: GENERALLY

Section 303(e) builds on this structure by obliging each state to operate "a continuing planning process" approved pursuant to the provision. Approval by the Administrator (of the process, not the plan) is dependent upon satisfaction of a number of criteria, not unlike the state implementation plans under the Clean Air Act. These include a showing that the process will yield a plan with adequate authority for intergovernmental cooperation,[35] implementation of revised or new water quality standards,[36] disposition of all residual waste from any water treatment processing,[37] setting of the "total maximum daily load" for priority rivers,[38] and preparation of an inventory and priority ranking of needs for the construction of waste treatment works.[39]

EPA has administered the section 303(e) planning provisions with gusto, effectively using them to replace section 208 areawide planning. Section 303(e) gave the Administrator no specific directions on implementing regulations but they arrived in mid-1974 in considerable detail.[40] The "continuing planning process" is defined as "a time-phased" process by which a state develops "the State strategy, to be updated annually, which sets the State's major objectives, approach and priorities for preventing and controlling pollution over a five year period." [41] The strategy must contain a statewide assessment of water quality problems and causes, a listing of geographical priorities, a scheduling of program actions, an expression of intention on the extent to which nonpoint sources of pollution will be addressed, and a ranking of each segment.[42] (A "segment", for planning purposes, means those waters having common hydrologic characteristics or flow regulation patterns, common natural, physical, chemical and

---

35. Section 303(e)(3)(E), 33 U.S.C.A. § 1313(e)(3)(E).

36. Section 303(e)(3)(F), 33 U.S.C.A. § 1313(e)(3)(F).

37. Section 303(e)(3)(G), 33 U.S.C.A. § 1313(e)(3)(G).

38. Section 303(e)(3)(C), 33 U.S.C.A. § 1313(e)(3)(C).

39. Section 303(e)(3)(H), 33 U.S.C.A. § 1313(e)(3)(H).

40. 39 Fed.Reg. 19635 (1974), 40 CFR pt. 130; 39 Fed.Reg. 19639 (1974), 40 CFR pt. 131. Substantial changes in parts 130 and 131 were proposed in 40 Fed.Reg. 29882 (1975) and adopted in id. at 55334. The 1975 revisions were designed to combine a state's 303(e) and 208 planning responsibilities. 40 CFR § 131.1(b).

41. 40 CFR § 130.1(c)(1). The definition continues:
(2) Individual State water quality management plans, which provide recommendations on water quality goals, define specific programs, priorities and targets for preventing and controlling water pollution in individual basins (or other approved planning areas) and establish policies which guide decision making over at least a twenty year span of time (in increments of five years).
(3) The annual State program plan required under Section 106 of the Act, which establishes the program objectives, identifies the resources committed for the State program each year, and establishes a mechanism for reporting progress toward achievement of program objectives.

42. Id. § 130.20.

biological characteristics and processes, and common reactions to external stresses, notably pollution.[43])

At the heart of the state strategy is the "state water quality management plan." This is defined, at a level of generality, as "a management document which identifies the water quality problems of a particular basin or other approved planning area and sets forth an effective management program to alleviate those problems and preserve water quality to all intended uses."[44] Its purpose, quite clearly, is to serve as a springboard for action on water quality management decisions and control programs. The term "basin" to which a water quality management plan applies, means the streams, rivers and lakes and total land and water surface area of an administratively defined basin unit.[45] That is to say, a "basin" is an administrative creation not necessarily responsive to hydrologic realities.

The generalities of a water quality management plan are reduced to specifics by the regulations,[46] which as currently drafted draw upon the provisions of both sections 303(e) and 208. A state is obliged to develop inventories of industrial and municipal sources and use its municipal inventories for purposes of construction grants.[47] It must classify each segment of water within a basin as a water quality or effluent limited segment.[48] A water quality limited segment is one where water quality standards are not expected to be met even after application of the section 301 effluent limitations.[49] An effluent limited segment is one where water quality standards predictably will be met by applying the various "best technology" effluent standards of section 301.[50] For each water quality segment, a state must identify the total allowable maximum daily load of pollutants during critical flow conditions and allocate them among point sources with a gross allotment for nonpoint sources.[51] Indeed, the plan must go further to include "schedules of compliance or target abatement dates for all significant dischargers, nonpoint source control measures, residual and land disposal controls and stormwater system needs, including

---

43. Id. § 130.2(n).

44. Id. § 131.1(c); see id. § 130.2(f). Formerly, EPA used the term "basin plan" instead of "water quality management plan." See id. § 131.100(b). This characterization was abandoned in the 1975 revisions, perhaps because of confusion between the section 303(e) "basin plan" and the section 209 "Level B basin plans" which serve entirely different purposes.

45. Id. § 130.2(m).

46. Unless otherwise indicated, the required plan contents referred to are found in id. § 131.11.

47. Id. § 131.11(c).

48. Id. § 131.11(b).

49. Id. § 130.2(n)(i); see § 4.8 above.

50. 40 CFR § 130.2(n)(2).

51. Id. § 131.11(f), (g). Id. § 131.11(f)(4) reads:
Where predictive mathematical models are used in the determination of total maximum daily loads, an identification and brief description of the model, and the specific use of the model [must be included in the management plan].

Sec. 4.9 PLANNING PROVISIONS: GENERALLY

major interim and final completion dates, and terms or conditions that are necessary to assure an adequate tracking of progress toward compliance."[52] By pinning down specific sources to identifiable loads and control requirements, a water quality management plan thus serves a function indistinguishable from an implementation plan under the Clean Air Act.[53]

Other noteworthy features of state water quality management plans include projections of demographic and economic growth and of municipal and industrial wasteloads,[54] recommendations for revisions of water quality standards (which in some respects might offend the anti-degradation policies of the Act),[55] an assessment of urban and industrial stormwater systems[56] and residual wastes control needs,[57] an assessment of nonpoint sources[58] and their control needs,[59] and a description of existing state and local regulatory programs.[60] With respect to nonpoint sources, a water quality management plan must include "an identification and evaluation of all measures necessary to produce the desired level of control through application of the best management practices (or more stringent control measures, as appropriate)."[61] The definition of "best management practices," which is purely an administrative creation, is accommodating and vague: "a practice, or combination of practices, that is determined by a State after problem assessment, examination of alternative practices, and appropriate public participation to be practicable and most effective in preventing or reducing the amount of pollution generated by diffuse sources to a level compatible with water quality goals."[62] Behind the words is a serious issue: the planning provisions of federal law, specifically section 208, require the development of enforceable regulatory programs to control nonpoint sources of pollution.[63] The adequacy of EPA's regulations and the ensuing state plans will be measured against that legal reality.

As indicated above, the section 303(e) continuing planning process has produced few tangible benefits. From the outset, EPA's Water Strategy Paper confirmed as a "first objective" the completion of the basin (now the water quality management) plans.[64] The plans have had their "greatest impact" to date "in setting priorities

---

52. Id. § 131.11(m).

53. See § 3.5 above.

54. 40 CFR § 131.11(c).

55. Id. § 131.11(e); see § 4.8 above.

56. 40 CFR § 131.11(1).

57. Id. § 131.11(k).

58. Id. § 131.11(c).

59. Id. § 131.11(j).

60. Id. § 131.11(n).

61. Id. § 131.11(j)(1).

62. Id. § 130.2(p).

63. The argument is developed in Donley, Moss, Outen & Speth, supra note 1. Compare § 4.4 above (nonpoint sources).

64. App. at A–1 (1974).

for construction grants, in issuing permits based on the classification of stream segments (as either 'water quality limited' or 'effluent limited' segments), and in determining waste load allocations for particular river stretches."[65] Many of the plans were poorly done, however, the product of inadequate staffing, unclear guidance and uncertain goals.

c. *Areawide Planning*

Although EPA probably has not exceeded its statutory boundaries by combining the section 303(e) and 208 planning responsibilities,[66] it should be acknowledged that section 208 details planning obligations far beyond those set forth in section 303(e). EPA regulations and the resultant state plans ultimately must satisfy the more stringent standards. There is near unanimity on section 208: it was meant to be the "key"[67] to the water pollution planning effort, and EPA has faltered badly in enforcing it.[68]

Section 208 establishes, under strict time requirements, a process for designation by state governors (with some exceptions) and approval by the Administrator of an organization "capable of developing effective areawide waste treatment management plans" for each area with "substantial water quality control problems."[69] Designated organizations, within a year, are then required to have in operation a continuing areawide waste treatment management planning process. It was the expectation of Congress that waste management agencies would be designated covering the entire area of a state[70] (and a court has so held[71]) although this sentiment is obscured by the statutory language singling out areas with "substantial water quality problems."

Section 208(c)[72] prescribes a number of conditions regarding adequate authority before the Administrator can accept a designated management agency—mostly relating to powers to design and construct treatment works, raise revenues, incur indebtedness, and the

---

65. Draft Report on Environmental Impact, supra note 1, at V–108.

66. 40 CFR § 131.1(b). Formerly, the section 303(e) continuing planning process and section 208 areawide planning were separately addressed by 40 CFR pts. 130, 131 and id. pt. 126, respectively.

67. Edelman, supra note 32, at 12.

68. A conclusion supported, in varying degrees, by Edelman, supra note 32, and all sources cited in note 1, supra.

69. Section 208(a)(2), 33 U.S.C.A. § 1288(a)(2). The finer nuances of the designation provisions are explored in Natural Resources Defense Council, Inc. v. Train, 396 F.Supp. 1386, 5 ELR 20405 (D.C.D.C.1975).

70. Comm. on Public Works, Federal Water Pollution Control Act Amendments of 1971, S.Rep. No. 414, 92d Cong., 1st Sess. (1971); 118 Cong. Rec. 33712 (1972) (remarks of Sen. Tunney).

71. Natural Resources Defense Council, Inc. v. Train, 396 F.Supp. 1386, 5 ELR 20405 (D.C.D.C.1975).

72. 33 U.S.C.A. § 1288(c).

Sec. 4.9 PLANNING PROVISIONS: GENERALLY

like. Section 208(b) [73] requires the submission of areawide waste treatment management plans by designated organizations not later than two years after the planning process is in operation. The plans must "contain alternatives for waste treatment management, and be applicable to all wastes generated within the area involved." [74] They must identify treatment works necessary to meet the anticipated municipal and industrial waste treatment needs of the area over a twenty-year period; [75] establish construction priorities; [76] prescribe a regulatory program for point and nonpoint sources within the area; [77] identify the economic, social and environmental impact of carrying out the plan within the time prescribed as necessary; [78] include processes for identifying and controlling nonpoint sources; [79] and so on. The plan requirements are more than precatory: several of the nonpoint source provisions require controls "to the extent feasible" which may be read as requiring resort to proven control practices (or, in EPA's words, the "best management practices").

Several important consequences follow if and when an areawide agency is designated, approved, and prepares and submits a plan which also is approved: no permits shall be issued for a point source in conflict with the plan;[80] section 201 grants go only to the designated agency and for works in conformity with the plan.[81] The plan calls for a description of what must be done and how it will be done and then, like any rule of law, holds the maker to his promise. The only court to consider section 208 assessed it, appropriately, as the "critical" feature of a "far-reaching" Act:

> Section 208 charts a course not only for the cleaning up of polluted waters but also for the prevention of future pollution by identifying problem sources, regulating construction of certain industrial facilities, and developing processes to control run-off sources of pollution. While [section] 208 focuses on 'urban-industrial' areas with substantial water quality control difficulties, it also directs attention to other geographical locations with water pollution problems, such as forests, mining areas, farms, and salt water inlets. As a 'bottom line' for the [section] 208 waste treatment management activities, the Act prescribes a 1983 goal of clean waterways. The period between October 18,

---

73. Id. § 1288(b).

74. Section 208(b)(1), 33 U.S.C.A. § 1288(b)(1).

75. Section 208(b)(2)(A), 33 U.S.C.A. § 1288(b)(2)(A).

76. Section 208(b)(2)(B), 33 U.S.C.A. § 1288(b)(2)(B).

77. Section 208(b)(2)(C), 33 U.S.C.A. § 1288(b)(2)(C).

78. Section 208(b)(2)(E), 33 U.S.C.A. § 1288(b)(2)(E).

79. Sections 208(b)(2)(F)–(K), 33 U.S.C.A. §§ 1288(b)(2)(F)–(K).

80. Section 208(e), 33 U.S.C.A. § 1288(e).

81. Section 208(d), 33 U.S.C.A. § 1288(d)

1972 and July, 1976 is mainly a planning and development stage. The remaining seven years are for implementing plans and eliminating the more difficult and persistent sources of water pollution.[82]

For some time EPA did little to encourage section 208 planning and a great deal to undermine it. Implementing regulations, due in January of 1973 arrived in September of 1973.[83] They clarify section 208 both procedurally (for example, by adding a public hearing requirement in connection with the areawide agency designation [84]) and substantively (for example, by defining, "a substantial water quality control problem" [85]). They also add to the list of the legislative criteria for an area designation (by indicating a "preference" will be given to areas of "urban-industrial concentrations" [86]). Criteria such as these resulted in snail's pace designations (85 designated section 208 areas, leaving 95 per cent of the nation's waterways undesignated), until a court decision [87] in June of 1975 read section 208(a)(6) [88] as requiring the state to act as the section 208 planning agency for non-designated portions of the state in the same manner as organizations that had been designated.

Limited expenditures implementing section 208 is further indicative of an administrative downplaying of the section. The probable explanation [89] is that section 208 planning is to be 100 per cent federally financed for each fiscal year through June 30, 1975 and 75 per cent thereafter.[90] This is to be contrasted with the section 303(e) continuing planning process, which has no direct federal grants, and is financed if at all through section 106 grants to support state programs. EPA's extended lack of enthusiasm about section 208 is to be contrasted with that of the Congress, which went so far as to make the Administrator's approval of a grant proposal a contractual obligation of the United States.[91] It has been suggested by a knowledge-

---

82. Natural Resources Defense Council, Inc. v. Train, 396 F.Supp. 1386, 1389–90, 5 ELR 20405, 20406 (D.C.D.C. 1975), citing EPA, Water Quality Strategy Paper 10–11 (1974).

83. 38 Fed.Reg. 25681 (1973), 40 CFR pt. 126. Section 208 planning is addressed also in the 1975 revisions. See note 40, supra.

84. 40 CFR § 126.30.

85. Id. § 126.10(b).

86. Id. § 126.10(a).

87. Natural Resources Defense Council, Inc. v. Train, 396 F.Supp. 1386, 5 ELR 20405 (D.C.D.C.1975).

88. 33 U.S.C.A. § 1288(a)(6), reads as follows:
The State shall act as a planning agency for all portions of such State which are not designated under paragraphs (2), (3) or (4) of this subsection.

89. See Edelman, supra note 32, at 12.

90. Section 208(f)(2), 33 U.S.C.A. § 1288(f)(2). EPA originally opposed the 100 per cent funding provision See Comm. on Public Works, Federal Water Pollution Control Act Amendments of 1972, H.R.Rep. No. 911, 92d Cong., 2d Sess. 154 (1972).

91. Section 208(f)(3), 33 U.S.C.A. § 1288(f)(3). Compare § 4.10 below (dis-

Sec. 4.10   FACILITIES & CONSTRUCTION GRANTS   435

able commentator that congressional authorization for appropriations under section 208 were mandatory in the sense that all sums authorized should have been made available for section 208 grants.[92] But the mandatory language of section 205 (sums authorized to be appropriated "shall be allotted" for section 201 construction grants), so important to the rationale of cases mandating allotments for purposes of section 201,[93] is missing from section 208.

d. *Facility Planning*

Almost by default, the fulcrum of water pollution planning activity has gravitated towards the construction grants program. The power to award grants for the construction of treatment works under section 201(g)(1)[94] vests EPA, coincidentally, with extraordinary leverage over areawide planning activities. Federally funded treatment works, moreover, not only must be planned in light of available alternatives, in the procedural tradition of the National Environmental Policy Act,[95] but also must embrace the best alternatives, if any there be, to discharges through conventional sewage treatment plants. The construction of new treatment works is a classic example of a major federal action that must hew closely to a number of strict substantive requirements.

§ 4.10   Planning: Facilities and Construction Grants

That the doers usually best the planners is illustrated convincingly by the impact of the federal grants program for the construction of sewage treatment works.[1] The program is huge, highly visible in consequence if not in the way it works, and far-reaching in

cussing the contractual obligation features of the construction grants program).

92. Edelman, supra note 32, at 12: Whatever the motivation, the decision not to fund section 208 in fiscal year 1973 and to provide for only $25 million in fiscal year 1974 is unfortunate. This is particularly so because, in the judgment of many, the law mandates—and I stress mandates—a total of $150 million for those two fiscal years. If the courts were able to find EPA in violation of the law as to the construction grant program, then the same result will have to follow with respect to section 208. Section 208 was written to follow the construction grant program.

93. See, e. g., Train v. City of New York, 420 U.S. 35, 95 S.Ct. 839, 43 L.Ed.2d 1 (1975).

94. 33 U.S.C.A. § 1288(g)(1).

95. See §§ 7.3, 7.4 below.

1. The leading analyses include Touche, Ross & Co., Institutional Assessment of the Implementation of the Construction Grants Program Under Public Law 92–500, July 1975 (a report for the National Commission on Water Quality) [hereinafter cited as Construction Grants Program Assessment]; and National Commission on Water Quality, Staff Draft Report on Water Quality Analysis and Environmental Impact Assessment of Public Law 92–500, Jan. 1976, at V–35 to –93 (borrowing heavily from the Construction Grants Program Assessment) [hereinafter cited as Draft Report on Environmental Impact].

practical importance. The 1972 Amendments contain a "firm commitment"[2] of substantial sums for the clean-up effort—$5 billion for fiscal year 1973, $6 billion for 1974 and $7 billion for 1975. While actual expenditures will fall short of these ambitious aims (an estimated $2.3 billion will have been spent by the end of the 1976 fiscal year) (September 30, 1976),[3] the program represents the fulcrum of planning actually undertaken to combat regional water pollution problems and the foundation of facilities that are built to realize those plans. Despite these efforts, only 40 to 50 per cent of municipal waste treatment plants will meet the secondary treatment effluent requirements by July 1, 1977.[4]

Discussion of the construction grants program will be organized as follows: (1) an overview of Title II; (2) the mechanics of facility planning and construction; (3) substantive requirements for federally funded facilities; and (4) planning of multi-purpose federal projects.

a. *Overview of Title II*

Section 201(c)[5] calls for planning and waste treatment management, to the extent practicable, "on an areawide basis" so as to "provide control or treatment of all point and nonpoint sources of pollution including in place or accumulated pollution sources." The means to this end are the provisions for federal grants to state, local and regional agencies "for the erection, building, acquisition, alteration, remodeling, improvement or extension of treatment works . . . ."[6] Grants are now conditioned, according to language representing a basic premise of the Act,[7] upon the applicant satisfactorily demonstrating to the Administrator that—

> (A) alternative waste management techniques have been studied and evaluated and the works proposed for grant assistance will provide for the application of the best practicable waste treatment technology over the life of the works consistent with the purposes of this title; and

> (B) as appropriate, the works proposed for grant assistance will take into account and allow to the extent practicable the application of technology at a later date which will provide for the reclaiming or recycling of water or otherwise eliminate the discharge of pollutants.

2. Train v. City of New York, 420 U.S. 35, 45, 95 S.Ct. 839, 845, 43 L.Ed.2d 1, 8 (1975).

3. Draft Report on Environmental Impact, supra note 1, at V–36.

4. See 6 BNA, Environment Rep.—Current Developments 479 (1975).

5. 33 U.S.C.A. § 1281(c).

6. Section 201(g)(2), 33 U.S.C.A. § 1281(g)(2).

7. Ibid.

Sec. 4.10 FACILITIES & CONSTRUCTION GRANTS 437

Approval of a grant is conditioned also upon satisfaction of a number of other criteria. Most of these appear in section 204,[8] which calls for a determination that the works conform to areawide and statewide plans (this assumes of course that the planning eventually will catch up to the construction [9]) and for a decision "that the size and capacity of [the] works relate directly to the needs to be served by [the] works." [10] The latter provision, among others, gives EPA adequate discretion to interdict federal financing of facilities grossly in excess of predictable needs with resultant subsidies for local growth ambitions.[11] Section 204 also contains a number of requirements regarding competent management and the establishment of a system of charges to assure that the recipient of waste treatment services pays a proportionate share of the costs of operation and maintenance.

Section 202 [12] establishes the federal share of grants for sewage treatment works at 75 per cent of the costs of construction. Section 203 [13] calls for each grant applicant to submit to the Administrator for his approval plans, specifications and estimates for each proposed project for the construction of treatment works. The term "construction" is defined broadly in the Act to include preliminary planning and administration associated with construction.[14] The term "treatment works" is expanded far beyond its meaning in earlier legislation to include any device, system or method for treating, recycling, or reclaiming liquid municipal sewage or industrial wastes or for treating or separating storm water runoff.[15] Specifically, the

---

8. 33 U.S.C.A. § 1284.

9. See § 4.9 above.

10. Section 204(a)(5), 33 U.S.C.A. § 1284(a)(5).

11. See Council on Environmental Quality, Interceptor Sewers and Suburban Sprawl, Sept. 1974 (prepared by Urban Systems Research and Engineering, Inc.) (analyzing 52 EPA sewage construction grants and finding substantial excess capacity with resultant land use implications).

12. 33 U.S.C.A. § 1282.

13. Id. § 1283.

14. Section 212(1), 33 U.S.C.A. § 1292 (1) reads:
The term 'construction' means any one or more of the following: preliminary planning to determine the feasibility of treatment works, engineering, architectural, legal, fiscal, or economic investigations or studies, surveys, designs, plans, working drawings, specifications, procedures or other necessary actions, erection, building, acquisition, alteration, remodeling, improvement, or extension of treatment works, or the inspection or supervision of any of the foregoing items.

15. Section 212(2)(A), 33 U.S.C.A. § 1292(2)(A), reads:
The term 'treatment works' means any devices and systems used in the storage, treatment, recycling, and reclamation of municipal sewage or industrial wastes of a liquid nature to implement section 1281 of this title, or necessary to recycle or reuse water at the most economical cost over the estimated life of the works, including intercepting sewers, outfall sewers, sewage collection systems, pumping, power, and other equipment, and their appurtenances; extensions, im-

"treatment works" which can be built with federal funds include "sewage collection systems" (embracing the main lines but not the connection lines to households and others) and "site acquisition of the land that will be an integral part of the treatment process or is used for ultimate disposal of residues resulting from such treatment." The inclusion of land purchase costs in federal construction grants is essential to any significant shift away from conventional treatment to land treatment.[16]

Upon the Administrator approving the plans, specifications and estimates submitted, his approval "shall be deemed a contractual obligation of the United States for the payment of its proportional contribution to such project."[17] Thus, the 1972 water pollution amendments, in the name of a better environment, adopt the financing procedure of the Highway Trust Fund, which some would say has not led to a better environment. The Conference Report specifically acknowledges an indebtedness to the highway funding provisions and explains that "a complete and thorough change" in the mechanics of the administration of the grant program has been wrought to assure states and communities "an orderly flow of Federal payments."[18] Section 205[19] mandates the allotment (but not the obligation) among the states of sums appropriated for the construction of treatment works under the grant program in accordance with a "needs" formula. Section 207[20] contains the original $18 billion authorization.[21] Section 206[22] provides a retroactive windfall,

provements, remodeling, additions, and alterations thereof; elements essential to provide a reliable recycled supply such as standby treatment units and clear well facilities; and any works, including site acquisition of the land that will be an integral part of the treatment process or is used for ultimate disposal of residues resulting from such treatment.

See section 212(2)(B), 3 U.S.C.A. § 1292(2)(B).

16. See EPA, Survey of Facilities Using Land Application of Wastewater (1973).

17. Section 203(a), 33 U.S.C.A. § 1283(a).

18. Comm. of Conference, Federal Water Pollution Control Act Amendments of 1972, H.R.Rep. No. 1465, 92d Cong., 2d Sess. 111 (1972) [hereinafter cited as Conference Report]. Despite the similarities, there are also substantial differences between the highway and sewage treatment plant construction programs. In contrast to the highway program (where the state has a major role in financing and program operation), the sewage construction grants program depends heavily upon localities for planning, partial funding, construction and maintenance. Nor does the sewage grant program have anything comparable to the assured source of funding provided by gasoline tax and related revenues earmarked for the federal highway trust fund. See Draft Report on Environmental Impact, supra note 1, at V–36.

19. 33 U.S.C.A. § 1285.

20. Id. § 1287.

21. Sections 205 and 207 are definitively interpreted in Train v. City of New York, 420 U.S. 35, 95 S.Ct. 839, 43 L.Ed.2d 1 (1975) (ordering the allotment among the states, albeit not the obligation, of the full sums authorized).

22. 33 U.S.C.A. § 1286.

Sec. 4.10 FACILITIES & CONSTRUCTION GRANTS   439

called a "reimbursement", for the sponsors of certain projects initiated after June 30, 1966 under less generous federal financing provisions than those appearing in the 1972 Amendments. The idea was "to establish a formula by which it would be possible to 'make whole' those who responded to the national need and to congressional urging to accelerate their local effort to clean up the Nation's waterways, but had not received as much money under the Federal grant program [for various reasons such as individual project limitations or inadequate appropriations] as they could have utilized to build facilities that qualified for a Federal grant." [23]

Section 210 [24] requires the Administrator to make "an annual survey to determine the efficiency of the operation and maintenance of treatment works constructed with grants made under this Act, as compared to the efficiency planned at the time the grant was made." This survey appears as part of the annual report required under section 516(a).[25] Indeed, it is subsumed by EPA's bi-annual surveys on national pollution control needs and construction costs which serve both as a barometer of total costs of achieving the goals of the Act and as a basis for allocation of construction grants.[26]

Section 211 [27] forbids any grant for "a sewage collection system" unless it is: (1) "for replacement or major rehabilitation of an existing collection system and is necessary to the total integrity and performance of the waste treatment works servicing [the] community," or (2) is "for a new collection system in an existing community with sufficient existing or planned capacity adequately to treat [the] collected sewage and is consistent with section 201." The Congress was concerned "that one of the reasons for delays in initiating construction of waste treatment facilities was due to the inability of public agencies to arrange for the financing of collection systems." [28] It was unconvinced that various programs to assist communities in financing collection systems (under the auspices of the Farmer's Home Administration, Economic Development Administration and the Department of Housing and Urban Development) worked smoothly to the advantage of water pollution control efforts. Congress also was aware of unnecessarily large sewage treatment plants being built to accommodate excessive volumes of water infiltrating into dilapidated collection systems.[29] Far wiser and cheaper

---

23. Comm. on Public Works, Federal Water Pollution Control Act Amendments of 1971, S.Rep. No. 414, 92d Cong., 1st Sess. 32 (1971) [hereinafter cited as Senate Report].

24. 33 U.S.C.A. § 1290; see Comm. on Public Works, Federal Water Polluton Control Act Amendments of 1972, H.R.Rep. No. 911, 92d Cong., 2d Sess. 98 (1972) [hereinafter cited as House Report].

25. 33 U.S.C.A. § 1376(a).

26. See Construction Grants Program Assessment, supra note 1, at III–A–1 to –18.

27. 33 U.S.C.A. § 1291.

28. House Report, supra note 24, at 99.

29. Id. at 99–100. For definitions of infiltration and inflow, see notes 49 & 50, infra.

it is to rehabilitate the collection system than to accommodate the treament works to the existing system. The solution was to expand the definition of "treatment works" to include "collection systems" and give EPA responsibility for funding both types of facilities. Grant approval is now conditioned upon a determination by the Administrator "that each sewer collection system discharging into [a] treatment works is not subject to excessive infiltration." [30]

Extending grant coverage to collection systems presents possibilities of abuse Congress was anxious to minimize. Limiting the aid to rehabilitation of existing systems or new systems for existing communities with adequate sewage capacity is designed to restrict the benefits to situations where collection system expenditures are an indispensable part of a community sewage treatment problem. There was no intention for the taxpayer to shoulder responsibility for connecting up private industry with existing systems, for ordinary repairs and maintenance of existing systems, or for new systems for new communities or subdivisions better treated as part of the development costs.[31]

b. *Mechanics of Facility Planning and Construction*

A leading analysis [32] summarizes the construction grant program as follows: "Grant funds are authorized by Congress and distributed to states on the basis of a bi-annual survey of treatment facility construction needs conducted by EPA. Localities may request financial assistance in order to prepare either a facility plan for a waste treatment project (requiring a 'Step 1' grant), or design specifications for a project (requiring a 'Step 2' grant), or for actual construction of the treatment facility (requiring a 'Step 3' grant). States rank competing fund requests from localities according to priority criteria which include the severity of the water pollution, amount of population affected, funds availability, and other relevant 'need' parameters. Grant applications for projects high enough on the state priority list to receive federal funding are reviewed by the state and forwarded to an EPA region for further review and possible approval of the application."

The initial preparation of the facilities plan is the single most important step in the legal system seeking to control water pollution from municipal treatment plants. Planning at the earlier stages is fluid and uncommitted.[33] By contrast, issuance of the discharge permit, according to one count,[34] represents the twenty-seventh point

30. Section 201(g)(3), 33 U.S.C.A. § 1281(g)(3).

31. See Senate Report, supra note 23, at 28–30; House Report, supra note 24, at 91–92.

32. Construction Grants Program Assessment, supra note 1, at II–2; see

40 CFR § 35.915 (state determination of project priority list).

33. See § 4.9 above.

34. Construction Grants Program Assessment, supra note 1, at III–G–16.

Sec. 4.10   FACILITIES & CONSTRUCTION GRANTS

of decision beginning with the local determination to initiate a waste treatment project and ending with the issuance of a permit to an operating facility. While members of the public and attorneys tend to focus upon the adjudicatory proceedings at the permit stage, options will have been narrowed drastically by decisions undertaken at the planning, design and construction levels. Technological momentum very nearly can render the law a superfluity.

The facility planning process may begin with a preapplication conference.[35] An application for a Step 1 grant must be supported by a "plan of study" which presents "(i) the proposed planning area; (ii) an identification of the entity or entities that will be conducting the planning; (iii) the nature and scope of the proposed Step 1 project, including a schedule for the completion of specific tasks; and (iv) an itemized description of the estimated costs for the project."[36] The plan of study serves as the plans, specifications and estimates to which the Administrator must give his approval under the Act.[37] Upon approval of the Step 1 grant, the facility plan is prepared. Public hearings are required at the beginning of the process and prior to adoption of the plan.[38] This is the last formal opportunity for public participation prior to the permit proceedings (with the possible exception of the holding of a hearing if an environmental impact statement is prepared). Step 2 (design) and Step 3 (construction) grants can be issued under certain circumstances prior to completion of a facilities plan,[39] which is just another example of the incessant pressures to put the construction cart ahead of the planning horse.

As described in the regulations,[40] the facilities plan represents a far-reaching effort to plan for treatment works that can meet the effluent requirements of the Act. The process requires "a systematic evaluation of feasible alternatives"[41] and calls for the ultimate application at "a minimum" of the "best practicable waste treatment technology,"[42] administratively defined, which of course is the basic criterion for grant approval under section 201(g). Also required is a description of the selected complete waste treatment system "of which the proposed treatment works is a part. The description shall cover all elements of the system, from the service area and collection sewers, through treatment, to the ultimate discharge of treated wastewaters and disposal of sludge."[43] By authoritative

---

35. 40 CFR § 35.920–2.

36. Id. § 35.920–3.

37. Section 203(a), 33 U.S.C.A. § 1283(a).

38. 40 CFR § 35.917–5.

39. Id. § 35.917.

40. Id. §§ 35.917, 35.917–1.

41. Id. § 35.917(b).

42. Id. § 35.917–1(d)(5).

43. Id. § 35.917–1(b).

account,[44] the most demanding aspects of the facilities plan are those calling for infiltration/inflow documentation,[45] a cost-effectiveness analysis of alternatives to the treatment works and the system of which it is a part,[46] and an environmental assessment.[47]

The infiltration/inflow documentation is an administrative elaboration of the statutory requirement that "each sewer system" discharging into a federally funded treatment works not be "subject to excessive infiltration."[48] For these purposes, infiltration takes its customary meaning of water seeping into the sewer system from the ground through defective pipes[49] while inflow includes discharges into the system from ordinary service connections and drains, usually as the result of a storm.[50] The purpose of the analysis is to determine where there is "excessive" infiltration/inflow.[51] This, in turn, calls for a judgment about the relative costs of rehabilitation of the sewer system versus the cost of transporting and treating the combined contributions to the system.[52] If necessary, rehabilitation work on the sewers to eliminate excessive infiltration/inflow must be incorporated in the facilities plan.[53]

The cost-effectiveness analysis has its statutory origins in the definition of "treatment works" which requires, in connection with grant applications to abate pollution from municipal systems, the submission of "adequate data and analysis demonstrating [the] proposal to be, over the life of the works, the most cost efficient alternative to comply with sections 301 or 302 of this Act, or the requirements of section 201 of this Act."[54] A cost-effectiveness analysis means simply a study to determine whether a particular waste treatment system or component part requires the minimum commitment

---

44. Construction Grants Program Assessment, supra note 1, at III–B–18; Draft Report on Environmental Impact, supra note 1, at V–39.

45. 40 CFR §§ 35.917–1(c), 35.927.

46. Id. § 35.917–1(d); see id. subpt. E, app. A (Cost Effectiveness Analysis Guidelines).

47. Id. §§ 35.917–1(7), 6.56.

48. Section 201(g)(3), 33 U.S.C.A. § 1281(g)(3).

49. 40 CFR § 35.905–9 defines "infiltration" as follows:
The water entering a sewer system, including sewer service connections, from the ground, through such means as, but not limited to, defective pipes, pipe joints, connections, or manhole walls. Infiltration does not include, and is distinguished from, inflow.

50. Id. § 35.905–11 defines "inflow" as follows:
The water discharged into a sewer system, including service connections from such sources as, but not limited to, roof leaders, cellar, yard and area drains, foundation drains, cooling water discharges, drains from springs and swampy areas, manhole covers, cross connections from storm sewers and combined sewers, catch basins, storm waters, surface run-off, street wash waters or drainage. Inflow does not include, and is distinguished from, infiltration.

51. Id. § 35.927–1(a).

52. Id. § 35.927–2.

53. Id. § 35.927–3.

54. Section 212(2)(B), 33 U.S.C.A. § 1292(2)(B).

Sec. 4.10 FACILITIES & CONSTRUCTION GRANTS 443

of resources over time to meet given legal requirements.[55] Both out-of-pocket dollar costs and social and environmental costs must be taken into account, which presents immediate quantification problems.[56] The cost-effectiveness analysis is conceived as requiring a thorough consideration of alternatives, as does the environmental assessment. The latter requirement (which is considered a part of the overall cost-effectiveness study) calls for a mini-environmental impact statement delving into effects and alternatives.[57] Together, the cost-effectiveness analysis and the environmental assessment are supposed to promote the selection of the best waste treatment alternative.

Both state agencies and the regional EPA offices have well defined roles in reviewing facility plans. The state (assuming it has been delegated the power to certify [58]) must review the plan and certify that it conforms to regional planning and other requirements for an adequate facilities plan.[59] EPA review follows [60] and, upon approval of the facilities plan, the groundwork is laid for awards of the Step 2 (specification) and Step 3 (construction) grants. Section 511(c)(1) [61] of the Act makes clear that the environmental impact statement and other requirements of the National Environmental Policy Act apply to section 201 grant activity. Ideally, the best occasion for EPA to prepare an environmental impact statement is in the course of reviewing a facilities plan or prior to the award of a Step 2 grant. The reason for this is that options are as fluid as they ever will be while the facilities plan is undergoing scrutiny be-

---

55. 40 CFR subpt. E, app. A(d)(2); see Zener, The Federal Law of Water Pollution Control, in Environmental Law Institute, Federal Environmental Law 682, 696–702 (E. L. Dolgin & T. G. P. Guilbert eds. 1974) (discussing possible differences between cost-benefit balancing, cost effectiveness analysis or other reasonable cost tests).

56. Id. subpt. E, app. A(f). Compare § 7.5 below.

57. 40 CFR §§ 6.56, 6.32. On the occasional fine line between environmental assessments and environmental impact statements, see Hanly v. Kleindienst (II), 471 F.2d 823, 2 ELR 20717 (2d Cir. 1972), cert. denied 412 U.S. 908 (1973) (especially Friendly, C. J., dissenting).

58. 40 CFR § 35.912.

59. Id. § 35.917–7.

60. Ibid.

61. 33 U.S.C.A. § 1371(c)(1), reads, in pertinent part:
> Except for the provision of Federal financial assistance for the purpose of assisting the construction of publicly owned treatment works as authorized by section 201 of this [Act], . . ., no action of the Administrator taken pursuant to this [Act] shall be deemed a major Federal action significantly affecting the quality of the human environment within the meaning of the National Environmental Policy Act of 1969 . . . .

While this provision speaks to federal grants "for the purpose of assisting the construction" of treatment works, there is no indication that the NEPA analysis should await Step 3 construction grants. Section 511(c) should be read generally as inviting the application of NEPA to all section 201 federal funding activity that could lead to the construction of a treatment works. Compare § 7.7 below.

fore an irrevocable commitment to a certain technology of fixed design. Actually, EPA impact statements often are delayed until much later in the construction grants process and usually are not prepared at all. Only four percent of the projects funded have resulted in the preparation of an EIS,[62] which suggests a gross underutilization of NEPA taking into account its low threshold requirements.[63]

Recitation of the specifics of the facility planning process may mislead by presenting a false sense of order. While the legal content is persuasive on paper, its implementation is hazardous: the plan can fall victim to hazy instructions, intergovernmental squabbling, unrecorded waivers, inflexible application, lack of innovation in response, government officials who don't know what they want, consulting engineers who have narrow specialties to sell.[64] Disorder may be compounded further by the facts that EPA regional offices administer what amounts to separate grant construction programs, that the lapse of time between planning and ultimate construction may run from ten to even fifteen years, that many facilities were planned and partly constructed under earlier versions of the Act and that major projects may involve many (sometimes scores) of separate grants for various component parts.[65]

Of all the practical barriers to implementation of the noble aims of the grants construction program, none is more important than the emergence of a shadow government of consultants who make decisions on how the money will be spent and what will be built. As with advisory committees where advisors may become *de facto* decisionmakers,[66] a substantial delegation of power may occur in the process of planning and building sewage treatment plants. The consulting and construction engineering firms hired by local governments, by reason of past experience and perhaps self-interest, have points of view that quickly may become government policy. These subgovernments can sell the same prescription time and again (only five firms in New York state, for example, handle fully 50 percent of the construction grant projects), and it may be based on misdiagnosis. The consultants, it is said, prefer advanced waste treatment and its byproducts of more construction, more contracts and more maintenance. Innovative or unusual options, including variations of land treatment,

---

62. EPA, Review of the Municipal Waste Water Treatment Works Program, Nov. 1974, at 22–26.

63. See § 7.6 below.

64. See Construction Grants Program Assessment, supra note 1, at III–B–11 to –28.

65. Some of these problems are detailed in Draft Report on Environmental Impact, supra note 1, at V–43 to –68.

66. § 1.11 above; see Snell, American Ground Transportation: A Proposal for Restructuring the Automobile, Truck, Bus and Rail Industries, Subcomm. on Antitrust and Monopoly of the Senate Comm. on the Judiciary, 93d Cong., 2d Sess. (Comm. Print 1974) (reporting on the dismantling of inner city trolley systems on the strength of advice from interested consultants).

Sec. 4.10 FACILITIES & CONSTRUCTION GRANTS

are as often as not laughed off. This phenomenon, if true, poses a serious threat to the success of the program but must be dealt with ultimately by the political process.

The Step 2 portion "of the construction grants process begins with the acceptance of the Step 2 grant by the municipality. The consulting engineer and architect hired by the city then prepare the plans and specifications based on the facility plan approved by EPA. When the plans and specifications are complete, the municipality forwards copies along with evidence of compliance with operations and maintenance requirements and a Step 3 grant application to the program agency. At the state level the package is reviewed by the engineering staff and other sections involved in the grants application process. In twenty-three states a certification agreement has been signed with EPA which enables the state to certify to EPA the technical and administrative accuracy of the plans and specifications." [67] Steps 2 and 3 are plainly important milestones on the road from plan to facility. Project designs prepared by consulting engineers "generally represent a uniform, standardized approach to the treatment of waste water. The similarity of treatment facilities applies to all geographic areas, regardless of local waste water, climate, soil and receiving water characteristics." [68] Thus are the options narrowed as the project proceeds from plan to permit.

c. *Substantive Requirements for Federally Funded Facilities*

No greater legal influence on the choice of facility design or method of treatment can be found than in EPA's administrative definitions of the effluent requirements that must be met by the facilities. In the case of publicly owned treatment plants, the statute mandates, not later than July 1, 1977, effluent limitations based upon "secondary treatment" [69] (or more stringent controls necessary to meet water quality standards [70]) and, not later than July 1, 1983, effluent limitations based upon "the best practicable waste treatment technology over the life of the works." [71] Actually, the "best practicable" standard also is a new source standard since it applies to the construction or modification of any facilities with federal grant funds authorized after June 30, 1974. EPA defines "secondary treatment" by numerical values for four familiar water quality parameters—biochemical oxygen demand (BOD), suspended solids, fecal coliform bacteria and acidity (pH).[72] Somewhat higher concentrations of BOD and

---

67. Construction Grants Program Assessment, supra note 1, at III–C–1.

68. Id. at III–C–6.

69. Section 301(b)(1)(B), 33 U.S.C.A. § 1311(b)(1)(B).

70. Section 201(b)(1)(C), 33 U.S.C.A. § 1311(b)(1)(C).

71. Sections 301(b)(2)(B), 201(g)(2)(A), 33 U.S.C.A. §§ 1311(b)(2)(B), 1281(g)(2)(A).

72. 38 Fed.Reg. 2298 (1973), 40 CFR § 133.102. A case-by-case exemption is provided for treatment works receiving combined storm water and sanitary sewage flows. 40 CFR § 133.103(a). For a discussion of the

suspended solids are allowed where the treatment works receives more than 10 percent of its design flow from industries for which less stringent effluent limitations have been promulgated.[73] Like the national ambient air quality standards, the "correct" numerical expression of "secondary treatment" is a subject over which continuous debate is probable.[74]

More important yet is the ultimate legal meaning that is accorded the "best practicable" standard. Thus far, EPA views the 1983 requirements as identical to the 1977 "secondary treatment" standards, while suggesting three options for achieving the 1983 "best practicable" standards—treatment and discharge, land application and wastewater reuse.[75] This formal expression of legal obligation must be considered against the background of other EPA utterances indicating that the grants program has downplayed land application in favor of treatment and discharge—a well publicized speech by the Administrator,[76] a letter from an assistant administrator to the regional administrators urging a closer consideration of land application,[77] and various technical publications.[78] If challenged, EPA will be hard pressed to defend its decision virtually to equate the 1977 and 1983 standards for municipal plants since the two-step tightening of the rules is a central premise of the legislation.

The "best practicable" standard of section 201(g)(2) surely requires a close look at alternatives; specifically mentioned is the "reclaiming or recycling of water." Reclamation means the use of effluent for groundwater recharge or in lakes or canals used for various purposes (including, conceivably, for drinking water purposes). Recycling means the land application or other processing of water so that it can be reused. The three basic approaches to land application are irrigation (where typically the wastewater is sprayed over certain crops), overland flow (where the wastewater flows in a sheet over the ground surface) and infiltration-percolation (where the

legality of the exemption, see § 4.12 below.

73. 40 CFR § 133.103(b).

74. See Draft Report on Environmental Impact, supra note 1, at V–69 to –71.

75. EPA, Alternative Waste Management Techniques for Best Practicable Waste Treatment, Oct. 1975 (published as guidelines under section 304(d)(2), 33 U.S.C.A. § 1314(d)(2)) [hereinafter cited as Best Practicable Waste Treatment Document].

76. Remarks by Russell E. Train, EPA Technology Transfer Design Seminar on Land Treatment of Municipal Wastewater Effluents, Atlanta, Ga., Apr. 23, 1975.

77. Memo on Land Treatment from EPA Deputy Administrator John Quarles to EPA Regional Administrators, Nov. 1, 1974.

78. E. g., Pound & Crites, Wastewater Treatment and Reuse by Land Application, Environmental Protection Agency, Aug. 1972 (2 vols.); Pound, Crites & Griffes, Costs of Wastewater Treatment By Land Application, Environmental Protection Agency, June 1975; Demirjian, Muskegan County Wastewater Management System, Prepared for EPA Design Seminar for Land Treatment of Municipal Wastewater Effluents, Oct. 1975.

Sec. 4.10 FACILITIES & CONSTRUCTION GRANTS

wastewater is spread in a basin and allowed to percolate through the soil [79]). Reuse is a generic term covering reuse of wastewater effluent for everything from industrial treatment to groundwater recharge to drinking water.[80]

More important than the question of whether the alternatives must be studied in connection with a section 201 grant is whether the "best" one must be selected. The answer seems to be yes: the "best practicable" standard is one that should extend "over the life of the works," suggesting that the best treatment choices be reflected in the design of the facility. Several provisions explicitly "encourage" improved waste treatment methods with an emphasis on recycling of sewage pollutants and reclamation of wastewater.[81] The legislative history is laden with warm references to new and improved disposal methods, particularly land treatment.[82] Not to be overlooked either is the 1985 no discharge goal which should be read as indicating that the construction grants program is framed with a "purpose to assist in development of waste treatment management treatment plants and practices to eliminate the discharge of pollutants."[83] Section 201 presupposes "other ways" and "better ways" than building "the same old waste treatment plants."[84]

---

79. Pound & Crites, supra note 78, passim.

80. Best Practicable Waste Treatment Document, supra note 75, at 32.

81. Sections 201(d), (e), (f), 33 U.S.C.A. §§ 1281(d), (e), (f).

82. E. g., Senate Report, supra note 23, at 24-25 ("conventional treatment is at best an interim solution; such facilities are easily overtaxed, their life expectancy is relatively short, and by themselves do not solve the problem of residual waste; i. e., sludge and other pollutants removed from the effluent . . . Alternative waste treatment methods, which [require] the return of pollutants to natural cycles, are new only in the sense that they have re-emerged for application. This method is commonly associated with the Muskegan [Michigan] project . . . The Committee emphasizes that the policy in Section 201, read with the policy stated in Section 101 [the no-discharge policy], requires the Administrator to direct his research and development authority under sections 104 and 105 to carry out those policies. This statement of policy, coupled with a requirement to consider alternatives as a condition to Federal assitance, is intended to overcome the resistance and lethargy present in many planners in the Federal agency, State agencies and in private consulting firms"); 118 Cong. Rec. 33754-55 (1972) (Rep. Harsha) ("It is the intent of the managers that the language in § 201(b) and 201(g)(2)(A) requires that all planning and constructions receiving Federal grant funds after the dates provided in the conference report shall be required to consider alternative advanced techniques. It is intended that there be a showing to the Administrator prior to his making any grant for treatment works construction, that the alternative advance waste management techniques have been studied and evaluated and that the selection of the treatment techniques to be used in any new or modified treatment works will reflect advance waste treatment management technology where it is practicable").

83. Conference Report, supra note 18, at 109.

84. Edelman, Legislative Goals and Constraints for Water Quality Planning, a speech reprinted in The

As with any "best technology" standard, questions must be answered about the state of the art and the relevance of economics. Section 201(g)(2) should be read as requiring only that the technology be adequately demonstrated [85] and that costs not be wholly out of line with benefits achieved.[86] In appropriate cases, the 1983 "best practicable" standard requires selection of environmentally superior treatment methods. It might also be read as shifting to the applicant (and ergo to the agency approving the application) the burden of justifying the choice of conventional treatment and discharge technology and of explaining whether and how the 1985 no discharge goal will be met. While the 1983 "best practicable" standard requires adequate investigation and explanation, it also sets unmistakable substantive boundaries on the treatment choices of the near future.

d. *Planning of Multi-purpose Federal Projects*

Additional facility planning provisions wholly unrelated to the construction grants program are found elsewhere in the Act. Indeed, section 102(b) [87] revises pollution dilution thinking that had become a near fixation in federal water pollution programs. Section 2(b) of the Federal Water Pollution Control Act of 1961 [88] made low-flow augmentation an important part of the federal law of multi-purpose project planning. Low-flow augmentation means the releasing of water from dams to maintain stream flow and the capacity of the water to assimilate wastes. Instead of adjusting the medium (the water), it is similarly possible to adjust the source of the pollutants during low stream flows (by holding wastes in treatment ponds, intensive treatment, temporary curtailment, and the like [89]). This practice is the water pollution version of the intermittent control strategies so heatedly debated under the Clean Air Act.[90] Whether it is the water or the sources that are adjusted, low-flow augmentation or intermittent controls are difficult to reconcile with policies demanding maximum control at the source.

The articulation of the low-flow augmentation principle in the 1961 Act shows an awareness of more water being used as an excuse for fewer controls: the old section 2(b) required the Corps of Engineers, Bureau of Reclamation or other agency, in the survey or planning of any reservoir, to give consideration "to inclusion of storage or the regulation of streamflow for the purpose of water quality control, except that any such storage and water releases

---

Potomac, May 10, 1973, at 9 (published by the Interstate Commission on the Potomac River Basin).

85. See § 3.10 above.

86. 118 Cong.Rec. 33694 (1972) (Sen. Muskie); Zener, supra note 55, at 696–702.

87. 33 U.S.C.A. § 1252(b).

88. Pub.L. No. 87–88, 75 Stat. 204.

89. See Roberts, River Basin Authorities: A National Solution to Water Pollution, 83 Harv.L.Rev. 1527, 1542–44 (1970).

90. See § 3.8 above.

Sec. 4.10   FACILITIES & CONSTRUCTION GRANTS   449

shall not be provided as a substitute for adequate treatment or other methods of controlling waste at the source." The sponsoring agency was obliged to make a judgment about the "need for and the value of storage" for water quality purposes and the views of the Secretary of HEW on the subject were to be included in any report to the Congress proposing authorization or construction of a reservoir. A value was to be assigned to this low-flow augmentation function and taken into account in determining the benefits of the entire project (including obviously such values as flood control, power production, recreation, maintaining navigation depths).

The 1972 Amendments do not work radical changes in the legislation although the Conference Report states unequivocally that the legislation "bans pollution dilution as an alternative to waste treatment" while acknowledging that "stream flow augmentation may be useful as a means of reducing the environmental impact of runoff from non-point sources." [91] Section 102(b)(1) repeats verbatim the provision in the 1961 Act requiring that consideration be given to including storage in a reservoir for streamflow purposes while insisting that it is not a substitute for adequate control at the source. One change from the 1961 Act is that "the need for, the value of, and the impact of" storage for water quality control is determined, not by the sponsoring agency, but by the Administrator of EPA, "and his views on these matters shall be set forth in any report or presentation to Congress proposing authorization or construction of any reservoir including such storage." [92] Another important change illuminated not at all by the legislative history forbids the grant of a Federal Power Commission license for certain hydroelectric power projects (most likely a pumped storage project where water is stored in a reservoir and released to generate power during peak load periods) unless the EPA Administrator recommends the inclusion of storage to regulate streamflow for water quality purposes "and such reservoir storage capacity shall not exceed such proportion of the total storage required for the water quality control plan as the drainage area of such reservoir bears to the drainage area of the river basin or basins involved in such water quality control plan." This accomplishes two objectives: (1) the Administrator is given a veto power over all low-flow augmentation for water quality purposes of FPC-licensed projects; (2) regardless of the views of the Administrator, storage capacity for water quality purposes is limited, perhaps to prevent partial or temporary depletion of the watercourse below.

The status of low-flow augmentation for water quality purposes is diminished but not dead. It is not legally sufficient for a source

91. Conference Report, supra note 18, at 101.

92. Section 102(b)(3), 33 U.S.C.A. § 2282(b)(3). Regulation of stream flow for purposes other than water quality (i. e., navigation, salt water intrusion, recreation) remains in the hands of the sponsoring agencies. Section 102(b)(2), 33 U.S.C.A. § 2282(b)(2).

to point to it as an excuse for avoiding or alleviating controls on its effluent. It is a permissible factor of value to be included in assessing a multi-purpose water project and thus might serve to justify projects that otherwise are objectionable on environmental grounds. But this is dependent upon a favorable determination by the Administrator of EPA who might be assumed to be more skeptical of the values of pollution flushing than the Corps of Engineers or the Bureau of Reclamation. Any Federal Power Commission authorization of storage capacity for water quality purposes is dependent wholly upon an EPA recommendation but this does not mean that a disapproval will necessarily defeat a project that conceivably can be justified economically on other grounds.[93] The courts should be more demanding in examining project justifications whose rationales have changed suddenly to recruit new explanations to replace the pollution dilution justification that will not be so readily forthcoming under the 1972 amendments.

Low-flow augmentation as an aspect of water quality management deserves the downgrading it has received. It is a complex and unpredictable management tool.[94] To succeed, it requires close cooperation among waste sources with the same low likelihood of success that afflicts intermittent control systems for air pollution. Releases must be coordinated with waste releases from downstream sewage plants and water removals from downstream industries: "it is not only a question then of assuring that a minimum and average flow can be maintained, but also one of making the water available in a proper time pattern."[95] So long as the water is available for dilution purposes, there is a temptation to use it, regardless of legal directives to exhaust alternatives at the source. This temptation for private sources grows to the extent public authorities can be persuaded to invest in low-flow augmentation.[96]

---

93. See N.Y. Times, Apr. 16, 1973, at 66, col. 1, reporting on the FPC staff position, taken in a draft impact statement on the proposed Blue Ridge project (on the New River on the Virginia-North Carolina border), that the project could be justified solely upon power production grounds although the pending application and early history indicated that a good deal of the reservoir capacity was needed for pollution flushing purposes. See also Ohio ex rel. Brown v. Callaway, 497 F.2d 1235, 4 ELR 20492 (6th Cir. 1974) (failure to obtain EPA certification); Save Our Invaluable Land, Inc. v. Needham, 542 F.2d 539, 6 ELR 20800 (10th Cir. 1976) (refusing to apply section 102(b)(3) to project funded before 1972 Amendments).

94. See R. K. Davis, The Range of Choice in Water Management: A Study of Dissolved Oxygen in the Potomac Estuary (1967); A. Kneese, Water Pollution: Economic Aspects and Research Needs 38–40 (Resources for the Future, 1962); Dep't of HEW, Public Health Service, Symposium on Streamflow Regulation for Quality Control (1963).

95. C. J. Meyers and A. D. Tarlock, Selected Legal and Economic Aspects of Environmental Protection 176 (1971), citing Kelnhofer, Metropolitan Planning and River Basin Planning: Some Interrelations 54–59 (Water Resources Center, Ga. Inst. of Technology, 1968).

96. See ibid. for an interesting explanation of a dispute between the City

§ 4.11 Effluent Standards: National Pollutant Discharge Elimination System Generally

The effluent standards at the heart of the 1972 Amendments fall into several categories: (1) water quality related effluent limitations (section 302);[1] (2) effluent standards for toxic pollutants (section 307);[2] (3) pretreatment standards (section 307), which are effluent standards for sources discharging into treatment works rather than directly into watercourses;[3] (4) standards of performance for new sources (section 306),[4] comparable to those under the Clean Air Act; (5) standards of performance for existing sources, both industrial and publicly owned treatment works (section 301).[5]

The Act defines an effluent limitation consistently with the conventional understanding of an effluent standard: "any restriction established by a State or the Administrator on quantities, rates, and concentrations of chemical, physical, biological and other constituents which are discharged from point sources into navigable waters, the waters of the contiguous zone, or the ocean, including schedules of compliance." [6] A "schedule of compliance" means "a schedule of remedial measures including an enforceable sequence of actions or operations leading to compliance with an effluent limitation, other limitation, prohibition, or standard." [7] Under these definitions, a pretreatment standard for sources discharging directly into a treatment works arguably is not, strictly speaking, an "effluent limitation" but the point is of no consequence for purposes of citizen lawsuits.[8]

---

of Atlanta and the U. S. Army Corps of Engineers over administration of the Buford Dam:

> Corps officials queried about [why Atlantic officials did not try to get a larger allocation of water when the dam was designed] said they did not think Atlanta could have bought storage space in the project . . . . If Buford had been designed to release a daily minimum of 1600 [cubic feet per second] for Atlanta, the computed benefits for this water would have been only about $160,000 annually, as against a power revenue loss of $700,000 annually. On that basis, it was pointed out, the Buford project would not have proved feasible economically. Alternatively, if Atlanta had been asked to pay all the added cost of enlarging the dam to accommodate her storage needs, it would have cost her about $10 million, a sum that the City would not have been willing to consider.

1. 33 U.S.C.A. § 1312; see § 4.8 above.

2. 33 U.S.C.A. § 1317; see § 4.14 below.

3. 33 U.S.C.A. § 1317; see § 4.15 below.

4. 33 U.S.C.A. § 1316; see § 4.13 below.

5. 33 U.S.C.A. § 1311; see §§ 4.12, 4.13 below.

6. Section 502(11), 33 U.S.C.A. § 1362 (11).

7. Section 502(17), 33 U.S.C.A. § 1362 (17).

8. An "effluent standard or limitation" for purposes of citizen suits is defined specifically to include a pretreatment standard. Section 505(f), 33 U.S.C.A. § 1365(f).

It must be remembered that the basic premise of the 1972 Amendments, borrowed from the Rivers and Harbors Act of 1899, is that "the discharge of any pollutant by any person shall be unlawful." [9] The exceptions are for sources brought, one way or another, under the permit enforced effluent limitations of the Act. The centerpiece of the permit requirements is the National Pollutant Discharge Elimination System, established by section 402.[10] Subsection 402(a)(1) authorizes the Administrator, after opportunity for public hearing, to issue a permit for the discharge of any pollutant so long as the source meets the "best technology" and related effluent limitations [11] or, prior to their implementation, "such conditions as the Administrator determines are necessary to carry out the provisions of this Act." Section 402 continues in force the handful of permits that had been issued under the Refuse Act Permit Program,[12] makes clear that no permits in the future are to be issued under Section 13 of the Refuse Act,[13] allows for delegation of the permit program to states demonstrating adequate authority to administer it [14] and binds the Administrator's permit program to the same statutory terms and conditions against which the adequacy of the state programs is measured.[15]

Thus, the NPDES program anticipates initial federal administration and a gradual delegation of authority to states demonstrating a capacity to administer their own programs, subject theoretically to a withdrawal of approval if a state's program falls short of legal requirements.[16] Approval of state water pollution permit programs, not unlike the approval of the implementation plans under the Clean Air Act, is dependent upon a demonstration of "adequate authority" in several respects, including the power to issue permits, enforce them, insure that municipal permits require notice to the agency of new introductions of pollutants into the treatment works, and so on.[17] As of November 21, 1975, twenty-six state permit programs had been approved, with prospects of NPDES delegation ultimately extending

9. Section 301(a), 33 U.S.C.A. § 1311(a)(1).

10. 33 U.S.C.A. § 1342.

11. Specifically mentioned are sections 301 (existing sources), 302 (water quality related effluent limitations), 306 (standards of performance for new sources), 307 (toxic and pretreatment effluent standards), 308 (inspections, monitoring and entry) and 403 (ocean discharge criteria).

12. Section 402(a)(4), 33 U.S.C.A. § 1342(a)(4). The Corps of Engineers had received 20,000 permit applications but had issued only 21 permits by the time the RAPP permit program was superseded by NPDES. National Water Quality Commission, Staff Draft Report on Water Quality Analysis and Environmental Impact Assessment of Public Law 92–500, Jan. 1976 at V–14 [hereinafter cited as Draft Report on Environmental Impact].

13. Section 402(a)(5), 33 U.S.C.A. § 1342(a)(5).

14. Section 402(b), 33 U.S.C.A. § 1342(b).

15. Section 402(a)(3), 33 U.S.C.A. § 1342(a)(3).

16. Section 402(c), 33 U.S.C.A. § 1342(c).

17. Sections 402(b)(1)–(9), 33 U.S.C.A. §§ 1342(b)(1)–(9).

Sec. 4.11　EFFLUENT STANDARDS: GENERALLY

to approximately forty states.[18] In short, NPDES has become substantially a state administered program.

Because the states have an important role in issuing permits, the question of uniformity of conditions becomes paramount. Section 301(b)(2)(A) [19] speaks of technology based effluent limitations for "categories and classes of point sources." Section 304(b)(1)(A) [20] requires the promulgation of guidelines within one year of enactment which, among other things, identify the degree of effluent reduction attainable through application of the 1977 and 1983 technology based effluent limitations "for classes and categories of point sources." Neither section 301 nor section 304 offers further enlightenment on the meaning of "classes and categories" of point sources although section 306,[21] dealing with standards of performance for new sources, does list twenty-seven categories of industrial sources.[22] EPA has designated guidelines for these twenty-seven categories as Group I (further subdivided into Phases I and II) and has designated additional categories not mentioned in section 306 as Group II. The Group I guidelines were due within one year of enactment and all other guidelines, with some exceptions, were ordered published before December 31, 1974.[23] (Prior to that date, the pendency of a permit application precluded a finding of a section 301 violation.[24] Obviously, "Congress contemplated that the task of evaluating permit applications and issuing permits would be completed by that date." [25]) In the guidelines published thus far, EPA has identified "more than 200 categories and subcategories of industrial processes (based on plant

---

18. Draft Report on Environmental Impact, supra note 12, at V-21.

19. 33 U.S.C.A. § 1311(b)(2)(A).

20. Id. § 1314(b)(1)(A).

21. Id. § 1316.

22. These are:
    pulp and paper mills;
    paperboard, builders paper and board mills;
    meat product and rendering processing;
    dairy product processing;
    grain mills;
    canned and preserved fruits and vegetable processing;
    canned and preserved seafood processing;
    sugar processing;
    textile mills;
    cement manufacturing;
    feedlots;
    electroplating;
    organic chemicals manufacturing;
    inorganic chemicals manufacturing;
    plastic and synthetic materials manufacturing;
    soap and detergent manufacturing;
    fertilizer manufacturing;
    petroleum refining;
    iron and steel manufacturing;
    nonferrous metals manufacturing;
    phosphate manufacturing;
    steam electric powerplants;
    ferroalloy manufacturing;
    leather tanning and finishing;
    glass and asbestos manufacturing;
    rubber processing; and
    timber products processing.

23. Natural Resources Defense Council, Inc. v. Train, 166 U.S.App.D.C. 312, 510 F.2d 692, 5 ELR 20046 (1974).

24. Section 402(k), 33 U.S.C.A. § 1343(k).

25. 166 U.S.App.D.C. at 327, 510 F.2d at 707, 5 ELR at 20054 (footnote omitted).

age and size, manufacturing process, raw material use, etc.) which will require discrete effluent limitations." [26] Most of the guidelines have been challenged in court.

A useful summary [27] explains how the interrelationship of sections 301 and 304 has been debated on jurisdictional grounds: "Section 301 states existing point sources must, by 1977 and 1983 respectively, achieve 'effluent limitations' which require application of the 'best practicable control technology currently available' and the 'best available technology economically achievable.' Neither the EPA Administrator nor anyone else is, however, explicitly authorized to promulgate regulations establishing such limitations. Section 304, on the other hand, requires the Administrator to publish 'regulations, providing guidelines for effluent limitations.' These guidelines identify for particular point source categories, 'the degree of effluent reduction attainable' through application of the 1977 and 1983 technologies, and must specify the factors, including, inter alia, cost of effluent reduction and age of equipment and facilities involved, which are to be taken into account in giving content to these general technological criteria. A related provision, § 509(b)(1),[28] makes the Administrator's approval or promulgation of any effluent limitation under § 301 reviewable in the appropriate U. S. Court of Appeals; guidelines promulgated solely under § 304 are, on the other hand, reviewable in the first instance in federal district court." EPA's effluent limitations guidelines for several industries recited both sections 301 and 304 as the source of authority, prompting attacks in the courts. Three federal district courts [29] dismissed challenges on the ground that section 301 effluent limitations are reviewable only in the Courts of Appeals. Then, the Eighth Circuit [30] ruled the Administrator had no power under section 301 to promulgate uniform effluent limitations for existing sources and thus the guidelines, supported only by section 304, were reviewable in the district court. More recently, the

---

26. Draft Report on Environmental Impact, supra note 12, at V–17; see id. at V–19 for a table of Federal Register dates of proposed and promulgated effluent limitation guidelines.

27. Comment, National Uniformity Under the Water Act: Two Circuits Uphold EPA's Authority to Issue Effluent Limitations Under § 301, 6 ELR 1008, 1009 (1976).

28. 33 U.S.C.A. § 1369(b)(1) (footnote added).

29. American Paper Inst. v. Train, 381 F.Supp. 553, 4 ELR 20815 (D.D.C. 1974, aff'd —— U.S.App.D.C. ——, 543 F.2d 328 (1976); E. I. duPont de Nemours & Co. v. Train, 383 F.Supp. 1244, 4 ELR 20855 (W.D.Va.1974), aff'd 528 F.2d 1136, 6 ELR 20116 (4th Cir. 1975), aff'd —— U.S. ——, 97 S.Ct. 965, 51 L.Ed.2d 204 (1977) (holding court of appeals has jurisdiction under section 509 without deciding whether Administrator has the power under section 301 to issue regulations); American Petroleum Inst. v. Train, 5 ELR 20298 (D.C.Colo.), aff'd 526 F.2d 1343 (10th Cir. 1975).

30. CPC Int'l, Inc. v. Train, 515 F.2d 1032, 5 ELR 20392 (8th Cir. 1975), on remand Grain Processing Corp. v. Train, 407 F.Supp. 96, 6 ELR 20200 (S.D.Iowa 1976) (invalidating several aspects of EPA's corn wet milling industry guidelines).

Sec. 4.11 EFFLUENT STANDARDS: GENERALLY

Third,[31] Fourth[32] and Seventh[33] Circuits have disagreed with the Eighth Circuit, holding that the Administrator is empowered under section 301 to issue effluent limitations binding on individual permits. All four circuit court opinions are well reasoned although the Third, Fourth, and Seventh Circuits happen to be right.

The reasons for the vigorous contesting of EPA's rulemaking powers under section 301 go back to the degree of uniformity expected in the permits. The Third Circuit was told, quite explicitly, that some of the plants affected by EPA's single number iron and steel manufacturing point source guidelines had "local problems which can be fully appreciated only by a local permit-issuing authority"[34]—for example, that the plants were very old, were major employers and would be forced to close to meet the standards. Maximum local autonomy was thought to be assured by denying EPA the power to lay down the specifics under section 301. This argument in large part contradicts the thrust of the 1972 Amendments which have a strong bias in favor of uniformity to ease administration and enforcement and prevent threats of shutdown from justifying nonenforcement of water pollution laws. Debate on the floor of the House[35] and Senate[36] and the Conference Report[37] strongly indicate that uni-

---

31. American Iron & Steel Inst. v. EPA, 526 F.2d 1027, 6 ELR 20068 (3d Cir. 1975).

32. E. I. duPont de Nemours & Co. v. Train, 528 F.2d 1136, 6 ELR 20116 (4th Cir. 1975), aff'd — U.S. —, 97 S.Ct. 965, 51 L.Ed.2d 204 (1977).

33. American Meat Inst. v. EPA, 526 F.2d 442, 6 ELR 20029 (7th Cir. 1975).

34. 526 F.2d at 1036, 6 ELR at 20070; see Grain Processing Corp. v. Train, 407 F.Supp. 96, 6 ELR 20200 (S.D. Iowa 1976) (holding that EPA's single number guidelines are inconsistent with the purpose of the Act to allocate responsibility to the states).

35. 118 Cong.Rec. 33758 (1972) (Rep. Dingell) (discussing Conference Report):
    Thus, a plant-by-plant determination of the economic impact of an effluent limitation is neither expected, nor desired, and in fact, it should be avoided.

36. Id. at 33697. (Sen. Muskie) (discussing Conference Report):
    The Conferees intend that the factors described in Section 304(b) be considered only within classes or categories of point sources and that such factors not be considered at the time of the application of an effluent limitation to an individual point source within such category or class . . . . Except as provided in Section 301(c) of the Act [addressing variances from the 1983 standards], the intent is that effluent limitations applicable to individual point sources be as uniform as possible. The Administrator is expected to be precise in his guidelines so as to assure that similar characteristics, regardless of their location or the nature of the water into which the discharge is made, will meet similar effluent limitations.

37. Comm. of Conference, Federal Water Pollution Control Act Amendments of 1972, H.R.Rep. No. 1465 92d Cong., 2d Sess. 121 (1972) [hereinafter cited as Conference Report]:
    The conferees intend that the Administrator, or the State, as the case may be, will make the determination of the economic impact of an effluent limitation on the basis of classes and categories of point sources, as distinguished from a plant-by-plant determination.

formity is to be achieved through the guidelines with minimal debate on a plant-by-plant basis. The strongest assurance of this uniformity is section 402(d)(2),[38] which gives the Administrator power to veto a state approved permit "as being outside the guidelines and requirements of this Act." This power to veto individual permits is not at all inconsistent with a power to make rules to fill in the meaning of the various "best technology" definitions of section 301, and to do so with some specificity.

The debate over the Administrator's section 301 rulemaking power is hardly worth the effort.[39] The reason for this is that under section 304(b) the Administrator promulgates guidelines that are meant to restrict the discretion of the permit issuers. Specifically, the guidelines must identify "the degree of effluent reduction attainable" by application of the two best technology standards to point source categories.[40] They also must "specify factors to be taken into account in determining" control measures under the 1977 and 1983 standards applied to point sources within these categories.[41] These factors include cost, the age of equipment and facilities, the process employed, engineering aspects of various types of control techniques, and non-water quality environmental impact. While these factors are "to be taken into account," presumably by the permit issuer, it does not follow that there is freedom to ignore prescribed effluent limits. The economic and other factors are "taken into account" in writing the compliance schedule necessary to meet the limits. The strong legislative history favoring uniformity for similar sources with similar problems [42] suggests that section 304(b) guidelines should establish at

38. 33 U.S.C.A. § 1342(d)(2).

39. American Meat Inst. v. EPA, 526 F.2d 442, 449 n. 14, 6 ELR 20029, 20031 n. 14 (7th Cir. 1975) (questioning whether a rejection of section 301 rulemaking powers would require "a radical change" in the way the Act is now administered).

40. Sections 304(b)(1)(A), (2)(A), 33 U.S.C.A. §§ 1314(b)(1)(A), (2)(A).

41. Sections 304(b)(1)(B), (2)(B), 33 U.S.C.A. §§ 1314(b)(1)(B), (2)(B).

42. Notes 35–37, supra; see Comm. on Public Works, Federal Water Pollution Control Act Amendments of 1971, S.Rep.No.414, 92d Cong., 1st Sess. 50 (1971); 118 Cong.Rec. 33696 (1972) (Sen. Muskie) ("It is assumed, in any event, that 'best practicable technology' will be the minimal level of control imposed on all sources within a category or class during the period subsequent to enactment and prior to July 1, 1977"); Natural Resources Defense Council, Inc. v. Train, 166 U.S.App.D.C. 312, 327, 510 F.2d 692, 707, 5 ELR 20045, 20054 (1974) ("These [section 304] guidelines are intended to assist in the establishment of section 301(b) limitations that will provide uniformity in the permit conditions imposed on similar sources within the same category by diverse state and federal permit authorities") (footnote omitted); Comm. on Public Works, Federal Water Pollution Control Act Amendments of 1972, H.R.Rep.No.911, 92d Cong., 2d Sess. 108 (1972) ("the Committee intends that the degree of reduction [under section 304] be specified in objective terms and that the incorporation of a specific process shall not be required. This means that the Administrator shall not prescribe a specific design or process to meet the requirements of [best technology] but instead shall set out effluent limitations which are consistent with such [best technology]").

Sec. 4.11 EFFLUENT STANDARDS: GENERALLY

least maximum levels of discharge for sources within a given category. This indicates that section 304(b) and section 301 guidelines cover largely the same territory and that regulations under either section can impose a ceiling on effluent discharges covered by a permit. The Third Circuit in *American Iron & Steel Institute* [43] essentially agrees, while insisting that sections 301 and 304 can be reconciled: "the section 301 limitations represent both the base level or minimum degree of effluent *control* permissible and the ceiling (or maximum amount of effluent discharge) permissible nationwide within a given category, and the section 304 guidelines are intended to provide precise guidance to the permit-issuing authorities in establishing a permissible level of discharge that is more stringent than the ceiling."

NPDES is now a functioning reality. As of June 30, 1975, more than 20,000 industrial permits had been issued (out of a total in excess of 40,000).[44] Theoretically, publication of the guidelines was supposed to precede issuance of the permits. This often did not happen which helps explain why conditions in a permit issued to a discharger may deviate from the guidelines for the relevant industrial category. Other reasons [45] for a lack of congruity between guidelines and permits within a class include neglect and oversight, the process may not fit exactly within the guidelines, state water quality standards may require different conditions, the state may request additional conditions or parameters in its section 401 [46] certification, the guidelines themselves may allow deviations, the permitting authority improperly may apply economic or technical factors to relax conditions.

Speaking theoretically, the content of the 1977 "best practicable" and 1983 "best available" effluent limitations for existing industrial sources should be defined by regulation prior to the issuance of a permit to an individual source. This means that claims of economic or technological infeasibility generally have no place in a permit proceeding since they involve a challenge to the underlying regulations.[47] There are two exceptions to this rule, one of them statutory, the other administrative, both emphasizing the narrow role of the economic

---

43. 526 F.2d at 1045, 6 ELR at 20074 (emphasis in original).

44. Draft Report on Environmental Impact, supra note 12, at V-24.

45. Id. at V-26; Energy and Environmental Analysis, Inc., Assessment of the National Pollutant Discharge Elimination System of Public Law 92-500, undated (a report for the National Commission on Water Quality) [hereinafter cited as NPDES Assessment]. See also Comptroller General, Implementing the National Water Pollution Control Permit Program: Progress and Problems, Report to the Subcomm. on Investigation and Review of the House Comm. on Public Works and Transportation (1976).

46. 33 U.S.C.A. § 1341.

47. Cf., e. g., Nader v. Nuclear Regulatory Comm'n, 168 U.S.App.D.C. 255, 266-67, 513 F.2d 1045, 1056-57, 5 ELR 20342, 20346 (1975); Union of Concerned Scientists v. Atomic Energy Comm'n, 163 U.S.App.D.C. 64, 85, 499 F.2d 1069, 1090, 4 ELR 20605, 20615 (1974). As indicated above (p. 456), these factors may be pertinent to the terms of a compliance schedule aimed at achieving the prescribed limits.

and technological defenses. Section 301(c) [48] is an outright variance provision authorizing modification of the requirements of the 1983 "best available" technology standard for any industrial point source seeking a permit after July 1, 1977, "upon a showing by the owner or operator of such point source satisfactory to the Administrator that such modified requirements (1) will represent the maximum use of technology within the economic capability of the owner or operator; and (2) will result in reasonable further progress toward the elimination of the discharge of pollutants." This is one of those provisions that takes away by giving: the discharger has the burden, and it is a heavy one, that is met by showing the proposed controls will bankrupt the proprietor not merely render a particular source uneconomic in operation. Section 301(c) thus is an escape route only for poor proprietors and not necessarily uneconomic operations.[49] By confirming the variance relief from the 1983 "best available" standard, the statute just as clearly denies that relief to those seeking a reprieve from the 1977 "best practicable" standard.

An administrative variance from both the 1977 and 1983 effluent standard is routinely included in the guidelines for individual industry categories for any individual discharger demonstrating that factors relating to its equipment or facilities are "fundamentally different" from the factors considered in establishing the guidelines.[50] This type of provision, which has been approved by appellate courts,[51]

48. 33 U.S.C.A. § 1311(c). The only other cost-justified variance provision in the Act is found in section 302, 33 U.S.C.A. § 1312, dealing with water quality related effluent limitations. See § 4.8 above. Section 306 (on new source performance standards) omits a cost-based variance procedure that had appeared in both Senate and House bills. S. 2770, § 306(b)(1)(C), 92d Cong., 1st Sess. (1971); H.R. 11896, § 306(b)(1)(C), 92d Cong., 2d Sess. (1972). This strengthens the conclusion that where cost-based variance provisions did not appear in the Act, "the omission was deliberate." Zener, The Federal Law of Water Pollution Control, in Environmental Law Institute, Federal Environmental Law 682, 701 (E. L. Dolgin & T. G. P. Guilbert eds. 1974).

49. A technical argument the other way is that an owner or operator means any person who owns or otherwise controls a source. See section 306(a)(4), 33 U.S.C.A. § 1316(a)(4). Therefore, when the statute speaks of the "economic capability" of the operator it is referring to his capability with respect to the particular source at issue. This seems an inadequate justification to excuse compliance by a rich company that happens to be operating a poor plant. Cf. Denver & Rio Grande R. R. v. Peterson, 30 Colo. 77, 88, 69 P. 578, 581 (1902) ("The care required of a warehouse man is the same, whether he be rich or poor").

50. E. g., 40 CFR § 405.12 (dairy products processing; receiving stations subcategory); id. § 406.12 (grain mills; corn wet milling subcategory); id. § 407.12 (canned and preserved fruits and vegetables; apple juice subcategory); id. § 408.12 (canned and preserved seafood processing; farm raised catfish processing subcategory).

51. Natural Resources Defense Council, Inc. v. Train, 166 U.S.App.D.C. 312, 330, 510 F.2d 692, 710, 5 ELR 20046, 20055 (1974) (by implication); Natural Resources Defense Council, Inc. v. EPA, 537 F.2d 642, 6 ELR 20461 (2d Cir. 1976); E. I. Dupont de Nemours & Co. v. Train, 541 F.2d 1029, 6 ELR 20371 (4th Cir. 1976), aff'd —— U.S. ——, 97 S.Ct. 965, 51 L.Ed.2d 204 (1977) (stating that guidelines should be presumptively applicable in permit proceedings). The Court's decision in duPont makes

Sec. 4.11 EFFLUENT STANDARDS: GENERALLY

is easily defended. Rather than a variance, it is better viewed as a declaration of inapplicability. In making law for the usual case in its guidelines, the agency did not mean to lay down standards for a facility fundamentally different from the ones considered. Generic lawmaking, however determined, cannot anticipate all the concrete cases.

A third instance where economic and technical arguments can be freely made in permit proceedings is the case, not at all unusual, where no guidelines speak to the situation. Like the cases of facilities "fundamentally different" from those in the relevant industry subcategory, this is a situation where the agency has not yet got around to filling in the details of the meaning of the 1977 "best practicable" standard or the 1983 "best available" standard. Just as the state of the art and the demands of economics could be argued by a source at the rulemaking stage,[52] the same arguments can be made at the adjudicatory stage if the agency has not attempted to define the scope of the various "best technology" standards. There is no question that both the 1977 and 1983 standards applicable to existing industrial sources involve consideration of both economic and technical factors.[53] In situations where implementing action has not been taken, permits can be issued subject to "such conditions as the Administrator determines are necessary to carry out the provisions of this Act."[54] The content of these permits is said to be governed by the Administrator's best practicable judgment[55] although this judgment, good or bad, is unconfined by administrative standards.

Assuming no delegation to the state has yet occurred, the permit issuance process can be parsed into ten separate steps (securing an application, completing it, filing it, formulating a draft permit, certification approval by the state of the EPA prepared permit, public notice, public hearing, formulation of a final draft permit, certification approval by the state of the final version of the permit, issuance).[56] The reciprocal powers of both the state and EPA to veto and prescribe conditions continue both before and after delegation.[57] EPA regulations allow each regional administrator to act on requests for adjudicatory hearings in connection with the issuance of NPDES permits.[58] Some 1500 of these hearings were pending by the end of 1975, which is indicative of their legal significance. An NPDES ad-

---

clear that the Act does not permit variances from the new sources performance standards. — U.S. —, 97 S.Ct. at 979–80, 51 L.Ed.2d at 223. See also Bethlehem Steel Corp. v. Train, 544 F.2d 657, 7 ELR 20019 (3d Cir. 1976), cert. denied — U.S. — (1977).

52. See § 4.12 below.

53. Ibid.

54. 33 U.S.C.A. § 1342(a)(1).

55. NPDES Assessment, supra note 45 at 184, 187–89.

56. Draft Report on Environmental Impact, supra note 12, at V–22; see 40 CFR pt. 125 (containing the NPDES regulations).

57. Sections 401(a)(1), (d), 402(d), 33 U.S.C.A. §§ 1341(a)(1), (d), 1312(d).

58. See note 58 on p. 460.

judicatory proceeding has some of the attributes of a familiar trial-type hearing (rights of intervention [59] and cross-examination [60]) but by no means all of them (no subpoena or discovery rights are afforded).[61] The proceedings are conducted before a Presiding Officer who is appointed by the Regional Administrator or Administrator.[62] The Presiding Officer's functions are mostly but not entirely ministerial. He certifies the record of a proceeding to the Regional Administrator who makes the initial decision in a case.[63] He also must certify issues of law to the General Counsel for decision.[64] The Presiding Officer does make legal decisions by ruling on offers of proof, motions to strike and the like, but his authority (as well as the continuity of the proceedings) is dependent upon securing the opinion of the General Counsel on issues of construction of the Act and the regulations. The Administrator, on his own initiative or upon petition of a party, may review the initial decision of the Regional Administrator. Judicial review of the final decision to issue or to deny a permit is available in the relevant Circuit Court of Appeals.[65]

Opinions of the EPA General Counsel on legal issues certified from adjudicatory hearings are an already active and expanding source of law on the subject of water pollution.[66] The General Counsel has made important decisions on procedural issues, by ruling that judicial review of the guidelines will not suspend their effect in permit proceedings,[67] that guideline limitations cannot be attacked collaterally as too stringent by a permittee,[68] that a state's Load Allocation Summary, prepared pursuant to Section 303(d) of the Act,[69] could be relied upon to set discharge limits,[70] that public participation in adjudicatory hearings is appropriate;[71] on substantive matters, by ruling that the July 1, 1983 goal of swimmable/fishable water is enforce-

58. 40 CFR § 125.36(b); see Dyecraftsmen, Inc. v. EPA, —— F.2d —— (1st Cir. 1976) (no hearing required where there are no material issues of fact).

59. 40 CFR § 125.36(d).

60. Id. § 125.36(i)(4).

61. This omission has been challenged in court on procedural due process grounds. Compare § 1.10 above (discussing use of the Freedom of Information Act as a supplement to truncated agency discovery rights).

62. Id. §§ 125.36(i)(2), (a)(6).

63. Id. § 125.36(l).

64. Id. § 125.36(m).

65. See Mianus River Preservation Comm. v. Administrator, 541 F.2d 899, 6 ELR 20597 (2d Cir. 1976) (finding lack of jurisdiction in a court of appeals to review a NPDES permit issued by a state authority).

66. The thirty-fourth decision in the series was issued on November 20, 1975. These are cited as NPDES Decisions of the General Counsel.

67. NPDES Decision of the General Counsel No. 3, Dec. 23, 1974 (U. S. Steel Corp.).

68. Ibid; NPDES Decision of the General Counsel No. 32, Oct. 14, 1975 (Youngstown Sheet & Tube Co.).

69. 33 U.S.C.A. § 1313(d); see § 4.8 above.

70. NPDES Decision of the General Counsel No. 27, Aug. 4, 1975 (Inland Steel Co.).

71. NPDES Decision of the General Counsel No. 29, Sept. 4, 1975 (Peabody Coal Co.).

Sec. 4.11 EFFLUENT STANDARDS: GENERALLY

able through permit conditions,[72] that a new source in fact is treated as an existing source for regulatory purposes if not covered by standards of performance under section 306,[73] that irrigation return flow is subject to the permit requirements,[74] that a municipal treatment works discharging directly into the ocean is not exempt from the 1977 secondary treatment requirements,[75] that "navigable waters" probably extends to a private lake impounded by a power company for cooling water purposes [76] but not to a creek whose entire flow is used for irrigation on a single ranch,[77] that data submitted in compliance with monitoring obligations can be used for enforcement purposes;[78] and, particularly, on conditions appearing in the permits, by ruling that a permit may allow for malfunctions [79] or include a force majeure clause,[80] that conditions in a prior Refuse Act consent decree are entitled to weight but are not controlling,[81] that conditions in a state consent decree can be disregarded [82] unless the state insists on them in a certification,[83] that a permit may require the presence of one qualified operator at the site of a privately owned treatment works plant even though the facility can comply without an operator being present,[84] that a permit must include all conditions recommended by the Corps of Engineers to protect anchorage and navigation,[85] can control well injections [86] but not the disposal of sewage sludge unless it threatens navigable waters,[87] can limit toxic pollutants before they

---

72. NPDES Decision of the General Counsel No. 2, Dec. 30, 1974 (U.S. Pipe and Foundry Co.).

73. NPDES Decision of the General Counsel No. 4, Apr. 4, 1975 (St. Regis Paper Co., International Paper Co.).

74. NPDES Decision of the General Counsel No. 21, June 27, 1975 (Riverside Irrigation District et al.).

75. NPDES Decision of the General Counsel No. 12, May 7, 1975 (Greater Anchorage Borough).

76. NPDES Decision of the General Counsel No. 7, Apr. 8, 1975 (Central Illinois Public Service Co.).

77. NPDES Decision of the General Counsel No. 30, Sept. 18, 1975 (City of Ely, Nevada).

78. NPDES Decision of the General Counsel No. 15, May 30, 1975 (Heinz, USA).

79. NPDES Decision of the General Counsel No. 1, Sept. 5, 1974 (Marathon Oil Co.).

80. NPDES Decision of the General Counsel No. 8, Apr. 8, 1975 (Jones & Laughlin Steel Corp.).

81. NPDES Decision of the General Counsel No. 2, Dec. 30, 1974 (U. S. Pipe & Foundry Co.).

82. NPDES Decision of the General Counsel No. 22, July 3, 1975 (U. S. Steel Corp.).

83. Ibid.

84. NPDES Decision of the General Counsel No. 19, June 27, 1975 (Greenbriar, Md., Sewage Treatment Plant).

85. NPDES Decision of the General Counsel No. 17, June 16, 1975 (U. S. Steel Corp.); NPDES Decision of the General Counsel No. 28, Aug. 11, 1975 (Zitmann Coal Co., Consolidation Coal Co.) (EPA cannot go beyond conditions prescribed by the Corps).

86. NPDES Decision of the General Counsel No. 6, Apr. 8, 1975 (E. I. DuPont de Nemours & Co.).

87. NPDES Decision of the General Counsel No. 33, Oct. 21, 1975 (Blue Plains Sewage Treatment Plant, Washington, D. C.).

are the subject of a proceeding under section 307.[88] The General Counsel seeks only a "rational connection" between a permit condition and an assurance of compliance with the effluent limitations of the Act.[89] The subject promises to be a fertile field of litigation.

Little need be said about the noncontroversial or standard permit conditions. Typically, they include effluent limitations for key parameters (biochemical oxygen demand [5-day], suspended solids, pH, perhaps fecal foliform or total phosphorus). These are expressed as average effluent concentrations over time and sometimes as average loadings. (Obviously, the longer the period over which averaging is permitted—30 days, say, instead of 24 hours—the wider the permissible fluctuations within those averages.) Provisions are included for schedules of compliance, facility operation, monitoring and reporting (typically, self-monitoring not third party or continuous monitoring). Once again, conditions on minimum frequency of analysis (monthly or daily, daily or hourly) and sample type (composite, which is an average of a number of samples, or grab, which anticipates analysis of a single sample of the effluent stream) can determine whether the quality of the effluent is closely monitored. Composite samples infrequently taken can obscure wide fluctuations in the quality of the effluent. It is not unusual for permits to require sampling and reporting on a number of parameters (for example, heavy metals) not addressed in the effluent limitations. Other permit conditions may address recording of samples, disposal of solids, system overflows or upsets, long range planning or study obligations. Even the boilerplate clauses can come under scrutiny in a contested case.

§ 4.12 Effluent Standards: Industrial Sources

The 1972 Amendments draw a clear distinction between existing and new industrial sources. For existing sources, section 301(b) contains a loose description of phase one and phase two effluent limitations, to be achieved by July 1, 1977 and July 1, 1983, respectively. The phase one standard requires the application of "the best practicable control technology currently available" as defined by the Administrator [1] while phase two calls for application of "the best available technology economically achievable" for a category or class of point sources "which will result in reasonable further progress toward

---

88. See NPDES Decision of the General Counsel No. 13, May 19, 1975 (Commonwealth Edison Co.); NPDES Decision of the General Counsel No. 14, May 21, 1975 (Indianapolis Power & Light Co.); NPDES Decision of the General Counsel No. 33, Oct. 21, 1975 (Blue Plains Sewage Treatment Plant, Washington, D. C.).

89. NPDES Decision of the General Counsel No. 19, June 27, 1975, at 4 (Greenbriar, Md., Sewage Treatment Plant).

1. Section 301(b)(1)(A), 33 U.S.C.A. § 1311(b)(1)(A).

Sec. 4.12   **INDUSTRIAL SOURCES**   463

the national goal of eliminating the discharge of all pollutants."[2] As discussed above,[3] the NPDES permits under section 402 contain the compliance schedules setting forth a phased agenda of action designed to enable the source to meet the standards by the two statutory deadlines.

Also discussed above[4] but deserving repetition is the basic structure for meeting the deadlines: the responsibility for fleshing out the "best practicable" and "best available" standards is that of the Administrator who must publish guidelines for effluent limitations under section 304(b). The purpose of the guidelines is "to assist in the establishment of section 301(b) limitations that will provide uniformity in the permit conditions imposed on similar sources within the same category by diverse state and federal permit authorities."[5] It was the contemplation of Congress that the "guidelines would precede individual permits"[6] and not that the tail would wag the dog by issuing the permits before the guidelines. The Act is structured so that the principal guidelines were to be issued within one year.[7] Most of the permits based on the guidelines were to be issued by December 31, 1974, when the pendency of a permit application no longer would be a bar to a finding of violation,[8] leaving thirty months lead time for affected industries to meet the phase one July 1977 "best practicable" deadline. The Court of Appeals for the District of Columbia has read the Act this way, but did not catch up to the process until late in 1974, ordering the Administrator to publish the 304(b)(1)(A) guidelines for major categories of point sources by the end of the year unless he offered a suitable justification for abstention or delay.[9]

Judge Leventhal has praised the procedures followed by EPA in developing industrial effluent guidelines,[10] which have consisted, first, of securing technical analyses from consultants for each point source category for which guidelines are being developed, then soliciting comments on the preliminary technical analyses.[11] Typically, this process has yielded standards not only for the "best practicable" and "best available" tests for a particular industry but also the new source

---

2. Section 301(b)(2)(A), 33 U.S.C.A. § 1311(b)(2)(A).

3. See § 4.11.

4. Ibid.

5. Natural Resources Defense Council, Inc. v. Train, 166 U.S.App.D.C. 312, 327, 510 F.2d 692, 707, 5 ELR 20046, 20054 (1974).

6. 166 U.S.App.D.C. at 331, 510 F.2d at 711, 5 ELR at 20056.

7. See section 304(b), 33 U.S.C.A. § 1314(b).

8. Section 402(k), 33 U.S.C.A. § 1342(k).

9. Natural Resources Defense Council, Inc. v. Train, 166 U.S.App.D.C. 312, 510 F.2d 692, 5 ELR 20046 (1974).

10. 166 U.S.App.D.C. at 332–33 n.105, 510 F.2d at 712–13 n.105, 5 ELR at 20057 n.105.

11. See Effluent Limitations Guidelines and Standards for New Sources, Advance Notice of Public Review Procedures, 38 Fed.Reg. 21202–06 (1973).

standards under section 306, and pretreatment standards under section 307.[12] Each industry category and subcategory is dealt with separately in the regulations, and the history of each regulation represents a separate series of studies, judgments and trade-offs.[13] The widespread efforts to seek court review of the guidelines (most of them are pending as of this writing) will add further, if predictable, gloss to the hard look or close scrutiny doctrine [14] which has become synonymous with judicial review of agency decision-making on technological and environmental issues.

Of overriding concern is the extent to which technological or economic limitations can be invoked to delimit a particular standard. Taking the technological question first, the 1977 "best practicable" standard normally "is based on the average performance of the best existing plants," [15] yet the legislative history indicates that even for this milder standard the Administrator was given a mandate "to press technology," [16] up to the point of requiring "higher levels of control than any currently in place." [17] This is not too demanding a concession in light of the historical recognition that an industrywide custom may fail as a defense even in a negligence case because "a whole calling may have unduly lagged in the adoption of new and available devices." [18] Under the 1983 "best available" standard the Administrator clearly must push for the adoption of technology not in routine use and often not in use at all. The House Committee meant by the term "those plant processes and control technology which, at the pilot plant, semi-works, or other level, has demonstrated both technological performance and economic viability at a level sufficient to reasonably justify the making of investments in such new facilities." [19] The Senate Committee saw the question as whether a certain performance level was "attainable." [20] If industry performance was a factor at all, it was only the "best performer" who represented the

12. See § 4.14 below.

13. See 40 CFR subch. N (Effluent Guidelines and Standards).

14. See § 1.5 above.

15. American Meat Inst. v. EPA, 526 F.2d 442, 453, 6 ELR 20029, 20033 (7th Cir. 1975); Tanners' Council of America, Inc. v. Train, 540 F.2d 1188, 1191, 6 ELR 20379, 20380 (4th Cir. 1976) (same).

16. Comm. on Public Works, Federal Water Pollution Control Act Amendments of 1971, S.Rep.No.414, 92d Cong., 1st Sess. 42 (1971) [hereinafter cited as Senate Report].

17. 118 Cong.Rec. 33696 (1972) (Sen. Muskie); see E. I. DuPont de Nemours & Co. v. Train, 541 F.2d 1018, 1031, 6 ELR 20371, 20375 (4th Cir. 1976), aff'd — U.S. —, 97 S.Ct. 965, 51 L.Ed.2d 204 (1977).

18. The T. J. Hooper, 60 F.2d 737, 740 (2d Cir. 1932).

19. Comm. on Public Works, Federal Water Pollution Control Act Amendments of 1972, H.R.Rep.No.911, 92d Cong., 2d Sess. 103 (1972) (discussing the "best available demonstrated technology" term appearing in H.R. 11896, § 301). [hereinafter cited as House Report]

20. Senate Report, supra note 16, at 42.

"minimum" demands of the 1983 standard.[21] The agency, indeed, may look beyond the "best performer" and beyond a pilot plant to "technologies that have not been applied as long as the record demonstrates that there is a reasonable basis to believe that the technology will be available by 1983."[22] Another "basic difference" between the 1977 and 1983 standards is said to be that the more stringent of the two requires that "the total plant" be considered, not only "the control techniques used at the actual discharge of the point source."[23] Thus, the 1983 "best available" standard is more demanding because it depends less on actual use, relies more on predictions or on pilot plant or other experimental uses offering slimmer assurances of reliability, and imposes a stronger obligation to overcome problems by revising entire plant processes not only controls at the source.

Economic differences between the two standards are clearly recognizable but ambiguously defined. The assessment of the "best practicable" 1977 standard, among other factors,[24] must "include consideration of the total cost of application of technology in relation to the effluent reduction benefits to be achieved from such applications." The better reading of this provision is that it requires not a strict cost-benefit analysis (in the sense that every dollar spent on technology must return at least a dollar in enhanced water quality) nor a cost-effectiveness analysis (in the sense that predetermined controls should be achieved by getting the biggest bang for the buck) but rather only a cost-sensitive analysis (in the sense that the costs of removal should not "far exceed any reasonable benefit to be achieved"[25]). The inquiry should proceed on a category or class, not on a plant by plant, basis.[26]

21. 118 Cong.Rec. 33696 (1972) (Sen. Muskie).

22. Tanners' Council of America, Inc. v. Train, 540 F.2d 1188, 1195, 6 ELR 20379, 20381 (4th Cir. 1976); see E. I. duPont de Nemours & Co. v. Train, 541 F.2d 1018, 1030, 6 ELR 20371, 20374 (3d Cir. 1976), aff'd, — U.S. —, 97 S.Ct. 965, 51 L.Ed.2d 204 (1977) (stating that a cost "balancing" is required for the 1977 but not the 1983 standard). See also National Commission on Water Quality, Staff Draft Report on Water Quality Analysis and Environmental Impact Assessment of Public Law 92–500, Jan. 1976, at II–136 to –159 (discussing innovative technologies and the prospects for eliminating all discharges from various industries).

23. House Report, supra note 19, at 102–03.

24. Both the 1977 and 1983 standards (subsections 304(b)(1)(B), (b)(2)(B)) require the technological assessment to take into account:
the age of equipment and facilities involved, the process employed, the engineering aspects of the application of various types of control techniques, process changes, non-water quality environmental impact (including energy requirements), and such other factors as the Administrator deems appropriate.

25. House Report, supra note 19, at 103; see 118 Cong.Rec. 33696 (1972) (Sen. Muskie); Zener, The Federal Law of Water Pollution Control, in Environmental Law Institute, Federal Environmental Law 682, 696–702 (E. L. Dolgin & T. G. P. Guilbert eds. 1974).

26. American Iron & Steel Inst. v. EPA, 526 F.2d 1027, 1051, 6 ELR 20068, 20077 (3d Cir. 1975).

The 1983 standard is not divorced from economics, either. It calls, after all, for "the best available technology economically achievable." The guidelines direct the Administrator to take into account "the cost of achieving such effluent reduction." [27] These requirements should be read, in the words of the House Committee, to require only a showing that the technology has demonstrated an "economic viability at the level sufficient to reasonably justify the making of investments in such new facilities." [28] This necessitates not a cost-benefit analysis nor assessment. It requires only a consideration of costs by the Administrator in a reasoned way.[29] If an industry can afford the technology, has access to market power to pass the costs along, and that technology is not demonstrably exorbitant, it is "economically achievable."

A third and distinctive effluent standard for industrial sources of water pollution is found in the new source performance provisions of section 306.[30] This section parallels a comparable section in the Clean Air Act in many ways but differs from it in other important respects.[31] A "new source", for purposes of water pollution law, means any source upon which construction is commenced after the publication of proposed regulations prescribing a standard of performance that is ultimately promulgated.[32] The provisions suffer from the same deficiency as the Clean Air Act by linking the standards to affirmative bureaucratic action that may be slow to materialize. An attempt to avoid this hiatus in the water pollution law takes the form of requiring the Administrator to list within ninety days twenty-seven categories of sources and, within a year thereafter, propose regulations establishing standards of performance for these sources.[33] The deadline was not met and, although most major categories are now covered by standards, there continues to be a distinct gap between new sources in fact and new sources in law.

The term "construction" is defined in the Act [34] and thus reduces the area of controversy over when new source performance standards apply. Policy reasons point strongly to an interpretation that minimizes the escape route for sources arguing that "construction" was under way before the regulations took effect: a source not having its processes or control technology set in concrete is the source from

---

27. Section 304(b)(2)(B), 33 U.S.C.A. § 1314(b)(2)(B).

28. House Report, supra note 19, at 103.

29. FMC Corp. v. Train, 539 F.2d 973, 6 ELR 20382 (4th Cir. 1976); cf. Portland Cement Ass'n v. Ruckelshaus, 158 U.S.App.D.C. 308, 486 F.2d 375, 3 ELR 20642 (1973), cert. denied 417 U.S. 921 (1974).

30. 33 U.S.C.A. § 1316.

31. See § 3.10 above.

32. Section 306(a)(2), 33 U.S.C.A. § 1316(a)(2).

33. Section 306(b)(1)(A), 33 U.S.C.A. § 1316(b)(1)(A), requires the list to include, at a minimum, the twenty-seven categories set forth in § 4.11 n. 22 above.

34. Section 306(a)(5), 33 U.S.C.A. § 1316(a)(5).

Sec. 4.12 INDUSTRIAL SOURCES 467

which a maximum effort should be expected. Some sympathy is due existing sources where tighter standards typically mean expensive retrofit and remodeling. The truly new source should reflect the showcase technology.

The conferees affirmatively acted to exclude "modifications" from the reach of the new source provisions but this should not be read as a weakness. The reason for the exclusion was that the two steps of effluent standards for existing sources were thought to render "superfluous" or "redundant" any interim controls imposed under the new source standards.[35] This is an affirmation of the presumed strength of the "best practicable" and "best available" standards not of the weakness of the new source standards. Obviously any existing source undergoing major modifications should look ahead to the statutory deadlines (and would need a new permit in any event which could incorporate schedules of compliance assuring that foresight).

The definition of "standard of performance" [36] in the 1972 amendments differs slightly from its counterpart in the Clean Air Act:

> a standard for the control of the discharge of pollutants which reflects the greatest degree of effluent reduction which the Administrator determines to be achievable through application of the best available demonstrated control technology, processes, operating methods, or other alternatives, including, where practicable, a standard permitting no discharge of pollutants.

Section 306(b)(1)(B) [37] makes clear that in establishing or revising new source standards, "the Administrator shall take into consideration the cost of achieving such effluent reduction, and any non-water quality environmental impact and energy requirements."

This new source standard is more demanding than the one under the Clean Air Act because it requires serious consideration (is it "practicable?" of a no discharge standard. New sources built in the late 1970's will be operating in 1985 so the new source standard for all practical purposes is the last chance for implementation of the 1985 no discharge goal. Sources not intending to meet the goal at least should be obliged to show why it is unworkable or unwise. Technological impossibility or economic infeasibility are arguments that are pertinent but they must overcome a statutory presumption favoring no discharge by 1985. Especially is this true since a new source constructed in accordance with the section 306 standards may be exempted from more stringent standards for ten years or the period of depreciation of the facility, whichever ends first.[38]

35. Comm. of Conference, Federal Water Pollution Control Act Amendments of 1972, H.R.Rep. No. 1465, 92d Cong., 2d Sess. 128 (1972).

36. Section 306(a)(1), 33 U.S.C.A. § 1316(a)(1).

37. 33 U.S.C.A. § 1316(b)(1)(B).

38. Section 306(d), 33 U.S.C.A. § 1316(d).

In important particulars, of course, the new source standards for water and air discharges require a similar inquiry. A technology may be "demonstrated" if based upon a reasonable prediction of prior developments, and cost factors need only be considered in a reasoned way,[39] disqualifying the exorbitantly costly but certainly requiring no strict cost-benefit analysis. It is certainly not easy to express the differences between the "best available demonstrated control technology" new source standard and the "best available technology economically achievable" existing source standard for 1983 other than to say that the new source standard should reach farther, require more in the way of extending the frontiers of technology, accord less sympathy to cost considerations. New sources are presumed to be models of pollution control. Ordinarily, new sources should eliminate or drastically curtail wastewaters; if impossible, the discharge should have pollutant concentrations no greater than those found in the source of supply.

The existing new source and pretreatment standards are undergoing the close scrutiny associated with judicial review of EPA decision-making. The agency's discretion has been affirmed in some respects: by allowing the use of single numbers in effluent limitation guidelines for subcategories,[40] by making clear that the 1977 standards may require more than end-of-the-pipe controls,[41] by permitting the setting of standards without an examination of all plants within a pertinent subcategory,[42] by affording great latitude in selecting pollution parameters,[43] statistical methodology [44] and assumptions used in a cost analysis,[45] by upholding projections of bold improvements for the 1983 standards on the ground that overoptimism can be corrected later.[46] The agency's discretion has been confined in other respects: by reading the obligation to consider the "age" of the plants as requiring an analysis of the cost and feasibility of retrofitting existing facilities,[47] by requiring the inclusion of variance provisions in new source standards,[48] by insisting that section 304(c) guidelines be de-

---

39. Cf. Portland Cement Ass'n v. Ruckelshaus, 158 U.S.App.D.C. 308, 486 F.2d 375, 3 ELR 20642 (1973), cert. denied 417 U.S. 921 (1974).

40. E. I. duPont de Nemours & Co. v. Train, 541 F.2d 1018, 1029–30, 6 ELR 20371, 20374 (4th Cir. 1976), aff'd —— U.S. ——, 97 S.Ct. 965, 51 L.Ed.2d 204 (1977). Contra, American Iron & Steel Inst. v. EPA, 526 F.2d 1027, 1046–47, 6 ELR 20068, 20075 (3d Cir. 1975); Grain Processing Corp. v. EPA, 407 F. Supp. 96, 6 ELR 20200 (S.D.Iowa 1976).

41. E. I. duPont de Nemours & Co. v. Train, 541 F.2d 1018, 1030, 6 ELR 20371, 20374 (4th Cir. 1976), aff'd —— U.S. ——, 97 S.Ct. 965, 51 L.Ed.2d 204 (1977).

42. FMC Corp. v. Train, 539 F.2d 973, 6 ELR 20382 (4th Cir. 1976).

43. Ibid.

44. Ibid.

45. Ibid.

46. Ibid.

47. American Iron & Steel Inst. v. EPA, 526 F.2d 1027, 1048, 6 ELR 20068, 20076 (3d Cir. 1975).

48. E. I. duPont de Nemours & Co. v. Train, 541 F.2d 1018, 1029, 6 ELR 20371, 20374 (4th Cir. 1976), rev'd on this ground —— U.S. ——, 97 S.Ct. 965, 51 L.Ed.2d 204 (1977).

tailed and specific not vague and hortatory,[49] by disallowing the establishment of an effluent limitation for a pollution parameter not subject to treatment under the agency's own technological model.[50] Above all, application of the hard look doctrine [51] requires carefully justified results every step of the way. Assumptions must be spelled out, inconsistencies explained, methodologies disclosed, contradictory evidence rebutted, record references solidly grounded, guesswork eliminated and conclusions supported in a "manner capable of judicial understanding." [52] While EPA must provide a basis in reason for abandoning a prior practice or methodology [53] or for concluding that a technology workable in one industry is transferable to another,[54] the agency has no obligation to rebut heavily qualified or conclusory charges of infeasibility [55] or undocumented assertions that performances by plants with unrepresentative engineering characteristics were relied upon to set the standards.[56] Cost considerations must be closely reasoned, and a remand may be in order if EPA has relied upon stale data or failed to develop separate operating and capital cost figures for both new and existing plants.[57] The remedies, too, follow the hard look pattern,[58] with the possibility of the court retaining jurisdiction while the agency reconsiders certain matters under a tight timetable.[59]

At an NPDES adjudicatory hearing where the guidelines are applied to individual sources, potential issues duplicate those ordinarily

49. FMC Corp. v. Train, 539 F.2d 973 (4th Cir. 1976).

50. Ibid.

51. See § 1.5 above; CPC Int'l, Inc. v. Train (II), 540 F.2d 1329 (8th Cir. 1976); American Frozen Food Inst. v. Train, — U.S.App.D.C. —, 539 F.2d 107 (1976); American Paper Inst. v. Train, — U.S.App.D.C. —, 543 F.2d 328 (1976); National Renderers Ass'n v. EPA, 541 F.2d 1281 (8th Cir. 1976); American Petroleum Inst. v. EPA, 540 F.2d 1023 (10th Cir. 1976).

52. E. I. duPont de Nemours & Co. v. Train, 541 F.2d 1018, 1030, 6 ELR 20371, 20378 (4th Cir. 1976). Judge Rives' opinion in duPont is an important contribution to the understanding of judicial review of technological decision-making by the agencies.

53. American Meat Inst. v. EPA, 526 F.2d 442, 459, 6 ELR 20029, 20036 (7th Cir. 1975).

54. 526 F.2d at 465 n. 49; 6 ELR at 20039 n. 49; CPC Int'l, Inc. v. Train, 515 F.2d 1032, 1048–50, 5 ELR 20392, 20399–400 (8th Cir. 1975) (EPA cannot rely on a "presumption of transferability"; "concrete data, test results, literature, or expert opinion" must be provided to support the EPA's "feelings, anticipations and prophecies") (footnote omitted).

55. American Meat Inst. v. EPA, 526 F.2d 442, 456, 6 ELR 20029, 20034–35 (7th Cir. 1975).

56. American Iron & Steel Inst. v. EPA, 526 F.2d 1027, 1049, 6 ELR 20068, 20076 (3d Cir. 1975).

57. CPC Int'l, Inc. v. Train, 515 F.2d 1032, 1051, 5 ELR 20392, 20400 (8th Cir. 1975); see Grain Processing Corp. v. Train, 407 F.Supp. 96, 6 ELR 20200 (S.D. Iowa 1976) (on remand).

58. See § 1.5 above.

59. CPC Int'l, Inc. v. Train, 515 F.2d 1032, 1052, 5 ELR 20392, 20400 (8th Cir. 1975); see Grain Processing Corp. v. Train, 407 F.Supp. 96, 6 ELR 20200 (S.D. Iowa 1976) (on remand).

arising in municipal permit proceedings.[60] The ambiguity of the Act and the judicial decisions on the scope of economic and technical defenses means they are likely to be explored in various ways at the permit stage.[61] Toxic pollutants are another likely candidate for controversy regardless of whether EPA has taken action to impose toxic pollutant effluent standards.[62] While the impact statement requirement of the National Environmental Policy Act applies to grants of assistance to construct municipal treatment works, it does not ordinarily apply to NPDES permit decisions.[63] As a practical matter this means that NEPA related issues are more likely to arise in the context of a municipal than an industrial permit proceeding. A significant exception to this rule of thumb applies in the case of the issuance of an NPDES permit to a new industrial source (as defined by section 306 [64]), which is subject to the normal standards of NEPA.[65]

§ 4.13 Effluent Standards: Municipal Sources

Existing publicly owned treatment works must meet two effluent standard deadlines of consequence: (1) "secondary treatment" by July 1, 1977;[1] and (2) "best practicable waste treatment technology over the life of the works" by July 1, 1983.[2] The Act does not clearly distinguish between new and existing publicly owned sources, as it does for industrial sources, but it is clear that no federal grant shall be approved after June 30, 1974 for the building or alteration of a treatment works unless the "best practicable" standard is met. A workable rule of thumb, therefore, is that new and modified treatment works must meet immediately the "best practicable" effluent standard applicable to existing plants by 1983.[3] New sources also "must

---

60. §§ 4.11 above, 4.13 below.

61. See § 4.11 above.

62. See § 4.15 below.

63. 33 U.S.C.A. § 1371(c)(1).

64. Id. § 1316.

65. Id. § 1371(c)(1).

1. Section 301(b)(1)(B), 33 U.S.C.A. § 1311(b)(1)(B).

2. Ibid. More fully stated, the standard requires that:
   alternative waste management techniques have been studied and evaluated and the works proposed for grant assistance will provide for the application of the best practicable waste treatment technology over the life of the works consistent with the purposes of this title.

Section 201(g)(2)(A), 33 U.S.C.A. § 1281(g)(2)(A). Further insight into the meaning of "best practicable waste treatment technology" is provided by section 201(b), 33 U.S.C.A. § 1281(b), reading in full as follows:
   Waste treatment management plans and practices shall provide for the application of the best practicable waste treatment technology before any discharge into receiving waters, including reclaiming and recycling of water, and confined disposal of pollutants so they will not migrate to cause water or other environmental pollution and shall provide for consideration of advanced waste treatment techniques.

3. Close questions of line drawing may be involved where one aspect of a treatment works project is approved by the Administrator under section 203 prior to June 30, 1974, making it subject to the "secondary treatment"

Sec. 4.13　　　MUNICIPAL SOURCES　　　471

allow to the extent practicable the application of technology at a later date which will provide for the reclaiming or recycling of water or otherwise eliminate the discharge of pollutants."[4] Thus the construction of new treatment works theoretically proceeds upon the assumption that the 1985 no discharge goal is to be taken seriously.

Objective analysis is less sanguine about the success of the municipal permit program than the industrial permit program. It appears that only 50 percent of all municipal permittees will meet the July 1, 1977 secondary treatment deadline.[5] The permits have been described as rubber-stamping current plant performance even when deficient.[6] The reasons are many: lack of credibility of sanctions against municipal sources, indifferent performances by consulting engineers, inadequate direction, inflexibility in application, and no small assortment of engineering and technical problems. Municipal plant operators have lobbied strongly against the secondary treatment requirement, believing it to be unrealistic as applied to plants discharging into ocean waters. The 1985 no discharge goal is considered genuinely preposterous by many members of the same fraternity, and the ideal of no discharge has had no discernible effect upon practice or planning.

One interesting feature of the "best practicable" standard for municipal plants is that the identical formulation is used to define the municipality's planning obligations in seeking grants under section 201 and its operating obligations as a permittee to meet certain effluent standards.[7] This lends support to the argument that satisfaction of the effluent limitations by a municipality is dependent upon the availability of grant money to pay for necessary controls.[8] The answer is that the section 301 limitations are nowhere made conditional upon any particular funding and that Congress was unlike-

standard, and another aspect of the project is approved after June 30, 1974, making it subject to the "best practicable" standard. Interpreted in light of the 1985 no discharge goal, the close cases should be resolved in favor of the "best practicable" coverage on the theory that if major modifications or components of a facility are to be undertaken after June 20, 1974 they certainly should be responsive to a no discharge goal scheduled to take effect in little more than a decade.

4. Section 201(g)(2)(B), 33 U.S.C.A. § 1281(g)(2)(B).

5. National Commission on Water Quality, Staff Draft Report on Water Quality Analysis and Environmental Impact Assessment of Public Law 92–500, Jan. 1976, at 24–25 [hereinafter cited as Draft Report on Environmental Impact].

6. Energy & Environmental Analysis, Inc., Assessment of the National Pollutant Discharge Elimination System of Public Law 92–500, undated, at 14 (prepared for the National Commission on Water Quality) [hereinafter cited as NPDES Assessment].

7. Compare section 201(g)(2)(A), 33 U.S.C.A. § 1281(g)(2)(A) with section 301(b)(2)(B), 33 U.S.C.A. § 1311(b)(2)(B).

8. State Water Control Bd. v. Train, —— F.Supp. ——, 6 ELR 20243 (E.D.Va.1976) (rejecting claim in a declaratory judgment action; reserving decision on whether good faith and impossibility of compliance for want of federal funding can be raised suc-

ly to extend to municipalities a form of cost-based variance it withheld from industries. Use of the same language to define pre-grant planning and post-grant discharge also confirms the view that the planner's obligation to identify the "best practicable" technology is synonymous with the operator's obligation to implement it.[9] This means a municipality's obligation to investigate alternatives is not merely a procedural exercise but can lead to a decidedly substantive burden.

EPA has undertaken to define "secondary treatment"[10] and, with less assurance, "best practicable treatment over the life of the works."[11] The decision virtually to equate the two standards is a severe putdown for the 1983 "best practicable" test. An attack, properly focused, might very well succeed in demonstrating to the courts that the Administrator exceeded the scope of his assignment by diluting so severely the substantive demands of the 1983 standard. Until and unless that happens, the major arena of municipal water pollution will be at the point of application of the standards to individual plants. How to regulate discharges from combined sewers and storm sewers presents a special problem. Combined sewers are designed to transport both storm water and sanitary sewage. Sometimes during normal weather and often during wet weather (when flows to the treatment plant are heavy) combined flows are bypassed, resulting in direct discharges of raw sewage from overflow points into receiving waters. EPA's "secondary treatment" regulations state, quite frankly, that treatment works receiving combined flows during wet weather may not be capable of meeting percentage removal requirements and that controls, if any, should be determined on a case-by-case basis.[12] EPA also has made clear that its NPDES policy aims to "minimize discharge of pollutants . . . from combined sewer overflows,"[13] if this can be called a policy. Elsewhere, it is said that overflow points will not be governed by separate effluent standards but will be adjudged by reference to whether they cause violations of the water quality standards.[14] It seems unarguable that combined sewage overflow points are point sources

cessfully as a defense in an enforcement proceeding).

9. See § 4.10 above, construing section 201 as requiring selection of the best course of action identified in the environmental assessment process.

10. 40 CFR pt. 133.

11. Id. § 133.102; see § 4.10 nn. 72–75 above.

12. 40 CFR § 133.103(a).

13. Memo from James L. Agee to Regional Administrators, NPDES Permits for Municipal Facilities with Combined Sewer Overflows and Bypasses, Sept. 16, 1974 (Program Guidance Memorandum No. 21); see NPDES Assessment, supra note 6, at 272; Metcalf & Eddy, Inc., Assessment of Technologies and Costs for Publicly Owned Treatment Works Under Public Law 92–500, Apr. 1975, at 6B–1 to –13 (report to the National Commission on Water Quality).

14. EPA, Water Quality Strategy Paper (2d ed. 1974).

subject to the effluent limitations of the Act. As point sources, they almost certainly are governed by the "secondary treatment" and "best practicable" effluent limitations applicable to publicly owned treatment works. The only possible escape route from this conclusion, which EPA has argued,[15] is that combined sewer overflows are not part of the "treatment works" to which the effluent limitations apply. The statutory definition of "treatment works",[16] however, suggests otherwise.

A related but distinctive issue is the question of the standards that apply to runoff from separate storm sewers. A separate storm sewer means a publicly owned system of pipes in an urbanized area operated for purposes of collecting and conveying storm runoff uncontaminated by industrial or commercial waste.[17] EPA's original decision to exempt separate storm sewers from the NPDES program [18] was invalidated in the courts.[19] The agency's response was to publish proposed regulations simply authorizing the owner or operator of a separate storm sewer to discharge, subject only to a reminder that conditions might later be imposed or a regular NPDES permit required.[20] This was accompanied by a frank acknowledgement that "EPA has no reason to believe that effluent limitations guidelines for separate storm sewers will be forthcoming in the foreseeable future." [21] For separate storm sewers, an argument can be made that the problem is actually one of nonpoint source runoff that has accidentally been reduced to a discrete conveyance, and therefore the effluent limitations policies of section 301 are inapropos. Also, despite the expansive definition of "treatment works" [22] EPA probably has the discretion to single out nonsewage related pollution for separate treatment.

The dimensions of combined sewer overflows and storm sewer discharges are little appreciated.[23] An NPDES permit may identify as many as fifty or sixty point sources, imposing effluent limitations on but a single source. Even major discharge points at the plant, used to divert excess flows during wet weather, may not be constrained seriously by applicable permits. Some overflow points may be the subject of study, others ignored altogether. Treatment options are difficult, expensive to implement, and therefore not undertaken.

15. Ibid.

16. Sections 212(2)(A), (B), 33 U.S.C.A. §§ 1292(2)(A), (B).

17. 40 Fed.Reg. 56932, 56935, 56936 (Dec. 5, 1975), 40 CFR §§ 124.83(a)(1), 125.52(a)(1).

18. 40 CFR § 125.4(f).

19. Natural Resources Defense Council, Inc. v. Train, 396 F.Supp. 1393, 5 ELR 20401 (D.C.D.C.1975).

20. 40 Fed.Reg. 56932, 56935, 56936 (Dec. 5, 1975), 40 CFR §§ 124.83(c), 125.52(c).

21. 40 Fed.Reg. at 56935.

22. Sections 212(2)(A), (B), 33 U.S.C.A. §§ 1292(2)(A), (B).

23. See Comptroller General, Need to Control Discharges from Sewers Carrying Both Sewage and Storm Runoff (1973).

There is simply a large gap between the single discharge point legal model and multiple discharge reality. The courts and the Congress both are likely intervenors on the subjects of storm sewers and combined sewer overflow.

Another critical constituent of the municipal permit program is the extent to which an NPDES permit may include no-growth or slow-growth provisions. Section 402(h) of the Act [24] makes clear that the permitting authority, in the event an NPDES permit condition is violated, "may proceed in a court of competent jurisdiction to restrict or prohibit the introduction of any pollutant into [the] treatment works by a source not utilizing [the] treatment works prior to the finding that [the] condition was violated." This power to control the introduction of new pollutants to the point of prohibition is a recognition of the simple fact of life that a permit to discharge should be responsive equally to the principal variables of the plant, which include not only the capabilities of the treatment facility (design factors and operational performance) but also prominently the rate and composition of the influent. In an appropriate case, it would appear also that the NPDES permit itself could prohibit the operator from authorizing further sewer hookups onto an overloaded facility. The EPA General Counsel has ruled that a permit may not contain a hookup ban,[25] reasoning that a moratorium on connections may be imposed only by a court and then only after a permit violation has occurred. But the issue may be one largely of semantics and form: permitting authorities need not sit idly by approving discharges from an oft overloaded facility that is in violation of water quality standards. Limitations on the rate and quantity of flow may be reasonably related to water quality, and limitations on the influent are reasonably related to the rate and quantity of flow. Needless to say, if NPDES municipal permits become (they are not now) seriously implicated in sewer hookup (and ergo growth) policies, the issue is comparable in magnitude to the no significant deterioration policy under the Clean Air Act.[26]

If the sewer ban theory is accepted, the range of permit conditions embraced by the need to control the influent and perforce the sources of that influent range from the mild to the extreme: (1) a mere warning notice that if certain permit provisions are violated (such as flow limitations) action will be taken immediately under section 402(h) to cut off further contributions to the system; (2) a reporting obligation on the permittee triggered by an occasion such as the average actual flow approaching a specified percentage (say 85 percent) of the maximum allowable rate; (3) in the event of a trigger report

---

24. 33 U.S.C.A. § 1342(h).

25. NPDES Decision of the General Counsel No. 33, Oct. 21, 1975 (Blue Plains Sewage Treatment Plant, Wash., D.C.) [hereinafter cited as NPDES Decision]. The author is an attorney of record in the case.

26. See §§ 2.17 (land development), 3.12 (no significant deterioration) above.

under (2), the permittee might be required to prepare a schedule of connections to the collection system or interceptors, tracking regularly the rate of actual hookups against the proposed schedule; this plan might include a cutoff point forbidding all further connections unless capacity is increased; (4) a moratorium against further connections; in this event, some user increases might be allowable if water conservation, reduced infiltration, user charges, or pretreatment requirements brought about other inflow reductions. Presumably the power to impose a sewer moratorium includes also the lesser included option of dividing the allowable capacity (i. e., allocating the shortages) among different jurisdictions using a facility.

An overriding practical question under the 1972 Act is the extent to which the laxity or complexity of administration of the law elsewhere can be overcome in a section 402 permit proceeding. A good illustration is whether the land treatment or related alternative that is not seriously considered in the grant application process [27] can be litigated (and, if justified, expressed as a permit condition) in an NPDES adjudicatory hearing. Once again, the EPA general counsel has answered the question in the negative,[28] reasoning that except through the grant provisions of section 201, EPA is not authorized to dictate what sewage method disposal a particular plant should follow. There is room for arriving at a different conclusion, both under the National Environmental Policy Act and the 1972 Amendments. NEPA very well might require a consideration of alternatives in connection with the decision to issue a permit,[29] and the 1972 Amendments might require selection of the best alternative (including a land treatment component [30]). If a better land treatment system is enforceable at the grants stage, it may also be enforceable at the permit stage. The Administrator may issue a permit, after all, "upon

---

27. See § 4.10 above.

28. NPDES Decision, supra note 25.

29. Under Section 511(c)(1) of the Act, 33 U.S.C.A. § 1371(c)(1), EPA is exempted from preparing impact statements on all aspects of the water quality program, except for the issuance of discharge permits for new sources and the making of grants for publicly owned waste treatment works. But being exempt from the impact statement requirements of Section 102(2)(C) of NEPA is not the same thing as being exempt from all requirements of NEPA, including sections 101 and 102(2)(E) (formerly 102 (2)(D)), which have been interpreted to be of substantive import to an administrative agency's powers. See Calvert Cliffs' Coordinating Comm. v. Atomic Energy Comm'n, 146 U.S.App. D.C. 33, 449 F.2d 1109, 1 ELR 20346 (1971), cert. denied 404 U.S. 942 (1972). Under this view, the Administrator must consider the environmental consequences of granting a section 402 permit and may deny or condition it upon the taking of steps to minimize adverse effects (such as a requirement that wastewater be disposed of on land). Cf. Zabel v. Tabb, 430 F.2d 199, 1 ELR 20023 (5th Cir. 1970), cert. denied 401 U.S. 910 (1971). For differing views on this and related subjects, compare Zener, The Federal Law of Water Pollution Control in Environmental Law Institute, Federal Environmental Law 682, 774–84 (E. L. Dolgin & T. G. P. Guilbert eds. 1974) with Anderson, the National Environmental Policy Act, in id. at 238, 257–60.

30. See § 4.7 above.

condition that such discharge will meet either all applicable requirements under [Section 301 of this Act], or prior to the taking of necessary implementing actions relating to all such requirements, such conditions as the Administrator determines are necessary to carry out the provisions of this Act." The "requirements" of section 301, to be sure, include the identical standard [31] under which the Administrator is empowered to order selection of a land treatment system, and the "provisions of this Act" obviously embrace the same standard. The argument the other way is an intensely practical one: what use is a reconsideration of alternatives long after the technology has been selected, paid for and partly built? In all likelihood, the permit powers for municipal treatment works will be construed as accommodating all conditions reasonably related to the introduction, treatment and disposal of the pollutants the facility is supposed to treat.

The NPDES permit program for municipal plants is being administered so poorly, even as compared to the evolution of the industrial permits, that the adjudicatory hearings leading eventually to judicial review will become an important source of law. Initially, it is important for the principals to keep in mind that the general requirements of section 402 [32] for permit issuance apply *a fortiori* to permit modifications or suspensions. It is the administrative way sometimes to slip into major redefinitions of legal obligations without bothering to retrace the prescribed steps. Another common procedural misstep, surprising because it is so obvious, is for a permit to issue without the necessary state certification of compliance with water quality standards (or a clearly indicated waiver).[33] The certification, or lack thereof, is highly pertinent to what is likely to become a major issue at the hearing—whether the anticipated discharges conform to existing water quality standards. Mentioned above [34] are some of the proof problems involved in establishing violations of the standards, particularly the narrative criteria which may ban "nuisance" or "eutrophic" conditions or may protect a use for "recreational" purposes. The significant step in the chain of evidence between proven violations and required effluent limitations for a given source may be provided by a number of planning or study documents that have accumulated with discouraging regularity for many years of water pollution control programs. The most obvious is a waste load allocation developed under section 303(d) for water quality limited segments.[35] This may state unequivocally that source Y must meet effluent standards of X pounds per day of Z pollutant to achieve water quality aims. A similar link between water quality and effluent controls may be supplied by other types of documents—technical studies, regional agreements,

---

31. Compare note 7, supra.

32. 33 U.S.C.A. § 1342; see 40 CFR § 125.22.

33. 33 U.S.C.A. § 1341(a)(1); see 40 CFR § 125.15(a).

34. § 4.8 above.

35. §§ 4.8, 4.9 above.

environmental impact statements, obligations imposed by enforcement conferences under earlier versions of the Act. It is important to remember that water quality standards themselves should not be revised *de facto* in the course of an adjudicatory hearing. There is a separate procedure for this eventuality [36], and it does not permit economic or technical feasibility arguments on the content of the standards [37].

Another issue of inescapable significance is whether the permit proposed for issuance conflicts with plans developed under sections 303(e) or 208 [38]. This issue is easy enough where there is extant a document officially entitled a section 303(e) basin plan or water quality management plan, approved by EPA. Even where there is no plan as yet officially "approved," [39] there is room for argument that the permits must anticipate planning obligations that are just around the corner. The Administrator, after all, has a general authority to prescribe permit conditions necessary and appropriate to fulfilling the aims of the Act.[40]

Thus the NPDES hearings for municipal treatment works involve some issues of special pertinence to municipal sewage treatment —the combined sewage and moratorium issues, the alternative of land treatment, and certain toxic substances (including heavy metals from street runoff and chlorine). They involve other issues of particular importance occurring with equal frequency in industrial permit proceedings—state certification, compliance with water quality standards and developed plans. And they involve the routine—facility operation, monitoring, reporting and study provisions.

§ 4.14 Effluent Standards: Pretreatment

A regulatory system that came down hard on direct discharge into United States' waters by industrial and municipal point sources would be incomplete if it neglected industrial sources discharging directly into publicly owned treatment works. The fact remains that the quality of the effluent from a sewage treatment plant is dictated greatly by the quality and quantity of the influent. Industries may prefer to discharge into municipal systems for many reasons— economies of scale, avoiding the costs of their own permit or monitoring programs, taking advantage of federal and local subsidies in the construction and operation of the facility.[1]

36. 33 U.S.C.A. § 1313(c); see 40 CFR § 130.17.

37. § 4.8 above.

38. § 4.9 above; see 40 CFR § 130.32.

39. 33 U.S.C.A. § 1288(b)(3) (section 208 areawide waste treatment management plan).

40. Id. §§ 1342(a)(1), (2).

1. National Commission on Water Quality, Staff Draft Report on Water Quality Analysis and Environmental Impact Assessment of Public Law 92–900, Jan. 1976, at V–93 to –94, citing EPA, Economic Report: Alternative Methods of Financing Wastewater Treatment (1973) [here-

There is considerable law on the subject of whether and when users can discharge into a treatment works. It takes the form of little noticed municipal regulations governing the quantity and quality of effluent that can be introduced into a system. Violators run the risk not only of the penalties prescribed by local regulation but also that a given offense may be deemed significant in establishing violations of the law of nuisance or riparian rights.[2] These rules governing use of just about every municipal treatment system in the country remain the pretreatment effluent standards of the longest duration and greatest contemporary significance. The 1972 Amendments bring federal regulators into the picture, while preserving maximum state and local autonomy.[3] The Administrator is directed to publish proposed pretreatment regulations, hold hearings on them, and promulgate standards for the introduction of pollutants into publicly owned treatment works.[4] The regulations may deal with two types of pollutants: (1) those "determined not to be susceptible to treatment by [the] works" and (2) those which "would interfere with the operation of [the] treatment works." It was the intention of Congress that the pretreatment standards would be "national in scope," addressing "the most significant pretreatment problems",[5] not preempting the details of existing pretreatment standards.

The generic regulations[6] classify pollutants either as incompatible or compatible (such as biochemical oxygen demand, suspended solids, pH and fecal coliform bacteria) as well as others the treatment works was designed to treat (for example, phosphorus or nitrogen[7]). Generally, pretreatment is not required for compatible pollutants unless a state or municipality demands it[8] and is required for incompatible pollutants introduced into a system by a major contributing industry (defined as one having a flow of 50,000 gallons or more per average work day or a flow greater than 5 percent of the flow carried by the system).[9] The pretreatment effluent stand-

inafter cited as Draft Report on Environmental Impact].

2. Springer v. Joseph Schlitz Brewing Co., 510 F.2d 468 (4th Cir. 1975).

3. Section 307(b)(4), 33 U.S.C.A. § 1317(b)(4), reads:
Nothing in this subsection shall affect any pretreatment requirement established by any State or local law not in conflict with any pretreatment standard established under this subsection.

4. Section 307(b)(1), 33 U.S.C.A. § 1317(b)(1).

5. Comm. on Public Works, Federal Water Pollution Control Act Amendments of 1972, H.R.Rep. No. 911, 92d Cong., 2d Sess. 113 (1972) [hereinafter cited as House Report].

6. 40 CFR pt. 128. They were reproposed in July of 1975 as 40 CFR pt. 403.

7. 40 CFR §§ 128.121, 128.122.

8. Id. § 128.132.

9. Id. § 128.124. A source also can qualify as a "major contributing industry" if it has in its waste a toxic pollutant, defined in section 307(a), 33 U.S.C.A. § 1317(a), or if it is found in connection with the issuance of an NPDES permit to have "significant impact" on the treatment works.

ard is, by administrative decree, the "best practicable" standard unless above average efforts are required by the NPDES permit for the treatment plant.[10] The Act directs the Administrator to promulgate pretreatment standards for new sources discharging into a treatment works simultaneously with the promulgation of section 306 standards of performance "for the equivalent category of new sources".[11] The specifics appear in the regulations for each industry category or subcategory.

The overriding policy of the pretreatment standards, it should be remembered, is to assure that the direct discharge requirements are not compromised by an industry's choice to use the service of a publicly owned treatment works. EPA's General Counsel has pointed out that "pretreatment standards could be formulated to insure that any industrial effluent entering the navigable waters after passing through a public treatment works will undergo the same degree of pollutant reduction, either at the industrial plant or at the treatment works, or by a combination of both, that the effluent would be required to receive if discharged directly into the navigable waters."[12] Not only could the standards be so formulated and applied, they ought to be: an industry's choice of direct discharge or utilization of a publicly owned treatment works should be based solely upon considerations of cost and that choice should be environmentally neutral.[13]

Pretreatment, like new and existing source standards, are strictly scrutinized under the hard look doctrine.[14] Thus, a general ban against excessive flow rates [15] is condemned on vagueness grounds, and EPA is required "to define in a reasonably specific manner what it considers to be an excessive discharge to a municipal plant over relatively short periods of time."[16] Fair procedure and reasoned results are indispensable.

The issue of allocating costs among industry users and the public is an important and controversial one: it led to specific requirements in the Act conditioning the approval of grants for treatment works upon provisions for industry users to contribute their pro rata share of the cost of construction,[17] and adopting a "system of charges" to assure that each recipient of services "will pay its proportionate share

10. 40 CFR § 128.133.

11. Section 307(c), 33 U.S.C.A. § 1317(c). The new source pretreatment standards "shall prevent the discharge of any pollutant into such treatment works, which pollutant may interfere with, pass through, or otherwise be incompatible with such works."

12. Zener, The Federal Law of Water Pollution Control, in Environmental Law Institute, Federal Environmental Law 682, 743–44 (E. L. Dolgin & T. G. P. Guilbert eds. 1974).

13. See id. at 744.

14. See §§ 1.5, 4.12 above.

15. 40 CFR § 128.131(d).

16. CPC Int'l, Inc. v. Train, 515 F.2d 1032, 1052, 5 ELR 20392, 20401 (8th Cir. 1975).

17. Section 204(b)(1)(B), 33 U.S.C.A. § 1284(b)(1)(B).

of the costs of operation and maintenance (including replacement)." [18] This brings into being a system of user charges, which can be defined as a charge levied on the users of treatment works to recover the cost of operation and maintenance of the system. A typical problem of the past has been user charges based on volume not strength of the wastes so that a user industry (such as a dairy) might be substantially subsidized by other users of the system.[19]

Perhaps no single issue in the pollution field has received greater sustained academic interest than the use of charges or other fees to discourage polluters or allocate costs among them.[20] EPA's regulations on user charges and industrial cost recovery have foreclosed none of the imaginative options for using a system of charges as a deterrent to pollution.[21] Regulation, not fees and charges, largely has preempted the field of pollution control. But charges for the users of treatment works afford an excellent laboratory for testing theories of a long line of distinguished economists who believe that pollution should be taxed not regulated.

The statute makes clear that pretreatment standards "shall specify a time for compliance not to exceed three years from the date of promulgation." [22] A compliance schedule presumably can be negotiated separately with a source by the operator of a treatment works; by contrast, important contributors to municipal plants may have a compliance schedule written for them directly into the NPDES permit for the treatment works. Section 402(b)(8)[23] makes clear that any permit for a discharge from a publicly owned treatment works should include conditions requiring notice to the permitting agency of new or increasing volumes of pollutants introduced into the works. The conferees agreed, stretching the language of this provision somewhat, "that each municipal waste treatment plant permit must iden-

---

18. Section 204(b)(1)(A), 33 U.S.C.A. § 1284(b)(1)(A).

19. There has been considerable litigation over the proper bases for sewer-use rates. See Annot., Validity and Construction of Regulation By Municipal Corporation Fixing Sewer-Use Rates, 61 ALR3d 1236 (1975).

20. Leading authorities include Coase, The Problem of Social Cost, 3 J.L. & Econ. 1 (1960); J. H. Dales, Pollution, Property & Prices (1968); A. C. Pigou, The Economics of Welfare (4th ed. 1932). A good contemporary collection of materials is found in E. H. Hanks, A. D. Tarlock & J. L. Hanks, Cases and Materials on Environmental Law and Policy 873–902 (1974).

21. 38 Fed.Reg. 22523 (1973), 40 CFR pt. 40. Even where sewer charges must be reasonably commensurate with the burden placed upon the sewer system, rate refinements can single out the worst polluters. See e. g., Boynton v. Lakeport Municipal Sewer Dist., 28 Cal.App.3d 91, 104 Cal.Rptr. 409 (1972); Larsen Baking Co. v. State, 30 A.D.2d 400, 292 N.Y.S.2d 145, aff'd 24 N.Y.2d 1036, 303 N.Y.S.2d 80, 250 N.E.2d 346 (1968) (surcharge based upon concentration); Municipal Authority v. Bloomsberg Coop. Canners, Inc., 203 Pa.Super. 393, 199 A.2d 502 (1964) (surcharge based upon biochemical oxygen demand).

22. Section 307(b)(1), 33 U.S.C.A. § 1317(b)(1).

23. 33 U.S.C.A. § 1342(b)(8).

tify any industrial users and the quality or quantity of effluents introduced by them."[24] It would appear that the proper scope of a discharge permit for publicly owned treatment works might extend not only to making note of the major sources of influent but putting those sources on a compliance schedule necessary to meet the obligations of the municipal discharger.

Pretreatment standards also are enforceable by the Administrator directly against the user of the treatment works,[25] as are the inspection, monitoring and entry provisions of section 308.[26] Somewhat unusual requirements that may be imposed upon dischargers into treatment works involve "treatability studies"[27] on those pollutants whose susceptibility to treatment is not known. The requirement that pretreatment standards preclude pollutants from interfering with, passing through or acting incompatibly with a treatment works perforce includes an authority to require a discharger to sustain the burden of proof on compatibility. EPA generic regulations prohibit the introduction of only obviously unacceptable wastes—those creating a fire hazard, corrosive structural damage, obstruction to the flow of sewers, and excessive flows that upset the treatment process.[28]

EPA walks a tightrope with its pretreatment standards. Joint treatment at a single facility offers substantial advantages—more dependable flow rates, economies of scale, better use of manpower and land, more efficient disposal of sludges.[29] Pretreatment standards too toughly written foreclose these gains. On the other hand, standards too laxly drafted encourage free rides, interference with the treatment system, and implication of public authorities in private acts of pollution.[30]

§ 4.15 Effluent Standards: Toxic Pollutants

Potentially far-reaching substantive laws often are saddled with extraordinary procedural preliminaries, reflecting a legislative judg-

---

24. Comm. of Conference, Federal Water Control Act Amendments of 1972, S.Rep. No. 1236, 92d Cong., 2d Sess. 130 (1972).

25. Section 309(a)(1), 33 U.S.C.A. § 1319(a)(1).

26. Section 402(b)(9), 33 U.S.C.A. § 1342(b)(9); see Conference Report, supra note 24, at 130.

27. House Report, supra note 5, at 113.

28. 40 CFR § 128.131; see note 16, supra.

29. See Draft Report on Environmental Impact, supra note 1, at V-94, quoting EPA, Guidelines for Pretreatment of Pollutants Introduced into Publicly Owned Treatment Works (1973).

30. See Environmental Defense Fund v. Montrose Chem. Corp., Civ. No. 70-2389 ALS (M.D.Cal.1970) (charging the company and the Los Angeles County Sanitation District, respectively, with discharging and authorizing the discharge of DDT compounds into a public sewer system and ultimately into the coastal waters of Santa Monica Bay) (dismissed as moot on June 17, 1971 after defendant ceased all discharges and began to dispose of wastes at a land fill) (the author was co-counsel in the case).

ment of sorts that a tough law ought to be difficult to implement. The toxic pollutant provisions of the Federal Water Pollution Control Act are illustrative. The major procedural events, if not the more subtle pitfalls, are spelled out in section 307 [1] of the Act: (1) within ninety days of enactment the Administrator is to publish a list including "any toxic pollutant" or combination of pollutants for which an effluent standard will be established; [2] (2) within one hundred and eighty days after publication of the list he must publish a "proposed effluent standard" for each pollutant listed along with a notice of public hearing on the proposed standard; [3] (3) a public hearing "on the record" must be held to determine whether a modification of the standard is justified; [4] (4) within six months after publication of the proposed standard a final standard must be promulgated,[5] to become effective no more than one year from the date of promulgation.[6]

Section 307 calls for "rigid controls" [7] based on the understanding that the need for the regulation of toxic pollutants is "especially urgent." [8] The definition of a "toxic pollutant" is broadly written to condemn all agents that injure biological organisms.[9] Indeed, the administrative challenge is how to single out on defensible grounds for regulation under section 307 the leading candidates among thousands of potentially toxic pollutants.[10] A toxic pollutant regulation,

1. 33 U.S.C.A. § 1317.

2. Section 307(a)(1), 33 U.S.C.A. § 1317(a)(1).

3. Section 307(a)(2), 33 U.S.C.A. § 1317(a)(2).

4. Ibid.

5. Section 307(a)(2), (3), 33 U.S.C.A. §§ 1317(a)(2), (3).

6. Section 207(a)(6), 33 U.S.C.A. § 1317(a)(6).

7. Comm. on Public Works, Federal Water Pollution Control Act Amendments of 1971, S.Rep. No. 414, 92d Cong., 1st Sess. 13 (1971) [hereinafter cited as Senate Report].

8. Id. at 61.

9. It means, according to section 502 (13), 33 U.S.C.A. § 1362(13):
 those pollutants, or combination of pollutants, including disease-causing agents, which after discharge and upon exposure, ingestion, inhalation or assimilation into any organism, either directly from the environment or indirectly by ingestion through food chains, will, on the basis of information available to the Administrator, cause death, disease, behavioral abnormalities, cancer, genetic mutations, physiological malfunctions (including malfunctions in reproduction) or physical deformations, in such organisms or their offspring.

10. The Department of Health, Education, and Welfare has identified some nine thousand substances potentially toxic in certain concentrations under certain conditions. National Institute of Occupational Safety and Health, Toxic Substances List, June 1973. Data on effects is extremely limited: "Information is virtually nonexistent on effects of toxic substances on living systems at the population or community level and in the field. Most available studies of toxic substances have been conducted in the laboratory, normally with a single species and almost always under rigidly controlled conditions. It is difficult to determine the extent to which this information can be used to evaluate field conditions, or to project ecosystem impacts following removal of toxic substances from the systems." National Commission on Water Quali-

moreover, may extend to "a combination" of pollutants,[11] which means the potential regulatory net is wider yet. It has been urged in court, for example, that the effluents from all pesticide manufacturing and formulating facilities, because of their toxicity and complexity, should be brought under section 307.[12]

A pollutant ultimately subject to regulation under section 307(a) confronts a far tougher regime than the various "best technology" effluent standards for conventional discharges. Control without regard to feasibility or cost is a theme from the common law [13] struck clearly in modern regulation of toxic pollutants. In the first place, in neither developing a standard nor enforcing it are economic factors considered pertinent. Section 307 nowhere mentions economics as a consideration, and the House Report contains an express disavowal: "Less stringent standards for an industry will not be established simply because it is more expensive to treat wastes to eliminate or reduce toxic discharges in one industry than in another. The Committee considers that the discharge of toxic pollutants are much too dangerous to be permitted on merely economic grounds." [14] Even the one year allowed between the date of promulgation and the date a regulation takes effect, which could be read as a slight bow to economic or technological practicalities, instead should be understood as an "absolute maximum time" with compliance required "as early as possible within this limit." [15]

Nor do technological difficulties justify a relaxation of effluent standards for toxic pollutants. The Administrator must adhere to identical criteria in publishing the list and proposing a standard, and these factors dwell exclusively on the power of the pollutant to inflict a hurt: "the toxicity of the pollutant, its persistence, degradability, the usual or potential presence of the affected organisms in any waters, the importance of the affected organisms and the nature and extent of the effect of the toxic pollutant on such organisms." [16] No escape route can be found in section 307 resembling the two-year administrative waivers or the presidential exemption on national security grounds found in the hazardous air pollutant provisions of the Clean Air Act.[17] The only glimmer of sympathy for technological

ty Staff Draft Report on Water Quality Analysis and Environmental Impact Assessment of Public Law 92-500, Jan. 1976, at I-25.

11. Section 307(a)(1), 33 U.S.C.A. § 1317(a)(1).

12. See complaint in Natural Resources Defense Council, Inc. v. Train, Civil No. 2153-73 (D.D.C., filed May 23, 1974). See also note 41, infra (settlement agreement).

13. § 2.4 above.

14. Comm. on Public Works, Federal Water Pollution Control Act Amendments of 1972, H.R.Rep. No. 911, 92d Cong., 2d Sess. 112-13 (1972).

15. Senate Report, supra note 7, at 61.

16. Section 307(a)(1) (criteria for publishing the list), repeated verbatim in section 307(a)(2) (criteria for publishing a proposed standard). 33 U.S.C.A. § 1317(a)(1), (2).

17. See § 3.11 above.

difficulties in controlling toxic pollutants is a provision allowing the Administrator to distinguish between categories of sources in setting standards [18] and therefore to treat differently, for example, a plant processing cadmium ore from a plant in which cadmium appears as a trace impurity in its discharge.[19] But the legislative history makes clear that these lines should not turn on whether it costs more for one or another industry to control,[20] which suggests that the Administrator must seek to justify different standards for the same pollutant on the ground of differences in effect. (This is not out of the question in light of possible synergistic effects (working together) of different constituents of the same effluent.)

Section 307 reflects in other ways the stringency of the regulatory scheme. The Administrator explicitly is given a choice between an effluent standard "or a prohibition," which of course is outright absolutism reflected in a standard of zero release. More important is the statutory directive that an effluent standard must be promulgated at a level providing "an ample margin of safety." This should be read as giving the Administrator an edge in the scientific debate on effects, allowing him to protect against potential hazards not yet uncovered by research or those suggested only tentatively or ambiguously by recorded data.[21] The "margin of safety" must be scientifically defensible, of course, not a basis for control by surmise.

With economics and technology ostensibly excluded from the debate, early legal action focused on procedures for selection and methods for determining effects of various pollutants. Faced with a definition of "toxic pollutant" of great breadth and dicta in the legislative history that the definition was intended to encompass only "a limited number of pollutants," [22] the Administrator was slow to decide. The first list, containing nine substances, was published on September 7, 1973,[23] eight months late and under court order.[24] Addi-

18. Section 307(a)(5), 33 U.S.C.A. § 1317(a)(5).

19. Senate Report, supra note 7, at 61.

20. See text accompanying note 14, supra.

21. See discussion of the "margin of safety" language pertaining to national ambient air quality standards in § 3.4 above.

22. Senate Report, supra note 7, at 60.

23. 38 Fed.Reg. 24342. The pollutants covered are:
   1. Aldrin-dieldrin;
   2. Benzidine and its salts;
   3. Cadmium and all cadmium compounds;
   4. Cyanide and all cyanide compounds;
   5. DDD–DDE–DDT;
   6. Endrin;
   7. Mercury and all mercury compounds;
   8. Polychlorinated biphenyls (PCB's);
   9. Toxaphene (chlorinated camphene).

The proposed list was published on July 6, 1973, id. at 18044. Proposed standards for the nine substances were published on December 27, 1973, id. 35388. This publication notes clearly that the standards "are not based upon economic considerations or upon the availability of treatment technology." Simultaneously, a notice of hearing was published.

24. Natural Resources Defense Council, Inc. v. Fri, 3 ELR 20587 (D.D.C. 1973) (Decree and Stipulation).

tional litigation ensued, raising claims that the Administrator had applied improper criteria and was moved by extra-record influences to exclude certain substances from the list (including lead, arsenic, asbestos, chromium and zinc). The immediate result [25] of the lawsuit was a determination that the district court had dismissed the matter initially without considering the entire administrative record. The case was remanded for the filing of a supplemental complaint to be considered in light of the complete administrative record.

Early administrative action was equally inconclusive. The nine pollutants initially listed were the subject of extensive consideration at the adjudicatory hearing that must follow any proposed standards (the parties included thirty-four industries and trade associations and two environmental groups).[26] Surprisingly, an important evidentiary ruling leading to the exclusion of several affidavits of EPA witnesses was sustained in an appeal to the Administrator, necessitating yet another hearing.[27] The reason assigned for excluding admittedly important evidence (one affidavit was described as representing "one of the most comprehensive summaries of the relevant chemical and toxicological data on cyanides ever produced"[28]) is that the statute is said to anticipate that "the standards as proposed be premised upon as thorough and complete a basis for promulgation as can be made by the agency prior to the hearing stage."[29] Thus, the hearing could not be used by the EPA staff to repair deficiencies in the data base supporting the standards originally proposed by presenting broad rebuttal evidence. Parties objecting to the standards, according to the theory, must be given a clear indication of what is contemplated before undertaking their burden of showing that a modification is justified. The statute says that this burden is not sustained unless the Administrator finds "based upon a preponderance of the evidence" adduced at the hearing that a modification is in order.[30] With all respect to the procedural sensitivities of the Administrator, the matter could have been handled more adroitly (by admitting the evidence and granting a continuance). The ferocity with which the agency turned on its only pending section 307 proceeding suggests a distinct distaste for both the procedure and its contemplated results. In any event, it can be said fairly that the better part of the first three years of experience with the toxic pollutant provisions of the 1972 Amend-

25. Natural Resources Defense Council, Inc. v. Train, 519 F.2d 287, 5 ELR 20578 (D.C. Cir. 1975).

26. In re: Proposed Effluent Standards for Aldrin-Dieldrin et al., Environmental Protection Agency, FWPCA § 307, Dkt. No. 1. EPA regulations governing the conduct of these hearings are found in 40 CFR pt. 104; see 39 Fed.Reg. 8325 (Mar. 5, 1974). Compare note 47, infra.

27. In re: Proposed Effluent Standards for Aldrin-Dieldrin, supra note 26, Order of the Deputy Administrator, Aug. 16, 1974.

28. Id., Appeal by Respondent, at 11.

29. Id., Order of the Administrator, at 7.

30. Section 307(a)(2), 33 U.S.C.A. § 1317(a)(2).

ments were consumed by straightening out the procedures under which toxic pollutants are to be regulated.

With section 307 stalled in a procedural thicket, a question arises over the extent to which the regulation of hazardous pollutants not formally listed under section 307 may proceed under other provisions of the Act. The answer is that toxic pollutants are subject to regulation under many provisions of the Act. Section 101(a)(3)[31] affirms a "national policy" that "the discharge of toxic pollutants in toxic amounts be prohibited." The policy can be implemented not only under section 307(a) but also under sections 301 (effluent limitations for point sources),[32] 302 (water quality related effluent standards),[33] 303 (water quality standards),[34] 306 (new sources),[35] 307(b) (pretreatment standards),[36] 311 (oil and hazardous substances regulation),[37] and even 318 (discharges associated with an approved aquaculture project).[38] Indeed, two of the better known toxic water pollutant incidents—contamination of the Hudson River by polychlorinated biphenyls[39] and pollution of Lake Superior by asbestos tailings[40] —have proceeded principally as water quality standard cases. Obviously, however, if toxic substances are regulated under provisions of the Act other than section 307, any applicable justifications of cost or technology must be met. For example, if controls on, let us say, chlorine in the effluent are justified under the 1983 "best available technology" standard, the cost and technological limitations of that standard must be satisfied. On the other hand, evidence of extreme toxicity or of widespread adverse effects are relevant to the choice of whether this control is too costly or that one based upon an unproven or speculative technology.

A landmark of sorts in the evolution of toxic pollutant standards occurred in March of 1976 with the approval of a settlement agreement resolving a number of pending lawsuits.[41] The agreement commits the Administrator to developing and promulgating standards for a large number of point source categories discharging a wide range of

31. 33 U.S.C.A. § 1251(a)(3).

32. Id. § 1311.

33. Id. § 1312.

34. Id. § 1313.

35. Id. § 1316.

36. Id. § 1317(b).

37. Id. § 1321; see § 4.17 below.

38. 33 U.S.C.A. § 1328.

39. In re General Elec. Co., 6 ELR 30007 (N.Y. Dep't of Environmental Conservation 1976).

40. See Reserve Mining Co. v. EPA, 514 F.2d 492, 5 ELR 20596 (8th Cir. 1975).

41. Natural Resources Defense Council, Inc. v. Train, Civil No. 2153–73 (D.D.C. Mar. 30, 1976) (the signatories to the agreement represented the Natural Resources Defense Council, Inc.; Environmental Defense Fund, Inc.; Businessmen for the Public Interest, Inc.; National Audubon Society, Inc.; Citizens for a Better Environment, Inc.; Environmental Protection Agency; National Coal Association) [hereinafter cited as Settlement Agreement].

Sec. 4.15 TOXIC POLLUTANTS

toxic pollutants. What is anticipated is a conventional development of existing, new and pretreatment effluent limitations, standards and guidelines under Sections 301, 304 and 306 of the Act.[42] The Administrator is expected to gather information, through the use of contractors and otherwise, "relating to technology, ecological and public health effects, and economic impact" of the regulations.[43] Various procedural obligations are imposed—Federal Register publication, progress reports, explanations of certain actions. The agreement imposes other constraints—for example, effluent limitations must cover at least 95 percent of the point sources within a category;[44] and it leaves room for discretion—for example, the Administrator may exclude a pollutant from regulation if he decides equally stringent protection already is afforded by existing regulations, if the pollutant is present in the discharge solely because it is found in the intake waters, or if it is present only in trace amounts not having toxic effects.[45]

This settlement is decidedly a two-way street. While there is public advantage to having the Administrator locked in at least to a program of toxic pollutants regulation, it is clear that this commitment will proceed on a course other than that prescribed by the demanding charter of section 307. While the agreement does require 307 action for a limited number of pollutants (aldrin/dieldrin, DDT (DDD, DDE), endrin, toxaphene, benzidine and PCB's[46]) and leaves open the possibility for other pollutants,[47] it is clear that regulation proceeds for the most part under the ordinary new and existing source standards where economic and technical defenses are much in vogue.[48] Thus lead, mercury and cadmium, to mention but three toxic elements randomly selected from the list, will be dealt with under the same set of criteria that served to guide controls over BOD and nontoxic suspended solids. Section 307 is confined accordingly to a little used emergency instrument. Whether the negotiated settlement represents the final internment of section 307 or its rising from the grave will be adjudged by future action.

Theoretically, the regulation of toxic discharges is treated, not as an afterthought, but as a central premise of the 1972 Amendments. Despite this, the subject remains the stepchild of federal water pollution control policy. While predictions are hazardous, it does not appear implausible that the law in the future will take a greater inter-

---

42. § 4.12 above.

43. Settlement Agreement, supra note 41, ¶E, at 10.

44. Id., ¶D.

45. Id., ¶F, at 13.

46. Id., ¶K, at 19; see 41 Fed.Reg. 23576 (June 10, 1976). Compare § 8.10 below.

47. Settlement Agreement, supra note 41, ¶I, at 17; see 41 Fed.Reg. 1765 (Jan. 12, 1976), proposing 40 CFR pt. 104 (Public Hearings on Effluent Standards for Toxic Pollutants).

48. § 4.12 above.

est in reaching toxic discharges than it has thus far. There is something absurd in the proposition that the "cleaning up" of the Hudson River may proceed apace by discouraging the dumping of leaves (which have a biological oxygen demand) or the discharge of soil (which contributes to suspended solids) but neglecting the polychlorinated biphenyls which can contaminate or destroy marine life tempted to return to the river.[49]

§ 4.16 Ocean Dumping

The regulation of ocean dumping in the United States has origins as far back as 1886.[1] In recent years, a series of important studies awakened interest on the subject.[2] Today, the key statute is the Marine Protection, Research, and Sanctuaries Act of 1972,[3] known popularly as the Ocean Dumping Act. The 1972 Amendments to the Federal Water Pollution Control Act also retain an ambiguous role. This section addresses (1) coverage of the Ocean Dumping Act; (2) issuance of permits and selection of sites; (3) overlap between the Act and FWPCA; and (4) enforcement.

a. *Coverage*

The Marine Protection Act has three titles. The first establishes a permit program, administered by EPA, for the transportation and dumping of material into ocean waters. Title II creates a research program, under auspices of the Secretary of Commerce, that includes among its objectives the coordination of studies "for the purpose of determining means of minimizing or ending all dumping of materials

---

49. See Comment, Federal Toxic Controls: The Patchwork Attack on PCB's, 6 ELR 10056 (1976); § 8.10 below (Toxic Substances Control Act).

1. Act of Aug. 5, 1886, ch. 929, 24 Stat. 310.

2. Council on Environmental Quality, Ocean Dumping—A National Policy (1970); Environmental Protection Agency, Solid Waste Management Office, Ocean Disposal of Barge-Delivered Liquid and Solid Wastes from U. S. Coastal Cities (1971); National Academy of Sciences-National Academy of Engineering, Waste Management Concepts for the Coastal Zone (1970). Until 1972, ocean dumping in only three port areas (New York City, Baltimore, Hampton Roads, Va.) was subject to regulation under the Supervisory Harbors Act of 1888, 25 Stat. 209, 33 U.S.C.A. §§ 441–51.

3. Pub.L. No. 92–532, 86 Stat. 1052, 33 U.S.C.A. § 1401 et seq. Minor amendments were adopted in 1974 to bring the Act into conformity with the Convention on the Prevention of Marine Pollution by Dumping of Wastes and Other Matter. Pub.L. No. 93–254, 88 Stat. 50. Recent oversight hearings include Hearings on Marine Protection, Research, and Sanctuaries Act of 1972, Before the Subcomm. on Ocean and Atmosphere of the Senate Comm. on Commerce, S.Doc. No. 32, 94th Cong., 1st Sess. (1975); Joint Hearings on Ocean Dumping Before the Subcomm. on Fisheries and Wildlife Conservation and the Environment and the Subcomm. on Oceanography of the House Comm. on Merchant Marine and Fisheries, H.R.Doc. No. 10, 94th Cong., 1st Sess. (1975); Joint Hearings on Ocean Dumping—Part 2, Before the Subcomm. on Fisheries and Wildlife Conservation and the Environment and the Subcomm. on Oceanography of the House Comm. on Merchant Marine and Fisheries, H.R. Doc. No. 25, 94th Cong., 2d Sess. (1976).

Sec. 4.16   OCEAN DUMPING   489

within five years of the effective date of this Act." [4] Title III authorizes the Secretary of Commerce, after consultation, to designate as "marine sanctuaries" undefined areas of ocean and other waters "which he determines necessary for the purpose of preserving or restoring such areas for their conservation, recreational, ecological, or esthetic values." [5] The consequences of designating a marine sanctuary are potentially important because "any activities" within a designated area may proceed only with the approval of the Secretary and consistently with regulations he promulgates.[6] A designation is allowed within the territorial limits of any state only upon the approval of the governor.[7]

The Act prohibits entirely the ocean dumping of radiological, chemical and biological warfare agents and high-level radioactive waste.[8] Permits are allowed for three distinct activities: (1) the transportation of any material from the United States for the purpose of dumping it into ocean waters;[9] (2) the dumping of any material transported from outside the United States into the territorial sea of the United States (a belt adjacent to the coast extending for three miles according to traditional international law) or the contiguous zone (extending twelve miles seaward from the base line from which the territorial sea is measured);[10] (3) the transporting of any material by a U. S. agency or U. S. registered vessel from outside of the United States for the purpose of dumping it into ocean waters.[11] "Material" is defined comprehensively in the Act [12] and is intended to be synonymous with the term "pollutant" appearing in the Federal Water Pollution Control Act.[13] "Ocean waters", means those waters of the open seas lying seaward of land,[14] within or outside the territorial sea.

Several types of dumping are exempted from the Act in the definition of "dumping" (which means a disposition of material): [15]

> (1) discharges from outfall structures subject to the permit provisions of other legislation (Federal Water Pollution Control Act, Atomic Energy Act, Rivers and Harbors Act of 1899); (2) a "routine discharge" of effluent incidental to the propulsion of, or

---

4. Section 203, 33 U.S.C.A. § 1443.

5. Section 302, 33 U.S.C.A. § 1432.

6. Section 302(f), 33 U.S.C.A. § 1432 (f). The regulations permit "multiple uses" within designated areas. 39 Fed. Reg. 23254 (1974), 15 CFR pt. 922.

7. Section 302(b), 33 U.S.C.A. § 1432(b).

8. 33 U.S.C.A. § 1412(a).

9. Section 101(a), 33 U.S.C.A. § 1412 (a).

10. Ibid.

11. Ibid.

12. 33 U.S.C.A. § 1402(c).

13. Comm. on Commerce, Marine Protection and Research Act of 1971, S. Rep. No. 451, 92d Cong., 1st Sess. 17 (1971).

14. 33 U.S.C.A. § 1402(b).

15. Id. § 1402(f).

operation of, motor-driven equipment on vessels; (3) the construction of a fixed structure or artificial island for a purpose other than disposal when the placement is otherwise regulated by a federal or state law or program (thus exempting oil exploration and drilling); (4) the deposit of oyster shells or other materials made for the purpose of maintaining fisheries resources if the deposit is otherwise regulated by a federal or state program. Additional exemptions apply to the dumping of fish wastes except in enclosed waters "or where the Administrator finds that such deposits could endanger health, the environment or ecological system in a specific location," [16] and to the dumping of materials "in an emergency to safeguard life at sea." [17]

Still other exemptions result from the decision to exclude sewage (and to a limited extent oil) from the definition of "material".[18] The purpose of the exclusion, quite clearly, was the belief that those two pollutants were regulated adequately by FWPCA.[19] One observer sees a problem in that the partial exclusion of oil from coverage has the "unintended effect" of not providing "clear regulatory authority for oily wastes loaded onshore for the purpose of ocean dumping." [20] It appears to this author that regulatory authority under the Ocean Dumping Act scarcely could be clearer [21] although Section 311 of FWPCA [22] would apply also.

b. *Issuance of Permits and Selection of Sites*

The power to dispense permits is vested in the Administrator of EPA, except that the Secretary of the Army has principal authority to issue permits "for the transportation of dredged material for the purpose of dumping it into ocean waters." [23] In permitting the dumping of dredged material, the Secretary applies the same criteria for evaluating permits as does the Administrator and is specifically invited to make an "independent determination" as to the need for the

---

16. Section 102(d), 33 U.S.C.A. § 1412(d).

17. Section 105(h), 33 U.S.C.A. § 1415(h). This provision is not an express exemption from the Act but only an exemption from all penalty provisions.

18. 33 U.S.C.A. § 1402(c).

19. See Comm. on Merchant Marines and Fisheries, Marine Protection, Research, and Sanctuaries Act of 1971, H.R. Rep. No. 361, 92d Cong., 1st Sess. 16 (1971) [hereinafter cited as House Report].

20. Lettow, The Control of Marine Pollution, in Environmental Law Institute, Federal Environmental Law 596, 654 (E. L. Dolgin & T. G. P. Guilbert eds. 1974).

21. 33 U.S.C.A. § 1402(c), in the definition of "material", states that "oil within the meaning of section 1321 of this title shall be included only to the extent that such oil is taken on board a vessel or aircraft for the purpose of dumping." The Administrator, under the Ocean Dumping Act, forbids the dumping of various wastes containing oil "insofar as these are not regulated" under FWPCA. 40 CFR § 227.22(d).

22. 33 U.S.C.A. § 1321.

23. Section 103(a), 33 U.S.C.A. § 1413(a). Compare § 4.6 above (disposal of dredged and fill material).

dumping, other possible methods of disposal, and appropriate locations for it.[24] Prior to issuing any permit the Secretary must notify the Administrator who can exercise a veto power over conditions or the site.[25] If the Secretary determines that "there is no economically feasible method or site available," other than one whose utilization would offend the governing criteria, he is required to so certify and request a waiver from the Administrator. The Administrator must grant the waiver within thirty days unless he finds that the dumping of the material "will result in an unacceptably adverse impact on municipal water supplies, shell-fish beds, wildlife, fisheries (including spawning and breeding areas), or recreational areas."[26] Thus the EPA Administrator must took twice at a dredge disposal site, if the Secretary of the Army insists, but he can still say no. The conferees, cognizant of the potential for serious conflict between the Corps of Engineers and EPA, struggled before surfacing with this compromise procedure, and repeatedly urged the potential adversaries to strive mightily to resolve their differences.[27]

---

24. Section 103(b), 33 U.S.C.A. § 1413 (b). Expressly made applicable are the criteria of 33 U.S.C.A. § 1412(a) reading in part:

> the Administrator may issue permits . . . where the Administrator determines that such dumping will not unreasonably degrade or endanger human health, welfare, or amenities, or the marine environment, ecological systems, or economic potentialities. The Administrator shall establish and apply criteria for reviewing and evaluating such permit applications, and, in establishing or revising such criteria, shall consider, but not be limited in his consideration to, the following:
>
> (A) The need for the proposed dumping.
>
> (B) The effect of such dumping on human health and welfare, including economic, esthetic, and recreational values.
>
> (C) The effect of such dumping on fisheries resources, plankton, fish, shellfish, wildlife, shore lines and beaches.
>
> (D) The effect of such dumping on marine ecosystems, particularly with respect to—
>
> (i) the transfer, concentration, and dispersion of such material and its byproducts through biological, physical, and chemical processes,
>
> (ii) potential changes in marine ecosystem diversity, productivity, and stability, and
>
> (iii) species and community population dynamics.
>
> (E) The persistence and permanence of the effects of the dumping.
>
> (F) The effect of dumping particular volumes and concentrations of such materials.
>
> (G) Appropriate locations and methods of disposal or recycling, including land-based alternatives and the probable impact of requiring use of such alternate locations or methods upon considerations affecting the public interest.
>
> (H) The effect on alternative uses of oceans, such as scientific study, fishing, and other living resource exploitation, and non-living resource exploitation.
>
> . . .

25. Section 103(c), 33 U.S.C.A. § 1413 (c).

26. Section 103(d), 33 U.S.C.A. § 1413 (d).

27. Comm. of Conference, Marine Protection, Research, and Sanctuaries Act of 1972, H.R.Rep. No. 1546, 92d Cong., 2d Sess. 15–16 (1972) [hereinafter cited as Conference Report].

The Secretary of the Army's powers under Section 103 of the Ocean Dumping Act and Section 404 of FWPCA are duplicative in several respects.[28] Some situations are covered by one act and not the other (section 404's applicability to dumping into "navigable waters", for example, covers many inland waters not considered "ocean waters"). Where both apply, there are procedural differences: section 404 conditions site disapproval by the Administrator of EPA upon compliance with notice, hearing, and written findings requirements; section 103 requires a response within thirty days from a waiver request by the Corps of Engineers. But the criteria for an administrative veto of a site by the Administrator of EPA are indistinguishable substantively ("unacceptably adverse impact" on listed uses under section 103,[29] "unacceptable adverse effect" on the same uses under section 404 [30]).

The EPA Administrator influences ocean disposal of nondredged materials in two important ways: he administers the permit program and designates recommended sites for dumping and critical areas unsuitable for dumping. Permits may be issued only "after notice and opportunity for public hearings" [31] although the Administrator has made clear that a hearing on the issuance of the permit (unlike the hearing on whether a penalty should be imposed for violating it) involves no rights of cross-examination.[32] Resort to the regulations is necessary for further information on the contents of a permit application,[33] processing fees,[34] and the time limits on the Administrator's decision.[35] The statute makes clear that information "received by the Administrator . . . as a part of any application or in connection with any permit granted . . . shall be available to the public as a matter of public record, at every stage of the proceeding." [36] It is clear also that the Administrator can deny or condition a permit if the applicant does not sustain its burden of providing adequate information (presumably including studies the Administrator deems necessary),[37] or its burden of demonstrating the dumping will have no adverse effects.[38]

28. See § 4.6 above.

29. 33 U.S.C.A. § 1413(d).

30. Id. § 1314(c).

31. Id. § 1412(a).

32. Compare 40 CFR § 222.8 with id. § 226.2; see 41 Fed.Reg. 26644 (June 28, 1976), proposing revisions of 40 CFR pts. 220–29 (advancing substantial changes of the ocean dumping regulations).

33. 40 CFR § 221.1.

34. Id. § 221.5.

35. Id. §§ 222.1–.2.

36. Section 104(f), 33 U.S.C.A. § 1414(f).

37. Section 104(e), 33 U.S.C.A. § 1414(e); see House Report, supra note 19, at 21.

38. In re City of Philadelphia, Interim Ocean Disposal Permit No. PA 010, Decision of the Administrator, Sept. 25, 1975, 5 ELR 30003, 30004 ("even assuming that no harm has occurred at this point in time, the City has not shown that its continued dumping [of sewage sludge] will not contribute to a general deterioration of the ocean

The issuance of ocean dumping permits, no less than permits under the National Pollutant Discharge Elimination System, raises questions about the criteria for issuance and the scope of conditions that may be included in the permit. A safe generality is that ocean dumping permits are water quality limited and not technology limited. The statute authorizes the issuance of a permit "where the Administrator determines that such dumping will not unreasonably degrade or endanger human health, welfare or amenities, or the marine environment, ecological systems, or economic potentialities." [39] Some content is added to this gentle reminder by a requirement that "no permit shall be issued for a dumping of material which will violate applicable water quality standards." [40] And the Administrator is required to establish and apply criteria, which have been published,[41] focussing almost exclusively on the effects of the dumping. In addition to effects, the Administrator's criteria must give consideration to "the need" for the dumping and the availability of waste disposal alternatives, including the impact of alternatives.

The statute gives small solace to technological or cost considerations as a justification for continued ocean dumping. The only clear reference to economics in the Act is that inviting the Administrator to determine whether the dumping will "unreasonably degrade . . . economic potentialities." This appears aimed not at the economic straits of the dumper but the economic potential of the dump (from the point of view of the development of fisheries, and so on). The necessity for evaluating the "need" for dumping and alternatives to it presumably invites some allowance for economic factors although a permit can be denied on environmental grounds alone. The legislative history accords a greater sympathy to economic constraints than does the Act but even this language is confined to the special problem of dredged materials.[42] The extent of the prohibition against ocean dumping thus is measured principally by the extent of the adverse effects, with the burden on the permit applicant to prove they are tolerable. The denial of a permit certainly need not be defended on

or that such deterioration will not eventually cause adverse effects"). If the applicant produces insufficient data, an environmental impact statement prepared by EPA also may be deficient and the action thus enjoinable. See text accompanying notes 66–68 infra.

39. Section 102(a), 33 U.S.C.A. § 1412(a), quoted in note 24, supra.

40. Ibid.

41. 40 CFR pt. 227.

42. The Conference Report, supra note 27, at 17, contains language identical to that appearing in the Conference Report on Section 404 of FWPCA (at 142), quoted in § 4.6 n. 60 above:

It is expected that until such time as economic and feasible alternative methods for disposal of dredge material are available, no unreasonable restrictions shall be imposed on dredging activities essential for the maintenance of interstate and foreign commerce, and that, consistent with the intent of this Act, the disposal activities of private dredgers and the Corps of Engineers will be treated similarly.

cost-benefit grounds in the sense that costs for alternative methods of disposal must be offset by gains to the ocean environment.

Pursuant to his authority to establish various categories of permits,[43] the Administrator has promulgated regulations [44] authorizing issuance of (1) general permits; (2) special permits; (3) emergency permits; (4) interim permits; and (5) research permits. General permits authorize the dumping of certain non-toxic materials (such as galley wastes) in small quantities at designated sites. They cover dumping that is low in controversy and of "minimal adverse environmental impact," according to the specific statutory authorization.[45] Special permits cover most other types of dumping, must have a fixed expiration date (no later than three years from the date of issuance), and call for more precision in describing the material to be dumped and the location.[46]

The categories of emergency and interim permits create problems. An emergency is defined in a way to allow the dumping of prohibited materials under circumstances none too emergent. It permits the dumping of certain material "which poses an unacceptable risk relating to human health and admits of no other feasible solution." An "emergency" refers to "situations requiring action with a marked degree of urgency, but is not limited in its application to circumstances requiring immediate action." [47] The problem with the category is that it comes close to amending the criteria for issuance and, in any event, is susceptible to abusive application.

The "interim permit" for all practical purposes is a variance procedure allowing the dumping of otherwise prohibited materials or of materials in excess of permissible concentrations upon the satisfaction of certain conditions; [48] these include the preparation of an environmental assessment [49] and the development and active pursuit of an implementation plan designed to eliminate the discharge or bring it within permissible limits. Cost and technological considerations are among those factors to be considered in the decision of whether or not to grant an interim permit. A permit of this category must expire within one year, and cannot be renewed, but this is hardly draconian since a new interim permit may be issued upon another application.

The Administrator's variance procedure, under the alias of an interim permit, creates two difficulties. The first is that it may be

---

43. Section 102(b), 33 U.S.C.A. § 1412(b).

44. 40 CFR § 220.3.

45. Section 104(c), 33 U.S.C.A. § 1414(c).

46. 40 CFR § 220.3(b).

47. Id. § 220.3(c).

48. Id. § 220.3(d).

49. Ocean dumping, both public and private, may require the preparation of an environmental impact statement under the National Environmental Policy Act. See Natural Resources Defense Council, Inc. v. Callaway, 524 F.2d 79, 5 ELR 20640 (2d Cir. 1975).

applied to grant permits upon an inadequate information base which the statute clearly discourages. Second, and more important, it requires some imagination to justify the creation of a variance procedure premised upon cost and technological considerations [50] when the statute of its origin creates no such procedure and places cost and technological limits low on the list of priorities. At the same time, it is impossible to read the Ocean Dumping Act as mandating a "cold turkey" solution to the problem of ocean dumping. By creating the interim permit or variance procedure, the Administrator undoubtedly had not transgressed the limits of his assigned discretion. The serious question is whether the procedures will be applied largely to condone present practices or to move towards a phase-out of ocean dumping.[51]

A research permit may issue when the Administrator "determines the scientific merit of the proposed project outweighs the potential damage that may occur from the dumping." [52] The applicant must provide a "detailed statement" of the probable environmental impact of the project. Reasonable grounds exist for the separate treatment of research permits: indeed, dumping in connection with research may be the *sine qua non* of adequate information for a special permit. The administrative criterion is an interesting example of an enforceable legal limit upon the domain of scientific inquiry.

Permits must designate, at a minimum (1) the type of material authorized to be transported for dumping; (2) amount of the material; (3) location of the dumping site; (4) duration of the permit; and (5) any special provisions "for the monitoring and surveillance of the transportation and dumping" deemed necessary by the Administrator or the Secretary after consultation with the Coast Guard. A catch-all provision is included authorizing the addition of any other conditions the permitting authority deems appropriate.[53] This should be read as embracing any and all conditions reasonably related to the basic power of prohibiting or delimiting the ocean dumping of materials. Form permits presently in use require telephone notice of sailing to the U. S. Coast Guard two hours prior to vessel departure, a legible identification of the owner's name painted on both sides of the scow or boat, maintenance of a monthly transportation and dump-

---

50. 40 CFR § 220.3(e).

51. The Philadelphia case, note 38, supra, is an example of the Administrator using his powers to require a phase-out of ocean dumping of sludge by 1981. See Comment, Latent Risks of Ocean Dumping: EPA Administrator Affirms Philadelphia's Phase Out Order, 5 ELR 10213 (1975). See also In re City of New York, Interim Ocean Disposal Permit No. NY 009, Decision of the Regional Administrator, July 20, 1976 (ordering a phase-out of ocean dumping of sludge by Dec. 31, 1981); Maryland v. Train, 415 F.Supp. 116, 6 ELR 20496 (D.Md. 1976) (ordering EPA to hold public hearings on the continuation of the ocean dumping permit for Camden, New Jersey).

52. 40 CFR § 220.3(c).

53. Section 104(a), 33 U.S.C.A. § 1414(a).

ing log, and an analysis of a representative sample of the barge load.[54] In the future, permittees might be required to install certain navigational or surveillance equipment to make sure they can locate the site and monitor the effects of the dumping.

Applying the criteria on effects, the Administrator is authorized to designate recommended sites for dumping, which he has done.[55] When "he finds it necessary to protect critical areas," he "shall, after consultation with the Secretary [of the Army], also designate sites or times within which certain materials may not be dumped."[56] Critical areas are not defined in the Act but should be read as including especially fragile or productive areas. Thus the Administrator explicitly is given what amounts to a broad zoning power, which can be exercised on a permit by permit or a comprehensive rulemaking basis, to rule out of order all types of dumping within defined areas.

c. *Overlap Between the Act and FWPCA*

The Administrator's powers under the Ocean Dumping Act, like those of the Secretary of Army, are duplicated in various respects by the 1972 Amendments to the Federal Water Pollution Control Act.[57] Section 403[58] of FWPCA directs the Administrator to promulgate guidelines "for determining the degradation of the waters of the territorial seas, the contiguous zone, and the oceans," listing numerous effects substantially similar to those listed as pertinent to the evaluation of permits under Section 102(a)[59] of the Ocean Dumping Act. Section 403(c)(2) is somewhat more explicit than its sister statute on the absolute necessity for a permit to be justified by adequate data: "In any event where insufficient information exists on any proposed discharge to make a reasonable judgment on any of the guidelines established pursuant to this subsection no permit shall be issued under section 402 of this Act." This places a heavy burden of proof on applicants on a subject where the burden is not easily sustained, but it is not materially different from the situation existing under the Ocean Dumping Act.

Potential inconsistencies in the two laws are more disturbing. Most important is the question whether the technology-based "best practicable" and "best available" standards of FWPCA apply to ocean

54. See Environmental Protection Agency, Region II, Marine Protection, Research, and Sanctuaries Act (Ocean Disposal) Permit, undated.

55. 40 CFR pt. 227, editorial note.

56. Section 102(c), 33 U.S.C.A. § 1412(c).

57. For contrasting views on the significance of the overlap by two knowledgeable observers, compare Lettow, supra note 20, at 655–58 with Zener, The Federal Law of Water Pollution Control, in Environmental Law Institute, Federal Environmental Law 682, 738–41 (E. L. Dolgin & T. G. P. Guilbert eds. 1974). See also Miller, Ocean Dumping—Prelude and Fugue, 9 J. Maritime L. & Commerce 51, 61–74 (1973).

58. 33 U.S.C.A. § 1314.

59. Id. § 1412(a).

Sec. 4.16 OCEAN DUMPING 497

dumping permits. EPA believes that they do and has written the standards into its interim permit variance procedure.[60] The statutes should be read in harmony, to be sure, but this is the wrong way to do it: the criteria established under the Ocean Dumping Act should be read as setting standards akin to the water quality related effluent limitations of Section 302 [61] of the 1972 Amendments—something above and beyond the technology-based limitations. The defenses of high cost or the limits of technology must be found, if at all, in the provisions of the Ocean Dumping Act.

Another potential trouble spot is the extent to which state regulation survives in light of the strongly preemptive language of the Ocean Dumping Act and the nonpreemptive language of FWPCA.[62] This involves two separate questions, the first being whether states qualified to carry out permit programs under FWPCA can exercise this power over ocean dumping. Section 403(b)[63] of FWPCA anticipates that they can, while admonishing the Administrator of EPA to retain his veto power over the permits. Section 106(a) of the Ocean Dumping Act suggests they cannot. The conflict is best resolved by taking the Ocean Dumping Act at face value in its insistence that its permits take precedence. This is consistent with the heavily national and international flavor of the Act, the indication in both acts that EPA is to have the last word on ocean dumping, and the rather fortuitous fact that the Ocean Dumping Act was enacted five days later than the 1972 FWPCA Amendments.

Another aspect of the preemption question is addressed in the Ocean Dumping Act: "no State shall adopt or enforce any rule or regulation relating to any activity regulated by this subchapter." [64] This forecloses stricter state standards for dumping and probably also state prohibitions in areas approved by the Administrator although this is a closer question. But the state retains the veto power it has under Section 401 of the 1972 Amendments to disapprove federally permitted activity that would result in a violation of state standards.[65]

Another disparity between the two acts concerns applicability of the National Environmental Policy Act. The Ocean Dumping Act is

---

60. 40 CFR § 227.4; see Zener, supra note 57, at 739 n. 242.

61. 33 U.S.C.A. § 1312.

62. Compare Section 106(a) of the Ocean Dumping Act, 33 U.S.C.A. § 1416(a) ("After the effective date of this subchapter, all licenses, permits, and authorizations other than those issued pursuant to this title shall be void and of no legal effect, to the extent that they purport to authorize any activity regulated by this title, and whether issued before or after the effective date of this title") with Section 510 of FWPCA, 33 U.S.C.A. § 1370 (generally preserving state authority).

63. 33 U.S.C.A. § 1343(b).

64. Section 106(d), 33 U.S.C.A. § 1416(d).

65. See Lettow, supra note 20, at 656–57.

silent on the question, suggesting that NEPA applies,[66] while the 1972 Amendments specifically exempts permit issuance from the impact statement requirement.[67] Once again, the Ocean Dumping Act should take precedence, but this does not mean that environmental impact statements must be prepared in connection with the issuance of each permit if, for example, effects can be said to be insignificant.[68]

d. *Enforcement*

Enforcement provisions under the Ocean Dumping Act [69] parallel those in the 1972 Amendments: [70] each violation of any provision or permit may result in a civil penalty of not more than $50,000 or revocation or suspension of the permit, to be imposed only after notice and hearing. A knowing violation is a criminal offense, whch may result in another $50,000 fine or imprisonment for not more than one year, or both. The Attorney General can sue to enjoin violations. A vessel used in a violation is liable in rem for any civil penalty assessed or criminal fine imposed, provided the owner or charterer was privy to the violation. Citizen suits are provided for, with a sixty day notice provision and the possibility of a party winning an award of costs (including reasonable attorney and expert witness fees).[71]

Of course the imposition of sanctions is dependent upon meaningful detection and surveillance. Responsibility for this under the Act is vested in the Coast Guard, which "shall conduct surveillance and other appropriate enforcement activity to prevent unlawful transportation of material for dumping, or unlawful dumping." [72] The Coast Guard must supply to the Administrator and the Attorney General, as appropriate, "such information of enforcement activities and such evidentiary material assembled as they may require in carrying out their duties relative to penalty assessments, criminal prosecutions, or other actions involving litigation pursuant to the provisions" of the Act.[73] The Coast Guard has its own operational guidelines for surveillance, ranging from escorting vessels containing toxic wastes to aircraft overflight to routine boarding and inspection.[74] The modest number of violations found [75] may be indicative not so much of an absence of violations but an absence of detection of violations by spot-checking. For this reason the Coast Guard is being urged to "include incorporation of high-accuracy navigation systems on surveillance

66. Note 49, supra.

67. Section 511(c)(1), 33 U.S.C.A. § 1371(c)(1).

68. See § 7.6 below.

69. Section 105, 33 U.S.C.A. § 1516.

70. See § 4.21 below.

71. See § 1.13 above.

72. Section 107(c), 33 U.S.C.A. § 1417(c).

73. Ibid.

74. See Third Coast Guard District Instruction 5922.5, Sept. 14, 1973.

75. EPA, Draft Second Annual Report on Administration of the Ocean Dumping Permit Program, Sept. 1974, at 18 (reporting four formal enforcement actions pending before EPA).

Sec. 4.17   OIL POLLUTION: PROHIBITIONS, ETC.

units, the collection and analysis of samples at, near, or on the routes to dumpsites, or development of remote airborne sensors." [76] Not to be overlooked either is the possibility that law enforcement will not catch up to the commerce and technology of ocean dumping for the foreseeable future.

§ 4.17 Oil Pollution: Prohibitions, Penalties and Cleanup

Liability for oil spills and regulation discouraging them is a confusing amalgam of common law and admiralty principles, international treaties, state and federal statutes. As this text is being written, Congress is considering yet another major reworking of the regulatory and liability scheme.[1]

We begin with Section 311 [2] of the 1972 amendments to FWPCA. The enactment is "basically the same" [3] as the existing law on oil pollution, which first appeared in the Water Quality Improvement Act of 1970. It deals comprehensively with (1) prohibitions, (2) penalties, and (3) cleanup of oil spills, and very little or not at all with (4) regulation, including ship design and traffic controls, and (5) liability for oil spill damage.

a. *Prohibitions*

The welter of words in section 311 obscures a very straight-forward approach to the problem of pollution by oil and other hazardous substances. The congressional expression of policy could not be clearer: "it is the policy of the United States that there should be no discharges of oil or hazardous substances into or upon the navigable waters of the United States, adjoining shorelines, or into or upon the waters of the contiguous zone." [4] The means of implementation is subsection 311(b)(3), which states that "[t]he discharge of oil or hazardous substances into or upon" these same waters "in harmful quantities as determined by the President . . . is prohibited." [5] (This is scarcely a radical innovation since the Oil Pol-

---

76. Walker, Enforcement of the Marine Protection, Research and Sanctuaries Act of 1972, at 8 (unpublished paper prepared for a course in environmental law, Georgetown U.Law Center, Fall 1974).

1. See S.1754, 94th Cong., 1st Sess. (1975); 121 Cong.Rec. S8274-78 (daily ed. May 15, 1975) (remarks of Sen. Magnuson upon introduction of S.1754).

2. 33 U.S.C.A. § 1321.

3. Comm. of Conference, Federal Water Pollution Control Act Amendments of 1972, H.R.Rep. No. 1465, 92d Cong., 2d Sess. 132 (1972) [hereinafter cited as Conference Report].

4. Section 311(b)(1), 33 U.S.C.A. § 1321(b)(1).

5. 33 U.S.C.A. § 1321(b)(3). There are two exceptions to this directive: "(A) in the case of such discharges of oil into the waters of the contiguous zone, where permitted under Article IV of the International Convention for the Prevention of the Pollution of the Sea by Oil, 1954, as amended, and (B) where permitted in quantities and at times and locations or under such circumstances or conditions as the President may, by reg-

lution Act of 1924 forbade "discharges of oil by any method . . . into or upon the coastal waters of the United States," unless permitted as not "deleterious" to health or seafood in regulations issued by the Secretary of War.[6]) The President through the Environmental Protection Agency has determined by regulation that oil discharges in harmful quantities include, with a few minor exceptions, all those that violate water quality standards or "[c]ause a film or sheen upon or discoloration of the surface of the water or adjoining shorelines or cause a sludge or emulsion to be deposited beneath the surface of the water or upon the adjoining shorelines."[7] The sheen test has been sustained in the courts, partly on grounds of ease of administration ("If you can see the spill, report it!"), over objections that it construed too liberally the statutory definition of "harmful quantities."[8]

This is stiff medicine: it approaches a no discharge policy for oil spills in the waters of the United States. Equating a "harmful discharge" with that which causes a sheen reaches spills of a few gallons or less. Protection extends not only to the broadly defined "waters of the United States"[9] but also to "adjoining shorelines," as the statute clearly says. Oil[10] and discharge[11] also are broadly defined. Discharges can come from any vessel,[12] onshore facility[13] or offshore

ulation, determine not to be harmful. Any regulation issued under this subsection shall be consistent with maritime safety and with marine and navigation laws and regulations and applicable water quality standards." The second exception is not an exception at all but rather a grant of rulemaking power to implement the general directive against "harmful" discharges. This would authorize, for example, a permit program for the ocean dumping of oily wastes. See § 4.16 nn. 20, 21 above.

6. Act of June 7, 1924, ch. 316, §§ 1–5, 7, 8, 43 Stat. 604–06.

7. 40 CFR § 110.3; see id. pt. 110.

8. E. g., United States v. Boyd, 491 F.2d 1163, 1172, 3 ELR 20434, 20437 (9th Cir. 1973); United States v. Kennecott Copper Corp., 523 F.2d 821, 5 ELR 20707 (9th Cir. 1975) (requiring the reporting of a spill even though it could not be seen); United States v. Beatty, Inc., 401 F.Supp. 1040 (W.D.Ky.1975); United States v. Eureka Pipeline Co., 401 F.Supp. 934 (N.D.W.Va.1975).

9. See § 4.3 above; United States v. Ashland Oil & Transp. Co., 504 F.2d 1317, 4 ELR 20784 (6th Cir. 1974).

10. Section 311(a)(1), 33 U.S.C.A. § 1321(a)(1), reads:
'oil' means oil of any kind or in any form, including, but not limited to, petroleum, fuel oil, sludge, oil refuse, and oil mixed with wastes other than dredged spoil.

11. Section 311(a)(2), 33 U.S.C.A. § 1321(a)(2), reads:
'discharge' includes, but is not limited to, any spilling, leaking, pumping, pouring, emitting, emptying, or dumping . . . .

12. Section 311(a)(3), 33 U.S.C.A. § 1321(a)(3), reads:
'vessel' means every description of watercraft or other artificial contrivance used, or capable of being used, as a means of transportation on water other than a public vessel . . . .

13. Section 311(a)(10), 33 U.S.C.A. § 1321(a)(10), reads:
'onshore facility' means any facility (including but not limited to, motor vehicles and rolling stock) of any

facility,[14] all three of which are broadly defined. They include clearly trucks, pipelines,[15] drilling platforms. The only significant exclusion, expressed in the legislative history, is for a discharge from any onshore or offshore facility and which "is not in harmful quantities and is pursuant to, and not in violation of, a permit issued" to the facility under Section 402 of the Act.[16] NPDES permits should not be issued to permit a sheen.

b. *Penalties*

This no discharge policy, moreover, is backed by no sympathy sanctions. Any owner or operator of a vessel or facility from which oil or a hazardous substance is discharged "shall be assessed a civil penalty . . . of not more than $5,000 for each offense." [17] This is a strict liability offense complete without regard to the fault or culpability of the actor. It represents no small advance over the Water Quality Improvement Act of 1970 where liability turned upon a showing that oil was "knowingly discharged" [18] and even the Senate version of the 1972 FWPCA Amendments which tied liability to an act "wilfully or negligently" [19] committed. A symbolic if not a practical illustration of the stringency of the 1972 Act is that some penalty must be imposed for each violation regardless of its severity.[20] A procedure also is available to withhold clearance from any vessel whose owner or operator is subject to civil penalties,[21] which means that the ship can be prevented from leaving port. The sanctions are made more credible yet by obliging the person in charge of a vessel or facility, under threat of criminal penalties, "immediately [to] notify the appropriate agency of the United States Government of such discharge." [22] Information obtained by the notification cannot be used against the person giving it in a criminal proceeding.

kind located in, on, or under, any land within the United States other than submerged land . . . .

14. Section 311(a)(11), 33 U.S.C.A. § 1321(a)(11), reads:
'offshore facility' means any facility of any kind located in, on, or under, any of the navigable waters of the United States other than a vessel or a public vessel . . . .

15. United States v. Ashland Oil & Transp. Co., 504 F.2d 1317, 4 ELR 20784 (6th Cir. 1974).

16. Conference Report, supra note 3, at 134.

17. Section 311(j), 33 U.S.C.A. § 1321 (j).

18. Pub.L. No. 91–224, § 11(b)(5), 84 Stat. 91.

19. Comm. on Public Works, Federal Water Pollution Control Act Amendments of 1971, S.Rep. No. 414, 92d Cong., 1st Sess. 66 (1971).

20. This requirement has caused some consternation within the U. S. Coast Guard, which is charged with enforcing the Act. See Proceedings of the Civil Penalties Conference, Oct. 10–11, 1973, at 25.

21. Section 311(b)(6), 33 U.S.C.A. § 1321(b)(6).

22. Section 311(b)(5), 33 U.S.C.A. § 1321(b)(5), reads:
Any person in charge of a vessel or of an onshore facility or an offshore facility shall, as soon as he has knowledge of any discharge of oil or a hazardous substance from such vessel or facility in violation of [section 311(b)(3)], im-

The Coast Guard, as the entity responsible for detecting violations [23] and assessing and imposing civil penalties, conducts informal penalty procedures on detected spills.[24] Most districts have a practice to close a case at a stated amount through service of a letter giving notice of the amount and scheduled hearing. Hearings are held before Hearing Officers, and appeals may be taken to the District Commander and then to the Commandant. (Of sixty-seven cases appealed to the Commandant during the first part of 1974 only one resulted in a reversal and one other in a mitigation of penalty.[25]) Cases of nonpayment are referred to the U. S. Attorney who must seek to collect in a civil suit where the defendant is entitled to a trial *de novo*.

The elements of the civil penalty offense are clear. The Coast Guard must prove by a preponderance of the evidence that (1) a discharge occurred; (2) it was of a harmful quantity; (3) it entered into or upon the navigable waters of the United States or adjoining shorelines or the waters of the contiguous zone (it is unnecessary to show that the oil actually reached a navigable tributary [26]); (4) it emanated from a specific vessel or facility, which is usually established by the self-reporting compelled under the Act;[27] and (5) the person charged is the owner or operator of the facility, which sometimes raises difficulties because of the various charter arrangements prevalent in the shipping industry. The operator, in any event, is the person having overall control of the vessel.

The criteria for assessing penalties raise only a few difficulties. "In determining the amount of the penalty, or the amount agreed upon in compromise," according to the statute, the Secretary (through the Commandant of the Coast Guard) shall give consideration to "the appropriateness of [the] penalty to the size of the business of the owner or operator charged, the effect on the owner or

---

mediately notify the appropriate agency of the United States Government of such discharge. Any person who fails to notify immediately such agency of such discharge shall, upon conviction, be fined not more than $10,000, or imprisoned for not more than one year, or both. Notification received pursuant to this paragraph or information obtained by the exploitation of such notification shall not be used against any such person in any criminal case, except a prosecution for perjury or for giving a false statement.

23. See section 311(b)(6), 33 U.S.C.A. § 1321(b)(6); U. S. Coast Guard, Polluting Incidents In and Around U. S. Waters: Calendar Year 1972 (this report is prepared on an annual basis).

24. See 46 CFR § 2.50–20. For further details, see Bartlett, Coast Guard Enforcement of the Federal Water Pollution Control Act of 1972, Section 311(b)(6), (unpublished paper completed for a seminar on environmental law, Georgetown U. Law Center, May 1974).

25. Bartlett, supra note 24, at 12.

26. United States v. Ashland Oil & Transp. Co., 504 F.2d 1317, 4 ELR 20784 (6th Cir. 1974).

27. See note 22, supra.

Sec. 4.17 OIL POLLUTION: PROHIBITIONS, ETC.

operator's ability to continue in business, and the gravity of the violation." [28] The Commandant has made clear that the judgment about the gravity of the violation should take into consideration the amount of oil discharged, the culpability and prior record of the offender, but not whether cleanup efforts were undertaken.[29] Since the Act elsewhere makes the owner or operator liable for the cost of cleanup,[30] it seems appropriate to disallow efforts to avoid those costs by a *pro tanto* reduction of the fine. The argument the other way, not unpersuasive either, is that the gravity of the violation is reduced to the extent cleanup efforts mitigate effects. Regardless of what criteria exist, they are applied by the Coast Guard to produce penalties in an average amount substantially below the statutory maximum of $5,000 per offense.[31]

The penalty procedure has come close to foundering on several legal shoals. As of May 1974, the Coast Guard did not advise a violator how the statutory criteria were applied in a given case and thus approached the forbidden due process grounds that proved temporarily fatal to the penalty provisions of the Coal Mine Health and Safety Act.[32] This is a procedural matter easily corrected.

Virtually every clause of the self-reporting provisions [33] has been construed judicially: The obligation to notify arises "immediately," to encourage containment or other mitigation action, not some time thereafter.[34] The "person in charge" who must notify includes lower level employees who are in a position to know.[35] The purpose of the provision, after all, is "to bring onto the side of the Government, even as against his own employer the man (or woman) most likely to be closest to or earliest at the site of the polluting incident"—the

---

28. Section 311(b)(6), 33 U.S.C.A. § 1321(b)(6); see United States v. Eureka Pipeline Co., 401 F.Supp. 934 (N.D.W.Va.1975) (rejecting defense that making the size of the penalty partly dependent on an ability to pay was a denial of equal protection of the laws).

29. Commandant Instruction 5922.11A. A Commandant Instruction constitutes the official policy of the Coast Guard, and directs that certain action be taken.

30. Section 311(f), 33 U.S.C.A. § 1321 (f).

31. In 1972, 1611 cases were processed for violation. Of these, 751 resulted in no penalty; 347 yielded a total assessment of $189,665. As of May 1974, the remaining cases were pending before United States Attorneys or the Coast Guard. Bartlett, supra note 23, at 15 n. 47.

32. Nat'l Independent Coal Operators Ass'n v. Morton, 357 F.Supp. 509 (D.C.D.C.1973), rev'd 161 U.S.App. D.C. 68, 494 F.2d 987 (1974), aff'd 423 U.S. 388, 96 S.Ct. 809, 46 L.Ed. 2d 580 (1976).

33. See note 22, supra.

34. United States v. Ashland Oil & Transp. Co., 504 F.2d 1317, 4 ELR 20784 (6th Cir. 1974) (overnight delay of fifteen hours); United States v. Kennecott Copper Corp., 523 F.2d 821, 5 ELR 20707 (9th Cir. 1975) (3 day delay).

35. E. g., United States v. Skil Corp., 351 F.Supp. 295, 3 ELR 20841 (N.D. Ill.1972).

janitor, night guard or supervisor.[36] Notification must be forthcoming not only where there is actual "knowledge" of a spill, communicated by a sheen or otherwise, but also where the circumstances support the conclusion that the person in charge should have known.[37] The "appropriate agency" to notify encompasses "any federal agency concerned with water and environmental pollution or navigable waters" (including obviously, the Coast Guard and the EPA).[38] The courts are divided over whether the "person" entitled to use immunity includes a corporation or only the flesh and blood "person in charge" who is obliged to report.[39] The better view is that the immunity provision, which is designed to honor the Fifth Amendment privilege against self-incrimination, protects individuals only. Otherwise, simple compliance with the reporting requirements would exempt a corporation from all Refuse Act and FWPCA liability for any discharges of oil or hazardous substances.

More serious is the objection that the civil penalty is in reality a criminal fine and that the self-reporting provisions of the Act therefore violate the Fifth Amendment privilege against self-incrimination. The courts are divided on the proposition,[40] with the better result favoring the constitutionality of section 311(b)(5). In the first place, although the question is a close one, the strict liability features and regulatory purposes of the penalties support a characterization of them as civil under traditional criteria.[41] Even if they are considered criminal, there is authority for the view[42] that

36. United States v. Skil Corp., 351 F. Supp. at 298, 3 ELR at 20842.

37. United States v. Kennecott Copper Corp., 523 F.2d 821, 5 ELR 20707 (9th Cir. 1975).

38. United States v. Kennecott Copper Corp., 523 F.2d at 824, 5 ELR at 20708; see 33 CFR § 153.105.

39. Compare United States v. Mobil Oil Corp., 464 F.2d 1124, 2 ELR 20456 (5th Cir. 1972) and United States v. Republic Steel Corp., 491 F.2d 315, 4 ELR 20276 (6th Cir. 1975) (following *Mobil Oil*) and United States v. United States Steel Corp., 2 ELR 20575 (W.D.Pa.1972) (allowing prosecution only if government's evidence was not obtained from notification) with United States v. Skil Corp., 351 F.Supp. 295, 3 ELR 20841 (N.D.Ill. 1972).

40. Compare United States v. Le Boeuf Bros. Towing Co., 377 F.Supp. 558 (E.D.La.1974), rev'd 537 F.2d 149, 6 ELR 20708 (5th Cir. 1976) (invalidating the notification provision) with United States v. W. B. Enterprises, Inc., 378 F.Supp. 420 (S.D.N.Y.1974) (upholding it) and United States v. Eureka Pipeline Co., 401 F.Supp. 934 (N.D.W.Va.1975) (same).

41. Kennedy v. Mendoza-Martinez, 372 U.S. 144, 168–69, 83 S.Ct. 554, 567–68, 9 L.Ed.2d 644, 660–62 (1963); see United States v. Mar-Tee Contractors, Inc., — F.Supp. —, 6 ELR 20417 (D.C.N.J.1976) (rejecting double jeopardy defense to criminal prosecution for oil spill after imposition of civil penalty). See also United States v. Baltimore & Carolina Line Inc., 382 F.2d 208 (4th Cir. 1967) (holding a fixed $100 penalty for negligent vessel operation to be a civil, not a criminal, sanction).

42. California v. Byers, 402 U.S. 424, 91 S.Ct. 1535, 29 L.Ed.2d 9 (1971) (upholding self-reporting under a state hit-and-run statute); Soper, The Constitutional Framework of Environmental Law, in Environmental Law Institute, Federal Environmental Law 20, 45–50 (E. L. Dolgin & T. G. P. Guilbert eds. 1974); Comment, Water

self-reporting nonetheless may be required if justified by noncriminal governmental purposes (such as the need for a quick cleanup). It would be unfortunate if one of the few efficient penalty systems in government regulation were nullified eventually on constitutional grounds not fairly applicable.

c. *Cleanup*

Hand in hand with the penalty scheme are the cleanup provisions. These are four in number: (1) preparation and publication of a National Contingency Plan for the removal of oil and hazardous substances and the prevention of spills;[43] (2) authorization of the United States to take summary action (including the removal and destruction of a vessel) "whenever a marine disaster in or upon the navigable waters of the United States has created a substantial threat of a pollution hazard to the public health or welfare of the United States, including, but not limited to, fish, shellfish, and wildlife and the public and private shorelines and beaches";[44] (3) authorization of the President to require the United States attorney in the relevant judicial district to seek judicial relief to abate any "imminent and substantial threat";[45] (4) imposition of costs of cleanup, within limits, upon the responsible owner or operator.[46]

The National Contingency Plan, developed by the Council on Environmental Quality, is in effect.[47] It is an elaborate plan for coordinating the activities of different government agencies to protect the environment from the damaging effects of spills. It also encourages the principal cleanup effort to be undertaken by the source of the spill.

Section 311 provides that an owner or operator shall be liable for actual costs incurred for the containment, dispersal and removal of oil under the National Contingency Plan. There are four exceptions: where an owner or operator can prove that a discharge was caused "solely by (A) an act of God, (B) an act of war, (C) negligence on the part of the United States Government, or (D) an act or omission of a third party without regard to whether any such act or omission was or was not negligent, or any combination of

Act's Oil Spill Notification Survives Constitutional Challenges, 6 ELR 10011 (1976).

43. Sections 311(c), (j), 33 U.S.C.A. § 1321(c), (j).

44. Section 311(d), 33 U.S.C.A. § 1321(d). Under this provision the owners of the Argo Merchant, which ran aground approximately 25 miles off Nantucket Island, Mass., are unlikely to be held liable for the more than $1 million spent by the U. S. Coast Guard to clean up the resulting spill of 7.5 million gallons of heavy industrial oil. See Wash. Post, Dec. 12, 1976, § A, at 1, col. 5. Compare note 4, supra.

45. Section 311(e), 33 U.S.C.A. § 1321(e).

46. Sections 311(f), (g), 33 U.S.C.A. § 1321(f), (g).

47. 40 Fed.Reg. 6282 (1975), 40 CFR pt. 1510. Further amendments were proposed in 41 Fed.Reg. 2396 (1976).

the foregoing causes." [48] There are limitations on this liability: not to exceed $100 per gross ton of the vessel or $14,000,000, whichever is less; not to exceed $8,000,000 for a discharge from an onshore or offshore facility. In all cases, the limitations can be overcome and liability imposed for the full amount of the costs if the United States can sustain a burden of showing that the discharge "was the result of willful negligence or willful misconduct within the privity and knowledge of the owner." [49] Any vessel over three hundred gross tons must maintain evidence of financial responsibility to meet its potential cleanup liabilities.[50] These filings are kept at the Federal Maritime Commission,[51] and are of no particular interest.

d. *Other Hazardous Substances*

One "major change" [52] wrought by the 1972 Amendments is the inclusion of other hazardous substances in the existing legal structure governing oil. Hazardous substances are treated like oil for purposes of financial responsibility, cleanup, compulsory notification and civil penalties. Hazardous substances, like oil, are not to be discharged into the waters "in harmful quantities as determined by the President." There is one problem: a substance does not become a "hazardous substance" until it is designated as such by the Administrator of EPA.[53] The guideline to be applied is whether a substance presents "an imminent and substantial danger to the public health or welfare, including, but not limited to, fish, shellfish, wildlife, shorelines, and beaches." [54] Late in 1975 the Administrator proposed [55] that 301 separate substances be designated "hazardous" under section 311. Also proposed for the same substances were designations of removability, determinations of harmful quantities and the fixing of penalty rates. Any quantity of a designated substance, according to the proposals,[56] is a "harmful quantity" if discharged into certain "special" waters (drinking water reservoirs, part of a designated National Wildlife Refuge System, National Forest Wilderness, National Park System or National Wilderness Preserve System). It goes without saying that the ultimate extension of section 311 to spills of hundreds of substances other than oil will represent a quantum leap in environmental law.

48. Sections 311(f)(1) (vessels), (f)(2) (onshore facility), (f)(3) (offshore facility), 33 U.S.C.A. § 1321(f)(1)–(3).

49. Ibid.

50. Section 311(p)(1), 33 U.S.C.A. § 1321(p)(1).

51. See 46 CFR pt. 542.

52. Lettow, The Control of Marine Pollution, in Environmental Law Institute, Federal Environmental Law 596, 610 (E. L. Dolgin & T. G. P. Guilbert eds. 1974).

53. Section 311(a)(14), 33 U.S.C.A. § 1321(a)(14).

54. Section 311(b)(2)(A), 33 U.S.C.A. § 1321(b)(2)(A).

55. 40 Fed.Reg. 59960 (1975), 40 CFR pts. 116–19.

56. 40 Fed.Reg. 59991 (1975), 40 CFR § 118.4.

§ 4.18 **Oil Pollution: Regulation**

The regulation of facilities involved in the handling and transfer of oil has proceeded apace. The Oil Pollution Act of 1924 was quite specific: "The Secretary of War is authorized and empowered to prescribe regulations for the loading, handling and unhandling of oil."[1] Not quite fifty years later administrative rules came into being but they did not arrive until after repeal of the 1924 Act. The source of today's regulation is subsection 311(j)[2] of the 1972 Amendments, which is the only broadly based regulatory authority in the oil and hazardous substances section. The subsection reads, in part: "Consistent with the National Contingency Plan . . . , the President shall issue regulations consistent with maritime safety and with marine and navigation laws" on various topics,[3] including prominently "procedures, methods, and equipment" to prevent discharges of oil and hazardous substances from vessels and from onshore facilities and offshore facilities. The references to "methods" and "equipment" quite clearly put the government in the business of prescribing methods of operation and control technology to contain oil and hazardous substance spills.

a. *Section 311(j) Regulations*

Under this provision the President delegated his powers partly to the Coast Guard for vessels and transportation-related onshore and offshore facilities, and partly to EPA for non-transportation related onshore and offshore facilities.[4] The EPA regulations[5] require the owner and operator of each facility that reasonably could be expected to discharge oil in harmful quantities to prepare a Spill Prevention Control and Countermeasure Plan containing minimum prevention facilities, restraints against drainage, an oil spill contingency plan, and so on. Considerable discretion is left to the operator under these regulations, with the exception of some detailed design specifications dealing with bulk storage tanks.[6]

The Coast Guard regulations,[7] on the other hand, "are filled with detailed standards covering equipment requirements, construc-

1. Section 3, 43 Stat. 604, 606.

2. 33 U.S.C.A. § 1321(j).

3. The regulations may deal with (1) establishing procedures for the removal of discharged oil and hazardous substances; (2) establishing criteria for the development of local and regional oil and hazardous substance removal contingency plans, and (3) the inspection of vessels carrying cargoes of oil and hazardous substances and the inspection of cargoes to reduce the likelihood of discharges.

4. Exec. Order No. 11548, 35 Fed.Reg. 11577 (1970), superseded by Exec. Order No. 11735, 38 Fed.Reg. 21243 (1973) (not affecting original allocation of responsibilities).

5. 50 CFR pt. 112.

6. 40 CFR § 112.7(e)(2), and others.

7. 33 CFR pts. 154 (large oil transfer facilities), 155 (vessel design and operations), 156 (oil transfer operations).

tion rules, and procedures for the operational transfer of oil to or from any vessel." [8] Generally, each facility that is covered [9] under the oil transfer provisions must submit a letter of intent to operate to the Captain of the Port not less than 60 days before it commences business.[10] The purpose is to give Coast Guard personnel an opportunity to inspect facilities directly; the letter of intent procedure was adopted specifically in lieu of a permit program.[11]

An imperfect analogue to this inspection and approval procedure is found in the Nuclear Regulatory Commission's staff oversight of the licensing of nuclear reactors. The operator of an oil transfer facility must submit an operations manual with the letter of intent—comparable to a license application to the NRC—describing operations procedures in detail. The Captain of the Port may require the facilities operator to amend the manual for noncompliance with regulatory requirements. These include detailed specifications regarding necessary equipment (hoses, closure devices, containment equipment), lighting, communications, recordkeeping and personnel.[12] The Captain of the Port has broad powers to suspend operations "if he finds that there is a condition requiring immediate action to prevent the discharge or threat of discharge of oil," [13] or to waive compliance with any of the regulations.[14] This form of administration, so common these days, makes the law peculiarly sensitive to the length of the administrator's foot.

The regulations on vessel design and operations are cut from the same cloth. The requirements are specific: the most important are those forbidding operation of a tank vessel with a capacity of 250 or more barrels without a means of removing oil from each container without discharging it into the water; [15] and those forbidding operation of a vessel of 100 or more gross tons unless it has a capacity to retain on board all oily waste and oily bilge slops.[16] Detailed requirements address the subjects of personnel qualifications, oil transfer procedures, adequate lighting, recordkeeping and so on.[17] The Captain of the Port has the power to suspend opera-

8. Lettow, The Control of Marine Pollution, in Environmental Law Institute, Federal Environmental Law 596, 634 (E. L. Dolgin & T. G. P. Guilbert eds. 1974).

9. The provisions apply to each onshore and offshore facility, when it transfers oil in bulk to or from any vessel that has a capacity of 250 or more barrels of oil except when it transfers—
   a. Lubricating oil for use on board a vessel; or
   b. Nonpetroleum based oil to or from a vessel other than a tank vessel.

10. 33 CFR § 154.100.

11. Id. § 154.320.

12. See id. §§ 154.500–.770.

13. Id. § 154.140.

14. Id. § 154.330.

15. Id. § 155.310.

16. Id. § 155.330.

17. Id. §§ 155.700–820; id. pt. 156.

tions [18] or to waive each and every requirement,[19] which makes the program entirely dependent upon the integrity of the regulator.

b. *Other Regulatory Statutes*

Two other statutes affect in vastly different but interrelated ways the design and operation of vessels principally responsible for oil pollution—the Ports and Waterways Safety Act of 1972 [20] and the Merchant Marine Act of 1970.[21] Before turning to the specifics of these sometimes schizophrenic laws, a reminder about remedial options is in order. The discussion of common law nuisance principles makes clear the differences, and sometimes the tension, between operational and technological controls.[22] Similar influences are found in efforts to control two major causes of oil pollution by vessels—casualty spills and intentional discharges from ballasting operations.[23] One way to reduce spills from tanker groundings or collisions is to improve traffic controls, an option provided for in the Ports and Waterways Safety Act. Another operational control technique, widely espoused and used, is the so-called "Load-On-Top" procedure, invoked to combat the common problem where empty tankers returning from a voyage pump seawater into tanks to provide stability, discharging it contaminated with oil during deballasting. The "Load-On-Top" allows time for oil and water in the tank to separate by normal operation of gravity, then calls for pumping the water overboard. The oily slop is retained on board and the next cargo loaded "on top" of it. Like intermittent controls on power plants or smelters,[24] the "Load-On-Top" practice rests on the shaky foundations of individual conscience, operator competence, sound training and good luck. As with power plants and copper smelters, technological modifications of the tankers themselves are advanced as alternatives—principally, double bottoms to protect against major casualties and segregated ballast (where oil and water never meet) to avoid intentional discharges from tank cleaning.[25]

18. Id. § 155.130.

19. Id. §§ 155.110, 156.107.

20. Pub.L. No. 92–340, 86 Stat. 427, 46 U.S.C.A. § 390 et seq.

21. Pub.L. No. 91–469, 84 Stat. 1018, 46 U.S.C.A. §§ 1151–61.

22. § 2.11 above.

23. The third identifiable cause is terminal spills. Of the three, ballasting operations probably account for "the greatest annual volume of oil discharged into the sea by ships" (1 million of 1.4 million tons annually).
Humble, Progress in Control of Marine Pollution, in 1972 Proceedings of the American Merchant Marine Conference 35.

24. See § 3.8 above.

25. For a discussion of some of the design alternatives, see Kinon, Kiss & Porricelli, Segregated Ballast VLCC's: An Economic Pollution Abatement Analysis, presented to the Chesapeake Section, Soc'y of Naval Architects and Marine Engineers, Jan. 11, 1973; Office of Technology Assessment, Oil Transportation by Tankers: An Analysis of Marine Pollution and Safety Measures (1975). See also Comm. on

The Ports and Waterways Safety Act is quite explicit in giving power to the Coast Guard to enforce technological and operational restrictions against tankers responsible for oil pollution. The legislative history puts the "emphasis on prevention." [26] An important part of that emphasis is traffic control and technological change (including segregated ballast and double bottoms). Section 101 [27] authorizes the Secretary of the Department in which the Coast Guard is operating to "establish, operate, and maintain vessel traffic services and systems for ports, harbors, and other waters subject to congested vessel traffic." The Coast Guard has initiated efforts to introduce traffic control systems in San Francisco Bay, Puget Sound and Houston-Galveston.[28] An increased federal presence in tanker trafficking will have two consequences on liability: it may result in liability being imposed on the government for negligent operations, and it may exempt tanker owners whose obligations under both the IMCO Civil Liability Convention and the cleanup provisions of Section 311 of FWPCA are relieved if the mishap can be assigned to government negligence.[29]

Section 201 of the Ports and Waterways Safety Act [30] extends broad rulemaking powers "for vessel safety" and "for the protection of the marine environment" to the Secretary of Transportation, including the authority to prescribe any rules "as may be necessary with respect to the design and construction, alteration, repair and maintenance of vessels, including, but not limited to, the superstructures, hulls, places for stowing and carrying cargo, fittings, equipment, appliances, propulsive machinery, auxiliary machinery and boilers . . . ." To the disappointment of some, the Coast Guard has been reluctant to use its powers to force modifications in tanker vessels beyond those called for in the section 311(j) regulations and the various international conventions dealing with oil pollution. Early in 1973, the Coast Guard issued an advance notice of proposed rulemaking that would have required segregated bal-

Commerce, Navigable Waters Safety and Environmental Quality Act of 1972, S.Rep. No. 724, 92d Cong., 2d Sess. 11–14 (1972) [hereinafter cited as Senate Report on Ports and Waterways Safety].

26. Id. at 4.

27. 46 U.S.C.A. § 1221.

28. Goldsmith, Puget Sound: The Evolution of a Vessel Traffic System (unpublished paper, prepared for a course in environmental law, Georgetown U. Law Center, Fall 1972); U.S. Coast Guard, Operating Manual: Puget Sound Vessel Traffic System, Sept. 1974; U.S. Coast Guard, Operating Manual: Houston-Galveston Vessel Traffic System, Feb. 1975. Section 402 of the Trans-Alaska Oil Pipeline Authorization Act, Pub.L. No. 93–153, 87 Stat. 589 (1973), mandates the establishment of a traffic control system for Prince William Sound and Valdez, Alaska.

29. Compare IMCO Convention on Civil Liability for Oil Pollution Damage, Nov. 29, 1969, art. III(2), 2 ELR 40307 (1972) with sections 311(f)(1), (2), (3), 33 U.S.C.A. § 1321(f)(1), (2), (3). For a brief discussion of the IMCO Conventions, see text accompanying notes 61–64, infra.

30. 46 U.S.C.A. § 391a.

last and double bottoms on future tank ships.[31] When proposed again in 1974,[32] the regulations had been modified substantially to require only segregated ballast for new vessels of 70,000 deadweight tons or more engaged in domestic trade. While regulations of this type will reduce the intentional pollution of the sea as a result of tank cleaning, pollution by accident (collision, grounding, structural failure) is not likely to be minimized significantly. For this reason, continuation of the debate over double bottoms and other structural changes to protect against catastrophe is certain.[33]

Working occasionally at cross-purposes with the objectives of Ports and Waterways Safety Act is the Merchant Marine Act of 1970 [34] which establishes for U. S. shipbuilders a tanker subsidy program, now administered by the Maritime Administration in the Department of Commerce. Without going into the details of the program,[35] it is sufficient to say that something in the neighborhood of fifty percent of the costs of a fleet of 50 or so crude oil carriers will

---

31. 38 Fed.Reg. 1748 (1973); see 39 Fed.Reg. 2467 (1973) (Coast Guard announcement that it would await the results of the October 1973 IMCO International Conference on Marine Pollution before proceeding further).

32. 39 Fed.Reg. 24150 (1974), proposing 33 CFR pts. 151, 157; see letter from Rebecca W. Hanmre, Acting Director, Office of Federal Activities, EPA, to Executive Secretary, Marine Safety Council, U.S. Coast Guard, Dec. 5, 1975 (commenting critically on the proposed rulemaking).

33. For a statement of the Coast Guard's position, see The Coast Guard's Approach to Tanker Pollution Abatement, Mar. 3, 1975, at 1, 4:
   Categorically stated, the Coast Guard is not opposed to double bottom construction of oil tankers. The Coast Guard is opposed to mandatorily, either legislatively or by a regulation, requiring that tankers be constructed with full length double bottoms because it would deny the possibility of other combinations of construction and operating standards for oil tankers which may provide better protection for our marine environment.
   . . .
   For reasons cited above, the Coast Guard is convinced that it is far more cost effective to place primary emphasis upon accident prevention features rather than construction features for mitigation of outflows. An exception would be those new tankers requiring segregated ballast to control operational pollution where attempts are continuing to identify an optional distribution as defensive space.
   Another frequently raised point is: Why aren't tankers required to have twin screws, twin rudders, bow thrusters, greater backing power, and controllable pitch propellers? Wouldn't all of these things reduce the risk of pollution from tanker accidents? These construction requirements might be able to improve the maneuvering capability of tankers somewhere in the range of 5 to 30 percent. Wouldn't this result in less pollution? The available evidence does not seem to indicate it would.

34. Pub.L. No. 91–469, 84 Stat. 1018, 46 U.S.C.A. §§ 1151–61.

35. For an outline of the program and its environmental effects, see Maritime Subsidy Board, In re Environmental Review of the Maritime Administration Tanker Construction Program, Dkt. No. A–75, Aug. 13, 1973; see Maritime Administration, Final Environmental Impact Statement on the Maritime Tanker Construction Program (1973); Maritime Administration, Economic Viability Analysis of the Maritime Tanker Construction Program (1973).

be financed in the next decade by the U. S. government. These "new sources" of oil pollution will be in service for some twenty-five years and will be of a design difficult if not impossible to retrofit for pollution control purposes. It is fair to suggest that a new generation of tankers should be designed to reflect the "best technology" to control its effluent (including segregated ballast and double bottoms if that is the prescription). The Maritime Administration is slow to see it that way although litigation compelled the agency to open its decision-making process to the demands of the National Environmental Policy Act.[36] Some steps have been taken to mandate for subsidized tankers certain pollution abatement and collision avoidance features in the Mar Ad Standard Specifications for Merchant Ship Construction.[37] But the fact remains these new tankers will be less than the "best" known to the law of pollution control.

A potentially powerful but as yet latent regulatory scheme for controlling and preventing oil pollution is found in the Deepwater Port Act of 1974.[38] A deepwater port is an offshore tanker moorage where oil can be unloaded and piped ashore. Enacted in the expectation that domestic deepwater ports will be needed to accommodate the international oil trade, the legislation sets up a licensing mechanism, administered by the Secretary of Transportation, to control the selection of sites. Environmental considerations weigh heavily in the decision to locate a port.[39] A strict liability scheme is established for oil spills.[40] "Subject to recognized principles of international law," the Secretary must promulgate regulations governing "vessel movement, loading and unloading procedures" to prevent pollution and otherwise minimize environmental effects.[41] While these powers are not unimportant, they fall short of the sweeping authority over vessel movement and design found in the Ports and Waterways Safety Act of 1972. The reference to "recognized principles of international law" also gives the Secretary a statutory justification, not found in the 1972 Act, for conforming regulations under the Deepwater Port Act to the mild precautions of international law.

36. Environmental Defense Fund, Inc. v. Peterson, 4 ELR 20298 (D.D.C. 1973); see Huffman, The Opportunities for Environmentalists in the Settlement of NEPA Suits, 4 ELR 50001 (1974).

37. See Decision of the Maritime Subsidy Board, supra note 35.

38. Pub.L. No. 93–627, 88 Stat. 2126, 33 U.S.C.A. § 1501–24; see Meltz, Deepwater Port Act of 1974: Half Speed Ahead, 5 ELR 50043 (1975).

39. See section 6, 33 U.S.C.A. § 1506.

40. See section 18, 33 U.S.C.A. § 1518.

41. Section 10(a), 33 U.S.C.A. § 1510(a). Under section 4(c)(5), 33 U.S.C.A. § 1504(c)(5), the issuance of a license is dependent upon the Secretary determining "that the applicant has demonstrated that the deepwater port will be constructed and operated using best available technology, so as to prevent or minimize adverse impact on the marine environment." See 40 Fed.Reg. 52563 (1975) (Environmental Review Criteria).

c. *Offshore Drilling*

A separate and distinct regulatory system for some types of oil spills is found in the Outer Continental Shelf Lands Act of 1953,[42] which authorizes the Secretary of the Interior to grant oil and gas leases "on submerged lands of the Outer Continental Shelf"[43] not reserved to the states by the Submerged Lands Act of 1953.[44] The Outer Continental Shelf is the gently sloping plain underlying the seas adjacent to most land masses, extending seaward to the point where there is a marked increase in the gradient of the decline leading to the ocean bottom.[45] The Continental Shelf, in some places like the Gulf of Mexico, may extend as much as 200 miles from shore. The Submerged Lands Act reserves to the states jurisdiction over oil and gas (and other) resources offshore to a distance of three geographical miles (about 3.45 land miles) for most states, nine geographical (10.5 land) miles for Texas and Florida.[46] Recently, the Supreme Court unanimously rejected attempts by several states to assert authority over the seabed of the Outer Continental Shelf beyond the areas reserved to them by the Submerged Lands Act.[47]

The principal statutory mandate of the Outer Continental Shelf Lands Act is a loose directive to the Secretary of the Interior to prescribe rules and regulations deemed "necessary and proper in order to provide for the prevention of waste and conservation of the natural resources of the Outer Continental Shelf, and the protection of correlative rights therein."[48] This includes the power to suspend operations or production and insist upon a wide range of environmental protection measures.[49] The environmental protection regulations are administered by the U. S. Geological Survey.[50] They con-

---

42. 67 Stat. 462, 43 U.S.C.A. §§ 1331–43.

43. 43 U.S.C.A. § 1333(e)(1).

44. 67 Stat. 29, 43 U.S.C.A. §§ 1301–15.

45. 43 U.S.C.A. § 1331(a); United States v. Louisiana, 363 U.S. 1, 5 n. 3, 80 S.Ct. 961, 966 n. 3, 4 L.Ed.2d 1025, 1032 n. 3 (1960). President Truman's unilateral claim for the United States, as against the rest of the world, to the mineral sources in the submerged lands of the Continental Shelf adjacent to our coasts (Presidential Proclamation No. 2667, Sept. 28, 1945, 10 Fed.Reg. 12303, 59 Stat. 884) for all practical purposes is accepted internationally under the 1958 Geneva Convention on the Continental Shelf, Apr. 29, 1958, 15 U.S.T. 471, T.I.A.S. No. 5578 (1964), which allows the coastal state to exploit resources on the shelf "to a depth of 200 meters or, beyond that limit, to where the depth of the superjacent waters admits of the exploitation of the natural resources." Id., art. 1. For the geological problems with a 200 meters limit, see Hedberg, Ocean Boundaries and Petroleum Resources, 191 Science 1009 (1976).

46. United States v. Louisiana, 363 U.S. 1, 80 S.Ct. 961, 4 L.Ed.2d 1025 (1960); United States v. Florida, 363 U.S. 121, 80 S.Ct. 1026, 4 L.Ed.2d 1096 (1960).

47. United States v. Maine, 420 U.S. 515, 95 S.Ct. 1155, 43 L.Ed.2d 363 (1975).

48. 33 U.S.C.A. § 1334(a)(1).

49. Gulf Oil Corp. v. Morton, 493 F.2d 141, 4 ELR 20086 (9th Cir. 1973); Union Oil Co. v. Morton, 512 F.2d 743, 5 ELR 20218 (9th Cir. 1975).

50. 30 CFR pt. 250.

tain general prohibitions against polluting the environment [51] and specific directives for pollution control and waste disposal.[52] Additional legal requirements can be found in general USGS orders governing operations in a particular area. The regulations impose strict liability for cleanup and removal costs [53] but, beyond this, liability questions are governed by state or maritime law.[54] Government decisions to lease are plainly "major Federal actions" for purposes of the National Environmental Policy Act, and leasing decisions are sharply contested in the courts.[55]

Even within the rude confines of the Outer Continental Shelf Lands Act, the Secretary clearly has the power to attach and enforce lease conditions reasonably related to the protection of the marine environment, up to and including suspending operations and production "in the interest of conservation" to allow Congress time to consider legislation cancelling the leases.[56] Although the Secretary may have legitimate environmental grounds for suspending operations, however, he must carefully explain his reasons for doing so, not merely waive an environmental flag.[57] A suspension must be terminable on the occurrence of events anticipated within a reasonable time and, if it is not, may ripen into a taking of the lessee's property rights which is beyond the scope of the Administrator's power.[58] In the near future, Congress may take a hand in fleshing out the Secretary's responsibility to protect the environment in light of increasing interest in federal OCS leasing.[59] Ultimately, here as elsewhere, the force of the law will turn not so much upon questions of power but upon the integrity of its administration.[60]

51. Id. § 250.43.

52. Ibid.

53. Id. § 250.43(b).

54. See § 4.19 below.

55. E. g., Natural Resources Defense Council, Inc. v. Morton, 148 U.S.App. D.C. 5, 458 F.2d 827, 2 ELR 20029 (1972); Sierra Club v. Morton, 510 F.2d 813, 5 ELR 20249 (5th Cir. 1975); California v. Morton, 404 F.Supp. 26, 6 ELR 20088 (C.D.Cal.1975); Southern Cal. Ass'n of Governments v. Kleppe, 413 F.Supp. 563, 6 ELR 20115 (D.D.C.1975).

56. Gulf Oil Corp. v. Morton, 493 F.2d 141, 144, 4 ELR 20086, 20087 (9th Cir. 1973) ("a careful reading of the statutes leads us to the conclusion that Congress authorized the Secretary to suspend operations under existing leases whenever he determines that the risk to the marine environment outweighs the immediate national interest in exploring and drilling for oil and gas"); see Santa Barbara v. Hickel, 426 F.2d 164 (9th Cir. 1970) (county has no right to a public hearing prior to the allowance of additional drilling under previously suspended leases).

57. Union Oil Co. v. Morton, 512 F.2d 743, 5 ELR 20218 (9th Cir. 1975).

58. Union Oil Co. v. Morton, 512 F. 2d at 750–51, 5 ELR at 20220–21.

59. Bills include S.521 and S.1186, 93d Cong., 1st Sess. 1975; see Hearings on Offshore Oil Development Administration, Before the Subcomm. on Minerals, Materials, and Fuels of the Senate Comm. on Interior and Insular Affairs, 93d Cong., 1st Sess. (1975).

60. See General Accounting Office, Improved Inspection and Regulation Could Reduce the Possibility of Oil

d. *International Regulation*

Much mooted but of limited practical effect on the subject of oil spills are the efforts of the International Governmental Maritime Consultative Organization (IMCO) which is a specialized agency of the United Nations established to deal with a variety of maritime affairs. Through its operating arms, IMCO is responsible for the 1954 International Convention for the Prevention of Pollution of the Sea by Oil and the 1973 International Convention for the Prevention of Pollution from Ships.[61] The 1954 Convention[62] forbade some types of discharges (with a content of 100 parts per million or more) from some types of tankers in some areas (namely, "prohibited zones," typically extending 50 miles from the nearest land). Enforcement, such as it was, was dependent upon the keeping of oil discharge record books by the skipper of each member vessel, and enforcement by the flag state, the latter being aptly described as "no enforcement at all,"[63] and the former as something less than that. The 1973 Convention[64] tightens up several provisions and calls for the mandatory installation of effluent monitoring and control systems and segregated ballast (so that oil and water do not mix) on new tankers of 10,000 deadweight tons or greater. But it lacks meaningful enforcement mechanisms and in any event will not take effect until twelve months after at least fifteen states, with combined merchant fleets constituting not less than half of the gross tonnage of the world's merchant shipping, have submitted articles of acceptance with IMCO. It would appear that the Coast Guard's domestic role as regulator is not in imminent danger of being preempted by international authority. One wonders, then, why the Coast Guard is extremely reluctant to forge ahead of the mild international constraints in fashioning rules for domestic shipping.

e. *State Regulation*

Widespread public concern over oil pollution has prompted an increasing number of state legislatures to enact laws combining strict liability with strict regulation of oil carriers and terminal facilities.[65]

Spills on the Outer Continental Shelf, June 1973.

61. Important references include Benkert, The Impact of the 1973 I. M. C. O. Convention on the Maritime Industry, 1974 Marine Technology 1; Dinstein, Oil Pollution by Ships and Freedom of the High Seas, 35 Maritime L. 363 (1972); Mendelsohn, Ocean Pollution and the 1972 United Nations Conference on the Environment, 3 J. Maritime L. 385 (1972); R. M. Hallman, Towards An Environmentally Sound Law of the Sea (1974) (Report of the International Institute for Environment and Development).

62. Convention for the Prevention of Pollution of the Sea by Oil, May 12, 1954, 12 U.S.T. 2989, T.I.A.S. No. 4900 (1961).

63. U. S. Coast Guard, Draft Environmental Impact Statement on the 1973 Convention, June 1973, at 78.

64. See Benkert, note 61, supra.

65. E. g., California, Miller Anti-Pollution Act of 1971, Ann.Cal.Harb. & Navig.Code § 293; Connecticut, Gen. Stat.Ann. § 25–54ee; Maryland, Ann. Nat.Res.Code § 8–1409; Massachusetts, Ann.Laws of Mass. ch. 21, § 27 (10); Michigan, Watercraft Pollution

The Washington Tanker Act,[66] for example, seeks to protect local waters by requiring oil tankers of a certain size (greater than 50,000 deadweight tons) to take on a Washington state licensed pilot while navigating in Puget Sound, by prohibiting very large crude carriers (greater than 125,000 deadweight tons) from entering the Sound altogether, and by requiring other tankers to possess standard safety features while navigating in the Sound, including twin screws (which improve maneuverability), double bottoms, collision avoidance radar and other navigational position location systems. The validity of these laws obviously is a close question. The Washington statute offers an excellent test case,[67] involving as it does an industry that is truly international and in need of uniform regulation and a state resource (Puget Sound) that is fragile, unique, highly productive, and in need of protection. One legal issue raised by this type of legislation is whether it constitutes an unreasonable burden on commerce. State attempts to ban tankers that threaten local resources raise the same genre of questions as do state attempts to protect local interests by banning imported garbage,[68] nonreturnable beverage containers[69] or detergents.[70] This "calls for an analysis of the justification for the ban, its effects and whether less restrictive alternatives are available."[71] Under these tests it would be difficult to invalidate local traffic restrictions or a requirement that a local pilot be taken on board to assist in navigation. The navigational design requirements and particularly the ban on large vessels are more difficult to justify. Yet, if as appears likely, the transportation of oil can proceed within these requirements, the Washington law stands a chance of surviving. Surely a state's power to protect its citizens from ecological disaster is not contracted indefinitely as an international technology becomes ever more inflexible.

A second question raised by state laws like that of Washington's is preemption. Under the Ports and Waterways Safety Act the Coast Guard clearly is given authority to regulate oil tanker design and

---

Control Act of 1970, Mich.Comp.Laws § 323.337; New Jersey, N.J.S.A. § 23:5–28; see § 4.19 n. 31 below (citing the Florida, Maine and Washington statutes).

66. Rev.Code Wash. § 88.16.170 et seq.

67. Atlantic Richfield Co. v. Evans, —— F.Supp. ——, 7 ELR 20071 (W.D. Wash.1976) (per curiam) (3-judge court), cert. granted —— U.S. —— (1977).

68. Hackensack Meadowlands Dev. Comm'n v. Municipal Sanitary Landfill Authority, 68 N.J. 451, 348 A.2d 505, 6 ELR 20356 (1975), vacated and remanded sub nom. Philadelphia v. New Jersey —— U.S. ——, 97 S.Ct. 987, 51 L.Ed.2d 224 (1977).

69. American Can Co. v. Oregon Liquor Control Comm'n, 15 Or.App. 618, 517 P.2d 691, 4 ELR 20218 (1973).

70. Soap & Detergent Ass'n v. Chicago, 357 F.Supp. 44, 3 ELR 20228 (N.D.Ill.1973) rev'd sub nom Proctor & Gamble, Inc. v. Chicago, 509 F.2d 69, 5 ELR 20146 (7th Cir. 1975), cert. denied 421 U.S. 978.

71. § 6.7 below (discussing the New Jersey garbage ban).

movement.[72] Active regulation by the Coast Guard manifestly would preempt inconsistent state regulation.[73] The question ultimately boils down to how pervasive Congress intended the federal presence to be.[74] It is not clear, however, that Congress intended to preempt something (state law) with nothing (an unfulfilled expectation of federal regulation).[75] The national legislature is quite likely to act again to spell out the permissible reach of state law in this delicate and evolving area.

§ 4.19 Oil Pollution: Compensation

In recent years, Congress has given consideration to a comprehensive compensation system for damages and cleanup costs occasioned by oil pollution of the marine environment.[1] Meanwhile, the rules governing compensation for oil spill damage, in ascending order of significance, are found in (1) federal maritime law, both statutory and common law; (2) state law, where recent statutory developments have supplemented considerably available common law remedies; (3) international law; and (4) voluntary compensatory arrangements,

---

72. Pub.L. No. 92–340, § 201, 86 Stat. 430, 46 U.S.C.A. § 391a(7).

73. See Northern States Power Co. v. Minnesota, 447 F.2d 1143, 1 ELR 20451 (8th Cir. 1971), aff'd mem. 405 U.S. 1035, 92 S.Ct. 1307, 31 L.Ed.2d 576 (1972).

74. The preemption effect of the Ports and Waterways Safety Act is unclear. See section 102(b), 46 U.S.C.A. § 1222(b) ("Nothing contained in this title . . . prevent[s] a State or political subdivision thereof from prescribing for structures only higher safety equipment requirements or standards than those which may be prescribed pursuant to this title"). The title (Title I) referred to in this provision, however, relates to structures on or in navigable waters and does not concern vessel design or regulation (Title II). See also § 4.19 below (discussing limited preemptive effect of FWPCA as interpreted by Askew v. American Waterways Operators, Inc., 411 U.S. 325, 93 S.Ct. 1590, 36 L.Ed.2d 280 (1973)).

75. Cf. J. Esposito, Vanishing Air 148–49 (1970) (discussing an attempt by John H. Schaffer, former Administrator of the Federal Aviation Administration, to head off state regulation of air pollution from aircraft with a speech promising federal regulation).

1. See S. 1754, 94th Cong., 1st Sess. (1975); S. 2162, 94th Cong., 1st Sess. (1975); 121 Cong.Rec. S8274–78 (daily ed. May 15, 1975) (remarks of Senator Magnuson upon introduction of S. 1754). See also Message from the President of the United States, Comprehensive Oil Pollution Liability and Compensation, H.R.Doc. No. 214, 94th Cong., 1st Sess. (1975); Dep't of Justice, Methods and Procedures for Implementing a Uniform Law Providing Liability for Cleanup Costs and Damages Caused by Oil Spills from Ocean Related Sources, Senate Comm. on Commerce, 94th Cong., 1st Sess. (Comm. Print 1975); Hearings on Oil Pollution Liability, Before the Subcomm. on Coast Guard and Navigation of the House Comm. on Merchant Marine and Fisheries, H.R. Doc. No. 21, 94th Cong., 1st & 2d Sess. (1976); Wood, Toward Compatible International and Domestic Regimes of Civil Liability for Oil Pollution of Navigable Waters, 5 ELR 50116 (1975); Mendelsohn, Maritime Liability for Oil Pollution—Domestic and International Law, 38 Geo.Wash. L.Rev. 195 (1968); Note, Civil Liability for Oil Pollution, 10 Hous.L. Rev. 394 (1973).

with the latter two categories offering little by way of meaningful relief from oil spill damage.

a. *Federal Law*

Admiralty jurisdiction of the federal courts extends to tortious acts occurring upon navigable waters of the United States and bearing a significant relationship to a traditional maritime activity.[2] This includes, quite clearly, damage caused by vessel spills of oil and hazardous substances on navigable waters,[3] reaching, by reason of the Admiralty Extension Act,[4] instances where the actual injury is sustained on land. Similarly, all damage proximately caused by oil spill accidents at fixed structures for offshore drilling are governed by general maritime law although an ambiguous reference to the law of the adjacent state in the Outer Continental Shelf Lands Act[5] complicates the choice of the governing law. In any event, recovery has been allowed for lost recreational[6] and commercial fishing[7] opportunities and for damages to pleasure boats[8] although not for the loss by boat owners of the opportunity to navigate in the Santa Barbara Channel.[9] It is clear also that a state may sue *parens patriae* on behalf of its citizens as a trustee of its natural resources to collect for environmental damage caused by oil pollution.[10]

2. Executive Jet Aviation, Inc. v. Cleveland, 409 U.S. 249, 93 S.Ct. 493, 34 L.Ed.2d 454 (1970).

3. State Dep't of Fish & Game v. S. S. Bournemouth, 307 F.Supp. 922 (C.D. Cal.1969); State Dept. of Fish & Game v. S. S. Bournemouth, 318 F. Supp. 839 (C.D.Cal.1970); G. Gilmore & C. Black, The Law of Admiralty 21 (1957).

4. 62 Stat. 496, 46 U.S.C.A. § 740.

5. 67 Stat. 462, 43 U.S.C.A. § 1333(a)(2); see Oppen v. Aetna Ins. Co., 485 F.2d 252, 3 ELR 20808 (9th Cir. 1973); Union Oil Co. v. Oppen, 501 F.2d 558, 4 ELR 20618 (9th Cir. 1974).

6. In re New Jersey Barging Corp., 168 F.Supp. 925 (S.D.N.Y.1959) (applying federal maritime law).

7. Union Oil Co. v. Oppen, 501 F.2d 558, 4 ELR 20618 (9th Cir. 1974) (suggesting federal maritime law applies but finding no differences if California law applied).

8. Oppen v. Aetna Ins. Co., 485 F.2d 252, 3 ELR 20808 (9th Cir. 1973).

9. Oppen v. Aetna Ins. Co., supra note 8 (reserving decision on whether federal maritime or state law applies) (under state nuisance law recovery is disallowed on ground that plaintiffs' damages are not different in kind from those suffered by the public at large; see § 2.2 above).

10. Maine v. M/V Tamano, 357 F.Supp. 1097, 3 ELR 20567 (D.C.Me.1973); Maryland v. Amerada Hess Corp., 350 F.Supp. 1060, 2 ELR 20606 (D.C. Md.1972); California Dept. of Fish & Game v. S. S. Bournemouth, 307 F. Supp. 922, 318 F.Supp. 839 (C.D.Cal. 1970); cf. North Dakota v. Minnesota, 263 U.S. 365, 44 S.Ct. 138, 68 L.Ed. 342 (1923) (*parens patriae* suit to restrain drainage changes increasing the flow of water in an interstate stream); New York v. New Jersey, 256 U.S. 296, 41 S.Ct. 492, 65 L.Ed. 937 (1921) (suit to enjoin sewage discharges into New York harbor); Georgia v. Tennessee Copper Co., 206 U.S. 230, 27 S.Ct. 618, 51 L.Ed. 1038 (1910) (interstate air pollution); Kansas v. Colorado, 206 U.S. 46, 27 S.Ct. 655, 51 L.Ed. 956 (1907) (diversion of water from an interstate stream); Missouri v. Illinois, 180 U.S. 208, 21 S.Ct. 331, 45 L.Ed. 497 (1901) (pollution by sewage of the Mississippi River). Compare § 2.16 above (public trust doctrine).

Success in a lawsuit for oil spill damages is complicated by predictable barriers—finding a defendant, overcoming subtle causation and burden of proof problems. It is further hampered by two severe limitations upon the scope of relief available in admiralty. The first flows from the Limited Liability Act of 1851,[11] which usually limits the liability of the owner of a vessel to the value of the ship and her "freight pending" when the ship causes injury without his "privity or knowledge." The absurdity of this long-standing doctrine was applied with a vengeance to limit the owner's liability to United States claimants in the *Torrey Canyon* disaster to the grand sum of fifty dollars—the value of one surviving lifeboat.[12]

A second barrier in admiralty jurisdiction is that the traditional statement of liability to persons and property not associated with the vessel requires proof of negligence or a breach of warranty of seaworthiness of the vessel (which amounts to the same thing as negligence).[13] This often means the scope of recovery under federal law will be coextensive with that afforded by state law, and it certainly means that state tort principles (both common law and statutory) will influence the content of federal maritime law.[14] But there is a divergence, and it is becoming more pronounced to the detriment of those whose remedies are limited to federal law, with the widespread adoption of state statutes imposing liability without regard to fault for damages caused by oil pollution.[15]

The extent to which the state strict liability laws can be enforced against activities within admiralty jurisdiction was raised in Askew v. American Waterways Operators, Inc.,[16] which held that the Florida Act imposing strict liability for certain oil spill damage was neither federally preempted nor an unconstitutional intrusion upon federal maritime authority. *Askew* has been criticized for neglecting to answer a number of questions not before the Court: Can Florida impose damages above the maximum of the federal Limited Liability Act? Can Florida extend its strict liability to all oil pollution-caused damages in its territorial waters or only to the area encompassed by the Admiralty Extension Act? Can Florida regulate, let us say,

---

11. 9 Stat. 635, now codified with amendments in 46 U.S.C.A. § 183.

12. In re Barracuda Tanker Corp., 281 F.Supp. 228 (S.D.N.Y.1968); see In re Harbor Towing Corp., 335 F.Supp. 1150, 2 ELR 20310 (D.C.Md.1971) (applying limitation of liability to an oil spill in Baltimore harbor).

13. See The Clara, 102 U.S. 200, 26 L.Ed. 145 (1880); Maryland v. Amerada Hess Corp., 350 F.Supp. 1060, 2 ELR 20606 (D.C.Md.1972) (refusing to apply seaworthiness doctrine in an oil spill case).

14. Oppen v. Aetna Ins. Co., 485 F.2d 252, 3 ELR 20808 (9th Cir. 1973); Union Oil Co. v. Oppen, 501 F.2d 558, 4 ELR 20618 (9th Cir. 1974); see Shutler, Pollution of the Sea by Oil, 7 Hous.L.Rev. 415, 434 (1970); Comment, Oil Pollution of the Sea, 10 Harv.Int'l L.J. 316, 347 (1969); Comment, A Reinforced Admiralty Remedy for Oil Spill Damage, 3 Law & Pol.Int'l Bus. 210 (1971).

15. See note 31, infra.

16. 411 U.S. 325, 93 S.Ct. 1590, 36 L.Ed.2d 280, 3 ELR 20362 (1973).

containment equipment inconsistently with the Coast Guard? But the Court did make clear Florida could impose strict liability for damages to some property interests, could require evidence of financial responsibility of a terminal facility or vessel, and could collect its costs in cleaning up the spillage. A crucial determinant of the decision was Section 311(o)(2) [17] of the 1972 FWPCA Amendments which makes clear that the section was not intended to preempt states or localities from imposing "any requirement or liability" with respect to the discharge of oil or hazardous substances into the waters of a state.

In the future, the preemption debate will proceed, as it should, on a case by case basis. The most important question of whether the states can ignore the federal Limited Liability Act surely is not answered decisively by a Congress of a century ago which we now know meant that the U. S. victims of the Torrey Canyon must be content with dividing up the proceeds of a fifty dollar lifeboat. Congress has spoken more recently and has said that oil should not be discharged upon navigable waters and the adjoining shorelines.[18] It would be difficult to read that expression as disavowing state laws seeking to saddle offenders of that advice with the costs of their transgressions. Indeed, it would be difficult to read it any way other than as approving state created remedies without regard to the ancient Limited Liability Act.

Three recent federal statutes address in various ways the oil spill liability problem. The provisions in the FWPCA allowing the government, within limits, to recover the costs of cleanup [19] are no help to an injured private party. One unsuccessful attempt has been made to imply a remedy from section 311 in favor of a private party damaged by a discharge from a pipeline and enforce it under the citizen suit provisions.[20] While an implied remedy is plausible, it is more likely the federal courts will await specific instruction from the Congress. The most important contribution of Section 311 of the FWPCA on the oil spill liability question is that it clearly preserves state remedies and may invite state supplementation of the Limitation of Liability Act.

Congress has enacted two explicit partial remedies for oil pollution damage, while disavowing a general intention to preempt. Sec-

---

17. 33 U.S.C.A. § 1321(o)(2), reads in full:

Nothing in this section shall be construed as preempting any State or political subdivision thereof from imposing any requirement or liability with respect to the discharge of oil or hazardous substance into any waters within such state.

18. Section 311(b)(1), 33 U.S.C.A. § 1321(b)(1); see § 4.17 above.

19. See § 4.17 above.

20. Weltner v. Producers Pipeline Co., —— F.Supp. —— (D.Kan.1975). Compare § 1.13 above (citizen suits).

tion 204 of the Trans-Alaska Pipeline Authorization Act [21] sets up a Trans-Alaska Pipeline Liability Fund that may sue or be sued in its own name. It is administered by the holders of the trans-Alaska pipeline right-of-way and funded by a fee of five cents per barrel assessed against the owner of the oil at the time it is loaded from the pipeline onto a vessel. The Fund, in certain circumstances, and the right-of-way holders are made strictly liable for damages "in connection with or resulting from activities along or in the vicinity of the proposed Trans-Alaskan pipeline" and "for all damages, including cleanup costs, sustained by any person or entity, public or private, including residents of Canada, as a result of discharges of oil" from vessels loaded at the terminal facilities of the pipeline.[22] Defenses paralleling those in Section 311 of FWPCA apply in the event of act of war, negligence of a government entity or of the damaged party.[23]

Ceilings on strict liability of fifty million and one hundred million dollars, respectively, are set for pipeline-related damage and vessel-related damage. Vessel liability is limited to $14 million per incident, with claims beyond that to the limits of the ceiling payable out of the Liability Fund. The TAP compensation system approaches strict liability for victims with the good fortune of having their misfortune traceable to oil carried by the Trans-Alaska pipeline.

A second *ad hoc* congressional venture into compensation for oil pollution damage is found in the Deepwater Port Act of 1974.[24] The Act gives the Secretary of Transportation a licensing authority to regulate the siting of deepwater ports but touches tangentially the liability question. The Act establishes a Deepwater Port Liability Fund, patterned after the TAP Fund, to be administered by the Secretary and supported by a fee of two cents per barrel assessed against the owner of any oil loaded or unloaded at the deepwater port.[25] Subject to another set of limitations and exceptions, the owner and operator of a vessel and the licensee of a deepwater port are strictly liable for cleanup costs and damages resulting from oil discharges from vessels moored at the port or within a "safety zone" around it. The Fund is strictly liable for costs and cleanup not compensated by others. Damages are defined broadly to include all losses (except cleanup costs) "suffered by any person, or involving real or personal property, the natural resources of the marine environment, or the coastal environment of any nation, including damages claimed without regard to any ownership of any affected lands, structures, fish, wildlife, or biotic or natural resources." [26] This might very well be read

21. Pub.L. No. 93–153, § 204(c)(4), 87 Stat. 587 (1973), 43 U.S.C.A. § 1653 (c)(4).

22. Pub.L. No. 93–153, §§ 204(a)(1), (c)(1), 87 Stat. 586, 43 U.S.C.A. §§ 1653 (a)(1), (c)(1).

23. 43 U.S.C.A. § 1653(c)(2).

24. Pub.L. No. 93–627, 88 Stat. 2126, 33 U.S.C.A. §§ 1501–24.

25. Sections 18(f)(1), (3), 33 U.S.C.A. §§ 1517(f)(1), (3).

26. Section 18(m)(2), 33 U.S.C.A. § 1517(m)(2).

as abandoning or narrowing proximate cause limitations on damages and to allow recovery for prospective economic losses not otherwise protected. The Attorney General (and in some instances private persons) may maintain a class action for damages in appropriate cases.[27] Another interesting provision authorizes the Secretary of Transportation to act "on behalf of the public as trustee of the natural resources of the marine environment" to recover damages in court.[28] Yet another provision, which may prove to be the most productive in the long run, directs several agencies under the auspices of the Attorney General "to study methods and procedures for implementing a uniform law providing liability for cleanup costs and damages from oil spills from Outer Continental Shelf operations, deepwater ports, vessels, and other ocean related sources."[29] A comprehensive legal treatment of oil spill liability is on the horizon, even if it results in approving the fragmentation inherent in a federal system and sporadic national legislative efforts.

b. *State Law*

At the state level, damages from spills of oil and other hazardous substances are governed by traditional negligence or, more likely, strict liability for abnormally dangerous activities.[30] Common law doctrines are being supplemented substantially by the adoption of statutes imposing strict liability for oil pollution damage.[31] A familiar technique is to impose strict liability and assure recovery for damaged claimants by requiring oil tanker owners to establish proof of financial responsibility within the state. After *Askew*,[32] these laws have good prospects of survival unless a clear conflict with a federal directive can be found.

Another approach, originating in the State of Maine, is to impose fees upon oil terminal operators to support funds used for cleanup and compensation purposes. These funds have survived challenges

---

27. Sections 18(i)(1), (2), 33 U.S.C.A. §§ 1517(i)(1), (2); see note 10, supra.

28. Section 18(i)(3), 33 U.S.C.A. § 1517(i)(3). Compare § 2.16 above (public trust doctrine).

29. Section 18(n)(1), 33 U.S.C.A. § 1517(n)(1); see Dep't of Justice, Methods and Procedures for Implementing a Uniform Law Providing for Cleanup Costs and Damages Caused by Oil Spills from Ocean Related Sources, Senate Comm. on Commerce, 94th Cong., 1st Sess. (Comm. Print 1975).

30. Green v. General Petroleum Corp., 205 Cal. 328, 270 P.2d 952 (1928) (blow-out of an oil well); see Union Oil Co. v. Oppen, 501 F.2d 558, 563 n. 3, 4 ELR 20618, 20620 n. 3 (9th Cir. 1974) (reserving question of strict liability); § 2.14 above.

31. Florida, Pollution Spill Prevention and Control Act, Fla.Stat.Ann. § 376.011 et seq.; Maine, Oil Discharge Prevention and Pollution Control Act, Me.Rev.Stat.Ann. ch. 38, § 541 et seq.; Washington, Oil Spill Act, Rev.Code Wash. ch. 90.48. Compare Lansco, Inc. v. Dep't of Environmental Protection, 138 N.J.Super. 275, 350 A.2d 520, 6 ELR 20247 (1975) (holding insurer liable for strict liability cleanup costs of an oil spill). See Bergman, No Fault for Oil Pollution, 5 J. Maritime L. & Com. 1 (1973).

32. Note 16, supra.

in the courts.³³ They obviously avoid the problem of applying a different liability regime to a vessel owner engaged in international trade. Maine accomplishes the same result, however, by imposing vicarious liability upon an oil terminal for discharges from any tanker destined for the terminal from the time the vessel enters the United States contiguous zone (the 12 mile limit).³⁴ Because the terminal operator is in a position to pass the costs along and include them in the ultimate cost of the product, imposing liability for the conduct of another seems grounded on sufficient rationality to overcome due process objections.

c. *International Law and Voluntary Agreements*

A comprehensive treatment of liability for oil spill damage is found in two treaties drafted under the auspices of the Intergovernmental Maritime Consultative Organization (IMCO), a specialized agency of the United Nations influenced in no small part by the international petroleum industry. The treaties are the International Convention on Civil Liability for Oil Pollution Damage, entered into force on June 19, 1975, and the International Convention on the Establishment of an International Fund for Oil Pollution Damage.³⁵ The Liability Convention would impose strict liability (with exceptions for extreme natural phenomena, government negligence in maintaining navigation aids, and the like) within limitations for damages caused by oil pollution from some ships (another exception for state-operated noncommercial vessels) provided an action is brought within three years. The most controversial feature of the Civil Liability Convention is that it would provide the exclusive remedy for oil pollution damage, thus preempting parts of Section 311 of the FWPCA dealing with cleanup damage and state law governing other liabilities. It of course makes no more sense to preempt state law with a half-baked federal remedy than it does to preempt both state and federal law with a half-baked international remedy. That is a judgment the Congress presumably will reach after it completes deliberations on the matter.³⁶ The IMCO Conventions in any event must be watched, for

33. Portland Pipe Line Corp. v. Environmental Improvement Comm'n, 307 A.2d 1, 3 ELR 20616 (Me.1973), appeal dismissed, 414 U.S. 1035 (1973); Mobil Oil Corp. v. Huntington, 72 Misc.2d 530, 339 N.Y.S.2d 139 (1972).

34. Me.Rev.Stat.Ann. ch. 38, § 552.

35. The text of the Liability Conventions is reproduced in 6 ELR 40306 (1976). See Doud, Compensation for Oil Pollution Civil Liability and Compensation Fund Conventions, 4 J. Maritime L. & Com. 525 (1973). A third treaty, the International Convention Relating to Intervention on the High Seas in Cases of Oil Pollution Damage, permits states that are parties to "take such measures on the high seas as may be necessary" to prevent or mitigate "grave and imminent danger to their coastline" by oil pollution. Except in cases of "extreme urgency requiring measures to be taken immediately," consultation with affected states and independent experts is required. Arts. 1, 3(d), 6 ELR 40301 (1976).

36. See Hearings on the International Compensation Fund for Pollution Damage, Before the Subcomm. on

when they enter into force, their requirements will apply to U. S. flag tankers "which must enter ports of nations party to the conventions to pick up oil for import into the U. S." [37]

Voluntary efforts of tanker owners scarcely represent a rule of law but they help complete the picture on oil spill compensation systems, to the extent they exist. In the wake of the *Torry Canyon* disaster, several major oil companies sponsored an arrangement that became known as the Tanker Owner's Voluntary Agreement Concerning Liability for Oil Pollution (TOVALOP) [38] and is now subscribed to by over 90 percent of the world's privately owned tanker tonnage. Each tanker owner under TOVALOP agrees either to clean up oil negligently discharged by one of its tankers or to compensate a national government for expenses reasonably incurred in cleaning up the spill. Supplementing TOVALOP is the Contract Regarding an Interim Supplement to Tanker Liability for Oil Pollution (CRISTAL), which requires cargo owners to contribute to a fund for reimbursing tanker owners for cleanup expenses and, to a limited extent, others suffering damage from an oil spill. Under neither TOVALOP nor CRISTAL will payments be made for fire, explosion, consequential loss or ecological impairment.[39] It cannot be said the agreements were conceived to compensate for environmental damage.

§ 4.20 Thermal Pollution

Thermal pollution can be defined as a man-induced alteration of natural water temperatures.[1] Other than the fact that there is more of it than most other pollutants, thermal pollution is hardly unusual—subtle in effects, difficult and expensive to control, partly due to the water volumes involved. The magnitude of the problem

---

Oceans and International Environment of the Senate Comm. on Foreign Relations, 93d Cong., 1st Sess. (1973). The Senate Foreign Relations Committee, however, has reported the Civil Liability Convention to the full Senate with the recommendation that advice and consent be given, subject to the proviso that the Senate should not take action until it acts also on the Fund Convention. See Senate Comm. on Foreign Relations, 1969 Oil Pollution Conventions and Amendments, Exec.Rep. No. 9, 92d Cong., 1st Sess. 5 (1971).

37. Lettow, The Control of Marine Pollution, in Environmental Law Institute, Federal Environmental Law 596, 625 (E. L. Dolgin & T. G. P. Guilbert eds. 1974); see id. at 615–25 for a detailed discussion of the conventions.

38. The TOVALOP agreement can be found in Hearings on S.7 and S.544, Before the Subcomm. on Air and Water Pollution of the Senate Comm. on Public Works, 91st Cong., 1st Sess. 261–65 (1969); see Becker, A Short Cruise on the Good Ships TOVALOP and CRISTAL, 5 J. Maritime L. & Com. 609 (1974).

39. TOVALOP, art. IV(A).

1. See generally Hearings on Thermal Pollution Before the Subcomm. on Air & Water Pollution of the Senate Comm. on Public Works, 90th Cong., 2d Sess. (1968). Compare Judge Coffin's statement in New Hampshire v. Atomic Energy Comm'n, 406 F.2d 170, 171 (1st Cir. 1969) ("Thermal pollution is used to designate the effects on a river—its water, flora, and fauna—of the injection of heated water").

Sec. 4.20   THERMAL POLLUTION   525

is illustrated aptly by two oft-cited figures: the amount of cooling water required for the 1990 capacity of steam-electric plants will amount to one-half to three-fourths of the average daily water runoff of the United States;[2] the total U. S. runoff would be warmed about ten degrees fahrenheit if the 1990 steam-electric plant capacity operates universally with once-through cooling (essentially without controls).[3] Under the law, thermal pollution historically has been treated like other pollution; raising the temperature of a river less than one degree fahrenheit is an enjoinable offense at behest of a downstream riparian user, who happens to use the water to make ice.[4] This section addresses briefly: (1) the effects of and control options for thermal pollution, (2) the common law and other miscellaneous legal controls, (3) the general provisions of the Federal Water Pollution Control Act (FWPCA), and (4) Section 316 of FWPCA, which is a unique thermal pollution variance provision.

a. *Effects and Control Options*

As with most environmental problems, judging the impact of a thermal discharge is a multidisciplinary venture. Obviously, the effects of a particular source depend upon its location, the amount, temperature and frequency of its discharge, its efficiency and size, and whether the water is used directly or recycled.[5] Temperature, it has been said, is "a catalyst, a depressant, an activator, a restrictor, a stimulator, a controller, a killer" and ergo "one of the most important and most influential water quality characteristics to life in water."[6] As a pollutant, heated water works in subtle ways:[7] it may effect development, metabolism and reproduction rates; it may decrease dissolved oxygen and increase the toxic effects of certain materials to fish; and it can present barriers to migration. Because fish are able to adapt to higher temperatures more rapidly than lower temperatures, fatalities may be caused by sudden decreases in temperatures brought about, for example, by the shutdown of a power plant.[8]

2. See S. Mathur, Waste Heat From Steam-Electric Generating Plants Using Fossil Fuels and Its Control 54 (1968) (published by the Federal Water Pollution Control Administration).

3. See M. M. Zarubica, Environmental Assessment of Alternative Thermal Control Strategies for the Electric Power Industry 101 (1974) (published by Environmental Protection Agency) [hereinafter cited as Environmental Assessment].

4. Sandusky Portland Cement Co. v. Dixon Pure Ice Co., 221 F. 200 (7th Cir. 1915).

5. Environmental Assessment, supra note 3, at 14–15.

6. Federal Water Pollution Control Administration, Laboratory Investigation No. 6: Temperature and Aquatic Life iv (1967) [hereinafter cited as Temperature and Aquatic Life]. This volume contains a substantial bibliography.

7. Id. at v–vii; see Environmental Protection Agency, Biologically Allowable Thermal Pollution Limits (1974).

8. See State v. Jersey Central Power & Light Co., 69 N.J. 102, 351 A.2d 337, 6 ELR 20352 (1976).

As with other pollutants,[9] heated water is a resource out of place. The bane of the downriver icemaker can be the boon of the downriver shipper whose business slows with the coming of the winter freeze. A great deal has been written about the potential beneficial uses of waste heat:[10] space heating and domestic hot water; warm water irrigation and aquaculture projects; melting of ice and snow on roadways; wastewater treatment, which works more efficiently at higher temperatures. In many ways heated effluent from an industrial facility resembles the polluted influent to a sewage treatment plant: a great deal more can be done with the resource than subjecting it to treatment and returning it to the watercourse. Unfortunately, the reuse of waste hot water, like resource recovery generally,[11] is in its infancy. The resource is imperfect; there is too much of it and temperatures are too low for many uses; and the costs of transportation are formidable.

Technological solutions are themselves imperfect. It is commonly acknowledged that thermal pollution is largely a problem of steam-electric power plants (accounting for 80 percent of the volume used for cooling)[12] and is especially acute for nuclear power plants (whose lower efficiencies account for more waste heat). Treatment technology can be grouped roughly into three categories:[13] (1) once-through cooling; (2) mitigation processes; and (3) closed cycle. Once-through cooling might as well be called once-through heating, and amounts to no control at all. The water is drawn from a river, ocean, or lake, passed across the condenser, and returned to the source from whence it came. The cooling that occurs is the result of natural phenomena such as dilution and radiation to the atmosphere. Mitigation processes are well established and include cooling ponds and lagoons (where water is retained and cooled prior to release or reuse), spray systems (which cool by evaporation), diffusers (which disperse or direct discharges to minimize effects), and wet towers (which also cool by evaporation through the release of heat to the atmosphere). So-called dry cooling, which is a rarity for economic reasons (none is presently in use in the United States), involves the

---

9. § 1.1 above.

10. E. g., Environmental Assessment, supra note 3, at 120–54; R. Stewart & S. Bjornssun, Conference Report: Beneficial Uses of Thermal Discharges (1969).

11. § 6.1 below.

12. D. Rimberg, Utilization of Waste Heat from Power Plants 29 (1974).

13. See, e. g., F. Parker & P. Krenkel, Engineering Aspects of Thermal Pollution (1969); Massachusetts Institute of Technology, Power Generation and Environmental Change 349 et seq. (A. Berkowitz & A. Squires eds. 1971); Environmental Assessment, supra note 3, at 24–31; Bloom, Heat—A Growing Water Pollution Problem, 1 BNA Environmental Rptr., Mono.No.4 (1970); Burns & Roe, Inc., Best Technology Available for the Location, Design, Construction, and Capacity of Cooling Water Intake Structures for Minimizing Adverse Environmental Impact (1976).

retention of cooling water "in a closed system and heat is dissipated to the air as in an automobile radiator." [14]

Control options have environmental as well as economic disadvantages. Cooling water cannot be recycled through towers and ponds "indefinitely" because chemicals collect by leaching and from additives.[15] To avoid overconcentration, some of the water is bled off (the discharge is called blowdown), and replaced by fresh water. This process "creates a potential massive water pollution problem associated with the use of blowdown chemicals (the organic and inorganic compounds that are employed to poison organisms in the cooling system and to clean parts of the system which may become fouled by chemical reactions). These chemicals often are highly toxic and can perform more harm than that which can be attributed to thermal pollution." [16] Other problems abound. Cooling ponds are generally low in consumptive use but require large amounts of land. Spray systems lose substantial amounts of water through evaporation and must be subjected to frequent defouling. Wet cooling towers, which are used widely, are notorious eyesores and are high in consumptive use (at least two percent of the circulated flow),[17] which is no small penalty especially in arid areas. They also contribute to air pollution by fogging, drifting salt (from site locations using salt water), and other impurities.

b. *Common Law and Other Miscellaneous Legal Controls*

It is safe to say that common law remedies have had no impact whatsoever on thermal pollution control decisions although theoretically the doctrines are perfectly viable.[18] The old icemaking case [19] indicates that the riparian rights doctrine (or alternatively a nuisance theory [20]) serves to forbid upstream thermal discharges that interfere unreasonably with downstream uses. That lawsuits are almost unheard of is explicable on the usual grounds that inhibit the use-

14. National Water Comm'n, Review Final Report 5–108 (1972).

15. Environmental Assessment, supra note 3, at 26.

16. Ibid.

17. Human & Ecologic Effects of Nuclear Power Plants 450 (L. Sogan ed. 1974).

18. E. g., Edwards, Legal Control of Thermal Pollution, 2 Nat.Res.L. 1 (1969); Jost, Cold Facts on Hot Water: Legal Aspects of Thermal Pollution, 1969 Wis.L.Rev. 253 (1969); Maloney, More Heat than Light: Thermal Pollution Versus Heat Energy Utilization, 25 U.Fla.L.Rev. 693 (1972); Thomas, Thermal Discharges: A Legal Problem, 38 Tenn.L.Rev. 369 (1971); Comment, Thermal Electric Power and Water Pollution: A Siting Approach, 46 Ind.L.J. 61 (1970); Comment, Thermal Pollution: "The Dishonorable Discharge" —New York's Criteria Governing Heated Liquids, 34 Albany L.Rev. 539 (1970).

19. Sandusky Portland Cement Co. v. Dixon Pure Ice Co., 221 F. 200 (7th Cir. 1915). For additional common law authorities, see Thomas, supra note 18, at 375–80.

20. See § 2.15 (discussing coalescence of riparian rights and nuisance doctrines).

fulness of common law remedies,[21] not the least of which is an inability to link up diminished marine life in the watercourse to defendant's upstream activities.

The frustrations of resorting to traditional common law remedies and their statutory supplements to correct thermal pollution is typified by the recent decision of the Supreme Court of New Jersey in State v. Jersey Central Power & Light Co.,[22] where the shutdown of a nuclear power plant caused a precipitous drop in water temperature and the eventual destruction of more than 500,000 menhaden. The court unanimously excused the defendant on three independent grounds, none of them particularly persuasive. First, it was reasoned that the fish were killed by a natural condition and not by defendant's operations. This is a simplistic view of cause in fact that overlooks the biological certainty that the fish will be attracted to heated water where they are vulnerable to rapid temperature changes. Second, the court concluded that the pumping of water into tidal areas was not the dumping of "debris, hazardous, deleterious, destructive or poisonous substances of any kind" within the meaning of a state statute.[23] While pumping heated water is not traditionally within the category of abnormally dangerous activities for which strict liability is imposed,[24] the purpose of the statute arguably reaches discharges that injure, obstruct or offend—aims fully encompassing thermal pollution.[25] The third ground for the decision was that the federal Atomic Energy Act preempted state liability rules under the circumstances. Whatever the reach of federal authority over radiation hazards,[26] it does not appear to comprehend immunity for environmental damage occasioned by plant operations.[27]

A once viable, but now limited, tool for controlling thermal pollution is the Rivers and Harbors Act of 1899.[28] Section 13 of the statute forbids the dumping of "refuse" into navigable waters, and a hot water discharge is quite clearly "refuse."[29] Section 13 was

21. Johnson, The Changing Role of Courts in Water Quality Management, in Water Resources Management and Public Policy 200 (H. Campbell & F. O. Sylvester eds. 1968).

22. 69 N.J. 102, 351 A.2d 337, 6 ELR 20352 (1976).

23. 23 N.J.S.A. § 5–28 is quoted in full in the opinion of the Appellate Division. Dep't of Environmental Protection v. Jersey Central Power & Light Co., 133 N.J.Super. 375, 336 A.2d 750, 5 ELR 20370 (1975).

24. § 2.14 above.

25. Cf. Rodgers, Industrial Water Pollution and the Refuse Act: A Second Chance for Water Quality, 119 U.Pa. L.Rev. 761, 769–77 (1971) (discussing the meaning of "refuse" in the federal Rivers and Harbors Act).

26. Northern States Power Co. v. Minnesota, 447 F.2d 1143 (8th Cir. 1971), aff'd mem. 405 U.S. 1035, 92 S.Ct. 1307, 31 L.Ed.2d 576 (1972).

27. See 42 U.S.C.A. § 2021(k); Estep & Adelman, State Control of Radiation Hazards: An Intergovernmental Relations Problem, 60 Mich.L.Rev. 41 (1961).

28. § 4.5 above.

29. 33 CFR § 209.131(d)(1); see United States v. Florida Power & Light Co.,

instrumental in the settlement of the Biscayne Bay case where nuclear units built by Florida Power and Light Company were said to jeopardize marine life in the extremely shallow waters in Biscayne Bay off Miami. The ensuing legal struggle involved, among other things, a proposal by the utility to pipe its discharges into deeper water,[30] an unsuccessful attempt to resist condemnation for the project on the grounds that it would harm natural resources,[31] and a shareholder suit charging a wasting of corporate assets by executive decisions that would bring retaliation against thermal pollution of the Bay.[32] The Federal Water Pollution Control Act Amendments of 1972 limit the application of section 13 to nonpoint source discharges and certain types of unauthorized discharges.[33] Section 13 is no longer a significant tool against thermal discharges from point sources operating pursuant to permits, which clearly cover most of the problem.

Another on-again, off-again source of thermal pollution law is found in the licensing powers of the Nuclear Regulatory Commission (NRC) over nuclear power plants.[34] The First Circuit held in 1969 [35] that the Commission's congressional charter under the Atomic Energy Act of 1954 did not allow it to consider thermal effects in the licensing process. After the coming of the National Environmental Policy Act in 1970, the position was repudiated in the well known case of Calvert Cliffs' Coordinating Committee v. Atomic Energy Commission,[36] which held that the AEC (predecessor to the Nuclear Regulatory Commission) was required to consider thermal effects in its decisions on individual plants, even to the point in appropriate cases of "demanding water pollution controls from its licensees which are *more strict* than those demanded by" applicable water quality standards.[37] The narrow holding of Calvert Cliffs, al-

---

311 F.Supp. 1391 (S.D.Fla.1970) (refusing a preliminary injunction against the discharge of heated water into Biscayne Bay on the ground that the government failed to show irreparable damage to the bay, although deciding that hot water was "refuse"). The case later was settled by consent decree.

30. See Nuclear Power: Thermal Pollution and Radiation, Address by Dan Paul, Paul & Thompson, Miami, Florida, American Bar Ass'n 1971 Annual Meeting, July 6, 1971, at 33; cf. § 3.8 above (discussing the tall stack strategy).

31. Seadade Indus., Inc. v. Florida Power & Light Co., 23 Fla.L.Rep. 465, 245 So.2d 209 (1971).

32. Discussed in Paul, supra note 30, at 37–39.

33. § 4.5 above.

34. See generally Green & Fridkis, Radiation and the Environment, in Environmental Law Institute, Federal Environmental Law 1022 (E. L. Dolgin & T. G. P. Guilbert eds. 1974).

35. New Hampshire v. Atomic Energy Comm'n, 406 F.2d 170 (1st Cir. 1969).

36. 146 U.S.App.D.C. 33, 449 F.2d 1109, 1 ELR 20346 (1971), cert. denied, 404 U.S. 942 (1972).

37. 146 U.S.App.D.C. at 48, 449 F.2d at 1124, 1 ELR at 20354 (emphasis in original). A NEPA action leading to an agreement to construct a closed-cycle cooling system for two units of the Quad Cities Nuclear Power Station is reported in Izaak Walton League v. Schlesinger, 2 ELR 20388 (D.C.D.C.1971).

lowing the Commission to improve upon existing standards, was overruled legislatively by Section 511(c)(2) of the Federal Water Pollution Control Act Amendments of 1972.[38] That provision forbids any agency (including the Nuclear Regulatory Commission) from attacking collaterally or supplementing an effluent limitation established under the FWPCA. Like any rule of preclusion, this prevents the Commission's administrative decision-makers (usually the Atomic Safety and Licensing Board or the Atomic Safety and Licensing Appeals Board) from rewriting effluent limitations and schedules of compliance for thermal discharges established by the Environmental Protection Agency or an appropriate state agency. But the Commission is free to act if, for one reason or another, the environmental agency has not addressed the question or addressed it narrowly, or if an approved thermal discharge is relevant in other ways (for example, by affecting adversely the stability of the site).

More importantly, the Commission is empowered to deny or condition nuclear power plant construction or operating permits to protect environmental values.[39] This means, as a practical matter, that the NRC permits prescribe construction or operational conditions necessary to achieve effluent limitations or water quality standards set by other agencies. Nothing could be clearer, for example, than this direction with regard to units of the Indian Point Nuclear Power Station on the Hudson River: "Operation . . . with its presently designed once-through cooling system shall be permitted until May 1, 1978. Operation after this date shall be permitted only after a closed cycle cooling system has been installed and placed in operation."[40] The basis for the decision was to enforce compliance with the New York State water quality standards.[41]

The temperature criteria in the state water quality standards represent the law of thermal pollution in its most pervasive form.[42] Drafting standards, to be sure, is "a complex scientific problem. If once-through cooling water is discharged into the stream, the phenomenon will be localized because the thermal discharge will be dissipated over time at the interface of the surface and the atmosphere, although this may require eight to ten miles of flow. However, if the discharge has a sufficiently high temperature it may have an

38. 33 U.S.C.A. § 1371(c)(2).

39. 10 CFR § 2.104(b)(3); see 38 Fed. Reg. 2679 (1973) (NRC Interim Policy Statement on Implementation of the Federal Water Pollution Control Act Amendments of 1972).

40. In re Consolidated Edison Co. (Indian Point Station, Unit No. 2), Dkt. No. 50–247, Initial Decision, Atomic Safety and Licensing Board, CCH Atomic Energy Rptr. ¶ 11,256.09 (Sept. 25, 1973).

41. Ibid.

42. For a compilation of state water quality standards, see BNA, Environment Rptr.—State Water Laws 621.0901–.0923. The status in 1970 of the state temperature criteria is addressed in Bloom, supra note 13. Compare § 4.8 above (water quality standards).

immediate detrimental ecological impact."[43] The state standards, which remain effective under Section 303 of the Federal Water Pollution Control Act,[44] typically contain restrictions on discharge temperatures and on temperature increases for receiving water streams (e. g., no more than 5° F increase in the prevailing temperature) and lakes (e. g., no more than a 3° F increase above normal temperatures in the epilimnion, the highest of three levels in lake water, and no discharges at all into the hypolimnion, the lowest of the three levels where temperatures are stable because they are unaffected by sunlight and wind). Certain bodies of water may be ruled off limits for thermal discharges, such as those critical to cold-water biota (inland trout streams, headwaters of salmon streams). Probably the most serious issue under the state thermal pollution standards is whether to permit a mixing zone in connection with thermal discharges. A mixing zone is simply an area within a watercourse in the vicinity of a discharge point where thermal standards are exceeded. Obviously, if the policy decision is made to permit these geographical variances a further effort is needed to adjust mixing zones to minimize their interference with marine life.[45]

c. *Federal Water Pollution Control Act*

With the exception of the variance provisions of section 316,[46] thermal pollution is accorded no special treatment under the Federal Water Pollution Control Act. Heat, for example, is mentioned in the definition of "pollutant."[47] Generally, the technology based standards for new[48] and existing[49] sources apply. Only three categories of sources, however, are affected by temperature criteria—beet sugar processing, cement manufacturing, and, of course, steam-electric power plants. The beet sugar processing new source standard calls for no discharge,[50] while both the 1977 and 1983 existing source standards prohibit discharges in excess of 90° F.[51] All three standards for cement manufacturing plants allow only those discharges not exceeding a 3° C rise above inlet water temperatures.[52]

43. C. J. Meyers & A. D. Tarlock, Water Resource Management 967 (1971).

44. 33 U.S.C.A. § 1313. Under § 1313 (d) the states must designate water quality limited segments where effluent controls for thermal pollution "are not stringent enough to assure protection of a balanced indigenous population of shellfish, fish, and wildlife." See § 4.8 above.

45. The concept of highly polluted sacrifice areas is a disagreeable one, cf. § 3.12 above (no significant deterioration), although it is implemented occasionally. A storm of protest, for example, followed suggestions by a committee of the National Academy of Sciences that stripmining in the West might require the designation of national sacrifice areas. See NAS, Rehabilitation Potential of Western Coal Lands 85–86 (1974).

46. 33 U.S.C.A. § 1326.

47. Section 502(b), 33 U.S.C.A. § 1362 (b).

48. § 4.12 above.

49. Ibid.

50. 40 CFR § 409.15.

51. Id. §§ 409.12, 409.13.

52. Id. §§ 411.12, 411.13, 411.15.

The standards for steam-electric power plants are a good deal more elaborate and are under attack in the courts.[53] Basically, the EPA regulations recognize four types of cooling water control technologies: (1) once-through cooling, (2) recirculating cooling (spray systems, wet or drying cooling towers), (3) cooling ponds (off-channel reservoirs which do not impede the flow of a navigable stream) and (4) cooling lakes (man-made impoundments which do impede stream flow). The regulations do not impose any 1977 best practicable technology thermal limitations but do call for compliance with the best available technology limitations by 1981. Those standards require that no heat may be discharged into navigable waters. Compliance can be accomplished by installing cooling towers or cooling ponds but not cooling lakes. New sources also must use cooling towers or cooling ponds. There are a number of exemptions for operators who can demonstrate (1) present use of a cooling lake; (2) that a cooling lake is under construction; (3) that sufficient land for cooling towers is unavailable; and (4) that cooling towers would be an aviation hazard. Also exempt are certain administratively defined "old units" and "small units." For these plants EPA has determined that the cost of retrofit would not be worth the benefits either because of the short useful life of the plant or the limited impact of its discharge.

While the effluent limitations undergo continuing judicial and administrative scrutiny, NPDES permits will be issued. No permit can be granted without limitations necessary to meet state water quality standards.[54] State certification under section 401 assures a state veto of discharges that offend applicable thermal standards.[55]

d. *Section 316*

Superimposed on the conventional water pollution regulatory requirements is a special variance procedure acknowledging the intractable peculiarities of thermal pollution. The provision originated in the House bill, which contained a requirement that the Administrator issue thermal discharge regulations recognizing "that the optimum method of control of any thermal discharge may depend upon local conditions, including the type and size of the receiving body of water."[56] The obligation to issue regulations was dropped in Conference, but a compromise measure emerged retaining the

---

53. Id. pt. 423. The regulations were challenged in Appalachian Power Co. v. Train, 545 F.2d 1351 (4th Cir. 1976) by 74 petitioners representing all facets of the electrical utility industry accounting for over 50 per cent of the Nation's electrical generating capacity. An especially effective presentation of the utility's position appears in the Brief and Reply Brief for Petitioners, authored principally by George C. Freeman, Jr., of the Richmond, Virginia firm of Hunton, Williams, Gay & Gibson.

54. 33 U.S.C.A. § 1311(b)(1)(C).

55. Id. § 1341.

56. H.R. 11896, § 216, at 46.

House preference for a case by case adjudication on issues of thermal pollution. Section 316 [57] allows the owner or operator of any source otherwise subject to the effluent standards for new or existing sources to prove to the satisfaction of the Administrator (or the state) "that any effluent limitation proposed for the thermal component of any discharge from [the] source will require effluent limitations more stringent than necessary to assure the protection and propagation of a balanced, indigenous population of shellfish, fish, and wildlife in and on the body of water into which the discharge is to be made . . . ." By its terms, the burden relates not to the costs of control but to the necessity for it. If this burden is carried, the permitting authority imposes an effluent limitation on the source "that will assure the protection and propagation of a balanced, indigenous population of shellfish, fish, and wildlife in and on that body of water."

The key legal propositions under Section 316 of the FWPCA are: (1) there must be an "opportunity for public hearing" on the issue; (2) the operator of the source has the burden of showing that the proposed effluent limitation for controlling the thermal component is "more stringent than necessary" to protect indigenous fish and wildlife; and (3) the standards proposed initially must conform to the various "best technology" provisions for new and existing sources under sections 306 and 301. Section 316(b) also makes clear that "the location, design, construction, and capacity of cooling water intake structure [should] reflect the best technology available for minimizing adverse environmental impact." [58] This means that not only the technology for minimizing the effects of heated water but also the methods of extraction must satisfy the "best technology" principle.[59] Thus, the section presumes the propriety of technology-based standards to combat thermal pollution but permits relaxation if less than the best is proven sufficient.

Carrying the burden of proving no damage from projected operations is more difficult even than proving credible risks of damage from present operations.[60] The question of who has the burden is one of the most difficult and decisive questions of modern environmental law.[61] It involves issues of full disclosure, margins of safety, and responsibility for risks of error. The administration

---

57. 33 U.S.C.A. § 1326; see Environmental Protection Agency, Section 316(a) Technical Guidance—Thermal Discharges (Sept. 30, 1974) (draft).

58. 33 U.S.C.A. § 1326(b).

59. See authorities collected in Thomas, supra note 18, at 369 n.3.

60. § 3.18 above.

61. See, e. g., Blank, The Delaney Clause: Technical Naivete and Scientific Advocacy in the Formulation of Public Health Policies, 62 Calif.L.Rev. 1084 (1974); Gelpe & Tarlock, The Uses of Scientific Information in Environmental Decisionmaking, 48 S.Cal.L.Rev. 371, 412–27 (1974); Tarlock, A Comment on Meyer's Introduction to Environmental Thought, 50 Ind.L.J. 454 (1975).

of section 316 offers a proving ground of how burden theories work in fact.[62]

§ 4.21 Enforcement

Federal water pollution enforcement authority is influenced strongly by the Clean Air Act,[1] and suffers from many of its weaknesses. Under the Federal Water Pollution Control Act the citizen,[2] the Environmental Agency, and the states share enforcement powers. As with the Clean Air Act,[3] the emphasis is upon administrative remedies, and these embrace "informal communications including letters and phone calls; formal remedies, including orders and permit modifications; and ancillary remedies, such as publicity, blacklisting and referral for judicial action."[4] This section discusses: (1) the miscellaneous enforcement powers of EPA, (2) special problems of enforcement against municipal treatment works and federal facilities, and (3) state enforcement powers. Considered elsewhere is enforcement under the Rivers and Harbors Act[5] and the oil pollution provisions.[6]

a. *Miscellaneous Powers*

The FWPCA extends to the Administrator broad powers to require the keeping of records and monitoring and to gain entry in pur-

---

62. Section 316 presents interpretation problems of lesser moment. There has been disagreement, for example, over whether the assurance of protection for "a balanced, indigenous" population of fish extends to species planted in a man-made cooling lake. See also EPA, Decision of the General Counsel No. 7 (Apr. 8, 1975) (holding that EPA may regulate discharges into any private lake which constitutes "navigable waters" as defined in FWPCA § 502(7), 33 U.S.C.A. § 1362(7)).

1. § 3.19 above.

2. § 1.13 above.

3. § 3.19 above.

4. Environmental Law Institute, Enforcement of Federal and State Water Pollution Controls 7 (1975) (prepared for the National Commission on Water Quality) [hereinafter cited as ELI Enforcement Report]. See also Arnold, Effluent Limitations and NPDES: Federal and State Implementation of the Federal Water Pollution Control Act Amendments of 1972, 15 B.C.Ind. & Com.L.Rev. 767 (1974); Davis & Glasser, Discharge Permit Program Under the Federal Water Pollution Control Act of 1972 —Improvement of Water Quality Through the Regulation of Discharges from Industrial Facilities, 2 Urban L.J. 179 (1974); Dickens, Law Making and Enforcement—A Case Study, 37 Modern L.Rev. 297 (1974); Hall, Litigation Under the Federal Water Pollution Control Act Amendments of 1972, 4 ELR 50109 (1974); Ipsen & Raisch, Enforcement Under the Federal Water Pollution Control Act Amendments of 1972, 9 Land & Water L.Rev. 369 (1974); Lindholm, Federal Water Pollution Control Act Amendments of 1972 . . . The Great Cleansing or Being Taken to the Cleaners?, 30 Mo.Bar J. 23 (1974); Wenner, Federal Water Pollution Control Statutes in Theory and Practice, 4 Environmental Law. 251 (1974); Note, Deficiencies in the Regulatory Scheme of the Federal Water Pollution Control Act Amendments of 1972, 19 St. Louis U.L.J. 208 (1974).

5. § 4.5 above.

6. § 4.17 above.

suit of his enforcement and other authority.[7] The language used closely tracks the language of the Clean Air Act, and the powers granted are not limited severely by constitutional considerations forbidding unreasonable searches and self-incrimination.[8] Provisions for delegating enforcement powers to the states are available,[9] as they are under the Clean Air Act. EPA monitors state performance in conjunction with grants issued under section 106 [10] and in overseeing the state assumption of permit granting powers under section 402(b).[11] It is reported authoritatively that "EPA routinely relies on state agencies for compliance monitoring, although it knows that some states themselves are unable to monitor with sufficient frequency and reliability."[12]

Under FWPCA, as under the Clean Air Act, the Environmental Protection Agency is empowered to convene conferences in certain circumstances, take over enforcement authority in states with widespread nonenforcement, and intervene in emergencies.[13] The elaborate conference procedures of early federal pollution laws were born in the Federal Water Pollution Control Act Amendments of 1956.[14] While the conference mechanism was put to use far more readily in water pollution cases than in air pollution cases (altogether fifty-nine water pollution abatement conferences were initiated [15]), the results

7. Section 308, 33 U.S.C.A. § 1318; see Brown & Duncan, Legal Aspects of a Federal Water Quality Surveillance System, 68 Mich.L.Rev. 1131 (1970).

8. § 3.19 above.

9. Section 308(c), 33 U.S.C.A. § 1318(c).

10. 33 U.S.C.A. § 1256(e)(1), conditions program grants on
   the establishment and operation of appropriate devices, methods, systems, and procedures necessary to monitor, and to compile and analyze data on (including classification according to eutrophic condition), the quality of navigable waters and to the extent practicable, ground waters including biological monitoring; . . . .
   Compare § 4.3 above (groundwater).

11. State administration of the NPDES permit program is conditioned on, among other things, a finding by the Administrator that a state has "adequate authority" to "inspect, monitor, enter, and require reports to at least the same extent as required in section 1318 of this title; . . . ."

12. ELI Enforcement Report at 26 (footnote omitted).

13. All three of these powers are discussed in § 3.19 above.

14. Act of July 9, 1956, ch. 518, 70 Stat. 498 (1956). A leading article on the history of federal water pollution abatement efforts is Barry, The Evolution of the Enforcement Provisions of the Federal Water Pollution Control Act: A Study of the Difficulty in Developing Effective Legislation, 68 Mich.L.Rev. 1103 (1970).

15. Environmental Protection Agency, The First Two Years: A Review of EPA's Enforcement Program 17, 38–48, 216–26 (1973). Detailed summaries of these enforcement conferences are found in Hearings on Water Pollution Oversight, Before the House Comm. on Public Works, 92d Cong., 1st Sess. 210–26 (1971). Discussions of individual conferences are found in D. Zwick & M. Benstock, Water Wasteland 119–96 (1971); J. Fallows, The Water Lords 195–204 (1970); N. W. Hines, Public Regulation of Water Quality in the United States (1971) (prepared for the National Water Commission).

were similarly frustrating. The published proceedings and backup reports are useful today mainly as historical commentary on water quality problems that still persist. All that remains of the conference procedures in the 1972 FWPCA Amendments is a provision directing the Administrator to convene a conference and to hold a hearing to explore issues of water pollution that endanger the health or welfare of persons in a foreign country.[16]

The FWPCA gives the EPA Administrator the same power he has under the Clean Air Act to exercise a period of "federally assumed enforcement" within a state upon a finding of "widespread" permit violations.[17] A federal takeover would be a gross institutional insult, comparable to a withdrawal of approval to administer the NPDES permit program.[18] It is an insult unlikely to be inflicted for a variety of reasons: great political and resource costs to EPA; no substantial augmentation of powers already available; possible crippling of the state program due to loss of section 106 program funds which can be devoted to state compliance monitoring.

Also unused, but of greater potential relevance, is the power of the Administrator to intervene in an emergency to protect the health or economic livelihood of people faced with a water pollution hazard.[19] The provision is intended to supplement, not short-circuit, the normal regulatory routine. But the fact remains that it permits the leap-frogging of administrative procedures to secure immediate judicial relief to correct a pollution problem. More than a few of the better known water pollution incidents might qualify as a section 504 emergency (mercury, asbestos, kepone, polychlorinated biphenyls). That section 504 has never been invoked indicates that it duplicates in part remedies available elsewhere and that its principal function is to act as the big stick held by EPA in negotiations. An absence of reported cases is not a fair indicator of statutory impotency.

16. Section 310, 33 U.S.C.A. § 1320.

17. Section 309(a)(2), 33 U.S.C.A. § 1319(a)(2).

18. Section 402(c)(3), 33 U.S.C.A. § 1342(c)(3).

19. Section 504, 33 U.S.C.A. § 1364, reads:
Notwithstanding any other provisions of this chapter, the Administrator upon receipt of evidence that a pollution source or combination of sources is presenting an imminent or substantial endangerment to the health of persons or to the welfare of persons where such endangerment is to the livelihood of such persons, such as inability to market shellfish, may bring suit on behalf of the United States in the appropriate district court to immediately restrain any person causing or contributing to the alleged pollution to stop the discharge of pollutants causing or contributing to such pollution or to take such other action as may be necessary.

Compare Reserve Mining Co. v. Environmental Protection Agency, 514 F.2d 492, 527–29, 5 ELR 20596, 20610–12 (8th Cir. 1975) (interpreting the pre-1972 requirement that a discharge "endanger . . . the health or welfare of persons"); § 3.18 above (interpreting fuel additive provisions of the Clean Air Act).

The remaining enforcement powers under section 309 are patterned closely on the air pollution model.[20] EPA has the power to impose administrative compliance orders, to seek injunctive relief directly in the courts, and to make referrals for criminal prosecution. Section 309 provides an important additional remedy for water pollution violations not available under the Clean Air Act—civil monetary penalties imposed in judicial (not administrative) proceedings. Much of the dogma on enforcement applies to EPA's endeavors under the FWPCA: a coordination of efforts with state authorities and the Justice Department is required,[21] and this consultation determines the action to be taken. An agenda of violations can bring enforcement action—noncompliance with any condition or limitation in a permit implementing various provisions of the Act (discharges contrary to effluent or water quality standards, new source and toxic effluent standards, monitoring obligations). Section 309 is replete with mandatory language ("shall proceed," "shall issue an order," "shall bring a civil action"), which should be understood as expressing congressional disapproval of tolerant administrative policies historically quite common as regards pollution violations.[22] Interestingly, the mandatory language was invoked first in court defensively by a discharger arguing that a civil action must precede the institution of a criminal prosecution. The argument was rejected,[23] quite properly, for the language should be read as narrowing the discretion to excuse substantive violators rather than dictating the choice of remedy. EPA has issued guidelines [24] further spelling out important matters such as the handling of communications with violators, referrals to the U. S. Attorney, and the circumstances in which state enforcement is to be accorded priority. A statement of policy issued by the Justice Department [25] offers guidance on conditions for settling FWPCA litigation (a proposed settlement is held open for public comment for a period of 30 days before final submission to the court).

Criminal penalties are unlikely to be any more effective in enforcing water pollution laws than they are in enforcing other regula-

---

20. § 3.19 above.

21. See ELI Enforcement Report ch. VI (Inter- and Intra-Governmental Relations).

22. See D. Zwick & M. Benstock, supra note 15, at 305–39; Glenn, The Crime of "Pollution", The Role of Federal Water Pollution: Criminal Sanctions, 11 Am.Crim.L.Rev. 835, 836–38 (1973).

23. United States v. Phelps Dodge Corp., 391 F.Supp. 1181, 5 ELR 20308 (D.Ariz.1975); cf. ELI Enforcement Report 217–20 (discussing a related question of whether a civil action may be brought after an administrative order has been issued by EPA; the conclusion is that all of the section 309 remedies are independent and nonexclusive).

24. Environmental Protection Agency, Guidelines for Water Pollution Enforcement (July 23, 1973), supplemented and revised by Memorandum to Directors, Enforcement Division, from Assistant Administrator for Enforcement and General Counsel, Mar. 20, 1974.

25. 28 CFR § 50.7.

tory objectives, although their deterrent value is always a subject of speculation.[26] Under section 309(c) [27] the federal crime of water pollution is defined broadly (reaching violations of the key effluent limitation provisions or of any permit condition or limitation implementing those sections). Culpability elements are relatively low (convictions may be had for violations "willfully or negligently" committed), and penalties are stiff (for first offenders, a maximum penalty of $25,000 per day of violation and one year's imprisonment; for subsequent offenders, the maximum is doubled).[28] In the first three years under the Act, fourteen cases in five EPA regions have been referred to the U.S. Attorneys for prosecution, all of them for discharging without a permit.[29] The principal legal issue that has emerged is the degree of culpability that must be proven to demonstrate that an offense was committed "negligently." [30]

Civil enforcement actions filed under FWPCA often combine requests for injunctive relief and the imposition of civil penalties.[31] The issuance of injunctions is governed by traditional equitable considerations including the degree of injury, the culpability of the violator, and the possible economic impact of any decree.[32] The Reserve Mining litigation, in particular, makes clear that the economic dislocation occasioned by a shutdown is a factor to be weighed in selecting a remedy.[33] The range of remedies is broad, and may include a direc-

26. See Glenn, supra note 22.

27. 33 U.S.C.A. § 1319(c).

28. The statute prescribes a minimum penalty of $2,500 per day of violation. This has been circumvented in one case, upon the recommendation of the U. S. Attorney, by fining the convicted discharger the statutory minimum and then suspending all but a fraction of the penalty. See United States v. Mahaska Bottling Co., Crim. No. 75–33 (N.D.Iowa 1975), discussed in ELI Enforcement Report at 239 & n. 75.

29. ELI Enforcement Report at 238.

30. EPA has argued for a standard of "the failure to use ordinary care under the circumstances." One court has instructed the jury that an offense is committed negligently "if done wantonly and recklessly, manifesting an utter disregard for the law and the rights and safety of others." United States v. American Beef Packer, Crim.No. 74–0–30 (D.Nev.1974) (resulting in an acquittal), discussed in ELI Enforcement Report at 241. The correct charge is a middle ground asking the jury to determine whether defendant's conduct constituted a "gross deviation from the standard of care that a reasonable person would observe in the actor's situation." Model Penal Code § 2.02(2)(d) (Proposed Official Draft 1962).

31. See ELI Enforcement Report at 216–17, 227–28. See also United States v. Buntin, Civil No. 76–64 NACV (M.D.Tenn.1976) (imposing a civil fine of $4,904.20 on a private homeowner as a consequence of a leaking heating oil tank discharging into a creek).

32. Compare § 2.11 above.

33. Reserve Mining Co. v. EPA, 514 F.2d 492, 537, 5 ELR 20596, 20616 (8th Cir. 1975) (holding that Reserve Mining must be afforded "a reasonable time to construct facilities to accomplish an abatement of its pollution" in order to avoid "hardship to employees and great economic loss incident to an immediate plant closing").

Sec. 4.21 ENFORCEMENT 539

tion for cleanup and restoration of the waters affected,[34] backed ultimately by contempt penalties,[35] and even the placement of a polluting facility in receivership.[36] Some courts may be disposed to exercise their discretion in favor of loose controls and lax timetables, however, and this factor is taken into account in some EPA regions by officials who forego requesting injunctive relief to avoid court supervised settlements resulting in permit modifications.[37] The Justice Department takes the position that settlements should not include "any modification of the terms of the permit either as to the amount of pollutants discharged or as to any schedule of compliance."[38] An undertaking to abide by the terms of a permit is a subject of negotiation, and represents an added burden encouraging compliance because of the possible need for enforcement by contempt. The Justice Department is quite correct in resisting the transformation of the judicial enforcement arena into a forum for pleading economic and technical hardship. The proper forum for these claims is during direct review of the guidelines and to a lesser extent in the permit proceedings.[39] Judicial participation in enforcement should discourage collateral attacks and confine the inquiry to whether there is a violation of a standard or condition and what the punishment or corrective remedy should be.

Section 309(d)[40] provides for judicially imposed civil penalties, which ought to be imposed on a strict liability basis in light of the absence of language of culpability in the provision and the liability without fault analogues found elsewhere in the law.[41] Controversy has

34. See ELI Enforcement Report at 229 & n. 55, where the court ordered the removal of cow carcasses dumped into a pit that drained into a reservoir serving as a drinking water supply for fifty-five communities. Interestingly, EPA Region VIII is the only region where restorative relief is sought regularly.

35. One water pollution case reportedly has resulted in imprisonment for contempt. Pennsylvania v. Dallas Corp. (Luzerne County Ct.Pa.1974), reported in National Ass'n of Attorneys General, Environmental Control Newsletter, Oct. 1974, at 7.

36. New Jersey Dep't of Health v. Jersey City, C34-47-67 (Hudson County Ct.N.J.), reported in ELI Enforcement Report at 249 n. 91.

37. Id. at 231.

38. Statement by Martin Green, Chief, Pollution Control Section, Land and Natural Resources Division, Department of Justice, in 13 Land & Natural Resources Div. J. 53 (1975).

39. §§ 4.11–.13 above; see section 509(b)(2), 33 U.S.C.A. § 1369(b)(2) ("Action of the Administrator with respect to which review could have been obtained under paragraph (1) of this subsection shall not be subject to judicial review in any civil or criminal proceeding for enforcement").

40. 33 U.S.C.A. § 1319(d), reads:
Any person who violates sections 1311, 1312, 1316, 1317, or 1318 of this title, or any permit condition or limitation implementing any of such sections in a permit issued under section 1342 of this title, by the Administrator, or by a State, and any person who violates any order issued by the Administrator under subsection (a) of this section, shall be subject to a civil penalty of not to exceed $10,000 per day of such violation.

41. Compare § 4.17 above (oil pollution); § 8.9 below (pesticide violations).

arisen over whether a penalty "of not to exceed $10,000 per day of such violation" imposes a ceiling of $10,000 per day per violation or $10,000 per day for all violations. EPA and the Justice Department have opted for the former reading,[42] although the issue is a virtual toss-up. Even on the narrower reading circumstances are likely to support substantial penalties since many violations are continuing ones, and subject to multiplication. The practical question is whether officials will ask for, and courts impose, monetary penalties amounting to more than absurdly tiny fractions of a corporate defendant's earned income.[43] An attack on the FWPCA's civil penalty provisions as being criminal in effect is certain to be made but unlikely to succeed.[44] In any case, it remains for the courts to articulate the permissible criteria for the imposition of civil penalties.

The Federal Water Pollution Control Act follows the Clean Air Act by imposing on the Administrator the obligation to correct violations by entering an enforcement order that specifies "a time for compliance, not to exceed thirty days, which the Administrator determines is reasonable, taking into account the seriousness of the violation and any good faith efforts to comply with applicable requirements."[45] EPA's authority to issue administrative orders has been delegated to the regions, and raises the problem of a *de facto* variance proceeding like that evolving under the Clean Air Act.[46] Indeed, there is scant justification under the schema of FWPCA to create any administrative mechanism for extending compliance obligations that are negotiated fully during the permit proceedings. The greatest protection against the use of formal administrative orders as variances of indefinite duration is the 30-day limit on compliance, although EPA has stretched this concept by suggesting that "multiple" orders might issue for an extended enforcement program.[47] EPA "normally limits its use of 309 orders to violations of federally-issued permits. When

---

42. See ELI Enforcement Report at 221–22, discussing United States v. Detrex Chem. Indus., Crim.No. C74–259 (N.D.Ohio 1974).

43. Cf. In re Virginia Elec. & Power Co. (North Anna Power Station Units 1 and 2), Constr. Permit Nos. CPPR–77, –78, Decision of the Atomic Safety and Licensing Appeal Bd., ALAB 324, 3 NRC 347 (1976), where VEPCO was fined $17,500 for material false statements in its formal submissions to the Atomic Energy Commission. Based on VEPCO's net earnings in 1975 of approximately $154,732,000, VEPCO, 1975 Annual Report 13 (1976), the fine roughly is equivalent to imposing a $1.70 penalty on an individual with a net income of $15,000. This is a substantial fine by NRC standards. The fine subsequently was increased to $32,500.

See Decision of the Commission, NRCI 76/11, 480 (1976), petitions for review pending VEPCO v. Nuclear Regulatory Comm'n, Civil No. 76–2275 (4th Cir.). See also § 1.13 n. 94 above.

44. The issue is discussed in connection with oil pollution penalties. § 4.17 above.

45. 33 U.S.C.A. § 1319(a)(4).

46. § 3.19 above; see Bethlehem Steel Corp. v. Train, 544 F.2d 657, 7 ELR 20019 (3d Cir. 1976), cert. denied —— U.S. —— (1977).

47. Memorandum to Directors, Enforcement Division, from Assistant Administrator for Enforcement and General Counsel, Mar. 20, 1974, quoted in pertinent part in ELI Enforcement Report at 178.

a region encounters a violation of a state-issued permit, it usually notifies both the state and the discharger pursuant to [section] 309(a)(1). According to that provision, however, EPA must issue its own order (or proceed with a judicial remedy) if the state fails to take 'appropriate enforcement action' within thirty days."[48] As in the case of administrative orders issued under the Clean Air Act,[49] the subject of administrative remedies under FWPCA deserves continuing study and analysis.

Apart from the traditional agenda of enforcement powers, the FWPCA anticipates enforcement in other ways, both by formal and informal means. The NPDES permit program is an enforcement device of considerable moment, which should prescribe for individual sources precise substantive obligations and compliance schedules.[50] Water pollution violators may be ineligible for federal contracts, grants, and loans.[51] The withholding of construction grants occasionally was used as an enforcement device even before enactment of the 1972 Amendments.[52] Most importantly, an understanding of EPA's enforcement efforts requires a recognition that negotiation, persuasion, and bargaining have been the preferred methods of resolving water pollution conflicts for decades.[53] While this process is open to heavy criticism on grounds of procedure, appearance, and result, it is a legal reality that deserves attention in no less a degree than the occasional formal adversarial clashes.

b. *Municipal Treatment Works and Federal Facilities*

Municipal sewage treatment plants always have presented unique enforcement challenges because their owners are not as easily fined, jailed, or shut down as are their private counterparts. Added to this is the practical point that progress in controlling water pollution at the local level substantially is determined by the flow of federal money, undercutting the normal incentives for enforcement. It has been held that interruptions of federal grant money are no justification for a failure to meet effluent requirements,[54] but the con-

---

48. ELI Enforcement Report at 179. What an "appropriate enforcement action" may be is anyone's guess, although it certainly anticipates action of some kind. See also Mianus River Preservation Comm. v. Administrator, 541 F.2d 899 (2d Cir. 1976) (dismissing for lack of jurisdiction a petition to review in the court of appeals a permit modification approved by state authorities exercising delegated NPDES powers).

49. § 3.19 above.

50. §§ 4.11– .13 above.

51. Section 508(c), 33 U.S.C.A. § 1368 (c); cf. 42 U.S.C.A. § 1857h–4 (a similar provision under the Clean Air Act). Implementing regulations applicable to both air and water violators are published in 40 Fed.Reg. 17124 (1975), adding 40 CFR pt. 15; see § 4.2 n. 70 above.

52. ELI Enforcement Report at 189.

53. See generally N. W. Hines, supra note 15.

54. Virginia State Water Quality Bd. v. Train, 6 ELR 20243 (E.D.Va.1976) (specifically reserving decision, however, on whether a lack of promised federal funding may support an impossibility defense in an enforcement proceeding).

straints on enforcement remain. EPA generally does not recommend enforcement action against municipalities whose cleanup efforts lag for want of federal money, and some regions appear to have a flat policy of not recommending enforcement actions against municipal dischargers. For this and other reasons, control of water pollution from municipal sewage treatment works has not been featured under FWPCA.[55]

The states have struggled with municipal dischargers for years, with mixed success. There are spectacular instances of equitable relief, including the placement of a treatment works in receivership,[56] and several other examples of cleanup injunctions despite pleas of hardship and poverty.[57] But the discovery of effective remedies has been elusive, and a policy of accommodation is often the easy way out. Professor Currie points out the lack of success in Illinois in seeking to impose monetary penalties against municipal governments or their responsible officers.[58]

Authorities in Illinois, however, also have discovered and invoked [59] the single enforcement tool that stands a chance of overcoming the immunities of local government water polluters—the sewer hookup ban or moratorium on new connections. That sewage treatment, and especially collection systems, may subsidize and direct local growth ambitions is a matter of record.[60] Placing limits on the availability of these facilities can freeze or deter future growth just as dramatically. Unfortunately, land use decisions affecting growth often are not confronted directly by local governments but rather are thrashed out coincidentally in debates over capacity, design and reach of a sewage treatment works. Where system capacity is exceeded, the justification for a moratorium is easily discovered: "Prohibiting additional connections after the lagoon is in operation while effluent standards are violated speaks for itself. Additional sewage should not be introduced into a plant that can not adequately process its present load." [61] Clearly, a sewer moratorium hits hard at

---

55. § 4.13 above.

56. New Jersey Dep't of Health v. Jersey City, C34–47–67 (Hudson County Ct.N.J.), reported in ELI Enforcement Report at 249 n. 91. Maryland has created a state corporation with authority to build sewage treatment facilities and pass the charges on to local government. Md.Nat.Res. Code Ann. § 3.101 et seq. This statutory receivership has not been invoked.

57. Dep't of Health v. Passaic Valley Sewerage Comm'n, 100 N.J.Super. 540, 242 A.2d 675 (1967), aff'd per curiam 105 N.J.Super. 565, 253 A.2d 577 (1968); Derby v. Water Resources Comm'n, 148 Conn. 584, 172 A.2d 907 (1961).

58. Enforcement Under the Illinois Pollution Law, 70 Nw.U.L.Rev. 389, 429–30, 433–34 (1975).

59. Id. at 435–43.

60. Council on Environmental Quality, Interceptor Sewers and Suburban Sprawl (1974) (a 2-volume study prepared by Urban Systems Research and Engineering, Inc.). Compare § 2.17 above (land development controls).

61. Citizens Utilities Co. v. Pollution Control Bd., 9 Ill.App.3d 158, 162, 289 N.E.2d 642, 645 (2d Dist. 1972).

the interests of both local governments (which may be hurt by reductions in tax revenues, increased unemployment, and other impacts) and their citizens (who have made expenditures in reliance upon an ability to connect). This particular version of the no-growth debate has been contested hotly in the courts wherever moratoria have been imposed, either by local governments themselves or by outside authorities seeking to control water pollution problems.[62]

Section 402(h) of the Act[63] gives the permitting agency, upon a finding that a NPDES permit condition is being violated, the power to go to court to secure a moratorium on future connections. EPA has never used this potent weapon, just as it has never used its authority to intervene in emergencies. Indeed, the EPA General Counsel has ruled that a permit may not contain a hookup ban,[64] "reasoning that a moratorium on connections may be imposed only by a court and then only after a permit violation has occurred. But the issue may be one largely of semantics and form: permitting authorities need not sit idly by approving discharges from an oft overloaded facility that is in violation of water quality standards. Limitations on the rate and quantity of flow may be reasonably related to water quality, and limitations on the influent are reasonably related to the rate and quantity of flow. Needless to say, if NPDES municipal permits become (they are not now) seriously implicated in sewer hookup (and ergo growth) policies, the issue is comparable in magnitude to the no significant deterioration policy under the Clean Air Act." [65]

---

62. See, e. g., Comm. for the Consideration of the Jones Falls Sewage System v. Train, 375 F.Supp. 1148 (D.C.Md.1974), aff'd 539 F.2d 1006 (4th Cir. 1976) (dismissing action against municipal defendants to compel imposition of sewer hookup moratorium); Robinson v. Boulder, — Colo. —, 547 P.2d 228, 6 ELR 20418 (1976) (city cannot refuse to extend sewer and water services to outlying residential developments for growth control purposes); Morshead v. Regional Water Quality Control Bd., 45 Cal.App.3d 442, 119 Cal.Rptr. 586 (1975) (upholding validity of a sewer hookup ban); Citizens Utilities Co. v. Pollution Control Bd., 9 Ill.App. 3d 158, 289 N.E.2d 642 (2d Dist. 1972) (upholding moratorium); Virginia Water Bd. v. Supervisors, 1 ERC 1482 (1970) (temporarily suspending moratorium). Compare § 2.17 above.

63. 33 U.S.C.A. § 1342(h) reads:
In the event any condition of a permit for discharges from a treatment works . . . which is publicly owned is violated, a State with a program approved under subsection (b) of this section or the Administrator, where no state program is approved, may proceed in a court of competent jurisdiction to restrict or prohibit the introduction of any pollutant into such treatment works by a source not utilizing such treatment works prior to the finding that such condition was violated.

64. NPDES Decision of the General Counsel No. 33, Oct. 21, 1975 (Blue Plains Sewage Treatment Plant, Wash., D. C.). The author is an attorney of record in the case.

65. § 4.13 above, citing § 3.12 above. Notwithstanding the advice of the General Counsel, some sewer connection bans have been incorporated in NPDES permits. See ELI Enforcement Report at 902 (Ohio).

The discrete problem of polluting federal facilities is addressed in Section 313 of FWPCA,[66] which is virtually identical to Section 118 of the Clean Air Act.[67] The heart of the obligation is that federal facilities are subject to state and local "requirements respecting control and abatement of pollution to the same extent that any person" is subject to these requirements. The Supreme Court has held that the "requirements" to which federal facilities are subject include state substantive water quality standards and presumably the effluent limitations but not the permit requirements which are the chief means of enforcing them.[68] Finding no "clear and unambiguous"[69] congressional expression that federal facilities are to be subjected to state permit requirements, the Court preferred to run the risk of an uneven enforcement of water pollution laws against private and public dischargers. As in its companion decision under the Clean Air Act,[70] the Court appears to have read the congressional will too narrowly and has invited awkwardness of administration in pursuit of no particular policy aim.

In one respect, the water pollution decision on federal facilities is less damaging than the air pollution decision. Under FWPCA the Environmental Protection Agency clearly has powers to administer a permit program, and it is presently exercising that power as regards federal facilities. It is reported that "some federal facilities might slip the 1977 compliance deadlines because issuance of their permits has been delayed. When interviewed in January [1975], EPA officials hoped to have all permits issued by March 1975 so that agencies could include in their FY 1977 budget requests (due in June 1975) funds for the projects necessary to meet the permit requirements."[71]

---

66. 33 U.S.C.A. § 1323, provides in part:

> Each department, agency or instrumentality of the executive, legislative and judicial branches of the Federal Government (1) having jurisdiction over any property or facility, or (2) engaged in any activity resulting, or which may result, in the discharge or runoff of pollutants shall comply with Federal, State, interstate and local requirements respecting control and abatement of pollution to the same extent that any person is subject to such requirements, including the payment of reasonable service charges.

As under Section 118 of the Clean Air Act, section 313 contains various provisions inviting presidentially approved exemptions.

67. § 3.19 above.

68. Environmental Protection Agency v. California ex rel. State Water Resources Control Bd., 426 U.S. 200, 96 S.Ct. 2022, 48 L.Ed.2d 578 (1976).

69. 426 U.S. at 211, 96 S.Ct. at 2028, 48 L.Ed.2d at 587. The court concluded "that the Federal Water Pollution Control Act Amendments of 1972 do not subject federal facilities to state NPDES permit requirements with the requisite degree of clarity." 426 U.S. at 227, 96 S.Ct. at 2035, 48 L.Ed.2d at 596. Executive Order No. 11752, 38 Fed.Reg. 34893 (1973) commits all federal facilities to comply with state and local substantive pollution standards but not their administrative procedures.

70. Hancock v. Train, 426 U.S. 167, 96 S.Ct. 2006, 48 L.Ed.2d 555 (1976).

71. ELI Enforcement Report at 322 (footnote omitted).

Sec. 4.21　　　　　　ENFORCEMENT　　　　　　　545

The power to enforce compliance is another matter. Under section 309 EPA may take various actions against any "person" violating a permit, but a "person" as defined elsewhere in the Act does not include a federal agency.[72] Several EPA regions indicate "they will issue administrative orders to non-complying federal facilities. But other regions indicate they will merely contact the violators and encourage them to make a better compliance effort. As for litigation to enforce permits and orders, EPA's authority to sue sister agencies is uncertain and it is EPA policy not to sue."[73] It is clear that any citizen, including a state, may sue to enforce compliance by a federal facility,[74] so a short-run effect of the decision excusing federal agencies from state permit requirements may be an increase in lawsuits by states recently disappointed in their efforts to exercise permit authority over federal facilities.

c. *State Enforcement Powers*

The legislative history of FWPCA makes clear that "the great volume of enforcement actions [is to] be brought by the State. It is clear that the Administrator [of EPA] is not to establish an enforcement bureaucracy but rather to reserve his authority for the cases of paramount interest."[75] While there is considerable evidence that states have been slow to use coercive techniques to abate water pollution,[76] it is also true that many states have the requisite authority for an effective enforcement program.[77] Several state laws grant enforcement powers substantially beyond those enjoyed by EPA, including the authority administratively to impose civil monetary penalties (several statutes have appeared setting $1,000 per day limits [78]),

72. Section 502(5), 33 U.S.C.A. § 1362 (5).

73. ELI Enforcement Report at 234 (footnote omitted).

74. Section 505, 33 U.S.C.A. § 1365.

75. Comm. on Public Works, Federal Water Pollution Control Act Amendments of 1971, S.Rep. No. 414, 92d Cong., 1st Sess. 64 (1971).

76. See, e. g., N. W. Hines, supra note 15.

77. See 1 F.Grad, Environmental Law: Pollution Control § 3.04, at 3–201 to –232 (summarizing existing state laws on water pollution); cf. id. § 3.-04, at 3–193 to –201 (summarizing interstate compacts on water pollution).

78. Alabama, 6 Code of Ala., tit. 22, § 140(12d)(o) ($100–$10,000); Alaska, Alas.Stat.Ann. § 46.03.790 (willful violation, not to exceed $1,000 and up to one year imprisonment); Arkansas, 7A Ark.Stat.Ann. § 82–1909 (a) (not to exceed $10,000 and up to one year imprisonment); California, Cal.Water Code Ann. § 13350(a) (intentional or negligent violation, not to exceed $6,000); Colorado, 11 Colo. Rev.Stat. § 25–8–609 (negligent or reckless violation, not to exceed $12,-000) (knowing or intentional violation, not to exceed $25,000); Connecticut, 12 Conn.Gen.Stat.Ann. § 25–54q(b) (willful or negligent violation, not to exceed $25,000); Delaware, 4 Del. Code Ann. ch. 7, § 6162(b)(1) ($1,000–$10,000); Florida, 14B Fla.Stat.Ann. § 403.121(1)(b) (not to exceed $5,000); Georgia, 6 Code of Ga.Ann. § 17–521.2 (not to exceed $1,000 for first day of violation and $500 for each additional day); Illinois, Ill.Ann.Stat. ch. 111½, § 1042(a) (Smith-Hurd) (not to exceed $10,000 and $1,000 for each day of violation); Iowa, 25 Iowa Code Ann. § 455B.49 (willful or negligent violation, not to exceed $10,000 for

and to sue for cleanup costs and damages to the environment.[79] States agencies have participated prominently in recent significant water pol-

first conviction and not to exceed $20,000 for any conviction thereafter); Kansas, 5 Kan.Stat.Ann. § 65–170d(a) (not to exceed $10,000); Kentucky, 9 Ky.Rev.Stat. § 224.994 (not to exceed $5,000) (willful violation, $1,000–$10,000 and up to one year imprisonment); Louisiana, 27 La.Rev. Stat. § 56:1444 ($100–$2,000 and up to one year imprisonment); Maine, 16 Me.Rev.Stat.Ann. ch. 38, § 453 ($200–$25,000); Maryland, Nat.Res. Code Ann. § 8–1416 (not to exceed $25,000 for first conviction and not to exceed $50,000 thereafter); Massachusetts, Mass.Gen.Laws Ann. ch. 21, § 42 ($2,500–$10,000); Michigan, 16 Mich.Comp.Laws § 323.10(2) ($2,500–$25,000 for first conviction and not to exceed $50,000 thereafter); Minnesota, 9 Minn.Stat.Ann. § 115.071(2) (negligent violation, $300–$25,000) (willful violation, $2,500–$25,000); Mississippi, 12 Miss.Code Ann. § 49–17–43(a) ($50–$3,000 and up to one year imprisonment); Missouri, 12 Ann. Mo.Stat. § 204.076(3) (willful or negligent violation) ($2,500–$25,000 for first conviction and not to exceed $50,000 thereafter); Montana, Rev.Codes of Mont.Ann. § 69–4823 (not to exceed $10,000); Nevada, Nev.Rev. Stat. § 445.331(1) (not to exceed $10,000); New Hampshire, 2 N.H.Rev. Stat.Ann. § 149:19(I) (not to exceed $25,000 and up to six months imprisonment); New Jersey, N.J.S.A. § 58:12–4.1 ($1,000–$3,000); New Mexico, 11 N.M.Stat.Ann. § 75–39–4.1 (P) ($300–$10,000); New York, N.Y. Environmental Conservation Laws § 71–1933(1) (McKinney) ($500–$10,000 and up to one year imprisonment); North Carolina, 3C Gen.Stat. of N.C. § 143–215.6(b)(1) (not to exceed $1,500); North Dakota, 12 N.D.Cent. Code Ann. § 61–28–08(1) (willful violation) (not to exceed $25,000 and up to one year imprisonment for first conviction, and not to exceed $50,000 and up to two years imprisonment thereafter); Ohio, Ohio Rev.Code Ann. § 6111.99(A) (not to exceed $25,000 and up to one year imprisonment); Oregon, Ore.Rev.Stat. § 468.942 (not to exceed $25,000 and up to one year imprisonment); Pennsylvania, 35 Pa. Stat.Ann. § 691.602(a) ($100–$1,000); South Carolina, 12 Code of Laws of S.C. § 63–195.35 ($500–$25,000); South Dakota, 13 S.D.Comp.Laws § 46–25–91 (not to exceed $25,000 and up to one year imprisonment); Tennessee, 12 Tenn.Code Ann. § 70–337 (a) ($50–$5,000); Texas, Tex.Water Code Ann. § 21.553 ($10–$1,000); Vermont, Vt.Stat.Ann. tit. 10, § 1275 (not to exceed $25,000 and up to six months imprisonment); Virginia, 9 Code of Va. § 62.1–44.32 (not to exceed $10,000); Washington, Rev.Code Wash.Ann. § 90.48.144(3) (not to exceed $5,000); West Virginia, 8 W.Va. Code § 20–5A–19 ($1,000–$10,000); Wisconsin, 20 Wis.Stat.Ann. § 147.21 (3) (not to exceed $25,000 for first conviction, and not to exceed $50,000 thereafter); Wyoming, 8 Wyo.Stat. § 35–502.49(c) (not to exceed $25,000 for first conviction, and not to exceed $50,000 thereafter). See also Council of State Governments, State Water Pollution Control Act § 21, in 33 Suggested State Legislation 36, 46 (1974) [hereinafter cited as Model State Act].

79. Alabama, 6 Code of Ala. tit. 22, § 140(12d)(p); Alaska, Alas.Stat.Ann. § 46.03.780; Arkansas, 7A Ark.Stat. Ann. § 82–1909(c) (not to exceed $5,000 per day of violation); California, Cal.Water Code Ann. § 13304 (a) (intentional or negligent violation); Connecticut, 12 Conn.Gen.Stat.Ann. § 25–54q(a) (willful or negligent, not to exceed $10,000 per day of violation); Florida, 14B Fla.Stat.Ann. § 403.141(1) (not to exceed $10,000 per day of violation); Georgia, 6 Code of Ga.Ann. § 17–521.1(1); Illinois, Ill. Ann.Stat. ch. 111½, § 1042(b) (Smith-Hurd) (reasonable value of fish or aquatic life destroyed); Kentucky, 9 Ky.Rev.Stat. § 224.110 (necessary to restock fish and wildlife); Louisiana, 27 La.Rev.Stat. § 56:1446; Maine, 16 Me.Rev.Stat.Ann. ch. 38, § 453; Maryland, Nat.Res.Code Ann. § 8–1416(d) ($500–$10,000 per day of violation); Massachusetts, Mass.Gen. Laws Ann. ch. 131, § 42 (twice the value of fish and wildlife destroyed); Michigan, 16 Mich.Comp.Laws § 323.-10(2); Mississippi, 12 Miss.Code Ann. § 49–17–43(b) (necessary to restock fish and wildlife); Nevada, Nev.Rev. Stat. § 445.331(3); New York, N.Y.

Sec. 4.21 ENFORCEMENT 547

lution litigation involving the pollutants PCB's,[80] mercury,[81] and asbestos,[82] among others.

State enforcement of water pollution laws, like state enforcement of air pollution laws, is a subject often addressed in the journals.[83] The case law is sufficiently well developed to support the conclusion that administrative decisions are given a close scrutiny in accordance with what are now established principles of environmental law.[84] Thus, general powers to regulate water pollution and make distinctions among sources are sustained usually in the face of police power,[85] delegation,[86] taking,[87] and discrimination[88] arguments. There

Environmental Conservation Laws § 71–1941(1) (McKinney); Oklahoma, Okl.Stat.Ann. tit. 82, § 937(b) (necessary to restock fish and wildlife); Oregon, Ore.Rev.Stat. § 468.745(1) (necessary to restock fish and wildlife); Pennsylvania, 35 Pa.Stat.Ann. § 691.605; South Carolina, § 63–195.-3511 (not to exceed $10,000 per day of violation); South Dakota, 13 S.D. Comp.Laws § 46–25–92 (not to exceed $10,000 per day of violation); Tennessee, 12 Tenn.Code Ann. § 70–338; Texas, Tex.Water Code Ann. § 21.-252 ($50–$1,000 per day of violation); Washington, Rev.Code Wash.Ann. § 90.48.142; West Virginia, 8 W.Va.Code § 20–5A–019a; Wisconsin, 20 Wis.Stat. Ann. § 147.23; Wyoming, 8 Wyo.Stat. § 35–502.49(b) (necessary to restock fish and wildlife). See also Model State Act § 20, comment.

80. In re General Elec. Co., 6 ELR 30001, 30007 (N.Y. Dep't of Environmental Conservation 1976).

81. State ex rel. Brown v. BASF Wyandotte Corp., 4 ELR 20520 (Ohio Ct.Common Pleas 1974).

82. Reserve Mining Co. v. Environmental Protection Agency, 514 F.2d 492, 5 ELR 20596 (8th Cir. 1975).

83. E. g., Arnold, supra note 4; Coggins, Regulation of Air and Water Quality in Kansas: A Critical Look at Legislative Ambiguity and Administrative Discretion, 21 Kan.L.Rev. 1 (1972); Esposito, Air and Water Pollution: What to Do While Waiting for Washington, 5 Harv.Civ.Rights L.Rev. 32 (1970); Freeborn, Illinois Environmental Law—The New Assault on Water Pollution, 24 De Paul L.Rev. 481 (1975); Hines, Nor Any Drop to Drink: Public Regulation of Water Quality, 52 Iowa L.Rev. 186 (1967); Laska, Water Pollution Control in Alaska: The Alaska Environmental Conservation Act of 1971, 4 U.C.L.A.–Alas.L.Rev. 263 (1975); Typer, Methods for State Level Enforcement of Air and Water Pollution Laws, 31 Tex.Bar J. 905 (1968); Note, Water Pollution—State Control Committee, 17 Vand.L.Rev. 1364 (1964); Note, Water Pollution Control Reform in Iowa: The Department of Environmental Quality Act of 1972, 8 Urban L.Ann. 241 (1974); Note Florida Courts and Water Pollution: A Floating Crap Game, 2 Environmental L. 189 (1971); Note, Water Pollution Control in New York, 31 Albany L. Rev. 50 (1967); Note, Water Quality Control in Georgia, 16 Mercer L.Rev. 469 (1965); Note, Water Pollution Control in Colorado, 36 U.Colo.L.Rev. 413 (1964); Note, Water Pollution Control in Idaho, 1 Idaho L.Rev. 111 (1964); Comment, Defenses to Orders and Actions of the Pennsylvania Department of Environmental Resources, 80 Dick.L.Rev. 265 (1976).

84. §§ 1.5, 3.19 above.

85. Hutchinson v. Valdosta, 227 U.S. 303, 33 S.Ct. 290, 57 L.Ed. 520 (1913); Bd. of Purification of Waters v. East Providence, 47 R.I. 431, 133 A. 812 (1926); Hines, supra note 83, at 212 (discussing hypothetical controls solely for aesthetic purposes). See also Soap & Detergent Ass'n v. Chicago, 357 F.Supp. 44, 3 ELR 20228 (N.D.Ill. 1973), rev'd sub nom. Proctor & Gamble, Inc. v. Chicago, 509 F.2d 69 (7th Cir. 1975), cert. denied 421 U.S. 978, 95 S.Ct. 1980, 44 L.Ed.2d 470.

86. See note 86 on page 548.

87. See note 87 on page 548.

88. See note 88 on page 548.

is a strict insistence upon procedural fairness, and enforcement efforts have been frustrated on grounds of inadequate notice [89] and opportunity for hearing,[90] denial of the right of cross-examination,[91] non-compliance with environmental laws,[92] and other failures of proof.[93] The administrative schemes often anticipate prior action by an agency so enforcement actions may run into objections of primary jurisdiction.[94] Remands to supplement the record are not uncommon.[95]

If the administrative agency acts on a full record and pays attention to procedural details, the state courts generally will not interfere with discretionary judgments.[96] Review may be strict, however,

86. Utica v. Water Pollution Control Bd., 5 N.Y.2d 164, 182 N.Y.S.2d 584, 156 N.E.2d 301 (1959). Contra, State Water Pollution Control Bd. v. Salt Lake City, 6 Utah 2d 247, 311 P.2d 370 (1957).

87. United States v. 531.13 Acres of Land, 366 F.2d 915 (4th Cir. 1966), cert. denied 385 U.S. 1025 (1967); Potomac Sand & Gravel Co. v. Governor, 266 Md. 358, 293 A.2d 241 (1972), cert. denied 409 U.S. 1040; Vermont Woolen Corp. v. Wackerman, 122 Vt. 219, 167 A.2d 533 (1961). Contra, Pittsburgh Coal Co. v. Sanitary Water Bd., 4 Pa.Comm. 407, 286 A.2d 459, 2 ELR 20339 (1972).

88. Stock v. State, 3 ELR 20569 (Alas. Super.Ct.1973), aff'd 526 P.2d 3 (Alas. Sup.Ct.1974); Vermont Woolen Corp. v. Wackerman, supra note 87; Diamond v. Mobil Oil Co., 65 Misc.2d 75, 316 N.Y.S.2d 734 (Sup.Ct. Erie County 1971). Contra, Sigety v. State Bd. of Health, 482 P.2d 574, 1 ELR 20258 (Mont.1971) (invalidating mining regulation law on equal protection and other grounds because of exemptions for several types of mining).

89. Commonwealth v. Toro Dev. Co., 2 Pa.Comm. 429, 1 ELR 20367 (1971) (sustaining objections of lack of specificity in complaint charging non-point source pollution by the washing of soil).

90. St. Regis Paper Co. v. State, 237 So.2d 797 (Fla.Dist.Ct.App.1970), modified 257 So.2d 253 (Fla.Sup.Ct. 1971) (civil penalty proceeding).

91. L. A. Darling Co. v. Water Resources Comm'n, 341 Mich. 654, 67 N.W.2d 890 (1955) (also a lack of sworn witnesses, no identification of exhibits or of the materials relied upon, and no findings were made) (denial of procedural due process).

92. Roswell v. New Mexico Water Quality Control Comm'n, 84 N.M. 561, 505 P.2d 1237, 3 ELR 20181 (1972); Stempel v. Dep't of Water Resources, 82 Wash.2d 109, 508 P.2d 166, 3 ELR 20685 (1973).

93. A. P. Weaver & Sons v. Sanitary Water Bd., 3 Pa.Comm. 499, 284 A.2d 515, 2 ELR 20120 (1971) (revocation of mine drainage permit) (no allowance of right of cross-examination; insufficient proof of causation). Compare Providence Journal Co. v. Shea, 110 R.I. 342, 292 A.2d 856, 2 ELR 20500 (1972) (requiring public access to the water pollution files of the Department of Health).

94. Sierra Club v. Sanitary Water Bd., 3 Pa.Comm. 110, 281 A.2d 256, 1 ELR 20494 (1971); White Lake Improvement Ass'n v. Whitehall, 22 Mich. App. 262, 177 N.W.2d 473 (1970); § 1.9 above.

95. In re Int'l Acceptance Corp., 1 ELR 20411 (Del.Super.Ct.1971); North Shore Sanitary Dist. v. Pollution Control Bd., 2 Ill.App.3d 797, 277 N.E.2d 754, 2 ELR 20144 (1972).

96. Plymouth Village Fire Dist. v. Water Pollution Comm'n, 103 N.H. 169, 167 A.2d 677 (1961); Bd. of Health

if the administrative decision is viewed as a question of law.[97] Whatever the standard of review, courts may choose to look skeptically at agency decisions with which they disagree. A good example is the case of North Suburban Sanitary Sewer Dist. v. Water Pollution Control Comm'n,[98] where the Minnesota Supreme Court reviewed a voluminous administrative record and upset an application of administrative standards forbidding the construction of a sewage treatment plant on the Mississippi River. The plant was thought to impose a remote but nonetheless serious risk to the integrity of Minneapolis' water supply. The case is an excellent example of a court confidently assessing risks that, while technological and scientific in origin, ultimately present a choice of policy.

The range of remedies invoked in water pollution enforcement cases is broad—civil[99] and criminal penalties,[1] and injunctions of great variety. Normal equitable considerations govern the choice of a decree,[2] including the economic impact on the source and the health consequences of the discharge.[3] The equitable defenses of estoppel, laches, and the like are theoretically but not practically available.[4] Orders may go into considerable detail on effluent limi-

v. Crew, 212 Md. 229, 129 A.2d 115 (1957); Derby v. Water Resources Comm'n, 148 Conn. 584, 172 A.2d 907 (1961); Dep't of Health v. Passaic Valley Sewerage Comm'n, 100 N.J.Super. 540, 242 A.2d 675 (1967), aff'd per curiam 105 N.J.Super. 565, 253 A.2d 577 (1968); Dep't of Water Resources v. A. H. Smith Sand & Gravel Co., 3 ELR 20581 (Md.Cir.Ct. 1973); Commonwealth v. Harmar Coal Co., 452 Pa. 77, 306 A.2d 308, 3 ELR 20336 (1973); State ex rel. Bar Realty Corp. v. Locker, 30 Ohio St.2d 190, 283 N.E.2d 164, 2 ELR 20375 (1972) (writ of mandamus may not issue to compel city officials to enforce water pollution laws); DeRham v. Diamond, 32 N.Y.2d 34, 343 N.Y.S. 2d 84, 295 N.E.2d 763, 3 ELR 20327 (1973) (reviewing state certification of compliance with water quality standards under a reasonable basis test); Chillisquaque Creek Watershed Ass'n v. Sanitary Water Bd., 2 Pa. Comwlth. 561, 280 A.2d 132 (1971); Sierra Club v. Sanitary Water Bd., 3 Pa.Comwlth. 110, 281 A.2d 256, 1 ELR 20494 (1971).

97. Pittsburgh Coal Co. v. Sanitary Water Bd., 4 Pa.Comwlth. 407, 286 A.2d 459, 2 ELR 20339 (1972) (operator of a mine may not be required to treat water seeping into mine from other sources) (court relies in part on taking principles).

98. 281 Minn. 524, 162 N.W.2d 249 (1968).

99. Notes 78, 79, supra.

1. Stock v. State, 3 ELR 20569 (Alas. Super.Ct.1973), aff'd 526 P.2d 3 (Alas. Sup.Ct.1974) (president of a corporation criminally liable if he knows of the violation and has authority to prevent it); State v. Kinsley, 103 N.J. Super. 190, 246 A.2d 764 (1968), aff'd 105 N.J.Super. 347, 252 A.2d 224.

2. Notes 31-36 above; § 2.11 above (nuisances); § 7.10 below (National Environmental Policy Act).

3. Diamond v. Mobil Oil Co., 65 Misc. 2d 75, 316 N.Y.S.2d 734 (Sup.Ct. Erie County 1971) (refusing injunction against large employer but indicating in dicta that injunction would be entered if health considerations were involved).

4. Moore v. Central Oklahoma Master Conservancy Dist., 441 P.2d 452 (Okl. 1968); Commonwealth v. Barnes & Tucker Co., 455 Pa. 392, 319 A.2d 871, 4 ELR 20545 (1974).

tations [5] and treatment obligations.[6] Ordinarily, as in the air pollution enforcement cases,[7] pleas of economic and technical hardship should be heard at the administrative level and not at the enforcement stage,[8] although sympathetic legislatures always can prolong the process by allowing de novo litigation when the matter goes to court.[9]

5. Rhodia, Inc. v. Harris County, 470 S.W.2d 415, 1 ELR 20413 (Tex.Ct.Civ.App.1971) (defendant enjoined during pendency of litigation from discharging arsenic concentrations in excess of one part per million); cf. Dep't of Water Resources v. A. H. Smith Sand & Gravel Co., 3 ELR 20581 (Md.Cir.Ct.1973) (upholding abatement order restricting settleable solids discharge to no more than 400 parts per million).

6. E. g., Derby v. Water Resources Comm'n, 148 Conn. 584, 172 A.2d 907 (1961).

7. § 3.19 above.

8. State v. Juneau, 238 Wis. 564, 300 N.W. 187 (1941); See 1 F. Grad, Environmental Law: Pollution Control § 3.04 at 3–231 to –232 (1975).

9. See ELI Enforcement Report at 203–04 (discussing various treatments of this question under state water pollution laws).

Chapter V

NOISE POLLUTION

§ 5.1 Background

Noise pollution is excessive sound.[1] Because it leaves no residue, it is generally considered to be one of the less serious pollutants. But a technological ill that is responsible for permanent hearing defects in four to five million people [2] and that subjects forty-four million others to annoying airport and highway noise [3] is not easily consigned to the trivial. That noise is not a silent, deadly killer but a raucous and easily recognizable invader of privacy perhaps explains why the subject is so popular a grievance in the common law reports.

Sources of noise pollution, like sources of air pollution, can be grouped into stationary and mobile sources although the distinction that is drawn usually for regulatory and analytical purposes is that between transportation and nontransportation sources. Transportation sources include prominently aircraft and highway and recreational vehicles while nontransportation sources embrace a wide range of industrial plants, construction equipment, household appliances, and the like.

A few generalities about noise pollution are appropriate. First, it is acknowledged that with few exceptions technology is available to control noise within tolerable limits.[4] The debate thus focuses more readily on the economic question of whether the benefits to be gained justify the investment. A second distinction of excessive noise is that while anyone can recognize it, measuring and describing it is quite another matter. The "bewildering array of terminology," says one sophisticated reporter, is "complex and confusing even to those well versed in acoustics." [5] So we have decibels (dB) to measure sound

---

1. A more popular definition is that noise is unwanted sound. See Hearings on Noise Control Act of 1971 and Amendments, Before the Subcomm. on the Environment of the Senate Comm. on Commerce, S.Doc. No.48, 92d Cong., 1st Sess. 172 (1971) (statement of William Ruckelshaus, Administrator, Environmental Protection Agency). It is rejected here in favor of an objective standard not dependent upon the subjective response of the receptor.

2. Hearings on Noise Control, Before the Subcomm. on Public Health & Environment of the House Comm. on Interstate & Foreign Commerce, H.R. Doc.No.30, 92d Cong., 1st Sess. 137 (1971) (EPA, Summary Status Report).

3. House Comm. on Interstate & Foreign Commerce, Noise Control Act of 1972, H.R.Rep.No.842, 92d Cong., 2d Sess. 6 (1972). Compare § 5.8 n. 1 below.

4. Id. at 7.

5. EPA, Summary Report on Noise 8 (1971).

pressure, perceived noise decibels (PNdB) which take into account subjective responses to each of the octave bands, and effective perceived noise decibels (EPNdB) which add still greater refinement by judging the effects of tone and duration. Subjective loudness is a function of both magnitude or pressure (measured in decibels) and of frequency (the rate at which the sound pressure level oscillates with time).[6] Methods are used to extrapolate a pressure equivalency for sounds of various frequency by approximating the frequency response of the human ear (the A-weighting scale being the most popular), thus allowing a general expression of sound levels in decibel terms. By this route, decibels (dB(A)) measure noise for legal purposes as parts per million are used to measure sulfur dioxide in the atmosphere.

Noise, like the other pollutants, has been the subject of criteria documents describing fully adverse effects at various levels of exposure.[7] Generally, with the exception of sonic booms capable of property damage,[8] the principal known effects are personal injuries to human beings, both physiological (damage to ear, loss of hearing) and psychological (annoyances including interference with sleep, interruption of conversation, and others). Impairment of the quality of life is reflected in the diminution of property values in areas adversely affected.

The law of noise pollution is a ragged amalgam of common law doctrines, outdated anti-noise codes, prevalent at the local level, and modern regulatory schemes beginning to make their appearance in some locales, several states and, in selected instances, within the national government. Compensatory damages for noise related injuries are governed almost exclusively by common law doctrines of nuisance or trespass and variations such as condemnation by adverse possession.[9] Regulation is still in the primitive stages, even for aircraft which have been vulnerable to regulation at the federal level for a number of years.[10] Prospects for more regulation of both transportation and nontransportation sources are certain, reflecting the dogma of the times that market forces cannot keep pace with technological harms.

Noise pollution has achieved the status of a problem worthy of sustained legal consideration. The Secretary of Transportation's decision to permit the Concorde supersonic transport aircraft to make limited commercial flights to and from the United States over a period

6. See Findley & Plager, State Regulation of Nontransportation Noise: Law and Technology, 48 S.Cal.L.Rev. 209, 217–23 (1974).

7. EPA, Public Health and Welfare Criteria for Noise (1973); see EPA, Effects of Noise on People (1971); EPA, Information on Levels of Environmental Noise Requisite to Protect Public Health and Welfare with an Adequate Margin of Safety (1974).

8. See Laird v. Nelms, 406 U.S. 797, 92 S.Ct. 1899, 32 L.Ed.2d 499 (1972).

9. See § 5.3 below.

10. See § 5.7 below.

of sixteen months marks one of the most controversial and celebrated legal milestones in recent history.[11] Simultaneously, the Department of Labor, in virtual obscurity, was considering regulations of infinitely greater short-run, if not long-run, importance—occupational noise exposure standards applicable to commercial establishments throughout the United States.[12] Lofty debate and nitty-gritty struggles are the ingredients of a mature body of law.

§ 5.2 The Noise Control Act: A Summary

The Noise Control Act of 1972 [1] is neither as comprehensive nor as determined in prospects as the Clean Air Act or the Federal Water Pollution Control Act. It represents, nonetheless, a major attempt to define the federal role in noise control, one not likely to be revised radically in the foreseeable future. The Act was the product of familiar forces: national concern over the quality of life that also produced seminal enactments on air and water pollution; dissatisfaction with the *ad hoc* functioning of the common law; impatience with local and state regulation accused of letting a problem get out of hand; a scattering of regulatory authority among a number of federal agencies. Unique influences affecting Congress' deliberations included dissatisfaction with the role of the Federal Aviation Administration in controlling jet noise, which made the issue controversial in virtually every congressional district hosting an airport populated by jet traffic, and a recognition that the sometimes conflicting remedial options of control at the source and land use accommodation required an attempt to delineate carefully federal and state jurisdictional domains.

The 1972 Act reflects a number of ideas borrowed from other federal environmental laws such as a citizen suits provision (section 12) [2] and an authorization to establish a Low-Noise-Emission Product Advisory Committee (section 15),[3] with responsibilities comparable to those of the Low Emission Vehicle Certification Board created by the Clean Air Act.[4] Other concepts in the Act have roots in the

---

11. Dep't of Transp., The Secretary's Decision on Concorde Supersonic Transport, Feb. 4, 1976.

12. § 5.10 below.

1. Pub.L. No. 92–574, 86 Stat. 1232, 42 U.S.C.A. §§ 4901 et seq.; see Lake, Noise: Emerging Federal Control, in Environmental Law Institute, Federal Environmental Law 1150 (E. L. Dolgin & T. G. P. Guilbert eds. 1974); Note, The Noise Control Act of 1972 —Congress Acts to Fill the Gap in Environmental Legislation, 58 Minn. L.Rev. 237 (1973). Title IV of the Clean Air Amendments of 1970 was called the Noise Pollution and Abatement Act of 1970, 84 Stat. 1710, 42 U.S.C.A. § 1858. It directed the Administrator to establish an Office of Noise Abatement and Control within EPA and called for a study on noise "and its effect on public health and welfare." The study that resulted, EPA Report to the President and Congress on Noise (1971), contributed to enactment of the Noise Control Act.

2. 42 U.S.C.A. § 4911; see § 1.13 above.

3. 42 U.S.C.A. § 4914.

4. § 3.2 above; see 40 CFR pt. 203 (Low-noise-emission products).

common law, such as reliance in part upon the "best technology" formulation to define noise emission standards for new products (section 6(c)).[5]

The Act, following the pattern of related initiatives, authorizes the Administrator of EPA to conduct and to contract for research on noise effects, methods for measuring and monitoring noise, and means for controlling it (section 14(1)),[6] and to provide technical assistance to state and local governments for various purposes including the training of noise control personnel and the preparation of model state and local legislation (section 14(2)).[7] Also familiar are the provisions in the Act calling for the preparation of various studies which themselves become documents of legal significance; the Administrator is required to establish criteria for noise, which are basic cause and effect documents, and he was obliged, within twelve months of enactment, to "publish information on the levels of environmental noise the attainment and maintenance of which in defined areas under various conditions are requisite to protect the public health and welfare with an adequate margin of safety" (section 5(a)(2)).[8] Both the criteria and the levels documents are now published.[9] Public health and welfare are not defined in the Act but should take on the same meaning that they are given in the Clean Air Act,[10] and thus are intended to achieve a no-effects ambient noise level. EPA has read the Act this way by identifying 45dB(A) indoors and 55dB(A) outdoors in residential areas as the maximum levels below which no effects occur due to interference with speech or other activity.[11] A 5dB(A) margin of safety is provided to protect speech communication. EPA freely admits that these levels, even with a margin of safety, cannot protect against occasional noise annoyance.[12]

Another important series of reports required by the Act are documents on technology, costs, and alternative methods of noise control,[13] which are equivalent to the control techniques documents as-

---

5. 42 U.S.C.A. § 4905(c)(1); see § 2.6 above.

6. 42 U.S.C.A. § 4913(1).

7. Id. § 4913(2); see Council of State Governments, State Noise Control Act, 33 Suggested State Legislation 10 (1974).

8. 42 U.S.C.A. § 4904(a)(2).

9. See § 5.1 n. 7 above.

10. See § 3.4 above.

11. EPA, Information on Levels of Environmental Noise Requisite to Protect Public Health and Welfare with an Adequate Margin of Safety 22 (1974).

12. Id. at 24:

According to present data, this margin of safety protects the vast majority of the population against long-term annoyance by noise. It would reduce environmental noise to a level where it is least important among environmental factors that influence the population's attitude toward the environment. To define an environment that eliminates any potential annoyance by noise occasionally to some part of the population appears not possible at the present state of knowledge.

13. Section 5(b)(2), 42 U.S.C.A. § 4904 (b)(2); see, e. g., EPA, Background Document for Portable Air Compressors (1975); EPA, Noise in Rail

sociated with the Clean Air Act. Other publications identify products or classes of products which in the judgment of the Administrator "are major sources of noise." [14] Identification of a product as a major source of noise is expected to lead, within eighteen months, to proposed regulations and, within two years, to final regulations.[15] In June of 1974 EPA identified medium and heavy duty trucks and portable air compressors as major sources of noise.[16] In May of 1975 the list of the loud was expanded to include motorcycles, buses, wheel and track loaders and wheel and track dozers (earth-moving equipment), truck transport refrigeration units, and truck mounted solid waste compactors.[17] Future candidates include light trucks, motorboats, chain saws, tires, pneumatic and hydraulic tools, piledrivers, lawn care equipment, and auxiliary truck equipment.[18]

The 1972 Act authorizes federal regulatory initiatives in four important areas: (1) noise emission standards for four categories of sources (construction equipment, transportation equipment [recreational vehicles are included], any motor or engine, and electrical equipment);[19] (2) labeling of any product emitting noise capable of affecting adversely the public health or welfare or which is sold on the basis of its effectiveness in reducing noise;[20] (3) aircraft noise and sonic boom, which necessitated delicate compromises in defining the roles of the Federal Aviation Administration and the Environmental Protection Agency;[21] and (4) noise emission regulations for other transportation sources (railroads and motor carriers).[22]

Enforcement provisions of the 1972 Act are weak, particularly in comparison with similarly motivated legislation such as the Consumer Product Safety Act.[23] Subject to the Administrator's authority

Transit Cars: Incremental Costs of Quieter Cars (1974); EPA, Lawn Mowers: Noise and Cost of Abatement (1974); EPA, 1 Control of Motorcycle Noise: Technology and Cost Information (1973); EPA, 1 Control of Snowmobile Noise: Technology and Cost Information (1973).

14. Section (5)(b)(1), 42 U.S.C.A. § 4909(5)(b)(1); see notes 15–17, infra.

15. Sections 6(a)(2), (3), 42 U.S.C.A. § 4905(a)(2), (3).

16. 39 Fed.Reg. 22297 (1974). This report discusses the criteria for identifying products as major sources of noise. Proposed regulations for these two sources are found in 39 Fed.Reg. 38185 (1974), final regulations in 41 Fed.Reg. 2161 (1976), adding 40 CFR pt. 204 (portable air compressors) and 41 Fed.Reg. 15537 (1976), adding 40 CFR pt. 205 (medium and heavy trucks).

17. 40 Fed.Reg. 23105 (1975).

18. See Summary, 5 ELR 10111 (1975).

19. Section 6, 42 U.S.C.A. § 4905.

20. Section 8, 42 U.S.C.A. § 4907.

21. Section 7(b), amending Section 611 of the Federal Aviation Act of 1958, Pub.L. No. 90–411, 82 Stat. 395, 49 U.S.C.A. § 1431.

22. Sections 17, 18, 42 U.S.C.A. §§ 4916, 4917.

23. Pub.L. No. 92–573, 86 Stat. 1207, 15 U.S.C.A. §§ 2051–81.

to grant open-ended exemptions for various purposes,[24] section 10(a) prohibits a number of obvious violations: (1) distributing any product manufactured in violation of noise emission standards; (2) tampering with any noise control device or using a product after such a device has been rendered inoperative; (3) distributing any new product not in conformity with labeling requirements; (4) removing any notice or label affixed to a product prior to its sale to an ultimate purchaser; (5) importing any product in violation of regulations issued by the Secretary of the Treasury; and (6) failing to comply with a compliance order or other provisions governing the maintenance of records or the regulations affecting railroad or motor carrier noise emission standards.

The only remedy for violating the tampering provisions ((2) and (4) above) is the securing of a prohibitory injunction in the district courts by the United States or the issuance of an administrative order specifying such relief as the Administrator determines "is necessary to protect the public health and welfare." [25] (Another trip to court would be required to enforce the order.) For the other four prohibitions, the same injunctive and administrative remedies are available, with the addition of a misdemeanor provision (that could result in a fine of not more than $25,000 per day or imprisonment for not more than one year or both) if the proof establishes that the violation was "willfully or knowingly committed." It is a safe generality that enforcement under the Noise Control Act of 1972 will be a rare and endangered event. The content of the regulations will be the true measure of the Act.

One of the innovative features of the 1972 Act is section 4(a),[26] which directs federal agencies "to the fullest extent consistent with their authority under Federal laws administered by them" to carry out their programs "to further" the anti-noise policy objectives expressed in the Act. These include a congressional declaration that "it is the policy of the United States to promote an environment for all Americans free from noise that jeopardizes their health or wel-

---

24. Section 10(b)(1), 42 U.S.C.A. § 4909(b)(1), reads:
For the purpose of research, investigations, studies, demonstrations, or training, or for reasons of national security, the Administrator may exempt for a specified period of time any product, or class thereof, from paragraphs (1), (2), (3), and (5) of subsection (a) of this section, upon such terms and conditions as he may find necessary to protect the public health or welfare.

25. Section 11(d)(1), 42 U.S.C.A. § 4910(d)(1).

26. 42 U.S.C.A. § 4903(a), reads:
The Congress authorizes and directs that Federal agencies shall, to the fullest extent consistent with their authority under Federal laws administered by them, carry out the programs within their control in such a manner as to further the policy declared in section 4901(b) of this title.

This directive is supplemented by section 4(b), 42 U.S.C.A. § 4901(b), requiring federal facilities to comply with federal, state, interstate, and local noise control requirements unless exempted by the President.

fare."[27] This confirms not only a responsibility, comparable to that under the National Environmental Policy Act, to consider fully the effect of agency actions on community noise levels[28] but also imposes a substantive (and presumably judicially enforceable) obligation to do something about ("to further") anti-noise policy objectives.[29]

Another interesting feature of the Noise Control Act is section 4 (c)(2)[30] which in some respects goes beyond Section 309 of the Clean Air Act. Under section 309 the Administrator can act as a self-starting critic of other agency action thought to be "unsatisfactory from the standpoint of public health or welfare or environmental quality"; he may publish his determination and refer the matter to the Council on Environmental Quality.[31] Under section 4(c)(2), in the event the Administrator determines that another agency's regulation or proposed regulation respecting noise "does not protect the public health and welfare to the extent he believes to be required and feasible," he may request that agency to review the matter and report to him on the advisability of a revision. The other agency is required to respond, and both the request and the response are published in the Federal Register. The Administrator thus is given a roving commission to expose poorly conceived noise related regulatory initiatives issuing from any federal agency. While institutional constraints confine EPA's power to pillory sister agencies, there is room for constructive criticism. One example under the 1972 Act where this authority might prove useful is found in section 9[32] which directs the Secretary of the Treasury, after consulting with the Administrator, to issue regulations "to carry out the provisions of the Act with respect to new products imported or offered for importation."

While the Noise Control Act gives the Environmental Protection Agency important responsibilities, other federal agencies retain significant powers. The Federal Aviation Administration, within the Department of Transportation (DOT), and the independent Civil Aeronautics Board, have authority over jet noise.[33] The National Aeronautics and Space Administration has research responsibilities affecting aircraft noise abatement.[34] Airport planning is influenced

---

27. Id. § 4901(b).

28. See § 7.3 below.

29. Compare Section 7 of the Endangered Species Act of 1973, 16 U.S.C.A. § 1536; National Wildlife Federation v. Coleman, 529 F.2d 359, 6 ELR 20344 (5th Cir. 1976); §§ 7.5, 7.12 below.

30. 42 U.S.C.A. § 4903(c)(2). EPA has invoked section 4(c)(2) upon one occasion concerning the Department of Labor's proposed occupational noise exposure regulation. See 39 Fed.Reg. 43802 (1974). The Department of Labor's reply appears in 40 Fed.Reg. 12336 (1975). See §§ 6.10 (on occupational noise exposure), 8.3 (discussing a similar referral mechanism used in pesticides regulation) below.

31. 42 U.S.C.A. § 1857(h)–7; see § 7.2 below.

32. 42 U.S.C.A. § 4908.

33. See § 5.5 below.

34. See Hearings on Aeronautical Research and Development, Before the Subcomm. on Aeronautics and Space

greatly by DOT under the Airport and Airway Development Act of 1970.[35] DOT, through the Federal Highway Administration, also has substantive authority with regard to standards dealing with the noise characteristics of highways.[36] The Occupational Safety and Health Administration, in the Department of Labor, regulates occupational noise exposure.[37] Regulatory policies of the Department of Housing and Urban Development influence noise exposure in important ways.[38] Other agencies are part of the legal picture—the Department of Defense, the Department of Commerce's National Bureau of Standards, the General Services Administration (which buys the lawnmowers to be used by federal agencies)[39] and the Federal Railway Administration (which is considering proposals to limit noise levels within railroad workers' sleeping quarters[40]).

§ 5.3 Nontransportation Sources: Common Law

Among nontransportation sources, factories and business establishments produce a noisy and varied chorus. Professors Findley and Plager advise us that the hundreds of distinct industrial noises "can be classified into five broad categories: electromechanical noise (motors, generators, transformers); mechanical noise (unbalanced machinery, gears, bearings); noise from fluid flow (fans, blowers, compressors); combustion noise (furnaces and burn-off flares); and impact noise (punch presses, stamping machines, forging hammers)."[1] The list of nontransportation noise sources is expanded indefinitely by reference to anecdotal experience: "construction equipment, automobile race tracks, car washes, air conditioners, loudspeakers, power lawnmowers, dogs, and children."[2] Most commonly embroiled in controversy are three types of sources: (1) industrial sources (forges and foundries, power plants, oil refineries, cement plants); (2) indirect sources (drive-in restaurants and movies); and (3) residential sources (dogs, musical instruments, chain saws).

Nuisance litigation reflects faithfully the conflicts attending the wide range of nontransportation noise sources.[3] Thus, annotations

Technology of the House Comm. on Science and Astronautics, 92d Cong., 2d Sess. (1972).

35. See § 5.7 below.

36. See § 5.8 below.

37. See § 5.10 below.

38. See § 5.8 below.

39. See GSA, Federal Supply Schedule, Lawn & Garden Equipment, pt. II-A, at 97 (1976).

40. See 41 Fed.Reg. 2186–87 (1976).

1. Findley & Plager, State Regulation of Nontransportation Noise: Law and Technology, 48 S.Cal.L.Rev. 209, 215 (1974), citing Hearings on R72–2, Before the Illinois Pollution Control Board, In the Matter of Noise Pollution Control Regulations 147–49 (1972).

2. Ibid.

3. Authorities cited in the text following are collected in A. W. Reitze, Jr., Environmental Law, App. Three B–41 (2d ed. 1972). See also Lloyd, Noise as a Nuisance, 82 U.Pa.L.Rev. 567 (1934).

Sec. 5.3 NONTRANSPORT. SOURCES: COMMON LAW 559

can be found on noise from stockyards,[4] sundry business premises,[5] auto wrecking yards,[6] undertaking establishments,[7] oil refineries,[8] dance halls,[9] drive-in restaurants,[10] dairies,[11] drive-in movies,[12] truck terminals,[13] power plants,[14] taverns [15] and shooting ranges.[16] In recent years, the case law reflects continuing controversy over noise from industrial sources (coal-mine,[17] cement plant,[18] cotton gin,[19] auto shredding plant [20]), indirect sources attracting large numbers of vehicles and people (drive-in theatre,[21] gun club,[22] sporting events,[23] cemetery,[24] county fairgrounds,[25] snowmobile races [26]), and residential homeowners (dogs [27]).

Nuisance lawsuits involving noise from nontransportation sources faithfully apply the key factors controlling in nuisance litigation generally.[28] Indeed, noise is often but one among many environmental insults leading to the characterization of certain conduct as a nuisance.[29] Thus, the case law stresses the extent and degree of the

4. Annot., 18 A.L.R.2d 1035 (1951).

5. Annot., 23 A.L.R.2d 1289 (1952).

6. Annot., 26 A.L.R.2d 653 (1952).

7. Annot., 39 A.L.R.2d 1007 (1955).

8. Annot., 44 A.L.R.2d 1322 (1955).

9. Annot., 44 A.L.R.2d 1394 (1955).

10. Annot., 91 A.L.R.2d 575 (1963).

11. Annot., 92 A.L.R.2d 977 (1963).

12. Annot., 93 A.L.R.2d 1171 (1964).

13. Annot., 2 A.L.R.3d 1372 (1965).

14. Annot., 4 A.L.R.3d 902 (1965).

15. Annot., 5 A.L.R.3d 989 (1966).

16. Annot., 26 A.L.R.3d 661 (1969).

17. Severt v. Beckley Coals, Inc., 153 W.Va. 600, 170 S.E.2d 577 (1969).

18. Bates v. Quality Ready Mix, Inc., 261 Iowa 696, 154 N.W.2d 852 (1967).

19. Moore v. Coleman, 185 S.W. 936 (Tex.Civ.App.1916).

20. Harrison v. Indiana Auto Shredders Co., 528 F.2d 1107, 6 ELR 20179 (7th Cir. 1975).

21. Johnson v. Mount Ogden Enterprises, Inc., 23 Utah 2d 169, 460 P.2d 333 (1969).

22. Smith v. Western Wayne County Conservation Ass'n, 380 Mich. 526, 158 N.W.2d 463 (1968).

23. Corp. of the Presiding Bishop of the Church of Latter Day Saints v. Ashton, 92 Idaho 571, 448 P.2d 185 (1969); Kasala v. Kalispell Pee Wee Baseball League, 151 Mont. 109, 439 P.2d 65 (1968).

24. Sanders v. Roselawn Memorial Garden, 152 W.Va. 91, 159 S.E.2d 784 (1968).

25. People v. Romani, 3 ELR 20161 (Cal.Super.Ct. Placer County 1972).

26. Cf. Ironstone Corp. v. Zoning Hearing Bd., 2 ELR 20469 (Pa.Commonwealth Ct.1973) (zoning case).

27. Davoust v. Mitchell, 257 N.E.2d 332 (Ind.1970); see Fredericktown v. Osborne, 429 S.W.2d 17 (Mo.App.1968).

28. §§ 2.1–.11 above; see Lloyd, Noise as a Nuisance, 82 U.Pa.L.Rev. 567 (1934).

29. E. g., Harrison v. Indiana Auto Shredders Co., 528 F.2d 1107, 6 ELR 20179 (7th Cir. 1975) (noise, vibration and air pollution) (applying Indiana law); Transcontinental Gas Pipe Line Corp. v. Gault, 198 F.2d 196 (4th Cir. 1952) (noise and air pollution); Smith v. Staso Milling Co., 18 F.2d 736 (2d Cir. 1927) (air, water and noise pollution); Vowinckel v. N. Clark & Sons, 216 Cal. 156, 13 P.2d 733 (1932) (air and noise pollution);

560   NOISE POLLUTION   Ch. 5

hurt,[30] with a number of cases declining injunctive relief where the noise was thought to be only sporadic or intermittent,[31] or merely annoying without constituting a serious health hazard,[32] or speculative,[33] or not "substantial" enough to justify recovery under an objective test of whether it would injure a normal person.[34] Otherwise insignificant noises might nonetheless be actionable if the defendant is motivated by malice.[35] Similarly, in determining whether a noise nuisance exists, and particularly in fashioning an appropriate remedy, courts have stressed the value of defendant's enterprise,[36] the state of the art in controlling the annoyance,[37] and the impact of legislation

Ensign v. Walls, 323 Mich. 49, 34 N.W.2d 549 (1948) (odors, noise, rats, and occasionally escaped dogs from a dog breeding and boarding establishment).

30. § 2.4 above; Smith v. Western Wayne County Conservation Ass'n, 380 Mich. 526, 158 N.W.2d 463 (1968); Sakler v. Huls, 20 Ohio Op.2d 283, 183 N.E.2d 152 (Ct.C.P.1961). Upon occasion judicial notice has stretched the limits of scientific knowledge: "That the subjection of a human being to a continued hearing of loud noises tends to shorten life is, I think, beyond all doubt." Gilbough v. West Side Amusement Co., 64 N.J.Eq. 27, 28, 53 A. 289 (1903).

31. E. g., Rogers v. Elliott, 146 Mass. 349, 15 N.E. 768 (1888) (ringing of church bell eight times on Sunday not a nuisance despite peculiar vulnerability of invalid living across street); Patrick v. Smith, 75 Wash. 407, 134 P. 1076 (1913) (single explosion).

32. Harrison v. Indiana Auto Shredders Co., 528 F.2d 1107, 6 ELR 20179 (7th Cir. 1975).

33. Connecticut Bank & Trust Co. v. Mularcik, 22 Conn.Super. 415, 174 A.2d 128 (1961). But see Hooks v. Int'l Speedways, Inc., 263 N.C. 686, 140 S.E.2d 387 (1965) (allowing anticipatory injunction against operation of a dragstrip).

34. Rogers v. Elliott, 146 Mass. 349, 15 N.E. 768 (1888) (ringing of church bell annoying to invalid); Dorsett v. Nunis, 191 Ga. 559, 13 S.E.2d 371 (1941) (same); Warren Co. v. Dickson, 185 Ga. 481, 195 S.E. 568 (1938); Meeks v. Wood, 66 Ind.App. 594, 118 N.E. 591 (1918) (whistle annoying nervous invalid); Myer v. Minard, 21 So.2d 72 (La.App.1945) (nervous invalid annoyed by crowing rooster); Meyer v. Kemper Ice Co., 180 La. 1037, 158 So. 378 (1935) (hypersensitive to factory noise); Aldridge v. Saxey, 242 Or. 238, 409 P.2d 184 (1965) (invalid affected by noise from neighbor's dogs).

35. Gorman v. Sabo, 210 Md. 155, 122 A.2d 475 (1956); Collier v. Ernst, 31 Del.Co. 49 (Pa.1941) (defendant played airs on marimba designed to annoy passersby, such as "Jingle Bells" for plaintiff, thought to resemble Santa Claus, and "Anchors A Weigh" for a sailor; playing limited to reasonable hours and volume by injunction); Christie v. Davey, [1893] 1 Ch. 316 (1892) (defendant enjoined from retaliating against piano playing in a duplex house by blowing whistles and pounding trays).

36. § 2.5 above; see Harrison v. Indiana Auto Shredders Co., 528 F.2d 1107, 1121, 6 ELR 20179, 20185 (7th Cir. 1975) (giving weight to the benefits of recycling); Smith v. Staso Milling Co., 18 F.2d 736, 738 (2d Cir. 1927) ("If the plaintiff had filed his bill before the mill was built, the balance of convenience would have been different, and we should not have hesitated to stop what is yet recognized as only a project"); cf. Gilbough v. West Side Amusement Co., 64 N.J.Eq. 27, 53 A. 289 (1903) (stressing that noisy roller skating rink is not a public necessity).

37. § 2.6 above; Harrison v. Indiana Auto Shredders Co., 528 F.2d 1107, 1117, 6 ELR 20179, 20183 (7th Cir. 1975) (summarizing defense testimony as showing the facility was "the cleanest and quietest shredder possible"); see Dauberman v. Grant, 198 Cal. 586,

Sec. 5.3 NONTRANSPORT. SOURCES: COMMON LAW 561

upon various factors involved.[38] So, too, noise cases represent classic examples of land use conflicts, and the courts thus often scrutinize the character of the neighborhood [39] and the priority of uses [40] in determining whether there has been an unreasonable interference with the use and enjoyment of property.

Remedies in noise nuisance cases span the spectrum,[41] ranging from a complete shutdown of operations [42] to a denial of relief for

246 P. 319 (1926); Godard v. Babson-Dow Mfg. Co., 313 Mass. 280, 47 N.E. 2d 303 (1943) (noise and vibration nuisance enjoined upon the master's report indicating that alternative motors were readily available on the market); see id., 319 Mass. 345, 65 N. E.2d 555 (1946) (same case on contempt proceedings); Pelletier v. Transit-Mix Concrete Corp, 11 Misc. 2d 617, 624, 174 N.Y.S.2d 794, 802 (1958) (evidence establishes operation by the defendant "with the best and most modern equipment and in conformity with usual custom and proper practices").

38. § 2.11 above; see People v. Romani, 3 ELR 20161, 20162 (Cal.Super. Ct. Placer County 1972) (enjoining nighttime automobile racing at county fairgrounds but stating, "In the event the vehicles being raced are equipped in a manner to conform with the noise control standards set for motor vehicles by the State of California, then racing should be permitted in the evening hours"); Beane v. H. K. Porter, Inc., 280 Mass. 538, 182 N.E. 823 (1932) (zoning ordinance). See also Harrison v. Indiana Auto Shredders Co., 528 F.2d 1107, 6 ELR 20179 (7th Cir. 1975) (justifying denial of injunctive relief partly on grounds of conformity with noise and air pollution standards).

39. § 2.9 above; see Harrison v. Indiana Auto Shredders Co., 528 F.2d 1107, 1124–25, 6 ELR 20179, 20186 (7th Cir. 1975) (auto shredder in area zoned for industrial use for over fifty years; plaintiffs there first); Swetland v. Curtiss Airports Corp., 55 F.2d 201 (6th Cir. 1932); Brandes v. Mitterling, 67 Ariz. 349, 196 P.2d 464 (1948); Nair v. Thaw, 156 Conn. 445, 242 A.2d 757 (1968) (commercial air conditioning unit adjacent to luxury home in residential neighborhood; injunction issues); Phelps v. Winch, 309 Ill. 158, 140 N.E. 847 (1923) (dance pavilion in residential neighborhood; plaintiffs there first); Smith v. Western Wayne County Conservation Ass'n, 380 Mich. 526, 158 N.W.2d 463 (1968) (gun club in open and agricultural area; no injunction); DeAlbert v. Novah, 78 Ohio App. 80, 69 N.E.2d 73 (1946) (duck farm in rural area; no injunction); Kramer v. Sweet, 179 Or. 324, 169 P.2d 892 (1946); Burke v. Hollinger, 296 Pa. 510, 146 A. 115 (1929) (public garage in residential area bordering on a commercial district); Krocker v. Westmoreland Planing Mill Co., 274 Pa. 143, 117 A. 669 (1922) (planing mill in residential neighborhood; plaintiffs there first).

40. § 2.8 above; see Kentucky W. Virginia Gas Co. v. Lafferty, 174 F.2d 848 (6th Cir. 1949) (gas plant caused noise and shaking of plaintiffs' houses; plaintiffs who were there first entitled to damages for past and future diminution of the value of use; plaintiffs who acquired interests after operations began entitled to no recovery); Stevens v. Rockport Granite Co., 216 Mass. 486, 488, 104 N.E. 371, 373 (1914) ("No one can move into a quarter given over to foundries and boiler shops and demand the quiet of a farm"); see Irby v. Panama Ice Co., 184 La. 1082, 168 So. 306 (1936); Grzelka v. Chevrolet Motor Car Co., 286 Mich. 141, 281 N.W. 568 (1938); Eller v. Koehler, 68 Ohio St. 51, 67 N.E. 89 (1903); Schlotfelt v. Vinton Farmers' Supply Co., 252 Iowa 1102, 109 N.W.2d 695 (1961).

41. § 2.11 above.

42. Vowinckel v. N. Clark & Sons, 216 Cal. 156, 13 P.2d 733 (1932) (four [of nineteen] kilns closest to plaintiff's property ordered abated despite defendant's offer to erect a fireproof sound-absorbing wall around all four kilns); Krocker v. Westmoreland Planing Mill Co., 274 Pa. 143, 146, 117 A. 669, 670 (1922) ("The chancellor,

annoyances thought to be insubstantial.[43] Although specific technological commitments may be required in noise cases,[44] the most common type of equitable relief is operational in nature, requiring adjustments in the hours or methods of operation. The reason for this is that noise injuries often are not intolerable *per se* unlike, for example, exposures to toxic fumes, but become so only because of when and how the noise occurs. Thus, the defendant may be forbidden from conducting business at all during certain hours [45] or from using certain tools (such as hammers, drills, and riveting machines) during those hours.[46] He may be required to conduct business only inside a building with all windows securely closed,[47] relocate noisy machinery,[48] reduce shock and noise by using smaller charges of dynamite,[49] turn down the loud speaker system,[50] or avoid striking metal with metal.[51] Damages, if and when they are appropriate, are for loss of use and are measured in rental value.[52] Special damages are recoverable too, as in the case where noise from a drag strip caused chinchillas to chew their own fur rendering it worthless for pelting purposes,[53] and punitive damages in an appropriate case, as where

after a careful investigation, found there was no way the mill could be operated without being a nuisance to the plaintiffs").

43. See cases cited in notes 31–34, supra.

44. E. g., Harrison v. Indiana Auto Shredders Co., 528 F.2d 1107, 1125, 6 ELR 20179 (7th Cir. 1975); Anderson v. Souza, 38 Cal.2d 825, 845, 243 P.2d 497, 510 (1952) ("The advance of aeronautical science may make use of the field possible without injury to plaintiffs by aircraft that can operate without making unduly low and noisy flights. . . . Upon a proper showing of changed circumstances, the trial court may modify or dissolve the injunction"); Stevens v. Rockport Granite Co., 216 Mass. 486, 492, 104 N. E. 371, 375 (1914) (enjoining operation of surface mining equipment upon finding that "defendant may be able to cut off the noise from reaching the houses of plaintiffs in offensive volume by a fence or by such dust blowing devices as will enable the machines to be placed under cover . . ."). See also Spater, Noise and the Law, 63 Mich.L.Rev. 1373, 1378 (1965).

45. Bates v. Quality Ready Mix Co., 261 Iowa 696, 154 N.W.2d 852 (1967).

46. Collins v. Wayne Iron Works, 227 Pa. 326, 76 A. 24 (1910) (between the hours of 7 p. m. and 7 a. m.).

47. Ibid.

48. Quinn v. American Spiral Spring & Mfg. Co., 293 Pa. 152, 141 A. 855 (1928).

49. Beecher v. Dull, 294 Pa. 17, 143 A. 498 (1928).

50. Payne v. Johnson, 20 Wash.2d 24, 145 P.2d 552 (1944) (drive-in movie theatre; a better technology was known [individual speakers in vehicles] but was unavailable in wartime); cf. Stodder v. Rosen Talking Machine Co., 241 Mass. 245, 135 N.E. 251 (1922) (enjoined from playing in the entrance of a store any records so as to cause noise to be "appreciably audible or heard" in plaintiffs' nearby place of business); id., 247 Mass. 60, 141 N.E. 569 (1923) (contempt proceeding).

51. Pelletier v. Transit-Mix Concrete Corp., 11 Misc.2d 617, 174 N.Y.S.2d 794 (1958).

52. Harrison v. Indiana Auto Shredders Co., 528 F.2d 1107, 6 ELR 20179 (7th Cir. 1975).

53. Kohr v. Weber, 402 Pa. 63, 166 A. 2d 871 (1960).

noise from a blaring radio was directed at a neighbor as part of a calculated campaign of harassment.[54]

Noise nuisances are defended on familiar grounds.[55] Arguments that all possible technological and operational controls have been exhausted either can defeat injunctive relief altogether [56] or prompt the court to order a shutdown [57] or money damages [58] as the only satisfactory remedy. Pleas of economic hardship,[59] priority,[60] and compatability [61] of use are weighed in fashioning the details of equitable relief. Total defenses based on laches,[62] prescription, or estoppel [63] succeed rarely but apparently often enough to encourage continued resort to them.

§ 5.4 Nontransportation Sources: Regulation

For many years nuisance law has been supplemented by a host of anti-noise statutes and ordinances.[1] For the most part they are a sorry collection of restrictions or bans against "unreasonable," "un-

54. Gorman v. Sabo, 210 Md. 155, 122 A.2d 475 (1956).

55. § 2.9 above; Hammon, Defending a Noise Pollution Case, 20 Defense L.J. 587 (1971).

56. Pelletier v. Transit-Mix Concrete Corp., 11 Misc.2d 617, 174 N.Y.S.2d 794 (1958).

57. Sakler v. Huls, 20 Ohio Op.2d 283, 183 N.E.2d 152 (Ct.C.P.1961) (drag strip).

58. Herbert v. Smyth, 155 Conn. 78, 230 A.2d 235 (1967) (commercial dog kennel).

59. York v. Stallings, 217 Or. 13, 25–26, 341 P.2d 529, 535 (1959) (decree requiring defendant to "effectively eliminate" noise from the operation of its sawmill modified to forbid only noise which unreasonably interferes with plaintiffs' enjoyment of their property; case remanded to determine extent of and effect of remedying air pollution aspects of the nuisance).

60. Schlotfelt v. Vinton Farmers' Supply Co., 252 Iowa 1102, 109 N.W.2d 695 (1961) (feed-grinding and fertilizer sales business in residential neighborhood; plaintiff there first); Protokowicz v. Lesofski, 69 N.J.Super. 436, 174 A.2d 385 (1961) (denying money damages to plaintiffs who moved into residential area near coal and trucking business being conducted as nonconforming use); Benton v. Kernan, 130 N.J.Eq. 193, 21 A.2d 755 (1941).

61. Schlotfelt v. Vinton Farmers' Supply Co., supra note 60; York v. Stallings, 217 Or. 13, 341 P.2d 529 (1959).

62. Protokowicz v. Lesofski, 69 N.J. Super. 436, 174 A.2d 385 (1961) (rejecting laches on grounds that plaintiff had lodged numerous complaints and nuisance had become increasingly more aggravating); Herbert v. Smyth, 155 Conn. 78, 230 A.2d 235 (1967) (rejecting laches because plaintiff had made timely and persistent objections).

63. See Howard v. Robinette, 122 Ind. App. 66, 99 N.E.2d 110 (1951), transfer denied 230 Ind. 199, 102 N.E.2d 630 (1952); cf. Greater Westchester Homeowners' Ass'n v. Los Angeles, — Cal. Rptr. —, — P.2d — (Cal.Super.Ct. 1975) (airport noise case) (assumption of risk is no defense to nuisance action).

1. See Compilation of State and Local Ordinances on Noise Control, 115 Cong. Rec. 32188–259 (1969); Leisure Sub-Council, National Industrial Pollution Control Council, Leisure Time Product Noise, Schedule C (1971); Environmental Protection Agency, Laws and Regulatory Schemes for Noise Abatement 1–117 to –137 (1971).

usual," "loud and boisterous" and "raucous" noises, sometimes singling out especially offensive sources, sometimes not. A common denominator of this legislation is its unenforceability,[2] its common fate is to be ignored. This is changing, although slowly, with the enactment in urban areas of legal restrictions containing measurable performance standards for noise sources.[3] This section addresses regulation at the (1) state, (2) federal and (3) municipal levels.

a. *State Regulation*

It always was true at common law that judicially enforceable noise controls combined land use, operational, and source restrictions. Modern regulation reflects these influences,[4] and is nicely illustrated by the recently enacted schemes in Colorado,[5] New Jersey,[6] and Illinois.[7] All three establish ambient noise levels, with daytime and nighttime limits, dependent upon general land use classifications. None go so far as to impose specific limitations on source categories but, as any student of the air pollution laws knows, an ambient standard ultimately can be translated into source or operational controls or may lead to land use accommodations.

Professors Findley and Plager place the prevailing nontransportation source noise regulatory schemes into three categories [8] which tie the standards, respectively, to (1) the noise generating characteristics of the source; (2) the noise sensitivity of the receiver; or (3) a combination of the two. Category one is illustrated by the Colorado scheme which emphasizes control at the source and thus encourages technological or at least operational control measures. The statute [9] establishes four land use classifications: residential, commercial, light industrial, and industrial. For each classification there is a progressively less stringent dB(A) daytime and nighttime limit—50dB(A), for example, between 7:00 p. m. and 7:00 a. m. in a residential zone, rising to 80dB(A) during daylight hours in an

2. Laws on Noise Abatement, supra note 1, at 3–31 (reporting that only two cases had reached the appellate level).

3. See Comment, The New York City Noise Control Code: Not with a Bang but a Whisper, 1972–73 Fordham Urban L.J. 446; Note, Noise Abatement at the Municipal Level, 7 U.San Fran. L.Rev. 478 (1973).

4. See Findley & Plager, State Regulation of Nontransportation Noise: Law and Technology, 48 Cal.L.Rev. 209 (1974); EPA, Noise Source Regulation in State and Local Noise Ordinances (1975).

5. Colo.Rev.Stat.Ann. §§ 25–12–101 to –108.

6. N. J. Dep't of Environmental Protection, Noise Control Regulations ch. 29, § 7.29–1.1 et seq.

7. Illinois Pollution Control Board Rules and Regulations ch. 8 (Noise Regulations), July 26, 1973 [hereinafter cited as IPCB Rules]. See Illinois Coal Operators v. Illinois Pollution Control Bd., 59 Ill.2d 305, 319 N.E.2d 782 (1974) (rejecting arguments that Board exceeded authority in promulgating noise regulations and that different treatment of construction and surface mining industry constituted a denial of equal protection).

8. Supra note 4, at 258–65.

9. Colo.Rev.Stat.Ann. § 25–12–103.

Sec. 5.4 NONTRANSPORT. SOURCES: REGULATION

industrial zone. Violations of the limits "shall constitute prima facie evidence" that the source of the noise "is a public nuisance." [10] Measurement is to be made at a distance of 25 feet or more from the property line of the emitter. The scheme quite clearly links ambient noise to a source and thus strongly encourages source controls although not as explicitly perhaps as emission or performance standards imposed on individual sources found on the property (an intimidating challenge since a single industrial plant may emit noise from hundreds of individual sources). Characterizing a violator as a public nuisance means that both public and private parties are commissioned in the enforcement effort,[11] and they may seek remedies ranging from strict emission controls to a shutdown.[12]

The Colorado scheme is to be contrasted with that of New Jersey, which "has a regulatory scheme keyed solely to the classification of the receiver." [13] This sets up three land use classifications: residential, commercial, and industrial property.[14] Ambient standards are set for receivers: those in residential areas are protected from emitters in both commercial and industrial areas; those in commercial areas are protected from excessive noise from industrial or other commercial sources; residential emitters are unregulated. Measurements are made at the property line of the receiver. The result, of course, is a classic ambient scheme, subject to the difficulties of linking up a violation to an individual source. Although noise (which greatly diminishes over short distances) is not subject to complex atmospheric dispersion patterns like air pollution, it is evident the New Jersey scheme lends itself more easily to measuring the problem than controlling the sources.

EPA's Model Community Noise Ordinance [15] is another example of the New Jersey approach. This forbids any person from operating a source of sound that exceeds sound limits for broad receiving land use categories measured at the property boundary of the receiver.[16] Like the New Jersey approach, it thus requires connecting a violation to an individual source. It stresses compatible land use by forbidding construction of residences, hospitals or recreational facilities in high noise areas.[17] Violators are subject to criminal penalties, administrative abatement orders and citizen suits.[18] Specific prohibitions against creating a "noise disturbance" are aimed at both nontransportation (playing of musical instruments and loud-

10. Ibid. Compare § 2.10 above (discussing the effect of statutes and regulations on nuisance litigation).

11. § 2.2 above.

12. § 2.11 above.

13. Findley & Plager, supra note 4, at 264.

14. N. J. Dep't of Environmental Protection, Noise Control Regulations ch. 29, § 7.29–1.2.

15. Sept. 1975.

16. Id., art. VIII.

17. Id., art. X.

18. Id., art. XI.

speakers, harboring barking dogs, construction, drilling and demolition work) and transportation (operating motorboats) activities.[19] Interestingly, a "noise disturbance" is defined in the Model Community Noise Ordinance as "any sound which (a) endangers or injures the safety or health of humans or animals, or (b) annoys or disturbs a reasonable person of normal sensitivities, or (c) endangers or injures personal or real property."[20] That is a paraphrase of the definition of nuisance,[21] which confirms again that contemporary regulatory endeavors often refurbish longstanding common law doctrines.

Illinois[22] combines the New Jersey and Colorado approaches. Professors Findley and Plager explain: the regulations establish three classifications (denominated A, B and C) "roughly approximating residential, commercial, and industrial, applicable to both receivers and emitters. A series of tables list, for each specified receiving class, separate levels for sounds originating from the three classes of emitters. For example, Table 1 of the Illinois regulation specifies allowable levels of sound emitted to any receiving class A land from class C land, class B land, and class A land. Other tables provide similar listings for receiving class B land and receiving class C land. Measurements are made within the receiving class land, but not less than 25 feet from the noise source. Separate levels are provided for class A receiving property during nighttime hours."[23] It is said of this system that "it has the advantage of providing a mechanism for establishing levels which give the different classes of receivers the maximum feasible protection according to their needs and to the abilities of different classes of emitters to quiet down."[24] At the same time, it defines the legal protection afforded by reference not only to the extent of the noise and its effects but also its source, which seems demonstrably irrelevant in setting noise pollution standards. Thus, in Illinois class C emitters, consisting principally of industrial sources, "are given anywhere from a three to eight decibel forgiveness, depending on the sound frequency."[25] Put another way, a citizen suffering legal injury as a result of excessive noise from his neighbor is no longer injured if his neighbor happens to be an industrial plant.

The Illinois regulations define a property-line-noise source as any equipment or facility operating within the three classes of land and capable of emitting sound beyond the property line where it is located.[26] Owners and operators of property-line-noise sources are

19. Id., art. VI.

20. Id. § 3.2.20.

21. §§ 2.2, 2.3 above.

22. See note 7, supra.

23. Findley & Plager, supra note 4, at 265.

24. Id. at 263.

25. Id. at 282. Compare §§ 2.7, 2.8 above.

26. IPCB Rule 101(o).

Sec. 5.4 NONTRANSPORT. SOURCES: REGULATION

required to comply with the standards—new sources as they go into operation and existing sources over time.[27] Variances are available. Violators are subject to cease and desist orders and the imposition of monetary penalties in the ordinary course under the Illinois Environmental Protection Act.[28] By requiring affected sources to achieve compliance, the Illinois scheme is truly regulatory unlike, for example, the Colorado law which adds a few numbers to existing nuisance law. Even at that, the nuisance origins of the Illinois noise rules are clearly evident in the Environmental Protection Act which sets forth a purpose "to prevent noise which creates a public nuisance," [29] forbids a person from emitting noise beyond the boundaries of his property "that unreasonably interferes with the enjoyment of life or with any lawful business or activity," [30] and authorizes the Board to categorize and prescribe emission standards for noise sources "that unreasonably interfere with the enjoyment of life . . .." [31]

The land classification-based noise control schemes confront a number of hard questions beyond whether emitter-based or receptor-based standards are preferred. Some are predictable outgrowths of any regulatory effort: setting numerical limits, fixing points of measurement, choosing between single-event and time-averaged measurements, adopting nighttime standards, defining land use classifications. (How closely should they be tied to actual development or zoning requirements? How finely drawn?) Others are peculiar to noise regulation: should penalties or other forms of more stringent regulation be imposed for impulsive sound (of less than one second duration, such as from hammering) [32] or for prominent discrete tones (with easily identifiable frequency or pitch components, such as whistles and transformer hum) [33] generally deemed to be more annoying? Professors Findley and Plager [34] identify special economical and technological challenges for a wide variety of sources: construction sites, electrical generating and distribution equipment, oil refineries, natural gas pipeline compressor stations,[35] automobile and motorcycle

---

27. IPCB Rule 209.

28. Ill.Rev.Stat. ch. 111½, tits. IX, XII. The Illinois Environmental Protection Act is closely analyzed in D. P. Currie, Cases and Materials on Pollution ch. 3 (1975).

29. Ill.Rev.Stat. ch. 111½, § 1023.

30. Id. § 1024 reads as follows:
No person shall emit from the boundaries of his property any noise that unreasonably interferes with the enjoyment of life or with any lawful business or activity, so as to violate any regulation or standard adopted by the Board under this Act.

31. Id. § 1025.

32. See IPCB Rule 206.

33. See IPCB Rule 207. These are often referred to as pure tones.

34. Supra note 4, at 297–315.

35. The Federal Power Commission has siting authority over various natural gas facilities. Regulations require that noise be a consideration in site selection and that pumping stations be located in areas "where sound resonation would be minimal. Further acoustical treatment should also be considered." 18 CFR § 2.69(a)(3)(iii).

race tracks, forging plants, railroad marshalling yards, mobile farm machinery, lawn maintenance equipment and home air conditioners. Economic and technical difficulties in controlling these sources often result in outright exemptions under modest land use state standards although the common law of nuisance gives up not so easily.

There is an obvious analogue between the land use implications of noise, air, and water pollution standards although noise law rarely goes so far as a "no significant deterioration" policy.[36] Noise considerations alone obviously should not dictate land use patterns but neither should existing uses dictate the extent of controls. It is the latter problem, not the former, which is prominent today.

b. *Federal Regulation*

A significant federal role over nontransportation sources (at least potentially) is found in the 1972 Act. The labeling provisions of section 8 [37] anticipate regulations giving notice "to the prospective user of the level of the noise the product emits, or of its effectiveness in reducing noise, as the case may be." [38] The idea, of course, is to bring consumer purchasing power to bear on unacceptable products. The Administrator has broad authority to designate products which must be labeled (any product emitting noise capable of adversely affecting the public health or welfare or any product sold wholly or in part on the basis of its effectiveness in reducing noise).[39] These modest regulatory powers have not been implemented hastily. A proposal to require the labeling of hearing protectors has been several years in incubation.

A more substantial regulatory charter is found in section 6(a)(1),[40] which compels the Administrator to impose noise emission standards "for each product," which is "a major source of noise" identified in a section 5(b)(1)[41] report and for which standards are thought by the Administrator to be "feasible." This mandatory obligation to impose emission standards reaches products falling into four broad categories: construction equipment, transportation equipment (including recreational vehicles and related equipment), any motor or engine (including any equipment of which an engine or motor is an integral part), electrical or electronic equipment. This is a sweeping charter which will be decades in implementation since Congress' mandatory directives are not accompanied by an enforceable timetable. This law requires federal noise standards for "most of the noise-producing equipment of stationary sources such as factories" [42] and probably also new automatic car washing facilities and

---

36. § 3.12 above. Compare § 2.17 above (land development controls).

37. 42 U.S.C.A. § 4907.

38. Id. § 4907(b).

39. Id. § 4905(a).

40. Id. § 4905(a)(1).

41. Id. § 4904(b)(1).

42. Findley & Plager, supra note 4, at 249.

Sec. 5.4 NONTRANSPORT. SOURCES: REGULATION

large commercial air conditioning equipment.[43] (But not church bells or stock cars.[44]) In addition to mandatory regulation within these four broad categories, the Administrator also is given discretion to impose regulations for any other product for which "noise emission standards are feasible and are requisite to protect the public health and welfare."[45] The lack of timetables and the inclusion of precautions that regulation should proceed only if "feasible" add up to a legislative invitation to the Administrator to impose noise emission standards on transportation and nontransportation sources of his choosing at a pace he prefers.

The criteria for issuance of noise emission standards are not unfamiliar, and they will be subject to further elaboration in the courts under precedents established for air and water pollution regulations.[46] Any regulation prescribed for a product under the Act "shall include a noise emission standard which shall set limits on noise emissions from such product and shall be a standard which in the Administrator's judgment, based on criteria published under section 5, is requisite to protect the public health and welfare, taking into account the magnitude and conditions of use of such product (alone or in combination with other noise sources), the degree of noise reduction achievable through the application of the best available technology, and the cost of compliance."[47] Because the standard must be that which is "requisite to protect the public health and welfare", it certainly must be sufficient to prevent hearing loss and other physiological damage; the legal ideal, as EPA recognizes,[48] is to go further to achieve a no-effects level. The references to "best available technology" and "cost of compliance" should be read, as are related performance standards in air and water pollution legislation, as requiring only that the standards be achievable and economically within reason, not that they be achievable by technology in use and then only upon a cost-benefit justification.[49]

In promulgating noise emission standards, the Administrator also must give "appropriate consideration" to other laws designed to safeguard the health and welfare of persons, "including any standards under the National Traffic and Motor Vehicle Safety Act of 1966, the

---

43. Hearings on S.1016, S.3342 and H.R.11021, Before the Sub.Comm. on Air & Water Pollution, of the Senate Comm. on Public Works, 92d Cong., 2d Sess. 345 (1972) (Additional Information Supporting EPA Statement on Noise Control Legislation).

44. Comm. on Public Works, Environmental Noise Control Act of 1972, S. Rep. No. 1160, 92d Cong., 2d Sess. 6 (1972) [hereinafter cited as Senate Report].

45. Section 6(b), 42 U.S.C.A. § 4905(b).

46. §§ 1.5, 3.16, 4.12 above.

47. Section 6(c), 42 U.S.C.A. § 4905(c).

48. § 5.2 & nn. 8–12 above.

49. §§ 3.10, 4.12 above; Portland Cement Ass'n v. Ruckelshaus, 158 U.S.App.D.C. 308, 486 F.2d 375, 3 ELR 20642 (1973), cert. denied 417 U.S. 921 (1974).

Clean Air Act, and the Federal Water Pollution Control Act." [50] This obviously means that the Administrator should fashion noise emission standards to avoid compromising safety, air and water pollution controls. Statutory language elsewhere allowing the Administrator to decline to adopt regulations adjudged not to be "feasible" [51] should be read only as authorizing no standards at all for certain products impossible of regulation (if any there be) not as attaching a general "feasibility" requirement to standards that are issued. The legislative direction in section 6(c)(1) that noise standards be "performance standards" means that the Administrator should prescribe results only, leaving to the manufacturer the decision on how best to get there.

As indicated above,[52] the regulatory scheme anticipates, first, an identification of classes of products as "major sources of noise" and, second, the promulgation of final emission standards within two years thereafter. EPA's identification of "major sources" has concentrated on transportation sources: medium and heavy duty trucks and portable air compressors in June of 1974; and motorcycles, buses, wheel and track loaders and wheel and track dozers, truck transport refrigeration units and truck mounted solid waste compactors in May of 1975. Future candidates include both transportation (light trucks, motor boats, tires, other truck equipment) and nontransportation sources (chain saws, pneumatic and hydraulic tools, piledrivers and lawn care equipment [rotary power mowers, riding mowers, tillers, edgers, snow and leaf blowers]). It goes without saying that large numbers of consumer products are within reach of the Act: by the end of 1970, for example, 2.5 million motorcycles, 4 million outboard motors, and 2.5 million chain saws were in use in the United States.[53]

The noise emission standards ultimately adopted [54] for portable air compressors (designed to power pneumatic tools and other equipment at a construction site) are indicative of both administrative methodology and legal issues to be expected in the evolution of federal noise emission standards. The process hews closely to that established for water pollution emission standards—the preparation of a background document disclosing the information base, accumulation of additional data through extended rulemaking proceedings, ultimate promulgation accompanied by a detailed statement that will be strictly scrutinized in the courts under hard look principles.[55] The central

50. Section 6(c), 42 U.S.C.A. § 4905(c).

51. Sections 6(a)(1), (b), 42 U.S.C.A. § 4905(a)(1), (b).

52. § 5.2 & nn. 14–18 above.

53. Leisure Sub-Council, supra note 1, at 8. See id. at 16, Schedule A (Recreation Equipment Noise Summary Table).

54. The standards were proposed in 39 Fed.Reg. 38186 (1974), adopted in 41 Fed.Reg. 2162 (1976), adding 40 CFR pt. 204.

55. §§ 1.5, 4.12 above.

Sec. 5.4   NONTRANSPORT. SOURCES: REGULATION   571

features of the air compressor noise standards address subjects that all have been subjected to judicial review earlier in environmental cases—economic and technological feasibility of the standards themselves,[56] testing methodology,[57] exemptions or variances.[58]

Enforcement provisions appearing in the air compressor regulations are symptomatic of weaknesses in the Act.[59] The manufacturer must warrant to the ultimate purchaser that the product "is designed, built and equipped so as to conform at the time of sale" with the regulation.[60] This design or production warranty is not supplemented by a performance warranty over the life of the product, so it is safe to assume that the noise warranties will prove as ineffective as the auto emission warranties before them.[61] The air compressor regulations contain various provisions on labeling,[62] selective testing by EPA,[63] instructions on anti-tampering,[64] cessation of distribution,[65] and recalling and remedying any compressor of a category found to have failed the tests.[66] (This is to be distinguished from recalling or repairing a compressor that does not meet the standards.) The absence of civil penalty provisions are due to their omission from the Act.

In future years, no issue is likely to confound the regulation of noise sources more than preemption. The Act allows a state or political subdivision to impose new product noise limits identical to those prescribed by federal law [67] and thus participate in enforcement. This is no small concession since local enforcement can achieve re-

---

56. 40 CFR § 204.52 (requiring the product to be designed and built to meet a 76 dB(A) average sound level at any time during its life when measured as proscribed by the regulations); § 3.14 above.

57. 40 CFR § 204.55; International Harvester Co. v. Ruckelshaus, 155 U.S.App.D.C. 411, 478 F.2d 615 (1973), cert. denied 417 U.S. 921 (1974).

58. 40 CFR § 204.5; E. I. DuPont de Nemours v. Train, 541 F.2d 1018, 6 ELR 20371 (4th Cir. 1976, rev'd in part — U.S. —, 97 S.Ct. 965, 51 L. Ed.2d 204 (1977).

59. Discussed briefly in § 5.2 above.

60. Section 6(d)(1), 42 U.S.C.A. § 4905 (d)(1); 40 CFR § 204.58–1.

61. § 3.15 above.

62. 40 CFR § 204.56.

63. Id. § 204.55–9. Initially all testing is done by the manufacturer in accordance with prescribed procedures. The Administrator intervenes only as an auditor.

64. Id. § 204.58–3 (to be included in the owner's manual).

65. Id. § 204.57–11.

66. Id. § 204.57–13.

67. Section 6(e)(1), 42 U.S.C.A. § 4905 (e)(1), reads:
No State or political subdivision thereof may adopt or enforce—
(A) with respect to any new product for which a regulation has been prescribed by the Administrator under this section, any law or regulation which sets a limit on noise emissions from such new product and which is not identical to such regulation of the Administrator; or
(B) with respect to any component incorporated into such new product by the manufacturer of such product, any law or regulation setting a limit on noise emissions from such component when so incorporated.

sults that by no means are assured by federal enforcement—notably, compliance by a product for the duration of its useful life. Regulation "not identical" is explicitly preempted, although regulation of sources free of federal rules is permissible, and ought to be.[68]

A difficult problem arises because the Act explicity reserves to states and municipalities the power to enforce controls "on environmental noise (or one or more sources thereof)" through "the licensing, regulation, or restriction of the use, operation or movement of any product or combination of products."[69] "Environmental noise" means "the intensity, duration, and the character of sounds from all sources."[70] This is an eminently sensible acknowledgement of the difference between source controls and land use controls: a federally regulated "quiet" chain saw might be unsuitable for a locally zoned hospital grounds. But there will be difficult questions of drawing lines when local "use" regulation perforce requires tighter decibel limits on a product, as, for example, required modifications of federally regulated air conditioners, additional acoustic equipment on a federally regulated car wash,[71] broad prohibitions against use of federally sanctioned piledrivers or snowmobiles.[72] It is an open question whether a state or municipality may ban, on grounds of excessive noise, a federally regulated product although Senator Muskie assumed it could not be done in a statement critical of the 1972 legislation.[73] The argument the other way is that the Act's reservation of "use" control to the states means "no use" where justified by local

---

68. The Minnesota noise emission standards on snowmobiles, for example, remain effective in the absence of preempting federal standards. See Minn.Stat.Ann. § 84.871.

69. Section 6(e)(2), 42 U.S.C.A. § 4905 (e)(2), reads:
   Subject to sections 4916 and 4917 of this title [dealing with railroad and motor carrier emission standards], nothing in this section precludes or denies the right of any State or political subdivision thereof to establish and enforce controls on environmental noise (or one or more sources thereof) through the licensing, regulation, or restriction of the use, operation, or movement of any product or combination of products.

Compare Allway Taxi, Inc. v. City of New York, 340 F.Supp. 1120, 2 ELR 20400 (S.D.N.Y.1972) (construing preemption provisions of the Clean Air Act); Chrysler Corp. v. Tofany, 419 F.2d 499 (2d Cir. 1969). The leading environmental preemption cases are discussed thoughtfully in Soper, The Constitutional Framework of Environmental Law, in Environmental Law Institute, Federal Environmental Law 20, 91–100 (E. L. Dolgin & T. G. P. Guilbert eds. 1974).

70. Section 3(11), 42 U.S.C.A. § 4902 (11).

71. These two examples are illustrative of permissible local regulation in EPA's view. See Findley & Plager, supra note 4, at 250.

72. See Ironstone Corp. v. Zoning Hearing Bd., 291 A.2d 310, 5 Pa. Comm. 420, 2 ELR 20469 (1972) (upholding zoning exclusion of snowmobile races). The "ambiguous" legislative history is collected in Opinion of the EPA Office of General Counsel, Pre-emption, August 24, 1973, in 1 EPA, Collection of Legal Opinions 265, 266 (1974).

73. See 118 Cong.Rec. 35389 (1972). Rep. Paul Rogers flatly disagrees. 118 Cong.Rec. 6039 (1972).

policies, leaving a manufacturer only the last-resort claim that a specific ban is an unconstitutional burden on commerce.

The legislative history suggests that Congress wanted the best of all possible worlds, with localities exercising wide authority but not in a way to discourage the sale of new products: "At a minimum, States and local governments may reach or maintain levels of environmental noise which they desire through (a) operational limits or regulations on products in use (such as speed or road limits or prohibitions of use in given areas or during given hours); (b) quantitative limits on environmental noise in a given area which may be enforced against any source within the area, including zones adjacent to streets and highways; (c) regulations limiting the environmental noise which may exist at the boundary of a construction site, (d) nuisance laws; or (e) other devices tailored to the needs of differing localities and land uses which do not amount to a burden manufacturers must meet to continue in business." [74] States and municipalities should feel free to impose noise controls consistently with their policy dictates, recognizing that a strong presumption of validity will protect their efforts to experiment with remedies, protect against effects as yet unknown, and bring temporary relief to a deteriorating situation.[75]

c. *Municipal Regulation*

The wide range of local autonomy preserved by the Noise Control Act is annotated specifically in the legislative history. The House Report, for example, refers favorably to the Chicago Noise Ordinance's[76] curfew provisions and ban against operation of heavy vehicles on private property for more than two consecutive minutes within 150 feet of residential property.[77] Obviously, regulatory options are substantial.[78] They include prominently land use classifications, symptomatic of state regulation discussed above. EPA's Model Community Noise Ordinance,[79] for example, is recommended for communities with populations of 100,000 or more.

Perhaps best known among the municipal regulatory efforts are the Chicago[80] and New York[81] ordinances. Among the innovations in the Chicago legislation are prohibitions against the selling or leasing of a wide variety of equipment not meeting noise emission stan-

---

74. Senate Report, supra note 44, at 8.

75. See Soper, supra note 69, at 99–100.

76. Chicago Municipal Code ch. 17, art. IV.

77. Comm. on Interstate and Foreign Commerce, Noise Control Act of 1972, H.R. Rep. No. 842, 92d Cong., 2d Sess. 8–9 (1972).

78. See Greenwald, Law of Noise Pollution, 1 BNA Environment Rep., Monograph No. 1 (1970).

79. Note 15, supra.

80. Chicago Municipal Code ch. 17, art. IV.

81. N.Y.City Admin.Code § 1403.3.

dards that are gradually tightened over time.[82] Major categories of nontransportation sources are covered, including construction equipment (rotary drills and augers, power shovels, cranes, trenchers, compactors, scrapers, pavement breakers, compressors but not pile drivers), commercial equipment (chain saws, log chippers, powered hand tools), and residential equipment (lawn mowers, lawn and garden tools, riding tractors, snow removal equipment). Chicago has a land use classification scheme encouraging control at the source by imposing performance standards (in dB(A)'s measured at the boundary line) for individual or combined plant operations within certain commercial districts,[83] and by imposing similar performance standards at the boundaries of an individual lot within residential districts.[84]

By contrast, New York City opts for a classic ambient approach by inviting an administrative creation of ambient noise quality zones covering the entire geographical area of the city.[85] This may include, in certain circumstances, the identification of noise sensitive zones [86] which may represent areas of strict nondegradation [87] or indeed eradication of existing noise sources. New York, like Chicago, prescribes performance or emission standards for both transportation and nontransportation sources (including circulation devices, refuse compacting vehicles, emergency signal devices and paving breakers [88]). New York has an elaborate enforcement arsenal (including provisions for citizen complaints, criminal and administrative remedies which may extend to orders to install certain apparatus [89]) although judging from noise levels within the city there is a tolerance policy applicable to many offenders.

Despite the advances represented by the Chicago and New York regulatory efforts, there is a need reflected in both ordinances to retain the specific and generic proscriptions of nuisance law. Thus, New York makes clear that certain well known types of nuisance activity is discouraged—allowing "unnecessary noise" from barking dogs or talking parrots,[90] operating a burglar alarm that does not terminate automatically within fifteen minutes of being activated,[91] playing commercial phonographs in public places.[92] Indeed, New York goes further to proclaim a general ban against causing or permitting "un-

---

82. Chicago Municipal Code § 17–4.8.
83. Id. § 17–4.12.
84. Ibid.
85. N.Y.City Admin.Code §§ 1403.3–6.01.
86. Id. §§ 1403.3–4.21.
87. Cf. § 3.12 above (no significant deterioration under the Clean Air Act).
88. N.Y.City Admin.Code § 1403.3–5.13 to 5.21.
89. Id. § 1403.3–8.01 to –8.25.
90. Id. § 1403.3–4.07.
91. Id. § 1403.3–4.05.
92. Id. § 1403.3–4.03.

necessary noise,"[93] while Chicago backs up its legal specifics with generic prohibitions against "boisterous" conduct within residential properties[94] and making "any noise of any kind" that is "distinctly and loudly audible" upon a public way.[95] These holdover provisions reflect an abiding conviction that the means of assaulting another by noise outrun attempts to catalogue them.

§ 5.5 Transportation Sources (Aircraft): Common Law

The common law of aircraft noise has roots deep in the concepts of trespass and nuisance.[1] It is complicated by several factors, however, not the least of which is sovereign immunity,[2] due to extensive governmental involvement in airport and air traffic operations. Ironically, sovereign immunity has posed no insuperable barriers to tort liability for noise related damage although it has forced a revision of theories—with inverse condemnation generally replacing trespass and nuisance.[3] (Inverse condemnation means that the government in fact has taken property although not formally exercising the power of eminent domain). The resulting legal actions have focused heavily upon the land use decisions of airport operators to the exclusion of the technological judgments of the carriers and aircraft manufacturers. That the common law of compensation for aircraft noise is today treated as a land use and not a technological problem is perhaps best illustrated by the fact that the decade of the 1960's saw a single judgment (for $12,500) entered in a noise case against a manufacturer.[4]

The modern law begins with United States v. Causby,[5] which held in 1946 that continuous low-altitude overflights by military aircraft, ruining plaintiff's chicken business and making life otherwise miserable, amounted to a wrongful taking of private property requiring compensation under the Fifth Amendment. Six years later the Supreme Court imposed liability for a taking not on the owner or opera-

93. Id. § 1403.3–3.01.

94. Chicago Municipal Code § 17–4.5.

95. Id. § 17–4.2.

1. See Prosser, Law of Torts 69–73 (4th ed. 1971); Anderson, Some Aspects of Airspace Trespass, 27 J. Air L. & Com. 341 (1960); §§ 2.1–2.13 above.

2. §§ 1.7, 1.8 above.

3. Leading articles include Kramon, Noise Control: Traditional Remedies and a Proposal for Federal Action, 7 Harv.J.Legis. 533 (1970); Hill, Liability for Aircraft Noise: The Aftermath of Causby and Griggs, 19 U. Miami L.Rev. 1 (1964); Ross, Inverse Condemnation Absent Overflight, 8 Nat.Res.J. 561 (1968); Russell, Aircraft/Airport Noise: Current Legal Remedies and Future Alternatives, 17 Ins. Counsel J. 92 (1975); Spater, Noise and the Law, 63 Mich.L.Rev. 1373 (1965); Tenzel, Jet Aircraft Noise: Problems and Their Solutions, 13 N.Y.For. 465 (1967); Tondel, Noise Litigation at Public Airports, 32 J. Air L. & Com. 387 (1966). Some of these and other leading articles are collected in Noise Pollution and the Law (J. L. Hildebrand ed. 1970).

4. Reported in T. Berland, The Fight for Quiet 284 (1970).

5. 328 U.S. 256, 66 S.Ct. 1062, 90 L.Ed. 1206 (1946).

tor of the planes but on the local manager of the airport in Pittsburgh, Pennsylvania, saying that "by constitutional standards" it did not acquire enough private property when it designed the facility.[6] Justices Black and Frankfurter, dissenting, argued that responsibility for the taking should be assigned to the federal authorities whose presence affected every takeoff and landing at the Greater Pittsburgh Airport.[7] The majority's rejection of this suggestion set the law upon a course still adhered to today. That course leads to legal responsibility for the local government as the operator of the airport, not the airlines as users nor the federal authorities as regulators.[8]

How much noise is too much calls for a careful but not unfamiliar analysis. The Supreme Court said in *Causby* that inconveniences caused by airplanes "are normally not compensable under the Fifth Amendment" and flights are not a taking "unless they are so low and so frequent as to be a direct and immediate interference with the enjoyment and use of the land." [9] This, of course, is the language of nuisance,[10] as is the measure of damages proposed: [11] "It is the owner's loss, not the taker's gain, which is the measure of the value of the property taken . . . . And that value may reflect the use to which the land could readily be converted, as well as the existing use." [12]

A strong case can be made that the protection afforded by the law of inverse condemnation, where applicable, and the law of nuisance should be coextensive although the prevailing dogma is that the taking theory is narrower,[13] protecting only against aggravated nuisances. The airport noise cases are rife with the concepts of nuisance law, regardless of the particular theory invoked. Thus, liability has been denied on the ground that the injuries suffered were insubstantial,[14]

---

6. Griggs v. Allegheny County, 369 U.S. 84, 90, 82 S.Ct. 531, 534, 7 L.Ed.2d 585, 589 (1962).

7. 369 U.S. at 91, 82 S.Ct. at 535, 7 L.Ed.2d at 590.

8. See Illinois ex rel. Scott v. Butterfield, 396 F.Supp. 632, 5 ELR 20587 (N.D.Ill.1975) (dismissing nuisance claim against federal government in airport noise case on ground that proper defendant was the city of Chicago).

9. United States v. Causby, 328 U.S. 256, 266, 66 S.Ct. 1062, 1068, 90 L.Ed. 1206, 1213 (1946).

10. § 2.3 above. Compare § 2.17 above (discussing the nuisance theory of taking).

11. § 2.11 above; see § 2.13 above (trespass).

12. 328 U.S. at 261, 66 S.Ct. at 1065–66, 90 L.Ed. at 1210.

13. See Nestle v. Santa Monica, 6 Cal. 3d 920, 101 Cal.Rptr. 568, 496 P.2d 480, 2 ELR 20417 (1972); Thornburg v. Port of Portland, 233 Or. 178, 376 P.2d 100 (1962), appeal on remand 244 Or. 69, 415 P.2d 750 (1966); Ferguson v. Keene, 108 N.H. 409, 238 A.2d 1 (1968), appeal on remand 111 N.H. 222, 279 A.2d 605 (1971) (finding no inverse condemnation for lack of an overflight but allowing recovery on a nuisance theory). The highway noise cases are especially prone to look for more than what would satisfy conventional nuisance principles. See § 5.6 below.

14. Mock v. United States, 164 Ct.Cl. 473, 475 (1964) (otherwise claims would "flood the court"); United States v. 3276.21 Acres of Land, 222

Sec. 5.5 AIRCRAFT 577

authorized by law,[15] or balanced unfavorably against the social utility of the airport enterprise.[16] Liability has been imposed if plaintiff was there first carrying on business consistently with prevailing land use patterns.[17] Damages are measured by the traditional nuisance test of diminution of market value supplemented by a sum for annoyance and discomfort even in the absence of physical illness.[18] The balancing process, used appropriately,[19] generally precludes injunctive relief against airport operations, particularly those of the government,[20] although there have been injunctions against private airport operations,[21] enforcing a wide range of equitable conditions.[22] One recent case approves the use of an anticipatory injunction against a private airport planned for a residential area.[23] A striking excep-

F.Supp. 887, 891 (S.D.Cal.1963); Kirk v. United States, 451 F.2d 690, 1 ELR 20615 (10th Cir. 1971), cert. denied 406 U.S. 963 (1972); Maynard v. United States, 430 F.2d 1264 (9th Cir. 1970); Aaron v. Los Angeles, 40 Cal.App.3d 471, 115 Cal.Rptr. 162 (1974), cert. denied 419 U.S. 1122 (1975) (dictum); § 2.4 above.

15. Atkinson v. Dallas, 353 S.W.2d 275 (Tex.Civ.App.1961), cert. denied 370 U.S. 939 (1962); Loma Portal Civic Club v. American Airlines, Inc., 61 Cal.2d 582, 39 Cal.Rptr. 708, 394 P.2d 548 (1964); see Tondel, supra note 3, at 397–98; § 2.10 above.

16. See Virginians for Dulles v. Volpe, 344 F.Supp. 573, 2 ELR 20360 (E.D. Va.1972), rev'd 541 F.2d 442, 6 ELR 20581 (4th Cir. 1976); Mallen, The Supersonic Transport's Sonic Boom Costs: A Common Law Approach, 37 Geo.Wash.L.Rev. 683, 700–18 (1969); § 2.3 above.

17. Seagraves v. Portland City Temple, 522 P.2d 893, 5 ELR 20507 (Or.1974) (en banc); §§ 2.7, 2.8 above. But cf. Greater Westchester Homeowner's Ass'n v. City of Los Angeles, 6 ELR 20051 (Cal.Super.Ct.L.A.County 1975) (allowing recovery despite priority of use by jet airplanes on ground that assumption of risk is not a defense to a nuisance action).

18. Greater Westchester Homeowners' Ass'n v. City of Los Angeles, supra note 17; § 2.11 above. It has been suggested that diminution of market value need not be shown if there has been a substantial interference with the use and enjoyment of land. See Russell, supra note 3.

19. See § 2.11 above; Thornburg v. Portland, 244 Or. 69, 415 P.2d 750 (1966).

20. Thompson v. Atlanta, 219 Ga. 190, 132 S.E.2d 188 (1963); Amherst v. Niagara Frontier Port Authority, 40 Misc.2d 116, 242 N.Y.S.2d 831 (1963); Schwab v. Burgese, 407 Pa. 531, 180 A.2d 921 (1952); Atkinson v. Dallas, 353 S.W.2d 275 (Tex.Civ.App.1961), cert. denied 370 U.S. 939 (1962). See also McKee v. Akron, 176 Ohio.St.2d 282, 199 N.E.2d 592 (1964) (odor from sewage treatment plant; court rejects analogy to aircraft noise).

21. Brandes v. Mitterling, 67 Ariz. 349, 196 P.2d 464 (1948); Loma Portal Civic Club v. American Airlines, Inc., 61 Cal.2d 582, 39 Cal.Rptr. 708, 394 P.2d 548 (1964); Barrier v. Troutman, 231 N.C. 47, 55 S.E.2d 923 (1949); Hyde v. Somerset Air Serv., 1 N.J. 346, 61 A.2d 645 (1948); Maitland v. Twin City Aviation Corp., 254 Wis. 541, 37 N.W.2d 74 (1949); see Parachutes, Inc. v. Lakewood, 121 N.J. Super. 48, 296 A.2d 71, 3 ELR 20225 (1972) (per curiam) (upholding municipal ordinance forbidding sounds of over 50 decibels at night, 60 during the day, applied to airplanes hovering and cruising at low altitudes for sport parachuting). See also Swetland v. Curtis Airports Corp., 55 F.2d 201 (6th Cir. 1932).

22. Seagraves v. Portland City Temple, 522 P.2d 893, 5 ELR 20507 (Or.1974) (en banc) (affirming injunction forbidding turns after takeoff over plaintiffs' property and barring charitable instruction or recreational rides).

23. See Camp v. Warrington, 227 Ga. 674, 182 S.E.2d 419, 2 ELR 20081

tion to the general rule protecting governmental defendants from injunctive relief is the decree in Hanover v. Morristown,[24] a suit brought by several individuals and communities to enjoin a runway extension. The court denied the requested relief but granted an experimental order banning night jet flights and prescribing a preferential runway system to go into effect upon completion of certain improvements.

One difference between the inverse condemnation and nuisance theories that has spawned distinct federal and state rules in aircraft noise cases is the requirement in some taking cases that a direct overflight of the affected property be alleged and proven. This absurdity has no basis either in the state of the technology or its impact on people (sideline noise may be more severe) but has been defended vigorously in a leading article [25] and a leading case, Batten v. United States,[26] on the ground the right protected is not freedom from noise but rather the integrity of the airspace above plaintiff's property. This trespassory theory of inverse condemnation is the prevailing view in the federal courts [27] although there is little to sustain it except that it is a handy vehicle for discouraging claims. The state cases generally go the other way,[28] drawing no distinction between overflights and nearby flights and thus bringing the concepts of nuisance and inverse condemnation closer together. One reason for the difference is that state constitutions often permit recovery of compensation for property "taken or damaged" for a public purpose, thus justifying a broader protection for property owners afflicted by aircraft noise.[29]

(1971) (affirming denial of motion to dismiss).

24. 108 N.J.Super. 461, 261 A.2d 692 (1969). The federal government instituted suit in the federal court challenging the injunction granted by the state court. See Draft Report on Legal and Institutional Analysis of Aircraft and Airport Noise and Apportionment of Authority Between Federal, State and Local Governments, prepared for the EPA Aircraft/Airport Noise Report Study, June 1973, at I–2–61. The judgment in the Hanover v. Morristown case and the complaint filed in the federal court attacking it are reprinted in 118 Cong.Rec. 35391–93 (1972).

25. Spater, supra note 3, at 1393–95.

26. 306 F.2d 580 (10th Cir. 1962).

27. Avery v. United States, 165 Ct.Cl. 357, 366, 330 F.2d 640, 645 (1964); Bellamy v. United States, 235 F.Supp. 139, 140 (D.C.S.C.1964); Leavell v. United States, 234 F.Supp. 734, 739 (D.C.S.C.1964); Neher v. United States, 265 F.Supp. 210, 216 (D.C. Minn.1967); Schubert v. United States, 246 F.Supp. 170, 171 (S.D.Tex.1955) (not only must there be an overflight but it must be less than 500 feet above the surface).

28. Thornburg v. Port of Portland, 233 Or. 178, 376 P.2d 100 (1962), appeal on remand, 244 Or. 69, 415 P.2d 750 (1966); Martin v. Port of Seattle, 64 Wash.2d 309, 391 P.2d 540 (1964); Henthorner v. Oklahoma City, 453 P.2d 1013 (Okl.1969); Johnson v. Greenville, 222 Tenn. 260, 435 S.W.2d 476 (1968); State v. Columbus, 3 Ohio St.2d 154, 209 N.E.2d 405 (1965), cert. denied 382 U.S. 925; Jacksonville v. Schumann, 167 So.2d 95 (Fla.Ct.App. 1964), cert. denied 172 So.2d 597 (1965). Compare Alevizos v. Metropolitan Airports Comm'n, 298 Minn. 471, 216 N.W.2d 651 (1974).

29. See Martin v. Port of Seattle, supra note 28.

The inverse condemnation theory is being overworked in the aircraft noise cases. The law of eminent domain usually does not provide compensation for a moderate reduction in property values attributable to the exercise of a public purpose, and sometimes not for a severe reduction.[30] Extending the concept on a "jet noise basis only" detracts from the dignity and consistency of decision-making; contracting it by requirements such as the overflight rule adds to the confusion and does so for policy reasons that are indecipherable. Far better it would be if the cases were analyzed under nuisance principles which provide the flexibility and familiarity necessary for full and complete relief. There is an encouraging trend in the case law to take sensible positions on issues important to a nuisance analysis: a refusal to balance the utility of the airport against the rights of individuals,[31] except where the question of remedy is concerned;[32] flexibility in applying the substantiality of the injury requirement;[33] reliance upon administrative standards[34] or legislative expressions[35] to define the extent of the hurt; a willingness to examine remedies

---

30. See F. Bosselman, D. Callies & J. Banta, The Taking Issue (1973); § 2.17 above.

31. Alevizos v. Metropolitan Airports Comm'n, 298 Minn. 471, 216 N.W.2d 651 (Minn.1974); Thornburg v. Port of Portland, 244 Or. 69, 415 P.2d 750 (1966).

32. Hanover v. Morristown, 108 N.J. Super. 461, 261 A.2d 692 (1969).

33. Compare Aaron v. Los Angeles, 40 Cal.App.3d 471, 115 Cal.Rptr. 162 (1974), cert. denied 419 U.S. 1122 (1975) (considering insubstantial damage noncompensable) with Martin v. Port of Seattle, 64 Wash.2d 309, 391 P.2d 540 (1964) (considering the slightest diminution in property value to be compensable).

34. Aaron v. Los Angeles, supra note 33, was a pioneering effort in using FAA-proposed standards for a noise exposure forecast (NEF) for airport environments in litigation concerned with effects. Compare Virginians for Dulles v. Volpe, 344 F.Supp. 573, 2 ELR 20360 (E.D.Va.1972), rev'd on other grounds 541 F.2d 442, 6 ELR 20581 (4th Cir. 1976) (treating NEF contours as a planning device not a noise standard). The FAA restricted use of the NEF concept under pressure from airport operators concerned about it being used against them in litigation. See Rodgers, Corporate Country 226–30 (1973). See also Jacksonville v. Schumann, 167 So.2d 95 (Fla.Ct.App.1964), cert. denied 172 So.2d 597 (1965) (plaintiffs' property was, according to an FAA designation, within an "Area Recommended for Non-Residential Development and the Exclusion of Places of Public Assembly").

35. For a discussion of the concept of legalized nuisance, see § 5.6 below. The leading case of Nestle v. Santa Monica, 6 Cal.3d 920, 938 n. 16, 101 Cal.Rptr. 568, 580 n. 16, 496 P.2d 480, 492 n. 16 (1972), quoting Hassell v. San Francisco, 11 Cal.2d 168, 78 P.2d 1021 (1938), makes clear that legislative authorization of nuisances is not lightly implied:

> A statutory sanction cannot be pleaded in justification of actions which by the general rules of law constitute a nuisance, unless the acts complained of are authorized by the express terms of the statute under which the justification is made, or by the plainest and most necessary implication from the powers expressly conferred, so that it can be fairly stated that the legislature contemplated the doing of the very act which occasions the injury.

See Greater Westchester Homeowners v. City of Los Angeles, 6 ELR 20051 (Cal.Super.Ct.L.A.County 1975) (same).

that include consideration of the aircraft and their use as well as their impact upon property values.[36] Despite claims of financial ruin by airport operators, several states,[37] led by California,[38] have adopted explicitly a nuisance theory for treating aircraft noise disputes.

No miracles are claimed for nuisance law in aircraft noise cases. The doctrine often is criticized as inadequate by commentators [39] favoring one or another regulatory initiative to curtail noise abuses. Nuisance law cannot fill the void caused by half-hearted regulation of the carriers. It does not, except on a case by case basis, decisively answer the question of what damages are compensable.[40] It is frustrated in different jurisdictions by the doctrine of sovereign immunity.[41] But the law of nuisance helps explain the cases and promises some guidance for future conduct.

The *Causby-Griggs* determination to look at the airport operator and not the carriers discourages direct litigation against the airlines and aircraft manufacturers. There is no reported action, for example, by claimed third party beneficiaries of the noise specifications in the contracts between manufacturers and carriers. No one has made a claim as an adversely affected bystander under the products liability provisions of the Restatement, Second, Torts § 402A.[42] Airport users

---

36. Hanover v. Morristown, 108 N.J. Super. 461, 261 A.2d 692 (1969); Seagraves v. Portland City Temple, 522 P.2d 893, 5 ELR 20507 (1974) (en banc).

37. Hanover v. Morristown, supra note 36; Ferguson v. Keene, 108 N.H. 409, 238 A.2d 1 (1968), appeal on remand 111 N.H. 222, 279 A.2d 605 (1971) (holding that there could be no inverse condemnation recovery without overflight but allowing those not directly overflown to recover under a nuisance theory).

38. Nestle v. Santa Monica, 6 Cal.3d 920, 101 Cal.Rptr. 568, 496 P.2d 480 (1972); see Berger, The California Supreme Court—A Shield Against Governmental Overreaching: Nestle v. City of Santa Monica, 9 Calif.W.L. Rev. 199 (1973); Note, Inverse Condemnation and Nuisance: Alternative Remedies for Airport Noise Damage, 24 Stan.L.Rev. 703 (1975).

39. E. g., Kramon, Noise Control: Traditional Remedies and a Proposal for Federal Action, 7 Harv.J.Legis. 533 (1970); Baxter, The SST: From Watts to Harlem in Two Hours, 21 Stan.L.Rev. 1, 50 (1968); Haar, Airport Noise and the Urban Dweller: A Proposed Solution, 36 Appraisal J. 551 (1968); Hildebrand, Noise Pollution: An Introduction to the Problem and an Outline for Future Legal Research, 70 Colum.L.Rev. 652, 655 (1970); Note, Airplane Noise: Problem in Tort Law and Federalism, 74 Harv. L.Rev. 1581 (1961). For more sanguine views of the possibilities of nuisance law, see Berger, Nobody Loves an Airport, 435 Calif.L.Rev. 631, 637–39 (1970); Fadem & Berger, A Noisy Airport Is A Damned Nuisance! 3 Sw.U.L.Rev. 39, 44 (1971); Stoebuck, Condemnation by Nuisance; The Airport Cases in Retrospect and Prospect, 71 Dick.L.Rev. 207 (1967).

40. See Batten v. United States, 306 F.2d 580, 587 (10th Cir. 1962) (Murrah, C. J., dissenting) (suggesting that the test is whether "the interference is of sufficient magnitude to cause us to conclude that fairness and justice as between the State and the citizen, requires the burden imposed to be borne by the public and not by the individual alone").

41. Cf. Laird v. Nelms, 406 U.S. 797, 92 S.Ct. 1899, 32 L.Ed.2d 449 (1972).

42. Cf. Piercefield v. Remington Arms Co., 375 Mich. 85, 133 N.W.2d 129 (1965) (allowing recovery to bystander injured by exploding shotgun shell).

may be drawn into noise controversies as a result of indemnity agreements in leases they have entered into with various airport operators.[43] Arguably, some state statutes imposing strict liability for damage on the ground caused by aircraft could be invoked in noise cases.[44] But a faithful report on the law of compensation for aircraft noise must begin and end with inverse condemnation and nuisance and the controversy surrounding the two theories.

§ 5.6 Transportation Sources (Railroads, Motor Vehicles): Common Law

Noise sufferers next to highways and railroad rights-of-way are virtually without monetary remedy today although there is some evidence the glacier is beginning to thaw. A 1965 article concluded that case law in twenty-one of twenty-two states having the "damaged" or equivalent language in their constitutions uniformly held that property owners adjacent to railroad or highway rights-of-way were required to bear without redress depreciation of property values due to noise pollution.[1] We are told, matter of factly, that the unsuccessful railway cases are characterized by claims of "cracked walls, broken windows, and interrupted sleep."[2] The most popular rationale for nonrecovery is that of "legalized nuisance," having its origins in Richards v. Washington Terminal,[3] and expressed as follows in the oft-quoted case of Bennett v. Long Island R. R.:[4]

> The rumble of trains, the clanging of bells, the shriek of whistles, the blowing off of steam, the discordant squeak of wheels in going around the curves, the emission of smoke, soot and cinders, all of which accompany the operation of steam cars, are undoubtedly nuisances to the neighborhood dwellings in the popular sense, but as they are necessarily incident to the maintenance of the road, they do not constitute nuisances in the legal sense, but are regarded as protected by the legislative authority which created the corporation and legalized its corporate operations.

---

43. Greater Westchester Homeowners Ass'n v. City of Los Angeles, 11 Av. Cas. 18,374 (Cal.Super.Ct.1970) (denying airlines' motion for summary judgment under indemnity agreements); see Berger, supra note 38, at 249–51, 257–58 & n. 277.

44. N.J.Stat.Ann. § 6:2–7 (making the owner of the aircraft "absolutely liable for injuries to persons or property on the land or water beneath, caused by ascent, descent or flight of the aircraft . . ..")

1. Spater, Noise and the Law, 63 Mich. L.Rev. 1373, 1401–05 & nn. 110–12 (1965).

2. Id. at 1403.

3. 233 U.S. 546, 34 S.Ct. 654, 58 L.Ed. 1088 (1913). Compare § 2.10 above.

4. 181 N.Y. 431, 436, 74 N.E. 418, 420 (1905); see Lombardy v. Peter Kiewit Son's Co., 266 Cal.App.2d 599, 72 Cal.Rptr. 240 (1968), appeal dismissed 394 U.S. 813 (1969); Deaconess Hospital v. State Highway Comm'n, 66 Wash.2d 378, 403 P.2d 54 (1965).

Nor does the legal nature of such annoyances change as traffic increases them in volume or extent.

Other popular reasons for denying recovery are that the plaintiff has suffered no injury different in kind to allow him to sue for a public nuisance,[5] that noise damage is not sufficiently substantial to justify relief,[6] or that litigation successes "would bring to an effective halt" the construction, operation and maintenance of access roads and highways within a given state.[7]

It is time enough for the "cracked walls, broken windows and interrupted sleep" to rise to the level of a compensable hurt. The principle of the airport cases, if it can be discovered and described, extends to highways and railroad rights-of-way. The legalized nuisance explanation thoroughly begs the question of a constitutional taking since obviously the legislature cannot approve what the constitution forbids. It is, moreover, preposterous to suggest that by endorsing the activities of railroading and highway travel a legislature also intends to create a permanent liability exemption for damages caused by the manner of operation.[8] The "special injury" requirement is put in doubt by the modern law of standing.[9] Recently, several courts have put a foot in the door by allowing recovery of the "full damage" attributable to highway noise impact on property remaining after parts of it had been taken to complete the project.[10] This is an example of the physical appropriation theory of the law of taking.[11] A 1960 California Supreme Court case [12] disallowing recovery for noise damage to persons or property unless a "sliver" of the owner's land was con-

---

5. Mathewson v. State Throughway Authority, 11 A.D.2d 782, 204 N.Y.S.2d 904 (1960), aff'd mem. 9 N.Y.2d 788, 215 N.Y.S.2d 86, 174 N.E.2d 754 (1961); Thomsen v. State, 284 Minn. 468, 474, 170 N.W.2d 575, 580 (1969) (stating that the court must decide whether property "has been so unfairly, directly, substantially and peculiarly injured" as to amount to a taking in a constitutional sense), modified expressly in Alevizos v. Metropolitan Airports Comm'n, 298 Minn. 471, 498, 216 N.W.2d 651, 660 (1974); State Highway Dep't v. Touchberry, 248 S.C. 1, 148 S.E.2d 747 (1966).

6. Lombardy v. Peter Kiewit Son's Co., 266 Cal.App.2d 599, 72 Cal.Rptr. 240 (1968), appeal dismissed 394 U.S. 813 (1969); Richmond County v. Williams, 109 Ga.App. 670, 137 S.E.2d 343 (1964); cf. Cheek v. Floyd County, 308 F.Supp. 777 (N.D.Ga.1970).

7. Northcutt v. State Road Dep't, 209 So.2d 710 (Fla.Ct.App.1968), cert. denied 219 So.2d 687 (1969).

8. §§ 2.10, 5.5 n. 35 above.

9. § 2.2 above.

10. State v. Elizabeth Bd. of Educ., 116 N.J.Super. 305, 282 A.2d 71 (1971) (granting an award in excess of $160,000 for soundproofing, landscape work and air conditioning); see United States v. Certain Parcels of Land, 252 F.Supp. 319 (W.D.Mich.1966); Dennison v. State, 28 A.D.2d 28, 281 N.Y.S.2d 257 (1967); State Highway Comm'n v. Colonial Inn, Inc., 246 Miss. 422, 149 So.2d 851 (1963); Randall v. Milwaukee, 212 Wis. 374, 249 N.W. 73 (1933).

11. § 2.17 above.

12. People v. Symons, 54 Cal.2d 855, 9 Cal.Rptr. 363, 357 P.2d 451 (1960).

Sec. 5.7 AIRCRAFT: REGULATION

demned has been given a rough reception by the commentators [13] and courts [14] alike. As was said in People v. Volunteers of America: [15]

> It is difficult to justify principles of law which permit consideration of the well being of Mr. and Mrs. Causby's chickens . . . ; but refuse to permit consideration of the mental, physical and emotional distress of the present and prospective occupants of defendants' residences, insofar as that distress, and the noise which occasions it, is reflected in a diminution of the value of the property.

Recognition of the irony and injustice of disallowing recovery in highway and railway noise cases is the required catalyst. Courts in at least a few states are convinced that the rules as to aircraft noise can be applied equally to other types of transportation noise.[16] A promise of relief is extended to any property owner "who can show a direct and substantial invasion of his property rights of such a magnitude he is deprived of the practical enjoyment of the property and that such invasion results in a definite and measurable diminution of the market value of the property." [17] The observations of a respected observer on airport noise apply equally to highways, railways and raceways: "Quiet, like the land on which runways are constructed, is a commodity; and if the airlines and air travelers consume it, they should pay for it." [18] Then it is time for the harder questions of when, how and how much.

§ 5.7 Transportation Sources (Aircraft): Regulation

No acoustical consultant is needed to demonstrate that noise from jet aircraft can be controlled in three ways: [1] at the source, by jug-

---

13. Berger, The California Supreme Court—A Shield Against Governmental Overreaching: Nestle v. City of Santa Monica, 9 Calif.W.L.Rev. 199, 226–27 (1973); Tondel, Government Liability for Non-Physical Damage to Land, 2 Urban L. 315 (1970); Van Alstyne, Just Compensation for Intangible Detriment; Criteria for Legislative Modifications in California, 16 U.C.L.A.L.Rev. 491, 505 (1969). A useful article collecting the highway noise cases and others is Harrison, Use and Enjoyment of Land—Compensation for Noise Damage, 4 Nat. Res.Law. 429 (1970).

14. See cases cited in Berger, supra note 13, at 227 nn. 144–45.

15. 21 Cal.App.3d 111, 127, 98 Cal.Rptr. 423, 434–35 (1971).

16. E. g., Aaron v. City of Los Angeles, 40 Cal.App.3d 471, 115 Cal.Rptr. 167 (1974), cert. denied 419 U.S. 1122 (1975) (airport case); Alevizos v. Metropolitan Airports Comm'n, 298 Minn. 471, 216 N.W.2d 651 (1974) (airport case); Board of Educ. v. Palmer, 88 N.J.Super. 378, 212 A.2d 564 (App.Div.1965), rev'd on other grounds 46 N.J. 522, 218 A.2d 153 (1966).

17. Alevizos v. Metropolitan Airports Comm'n, 298 Minn. 471, 493, 216 N.W. 2d 651, 662 (1974).

18. Haar, Airport Noises and the Urban Dweller, Speech to the Practicing Law Institute, May 10, 1968, at 20.

1. For a comprehensive discussion of the regulatory aspects of noise control, see Lake, Noise: Emerging Federal Control, in Environmental Law Institute, Federal Environmental Law 1150 (E. L. Dolgin & T. G. P. Guilbert eds. 1974).

gling the timing and direction of takeoff and landing operations (this is the intermittent control system of the airways [2]), or at the receptor (by moving him out of the way, furnishing him with earmuffs, or thickening the plaster on the walls of his home). Regulation, as it is wont, has touched every part of this system, none of it effectively. The nuisance and inverse condemnation lawsuits discussed above [3] are concerned largely with moving the receptor out of the way, albeit at the expense of the airport operator.

a. *Source Regulation*

Probably since 1958 [4] and certainly since 1968 [5] the Federal Aviation Administration has possessed authority to impose noise emission standards on aircraft. The 1968 amendments authorized the Administrator of the FAA, in broad terms, to prescribe rules and regulations "necessary to provide for the control and abatement of aircraft noise and sonic boom, including the incorporation of limitations into certificates authorized under the Act." [6] While the 1968 legislative authorization clearly anticipated traffic controls as a noise reduction alternative, Congress expected the authority to be used principally to control noise at the source through noise emission standards incorporated into aircraft type certificates.[7] (The type certificate covers all aircraft of similar design [8].) Indeed, the legislative history shows a desire to require the "full application of noise reduction technology." [9] This determination was moderated somewhat by loosely written criteria obliging the Administrator to consider several factors in setting standards, including whether a regulatory proposal was "economically reasonable, technologically practicable and appropriate for the particular type of aircraft, aircraft engine appliance, or certificate to which it will apply." [10]

2. Compare § 3.8 above.

3. § 5.5.

4. The Federal Aviation Act of 1958 directed the FAA "to prescribe air traffic rules and regulations governing the flight of aircraft . . . for the protection of persons and property on the ground . . ." Pub.L. No. 85–726, § 307(c), 77 Stat. 749.

5. Section 611 of the Federal Aviation Act, Pub.L. No. 90–411, § 1, 82 Stat. 395, 49 U.S.C.A. § 1431.

6. Lake, supra note 1, at 1155 n. 14: "A type certificate is issued when the FAA approves the design and construction of a new type of aircraft which has not been previously marketed. The type certificate is followed by a production certificate, which authorizes the manufacturer of duplicates of the aircraft. Finally, as each copy of the aircraft is shown to conform to the type certificate, it is issued an airworthiness certificate which entitles it to be flown in air commerce." See 49 U.S.C.A. § 1432.

7. See Comm. on Commerce, Aircraft Noise Abatement Act of 1968, S.Rep. No. 1353, 90th Cong., 2d Sess. 2, 4 (1968) [hereinafter cited as 1968 Senate Report].

8. 14 CFR § 1.1; note 6, supra.

9. 1968 Senate Report, supra note 7, at 2.

10. Pub.L. No. 90–411, § 1(d)(4), 82 Stat. 395, 49 U.S.C.A. § 1431(d)(4).

For a number of reasons (not excluding regulatory torpor), the 1968 amendments did not do the job. Five years after their enactment a panel quite sympathetic to the airlines was moved to observe that "noise is the most explosive problem facing aviation today." [11] Not the least of the difficulties are limitations upon operations and growth prompted in part by local dissatisfaction with federal efforts to control noise at the source. The Noise Control Act of 1972 marks a serious legislative attempt to improve the regulatory mechanism. One drastic change was rejected: on the floor of both houses unsuccessful efforts were made to strip FAA of its principal authority over aircraft noise and vest the power in EPA.[12] Four major revisions were adopted. The first forbids FAA from granting an exemption from any standard without EPA approval absent a safety emergency.[13] The second bars FAA from issuing an original type certificate "for any aircraft for which substantial noise abatement can be achieved by prescribing standards and regulations in accordance with this section" unless the Administrator prescribes standards for the aircraft which "protect the public from aircraft noise and sonic boom, consistent with the considerations set forth in the Act." The purpose of the provision is to compel the issuance of noise standards for new aircraft. The mandate is trimmed considerably by leaving the final choice to the Administrator of the FAA and allowing his discretion to roam across a wide landscape, including the vague 1968 criteria of whether any proposed standard "is economically reasonable, technologically practicable, and appropriate" for the aircraft to which it will apply.[14]

The preamble of section 611 also was changed by the 1972 Act to read "in order to afford present and future relief and protection to the public health and welfare from aircraft noise and sonic boom" from its previous reading which was "in order to afford present and future relief and protection to the public from unnecessary aircraft noise and sonic boom." This is significant, justifying regulatory authority to protect against adverse effects by use of the familiar "public health and welfare" language of the air pollution laws.[15] It is a justification more soundly based than the 1968 commitment to relieve the public from "unnecessary" noise.

---

11. Report of the Aviation Advisory Commission, The Long Range Needs of Aviation III–37 (1973).

12. 118 Cong.Rec. 6058 (1972); 118 Cong.Rec. 35411 (1972).

13. Section 116(b)(1), 49 U.S.C.A. § 1431(b)(1), reads, in part:
No exemption with respect to any standard or regulation under this section may be granted under any provision of this [Act] unless the FAA shall have consulted with EPA before such exemption is granted, except that if the FAA determines that safety in air commerce or air transportation requires that such an exemption be granted before EPA can be consulted, the FAA shall consult with EPA as soon as practicable after the exemption is granted.

14. Section 166(d)(4), 49 U.S.C.A. § 1431(d)(4).

15. Compare § 3.4 above.

The fourth substantial revision wrought by the 1972 Act is the creation of a tortuous six-step procedure under which EPA can cajole and harass FAA but not overrule it. Here is what happens: (1) EPA submits to the FAA proposed regulations to provide control and abatement of aircraft noise and sonic boom "as EPA determines is necessary to protect the public health and welfare"; [16] (2) within 30 days of the submission, the FAA must publish the proposed regulations in a notice of proposed rulemaking; (3) within 60 days of the publication of notice the FAA must commence a hearing; (4) within a "reasonable time" after conclusion of the hearing the FAA either must prescribe regulations substantially as submitted, modify them, or publish in the Federal Register a notice that it is rejecting the EPA submissions "together with a detailed explanation" of the reasons why; (5) if EPA "has reason to believe" the FAA's action "does not protect the public health and welfare from aircraft noise and sonic boom, consistent with the considerations listed" in the Act, EPA must consult with the FAA and "may request the FAA to review, and report to EPA on the advisability of prescribing the regulation originally proposed by EPA"; this request also is to be published in the Federal Register together with "a detailed statement of the information on which it is based"; (6) the FAA "shall complete the review as requested and shall report to EPA", again publishing the response in the Federal Register. The FAA report must contain a "detailed statement" of findings and conclusions and indicate whether an environmental impact statement has been filed.

A recitation of the procedure should suffice to show that the shotgun wedding of FAA and EPA, complete with a public washing of dirty linen, is unlikely to produce an enduring marriage. At best, it represents a temporary legislative compromise. The issue of who writes the aircraft noise standards is likely to be a recurring one in the Congress.

Section 7 [17] of the 1972 Act called upon the Administrator to conduct a study of the adequacy of the FAA's flight and operational noise controls. The study is now extant,[18] and contains a useful summary of the rulemaking initiatives on both source and operational con-

---

16. Section 166(c)(1), 49 U.S.C.A. § 1431(c)(1). Compare § 8.7 below (discussing EPA's obligation to consult with Department of Agriculture in connection with pesticide cancellation decisions). As of May 1976, EPA had submitted seven proposals to FAA dealing with source and operation regulations. Hearings have been held on all of the proposals, but action has been taken on none. EPA, Noise Control Program Progress to Date 8–9 (1976).

17. 42 U.S.C.A. § 4906.

18. Report on Aircraft-Airport Noise to the Senate Comm. on Public Works, S.Doc. No. 8, 93d Cong., 1st Sess. (Comm.Print 1973) [hereinafter cited as EPA Aircraft-Airport Noise Report]. Another review of the FAA's regulatory efforts is found in Aircraft/Airport Noise Report Study, Task Group 5, Draft Report on Review and Analysis of Present and Planned FAA Noise Regulatory Actions and Their Consequences Regarding Aircraft and Airport Operations, for the Environmental Protection Agency (1973).

trols. The familiar distinction between new and existing sources is found in the FAA's rulemakings, both those adopted and those neglected.[19]

i. *New Sources*

The FAA's equivalency of new source performance standards for aircraft were adopted in 1969 and now represent the major regulatory effort [20] on noise emissions from aircraft considered "most likely to raise the aircraft noise levels in airport neighborhoods." [21] These include all subsonic commercial aircraft (both jet and propeller) and all subsonic jet aircraft (including small personal and business jets). The basic promise of FAR 36 is that aircraft noise at the source is best controlled by addressing the certificates authorizing the production of a line of aircraft of similar design. There is no warranty or recall provision. There are no effective sanctions for noncompliance by individual aircraft once the type certificate issues.

FAR 36 makes a "significant contribution" in the form of three appendices "that have come to be used as standards or recommended practices in the measurement and evaluation of aircraft noise." [22] Appendix A, not unlike the certification procedures for automobiles under the Clean Air Act,[23] prescribes conditions "under which noise type certification tests for aircraft must be conducted and the noise measurement procedures that must be used." [24] Appendix B describes

---

19. The FAA noise emission regulations, notices of proposed rulemaking NPRM) and advance notices of proposed rulemaking (ANPRM) include the following:

(1) Federal Aviation Regulation (FAR) Part 36: Noise Standards: Aircraft Type Certification, 34 Fed. Reg. 453 (1969), 14 CFR pt. 36.

(2) ANPRM 70-33, Civil Supersonic Aircraft Noise Type Certification Standards, 35 Fed.Reg. 12555 (1970).

(3) ANPRM 70-44, Civil Airplane Noise Reduction Retrofit Requirements, 35 Fed.Reg. 16981 (1970).

(4) NPRM 71-26, Noise Type Certification and Acoustical Change Approvals, 35 Fed.Reg. 18584 (1971).

(5) NPRM 72-19, Newly Produced Airplanes of Older Type Design; Proposed Application of Noise Standards, 37 Fed.Reg. 14814 (1972).

(6) ANPRM 73-3, Civil Airplane Fleet Noise (FNL) Requirements, 38 Fed.Reg. 2769 (1973), reproposed in NPRM 74-14, 39 Fed.Reg. 11302 (1974), revised and adopted 41 Fed. Reg. 56045 (1976), adding 14 CFR pt. 36, subpt. E.

(7) Federal Aviation Regulation (FAR) Part 91.55: General Operating and Flight Rules: Civil Aircraft Sonic Boom, 38 Fed.Reg. 8054 (1973), 14 CFR pt. 91.55.

(8) NPRM 75-15, Civil Supersonic Airplanes; Noise Requirements Submitted to FAA by EPA, 40 Fed. Reg. 14093 (1975).

(9) NPRM 75-37, Subsonic Transport Category Large Aircraft and Subsonic Turbojet Powered Airplanes; Proposed Noise Reduction Stages and Acoustical Change Requirements, 40 Fed.Reg. 51476 (1975).

20. 14 CFR pt. 36; see Lake, supra note 1, at 1156–71.

21. 34 Fed.Reg. 453, 454 (1969).

22. EPA Aircraft-Airport Noise Report, supra note 18, at 34.

23. § 3.14 above.

24. EPA Aircraft-Airport Noise Report, supra note 18, at 34.

the method to compute the effective perceived noise level (EPNL). Appendix C provides the "noise criteria levels, noise measuring points, and airplane flight test conditions for which compliance must be shown with noise levels" [25] measured and evaluated as prescribed in appendices A and B. The prescribed noise levels are not the same for each type of aircraft. There is a sliding scale of limits with heavier aircraft allowed to produce more noise. For the heaviest airliners, the maximum noise output is 107 EPNdB.

FAR 36 has several gaps: (1) it does not cover potentially significant noise producers like the SST's or the nontransport, nonjet aircraft designed for vertical or short takeoff and landing (V/STOL); [26] (2) it provides exceptions for aircraft with certifications pending at the time of adoption, including the Boeing 747, which permitted the subsequent production of some planes that need not meet the standards; (3) it abandoned a "noise floor" or "objective" of 80 EPNdB for all new aircraft originally proposed as a "reasonable boundary between noise levels that are high enough to interfere with communications and to obstruct normal life in homes or other buildings that are not designed with specific acoustical objectives, and lower noise levels which, while not completely benign, nevertheless allow those activities to proceed." [27] A reason for abandoning the floor was said to be "that the number 80 EPNdB might be misconstrued as being a value that is Federally determined to be 'acceptable' in a given local airport environment." [28] This is the same form of bureaucratic trepidation that encouraged the FAA to drop the NEF noise imprint standards because they might be used in litigation.[29] The agency should tend to the business of regulating without worrying about how others construe their actions. Finally, FAR 36 originally permitted compliance with standards "to be shown by tests at sea level and at any single temperature." This allowed an airplane to be approved "even though it might be incapable of complying with the applicable noise limits under other conditions under which the airplane is au-

---

25. Ibid.

26. In 1970 the FAA, in response to a petition filed by the Environmental Defense Fund, issued an advance notice of proposed rulemaking to establish noise standards for SST's. 35 Fed. Reg. 12555 (1970). On January 14, 1976, EPA transmitted to FAA an SST noise proposal "that would apply FAR 36 standards to any aircraft, including supersonics that did not have flight time before December 31, 1974, the cutoff date now applicable to United States subsonic planes." Dep't of Transp., The Secretary's Decision on the Concorde Supersonic Transport, Feb. 4, 1976, at 16 n. 27 [hereinafter cited as 1976 Concorde Decision].

27. 34 Fed.Reg. at 456. The 80 EPNdB level was not a strict standard for new aircraft but only one to be adhered to the extent this level was "economically reasonable, technologically practicable and appropriate" for a particular aircraft. Ibid.

28. 34 Fed.Reg. 18361 (1969).

29. § 5.5 n. 34 above; see text accompanying notes 92–93, infra.

Sec. 5.7 **AIRCRAFT: REGULATION** 589

thorized to operate under the FAA's airworthiness regulations." [30] This, of course, is the familiar problem of whether assembly line testing brings about compliance by the vehicle in use. A rulemaking to correct this situation was initiated [31] but long delayed.

ii. *Existing Sources*

The FAA's rulemakings to control noise from existing sources are much criticized. EPA affirms without apparent contradiction that "currently available technology" is capable of being translated into equipment that, together with employment of noise abatement flight procedures, can decrease significantly "the noise impact from aircraft . . . . Current source noise abatement technology can be applied as a retrofit option for existing aircraft, as a modification to newly produced airplanes of older type designs, and also, be included in the design and development of new aircraft systems." [32] One common proposal on retrofit involves treating acoustically the jet engine and its nacelle (housing) with sound absorption material. Back in 1970, the FAA initiated an advanced notice of proposed rulemaking to inquire into how best to quiet down the sizeable current fleet not covered by FAR 36 (about three-fourths of all large jet aircraft), which includes all commercial jetliners except the new wide-bodied airplanes (747's, DC–10's, L–1011's), notably the 707's and DC–8's, the smaller Boeing 727 and 737 and the McDonnel-Douglas DC–9.[33] The problem with this advanced notice on retrofit is that it proposed no firm action, and resulted in none.

It did generate considerable comment.[34] A second-grader: "I hope you will put mufflers in all the jets. My teacher yells when 707 jets come over us. . . . I cannot stand it one more day." An optimist: "My husband and I were very happy to learn . . . that we have finally located the correct department to complain about the noise and disturbance of the jet planes." A pessimist: "I feel all levels of government have let us down and I am bitter . . . . Financially, we are ruined. That is what noise from jets has done to us." An insomniac: "I am constantly awakened between two and three in the morning." An engineer outside of the industry: "[T]here is technology now available that will enable these rules to be met at reasonable cost." An airport operator: "We must conclude that the FAA at the national level has accomplished little to alleviate the aircraft noise problem . . . ." A spokesman for the manufacturers: "[I]t is the AIA [Aerospace Industries Association] view that the necessary studies and information required to reach . . . de-

30. Lake, supra note 1, at 1163.

31. NPRM 71–26, Noise Type Certification and Acoustical Change Approvals, 36 Fed.Reg. 18584 (1971).

32. Aircraft-Airport Noise Report, supra note 18, at 30.

33. ANPRM 70–44, Civil Airplane Noise Reduction Retrofit Requirements, 35 Fed.Reg. 16981 (1970).

34. Examples are taken from the FAA files, Dkt. No. 10664, ANPRM, supra note 33.

cisions are presently not in hand." The Air Transport Association: "[I]t is our carefully considered position that there should not be a noise retrofit requirement for currently certificated turbofan and turbojet aircraft. Until the value to the public of a retrofit program has been demonstrated and proven to be economically reasonable and technically feasible, such a program would be meaningless."

Drawing on this advice the FAA Administrator gradually wound down the retrofit issue. In October 1971 he said a proposed rule on retrofitting the 727's, the 737's and the DC–9's would be released "imminently." [35] In May of 1972 he told the Aerospace Industries Association it would cost "considerably more than one million each to retrofit either a DC–8 or 707 . . . . Considering the size of the fleet, admirable as it may be, I just don't believe our airlines can absorb such costs nor do I personally believe such a program would be, in the long term, in the best interest of this nation." [36] It appears that this judgment ultimately may control the outcome of the retrofit issue.

Early in 1973 a new approach on the retrofit problem was unveiled by the FAA in another advance notice of proposed rulemaking entitled "Civil Airplane Fleet Noise (FNL) Requirements." [37] The agency explained that "the FNL concept is designed to permit an air carrier the alternative of modifying existing airplanes, replacing them with others having lower noise levels, or a combination of these actions." [38] It was said not to "imply a rejection of the retrofit program," [39] although clearly it does by looking more towards results (noise reductions) than the methods by which those results are achieved (redesigning existing fleets). The FNL proposed rules are basically three: (1) each commercial air fleet must freeze its noise level at or below the current level; (2) each fleet must reduce its noise level by July 1, 1976; (3) every airplane in each fleet must meet FAR 36 noise standards by July 1978. EPA says that "the concept and structure of the FNL proposal is adequate to effectively exploit the current technology (nacelle retrofit), to encourage the use of near future technology (refan retrofit)" (which involves modification of the principal existing engines) and "to provide incentives for the phaseout of aircraft not amenable to retrofit by the introduction of new quieter wide-body aircraft. . . . " [40] On the other hand, there are problems with the FNL proposal: it exempts airplanes en-

---

35. New York Times, Oct. 14, 1971, at 89, col. 5.

36. Speech of John Shaffer, Before the Aerospace Industry Association 28th Annual Conference, May 10, 1972.

37. ANPRM 73–3, 38 Fed.Reg. 2769 (1973), reproposed in NPRM 74–14, 39 Fed.Reg. 11302 (1974), revised and adopted 41 Fed.Reg. 56045 (1976) adding 14 CFR pt. 36, subpt. E.

38. Id. at 2770.

39. Ibid.

40. Aircraft-Airport Noise Report, supra note 18, at 36.

gaged in foreign overseas and interstate air commerce; it has no requirements for sideline noise as distinguished from takeoff and approach noise; it is difficult if not impossible to determine total fleet noise, much less detect violations and implement enforcement.[41] Even with these limitations, the third anniversary of the FNL proposal has come and gone with the FAA still delaying action on it.

As the retrofit debates proceed in the years ahead, it is useful to acknowledge that modern environmental regulation is least effective (and sometimes nearly helpless) against existing as distinguished from new sources. Existing sources are economically, technologically, politically and perforce legally difficult to revise. They are backed by strong constituencies, support important segments of the economy and resist easy redesign. New sources are free of much of this technological momentum. Building a new plane or constructing a new oil tanker that will not meet present or predicted environmental standards is a special form of perversity. Dirty and noisy existing sources are more sympathetic subjects because of the economics and the technology, both of which are accorded weight under law.

b. *Operations Regulation*

i. *Federal Law*

If, for one reason or another, source controls are frustrated or prove inadequate, regulation is likely to focus on another part of the system. With jet noise it is the operation of the planes. The FAA has adopted two Federal Aviation Regulations (FAR's) and two Advisory Circulars (AC's) related to flight and operational noise controls.[42] (Advisory circulars inform the public of nonregulatory material of interest but are not binding.) These accomplish the following: (1) FAR 91-55 [43] prohibits flights at speeds in excess of Mach 1 and thus prevents sonic boom, unless an exemption is expressly allowed; (2) FAR 91-87 [44] regulates airports with operating control towers and contains several provisions of protential benefit to noise sufferers, including a direction that a minimum altitude of 1500 feet be maintained by turbine powered or large aircraft (except on takeoff or landing) and a requirement that pilots of these aircraft use, whenever possible, the preferential noise abatement runways designated by the FAA; (3) AC 90-59 describes the FAA's much touted "Keep-em-High" program under which controllers issue clearances to keep noisy aircraft as high as possible; the program does not require the use of any

---

41. Compare § 3.4 above (discussing difficulties in enforcing long term ambient air quality standards).

42. The text follows closely the discussion in EPA Aircraft-Airport Noise Report, supra note 18, at 14–15. One measure of the ineffectiveness of these regulations is that they have been extant for many years while the noise problem has worsened. See Tondel, Noise Litigation at Public Airports, 32 J. Air. L. & Com. 387, 394 (1966), discussing operational regulations.

43. 14 CFR § 91.55.

44. Id. § 91.87.

noise abatement takeoff or approach procedure; (4) AC 91–36 encourages pilots flying in visual weather conditions to maintain at least 2000 feet altitude above noise sensitive areas.

Despite the assumption that operating procedures to minimize noise exposures would be readily agreed upon, EPA has found that "existing FAA flight and operational controls do not adequately protect the public health and welfare from aircraft noise." [45] Various recommendations have been made, including improved noise abatement takeoff and approach procedures and increased minimum altitudes.[46]

Benefits to be achieved from operational controls are limited, not the least by safety considerations. Consistent performance is not to be expected: climb steeply at full throttle to relieve the people downstream is one idea. No, says another school of thought, reduce thrust and climb gradually to help the people close in. Keep shifting the traffic to stay one jump ahead of the complaints. Cut the power when flying over the noise monitoring station, but make up the difference over somebody else. A systems analysis of noise control that focuses not on the aircraft but on the pilot or the manager of the airport also is likely to be resented (the Airport Operators Council International has supported retrofit for many years [47]) and is difficult to enforce. An example is the total failure to apply sanctions to enforce the 10 p. m. jet curfew at National Airport in Washington, D.C.,[48] which is operated by the FAA.[49]

Another source of operational (and other) restrictions can be found in the power of the FAA to impose operations specifications on licensed carriers.[50] The environmental impact statement on British Airways' and Air France's request for an amendment to their operations specifications authorizing them to operate the Concorde in commercial service into and out of the United States addresses three possible conditions: restrictions on arrival and departure times; restrictions on number of flights on an airport or carrier basis; additional operating procedures (such as requiring a power reduction or

---

45. Aircraft-Airport Noise Report, supra note 18, at 14.

46. Id. at 14–26; see Aircraft/Airport Noise Report Study, Task Group 2, Draft Report on Operations Analysis Including Monitoring, Enforcement, Safety and Costs for the Environmental Protection Agency, June 1, 1973.

47. Resolution No. 5, General Membership Meeting, Nov. 1970, adopted by U.S. members only.

48. Virginians for Dulles v. Volpe, 344 F.Supp. 573, 2 ELR 20360 (E.D.Va. 1972), rev'd 541 F.2d 442, 6 ELR 20581 (4th Cir. 1976).

49. See FAA, Washington National Airport Noise Abatement Procedures, effective June 1, 1970 (airlines also are required to use a thrust reduction during climbout and to follow the Potomac River on approach).

50. See 14 CFR pt. 129.

a reduced climb gradient).[51] Eventually, the Secretary of Transportation ordered a provisional amendment of the specifications to permit the carriers to commence commercial service for a limited period of time (16 months) with a limited number of flights (2 per day by each carrier into John F. Kennedy Airport, 1 per day by each carrier into Dulles International Airport) subject to other restrictions on timing (no flight before 7 a. m. local time or after 7 p. m. local time) and operations (thrust cut-back on departure if imposed by the FAA and no flights at supersonic speed over the United States).[52] The power to control operations specifications provides significant leverage over international carriers whose operations are but lightly touched by international law on the subject of noise.[53]

The Civil Aeronautics Board (CAB) exercises broad authority over air commerce [54] including (1) certifying new carrier air routes and (2) regulating fares charged for air transportation. These powers influence aircraft operations and ergo noise. It is clear that the CAB is obliged to consider environmental factors in its decision-making, both before [55] and particularly after [56] passage of the National Environmental Policy Act. This is accomplished on a case by case basis in proceedings for an application by an air carrier for a certificate of public convenience and necessity to provide service.[57] The agency has refused to act on a petition urging action to combat the cumulative effects of noise through methods other than certification proceedings.[58] Mr. Lake points out [59] that section 401(e)(4) of the Federal Aviation Act prevents the CAB from conditioning a certificate in such a way as to "restrict the right of an air carrier to add to or change schedules [and] equipment . . . as the development of the business and the demands of the public shall require." [60]

This provision is designed to free management from day to day regulatory supervision but obviously hampers the agency from a thorough evaluation of noise effects and thus clearly conflicts with the

51. Federal Aviation Administration, Final Environmental Impact Statement on Concorde Supersonic Transport Aircraft, Sept. 1975, vol. 1, at V–1 to –5.

52. 1976 Concorde Decision, supra note 26, at 3–4.

53. See id. at 9–12, summarizing pertinent international law.

54. 49 U.S.C.A. §§ 1371(d)(1), 1373–76.

55. Palisades Citizens Ass'n v. Civil Aeronautics Bd., 420 F.2d 188 (D.C. Cir. 1969).

56. CAB, Policy Statement Implementing the National Environmental Policy Act of 1969, 14 CFR § 399.110.

57. See Lake, supra note 1, at 1173 n. 105 for citations of proceedings considering the noise issue. Compare § 4.20 above (discussing consideration of thermal pollution issues in Nuclear Regulatory Commission licensing proceedings).

58. CAB, Order Dismissing Complaint of Natural Resources Defense Council, 1 ELR 30045 (1971).

59. Supra note 1, at 1173.

60. 49 U.S.C.A. § 1371(e)(4).

National Environmental Policy Act.[61] CAB does have the power to suspend or alter a certificate in the public interest [62] if changes in schedule or equipment increase the din unacceptably but the likelihood of this blunderbuss being invoked is infinitesimal. The Board has denied a hearing on a petition to decertify one or more of the carriers serving Los Angeles International Airport because noise and air pollution had reached unacceptable levels.[63] The drastic remedy of the shutdown is out of the question as applied by an agency which as a matter of "historical fact" [64] was conceived by the airlines.

ii. *Local Law*

A perplexing legal question is the extent to which municipal airport operators can insist upon curfew, preferential runway, operational or other restrictions to reduce noise that can lead ultimately to an inverse condemnation suit. This issue has been litigated for many years on preemption and burden on commerce grounds with the decisions usually but not always favoring the carriers over the regulating authority.[65] The Supreme Court had an opportunity recently to clarify the situation but ended up adding to the confusion. In a 5–4 decision the Court in Burbank v. Lockheed Air Terminal [66] struck down, on preemption grounds, an ordinance of Burbank, Cali-

---

61. See § 7.6 below. Generally, clearly conflicting statutory mandates prevail over NEPA. E. g., United States v. Kosanke Sand Corp., 12 IBLA 282, 3 ELR 30017 (1973) (en banc) (General Mining Act of 1872 found to conflict with NEPA).

62. 49 U.S.C.A. § 1371(g).

63. CAB, Order No. 72–2–41 (Feb. 11, 1972).

64. Speech of Secor Brown, Chairman, Civil Aeronautics Board, Oct. 29, 1970, at 10.

65. American Airlines, Inc. v. Audubon Park, 407 F.2d 1306 (6th Cir.) (per curiam), cert. denied 396 U.S. 845 (1969) (invalidating limitation on elevation); Allegheny Airlines, Inc. v. Cedarhurst, 132 F.Supp. 871, 57 (D.C.N.J.1958) (refusing to permit local regulation of flight patterns); Port of New York Authority v. Eastern Airlines, Inc., 259 F.Supp. 142 (E.D.N.Y.1966) (allowing operator to ban jets from using one runway at LaGuardia); American Airlines v. Hempstead, 272 F.Supp. 226 (E.D.N.Y.1967), aff'd on other grounds 398 F.2d 369 (2d Cir. 1968), cert. denied 393 U.S. 1017 (1969) (disallowing local attempt to regulate flight patterns); Loma Portal Civil Club v. American Airlines, Inc., 61 Cal.2d 582, 39 Cal.Rptr. 708, 394 P.2d 548 (1964) (sustaining state action affecting flight operations not in conflict with federal law); Air Transport Ass'n v. Inglewood, 2 ELR 20596 (C.D. Cal.1972); Cook v. Priester, 3 ELR 20183 (Ill.Cir.Ct.Cook County 1972) (invalidating county ordinance attempting to regulate flight patterns and aircraft weight); People v. Altman, 61 Misc.2d 4, 304 N.Y.S.2d 534 (Dist.Ct.1969) (no federal preemption); see Lesser, The Aircraft Noise Problem: Federal Power but Local Liability, 3 Urban Law. 175 (1971); Danforth, Mercury's Children in the Urban Trap: Community Planning and Federal Regulation of the Jet Noise Source, 3 Urban Law. 206 (1971); Sax, Takings and the Police Power, 74 Yale L.J. 36 (1964); Annot., 36 ALR 3d 1310 (1971). See also Opinion of the Justices, 359 Mass. 778, 271 N.E.2d 354 (1971) (advising that legislature could not enact constitutionally a statute prohibiting landing of any commercial supersonic aircraft within the commonwealth).

66. 411 U.S. 624, 93 S.Ct. 1854, 36 L.Ed.2d 547 (1973).

Sec. 5.7　　　　AIRCRAFT: REGULATION　　　　595

fornia, making it unlawful for a so-called pure jet aircraft to take off from the Hollywood-Burbank Airport between 11 p. m. one day and 7 a. m. the next. The Court created acute confusion with a footnote pointing out that the authority a municipality may have "as a landlord is not necessarily congruent with its police power."[67] Since the Hollywood-Burbank airport is the only major domestic airport privately owned, a subsequent affirmation that the proprietor has broader authority than the local regulator could undercut thoroughly the *Burbank* decision.[68] Another confusing aspect of the decision is that it can be read as preempting a wide range of the operator's powers necessary to control noise problems not about to be controlled at the source. The Court quoted a statement of Senator Tunney's indicating the expected range of federal regulation under the 1972 Act that may be suggestive also of the scope of preemption:

> [regulations to be considered by EPA for recommendation to FAA would include] proposed means of reducing noise in airport environments through the application of emission controls *the number, frequency, or scheduling of flights* [as well as] on aircraft, the regulation of flight patterns *and modifications in . . . the imposition of curfews on noisy airports,* the imposition of flight path alterations in areas where noise was a problem, the imposition of noise emission standards on new and existing aircraft—with the expectation of a retrofit schedule to abate noise emissions from existing aircraft—*the imposition of controls to increase the load factor on commercial flights, or other reductions in the joint use of airports,* and such other procedures as as may be determined useful and necessary to protect public health and welfare.[69]

Mr. Justice Rehnquist, in dissent, points out that the 1972 Act discloses no preemptive intent and reflects an affirmative purpose to preserve a municipality's power to regulate airport operations in the interest of noise control.[70] He quite properly reads the Act as establish-

---

67. 411 U.S. at 635–36 n. 14, 93 S.Ct. at 1861 n. 14, 36 L.Ed.2d at 555 n. 14.

68. See National Aviation v. Hayward, 418 F.Supp. 417, 6 ELR 20649 (N.D. Cal.1976) (sustaining ordinance prohibiting aircraft operations producing noise levels above 75dB(A) between 11:00 p.m. and 7:00 a.m.) (distinguishing Burbank as a nonproprietor case).

69. 411 U.S. at 637, 93 S.Ct. at 1861, 36 L.Ed.2d at 555–56, quoting 118 Cong.Rec. 37317 (1972) (emphasis supplied by Court).

70. 411 U.S. at 652, 93 S.Ct. at 1869, 36 L.Ed.2d at 564–65. Examples of cases sustaining these powers are Stagg v. Municipal Court, 2 Cal.App. 3d 318, 82 Cal.Rptr. 578, 2 ELR 20083 (1969) (curfew); Hanover v. Morristown, 108 N.J.Super. 461, 261 A.2d 692 (1969), aff'd 121 N.J.Super. 536, 298 A.2d 89 (App.Div.1972) (imposition of noise suppression controls and curfew); Port of New York Authority v. Eastern Airlines, Inc., 259 F.Supp. 745 (E.D.N.Y.1966) (exclusion of certain aircraft from an airport or a runway on noise grounds); cf. Aircraft Owners & Pilots Ass'n v. Port Authority, 305 F.Supp. 93 (E.D.N.Y.1969) (upholding takeoff fee schedule disfavoring small aircraft in order to reduce congestion).

ing exclusive federal control of the technological methods for reducing the output of noise by jet aircraft, but that is "a far cry from saying that it prohibited any local regulation of the times at which the local airport might be available for use of jet aircraft." [71] Also, it is one thing to say that federal authorities might move to impose a 10 p. m. curfew (as they have at National Airport) but quite another to say that the states cannot do so if the federal government does nothing. Add to this the appealing suggestion that it is preposterous to hold the operator for unconstitutional takings yet deny him the means to protect himself, and it is difficult to resist the conclusion that *Burbank* was wrongly decided.

It is likely that *Burbank* will be contained. In the future, the federal presence assures preemption of regulations at the source and perhaps local police power bans against federally certified aircraft.[72] But selective means for protecting communities against noisy operations are likely to survive: perhaps landing fees or head taxes to shift the costs of compensation; [73] preferential runways and other controls over approach and departure flight paths; curfews and similar limits to protect the population during sensitive time periods; elimination or reductions in engine runup tests on the ground or requirements that runups be conducted at specified locations.

The boldest state effort to control aircraft operations and surrounding land use is reflected in the California Noise Standards,[74] adopted in 1970 and quickly embroiled in litigation. They are summarized by the court in Air Transport Ass'n v. Crotti: [75] "[he objective of the regulations is to achieve] a gradual reduction of noise to be suffered at airports operating under California permits to a level at which no residential community is exposed to more than 65dB as of December 31, 1985 . . .; that level is designated as the Community Noise Equivalent Level (CNEL). By that date, absent the granting of a variance . . ., no incompatible land use is to exist within the 65dB Noise Impact Boundary (residential usage is not a compatible

---

71. 411 U.S. at 651, 93 S.Ct. at 1868, 36 L.Ed.2d at 563–64.

72. Fairfax County, Virginia, has banned flights by the Concorde into Dulles, which is operated by the federal government. Code of the County of Fairfax, Virginia § 108–4–6. The measure was ruled invalid. Fairfax County Bd. of Supervisors v. McLucas, Civil No. 76–467 (E.D.Va.1976). But a denial of landing rights to the Concorde by the New York Port Authority, the proprietor of JFK would be another matter. The Secretary's Concorde Decision, supra note 26, at 3 n. 6, explicitly recognizes that "the situation with respect to JFK may be complicated by the fact that under federal policy that has hitherto prevailed a local airport proprietor has had authority under certain circumstances to refuse landing rights."

73. Cf. Aircraft Owners & Pilots Ass'n v. Port Authority, 305 F.Supp. 93 (E.D.N.Y.1969).

74. 4 Cal.Admin.Code § 5011 ("Methodology for Controlling and Reducing Noise Problems").

75. 389 F.Supp. 58, 61, 5 ELR 20236, 20237 (N.D.Cal.1975) (three-judge court).

one within the Noise Impact Boundary). Airports with a noise problem are responsible for establishing the Noise Impact Boundary by monitoring and measuring aircraft noise emissions . . . ." The means available to the airport proprietors to meet their noise reduction obligations run the gamut of available operational and land use controls:[76]

> (a) Encouraging use of the airport by aircraft classes with lower noise level characteristics and discouraging use by higher noise level aircraft classes;
>
> (b) Encouraging approach and departure flight paths and procedures to minimize the noise in residential areas;
>
> (c) Planning runway utilization schedules to take into account adjacent residential areas, noise characteristics of aircraft and noise sensitive time periods;
>
> (d) Reduction of the flight frequency, particularly in the most sensitive time periods and by the noisier aircraft;
>
> (e) Employing shielding for advantage, using natural terrain, building, . . . and
>
> (f) Development of compatible land use within the noise impact boundary.

The Code does not require a licensed airport to adopt any of the suggested noise reduction strategies. Airport authorities "are left to choose among the suggested means at their own discretion, tailoring their own programs to their peculiar needs and inclinations. Furthermore, airport authorities are left free to design and employ other noise control measures beyond those suggested in the Code."[77]

In addition to the long term ambient goals, California also sought to establish maximum Single Event Noise Exposure Levels (SENEL). This was responsive to the easily comprehended point that while the average may be well below tolerance levels it is made up of single events representing unacceptable exposures.[78] CNEL thus stresses limited operational controls and land use accommodations while SENEL was aimed at noisy sources in flight.

The three-judge court in *Crotti,* holding that *Burbank* was a police power and not a proprietor case, rejected an attack on the face of the land use and operationally oriented CNEL although noting that the authority to reduce flight frequency "appears suspect"[79] (it had not been implemented by any airport). The SENEL provisions, on the other hand, involving the regulation of noise levels when an aircraft is in "direct flight" and the levying of criminal fines for viola-

---

76. 4 Cal.Admin.Code § 5011.

77. 389 F.Supp. at 61–62, 5 ELR at 20237.

78. Compare § 4.11 above (discussing averaging in connection with water pollution sampling).

79. 389 F.Supp. at 65, 5 ELR at 20238.

tion, "are a per se unlawful exercise of police power into the exclusive federal domain of control over aircraft flights and operation . . . .[80]" Thus the message is that the states can regulate totally the use of the land, partially the operations of the aircraft, and not at all the technology that produces the problem.

c. *Land Use*

Although inverse condemnation is an ad hoc regulator with heavy hand, land use restrictions in the traditional sense are common guardians of the airport environment. They are found in both federal and local law as the California Noise Standards eloquently attest.

i. *Federal Law*

The Airport and Airway Development Act of 1970,[81] which has origins going back to the Federal Airport Act of 1946,[82] contains the airport version of the federal highway trust fund. It sets up a grant program to finance airport facilities. No airport development project can be approved by the Secretary of Transportation (acting through the FAA) "unless he is satisfied that fair consideration has been given to the interest of communities in or near which the project may be located."[83] Project approval is dependent upon the sponsoring agency certifying that public hearings have been afforded "for the purpose of considering the economic, social, and environmental effects of the airport location and its consistency with the goals and objectives of such urban planning as has been carried out by the community."[84] It is declared to be national policy that airport development projects "shall provide for the protection and enhancement of the natural resources and the quality of environment of the Nation."[85] The Secretary of Transportation is required to consult with other agencies of the government about possible adverse environmental effects of any project involving airport location, a major runway extension or runway location, "and shall authorize no such project found to have adverse effect unless [he] shall render a finding, in writing, following a full and complete review, which shall be a matter of public record, that no feasible and prudent alternative exists and that all possible efforts have been taken to minimize such adverse effect."[86] This is strong medicine, imposing a substantive obligation more unequivocal than

---

80. Ibid.

81. Pub.L. No. 91–258, 84 Stat. 235, 49 U.S.C.A. § 1701 et seq.; see Dworkin, Planning for Airports in Urban Environments, 5 Transp.L.J. 183 (1973).

82. 60 Stat. 170.

83. Section 16(c)(3) of the Airport and Airway Development Act of 1970, 49 U.S.C.A. § 1716(d)(1).

84. Id. § 1716(c)(1).

85. Id. § 1716(c)(4).

86. Ibid; cf. Citizens to Preserve Overton Park v. Volpe, 401 U.S. 402, 91 S.Ct. 814, 28 L.Ed.2d 136 (1971) (construing similar provisions in the Department of Transportation Act of 1966 and the Federal-Aid Highway Act of 1968).

that found in the National Environmental Policy Act.[87] The rapidly accumulating case law, usually involving claims under both NEPA and the Airport and Airway Development Act, is discussed elsewhere.[88]

Another potentially important federal land use lever in the Airport and Airways Development Act is the requirement that all federally funded airport development "shall be in accordance with standards established by the Secretary, including standards for site location, airport layout, grading, drainage, seeding, paving, lighting and safety of approaches."[89] It has been suggested, understandably, that this language contemplates that the FAA "will prescribe standards for airport location and layout, based on noise and other considerations."[90] But no meaningful standards have been proposed, with the consequence that local sponsors of airport projects are without federal guidance on how to design for minimum noise impact.[91]

Typical of what could be done is the so-called noise exposure forecast (NEF) for airport environments, which has become an embarassing chapter in the noise control efforts of the FAA. Developed for the agency in the late 1960's by the well known noise consultants, Bolt, Beranek and Newman,[92] the NEF procedures provide a means for predicting the impact of noise on people (at least on those who complain) and on land use. It is developed by utilizing a number of different operations (takeoffs, landings, ground runups) by different aircraft. The result is recorded on an overlay of an airport map to depict graphically the noise radiating over surrounding areas from the airport runways. NEF 30 translates into seriously affected residential uses; NEF 40 recommends no residential usage under any circumstances; less than 30 anticipates no serious problems. Although NEF maps have been prepared for over thirty civil airports in the country (including O'Hare in Chicago and JFK in New York), the concept has not been used either as an official guideline for projecting noise problems or as a means of conditioning federal grants on land use compatability. The principal reasons for downplaying the technique were objections from airport operators fearful the NEF's would be used against them in litigation.[93]

87. § 7.12 below; see Life of the Land v. Brinegar, 485 F.2d 460, 472, 3 ELR 20811, 20817 (9th Cir. 1973) (quoting *Overton Park* in support of conclusion that Secretary only must "reasonably believe" there are no feasible alternatives).

88. § 5.9 below.

89. Section 16(a), 49 U.S.C.A. § 1716 (a).

90. Lake, supra note 1, at 1175.

91. See Hearings on H.R. 5275 and Other Bills, Before the Subcomm. on Public Health and the Environment of the House Comm. on Interstate and Foreign Commerce, 92d Cong., 1st Sess. 380–81 (1971).

92. P. E. Bishop & R. D. Horonjeff, Procedures for Developing Noise Exposure Forecast Areas for Aircraft Flight Operations (1969).

93. See Lake, supra note 1, at 1176–78.

A federal planner perhaps more important than the FAA is the Department of Housing and Urban Development (HUD) which has a policy prohibiting HUD support for housing construction in areas adversely affected by noise.[94] The circular expressing this policy establishes three categories of noise exposure (acceptable, discretionary and unacceptable) defined numerically in dB(A)'s and, in the case of airport environs, NEF and similar zones. The discretionary category is further subdivided into a "normally acceptable" range and "normally unacceptable" range. The major provisions are summarized by Mr. Lake:[95] "HUD assistance for new construction will not be approved for a site whose noise exposure is in the unacceptable category, unless an exception is made. . . . Assistance will be extended for sites in the normally unacceptable range of the discretionary category only if noise attenuation measures are taken, an environmental impact statement under NEPA is prepared, and the site is approved by a regional administrator or higher HUD official. Assistance for clearly acceptable sites may be approved routinely at the lowest possible levels within field offices." The HUD Noise Circular is important, and like all law of significance spawns gloss and exceptions best known at the administrative level where they are applied.

ii. *Local Law*

Taking by inverse condemnation[96] is not the only nor indeed the most significant local land use regulation of the airport environment. Local or regional zoning measures often address, to mention the two most common examples, height restrictions on structures to make approaches obstruction free and restriction on uses that may be made in the vicinity of an airport (such as the exclusion of schools, hospitals or residences). The latter are clearly highly significant for noise purposes. A recent synthesis[97] identifies nineteen reported decisions dealing with the validity of airport zoning, twelve ruling that the particular ordinance in question amounted to a taking,[98] seven

---

94. HUD, Circular 1390.2, Noise Abatement and Control: Departmental Policy, Responsibilities, and Standards, Aug. 4, 1971. A useful source document is HUD Final Environmental Impact Statement, Proposed HUD Circular, Noise Abatement and Control: Departmental Policy, Responsibilities, and Standards (1971).

95. Lake, supra note 1, at 1203 (footnotes omitted).

96. § 5.5 above.

97. Aircraft/Airport Noise Report Study, Task Group 1, Draft Report on Legal and Institutional Analysis of Aircraft and Airport Noise and Apportionment of Authority Between Federal, State and Local Governments, Environmental Protection Agency, June 1973, at 1–2–50 to –55.

98. Mutual Chem. Co. v. Mayor and City Council of Baltimore, 1 Av.Cas. 804 (Md.Cir.Ct.Baltimore City 1939); Yara Engin. Corp. v. Newark, 132 N.J.L. 370, 40 A.2d 559 (1945); Dutton v. Mendocino County, 1949 U.S. Aviation Rep. 1 (Cal.Super.Ct. Mendocino County 1948); Banks v. Fayette County Bd. of Airport Zoning Appeals, 313 S.W.2d 416 (Ky.Ct.App.1958); Kissinger v. Los Angeles, 161 Cal.App.2d 254, 327 P.2d 10 (1958); Sneed v. Riverside County, 218 Cal.App.2d 205, 32 Cal.Rptr. 318 (1963), cert. denied 379 U.S. 487

upholding the zoning restrictions as reasonable exercises of police power.[99] The message seems to be that it is every bit as difficult to erode property values by direct zoning as it is to erode them by bringing in more aircraft without bothering to zone.

Local land use restrictions take other forms: the California Noise Standards, discussed above,[1] have a strong land use component. State environmental policy acts may contribute to improved planning of airport expansions to combat noise.[2] The land use classification schemes discussed in connection with nontransportation sources above [3] apply also to noise from transportation sources such as aircraft. Fortunately, the alternative of treating the technological problem of jet noise by soundproofing the homes of the sufferers has gained no more adherents than has the suggestion of combating air pollution by developing more resistant species of plants. The authorities recognize that control at the source and land use accommodations are the more practical ways to control noise.[4]

§ 5.8 Transportation Sources (Railroads, Motor Vehicles): Regulation

Nearly 100 million people in the United States are exposed to urban transportation noise above levels EPA identifies as necessary to protect public health and welfare with an adequate margin of safety.[1] While aircraft are a sizeable part of the problem,[2] ground vehicles have a more pervasive impact. By far the most numerous source, the automobile, is usually least offensive although noise from

(1965); Roark v. Caldwell, 87 Idaho 557, 394 P.2d 641 (1964); Jackson Municipal Airport Authority v. Evans, 191 So.2d 126 (Miss.1966); Shipp v. Louisville & Jefferson County Air Bd., 431 S.W.2d 867 (Ky.Ct.App.1968), cert. denied 393 U.S. 1088 (1969); Hageman v. Wayne Township Bd. of Trustees, 20 Ohio App.2d 12, 251 N.E. 2d 507 (1969); Peacock v. County of Sacramento, 271 Cal.App.2d 845, 77 Cal.Rptr. 391 (1969). Compare § 2.17 above (discussing the taking theories).

99. Harrell's Candy Kitchen v. Sarasota-Manatee Airport Authority, 111 So.2d 439 (Fla.1959); Waring v. Peterson, 137 So.2d 268 (Fla.Dist.Ct.App. 1962); Baggett v. Montgomery, 276 Ala. 166, 160 So.2d 6 (1963); Smith v. County of Santa Barbara, 243 Cal. App.2d 126, 52 Cal.Rptr. 292 (1966); Morse v. County of San Luis Obispo, 247 Cal.App.2d 600, 55 Cal.Rptr. 710 (1967); Hickory v. Chadderton, 43 Pa. D. & C.2d 319 (Common Pleas, Mercer County 1967); Willoughby Hill v. Corrigan, 29 Ohio St.2d 39, 278 N.E.2d 658, cert. denied sub nom.,

Chongris v. Corrigan, 409 U.S. 919 (1972).

1. See text accompanying notes 74–80 supra.

2. See Secretary of Environmental Affairs v. Massachusetts Port Authority, —— Mass. ——, 323 N.E.2d 329, 5 ELR 20200 (1975); § 5.9 below.

3. § 5.4 above.

4. Note, A Model Ordinance to Control Noise Through Building Code Performance Standards, 9 Harv.J.Legis. 66, 67 (1971); Cleary, Gottlieb, Steen & Hamilton, Legal Aspects of Required Soundproofing in High Noise Areas Near John F. Kennedy International Airport, Feb. 1970 (an unpublished legal memorandum prepared for the Tri-State Transportation Commission).

1. 41 Fed.Reg. 15538, 15544 (1976). Compare § 5.1 nn. 2 & 3 above.

2. §§ 5.5, 5.7 above.

passenger cars may reach disturbing levels "due to the cumulative effect of exhaust and air intake systems, the engine, interaction of tires with road surface, and the aerodynamic 'swish' of" the moving vehicles.[3] A typical truck generates between "10 to 32 times" the sound pressure produced by a properly maintained automobile.[4] In comparative terms, one motorcycle is as noisy as thirty passenger cars passing by simultaneously.[5] Buses, although significantly quieter than trucks, present obvious problems in urban areas. Noise from snowmobiles is especially annoying when it occurs, as it often does, in quiet environments. Since the days of Richards v. Washington Terminal Co.,[6] noisy railways has received the attention of the law, albeit not its close scrutiny.

a. *Planning Controls*

By manipulating highway location and design, it is possible to reduce "the subjective loudness of future traffic noise by as much as a factor of two to four."[7] Section 136 of the Federal-Aid Highway Act of 1970[8] initiates regulation of highway design for noise purposes by requiring the Secretary of Transportation to develop and promulgate "standards for highway noise levels compatible with different land uses." After July 1, 1972, the Secretary is directed to condition approval of plans and specifications for proposed projects on any federal-aid system upon a determination "that [the] plans and specifications include adequate measures to implement the appropriate noise level standards."

The highway design noise regulations, now in effect,[9] set "design noise levels" to be treated by the Federal Highway Administration as generally acceptable for different types of "developed" land use near highways. These include "three standards for exterior noise: 60dB(A) for areas in which 'serenity and quiet are of extraordinary significance,' such as amphitheatres and some parks; 70dB(A) for the exteriors of residences, hotels, public build-

---

3. Columbia University Legislative Drafting Research Fund, The Automobile and the Regulation of Its Impact on the Environment at 10–1 to –2 (1975) [hereinafter cited as Columbia University Automobile Study].

4. Id. at 10–2, citing authorities.

5. Id. at 10–21 n. 34, citing Lyon, Automotive Noise Propagation in Open Areas (Lecture No. 17 in series Noise and Vibration in Transportation Systems, Apr. 9, 1970) and Organization for Economic Cooperation and Development, Urban Traffic Noise: Strategy for an Improved Environment (1969).

6. 233 U.S. 546, 34 S.Ct. 654, 58 L. Ed. 1088 (1914).

7. Kugler & Anderson, Automotive Noise—Environmental Impact and Control, at 23 (undated).

8. Pub.L. No. 91–605, 84 Stat. 1734, 23 U.S.C.A. § 109(i).

9. Policy and Procedure Memorandum (PPM) 90–2, 23 CFR pt. 772. The regulations are discussed thoroughly in Lake, Noise: Emerging Federal Control, in Environmental Law Institute, Federal Environmental Law 1150, 1194–201 (E. L. Dolgin & T. G. P. Guilbert eds. 1974). See also 41 Fed. Reg. 16933 (1976) (proposing procedures for abatement of highway construction noise).

ings and outdoor recreation areas; and 75dB(A) for other developed land uses. There is also a design noise level of 55dB(A) for the interiors of homes and other occupied buildings. No limit applies to highways abutting undeveloped lands." [10] The design noise levels selected are based not on an annoyance factor but on a judgment of the extent of speech interference. A noise level of 55dB(A) for the interior of homes, for example, would permit communication by normal voice between persons eleven feet apart; at 60dB(A) a normal communication could be conducted by persons six and a half feet apart, which raises some doubt about whether the person sitting at the rear of the amphitheatre will be able to hear the performance.

The highway design noise regulations are hedged by the usual agenda of exceptions: the numerical design levels are not absolute limits but rather can be exceeded no more than ten percent of the time for one hour a day during the "design year" (usually twenty years in the future) when most traffic noise will occur.[11] This is another illustration of a problem familiar to environmental law: the inseparability of the standards themselves and the methodology for determining compliance. The highway design standards also allow for variances, although they are not so denominated, if existing noise levels from nonhighway sources are comparable to the predicted traffic noise levels [12] or if noise abatement measures are otherwise deemed to be "impracticable." [13] The first exception presupposes that a noisy environment is unlikely to improve; the second makes noise abatement entirely a matter of administrative discretion. If predicted noise exceeds design levels and is not excused by the variance provisions, the plans for the highway project should be revised to include abatement measures. These may embrace relocation, depressing or elevating the roadway, shielding by earth berms or walls of vegetation (which is not very effective). Other abatement measures include the acquisition of property for buffer zones (either in fee or lesser interests) and, in some circumstances, the soundproofing of buildings.[14] While the Federal Highway Administration's noise design regulations can reduce the grosser effects of traffic noise on some new highways, they also may be significant in defining maximum exposures in highway noise taking cases.[15] The argument that property is taken without compensation is quite persuasive if traffic noise from the new highway exceeds levels thought to oblige state authorities to acquire adjoining property for a buffer zone.

The noise guidelines of the Department of Housing and Urban Development [16] are applicable equally to stationary and transporta-

10. Lake, supra note 9, at 1196.

11. 23 CFR § 772.2(f).

12. Id. § 772.3(c).

13. Id. § 772.4(a).

14. Id. § 772.7(b).

15. § 5.6 above.

16. Noise Abatement and Control Standards, Circular No. 1390.2, Aug. 4, 1971.

tion sources of noise. While they alone cannot assure quieter highways and railways, they can put a ceiling on the problem by foreclosing federal assistance for new construction of housing in unacceptably noisy areas.

b. *Operational and Source Controls*

Even with the arrival of the Noise Control Act of 1972, noise regulation at the source is governed mostly by state law.[17] A common operational restriction is a limit on the use of horns or sirens, usually expressed as a vague ban against "any unnecessary or unreasonably loud" usage.[18] Other operational restrictions range from limits on the size of bells on vehicles selling ice cream products [19] to prohibitions against carrying metal on vehicles loaded so as to cause unnecessary noise.[20] Of far greater practical importance are outright bans against use of noisy vehicles in noise sensitive areas. Section 4(c) of the Wilderness Act of 1964,[21] for example, affirms, subject to exceptions, that "there shall be no temporary road, no use of motor vehicles, motorized equipment or motorboats, [and] no other form of mechanical transport" within a wilderness area. Land management agencies, both state and federal, pursue similar policies with special attention being paid to off-road vehicles (such as snowmobiles and motorcycles).[22]

Virtually all states have muffler statutes which, like the horn statutes, are vaguely written directives requiring that every motor vehicle be equipped with a muffler "in good working order" to prevent "excessive or unusual noise."[23] Several states extend these subjective bans against muffler noise to the motor vehicle generally. Connecticut forbids the operation of a motor vehicle making "unnecessary noise."[24] Kentucky requires that vehicles be operated

---

17. See Hildebrand, Noise Pollution: An Introduction to the Problem and an Outline for Future Legal Research, 70 Colum.L.Rev. 652 (1970); Ware, The States and Motor Vehicle Noise: Present Regulation, Trends in the Law and the Impact of Federal Legislation (unpublished paper completed for a course in environmental law, Georgetown U.Law Center, Fall 1972); Environmental Protection Agency, Laws and Regulatory Schemes for Noise Abatement 1–60 to –71 and 1–97 to –137 (1971); Columbia University Automobile Study, supra note 3, ch. 10; Comment, Constitutionality of the Auto Muffler Statutes: Comments on Noise Pollution Laws, 48 J.Urban L. 755 (1971).

18. E. g., Ala.Code tit. 36, § 36.

19. Md.Ann.Code art. 66½, § 293.

20. N.J.Stat.Ann. § 39:4–78.

21. 16 U.S.C.A. § 1133(c).

22. See e. g., Bureau of Outdoor Recreation, Dep't of the Interior, Draft Environmental Impact Statement, Departmental Implementation of Executive Order 11644 Pertaining to Use of Off-Road Vehicles on Public Lands (1976).

23. E. g., Ala.Code tit. 36, § 39; Ariz. Rev.Stat.Ann. § 28–955; Ark.Stat. Ann. § 75–726; see People v. Byron, 17 N.Y.2d 64, 268 N.Y.S.2d 24, 215 N.E.2d 345 (1966).

24. Conn.Gen.Stat.Ann., tit. 14, § 14–80(e).

with "a minimum of noise"[25] while Oregon forbids operation with "any greater noise than is reasonably necessary."[26] The next, and obvious, legislative move is to attach an objective decibel limit as a ceiling on permissible noise. New York took this step in 1965, fixing 88dB(A) measured roughly at a distance of fifty feet from the center of the lane in which the vehicle is traveling.[27] California[28] and several other states[29] soon followed suit. Presently, California forbids the operation of motor vehicles (with the exception of motorcycles and vehicles in excess of 6000 pounds) emitting sound in excess of 76dB(A) at speeds under 45 miles per hour.[30] Measurements are made fifty feet from the center lane of travel.

In 1971, California went one step further to prohibit the sale of new motor vehicles exceeding prescribed noise levels.[31] For a motor vehicle in excess of 6000 pounds the following standards are imposed gradually as follows: 88dB(A) for a vehicle manufactured after 1967 and before 1973; 86dB(A) for a vehicle manufactured after 1972 and before 1975; 83dB(A) for a vehicle manufactured after 1974 and before 1978; 80dB(A) for a vehicle manufactured after 1977 and before 1988; and 70dB(A) for all vehicles manufactured after 1987. A similar gradually tightening scale is imposed for any other motor vehicle (motorcycles excepted): 86dB(A) after 1967 and before 1973; 84dB(A) after 1972 and before 1975; 80dB(A) after 1974 and before 1978; 75dB(A) after 1977 and before 1988; 70dB(A) for all motor vehicles manufactured after 1987. Inevitably, any attempt by the states to impose noise emission standards on new motor vehicles increases the pressure for uniform federal legislation, which arrived with enactment of the Noise Control Act of 1972. Federal auto noise emission standards prescribed by EPA will make a belated appearance sometime before the end of the decade.[32]

State regulations of noise from motorcycles follow the same pattern as that for other motor vehicles. Motorcycles are generally subject to the statutes governing autos and trucks. Some states have muffler laws applying only to motorcycles.[33] A few impose

25. Ky.Rev.Stat. § 189.140.

26. Or.Rev.Stat. § 483.448(3).

27. N.Y.Veh. & Traf.Law § 386 (McKinney).

28. Cal.Vehicle Code § 23130.

29. E. g., Colo.Rev.Stat.Ann. § 25–12–103; Conn.Gen.Stat.Ann. § 14–80a; Idaho Code Ann. § 49–835; Ind.Ann. Stat. § 47.2230(a); Minn.Stat.Ann. § 169.691. Predictably, several state legislatures have given administrators the power to impose noise standards on the operation of motor vehicles.

E. g., N.J.Stat.Ann. § 13:1G–6; Nev. Rev.Stat. § 484.610; N.D.Cent.Code § 23–01–17.

30. Cal.Vehicle Code § 23130.

31. Id. § 27160.

32. See National Observer, Sept. 25, 1976, at 11, col. 1 (reporting that regulations are "at least a year away").

33. E. g., N.J.Stat.Ann. § 39:3–76; Nev. Rev.Stat. § 486.321; Wash.Rev.Code § 46.37.390(3).

specific decibel limits on motorcycles operated within the state (typically with a measurement distance of fifty feet).[34] California goes further [35] to impose a sliding scale of standards for motorcycles sold within the state: 88dB(A) for those manufactured in the years 1970 to 1972; 86dB(A) for 1973 to 1974; 80dB(A) for 1975 to 1977; 75dB(A) for 1978 to 1987; 70dB(A) thereafter. The eventual fate of the California motorcycle noise emission standards, like those for trucks and autos, is likely to depend upon whether federal regulatory authorities move to preempt the field.

Although most of the older noise laws antedate the snowmobile, a few states confront the problem with traditional generalities. Maine, for example, requires that all snowmobiles be operated with an "adequate" muffler.[36] Wisconsin forbids operation that causes excessive or unusual noise.[37] A more useful regulatory option is the imposition of decibel limits on snowmobiles operated or sold within a state. The standards adopted vary widely: snowmobiles cannot be sold in Montana unless the vehicle conforms to 85dB(A) at fifteen feet; [38] in Colorado 84dB(A) at fifty feet; [39] in Michigan [40] and California [41] 82dB(A) at fifty feet; in Massachusetts [42] and New York [43] 73dB(A) at fifty feet. State statutes also contain various operational restrictions: Michigan,[44] for example, prohibits the operation of a snowmobile within one hundred feet of a dwelling between midnight and 6 a. m. at speeds greater than the minimum required to maintain forward movement.

Enforcement of state laws restricting noise from transportation sources is notoriously weak.[45] Operational restrictions, almost by definition, are enforceable only upon an accidental meeting of violator and enforcer, a species largely extinct.[46] Predictably, frustration in securing relief from difficult-to-enforce operational limits leads to efforts to control at the source. Source controls imposed

---

34. Cal.Vehicle Code §§ 23130, 23130.5, 27160; Ind.Ann.Stat. § 47–2230(a); Minn.Stat.Ann. §§ 169.691–.692.

35. Cal.Vehicle Code § 23130.5.

36. Me.Rev.Stat. tit. 12, § 1978(6). The six states regulating noise from boats also do so by relying upon various muffler statutes. See Laws and Regulatory Schemes, for Noise Abatement, supra note 17, at 1–72.

37. Wis.Stat.Ann. § 350.11.

38. Mont.Rev.Code Ann. § 53–1020(3).

39. Colo.Rev.Stat.Ann. § 25–12–103.

40. Mich.Comp.Laws § 257.1515(f).

41. Cal.Vehicle Code § 27160.

42. Mass.Ann.Laws ch. 90B, § 24.

43. N.Y.Parks & Rec.Law § 25.17 (McKinney).

44. Mich.Comp.Laws § 257.1515(g).

45. See Columbia University Automobile Study, supra note 3, at 10–10; Laws and Regulatory Schemes, for Noise Abatement, supra note 17, at 3–24 to –32.

46. See Laws and Regulatory Schemes for Noise Abatement, supra note 17, at 3–25, reporting that six two-man monitoring teams represent the entire enforcement commitment in the State of California.

by many jurisdictions in turn are often a precursor to federal entry into the field.

Noise from transportation sources can be regulated by Sections 6, 17 and 18 of the Noise Control Act of 1972.[47] The general powers to establish noise emission standards for products under section 6(a)(1)(C)[48] explicitly extend to "transportation equipment (including recreational vehicles and related equipment)." This means that any federal standards for snowmobiles, boats, buses and motorcycles will be addressed under the general provisions of section 6, and will be subject to limited preemption under subsection 6(e).[49]

Sections 17 and 18, respectively, deal with rail carrier and motor carrier noise emission standards in language that is virtually identical. Using section 17 for purposes of illustration, several ambiguities are apparent. The EPA Administrator is directed to propose standards setting limits on noise emissions "resulting from operation of the equipment and facilities of surface carriers engaged in interstate commerce by railroad which reflect the degree of noise reduction achievable through the application of the best available technology, taking into account the cost of compliance."[50] The "equipment and facilities" to which federal regulations may be applied are undefined in the Act but obviously embrace a wide range of railroad operations. Section 17 does not state that railroad noise emission standards must benefit health and welfare, and the EPA General Counsel says they need not,[51] although agency initiatives recite that in excess of 2 million people are exposed to railroad traffic noise at or about 55dB(A) and that its regulatory strategy could provide relief for more than a half million people.[52] The "best available technology" is undefined in the Act but should require only a reasoned judgment that the equipment needed to do the job will be available when the regulations take effect.[53] The direction that costs be taken into account does not require a cost-benefit analysis but only that costs be considered by the Administrator in a reasoned way.[54] The legislation authorizing railroad noise emission standards is complicated further by two additional unusual provisions—one giving the EPA Administrator substantial leeway in defining the preemptive effect of his own regulations,[55] an-

47. 42 U.S.C.A. §§ 4905, 4916, 4917.

48. Id. § 4905(a)(1)(C).

49. See § 5.4 above.

50. 42 U.S.C.A. § 4916(a)(1).

51. EPA Opinion of the General Counsel, Health and Welfare Criteria for Section 18, in 1 EPA Collection of Legal Opinions 263 (1974).

52. 41 Fed.Reg. 2183, 2190 (1976).

53. Id. at 2184; EPA Opinion of the General Counsel, Definition of "Best Available Technology", in 1 EPA Collection of Legal Opinions 256 (1974); §§ 3.10, 4.12 above.

54. §§ 3.10, 4.12 above.

55. 42 U.S.C.A. § 4916(c)(2), reads as follows:
Nothing in this section shall diminish or enhance the rights of any State or political subdivision thereof to establish and enforce stan-

other vesting the Secretary of Transportation with primary enforcement responsibilities.[56]

The Administrator proposed in 1974 [57] and promulgated in 1976 [58] railroad noise emission standards pointing up many of the legal difficulties apparent on the face of the authorizing legislation. The regulations set separate standards for locomotives (the only ones excluded are the old steam engines, used mostly for display, and the new gas turbine powered engines, used primarily for demonstration and experimental purposes) and for rail car operations, which is understood to include other types and sources of train noise. For stationary locomotives manufactured before December 31, 1979, the standards forbid operation at sound levels in excess of 93dB(A) at any throttle except idle and 73dB(A) at idle; for stationary locomotives manufactured after December 31, 1979 the standards are lowered to 87dB(A) and 70dB(A), respectively.[59] As for locomotives under moving conditions, the standard for those manufactured before December 31, 1979 is 93dB(A) and for those manufactured thereafter is 90dB(A).[60] The rail car operation standards, effective December 31, 1976, are 88dB(A) at rail speeds up to 45 miles per hour and 93dB(A) at greater speeds.[61]

The railroad noise regulation is limited despite some industry efforts to broaden its coverage and perforce its preemptive effect. Interurban subway systems are exempted because they are not "common carriers." [62] A wide variety of noisy railroad "equipment and facilities" is exempted, usually for the reason that state and local regulation is thought more suitable. Untouched by federal regulation are the use of horns, bells, whistles and other warning devices, railroad office buildings, assorted fixed facilities (such as repair and maintenance shops, terminal and marshalling yards which are akin to non-

dards or controls on levels of environmental noise or to control, license, regulate, or restrict the use, operation or movement of any product if the Administrator, after consultation with the Secretary of Transportation, determines that such standard, control, license, regulation or restriction is necessitated by special local conditions and is not in conflict with regulations promulgated under this section.

56. 42 U.S.C.A. § 4916(b), reads as follows:
The Secretary of Transportation, after consultation with the Administrator, shall promulgate regulations to insure compliance with all standards promulgated by the Administrator under this section. The Secretary of Transportation shall carry out such regulations through the use of his power and duties of enforcement and inspection authorized by the Safety Appliance Acts, the Interstate Commerce Act, and the Department of Transportation Act. Regulations promulgated under this section shall be subject to the provisions of sections 4909, 4910, 4911, and 4915 of this title.

57. 39 Fed.Reg. 24579 (1974).

58. 41 Fed.Reg. 2183 (1976), 40 CFR pt. 201.

59. 40 CFR § 201.11.

60. Id. § 201.12.

61. Id. § 201.13.

62. Id. § 201.1(b).

Sec. 5.8   RAILROADS, MOTOR VEHICLES: REG.   609

transportation sources such as machine shops, foundries and forges), special purpose equipment (bolt machines, brushcutters, compactors, cranes, derricks, piledrivers and other equipment used for maintaining rights of way). Section 17(c)(1) [63] makes clear that no state or local government can adopt or enforce any standard other than an identical one on noise emissions "resulting from the operation of the same equipment or facility" covered by federal standards. Quite clearly, this bars the states from imposing stiffer standards on locomotives. But the preemptive effect of the general rail car standard is less certain because it does not identify carefully the "equipment and facility" causing the problem. EPA's opinion, which is entitled to weight,[64] is that the federal regulations preempt local regulation "of the noise from refrigerator units on refrigerator cars, auxiliary power units on locomotives, and the noise caused by the condition of track. The noise caused by retarders, however, is a separate source of noise which will not be present during compliance measurement for the rail car standard, and as such is not subject to preemption." [65] EPA properly recognizes that substantial local powers survive federal regulatory initiatives, even where insistence on local land use standards—for example, that no school may be exposed to exterior noise levels in excess of 55dB(A)—may require design modification of locomotives or rail cars.[66]

EPA reads the "best available technology" criterion as requiring two substantial modifications in the regulations as proposed originally. The first relaxes the 1980 locomotive idle standard from 67dB(A) to 70dB(A) [67] (permitting roughly a doubling of noise) on the ground that available muffler technology could not solve the problem on certain locomotive models.[68] This is a generous concession to locomotives not yet manufactured. The second modifies the requirement that the entire fleet be obliged to conform to lower noise levels four years after promulgation of the final regulation. The reason invoked is the costliness and technical difficulties of retrofitting.[69] The result is that existing locomotives are mildly controlled, and new locomotives more strictly controlled, except that new locomotives are not considered new unless they are manufactured after December 31, 1979.[70] The railroad noise emission standards contain some criteria for measurement [71] but absolutely nothing on compliance or enforcement. The

63. 42 U.S.C.A. § 4916(c)(1); § 1.13 above (citizen suits).

64. See note 55, supra.

65. 41 Fed.Reg. 2193 (1976); see id. at 2192–93 for a useful discussion of preemption; cf. Chrysler Corp. v. Tofany, 419 F.2d 499 (2d Cir. 1969).

66. See 41 Fed.Reg. 2193 (1976) (leaving open the question of whether such a regulation would be preempted).

67. 40 CFR § 201.11(b).

68. See 41 Fed.Reg. 2192 (1976).

69. Ibid.

70. 40 CFR §§ 201.11, 201.12.

71. Id. §§ 201.20–.24.

latter requirements must be imposed in a separate rulemaking by the Department of Transportation [72] although they are enforceable by EPA and citizens under the modest enforcement provisions of the Noise Control Act [73] when they take effect. This thoroughly unsatisfactory compliance arrangement at the federal level is reason enough for state and local governments to adopt identical regulations for purposes of enforcing them.

Section 18 of the Noise Control Act directs the Administrator to publish proposed noise emission regulations for motor carriers within nine months after passage of the Act and to promulgate final regulations within ninety days thereafter.[74] EPA chose to ignore these deadlines, perhaps for the reason that the provision is hobbled by the same weaknesses that afflict the statutory basis for railroad noise emission standards (the most serious being that the Secretary of Transportation must promulgate regulations to insure compliance).[75] Regulations under section 18 are supposed to be "in addition to" [76] any regulations proposed under section 6, but section 6 has turned out to be the principal source of authority invoked.

EPA proposed in 1974 [77] and adopted in 1976 [78] noise emission standards for medium and heavy trucks (weighing in excess of 10,000 pounds). Every new vehicle manufactured for distribution in commerce must conform to noise emission standards and meet certain other requirements (such as labeling and compliance with verification procedures).[79] Measured at fifty feet from the vehicle, the standards and effective dates are: 83dB(A) effective January 1, 1978, 80dB(A) effective January 1, 1982. These standards are less stringent than those prescribed in California,[80] and EPA candidly asserts that its technology based requirements "are not sufficiently protective of public health and welfare." [81] The agency promises a further reduction in prescribed noise levels to take effect in 1985.[82]

In content, EPA's truck noise standards are not dissimilar to its air compressor standards [83] and conform to well established patterns of regulation. There are general provisions on inspection and moni-

---

72. Note 56, supra; see EPA Opinion of the General Counsel, EPA Enforcement Responsibilities, in 1 EPA Collection of Legal Opinions 253, 255 (1974) (pointing out that the Interstate Commerce Act and the Department of Transportation Act do not provide penalties for violation of noise emission standards).

73. 42 U.S.C.A. §§ 4909, 4910, 4911, 4915.

74. Id. § 4917(a)(1), (2).

75. Id. § 4917(b).

76. Id. § 4917(a)(1).

77. 39 Fed.Reg. 38338 (1974).

78. 41 Fed.Reg. 15537 (1976), 40 CFR pt. 205.

79. 40 CFR § 205.55–1.

80. See note 31, supra.

81. 41 Fed.Reg. 15538 (1976).

82. Ibid.

83. See § 5.4 above.

Sec. 5.9 NATIONAL ENVIRONMENTAL POLICY ACT

toring,[84] exemptions[85] and maintenance of records.[86] Testing procedures are prescribed in some detail,[87] as is a production verification procedure by the manufacturer[88] and enforcement auditing by EPA.[89] Compliance is sought to be assured by a prohibition on distribution of nonconforming vehicles[90] and, to a lesser extent, requirements on warranties,[91] anti-tampering,[92] maintenance instructions[93] and recall.[94] These regulations undoubtedly will influence the content of later federal initiatives on motorcycles, snowmobiles and buses, and must eventually be reconciled with state action under preemption principles.

§ 5.9 Transportation Sources: National Environmental Policy Act

In the few short years since passage of the National Environmental Policy Act (NEPA), activities at many of the major airports in the country have been challenged in lawsuits raising NEPA claims (which are usually joined with claims under the Airport and Airway Development Act). NEPA of course deals with all types of governmental actions and all kinds of environmental hurts.[1] But where the action is a major expansion of airport operations (the typical fact situation), the principal consequence is likely to be greatly increased noise exposures. The NEPA airport cases where noise is a dominant issue are discussed here separately. The highway cases where noise is usually but one among many factors are not singled out for extensive treatment.

Although the Federal Aviation Administration, like most other federal agencies, was slow to recognize that its grant construction program routinely would require the preparation of impact statements,[2] the airport cases conform to the general understanding that the impact statement requirements are triggered by a wide range of activities with potential environmental effects.[3] One early NEPA case (which is quite clearly wrong) held that the introduction of noisier stretch jets (Boeing 737's) into Washington, D. C.'s National Airport was not a "major federal action" for NEPA purposes.[4] In

---

84. 40 CFR § 205.4.

85. Id. § 205.5–.5–7.

86. Id. § 205.53.

87. Id. §§ 205.54–.54–1.

88. Id. §§ 205.55–.55–12.

89. Id. §§ 205.56–.57–9.

90. Id. § 205.57–9; see § 205.55–10.

91. 40 CFR § 205.58–1. Compare § 3.15 above.

92. 40 CFR § 205.58–2.

93. Id. § 205.58–3.

94. Id. § 205.59.

1. Ch. 7 below.

2. See Turner, An Evaluation of FAA's Compliance with the National Environmental Policy Act of 1969 (unpublished paper prepared for a course in environmental law, Georgetown U.Law Center, Fall 1974).

3. § 7.6 below.

4. Virginians for Dulles v. Volpe, 344 F.Supp. 573, 2 ELR 20360 (E.D.Va. 1972), rev'd —— F.2d ——, 6 ELR

the intervening years, however, NEPA or its state equivalents [5] have been applied routinely to runway extensions,[6] construction of a new control tower,[7] land acquisitions,[8] pavement rehabilitation, apron expansion, lighting improvements,[9] and so on,[10] even where a purpose and expected consequence of the airport project is an overall reduction in noise exposure.[11] One useful rule of thumb for determining the necessity for preparing an impact statement is whether "some residential areas might suffer from significant noise exposure" as a result of the project proposed and undertaken.[12]

An issue unique in certain respects to the airport cases is to determine when a project becomes sufficiently "federal" to trigger the impact statement requirements.[13] A First Circuit decision,[14] later distinguished by the same court,[15] refused to enjoin construction activities by a nonfederal applicant for aid under AADA on the ground that FAA approval of an airport layout plan without a firm commitment to fund did not trigger the impact statement requirements. This has been read flatly by one district court to mean that there is no "federal" action for NEPA purposes under AADA until the execution of a grant agreement assuring assistance to local authorities carrying out the construction.[16] Another district court has held a project to be "federalized" earlier in time upon the FAA's receipt of the applicant's request for federal money.[17] The lesson is that an action be-

20581 (4th Cir. 1976). See also Petterson v. Froehlke, 354 F.Supp. 45, 2 ELR 20747 (D.C.Or.1972) (refusing to apply NEPA to airport expansion project initiated before passage of the Act).

5. § 7.11 below.

6. Secretary of Environmental Affairs v. Massachusetts Port Authority, —— Mass. ——, 323 N.E.2d 329, 5 ELR 20200 (1975).

7. Friends of the Earth, Inc. v. Coleman, 518 F.2d 323, 5 ELR 20428 (9th Cir. 1975).

8. Sierra Club v. Los Angeles, 3 ELR 20340 (Cal.Super.Ct.L.A.County 1972).

9. Citizens Airport Comm. v. Brinegar, 5 ELR 20385 (N.D.N.Y.1975).

10. E. g., Illinois ex rel. Scott v. Butterfield, 396 F.Supp. 632, 5 ELR 20587 (N.D.Ill.1975) (upholding NEPA claims against both FAA and CAB for undertaking various actions increasing the capacity of O'Hare International Airport to accommodate additional aircraft); Nader v. Butterfield, 373 F.Supp. 1175, 4 ELR 20431 (D.C.D.C.1974) (requiring preparation of EIS to accompany installation of x-ray search devices at airport terminals).

11. Life of the Land v. Brinegar, 485 F.2d 460, 3 ELR 20811 (9th Cir. 1973), cert. denied 416 U.S. 961 (1974).

12. Secretary of Environmental Affairs v. Massachusetts Port Authority, —— Mass. ——, ——, 323 N.E.2d 329, 344, 5 ELR 20200, 20203 (1975).

13. § 7.7 below.

14. Boston v. Volpe, 464 F.2d 254, 2 ELR 20501 (1st Cir. 1972).

15. Silva v. Romney, 473 F.2d 287, 290 n. 5, 3 ELR 20082, 20083 n. 5 (1st Cir. 1973).

16. Boston v. Brinegar, 6 ERC 1961 (D.C.Mass.1974), dismissed as moot 512 F.2d 319, 5 ELR 20241 (1st Cir. 1975).

17. Citizens Airport Comm. v. Brinegar, 5 ELR 20385 (N.D.Ill.1975).

comes federal under the grant provisions of the Airport and Airway Development Act somewhere along a spectrum beginning with the inspiration to seek federal assistance and extending to the filing of a letter of intent by the applicant, tentative approvals by the FAA, and actual consummation of the grant agreement. It goes without saying that the timing question should be answered by reference to NEPA policies, which argue for early application, not dry formalities.[18]

Because major airport expansions are unlikely to proceed without the injection of federal monies at some point, the question of whether injunctions can issue against locally funded aspects of a partly federally funded project is likely to recur. The Ninth Circuit [19] recently has approved the First Circuit's decision in *City of Boston* by refusing to stop work on locally funded improvements (a terminal and parking garage) that were part of a development program at the San Francisco International Airport that admittedly would aggravate noise exposures. The court strains for a rationale (finding a "substantial functional complementarity" falling short of "functional interdependence" between the locally and federally funded projects [20]) but rests ultimately on the discretionary ground that the federal tail should not wag the local dog by reading NEPA as authorizing injunctions against a wide range of airport improvement projects with a low level of federal financial support (less than 10 percent overall).[21]

Another central issue under NEPA of special pertinence in the airport development cases is the question of who prepares the environmental impact statement.[22] The FAA is inclined to delegate substantial statement preparation responsibilities to the local sponsor of the project, the airport operator.[23] Airport managers, in turn, usually lack staff capabilities for scrutinizing the environmental effects of their actions; they hire outside consultants to do the job. There is thus often a double delegation (from FAA to airport operator to private consultant) that strains the statutory requirement that the statement be prepared by the responsible federal official. Although airport cases have sustained these delegations subject only to assurances that FAA officials "participated" in the EIS preparation,[24] the practice may be legally vulnerable, particularly if the statement is written by a firm with a financial interest in the success of the project.[25]

18. § 7.7 below.

19. Friends of the Earth, Inc. v. Coleman, 518 F.2d 323, 328, 5 ELR 20428, 20429 (9th Cir. 1975), citing Friends of the Earth, Inc. v. Coleman, 513 F.2d 295, 5 ELR 20259 (9th Cir. 1975).

20. 518 F.2d at 329, 5 ELR at 20429-30.

21. See § 7.10 below.

22. § 7.8 below.

23. See Turner, supra note 2.

24. Life of the Land v. Brinegar, 485 F.2d 460, 3 ELR 20811 (9th Cir. 1973), cert. denied 416 U.S. 961 (1974).

25. § 7.8 below; cf. Bayside Timber Co. v. Board of Supervisors, 20 Cal. App.3d 1, 97 Cal.Rptr. 431 (1971) (invalidating delegation of rulemaking powers regarding protection of forest lands to private timber industry).

The general procedural [26] lessons of NEPA were applied rigorously in a recent action to halt, principally on grounds of increased noise exposure, a third parallel runway at Detroit's Metropolitan Wayne County Airport.[27] In enjoining further federal participation in planning, funding or construction of the runway pending compliance with NEPA, the court made clear that the EIS was deficient in several respects: it omitted figures as to actual airport traffic operations and FAA sponsored forecasts; included unexplained inconsistencies in the fleet mix used to predict cost saving; embraced undefined terms and unsupported conclusions. The two methodologies in the EIS used to predict the noise impact of the proposed runway (neither one of them the NEF contours)[28] were inadequate by arbitrarily selecting 85dB(A) as a threshold of unacceptability, by failing to disclose projected noise exposures above 85dB(A), and especially by failing to explain the significance of the numbers recorded:

> A more basic defect is the total lack of information as to what the CNR contours mean in terms of an acceptable human environment. The nontechnical reader should be advised of existing governmental standards, such as the site exposure guidelines of H.U.D., so that an informed analysis would be possible. As presented in the EIS, the CNR contours are meaningless numbers to the nonscientist with no guidelines to analyze the data presented in terms of acceptability for a human environment.[29]

The Airport and Airway Development Act includes provisions that are clearly substantive, going beyond the familiar procedural protection of NEPA. Section 16(c)(3) suggests mildly that "no airport development project may be approved by the Secretary unless he is satisfied that fair consideration has been given to the interest of communities in or near which the project may be located." [30] This probably means only that the Secretary must study the impact and consider it.[31] Section 16(c)(4) goes considerably further by establishing a "national policy" that airport development projects authorized by the Act "shall provide for the protection and enhancement of the natural resources and the quality of the environment of the Nation." In carrying out this policy, the Secretary of Transportation is obliged to consult other agencies with regard to effects and can authorize no project found to have adverse effects unless he renders "a finding, in writing, following a full and complete review, which shall be a matter of public record, that no feasible and prudent alternative exists and that all possible steps have been taken to minimize such

---

26. §§ 7.3, 7.4 below.

27. Romulus v. Wayne, 392 F.Supp. 578, 5 ELR 20302 (E.D.Mich.1975).

28. See § 5.7 above.

29. 392 F.Supp. at 594, 5 ELR at 20307 (footnote omitted).

30. 49 U.S.C.A. § 1716(c)(3).

31. See Citizens Airport Comm. v. Volpe, 351 F.Supp. 52, 3 ELR 20021 (E.D.Va.1972).

adverse effect." [32] This normally requires an examination of all alternatives, the selection of one that is least harmful to the affected community,[33] and the exhaustion of all means for minimizing noise effects. The importance of the substantive lever undoubtedly will be demonstrated in future legal struggles over the location and expansion of airports.

Increased noise exposure is a common component of NEPA highway cases.[34] The impact statement vehicle may be useful in forcing agencies to come to grips with highway design noise standards.[35] In one case,[36] resolved by consent, a state turnpike authority agreed to develop noise standards and implementation plans, in consultation with plaintiffs' consultants, and to implement those standards within six months of completion of a highway widening project. NEPA promises to elevate consideration of noise effects beyond the traditional treatment by afterthought or total neglect.

§ 5.10 Occupational Noise Exposure

Noise in the workplace is an environmental hazard of the highest order. One estimate is that the number of workers in the country experiencing noise conditions potentially dangerous to hearing is in excess of 6 million and possibly may be as high as 16 million.[1] Another is that approximately fifty percent of the machinery used in heavy industry produces noise levels high enough to cause hearing losses to exposed workers.[2] Simply put, the hazard adversely affects millions of people and will cost billions of dollars to alleviate.[3]

For a number of years, several federal agencies (including the Air Force, the Departments of the Army and Navy, and the Atomic Ener-

---

32. 49 U.S.C.A. § 1716(c)(4); see § 7.-12 below.

33. Citizens Airport Comm. v. Volpe, 351 F.Supp. 52, 3 ELR 20021 (E.D.Va. 1972).

34. E. g., I–291 Why? Ass'n v. Burns, 372 F.Supp. 223, 253–60, 4 ELR 20230, 20242–46 (D.C.Conn.1974); Civic Improvement Comm. v. Volpe, — F. Supp. —, 6 ELR 20797 (W.D.N.C. 1976); see § 7.12 n. 83 below (citing federal highway NEPA cases).

35. § 5.8 above.

36. See Concerned Citizens of East Brunswick, Inc. v. New Jersey Turnpike Authority, 2 ELR 20109 (N.J.Super.1972) (jurisdictional basis for action not disclosed; apparently not based on NEPA).

1. Occupational Safety and Health Administration, Draft Environmental Impact Statement on Proposed Noise Regulation 2 (1975) (citing authority) [hereinafter cited as OSHA Draft EIS].

2. See ibid (citing authority).

3. See id. at 50 (reporting estimates that the capital costs of attaining an average exposure level of 90dB(A) would be 13 billion dollars; the additional cost of attaining an 85dB(A) level would be about 18 billion dollars). The estimates are based upon a report by Bolt, Beranek & Newman, Inc., Impact of Noise Control at the Workplace, undated (submitted to the U. S. Department of Labor). Occupational noise injuries occasionally are resolved in court. See Sampson v. Schultz, 242 So.2d 363 (La.App. 1970) (allowing recovery).

gy Commission, now the Nuclear Regulatory Commission) have pursued regulatory programs designed to protect employees from excessive noise exposures.[4] Historically, far and away the most important provision is the Walsh-Healey Public Contracts Act of 1936 which states that federal contracts shall not be performed in surroundings or under working conditions "which are unsanitary or hazardous or dangerous to the health or safety of employees" engaged in the performance of the contract.[5] For several decades, this statute was implemented by vague regulations proscribing "excessive noise,"[6] comparable to state and local prohibitions against various noise nuisances.[7] In 1969, however, the Department of Labor promulgated a regulation establishing 90dB(A) as a maximum average exposure over an 8 hour day.[8] These regulations which are still in effect (as of July 1976) permit higher exposures for shorter time periods (100dB(A) over 2 hours, 110dB(A) over one half hour and so on) and impose a ceiling on impulsive or impact noise of 140dB(A).[9] Employers are required to use "feasible administrative or engineering controls" to keep sound levels below permissible levels.[10] If these controls do not suffice, employers must provide and require use of personal protective equipment for employees and administer a program of hearing conservation.[11] The debate over controls at the source and immunizing the receptor of course is a longstanding one in environmental law.

Despite exclusions, the Walsh-Healey noise rules are said to reach some 27 million workers in 70,000 plants.[12] These limitations applying to workers on federal supply contracts, moreover, were extended in 1971 to workers on federal construction contracts by action of the Secretary of Labor[13] under provisions of the Construction Safety Act.[14] Also in 1971, the Secretary of Interior, acting under the Coal Mine Health and Safety Act of 1969, extended the Walsh-Healey Act noise regulations to underground and surface coal mine operations.[15]

4. For a summary, see Environmental Protection Agency, Laws and Regulatory Schemes for Noise Abatement 1–28 to –39 (1971).

5. 49 Stat. 2036, 41 U.S.C.A. § 35(e).

6. See National Institute for Occupational Safety and Health, Criteria for a Recommended Standard: Occupational Exposure to Noise II–1 (1972) [hereinafter cited as NIOSH Noise Study].

7. See § 5.4 above.

8. 34 Fed.Reg. 7946 (1969), as amended, 35 Fed.Reg. 1015 (1970), 41 CFR § 50–204.10.

9. 41 CFR § 50–204.10(d).

10. Id. § 50–204.10(b).

11. Ibid.

12. D. Lipscomb, Noise: The Unwanted Sounds 249 (1974).

13. 36 Fed.Reg. 7340 (1971).

14. 40 U.S.C.A. §§ 327 et seq. Section 333(a) makes it a condition of each contract that no contractor require any laborer "to work in surroundings or under working conditions which are unsanitary, hazardous, or dangerous to his health or safety . . . ."

15. 36 Fed.Reg. 12739 (1971).

Sec. 5.10 OCCUPATIONAL NOISE EXPOSURE

Despite these good intentions, however, a 1972 study concluded that approximately 14 percent of all workers in manufacturing are exposed to noise levels above the 90dB(A) standard.[16]

Enactment of the Occupational Safety and Health Act in 1970 (OSHA)[17] led eventually to a major reconsideration of the federal occupational noise exposure standards which five years later had not come close to running its course. The Walsh-Healey Act standards immediately became applicable to all covered employees when the OSHA took effect in 1970.[18] This is not an insignificant event since the range of remedies applicable to OSHA violations (civil and criminal penalties, among others) go far beyond mere removal of a contractor from a bidder's list.[19] Presently under way is a major rulemaking that could lead to widespread changes in occupational noise standards. Following procedures prescribed by the Act,[20] the National Institute for Occupational Safety and Health (NIOSH) in the Department of Health, Education, and Welfare developed a criteria document for noise which in August of 1972 was submitted to the Occupational Safety and Health Administration in the Department of Labor. The NIOSH Noise Study[21] recommended that noise exposure in the workplace not be allowed to exceed a 90dB(A) average, 85dB(A) for new installations; that a ceiling on exposure be set at 115dB(A); that medical surveillance be undertaken on employees subject to high noise levels and those whose occupational exposure is controlled by personal protective equipment, and that administrative or engineering controls be utilized to achieve desired limits, permitting the use of personal protective equipment (i. e., ear protectors) "only until" engineering and administrative controls can be implemented.[22] After the NIOSH submission the Secretary of Labor appointed a Standards Advisory Committee on Noise pursuant to Section 7(b) of the Act.[23] The committee considered a number of issues relating to the NIOSH report and transmitted recommendations for a revised standard to the Occupational Safety and Health Administration in December of 1973.

In 1974, OSHA proposed a new noise rule reflecting the recommendations of both NIOSH and the noise advisory committee.[24] OSHA proposes to retain the 90dB(A) eight hour average sound level, es-

---

16. NIOSH Noise Study, supra note 6, preface.

17. Pub.L. No. 91–596, 84 Stat. 1590, 29 U.S.C.A. §§ 651–78, as amended.

18. 29 U.S.C.A. § 653(b)(2); see 36 Fed.Reg. 10518 (1971), 41 CFR § 50–204.10; 37 Fed.Reg. 20501 (1972).

19. See Laws and Regulatory Schemes for Noise Abatement, supra note 4, at 1–31.

20. 29 U.S.C.A. §§ 669(a), 671.

21. Supra note 6, at I–1 to –19.

22. Id. at I–9.

23. 29 U.S.C.A. § 656(b).

24. 39 Fed.Reg. 27773 (1974), proposing 29 CFR § 1910.95.

tablish a maximum sound level of 115dB(A) (with a limited number of 140dB impulses), require monitoring of and a conservation program for employees subject to high noise levels, and allow personal protective equipment only as a least favored alternative to engineering and administrative controls. That technological controls be exhausted before the earmuffs are handed out is a course preferred not only at common law [25] but also by the Occupational Safety and Health Act.[26] Any final regulation on the subject must be set at a level "which most adequately assures, to the extent feasible, on the basis of the best available evidence, that no employee will suffer material impairment of health or functional capacity." [27] The OSHA noise rulemaking has undergone extensive hearings. Perhaps the most crucial issue, which must be addressed in the final regulations, is the recommendation of EPA (made pursuant to Section 4(c)(2) of the Noise Control Act [28]) that an eight hour 85dB(A) standard will better protect against hearing impairment risk. The final regulations must represent a classic balancing of actual and presumed effects, economic costs and technological feasibility, and ultimately will be subjected to closely reasoned review in the courts under standards now familiar in modern technological conflicts.[29]

25. § 2.6 above.

26. 29 U.S.C.A. § 654(a)(1); see American Smelting & Ref. Co. v. Occupational Safety & Health Review Comm'n, 501 F.2d 504 (8th Cir. 1974).

27. 29 U.S.C.A. § 655(b)(5).

28. 42 U.S.C.A. § 4903(c)(2).

29. § 1.5 above.

Chapter VI

SOLID WASTE/RESOURCE RECOVERY

§ 6.1 Background

Solid waste can be defined as useless, unwanted or discarded material with insufficient liquid content to be free flowing.[1] Solid waste management means a systematic "control of the generation, storage, collection, transport, separation, processing, recovery and disposal of solid waste."[2] Traditionally, solid waste management has meant no more than seeing to it that the garbage gets picked up and taken to the dump. Resource recovery is the process of obtaining energy or material resources from solid waste. The energy values of solid waste make it a promising fuel of the future.[3] Recovery of materials is called salvage or reclamation.[4] Recovered materials are either reused (reintroduced into the economic stream without substantial change) (i. e., soft drink bottles) or recycled (transformed into new products so that the original products lose their identity) (i. e., aluminum soft drink cans).[5] Generally, resource recovery is a good thing for the environment because available evidence indicates that "compared with virgin material extraction and processing, [it] results in less atmospheric emissions, [waterborne] wastes, mining and solid wastes, and energy consumption."[6]

---

1. National Ass'n of Counties, Basic Issues on Solid Waste Management Affecting County Government, May 1973, app. E, at 40 (definition of terms) (published under auspices of U. S. Environmental Protection Agency) [hereinafter cited as Basic Issues on Solid Waste Management]; State Solid Waste Management and Resource Recovery Incentives Act § 3 (33), in 32 Council of State Governments, Suggested State Legislation 63 (1972) [hereinafter cited as Model State Act].

2. Basic Issues on Solid Waste Management, supra note 1, app. E, at 40; see 42 U.S.C.A. § 6903(28).

3. Environmental Protection Agency, Energy Conservation Through Improved Solid Waste Management 11–13 (1974).

4. Basic Issues on Solid Waste Management, supra note 1, app. E, at 40.

5. Ibid; see Model State Act § 3(20).

6. Environmental Protection Agency, First Report to Congress on Resource Recovery and Source Reduction, at ix (3d ed. 1974); see Midwest Research Institute, Resource Recovery: The State of Technology (1973) (prepared for the Council on Environmental Quality) [hereinafter cited as Resource Recovery Technology Study]; Council on Environmental Quality, Fourth Ann.Rep. 204 (1973) ("making 1000 tons of steel reinforcing bars from scrap instead of from virgin ore takes 74 percent less energy and 51 percent less water, creates 86 percent less air pollution emissions, and generates 97 percent less mining wastes") (citing authority.)

The dimensions of the solid waste problem are vaguely familiar:[7] of the 4.3 billion tons of solid wastes generated in the United States in 1969, most of it originated from agricultural activities. The more than two billion tons of agricultural wastes produced each year include "animal and slaughterhouse wastes, useless residues from crop harvesting, vineyard and orchard prunings, and greenhouse wastes."[8] Cattle and other animals on concentrated feedlots generate enormous quantities of manure "that cannot readily and safely be assimilated by the soil."[9] A second major category is mineral solid wastes which are produced in vast quantities (1700 million tons) by mining, milling and processing industries. These include "slag heaps, culm piles, and mill tailings [which] accumulate near extraction or processing operations."[10] Eight major industries are responsible for 80 percent of the total—copper, "followed by iron and steel, bituminous coal, phosphate rock, lead, zinc, alumina and anthracite."[11] More than 100 million tons of other industrial solid wastes are generated each year, with the quantities rapidly increasing:[12] fly ash from coal burning electrical utilities, various sludges and slags,[13] scrap metal, paper, plastics, bales of rags and drums of other refuse.

The most familiar category of solid wastes, representing perhaps 6 percent of the total or 250 million tons per year, can be classified as residential, commercial or institutional wastes.[14] The constituents are familiar and include "30 million tons of paper and paper products; 4 million tons of plastics; 100 million tires; 30 billion bottles; 60 billion cans; millions of tons of demolition debris, grass and tree trimmings, food wastes, and sewage sludge; and millions of discarded automobiles and major appliances."[15] To manage this waste, we spend some $6 billion annually, most of it for collecting the waste and transporting it somewhere else to be dumped or burned.[16] The "final disposal point" for an estimated 90 percent of all collected solid wastes in the country is 1400 open dumps or landfills; the remaining 10 percent is disposed of by incineration.[17] In 1970, as many as 90 percent of the dumps and 75 percent of the municipal incinerators were said to be "inadequate", and major water, air and land polluters.[18]

7. See Council on Environmental Quality, First Ann.Rep. 107 (1970).

8. Ibid.

9. Id. at 107–08.

10. Id. at 108.

11. Ibid.

12. Ibid.

13. See § 6.7 below.

14. CEQ, First Ann.Rep. 107 (1970).

15. Id. at 108.

16. Compare Comm. on Interstate and Foreign Commerce, Resource Recovery Act of 1970, H.R.Rep. No. 1155, 91st Cong., 2d Sess. 2 (1970) ($4.5 billion cost estimate) [hereinafter cited at House Report] with § 6.8 n. 2 below (estimating annual collection and disposal costs to be $6 billion).

17. CEQ, First Ann.Rep. 110 (1970).

18. House Report, supra note 16, at 2.

Pollution sources commonly associated with solid waste disposal are reflected faithfully in the case law and legislation. Two of the better known air [19] and water [20] pollution conflicts involve, respectively, agricultural (feedlot) and mineral (tailings) solid wastes. Disposal sites pollute in several ways. First, the town dump may be an aesthetic nuisance, a visual pollutant. That was the premise of the federal Highway Beautification Act of 1965,[21] which included as a major aim the screening of junkyards. A second problem not so easily covered up is the transmission of disease agents from the site principally by vectors (transporting agents such as insects, humans, birds, household pets and, of course, rats). Wind and water also may carry disease from a site. Leachate is the name given to the water moving from a disposal site with impurities picked up either in solution or suspension.[22] Until very recently, solid waste managers gave "primary emphasis" to these biological pollution problems, stressing disease agents carried by vectors and giving vector control a high priority.[23] There is now a "greater emphasis upon the dangers of natural elements and man-made compounds transported from a site by natural carriers." [24] Leachate emanating from a site may contain not only biological pathogens but "more subtle factors resulting in groundwater supply degradation such as elements of trace metals, persistent pesticides, and other organic compounds." [25] Recent concern with the disposal of toxic wastes [26] reflects the maturation of solid waste management and the expansion of its horizons from ugliness and litter to rats and flies to the complex chemical constituents of modern life.

The technology and economics of resource recovery resist generality and often turn upon the particular constituency of the solid waste stream under consideration (that is, scrap metal, beverage containers, paper, plastics). A leading study [27] points out that two methods for recovering resources from mixed municipal wastes are fully developed and occasionally practiced—composting and energy recovery. Composting plants produce a humus material from the organic portion of mixed wastes. Success in the United States has been limit-

---

19. Spur Indus., Inc. v. Del E. Webb Dev. Co., 108 Ariz. 178, 494 P.2d 700, 2 ELR 20390 (1972) (en banc).

20. United States v. Reserve Mining Co., 514 F.2d 492, 5 ELR 20596 (8th Cir. 1975).

21. Pub.L. No. 89–285, 79 Stat. 1030, 23 U.S.C.A. § 136.

22. See Council of State Governments, The State's Role in Solid Waste Management: A Task Force Report 51 (1973) (reprinted by the Environmental Protection Agency).

23. Ibid.

24. Ibid.

25. Id. at 6; see § 4.3 above (ground water).

26. Environmental Protection Agency, Report to Congress on the Disposal of Hazardous Wastes (1974); § 6.10 below.

27. See Resource Recovery Technology Study, supra note 6. The definitions of the five resource recovery processes discussed in text are drawn from id. at 6.

ed not by the capabilities of technology but by a lack of markets for the compost.[28] Energy recovery processes capture the energy content of mixed municipal wastes, in the form either of steam, electricity or fuel. Well known is the joint effort of the City of St. Louis and the Union Electric Company to use refuse as a supplemental fuel for electrical power generation.[29] Some heat recovery systems are fully operational in the United States—for example, the City of Ansonia, Connecticut, uses heat recovered from incineration to dry sludge from the city's water pollution control plant.[30] Three other resource recovery processes are at various stages of development, some quite advanced—materials recovery, pyrolysis and chemical conversion. Materials recovery, as the name suggests, involves extraction of the basic materials, such as paper, metals and glass, from mixed municipal wastes. Well advertised processes in this category include the Black Clawson system in Franklin, Ohio, which has proven capable of recovering paper pulp and magnetic metals from municipal refuse, and the Bureau of Mines process at College Park, Maryland, which reclaims metals from incinerator residues on a continuous basis.[31] Pyrolysis processes rely on thermal decomposition of mixed municipal wastes in controlled amounts of oxygen, producing byproducts such as oil, gas, tar and acetone.[32] Chemical conversion processes function by converting the wastes chemically into protein and other organic products.

The "most obvious" finding of a leading economic study "is that resource recovery systems are not self-sustaining economic operations" under the conditions posited.[33] There is an important proviso, however: "where incineration, remote landfill, or other high-cost waste disposal is necessary, resource recovery offers an economically viable alternative. Most resource recovery systems show lower costs than conventional incineration (without resource recovery); several have net costs (for large capacity plants) low enough to compete with landfill, if the recovered products can be sold at or above the assumed prices."[34] According to this study, the process ranking by lowest net cost is fuel recovery, followed by materials recovery, pyrolysis, composting, steam generation with incinerator residue recovery, steam recovery, incinerator residue recovery and electrical energy generation. Needless to say, the low cost aspects of land disposal of solid waste have been overstated traditionally by external environmental costs which only now are being corrected.

28. Environmental Protection Agency, Composting of Municipal Solid Wastes in the United States (1971).

29. Environmental Protection Agency, St. Louis/Union Electric Refuse Firing Demonstration Air Pollution Test Report, Aug. 1974.

30. Resource Recovery Technology Study, supra note 6, at 7.

31. Id. at 10–11.

32. Id. at 6, 11–15.

33. Id. at 3.

34. Ibid.

§ 6.2 Common Law

The town dump was and is the epitome of a public nuisance. With federal and even state statutory law today intruding only modestly upon the domain of solid waste, nuisance law retains a strong influence. The general principles [1] are prominently at work: courts, in the balancing process, will be sensitive to the degree of injury caused, inclined to overlook mere aesthetic objections [2] or minor intrusions such as occasional smoke or sparks or trash blowing onto plaintiff's land,[3] but determined to correct severe problems such as the causing of plaintiff's property to become "uninhabitable" because of foul stenches and odors, frequent fires, infestation by insects and rodents, inundation by flooding, constant invasion by trash.[4] Relief is likely to be forthcoming if the wastes are especially toxic [5] or if intervention by public health authorities lends credibility to health hazard claims.[6] Attempts to gain anticipatory relief against a planned dump, on the other hand, are usually [7] but not always [8] unsuccessful because of the perpetual problem of estimating damage before the fact. The value of defendant's enterprise typically is weighed against plaintiff's injuries, with injunctions unlikely where defendant performs an im-

---

1. §§ 2.1-.12 above.

2. Mahlstadt v. Indianola, 251 Iowa 222, 100 N.W.2d 189 (1959); Bohley v. Crofoot, 7 Ohio L.A. 667 (1929) (dictum); cf. State v. Brown, 250 N.C. 54, 108 S.E.2d 74 (1959) (overturning convictions for violating a statute requiring the screening of junkyards as beyond the police power of the state).

3. Jezowski v. Reno, 71 Nev. 233, 286 P.2d 257 (1955).

4. Steifer v. Kansas City, 175 Kan. 794, 267 P.2d 474 (1954); Davis v. Kansas City, 204 Kan. 524, 464 P.2d 154 (1970) (dump was source of smoke, fumes, wild dogs and rats); Lenari v. Kingston, 342 Mass. 705, 175 N.E.2d 384 (1961) (indicating that smoke, odors, flies and rodents from dump coming onto plaintiff's property may be a nuisance but reversing for findings on whether offensive conditions continued to exist and whether reasonable means to abate them had been exhausted); Reno v. Fields, 69 Nev. 300, 250 P.2d 140 (1952) (loose material blown onto plaintiffs' property); Bloss v. Canastota, 35 Misc.2d 829, 232 N.Y.S.2d 166 (1962) (massive rat infestation of plaintiffs' farm causing disease in dairy herd, a high bacteria count in milk produced, damage to buildings and crops).

5. Curry Coal Co. v. M. C. Arnoni Co., 439 Pa. 144, 266 A.2d 678 (1970) (noxious industrial sludge) (trespass theory) (dicta); cf. In re Kurtz, 68 Cal. 412, 9 P. 449 (1886) (large quantities of offensive solid and liquid filth allowed to accumulate in a flume ditch) (conviction for maintaining a public nuisance); Bloss v. Canastota, 35 Misc.2d 829, 232 N.Y.S.2d 166 (1962).

6. Bd. of Commissioners v. Dep't of Pub. Health, 229 Ga. 173, 190 S.E.2d 39 (1972); Commissioner of Pub. Health v. Bd. of Health, 350 Mass. 507, 215 N.E.2d 745 (1966); Clayton v. Mayfield, 82 N.M. 596, 485 P.2d 352, 1 ELR 20491 (1971).

7. Myers v. Hagertown, 214 Md. 312, 135 A.2d 147 (1957); O'Brien v. Greenburgh, 239 App.Div. 555, 268 N.Y.S. 173 (1933).

8. Brainard v. West Hartford, 140 Conn. 631, 103 A.2d 135 (1954); Harris v. Skirving, 41 Wash.2d 200, 248 P.2d 408 (1952).

portant recycling service [9] or where regional waste disposal is dependent upon maintenance of the facility,[10] and more likely where the community suffers no substantial loss and the defendant can use his property productively for something else.[11]

Land use values inherent in nuisance law operate to bar dumps from residential neighborhoods,[12] particularly if plaintiffs were there first,[13] and allow them in rural areas.[14] The state of the art is an important factor also, with the courts usually insisting that the best technology [15] and procedures [16] be followed and rejecting slipshod or half-hearted measures to control adverse environmental effects.[17] When available control measures are exhausted, the court must still face the question of whether to order a shutdown of operations [18] or allow them to continue upon payment of damages or upon the understanding that defendant's obligations have been fully met.[19]

Decrees issued in the waste disposal nuisance cases have been sensitive to the technological and operational alternatives to a shut-

9. Harrison v. Indiana Auto Shredders Co., 528 F.2d 1107, 6 ELR 20179 (7th Cir. 1975).

10. See Smith v. Ann Arbor, 303 Mich. 476, 6 N.W.2d 752 (1942) (dissolves absolute injunction in favor of a limitation on operations because city had no other place to dispose of solid waste).

11. Cf. Mile Road Corp. v. Boston, 345 Mass. 379, 187 N.E.2d 826 (1963) (statute prohibiting dump in certain areas not an unconstitutional taking as applied to plaintiff because there is no showing that land cannot be filled and put to other use).

12. See Bresett v. Ogdensburg, 14 Misc.2d 912, 180 N.Y.S.2d 908 (1958) (granting temporary injunction).

13. Dale v. Bryant, 75 Ohio L.Abs. 401, 141 N.E.2d 504 (1957) (enjoining operation of a new automobile salvage business in an established residential neighborhood); cf. Northwest Home Owners Ass'n v. Detroit, 298 Mich. 622, 299 N.W. 740 (1941) (incinerator in residential neighborhood). Contra, O'Brien v. Greenburgh, 239 App.Div. 555, 268 N.Y.S. 173 (1933) (denying anticipatory relief).

14. Cf. Zengerle v. Bd. of County Commissioners, 262 Md. 1, 276 A.2d 646 (1971) (upholding conditional use permit and variance to use land zoned for agricultural purposes as a sanitary landfill).

15. McDonald v. City of New York, 36 F.2d 714, 716 (2d Cir. 1929) ("The interest of shipping to be free from dust and cinders is not in our judgment so important as to deny the city power to dispose of its rubbish by water, provided it was the best means available to reduce the annoyance") (L. Hand, J.).

16. Storm v. City of New York, 135 Misc. 622, 625, 238 N.Y.S. 143, 146 (1917) ("The general health and comfort of the inhabitants of the city require the operation of dumps, and if the manner and method adopted in the conduct of such operations are in keeping with the best known methods, . . . the right to do so must be supported"); Davis v. Kansas City, 204 Kan. 524, 464 P.2d 154 (1970).

17. See Wilson v. Portland, 153 Or. 679, 58 P.2d 257 (1936).

18. Mitchell v. Hines, 305 Mich. 296, 9 N.W.2d 547 (1943) (injunction affirmed where proof failed to reveal any method of feeding garbage to pigs on a commercial scale that would not constitute a nuisance).

19. McDonald v. City of New York, 36 F.2d 714 (2d Cir. 1929); cf. Crandall v. Biergans, 2 ELR 20238 (Mich.Cir. Ct. Clinton Co. 1972).

down. Thus, defendants have been directed to operate a dump in accordance with the sanitary landfill method [20] (where waste is spread in thin layers, compacted to the smallest practical volume, and covered with soil at the end of each working day),[21] to maintain certain slope grades, to revegetate final slopes, to undertake a vector control program,[22] to burn rubbish only in quantities and at times when it is possible to avoid adverse effects,[23] to cease burning garbage in an incinerator until emissions are controlled,[24] to stop using metal containers to transport offal and garbage to a commercial hograising farm,[25] to refrain from processing garbage between the hours of 11 p. m. and 2 a. m.,[26] to control fires, treat animal and industrial wastes and hire a custodian,[27] and to retain consultants to evaluate commercial offers for recycling.[28]

Statutes and regulatory schemes weigh heavily in solid waste disposal nuisance cases, both the older zoning legislation and more recent environmental laws addressing solid waste disposal directly. Thus municipalities may be disabled from moving against landfill operations somehow sanctioned by state law.[29] Although courts will defer to administrative orders and regulations,[30] there is a pronounced reluctance to find nuisance law preempted by regulatory schemes.[31] Within broad constitutional limits the legislature can determine whether

20. Commissioner of Pub. Health v. Bd. of Health, 350 Mass. 507, 215 N.E.2d 745 (1960); cf. United States v. Michallian, 2 ELR 20463 (S.D.N.Y. 1972) (consent decree) (claims arising under Rivers and Harbors Act).

21. See Environmental Protection Agency, Suggested Solid Waste Management Ordinance for Local Government, Mar. 1974, at 2.

22. See Commonwealth v. Haines, 55 Pa.D. & C.2d 204, 85 York 161 (1972) (conditions originally imposed by consent decree).

23. Smith v. Ann Arbor, 303 Mich. 476, 6 N.W.2d 752 (1942).

24. Northwest Home Owners Ass'n, Inc. v. Detroit, 298 Mich. 622, 299 N.W. 740 (1941) (burning of rubbish not protected from nuisance claim on ground of prescriptive right).

25. Mercer v. Brown, 190 So.2d 610 (Fla.Dist.Ct.App.1966).

26. Ibid.

27. Bloss v. Canastota, 35 Misc.2d 829, 232 N.Y.S.2d 166 (1962).

28. United States v. Michallian, 2 ELR 20463 (S.D.N.Y.1972) (consent decree) (claims arising under Rivers and Harbors Act).

29. Valley View v. Rockside Hideway Sanitary Landfill, Inc., 32 Ohio Misc. 135, 289 N.E.2d 598 (1972); Oronoco v. Rochester, 293 Minn. 468, 197 N. W.2d 426 (1972); Waterford Processing & Reclaiming Co. v. Township of Waterford, 25 Mich.App. 507, 181 N. W.2d 675 (1970); O'Connor v. Rockford, 52 Ill.2d 360, 288 N.E.2d 432 (1972).

30. Hewlett v. Hempstead, 3 Misc.2d 945, 133 N.Y.S.2d 690 (1954) (operation of incinerator permissible under zoning ordinance); Bath, Inc. v. Pollution Control Bd., 10 Ill.App.3d 507, 294 N.E.2d 778 (1973) (holding valid certain regulations of the Pollution Control Board); Commissioner of Pub. Health v. Bd. of Health, 350 Mass. 507, 215 N.E.2d 745 (1966) (holding that the Department of Public Health has authority to order that a dump be conducted in accordance with sanitary landfill methods or, failing that, to shut down).

31. State v. Huntington, 67 Misc.2d 875, 325 N.Y.S.2d 674 (1971).

certain landfill practices are permissible or enjoinable or certain sites acceptable or not. Often, contemporary legislation on solid waste repeats a prohibition against maintaining a "public nuisance" or "nuisance conditions," [32] reflecting a judgment of sorts that the common law is the best hedge against an improperly operated landfill.

Defenses in common law solid waste cases conform to familiar patterns of nuisance law.[33] The basic arguments of technological infeasibility and economic hardship are subsumed in the overriding question of whether a nuisance is proven. Factors important to determining a nuisance [34]—degree of the hurt, social value of the enterprise, the state of control technologies, character of the neighborhood, who was there first—may be as useful defensively as they are offensively. Separate doctrinal defenses of estoppel, laches and the like are usually the last resort of a losing party.[35] Far more likely to succeed is an argument that the municipal operator of a solid waste landfill is protected by sovereign immunity [36] although the better view calls for equal treatment of public and private operators.[37]

Nuisance litigation over solid waste, like nuisance lawsuits generally, need not be called nuisance: the landfill and waste disposal cases, on facts quite alike, may be litigated on numerous theories—trespass,[38] strict liability,[39] negligence,[40] inverse condemnation,[41] statutory public nuisance,[42] the public trust doctrine,[43] zoning [44], even the Rivers and Harbors Act of 1899 [45] and the National Environmental

32. See § 6.7 n. 19 below.

33. § 2.9 above.

34. §§ 2.4–.8 above.

35. § 2.9 above.

36. Ethridge v. Lavonia, 101 Ga.App. 190, 112 S.E.2d 822 (1960); Osborn v. Akron, 171 Ohio 361, 171 N.E.2d 492 (1960).

37. Greer v. Lennox, 79 S.D. 28, 107 N.W.2d 337 (1961); West Point v. Meadows, 236 Miss. 394, 110 So.2d 372 (1959); § 1.7 above.

38. Curry Coal Co. v. M. C. Arnoni Co., 439 Pa. 114, 266 A.2d 678 (1970).

39. Cf. Osborn v. Whittier, 103 Cal. App.2d 609, 230 P.2d 132 (1951) (based on statute).

40. Curry Coal Co. v. M. C. Arnoni Co., 439 Pa. 114, 266 A.2d 678 (1970) (plaintiffs unsuccessful on negligence theory; case remanded for trial on trespass theory).

41. E. g., Jacobs v. Seattle, 93 Wash. 171, 160 P. 299 (1916) (garbage incinerator); Glace v. Pilot Mountain, 265 N.C. 181, 143 S.E.2d 78 (1965) (awarding damages for impairment of property value of a residence caused by nearby municipal sewage lagoon).

42. Cf. Arneil v. Schnitzer, 173 Or. 179, 144 P.2d 707 (1944) (fire hazard).

43. Stephenson v. County of Monroe, 43 A.D.2d 897, 351 N.Y.S.2d 232, 4 ELR 20364 (1974) (public trust doctrine bars county from siting a landfill in a public park without express legislative approval); § 2.16 above.

44. Bd. of County Commissioners v. Thompson, 177 Colo. 277, 493 P.2d 1358, 2 ELR 20423 (1972) (upholding county zoning ordinance prohibiting the use of land zoned agricultural for the storage of junk).

45. United States v. Michallian, 2 ELR 20463 (S.D.N.Y.1972) (consent decree); see United States v. Berkeley, Civil No. C–75–1962 SAW (N.D.Cal. 1975).

Policy Act.[46] The cases illustrate also how closely connected are pollution problems: land use disputes over sites; noise pollution from the operation of equipment and transportation of wastes; water pollution if wastes are dumped without burning; air pollution if they are controlled by burning. Even splendid recycling efforts where garbage is turned into food may be subject to injunction as nuisances.[47]

§ 6.3 Solid Waste Disposal Act: A Summary

a. *The Early Years*

Prior to 1976, the direct role of the national government in solid waste management was modestly conceived and underwent little of the inexorable growth experienced in the fields of air and water pollution. Early efforts were nongovernmental: in the nineteenth century, the American Public Health Association undertook a study of the existing garbage disposal system.[1] In the 1920's a solid waste classic was published,[2] stressing the public health and siting problems of the disposal of municipal refuse. By 1939, a board of experts appointed by the U. S. Surgeon General had laid down principles for sound landfill practices;[3] present federal regulation goes only slightly beyond this policy plateau. By the early 1960's the federal effort still was confined narrowly to conducting studies (of sanitary landfill and composting practices) and providing limited technical assistance. A major accomplishment was said to be[4] the provision of federal assistance to the American Public Works Association to help prepare two manuals[5] still serving today as "major guidelines" for the design and evaluation of refuse collection and disposal systems.[6]

In 1965, a presidential message urging "better solutions to the disposal of solid wastes"[7] was followed by enactment of the Solid Waste Disposal Act of 1965[8] as part of the amendments to the Clean

---

46. Comm. for Green Foothills v. Froehlke, 3 ELR 20861 (N.D.Cal.1973) (refusing to enjoin, after balancing equities, filling of marshland by sanitary landfill).

47. Mitchell v. Hines, 303 Mich. 290, 9 N.W.2d 547 (1943).

1. Environmental Protection Agency, Initiating a National Effort to Improve Solid Waste Management 9 (1971) [hereinafter cited as Initiating a National Effort].

2. R. Hering & S. A. Greeley, Collection and Disposal of Municipal Refuse (1921).

3. 1 F. Grad, Environmental Law § 4.02, at 4–39 n. 3 (1975), citing note to N.Y.C. Health Code § 153.23.

4. Initiating a National Effort, supra note 1, at 11.

5. Municipal Refuse Disposal (3d ed. 1970); Refuse Collection Practice (3d ed. 1966).

6. Initiating a National Effort, supra note 1, at 11.

7. Special Message to the Congress on Conservation and Restoration of Natural Beauty, Feb. 8, 1965, in 1 Public Papers of the Presidents of the United States, Lyndon B. Johnson 1963 (1966).

8. Pub.L. No. 89–272, 79 Stat. 992.

Air Act. The 1965 Act authorized limited research and grant programs. It contained bold and stirring acknowledgements of the problem in the findings and purposes clause: technological progress and improvement in methods of manufacture, packaging and marketing of consumer products "has resulted in an ever-mounting increase, and in a change in characteristics, of the mass of material discarded by the purchaser"; economic activities of all types "have resulted in a rising tide of scrap, discarded and waste materials"; "inefficient and improper methods of disposal" produce scenic blights, health hazards, depressed land values, and "create public nuisances"; and the failure or inability "to salvage and reuse" waste materials economically "results in the unnecessary waste and depletion of our natural resources." [9] The discussion here addresses the general provisions of the Act particularly as amended by the Resource Recovery Act of 1970 and the Resource Conservation and Recovery Act of 1976. The following section deals more closely with the solid waste collection and disposal and resource recovery guidelines.

Section 204 [10] of the 1965 Act brought into being a demonstration grant program directing the Secretary of Health, Education and Welfare (now the Administrator of the Environmental Protection Agency) to support, and promote the coordination of, "research, investigations, experiments, training, demonstrations, surveys and studies relating to the operation and financing of solid-waste disposal programs, the development and application of new and improved methods of solid-waste disposal (including devices and facilities therefor), and the reduction of the amount of such waste and unsalvageable waste materials." The definitions under the Act conformed to the dogma: [11] solid waste meant "garbage, refuse, and other discarded solid materials, including solid-waste materials resulting from industrial, commercial and agricultural operations, and from community activities, but does not include solids or dissolved material in domestic sewage or other significant pollutants in water resources, such as silt, dissolved or suspended solids in industrial waste water effluents, dissolved materials in irrigation return flows or other common water pollutants." [12] Solid-waste disposal was defined to include "the collection, storage, treatment, utilization, processing or final disposal of solid waste." [13]

The second major program authorized by the 1965 Act dealt with grants to state or interstate agencies of not to exceed 50 per cent "of the cost of making surveys of solid-waste disposal practices and problems" within the jurisdictional areas of the states or agencies, "and of developing solid-waste disposal plans for such areas." [14] A num-

9. Section 202, 79 Stat. 997 (1965).
10. 79 Stat. 998 (1965).
11. § 6.1 above.
12. Section 203(4), 79 Stat. 998 (1965).
13. Section 203(5), 79 Stat. 998 (1965).
14. Section 206(a), 79 Stat. 999 (1965).

ber of eligibility requirements were prescribed, including "satisfactory assurance that the planning of solid-waste disposal will be coordinated, so far as practicable, with other related state, interstate, regional, and local planning activities, including those financed in part with funds pursuant to section 701 of the Housing Act of 1954." [15]

b. *The 1970 Legislation*

The Resource Recovery Act of 1970 [16] amended the Solid Waste Disposal Act in important particulars, notably by changing the legislative emphasis from disposal to recovery and by specifying a series of studies that were to lay the groundwork for future legislative action. Thus, the statement of purposes of the Resource Recovery Act expressed a desire "to promote the demonstration, construction and application of solid waste management and resource recovery systems which preserve and enhance the quality of air, water and land resources"; and "to promote a national research and development program for improved management techniques, more effective organizational arrangements, and new and improved methods of collection, separation, recovery and recycling of solid wastes, and the environmentally safe disposal of nonrecoverable residues." [17] Definitions were added consistently with established patterns of usage: "recovered resources" means "materials or energy recovered from solid waste." [18] A "resource recovery system" means "a solid waste management system which provides for collection, separation, recycling and recovery of solid wastes, including disposal of nonrecoverable waste residues." [19]

The 1970 Act expanded the Administrator's section 204 demonstration grant authority beyond solid waste disposal practices to include "the development and application of new and improved methods of collecting and disposing of solid waste and processing and recovering materials and energy from solid wastes" and "the identification of solid waste components and potential materials and energy recoverable from such waste components." [20] The Administrator also was directed to conduct research and investigations to reduce the amount of waste and "unsalvageable waste materials." [21] Similarly, the planning grant program provisions were expanded to cover up to 75 percent of the cost of "developing and revising solid waste disposal plans as part of regional environmental protection systems for

15. Section 206(c), 79 Stat. 1000 (1965).

16. Pub.L. No. 91–512, 84 Stat. 1227.

17. Sections 202(b)(1), (3), 84 Stat. 1227–28 (1970) (now sections 1003(6), (7), 42 U.S.C.A. §§ 6902(6), (7)).

18. Section 203(9), 84 Stat. 1228 (1970) (now section 1004(22), 42 U.S.C.A. § 6903(22)); see § 6.1 above.

19. Section 203(10), 84 Stat. 1228 (1970) (now section 1004(23), 42 U.S.C.A. § 6903(23)).

20. Sections 204(a)(4), (5), 84 Stat. 1228 (1970) (now sections 8001(6), (7), 42 U.S.C.A. §§ 6981(6), (7)).

21. Section 204(a)(3), 84 Stat. 1228 (1970) (now section 8001(5), 42 U.S.C.A. § 6981(5)).

such areas, providing for recycling or recovery of materials from wastes whenever possible and including planning for the reuse of solid waste disposal areas and studies of the effect and relationship of solid waste disposal practices on areas adjacent to waste disposal sites." [22] Grants also were made available to support resource recovery studies [23] and proposals for demonstration resource recovery systems.[24] The solid waste plans were meant to be regional or statewide in scope, although not so ambitious as the section 208 plans under the Federal Water Pollution Control Act.[25] A grant application to develop a solid waste plan was supposed to indicate "the manner in which provision will be made to assure full consideration of all aspects of planning essential to areawide planning for proper and effective solid waste disposal consistent with the protection of public health and welfare, including such factors as population growth, urban and metropolitan development, land use planning, water pollution control, air pollution control, and the feasibility of regional disposal and resource recovery programs." [26] In the more than ten years the solid waste disposal planning grants have been available, a large number of plans were developed for many regions of the country.[27] Although their quality is not generally acknowledged to be high, and while most of them are gathering dust on backroom shelves, they can be of legal significance and are sometimes the only available comprehensive source on the subject.

A demonstration grant program authorized by the 1965 Act also was expanded by the 1970 amendments. Grants could be extended to municipalities "for the demonstration of resource recovery systems or for the construction of new or improved solid waste disposal facilities." [28] Any grant for the demonstration of a resource recovery system, among other requirements, must be consistent with any areawide solid waste treatment management plan and with EPA's recycling guidelines [29] and must be "designed to provide areawide re-

22. Section 207(a)(2), 84 Stat. 1229–30 (1970).

23. Section 205, 84 Stat. 1228–29 (1970) (now section 8005, 42 U.S.C.A. § 6985).

24. Section 207(a)(3), 84 Stat. 1230 (1970).

25. § 4.9 above.

26. Section 207(b)(2), 84 Stat. 1230 (1970).

27. See Council on Environmental Quality, Sixth Ann.Rep. 93–95 (1975); see, e. g., Environmental Protection Agency, California Solid Waste Management Study and Plan (1971); Environmental Protection Agency, Kentucky Solid Waste Management Plan Status Report 1970 (1971); Environmental Protection Agency, New York Solid Waste Management Plan Status Report 1970 (1971); Environmental Protection Agency, Oregon Solid Waste Management Plan Status Report 1969 (1971).

28. Section 208(a), 84 Stat. 1230 (1970) (now section 8006(a), 42 U.S.C.A. § 6986(a)).

29. These guidelines were prescribed by section 209, 84 Stat. 1232 (1970) (as revised, now section 1008, 42 U.S.C.A. § 6907) and are discussed in § 6.4 below.

source recovery systems." [30] Any grant for the construction of an improved solid waste facility must be consistent with regional plans and the recycling guidelines, and must advance "the state of the art by applying new and improved techniques in reducing the environmental impact of solid waste disposal, in achieving recovery of energy or resources, or in recycling useful materials." [31] The federal share of a demonstration or improved facility is defined (generally not more than 75 per cent [32]), and the Act perforce defines the "construction" [33] for which assistance is available.

The legislative history strongly insists that the facility construction program is not a general "grant-in-aid program" but rather an "experimental one designed to assist in the financing of advanced solid waste disposal facilities".[34] The demonstration grants are supposed "to stimulate innovative systems" deemed "clearly superior with respect to the systems of resources recovery proposed, the economics of the system, and the potential for general application for solution of myriad waste problems." [35] Congress consistently has favored the innovative and selective approach instead of following the path of the water pollution program by opting for a construction grants program with a consequent "massive commitment to presently available technology oriented towards disposal." [36] Technological and process breakthroughs have been modest, however,[37] and the

---

30. Section 208(b)(1), 84 Stat. 1230 (1970) (now section 8006(b)(1), 42 U.S.C.A. § 6986(b)(1)).

31. Section 208(c)(1), 84 Stat. 1230–31 (1970) (now section 8006(c)(1), 42 U.S.C.A. § 6986(c)(1)), reads in full as follows:
   A grant under this section for the construction of a new or improved solid waste disposal facility may be made only if—
   (A) a State or interstate plan for solid waste disposal has been adopted which applies to the area involved, and the facility to be constructed (i) is consistent with such plan, (ii) is included in a comprehensive plan for the area involved which is satisfactory to the Secretary for the purposes of this chapter, and (iii) is consistent with the guidelines recommended under section 209 [as revised, now section 1008, 42 U.S. C.A. § 6907] of this title, and
   (B) the project advances the state of the art by applying new and improved techniques in reducing the environmental impact of solid waste disposal, in achieving recovery of energy or resources, or in recycling useful materials.

32. Sections 208(b)(2), (c)(2), 84 Stat. 1230, 1231 (1970) (now sections 8006(b)(2), (c)(2), 42 U.S.C.A. §§ 6986(b)(2), (c)(2)).

33. Section 203(6), 79 Stat. 998 (1965) (now section 1004(2), 42 U.S.C.A. § 6903(2)).

34. Comm. on Interstate and Foreign Commerce, Resource Recovery Act of 1970, H.R.Rep. No. 1155, 91st Cong., 2d Sess. 5 (1970).

35. Comm. on Public Works, Resource Recovery Act of 1970, S.Rep. No. 1034, 91st Cong., 2d Sess. 10–11 (1970).

36. Id. at 9.

37. Comptroller General, Report to the Congress: Need for Federal Agencies to Improve Solid Waste Management Practices 34 (1972). See also Comptroller General, Report to the Congress: Using Solid Wastes to Conserve Resources and to Create Energy (1975).

truck, the bulldozer and the dump continue to dominate the solid waste horizon.

The preceding discussion of available grant mechanisms under the Solid Waste Disposal Act has a decidedly fictional ring when amounts expended are compared to the commitments expressed. For fiscal year 1977, for example, covering the period October 1, 1976 through September 30, 1977, the administrative intention was to award grants only under section 204 [38] of the Act to support state and local programs.[39] No plans were underway within EPA's Office of Solid Waste Management Programs to make grant awards under sections 210 [40] (training projects), 208 [41] (resource recovery demonstrations), 207 [42] (planning) or 205 [43] (resource recovery studies). That several sections of the Solid Waste Disposal Act were virtual dead letters is one indicator, among many,[44] that solid waste and recycling long remained the stepchild of federal environmental programs.

The study provisions of the Resource Recovery Act are important illustrations of how Congress often commissions the executive to undertake fact gathering missions that can lead to further legislation. Section 212 [45] of the Act called for "a comprehensive report and plan for the creation of a system of national disposal sites for the storage and disposal of hazardous wastes, including radioactive, toxic chemical, biological and other wastes which may endanger public health or welfare." The report was submitted to Congress,[46] resulted in proposed legislation,[47] and eventually a serious regulatory regime with the arrival of the Resource Conservation and Recovery Act of 1976.[48]

The most comprehensive reporting provisions in the Resource Recovery Act of 1970 were found in section 205 [49] which required

38. 84 Stat. 1228 (1970) (now section 8001, 42 U.S.C.A. § 6981).

39. Letter to author from Thomas M. Canfield, Director, Program Analysis Staff, Office of Solid Waste Management Programs, EPA, June 16, 1976.

40. 84 Stat. 1232 (1970) (now section 7007, 42 U.S.C.A. § 6977).

41. Id. at 1230 (now section 8006, 42 U.S.C.A. § 6986).

42. Id. at 1229.

43. Id. at 1228 (now section 8005, 42 U.S.C.A. § 6985).

44. For fiscal year 1974, for example, $216 million were authorized for EPA's solid waste program; however, EPA only requested an appropriation of $5.7 million, and although $23.7 million actually were appropriated by Congress, only $17.3 million were expended for solid waste activities. Hearings on Waste Control Act of 1975, Before the Subcomm. on Transportation and Commerce of the House Comm. on Interstate and Foreign Commerce, H.R. Doc. No. 28, 94th Cong., 1st Sess. 766 (1975).

45. 84 Stat. 1233 (1970).

46. Environmental Protection Agency, Report to Congress on The Disposal of Hazardous Wastes (1974).

47. S. 1086, 93rd Cong., 1st Sess. (1973); H.R. 4873, 92d Cong., 1st Sess. (1973).

48. § 6.10 below.

49. 84 Stat. 1228 (1970) (now section 8005, 42 U.S.C.A. § 6985).

"from time to time, but not less frequently than annually," comprehensive reports to the President and the Congress on a number of topics, including: "means of recovering materials and energy from solid waste . . . ."; "changes in current product characteristics and production and packaging practices which would reduce the amount of solid waste"; "the use of Federal procurement to develop market demand for recovered resources"; and "the necessity and method of imposing disposal or other changes in packaging, containers, vehicles, and other manufactured goods, which . . . would reflect the cost of final disposal, the value of recoverable components of the item, and any uncontrolled disposal . . . ."

This is clearly a broad enough charter to justify reports igniting several legislative fires, if that were desired. But the first report was long delayed and was criticized when it arrived as slighting "most of these controversial subjects." [50] There are four major findings of the first report: [51] (1) "the use of recycled materials appears to result in a reduction in atmospheric emissions, generated waste and energy consumption levels, when compared with virgin material utilization"; (2) "the recovery of materials from waste depends largely on economics" and "artificial economic advantages" such as depletion allowances and capital gains treatment "appear to have been major contributors to this economic situation"; (3) technology is "sufficient" to allow materials to be extracted from "mixed municipal wastes"; however, cost of extraction is "high", making recovery processes attractive "only in areas where high disposal costs prevail and favorable local markets exist for the materials"; (4) "recovery of materials (as opposed to energy) from mixed municipal wastes, while conceptually the best alternative to disposal, cannot be instituted on a large scale without a substantial reduction in processing costs and/or upgrading in quality (which is simply unattainable given reasonable projection of technology) and/or a major reordering in the relative prices of virgin and secondary materials, so that secondary materials become economically more attractive." The first report concludes that "additional federal incentives for recycling are not considered desirable at this time", and recommends more study.[52]

The Environmental Protection Agency's second 205 report [53] provides more study and recommends "that EPA continue to study and evaluate product controls in an attempt to identify measures that would lead to increased overall efficiency of resource utilization, pollution control and waste management." Possible product controls for

50. Bryson, Solid Waste and Resource Recovery, in Environmental Law Institute, Federal Environmental Law 1290, 1296 (E. L. Dolgin & T. G. P. Guilbert eds. 1974).

51. Environmental Protection Agency, First Report to Congress on Resource Recovery and Source Reduction 5 (1973).

52. Id. at x.

53. Second Report to Congress on Resource Recovery and Source Reduction (1974).

reducing sources of solid waste "could include regulation of product lifetime, reusability, consumption level, and material or energy intensity." Potential regulatory mechanisms, identified in the report, embrace "taxes or charges, deposits, bans, and design regulation," including the regulation of reclaimability and recycled material content.[54] EPA's second and third [55] reports and other publications [56] contain commentaries on resource recovery efforts and source reduction regulation, aimed prominently at packaging materials, beverage containers, rubber tires and automobile hulks.[57]

Title II of the Resource Recovery Act of 1970 was known as the National Materials Policy Act of 1970 which created a National Commission on Materials Policy with a broad charter to study the relationship between materials policies, population size and environmental quality.[58] Materials are defined broadly to include "natural resources intended to be utilized by industry for the production of goods, with the exclusion of food." [59] The Commission's final report is now a matter of public record.[60] Its recommendations touch gingerly on a number of topics—favoring consumer product standards that improve service life and recyclability, the rezoning of urban fringe areas to accommodate waste processing, recycling and disposal, opposing delays in the oil shale and offshore oil leasing programs and executive land withdrawals that unnecessarily hamper mining activities.[61] The Commission's recommendations are unlikely to influence seriously recycling or solid waste disposal policies.

Somewhat more useful are the Environmental Protection Agency's strategy papers on its solid waste management programs,[62] comparable to its water pollution control strategy papers.[63] These afford

---

54. Id. at xiii.

55. Third Report to Congress on Resource Recovery and Waste Reduction (1975).

56. E. g., Environmental Protection Agency, Analysis of Federal Programs Affecting Solid Waste Generation and Recycling (1972); Environmental Protection Agency, The Automobile Cycle: An Environmental and Resource Reclamation Problem (1972); Environmental Protection Agency, Solving the Abandoned Car Problem in Small Communities (1974); Environmental Protection Agency, Salvage Markets for Materials in Solid Wastes (1972); Environmental Protection Agency, Resource and Environmental Profile Analysis of Nine Beverage Container Alternatives: Final Report (1974); Environmental Protection Agency, Scrap Tires as Artificial Reefs (1974); Environmental Protection Agency, Feasibility Study of the Disposal of Polyethylene Wastes (1971).

57. § 6.9 below.

58. 84 Stat. 1234 (1970).

59. Section 206, 84 Stat. 1235 (1970).

60. National Commission on Materials Policy, Material Needs and the Environment: Today and Tomorrow (1973).

61. Id., app. R (Compendium of Recommendations).

62. See, e. g., Office of Solid Waste Management Programs, Solid Waste Management Strategy, Oct. 31, 1974 [hereinafter cited as 1974 Strategy Paper].

63. See § 4.2 above.

general policy guidance and may afford insights into how regulations will be interpreted. EPA assumes that the federal solid waste management program "will continue to evolve in a generally regulatory direction related to waste *treatment* and *disposal* activities while in the resource recovery activities the Federal role will consist of implementation stimulation through technical assistance, information dissemination, planning activities, and demonstrations." [64] The thrust of the program for fiscal year 1975, for example, was said to include "developing a data base on hazardous wastes; demonstration programs to advance certain treatment and disposal methods; developing a hazardous waste regulatory strategy; augmenting knowledge on the inter-media effects of land disposal; consolidating technical/economical data on all aspects of solid waste management; and technical assistance support to improve local practices." [65]

c. *Resource Conservation and Recovery Act of 1976*

Late in 1976, the Congress approved a comprehensive overhaul of the Solid Waste Disposal Act [66] that elevated federal solid waste and recycling programs to a level of sophistication long achieved in the fields of air and water pollution. For the first time serious regulatory measures appeared—a qualified prohibition on the open dumping of solid or hazardous wastes,[67] and a comprehensive scheme for managing hazardous wastes.[68] They are supported by a conventional collection of enforcement techniques borrowed from air and water pollution laws [69]—power in the EPA Administrator to issue compliance orders [70] and move against imminent hazards,[71] and citizen suit provisions.[72] The section 207 planning grant provisions are rewritten thoroughly along the lines of the section 208 areawide planning provisions of the Federal Water Pollution Control Act [73] to accommodate regional plans for solid waste management and systems for re-

---

64. 1974 Strategy Paper, supra note 62, at 4 (emphasis in original).

65. Id. at 2.

66. Pub.L. No. 94–580, 90 Stat. 2795, 42 U.S.C.A. § 6901 et seq. For some of the legislative history, see Comm. on Public Works, Solid Waste Utilization Act of 1976, S.Rep. No. 988, 94th Cong. 2d Sess. (1976); Comm. on Interstate and Foreign Commerce, Resource Recovery and Conservation Act of 1976, H.R.Rep. No. 1491, 94th Cong., 2d Sess. (1976); 122 Cong.Rec. S11061–105 (daily ed. June 30, 1976); 122 Cong.Rec. H11147–82 (daily ed. Sept. 27, 1976).

67. Section 4005(c), 42 U.S.C.A. § 6945 (c), reads in part:
Any solid waste management practice or disposal of solid waste or hazardous waste which constitutes the open dumping of solid waste or hazardous waste is prohibited, except in the case of any practice or disposal of solid waste under a timetable or schedule for compliance established under this section.

68. Sections 3001–11, 42 U.S.C.A. §§ 6921–31; see § 6.10 below.

69. §§ 3.20, 4.21 above.

70. Section 3008(a), 42 U.S.C.A. § 6928 (a).

71. Section 7003, 42 U.S.C.A. § 6973.

72. Section 7002, 42 U.S.C.A. § 6972.

73. § 4.9 above.

source recovery and resource conservation.[74] The section 209 guideline provisions [75] also are rewritten, with one of the most important changes being a directive to the EPA Administrator to develop within a year "minimum criteria" defining the open dumping which is prohibited under section 4005.[76] The 1976 amendments espouse several other important new policies—the development of sound disposal and resource recovery practices for mining waste and sludge,[77] a boost to the use of federal procurement powers in the interests of recycling,[78] assistance for solid waste management in rural communities,[79] a direction to the Secretary of Commerce to encourage "greater commercialization of proven resource recovery technology," [80] an unequivocal waiver of sovereign immunity for federal facilities,[81] and another major study of all aspects of resource conservation.[82]

A key to the Resource Conservation and Recovery Act of 1976 is section 4008,[83] which authorizes the Administrator to provide financial assistance for state plans and programs. In order to qualify a plan or program must include, among other things, adequate authority to assure the consistency of local and areawide plans with state plans, to enforce the section 4005 prohibition on open dumping, and to place noncomplying municipalities on compliance schedules.[84] Section 4006 contains provisions for designating agencies and areas for purposes of areawide solid waste management planning.[85] Ideally, areawide solid waste management plans will be developed by the same agency producing the section 208 plans under the Federal Water Pollution Control Act.[86] Within a year after the Administrator has published guidelines for the identification of solid waste management regions under section 4002(a),[87] the governor of each state is required to identify the agency, or agencies, responsible for developing and implementing the state plan.[88] No time limit is provided for adoption of a state plan. The amendments also set forth the mini-

---

74. The term "resource conservation" is defined by the 1976 amendments as the "reduction of the amounts of solid waste that are generated, reduction of overall resource consumption, and utilization of recovered resources." Section 1004(21), 42 U.S.C.A. § 6903(21).

75. Now section 1008, 42 U.S.C.A. § 6907; see § 6.4 below.

76. Section 1008(a)(3), 42 U.S.C.A. § 6907(a)(3).

77. Sections 8002(f), (g), 42 U.S.C.A. §§ 6982(f), (g).

78. Section 6002, 42 U.S.C.A. § 6962.

79. Section 4009, 42 U.S.C.A. § 6949.

80. Section 5001, 42 U.S.C.A. § 6951.

81. Section 6001, 42 U.S.C.A. § 6961.

82. Section 8005, 42 U.S.C.A. § 6985.

83. 42 U.S.C.A. § 6948; see section 4007, 42 U.S.C.A. § 6947.

84. Section 4003, 42 U.S.C.A. § 6943; see note 89, infra.

85. 42 U.S.C.A. § 6946.

86. See id. § 6946(b)(1). Compare § 4.9 above.

87. 42 U.S.C.A. § 6942(a).

88. See sections 4006(a), (b)(1), 42 U.S.C.A. §§ 6946(a), (b)(1).

mum requirements a state plan must comply with in order to receive the necessary approval for federal financial assistance.[89]

Implementation of these areawide plans, once developed, is said to rest in the hands of local or regional agencies.[90] The fact of the matter is the process of designation and plan development is bound to be slow and arduous, and it precedes any serious implementation.[91] Let us not forget that the first generation of plans developed under the Solid Waste Disposal Act have proven to be mainly a paper exercise.[92] A prescription for a more ambitious collection of planning documents offers no panacea. Indeed, the presumption of futility can be overcome only by demonstrable progress.

§ 6.4 Federal Guidelines: Disposal and Resource Recovery

Under section 1008 of the Solid Waste Disposal Act, as amended in 1976, the Administrator is obliged to publish "suggested guidelines for solid waste management."[1] The guidelines, by reason of the defi-

---

89. Section 4003, 42 U.S.C.A. § 6943, reads:

In order to be approved under section 4007, each State plan must comply with the following minimum requirements—

(1) The plan shall identify (in accordance with section 4006(b)) (A) the responsibilities of State, local, and regional authorities in the implementation of the State plan, (B) the distribution of Federal funds to the authorities responsible for development and implementation of the State plan, and (C) the means for coordinating regional planning and implementation under the State plan.

(2) The plan shall, in accordance with section 4005(c), prohibit the establishment of new open dumps within the State, and contain requirements that all solid waste (including solid waste originating in other States, but not including hazardous waste) shall be (A) utilized for resource recovery or (B) disposed of in sanitary landfills (within the meaning of section 4004(a)) or otherwise disposed of in an environmentally sound manner.

(3) The plan shall provide for the closing or upgrading of all existing open dumps within the State pursuant to the requirements of section 4005.

(4) The plan shall provide for the establishment of such State regulatory powers as may be necessary to implement the plan.

(5) The plan shall provide that no local government within the State shall be prohibited under State or local law from entering into long-term contracts for the supply of solid waste to resource recovery facilities.

(6) The plan shall provide for such resource conservation or recovery and for the disposal of solid waste in sanitary landfills or any combination of practices so as may be necessary to use or dispose of such waste in a manner that is environmentally sound.

90. Section 4006(c)(3), 42 U.S.C.A. § 6946(c)(3), reads:

Implementation of interstate regional solid waste management plans shall be conducted by units of local government for any portion of a region within their jurisdiction, or by multijurisdictional agencies or authorities designated in accordance with State law, including those designated by agreement by such units of local government for such purpose.

91. Compare § 4.9 above (discussing the planning provisions of the Federal Water Pollution Control Act).

92. See text accompanying note 27, supra.

1. Section 1008(a), 42 U.S.C.A. § 6907(a).

nition of solid waste management,[2] may reach "the collection, source separation, storage, transportation, transfer, processing, treatment, and disposal of solid waste." They are intended to "describe levels of performance, including appropriate methods and degrees of control, that provide at a minimum" for the "protection of public health and welfare."[3] The guidelines are mostly advisory except that they govern solid waste disposal activities directly engaged in by federal agencies or controlled by them through contract, permit or lease.[4] In important particulars, the Administrator's power to prescribe guidelines under the Resource Conservation and Recovery Act of 1976 is simply a restatement of an authority bestowed initially by the Resource Recovery Act of 1970.[5] The most significant new power extended by the 1976 amendments is that granted to the Environmental Protection Agency Administrator to lay down "minimum criteria" for defining the open dumping of solid or hazardous waste prohibited under section 4005.[6] For all practical purposes, these criteria will amount to federal performance standards enforceable by public authorities and citizens alike.

The EPA guidelines, which are aimed principally at the activities of federal agencies, are aptly targeted. The federal government happens to be one of "the largest single institutional consumers in the Nation", responsible for generating "tremendous volumes of solid

---

2. Section 1004(28), 42 U.S.C.A. § 6903(28).

3. Section 1008(a)(2), 42 U.S.C.A. § 6907(a)(2), provides that suggested guidelines shall—
    not later than two years after the enactment of this section describe levels of performance, including appropriate methods and degrees of control, that provide at a minimum for (A) protection of public health and welfare; (B) protection of the quality of ground waters and surface waters from leachates; (C) protection of the quality of surface waters from runoff through compliance with effluent limitations under the Federal Water Pollution Control Act, as amended; (D) protection of ambient air quality through compliance with new source performance standards or requirements of air quality implementation plans under the Clean Air Act, as amended; (E) disease and vector control; (F) safety; and (G) esthetics; and
    . . . .

4. Section 6004, 42 U.S.C.A. § 6964 (formerly section 211).

5. The former section 209(a) authorized the Administrator of EPA to "recommend to appropriate agencies and publish in the Federal Register guidelines for solid waste recovery, collection, separation, and disposal systems (including systems for private use), which shall be consistent with public health and welfare, and air and water quality standards and adaptable to appropriate land-use plans." 84 Stat. 1227, 1232 (1970). Conceivably, the absence of specific authority in the 1976 amendments to prescribe guidelines for "recovery" systems could be read as limiting the power approved in 1970. This would be a perversion of a change intended "to broaden the scope of the information and solid waste management guidelines authorized by the Resource Recovery Act of 1970." Comm. on Public Works, Solid Waste Utilization Act of 1976, S.Rep. No. 988, 94th Cong., 2d Sess. 12 (1976). The expansive statutory definition of solid waste management is likely to support guidelines aimed at improved resource recovery and source reduction.

6. Section 1008(a)(3), 42 U.S.C.A. § 6907(a)(3).

Sec. 6.4   FEDERAL GUIDELINES

waste", often with a "very poor record of solid waste management." [7] In 1970, Congress was determined that the federal agencies "take the lead" [8] in overcoming the reluctance to invest funds necessary to control solid waste pollution. Indeed, the obligation was seen as requiring each federal agency "to use the most advanced technology and management systems available to properly manage solid waste with maximum recovery of materials and energy." [9]

Standards governing federal dumping practices go back at least to 1966 with Executive Order 11282,[10] which directed that refuse from federal activities not be left in open dumps without being covered with inert matter within a reasonable period of time. Several years later a comprehensive report by the General Accounting Office [11] found widespread neglect: of 651 solid waste disposal sites within the scope of the study, 91 percent failed to meet federal standards for sanitary landfill; [12] over 60 percent were open dumps; [13] of the 131 sites actually visited, 24 had dumps in contact with groundwaters, streams, or swamps; 7 of 8 incinerators did not meet federal emission standards. That there are problems even with a policy of closing dumps is illustrated anecdotally by the situation in Yellowstone National Park where the Park Service, contrary to the advice of its consultants, precipitously shut down dumps constituting a major food supply for the grizzly bear population. The resultant increase in bear-man conflicts necessitated greater "control" efforts against grizzly bears and population reductions of an arguably endangered species.[14] It can be assumed that the incomplete compliance of federal agencies with solid waste disposal guidelines is not motivated principally by a desire to perpetuate endangered species.

In 1976, Congress responded to this unimpressive environmental record of federal facilities by going beyond the guidelines to effectuate an unequivocal waiver of sovereign immunity. The consequence is to subject federal facilities to the constraints both of the federal guidelines and of state and local legal regimes applicable to privately operated facilities. Thus federal agencies having jurisdiction over solid waste management facilities "shall be subject to, and comply with, all Federal, State, interstate, and local requirements, both substantive and procedural (including any requirement for permits or

7. Comm. on Public Works, Resource Recovery Act of 1970, S.Rep. No. 1034, 91st Cong., 2d Sess. 14 (1970) [hereinafter cited as Senate Report].

8. Id. at 15.

9. Ibid.

10. 31 Fed.Reg. 7663 (1966).

11. Comptroller General, Report to the Congress: Need for Federal Agencies to Improve Solid Waste Management Practices (1972) [hereinafter cited as GAO Report].

12. Id. at 2. The standards referred to are found in U. S. Public Health Services, The Sanitary Landfill (1969). The section 1008 solid waste guidelines adhere to and expand upon the standards found in this publication.

13. GAO Report, supra note 11, at 2.

14. L. Regenstein, The Politics of Extinction ch. 5 (1974).

reporting or any provision for injunctive relief and such sanctions as may be imposed by a court to enforce such relief), respecting control and abatement of solid waste or hazardous waste disposal in the same manner, and to the same extent, as any person is subject to such requirements, including the payment of reasonable service charges." [15] This formulation rejects, and properly so, the Supreme Court's interpretation of the air and water pollution acts that protects federal facilities from compliance with state permit requirements.[16]

a. *Disposal and Collection Guidelines*

Section 1008 guidelines may reach not only "disposal" systems such as landfills and incinerators but also solid waste collection, source separation and processing activities. A considerable body of administrative law is promised; much of it has arrived. Two published guidelines deal with conventional patterns of collection and disposal—"Guidelines for the Storage and Collection of Residential, Commercial and Institutional Solid Waste" [17] and "Thermal Processing and Land Disposal of Solid Waste Guidelines." [18] Four others address various aspects of resource recovery and recycling—"Guidelines for Procurement of Products that Contain Recycled Material",[19] "Beverage Container Guidelines",[20] "Guidelines for Resource Recovery Facilities",[21] and "Source Separation for Materials Recovery Guidelines".[22]

The land disposal guidelines are the most important since they strongly encourage sanitary landfilling of a large volume of federally controlled solid wastes. A sanitary landfill is defined carefully [23] as "a land disposal site employing an engineered method of disposing of solid wastes on land in a manner that minimizes environmental hazards by spreading the solid wastes in thin layers, compacting the solid wastes to the smallest practical volume, and applying and compacting cover material at the end of each operating day." Hazardous, agricultural and mining wastes are exempted.[24] The guidelines address the subjects of wastes that ought to be excluded from a facility,

---

15. Section 6001, 42 U.S.C.A. § 6961. Under the provision the President may exempt a facility "if he determines it to be in the paramount interest of the United States to do so." Ibid.

16. §§ 3.19, 4.21 above, discussing Hancock v. Train, 426 U.S. 167, 96 S.Ct. 2006, 48 L.Ed.2d 555 (1976) and Environmental Protection Agency v. California ex rel. State Water Resources Control Bd., 426 U.S. 200 96 S.Ct. 2022, 48 L.Ed.2d 578 (1976).

17. 41 Fed.Reg. 6766 (1976), 40 CFR pt. 243.

18. 39 Fed.Reg. 29328 (1974), 40 CFR pts. 240, 241.

19. 41 Fed.Reg. 2355 (1976), 40 CFR pt. 247; see § 6.5 below.

20. 40 Fed.Reg. 52968 (1975), 40 CFR pt. 244; see § 6.9 below.

21. 41 Fed.Reg. 41208 (1976), 40 CFR pt. 245.

22. 41 Fed.Reg. 16950 (1976), 40 CFR pt. 246.

23. 40 CFR § 241.101(s).

24. Id. § 241.100.

Sec. 6.4   FEDERAL GUIDELINES   641

site selection, design and operational procedures. The format is to prescribe vaguely written mandatory requirements accompanied by somewhat more specific recommended procedures by which the obligations may be met. A sample of the requirements: a land disposal site must be operated so "to provide adequate protection to ground and surface waters used as drinking water supplies,"[25] must be designed and operated "in an aesthetically acceptable manner,"[26] must control decomposition gases "to avoid posing a hazard to occupants of adjacent property,"[27] must maintain conditions "unfavorable" to the breeding of vectors,[28] and must apply cover material "as necessary" to minimize fire hazards, infiltration or precipitation, odors and blowing litter; control gas venting and vectors; discourage scavanging; and provide a pleasing appearance.[29] The recommended procedures embrace conventional sanitary landfill practices, as by prohibiting burning,[30] urging daily cover (usually by soil) of the compacted wastes,[31] and the diversion of surface water runoff from the working face (where the wastes are discharged, spread and compacted prior to the placement of cover) by means of trenches and conduits.[32]

The vagueness of the solid waste disposal guidelines is only one reason for questioning their enforceability. The 1970 Act anticipated additional action by the President, which was long delayed, to "insure compliance" with the guidelines by executive agencies.[33] Some doubt exists also about the binding effect of the guidelines. They are clearly advisory to nonfederal, state, regional and local agencies.[34] They are clearly binding on federal executive agencies to the extent they engage directly in solid waste disposal activities themselves or permit the use of federal property for solid waste disposal.[35] The guidelines themselves qualify federal responsibility by insisting that implementation "can be expected only in those situations where the Federal agency is able to exercise direct management control over the proc-

25. Id. § 241.204–1.

26. Id. § 241.208–1.

27. Id. § 241.206–1.

28. Id. § 241.207–1.

29. Id. § 241.209–1.

30. Id. § 241.205–3(a).

31. Id. § 241.209–3(a). EPA recognizes "the application of daily, intermediate and final cover as the most efficient operating practice based on current knowledge for meeting the [cover] requirement as stated." But the guidelines do not preclude other practices. 39 Fed.Reg. 29329 (1974).

32. 40 CFR § 241.204–3.

33. Section 211(a)(4), 84 Stat. 1233 (1970) (now section 6004(a)(4), 42 U.S.C.A. § 6964(a)(4)). Implementing action was taken in Exec. Order No. 11752, 38 Fed.Reg. 34793 (1973).

34. Section 209(a), 84 Stat. 1232 (1970) (as revised, now section 1008(a), 42 U.S.C.A. § 6907(a)). EPA has declined to recommend its storage and collection guidelines to all contractors and grantees of the federal government. 41 Fed.Reg. 6766 (1976). Compare section 1008(a)(3), 42 U.S.C.A. § 6907(a)(3).

35. Section 211, 84 Stat. 1233 (now section 6004, 42 U.S.C.A. § 6964).

essing and disposal operations." [36] This interpretation excludes a wide variety of situations where a federal agency uses the local landfill like anybody else, presumably under a contractual arrangement. The statute, with some effort, can be read as requiring that a federal agency contracting to dispose of solid waste must insist upon compliance with the guidelines.[37] Despite these questions about enforceability and reach, the solid waste disposal guidelines are bound to be influential. In particular, they shoud be helpful in nuisance cases searching for a frame of reference.

EPA's guidelines for the storage and collection of residential, commercial and institutional solid waste [38] closely follow the pattern of the disposal guidelines. Hazardous, infectious, agricultural, mining and industrial solid wastes and sludges are exempted.[39] Vague mandatory requirements are supplemented by somewhat more specific recommendations. Thus, the requirements affirm that solid wastes shall be "stored in such a manner that they do not constitute a fire, health or safety hazard or provide food or harborage for vectors, and shall be contained or bundled so as not to result in spillage," [40] shall be "collected with frequency sufficient to inhibit the propagation or attraction of vectors and the creation of nuisances," [41] and that the collection vehicle operator shall be responsible for creating "no undue disturbance of the peace and quiet in residential areas in and through which he operates." [42] The recommendations go into greater detail on methods of storage, standards to be met by collection vehicles and frequency of collection.

The collection guidelines, like the disposal guidelines, raise issues of coverage. The guidelines exempt federally generated waste collected by local systems beyond federal managerial control.[43] Also exempted are locally generated wastes disposed of on federal land.[44] The latter exclusion is an arguably correct reading of section 6004(a)(3),[45] but cannot be defended on the broader ground that the dis-

36. 40 CFR § 241.100.

37. One textual argument is that if any agency has "jurisdiction over any real property or facility the operation or administration of which" involves the agency in solid waste disposal activities, then compliance with the section 1008 guidelines is required. See Section 211(a)(1)(A), 84 Stat. 1233 (1970) (now section 6004(a)(1)(A), 42 U.S.C.A. § 6964(a)(1)(A)). This can be read as reaching the situation where the agency disposes of its solid waste by contract as well as the case where it exercises "direct management control."

38. 40 Fed.Reg. 29404 (1975) (proposed), 41 Fed.Reg. 6766 (1976) (adopted), 40 CFR pt. 243.

39. 40 CFR § 243.100(b).

40. Id. § 243.200–1(a).

41. Id. § 243.203–1.

42. Id. § 243.204–1.

43. Id. § 243.100(c).

44. See 41 Fed.Reg. 6766 (1976).

45. Section 211(a)(3), 84 Stat. 1233 (1970) (now section 6004(a)(3), 42 U.S.C.A. § 6964(a)(3)), reads as follows: Each Executive agency which permits the use of Federal property for purposes of disposal of solid waste shall insure compliance with such guidelines and the purposes

posal guidelines alone are binding on federal agencies. To be sure, the heading of section 6004 reads "Applicability of Solid Waste Disposal Guidelines to Executive Agencies" but the text refers generally to federal agencies insuring compliance with "the guidelines recommended under section 1008," which of course include the collection, separation and recycling guidelines.[46] No discernible policy reason suggests that federal agencies should meet the guidelines while disposing of solid waste but ignore them while storing and collecting it.

Another controversial collection guideline permits noncompliance by federal agencies for reasons of costs and technological inhibitions, provided a detailed report on the subject is submitted to the Administrator of EPA.[47] It is not clear whether or to what degree the legislative charter of section 1008, authorizing the promulgation of guidelines providing for "the protection of public health and the environment," makes allowance for the demands of economics and technology.

b. *Resource Recovery*

The Environmental Protection Agency's resource recovery facilities guidelines,[48] like the disposal and collection guidelines, apply to residential, commercial and institutional solid wastes and exclude mining, agricultural and industrial wastes.[49] The idea is to put federal agencies in the business of resource recovery and recycling as they are now firmly involved in collection and disposal. Under the guidelines resource recovery facilities must be established if any single federal facility generates, collects or disposes of 100 tons or more of solid waste per day or if a single facility within a Standard Metropolitan Statistical Area generates 50 tons or more per day and combines with other federal facilities within the SMSA to produce 100 tons or more per day.[50] A "resource recovery facility" means "any physical plant that processes residential, commercial, or institutional solid wastes biologically, chemically, or physically, and recovers useful products, such as shredded fuel, combustible oil or gas, steam, metal, glass, etc. for recycling."[51] The facilities guidelines are not meant to lock the agencies into specific resource recovery options, and therefore, prior to a specific commitment, recommend market studies for recycled materials[52] and an analysis of available recovery

of this Act in the disposal of such waste.

It is possible that in the context of discussing disposal directly, "such guidelines" means only the disposal guidelines. It is also possible that, in the context of the entire section, "such guidelines" refers to all guidelines recommended under Section 209, 84 Stat. 1232 (1970) (as revised, now section 1008, 42 U.S.C.A. § 6907).

46. Section 211(a)(1), 84 Stat. 1233 (1970) (now section 6004(a)(1), 42 U.S.C.A. § 6964(a)(1).

47. 40 CFR § 243.100(i).

48. 41 Fed.Reg. 41208 (1976), 40 CFR pt. 245.

49. 40 CFR § 254.100(a).

50. Id. §§ 245.200–1(a), (b).

51. Id. § 245.101(l).

52. Id. § 245.200–3(b).

technologies.[53] The proposed guidelines contain no deadline for implementation and, without one, compliance is not to be expected soon.

EPA's source separation guidelines [54] are meant to aid resource recovery efforts, wherever implemented. Source separation, properly implemented, conserves resources, cuts down on waste disposal and avoids contamination of high value materials that can be sold for recycling. The requirements sections of the guidelines [55] oblige facilities of a certain size to separate and sell for purposes of recycling certain high grade paper (computer print-out, typing and tablet sheets),[56] used newspapers and corrugated containers. "In areas where markets are available," it is recommended "that glass, cans and mixed paper be separated at the source of generation and separately collected for the purpose of recycling." [57] Market studies are recommended [58] and economic analyses suggested "which [compare] the costs of the present waste collection and disposal system with the proposed segregated systems." [59] EPA specifically declined an invitation to require the implementation of separation programs only when they are self-supporting [60] although it does permit agency noncompliance for "inability to sell the recovered materials due to lack of market, and costs so unreasonably high as to render source separation for materials recovery economically impracticable." [61] The collection guidelines require each agency within a year to make "a final determination as to what actions shall be taken to adopt the requirements of these guidelines," [62] and sixty days thereafter to report to the Administrator on actions taken.

Other important contributions of the guidelines are discussed elsewhere: the beverage container guidelines [63] represent an important source reduction effort by federal agencies being pursued seriously at the state and local level.[64] The guidelines for procurement of products containing recycled materials [65] are an important component of the federal government's indirect presence on solid waste and resource recovery issues.[66]

---

53. Id. § 245.200–3(c).

54. 41 Fed.Reg. 16950 (1976), 40 CFR pt. 246.

55. 40 CFR §§ 246.200–1 (high-grade paper), 246.201–1 (used newspapers), 246.202–1 (corrugated containers).

56. See id. § 246.101(o).

57. Id. § 246.201–3.

58. Id. §§ 246.200–2, 246.201–4, 246.-202–3.

59. Id. §§ 246.200–8, 246.201–7, 246.-202–6.

60. 41 Fed.Reg. 16950 (1976), citing the insistence in the Senate Report, supra note 7, at 12, that federal agencies "must take the lead in overcoming the reluctance to invest funds necessary to control solid waste pollution."

61. 40 CFR § 246.100(f).

62. Id. § 246.100(e)(1).

63. 40 Fed.Reg. 52968 (1975), 40 CFR pt. 244.

64. §§ 6.7, 6.8 below.

65. 41 Fed.Reg. 2355 (1976), 40 CFR pt. 247.

66. § 6.5 below.

§ 6.5 Indirect Federal Role

While federal regulatory responsibility for waste disposal and recycling is minimal, the federal presence is nonetheless substantial. Pertinent legal authority can be aligned loosely under (1) ad hoc regulation; (2) other incidental influences on resource use decisions; and (3) energy conservation. The first two categories are discussed in this section; the third is discussed elsewhere.[1]

a. *Ad Hoc Regulation*

Offensive land disposal practices obviously are within reach of Section 13 of the Rivers and Harbors Act of 1899, which forbids the depositing of material on the banks of any navigable water where it "shall be liable to be washed into such navigable water."[2] Runoff from land disposal sites constitutes a direct discharge of pollutants forbidden under section 13[3] and under Section 301[4] of the Federal Water Pollution Control Act.

While these discharges may be attacked on an ad hoc basis, the power to impose systematic federal regulations on solid waste disposal sites polluting surface waters is generally lacking under FWPCA. A dump creating water pollution by runoff is probably not a "point source" subject to the permit provisions unless it discharges fortuitously through a discrete "ditch", "pipe" or "channel".[5] Runoff from nonpoint sources is reached only under the planning provisions of the Act, notably section 208, which requires each areawide waste treatment management plan to include "a process to control the disposal of pollutants on land or in subsurface excavations within such area to protect ground and surface water quality."[6]

Groundwater contamination by leachate from waste disposal sites is generally thought to be beyond the reach of federal regulation under the Federal Water Pollution Control Act.[7] Limited regulatory authority over underground injection and the disposal of pesticides and pesticide containers, respectively, is found in the Safe Drinking Water Act of 1974 and the Federal Environmental Pesticide Control Act.[8] The Safe Drinking Water Act also gives the EPA

---

1. § 6.6 below.

2. 33 U.S.C.A. § 407; see United States v. Esso Standard Oil Co., 375 F.2d 621 (3d Cir. 1967).

3. See § 4.5 above.

4. 33 U.S.C.A. § 1311. Direct dumping would be forbidden also by Section 10 of the Rivers and Harbors Act and FWPCA's dredge and fill provisions. See §§ 4.5, 4.6 above. See also Hearings on Resource Conservation and Recycling, Before the Subcomm. on Science, Technology and Commerce of the Senate Comm. on Commerce, S.Doc. No. 56, 93d Cong., 2d Sess., pt. 3, at 911 (1974) (indicating that the Corps of Engineers asserts jurisdiction over 170 solid waste disposal sites in the San Francisco Bay area alone).

5. See § 4.4 above.

6. Section 208(b)(2)(K), 33 U.S.C.A. § 1288(b)(2)(K); see § 4.9 above.

7. See § 4.3 above.

8. Ibid; see § 6.10 below (hazardous wastes).

Administrator limited emergency powers to prevent contamination of a public water system which "may present an imminent and substantial endangerment to the health of persons." [9] Nonetheless, legal authority over groundwater pollution remains principally in state and local hands.

As a practical matter, federal authority reaches farther than it does theoretically: historically, wetlands have attracted disposal and dumping of all sorts. United States Attorneys' and Corps of Engineers' offices across the country often have intervened under their Rivers and Harbors Act and dredge and fill authorities.[10] The cases often are resolved without a filing or settled shortly thereafter. The consent decree signed by Judge Frankel of the Southern District of New York, preventing pollution of the Hudson River by Westchester County, is the most detailed court order on sanitary landfilling yet recorded.[11] It contains a number of unique provisions on cover, compaction, handling of industrial wastes, restoration and the retention of consultants to investigate effects on groundwater, the construction of a dike to contain leachate and other refuse, selection of alternative sites and identification of markets for recycled materials.[12]

b. *Other Incidental Influences on Resource Use Decisions*

Many economic practices of federal agencies are suspected of favoring the use of primary or virgin raw materials over secondary or recycled materials: procurement and tax policies, freight rates, labeling requirements, incentives for mineral discovery, municipal waste disposal subsidies. Of these, procurement policies deserve special mention. Government purchasing power has been recognized for many years as an important component of the struggle against air and water pollution.[13] The study provisions of the Resource Recovery Act of 1970 specifically called for an investigation of "the use of Federal procurement to develop market demand for recovered resources." [14] Several studies were carried out, and resulted in a finding that "purchasing specifications constitute a barrier to increased resource recovery because recycled materials are often excluded." [15]

The Environmental Protection Agency's guidelines for the procurement of products that contain recycled material [16] are intended

---

9. Section 1431, 42 U.S.C.A. § 300i.

10. See §§ 4.5, 4.6 above.

11. United States v. Michaelian, 2 ELR 20463 (S.D.N.Y.1972) (consent decree).

12. See, e. g., Muchow, Recycling of Solid Waste: Legal Impediments and a Program for Reform, 59 Cornell L. Rev. 440 (1974). In recent years congressional hearings on resource recovery generally and federal agency policies specifically have been legion.

13. Exec. Order No. 11738, 38 Fed. Reg. 25161 (1973), superseding Exec. Order No. 11602.

14. Section 205(a)(4), 84 Stat. 1228.

15. 41 Fed.Reg. 2356 (1976), citing, among other studies, Arthur D. Little, Inc., Can Federal Procurement Practices Be Used to Reduce Solid Wastes? (1974).

16. 41 Fed.Reg. 2356 (1976), adding 40 CFR pt. 247.

Sec. 6.5   INDIRECT FEDERAL ROLE   647

to help tear down these barriers. Recycled material means "a material that can be utilized in place of a raw or virgin material in manufacturing a product and consists of materials derived from post consumer waste, industrial scrap, material derived from agricultural wastes and other items . . . ."[17] The guidelines require nothing, however, and are content to recommend in general terms better ways of conducting the government's business. Thus, all agencies are urged to eliminate from their procurement specifications virgin material requirements and recycled material exclusions "unless performance standards would not be satisfied."[18] All agencies are called upon to revise specifications used in purchasing personal and real property "so that all specifications require the inclusion of recycled material to the maximum extent practicable."[19] The revised specifications "should require the recycled material contained in the products to be post-consumer waste whenever practicable or that the recycled material specified contain the highest percentage of post-consumer waste that is practicable."[20] Agencies generating energy and having the necessary technical capability "should use solid-waste-derived fuel to the maximum extent practicable."[21]

It is recognized that while government purchases of key secondary commodities (paper, iron and steel, nonferrous metals, glass, plastics, rubber) are not sufficiently large to create major new markets, United States agency specifications do have a ripple effect as others follow suit. Progress to date has not been encouraging[22] although the potential is waiting to be tapped—for example, by Defense Department purchase of recycled oil, Post Office use of retreaded tires, and so on.[23] Perhaps best known of the federal government's procurement levers, and the one serving as an inspiration for EPA's recycling guidelines,[24] is the General Services Administration's program requiring some reclaimed fiber in paper of various classifications purchased by the United States.[25] These specifications typically require a small per-

17. 40 CFR § 247.101(g). Post consumer waste means "a material or product that has served its intended use and has been discarded for disposal after passing through the hands of a final user." Id. § 247.101(e).

18. Id. §§ 247.200–1(a), (b).

19. Id. § 247.200–1(c).

20. Id. § 247.200–1(f).

21. Id. § 247.202–1.

22. Bryson, Solid Waste and Resource Recovery, in Environmental Law Institute, Federal Environmental Law 1290, 1304–05 (E. L. Dolgin & T. G. P. Guilbert eds. 1974).

23. The General Services Administration uses very few recapped tires and very little used motor oil while the Defense Department uses both. See General Accounting Office, Report to Congress: Need for Federal Agencies to Improve Solid Waste Management Practices 21 (1972).

24. See 41 Fed.Reg. 2356 (1976).

25. To date, reclaimed fibers are required by 86 purchase specifications (including toilet tissue, paper towels, fiberboard boxes, egg cartons, Kraft paper, envelopes and file folders). Specifications for thermal insulation, plastic piping and roofing felt also encourage the inclusion of recycled materials. Federal Supply Service,

centage of recycled paper from post-consumer waste (such as newspapers, magazines and other fibrous materials recycled from municipal solid waste) and a somewhat larger percentage from converting and fabrication wastes (such as rejected paperstock or other paper mill wastes). The GSA specifications are not particularly demanding; they are set so as to maintain competitive bidding. They require only token contributions of post-consumer waste, which presents the most difficult recycling problems, and are unenforceable in any event; it is impossible, in fact, to determine compliance by testing the paper and products.[26] Unfortunately, while a panel of the National Academy of Sciences has recommended that half of the new capacity pulp and paper plants over the next fifteen years be accommodated to waste material,[27] the trend is the other way. Federal leadership of recycling efforts through the procurement powers is unlikely to be felt keenly unless Congress commits itself to significant economic incentives for the use of recycled materials. By way of illustration, the Noise Control Act authorizes federal buyers to spend up to 125 percent of the otherwise prevailing retail price payable for low-noise-emission products.[28] The Resource Conservation and Recovery Act of 1976 encourages recycling in terms somewhat less insistent. Section 6002 [29] obliges each procuring agency [30] with respect to the purchase or acquisition of an item, or a quantity of items, having a purchase price exceeding $10,000 [31] to procure those items "composed of the highest percentage of recovered materials practicable consistent with maintaining a satisfactory level of competition." [32]

General Services Administration, Fact Sheet on Recycled Paper, Mar. 3, 1975 (with enclosures).

26. See W. Franklin, Paper Recycling: The Art of the Possible 1970–1985, 110–13, 159 (1973) (indicating that when conducting blind performance tests on recycled paper as compared to nonrecycled paper, researchers are unable to determine which samples contain recycled fibers).

27. See New York Chamber of Commerce, Paper Recycling: A Business Perspective 17 (1972).

28. 42 U.S.C.A. § 4914(c)(1). Whether one discrimination justifies another is a separate question. Section 383 of the Energy Policy and Conservation Act of 1975, Pub.L. No. 94–163, 89 Stat. 940, 42 U.S.C.A. § 6363, strongly affirms a congressional purpose to encourage the recycling of used oil and reduce the consumption of new oil. On the subject of procurement, however, the Act only goes so far as to direct federal officials to revise policies to encourage procurement of recycled oil for military and nonmilitary federal uses if recycled oil is available at prices competitive with new oil procured for the same end use. 42 U.S.C.A. § 6363(f).

29. 42 U.S.C.A. § 6962.

30. A "procuring agency" is defined to mean "any Federal agency, or any State agency, or agency of a political subdivision of a State which is using appropriated Federal funds for such procurement, or any person contracting with any such agency with respect to work performed under such contract." Section 1004(17), 42 U.S.C.A. § 6903(17).

31. Section 6002(a), 42 U.S.C.A. § 6962 (a).

32. Section 6002(c)(1)(A), 42 U.S.C.A. § 6962(c)(1)(A). A decision not to procure items composed of recycled

The Office of Procurement Policy in the Executive Office of the President is directed to coordinate policies for federal procurement in such a way "as to maximize the use of recovered resources" and to report annually to the Congress on implementation.[33] All federal agencies are directed to revise their procurement regulations to maximize the use of recovered resources [34] and to eliminate specifications requiring the use of virgin goods and materials.[35] Contracting officers also are directed to require suppliers to certify the total percentage of recycled materials utilized for the performance of the contract.[36]

Tax laws offer another example of policies that may tilt resource use decisions towards virgin materials.[37] Most often cited are the depletion allowances for certain minerals—lead, nickel, oil, copper and other metallic ores.[38] The rerefined oil industry, to mention but one conspicuous example, does not enjoy benefits comparable to those entitled to oil depletion allowances.[39] Indeed, the image of the rerefiner as a poor fellow with a truck is not all that misleading, and contrasts strikingly with associations brought to mind by the major oil companies whose stock in trade is the virgin resource.

The capital gains tax treatment of virgin timber resources [40] is another provision singled out for perpetuating heavy reliance upon the virgin resource and consequent economic disinterest in the post-consumer resource. The debate over the extent to which these tax laws hinder recycled materials markets is longstanding and is likely to continue. A recent report by the Environmental Law Institute "measures the size of income tax subsidies enjoyed by certain virgin raw materials, calculates the impact which these subsidies may have on the market price of virgin-based products, and estimates the impacts of the price effects on the amount of recycled resources in use. It concludes that tax subsidies alone have little impact on recycling

---

materials must be made on the basis that the items—
(i) are not reasonably available within a reasonable time;
(ii) fail to meet the performance standards set forth in the applicable specifications or fail to meet the reasonable performance standards of the procuring agencies; or
(iii) are only available at an unreasonable price.

33. Section 6002(f), 42 U.S.C.A. § 6962(f).

34. Section 6002(d)(2)(C), 42 U.S.C.A. § 6962(d)(2)(C).

35. Section 6002(d)(2)(B), 42 U.S.C.A. § 6962(d)(2)(B).

36. Section 6002(c)(1)(C), 42 U.S.C.A. § 6962(c)(1)(C). Compare note 26, supra.

37. See Hearings on the Economics of Recycling Waste Materials, Before the Subcomm. on Fiscal Policy of the Joint Economic Comm., 92d Cong., 1st Sess. (1971) [hereinafter cited as 1971 Joint Hearings].

38. Environmental Protection Agency, Analysis of Federal Programs Affecting Solid Waste Generation and Recycling 4–6 (1972).

39. Environmental Protection Agency, Waste Oil Study: Preliminary Report to the Congress, Apr. 1973, at 49.

40. Int.Rev.Code of 1954, § 631.

and conservation of depletable resources." [41] Of course, tax policies exist for reasons other than their coincidental impact on the use of recycled materials. Perhaps because of this, before the Congress for several years spokesmen for the National Association of Secondary Materials Industries have refrained from urging the abolition of tax advantages for virgin producers in favor of comparable advantages for recyclers.[42] Skeptical staffers refer to the phenomenon as the double pickpocket theory of tax reform.

Less well known but of considerable importance are provisions in the tax laws influencing investments in resource recovery facilities. Section 169 of the Internal Revenue Code permits rapid amortization of facilities which serve an add-on air and water pollution control function.[43] The narrow definition of qualifying facilities [44] tends to discourage investments in resource recovery systems. Similarly, Section 103(c) [45] of the Internal Revenue Code permits industry to finance the cost of air and water pollution control facilities through the mechanism of tax exempt municipal bonds. This time it was the Treasury Department, not the Congress, that insisted upon a narrow definition of qualifying facilities to prevent huge revenue losses.[46] The limitation confines the benefits of tax exempt financing to cruder end-of-the-pipe treatment instead of more sophisticated advanced processing or resource recovery.

A third important policy influencing recycled materials usage is that of freight rates. One study insists, for example, that ocean freight rates from west coast ports "effectively may preclude wastepaper from being competitive with virgin pulpwood in foreign markets." [47] More exports has meant a greater domestic wastepaper

41. Comment, Federal Tax Policy Has Only Modest Impact on Recycling, Environmental Law Institute Study Concludes, 6 ELR 10041 (1976). The report estimates that "the long-run impact of current virgin material tax subsidies may reduce the quantities of materials which would otherwise be recycled by as much as the following: paper—1.5 percent, steel—3 to 6 percent, copper—0.9 percent, lead—0.8 percent, and aluminum—1.7 percent." Id. at 10042.

42. See Hearings on Resource Conservation and Recycling, Before the Subcomm. on Environment of the Senate Comm. on Commerce, S.Doc. No. 56, 93d Cong., 1st Sess. 362–82 (1973) (statement of M. J. Mighdoll, Executive Vice President, National Association of Secondary Materials Industries).

43. Int.Rev.Code of 1954, § 169.

44. Id. § 169(d) reads:
The term 'certified pollution control facility' means a new identifiable treatment facility which is used in connection with a plant or other property in operation before January 1, 1969, to abate or control water or atmospheric pollution or contamination by removing, altering, dispensing or storing of pollutants, contaminants, waste or heat
. . . .

45. Id. § 103(c).

46. 40 Fed.Reg. 36371 (1975), proposing to amend Income Tax Regs. § 1.103–8; see Hearings on the Tax Reform Act of 1975, Before the House Comm. on Ways and Means, 94th Cong., 1st Sess. 14 (1975).

47. Hearings on Resource Conservation and Recycling, Before the Subcomm. on Environment of the Senate Comm.

recovery rate.[48] Claiming discrimination, shippers of wastepaper from the United States west coast to the Far East in 1972 challenged the governing rate structure in what became a major adjudicatory proceeding before the Federal Maritime Commission.[49] Evidence adduced at the hearing establishes that sometimes the costs of shipping wastepaper would be twice that of shipping an equivalent load of virgin woodpulp. Thus far, however, legal decision-makers have not been moved to invalidate these gross disparities under pertinent provisions of the Shipping Act.[50] Decision has been long delayed on the ground that the decision in Aberdeen & Rockfish R.R. v. Students Challenging Regulatory Agency Procedures (SCRAP II)[51] necessitated another environmental impact assessment to remedy defects in the analysis initially prepared by the Commission.[52]

For several years, the debate over the effect of freight rates on recycling has focused on the policies of the Interstate Commerce Commission. As with the shipping rates of the Federal Maritime Commission, there is no question that ICC railroad freight rates work to the disadvantage of the shippers of secondary materials who at times pay as much as thirty to forty percent more for services along the same route than their primary materials competitors.[53] Although the proposition is one of those subject to perpetual debate, the Environmental Protection Agency is convinced that freight rates make a difference in secondary materials markets: "For lower value secondary materials such as scrap iron, wastepaper, glass cullet, and scrap rubber, the freight rate is a substantial fraction of the overall delivered cost. For these materials a significant adjustment of freight rates could cause a significant price change and, if the demand is elastic, a corresponding change in consumption."[54]

The well known *SCRAP* litigation, challenging ICC rate policies, has produced important decisions on the law of standing[55] and the

on Commerce, S.Doc.No. 56, 93d Cong., 1st Sess. 221 (1973) (statement of Samuel Hale, Jr., Deputy Assistant Administrator, Solid Waste Management Program, EPA) [hereinafter cited as 1973 Senate Recycling Hearings].

48. Environmental Protection Agency, Trends in Wastepaper Exports and Their Effects on Domestic Markets 16–17 (1974).

49. FMC Dkt. No. 72–35, Pacific Westbound Conference—Investigation of Rates, Sales and Practices Pertaining to the Movement of Wastepaper from United States West Coast to the Far East.

50. 46 U.S.C.A. §§ 814–16.

51. 422 U.S. 289, 95 S.Ct. 2336, 45 L.Ed.2d 191 (1975); see § 7.7 below.

52. 40 Fed.Reg. 50750 (1975).

53. 1971 Joint Hearings, supra note 37, at 16 (statement of M. J. Mighdoll, National Association of Secondary Materials Industries).

54. 1973 Senate Recycling Hearings, supra note 47, at 243 (statement of Samuel Hale, Jr., Deputy Assistant Administrator, Solid Waste Management Program EPA).

55. United States v. Students Challenging Regulatory Agency Procedures (SCRAP) (I), 412 U.S. 669, 93 S.Ct. 2405, 37 L.Ed.2d 254 (1973); see § 1.6 above. A thorough discussion

meaning of the National Environmental Policy Act [56] but precious little on the underlying issues of rate discrimination and recycling. It is perhaps significant that environmental values now must be weighed at points in the course of the ratemaking process but, apart from a few delays, substantial relief to the complainants has not been forthcoming in the principal rulemaking [57] around which the SCRAP litigation swirled. In other proceedings, the ICC has granted hold-downs on tariffs on certain scrap commodities when the railroads had petitioned for general rate increases.[58] The ICC also has attempted to mitigate the secondary materials industry's railroad freight rate barriers by establishing wide-open licensing privileges for motor carriers transporting waste products for reuse.[59] It is now possible for any truck to obtain a license without fee to carry post-consumer waste materials in interstate commerce.[60]

A fourth example of a federal policy working indirectly to discourage recycling is the Federal Trade Commission's requirements that certain rerefined oils be labeled as "used oil." Section 383 [61] of the Energy Policy and Conservation Act of 1975 strongly affirms a purpose of encouraging the recycling of used oil and towards that end directs the National Bureau of Standards to develop test procedures "for the determination of substantial equivalency of re-refined or otherwise processed used oil . . . with new oil for a particular end use." [62] The Bureau of Standards must report on its procedures within ninety days to the Federal Trade Commission, which then promulgates rules on test procedures for determining "substantial equivalency" and labeling standards applicable to containers of recycled oil.[63] The labeling standards must permit "any container of recycled oil to bear a label indicating any particular end use for which a determination of substantial equivalency has been made . . . . ." [64]

of the early phases of the *SCRAP* litigation is found in 1 F. Grad, Environmental Law § 4.5, at 4–79 to –90 (1975).

56. Aberdeen & Rockfish R. R. v. SCRAP (II), 422 U.S. 289, 95 S.Ct. 2336, 45 L.Ed.2d 191 (1975); §§ 7.6, 7.7 below.

57. ICC Dkt. Ex Parte No. 281, Increased Freight Rates, 1972, 341 ICC 288. In Ex Parte No. 270 the ICC has initiated an investigation into the entire basic rate structure. See also Regional Rail Reorganization Act of 1973, § 603, 45 U.S.C.A. § 793; Railroad Revitalization and Regulatory Reform Act of 1976, § 204, 45 U.S.C.A. § 793 note.

58. ICC Dkt. Ex Parte No. 267, Increased Freight Rates, 1971.

59. ICC Dkt. Ex Parte No. MC–85; see Chemical Leaman Tank Lines, Inc. v. United States, 368 F.Supp. 925 (D.Del.1973), 53 Tex.L.Rev. 539 (1975) (discerning no rational basis for a general finding that carriers of recyclable waste products serve the public interest).

60. Ibid.

61. 42 U.S.C.A. § 6363; see note 28, supra.

62. Section 383(c), 42 U.S.C.A. § 6363 (c).

63. Section 383(d)(1)(A), 42 U.S.C.A. § 6363(d)(1)(A).

64. Section 383(d)(1)(B), 42 U.S.C.A. § 6363(d)(1)(B).

It was the conferees' understanding,[65] repeated in the statute,[66] that the FTC's regulatory authority was circumscribed to prevent the Commission from requiring recycled oil, otherwise qualified, "to be labeled with any term, phrase or description which connotes less than substantial equivalency with new oil for a particular purpose."

Numerous other regulatory powers of various federal agencies affect waste disposal and resource recovery in direct and subtle ways.[67] Illustrative are the responsibilities of the Federal Highway Administration (clearing and demolition specifications), the Federal Trade Commission (packaging regulation and labeling), National Bureau of Standards (development of voluntary product standards), Office of Community Development in the Department of Housing and Urban Development (solid waste generation and salvage aspects of building techniques) [68] and various entities in the Department of the Interior (disposal practices of mining activities conducted on federal lands), and the Defense Department (procurement and stockpiling). These and other policies are fair game for debate and legal challenge if and when they discourage resource recovery.[69]

§ 6.6 Energy Conservation

The federal law of energy, which is vast [1] and growing at a pace astonishing even to observers of environmental law,[2] reaches the principal energy sources (oil, gas, coal, hydropower and nuclear) at most points of the energy supply system (extraction, processing, electricity production, transportation and ultimate consumption). Singled out for treatment here is the Energy Policy and Conservation Act of

---

65. Comm. of Conference, Energy Policy and Conservation Act, S.Rep. No. 516, 94th Cong., 1st Sess. 184 (1975).

66. Section 383(e)(2), 42 U.S.C.A. § 6363(e)(2).

67. Environmental Protection Agency, Analysis of Federal Programs Affecting Solid Waste Generation and Recycling (1972).

68. See Comptroller General, Need for Effective Controls of Timber-Cutting Practices in Pacific-Northwest Region (1966).

69. See Environmental Defense Fund, Inc. v. Mathews, 410 F.Supp. 336, 6 ELR 20369 (D.D.C.1976) (NEPA requires consideration of environmental factors in connection with Food and Drug Administration decision to authorize use of nonreturnable plastic beverage containers).

1. See Stoel, Energy, in Environmental Law Institute, Federal Environmental Law 928 (E. L. Dolgin & T. G. P. Guilbert eds. 1974).

2. See, e. g., Caldwell, Energy Crisis and Environmental Law: Paradox of Conflict and Reinforcement, 20 N.Y.L. Forum 751 (1975); Dreyfus & Grundy, Influence of the Energy Crisis upon the Future of Environmental Policy, 3 Environmental Affairs 252 (1974); Howard, Energy Crisis and its Impact upon Environmental Law, 20 N.Y.L.Forum 711 (1975); Plumlee, Perspectives in U. S. Energy Resource Development, 3 Environmental Affairs 1 (1974); Stang, Energy Legislation of the 93rd Congress—Policy Trends and Implications for the Future, 26 Oil & Gas Inst. 167 (1975). See also ALI–ABA, Environmental Law–V, 269 (1975) (listing 42 major energy laws enacted by the 93d Congress).

1975,[3] which as the name suggests is aimed at saving depletable resources that otherwise would be lost. Even the most ardent proponents of energy recovery from solid waste recognize that successful mining of the landfill would provide only a small percentage (less than 5) of the fuel needs of all utilities,[4] supplied mostly today by oil, gas and coal. The saving of fossil fuels in other ways has obvious environmental advantages. To mention but one plausible example, if by the 1980's new automobiles could improve fuel efficiency to an average of 20 miles per gallon, the reduction in gasoline demand would represent "four large oil refineries and numerous oil wells, pipelines and tankers." [5]

The Energy Policy and Conservation Act attacks the wasting of energy resources at several vulnerable points: (1) automotive fuel economy; (2) consumer products other than automobiles; and (3) industrial usage. The Act also addresses (4) state and federal energy conservation programs.

a. *Automotive Fuel Economy*

Pursuant to Section 10 of the Energy Supply and Environmental Coordination Act of 1974,[6] the Department of Transportation and the Environmental Protection Agency issued a joint report to Congress entitled "Potential for Motor Vehicle Fuel Economy Improvement." [7] The report's principal conclusion is that it is "practicable to achieve" with "little further price increase" a 20 percent "fuel economy improvement" in 1980 model year vehicles compared to those of 1974.[8] This report was instrumental in persuading the Congress to embrace legislation on automotive fuel economy, which appears as a new Title V to the Motor Vehicle Information and Cost Savings Act.[9]

The legislative framework for the auto fuel economy standards resembles closely that for the auto emission standards,[10] and it is reasonable to anticipate a similar evolution of regulations and case law. Section 502 [11] establishes an average fuel economy standard, expressed in miles per gallon, for passenger autos manufactured in any model

3. Pub.L. No. 94–163, 89 Stat. 871, 15 U.S.C.A. § 2001 et seq., 42 U.S.C.A. § 6201 et seq. See also Energy Conservation and Production Act, Pub.L. No. 94–385, 90 Stat. 1125, 42 U.S.C.A. § 6801 et seq. (containing reporting provisions on rate design and the formulation of energy conservation standards for newly constructed buildings).

4. EPA, Third Report to Congress on Resource Recovery and Waste Reduction 33–34 (1975).

5. Council on Environmental Quality, Fifth Ann.Rep. 105 (1974).

6. Pub.L. No. 93–319, 88 Stat. 261, 42 U.S.C.A. § 1857–6f.

7. Dep't of Transp. & Environmental Protection Agency, Report to the Congress: Potential for Motor Vehicle Fuel Economy Improvement (1974) [hereinafter cited as DOT–EPA Fuel Economy Report].

8. Id. at 1.

9. 15 U.S.C.A. § 1901 et seq.

10. See §§ 3.14, 3.15 above.

11. 15 U.S.C.A. § 2002.

year—18.0 for 1978, 19.0 for 1979, 20.0 for 1980, 27.5 for 1985 and thereafter. For the model years 1981–84, the standard is to be prescribed in a rulemaking by the Secretary of Transportation.[12] The term fuel economy means "the average number of miles traveled by an automobile per gallon of gasoline" or equivalent amount of other fuel, as fixed by the EPA Administrator.[13] Determining this average, which is a critical regulatory step, requires the Administrator to make separate calculations for domestically manufactured autos and captive imports (marketed in the U.S. but manufactured abroad), with each category required to meet the standard.[14] Fuel economy tests, expected to be conducted in conjunction with tests for the auto emission standards, shall be in accordance with "the procedures utilized by the EPA Administrator for model year 1975 (weighed 55 percent urban cycle, and 45 percent highway cycle), or procedures which yield comparable results."[15] This testing, which must account for differences between fuel economy and fuel consumption,[16] will be shrouded with the same uncertainties that often make the method of measurement the most important component of any technological standard.[17]

The Secretary of Transportation is given powers to exempt small manufacturers who meet certain conditions [18] and modify the standard applicable to any manufacturer for model year 1978, 1979 and 1980. This relaxation depends upon findings that "a Federal standards fuel economy reduction is likely to exist for [the] manufacturer for the model year to which the application relates" and that the manufacturer has "applied a reasonably selected technology." [19] The idea is to relax fuel economy standards applicable to any manufacturer whose fuel economy efforts are penalized by compliance with other laws such as emission or noise standards.[20] A "reasonably selected technology"

---

12. Section 502(a)(3), 15 U.S.C.A. § 2002(a)(3).

13. Section 501(b), 15 U.S.C.A. § 2001(b).

14. Sections 503(a)–(c), 15 U.S.C.A. §§ 2003(a)–(c).

15. Section 503(d), 15 U.S.C.A. § 2003(d).

16. See DOT–EPA Fuel Economy Report, supra note 7, at 17:
A certain percentage increase or decrease in fuel economy *does not equal* the same percentage decrease or increase in fuel consumption. For example, one car getting 20 mpg has 33 percent better fuel economy than one with 15 mpg. However, its fuel consumption is only 25 percent less. Thus the 33 percent increase in fuel economy gained from improving a 15 mpg car to 20 mpg provides only a 25 percent fuel savings per mile. (emphasis in original).

17. § 3.14 above; cf. Natural Resources Defense Council, Inc. v. Ruckelshaus, 359 F.Supp. 1028, 3 ELR 20787 (D.D.C.1972) (holding that EPA Administrator acted within his discretion in modifying test procedures for auto emission standards); Portland Cement Ass'n v. Train (II), 168 U.S.App.D.C. 248, 513 F.2d 506, 5 ELR 2034 (1975) cert. denied, 423 U.S. 1025.

18. Section 502(c), 15 U.S.C.A. § 2002(c).

19. Section 502(d), 15 U.S.C.A. § 2002(d).

20. See ibid.

means a technology determined by the Secretary to be "reasonable for a manufacturer to select, considering (i) the Nation's need to improve the fuel economy of its automobiles, and (ii) the energy savings, economic costs and lead-time requirements associated with alternative technologies practically available to such manufacturer."[21] The term "technology" must be read broadly and "may include such items as vehicle weight, engine displacement, transmissions, streamlining, radial tires, as well as technology specifically related to meeting Federal automobile standards."[22] But a technology cannot be "reasonably selected" unless it "minimizes" fuel economy reduction[23] for the obvious reason that a legal reward should not be extended to those who do not make the best effort to minimize the conflict between fuel economy and other auto standards.

The Secretary also may amend the average fuel economy standard specified for model years 1985 or thereafter (27.5) to a level which he determines is the "maximum feasible average fuel economy level" for the model year, except that any amendment raising the level in excess of 27.5 miles per gallon or lowering it below 26.0 miles per gallon requires the approval of each House of the Congress.[24] In language reminiscent of the suspension provisions of the Clean Air Act,[25] the Act requires[26] the Secretary to consider the following factors in determining maximum feasible fuel economy: (1) technological feasibility; (2) economic practicability; (3) the effect of other federal motor vehicle standards on fuel economy; and (4) the need of the Nation to conserve energy.

Consumer leverage against gas guzzlers is dependent largely upon success of a labeling program. The law requires each manufacturer to affix, and each dealer to maintain, "in a prominent place," a label on each auto manufactured in any model year after 1976.[27] The label must indicate the fuel economy of the automobile, estimated annual fuel costs associated with its operation and the range of fuel economy of comparable automobiles.[28] The EPA Administrator also must pre-

21. Section 502(d)(3)(A), 15 U.S.C.A. § 2002(d)(3)(A).

22. Comm. of Conference, Energy Policy and Conservation Act, S.Rep.No. 516, 94th Cong., 1st Sess. 156 (1975) [hereinafter cited as Conference Report].

23. Ibid.

24. Section 502(a)(4), 15 U.S.C.A. § 2002(a)(4).

25. See § 3.14 above.

26. Section 502(e), 15 U.S.C.A. § 2002(e).

27. Section 506(a)(1), 15 U.S.C.A. § 2006(a)(1).

28. Ibid. Labeling rules applicable to model year 1976 automobiles "shall require that a label be affixed" which discloses only the fuel economy of such automobile, in accordance with procedures established in the [Environmental Protection Agency] and [Federal Energy Administration] Voluntary Fuel Economy Labeling Program for Automobiles." Conference Report, supra note 22, at 151, citing 40 Fed.Reg. 26058 (1975) (establishing the voluntary labeling program).

Sec. 6.6 ENERGY CONSERVATION 657

pare a "simple and readily understandable booklet containing data on fuel economy of automobiles manufactured in each model year."[29] The fuel economy labeling requirements developed by the Administrator are likely to be strenuously contested if the octane labeling requirements before them are any indicator.[30] Violations of fuel economy labeling rules are treated as violations of the Automobile Information Disclosure Act and the Federal Trade Commission Act,[31] which means they are to be remedied mostly by cease and desist orders. The labels are not to be treated as warranties,[32] which presumably means they are idle puffing insofar as the buyer is concerned.

The fuel economy legislation contains none of the in-use quality controls associated with auto emissions—warranties, recall and certification.[33] Certain conduct is made unlawful, including the failure of a manufacturer to comply with any average fuel economy standards.[34] Civil penalties are prescribed for violations, pursuant to an elaborate procedure that will represent a major legal event when first invoked.[35]

Other features of the automotive fuel economy provisions are predictable—fuel economy standards are given a preemptive effect, with the exception of autos procured by local governments for their own use.[36] The federal government's procurement power is commissioned in the aid of fuel economy.[37] The Federal Trade Commission is directed to establish a program "for systematically examining fuel economy representations made with respect to retrofit devices."[38] A research effort by the Energy Research and Development Administration (ERDA) investigating advanced electric and hybrid automotive technologies also has been established.[39] The Administrator of ERDA

29. Section 506(b)(1), 15 U.S.C.A. § 2006(b)(1).

30. See Hearings on Consumer Fuel Disclosure Act of 1975, Before the Subcomm. on Consumers of the Senate Comm. on Commerce, 94th Cong., 1st Sess. 42–51 (1975) (testimony of Louis V. Lombardo, President, Public Interest Campaign). The FTC's power to require octane labeling was confirmed in National Petroleum Refiners Ass'n v. Federal Trade Comm., 157 U.S.App.D.C. 83, 482 F.2d 672 (1973), cert. denied 415 U.S. 951 (1974).

31. Section 506(c)(1), 15 U.S.C.A. § 2006(c)(1).

32. Section 506(d), 15 U.S.C.A. § 2006(d) reads:
Any disclosure with respect to fuel economy or estimated annual fuel cost which is required to be made under the provisions of this section shall not create an express or implied warranty under State or Federal law that such fuel economy will be achieved, or that such cost will not be exceeded, under conditions of actual use.

33. § 3.15 above.

34. Section 507, 15 U.S.C.A. § 2007.

35. Section 508, 15 U.S.C.A. § 2008.

36. Section 509, 15 U.S.C.A. § 2009.

37. Section 510, 15 U.S.C.A. § 2010.

38. Section 511, 15 U.S.C.A. § 2011.

39. Electric and Hybrid Vehicle Research, Development, and Demonstration Act of 1976, Pub.L. No. 94–413, § 4, 90 Stat. 1262, 15 U.S.C.A. § 2503.

is directed to promulgate performance standards and to contract for the purchase or lease of 2,500 electric or hybrid vehicles within two years and of 5,000 additional advanced vehicles within four and a half years to be used by federal agencies, state and local governments and other persons in order to demonstrate the feasibility of electric and hybrid automotive technologies.[40]

b. *Consumer Products Other Than Automobiles*

For consumer products other than automobiles, the Energy Conservation Act stakes out a regulatory program conforming closely to what has become the congressional model for treating technological and environmental ills. It is replete with deadlines and reporting requirements, vests considerable discretion in administrative authorities but confines it within bounds, defined by reference to technology and economics, and relies for enforcement on civil penalties and citizen suits.

The Act defines as a "covered product" thirteen major energy using consumer products—refrigerators and refrigerator freezers, freezers, dishwashers, clothes dryers, water heaters, room air conditioners, home heating equipment other than furnaces, television sets, kitchen ranges and ovens, clothes washers, humidifiers and dehumidifiers, central air conditioners and furnaces.[41] The Administrator of the Federal Energy Administration has discretion to expand the category of a "covered product."[42] Recognizing the inseparability of test methodologies and standards, the Act goes into considerable detail on the development of test procedures.[43] The Administrator of FEA is obliged to direct the National Bureau of Standards to develop test procedures for determining "(A) estimated annual operating costs of covered products . . ., and (B) at least one other useful measure of energy consumption of such products which the Administrator determines is likely to assist consumers in making purchasing decisions."[44] Any test procedures so developed "shall be reasonably designed to produce test results which reflect energy efficiency, energy use, or estimated annual operating cost of a covered product during a representative average use cycle (as determined by the Administrator), and shall not be unduly burdensome to conduct."[45] The idea is to calculate the energy consumption of a product, translate it into dollar terms, and present it so as to facilitate comparison shopping.

As with automobiles, a major regulatory premise for other products rests on labeling. Subject to some exceptions, the Federal Trade Commission is expected to prescribe labeling rules applicable to all

---

40. Id. § 7, 15 U.S.C.A. § 2506.

41. Sections 321(a)(2), 322(a), 42 U.S.C.A. §§ 6291(a)(2), 6292(a).

42. Section 322(b), 42 U.S.C.A. § 6292(b).

43. Section 323, 42 U.S.C.A. § 6293.

44. Section 323(a)(2), 42 U.S.C.A. § 6293(a)(2).

45. Section 323(b)(1), 42 U.S.C.A. § 6293(b)(1).

Sec. 6.6   ENERGY CONSERVATION   659

covered products.[46] The rules usually will require the labeling of each product so as to disclose its "estimated annual operating cost" and "information respecting the range of estimated annual operating costs for covered products to which the rule applies." [47] Alternatively, the rules may call for "a different useful measure of energy consumption" and a range appropriate for comparison purposes if a judgment is made [48] that the disclosure of estimated annual operating cost is not economically or technologically feasible or would not be likely to assist consumers in making purchasing decisions.[49]

The law goes beyond labeling to require the FEA Administrator to prescribe an "energy efficiency improvement target" for covered consumer products.[50] The targets must be designed so that "the aggregate energy efficiency" of the first ten categories of covered products (excluding only humidifiers, central air conditioners and furnaces) "which are manufactured in the calendar year 1980 will exceed the aggregate energy efficiency achieved by products of all such types manufactured in calendar year 1972 by a percentage which is the maximum percentage improvement which the Administrator determines is economically and technologically feasible, but which in any case is not less than 20 percent." [51] Within this awkward phrase lurks a host of administrative problems, including the assignment of efficiency improvements among product categories included in the average, the meaning of economic and technological feasibility, and the application of the mandated 20 percent improvement if it conflicts with the chosen economic and technical ceilings. Understandably, the FEA Administrator also is given authority to prescribe, within economic and technological limits, energy efficiency improvement targets for humidifiers, air conditioners and furnaces,[52] and to modify the targets he selects for any product.[53]

Reporting requirements are imposed upon manufacturers to help the Administrator determine whether the targets will be met.[54] If it appears that a target is "not likely to be achieved," the Administrator must initiate a proceeding to establish an energy efficiency standard for the product type. An energy efficiency standard is a performance standard prescribing a minimum level of energy efficiency for a prod-

46. Section 324, 42 U.S.C.A. § 6294.

47. Sections 324(c)(1)(A), (B), 42 U.S.C.A. §§ 6294(c)(1)(A), (B).

48. The assignment of decision-making authority between FEA and FTC is not altogether clear. Compare section 324(a)(2), 42 U.S.C.A. § 6294(a)(2) with section 324 (c)(1), 42 U.S.C.A. § 6294(c)(1).

49. Section 324(c)(1), 42 U.S.C.A. § 6294(c)(1).

50. Section 325(a)(1)(A), 42 U.S.C.A. § 6295(a)(1)(A).

51. Section 325(a)(1)(B), 42 U.S.C.A. § 6295(a)(1)(B).

52. Section 325(a)(2), 42 U.S.C.A. § 6295(a)(2).

53. Section 325(a)(3), 42 U.S.C.A. § 6295(a)(3).

54. Section 325(a)(4), 42 U.S.C.A. § 6295(a)(4).

uct by reference to the testing procedures.[55] It might establish, for example, a ceiling on annual operating costs for a particular product. As in setting the targets, the Administrator's discretion in establishing standards is hedged sharply. He must determine that the improvement in energy efficiency called for is "technologically feasible and economically justified" and that a labeling rule is "not likely to be sufficient" to bring about the maximum energy efficiency achievable.[56] This elevates labeling to the status of the most favored regulatory option. For purposes of setting standards, an improvement of energy efficiency is "economically justified" if "the benefits of reduced energy consumption, and the savings in operating costs throughout the estimated average life of the covered product, outweigh—

> (i) any increase to purchasers in initial charges for, or maintenance expenses of, the covered product which is likely to result from the imposition of the standard, (ii) any lessening of the utility or the performance of the covered product, (iii) any negative effects on competition." [57]

This provision calls for a systematic cost-benefit analysis (replete with an evaluation of incommensurables such as negative effects on competition) which the courts usually do not find in legislation authorizing the establishment of environmental performance standards.[58]

The Act makes unlawful several actions inconsistent with the statute's regulatory aims—distributing in commerce a new product contrary to the labeling rules or applicable energy efficiency standard,[59] rendering illegible any label,[60] and so on. As with the auto standards, enforcement relies chiefly upon civil penalty provisions, subject to a requirement that violations be committed knowingly and a ceiling of not more than $100 for each violation.[61] Provisions also are included for relief by way of injunction [62] and, under some circumstances, by citizen suit.[63] Preemption is addressed in a fashion giving the FEA Administrator discretion to determine whether a state energy efficiency standard is preempted by federal law.[64]

c. *Industrial Energy Conservation*

The Energy Conservation Act stops short of regulation and compulsion on the subject of industrial energy usage. The FEA Admin-

---

55. Sections 321(a), (b), 42 U.S.C.A. § 6291(a), (b).

56. Section 325(a)(4)(C), 42 U.S.C.A. § 6295(a)(4)(C).

57. Section 325(a)(4)(D), 42 U.S.C.A. § 6295(a)(4)(D).

58. See §§ 3.10, 3.14, 4.12 above.

59. Sections 332(a)(1), (5), 42 U.S.C.A. §§ 6302(a)(1), (5).

60. Section 332(a)(2), 42 U.S.C.A. § 6302(a)(2).

61. Section 333, 42 U.S.C.A. § 6303.

62. Section 334, 42 U.S.C.A. § 6304.

63. Section 335, 42 U.S.C.A. § 6305.

64. Section 327, 42 U.S.C.A. § 6297. Compare § 5.8 above (discussing EPA role in determining pre-emptive effect of federal noise regulation of transportation sources).

istrator is directed, in consultation with the Secretary of Commerce and the Administrator of the Energy Research and Development Administration, to initiate and maintain a program "to promote increased energy efficiency by American industry" and "to establish voluntary energy efficiency improvement targets for at least the 10 most energy-consumptive major energy-consuming industries."[65] Each target "shall be established at the level which represents the maximum feasible improvement in energy efficiency which [the] industry can achieve by 1980."[66] In making this determination, the Administrator shall consider, among other criteria, "the technological feasibility and economic practicability of utilizing alternative operating procedures and more energy efficient technologies."[67] The Administrator is given discretion to establish a target for any major energy-consuming industry outside of the top ten.[68] That a target is something to be commended and praised but not necessarily met is suggested by this explicit legislative assessment of its legal significance: "no liability shall attach, and no civil or criminal penalties may be imposed, for any failure to meet any industrial energy efficiency improvement target . . . . ."[69]

The Act also imposes mild reporting requirements on industrial energy users. Within ninety days of enactment, the Administrator was obliged to identify each major energy-consuming industry in the United States and establish "a priority ranking of such industries on the basis of their respective total annual energy consumption." Within each industry so identified, a further subdivision is required, singling out each corporation which consumes at least one trillion British thermal units of energy per year (a BTU is a heat measure serving as a common denominator for all sources of energy) and is among the top fifty energy consumers within each industry.[70] The chief executive officer of each of these large corporate users, if within an industry covered by an energy efficiency improvement target, must make annual reports "on the progress which the corporation has made in improving its energy efficiency."[71] Corporations with an "adequate voluntary reporting program", as determined by the Administrator, may be exempted from the reporting requirements.[72] The Administrator himself must report annually to the Congress and the President on the industrial energy efficiency program.[73]

---

65. Section 372, 42 U.S.C.A. § 6342.

66. Section 374(a)(2), 42 U.S.C.A. § 6344(a)(2).

67. Section 374(b)(2), 42 U.S.C.A. § 6344(b)(2).

68. Section 374(c), 42 U.S.C.A. § 6344(c).

69. Section 376(f), 42 U.S.C.A. § 6346(f).

70. Section 373, 42 U.S.C.A. § 6343. The ranking was issued in 41 Fed. Reg. 12766 (Mar. 26, 1976).

71. Section 375(a), 42 U.S.C.A. § 6345(a).

72. Section 376(g)(1), 42 U.S.C.A. § 6346(g)(1).

73. Section 375(c), 42 U.S.C.A. § 6345(c).

d. *State and Federal Energy Conservation Programs*

Drawing on the experience of the implementation plans under the Clean Air Act,[74] Congress also launched a program of federal guidance for state energy conservation plans in the Energy Policy and Conservation Act. Congress affirmed a purpose "to promote the conservation of energy and reduce the rate of growth of energy demand by authorizing the Administrator to establish procedures and guidelines for the development and implementation of specific State energy conservation programs and to provide Federal financial and technical assistance to States in support of such programs."[75] Federal guidelines are called for on two types of state plans—an energy conservation feasibility report and an energy conservation plan. The feasibility report must assess the feasibility of establishing a State energy conservation goal which shall consist of a reduction "of 5 percent or more in the total amount of energy consumed in [the] state in the year 1980 from the projected energy consumption for [the] state in the year 1980."[76] The feasibility report also must include a proposal for the development of a state energy conservation plan to achieve the goal.[77]

The state energy conservation plans may prove to be ambitious undertakings. Each plan, which may be submitted by a governor of a state for FEA approval, should spell out scheduled progress towards achievement of the state energy conservation goal and contain "a detailed description of the requirements, including the estimated cost of implementation and the estimated energy savings, associated with each functional category of energy conservation included in the state energy conservation plan."[78] To be eligible for federal funding, each state energy conservation plan shall include—

(1) mandatory lighting efficiency standards for public buildings;

(2) programs to promote the availability and use of carpools, vanpools and public transportation . . .;

(3) mandatory standards and policies relating to energy efficiency to govern the procurement practices of the [the] State and its political subdivisions;

(4) mandatory thermal efficiency standards and insulation requirements for new and renovated buildings;

(5) a traffic law or regulation which, to the maximum extent practicable consistent with safety, permits the operator of a motor

---

74. See §§ 3.5–.8 above.

75. Section 361(b), 42 U.S.C.A. § 6321(b).

76. Section 362(a)(1), 42 U.S.C.A. § 6322(a)(1).

77. Section 362(a)(2), 42 U.S.C.A. § 6322(a)(2). The Federal Administration Agency guidelines on the feasibility reports add very little to the statutory requirements. 41 Fed.Reg. 8335 (1976), adding 10 CFR pt. 420.

78. Sections 362(b)(1), (2), 42 U.S.C.A. §§ 6322(b)(1), (2).

Sec. 6.6   ENERGY CONSERVATION   663

vehicle to turn . . . right at a red stop light after stopping.[79]

State energy conservation plans also may include restrictions on the operation of public buildings and on the use of decorative or nonessential lighting, transportation controls (which are plans designed to reduce energy consumed in transportation),[80] public information programs and "any other appropriate method or programs to conserve and improve efficiency in the use of energy."[81] Standby plans for conserving energy "during a severe energy supply interruption" are eligible for separate funding.[82]

Unlike the Clean Air Act, the Energy Supply and Conservation Act is wholly dependent for compliance upon the carrot, not the stick. The FEA Administrator is without power to require the filing of state plans, much less substitute his own plans for those deemed inadequate. The Administrator is empowered to extend federal assistance to develop a state plan and to implement parts of it submitted to and approved by the Administrator.[83] The conferees expected that all approved plans would receive federal assistance, subject to the understanding that the Administrator would seek to allocate funds among states "to achieve the greatest aggregate savings in energy affecting the greatest number of people."[84] At the request of a governor, the Administrator must provide information and technical assistance, including model state laws and proposed regulations relating to energy conservation.[85] It is inevitable that the next several years will bring significant new direction to state laws taking aim at conserving valuable energy resources.[86]

The legislation that seeks to inspire energy conservation at the state level does not neglect the federal government. The President is directed to develop and implement mandatory standards on energy conservation and energy efficiency to govern the procurement policies and decisions of the agencies.[87] The President also is instructed to develop and implement a 10-year plan for energy conservation with

79. Section 362(c), 42 U.S.C.A. § 6322(c).

80. Section 366(8), 42 U.S.C.A. § 6326(8). Compare § 3.16 above (discussing transportation controls under the Clean Air Act).

81. Section 362(d), 42 U.S.C.A. § 6322(d).

82. Section 362(e), 42 U.S.C.A. § 6322(e).

83. Section 363(b)(1), 42 U.S.C.A. § 6323(b)(1).

84. Conference Report, supra note 22, at 179–80.

85. Section 363(a), 42 U.S.C.A. § 6323(a).

86. The Environmental Law Institute's Energy Conservation Project aims to develop a series of handbooks addressed to state and local officials and others on the subject of strategies for conserving energy. The Project publishes a newsletter, Energy Conservation Project Report, containing useful information. Illustrative is the article by Harwood, Planning for Energy Conservation, Project Rep. No. 5, Mar. 1976.

87. Section 381(a)(1), 42 U.S.C.A. § 6361(a)(1).

respect to buildings owned or leased by United States' agencies.[88] The FEA Administrator is directed to pursue a "responsible public education program" (to be distinguished presumably from an irresponsible one) to encourage energy conservation and energy efficiency and to promote vanpooling and carpooling arrangements.[89] Several agencies were given sixty days to report to the Congress on what they have been doing to conserve energy—the Civil Aeronautics Board, the Interstate Commerce Commission, the Federal Maritime Commission, the Federal Power Commission, and the Federal Aviation Administration.[90] Several specific steps were mandated to encourage the recycling of used oil, one of the conspicuous and embarrassing examples of domestic resource waste.[91]

§ 6.7 The State Role

Virtually all state governments today have responsibilities on the subject of solid waste.[1] Major categories of regulation are likely to be assigned to specialized agencies—timber removal to a department of forest practices, mining to a department of natural resources, solid waste along roadways to the highway department, wastes within public parks to the parks department, agricultural wastes to the department of agriculture.[2] Regulation of collectors or haulers also may be thoroughly dispersed: "[h]auling and disposal of septic tank sludges may be regulated by a separate health department agency; the hauling of diseased animal carcasses may be regulated by an agricultural department; the hauling of hazardous wastes may require special licenses from state departments of transportation or a public safety agency."[3] Further fragmentation may result from the separate legislative treatment of various aspects of the management system—storage, collection, transportation, processing, disposal, recycling. The consequence is not only a conflict among agencies, as where one authority permits open burning in contravention of another's regulations, but also a situation where "comprehensive" state management may be confined to the fraction of the problem represented by residential refuse, and principally the disposal part of that fraction. With

---

88. Section 381(a)(2), 42 U.S.C.A. § 6361(a)(2).

89. Section 381(b)(1), 42 U.S.C.A. § 6361(b)(1).

90. Section 382(a)(1), 42 U.S.C.A. § 6362(a)(1).

91. § 6.5 above.

1. Leading provisions of state law are reproduced in BNA, Environment Reporter: State Solid Waste—Land Use [hereinafter cited as BNA Solid Waste Reporter]. See generally, Massey, Solid Waste Management in North Dakota, 49 N.D.L.Rev. 499 (1973); Note, The Legal Framework of Solid Waste Disposal, 3 Ind.Legal Forum 415 (1970).

2. Council of State Governments, The States' Role in Solid Waste Management: A Task Force Report 18–19 (1973) [hereinafter cited as Council of State Governments Report].

3. Id. at 19. Compare § 6.10 below (hazardous wastes).

this understanding, we will look more closely at the state role as regards residential and commercial solid waste and resource recovery.

a. *Residential and Commercial Solid Waste*

Typically, regulatory legislation takes the form of assigning a statewide agency the power to issue permits to public and private landfill operators, promulgate regulations governing operation of facilities, inspect day to day operations, and apply mild sanctions to correct violations, usually after an administrative hearing.[4] Within this general framework, variations are substantial: licenses or permits may be wholly excused [5] or may require the filing of elaborate plans of operation and application forms.[6] Facilities reached by the licensing scheme may include not only solid waste disposal sites but resource recovery [7] and volume reduction plants (pulverizers, compactors, shredding and bailing plants),[8] incinerators,[9] composting plants,[10] sludge disposal [11] and other industrial solid waste disposal sites.[12] Statewide authority may reach transfer facilities, vehicles and sometimes the entire collection process.[13]

Regulation of operations may be content with excluding hazardous or bulk wastes, such as automobile hulks, from landfills altogether,[14] or may prescribe special provisions for their accommodation.[15] The statutes often ban open dumping,[16] forbid unacceptable methods of

---

4. State Solid Waste Management and Resource Recovery Incentives Act, in 32 Council of State Governments, Suggested State Legislation 63 (1973).

5. E. g., Vermont Solid Waste Law, Vt.Stat.Ann. tit. 24, §§ 2201–04.

6. Florida Resource Recovery and Management Regulations §§ 17–7.10–.11 (1975).

7. Delaware Solid Waste Authority Act, Del.Code Ann. tit. 7, § 6404(1).

8. Michigan Resource Recovery Act, Mich.Comp.Laws § 299.306(1) (defining "volume reduction plant").

9. Arkansas Solid Waste Disposal Regulations § 4 (1973).

10. Ibid.

11. Oregon Solid Waste Regulations § K (1974); see § 4.7 above.

12. Delaware Solid Waste Disposal Regulation § 7 (1974).

13. Delaware Solid Waste Authority Act, Del.Code Ann. tit. 7, § 6404 (defining functions of the Delaware Solid Waste Authority as including "the planning, design, construction, financing, management, ownership, operation and maintenance of solid waste disposal, volume reduction and resources recovery facilities and all related waste reception, transfer, storage, transportation and waste-handling and general support facilities . . .").

14. Alaska Solid Waste Management Regulations, Alas.Admin.Code tit. 18, § 60.030(3) (requires permittee to obtain approval of the Department of Environmental Conservation to process and dispose of hazardous waste). Compare § 6.9 below (discussing auto hulks).

15. Alabama Solid Wastes Disposal Act § 3(a); Code of Ala. tit. 22, § 348(a); Oklahoma Solid Waste Management Regulations § 5.0 (1974); Rhode Island Solid Waste Management Regulations § 5.4.5 (1975).

16. South Carolina Landfill Regulations § IV (1971); see § 6.3 nn. 84 & 89 above.

disposal,[17] preclude use of certain vulnerable sites,[18] and require the more salient protections of a sanitary landfill. General bans against maintaining nuisance conditions are common.[19] Usually by regulation,[20] state agencies spell out the requirements of a sanitary landfill, often in greater detail than the Environmental Protection Agency guidelines.[21] Provisions ordinarily address site selection (perhaps requiring hydrological and soil surveys or an environmental impact statement), operator qualifications, protection of ground and surface waters, litter and vector control, compaction and cover, protection against fire, limited access, scavenging prohibitions and a number of other requirements customarily associated with a properly maintained sanitary landfill.

Enforcement often is qualified substantially by liberal provisions for exemptions, variances and waivers.[22] A variance is available in Minnesota, for example, if the Pollution Control Agency finds "that by reason of exceptional circumstances strict conformity with any provisions of the regulations . . . would cause undue hardship, would be unreasonable, impractical or not feasible under the circumstances.[23]" Hazardous wastes may not be disposed of at ordinary landfills in Mississippi except with the approval of the health department.[24] Possible sanctions run the gamut,[25] ranging from no discernible penalties to criminal and civil sanctions, loss or modification of license, and administrative corrective orders.

Many state enactments have funding provisions, some functioning as classic waste disposal charges. Colorado's statute authorizes counties to create a solid wastes disposal site and facility fund "to pay the

17. Minnesota Solid Waste Disposal Regulations § SW–6 (1973).

18. Ohio Solid Waste Disposal Regulations § HE–24–04 (1968) (forbidding siting in locations creating a hazard to quality of ground or surface water or a health hazard).

19. E. g., Alaska Solid Waste Management Regulations, Alas.Admin. Code tit. 18, § 60.030(2) (requiring operator to control "nuisance conditions"); North Dakota Solid Waste Management Regulations, Dep't of Health Reg. No. 86, § 3.1 (1971) (requiring storage of solid waste so "that it cannot be considered a public nuisance"); Ohio Solid Waste Disposal Regulations § HE–24–07 (1968) (requiring a person planning to establish or expand a sanitary landfill to submit plans to the director of the department of health in sufficient detail "to assure" a landfill operated at the site "will not create a nuisance or health hazard").

20. See BNA Solid Waste Reporter, passim.

21. § 6.4 above.

22. E. g., Georgia Solid Waste Management Act, Code of Ga.Ann. § 43–1608 (exempting individual disposing of solid wastes "originating from his own residence onto land or facilities owned by him" provided the disposal of the wastes does not "thereby create a nuisance or adversely affect the public health").

23. Minnesota Solid Waste Disposal Regulations § SW–1 (1973).

24. Mississippi Solid Wastes Disposal Act of 1974, § 4, Miss.Code § 17–17–5.

25. E. g., Georgia Solid Waste Management Act, Code of Ga.Ann. §§ 43–1615, 43–1615.1 (providing for civil and injunctive remedies).

cost of land, labor, equipment and services needed in the operation of solid waste disposal sites and facilities." [26] Minnesota at one time imposed a flat user fee of 15 cents per cubic yard on solid waste material discharged at a solid waste disposal site.[27] New Jersey has gone so far as to authorize rate regulation of solid waste services.[28]

It is an axiom that solid waste and garbage belong in somebody else's backyard. The tendency of states and municipalities to protect themselves from alien effluent assures a continuing conflict among jurisdictions, sometimes across state lines. New Jersey's qualified prohibition against the importation for disposal of solid and liquid wastes originating outside its territorial limits thus far has survived in the courts.[29] It will be emulated widely and enforced, assuring some clarification by the United States Supreme Court in the near future. The principal federal issue is whether the burden imposed on commerce "is clearly excessive in relation to the putative local benefits." [30] This calls for an analysis of the justification for the ban, its effects and whether less restrictive alternatives are available. New Jersey's vulnerable wetlands and the availability of options to the principal invader, the City of Philadelphia, bodes well for the survival of the New Jersey ban. A gradual phaseout of foreign wastes of course would be still more likely to survive.[31] There is no single environmental right answer to local restrictions on out-of-state solid wastes, as where a heavily stripmined state bans out-of-state wastes that could be used for purposes of reclamation, so they are likely to be tested on a case by case basis.

Interstate conflicts over waste disposal are repeated with greater intensity within a single state. The principal difference is that the state legislature usually can deal decisively with local vetoes or state overrides of communities unwilling to tolerate the regional landfill. Occasionally, a state vests sweeping authority in a state agency to manage and control all solid waste facilities within the jurisdiction.[32] Sometimes a state forbids localities from excluding

26. Colorado Solid Waste Disposal Sites and Facilities Law, Colo.Rev. Stat. § 36–23–16.

27. Minnesota Solid Wastes Recycling Law, Minn.Rev.Stat. § 116F.07, repealed Laws 1974, ch. 78, § 2.

28. Solid Waste Utility Control Act of 1970, N.J.Rev.Stat. § 48:13A–4.

29. Hackensack Meadowlands Dev. Comm'n v. Municipal Sanitary Landfill Authority, 68 N.J. 451, 348 A.2d 505, 6 ELR 20356 (1975), vacated and remanded —— U.S. ——, 97 S.Ct. 378, 51 L.Ed.2d 224 (1977).

30. Pike v. Bruce Church, Inc., 397 U.S. 137, 142, 90 S.Ct. 844, 847, 25 L.Ed. 2d 174, 178 (1970); see Hudson County Water Co. v. McCarter, 209 U.S. 349, 28 S.Ct. 529, 52 L.Ed. 828 (1908).

31. A successful lawsuit challenging interstate pollution under a theory of federal common law likely would result in a gradual curtailment of the source. See § 2.12 above. Compare § 4.18 above (discussing state regulation of interstate activities threatening pollution by oil).

32. E. g., Connecticut Solid Waste Management Act, Conn.Gen.Stat.Ann. § 19–524a et seq.; Connecticut Solid

properly managed waste disposal and resource recovery activities.[33] Usually, a state assumes a supportive, not a preemptive, posture as regards local solid waste management activities.[34] The fact remains that jurisdictional relationships are tested severely by conflicts over whether state agencies can override a local veto on site approval [35] or modify locally imposed conditions of operation.[36]

The state role in solid waste management is likely to become more explicit, partly to combat "the long-standing [local] tradition of locating the dump as far as practical from urban populations." [37] A Council of State Governments' Task Force Report recently stressed the problem of "surrounding local governments setting up legal barriers to prevent the central city or other local governments from using their land for solid waste processing facilities and disposal sites." This was said not to be an issue so much of environmental protection as "it is a problem of the fear of depreciated property

Waste Management Services Act, Conn.Gen.Stat.Ann. § 19–524p et seq.; Delaware Solid Waste Authority Act, Del.Code Ann. tit. 7, § 6401 et seq.

33. Michigan Resource Recovery Act, Mich.Comp.Laws § 299.308(3) (permitting override of local zoning authority "if a municipality totally excludes provision in its zoning ordinance for a suitable site . . ."). Compare Connecticut Solid Waste Management Services Act, Conn.Gen. Stat.Ann. § 19–524ii(d) (forbidding statewide authority from establishing certain solid waste disposal areas "until *and* unless it has first obtained the written consent of the municipal authority concerned") (emphasis added); § 2.17 above (discussing state industrial siting laws which raise similar local veto-state override issues).

34. Council of State Governments Report, supra note 2, at 32:
> The Task Force recognized that local government should be responsible for providing or providing for adequate levels and qualities of solid waste collection and disposal services for all inhabitants in their jurisdictions in manners that protect the public health and in manners that are not detrimental to qualities of their local environments.

See Pennsylvania Solid Waste Management Act, Pa.Stat.Ann. tit. 35, § 6011 (Purdon) (reserving in State Department of Health the power to order correction of municipal solid waste disposal activities causing pollution or creating a nuisance).

35. See Oronoco v. Rochester, 293 Minn. 468, 197 N.W.2d 426 (1971); cf. Valley View v. Rockside Hideaway Sanitary Landfill Inc., 32 Ohio Misc. 135, 289 N.E.2d 598 (1972); Waterford Processing & Reclaiming Co. v. Township of Waterford, 25 Mich.App. 507, 181 N.W.2d 675 (1970).

36. Compare Municipal Sanitary Landfill Authority v. Hackensack Meadowlands Dev. Comm'n, 120 N.J.Super. 118, 293 A.2d 426 (1972) (no preemption) with Ringlieb v. Parsippany-Troy Hills, 59 N.J. 348, 283 A.2d 97 (1971) (preemption) and Upper Saddle River v. Goess Environment Serv. Corp., 123 N.J.Super. 375, 303 A.2d 103 (1973) (no preemption after a legislative overruling of *Ringlieb*); cf. People ex rel. Scott v. North Shore Sanitary Dist., 132 Ill.App.2d 854, 270 N.E.2d 133 (1971) (sanitary district not required to conform to city's zoning regulations in constructing expanded sewage treatment facility). See also Alsop, The Role of the Commonwealth in Managing Solid Waste Disposal, 8 Suffolk U.L.Rev. 557, 597 (1974) (a useful case study of state-local conflicts coming down on the side of "home rule, local veto and local accountability, subject to state environmental regulation").

37. Council of State Governments Report, supra note 2, at 17.

values and the long-standing attitude and fear of assuring the demeaned social status of people who must reside near the town dump." [38] Evolving state policies perforce will respond to local views on health and environmental values and local preferences on land use development although conflicts are inevitable.

An increasingly important component of the relationship between a state and its subdivisions is found in solid waste planning authority. Several states require municipalities and counties of a certain size to prepare and submit for approval solid waste management plans.[39] Requirements for a satisfactory plan vary widely but usually call for projections of future sites and population over a 10 or 15 year period, identification of present unsatisfactory sites and operational problems, and environmental or legal, such as zoning, limits on future expansion of facilities. Some plans must contain an analysis of "all refuse generated in the area including tonnage and classification" [40] and address "reduction, through recycling where possible, of the volume of solid wastes for ultimate disposal and the conservation of natural resources." [41] State agency disapproval of a local or regional plan has various consequences: the state authority might order implementation of an alternative plan, under threat of a mandamus action or civil penalties of up to $2500 per day; [42] it might adopt a plan of its own for the municipality which has the burden of implementation; [43] it might proceed against the municipality for creating or maintaining a nuisance; [44] it might simply take steps to negotiate a satisfactory plan.[45] Compliance or noncompliance with an approved plan also has various consequences on the issuance of permits,[46] the approval of grants [47] and the construction of new facilities.[48]

38. Ibid. Compare § 2.17 above (discussing exclusionary zoning).

39. E. g., Arkansas Solid Waste Management Act, Ark.Stat.Ann. §§ 82–2705, 82–2706; California Solid Waste Management and Resource Recovery Act of 1972, Ann.Cal.Gov.Code § 66780; Connecticut Solid Waste Management Act, Conn.Gen.Stat.Ann. § 19–524e; Florida Resource Recovery and Management Act, Fla.Stat.Ann. § 403.706; Georgia Solid Waste Management Rules § 391–3–4–.05 (1974); Michigan Solid Waste Disposal Act, Mich.Comp.Laws § 325.297b; Pennsylvania Solid Waste Management Act, Pa.Stat.Ann. tit. 35, § 6005 (Purdon); Washington Solid Waste Management Act, Rev.Code Wash.Ann. §§ 70.95.090–.110.

40. Michigan Solid Waste Regulations R 325.2786(a) (1973).

41. Id. R 325.2782(f).

42. Michigan Resource Recovery Act, Mich.Comp.Laws § 299.310.

43. Florida Resource Recovery and Management Act, Fla.Stat.Ann. § 403.706.

44. Pennsylvania Solid Waste Management Act, Pa.Stat.Ann. tit. 35, § 6011 (Purdon).

45. Georgia Solid Waste Management Act, Code of Ga.Ann. § 43–1606.

46. Pennsylvania Solid Waste Management Act, Pa.Stat.Ann. tit. 35, § 6007 (Purdon) (no county permit required of a municipality for a landfill operating pursuant to state solid waste management plan).

47. California Solid Waste Management and Resource Recovery Act of 1972, Ann.Cal.Gov.Code § 66782.

48. Connecticut Solid Waste Management Services Act, Conn.Gen.Stat. Ann. § 19–524r(9).

California's Solid Waste Management and Resource Recovery Act of 1972 [49] is illustrative of the modern genre. It brings together in the State Resources Agency (one of four superagencies) the Solid Waste Management Board comprised of seven appointed members,[50] the temporary State Solid Waste Management and Resource Recovery Advisory Council with twenty-five appointed members operating under the Board,[51] and the State Department of Health which provides basic staff and regulatory functions. The Board, in language reminiscent of Section 209 (now Section 1008) of the federal Solid Waste Disposal Act, is directed to "formulate and adopt state policy for solid waste management, including minimum standards for solid waste handling and disposal for the protection of air, water and land from pollution." [52] The state-local relationship is carefully defined: The Board's statewide standards "may include the location, design, operation, maintenance, and ultimate reuse of solid waste processing or disposal facilities, but shall not include aspects of solid waste handling or disposal which are solely of local concern and not determined by the board to be of statewide concern, such as, but not limited to, frequency of collections, means of collection and transportation, level of service, charges and fees, designation of territory served through franchises, contracts or governmental employees, and purely aesthetic considerations." [53] Each county, in cooperation with affected local jurisdictions, must prepare "a comprehensive, coordinated solid waste management plan, consistent with state policy and any appropriate regional or subregional solid waste management plan, for all waste disposal within the county and for all waste originating [in the county] which is to be disposed of outside [the] county." [54] No new solid waste transfer station or disposal site can commence operations not in conformity with a county plan previously approved without a finding by the Board, at a public meeting, "that the protection of the public health, or public need and necessity, require the immediate implementation of the sites." [55] Additionally, in the future no person "shall establish sites for solid waste disposal, transfer station, waste processing, or resource recovery not in conformance with the county solid waste management plan approved by the board." [56] Noncompliance may result in amending the plan to conform to the practice or, at the request of the

---

49. Ann.Cal.Gov.Code tit. 7.3.

50. Id. § 66740.

51. Id. § 66750.

52. Id. § 66770.

53. Id. § 66771.

54. Id. § 66780.

55. Id. § 66783.1.

56. Id. § 66784. Nonprofit and community recycling efforts are exempted. Ibid.

Board or any local government entity, a suit by the Attorney General to require that the practice conform to the plan.[57]

b. *Resource Recovery*

While state regulation and planning is confined for the most part to the familiar systems of disposal and sometimes collection, there has been no dearth of initiatives regarding resource recovery. Many states, either through general environmental policy acts [58] or narrowly drawn resource recovery statutes, explicitly tilt state policies in favor of waste reduction and resource recovery. In Michigan, it is an express policy that the resources of the state, including waste, be "recovered and recycled to the greatest extent practicable for continued use as a source of energy or materials."[59] In Connecticut, the legislature declares "that maximum resources recovery from solid waste and maximum recycling and reuse of such resources shall be considered environmental goals of the state." [60] California favors "maximum reutilization and conversion to other uses of the resources contained" in solid wastes,[61] while Minnesota is on record as encouraging "both the reduction of the amount and type of material entering the solid waste stream and the reuse and recycling of materials."[62] Several state agencies are given explicit charters to promote recycling and secondary materials industries.[63]

More than a dozen states are preparing and implementing statewide solid waste and resource recovery plans.[64] These include the

---

57. Ibid.

58. § 7.11 below.

59. Michigan Resource Recovery Act, Mich.Comp.Laws § 299.308, directs the newly created state resource recovery commission to:

 . . .

 (f) Study all facets of resource recovery and management, including laws and programs in other states, and recommend to the department rules; to insure that the resources of this state, including waste, are collected, disposed of, and managed in a manner consistent with environmental and economic concerns and are recovered and recycled to the greatest extent practicable for continued use as a source of energy or materials; and to provide to the greatest extent practicable for a reduction in materials or energy consumed in the production of materials which ultimately become solid waste.

60. Connecticut Solid Waste Management Services Act, Conn.Gen.Stat. Ann. § 19–524r(1).

61. Ann.Cal.Gov.Code § 66702.

62. Minnesota Solid Wastes Recycling Law, Minn.Rev.Stat. § 116F.01.

63. E. g., Connecticut Solid Waste Management Services Act, Conn.Gen. Stat.Ann. § 19–524u(5) (stating as a purpose of the Connecticut Resources Recovery Authority "assistance in the development of industries and commercial enterprises within the state of Connecticut based upon resources recovery, recycling and reuse"); Michigan Resource Recovery Act, Mich.Comp.Laws § 299.308(h) (directs the state resource recovery commission to "examine a source reduction of disposable materials manufactured from natural resources and promote the use of recycled materials by business and the general public").

64. EPA, Third Report to Congress on Resource Recovery and Waste Reduction 81–83 (1975). Compare § 6.3 above (discussing state plans developed under the Solid Waste Disposal Act). The older plans are oriented principally towards classical

planned construction and operation of facilities and changes in state laws to enhance resource recovery. The Connecticut plan, being implemented by the Connecticut Resources Recovery Authority (CRRA), is credited with being one of the most advanced. The plan "calls for the construction of 10 resource recovery facilities by 1985 that will process 84 percent of the State's waste." [65] The CRRA has been given $250 million bonding authority for facility construction.[66] The California statute also serves for purposes of illustration. One of the Solid Waste Management Board's most important functions is to adopt and modify the State Solid Waste Resource Recovery Program, initially submitted to the Board by the Resource Recovery Advisory Council.[67] The program is broadly conceived and includes such elements as guidelines and procedures for a state directed research and development program "to develop technologically and economically feasible systems" for "collecting, converting and recycling solid wastes" and for assuring the environmentally safe disposal of nonusable residues. The program calls for studies and demonstration projects on the recovery of useful energy and resources from solid waste, including identifying potential markets for recovered resources, using state procurement to develop market demand, changing current production and packaging practices to reduce the amount of solid waste generated at its source, exploring the advantages and disadvantages of imposing disposal taxes which "would reflect the cost of final disposal, the value of recoverable components of the item, and any social costs associated with the nonrecycling or uncontrolled disposal of such items". The program also anticipates pilot resource recovery projects at state institutions.[68]

State law has gone beyond the stage of precatory utterance and paper planning to enforce a wide variety of substantive policy changes. Restrictions on nonreturnable beverage containers are only the best known example.[69] Minnesota has an unusual pre-market clearance procedure which may lead to prohibitions against the sale of new packages or containers in the state shown to constitute "a solid waste disposal or environmental protection problem." [70] Washington imposes an annual assessment on the makers and sellers of various products, such as newspapers, magazines, food and drink containers, conspicuously found in litter.[71] This effluent charge is no less innovative because it was promoted as a preferable alternative by manufacturers anxious to discourage adoption of a statewide ban against

collection and disposal while the newer ones address more broadly the full cycle of use and reuse of materials.

65. Id. at 82.

66. Ibid.

67. Ann.Cal.Gov.Code, § 66785.

68. Ibid.

69. § 6.9 below.

70. Minnesota Solid Wastes Recycling Law, Minn.Rev.Stat. § 116F.06.

71. Washington Model Litter Control Act, Rev.Code Wash.Ann. §§ 70.93.-120, 70.93.130.

the sale of nonreturnable beverage containers.[72] In Florida, the responsible agency has been directed to "evaluate the amount of waste paper material recycled by the state and make all necessary modifications to [the] recycling program to insure that all waste paper materials are effectively and practicably recycled."[73] Ratemaking authorities in the same state are instructed to establish railroad and common carrier rates which "do not discriminate against the transport of solid waste, recovered resources, or recycled materials, and which . . . shall, whenever practicable, provide an incentive for resource recovery and recycling."[74]

While many states pioneer with solid waste and resource recovery innovations, they are unprepared to deny a federal role. One recent convocation of state authorities, not the first to share the view, was firm in the belief that federal money would make life easier. Federal funding assistance, according to the recorded dogma, "is needed to: improve the administrative and managerial capabilities within state and local governments; permit consideration and development of more efficient local area solid waste service systems; develop essential formal and on-the-job training programs to permit the development of personnel for managing and operating improved services; permit States to develop more adequate assistance programs for local governments; strengthen the regulatory functions of state government; stimulate intergovernmental coordination efforts and related activities needed to establish more effective local solid waste service systems; finally, federal funding is necessary to support state loan, loan insurance, or other state mechanisms developed to assist local governments to initiate the implementation of more effective solid waste service systems."[75] It has been observed before that a clamor by state and local managers for federal money often brings forth an unwelcome residue of federal regulation.

§ 6.8 The Local Role

The collection, transport, processing and disposal of solid wastes today remains largely in local hands. Nearly 50 percent of the environmental budgets of the nation's 48 largest cities is allocated to solid waste management.[1] Overall annual costs of collection and disposal may approach six billion dollars,[2] 80 percent of this devoted to

72. W. Rodgers, Corporate Country ch. 1 (1973).

73. Florida Resource Recovery and Management Act, Fla.Stat.Ann. § 403.714(3).

74. Id. § 323.08(6).

75. Council of State Governments Report, supra note 2, at 38.

1. National League of Cities & United States Conference of Mayors, Cities and the Nation's Disposal Crisis 3 (1973) [hereinafter cited as National League of Cities].

2. Ibid. The figures obviously are imprecise. Compare Council on Environmental Quality, First Ann.Rep. 108 (1970) ($3.5 billion) with Comm. on Interstate and Foreign Commerce,

collection and transport.[3] The profile of the collection and disposal industry is vaguely familiar: structurally, private firms collect as much as three-fourths of the nation's solid waste tonnage, typically under government franchising or contracting arrangements.[4] Technologically, "[t]he one significant advance has been the compactor truck. These closed-body vehicles now make up a large part of the 150,000 refuse collection trucks in the United States. With hydraulic presses, they compress waste, usually at a 3-to-1 ratio, thus saving vehicle space and cutting the number of trips necessary to cover collection routes. However, the compactor has disadvantages. Because refuse of different types is mixed and crushed, recyclables are lost or contaminated by unusable waste. It is also hazardous to operators."[5] During the trip from the curb to the landfill site, solid waste may be hauled to a transfer station, a facility where waste from several small vehicles is concentrated into a larger one for further hauling to the disposal site. At the transfer station, waste may be subject to processing, often by compaction, less likely by bailing (where volume is reduced by compressing the solid waste and binding it) or shredding (which includes other volume reduction processes transforming the waste into a homogeneous material by pulverization, grinding or milling).[6]

The location and operation of dumps and junkyards also is dictated mostly by local law. Land use values result in locating the landfill in places least valuable economically, "usually in some out-of-the-way place near the edge of the community. Stream banks, hillsides, gullies and quarries have been favorite places for the location of dumps. Another typical location has been in the area where the least-favored residents of the community live."[7] Putting the dump somewhere else is a consistent theme.

Local legal mechanisms for controlling the solid waste management system can be grouped into three categories: (1) nuisance law and zoning ordinances, which affect mostly siting and operation; (2) conventional regulation of collection, transportation and disposal; and (3) innovations aimed at source reduction and resource recovery.

Resource Recovery Act of 1970, H.R. Rep. No. 1155, 91st Cong., 2d Sess. 2 (1970) ($4.5 billion).

3. This 80 percent cost figure is repeated constantly in the literature. E. g., CEQ, First Ann.Rep. 108 (1970).

4. 1 Environmental Protection Agency, The Private Sector in Solid Waste Management 1.1 (1973).

5. CEQ, First Ann.Rep. 110 (1970).

6. Environmental Protection Agency, Decision-Makers Guide in Solid Waste Management 70–83 (1976) [hereinafter cited as 1976 Decision-Makers Guide].

7. Council of State Governments, The State's Role in Solid Waste Management: A Task Force Report 16 (1973) (reprinted by the Environmental Protection Agency).

a. *Nuisance Law and Zoning Ordinances*

Discussed earlier are the general principles of nuisance law and the impact of zoning ordinances upon them,[8] as well as their special application to waste disposal activities.[9] Common issues in the zoning cases involve efforts by a municipality to circumvent its own zoning laws [10] or keep somebody else's waste out of its jurisdiction.[11] Privately operated dumps and junkyards are treated harshly by the zoning laws.[12] Municipal undertakings seem to have an easier life legally because the operator is often the one writing the rules.[13] There is certainly very little law resembling the airport cases holding that various types of impositions upon adjoining property owners rise to the level of unconstitutional takings.[14] Of course landfills, unlike airports, do not require affirmative restrictions, such as height restrictions, on adjoining properties to assure freedom of operation although it is safe to assume that property use options can be cut as severely by the stench of an open dump as by the din of an airport.

b. *Conventional Regulations*

Local solid waste management ordinances obviously can include everything imaginable but in their more advanced forms prescribe a familiar administrative arrangement—a responsible agency, usually a Board of Health, with the power to promulgate regulations, issue permits, fix fees and conditions of service, and prescribe penalties. Generalities, of course, are dangerous, and local law may range from next to nothing in rural areas [15] to the loose licensing of garbage collection services to stricter bans against disposal practices.[16] While the state often becomes involved with facility or plan approval and

---

8. §§ 2.1–.10 above.

9. § 6.2 above.

10. Compare Hewlett v. Hempstead, 3 Misc.2d 945, 133 N.Y.S.2d 690 (Special Term 1954) (upholding construction of an incinerator in a residential area) with O'Brien v. Greenburgh, 239 App.Div. 555, 268 N.Y.S. 173 (1933) (forbidding construction of a garbage disposal plant in a residential area); Annot., 61 ALR2d 970 (1958) (a municipality generally is not subject to its own zoning laws).

11. E. g., Croton-on-Hudson v. Westchester, 38 A.D.2d 979, 331 N.Y.S.2d 883 (1972); Edgeboro, Inc. v. East Brunswick, 31 N.J.Super. 238, 106 A. 2d 337 (1954); Boone Landfill, Inc. v. Boone County, 51 Ill.2d 538, 283 N.E. 2d 890 (1972) (invalidating county ordinance prohibiting dumping of refuse not originating within the county). Compare § 6.7 above (discussing the local veto-state override issue).

12. E. g., Board of County Commissioners v. Thompson, 177 Colo. 277, 493 P.2d 1358, 2 ELR 20423 (1972); Hillsdale v. Hillsdale Iron & Metal Co., 358 Mich. 377, 100 N.W.2d 467 (1960); see text accompanying § 6.3 n. 61 above (reporting recommendation of the National Commission on Materials Policy that urban fringe zoning laws be relaxed to accommodate waste processing).

13. Note 10, supra.

14. § 5.5 above; see § 5.7 above. Compare § 6.2 n. 41 above.

15. Environmental Protection Agency, Improving Rural Solid Waste Management Practices (1973).

16. Environmental Protection Agency, Digest of Selected Local Solid Waste Management Ordinances (1972).

regulation of disposal practices,[17] the local or county agency may do these things and many more, particularly as regards the collection and transportation segments of the system. Municipal decision-makers often confront a wide range of issues on public or private ownership of facilities, operating revenues, scope of services and regulation throughout the system.[18] That these decisions are potentially subject to review in the courts is nowhere better demonstrated than by Teagen v. Bergenfield,[19] finding illegality in local waste collection practices that discriminated unfairly against large multi-family apartment complexes.

Local rules governing collection from residential homeowners may make significant differences economically and environmentally. Collection savings of 50 percent may be realized by abandoning backyard collection in favor of curbside collection.[20] Source separation, particularly of paper, is a critical component of successful efforts to recover materials from post-consumer waste.[21] Professor Grad summarizes [22] municipal law addressing the householder's obligations to sort and store solid waste and prepare it for collection: "Some municipal ordinances require the sorting and separate storage of ashes, paper, cans, bottles, and perishable, or kitchen wastes. Sanitary or health codes, as well as housing codes, may provide for the manner in which wastes are stored and readied for collection. Such regulations frequently deal with the number and kinds of waste receptables that must be provided, and in many instances these regulations are related to efforts to reduce rodent and other pest infestations or to avoid fire hazards. For some time, galvanized iron cans with fitting covers were favored because they were thought to be both rodent proof and fireproof when used for the storage of hot ashes. The collection of wastes in galvanized cans early in the morning creates a real noise pollution hazard, however, and in the sixties heavy gauge plastic garbage containers began to be favored in municipal legislation. In the early seventies, securely-tied heavy gauge disposable plastic bags became permissible, as well as securely-tied double-strength disposable paper bags. Disposable bags are lightweight and therefore speed up the collection process—and they are also less likely to cause injury to sanitation department personnel." The environmental assessment of paper and plastic bags thus far is positive, provided they do not contain potentially toxic polyvinyl chloride.[23]

17. § 6.7 above.

18. See 1976 Decision-Makers Guide, supra note 6.

19. 119 N.J.Super. 212, 290 A.2d 753 (1972); cf. Neptune City v. Avon-by-the-Sea, 61 N.J. 296, 294 A.2d 47, 2 ELR 20519 (1972) (discussed in § 2.16 above).

20. 1976 Decision-Makers Guide, supra note 6, at 25–26.

21. Id. at 38–47.

22. 1 Environmental Law § 4.02, at 4–27 to –28 (1975) (footnote omitted).

23. 1976 Decision-Makers Guide, supra note 6, at 34–35; see Soc'y of

A suggested ordinance based on a review of more than one hundred local legislative schemes [24] gives some idea of the likely direction of future local initiatives. It prescribes a detailed permit system for activities at various points in the waste management system—transportation, storage, collection, location and operation of a transfer station, resource recovery facility or incinerator.[25] It regulates the collection process by requiring set-out and removal of containers by the homeowner,[26] and imposing special conditions for the removal of bulk wastes (refrigerators, washers, and so on) [27] and dead animals.[28] It contains a number of prohibitions against such activities as littering,[29] casual picking or scavenging,[30] transporting solid waste in vehicles allowing it to escape,[31] or operating an open dump.[32] In fact, the purpose of the ordinance is to require mandatory conversion to sanitary landfills.

There is room for innovation even within the confines of traditional local solid waste management ordinances. Beaufort County, South Carolina collectors identify unsatisfactory containers in use with a red adhesive sticker: "This container is condemned for use of garbage and refuse by authority of the Beaufort County Health Department." [33] The idea is to prod households or businesses into providing satisfactory containers, surely an appropriate police power objective. A Los Angeles County Health Department sanitarian is empowered to secure a court order to compel a recalcitrant homeowner to clean up his property, else the county does it and sends the homeowner the bill.[34] This type of relief, widely known in other nations, is virtually unheard of in the United States: where is the last reported court order requiring a city to install adequate pollution control facilities on an offending source at the expense of the violator? Sanctions in solid waste ordinances include unenforceable misdemeanor provisions but also may embrace revocation or suspension of licenses, probationary periods of operation, forfeiture of bonds for noncompliance with conditions of operation, and civil penalties.

Plastics Indus., Inc. v. Occupational Safety & Health Administration, 509 F.2d 1301 (2d Cir.), cert. denied 421 U.S. 992 (1975).

24. Environmental Protection Agency, Suggested Solid Waste Management Ordinance for Local Government, 1974 (prepared under contract with the National Association of Counties Research Foundation) [hereinafter cited as Suggested Solid Waste Management Ordinance].

25. Id. tit. 7.

26. Id. tit. 12.

27. Id. tit. 14; see § 6.9 below.

28. Suggested Solid Waste Management Ordinance tit. 15.

29. Id. § 25.02.

30. Id. § 25.06.

31. Id. § 25.04.

32. Id. § 25.08.

33. See Environmental Protection Agency, Guidelines for Local Governments on Solid Waste Management 28–29 (1971).

34. Id. at 26.

c. *Innovations in Source Reduction and Resource Recovery*

There is a tendency even (or perhaps especially) among local solid waste administrators to expect the big problems of source reduction and recycling to be taken care of by somebody else, notably the federal government.[35] This view defines the local mission as picking up and disposing of nonhazardous wastes. Local governments can do more: resource recovery is likely to occur first in limited areas where market factors are particularly attractive. Use of solid waste as fuel practically is more viable in jurisdictions served by municipally owned electrical and solid waste utilities. The failure to separate post-consumer wastes inhibits some recycling endeavors but can be overcome in communities willing to undertake a separation program. The laboratory function of local innovations aimed at reducing the solid waste stream is well established—Bowie, Maryland's five cent deposit requirement for beverage containers,[36] New York City's tax on certain types of plastics in packaging,[37] North Hempstead, New York's paper recycling ordinance,[38] Madison, Wisconsin's composting and milling programs,[39] Franklin, Ohio's system for materials recovery[40], Latah County, Idaho's improved rural collection.[41] Unlike many air and water pollution problems whose solutions require extraordinary technological commitments, the solid waste chain is somewhat more vulnerable to individual imagination and community concern.

§ 6.9 Special Problems

A few issues of resource recovery and waste disposal are sufficiently emergent or annoying to inspire individualized treatment by the legislatures and courts. Grouped here are measures addressing (1) junked automobiles, (2) other bulk consumer goods, (3) nonreturnable beverage containers, and (4) miscellaneous consumer products.

---

35. See National Ass'n of Counties, Basic Issues on Solid Waste Management Affecting County Government 4.5 (1973) (reprinted by the Environmental Protection Agency).

36. Bowie Inn, Inc. v. Bowie, 2 ELR 20056 (Md.Cir.Ct. Prince George's County 1971) (upholding constitutionality of ordinance); see Hearings on Solid Waste Management Act of 1972, Before the Subcomm. on Environment of the Senate Comm. on Commerce, S.Doc. No. 60, 92d Cong., 2d Sess. 45–75 (1972) (statement of Ellis Yochelson, a participant in the Bowie campaign).

37. See Soc'y of Plastics Indus. v. City of New York, 68 Misc.2d 366, 326 N.Y.S.2d 788 (Sup.Ct.1971) (holding that the tax unconstitutionally discriminated against the plastics industry in favor of the paper board, fibre, glass and metal industries.)

38. See Business Publishers, Inc., Solid Waste Report, Aug. 9, 1971 (prohibiting the mixing of discarded newspaper with discarded materials).

39. See Dyszynski, Solid Waste Management in Madison, Wisconsin, in Report of the First National Conference on Composting—Waste Recycling 87 (1971).

40. 1976 Decision-Makers Guide, supra note 6, at 102–07.

41. U. S. Environmental Protection Agency, Problem-Solving in Solid Waste Management Through Federal-Local Cooperation 31–34 (1974).

a. *Junked Automobiles*

Singled out for investigation and study by the Resource Recovery Act of 1970 was the matter of "recommended incentives (including Federal grants, loans and other assistance) and disincentives to accelerate the reclamation or recycling of materials from solid wastes, with special emphasis on motor vehicle hulks. . . ."[1] The problem has been studied repeatedly,[2] and its dimensions are generally understood: nationwide, ten to thirty million junked automobiles mar the landscape and rest in automobile graveyards; an old car is abandoned at the rate of one every thirty minutes or so.[3] Overall, 8 of the approximately 9 million autos taken out of circulation each year are disposed of properly by dismantlers, processors and at solid waste disposal sites.[4] That leaves close to 1 million cars a year, however, that are simply abandoned, sometimes on private but usually on public property.

An abandoned car is a source of mineral resources (iron, copper, zinc, aluminum and lead) although the copper can be an unwanted contaminant making a hulk unappealing as a source of steel scrap.[5] Technologically, prospects for recycling old autos are good. During the 1960's commercial shredders were introduced and spread rapidly so that they now serve all areas of the United States except a small section of the northern Rocky Mountains.[6] Shredders reduce discarded autos to fist-size chunks suitable for processing by separators which bring about more rapid and complete removal of contaminants, assuring a higher quality scrap. Concurrently, the steel and foundry industries increased their use of electric furnaces and the continuous casting process, both of which generate considerable demand for acceptable scrap.[7] Presumably, the total inventory of scrap autos could be used were it not for the economics of moving the bundle of resources from the place of discard to where it is needed.

The auto wreckers who sell used parts at retail and the scrap processors who sell discarded metals to steel mills and foundries for

---

1. 84 Stat. 1228.

2. Useful studies include Environmental Protection Agency, The Automobile Cycle: An Environmental and Resource Reclamation Problem (1972) [hereinafter cited as EPA Auto Cycle Study]; Dep't of HEW, Automobile Scrapping Processes and Needs for Maryland (1970) [hereinafter cited as HEW Auto Scrapping Study]; Columbia University Legislative Drafting Research Fund, The Automobile and the Regulation of Its Impact on the Environment ch. 12 (1974) [hereinafter cited as Columbia University Auto Study]; Dep't of Commerce, Motor Vehicle Abandonment in U. S. Urban Areas (1967).

3. See Reichert, Recycling Abandoned Automobiles: Do Present Laws Act as Bottlenecks? 2 Env.L. 105 (1971), citing Phoenix Q. [No. 1] 3 (Apr. 1969).

4. EPA Auto Cycle Study, supra note 2, at 18–21.

5. Id. at 12–15.

6. National Industrial Pollution Control Council: Automotive Subcouncil, Junk Car Disposal 12–13 (1970) [hereinafter cited as NIPCC Junk Car Disposal Report].

7. See HEW Auto Scrapping Study, supra note 2.

remelting into new steel are indispensable segments of the recycling process. These businesses, to be sure, may do things in the wrong way or in the wrong place to become subject to nuisance laws,[8] mostly for air or noise pollution, although their value to the community will be weighed when remedies are considered.[9] Abandoned autos themselves, either in isolated repose or collective graveyards, are chiefly aesthetically offensive although some health hazard accusations have been aimed their way. Certainly it was the aesthetic effrontery that prompted the Congress to call for the screening of junkyards along federally-aided highways in the novel, albeit mostly unworkable, Highway Beautification Act of 1965.[10]

The principal legal challenge to maximizing the recycling of junked autos is to bring the force of the law to bear on the individual's decision to abandon the car which reduces greatly its chances of reentering the recycling stream. The obvious choice is to make it a crime to abandon an auto at an unauthorized site; criminal statutes are widely adopted,[11] often urged as appropriate [12] and rarely enforced for many of the same reasons that make unserviceable the laws forbidding the abandonment of beer cans.[13] A variation on the criminal sanction theme is to make the owner of record presumptively liable civilly for all costs of removal, storage and disposal.[14] This is a better idea although, as with many small claims, tracking down the owner may not be worth the effort.[15] Another administrative variation, better yet, is to condition the owner's future vehicle registrations upon payment of past obligations for disposing of an abandoned vehicle.[16] Variations of this principle have succeeded in bringing traffic ticket scofflaws to account, and it might work also to cover the costs of proper disposal of discarded autos. Possibilities of using the carrot instead of the stick were suggested in the President's 1970 Message on

---

8. David J. Joseph Co. v. Ashland, 223 Ky. 203, 3 S.W.2d 218 (1928); Mayor and City Council of Baltimore v. Price, 168 Md. 174, 177 A. 160 (1931); Middleton Iron & Steel Co. v. Evatt, 139 Ohio St. 113, 38 N.E.2d 585 (1941); Commonwealth v. Sitkin's Junk Co., 412 Pa. 132, 194 A.2d 199 (1963).

9. Harrison v. Indiana Auto Shredders Co., 528 F.2d 1107, 1121, 6 ELR 20179, 20183 (7th Cir. 1975).

10. 23 U.S.C.A. § 136; see Lamm & Yasinow, Highway Beautification Act of 1965: A Case Study in Legislative Frustration, 46 Denver L.J. 437 (1969).

11. E. g., N.Y.Vehi. & Traf.Law § 1224 (6) (McKinney) (fine not exceeding $100); Ill.Ann.Stat. ch. 95½, § 4–214 (Smith-Hurd) (fine $25–$100 plus disposition of the vehicle).

12. See NIPCC Junk Car Disposal Report, supra note 2, at 16 (government assistance needs mainly "to stress expediting of de-titling, encouragement of zoning and shielding regulations, and adoption of penalties for car abandonment").

13. See Columbia University Auto Study, supra note 2, at 12–11 to –12.

14. Indiana Abandoned Vehicle Act, Ind.Stat.Ann. § 9–9–1–6 (Burns).

15. See Dep't of Commerce, Motor Vehicle Abandonment in U.S. Urban Areas 25 (1967).

16. Indiana Abandoned Vehicle Act, Ind.Stat.Ann. §§ 9–9–13 to –16 (Burns).

the Environment [17] which asked the Council on Environmental Quality to study whether a bounty payment or similar incentive system could be used to encourage the scrapping of all junked autos. This system would function something like the returnable bottle system where a sum, say $30, would be payable upon purchase of a new car and returned to the person surrendering the vehicle for proper disposal, usually the owner or perhaps a scavenger or municipal government cleaning its streets of auto hulks.[18] The Council's report was mostly negative, concluding that it would be unfair to tax those who disposed of vehicles properly to subsidize those who did not and that the deterrent to abandonment was speculative at best.[19] Others have criticized the bounty idea,[20] on grounds it would be burdensome administratively and regressive in effect by requiring rich and poor alike to pay a substantial deposit with the purchase of a new car. A very important question is whether a deposit system will bring abandoned autos to scrap dealers, and we will never know the answer to that unless and until a particular jurisdiction shrugs off hypothetical objections to undertake the experiment.

A substantial uncertainty in the law placing an artificial ceiling on auto recycling has been the treatment of an abandoned car not as a resource free for the taking by the economically motivated but as personal property temporarily misplaced by the owner. Obviously, there are due process limits on the extent to which a municipality may snatch autos off the street and sell them to the shredder, just as there may be due process limits on jail sentences for poor people whose cars expire on public property [21] or on civil liabilities for rich people obliged to remove vehicles somebody else leaves on their land.[22] Due process protections for owners of abandoned autos may take the form of strict title and impoundment requirements. Titling requirements, in various particulars, may oblige a scrap dealer to secure a certificate of title and pay a transfer fee on every vehicle purchased for recycling.[23] Impoundment requirements may be equally cumbersome, calling for extended impoundment, actual notice and other precautions such as public auction before obviously abandoned auto hulks are taken to a reprocessor who pays the costs.[24] In a business where

---

17. Council on Environmental Quality, First Ann.Rep. 254, 266 (1970).

18. See H.R. 15860, 91st Cong., 2d Sess. (1970).

19. See Council on Environmental Quality, First Ann.Rep. 116 (1970).

20. Columbia University Auto Study, supra note 2, at 12–13 to –14.

21. Cf. Tate v. Short, 401 U.S. 395, 91 S.Ct. 668, 28 L.Ed.2d 130 (1971).

22. Leet v. Montgomery County, 264 Md. 606, 287 A.2d 491, 2 ELR 20242 (1972) (holding that county government's attempts to force landowner under nuisance theory to remove autos abandoned on his property without his consent constituted a taking without just compensation).

23. See Reichert, supra note 3, at 110–11.

24. Id. at 110–14.

a few dollars makes a difference, marginal costs added by title and impoundment laws may tip the balance against re-use of the hulk.

The chief legislative technique for overcoming title and impoundment obstacles is to fashion complete or partial exemptions for autos satisfying the definition of "abandoned vehicle". Legislative indicia of an "abandoned vehicle" are stated variously and include cars of dilapidated appearance,[25] without license plates,[26] unattended for an extended period (48 hours is common),[27] and those that are appraised at or below a certain value ($100 is a common ceiling).[28] Thus, "notification may be simplified for lower value vehicles, impounding periods shortened or eliminated, and titling requirements simplified or eliminated, when the vehicle is only fit for scrappage or dismantling."[29] Various forms of substantially abbreviated procedures, while difficult to evaluate in the abstract, are likely to survive in the courts.

The Council of State Governments' Suggested State Abandoned Vehicle Act[30] contains an unexceptional legislative scheme whose essential components are in effect in several states and likely to be followed elsewhere. The Act invokes both legal and scientific tradition by condemning abandoned vehicles as "a public nuisance" and as a "resource out of place."[31] It makes criminal the abandoning of a vehicle upon any highway or upon any public or private property without consent of the owner.[32] A vehicle is presumed abandoned if it is left unattended on a public highway or on public or private property for a period of time specified by the legislature.[33] Any police officer who has "reasonable grounds" for believing that a vehicle has been abandoned may have it removed to a garage for impoundment, at the expense of the owner.[34] Written notice to the owner and the lienholder of record is required, except that notice may be dispensed with for vehicles valued at less than $100 or those more than

25. E. g., 21 Del.Code Ann. tit. 21, § 4401(b) ("Any vehicle that is in such a state of disrepair as to be incapable of being operated in the manner for which it is designed"); N.C.Gen.Stat. § 153A–132(b) (1974) ("junked vehicles which are otherwise already deemed abandoned").

26. E. g., 21 Del.Code Ann. tit. 21, § 4401(b); N.Y.Veh. & Traf.Law § 1224(1)(a) (McKinney).

27. E. g., Ariz.Rev.Stat.Ann. § 28–1401 (1) (36 hours); Ill.Ann.Stat. ch. 95½, § 4–200(b) (Smith-Hurd) (20 to 24 hours on any highway or public place and 7 days on private property); Mich.Comp.Laws Ann. § 257–252(b) (48 hours); N.Y.Veh. & Traf.Law § 1224(1)(b), (c), (d) (McKinney) (24 hours on any highway or other public place where there is no legal parking, 48 hours where there is legal parking, 7 days on private property).

28. Ind.Ann.Stat. §§ 9–9–1.5–6 to .5–7 (Burns) ($100); N.Y.Veh. & Traf.Law § 1224(2) (McKinney) ($100 if no license plate affixed); Or.Rev.Stat. §§ 483.388, 483.395 ($100).

29. Columbia University Auto study, supra note 2 at 12–8.

30. 32 Suggested State Legislation 57 (1973).

31. Section 2(a); see § 1.1 above.

32. Sections 6(a), (b), 13.

33. Section 6(d).

34. Section 6(c).

eight years old.[35] Title to an unclaimed impounded vehicle vests in the state or local authority after passage of a specified period.[36] The vehicle can be disposed of to licensed dealers by contract or auction if valued at less than $100 or by public sale if valued at more than $100, and title conveyed by bill of sale.[37] Wreckers, processors, sellers of used accessories, junkyard operators and others are licensed by the state, subject to certain reporting requirements.[38] The most innovative feature of the Act is a provision to establish a revolving fund to finance a statewide "self sufficient" abandoned vehicle program.[39] Monies to be deposited in the fund can be raised by a combination of a refundable disposable tax on new or used vehicles, an inventory tax on licensed junkyards, wreckers and processors, special fees on vehicle title or registration and income from sales of impounded vehicles. Disbursements may be authorized for such causes as incentives or bounties to licensed operators or the last owner of record and subsidies to municipalities who collect, store or dispose of abandoned vehicles.[40]

b. *Other Bulk Consumer Goods*

A less dramatic but in some ways more intractable resource recovery problem is presented by bulk consumer goods other than autos. Presently in use in American households are some 350 million major appliances, and the numbers are increasing. In 1971, about 21 million appliances were discarded annually with refrigerators accounting for 20 percent of the total, washers 19 percent, water heaters 17 percent, dryers 8 percent, room air conditioners 7 percent and dishwashers 3 percent.[41] By 1980, discards will climb to 29 million annually and the mix will change: room air conditioners will account for 20 percent of the total, washers 16 percent, water heaters 14 percent, refrigerators 12 percent, dishwashers and dryers 7 percent each.[42] Bulk appliances occasionally are abandoned—who can miss the lonely refrigerator standing vigil on the hillside?—but for the most part are disposed of at conventional landfills. There, they take

---

35. Ibid.

36. Section 6(e).

37. Section 9.

38. Section 10.

39. Section 12.

40. For a discussion of two case studies of small communities cleaning up auto hulks, see Environmental Protection Agency, Solving the Abandoned Car Problem in Small Communities (1974). See also Comptroller General, Review of Appalachian Regional Commission's Contract with West Virginia's Rehabilitation Environmental Action Program (1975) (describing abandoned vehicle removal program under the Appalachian Regional Development Act of 1965); Hughes v. Alexandria Scrap Corp., 426 U.S. 794, 96 S.Ct. 2488, 49 L.Ed. 2d 220 (1976) (upholding Maryland law giving preferential treatment to in-state scrap processors in program to remove old automobile hulks).

41. National Industrial Pollution Control Council, Electric and Nuclear Subcouncil, The Disposal of Major Appliances 12 (1971) [hereinafter cited as Disposal of Major Appliances].

42. Ibid.

up landfill volume and remain as unreclaimed mineral resources—steel, copper, brass, aluminum, plastics, rubber, glass, porcelain and others.

The legal treatment of bulk consumer goods is unique mostly in the collection process. A pick-up service may be provided routinely, on a call basis, or not at all.[43] Often a householder may be required to remove refrigerator or freezer doors to qualify for pick-up.[44] In many areas of the country no pick-up service is offered, which means the homeowner must make arrangements to haul the hulk to a landfill himself or otherwise dispose of it, perhaps by leaving it in his basement or his backyard indefinitely. Prospects for recycling major appliances are not good: they are generally high in contaminants (enamel coating, copper and aluminum wiring and others) which lower their value as steel scrap.[45] The economics are discouraging: the "average auto hulk weighs about 2,000 pounds, and has been stripped to the point where it is almost 90 percent steel. The average appliance hulk weighs about 200 pounds, usually has not been stripped, and is 80 percent to 90 percent steel."[46] Notwithstanding this, the greatest prospect for reuse is at shredders which today are designed primarily to handle auto hulks, presently in abundant supply.[47] Penalties for improper disposal and incentives for reuse, mentioned in the discussion above on abandoned cars, apply equally to abandoned ranges, refrigerators and washing machines. Longer-lived products, which can be encouraged or mandated by law, also would bring about a reduction of waste at the source, "a form of recycling —without any materials collection, scrap processing, materials reprocessing, fabrication or distribution having taken place."[48] It also has been suggested that bulk appliance discards be preserved for future recycling by burying them at one location in open pits or abandoned mines. This aim is realized, perhaps coincidentally, by the separate treatment of bulk goods at some landfills.[49]

c. *Nonreturnable Beverage Containers*

The most conspicuous actor in the recycling arena is the beverage container. Back in 1958, the beer and soft drink you bought was sold mostly in returnable containers. Since then, there has been a

[43]. Environmental Protection Agency, Suggested Solid Waste Management Ordinance for Local Government, § 14, Mar. 1974.

[44]. Disposal of Major Appliances, supra note 41, at 13.

[45]. Environmental Protection Agency, Salvage Markets for Materials in Solid Wastes 54–55 (1972) [hereinafter cited as Salvage Markets Study].

[46]. Disposal of Major Appliances, supra note 41, at 20.

[47]. Id. at 21.

[48]. Salvage Markets Study, supra note 45, at 94.

[49]. E. g., Connecticut Solid Waste Management Regulations § 19–525–8 (1975); Maine Solid Waste Regulations § 408.2 (1975); Massachusetts Sanitary Landfill Regulations, Reg. 17 (1971); New Jersey Waste Management Regulations, N.J.Adm.Code § 2.6.2.3.

Sec. 6.9   SPECIAL PROBLEMS   685

technological revolution, so that today the consumer's beer and soft drinks comes mostly in nonreturnables. The 43.8 billion beverage containers made in the United States in 1969, according to one estimate,[50] may climb to 100 billion by 1980. One or two billion of these will end up as litter—enough to encircle the planet several times.[51] While beer and soft drink containers contribute only modestly to the conventional residential, commercial and institutional solid waste stream (perhaps 21 percent of all packaging wastes, 8 percent of total wastes),[52] its ubiquitous and offensive appearance has provided a legal rallying point.[53] As with abandoned cars, the objections to abandoned bottles and cans are mostly aesthetic although they also involve obvious health hazards.

Prospects for reusing beverage containers from the consumer waste stream and the spillover represented by litter are limited not so much by technological considerations[54] as by economic ones. Thus the demand for glass cullet and steel cans from municipal waste is virtually nonexistent, while that for the higher value aluminum cans is only slightly better.[55] The early 1970's brought forth a spate of industry sponsored bring-them-back programs and recycling centers, often as defensive gestures to ward off various ban-the-can and mandatory deposit proposals. There is some evidence that can and bottle recycling centers are half-way stations for containers on the way to the sanitary landfill,[56] and very little evidence that they can bring back into the resource chain any more than a tiny fraction of the beverage containers produced (5 percent of the bottles,[57] perhaps 13 percent of aluminum cans[58]).

As with abandoned automobiles, the act of abandoning cans and bottles on public and private property is prohibited by anti-litter laws in virtually every jurisdiction. Litter is a people problem, accord-

50. Council on Environmental Quality, First Ann.Rep. 117 (1970).

51. See Fenchuk, The Economics of Banning Throwaway Beverage Containers, in Hearings on Solid Waste Management Act of 1972, Before the Subcomm. on Environment of the Senate Comm. on Commerce, S.Doc. No.60, 92d Cong., 2d Sess. 382, 383–84 (1972).

52. Quarles, The Case for the Returnable Beverage Container, 5 ELR 50023 (1975), citing T. Bingham & P. Mulligan, The Beverage Container Problem: Analysis and Recommendations 55 (1972) (prepared under contract by Research Triangle Park) [hereinafter cited as Research Triangle Park Study]. See also Federal Energy Administration, Energy and Economic Impacts of Mandatory Deposits (1976).

53. Bottles and cans together on an item basis account for something over 20% of roadside litter. Research Triangle Park Study, supra note 52, at 25–29.

54. Salvage Markets Study, supra note 45, at 55; § 6.4 above.

55. Salvage Markets Study, supra note 45, at 52–53, 62, 69.

56. See Adams, A Recycling Nut Answers the Backlashers, Compost Science, July-Aug. 1971, at 31.

57. See N. Y. Times, Nov. 8, 1970.

58. Research Triangle Park Study, supra note 52, at 23.

ing to this view, which conforms to the expectation that the maker of the product thinks first of controlling the user rather than revising his manufacturing process.[59] Far and away the dominant anti-litter voice since its founding in 1953 by the brewers and bottle and can makers is Keep America Beautiful, which calls itself the National Public Service Organization for the Prevention of Litter. KAB publicity stresses the "three E's" of litter prevention—Education of the public, Enforcement of anti-littering laws and Equipment, notably more trash barrels. While few would suggest that anti-littering laws should be done away with, they hardly deserve acclaim for effectiveness. The combination of widespread violations, impossibility of detection, and continuous temptation [60] pretty well defeats the principal objective of seeing to it that the bottles and cans find their way to the landfill. Notwithstanding this, anti-litter measures are constantly advanced and occasionally adopted, often in response to sterner source reduction proposals. A good example in recent years is the enactment in Washington State of the Model Litter Control Act, consisting of a renovated fine system for litterers, provisions for anti-litter labeling messages on containers, requirements that vehicles operating in the state carry litter bags, and that commercial firms catering to the public use state-approved litter barrels.[61] The feature of the Washington State legislation attracting the most attention is a litter assessment tax on the gross sales of various consumer products thought to be reasonably related to the litter problem.[62] The tax is viewed and has functioned not as a source reduction measure but as a fund-raiser to support anti-litter public information programs.

In recent years source reduction legislation has been considered widely and enacted occasionally to contain the dispersal of beverage containers. The laws take various forms:[63] Minnesota [64] reserves a pre-marketing review power over all new packaging materials, and the authority to ban those that would constitute "a solid waste disposal or environmental protection problem." South Dakota [65] prohibits

59. Compare §§ 3.8 (intermittent controls), 3.15 (transportation controls), 4.18 (load on top), 5.7 (keep 'em high), above; § 8.3 (read the label) below.

60. One source estimates that litter fines assessed average a ludicrously low $100 per state per year. National Industrial Pollution Control Council, Minutes of Beverage Subcouncil, June 23, 1970, at 4.

61. Rev.Code Wash.Ann. § 70.93.010 et seq.

62. Id. §§ 70.93.120–.140.

63. See Research Triangle Park Study, supra note 52, ch. 4 (analyzing ten alternative proposals); Environmental Protection Agency, Resource and Environmental Profile Analysis of Nine Beverage Container Alternatives: Final Report (1974). In the November 1976 general elections, mandatory deposit referendums were approved by the voters of Maine and Michigan, but two similar proposals were rejected in Colorado and Massachusetts. See National Wildlife Federation, Conservation News, Nov. 15, 1976, at 2.

64. Minn.Solid Wastes Recycling Law, Minn.Stat.Ann. § 116F.06(2).

65. S.D.Comp.Laws § 34–16C–9.

the sale of beverage containers which are not reusable or biodegradable. Vermont,[66] Oregon[67] and several municipalities[68] require mandatory deposits on all beer and soft drink containers sold within the state. At a policy level, the merits and demerits of a mandatory deposit system have been debated as thoroughly as any single environmental issue.[69] Proponents point to energy savings,[70] job increases (mostly at the retail and distribution sectors),[71] lower prices for consumers,[72] a reduction in litter[73] and solid waste[74] with a consequent preservation of resources. Opponents cite job losses (mostly at the container manufacturing level),[75] sales declines, price increases, reduced tax revenues, an unchanged litter level and a curtailment of consumer freedom.[76] Choosing a mandatory deposit system in light of these competing claims seems well within the state's permissible police power, and has been held not to burden interstate commerce in

66. Vt.Stat.Ann. tit. 10, § 1522.

67. Or.Rev.Stat. §§ 459.810–459.890; see Comment, The Oregon Bottle Bill, 54 Or.L.Rev. 175 (1975); D. Waggoner, Oregon's Bottle Bill Two Years Later (1974).

68. E. g., City Council of Bowie, Maryland, Ordinance O–4–71 (Mar. 8, 1971).

69. A recent bibliography appears in 40 Fed.Reg. 52970 (Nov. 13, 1975). Extensive congressional hearings have been held over a period of several years. See Hearings on Solid Waste Management Act of 1972, Before the Subcomm. on Environment of the Senate Comm. on Commerce, S.Doc. No.60, 92d Cong., 2d Sess. (1972) [hereinafter cited as 1972 Senate Hearings]; Hearings on Resource Conservation and Recycling, Before the Subcomm. on Environment of the Senate Comm. on Commerce, S.Doc. No.56, 93d Cong., 1st Sess. (1973); Hearings on Nonreturnable Beverage Container Prohibition Act, Before the Subcomm. on Environment of the Senate Comm. on Commerce, S.Doc. No.120, 93d Cong., 2d Sess. (1974); Hearings on Waste Control Act of 1975, Before the Subcomm. on Transportation and Commerce of the House Comm. on Interstate and Foreign Commerce, H.R.Doc.No.28, 94th Cong., 1st Sess. (1975) [hereinafter cited as 1975 House Hearings].

70. Hannon, System Energy and Recycling: A Study of the Beverage Industry (1972), in 1972 Senate Hearings, supra note 69, at 302.

71. 1972 Senate Hearings, supra note 69, at 298–301 (testimony of Hugh Folk, Professor of Economics, U. of Illinois).

72. Hearings on Proposals to Prohibit Certain No-Deposit, No-Return Containers, Before the Subcomm. on Public Health and Welfare of the House Comm. on Interstate and Foreign Commerce, H.R.Doc.No.88, 91st Cong., 2d Sess. 18–19 (1970) (testimony of W. Roger Strelow, HEW) [hereinafter cited as Hearings on No-Return Containers].

73. Quarles, supra note 52, at 50025 (citing authorities).

74. Research Triangle Institute Report, supra note 52, at 153–55.

75. Midwest Research Institute, The National Economic Impact of a Ban on Nonrefillable Beverage Containers (1971). The Research Triangle Institute Report, supra note 52, at 58–59, predicts a national deposit measure in 1969 would cause the loss of approximately 60,500 jobs, primarily in the container manufacturing industries, and a gain of 60,800 jobs, primarily in the retail and product distribution sections.

76. See 1975 House Hearings, supra note 69.

a constitutional sense.[77] Some of the municipal mandatory deposit measures have been invalidated on grounds peculiar to local law.[78] The long run prospects for survival and emulation by other jurisdictions, however, is good.

After several years of indecision,[79] the federal Environmental Protection Agency is now committed to a phased-in system of returnable bottles on a national scale. One regulatory step it has initiated to enforce its view is to promulgate Guidelines for Beverage Containers under Section 209 (now Section 1008) of the Solid Waste Disposal Act.[80] These guidelines, which are binding only on federal agencies, would require that all soft drinks sold in beverage containers (including bottles and cans but not cups) [81] be sold only in returnable containers having a deposit value of at least five cents.[82] A dealer engaged in the sales is required to pay the refund value only on those containers of brands he sells.[83] Sales by vending machines are proposed to be covered although, if the machines are unattended, the five cent deposit may not be included in the price of the product provided the container has a refund value.[84] As with most of its guidelines,[85] EPA makes allowance for agencies who decide not to comply,[86] although this generosity well may be inconsistent with the spirit of the Act.[87]

d. *Miscellaneous Consumer Products*

The management of conventional solid wastes presents a wide range of other unique problems that sometimes are dealt with sepa-

77. American Can Co. v. Oregon Liquor Control Comm'n, 15 Or.App. 618, 517 P.2d 691, 4 ELR 20218 (1973).

78. See, e. g., Washington Coca Cola Bottling Co. v. Montgomery County, Equity No. 54916 (Md.Cir.Ct. Montgomery County 1976) (holding that the county imposed tax on nonreturnable beverage containers violated the Maryland Constitution, which vests the state legislature with the exclusive authority to impose regulatory taxes). Contra Allview, Inc. v. Howard County, 3 ELR 20223 (Md. Cir.Ct.1972) (rejecting state law attack on validity of county ordinance forbidding sale of beer and soft drinks in nonreturnable containers).

79. Compare Hearings on No-Return Containers, supra note 72, at 24 with 1972 Senate Hearings, supra note 69, at 229. See also 122 Cong.Rec. S11072–88 (daily ed. June 30, 1976) (containing debate and negative vote [60–26] on the Hatfield amendment that would have required the sale of beer and soft drinks in containers with a refund value of at least five cents; a provision to study a mandatory deposit program was adopted).

80. 41 Fed.Reg. 41202 (Sept. 21, 1976), 40 CFR pt. 244.

81. 40 CFR § 244.101(b).

82. Id. § 244.201(b).

83. Id. § 244.201(c).

84. See 41 Fed.Reg. 41203 (Sept. 21, 1976).

85. § 6.4 above.

86. 40 CFR § 244.100(f)(3) (requiring a report from noncomplying agencies).

87. 42 U.S.C.A. § 6964(a)(1) requires federal agencies to "insure compliance" with EPA-recommended guidelines. This mandatory legislative direction is circumvented when EPA includes in its guidelines provisions inviting noncompliance.

rately by law. Collection challenges are posed by residential complexes, multi-story buildings, and rural areas. Storage problems are presented acutely by food wastes. Disposal or reuse dilemmas are created by scrap automobile tires,[88] hospital wastes,[89] polyethylene plastics (accounting for 30 percent of total United States' plastic production),[90] and textiles, especially the synthetics,[91] to mention only a few examples.

§ 6.10 Hazardous Wastes

Hazardous wastes include any wastes posing a present or potential hazard to human health because of toxicity, nondegradability, persistence in nature or susceptibility to biological magnification.[1] They come in many forms (solids, sludges, slurries and liquids), and fall into categories that often overlap (inorganic toxic metals; salts, acids or bases; synthetic organics; flammables; explosives; pathological, biological and radioactive materials). Hazardous wastes are generated in substantial quantities, and the problem is growing: the Environmental Protection Agency estimates the annual total industrial waste stream to be some 260 million tons, of which perhaps 25 million tons are deemed hazardous; this figure is 2.5 times the level reported to Congress in 1974.[2] Air and water pollution control residuals are one of the prime sources of the hazardous wastes now mostly disposed of on land.

a. *Present Practice*

Disposal of hazardous wastes presently is best described as erratic:[3] on-site disposal is common. This consists of filling large lagoons with liquids or of stockpiling solids on industrial sites. The problem is postponed until environmental effects are felt, sometimes soon, sometimes not for decades. Illicit dumping is common—in sewers, streams, landfills, swamps, quarries, open fields. Often the

---

88. Environmental Protection Agency, Scrap Tires as Artificial Reefs (1974).

89. Dep't of HEW, Solid Wastes Handling in Hospitals (reprinted 1970).

90. Environmental Protection Agency, Feasibility Study of the Disposal of Polyethylene Plastic Waste (1971).

91. Salvage Markets Study, supra note 45, at 73–79.

1. Section 3(4) of S.1086 and H.R. 4873, 93d Cong., 1st Sess. (1973), the proposed Hazardous Waste Management Act of 1973, reprinted in Environmental Protection Agency, Report to Congress on the Disposal of Hazardous Wastes, Senate Comm. on Public Works, Doc.No.21, 93d Cong., 2d Sess. app. G (Comm.Print 1974) [hereinafter cited as EPA Hazardous Wastes Report]. Compare note 53, infra. Definitions of hazardous wastes vary widely in state legislation. See Model State Toxic Waste Disposal Act § 3(6), in 32 Council of State Governments, Suggested State Legislation 20 (1973).

2. See Hearings on Waste Control Act of 1975, Before the Subcomm. on Transportation and Commerce of the House Comm. on Interstate and Foreign Commerce, 94th Cong., 1st Sess. 769–72 (1975) [hereinafter cited as 1975 House Hearings].

3. Id. at 775.

immediate perpetrator is a low-bid contract hauler doing the dirty work for a reputable manufacturer or government enterprise.

Some firms specialize in the safe treatment and disposal of hazardous wastes.[4] Typically, they are uncommon (sometimes only one or two firms in major industrial states), economically marginal, often in continuous difficulty as air, water and land polluters. The facilities may amount to little more than a place where hazardous wastes are contained. Ingenuity may bring new markets but many of the wastes are simply kept there with the hope they will not escape during the next heavy rainfall. Technologically, according to the dogma, most hazardous wastes can be treated and disposed of properly.[5] There are some exceptions—radioactive wastes in gas or solid form, and some chemical wastes such as arsenic trioxide—which simply must be stored in secure containers and isolated indefinitely. Economically, the proper disposal of hazardous wastes may cost 30 to 40 times the alternatives that are environmentally less attractive.[6] It is primarily the cost factor that has led to a very sizeable black-market in the disposal of toxic wastes.

The consequences of haphazard disposal practices are duly recorded and include thousands of pollution incidents, many of them well known.[7] Illustrative are the recent controversies in Hopewell and Alexandria, Virginia, involving contamination by kepone and arsenic wastes, respectively.[8] Documented cases include [9] the hospitalization of several people in Minnesota who consumed water contaminated by a 30-year-old deposit of arsenic, the intoxication of workers by the on-site disposal of alkyl lead, massive water pollution caused by a dike collapsing and releasing approximately 400 acre-feet of fly ash waste, another rupturing dike releasing 2 billion gallons of slime composed of phosphatic clays and insoluble halides. There are numerous instances also of workers at landfill sites being injured by chemical and other wastes. Incidents such as these may lead to bans against hazardous wastes at landfill sites, which may be best able to handle

---

4. Environmental Protection Agency, Hazardous Waste Management Facilities in the United States (1974).

5. EPA Hazardous Wastes Report, supra note 1, at ix.

6. Council on Environmental Quality, Fifth Ann.Rep. 139 (1974).

7. E. g., Comm. on Interstate and Foreign Commerce, Resource Recovery and Conservation Act of 1976, H.R. Rep. 1491, 94th Cong., 2d Sess., 17–23 (1976) (describing 59 incidents in 20 states); EPA Hazardous Wastes Report, supra note 1, app. A; Walker, Where Have All the Toxic Chemicals Gone? 11 Ground Water No. 2 (1973).

8. See Wash.Post, Dec. 17, 1975, at A1, col. 5 (reporting that "detectable traces" of Kepone were discovered by EPA in air samples taken as far away as 16 miles from the Life Sciences plant in Hopewell and in water samples taken as far away as 40 miles); Wash.Post, Feb. 23, 1976, at A1, col. 4 (reporting that soil samples taken from property owned by the R. H. Bogle Chemical Co. contained as much as 27,700 ppm of arsenic; 100–200 ppm of arsenic is considered to be dangerous).

9. EPA Hazardous Wastes Report, supra note 1, app. A.

them, forcing disposal by chancier means. A hazardous wastes disposal problem familiar to many citizens is that of crankcase oil, which is inadequately disposed of in huge quantities for want of suitable disposal sites and of incentives.[10]

Close to twenty federal statutes have varying degrees of direct impact on the disposal of hazardous wastes,[11] including prominently the Clean Air Act,[12] the Federal Water Pollution Control Act[13] and the Federal Environmental Pesticide Control Act.[14] Sometimes Congress separately addresses certain kinds of wastes—sewage sludge from municipal plants,[15] pesticides and pesticide containers,[16] waste oils [17] and radioactive materials.[18] More often it acts to protect vulnerable resources—estuarine areas by the Rivers and Harbors Act,[19] ocean waters by the Marine Protection, Research and Sanctuaries Act,[20] drinking water supplies by the Safe Drinking Water Act.[21] Except in a fragmentary way, prior to 1976 there was no federal regulation of the land disposal of hazardous wastes. In its 1974 Report to the Congress, EPA proposed legislation on the subject,[22] which was enacted into law with the passage of the Resource Conservation

10. E. g., Cornell, Howland, Hayes & Merrifield, Seattle Area Oil Waste Disposal Facility Study (1969) (indicating that of the six million gallons of crankcase oil sold annually in the Seattle region less than half (2.5 million gallons) was refined); §§ 6.5, 6.6 above.

11. EPA Hazardous Wastes Report, supra note 1, at 15, mentions 17. Several others are not mentioned.

12. Ch. 3 above.

13. Ch. 4 above.

14. Ch. 8 below.

15. § 4.7 above.

16. § 8.3 below.

17. § 6.6 above.

18. See Comm. on Government Operations, Low-Level Nuclear Waste Disposal, H.R.Rep.No.1320, 94th Cong., 2d Sess. (1976); Hearings on Low-Level Radioactive Waste Disposal, 94th Cong., 2d Sess. (1976). The transportation and disposal of radioactive wastes is regulated by the Department of Transportation and the Nuclear Regulatory Commission (formerly the Atomic Energy Commission). See Gofman & Tamplin, Nuclear Power, Technology and Environmental Law, 2 Env.L.Rev. 57 (1971); Green, Radioactive Waste and the Environment, 11 Nat.Res.J. 281 (1971); Kubo & Rose, Disposal of Nuclear Wastes, 182 Science 1205 (1973); Moore, The Environmentalist and Radioactive Waste, 49 Chi.–Kent L.Rev. 55 (1972); Swan, Management of High-Level Radioactive Wastes: The AEC and the Legal Process, 1973 Law & Social Order 263; Note, Radioactive Waste: A Failure of Government Regulation, 37 Albany L.Rev. 97 (1972). The National Environmental Policy Act has been read to require consideration of the waste disposal problem in the licensing process. See Natural Resources Defense Council, Inc. v. Nuclear Regulatory Comm'n (Vermont Yankee), —— U.S.App.D.C. ——, 547 F.2d 633 (1976); Aeschliman v. Nuclear Regulatory Comm'n (Midland), —— U.S.App.D.C. ——, 547 F.2d 622, 6 ELR 20599 (1976); Natural Resources Defense Council, Inc. v. Nuclear Regulatory Comm'n (GESMO), 539 F.2d 824, 6 ELR 20513 (2d Cir. 1976). See also Nuclear Regulatory Comm'n, Environmental Survey of the Reprocessing and Waste Management Portions of the CWR Fuel Cycle (1976).

19. § 4.5 above.

20. § 4.16 above.

21. § 4.3 above.

22. Note 1, supra.

and Recovery Act of 1976. The approach recommended was essentially regulatory for nonradioactive wastes as opposed to government owned and operated facilities. EPA would identify hazardous wastes, establish standards for treatment and disposal and lay down guidelines for state implementation programs. As under FWPCA, the proposal envisaged delegation of enforcement authority to state officials. Further federal legislation was inevitable as the case studies on poisonings, rupturing waste ponds and indiscriminate dumping accumulated. One observer predicts eventual "cradle to grave" management of hazardous wastes, with a strong role for the federal government.[23]

Liability for injuries caused by the land disposal of hazardous wastes is exclusively the domain of state law. The common theories are negligence and strict liability for abnormally dangerous activities.[24] The trend towards strict liability may be accelerated by legislation.[25] An adequate program of regulation, according to one authority, "would require hazardous waste generators to report the types of quantities of waste which they generate, and would regulate temporary waste sinks (i. e., storage and transfer facilities), permanent sinks (i. e., reprocessing, treatment, and disposal facilities), and the transportation of hazardous wastes."[26] By these criteria, only three states (California, Oregon and Minnesota) are well along towards implementation of a comprehensive hazardous wastes management program.[27]

Altogether, twenty-five states assert a regulatory role over various aspects of the transportation, reprocessing, disposal cycle.[28] Ten states require permits of hazardous waste haulers.[29] Indiana, for example, requires a waste hauler permit for all persons carrying liquid industrial waste within the boundaries of the state.[30] No entity can allow the hauling of liquid waste from its site or accept it for disposal or treatment unless the carrier has a valid permit.[31] Loose controls are imposed on the spreading of waste oil for dust control purposes[32] and other dispositions threatening water quality. All trucks and tanks used for hauling are given numbers.[33] Records must be kept of all hauls, including "the date, source of waste, quan-

23. Lehman, Federal Program for Hazardous Waste Management, reprinted from Waste Age, Sept. 1974.

24. § 2.14 above.

25. E. g., Or.Rev.Stat. § 459.685.

26. 1975 House Hearings, supra note 2, at 775.

27. Ibid.

28. EPA Hazardous Waste Report, supra note 1, at 17.

29. 1975 House Hearings, supra note 2, at 775.

30. Indiana Industrial Waste Hauler Permit Regulation § II(a) (1974).

31. Id. §§ II(b), (c).

32. Id. § II(c). The spreading of waste oil on roadways for dust control is permissible "if done in a manner that precludes hazardous or nuisance conditions."

33. Id. § II(h).

tity, type and the point and method of disposal."[34] Similarly, those who use haulers to dispose of wastes are obliged to record "the date, the name of the waste hauler, and the quantity and type of waste removed."[35] These reporting requirements obviously are designed to determine how big the problem is and where it goes. They eventually should be supplemented by a requirement that disposal be made only at approved sites.

State regulations of the processing and disposal of hazardous wastes vary greatly. Some call for an administrative listing of hazardous wastes;[36] other do not. Hazardous wastes are defined variously. California has a category of "extremely hazardous waste", (capable of causing death or disabling personal injury), producers of which must notify the State Department of Public Health when they intend to dispose of it.[37] Regulatory techniques differ and may include public ownership and control of disposal sites,[38] the licensing or registration of sites,[39] and the issuance of permits to those disposing of wastes.[40] Standards governing disposal are occasionally specific[41] but are usually quite general, reflecting a lack of administrative familiarity with the problems. South Carolina, for example, insists that disposal of "waste sludge and slurries shall be done with special consideration of air and water pollution, and the health and safety of employees"; conditions are to be prescribed on a "case by case basis."[42] Several states simply reserve the right to decide whether hazardous wastes of certain types may be permitted in a sanitary landfill,[43] or must be disposed of elsewhere.[44] Only fourteen states designate land-

34. Id. § IV(a).

35. Id. § IV(b).

36. E. g., Oregon Solid Waste Management Law, Or.Rev.Stat. §§ 459.410(6)(b), 459.430(6); Pennsylvania Solid Waste Regulations, 25 Pa.Code § 75.231 (1973).

37. California Health & Safety Code § 25153.

38. Or.Rev.Stat. ch. 459, §§ 459.590, 459.595.

39. Id. § 459.510(2); Texas Regulation on Disposal of Industrial Solid Waste, Rule 310.1 (1970).

40. South Carolina Guidelines for Waste Disposal Permits (1972).

41. South Carolina Industrial Solid Waste Disposal Site Regulation § IX (1972) (prescribing conditions for land disposal of inert industrial solid waste); Delaware Solid Waste Disposal Regulation § 7 (1974).

42. South Carolina Industrial Solid Waste Disposal Site Regulation § VI (1972).

43. E. g., Pennsylvania Solid Waste Regulations, 25 Pa.Code §§ 75.116(a), (b), read as follows:

(a) The disposal of sewage solids, liquids and hazardous waste in a sanitary landfill shall not be permitted until the methods of disposal, suitability of the site and plan of operation have been reviewed and approved by the Department.

(b) sewage sludge shall be digested properly and dried to approximately eighty (80%) per cent moisture contents by weight. Septic system cleanings shall not be allowed except as approved by the Department.

Compare § 4.7 above (sewage sludge).

44. E. g., Florida Resource Recovery and Management Regulations § 17-7.04(3) (1975); Illinois Solid Waste Regulations, Rule 310(b) (1973);

fill sites as suitable for hazardous wastes.[45] Not all states purporting to regulate the disposal or reprocessing of hazardous wastes have in force what appears to be an obvious prohibition against the disposal of hazardous wastes at unauthorized sites or by disapproved methods. That the present regulatory system is more than a little porous is suggested strongly by the disclosure that several of the twenty-five states purporting to manage hazardous wastes do not have a single treatment and disposal facility within their borders.[46]

As with many pollution problems, common law liability rules are proven losers in influencing the choice of disposal alternatives for hazardous wastes. In many respects, these newly discovered land pollutants are refugees from air and water pollution regulatory schemes. The same principles of source reduction and the narrowing of treatment options undoubtedly will be carried over to those generating solid wastes. The movement in state legislatures might very well lead eventually to solid waste discharge permits, to be satisfied by adequate on or off-site treatment or by placing the wastes in the hands of a hauler who in turn can be held responsible.

b. *1976 Amendments*

The long awaited federal presence on hazardous waste disposal appeared in pretty much the expected form in the Resource Conservation and Recovery Act of 1976.[47] Under the Act the EPA Administrator must promulgate criteria for identifying hazardous wastes and publish a list designating certain materials as hazardous wastes.[48] There is no express provision that solid wastes containing substances designated as hazardous under the air [49] and water [50] pollution laws are to be deemed hazardous wastes for the purpose of the Resource Recovery Act; [51] however, it is apparent that a decision not to list such a substance would be subject to strict judicial scrutiny under the dictates of the "hard look" doctrine.[52] The statutory definition of "hazardous waste" is "a solid waste, or combination of solid wastes, which because of its quantity, concentration, or physical, chemical, or

Michigan Solid Waste Regulations, R 325.2723 (1973).

45. 1975 House Hearings, supra note 2, at 775.

46. EPA Hazardous Waste Report, supra note 1, at 17.

47. Pub.L. No. 94–580, 90 Stat. 2795, 42 U.S.C.A. § 6901 et seq.

48. Sections 3001(a), (b), 42 U.S.C.A. §§ 6921(a), (b). After publication of the initial list of hazardous wastes, the governor of any state may petition the Administrator to identify or list a material not included. Section 3001(c), 42 U.S.C.A. § 6921(c). The Administrator must act within 90 days following receipt of the petition, and if the Administrator denies the petition because of "financial considerations," he must provide a statement concerning such considerations. Ibid.

49. See § 3.11 above.

50. See § 4.15 above.

51. Compare S.3622, § 212(a), 94th Cong., 2d Sess. (1976).

52. See § 1.5 above.

infectious characteristics may—(A) cause, or significantly contribute to an increase in mortality or an increase in serious irreversible, or incapacitating reversible, illness, or (B) pose a substantial present or potential hazard to human health or the environment when improperly treated, stored, transported, or disposed of, or otherwise managed." [53]

The basic regulatory premise forbids disposal [54] of any designated hazardous waste, within six months [55] of the designation, except in accordance with a permit.[56] Within 18 months after enactment, the EPA Administrator must promulgate regulations requiring permits for those engaged in the disposal, treatment [57] or storage [58] of hazardous wastes.[59] A number of statutory conditions must be met prior to the issuance of a permit,[60] including satisfaction of reporting and record keeping requirements, development of a contingency plan "to minimize damage" from any disposal, and compliance with appropriate practices "for the management, treatment, storage, and disposal of hazardous wastes." As under the National Pollutant Discharge Elimination System of the Federal Water Pollution Control Act,[61] provision is made for delegating permit authority over hazardous wastes to states satisfying statutory criteria for a satisfactory permit program.[62] The Administrator must be given a copy of each state permit proposed to be issued and, within constraints, may exercise a veto power over it.[63] An explicit invitation for a state veto of fed-

53. Section 1004(5), 42 U.S.C.A. § 6903 (5). Solid or dissolved materials in domestic sewage and irrigation return flows, industrial discharges subject to permits under Section 402 of the Federal Water Pollution Control Act, and source, special nuclear or byproduct material as defined by the Atomic Energy Act of 1954 are not considered "solid waste". See section 1004(27), 42 U.S.C.A. § 6903(27).

54. Section 1004(3), 42 U.S.C.A. § 6903 (3), defines "disposal" as
the discharge, deposit, injection, dumping, spilling, leaking, or placing of any solid waste or hazardous waste into or on any land or water so that such solid waste or hazardous waste or any constituent thereof may enter the environment or be emitted into the air or discharged into any waters, including ground waters.

55. Section 3010(b), 42 U.S.C.A. § 6930 (b).

56. Section 2005(a), 42 U.S.C.A. § 6925 (a).

57. Section 1004(34), 42 U.S.C.A. § 6903(34), defines "treatment" as any method, technique, or process, including neutralization, designed to change the physical, chemical, or biological character or composition of any hazardous waste, so as to neutralize such waste or so as to render such wastes nonhazardous, safer for transport, amenable for resource recovery, amenable for storage, or reduced in volume.

58. Section 1004(33), 42 U.S.C.A. § 6903(33), defines "storage" as the containment of hazardous waste, either on a temporary basis or for a period of years, in such a manner as not to constitute disposal of such hazardous waste.

59. Section 3005(a), 42 U.S.C.A. § 6925 (a).

60. Sections 3004(2), (5), (7), 42 U.S.C.A. §§ 6924(2), (5), (7).

61. See § 4.11 above.

62. Section 3006(b), 42 U.S.C.A. § 6926 (b).

63. Ibid.

erally issued permits, comparable to that appearing in Section 401 of the Federal Water Pollution Control Act,[64] is missing from the hazardous waste permit requirements although it appears that the EPA Administrator may provide for a state veto in the implementing regulations.

Permit conditions, once imposed, are enforceable by citizen suits [65] and by the Administrator.[66] As under the air [67] and water [68] pollution laws, the Administrator's principal enforcement options include issuance of a civil compliance order or initiation directly of a civil enforcement action.[69] Any administrative order "shall state with reasonable specificity the nature of the violation, and shall specify a time for compliance and assess a penalty, if any, which the Administrator determines is reasonable taking into account the seriousness of the violation and any good faith efforts to comply with applicable requirements." [70] Knowing violations of an order are punishable by a fine of "not more than $25,000 per day of violation" or by imprisonment for not more than one year, or by both.[71]

64. 33 U.S.C.A. § 1341.

65. Section 7002(a)(1), 42 U.S.C.A. § 6972(a)(1).

66. Section 3008, 42 U.S.C.A. § 6928.

67. See § 3.19 above.

68. See § 4.21 above.

69. Section 3008(a)(1), 42 U.S.C.A. § 6928(a)(1).

70. Section 3008(c), 42 U.S.C.A. § 6928(c).

71. Section 3008(d), 42 U.S.C.A. § 6928(d).

Chapter VII

NATIONAL ENVIRONMENTAL POLICY ACT

§ 7.1 Introduction

The National Environmental Policy Act of 1969 [1] is the Sherman Act of environmental law. It is a seminal enactment that introduces federal courts to environmental questions comprehensively for the first time, expands the scope of judicial review of administrative action, injects new discipline and values into administrative decision-making, and strengthens the hand of the Congress in overseeing agency actions with adverse environmental effects. While NEPA can be credited with all these things and more, so too it can be written off as "a paper tiger." [2] It is the fate of significant legislation to fall short of its supporters' fondest aims.

NEPA contains none of the intricacies of the Clean Air Act or the Federal Water Pollution Control Act. It sets forth a ringing and vague statement of purposes.[3] Title I has five sections. Section 101(a),[4] which might as well be an extension of the purpose clause, declares it the "continuing policy of the Federal Government . . . to use all practicable means and measures . . . to create and maintain conditions under which man and nature can exist in productive harmony, and fulfill the social, economic, and other requirements of present and future generations of Americans." Section 101(b)[5]

1. Pub.L. No. 91–180, 83 Stat. 852, 42 U.S.C.A. §§ 4331 et seq.

2. Calvert Cliffs' Coord. Comm. v. Atomic Energy Comm'n, 146 U.S.App. D.C. 33, 38, 449 F.2d 1109, 1114, 1 ELR 20346, 20348 (1971), cert. denied 404 U.S. 942 (1972).

3. The purposes clause, 83 Stat. 852, reads in full as follows:
    The purposes of this Act are: To declare a national policy which will encourage productive and enjoyable harmony between man and his environment; to promote efforts which will prevent or eliminate damage to the environment and biosphere and stimulate the health and welfare of man; to enrich the understanding of the ecological systems and natural resources important to the Nation; and to establish a Council on Environmental Quality.

4. 42 U.S.C.A. § 4331(a).

5. The objectives identified in section 101(b), 42 U.S.C.A. § 4331(b), are that the Nation may—
    (1) fulfill the responsibilities of each generation as trustee of the environment for succeeding generations;
    (2) assure for all Americans safe, healthful, productive, and esthetically and culturally pleasing surroundings;
    (3) attain the widest range of beneficial uses of the environment without degradation, risk to health or safety, or other undesirable or unintended consequences;
    (4) preserve important historic, cultural, and natural aspects of our national heritage, and maintain, wherever possible, an environment which supports diversity, and variety of individual choice;
    (5) achieve a balance between population and resource use which

asserts that "it is the continuing responsibility of the Federal Government to use all practicable means, consistent with other essential considerations of national policy," to improve plans and programs towards achieving six general ends of environmental excellence, such as approaching maximum attainable recycling and achieving a balance between population and resource use.

Section 101(b) obviously is not intimidating in its specificity. The ends to be achieved are generally stated. Only "practicable" means to those ends must be pursued. And otherwise "practicable" means can be ignored if inconsistent "with other essential considerations of national policy." Lest vague objectives and uncertain means be equated with substantive law of no consequence, however, one should recall the definition of a private nuisance:[6] conduct unreasonably interfering with the use and enjoyment of another's property.

Section 102 directs that "to the fullest extent possible" all agencies of the federal government shall undertake eight types of actions designed to fulfill the objectives of the statute, including making available to other government entities information useful in enhancing environmental quality[7] and lending support to initiatives designed to maximize international cooperation in preventing a decline in worldwide environmental quality.[8] Best known among these calls to action[9] is section 102(2)(C) requiring the inclusion "in every recommendation or report on proposals for legislation and other major Federal actions significantly affecting the quality of the human environment" a detailed statement on, among other things, "the environmental impact of the proposed action." Prior to making any detailed statement, "the responsible Federal official shall consult with and obtain the comments of any Federal agency which has jurisdiction

will permit high standards of living and a wide sharing of life's amenities; and
    (6) enhance the quality of renewable resources and approach the maximum attainable recycling of depletable resources.

6. § 2.3 above.

7. Section 102(2)(G), 42 U.S.C.A. § 4332(2)(G), reads:
make available to States, counties, municipalities, institutions, and individuals, advice and information useful in restoring, maintaining and enhancing the quality of the environment.

8. Section 102(2)(F), 42 U.S.C.A. § 4332(2)(F), reads:
recognize the worldwide and long-range character of environmental problems and, where consistent with the foreign policy of the United States, lend appropriate support to initiatives, resolutions, and programs designed to maximize international cooperation in anticipating and preventing a decline in the quality of mankind's world environment.

9. The provisions and procedures that became section 102 are called "action-forcing designed to assure that all Federal agencies plan and work towards meeting the challenge of a better environment." Comm. on Interior and Insular Affairs, National Environmental Policy Act of 1969, S.Rep.No. 296, 91st Cong., 1st Sess. 9 (1969); see § 7.4 below.

by law or special expertise with respect to any environmental impact involved." The statement must be circulated to interested federal, state and local agencies and "shall accompany the proposal through the existing agency review processes."

Section 103 [10] has been called a "neglected but fertile provision" [11] which accords the agencies strong powers of self-analysis. Section 103 requires all agencies of the federal government to review their present statutory authority, administrative regulations and policies "for the purpose of determining whether there are any deficiencies or inconsistencies therein which prohibit full compliance with the purposes and provisions of this Act." Each agency was required to propose to the President not later than July 1, 1971 "such measures as may be necessary to bring their authority and policies into conformity with the intent, purposes, and procedures set forth in this Act." For the most part these "103 statements" restate NEPA, sometimes evading it, sometimes amending it, often interpreting it. Agency regulations implementing the Act of course are now widely in effect, and part and parcel of NEPA litigation.[12]

Sections 104 and 105 attempt to reconcile NEPA with the agencies' existing statutory mandates. Section 105 [13] makes clear that the policies and goals of the Act are "supplementary" to those set forth in "existing authorizations of Federal agencies." Conflicts there will be but a reconciliation must be sought. Case law gives rise to a distinction between the use of NEPA to expand powers incrementally but not to overthrow them entirely. Thus, NEPA adds a supplemental environmental criterion to the U. S. Corps of Engineers' general powers to issue dredge and fill permits,[14] the Atomic Energy Commission's (now the Nuclear Regulatory Commission's) authority to license the construction and operation of nuclear power plants,[15] the Securi-

---

10. 42 U.S.C.A. § 4333.

11. F. Anderson, NEPA In the Courts: A Legal Analysis of the National Environmental Policy Act 3 (1973) [hereinafter cited as NEPA in the Courts].

12. See 5 ELR 46001 et seq. (1975), reproducing verbatim the regulations of, among others, the Forest Service, Rural Electrification Administration, Soil Conservation Service, Atomic Energy Commission (now the Nuclear Regulatory Commission), Central Intelligence Agency, Army Corps of Engineers, Environmental Protection Agency, Law Enforcement Assistance Administration, Occupational Safety and Health Administration, National Aeronautics and Space Administration, National Science Foundation, Tennessee Valley Authority, Department of Transportation, Department of the Treasury and the Veterans Administration. For a full listing and citation of NEPA regulations prepared by nearly seventy entities of the federal government, see Council on Environmental Quality, Fifth Ann. Rep. 382–85, table 1 (1974). See also Andrews, NEPA in Practice: Environmental Policy or Administrative Reform? 6 ELR 50001 (1976).

13. 42 U.S.C.A. § 4335.

14. Zabel v. Tabb, 430 F.2d 199, 214, 1 ELR 20023, 20031 (5th Cir. 1970), cert. denied 401 U.S. 910 (1971); cf. United States v. Asbury Park, 340 F.Supp. 555, 563–64 n. 12, 2 ELR 20126, 20129 n. 12 (D.C.N.J.1972).

15. Calvert Cliffs' Coord. Comm. v. Atomic Energy Comm'n, 146 U.S. App.D.C. 33, 449 F.2d 1109, 1 ELR 20346 (1971), cert. denied 404 U.S. 942 (1972).

ties and Exchange Commission's organic powers to require registered companies to disclose information "in the public interest," [16] the Civil Aeronautic Board's powers to license activities resulting in increased traffic at an airport,[17] and the Food and Drug Administration's authority under the Food, Drug and Cosmetic Act to authorize the use of nonreturnable plastic beverage containers.[18] Similarly, NEPA is invoked in support of executive initiatives establishing the Refuse Act Permit Program, regulating the use of off-road vehicles on public lands, barring certain poisons in federal predator-control programs, modifying the multiple use concept of national forest management and regulating mining on national forest lands.[19] Yet at some point it must be recognized that if Congress wants particular action from an agency it should be more explicit than it was in enacting NEPA several years ago. This explains the negative responses of the general counsels of the Council on Environmental Quality, Environmental Protection Agency, Atomic Energy Commission and Federal Power Commission to a question put by Senator Baker: "do you interpret NEPA as expanding the statutory authority of a given agency to implement an alternative otherwise beyond its jurisdiction?"[20] This explains also the view expressed in some cases that "NEPA does not mandate action which goes beyond the agency's organic jurisdiction."[21] While NEPA authorizes a supplemental expansion of authority, it does not justify a gross extension; it embel-

16. Natural Resources Defense Council, Inc. v. Securities & Exch. Comm'n, 389 F.Supp. 689, 5 ELR 20074 (D.C. D.C.1974).

17. See Illinois ex rel. Scott v. Butterfield, 396 F.Supp. 632, 642, 5 ELR 20587, 20591–92 (N.D.Ill.1975) (NEPA reaffirms preexisting powers); cf. Palisades Citizens Ass'n, Inc. v. Civil Aeronautics Bd., 136 U.S.App.D.C. 346, 350, 420 F.2d 188, 192 (1969) (questions of environmental impact are proper "public interest" questions in the Board's certification inquiry).

18. Environmental Defense Fund, Inc. v. Mathews, 410 F.Supp. 336, 6 ELR 20369 (D.C.D.C.1976).

19. Anderson, The National Environmental Policy Act, in Environmental Law Institute, Federal Environment Law 238, 292 n. 198, 296 n. 209 (E. L. Dolgin & T. G. P. Guilbert eds. 1974) (citing authorities); cf. Natural Resources Defense Council, Inc. v. Morton, 388 F.Supp. 829, 5 ELR 20327 (D.D.C.1974) (NEPA supplements Secretary of Interior's powers under the Taylor Grazing Act).

20. Joint Hearings on the Operation of the National Environmental Policy Act of 1969, Before the Senate Comm. on Public Works and the Senate Comm. on Interior and Insular Affairs, S.Doc.No.H32, 92d Cong., 2d Sess. 394–410 (1972).

21. Gage v. Atomic Energy Comm'n, 156 U.S.App.D.C. 231, 237 n. 19, 479 F.2d 1214, 1220 n. 19, 3 ELR 20479, 20482 n. 19 (1973); see Milo Community Hospital v. Weinberger, 525 F.2d 144, 6 ELR 20027 (1st Cir. 1975); Kitchen v. Federal Communications Comm'n, 150 U.S.App.D.C. 292, 464 F.2d 801, 2 ELR 20534 (1972); cf. Flint Ridge Dev. Co. v. Scenic Rivers Ass'n, 426 U.S. 776, 96 S.Ct. 2430, 49 L.Ed.2d 205 (1976) (interpreting directive in 42 U.S.C.A. § 4332(2)(C) that agencies comply "to the fullest extent possible" with NEPA's environmental mandate); § 7.6 below. Compare § 5.7 above (discussing EPA–FAA relationship as regards aircraft noise); § 8.3 below (discussing EPA–DOA relationship on pesticide cancellation decisions).

lishes existing authority, but does not repudiate it. The line that is drawn depends upon such factors as the scope and specificity of the existing mandate, the logic of the extension, the degree of congressional attention given to the subject.

Section 104 [22] says that nothing in sections 102 and 103 "shall in any way affect the specific statutory obligations of any Federal agency (1) to comply with criteria or standards of environmental quality, (2) to coordinate or consult with any Federal or State agency, or (3) to act, or refrain from acting, contingent upon the recommendations or certification of any other Federal or State agency." The principal motivation for section 104 was to remove any inference that NEPA worked a change in the many arrangements where one agency is given an explicit role, such as a veto power, in decisions of another agency.[23]

While much of NEPA is a sleeper exceeding the boldest expectations of its creators, parts of it are clinkers fulfilling little of their potential. The best example is section 101(c)[24] reading: "The Congress recognizes that each person should enjoy a healthful environment and that each person has a responsibility to contribute to the preservation and enhancement of the environment." Despite a legislative history indicating the Congress deliberately refrained from giving federal courts jurisdiction to enforce this provision,[25] a case could be made that section 101(c) creates a federal right to a healthful environment enforceable under the general federal question jurisdiction.[26] So read, section 101(c) could support a vast body of federal case law defining the right to a healthful environment in terms comparable to common law nuisances. The few courts that have considered the point have rejected it summarily,[27] and no serious test case is underway; the Environmental Defense Fund, abandoning previous practice, no longer includes a section 101(c) claim in its major complaints. Section 101(c) seems destined for oblivion, along with the

---

22. 42 U.S.C.A. § 4334.

23. See NEPA in the Courts, supra note 11, at 7–8.

24. 42 U.S.C.A. § 4331(c).

25. Section 101(b) of S.1075, as passed by the Senate, stated, "Congress recognizes that each person has a fundamental and inalienable right to a healthful environment"; however, this was replaced in conference by the language in section 101(c) as enacted because the House conferees were concerned that the Senate version created a private right of action. Comm. of Conference, National Environmental Policy Act of 1969, H.R. Rep.No.765, 91st Cong., 1st Sess. 8 (1969).

26. Cf. J. I. Case Co. v. Borak, 377 U.S. 426, 84 S.Ct. 1555, 12 L.Ed.2d 423 (1964). See also 115 Cong.Rec. 40416 (1969) (remarks of Senator Jackson).

27. Pye v. Dep't of Transp. of Georgia, 513 F.2d 290, 5 ELR 20455 (5th Cir. 1975); Tanner v. Armco Steel Corp., 340 F.Supp. 532, 2 ELR 20246 (S.D. Tex.1972); Environmental Defense Fund, Inc. v. Hoerner Waldorf, 3 ELR 20794 (D.C.Mont.1970). Compare § 2.12 above (federal common law of nuisance).

likes of the federal constitutional right to a clean environment [28] for which this author at least believes there is no support whatsoever.

Title II of NEPA creates and defines the powers of the Council on Environmental Quality. Section 201 [29] directs the President to transmit to the Congress annually an Environmental Quality Report. These reports by now are a regular feature of the environmental literature with a reputation for excellence. Section 204 [30] gives the Council limited powers to investigate the quality of the environment, develop national policies to improve environmental quality, and to review programs and activities of the federal government to ascertain whether they are contributing to fulfillment of the goals of NEPA. Other powers relating to information-gathering and agency-coordinating are given to the Council by the Environmental Quality Improvement Act of 1970 [31] and Executive Order 11514,[32] implementing NEPA. The 1970 Act says that the Chairman of the Council shall aid the President by, among other things, "assisting the Federal departments and agencies in the development and interrelationships of environmental quality criteria and standards established through the Federal Government." [33] The Executive Order directs the Council to undertake various initiatives, including the coordination of "Federal programs related to environmental quality" and the issuance of guidelines to federal agencies "for the preparation of detailed statements on proposals for legislation and other Federal actions affecting the environment, as required by section 102(2)(C) of [NEPA]." [34]

These modest sources of authority have sustained an impressive list of accomplishments. The Council, to be sure, "has chosen the role of presidential advisor" [35] as distinguished from a free-lance ombudsman or agent of the Congress within the executive branch. While this posture sometimes constrains the Council to support publicly positions inconsistent with the dominant environmentalist view

---

28. Roberts, The Right to a Decent Environment; E=MC²: Environment Equals Man Times Courts Redoubling Their Efforts, 55 Cornell L.J. 674 (1970); Note, Toward a Constitutionally Protected Environment, 56 Va.L. Rev. 458 (1970). For an authoritative overview, see Soper, The Constitutional Framework of Environmental Law, in Environmental Law Institute, Federal Environmental Law 20, 100–16 (E. L. Dolgin & T. G. P. Guilbert eds. 1974).

29. 42 U.S.C.A. § 4341.

30. Id. § 4344.

31. Pub.L. No. 91–224, 84 Stat. 114, 42 U.S.C.A. §§ 4371–74.

32. 35 Fed.Reg. 4247 (1970), 3 CFR 286, 42 U.S.C.A. § 4321 note.

33. 42 U.S.C.A. §§ 4372(a), (b).

34. Section 3(b), supra note 32.

35. J. C. Davies III & C. F. Lettow, The Impact of Federal Institutional Arrangements, in Environmental Law Institute, Federal Environmental Law 126, 133 (E. L. Dolgin & T. G. P. Guilbert eds. 1974). The article contains an excellent short summary of the work of the Council. Id. at 130–36. Anderson, supra note 19, at 248–56, provides another insightful commentary on CEQ's "split personality," noting an "obvious conflict" between its roles as a confidential presidential advisor and as overseer of NEPA compliance by the agencies.

Sec. 7.1   INTRODUCTION   703

(support for the supersonic transport being the best example), the role of advisor and coordinator has advantages also. The Council generally is credited with, or blamed for, "the halt to construction of the Cross-Florida Barge Canal, rejection by the Secretary of Transportation of the California Minarets Road proposal, and delays in funding the Tocks Island project in the Delaware River Basin." [36] Occasionally, the Council position on a particular project will be of evidentiary significance in environmental litigation,[37] a circumstance that would occur more often if CEQ's advice were honored as expert opinion publicly available under Section 102(2)(C) of NEPA.[38]

The Council's "major task" is said to be "coordination and development" of the President's annual environmental message and legislative program.[39] While the great legislative ferment of the early 1970's is bound to slacken, CEQ can continue a valuable service as an environmental law revision commission, recommending changes compelled by experience. The Council's administrative law-making is important also, with the thrice revised Guidelines for Preparation of Environmental Impact Statements [40] being a significant trend setter.[41]

36. Davies & Lettow, supra note 35, at 135.

37. E. g., Comm. for Nuclear Responsibility, Inc. v. Schlesinger, 404 U.S. 917, 920, 92 S.Ct. 242, 245–6, 30 L.Ed.2d 191, 193–4 (1971) (Douglas, J.) (citing CEQ opposition to the Cannikin Nuclear Test); Warm Springs Dam Task Force v. Gribble, 417 U.S. 1301, 1307, 94 S.Ct. 2542, 2546, 41 L.Ed.2d 654, 658–9 (1974) (Douglas, Circuit Justice), stay aff'd per curiam 418 U.S. 910, 94 S.Ct. 3202, 41 L.Ed.2d 1156 (1974) (staying construction pending appeal largely on the basis of a letter from the General Counsel of CEQ to the Corps of Engineers stating that the project's environmental impact statement was clearly deficient); Comment, Supreme Court Ushers in New Era for CEQ in Warm Springs Case, 4 ELR 10130 (1974). See also letter from Mr. Gary Widman, CEQ General Counsel to Robert Elliott, HUD General Council, March 15, 1976, attached as exh. A to Appellant's Supplemental Memorandum on Mootness, Homeowners Emergency Life Protection Comm. v. Lynn, Civil No. 74–3301 (9th Cir.).

38. Section 102(2)(C), 42 U.S.C.A. § 4332(2)(C), states that "prior to making any detailed statement, the responsible Federal official shall consult with and obtain the comments of any Federal agency which has jurisdiction by law or special expertise with respect to any environmental impact involved." This "expert" commentary must be made available to the public, see ibid, but CEQ suggestions to agencies on major projects may be unpublished on the theory that they do not come from an agency with any "special expertise." See Davis & Lettow, supra note 35, at 134–35. There is certainly nothing in the legislative history nor plain meaning of section 102(2)(C) to suggest that advice from the President's principal environmental advisor should be silenced on grounds of incompetence. The purpose of the provision quite clearly is to force disclosure from the executive branch of authoritative commentary on environmental impact, and the views of CEQ qualify within that purpose. Compare § 1.10 above (Freedom of Information Act).

39. Davies & Lettow, supra note 35, at 134.

40. 40 CFR pt. 1500; see 42 U.S.C.A. § 5304(h) (giving CEQ power to approve HUD regulations implementing NEPA).

41. § 7.2 below.

Apart from general annual reports, Council studies on discrete topics occasionally play a role in major policy and legal initiatives. A report on ocean dumping [42] contributed to enactment of the Marine Protection, Research and Sanctuaries Act of 1972.[43] A CEQ-sponsored report on predator control [44] contributed to an executive order [45] to minimize environmental abuses from government programs. Reports on toxic substances,[46] offshore drilling,[47] and suburban sprawl [48] are pertinent to continuing legislative debate on those topics. Council studies on clearcutting [49] prompted a draft executive order but no final legal initiatives by the President on the subject.[50] Thus the Council on Environmental Quality, like the National Academy of Sciences [51] and the Office of Technology Assessment [52] is a significant source of the facts to which environmental law responds.

§ 7.2 The Implementing Institutions

The National Environmental Policy Act is tectonic legislation affecting relationships of governmental institutions in many subtle ways. A general discussion of these major influences will precede a voyage through the doctrinal details of the Act.[1] We will examine, in order, the roles under NEPA of (1) the Council on Environmental Quality, (2) the Environmental Protection Agency, (3) the other agencies, and (4) the Congress.

42. Ocean Dumping—A National Policy (1970).

43. § 4.16 above.

44. Advisory Committee on Predator Control, Predator Control—1971: A Report to the CEQ and the Department of the Interior.

45. Exec. Order No. 11643 (Feb. 8, 1972), rescinded by Exec. Order No. 11870 (July 18, 1975).

46. Toxic Substances (1971).

47. OCS Oil and Gas—An Environmental Assessment (1974); Comment, CEQ's Report on Outer Continental Shelf Oil and Gas Development: Recommendations for Institutional and Legal Modifications, 4 ELR 10070 (1974).

48. Interceptor Sewers and Suburban Sprawl (1974) (a 2-volume study prepared by Urban Systems Research and Engineering, Inc.).

49. L. James & V. Randolph, Clearcutting in the Public Forest (1971).

50. See Liroff, The Council on Environmental Quality, 3 ELR 50051, 50064 (1973).

51. § 1.12 above.

52. § 1.3 above.

1. This and succeeding chapters is indebted heavily to the considerable body of legal scholarship on NEPA. Leading efforts include F. R. Anderson, NEPA in the Courts: A Legal Analysis of the National Environmental Policy Act (1973) [hereinafter cited as NEPA in the Courts]; Anderson, The National Environmental Policy Act, in Environmental Law Institute, Federal Environmental Law 238 (E. L. Dolgin & T. G. P. Guilbert eds. 1974); Implementing NEPA's Substantive Goals: A Symposium, 6 ELR 50001 (1976).

a. *Council on Environmental Quality*

Although Senator Henry Jackson, known popularly as the father of NEPA, believed that the Office of Management and Budget (OMB) would play a role in coordinating agency compliance with the Act,[2] OMB has shown "remarkably little enthusiasm for NEPA."[3] It has gradually withdrawn from the fray, despite criticism,[4] leaving the Council on Environmental Quality as the undisputed overseer of agency compliance with NEPA. The chief legitimator of the Council's role is Executive Order 11514, issued March 5, 1970, mandating the issuance of guidelines to assist the agencies in preparing environmental impact statements.[5] Although the courts from time to time have questioned mildly CEQ's statutory authority to issue the guidelines,[6] the power probably can be found in the Environmental Quality Improvement Act of 1970[7] and section 204(3) of NEPA.[8] The question is largely academic, however, as the courts and the agencies have settled upon a course of deference to CEQ guidance and interpretations of NEPA.[9]

In pursuit of its oversight responsibilities, CEQ has prepared "three progressively more demanding sets of guidelines, has issued memoranda to agency counsel on adequate NEPA compliance, has initiated informal quality reviews of impact statements, and has conferred periodically with agency personnel on the adequacy of agency compliance."[10] The CEQ guidelines have become a crucial ingredient of the NEPA decision-making process.[11] Judicial innovations in in-

2. Hearings on S.1075, S.237 and S. 1752, Before the Senate Comm. on Interior and Insular Affairs, 91st Cong., 1st Sess. 116–17 (1969).

3. Anderson, supra note 1, at 250.

4. See Comptroller General of the United States, Report to the House Subcomm. on Fisheries and Wildlife Conservation: Improvements Needed in Federal Efforts to Implement the National Environmental Policy Act of 1969, at 51 (1972).

5. Protection and Enhancement of Environmental Quality § 3(h), Exec. Order No. 11575, 35 Fed.Reg. 4247 (1970).

6. E. g., Greene County Planning Bd. v. Federal Power Comm'n (I), 455 F. 2d 412, 421, 2 ELR 20017, 20021 (2d Cir. 1972), cert. denied 409 U.S. 849; Hiram Clarke Civic Club v. Lynn, 476 F.2d 421, 425, 3 ELR 20287, 20288–89 (5th Cir. 1973) (following *Greene County*).

7. Pub.L. No. 91–224, §§ 203(d)(5), (6), 84 Stat. 114, 42 U.S.C.A. §§ 4372 (d)(5), (6) give the chairman of CEQ the power to assist and advise the President on environmental matters by—

(5) assisting in coordinating among the Federal departments and agencies those programs and activities which affect, protect, and improve environmental quality.

(6) assisting the Federal departments and agencies in the development and interrelationship of environmental quality criteria and standards established through the Federal Government.

8. 42 U.S.C.A. § 4344(3).

9. See cases cited in notes 12, 40–42, infra.

10. Anderson, supra note 1, at 248; see CEQ, Environmental Impact Statements: An Analysis of Six Years' Experience by Seventy Federal Agencies (1976).

11. 40 CFR pt. 1500; see Liroff, The Council on Environmental Quality, 3 ELR 50051 (1973) (discussing the role of CEQ and the evolution of the oversight guidelines). The guidelines are published in 35 Fed.Reg. 7390, 1 ELR 46001 (1970), 35 Fed.Reg. 17224, 2

terpreting the Act sometimes inspire, and sometimes are inspired by, the guidelines.[12] The CEQ rules address many of the close questions under the Act—whether,[13] when [14] and how [15] an environmental impact statement should be prepared, by whom [16] and what it should contain.[17] The habits and standard procedures of the environmental impact statement (EIS) process today owe their existence in large part to the guidelines. Each agency and subdepartment components having EIS procedures must review and revise their procedures, in consultation with the Council, to bring them into conformity with the guidelines.[18] Agency regulations implementing the guidelines hew closely to the CEQ lead. The guidelines prescribe a variety of practices that are now habitually followed—a process of environmental assessment to determine whether a statement is required,[19] circulation of draft and final impact statements,[20] inclusion in the final statement of all substantive comments received on the draft,[21] distribution of the final statement to all persons commenting substantively on the draft and to those who request a copy,[22] preparation of initial environmental assessments concurrently with initial technical and economic studies on a project.[23]

The guidelines underscore and complement NEPA in important respects: they insist that each agency "shall interpret the provisions of NEPA" as a "supplement" to its existing authority and "as a mandate to view traditional policies and missions in the light of the Act's national environmental objectives." [24] Public information provisions are strengthened: each agency must develop an "early notice system" for informing the public on a decision to prepare a draft EIS and for soliciting comments;[25] maintain and make available to the public a list of administrative actions for which EIS' are being prepared;[26] prepare a "publicly available record" of neg-

ELR 46049 (1971), 38 Fed.Reg. 20549, 5 ELR 46003 (1975).

12. Conservation Soc'y of Southern Vermont v. Secretary of Transp. (I), 508 F.2d 927, 5 ELR 20068 (2d Cir. 1974), vacated 423 U.S. 809 (1975) (discussing CEQ accommodation with court interpretation); Environmental Defense Fund, Inc. v. Tennessee Valley Authority (Tellico Dam), 339 F.Supp. 806, 811, 2 ELR 20726 (E.D.Tenn. 1972); Environmental Law Fund v. Volpe, 340 F.Supp. 1328, 1331, 2 ELR 20225, 20226 (N.D.Cal.1972); Sierra Club v. Morton, 348 F.Supp. 219, 220, 2 ELR 20576 (N.D.Cal.1972).

13. 40 CFR §§ 1500.5, 1500.6; see § 7.6 below.

14. 40 CFR § 1500.2; see § 7.7 below.

15. 40 CFR §§ 1500.9–.11.

16. Id. § 1500.7; see § 7.8 below.

17. 40 CFR § 1500.8; see § 7.9 below.

18. 40 CFR § 1500.3.

19. Id. §§ 1500.6(c), 1500.11(f).

20. Id. §§ 1500.7, 1500.9, 1500.10.

21. Id. § 1500.10(a).

22. Id. § 1500.10(b).

23. Id. § 1500.2(b).

24. Id. § 1500.4; see § 7.1 above.

25. 40 CFR § 1500.6(c).

26. Id. §§ 1500.6(c)(1), (3).

Sec. 7.2   THE IMPLEMENTING INSTITUTIONS   707

ative determinations and the reasons the agency is not preparing an EIS for a specific action where one would be expected;[27] make available to the public under the Freedom of Information Act the statement, comments received, and any "underlying documents" including all intra-agency and inter-agency memoranda transmitting comments of federal agencies on the environmental impact of the proposed action.[28] CEQ is committed to publish weekly in the *Federal Register* lists of environmental statements received during the preceding week that are available for public comment.[29]

Public hearing provisions also are addressed in the guidelines. Agency procedures shall "include provision for public hearings on major actions with environmental impact, wherever appropriate, and for providing the public with relevant information, including information on alternative courses of action."[30] Criteria for deciding whether a hearing is appropriate include the expense and size of the proposal, degree of interest in it, and whether public involvement can be achieved by other means.[31] Draft EIS' should be made available to the public at least 15 days prior to the hearing.[32]

The Guidelines also install CEQ as a permanent referee over NEPA related matters: it offers advisory opinions to agencies interested in whether specific actions require impact statements;[33] is available for consultation on the revision of agency regulations;[34] assists in resolving questions of responsibility for statement preparation in cases of multi-agency actions;[35] requests the preparation and circulation of an EIS on a particular project, which can be refused by an agency only upon the preparation of "an environmental assessment and a publicly available record briefly setting forth the reasons for its determination."[36] CEQ commissions studies of selected cases and agency implementation of the NEPA process.[37] But CEQ's NEPA role is virtually all carrot and no stick: the Council does not disapprove agency procedures, environmental statements, or condemn neglect or footdragging in preparing statements. Criticism of statements that is forthcoming is "nonsystematic, *ex parte*",[38] and generally withheld from the public.[39]

27. Id. § 1500.6(c).

28. Id. § 1500.11(d). Under certain circumstances, Section 102(2)(C) of NEPA may require the disclosure of documents otherwise protected under the intra-agency communication exception to the Freedom of Information Act. See § 1.10 above.

29. 40 CFR § 1500.11(c).

30. Id. § 1500.7(d); see § 7.3 below (on NEPA procedures).

31. 40 CFR § 1500.7(d).

32. Ibid.

33. Id. § 1500.6(a).

34. Id. § 1500.3(a).

35. Id. § 1500.7(b); see § 7.8 below.

36. 40 CFR § 1500.11(f).

37. Council on Environmental Quality, Fifth Ann.Rep. 386–87 (1974).

38. NEPA in the Courts, supra note 1, at 13.

39. § 7.1 n. 30 above. For a case study mentioning CEQ's peripheral

Notwithstanding CEQ's disinclination to override and veto, it has by example influenced the direction of administrative and judicial interpretations of NEPA. Courts regularly cite the CEQ guidelines treating them for all practical purposes as indistinguishable from agency regulations;[40] of course under NEPA, as elsewhere, a "government agency is bound by its own regulations".[41] The leading case on the preparation of statements for research and development projects, to mention but one prominent example, draws repeatedly on the CEQ guidelines.[42]

Although they have become influential interpretive aids, the guidelines are not automatically embraced: courts have eschewed CEQ interpretations that an agency could substitute the applicant's draft impact statement for its own prior to an adjudicatory hearing;[43] that EPA was exempt from the impact statement process;[44] and that public controversy did not alone suffice to qualify a project as a "major federal action."[45] And, of course, some courts entertain doubts on the statutory justification for the guidelines,[46] calling them "merely advisory,"[47] while others apply them uncritically[48] or insist they can be ignored only for the "strongest reasons."[49]

b. *Environmental Protection Agency*

While CEQ has shied away from day to day evaluation of environmental impact statements, the Environmental Protection Agency

role in the evaluation of a project alleged to be environmentally indefensible, see Davis, A NEPA Settlement: Conservation Council of North Carolina v. Froehlke, 5 ELR 50079 (1975).

40. Conservation Soc'y of Southern Vermont v. Secretary of Transp. (I), 508 F.2d 927, 932, 5 ELR 20068, 20070 (2d Cir. 1974), vacated 423 U.S. 809 (1975) (relying upon a CEQ accommodation to an earlier court decision); Trout Unlimited v. Morton, 509 F.2d 1276, 1283 & n. 9, 5 ELR 20151, 20154 & n. 9 (9th Cir. 1974); Simmans v. Grant, 370 F.Supp. 5, 16, 4 ELR 20197, 20200–01 (S.D.Tex.1974) (interpreting guidelines on "significance" of the federal actions).

41. Silva v. Romney, 342 F.Supp. 783, 784, 2 ELR 20385 (D.C.Mass.1972), rev'd in part 473 F.2d 287, 3 ELR 20082 (1st Cir. 1973).

42. Scientists' Inst. for Pub. Information v. Atomic Energy Comm'n, 156 U.S.App.D.C. 395, 481 F.2d 1079, 3 ELR 20525 (1973); § 7.7 below.

43. Greene County Planning Bd. v. Federal Power Comm'n (I), 455 F.2d 412, 420, 2 ELR 20017, 20020 (2d Cir.), cert. denied 409 U.S. 849 (1972).

44. Anaconda Co. v. Ruckelshaus, 352 F.Supp. 697, 713, 3 ELR 20024, 20032 (D.C.Colo.1972), rev'd on other grounds 482 F.2d 1301, 3 ELR 20719 (10th Cir. 1973).

45. Hanly v. Kleindeinst (Hanly II), 471 F.2d 823, 830, 2 ELR 20717, 20720 (2d Cir. 1972), cert. denied 412 U.S. 908 (1973).

46. Note 6, supra.

47. Greene County Planning Bd. v. Federal Power Comm'n (I), 455 F.2d 412, 421, 2 ELR 20017, 20021 (2d Cir. 1972), cert. denied 409 U.S. 849.

48. See cases in note 40, supra.

49. Environmental Defense Fund, Inc. v. Tennessee Valley Authority (Tellico Dam), 339 F.Supp. 806, 811, 2 ELR 20044, 20046 (E.D.Tenn.1972); see Environmental Defense Fund, Inc. v. Corps of Engineers (Gillham Dam), 325 F.Supp. 728, 744, 1 ELR 20130, 20136 (E.D.Ark.1971).

under Section 309 of the Clean Air Act is given "a roving commission to review and comment in writing on the environmental impact of various activities to be taken by other federal departments and agencies."[50] This provision makes EPA "a general environmental busybody and gossip"[51] and a "self-starter" with a responsibility to "raise the red flag" over unsuitable environmental adventures.[52] The purpose of the provision is to provide mission-oriented federal agencies with "environmental expertise", however unwelcome it may be, so that "adequate consideration" may be given to environmental factors.[53]

Section 309[54] is noteworthy in several respects:[55] the duty to review and comment is obligatory which means it is enforceable under the citizen suit provisions. It is far reaching, extending to the environmental impact of "any matter" relating to EPA's authority which pretty well covers the entire legal landscape on environmental issues.[56] It explicitly includes proposed legislation and regulations of other agencies and newly authorized federal projects for construction regardless of whether they would be considered "major Federal actions" under Section 102(2)(C) of NEPA. The provision is truly self-starting which means that EPA can launch an inquiry without an invitation from another agency and despite a negative declaration by that agency on the necessity for an EIS. The inquiry is substan-

---

50. § 3.2 above.

51. Ibid.

52. Hearings on the Nomination of William Ruckelshaus as EPA Administrator, Before the Senate Comm. on Public Works, 91st Cong., 2d Sess. 45–46 (1970) (remarks of Sen. Muskie).

53. The text of 42 U.S.C.A. § 1857h–7 reads in full as follows:
Sec. 309(a) The Administrator shall review and comment in writing on the environmental impact of any matter relating to duties and responsibilities granted pursuant to this Act or other provisions of the authority of the Administrator, contained in any (1) legislation proposed by any Federal department or agency, (2) newly authorized Federal projects for construction and any major Federal agency action (other than a project for construction) to which section 102(2)(C) [of NEPA] applies, and (3) proposed regulations published by any department or agency of the Federal Government. Such written comment shall be made public at the conclusion of any such review.

(b) In the event the Administrator determines that any such legislation, action, or regulation is unsatisfactory from the standpoint of public health or welfare or environmental quality, he shall publish his determination and the matter shall be referred to the Council on Environmental Quality.

54. 42 U.S.C.A. § 1857h–7.

55. See Comment, Section 309 of the Clean Air Act: EPA's Duty to Comment on Environmental Impacts, 1 ELR 10147 (1971); Healy, The Environmental Protection Agency's Duty to Oversee NEPA's Implementation: Section 309 of the Clean Air Act, 3 ELR 50071 (1973) (containing a complete and full description of the section 309 process); Anderson, supra note 1, at 267–73.

56. See Senate Comm. on Public Works, National Air Quality Standards Act of 1970, S.Rep. No. 1196, 91st Cong., 2d Sess. 66 (1970) (indicating that matters "indirectly" related to EPA's authority are a proper subject of comment).

tive in the sense that the review and comment is directed to the "environmental impact" of proposals not merely to the analyses of statements. The comments are disclosed in every case and disclosed dramatically sometimes by publication, presumably in the Federal Register, and by reference to the Council on Environmental Quality if EPA determines that the proposed action "is unsatisfactory from the standpoint of public health or welfare or environmental quality."

Before addressing the implementation of section 309, its legal significance deserves mention: in this age of administrative government and interdisciplinary problem solving, conflicts among agencies are an important legal phenomenon. One of the great strengths of NEPA is that the commenting process routinely exposes disagreements among agencies. Sustaining an attack on a project or regulation on environmental grounds is enhanced by expert support, sometimes only a single letter, originating from a government agency. It is thus relevant to the courts that a power plant site is opposed by a responsible department,[57] or that proposed regulations [58] or construction projects [59] run into heavy criticism elsewhere within the government. Of course conflicts among agencies are resolved not only by the courts; it has been suggested that a section 309(b) referral to the Council on Environmental Quality by EPA should result in a suspension of the project and resolution within the executive branch, at the cabinet or presidential level.[60]

EPA has the staff potential to transform section 309 and NEPA into an effective instrument for screening environmentally unsatisfactory projects. The agency "got off to a slow start" [61] in implementing the provision for several reasons, not the least of which was the inherent hazards of a neophyte agency openly criticizing projects

57. Rhode Island Comm. on Energy v. General Serv. Administration, 397 F. Supp. 41, 58, 5 ELR 20685, 20689 (D.C.R.I.1975). See also Sierra Club v. Morton (Jim Bridger power plant), 379 F.Supp. 1254, 4 ELR 20690 (D.C. Colo.1974).

58. Ethyl Corp. v. Environmental Protection Agency, 5 ELR 20096, 20016–17, rev'd en banc — U.S.App.D.C. —, 541 F.2d 1, 6 ELR 20267 (1976), cert. denied — U.S. —. ("the collective scientific judgment in every department or agency of the government commenting on the first two EPA Health Documents and proposed regulations is dead against the Administrator's conclusion—and he did not risk this same fate with the Third Document").

59. Sierra Club v. Froehlke (Wallisville-Trinity River), 359 F.Supp. 1289, 1314, 3 ELR 20248, 20254 (S.D.Tex. 1973), rev'd and remanded 449 F.2d 982, 4 ELR 20731 (5th Cir. 1974); DiVosta Rentals, Inc. v. Lee, 488 F.2d 674, 4 ELR 20005 (5th Cir. 1973) (denial of a Rivers and Harbors Act permit not "arbitrary and capricious" when dredging proposal opposed by three agncies); see Healy, supra note 55, at 50076–77, discussing EPA's role in the Trans-Alaska pipeline case.

60. Comment, supra note 55, at 10150; Anderson, supra note 1, at 271. The Senate version of section 309(b)—Section 310(b) of S.4358—required CEQ to make "a determination" on a reference from EPA "and a recommendation to the President which shall be made public." The decision to excuse CEQ from publicly putting the President on the spot does not mean that a resolution by the President is not the appropriate response.

61. Healy, supra note 55, at 50076.

of well established government powers. Late in 1972 standards governing the 309 and NEPA reviews were prescribed;[62] for the most part, the normal NEPA commenting process serves as a substitute for an extraordinary intervention under section 309. EPA comments on the environmental impact of agency proposals fall into three categories: (1) lack of objection, (2) environmental reservations, and (3) environmentally unsatisfactory. Similarly, EPA reviews of the adequacy of impact statements fall into three categories: (1) adequate, (2) insufficient information, and (3) inadequate. The EPA practice is to conduct another review at the final impact statement stage if the first evaluation expresses environmental reservations or considers the project environmentally unsatisfactory, or if the draft statement was deemed insufficient or inadequate.[63] The idea is to monitor continuously the projects raising doubts. Normally, EPA opposition is ignored, withdrawn after further interagency consultation, or results in minor project modifications.

A valuable empirical study of EPA's environmental reviews indicates that during the period examined (December 1, 1972—May 30, 1973) EPA "found serious abuses of the NEPA process in roughly 8 percent of the draft impact statements, and major substantive shortcomings in 30 percent. Over 65 percent had substantial informational deficiencies."[64] There was little pursuit of section 309 duties beyond this point, however, with comment and the final review of projects being quite limited and referrals to CEQ nonexistent.[65] More recently, it has become apparent that section 309(b) referrals will be confined to selected issues of acute environmental importance.[66]

Obviously, the intensity of EPA review of federal actions will vary from time to time and region to region; there is little in section 309 to assure a thorough and detailed critique of agency action even when undertaken. Notwithstanding this, EPA 309–NEPA reviews, published in summary form in the Federal Register on a semimonthly basis for both proposed and final statements,[67] are valuable source material and potential evidence. It is important also to stress that Congress determined that federal action should be subject to expert commentary and mandatory disclosure prescribed by section 309. Judicial relief to enforce compliance with the provision is an expected consequence.[68]

62. EPA Order 1640.1, Review of Federal Action Impacting the Environment (Nov. 30, 1972).

63. Id. ¶ 4a.

64. Healy, supra note 55, at 50080.

65. Id. at 50080–81.

66. Comment, Section 309 of the Clean Air Act Revisited: EPA Makes Second Referral of "Environmentally Unsatisfactory" Federal Proposal to CEQ, 6 ELR 10059 (1976).

67. E. g., 41 Fed.Reg. 4059 (1976); 38 Fed.Reg. 33412 (1973).

68. Compare National Forest Preservation Group v. Butz, 343 F.Supp. 696, 2 ELR 20571 (D.Mont.1972) (refusing to enjoin an exchange of federal for private land despite EPA failure to

c. *The Other Agencies*

Fundamentally, NEPA is a directive to the agencies of the federal government to revise their procedures and amend their charters in pursuit of environmental values. While Congress and the courts intervene sporadically, sometimes dramatically, in the decision-making process, the vast majority of day to day judgments are dispatched by the administrative mill. That NEPA initially was received with hostility and administered grudgingly is a matter of record.[69] Cases in the future will disclose instances of the NEPA process serving as an ex post facto justification of what was destined to be.

Nonetheless, there is considerable empirical evidence to support the general impression that "almost all of the agencies have settled down to live with the Act."[70] There is, first of all, a response impressive in terms of sheer bulk: by June 30, 1974, four and a half years after NEPA was enacted, environmental impact statements had been prepared on 5,430 agency actions, final impact statements had been completed for 3,344 actions.[71] Implementing regulations have been issued by close to seventy agencies and departments.[72] While the production of paper is not a measure of compliance, studies of various agencies confirm a relaxation of the decision-making process to accommodate environmental considerations,[73] even among the poorer performers such as the Federal Aviation Administration[74] and the Bureau of Land Management.[75] NEPA is no harbinger of over-

comment under section 309) with Citizens Environmental Council v. Volpe, 364 F.Supp. 286, 3 ELR 20077 (D.C.Kan.1973) (refusing injunctive relief in a highway case without addressing the 309 claim).

69. Anderson, supra note 1, at 244–46. Judicial admonishment of the administrators is commonplace and caustic. See, e. g., Calvert Cliffs' Coord. Comm. v. Atomic Energy Comm'n, 146 U.S.App.D.C. 33, 41, 449 F.2d 1109, 1117, 1 ELR 20340, 20350 (1971), cert. denied 404 U.S. 942 (1972) (the Commission's "crabbed interpretation . . . made a mockery of the Act").

70. Anderson, supra note 1, at 246.

71. Council on Environmental Quality, Fifth Ann.Rep. 388 (1974).

72. Id. at 382–85, table 1; see note 73, infra.

73. See generally CEQ, Environmental Impact Statements: An Analysis of Six Years' Experience by Seventy Federal Agencies (1976). See also Cramton & Berg, Enforcing the National Environmental Policy Act in Federal Agencies, 18 Practical Law. 79 (1972); Debervoise & Madden, Impact of the National Environmental Policy Act upon Administration of the Federal Power Act, 8 Land & Water L.Rev. 93 (1973); Peterson & Kennan, The Federal Aid Highway Program: Administrative Procedures and Judicial Interpretation, 2 ELR 50001 (1972); Wood, A Prescriptive Analysis of the U.S. Navy's Program to Implement the National Environmental Policy Act, 5 ELR 50049 (1975); CEQ, An Evaluation of Implementation and Administration of NEPA by the Forest Service and the Bureau of Land Management (Prelim.Rep.1974); CEQ, A Study of the Implementation of NEPA by the United States Navy (1974).

74. See § 5.9 above.

75. CEQ, An Evaluation of Implementation and Administration of NEPA by the Forest Service and the Bureau of Land Management (Prelim.Rep.1974).

night reformation, as the literature attests,[76] but it has enhanced disclosure, broadened the perspective of decision-making and even changed results upon occasion.[77]

While there is considerable room for improvement,[78] agency regulations implementing NEPA add content to the Act and the case law interpreting it. They may specify types of agency actions giving rise to environmental impacts and categories of effects that must be considered. Requirements vary widely on the extent to which social, economic, and energy conservation effects must be considered. HUD calls for a discussion of the impact of the surrounding environment on the proposed project (for example, airport noise on a proposed hospital) and of the quality of the interior environment that will result. While many of the agency guidelines require consideration of the proposed action's impact on program goals and policies, only a few call for a discussion of impact on NEPA's substantive goals and objectives. Some 12 to 15 agencies are developing handbooks or manuals to assist design or data collection procedures in environmental impact statement analyses. The guidelines routinely demand citations of the sources of information and predictions used but with few elaborations: "Most do not require demonstration of the basis of impact predictions in sufficient detail that they could be independently validated; and most do not require identification of individual authorship of the impact statement, nor of the credentials of experts whose professional judgments provided the basis for impact predictions. This deficiency appears to encourage or at least permit superficial judgments and glib literature analogies." [79]

d. *The Congress*

By applying the impact statement requirement of Section 102 (2)(C) of NEPA to "every recommendation or report on proposals

76. Cramton & Berg, On Leading a Horse to Water: NEPA and the Federal Bureaucracy, 71 Mich.L.Rev. 511 (1972); Gillette, National Environmental Policy Act: How Well Is It Working? 176 Science 146 (1972); Murphy, National Environmental Policy Act and the Licensing Process: Environmentalist Magna Carta or Agency Coup de Grace?, 72 Colum.L. Rev. 963 (1972); Tarlock, Balancing Environmental Considerations and Energy Demands: A Comment on Calvert Cliffs Coordinating Comittee, Inc. v. AEC, 47 Ind.L.J. 645, 671–72 (1972); Note, The National Environmental Policy Act: A Sheep in Wolf's Clothing, 37 Brooklyn L.Rev. 139 (1970).

77. See CEQ, Fourth Ann.Rep. 247 (1973) (reporting that Corps of Engineers after NEPA reviews had dropped 24 projects, temporarily or indefinitely delayed 44 others, and modified significantly 197 more); Hearings on National Environmental Policy Act Oversight, Before the Subcomm. on Fisheries & Wildlife Conservation of the House Comm. on Merchant Marines & Fisheries, H.R. Doc. No. 14, 94th Cong., 1st Sess. 204–05 (1975) (statement of Russell Peterson, Chairman, CEQ) (giving other examples of NEPA impact on substance of projects).

78. Andrews, NEPA in Practice: Environmental Policy or Administrative Reform, 6 ELR 50001 (1976); Schindler, The Impact Statement Boondoggle, 192 Science 509 (1976).

79. Andrews, supra note 78, at 50003.

for legislation," Congress was presumed to be a major beneficiary as well as an enforcer of the Act. Both benefits and enforcement are scant. The fact is that impact statements on legislation are prepared irregularly, usually upon environmentally protective proposals less in need of EIS' than development oriented bills.[80] Congress is not alone in winking at the requirements: the CEQ guidelines require agencies to prepare impact statements prior to submission of their legislative proposals to the Office of Management and Budget for clearance.[81] But CEQ does not enforce the provision and neither does OMB which has resisted the responsibility thrust upon it by the guidelines.[82] The Environmental Protection Agency also has shown no interest in focusing its review powers under Section 309 of the Clean Air Act on proposed legislation.[83]

The principal responsibility for relaxing the legislative EIS requirement, however, must rest with the Congress. Only the Senate Committee on Public Works has amended its rules to make the submission of an EIS a precondition of committee action,[84] and there has been little pressure for enforcement from the committees or individual members. This is a poor show for an institution elsewhere on record as endorsing "early warning" systems, creating the Office of Technology Assessment,[85] and regularly criticizing the lack of timely information extended by the agencies. Properly drawn legislative impact statements fulfill splendidly the NEPA objectives of prediction, prevention, and before-the-fact analysis, but they will not become a regular feature of agency submissions until the Congress insists on them.

It is theoretically possible to secure judicial relief against an agency neglecting to prepare a legislative impact statement [86] but an injunction restraining the Congress from considering bills unaccompanied by a statement is wholly out of the question.[87] Subject to this understanding on enforcement, the NEPA Section 102(2)(C) phrase "every recommendation or report on proposals for legislation" should be read broadly to require EIS' for every formal submission to Congress proposing legislative action. This includes quite clearly

80. House Comm. on Merchant Marine and Fisheries, Administration of the National Environmental Policy Act of 1969, H.R.Rep. No. 316, 92d Cong., 1st Sess. 15–26 (1971); see Anderson, supra note 1, at 331–35.

81. 40 CFR § 1500.12.

82. See Anderson, supra note 1, at 334–35.

83. Healy, supra note 55, at 50078–79.

84. Rule 13, discussed in Anderson, supra note 1, at 333.

85. § 1.3 above.

86. See Anderson, supra note 1, at 332.

87. Joint Hearings on the Operation of the National Environmental Policy Act of 1969, Before the Senate Comm. on Public Works and the Senate Comm. on Interior and Insular Affairs, S.Doc. No. H32, 92d Cong., 2d Sess. 417 (1972) (remarks of Roger Cramton, Chairman, Administrative Conference).

appropriations requests [88] and reports submitted in furtherance of a legislative program although one court unfortunately drew a distinction between explicit proposals for legislation which require EIS' and longer range recommendations which do not.[89] Long range plans requiring legislative implementation over time are especially suitable for a NEPA analysis.[90]

Having relinquished the one tool that would afford systematic control over agency compliance with an important aspect of the Act, congressional oversight on NEPA pretty well follows the fragmentary pattern associated with most major legislative programs. Oversight hearings have been held, some treating the Act sympathetically,[91] others with hostility,[92] particularly in the wake of the *Calvert Cliffs* decision [93] which made clear for the first time that heavy sledding was in store for major government programs. During the 92d Congress scores of bills that would curtail NEPA were introduced,[94] but the expressed fear that government would be "stopped in its tracks" by this legislative monster met with a surprisingly limited congressional response. The only program exemption from NEPA granted in 1972 was that involving much of EPA's authority over the water quality program [95] while congressional reaction to the *Calvert Cliffs* decision was confined to a limited acceleration of the environ-

88. Scientists' Inst. for Pub. Information v. Atomic Energy Comm'n, 156 U.S.App.D.C. 395, 404, 481 F.2d 1079, 1088, 3 ELR 20525, 20528 (1973); Environmental Defense Fund, Inc. v. Tennessee Valley Authority (Tellico Dam), 468 F.2d 1164, 1181–82, 2 ELR 20726, 20729 (6th Cir. 1972); Sierra Club v. Morton, 395 F.Supp. 1187, 5 ELR 20383 (D.D.C.1975); Environmental Defense Fund, Inc. v. Froehlke (Truman Dam), 348 F.Supp. 338, 364, 2 ELR 20620, 20631 (W.D.Mo.1972), aff'd 477 F.2d 1033, 3 ELR 20382 (8th Cir. 1973); Comment, Sierra Club Seeks to Require NEPA Impact Statement on Annual Appropriations Proposals, 5 ELR 10071 (1975).

89. See Environmental Defense Fund, Inc. v. Volpe, Civ. No. 151–72, (D.D.C. 1972) (requiring no statement accompanying transportation needs reports required by statute to be submitted to Congress) ("Although the reports did not contain the actual language of legislative proposals, they did contain the secretary's recommendations to Congress concerning federal funding for states that had completed their part of the interstate network, his recommendations for the functional realignment of the federal-aid highway system, his estimate of future highway needs, and his recommendations for the federal highway program from 1976 to 1990." NEPA in the Courts, supra note 1, at 128.)

90. § 7.7 below.

91. See authorities collected in Anderson, supra note 1, at 274–75 n.129; Hearings on National Environmental Policy Act Oversight, supra note 77.

92. See Anderson, supra note 1, at 275 n.130.

93. Calvert Cliffs' Coord. Comm. v. Atomic Energy Comm'n, 146 U.S.App. D.C. 33, 449 F.2d 1109, 1 ELR 20346 (1971), cert. denied 404 U.S. 942 (1972); see Anderson, supra note 1, at 276 n. 136.

94. Library of Congress, Congressional Research Service, National Environmental Policy Act of 1969: An Analysis of Proposed Legislative Modifications, Senate Comm. on Interior and Insular Affairs, 93d Cong., 1st Sess. (Comm. Print 1973).

95. Federal Water Pollution Control Act Amendment of 1972, § 511(c)(1), 33 U.S.C.A. § 1371(c)(1).

mental review process for a few nuclear power plants.[96] In recent years, the much sought after NEPA exceptions have been accorded a few controversial projects [97] and programs,[98] particularly on the subject of energy, but nothing has occurred that would portend a wholesale retreat from the Act's blanket requirements. Congress may not have insisted upon conformity to the letter of the Act as written originally, but neither is it particularly inclined to major revisions.

§ 7.3 Review of Agency Decision-Making: General Procedures

Citizens to Preserve Overton Park v. Volpe [1] lays down the "substantial inquiry" test [2] for judicial review of administrative action under the Administration Procedures Act (APA). Many courts reflexively treat their reviewing powers under NEPA as governed by the APA—*Overton Park* tests,[3] while others treat NEPA issues as presenting federal questions reviewable under 28 U.S.C.A. § 1331, perhaps by standards even stricter than those of *Overton Park*.[4] Re-

---

96. Pub.L. No. 92–307, 86 Stat. 191 (1972), 42 U.S.C.A. § 2242.

97. E. g., Trans-Alaska Pipeline Authorization Act, Pub.L. No. 93–153, § 203(d), 87 Stat. 584 (1973), 43 U.S. C.A. § 1652(d) (Alaska pipeline construction and initial operation); Federal-Aid Highway Act of 1973, Pub.L. No. 93–87, § 154, 87 Stat. 250 (San Antonio freeway); Energy Supply and Environmental Coordination Act of 1974, Pub.L. No. 93–319, § 7(d), 15 U.S.C.A. § 793(d) (transmission facilities between Canada and United States in vicinity of Ft. Covington, New York); Act of Feb. 4, 1976, Pub. L. No. 94–207, § 2(b), 90 Stat. 28 (1976) (certain blackbird control activities).

98. Energy Supply and Environmental Coordination Act of 1974, § 7(c)(1), 15 U.S.C.A. § 793(c)(1) (action taken under the Clean Air Act); Federal Water Pollution Control Act Amendments of 1972, § 511(c)(1), 33 U.S.C.A. § 1371(c)(1) (action taken under FWPCA with the exception of grants for the construction of treatment works and issuances of permits for new sources); Disaster Relief Act of 1974, § 405, 42 U.S.C.A. § 5175 (disaster assistance having the effect of restoring facilities substantially as they existed prior to the disaster); Regional Rail Reorganization Act of 1973, § 601(c), 45 U.S.C.A. § 791(c) (all action taken before the effective date of the final system plan).

1. 401 U.S. 402, 91 S.Ct. 814, 28 L.Ed. 2d 136 (1971).

2. § 1.5 above.

3. E. g., Conservation Council of North Carolina v. Froehlke (I), 473 F.2d 664, 665, 3 ELR 20132 (4th Cir. 1973); Sierra Club v. Froehlke (Kickapoo River), 486 F.2d 946, 953, 3 ELR 20823, 20826 (7th Cir. 1973); Jicarilla Apache Tribe v. Morton, 471 F.2d 1275, 1281, 3 ELR 20045, 20047 (9th Cir. 1973); Hanly v. Kleindienst (Hanly II), 471 F.2d 823, 829–30, 2 ELR 20717, 20719 (2d Cir. 1972), cert. denied 412 U.S. 908 (1973); Environmental Defense Fund, Inc. v. Corps of Engineers (Gillham Dam), 470 F.2d 289, 300, 2 ELR 20740, 20745 (8th Cir. 1972); Calvert Cliffs' Coord. Comm. v. Atomic Energy Comm'n, 146 U.S.App.D.C. 33, 39, 449 F.2d 1109, 1115, 1 ELR 20346, 20348 (1971), cert. denied 404 U.S. 942 (1972).

4. E. g., Silva v. Lynn, 482 F.2d 1282, 3 ELR 20698 (1st Cir. 1973); Cape Henry Bird Club v. Laird, 359 F. Supp. 404, 3 ELR 2057 (W.D.Va.), aff'd 484 F.2d 453, 3 ELR 20786 (4th Cir. 1973); National Helium Corp. v. Morton (II), 486 F.2d 995, 1001–02, 4 ELR 20041, 20044 (10th Cir. 1973), cert. denied 416 U.S. 993 (1974) (imposing a rule of reason standard for reviewing the adequacy of the impact statement as distinguished from the underlying agency action).

Sec. 7.3 GENERAL REVIEW PROCEDURES

gardless of the route to decision, there is no question that NEPA accentuates the *Overton Park* tendency to require a "hard look"[5] by the courts at agency actions affecting the environment. This calls for, at a minimum, strict adherence to procedural requirements, carefully explained decision-making, and results not plainly indefensible.[6] How the agency reaches its decision and explains it can be classified as procedural. What it does and the wisdom of it is a substantive matter.

While a procedural-substantive dichotomy is imperfect in environmental law,[7] as elsewhere, it is a useful tool for looking at NEPA. Section 101 prescribes substantive results:[8] exploiting resources without degradation; exhausting opportunities to assure that federal actions do not compromise a safe and healthful environment; approaching the maximum attainable recycling of depletable resources; achieving a balance between population and resource use. Section 102 is concerned with methodology: it requires a systems analysis approach by the agencies and imposes disclosure obligations upon them,[9] with the section 102(2)(C) environmental impact statement requirement being the best known.[10] NEPA's concern with both results and methods is echoed in the case law: thus one court says "the goal" of NEPA is "a better environment"[11] while another insists the impact statement provision "was not directed solely or even primarily [against] adverse consequences to the environment" but rather "the failure of decision-makers to take environmental factors into account in the way that NEPA mandates."[12] Both are right—NEPA is aimed at the agencies' bad decisions as well as their bad manners.

While courts treat gingerly and some even disclaim an authority to disapprove agency actions on the merits,[13] the procedural provisions of Section 102 of NEPA are enforced with a vengeance. The legislative requirement of "consideration to the fullest extent possible," Judge Skelly Wright wrote in the extraordinary influential

---

5. Leventhal, Environmental Decisionmaking and the Role of Courts, 122 U.Pa.L.Rev. 509, 512 (1974). This valuable article develops the thesis that "in the environmental field the courts so far have been, if anything, fully vigilant to exercise rather than abdicate their supervisory role." Id. at 512.

6. § 1.5 above.

7. Leed, The National Environmental Policy Act of 1969: Is the Fact of Compliance a Procedural or Substantive Question, 15 Santa Clara Law. 303 (1975).

8. § 7.5 below.

9. See Environmental Defense Fund, Inc. v. Corps of Engineers (Tennessee-Tombigbee), 492 F.2d 1123, 1136, 4 ELR 20329, 20332–34 (5th Cir. 1974).

10. § 7.4 below.

11. Sierra Club v. Lynn, 502 F.2d 43, 60, 4 ELR 20844, 20851 (5th Cir. 1974), cert. denied 421 U.S. 944 (1975).

12. Jones v. District of Columbia Redev. Land Agency, 162 U.S.App.D.C. 366, 376, 499 F.2d 502, 512, 4 ELR 20479, 20483 (1974).

13. § 7.5 below.

Calvert Cliffs decision, "sets a high standard for the agencies, a standard which must be rigorously enforced by reviewing courts."[14] Compliance with section 102, particularly the environmental impact statement requirements, is mandatory unless an agency can point to a directly conflicting statutory mandate of which there are surprisingly few.[15] The "history of the environment", it is said, may well prove to be "the history of observance of procedural safeguards."[16]

NEPA thus has spawned a code of procedures for environmental decision-making: it is generally understood that the agency is obliged to evaluate environmental factors "before the planning and implementation process has advanced so far that it has become impracticable to make changes in the proposed plan."[17] This may mean that a public hearing is required[18] although most courts look to whether one is called for by existing agency procedures.[19] Any hearing probably need not involve adjudicatory procedures,[20] questioning from the floor[21] or a verbatim transcript[22] unless they are ordinarily made available by the agency. But where a hearing is held, it must be preceded by adequate notice[23] and the distribution of in-

---

14. Calvert Cliffs' Coord. Comm. v. Atomic Energy Comm'n, 146 U.S.App. D.C. 33, 38, 449 F.2d 1109, 1114, 1 ELR 20346, 20348 (1971), cert. denied 404 U.S. 942 (1972).

15. 146 U.S.App.D.C. at 39, 449 F.2d at 1115, 1 ELR at 20349; § 7.6 below; see Flint Ridge Dev. Co. v. Scenic Rivers Ass'n, 426 U.S. 776, 96 S.Ct. 2430, 49 L.Ed.2d 205 (1976).

16. Lathan v. Brinegar (II), 506 F.2d 677, 693, 4 ELR 20802, 20808 (9th Cir. 1974) (en banc), quoting McNabb v. United States, 318 U.S. 332, 347, 63 S.Ct. 608, 616, 87 L.Ed. 819, 827 (1943) (Frankfurter, J.).

17. Saunders v. Washington Metropolitan Area Transit Authority, 159 U.S. App.D.C. 55, 486 F.2d 1315, 4 ELR 20001 (1973) (per curiam).

18. Hanly v. Kleindienst (II), 471 F.2d 823, 2 ELR 20717 (2d Cir. 1972), cert. denied 412 U.S. 908 (1973) (dictum).

19. Aberdeen & Rockfish R. R. v. Students Challenging Regulatory Agency Procedure (SCRAP II), 422 U.S. 289, 320, 95 S.Ct. 2336, 2356, 45 L.Ed.2d 191, 214–15 (1975); Lathan v. Volpe (I), 4 ELR 20083, 20085 (9th Cir. 1973) (making clear that NEPA does not itself provide for public hearings and that none are required in the absence of independent authority, such as that found in the Federal-Aid Highway Act); see 40 CFR § 1500.7(d) (listing factors to be considered in determining need for public hearing).

20. E. g., Jicarilla Apache Tribe of Indians v. Morton, 471 F.2d 1275, 1286, 3 ELR 20045, 20048 (9th Cir. 1973); Bucks County Bd. of Commissioners v. Interstate Energy Co., 403 F.Supp. 805, 817, 6 ELR 20406, 20412 (E.D.Pa. 1975); cf. International Harvester v. Ruckelshaus, 155 U.S.App.D.C. 411, 427, 478 F.2d 615, 631, 3 ELR 20133, 20137–38 (1973) (arising under the Clean Air Act) (permits some cross-examination in the discretion of the presiding officer).

21. Cf. International Harvester v. Ruckelshaus, supra note 20.

22. See Lathan v. Volpe (I), 350 F. Supp. 262, 265, 2 ELR 20545, 20547 (W.D.Wash.1972).

23. Ecology Center of Louisiana, Inc. v. Coleman, 515 F.2d 860, 865, 5 ELR 20488, 20490 (5th Cir. 1975) (doctrine of administrative exhaustion does not apply where agency fails to notify properly parties of public hearing); Hanly v. Kleindienst (II), 471 F.2d 823, 836, 2 ELR 20717, 20723 (2d Cir. 1972), cert. denied 412 U.S. 908 (1973). See 40 CFR § 1500.9(b); cf. Fund for Animals v. Frizzell, 174

formation such as a draft environmental impact statement [24] to make the proceeding a valuable exercise.

With the exception of Section 102(2)(C) of NEPA, containing the impact statement requirement,[25] the procedural provisions of section 102 are rarely discussed in isolation. Nor need they be since several of the provisions speak with slightly differing degrees of emphasis to utilizing information from various disciplines,[26] conducting research,[27] cooperating with other agencies,[28] studying alternatives,[29] and making information available to the public.[30] But neither should the specifics of section 102 be ignored.

Section 102(2)(A) of NEPA requires federal agencies to "utilize a systematic, interdisciplinary approach which will insure the integrated use of the natural and social sciences and environmental design arts in planning and in decision-making which may have an impact on man's environment." Requiring an agency to "utilize" a systems approach which "will insure the integrated use" of certain types of information "in decision-making" has important connotations for how an agency gathers information and puts it to use. The purpose of serious interdisciplinary study is to assure that the environmental effects of a project are understood fully, and addresssed on the merits. Section 102(2)(A) lends strength to the argument that the agency must disclose and consider responsible opposing scientific opinions,[31] coordinate expertise within the agency,[32] expand its staff to accom-

U.S.App.D.C. 130, 136, 530 F.2d 982, 988, 6 ELR 20188, 20192 (1975) (per curiam) (interpreting Administrative Procedure Act).

24. Keith v. California Highway Commission, 4 ELR 20076, 20079 (9th Cir. 1973) (Hanley, J., dissenting) (interpreting Federal Highway Administration regulations) (the state has "the duty of developing the information necessary for full consideration of the possible effects of the proposed freeway on noise and air pollution. That information must then be made available to the public for consideration at a public hearing"); 40 CFR § 1500.7(d) (CEQ guidelines) (draft EIS should be made available to the public at least 15 days prior to a hearing).

25. § 7.4 below.

26. Sections 102(2)(A), (B), (C), (E), (H), 42 U.S.C.A. § 4332(2)(A), (B), (C), (E), (H). In August 1975 Congress amended NEPA by adding a new paragraph to section 102(2). Pub.L. No. 94–83, 89 Stat. 424. The new paragraph is designated 102(2) (D) and the old subsection 102(2)(D) is redesignated 102(2)(E) with subsequent redesignations for the remaining original paragraphs (now (F) through (I)). The change is confusing for the reason that the case law for several years has given personality to the original designations.

27. Section 102(2)(A), (B), (C), (E), 42 U.S.C.A. § 4332(2)(A), (B), (C), (E).

28. Section 102(2)(A), (B), (C), (G), (I), 42 U.S.C.A. § 4332(2)(A), (B), (C), (G), (I).

29. Section 102(2)(C), (E), 42 U.S.C.A. § 4332(2)(C), (E).

30. Section 102(2)(C), (G), 42 U.S.C.A. § 4332(2)(C), (G).

31. Comm. For Nuclear Responsibility v. Seaborg, 149 U.S.App.D.C. 380, 463 F.2d 783, 1 ELR 20469 (1971).

32. Simmans v. Grant, 370 F.Supp. 5, 20, 4 ELR 20197, 20203 (S.D.Tex. 1974) (section 102(2)(A) "necessitates closer coordination between engineer-

modate environmental evaluations,[33] respond to concerns raised by experts it retains,[34] sponsor research on important issues either as a pre-condition[35] or concurrently with[36] implementation of a project, answer or perhaps even defer to [37] expert criticism or recommendations from other agencies, actively seek out (as distinguished from passively absorbing) expert advice and opposing opinions,[38] or engage in actual consultation with other agencies.[39] On the other hand, the

ing, economic and environmental experts within an agency [in order to ensure that an appropriate balancing of interest may be reached] than appears to have occurred on this project to date").

33. Harlem Valley Transp. Ass'n v. Stafford, 500 F.2d 328, 337, 4 ELR 20638, 20642 (2d Cir. 1974).

34. Conservation Soc'y of Southern Vermont, Inc. v. Secretary of Transp. (I), 362 F.Supp. 627, 633–34, 3 ELR 20709, 20710 (D.C.Vt.1973), aff'd 508 F.2d 927, 5 ELR 20068 (2d Cir. 1974), vacated 423 U.S. 809 (1975); Sierra Club v. Froehlke (Wallisville-Trinity River), 359 F.Supp. 1289, 1338–39, 3 ELR 20248, 20265 (S.D.Tex. 1973), rev'd on other grounds 499 F.2d 982, 4 ELR 20731 (5th Cir. 1974).

35. Environmental Defense Fund, Inc. v. Hardin, 325 F.Supp. 1401, 1403, 1 ELR 20207, 20208 (D.D.C.1971): [Section 102(2)(A)] . . . makes the completion of an adequate research program a prerequisite to agency action. The adequacy of the research should be judged in light of the scope of the proposed program and the extent to which existing knowledge raises the possibility of potential adverse environmental effects.

36. Environmental Defense Fund v. Dep't of Transp., Civil No. 76–1105 (D.C.Cir. 1976); Environmental Defense Fund, Inc. v. Corps of Engineers (Tennessee-Tombigbee), 492 F.2d 1123, 1130, 4 ELR 20329, 20330–31 (5th Cir. 1974); Jicarilla Apache Tribe v. Morton, 471 F.2d 1275, 1281, 3 ELR 20045, 20047 (9th Cir. 1973). See also Natural Resources Defense Council, Inc. v. Callaway, 524 F.2d 79, 95–96 & n. 2, 5 ELR 20640, 20649 & n. 2 (2d Cir. 1975) (Mulligan, J., dissenting).

37. Akers v. Resor, 339 F.Supp. 1375, 2 ELR 20221 (W.D.Tenn.), 3 ELR 20157 (W.D.Tenn.1972) (should not include increased crop production as a benefit of flood control project without consulting with Department of Agriculture which has programs to pay farmers not to cultivate existing lands); Sierra Club v. Froehlke (Wallisville-Trinity River), 359 F.Supp. 1289, 1348, 3 ELR 20248, 20264 (S.D.Tex.1973) (requiring Corps of Engineers to defer to environmental evaluations of expert agencies in the absence of "clear and convincing evidence" that the reviewing agency was incorrect), rev'd and remanded 499 F.2d 982, 993, 4 ELR 20731, 20737 (5th Cir. 1974) ("in view of the [district court's] statement that when a conflict arises between the Corps and the agency making an evaluation that the Act obligates the Corps in most instances to 'defer' to that evaluation, we deem it not inappropriate to observe that the word as so employed must yield to the language of the Act which does not lend itself to a construction that the agency making the evaluation is vested with authority to veto the evaluation of the Corps") (footnote omitted).

38. Soc'y for Animal Rights, Inc. v. Schlesinger, 168 U.S.App.D.C. 1, 3, 512 F.2d 915, 917, 5 ELR 20221, 20223 (1975) (per curiam) (dissolving an injunction pending appeal prohibiting the Defense Department from spraying 10 million blackbirds) ("the public interest may well warrant . . . seeking the advice of impartial scientists before proceeding with the spraying").

39. Sierra Club v. Froehlke (Wallisville-Trinity River), 359 F.Supp. 1289, 1346, 3 ELR 20248, 20267 (S.D.Tex. 1973), rev'd on other grounds 499 F.2d 982, 4 ELR 20731 (5th Cir. 1974); Simmans v. Grant, 370 F.Supp. 5, 19, 4 ELR 20197, 20203 (S.D.Tex.1974).

Sec. 7.3 GENERAL REVIEW PROCEDURES 721

agency need not be paralyzed by conflicting expert opinions,[40] so long as they are fully disclosed; or undertake long-range research commitments as a pre-condition of action; [41] or hire a full stable of experts to consider a project or prepare an environmental impact statement so long as its doors are open to expert advice.[42]

Section 102(2)(B) requires each agency to "identify and develop methods and procedures, in consultation with the Council on Environmental Quality . . . , which will insure that presently unquantified environmental amenities and values may be given appropriate consideration in decision-making along with economic and technical considerations." The courts have invoked subsections 102(2)(A) or (B) to require a balancing of environmental factors on a par with dollars and technology,[43] to call for a quantification of environmental data where possible,[44] to compel consideration of this data and other environmental values in the impact statement,[45] to require solicitation of public opinion, perhaps including hearings, on the decision whether to prepare an impact statement for activity affecting values not easily quantified,[46] and to order a research effort on adverse ef-

40. Comm. for Nuclear Responsibility v. Seaborg, 149 U.S.App.D.C. 380, 383, 463 F.2d 783, 787, 1 ELR 20529, 20530 (1971) (per curiam); Citizens Against the Destruction of NAPA v. Lynn, 391 F.Supp. 1188, 1196, 5 ELR 20451, 20454 (N.D.Cal.1975) ("disagreement of experts, standing alone, will not serve to invalidate an EIS"); Cape Henry Bird Club v. Laird, 359 F.Supp. 404, 3 ELR 20571 (W.D.Va.), affirmed 484 F.2d 453, 3 ELR 20786 (4th Cir. 1973).

41. Lathan v. Volpe (II), 350 F.Supp. 262, 265, 2 ELR 20545, 20547 (W.D. Wash.1972) ("The proper response to comments which are both relevant and reasonable is to either conduct the research necessary to provide satisfactory answers, or to refer to those places in the impact statement which provide them").

42. Compare Environmental Defense Fund, Inc. v. Corps of Engineers (Tennessee-Tombigbee), 492 F.2d 1123, 4 ELR 20329 (5th Cir. 1974) (Corps assigned six-man scientific team to examine the project).

43. Environmental Defense Fund, Inc. v. Corps of Engineers (Tennessee-Tombigbee), 492 F.2d at 1132–33, 4 ELR at 20333; Calvert Cliffs' Coord. Comm. v. Atomic Energy Comm'n, 146 U.S.App.D.C. 33, 37 & n. 9, 449 F.2d 1109, 1113 & n. 9, 3 ELR 20346, 20348 & n. 9 (1971), cert. denied 404 U.S. 942 (1972).

44. Cf. I–291 Why? Ass'n v. Burns, 372 F.Supp. 223, 236, 4 ELR 20239, 20243 (D.C.Conn.1974), aff'd per curiam, 517 F.2d 1077, 5 ELR 20430 (2d Cir. 1975) (interpreting section 102(2)(C)); Environmental Defense Fund, Inc. v. Hardin, 325 F.Supp. 1401, 1403, 1 ELR 20207, 20208 (D.C. D.C.1971).

45. Environmental Defense Fund, Inc. v. Corps of Engineers (Gillham Dam), 325 F.Supp. 749, 756–57, 1 ELR 20130, 20140–41 (E.D.Ark.1971), aff'd 470 F.2d 289, 2 ELR 20740 (8th Cir. 1972); Environmental Defense Fund, Inc. v. Corps of Engineers (Tennessee-Tombigbee), 492 F.2d 1123, 1133, 4 ELR 20329, 20333 (5th Cir. 1974) (plaintiffs' "criticism of the one-sided economic use of environmental values is impressive" but the court finds no violation of subsection (B)); Calvert Cliffs' Coord. Comm. v. Atomic Energy Comm'n, 146 U.S.App.D.C. 33, 37, 449 F.2d 1109, 1113, 1 ELR 20346, 20347 (1971), cert. denied 404 U.S. 942 (1972).

46. Hanly v. Kleindienst (Hanly II), 471 F.2d 823, 835, 2 ELR 20717, 20723 (2d Cir. 1972). Compare Scenic Hudson Preservation Conference v. Federal Power Comm'n (II), 453 F.2d 463, 481, 1 ELR 20496, 20503 (2d Cir.

fects consistent with the "current state of the art" of relevant scientific inquiry.[47] It has been held, on the other hand, that subsection (B) "cannot be fairly read to command an agency to develop or define any general or specific quantification process. . . .[48] [It] requires no more than that an agency search out, develop and follow procedures reasonably calculated to bring environmental factors to peer status with dollars and technology in their decision-making."[49]

A third aspect of the scientific underpinnings of NEPA is section 102(2)(H) which directs each agency to "initiate and utilize ecological information in the planning and development of resource-oriented projects." This provision has been held to authorize environmentally related research not previously within the agency's jurisdiction,[50] which seems correct in light of the Act's charter expanding purposes. Section 102(2)(H) also substantiates the case for the courts' demanding mitigation measures concurrently with project construction. Utilizing ecological information in the planning and development of projects requires both ascertaining and correcting environmental losses.

Section 102(2)(F) requires each agency to "recognize the worldwide and long-range character of environmental problems and, where consistent with the foreign policy of the United States, lend appropriate support to initiatives, resolutions and programs designed to maximize international cooperation in the quality of mankind's world environment." This is not one of the stronger mandates of NEPA, and is rarely cited by the courts. It can be invoked as a supplementary justification for requiring an agency to consider the long-range or worldwide consequences of its actions,[51] or to conduct

1971), cert. denied 407 U.S. 926 (1972) (holding that subsection (A)'s interdisciplinary requirements were satisfied by the FPC's public hearing process).

47. Environmental Defense Fund, Inc. v. Hardin, 325 F.Supp. 1401, 1404, 1 ELR 20207, 20208 (D.C.D.C.1971); see Environmental Defense Fund, Inc. v. Corps of Engineers (Tennessee-Tombigbee), 348 F.Supp. 916, 928, 2 ELR 20536, 20540 (N.D.Miss.1972), aff'd 492 F.2d 1123, 4 ELR 20329 (5th Cir. 1974) (finding section 102(2)(B) satisfied if the methodology used "effectively measures life's amenities in terms of the present state of the art").

48. Environmental Defense Fund, Inc. v. Corps of Engineers (Tennessee-Tombigbee), 492 F.2d 1123, 1133, 4 ELR 20329, 20333 (5th Cir. 1974). The quotation continues:
Plaintiffs concede that compliance with this subsection does not require that every environmental amenity be reduced to an integer capable of insertion in a 'go-no go' equation. They must further acknowledge that many environmental values cannot be fixed even within a given project area, and that others are bound to vary in value from place to place and time to time.

49. Ibid.

50. See Environmental Defense Fund, Inc. v. Hardin, 325 F.Supp. 1401, 1404, 1 ELR 20207, 20208 (D.C.D.C.1971).

51. See Conservation Soc'y of Southern Vermont v. Secretary of Transp. (I), 508 F.2d 927, 934, 5 ELR 20068, 20071–72 (2d Cir. 1974), vacated 423 U.S. 809 (1975) (citing 102(2)(F) [formerly 102(2)(E)] in support of its conclusion to sustain the requirement of a broad EIS anticipating future developments).

research into possible effects over an extended period of time. This emphasis upon the longer range perspective is a valuable counterpoise to the tight time constraints on the impact statement requirements, and more compatible with the scientific method.

The scientific bases of the NEPA analysis, expressed in subsections 102(2)(A), (B), (F), and (H), have not been strongly observed.[52] The reasons are several: basic monitoring and survey data are generally lacking, and not obtainable within the tight timetables for EIS preparation. Expression of this data in a quantified way is very difficult and highly subjective if undertaken at all, which hinders a comparison of environmental values with economic ones. Synthesizing the data into "a complete and accurate description of a natural system" and predicting the impact of technology on that system "is a science (perhaps art) practiced by a few and not satisfactorily."[53] Ecological research, unlike that of other natural sciences like physics and chemistry, has not achieved a high predictive capability. Given the constraints, simulation modeling is not used impressively in implementing NEPA.

The hard question for the courts is whether to accept the state of the stagnant art and its uninspired expression in the current crop of EIS',[54] or to read NEPA as demanding a closer analysis. Section 102(2)(B), while prescribing no particular methodology, suggests an obligatory consideration of techniques that become widely adopted or demonstrably reliable.[55] A continued inability to quantify environmental amenities may prompt the courts to insist upon more extensive research obligations or mitigation measures to preserve or compensate for important incommensurables. Followup assessment and monitoring during implementation phases also may be prescribed to protect against a lack of predictive capability. The significance of subsections 102(2)(A) and (B) obviously turns upon whether they are read to require the agency only to tinker with a problem or exhaustively to consider and solve it. Likely to be correct is the prediction that the courts will invoke the section 102(2)(A) and (B) requirements in support of "an interdisciplinary, more scientific approach to back up their probing of basic decision-making under NEPA's substantive provisions, and to castigate agencies for deferring to intrenched perspectives and values."[56]

52. Carpenter, The Scientific Basis of NEPA—Is It Adequate?, 6 ELR 50014 (1976).

53. Id. at 50017.

54. Schindler, The Impact Statement Boondoggle, 192 Science 509 (1976).

55. For a discussion of the state of the art on environmental indices, see Congressional Research Service, National Environmental Policy Act of 1969, Environmental Indices—Status of Development Pursuant to Sections 102(2)(B) and 204 of the Act, Senate Comm. on Interior & Insular Affairs, 93d Cong., 1st Sess. (Comm. Print 1973).

56. Anderson, The National Environmental Policy Act, in Environmental Law Institute, Federal Environmental Law 238, 317 (E. L. Dolgin & T. G. P. Guilbert ed. 1974).

As the courts demand more scientifically from impact statements as a procedural matter, the scope of substantive review is likely to expand in reciprocal fashion.[57] A reliable quantification of environmental values invites a cost-benefit analysis. Better prediction of adverse effects demands mitigation. Proven unknowns call for protective measures or continued study or monitoring. A serious possibility of disaster suggests abandoning the project or at least postponing it until doubts are resolved.

Section 102(2)(E), formerly 102(2)(D), requires each agency to "study, develop and describe appropriate alternatives to recommended courses of any action in any proposal which involves unresolved conflicts concerning alternative uses of available resources." This provision obviously must be construed in conjunction with section 102(2)(C)(iii) which requires an impact statement to address "alternatives to the proposed action," and will be considered more fully in the section discussing the scope of the EIS requirement.[58] But its stringency deserves emphasis. It is, first of all, not limited to "major federal actions" as is 102(2)(C).[59] It is "supplemental to and more extensive in its commands"[60] than is section 102(2)(C)(iii), particularly insofar as it requires not only the study and description of appropriate alternatives but also that they be "developed." This directive imports not mere lipservice to and discussion of alternatives; it presumes a degree of serious consideration, perhaps some preliminary research, contingency planning, and the assignment of personnel and equipment to pursue the possibilities.[61] Section 102(2)(E) may require a discussion of alternatives not only in greater depth but also in wider range, perhaps including an indication of the "optimum" use of the resources at stake.[62]

Section 102(2)(G), formerly 102(2)(F), stresses the public information aspects of NEPA by requiring each agency to "make available to States, counties, municipalities, institutions, and individuals, advice and information useful in restoring, maintaining and enhancing the quality of the environment." It is conceivable, but unlikely, that this provision can be read as doing away with the principal Freedom of Information Act exemptions,[63] such as intra-agency

57. § 7.5 below.

58. § 7.9 below.

59. Hanly v. Kleindienst (Hanly II), 471 F.2d 823, 2 ELR 20717 (2d Cir. 1972), cert. denied 412 U.S. 908 (1973); Citizens for Reid State Park v. Laird, 336 F.Supp. 783, 2 ELR 20122 (D.C. Me.1972); see Trinity Episcopal School Corp. v. Romney, 523 F.2d 88, 5 ELR 20497 (2d Cir. 1975).

60. Environmental Defense Fund, Inc. v. Corps of Engineers (Tennessee-Tombigbee), 492 F.2d 1123, 1135, 4 ELR 20329, 20334 (5th Cir. 1974).

61. See Conservation Council of North Carolina v. Froehlke (I), 340 F.Supp. 222, 227–28, 2 ELR 20155, 20157 (M.D.N.C.), remanded 473 F.2d 664, 2 ELR 20259 (4th Cir. 1972).

62. Environmental Defense Fund, Inc. v. Corps of Engineers (Gillham Dam), 325 F.Supp. 749, 762, 1 ELR 20130, 20143 (E.D.Ark.1971).

63. § 1.10 above.

Sec. 7.4 IMPACT STATEMENT REVIEW PROCEDURES

communications, where they are invoked to withhold access to agency information relevant to environmental quality. A more probable interpretation of subsection 102(2)(G) is that it requires agencies to disclose information in their possession pertinent to an ongoing NEPA evaluation,[64] necessitates supplemental impact statements to accommodate recent information,[65] and substantiates further the general NEPA obligation of the agencies to "lay their cards on the table in full public view." [66]

Section 102(2)(I), formerly 102(2)(H), makes it mandatory for each agency to "assist the Council on Environmental Quality". This is meant to be helpful to CEQ alone. Specific instances of lack of cooperation, such as refusing to disclose pertinent information or to file environmental impact statements with CEQ, coincidentally may be useful to others in collateral attacks on agency actions under NEPA.

§ 7.4 Review of Agency Decision-Making: Environmental Impact Statement Procedures

Section 102(2)(C)[1] is the heart of NEPA. It combines the legislative objectives of full disclosure, consultation, and reasoned decision-making prescribed as the cutting edge of administrative reform. Discussed here are the general purposes and language of section 102(2)(C) and the courts' interpretation of them. Addressed elsewhere are specific questions concerning whether,[2] when,[3] and by whom[4] an environmental impact statement must be prepared, what it must contain,[5] and remedies available for violations.[6]

Section 102(2)(C) requires a "detailed statement" on the environmental impact of, and alternatives to, various federal actions.[7]

---

64. See I–291 Why? Ass'n v. Burns, 372 F.Supp. 223, 253–60, 4 ELR 20230, 20242–46 (D.C.Conn.1974), affirmed per curiam, 517 F.2d 1077, 5 ELR 20430 (2d Cir. 1975) (discussing noise and air quality studies commissioned the same day design approval for the highway was given) (no discussion of 102(2)(G)).

65. See Sierra Club v. Mason, 365 F. Supp. 47, 49, 4 ELR 20186, 20187 (D.C.Conn.1973).

66. Wisconsin v. Callaway, 371 F.Supp. 807, 811, 4 ELR 20296, 20298 (W.D. Wis.1974); see Natural Resources Defense Council, Inc. v. Securities & Exch. Comm'n, 389 F.Supp. 689, 695, 5 ELR 20074, 20076 (D.C.D.C.1974) (citing 102(2)(G) in support of determination that Commission violated APA in rulemaking proceeding regarding the disclosure of environmentally related information under the securities laws) ("*Congress* has determined that the dissemination of information to governmental units, institutions and individuals, can aid the purposes of NEPA") (emphasis in original).

1. 42 U.S.C.A. § 4332(2)(C).
2. § 7.6 below.
3. § 7.7 below.
4. § 7.8 below.
5. § 7.9 below.
6. § 7.10 below.
7. The subjects an impact statement must address bear repetition:
   (i) the environmental impact of the proposed action,

Numerous cases [8] invoke the obligation to prepare a "detailed statement" in support of the bedrock premise that NEPA is an "environmental full disclosure law." [9] The audiences addressed in any environmental impact statement are three: (1) the general public, both laymen and experts; [10] (2) other entities of government; [11] and (3) other persons within the issuing agency.[12] The interests of these groups are obvious: the citizen needs to know because he is the prime instrument for enforcing the Act. The President, the Congress, the Council on Environmental Quality, and the Environmental Protection Agency need to know because they have authority to review and redirect environmentally damaging activities. Other agencies need to know because they have special expertise brought explicitly into the decision-making process by NEPA. That an agency must talk clearly not only to others but also to itself is unremarkable if for no other reason than that a government enterprise today can resemble a sprawling megalopolis with a thorough breakdown in communication between its separate members.[13]

It is often said that the EIS requirement acts as an alarm bell [14] or that "notice of environmental consequences is all that is required." [15] This is true as far as it goes, but it is not enough for a statement to disclose only that something is amiss or that controversy exists. Notice must be accompanied by information allowing others

    (ii) any adverse environmental effects which cannot be avoided should the proposal be implemented,
    (iii) alternatives to the proposed action,
    (iv) the relationship between local short-term uses of man's environment and the maintenance and enhancement of long-term productivity, and
    (v) any irreversible and irretrievable commitments of resources which would be involved in the proposed action should it be implemented.

8. E. g., Monroe County Conservation Council, Inc. v. Volpe, 472 F.2d 693, 697, 3 ELR 20006, 20008 (2d Cir. 1972).

9. Environmental Defense Fund, Inc. v. Corps of Engineers (Gillham Dam), 325 F.Supp. 749, 759, 1 ELR 20130, 20141 (E.D.Ark.1971).

10. Environmental Defense Fund, Inc. v. Froehlke (Cache River), 473 F.2d 346, 350–51, 3 ELR 20001, 20003 (8th Cir. 1972); Calvert Cliffs' Coord. Comm. v. Atomic Energy Comm'n, 146 U.S.App.D.C. 33, 38, 449 F.2d 1109, 1114, 1 ELR 20346, 20348 (1971), cert. denied 404 U.S. 942 (1972).

11. Jones v. District of Columbia Redev. Land Agency, 162 U.S.App.D.C. 366, 375, 499 F.2d 502, 511, 4 ELR 20479, 20482 (1974); Natural Resources Defense Council, Inc. v. Grant, 341 F.Supp. 356, 364, 2 ELR 20185, 20188 (E.D.N.C.1972).

12. Environmental Defense Fund, Inc. v. Corps of Engineers (Tennessee-Tombigbee), 492 F.2d 1123, 1136, 4 ELR 20329, 20335 (5th Cir. 1974).

13. See Simmans v. Grant, 370 F.Supp. 5, 22, 4 ELR 20329, 20335 (5th Cir. 1974).

14. See Hearings on the Nomination of William Ruckelshaus as EPA Administrator, Before the Senate Comm. on Public Works, 91st Cong., 2d Sess. 45–46 (1970) (remarks of Sen. Muskie).

15. Iowa Citizens for Environmental Quality, Inc. v. Volpe, 487 F.2d 849, 853, 4 ELR 20056, 20058 (8th Cir. 1972).

Sec. 7.4 IMPACT STATEMENT REVIEW PROCEDURES

to make independent judgments about the project. Outsiders from the public and other agencies are commissioned by NEPA to be consultants in the decision-making process, and the consultant's judgment is only as useful as the information upon which it is based. A "detailed statement" is "that which is sufficient to enable those who did not have a part in its compilation to understand and meaningfully consider the facts involved." [16]

The form and scope of the EIS should serve the audiences addressed. It must be comprehensible to the layman and instructive to the expert. It "must be written in language that is understandable to the nontechnical minds and yet contain enough scientific reasoning to alert specialists within the field of their expertise." [17] This obligation to popularize scientific concepts is no small challenge,[18] and it is often not met by the anonymous authors of an EIS. CEQ urges that the statement be "an essentially self-contained instrument, capable of being understood by the reader without the need for undue cross references." [19] Underlying reports or documents considered during preparation, including cost-benefit analyses, should either be appended or identified in the document, along with an indication of how the information can be obtained.[20] Comprehensive bibliographies are recommended.[21] An EIS, on the other hand, need not be cluttered with backup data unnecessary to an understanding of the agency's reasoning process.[22] The more common affliction appears to be too little

---

16. Environmental Defense Fund, Inc. v. Corps of Engineers (Tennessee-Tombigbee), 492 F.2d 1123, 1136, 4 ELR 20329, 20335 (5th Cir. 1974); see Iowa Citizens for Environmental Quality v. Volpe, 487 F.2d 849, 851, 4 ELR 20056, 20057 (8th Cir. 1974) (the EIS "is to serve as a basis for consideration of environmental factors by the agency involved and is to provide a basis for critical evaluation by those not associated with the agency"), citing Environmental Defense Fund, Inc. v. Froehlke (Cache River), 473 F.2d 346, 350–51, 3 ELR 20001, 20003 (8th Cir. 1972); Environmental Defense Fund, Inc. v. Corps of Engineers (Gillham Dam), 470 F.2d 289, 297–99, 2 ELR 20740, 20743 (8th Cir. 1972); Calvert Cliffs' Coord. Comm. v. Atomic Energy Comm'n, 146 U.S.App.D.C. 33, 449 F.2d 1109, 1 ELR 20346 (1971), cert. denied 404 U.S. 942 (1972); Cummington Preservation Comm. v. Federal Aviation Administration, 524 F.2d 241, 5 ELR 20696 (1st Cir. 1975).

17. Environmental Defense Fund, Inc. v. Corps of Engineers (Tennessee-Tombigbee), 348 F.Supp. 916, 933, 2 ELR 20536, 20542 (N.D.Miss.1972), aff'd 492 F.2d 1123, 4 ELR 20329 (5th Cir. 1974), quoted with approval in several cases including Natural Resources Defense Council, Inc. v. Grant, 355 F.Supp. 280, 286, 3 ELR 20176, 20178 (E.D.N.C.1973).

18. Compare In re Virginia Elec. & Power Co. (North Anna Power Units 1 and 2), Constr. Permit Nos. CPPR–77, –78, ALAB 324, 3 NRC 347, aff'd NRCI 76/11, 480 (1976), petition for review pending VEPCO v. Nuclear Regulatory Comm'n, Civil No. 76–2275 (4th Cir.) (rejecting reasonable layman test in favor of a reasonable expert test for evaluating accuracy of representations in technical submissions to the Nuclear Regulatory Commission).

19. 40 CFR § 1500.8(b).

20. Ibid; § 1500.8(a)(7).

21. Id. § 1500.8(b).

22. Environmental Defense Fund, Inc. v. Armstrong, 352 F.Supp. 50, 55, 2 ELR 20735, 20737 (N.D.Cal.1972),

documentation rather than too much; the bases of impact predictions are rarely provided in sufficient detail for the reader to validate them independently.[23]

The requirement that the EIS be a self-contained instrument like a judicial opinion strengthens its role in rationalizing agency decisions affecting the environment. It is said that the EIS "must stand the test alone—i. e., in and of itself it must either meet the requirements of NEPA or fail."[24] Neither subsequent argument of counsel,[25] nor proof in court,[26] nor a hastily prepared supplement[27] can justify an EIS inadequate on its face. Strict adherence to form, like practicing the piano, is the way recommended to overcome engrained habits of agency decision-making. Once the EIS becomes less than a complete environmental decision, it is in danger of becoming just another bit of information along the way. That fate would fulfill little of NEPA's promise of full disclosure and methodological reform.

One authority on NEPA urges that care must be taken to confine the scope of the EIS to an assessment of environmental impacts.[28] It is true that balancing short-term uses against long-term productivity under 102(2)(C)(iv) requires some exploration of need and project justification in the impact statement. But "there is a danger that project justifications and economic and technical considerations will swallow up environmental impact analysis if the scope of the statement is expanded."[29] This should not happen if both purposes of NEPA are kept clearly in focus: full disclosure of environmental effects and a statement of reasons as to why those effects are acceptable and how they can be minimized. An exposition on project benefits may be needed to rationalize the consequences but the emphasis is on answering environmental questions.

aff'd 487 F.2d 814, 4 ELR 20001 (9th Cir. 1973), cert. denied 416 U.S. 974 (1974) ("the EIS need not be an exhaustive collection of various and sundry minute scientific details").

23. Andrews, NEPA in Practice: Environmental Policy or Administrative Reform, 6 ELR 50001, 50002 (1976).

24. Environmental Defense Fund, Inc. v. Corps of Engineers (Tennessee-Tombigbee), 492 F.2d 1123, 1130, 4 ELR 20329, 20331 (5th Cir. 1974).

25. Natural Resources Defense Council, Inc. v. Morton, 148 U.S.App.D.C. 5, 14, 458 F.2d 827, 836, 2 ELR 20029, 20033 (1972).

26. Greene County Planning Bd. v. Federal Power Comm'n (I), 455 F.2d 412, 420–21, 2 ELR 20017, 20020 (2d Cir.), cert. denied 409 U.S. 849 (1972) (the written testimony of the agency's staff "cannot replace a single coherent and comprehensive environmental analysis, which is itself subject to scrutiny during the agency review process").

27. Natural Resources Defense Council, Inc. v. Morton, 337 F.Supp. 170, 172, 2 ELR 20071, 20072 (D.C.D.C. 1972) (on remand). Supplemental data and statements are permissible so long as they are circulated among the agencies and considered prior to final action being taken. See Natural Resources Defense Council, Inc. v. Callaway, 524 F.2d 79, 91–92, 5 ELR 20640, 20646 (2d Cir. 1975).

28. Anderson, The National Environmental Policy Act, in Environmental Law Institute, Federal Environmental Law 238, 311–14 (E. L. Dolgin & T. G. P. Guilbert eds. 1974).

29. Id. at 312.

Sec. 7.4 IMPACT STATEMENT REVIEW PROCEDURES

Section 102(2)(C) says clearly that "[prior to making any detailed statement], the responsible Federal official shall consult with and obtain the comments of any Federal agency which has jurisdiction by law or special expertise with respect to any environmental impact involved." This is an important aspect of the interdisciplinary decision-making sought to be promoted by NEPA because the consultation must precede the statement which in turn must precede the action. The federal agencies having jurisdiction by law or special expertise over particular environmental impacts are listed in the CEQ guidelines.[30] The list is not necessarily exhaustive and obviously is not static. Consultation requires more than a cursory or ritualistic request for information and, depending on the circumstances, may call for meetings, follow-up inquiries, and continued deliberation of the questions raised.[31] An issue of considerable importance is whether the section 102(2)(C) consultation provisions afford agencies with environmental expertise a veto power over aspects of other agencies' actions.[32] The answer probably is in the negative although as a practical matter an agency going against the advice of an expert sister agency will have difficulty justifying its choice.[33] In particular, failure to implement mitigation measures recommended by other expert agencies may be subject to correction by the courts under the substantive provisions of NEPA.[34]

Section 102(2)(C) also provides for securing comments on the statement from federal, state and local agencies "which are authorized to develop and enforce environmental standards." These comments "shall accompany the proposal through the existing agency review processes" which means more than traveling in juxtaposition to the proposal as it undergoes agency review.[35] The purpose, quite clearly, is to require an agency to consider, evaluate and, if necessary, act

---

30. 40 CFR § 1500, App. II.

31. See Akers v. Resor, 3 ELR 20157, 20158 (W.D.Tenn.1972); Sierra Club v. Froehlke (Wallisville-Trinity River), 359 F.Supp. 1289, 1346, 3 ELR 20248, 20267 (S.D.Tex.1973), rev'd and remanded on other grounds 499 F.2d 982, 4 ELR 20731 (5th Cir. 1974); cf. Davis v. Coleman, 521 F.2d 661, 678–79, 5 ELR 20633, 20639 (9th Cir. 1975) (interpreting the word "consideration" in 23 U.S.C.A. § 128).

32. Sierra Club v. Froehlke (Wallisville-Trinity River), 359 F.Supp. 1289, 3 ELR 20248 (S.D.Tex.1973), rev'd 499 F.2d 982, 993, 4 ELR 20731, 20737 (5th Cir. 1974); cf. Sierra Club v. Froehlke (Meramec Park Lake Dam), 534 F.2d 1289, 1313, 6 ELR 20448, 20454 (8th Cir. 1976) ("consultation" under Section 7 of the Endangered Species Act "does not require acquiescence"). Compare § 7.3 n. 37 above.

33. See Conservation Council of North Carolina v. Costanzo (II), 398 F.Supp. 653, 661, 5 ELR 20666, 20669 (E.D. N.C.), aff'd 528 F.2d 250, 6 ELR 20116 (4th Cir. 1975) (reciting testimony that Corps of Engineers in that district had never overridden objection of another agency to the issuance of a permit). But see Sierra Club v. Callaway (Wallisville-Trinity River), 499 F.2d 982, 4 ELR 20731 (5th Cir. 1974).

34. § 7.5 below.

35. Calvert Cliffs' Coord. Comm. v. Atomic Energy Comm'n, 146 U.S.App. D.C. 33, 41–42, 449 F.2d 1109, 1117–18, 1 ELR 20346, 20350 (1971), cert. denied 404 U.S. 942 (1972).

upon qualified opinion from other agencies while developing a specific proposal. The methodology requires "a two-way discussion; a forced dialogue."[36] The physical act of the comments accompanying the proposal is designed to be the harbinger of reasoned decision-making by the agency. Case law indicates that expert opinion from sources other than environmental standard-setting agencies must be treated similarly, and that a failure to include responsible opposing scientific views in an environmental impact statement will render it inadequate.[37]

The environmental impact statement thus serves not only to give notice of environmental consequences but also to verify the genuineness of the decision-making process. The document should show who was consulted, what they said, and the agency's response. The consultation and consideration requirements of section 102(2)(C) (the comments "shall accompany the proposal through the existing agency review processes") tend to assure the reasoned results which courts today demand of the agencies.[38] Characterization of the EIS as a reasoned document are many: it must be "sufficient to permit a reasoned choice" ;[39] should treat the decision "as an impending choice to be pondered, [not] as a foregone conclusion to be rationalized" ;[40] must "include the results of the [agency's] own investigation and evaluation of alternatives so that the reasons for the choice of a course of action are clear";[41] should "explicate fully [the agency's] course of inquiry, its analysis and its reasoning";[42] and must "go beyond mere assertions and indicate its basis for them."[43]

The great majority of NEPA cases finding inadequacies in EIS' detect marked deviations from the 102(2)(C) requirements of a "detailed statement", consultation with other agencies, and deliberate decision-making. Although generalities do not decide concrete cases, they are worth repeating: the EIS is supposed to be a reasoned and a relatively complete effort. It is not conceived as a "promotional document" catering to "just the sort of tendentious decision-making the NEPA seeks to avoid."[44] Nor should it be a purely mechanical

---

36. Tierrasanta Community Council v. Richardson, 4 ELR 20309, 20311 (S.D. Cal.1973).

37. Comm. for Nuclear Responsibility v. Seaborg, 149 U.S.App.D.C. 380, 384, 463 F.2d 783, 787, 1 ELR 20469, 20470 (1971).

38. §§ 1.5, 7.3 above.

39. Natural Resources Defense Council, Inc. v. Morton, 148 U.S.App.D.C. 5, 14, 458 F.2d 827, 836, 2 ELR 20029, 20033 (1972).

40. I–291 Why? Ass'n v. Burns, 372 F.Supp. 223, 249, 4 ELR 20230, 20241 (D.Conn.1974), aff'd per curiam, 517 F.2d 1077, 5 ELR 20430 (2d Cir. 1975).

41. Environmental Defense Fund, Inc. v. Froehlke (Cache River), 473 F.2d 346, 350, 3 ELR 20001, 20002 (8th Cir. 1972).

42. Ely v. Velde, 451 F.2d 1130, 1139, 1 ELR 20612, 20615 (4th Cir. 1971).

43. Silva v. Lynn, 482 F.2d 1282, 1283, 3 ELR 20698 (1st Cir. 1973).

44. I–291 Why? Ass'n v. Burns, 372 F.Supp. 223, 253, 4 ELR 20230, 20242 (D.Conn.1974), aff'd per curiam 517 F.2d 1077, 5 ELR 20430 (2d Cir. 1975).

Sec. 7.4   IMPACT STATEMENT REVIEW PROCEDURES   731

exercise [45] or a "paperwork" justification.[46] On the other hand, a court must look only for "adequacy and completeness . . . not perfection," [47] nor "the impossible," [48] nor an "objection free" document.[49] An EIS need not be "exhaustive," [50] documenting each problem "from every angle to explore its potential for good or ill." [51] A court will not "fly speck" [52] an EIS nor sustain criticism that is viewed as "overly technical," "hypercritical," [53] "chronic faultfinding," [54] or reflecting "hindsight and sophisticated editing." [55] What is required is "full, fair, bona fide compliance." [56]

Environmental impact statements found inadequate by the courts customarily display serious lapses of disclosure and reasoned decisions. Thus, prominent indicia of a defective EIS include conclusions that are sweepingly vague,[57] unsupported in fact,[58] scientifically indefensible,[59]

---

45. Canal Authority of Florida v. Callaway, 4 ELR 20259, 20265 (M.D. Fla.1974).

46. Montgomery v. Ellis, 364 F.Supp. 517, 528, 3 ELR 20845, 20849 (N.D. Ala.1973).

47. National Helium Corp. v. Morton (II), 486 F.2d 995, 1004, 4 ELR 20041, 20045 (10th Cir. 1973).

48. Environmental Defense Fund, Inc. v. Tennessee Valley Authority (Tellico Dam), 492 F.2d 466, 468 n. 1, 4 ELR 20225 n. 1 (6th Cir. 1974) (per curiam).

49. Bucks County Bd. of Commissioners v. Interstate Energy Co., 403 F. Supp. 805, 814, 6 ELR 20406, 20410 (E.D.Pa.1975), citing Cape Henry Bird Club v. Laird, 359 F.Supp. 404, 412, 3 ELR 20571, 20574 (W.D.Va.), aff'd 484 F.2d 453, 3 ELR 20786 (4th Cir. 1973).

50. Iowa Citizens for Environmental Quality, Inc. v. Volpe, 487 F.2d 849, 852, 4 ELR 20056, 20057 (8th Cir. 1973).

51. Sierra Club v. Froehlke (Kickapoo River), 345 F.Supp. 440, 444, 2 ELR 20307, 20308 (W.D.Wis.1972), aff'd 486 F.2d 946, 3 ELR 20823 (7th Cir. 1973); see Natural Resources Defense Council v. Callaway, 524 F.2d 79, 88, 5 ELR 20640, 20644 (2d Cir. 1975) (EIS need not be "all-encompassing in scope" so that the task of preparing it would become "either fruitless or well nigh impossible").

52. Lathan v. Brinegar (II), 506 F.2d 677, 693, 4 ELR 20802, 20808 (9th Cir. 1974) (en banc).

53. Environmental Defense Fund, Inc. v. Tennessee Valley Authority (Tellico Dam), 492 F.2d 466, 468 n. 1, 4 ELR 20225 n. 1 (6th Cir. 1974) (per curiam).

54. Environmental Defense Fund, Inc. v. Froehlke (Truman Dam), 368 F. Supp. 231, 238, 4 ELR 20062, 20064–65 (W.D.Mo.1973), quoting Lathan v. Volpe (II), 350 F.Supp. 262, 266, 2 ELR 20545, 20547 (W.D.Wash.1972).

55. Nat'l Forest Preservation Group v. Butz, 485 F.2d 408, 412, 3 ELR 20783, 20784 (9th Cir. 1973).

56. Lathan v. Brinegar (II), 506 F.2d 677, 693, 4 ELR 20802, 20808 (9th Cir. 1974) (en banc).

57. Akers v. Resor, 3 ELR 20157, 20159 (W.D.Tenn.1972).

58. Simmans v. Grant, 370 F.Supp. 5, 21, 4 ELR 20197, 20202 (S.D.Tex.1975); Akers v. Resor, 3 ELR 20157, 20159 (W.D.Tenn.1972); Rankin v. Coleman, 394 F.Supp. 647, 661, 5 ELR 20626, 20629 (E.D.N.C.1975).

59. Romulus v. Wayne, 392 F.Supp. 578, 592, 5 ELR 20302, 20306 (E.D. Mich.1975) (airport noise case) ("[T]he choice of 85dB(A) as a threshold of unacceptability was highly misleading and did not conform to what is scientifically known about the effects of noise on humans").

wholly unquantified,[60] unexplained in comprehensible terms,[61] internally contradictory,[62] basically flawed,[63] obviously misleading [64] or incomplete,[65] excessively cryptic [66] or perfunctory,[67] argumentative,[68] genuinely preposterous,[69] dependent upon stale data [70] or biased procedures,[71] ignore important topics,[72] delete telling information,[73] exude

60. Romulus v. Wayne, 392 F.Supp. at 593, 5 ELR at 20306 (the EIS "does not quantify the increase in [noise] exposure to some areas and the exposure of formerly unexposed areas"); see Sierra Club v. Froehlke (Wallisville-Trinity River), 359 F.Supp. 1289, 1352–53, 3 ELR 20248, 20272 (S.D.Tex.1973), rev'd 499 F.2d 982, 4 ELR 20731 (5th Cir. 1974) (stressing the Corps' failure to use established techniques to predict estuarine damage).

61. Davis v. Coleman, 521 F.2d 661, 674, 5 ELR 20633, 20637 (9th Cir. 1974) (characterizing a negative declaration as "bureaucratic doubletalk"); Natural Resources Defense Council v. Callaway, 524 F.2d 79, 94, 5 ELR 20640, 20647–48 (2d Cir. 1975) (EIS leaves reader "completely in the dark" as to why one dumping site was "suddenly chosen" over another); Romulus v. Wayne, 392 F.Supp. at 594, 5 ELR at 20307.

62. Minnesota Pub. Interest Research Group v. Butz (II), 401 F.Supp. 1276, 1309–10, 6 ELR 20133, 20143 (D.C. Minn.1975), rev'd 541 F.2d 1292, 6 ELR 20736 (8th Cir. 1976) (criticizing shifting definitions and assumptions).

63. Minnesota Pub. Interest Research Group v. Butz (II), 401 F.Supp. at 1304, 6 ELR at 20142.

64. See Rhode Island Comm. on Energy v. General Serv. Administration, 397 F.Supp. 41, 49 n. 14, 5 ELR 20685, 20688 n. 14 (D.C.R.I.1975) (negative declaration; agency public statements explaining its action are characterized as "misleading").

65. Montgomery v. Ellis, 364 F.Supp. 517, 522, 3 ELR 20845, 20847 (N.D. Ala. 1973).

66. Appalachian Mtn. Club v. Brinegar, 394 F.Supp. 105, 118, 5 ELR 20311, 20315 (D.C.N.H.1975) ("While quantity does not connote quality, an assessment of alternatives that is limited to two pages raises a red flag that there has not been an examination to the 'fullest extent possible'"); McDowell v. Schlesinger, 404 F.Supp. 221, 251, 6 ELR 20224, 20238 (W.D.Mo.1975) ("extremely terse"; "perfunctory and superficial").

67. Breckinridge v. Schlesinger, —— F. Supp. ——, ——, 6 ELR 20111, 20113 (E.D.Ky.1975), rev'd 537 F.2d 864, 6 ELR 20597 (6th Cir. 1976).

68. Students Challenging Regulatory Agency Procedures v. United States (SCRAP II), 371 F.Supp. 1291, 1302, 4 ELR 20267, 20271 (D.C.D.C.1974), rev'd sub nom. Aberdeen & Rockfish R. R. v. SCRAP, 422 U.S. 289, 95 S.Ct. 2336, 45 L.Ed.2d 191 (1975) (criticizing the "combative, defensive and advocacy language and style" used in the EIS).

69. Brooks v. Volpe, 350 F.Supp. 269, 278, 2 ELR 20704, 20707 (W.D.Wash. 1972) (comparing impact of seven-lane highway to old wagon road "hardly comports with common sense, let alone objective research").

70. Romulus v. Wayne, 392 F.Supp. 578, 588, 5 ELR 20302, 20304 (E.D. Mich.1975) (airport noise case; "the failure to include figures *then* available as to actual operations and future forecasts prepared by the FAA was potentially misleading, both to the agency decision-makers, other reviewing agencies and the public") (emphasis in original) (footnote omitted).

71. Montgomery v. Ellis, 364 F.Supp. 517, 532, 3 ELR 20845, 20850 (N.D. Ala.1973) (Soil Conservation Service cost-benefit computation based on "artificial and unrealistic" interest rate and "unduly long" project life). See also Environmental Defense Fund, Inc. v. Corps of Engineers (Gillham Dam), 325 F.Supp. 749, 761, 1 ELR 20130, 20142 (E.D.Ark.1971).

72. Rankin v. Coleman, 394 F.Supp. 647, 661, 5 ELR 20626, 20632 (E.D. N.C.1975) (certain subjects "completely overlooked").

73. Breckinridge v. Schlesinger, —— F. Supp. ——, ——, 6 ELR 20111, 20113

arrogance,[74] callousness[75] or whimsy unresponsive to expert criticism,[76] or demonstrate a reluctant, begrudging compliance.[77] Courts are particularly demanding in scrutinizing statements prepared in connection with actions that offend local land use planning requirements,[78] exact heavy environmental consequences,[79] trigger other consequential developments,[80] are implemented in secrecy,[81] or undertaken by agencies not likely to be sympathetic to environmental concerns.[82] On the other hand, courts are likely to be satisfied with lesser detail and a more limited analysis in impact statements on actions having no unusual environmental effects[83] or limited in scale;[84] where the effects are more social than environmental,[85] or

(E.D.Ky.1975), rev'd 537 F.2d 864, 6 ELR 20597 (6th Cir. 1976) (surreptitious editing of study on effects of closing army depot).

74. Appalachian Mtn. Club v. Brinegar, 394 F.Supp. 105, 118, 5 ELR 20311, 20316 (D.C.N.H.1975) (EIS describes comments that action may have a major adverse impact as "specious").

75. Rhode Island Comm. on Energy v. General Serv. Administration, 397 F.Supp. 41, 58, 5 ELR 20685, 20693 (D.R.I.1975) (noting the agency's "utter disregard" for environmental concerns).

76. I-291 Why? Ass'n v. Burns, 372 F.Supp. 223, 254, 4 ELR 20230, 20243 (D.C.Conn.1974), aff'd per curiam 517 F.2d 1077, 5 ELR 20430 (2d Cir. 1975) (author of air pollution aspects of a highway EIS admitted to writing it "off the top of my head" without support of any empirical data).

77. Prince George's County v. Holloway, 404 F.Supp. 1181, 1184, 6 ELR 20109, 20110 (D.C.D.C.1975) (NEPA is not to be treated as a bureaucratic "annoyance").

78. Maryland-Nat'l Capital Park & Planning Comm'n v. Postal Serv., 159 U.S.App.D.C. 158, 164–65, 487 F.2d 1029, 1035–37, 3 ELR 20702, 20704 (1973); Ely v. Velde, 451 F.2d 1130, 1 ELR 20612 (4th Cir. 1971); Goose Hollow Foothills League v. Romney, 334 F.Supp. 877, 1 ELR 20492 (D.C. Or. 1971).

79. Nelson v. Butz, 377 F.Supp. 819, 821, 4 ELR 20840 (D.Minn.1974) ("where particularly unique aspects are affected, the EIS should note them in some detail"); Indian Lookout Alliance v. Volpe, 345 F.Supp. 1167, 1170, 3 ELR 20051, 20053 (S.D. Iowa 1972). See also Iowa Citizens for Environmental Quality, Inc. v. Volpe, 487 F.2d 849, 852, 4 ELR 20056, 20057 (8th Cir. 1973) ("'The extent of detail required must necessarily be related to the complexity of the environmental problems created by the project'") (quoting opinion of lower court).

80. Natural Resources Defense Council, Inc. v. Morton, 148 U.S.App.D.C. 5, 13, 458 F.2d 827, 835, 2 ELR 20029, 20032 (1972) ("When the proposed action is an integrated part of a coordinated plan to deal with a broad problem, the range of alternatives that must be evaluated is broadened"). See also Environmental Defense Fund, Inc. v. Corps of Engineers (Gillham Dam), 325 F.Supp. 749, 761, 1 ELR 20130, 20138 (E.D. Ark.1971).

81. McDowell v. Schlesinger, 404 F. Supp. 221, 252 n. 43, 6 ELR 20224, 20239 n. 43 (W.D.Mo.1975).

82. Leventhal, Environmental Decisionmaking and the Role of the Courts, 122 U.Pa.L.Rev. 509, 515, 525 (1974).

83. Rankin v. Coleman, 394 F.Supp. 647, 654, 5 ELR 20626, 20628 (E.D. N.C.1975) (adequacy of an EIS "must be viewed in terms of the size and scope of a project, the commitment of resources involved, and the extent and gravity of potential environmental impacts").

84. Ibid.

85. Nucleus of Chicago Homeowners Ass'n v. Lynn, 524 F.2d 225, 5 ELR 20698 (7th Cir. 1975), cert. denied

merely aesthetic,[86] or remote and speculative,[87] or extremely hypothetical when the outcome is practically pre-ordained;[88] where alternatives are clearly disadvantageous,[89] or there is little room for variation[90] or mitigation;[91] where problems can be corrected later[92] by the exercise of continuing regulatory control;[93] or where criticisms of the statement are mentioned for the first time at trial[94] thus detracting from their seriousness.

The proper contents of an EIS are outlined in the CEQ guidelines[95] which track the five subjects of inquiry identified in Section 102(2)(C) of the Act. Needless to say, the statements themselves do

424 U.S. 967 (1976); Natural Resources Defense Council, Inc. v. Tennessee Valley Authority, 367 F.Supp. 128, 3 ELR 20725 (E.D.Tenn.1973), aff'd per curiam, 502 F.2d 852, 4 ELR 20737 (6th Cir. 1974); cf. § 2.4 above (discussing leniency accorded social nuisances).

86. See Maryland Nat'l Capital Park & Planning Comm'n v. Postal Serv., 159 U.S.App.D.C. 158, 167–68, 487 F.2d 1029, 1038–39, 3 ELR 20702, 20705–06 (1973).

87. Sierra Club v. Morton, 510 F.2d 813, 824, 5 ELR 20249, 20253 (5th Cir. 1975); Trout Unlimited v. Morton, 509 F.2d 1276, 1283, 5 ELR 20151, 20154 (9th Cir. 1974) (one of the remote consequences was the collapse of the Teton Dam which occurred subsequently); accord, Warm Springs Dam Task Force v. Gribble, 378 F.Supp. 240, 245–46, 4 ELR 20661, 20663 (N.D.Cal.), order stayed pending appeal 417 U.S. 1301, 94 S.Ct. 2542, 41 L.Ed.2d 654 (Douglas, J., sitting as Circuit Justice), aff'd per curiam, 418 U.S. 910 (1974).

88. E. g., Daly v. Volpe, 514 F.2d 1106, 5 ELR 20257 (9th Cir. 1975); Sierra Club v. Morton, 510 F.2d 813, 5 ELR 20249 (5th Cir. 1975); Conservation Soc'y of Southern Vermont v. Brinegar (I), 508 F.2d 927, 5 ELR 20068 (2d Cir. 1974), vacated 423 U.S. 809 (1975); Environmental Defense Fund, Inc. v. Corps of Engineers (Tennessee-Tombigbee), 492 F.2d 1123, 4 ELR 20329 (5th Cir. 1974); Environmental Defense Fund, Inc. v. Corps of Engineers (Gillham Dam), 470 F.2d 289, 2 ELR 20740 (8th Cir. 1972).

89. Cummington Preservation Comm. v. Federal Aviation Administration, 524 F.2d 241, 244, 5 ELR 20696, 20698 (1st Cir. 1975) (need not discuss alternatives ruled out by scientific realities); cf. Natural Resources Defense Council, Inc. v. Morton, 148 U.S.App.D.C. 5, 15, 458 F.2d 827, 837, 2 ELR 20029, 20034 (1972) ("We do not suppose Congress intended discussion of the environmental impact of alternatives so remote from reality as to depend on, say, repeal of the antitrust laws"); Iowa Citizens for Environmental Quality, Inc. v. Volpe, 487 F.2d 849, 853, 4 ELR 20056, 20058 (8th Cir. 1973).

90. Groton v. Laird, 353 F.Supp. 344, 351, 3 ELR 20316, 20319 (D.C.Conn. 1972) (proposed action only known alternative).

91. Iowa Citizens for Environmental Quality, Inc. v. Volpe, 487 F.2d 849, 852, 4 ELR 20056, 20058 (8th Cir. 1973) (no need for exhaustive analysis where no "significant differences in environmental impact among alternatives").

92. Life of the Land v. Brinegar, 485 F.2d 460, 473, 3 ELR 20811, 20816 (9th Cir. 1973) (". . . if the size of the [replacement] habitats do indeed prove to be inadequate, there is no reason why adjustments could not be made even if the construction as planned proceeds to completion").

93. Sierra Club v. Morton, 510 F.2d 813, 828, 5 ELR 20249, 20255 (5th Cir. 1975) ("continuing control must be considered in determining the reasonableness of the impact statement").

94. Sierra Club v. Morton, 510 F.2d at 826, 5 ELR at 20254.

95. 40 CFR § 1500.8.

Sec. 7.4 IMPACT STATEMENT REVIEW PROCEDURES

not always conform to the CEQ credo or the courts' views of an adequate EIS. While the grounds for inadequacy defy summary restatement, some per se categories are slowly emerging. Fatal defects often involve major deviations from the terms of 102(2)(C) and the guidelines: (1) failure to consult;[96] (2) inadequate description of the project area[97] or the policy[98] being implemented; (3) inadequate discussion of the relationship of the project to land use plans;[99] (4) incomplete discussion of probable environmental impacts,[1] (5) its cumulative effects,[2] or (6) secondary impact such as induced population growth;[3] (7) inadequate discussion of how

---

96. Simmans v. Grant, 370 F.Supp. 5, 19, 4 ELR 20197, 20202 (S.D.Tex. 1974); James v. Lynn, 374 F.Supp. 900, 4 ELR 20675 (D.C.Colo.1974).

97. 40 CFR § 1500.8(a)(1); see Montgomery v. Ellis, 364 F.Supp. 517, 521, 3 ELR 20845, 20846 (N.D.Ala.1973) ("It would seem elemental for an environmental impact statement to describe . . . adequately the project in question so that those removed from the initial decisionmaking process may be appraised what type of project is being considered").

98. Minnesota Pub. Interest Research Group v. Butz (II), 401 F.Supp. 1276, 1303, 6 ELR 20133, 20142 (D.Minn. 1975), rev'd on other grounds 541 F. 2d 1292, 6 ELR 20736 (8th Cir. 1976).

99. 40 CFR § 1500.8(a)(2); see Tierransanta Community Council v. Richardson, 4 ELR 20309 (S.D.Cal.1973); Environmental Defense Fund, Inc. v. Tennessee Valley Authority (Tellico Dam), 339 F.Supp. 806, 809, 2 ELR 20044, 20045 (E.D.Tenn.1972) (quoting the EIS as evidencing a lack of careful research and planning: "While land use planning is far from complete, *broad conclusions* concerning the environmental impact . . . *can be made at the present time*") (emphasis added by court).

1. 40 CFR § 1500.9(a)(3); see Chelsea Neighborhood Ass'ns v. Postal Serv., 516 F.2d 378, 387, 5 ELR 20373, 20377 (2d Cir. 1975); Appalachian Mtn. Club v. Brinegar, 394 F.Supp. 105, 117, 5 ELR 20311, 20314 (D.C.N.H.1975); Nelson v. Butz, 377 F.Supp. 819, 821, 4 ELR 20840, 20841 (D.C.Minn.1974); Lathan v. Volpe (II), 350 F.Supp. 262, 266, 2 ELR 20545, 20547 (W.D.Wash. 1972).

2. 40 CFR § 1500.8(a)(3); see Natural Resources Defense Council, Inc. v. Grant, 355 F.Supp. 280, 287, 3 ELR 20176, 20179 (E.D.N.C.1973) (cumulative effects of sedimentation caused by other channelization projects); Jones v. Lynn, 477 F.2d 885, 891, 3 ELR 20358, 20360 (1st Cir. 1973) (cumulative effects of urban development); Natural Resources Defense Council, Inc. v. Callaway, 524 F.2d 79, 94, 5 ELR 20640, 20645 (2d Cir. 1975) (cumulative effects of ocean dumping); Prince George's County v. Holloway, 404 F.Supp. 1181, 6 ELR 20109 (D.C.D.C.1975) (cumulative effects of other government installations).

3. 40 CFR § 1500.8(a)(3); see Davis v. Coleman, 521 F.2d 661, 680–81, 5 ELR 20633, 20640 (9th Cir. 1975):

[the evaluation] contains no detailed discussion of the project's probable impact on growth, land use or the planning process in the Dixon-Kidwell area, no detailed consideration of the effect industrialization would have on the proposed recreational development along Putah Creek, no estimate of the increased demand for Davis city services which increased population would occasion, no indication that the effects on community cohesion and the tax base have been studied, and no scientifically supported estimate of the effects of industrialization on air and noise pollution or on the quality and sufficiency of Davis' water supply.

See also Council on Environmental Quality, Fifth Ann.Rep. 410–11 (1974) (stressing the importance of analyzing secondary effects); Appalachian Mtn. Club v. Brinegar, 394 F.Supp. 105, 115, 5 ELR 20311, 20314 (D.C. N.H.1975) ("The Final EIS turned a blind eye to the possible incidental environmental effects that could occur

avoidable effects will be mitigated;[4] (8) inadequate discussion of other interests and considerations of federal policy thought to offset adverse environmental consequences;[5] (9) inadequate discussion of alternatives;[6] (10) slighting of tradeoffs between immediate benefits and long-term costs;[7] (11) failure to identify irreversible and irretrievable commitments of resources;[8] and (12) failure to recite the "history of success or failure of similar projects."[9]

There is authority for the proposition that a party attacking the adequacy of an EIS need only make a *prima facie* showing of inadequacy whereupon the burden of persuasion shifts to the agency to sustain the adequacy of the statement.[10] The prevailing view is that plaintiff has the traditional burden of proving by a preponderance of the evidence that the EIS is inadequate.[11] As the courts occasionally

in Franconia Notch, located only thirteen miles south of the proposed construction"). Compare Trout Unlimited v. Morton, 509 F.2d 1276, 1283, 5 ELR 20151, 20154 (9th Cir. 1975) (need not discuss "remote possibilities" of secondary development in vicinity of a dam site) (the project, the Teton Dam, later suffered a catastrophic collapse); Life of the Land v. Brinegar, 485 F.2d 460, 469, 3 ELR 20811, 20815 (9th Cir. 1973) (need not discuss "speculative" demographic effects).

4. 40 CFR § 1500.8(a)(5); see Prince George's County v. Holloway, 404 F.Supp. 1181, 1187, 6 ELR 20109, 20110 (D.C.D.C.1975); Simmans v. Grant, 370 F.Supp. 5, 21, 4 ELR 20197, 20203 (S.D.Tex.1974); Montgomery v. Ellis, 364 F.Supp. 517, 523, 3 ELR 20845, 20848 (N.D.Ala.1973).

5. 40 CFR § 1500.8(a)(8); see Natural Resources Defense Council, Inc. v. Morton, 148 U.S.App.D.C. 5, 13, 458 F.2d 827, 835, 2 ELR 20029, 20032–33 (1972); Chemical Leaman Tank Lines, Inc. v. United States, 368 F.Supp. 925, 948–49 (D.C.Del.1973).

6. 40 CFR § 1500.8(a)(4); see § 7.9 below.

7. 40 CFR § 1500.8(a)(6); see Sierra Club v. Morton, 510 F.2d 813, 827, 5 ELR 20249, 20255 (5th Cir. 1975) (holding that a cost-benefit analysis is not required by 102(2)(C)(iv); "the use of a postulated economic equation to express these values is permissible and in many instances desirable, but it is not a *sine qua non*").

8. 40 CFR § 1500.8(a)(7); Scientists' Inst. for Pub. Information v. Atomic Energy Comm'n, 156 U.S.App.D.C. 395, 481 F.2d 1079, 3 ELR 20525 (1973); Nelson v. Butz, 377 F.Supp. 819, 821, 4 ELR 20840 (D.C.Minn. 1974) (inadequate discussion of effects of inundation of unique resources); see § 7.7 below.

9. Natural Resources Defense Council Inc. v. Grant, 355 F.Supp. 280, 288 (E.D.N.C.1973); see Sierra Club v. Morton, 510 F.2d 813, 824, 5 ELR 20249, 20253 (5th Cir. 1975).

10. Scherr v. Volpe, 466 F.2d 1027, 1034, 2 ELR 20453, 20456 (7th Cir. 1972); Simmans v. Grant, 370 F.Supp. 5, 12, 4 ELR 20197, 20199 (S.D.Tex. 1974) (citing superior resources and expertise possessed by federal agency); Sierra Club v. Froehlke (Wallisville-Trinity River), 359 F.Supp. 1289, 1334–35, 3 ELR 20248, 20263 (S.D.Tex. 1973), rev'd 499 F.2d 982, 4 ELR 20731 (5th Cir. 1974). See also Maryland-Nat'l Capital Park & Planning Comm'n v. Postal Serv., 159 U.S.App.D.C. 158, 168, 487 F.2d 1029, 1039, 3 ELR 20702, 20706 (1973) (agency must provide "convincing reasons" why EIS not required).

11. Sierra Club v. Morton, 510 F.2d 813, 818, 5 ELR 20249, 20250 (5th Cir. 1975); Environmental Defense Fund, Inc. v. Corps of Engineers (Tennessee-Tombigbee), 492 F.2d 1123, 1130–31, 4 ELR 20329, 1126 (5th Cir. 1974); Trinity Episcopal School Corp. v. Romney, 387 F.Supp. 1044, 1080 (S.D.N.Y.1974), aff'd 523 F.2d 88, 5 ELR 20497 (2d 1975); Boone v.

recognize,[12] the significance of the burden of persuasion issue turns upon the depth of pretrial discovery and the scope of the hearing before the court. The burden is tolerable for the unusual plaintiff who enjoys free access to government files. Where discovery is limited and grudgingly conceded, assigning the burden of rebutting a *prima facie* case to the party with ready access to the facts is appropriate. The burden of persuasion is one more weapon in the arsenal of courts intent upon taking a hard look at agency decision-making.[13]

Judicial review of agency compliance with NEPA, especially the procedural aspects, is consistently rigorous. Although courts are mindful of limitations on their powers to second-guess the agencies, they scarcely could be more demanding of the decision-making process if they were sitting in nuisance cases with absolute authority to shape the final outcome. The practice is to examine every scrap of evidence considered by the agency in making its decision, to probe deeply into the reasoning process, and to supplement the administrative record where necessary. Judge Leventhal cites the twenty-five day trial after remand in *Overton Park* [14] as an example of the "hard look doctrine in spades," [15] and there are several comparable cases arising under NEPA.[16] Discovery can be extensive—a deposition from the Secretary of Transportation, production routinely of the entire administrative record and explanations beyond it; [17] testimony

---

Tillatoba Creek Drainage Dist., 379 F. Supp. 1239, 1241 (N.D.Miss.1974).

12. See Sierra Club v. Froehlke (Wallisville-Trinity River), 359 F.Supp. 1289, 1334–35, 3 ELR 20248, 20264–65 (S.D.Tex.1973), reversed on other grounds 499 F.2d 982, 4 ELR 20731 (5th Cir. 1974). See also Calvert Cliffs' Coord. Comm. v. Atomic Energy Comm'n, 146 U.S.App.D.C. 33, 42–43, 449 F.2d 1109, 1118–19, 1 ELR 20346, 20351 (1971).

13. Cf. International Harvester Co. v. Ruckelshaus, 155 U.S.App.D.C. 411, 438, 478 F.2d 615, 642, 3 ELR 20133, 20142 (1973).

14. 335 F.Supp. 873 (W.D.Tenn.1972), rev'd 494 F.2d 1212 (6th Cir. 1974).

15. Leventhal, supra note 82, at 514.

16. E. g., Brooks v. Volpe, 319 F.Supp. 90, 1 ELR 20045 (W.D.Wash.1970), rev'd 460 F.2d 1193, 2 ELR 20139 (9th Cir.), on remand 350 F.Supp. 269, 2 ELR 20704 (W.D.Wash.), injunction granted 350 F.Supp. 287, 3 ELR 20211 (W.D.Wash.1972), injunction dissolved 380 F.Supp. 1287, 5 ELR 20001 (W.D.Wash.), aff'd 518 F.2d 17, 5 ELR 20444 (9th Cir. 1974); Environmental Defense Fund, Inc. v. Corps of Engineers (Gillham Dam), 325 F.Supp. 728, 749, 1 ELR 20130 (E.D.Ark.1972), 342 F.Supp. 1211, 2 ELR 20353 (E.D.Ark.), aff'd 470 F.2d 289, 2 ELR 20740 (8th Cir.); Natural Resources Defense Council, Inc. v. Grant, 341 F.Supp. 356, 2 ELR 20185 (E.D.N.C.1972), 355 F.Supp. 280, 3 ELR 20176 (E.D.N.C.1973).

17. Production of the administrative record of course is mandatory. Citizens to Preserve Overton Park, Inc. v. Volpe, 401 U.S. 402, 421, 91 S.Ct. 814, 825, 28 L.Ed.2d 136, 155 (1971). See, e. g., Chelsea Neighborhood Ass'ns v. Postal Serv., 516 F.2d 378, 389, 5 ELR 20373, 20378 (2d Cir. 1975) (studies cited by agency in support of conclusions contained in EIS); Silva v. Lynn, 482 F.2d 1282, 1283, 3 ELR 20698 (1st Cir. 1973) (citing Administrative Procedure Act, 5 U.S. C.A. § 706); Natural Resources Defense Council, Inc. v. Morton, 148 U.S.App.D.C. 5, 13, 458 F.2d 827, 836, 2 ELR 20029, 20033 (1972); Comm. for Nuclear Responsibility, Inc. v. Seaborg, 149 U.S.App.D.C. 385, 391,

at trial can be wide ranging—cross-examination of the administrative decision-maker or the draftsmen of the environmental impact statement. This often results in seemingly technical decisions requiring agencies to retrace the commenting procedures,[18] rewrite the EIS,[19] and otherwise reconsider projects [20] under circumstances where the outcome is unlikely to be influenced. The protagonists may be displeased: agencies ask why they should be put through a ritual and exposed to delay; complaining parties question the value of a paper victory. The answer is that requiring the government to turn square corners when dealing with the environment is thought to be the best assurance of a sound result.

§ 7.5 Review of Agency Decision-Making: Substance

Substantive judicial review under the National Environmental Policy Act is a subject much mooted in the journals.[1] Substantive

463 F.2d 788, 794, 1 ELR 20529, 20531 (1971) (adverse comments received from other federal agencies); Romulus v. Wayne, 392 F.Supp. 578, 588, 5 ELR 20302, 20304 (E.D.Mich. 1975) (raw data and future forecasts used by agency).

18. Natural Resources Defense Council, Inc. v. Morton, 337 F.Supp. 165, 167, 2 ELR 20028, 20029 (D.D.C.), aff'd 148 U.S.App.D.C. 5, 458 F.2d 827, 2 ELR 20029 (1972).

19. § 7.10 below.

20. E. g., Arizona Pub. Serv. Co. v. Federal Power Comm'n, 157 U.S.App.D.C. 272, 280, 483 F.2d 1275, 1283, 3 ELR 20776, 20778 (1973) (preparation of EIS or finding why EIS unnecessary); Greene County Planning Bd. v. Federal Power Comm'n (I), 455 F.2d 412, 422, 2 ELR 20017, 20021–22 (2d Cir. 1972), cert. denied 409 U.S. 349 (preparation of EIS in lieu of assessment prepared by applicant); Appalachian Mtn. Club v. Brinegar, 394 F.Supp. 105, 122, 5 ELR 20311, 20317 (D.C.N.H.1975); City of New York v. United States, 337 F.Supp. 150, 162–63, 2 ELR 20275, 20277 (E.D.N.Y.1972) (consideration of environmental issues adduced at trial).

1. E. g., Andrews, NEPA in Practice: Environmental Policy or Administrative Reform?, 6 ELR 50001 (1976); Arnold, The Substantive Right to Environmental Quality Under the National Environmental Policy Act, 3 ELR 50028 (1973); Briggs, NEPA as a Means to Preserve and Improve the Environment—The Substantive Review, 15 B.C.Ind. & Com.L.Rev. 699 (1974); Bue, Judicial Review as Reviewed by the Judiciary, 4 ELR 50148 (1974); Cohen & Warren, Judicial Recognition of the Substantive Requirements of the National Environmental Policy Act of 1969, 13 B.C.Ind. & Com.L.Rev. 685 (1972); Leventhal, Environmental Decisionmaking and the Role of the Courts, 122 U.Pa.L.Rev. 509, 527–29 (1974); Robie, Recognition of Substantive Rights Under NEPA, 7 Nat.Res.L. 387 (1974); Yarrington, Judicial Review of Substantive Agency Decisions: A Second Generation of Cases Under the National Environmental Policy Act, 19 S.D.L.Rev. 279 (1974); Comment, The Role of the Courts Under the National Environmental Policy Act, 23 Cath.U.L.Rev. 300 (1973); Comment, Judicial Review of Administrative Decisions Under the National Environmental Policy Act of 1969, 9 Land & Water L.Rev. 145, 155–63 (1974); Note, Substantive Review Under the National Environmental Policy Act: EDF v. Corps of Engineers, 3 Ecology L.Q. 173 (1973); Note, Scenic Hudson Revisited: The Substantial Evidence Test and Judicial Review of Agency Environmental Findings, 2 Ecology L.Q. 837 (1972); Note, The Least Adverse Alternative Approach to Substantive Review Under NEPA, 88 Harv.L.Rev. 735 (1975); Note, The National Environmental

review is used here to refer to the power of the courts to modify or nullify agency actions found offensive to the principles of NEPA. Judicial review of underlying agency action is a question separate and distinct from the procedural review of the adequacy of the impact statement although some courts tend to blur the two by faulting the impact statement on grounds that can be corrected only by modifying the project.[2] Defining the substantive standards for testing the legality of agency actions under NEPA poses a perplexing challenge for the courts. Several approaches are addressed: (1) the good faith test, (2) the miscellaneous standards of section 101, and (3) the balancing test, including its important components of cost-benefit analysis and best technology.

a. *Good Faith Test*

"Where NEPA is involved," according to a widely quoted statement on the scope of substantive review, "the reviewing court must first determine if the agency reached its decision after a full, good faith consideration and balancing of environmental factors."[3] Virtually all courts agree that NEPA at least requires a good faith consideration of environmental factors by the mission agency although few courts explain what the good faith requirement means and whether it adds anything to the procedural strictures of section 102(2). Taken literally, subjective good faith as a standard of review demands too much and too little. It asks too much of old line agencies by insisting they put aside their biases and dearly held aims in favor of alien values; and it demands too little by blinking at disaster because those responsible genuinely adhere to foolishness.

Policy Act: What Standard of Judicial Review, 39 J.Air L. & Com. 643 (1973); Note, Substance and Procedure in the Construction of the National Environmental Policy Act, 6 U.Mich.J.L.Ref. 491 (1973).

2. See Anderson, The National Environmental Policy Act, in Environmental Law Institute, Federal Environmental Law 238, 311–14 (E. L. Dolgin & T. G. P. Guilbert eds. 1974); e. g., Silva v. Lynn, 482 F.2d 1282, 1285, 1287, 3 ELR 20698, 20699 (1st Cir. 1973); Environmental Defense Fund, Inc. v. Froehlke (Cache River), 473 F.2d 346, 351, 3 ELR 20001, 20003 (8th Cir. 1972); Natural Resources Defense Council, Inc. v. Stamm, 4 ELR 20463 (E.D.Cal.1974); Natural Resources Defense Council, Inc. v. Grant, 355 F.Supp. 280, 289, 3 ELR 20176, 20179 (E.D.N.C.1973); Keith v. Volpe, 352 F.Supp. 1324, 1336, 2 ELR 20632, 20635 (C.D.Cal.1972). See also Maryland Nat'l Capital Park & Planning Comm'n v. Postal Serv., 159 U.S.App.D.C. 158, 171, 487 F.2d 1029, 1042, 3 ELR 20702, 20707 (1973) (dictum) (court may require stipulation that agency will modify project as condition for not enjoining action).

3. Environmental Defense Fund, Inc. v. Corps of Engineers (Gillham Dam), 470 F.2d 289, 300, 2 ELR 20740, 20745 (8th Cir. 1972), quoting Calvert Cliffs' Coord. Comm. v. Atomic Energy Comm'n, 146 U.S.App.D.C. 33, 39, 449 F.2d 1109, 1115, 1 ELR 20346, 20349 (1971). The quotation continues:

The Court must then determine, according to the standards set forth in §§ 101(b) and 102(1) of the Act, whether the actual balance of costs and benefits as struck was arbitrary or clearly gave insufficient weight to environmental values.

In practice, the good faith test is not particularly demanding. What is required is "good faith objectivity" rather than "subjective impartiality." [4] Bad faith is not proven by showing that an agency was committed to a project before it initiated its environmental study,[5] promoted the project by speeches [6] or letters [7] while environmental studies were underway, used data provided by an interested party,[8] refused to change its position after preparing an impact statement,[9] or decorated the EIS with "rhapsodic prose." [10] Bad faith usually is reserved in the decisions to describe conduct that would amount to a flagrant violation of NEPA's procedural provisions that would be readily reviewable in court—fraud in the preparation of a statement,[11] outright refusal to comply,[12] or a contemptuous effort evincing a "callous disregard" [13] of environmental consequences.

Quite correctly, the good faith test sometimes is equated in the case law with *Overton Park's* "substantial inquiry" [14] or Judge Leventhal's "hard look" [15] doctrine of judicial review.[16] Thus, it is said

---

4. Sierra Club v. Froehlke (Wallisville-Trinity River), 359 F.Supp. 1289, 1342, 3 ELR 20248, 20268 (S.D.Tex. 1973), rev'd on other grounds 499 F.2d 982, 4 ELR 20731 (5th Cir. 1974), quoting Environmental Defense Fund, Inc. v. Corps of Engineers (Gillham Dam), 470 F.2d 289, 296, 2 ELR 20740, 20743 (8th Cir. 1972).

5. Environmental Defense Fund, Inc. v. Corps of Engineers (Tennessee-Tombigbee), 492 F.2d 1123, 1129, 4 ELR 20329, 20331 (5th Cir. 1974); Jicarilla Apache Tribe v. Morton, 471 F.2d 1275, 1281, 3 ELR 20043, 20045 (9th Cir. 1973).

6. Environmental Defense Fund, Inc. v. Corps of Engineers (Gillham Dam), 470 F.2d 289, 295, 2 ELR 20740, 20742 (8th Cir. 1972), cert. denied 412 U.S. 931 (1973) (statement by district engineer in charge of project before a local Chamber of Commerce meeting that the dam definitely would be built).

7. Environmental Defense Fund, Inc. v. Corps of Engineers (Tennessee-Tombigbee), 492 F.2d 1123, 1129, 4 ELR 20329, 20331 (5th Cir. 1974) (the letters conveyed a "spirit of confidence" on the part of the writer that the project would proceed).

8. Florida Audubon Soc'y v. Callaway, 4 ELR 20251, 20254 (M.D.Fla.1974).

9. Daly v. Volpe, 514 F.2d 1106, 1111, 5 ELR 20257, 20258 (9th Cir. 1975).

10. Conservation Soc'y of Southern Vermont v. Secretary of Transp. (I), 362 F.Supp. 627, 633, 3 ELR 20709, 20711 (D.C.Vt.1973), aff'd 508 F.2d 927, 5 ELR 20068 (2d Cir. 1974, vacated 423 U.S. 809 (1975).

11. Sierra Club v. Froehlke (Wallisville-Trinity River), 359 F.Supp. 1289, 1342, 3 ELR 20248, 20268 (S.D.Tex. 1973), rev'd on other grounds 499 F.2d 982, 4 ELR 20731 (5th Cir. 1974) (the good faith test would preclude "consciously slanted or biased impact statements wherein intentional misrepresentation was attempted"), citing Environmental Defense Fund, Inc. v. Corps of Engineers (Gillham Dam), 342 F.Supp. 1211, 1214, 2 ELR 20353, 20354 (E.D.Ark.1972).

12. Jicarilla Apache Tribe v. Morton, 471 F.2d 1275, 1284, 3 ELR 20045, 20048 (9th Cir. 1973) ("There is no evidence of any attempt to avoid NEPA or any obstinate refusal to comply with NEPA").

13. I-291 Why? Ass'n v. Burns, 372 F.Supp. 223, 242, 4 ELR 20230, 20237 (D.C.Conn.1974), aff'd per curiam, 517 F.2d 1077, 5 ELR 20430 (2d Cir. 1975).

14. § 1.5 above.

15. Leventhal, supra note 1, at 528.

16. § 1.5 above.

that "good faith consideration" is demonstrated by an agency showing "that it has adequately weighed the relevant environmental factors in deciding whether and how to go forward with the project," or has evinced an attitude to "modify or drop the project if the environmental costs are sufficient to outweigh the benefits . . . ."[17] There is no question that NEPA requires a genuine consideration of environmental factors. Section 102(2) imposes a procedural straitjacket (written statements, consultation, consideration) which allows the courts to take a "hard look" at the agency decision-making while confining their review solely to procedural matters.[18] Properly viewed, the good faith test is simply a reaffirmation of the view that the courts will enforce the procedural requirements of NEPA with telling effect.[19]

b. *Miscellaneous Standards of Section 101*

There is, at the outset, no legislative barrier to judicial review of agency actions under the substantive provisions of NEPA since the Administrative Procedure Act precludes review only of matters "committed to agency discretion,"[20] and this exception applies under *Overton Park* only where there is "no law to apply."[21] Whatever can be said of the general directives of Section 101 of NEPA, they cannot be denigrated as nonlaw, particularly in light of the vague nuisance or public trust principles against which they must be considered.[22]

Despite this, judicial opinion is by no means universal that NEPA creates substantive rights enforceable in court.[23] The holdouts as-

17. Conservation Soc'y of Southern Vermont v. Secretary of Transp. (I), 362 F.Supp. 627, 633, 3 ELR 20709, 20711 (D.C.Vt.1973), affirmed, 508 F.2d 927, 5 ELR 20068 (2d Cir. 1974), vacated 423 U.S. 809 (1975).

18. §§ 7.3, 7.4 above.

19. Ibid.

20. 5 U.S.C.A. § 701(a)(2).

21. Citizens to Preserve Overton Park v. Volpe, 401 U.S. 402, 410, 91 S.Ct. 814, 821, 28 L.Ed.2d 136, 150 (1971).

22. Ch. 2 above.

23. NEPA is recognized as creating substantive rights in the following circuits: Environmental Defense Fund, Inc. v. Corps of Engineers (Tennessee-Tombigbee), 492 F.2d 1123, 4 ELR 20329 (5th Cir. 1974); Sierra Club v. Froehlke (Kickapoo River), 486 F.2d 946, 3 ELR 20823 (7th Cir. 1973); Silva v. Lynn, 482 F.2d 1282, 3 ELR 20698 (1st Cir. 1973); Conservation Council of North Carolina v. Froehlke, 473 F.2d 664, 3 ELR 20132 (4th Cir. 1973); Environmental Defense Fund, Inc. v. Corps of Engineers (Gillham Dam), 470 F.2d 289, 2 ELR 20740 (8th (Cir. 1972), cert. denied 412 U.S. 931 1973); Calvert Cliffs' Coord. Comm. v. Atomic Energy Comm'n, 146 U.S. App.D.C. 33, 449 F.2d 1109, 1 ELR 20346 (1971), cert. denied 404 U.S. 942 (1972); Environmental Defense Fund, Inc. v. Tennessee Valley Authority, 371 F.Supp. 1004, 4 ELR 20120 E.D.Tenn.1973), aff'd per curiam, 492 F.2d 466, 4 ELR 20225 (6th Cir. 1974); Conservation Soc'y of Southern Vermont v. Secretary of Transp. (I), 362 F.Supp. 627, 3 ELR 20709 (D.C.Vt. 1973), aff'd on other grounds 508 F.2d 927, 5 ELR 20068 (2d Cir. 1974), vacated 423 U.S. 809 (1975). Contra, Lathan v. Brinegar (II), 506 F.2d 677, 4 ELR 20802 (9th Cir. 1974) (substantive review only under the Administrative Procedure Act, 5 U.S.C.A.

signing NEPA strictly a procedural role are not necessarily unsympathetic to the aims of the legislation but rather are convinced that courts can fulfill their function by a close procedural review under the hard look doctrine.[24]

Enforceable standards are not difficult to discover in section 101(b),[25] particularly when read against the experience of the common law. The general directive to the agencies to "use all practicable means" to conform their plans to environmental values suggests the best technology standard of the nuisance cases.[26] The best control technology and the most environmentally sensitive management practices are standards by no means foreign to judicial experience.[27] Using "all practicable means" to "fulfill the responsibilities of each generation as trustee of the environment for succeeding generations" suggests the discipline of the public trust doctrine. This imposes discernible constraints on public resource use decisions,[28] including protecting current public uses, giving preferences to nonconsumptive uses and preventing the subordination of public uses to private development decisions.[29]

§ 706(2)(A)); National Helium Corp. v. Morton (II), 486 F.2d 995, 4 ELR 20041 (10th Cir. 1973).

24. See § 1.5 above.

25. 42 U.S.C.A. § 4331(b), reads:
In order to carry out the policy set forth in this chapter, it is the continuing responsibility of the Federal Government to use all practicable means, consistent with other essential considerations of national policy, to improve and coordinate Federal plans, functions, programs, and resources to the end that the Nation may—
(1) fulfill the responsibilities of each generation as trustee of the environment for succeeding generations;
(2) assure for all Americans safe, healthful, productive, and esthetically and culturally pleasing surroundings;
(3) attain the widest range of beneficial uses of the environment without degradation, risk to health or safety, or other undesirable and unintended consequences;
(4) preserve important historic cultural and natural aspects of our national heritage, and maintain, wherever possible, an environment which supports diversity and variety of individual choice;
(5) achieve a balance between population and resource use which will permit high standards of living and a wide sharing of life's amenities; and
(6) enhance the quality of renewable resources and approach the maximum attainable recycling of depletable resources.

26. § 2.6 above.

27. Ibid.

28. E. g., Sax, The Public Trust Doctrine in Natural Resource Law: Effective Judicial Intervention, 68 Mich. L.Rev. 471 (1970); § 2.16 above.

29. E. g., Illinois Central R.R. v. Illinois, 146 U.S. 387, 13 S.Ct. 110, 36 L.Ed. 1018 (1892) (conveyance of submerged lakefront property to railroad); Sierra Club v. Dep't of Interior, 376 F.Supp. 90, 4 ELR 20444 (N.D.Cal.1974) (maintenance and protection of Redwood National Park); Gewirtz v. Long Beach, 69 Misc.2d 763, 330 N.Y.S.2d 495, 2 ELR 20523 (1972), aff'd 45 A.D.2d 841, 358 N.Y.S. 2d 957 (1974) (access to public beach); Paepcke v. Pub. Bldg. Comm'n, 46 Ill. 2d 330, 263 N.E.2d 11, 1 ELR 20172 (1970) (construction of school in public park).

Sec. 7.5 AGENCY DECISION-MAKING: SUBSTANCE

The land-use connotations of nuisance law, protecting the character of neighborhoods and the priority of use,[30] can be found in the statutory assurance of "safe, healthful, productive, and esthetically and culturally pleasing surroundings". Thus, an EIS can be found inadequate for not discussing the nonconforming use aspects of a federal action,[31] and a court may yet rule out a federal siting decision that ignores sensible land use patterns. A nondegradation principle is found in the directive that beneficial uses of the environment must proceed "without degradation". While the content of nondegradation is elusive,[32] it certainly can be expressed in terms decidedly substantive: air and water quality levels must be maintained; development shall not be allowed; or resources shall be preserved in a natural state.[33] The legislative suggestion that federal development proceed without "risk to health or safety", like the nondegradation principle, could lead to paralysis if accepted literally. But it is certainly not startling to suggest that health values are held dearly,[34] and that federal projects flouting them must be stopped in their tracks or refashioned accordingly. Emphasis upon an environment "which supports diversity, and a variety of individual choice" could make a difference in an individual case, as could the reference to "the maximum attainable recycling of depletable resources" in subsection (6). Using best efforts or the best technology to achieve a desired end is perhaps the most important substantive obligation of nuisance law.[35] There is a hint of equal protection and equal opportunity in the obligation of federal agencies to use all practicable means to "achieve a balance between population and resource use" which will permit "a wide sharing of life's amenities". Federal sponsorship of special interest exploitation certainly is not encouraged by the provision.

The chief barrier to uninhibited substantive review of agency actions under NEPA is the Administrative Procedure Act which says that the reviewing court may set aside agency actions only if they are found to be "arbitrary, capricious, an abuse of discretion or otherwise not in accordance with law." [36] This gives the agency the benefit of the doubt that a private party does not enjoy. The arbitrary and capricious standard of review is a rough prescription for protecting executive decision-making from encroachment by the judiciary. The separation of powers cuts against an expansive substantive review. Some considerations go the other way. One of the great constraints upon substantive review of private actions under nuisance

---

30. §§ 2.7, 2.8 above.

31. See cases cited in § 7.4 n. 78 above.

32. § 3.12 above.

33. See Ass'n for the Protection of the Adirondacks v. MacDonald, 253 N.Y. 234, 170 N.E. 902 (1930) (discussing N.Y.Const. art. 7, § 7 (now art. 14, § 1) which states that the forest preserve "shall be forever kept as wild forest lands").

34. § 2.4 above.

35. § 2.6 above.

36. 5 U.S.C.A. § 706(2)(a).

law, for example, is the marketplace.[37] Expenditures to protect the public from pollution may not be ordered if the defendant will be driven out of business. Theoretically at least, an inability to pay is a poor excuse for agency actions impacting the environment.

c. *The Balancing Test*

The Supreme Court made it clear in *Overton Park* that the arbitrary and capricious standard allows a court only to consider "whether the decision was based on a consideration of relevant factors and whether there has been a clear error of judgment." [38] This language was picked up in *Calvert Cliffs* and, although the issue remained open for some time,[39] led eventually to a formulation that today approaches blackletter law on the scope of substantive review under NEPA: "The court must . . . determine, according to the standards set forth in §§ 101(b) and 102(1), whether the actual balance of costs and benefits as struck was arbitrary or clearly gave insufficient weight to environmental values." [40] *Calvert Cliffs* is perhaps best known for its dicta that "NEPA mandates a rather finely tuned and 'systematic' balancing analysis" [41] by the agencies.

Before addressing the problem of standards, it should be pointed out that courts for centuries have engaged in balancing the gravity of harm against the utility of conduct in nuisance cases. While there may be differences between the types of activity attacked as nuisances and major federal actions under NEPA, there also are similarities: nuisance litigation has concerned itself with the subtle science of effects, the state of the art of controls, and the complexities of modern industrial enterprises.[42] While nuisance litigation involves mostly private activity, reflecting the state of the economy, this is by no

37. § 2.5 above.

38. 401 U.S. 402, 416, 91 S.Ct. 814, 824, 28 L.Ed.2d 136, 153 (1971).

39. For a discussion of the early evolution of substantive review under NEPA, see Cohen & Warren, supra note 1. See also Yarrington, supra note 1.

40. Environmental Defense Fund, Inc. v. Corps of Engineers (Gillham Dam), 470 F.2d 289, 300, 2 ELR 20740, 20745 (8th Cir. 1972), quoting Calvert Cliffs' Coord. Comm. v. Atomic Energy Comm'n, 146 U.S.App.D.C. 33, 39, 449 F.2d 1109, 1115, 1 ELR 20346, 20349 (1971); see text accompanying note 3, supra.

41. 146 U.S.App.D.C. at 37, 449 F.2d at 1113, 1 ELR at 20348. The court elaborated on the theme:

NEPA mandates a case-by-case balancing judgment on the part of federal agencies . . . . The particular economic and technical benefits of planned action must be assessed and then weighed against the environmental costs; alternatives must be considered which would affect the balance of values. . . . In some cases, the benefits will be great enough to justify a certain quantum of environmental costs; in other cases, they will not be so great and the proposed action may have to be abandoned or significantly altered . . . . The point of the individualized balancing analysis is to ensure . . . that the optimally beneficial action is finally taken.
146 U.S.App.D.C. at 47, 449 F.2d at 1123, 1 ELR at 20353.

42. Ch. 2 above.

means universally true, with the solid waste disposal cases being one prominent example.[43] Nor are nuisance cases unfamiliar with the intrusion of administrative or legislative judgments [44] which means that separation of power questions may lurk beneath the surface. Nuisance litigation today on airport operations, sewage treatment plants and sanitary landfills must confront an administrative presence no less than NEPA litigation on the same subjects.

The development of substantive principles under NEPA has not moved greatly beyond *Calvert Cliffs'* analysis that the courts can upset agency decisions clearly mistaken in the balance of costs and benefits. The balancing process is vulnerable to criticism on the ground of the sheer impossibility of weighing the pros and the cons of a host of incommensurables,[45] but nuisance law is subject to similar criticism if the decision-making process is described definitively as involving simply a balance of the gravity of the harm against the utility of the conduct. The advantage of the balancing approach under NEPA, first by the agency, then by the courts, is not that it is particularly helpful in concrete cases but that it suggests a necessary process of identifying benefits, including the need for the project, and its costs, which clearly must precede any administrative or judicial determination about whether the project ought to go forward and, if so, with what modifications.

i. *Cost-Benefit Analysis*

It has been suggested that judicial review of agency projects under a strict cost-benefit analysis can afford clear judicial guidance in this standardless sea.[46] This is partly true although the utility of the approach is hampered by the recognition that NEPA, standing alone,[47] may not require the preparation of a cost-benefit analysis,[48] despite strongly encouraging a quantification of environmental values [49] and their expression whenever possible in cost-benefit formu-

---

43. § 6.2 above.

44. § 2.10 above.

45. See NEPA In the Courts, supra note 1, at 256–58; Murphy, The National Environmental Policy Act and the Licensing Process: Environmentalist Magna Carta or Agency Coup de Grace?, 72 Colum.L.Rev. 963, 977–81 (1972).

46. Note, 88 Harv.L.Rev., supra note 1, at 742–47.

47. See § 7.12 below for affirmation of the proposition that NEPA often does not stand alone.

48. Note, 88 Harv.L.Rev., supra note 1, at 743–45; Bucks County Bd. of Commissioners v. Interstate Energy Co., 403 F.Supp. 805, 6 ELR 20406 (E.D.Pa. 1975) (cost-benefit analysis not required where project is funded privately); see 403 F.Supp. at 816–17, 6 ELR at 20411 (collecting cases on whether NEPA requires preparation of a cost-benefit analysis). For a discussion of NEPA's effect on the preparation of cost-benefit analyses, see generally Note, Cost-Benefit Analysis in the Courts: Judicial Review Under NEPA, 9 Ga.L.Rev. 417 (1975); Note, Cost-Benefit Analysis and the National Environmental Policy Act of 1969, 24 Stan.L.Rev. 1092 (1972).

49. 42 U.S.C.A. § 4332(2)(B).

las.[50] Cost-benefit investigations also are difficult to pursue, dependent as they are upon predicting benefits and effects, quantifying them, expressing them in present values, and otherwise disguising subjective judgments.[51] Congress, in any event, may authorize a project that cannot be cost-justified.[52] Ultimately, even a serious cost-benefit undertaking asks only one, albeit the most important, question among many: whether the project should proceed. The issue of a shutdown always is an improbable one for the courts, even in nuisance cases where the question of power is conceded.[53] More likely the debate will involve not whether the dam will be built but the necessity for fish ladders, intake screens, and mitigation measures implemented concurrently with the project.[54]

Despite its limited application, the discussion over judicial enforcement of cost-benefit formulas is spirited. Authority is split over whether NEPA requires a cost-benefit analysis.[55] Authority is split further over whether courts can review an agency's cost-benefit decisions, once undertaken.[56] The better view is to require a cost-

---

50. See id. § 4332(2)(C)(iv).

51. E. g., C. Howe, Benefit-Cost Analysis for Water System Planning (1971); U.S. Water Resources Council, Summary and Analysis of Public Response to the Proposed Principles and Standards for Planning Water and Related Land Resources and Draft Environmental Statement (1972).

52. Oklahoma v. Guy F. Atkinson Co., 313 U.S. 508, 61 S.Ct. 1050, 85 L.Ed. 1487 (1941) (no right of judicial review of benefit-cost analysis under 33 U.S.C.A. § 701a); Sierra Club v. Froehlke (Kickapoo River), 486 F.2d 946, 3 ELR 20823 (7th Cir. 1973); Warm Springs Dam Task Force v. Gribble, 378 F.Supp. 240, 247, 4 ELR 20661, 20663 (N.D.Cal.), stay granted 417 U.S. 1301, 94 S.Ct. 2542, 41 L.Ed. 2d 654 (1974); Environmental Defense Fund, Inc. v. Froehlke (Truman Dam), 368 F.Supp. 231, 239, 4 ELR 20062, 20066 (W.D.Mo.1973), aff'd per curiam 497 F.2d 1340, 4 ELR 20686 (8th Cir. 1974) ("The questions of fact involved in connection with the ultimate resolution of conflicting data in regard to the determination of benefit-cost ratios are solely a matter for Congressional determination"); Cape Henry Bird Club v. Laird, 359 F.Supp. 404, 3 ELR 20571 (W.D.Va.), affirmed, 484 F.2d 453, 3 ELR 20786 (4th Cir. 1973). See also United States v. 2, 606. 84 Acres of Land in Tarrant County, Texas, 432 F.2d 1286 (5th Cir. 1970) cert. denied 402 U.S. 916 (1971).

53. § 2.11 above.

54. § 7.10 below.

55. Compare Environmental Defense Fund, Inc. v. Armstrong, 352 F.Supp. 50, 57, 2 ELR 20735, 20738 (N.D.Cal. 1972), aff'd 487 F.2d 814, 4 ELR 20001 (9th Cir. 1973), cert. denied 416 U.S. 974 (1974); Daly v. Volpe, 514 F.2d 1106, 1112, 5 ELR 20257, 20259 (9th Cir. 1975); Sierra Club v. Morton, 510 F.2d 813, 827, 5 ELR 20249, 20254–55 (5th Cir. 1975); Trout Unlimited v. Morton, 509 F.2d 1276, 1286, 5 ELR 20151, 20155 (9th Cir. 1974); Sierra Club v. Stamm, 507 F.2d 788, 794, 5 ELR 20209, 20211 (10th Cir. 1974); Warm Springs Task Force v. Gribble, 378 F.Supp. 240, 247, 4 ELR 20661, 20663 (N.D.Cal.1974), stay pending appeal 417 U.S. 1301, aff'd per curiam 418 U.S. 910 (1974) with Environmental Defense Fund, Inc. v. Tennessee Valley Authority, 371 F.Supp. 1004, 1010–11, 4 ELR 20120, 20222 (E.D.Tenn.1973), aff'd per curiam 492 F.2d 466, 4 ELR 20225 (6th Cir. 1974); Montgomery v. Ellis, 364 F.Supp. 517, 521, 3 ELR 20845, 20847 (N.D.Ala. 1973).

56. Compare Environmental Defense, Fund, Inc. v. Froehlke (Truman Dam), 368 F.Supp. 231, 240–41, 4 ELR 20062, 20066 (W.D.Mo.1973), aff'd 497 F.2d

benefit analysis if possible and where it is customary, and to review the decision under the arbitrary and capricious standard. It seems perfectly proper for the court to hold an agency to its professed methodology of decision-making no less than to its other regulatory commitments. A project may fail the cost-benefit justification if it rests upon arbitrary interest rates, absurd project lengths, or artificially puffed-up benefits.[57]

ii. *Maximum Mitigation*

A second approach to disciplined substantive decision-making under NEPA draws heavily on the nuisance analogue. The nuisance cases, it will be recalled, focus on the question of injury.[58] Once a substantial injury is established, the inquiry turns to the remedy where balancing principles are much in evidence.[59] There is considerable pressure in the nuisance cases to control adverse effects to the limits of technological and operational capability.[60] Section 101(b) of NEPA invites a similar approach: agencies are obliged "to use all practicable means, consistent with other essential considerations of national policy, to improve" their plans and actions to achieve environmental goals. The test of "all practicable means" does not differ markedly from, let us say, a test of "best practicable technology,"[61] and both are informed by the common

1340, 4 ELR 20686 (8th Cir. 1974); Cape Henry Bird Club v. Laird, 359 F. Supp. 404, 413, 3 ELR 20571, 20574 (W.D.Va.), aff'd 484 F.2d 453, 3 ELR 20786 (4th Cir. 1973); Environmental Defense Fund, Inc. v. Armstrong, 352 F.Supp. 50, 57, 2 ELR 20735, 20738 (N.D.Cal.1972), aff'd 487 F.2d 814, 4 ELR 20001 (9th Cir. 1973), cert. denied 416 U.S. 974 (1974); Environmental Defense Fund, Inc. v. Corps of Engineers (Gillham Dam), 325 F.Supp. 728, 741, 1 ELR 20130, 20134 (E.D. Ark.1970) with Environmental Defense Fund, Inc. v. Corps of Engineers (Tennessee-Tombigbee), 492 F.2d 1123, 1134, 4 ELR 20329, 20333-34 (5th Cir. 1974); Environmental Defense Fund, Inc. v. Froehlke (Cache River), 473 F.2d 346, 353, 3 ELR 20001, 20004 (8th Cir. 1972); Environmental Defense Fund, Inc. v. Tennessee Valley Authority, 371 F. Supp. 1004, 1014, 4 ELR 20120, 20124 (E.D.Tenn.1973), aff'd 492 F.2d 466, 4 ELR 20225 (6th Cir. 1974); Montgomery v. Ellis, 364 F.Supp. 517, 531, 3 ELR 20845, 20850 (N.D.Ala.1973); Sierra Club v. Froehlke (Wallisville-Trinity River), 359 F.Supp. 1289, 1363, 3 ELR 20248, 20273 (S.D.Tex.1973), rev'd on other grounds 499 F.2d 982, 4 ELR 20731 (5th Cir. 1974).

57. Concerned Residents of Buck Hill Falls v. Grant, 388 F.Supp. 394, 399, 5 ELR 20207, 20208 (M.D.Pa.1975), rev'd 537 F.2d 29 (3d Cir. 1976); Montgomery v. Ellis, 364 F.Supp. 517, 532, 3 ELR 20845, 20852 (N.D.Ala. 1973) ("In this case, however, use of such an historical and unrealistic interest rate and project life is clearly as a matter of law not within the reasonable zone of administrative discretion and, thus, should be subject to judicial review and reversal"); Sierra Club v. Froehlke (Wallisville-Trinity River), 359 F.Supp. 1289, 1363, 3 ELR 20248, 20273 (S.D.Tex.1973), rev'd on other grounds 499 F.2d 982, 4 ELR 20731 (5th Cir. 1974). See also Comment, Evolving Judicial Standards Under the National Environmental Policy Act and the Challenge of the Alaska Pipeline, 81 Yale L.J. 1592, 1600-01 (1972).

58. § 2.4 above.

59. § 2.11 above.

60. § 2.6 above.

61. Federal Water Pollution Control Act § 301(b)(1)(A), 33 U.S.C.A. § 1311 (b)(1)(A).

law "state of the art" cases.⁶² What is required is a maximum effort to minimize effects. The overriding qualifier—"consistent with other essential considerations of national policy"—is a narrow one, as pointed out by those commentators who stress that the use of the word "essential" makes clear that not every conflicting policy justifies a sacrifice of environmental values.⁶³ Indeed, while national policy will continue to call for use and consumption of natural resources and "major federal actions," it would be a rarity to discover an instance of an "essential consideration of national policy" that would call for a feckless use or an unnecessarily polluting one. Environmental values should be preserved if there is a way to do it.

A best technology or state of the art standard for substantive judicial review under NEPA is a demanding one. Where the issue is one of equipment, it calls for protecting the environment to the limits of technological feasibility.⁶⁴ Where the issue is one of design, it calls for the best alternative from an environmental perspective, consistent with realization of the aims of the action.⁶⁵ Where the issue is one of location, it calls for the least damaging alternative.⁶⁶ Where the issue is one of operation or management, it calls for the most environmentally sensitive practices. Where the issue is one of the extent of the damage expected, it calls for best efforts to avoid it and maximum efforts to mitigate it.

The case law is closing in on the "state of the art" approach. In the first place, strict enforcement of NEPA's procedural provisions assures a full discussion of alternatives and mitigation. Obviously, one purpose for this requirement is to give the agency an opportunity to rethink alternatives and maximize mitigation.⁶⁷ There is some evidence that this occurs: the litigation in Natural Resources Defense Council v. Morton⁶⁸ led to a decision refusing to lease for offshore oil development eight tracts close to a waterfowl refuge; the Alaska

---

62. § 2.6 above; cf. Davis v. Coleman, 521 F.2d 661, 676, 5 ELR 20633, 20638 (9th Cir. 1975) (while an agency need not foresee the unforeseeable, it "must use its best efforts to find out all that it reasonably can").

63. Cohen, supra note 1, at 693–94.

64. Cf. § 2.6 above.

65. See Note, 88 Harv.L.Rev., supra note 1.

66. But see Prince George's County v. Holloway, 404 F.Supp. 1181, 1183–84, 6 ELR 20109, 20110 (D.C.D.C.1975) (nothing in NEPA prevents the Navy from moving a program and its civilian personnel to a site that "is clearly the least desirable environmentally").

67. Environmental Defense Fund, Inc. v. Froehlke (Cache River), 473 F.2d 346, 352, 3 ELR 20001, 20003 (8th Cir. 1972) ("the option of mitigation" must not be "prematurely foreclosed"; a thorough analysis is necessary "in order to give decision-makers an opportunity to consider the possibility of delaying construction until a mitigation plan was put into effect").

68. 148 U.S.App.D.C. 5, 458 F.2d 827, 2 ELR 20029 (1972); § 7.19 below.

Sec. 7.5   AGENCY DECISION–MAKING: SUBSTANCE

pipeline was modified substantially; and there are other examples.[69] Courts often applaud agencies for undertaking "state of the art" mitigation measures concurrently with the action,[70] and are not content to let the matter rest with the agencies' good faith. Thus, steps are taken to assure that mitigation measures are reduced to firm commitments [71] or implemented in fact.[72] The weight of judicial opinion seems to be that the Act requires mitigation to be implemented concurrently with the action [73] and not left to the good faith of the promisor. This is fully consistent with using "all practicable means" to avoid degradation of the environment or other "undesirable" consequences, and with NEPA's incorrigible commitment to looking before the leap.

The disclosure and discussion of alternatives and mitigation required by NEPA procedures, coupled with a full evidentiary record developed by the court, provides the necessary predicates for substantive review. What is the judge to do if he sees a far less damaging alternative being ignored or a "state of the art" mitigation or control measure swept under the rug? And what is the court to

---

69. Illustrations of NEPA's effect on federal decision-making include: Department of Interior, decision in 1975 to defer proposed phosphate leasing on 25,000 acres of the Osceola National Forest, Florida, pending completion of a two year study by the U. S. Geological Survey; Atomic Energy Commission, cancellation of two major radioactive waste disposal site proposals at Lyons, Kansas and at the Savannah River, Georgia; Energy Research and Development Administration, reevaluation of surface radioactive waste storage facilities program; Department of Transportation, rejection of proposed extension of I–66 into Washington, D. C., later approved with modifications; Department of Defense, relocation of Atlantic Coast Maneuvering Range; General Services Administration, relocation of proposed site for the Kennedy Library and Museum in Boston, Massachusetts; and general program and project reevaluations by the Corps of Engineers, Soil Conservation Service, Forest Service, and Department of Housing and Urban Development. CEQ, Environmental Impact Statements: An Analysis of Six Years' Experience by Seventy Federal Agencies 21–25, D–1 to –4 (1976).

70. E. g., Life of the Land v. Brinegar, 485 F.2d 460, 473, 3 ELR 20811, 20815 (9th Cir. 1973) ("the replacement habitats at nearby Pearl Harbor Naval Station are being developed in conjunction with the project"); Jicarilla Apache Tribe v. Morton, 471 F.2d 1275, 1283 n. 13, 3 ELR 20045, 20048 n. 13 (9th Cir. 1973) ("The record is replete with instances of review and substantial alteration of the Navajo project to improve environmental control . . ."); Bucks County Bd. of Commissioners v. Interstate Energy Co., 403 F.Supp. 805, 814, 6 ELR 20406, 20410 (E.D.Pa.1975) ("Commission's in depth study demonstrates that 'all practical means' were used 'to prevent damage to the environment,' thereby fulfilling NEPA's substantive charge . . .").

71. Simmans v. Grant, 370 F.Supp. 5, 21, 4 ELR 20197, 20203 (S.D.Tex. 1974).

72. See Maryland-Nat'l Capital Park & Planning Comm'n v. Postal Serv., 159 U.S.App.D.C. 158, 171, 487 F.2d 1029, 1042, 3 ERL 20702, 20706 (1973).

73. See cases cited in note 70, supra; Sierra Club v. Froehlke (Wallisville-Trinity River), 359 F.Supp. 1289, 1339–40, 3 ELR 20248, 20266–67 (S.D. Tex.1973), rev'd on other grounds 499 F.2d 982, 4 ELR 20731 (5th Cir. 1974); Akers v. Resor, 339 F.Supp. 1375, 1380, 2 ELR 20221, 20223 (W.D.Tenn. 1972) (interpreting NEPA and the Fish and Wildlife Coordination Act).

do in the rare case where project costs clearly outweigh its benefits? A substantive judgment must be made and enforced, and the state of the art and cost-benefit tests inform this judgment in different ways.

The substantive predicate of NEPA often is unimportant because NEPA claims may be litigated concurrently with claims arising under other federal statutes with undisputed substantive content.[74] Already mentioned is the fact that strict procedural enforcement alone can bring about changes in results as the agencies see the light of day.[75] Thus, while the substantive content of NEPA is an issue fascinating to the commentators, its day to day significance remains to be demonstrated.

§ 7.6 The Recurring Issues: Whether

An issue perpetually in litigation is the threshold NEPA question of whether a particular proposal is a "major" federal action "significantly affecting the quality of the human environment."[1] Preparation of an environmental impact statement thus is dependent upon a showing that an undertaking is (1) major, (2) that it significantly affects the quality of the human environment, and (3) that it is federal. The issues of whether an action is major and has significant effects are separate and distinct[2] although in the great majority of cases the reasons for finding an action "major" establish also its significant effects. And there has not been, and is not likely to be, a holding exempting from the Act a minor federal action significantly affecting the quality of the human environment.[3]

74. § 7.12 below.

75. §§ 7.3, 7.4 above.

1. 42 U.S.C.A. § 4332(2)(C).

2. Hanly v. Mitchell (Hanly I), 460 F.2d 640, 644, 2 ELR 20216, 20218 (2d Cir.), cert. denied 409 U.S. 990 (1972). But see Minnesota Pub. Interest Research Group v. Butz (I), 498 F.2d 1314, 4 ELR 20700 (8th Cir. 1974) (en banc). For examples of cases holding the action major but not significant, see Wilson v. Lynn, 372 F.Supp. 934, 4 ELR 20476 (D.C.Mass.1974) (HUD mortgage insurance for building rehabilitation project); Groton v. Laird, 353 F.Supp. 344, 2 ELR 20316 (D.Conn.1972) (Navy housing project). Some courts indicate that section 102 (2)(C) imposes a single standard test. See, e. g., Citizens for Reid State Park v. Laird, 336 F.Supp. 783, 788, 2 ELR 20122 (D.Me.1972).

3. Minnesota Pub. Interest Research Group v. Butz (I), 498 F.2d at 1321–22, 4 ELR at 20703 ("to separate the consideration of the magnitude of the Federal action from its impact on the environment does little to foster the purposes of the Act, i. e., to attain the widest range of beneficial uses of the environment without degradation, risk to health and safety, or other undesirable and unintended consequences. . . . [I]f the action has a significant effect it is the intent of NEPA that it should be the subject of the detailed consideration mandated by NEPA; the activities of Federal agencies cannot be isolated from their impact on the environment"); see Davis v. Morton, 469 F.2d 593, 2 ELR 20578 (10th Cir. 1972); Cady v. Morton, 527 F.2d 786, 5 ELR 20445 (9th Cir. 1975); Davis v. Coleman, 521 F.2d 661, 673 n. 15, 5 ELR 20633, 20636 n. 15 (9th Cir. 1975) (approving Minnesota Pub. Interest Research Group v. Butz) (dictum).

Sec. 7.6   THE RECURRING ISSUES: WHETHER   751

Views differ on the standard applied to review agency threshold determinations under NEPA—Is an action major? Federal? Does it significantly affect the environment? Some courts view the agency determination as a factual question reviewable only under the arbitrary and capricious standard of the APA.[4] Others consider the agency judgment to involve mixed questions of law and fact reviewable under a "rational basis" test, "whereby the agency's decision will be accepted where it has 'warrant in the record' and a 'reasonable basis in law.'"[5] Still others, a distinct minority, deem the question of applicability to be purely a question of law reviewable *de novo* in the courts.[6] In the view of the author, the definitions of "major Federal actions significantly affecting the quality of the human environment" are legal questions. The record before the court, in any event, will include the entire administrative record and possible substantial supplementation.[7] The argument that administrative expertise deserves deference often is wide of the mark since the agency typically lacks expertise in—and may be positively hostile to—environmental values. When a court is suited institutionally to decide a legal question on a full factual record, the case for deferring to the agency remains to be made.

This section on applicability addresses (1) major actions and significant effects; (2) the federal requirement; and (3) exceptions to NEPA.

a. *Major Actions and Significant Effects*

There has been some attempt in the cases and the CEQ guidelines to generalize about applicability despite Chief Judge Friendly's warning that the word "significant"—and the same can be said for "major"—is especially chameleon-like, reflecting the color of its en-

---

4. E. g., Nucleus of Chicago Homeowners Ass'n v. Lynn, 524 F.2d 225, 229, 5 ELR 20698, 20699 (7th Cir. 1975), cert. denied 424 U.S. 967 (1976); Hanly v. Kleindienst (Hanly II), 471 F.2d 823, 828–30, 2 ELR 20717, 20719–20 (2d Cir. 1972), cert. denied 412 U.S. 908 (1973).

5. Hanly v. Kleindienst (Hanly II), 471 F.2d 823, 829, 2 ELR 20717, 20719 (2d Cir. 1972), cert. denied 412 U.S. 908 (1973), quoting National Labor Relations Bd. v. Hearst Publications, 322 U.S. 111, 131, 64 S.Ct. 851, 861, 88 L.Ed. 1170, 1185 (1944); see Davis v. Coleman, 521 F.2d 661, 673, 5 ELR 20633, 20636 (9th Cir. 1975); Minnesota Pub. Interest Research Group v. Butz (I), 498 F.2d 1314, 1320, 4 ELR 20700, 20702 (8th Cir. 1974) (en banc); Wyoming Outdoor Coord. Council v. Butz, 484 F.2d 1244, 1248, 3 ELR 20830, 20831 (10th Cir. 1973); Save Our Ten Acres v. Kreger, 472 F.2d 463, 467, 3 ELR 20041, 20042 (5th Cir. 1973); Hiram Clarke Civic Club v. Lynn, 476 F.2d 421, 424, 3 ELR 20287, 20288 (5th Cir. 1973) (following Save Our Ten Acres v. Kreger).

6. Scherr v. Volpe, 336 F.Supp. 882, 888, 2 ELR 20068, 20070 (W.D.Wis. 1971), aff'd 466 F.2d 1027, 1032, 2 ELR 20453, 20455 (7th Cir. 1972) (reserving decision on whether a failure to prepare an EIS is reviewable de novo); Natural Resources Defense Council, Inc. v. Grant, 341 F.Supp. 356, 366, 2 ELR 20185, 20189 (E.D. N.C.1972) (following the district court in Scherr v. Volpe); Kisner v. Butz, 350 F.Supp. 310, 321, 2 ELR 20709, 20715 (N.D.W.Va.1972).

7. E. g., Silva v. Lynn, 482 F.2d 1282, 3 ELR 20698 (1st Cir. 1973).

vironment: "it covers a spectrum ranging from 'not trivial' through 'appreciable' to 'important' and even 'momentous'." [8] A "major" action is "one that requires substantial planning, time, resources or expenditure." [9] A significant effect is one that has an "important or meaningful" consequence, directly or indirectly.[10] The "human environment" embraces "any of the many facets of man's environment," [11] including aesthetic [12] and social [13] effects.

Criteria for what is "major" or what effects are "significant" are many. Controversy is a barometer of community concern [14] just as is a lack of controversy.[15] The greater the quantitative injury, or threat of injury, the greater the likelihood of coverage.[16]

8. Hanly v. Kleindienst (Hanly II), 471 F.2d 823, 837, 2 ELR 20717, 20724 (2d Cir. 1972) (Friendly, C. J., dissenting), cert. denied 412 U.S. 908 (1973).

9. Natural Resources Defense Council, Inc. v. Grant, 341 F.Supp. 356, 366–67, 2 ELR 20185, 20189 (E.D.N.C. 1972); see Smith v. Cookeville, 381 F.Supp. 100, 5 ELR 20015 (M.D.Tenn. 1974); Citizens Organized to Defend the Environment v. Volpe, 353 F.Supp. 520, 3 ELR 20239 (S.D.Ohio 1972).

10. Natural Resources Defense Council, Inc. v. Grant, 341 F.Supp. 356, 367, 2 ELR 20185, 20189 (E.D.N.C. 1972).

11. Ibid.

12. Maryland Nat'l Capital Park & Planning Comm'n v. Postal Serv., 159 U.S.App.D.C. 158, 167–68, 487 F.2d 1029, 1038–39, 3 ELR 20702, 20705–06 (1973).

13. E. g., Hanly v. Mitchell (Hanly I), 460 F.2d 640, 647, 2 ELR 20216, 20220 (2d Cir.), cert. denied 409 U.S. 990 (1972). While aesthetic and social values clearly are within NEPA, there is authority for the proposition that judicial review of these values is circumscribed sharply, mostly due to problems of quantification and predictive analyses. Maryland Nat'l Capital Park & Planning Comm'n v. Postal Serv., 159 U.S.App.D.C. 158, 167–68, 487 F.2d 1029, 1038–39, 3 ELR 20702, 20705–06 (1973) ("[A] substantial inquiry or 'hard look' was not contemplated, as a matter of reasonable construction of NEPA, where the claim of NEPA application is focused on alleged esthetic impact and the matters at hand pertain essentially to issues of individual and potentially diverse tastes"); see Nucleus of Chicago Homeowners Ass'n v. Lynn, 524 F.2d 225, 5 ELR 20698 (7th Cir. 1975), cert. denied 424 U.S. 967 (1976); cf. § 2.4 above (discussing the common law social nuisance), § 2.17 above (exclusionary zoning). But see National Ass'n of Gov't Employees v. Rumsfeld, 413 F.Supp. 1224, 1229–30 (D. D.C.1976) (holding that social impacts alone not sufficient to trigger EIS requirements; "the primary concern [of NEPA] is the *physical* environmental resources of the nation") (emphasis in original).

14. See 40 CFR § 1500.6. Compare Hanly v. Kleindienst (Hanly II), 471 F.2d 823, 830, 2 ELR 20717, 20720 (2d Cir. 1972), cert. denied 412 U.S. 908 (1973) ("[T]he term 'controversial' apparently refers to cases where a substantial dispute exists as to the size, nature or effect of the major Federal action rather than to the existence of opposition to a use, the effect of which is relatively undisputed"); Southern Illinois Asphalt Co. v. Environmental Protection Agency, 15 Ill.App.3d 66, 303 N.E.2d 606, 3 ELR 20905 (1973) (Illinois Environmental Protection Act).

15. Cf. Soc'y for Animal Rights, Inc. v. Schlesinger, 168 U.S.App.D.C. 1, 512 F.2d 915, 5 ELR 20221 (1975) (expedited EIS accompanying Department of Defense proposal to eradicate approximately 10 million blackbirds held adequate where local communities exhibited general acceptance of proposal and attendant risks).

16. See, e. g., Maryland-Nat'l Capital Park and Planning Comm'n v. Postal

Sec. 7.6   THE RECURRING ISSUES: WHETHER   753

Other factors pertinent to applicability include the extent to which the action will cause adverse environmental effects in excess of those created by existing uses [17] or by prior practice; [18] whether more than one agency concurs in the conclusion that effects will be insignificant; [19] whether the action is consistent with local zoning requirements; [20] and the scope and size of the project and the extent of the investment in it.[21]

A rule of thumb is that close cases are resolved in favor of coverage. Actions may be "major" although expenditures are modest and planning minimal. Effects may be "significant" although of

Serv., 159 U.S.App.D.C. 158, 168 & n. 7, 487 F.2d 1029, 1039 & n. 7, 3 ELR 20702, 20706 & n. 7 (1973) (remanding for consideration of whether potential problems of water and oil runoff and increased traffic associated with bulk mail facility under construction necessitates the preparation of an EIS); Wisconsin v. Butz, 389 F.Supp. 1065, 5 ELR 20240 (E.D.Wis. 1975) (enjoining U. S. Forest Service herbicide application program within certain national forests pending completion of EIS); Nader v. Butterfield, 373 F.Supp. 1175, 4 ELR 20431 (D.C. D.C.1974) (holding FAA must prepare EIS or publish detailed reasons why a statement is unnecessary with regard to proposal to use x-ray devices in airport terminals to inspect passenger baggage); cf. § 2.4 above.

17. Hanly v. Kleindienst (Hanly II), 471 F.2d 823, 830–31, 2 ELR 20717, 20720 (2d Cir. 1972), cert. denied 412 U.S. 908 (1973); Julis v. Cedar Rapids, 349 F.Supp. 88, 3 ELR 20033 (N.D. Iowa 1972) (holding no EIS required where proposed highway project does not create a new highway location or result in a change in the characteristics of the area).

18. See, e. g., Rucker v. Willis, 484 F.2d 158, 3 ELR 20912 (4th Cir. 1973) (EIS unnecessary for Corps of Engineers' permit where affected area contains similar structures within the immediate vicinity of the project); Transcontinental Gas Pipeline Corp. v. Hackensack Meadowlands Dev. Comm'n, 464 F.2d 1358, 2 ELR 20495 (3d Cir. 1972) (EIS not required where FPC approval given to enlargement of existing liquified natural gas processing and storage facility); Maddox v. Bradley, 345 F.Supp. 1255, 2 ELR 20404 (N.D.Tex.1972) (no EIS required for Bureau of Reclamation proposal to fence boundary of property formerly used as grazing land for livestock to prevent encroachment upon area set aside for wildlife); Durnford v. Ruckelshaus, 3 ELR 20175 (N.D.Cal.1972) (no EIS required for EPA funding grant for pier-outfall project in area used for fishing).

19. See, e. g., Rucker v. Willis, supra note 18; Durnford v. Ruckelshaus, supra note 18.

20. See, e. g., Maryland-Nat'l Capital Park and Planning Comm'n v. Postal Serv., 159 U.S.App.D.C. 158, 487 F.2d 1029, 3 ELR 20702 (1973); Rucker v. Willis, 484 F.2d 158, 3 ELR 20912 (4th Cir. 1973). But cf. Groton v. Laird, 353 F.Supp. 344, 350, 3 ELR 20316, 20318 (D.C.Conn.1972) (". . . NEPA is not a sort of meta-zoning law. It is not designed to enshrine existing zoning regulations on the theory that their violation presents a threat to environmental values. NEPA may not be used by communities to shore up large lot and other exclusionary zoning devices that price out low and even middle income families"); § 2.17 above.

21. E. g., Sansom Comm. v. Lynn, 382 F.Supp. 1242, 5 ELR 20093 (E.D.Pa. 1974) (demolition of buildings in entire city block as a part of an urban renewal project extensively financed by HUD); Smith v. Cookeville, 381 F. Supp. 100, 110, 5 ELR 20015, 20018 (M.D.Tenn.1974) (proposed $1,000,000 conservation and development project receiving 55% funding from the Department of Agriculture).

short duration, largely hypothetical [22] or quite remote.[23] The "human environment" reaches just about everything important to people—not only pollution and natural resource use but also crime and crowding,[24] race relations,[25] unemployment,[26] and the availability of schools and housing.[27] Formulations popularized by the courts stretch the extensive reach of section 102(2)(C): an impact statement is required if a project "may cause a significant degradation of some human environmental factor"; [28] if it "could have a significant effect on the environment"; [29] if it *arguably* will have an adverse environmental impact"; [30] if it has a "potentially significant

---

22. See Hanly v. Kleindienst (Hanly II), 471 F.2d 823, 831, 2 ELR 20717, 20720–21 (2d Cir. 1972), cert. denied 412 U.S. 908 (1973) (dictum) ("Although the existing environment which is the site of the major Federal action constitutes one criterion to be considered, it must be recognized that even a slight increase in adverse conditions may sometimes threaten harm that is significant. One more factory polluting air and water in an area zoned for industrial use may represent the straw that breaks the back of the environmental camel").

23. Port of New York Authority v. United States, 451 F.2d 783, 2 ELR 20105 (2d Cir. 1971).

24. Hanly v. Mitchell (Hanly I), 460 F.2d 640, 647, 2 ELR 20216, 20220 (2d Cir.), cert. denied 409 U.S. 990 (1972) ("Noise, traffic, overburdened mass transportation systems, crime, congestion and even availability of drugs all affect the urban 'environment' and are surely results of the 'profound influences of . . . high-density urbanization and industrial expansion' "), quoting section 101(a).

25. Prince George's County v. Holloway, 404 F.Supp. 1181, 6 ELR 20109 (D.C.D.C.1975). But cf. Nucleus of Chicago Homeowners Ass'n v. Lynn, 524 F.2d 225, 231, 5 ELR 20598, 20700 (7th Cir. 1975), cert. denied 424 U.S. 967 (1976) ("To the extent that this claim can be construed to mean that HUD must consider the fears of neighbors of prospective public housing tenants, we seriously question whether such an impact is cognizable under NEPA"). Compare note 13, supra with Everett v. Paschall, 61 Wash. 47, 51, 111 P. 879, 880 (1910) (tuberculosis sanitarium enjoined as nuisance in a residential district; "[T]he question is not whether the fear is founded in science, but whether it exists; not whether it is imaginary, but whether it is real, in that it affects the movement and conduct of men. Such fears are actual, and must be recognized by the courts as other emotions of the human mind").

26. McDowell v. Schlesinger, 404 F. Supp. 221, 6 ELR 20224 (W.D.Mo. 1975) (relocation of air force units); see Breckinridge v. Schlesinger, —— F.Supp. ——, ——, 6 ELR 20111, 20115 (E.D.Ky.1975), rev'd 537 F.2d 864, 6 ELR 20597 (6th Cir. 1976) (closing and transfer of functions of army depot) (EIS required; court reserves decision on whether "human environment" includes socio-economic ramifications of federal actions such as unemployment and economic dislocation).

27. Prince George's County v. Holloway, 404 F.Supp. 1181, 6 ELR 20109 (D.C.D.C.1975) (consolidation and transfer of navy facilities).

28. Save Our Ten Acres v. Kreger, 472 F.2d 463, 467, 3 ELR 20041, 20042 (5th Cir. 1973).

29. Minnesota Pub. Interest Research Group v. Butz (I), 498 F.2d 1314, 1320, 4 ELR 20700, 20702 (8th Cir. 1974) (en banc).

30. Students Challenging Regulatory Agency Procedure v. United States (SCRAP I), 346 F.Supp. 189, 201 (D.C.D.C.1972) (three-judge court), rev'd on other grounds 412 U.S. 669, 93 S.Ct. 2405, 37 L.Ed.2d 254 (1973) (emphasis in original).

Sec. 7.6 THE RECURRING ISSUES: WHETHER 755

adverse effect"; [31] or "whenever it can be fairly argued on the basis of substantial evidence that the project may have a significant environmental impact." [32]

The courts' predisposition to look closely at agency decisions affecting the environment [33] makes coverage more likely. All agencies have procedures for dispensing with impact statement requirements in cases thought not to involve major actions with significant effects. These decisions on nonapplicability usually are called negative declarations and often involve a cursory analysis, known as an environmental assessment, of the impacts identified in Section 102 (2)(C) of NEPA. Several courts have held that in making a determination that an impact statement is not required, a federal agency is obliged to develop and produce a record facilitating judicial review.[34] The Second Circuit has gone so far as to require the agency to give public notice and perhaps even hold a hearing before making the threshold decision on whether to write an impact statement.[35] As Chief Judge Friendly points out in dissent, "The agency would do better to prepare an impact statement in the first instance."[36] This appears to be good advice since the reports offer many examples of agency negative declarations being repudiated in the courts after a thorough inquiry into what often turns out to be an embarrassingly thin administrative effort.[37]

What the courts do is a better barometer than what they say. The impact statement requirement obviously applies to "the trans-Alaskan oil pipeline, to the Cross-Florida Barge Canal, to the detona-

---

31. Hanly v. Kleindienst (Hanly II), 471 F.2d 823, 831, 2 ELR 20717, 20721 (2d Cir. 1972), cert. denied 412 U.S. 908 (1973).

32. No Oil, Inc. v. Los Angeles, 13 Cal.3d 68, 75, 82–86, 52 P.2d 66, 70, 75–78, 118 Cal.Rptr. 34, 38, 43–46 (1974) (interpreting California Environmental Quality Act).

33. §§ 1.5, 7.3, 7.4 above.

34. Hanly v. Mitchell (Hanly I), 460 F.2d 640, 647, 2 ELR 20216, 20220 (2d Cir.), cert. denied 409 U.S. 990 (1972). See also Nucleus of Chicago Homeowners Ass'n v. Lynn, 524 F.2d 225, 5 ELR 20698 (7th Cir. 1975), cert. denied 424 U.S. 967 (1976); Arizona Pub. Serv. Co. v. Federal Power Comm'n, 157 U.S.App.D.C. 272, 483 F.2d 1275, 3 ELR 20776 (1973); Silva v. Lynn, 482 F.2d 1282, 3 ELR 20098 (1st Cir. 1973); Country Club Bank v. Smith, 399 F.Supp. 1097 (W.D.Mo. 1975); Concerned Residents of Buck Hill Falls v. Grant, 388 F.Supp. 394, 4 ELR 20197 (E.D.Pa.1974), rev'd 537 F.2d 29 (3d Cir. 1976).

35. Hanly v. Kleindienst (Hanly II), 471 F.2d 823, 2 ELR 20717 (2d Cir. 1972), cert. denied 412 U.S. 908 (1973); see § 7.3 above.

36. 471 F.2d at 839, 2 ELR at 20723–24.

37. E. g., Rhode Island Comm. on Energy v. General Serv. Administration, 397 F.Supp. 41, 58, 5 ELR 20685, 20693 (D.R.I.1975) (negative declaration on disposal of surplus government property for construction of nuclear power plant; applicability of NEPA conceded; agency behavior represents an "utter disregard of environmental concerns"); Davis v. Coleman, 521 F.2d 661, 674, 5 ELR 20633, 20637 (9th Cir. 1975) (negative declaration on a proposed freeway interchange; declaration is characterized as "bureaucratic doubletalk" that "stands reality on its head").

tion of a 5-megaton nuclear warhead under Amchitka Island, Alaska, to the leasing of 380,000 acres of submerged lands for oil development in the Gulf of Mexico, to the cancellation of a national program to purchase irreplaceable helium, and to a nine-state program for spraying colonies of fire ants with insecticide".[38] Less obviously, an impact statement is required for:

—an ICC railroad abandonment authorization affecting service in New York and New Jersey;[39]

—an Economic Development Administration grant for construction of a 26-mile highway (7.5 miles of it upgrading an existing road) traversing the Santa Fe National Forest;[40]

—an ICC decision not to declare unlawful a surcharge applied to virgin and some recyclable commodities;[41]

—construction by the General Services Administration of a $4.5 million juvenile facility on a 206.43 acre site in a planned, low density residential area within the City of San Diego;[42]

—administration of the National Park Service's grizzly bear management program in Yellowstone Park;[43]

—HUD's changing the status of a 20-block urban renewal area from an industrial park project to a neighborhood development program;[44]

—a HUD loan of $3.5 million for construction of a 16-story high rise apartment building in an area containing no high rise projects in Portland, Oregon;[45]

—HUD's acquisition and holding of foreclosed properties and removal of occupants in Brooklyn, New York;[46]

38. F. R. Anderson, NEPA in the Courts: A Legal Analysis of the National Environmental Policy Act 76–77 (1973).

39. City of New York v. United States, 337 F.Supp. 150, 2 ELR 20275 (E.D. N.Y.1972) (three-judge court).

40. Upper Pecos Ass'n v. United States, 328 F.Supp. 332, 1 ELR 20228 (D.C.N.M.1971), aff'd 452 F.2d 1233, 2 ELR 20085 (10th Cir.) vacated 409 U.S. 1021 (1972).

41. Students Challenging Regulatory Agency Procedures v. United States (SCRAP II), 353 F.Supp. 317, 3 ELR 20308 (D.C.D.C.) (three-judge court), rev'd on other grounds 412 U.S. 669, 93 S.Ct. 2405, 37 L.Ed.2d 254 (1973).

42. Tierrasanta Community Council v. Richardson, 4 ELR 20309 (S.D.Cal. 1973).

43. Regenstein v. Anderson, Civil No. 2193–73 (D.D.C.1974) (by stipulation).

44. San Francisco Tomorrow v. Romney, 472 F.2d 1021, 3 ELR 20124 (9th Cir. 1973).

45. Goose Hollow Foothills League v. Romney, 334 F.Supp. 877, 1 ELR 20492 (D.C.Or.1971).

46. See Brotherhood Blocks Ass'n of Sunset Park v. Secretary of Housing & Urban Dev., 3 ELR 20351 (E.D. N.Y.1973) (denying motion for preliminary injunction while agreeing that plaintiffs raise substantial questions concerning NEPA's application).

Sec. 7.6   THE RECURRING ISSUES: WHETHER   757

—the Forest Service's modification and extension of contracts, and supervision of day to day timber cutting operations over an area of 29,000 acres within a national forest; [47]

—two proposed timber sales by the Forest Service which would result in the clearcutting of 670 acres in an area traversed only by "jeep roads" and inhabited by elk; [48]

—a proposal by the Bureau of Land Management to round up and exterminate between 130 and 260 wild horses on public grazing lands near Challis, Idaho; [49]

—the Navy's initiatives to construct 600 row-type, multi-family, four and five bedroom housing units on approximately 81 acres of land in an ecologically sensitive area; [50]

—the construction by the U.S. Postal Service of a bulk mail facility on a 63-acre tract in partial contravention of local zoning requirements; [51]

—ordinary standards promulgated under the Occupational Safety and Health Act; [52]

—construction of an incinerator at the Walter Reed Medical Center Annex; [53]

—the Corps of Engineers' condemnation of 247.37 acres of grazing land for a flood control project; [54]

—a federal block grant of $775,000 for a prison medical facility and prisoner reception center in a rural, historic area of Virginia; [55]

—issuance of a permit to a water discharger by the Corps of Engineers under the Refuse Act Permit Program; [56]

---

[47]. Minnesota Pub. Interest Research Group v. Butz (I), 498 F.2d 1314, 4 ELR 20700 (8th Cir. 1974) (en banc).

[48]. Wyoming Outdoor Coord. Council v. Butz, 484 F.2d 1244, 3 ELR 20830 (10th Cir. 1973).

[49]. American Horse Protection Ass'n v. Kleppe, — F.Supp. —, 6 ELR 20801 (D.C.D.C.1976). But see American Horse Protection Ass'n v. Frizzell, 403 F.Supp. 1206 (1975) (no EIS required for roundup of some 400 horses by BLM).

[50]. Fort Story—Its Future? v. Schlesinger, 5 ELR 20038 (E.D.Va.1974).

[51]. Maryland-Nat'l Park & Planning Comm'n v. Postal Serv., 159 U.S.App. D.C. 158, 487 F.2d 1029, 3 ELR 20703 (1973) (affirming denial of preliminary injunction but suggesting that some equitable relief would be appropriate).

[52]. Dry Color Mfr's Ass'n v. Dep't of Labor, 486 F.2d 98, 3 ELR 20855 (3d Cir. 1973) (dictum) (vacating emergency temporary OSHA standards on other grounds).

[53]. Montgomery County v. Richardson, 340 F.2d 591, 2 ELR 20140 (D.C.D.C. 1972).

[54]. United States v. 247.37 Acres of Land, 1 ELR 20513 (S.D.Ohio 1971), 2 ELR 20154 (S.D.Ohio 1972).

[55]. Ely v. Velde, 451 F.2d 1130, 1 ELR 20612 (4th Cir. 1971).

[56]. Kalur v. Resor, 335 F.Supp. 1, 1 ELR 20637 (D.C.D.C.1971); cf. Conservation Council of North Carolina v. Costanzo (II), 398 F.Supp. 653, 5

—a Corps of Engineers' project to clear 3000 acres of oxygen-consuming vegetation from 55 miles of the Gila River; [57]

—a loan by the Federal Housing Administration for the construction of a golf course and park; [58]

—the exchange of 10,200 acres of national forest land for 20,500 acres of land privately held by Big Sky of Montana, Inc., in anticipation of construction of a recreational development; [59]

—the U.S. Park Service's repair and expansion of the towpath along the C & O Barge Canal, an historic, recreational area in Washington, D.C.; [60]

—an annual budget proposal of the Department of the Interior for financing the National Wildlife Refuge System; [61]

—initial steps of construction by the Federal Highway Administration of the "Darien Gap Highway" through Panama and Columbia, South America; [62]

—issuance of air carrier certificates by the Civil Aeronautics Board for commercial air carriers into O'Hare Airport, in pursuit of a policy to establish O'Hare as a central airport for national and international commerce.[63]

Refusals to apply NEPA may be influenced by procedural questions, the equities between the parties and terms of the Act other than the threshold question of whether the evidence establishes a "major Federal [action] significantly affecting the quality of the human environment." Subject to this understanding, NEPA does not apply to:

—FAA approval of three flights into and out of Boston by the supersonic Concorde without a showing of possible future flights; [64]

—a small Soil Conservation Service project deepening the natural channel in Big Creek Slough over a total length of approximately 11 miles at a cost of more than $275,000; [65]

ELR 20666 (E.D.N.C.), aff'd 528 F.2d 250, 6 ELR 20116 (4th Cir. 1975) (issuance by the Corps of Engineers of a permit to construct a marina).

57. Sierra Club v. Laird, 1 ELR 20085 (D.Ariz.1970).

58. Texas Comm. on Natural Resources v. United States, 2 ELR 20574 (W.D.Tex.), vacated as moot 430 F. 2d 1315 (5th Cir. 1970).

59. Nat'l Forest Preservation Group v. Butz, 485 F.2d 408, 3 ELR 20783 (9th Cir. 1973).

60. Berkson v. Morton, 2 ELR 20659 (D.Md.1971).

61. Sierra Club v. Morton, 395 F.Supp. 1187, 5 ELR 20383 (D.C.D.C.1975).

62. Sierra Club v. Coleman, 405 F. Supp. 53, 6 ELR 20051 (D.C.D.C.1975).

63. Illinois ex rel. Scott v. Butterfield, 396 F.Supp. 632, 5 ELR 20587 (N.D. Ill.1975).

64. Massachusetts Air Pollution & Noise Abatement Comm. v. Brinegar, 499 F.2d 125, 4 ELR 20496 (1st Cir. 1974) (per curiam) (dismissing appeal from denial of request for a temporary restraining order).

65. Simmans v. Grant, 370 F.Supp. 5, 4 ELR 20197 (S.D.Tex.1974) (no sig-

Sec. 7.6   THE RECURRING ISSUES: WHETHER   759

—EPA funding of a combination sewer outfall and fishing pier project extending some 1200 feet into the ocean and costing close to $4 million that would upgrade a location without changing existing uses; [66]

—approval by the Secretary of Transportation of the crossing of an interstate highway by a huge stripmining shovel; [67]

—a $300,000 plus federal contribution to a project in Cedar Rapids, Iowa widening portions of an existing street from two to four lanes over a fourteen block area, installing traffic signals and a pedestrian overpass; [68]

—a HUD insured loan of $3.7 million for construction of a 272-unit apartment complex on a fifteen acre tract in Houston, Texas; [69]

—the Navy's construction of a 300-unit housing project involving essentially the same use as that envisaged by the town; [70]

—the granting of a certificate of public convenience and necessity by the ICC to a barge line to operate as a common carrier on the same waterways that it served before becoming a regulated carrier; [71]

—issuance of Corps of Engineers' permit for construction of a boating and fishing marina and pier extending 1000 feet into the Atlantic Ocean; [72]

—preliminary approval by the Comptroller of the Currency of the chartering of a national bank in Dade County, Florida; [73]

—a Rural Electrification Administration loan of $293,000 for construction of a 44 Kv transmission line approximately 12.2 miles in length crossing residential woodlands, a swamp, and farmland; [74]

nificant impact if mitigation measures implemented).

66. Durnford v. Ruckelshaus, 3 ELR 20175 (N.D.Cal.1972).

67. Citizens Organized to Defend the Environment v. Volpe, 353 F.Supp. 520, 3 ELR 20239 (S.D.Ohio 1972) (the court indicates the original approval of the project agreement permitting the use of the highway to facilitate stripmining operations would have been covered by NEPA).

68. Julis v. Cedar Rapids, 349 F.Supp. 88, 3 ELR 20033 (N.D.Iowa 1972).

69. Hiram Clarke Civic Club, Inc. v. Lynn, 476 F.2d 421, 3 ELR 20287 (5th Cir. 1973).

70. Groton v. Laird, 353 F.Supp. 344, 3 ELR 20316 (D.C.Conn.1972).

71. Union Mechling v. United States, 390 F.Supp. 411, 432–33 (W.D.Pa.1974) (3-judge court).

72. Rucker v. Willis, 484 F.2d 158, 3 ELR 20912 (4th Cir. 1973). Contra, Conservation Council of North Carolina v. Costanzo (II), 398 F.Supp. 653, 5 ELR 20666 (E.D.N.C.1975), aff'd 528 F.2d 250, 6 ELR 20116 (4th Cir.).

73. First Nat'l Bank v. Watson, 363 F. Supp. 466, 3 ELR 20612 (D.C.D.C. 1973). Contra, Billings v. Camp, 2 ELR 20687 (D.C.D.C.1972); Country Club Bank v. Smith, 399 F.Supp. 1097 (W.D.Mo.1975) (comptroller of the currency must develop a reviewable environmental record).

74. Mowry v. Central Elec. Power Coop., 3 ELR 20843 (D.C.S.C.1973).

—a recommendation of the Maryland-National Capital Park & Planning Commission to the District of Columbia City Council to close part of a public alley;[75]

—the Forest Service's set-aside program reserving timber sales for small businesses without changing either the manner or volume of timber harvested each year;[76]

—the Navy's plan to conduct a mock amphibious assault of 900 marines and to bivouac for 3 or 4 days in an ocean-front state park in Maine;[77]

—HUD insurance for a proposed 66-unit apartment building in Los Angeles;[78]

—a single train shipment of nerve gas from Bangor, Washington to Umatilla, Oregon;[79]

—issuance of a permit from the Federal Power Commission for a 7-acre addition to an existing 17-acre liquid natural gas facility on the company's privately owned 500 acre parcel in the New Jersey meadowland;[80]

—the Department of Interior's issuance of a small number of permits for private automobiles to travel on the Fire Island National Seashore;[81]

—a refusal by the Department of the Interior to object, under the terms of the Small Reclamation Projects Act of 1956, to a lease arrangement allowing a private corporation to use water pipeline facilities for non-irrigation purposes (the transport of well water to a proposed resort complex);[82]

—the Department of the Interior's imposition of restrictions on the use of motor vehicles within Backbay National Wildlife Refuge;[83]

75. Metropolitan Washington Coalition for Clean Air v. Dep't of Economic Dev., 373 F.Supp. 1096, 1098, 3 ELR 20887, 20888 (D.C.D.C.1973) ("[T]he thrust of this provision applies to federal action, and not mere recommendations regarding actions by state or local government").

76. Duke City Lumber Co. v. Butz, 382 F.Supp. 362, 5 ELR 20080 (D.C. D.C.1974), aff'd —— U.S.App.D.C. ——, 539 F.2d 220, 6 ELR 20629 (1976).

77. Citizens for Reid State Park v. Laird, 336 F.Supp. 783, 2 ELR 20122 (D.C.Me.1972).

78. Echo Park Residents Comm. v. Romney, 2 ELR 20337 (C.D.Cal.1971).

79. See Rodgers, Nerve Gas to the Northwest and Beyond, 1 Environmental Letters 111, 129–30 (1971).

80. Transcontinental Gas Pipeline Co. v. Hackensack Meadowlands Dev. Comm'n, 464 F.2d 1358, 2 ELR 20495 (3d Cir. 1972).

81. Biderman v. Morton, 507 F.2d 396, 5 ELR 20027 (2d Cir. 1974) (relying in part on defendant's assurance that an EIS would accompany a master plan being prepared for the area).

82. Molokai Homesteaders Coop. Ass'n v. Morton, 506 F.2d 572, 5 ELR 20024 (9th Cir. 1974).

83. See Coupland v. Morton, 5 ELR 20504, 20506 (E.D.Va.1975) (dictum)

Sec. 7.6   THE RECURRING ISSUES: WHETHER   761

—initiation by the Federal Trade Commission of an adjudicatory proceeding under the antitrust laws challenging the acquisition by a cement manufacturer of a sand and gravel subsidiary; [84]

—adoption by the Delaware River Basin Commission of charges for the use of surface waters where water demand is price inelastic; [85]

—Forest Service approval of exploratory mining operations involving construction of a bridge, road improvements, drilling, and storage of 4000 cubic yards of rock extracted from the site.[86]

b. *The Federal Requirement*

The third chameleon-like word at NEPA's threshold is the necessity for demonstrating the "Federal" character of the major action significantly affecting the quality of the human environment. The issue arises in three distinct contexts: (1) what degree of involvement by the national government is required to support a finding that an action is "Federal"; (2) when does an action initially nonfederal become federal for NEPA purposes; and (3) under what circumstances are nonfederal segments treated as part of an overall "federal" project. The first category raises issues strictly of applicability; the second involves both applicability and timing and will be dealt with below; [87] the third is concerned with scope of the EIS, and also will be discussed below.[88]

It is not implausible on the face of NEPA that the "major Federal actions" triggering the impact statement requirement could be limited to actions federally conceived, constructed and managed. But the case law, with a boost from the legislative history,[89] soon established that federal sanctioning of private, state or local activity could constitute

(impact statement was prepared although court was "unconvinced that such a statement is necessary").

84. Gifford-Hill & Co. v. Federal Trade Comm'n, 173 U.S.App.D.C. 135, 523 F.2d 730, 6 ELR 20019 (1975) (per curiam).

85. Morrisville v. Delaware River Basin Comm'n, 399 F.Supp. 469, 6 ELR 20021 (E.D.Pa.1975); cf. Cartwright Van Lines, Inc. v. United States, 400 F.Supp. 795, 6 ELR 20166 (W.D.Mo. 1975) (dictum) (no significant effect from application of ICC gateway rules).

86. Friends of the Earth, Inc. v. Butz, 406 F.Supp. 742, 6 ELR 20403 (D.C. Mont.1975).

87. See § 7.7 nn. 47–64 and accompanying text below.

88. § 7.9 below.

89. Comm. of Conference, National Environmental Policy Act of 1969, H.R.Rep. No. 765, 91st Cong., 1st Sess. 9–10 (1969); Senate Comm. on Interior and Insular Affairs, National Environmental Policy Act of 1969, S. Rep. No. 296, 91st Cong. 1st Sess. 8 (1969) ("examples of the rising public concern over the manner in which federal policies and activities have contributed to environmental decay and degradation may be seen in . . . federally sponsored or aided construction activity such as highways, airports, and other public works projects . . . [NEPA] is designed to deal with many of the basic causes of these increasingly troublesome and often critical problems of domestic policy").

"major federal action." Thus, federal licenses,[90] permits,[91] leases,[92] loans,[93] grants,[94] insurance,[95] contracts,[96] contract extensions and modifications,[97] conveyances,[98] assistance authorizations,[99] approvals of rights-of-ways,[1] or filings [2] in appropriate cases may require preparation of an impact statement although the federal presence is minimal. The federal touch was extremely light but nonetheless sufficient in Davis v. Morton,[3] involving the Secretary of the Interior's *pro forma* approval of a lease by Pueblo Indians of their land; in Ely v. Velde,[4] involving a no-strings-attached $775,000 block grant by the Law Enforcement Assistance Administration for 20 percent of the construc-

90. Calvert Cliffs' Coord. Comm. v. Atomic Energy Comm'n, 146 U.S.App. D.C. 33, 449 F.2d 1109, 1 ELR 20346 (1971), cert. denied 404 U.S. 942 (1972).

91. Kalur v. Resor, 335 F.Supp. 1, 1 ELR 20637 (D.C.D.C.1971); Conservation Council of North Carolina v. Costanzo (II), 398 F.Supp. 653, 5 ELR 20666 (E.D.N.C.1975), aff'd 528 F.2d 250, 6 ELR 20116 (4th Cir.); Natural Resources Defense Council, Inc. v. Morton, 388 F.Supp. 829, 5 ELR 20327 (D.C.D.C.1974) (livestock grazing).

92. Natural Resources Defense Council, Inc. v. Morton, 148 U.S.App.D.C. 5, 458 F.2d 827, 2 ELR 20029 (1972) (offshore oil development); Cady v. Morton, 527 F.2d 786, 5 ELR 20445 (9th Cir. 1975) (Bureau of Indian Affairs' approval of coal leases on Indian land).

93. Goose Hollow Foothills League v. Romney, 334 F.Supp. 877, 1 ELR 20492 (D.C.Or.1971); Texas Comm. on Natural Resources v. United States, 2 ELR 20574 (W.D.Tex.), vacated as moot 430 F.2d 1315 (5th Cir. 1970).

94. Ely v. Velde, 451 F.2d 1130, 1 ELR 20612 (4th Cir. 1971).

95. Silva v. Romney, 342 F.Supp. 783, 2 ELR 20385 (D.C.Mass.1972), rev'd in part on other grounds 473 F.2d 287, 3 ELR 20082 (1st Cir. 1973).

96. Port of Astoria v. Hodel, 5 ELR 20657 (D.C.Or.1975) (power sales contract); Wyoming Outdoor Coord. Council v. Butz, 484 F.2d 1244, 3 ELR 20830 (10th Cir. 1973) (timber sales contract).

97. Minnesota Pub. Interest Research Group v. Butz (I), 498 F.2d 1314, 4 ELR 20700 (8th Cir. 1974) (en banc).

98. Rhode Island Comm. on Energy v. General Serv. Administration, 397 F. Supp. 41, 5 ELR 20685 (D.C.R.I.1975) (conveyance of surplus land for the construction of a nuclear power plant; government concedes applicability).

99. Environmental Defense Fund, Inc. v. United States Agency for International Development, 6 ELR 20121 (D.C.D.C.1975) (stipulation).

1. Swain v. Brinegar, 517 F.2d 766, 5 ELR 20354 (7th Cir. 1975); Monroe County Conservation Council, Inc. v. Volpe, 472 F.2d 693, 3 ELR 20006 (2d Cir. 1972); Lathan v. Volpe (I), 455 F.2d 1111, 1 ELR 20602 (9th Cir. 1971); Pennsylvania v. Morton, 381 F.Supp. 293, 5 ELR 20008 (D.C.D.C. (1974). See also Wilderness Society v. Morton, 156 U.S.App.D.C. 121, 166–69, 479 F.2d 842, 887–90, 3 ELR 20085, 20100–01 (en banc), cert. denied 411 U.S. 917 (1973) (dictum); but see Trans-Alaska Pipeline Authorization Act, Pub.L. No. 93–153, § 203(d), 87 Stat. 584 (1973), 43 U.S. C.A. § 1652(d).

2. Scenic Rivers Ass'n v. Lynn, 520 F.2d 240, 5 ELR 20537 (10th Cir. 1975), rev'd 426 U.S. 776, 96 S.Ct. 2430, 49 L.Ed.2d 205 (1976).

3. 469 F.2d 593, 2 ELR 20758 (10th Cir. 1972).

4. 451 F.2d 1130, 1 ELR 20612 (4th Cir. 1971), on remand 356 F.Supp. 726, 3 ELR 20764 (E.D.Va.1973); Note, Ely v. Velde: The Application of Federal Environmental Policy to Revenue Sharing Programs, 1972 Duke L.J. 667 (1972).

Sec. 7.6 THE RECURRING ISSUES: WHETHER

tion cost of a state prison medical facility; and in McLean Gardens Civic Ass'n v. National Capital Planning Comm'n,[5] finding sufficient "federal" involvement by a commission whose role in reviewing and "approving" a rezoning request was advisory only.

That the precedents are not all one way is indicated by authority finding no "federal" involvement by general revenue sharing,[6] unrestricted subsidies,[7] some types of permits[8] and approvals to conduct business,[9] mere recommendations,[10] simple inaction where there is no duty to control nonfederal activity,[11] ministerial approvals of activity previously contracted for,[12] routine amendatory grants to cover rising costs,[13] and nondiscretionary conveyances of title to valuable mineral lands to persons qualifying under the General Mining Act of 1872.[14] Without attempting to explain or reconcile all the cases, the distinguishing feature of "federal" involvement is the ability to influence or control the outcome in material respects. The EIS process is supposed to inform the decision-maker. This presupposes he has judgment to exercise. Cases finding "federal" action emphasize authority to exercise discretion over the outcome.[15]

5. 2 ELR 20659 (D.C.D.C.), motion for stay of injunction and summary reversal denied per curiam, 2 ELR 20662 (D.C.Cir. 1972), further proceedings 390 F.Supp. 165 (D.C.D.C. 1974).

6. Carolina Action v. Simon, 389 F. Supp. 1244, 5 ELR 2045 (M.D.N.C. 1975); see 40 CFR § 1500.5(2).

7. Kings County Economic Community Dev. Ass'n v. Hardin, 478 F.2d 478, 3 ELR 20335 (9th Cir. 1973).

8. Rucker v. Willis, 484 F.2d 158, 3 ELR 20912 (4th Cir. 1973).

9. First Nat'l Bank v. Watson, 363 F. Supp. 466, 3 ELR 20612 (D.C.D.C. 1973) (approval of a national bank charter). But see Country Club Bank v. Smith, 399 F.Supp. 1097 (W.D.Mo. 1975) (Comptroller must issue a statement of reasons why an EIS is unnecessary). See also Gifford-Hill & Co. v. Federal Trade Comm'n, 389 F.Supp. 167 (D.D.C.1974), aff'd per curiam 173 U.S.App.D.C. 135, 523 F.2d 730, 6 ELR 20019 (1975) (promulgation of guidelines relating to vertical mergers in the cement industry).

10. Metropolitan Washington Coalition for Clean Air v. Dep't of Economic Dev., 373 F.Supp. 1096, 1098, 3 ELR 20887 (D.C.D.C.1973).

11. Biderman v. Morton, 507 F.2d 396, 5 ELR 20027 (2d Cir. 1974).

12. Citizens Organized to Defend the Environment v. Volpe, 353 F.Supp. 520, 541 & n. 28, 3 ELR 20239, 20247 & n. 28 (S.D.Ohio 1972); cf. Flint Ridge Development Co. v. Scenic Rivers Ass'n, 426 U.S. 776, 96 S.Ct. 2430, 49 L.Ed.2d 205 (1976) (mere acceptance of the filing of a disclosure statement).

13. O'Brien v. Brinegar, 379 F.Supp. 289, 4 ELR 20831 (D.Minn.1974).

14. United States v. Kosanke Sand Corp., 12 IBLA 282, 3 ELR 30017 (Dept. Inter. Bd. of Land App. 1973) (en banc).

15. Flint Ridge Development Co. v. Scenic Rivers Ass'n, 426 U.S. 776, 789-90, 96 S.Ct. 2430, 2435, 49 L.Ed.2d 205, 212 (1976) ("The Secretary has no power to evaluate the substance of the developer's proposal . . ."); Ely v. Velde, 451 F.2d 1130, 1137, 1 ELR 20612, 20614 (4th Cir. 1971) (the court considers "LEAA's overall involvement in the promotion and planning of the Center, as well as the cumulative impact of the proposed federal action"); Jones v. Lynn, 477 F.2d 885, 890, 3 ELR 20358, 20359 (1st Cir. 1973) ("We would be reluctant not to find a continuing major federal involvement so long as it was establish-

c. *Exceptions*

Exceptions to NEPA are surprisingly few; the Act applies to "all agencies of the Federal Government" and it requires them to comply "to the fullest extent possible." [16] A plea of impossibility is sustainable only upon a showing of a clearly contradictory statutory mandate.[17] Even if a clear conflict forbids partial compliance, such as with the commenting procedure, other requirements must be met "to the fullest extent possible." The impossibility exceptions, for the most part grudgingly conceded to assist speedy decision-making, have included a price increase granted by the Price Commission,[18] the promulgation of an Emergency Temporary Standard on carcinogens in the workplace issued by the Occupational Safety and Health Administration,[19] an emergency gas curtailment order of the Federal Power Commission,[20] the purchase of coal by the Tennessee Valley Authority,[21] and actions taken in haste under the Petroleum Allocation Act.[22]

A few cases, mostly from the early days of NEPA, suggest an open-ended exemption for agencies showing "substantial" compliance.[23] This view never gained wide acceptance. The overwhelm-

ed that HUD retained any significant discretionary powers as might permit it to effect an alteration of building or design plans to enhance the urban living environment").

16. 42 U.S.C.A. § 4332.

17. Flint Ridge Dev. Co. v. Scenic Rivers Ass'n, 426 U.S. 776, 96 S.Ct. 2430, 49 L.Ed.2d 250 (1976) (finding a conflict between NEPA and the Interstate Land Sales Registration Act); National Helium Corp. v. Morton (I), 326 F.Supp. 151, 156, 1 ELR 20157, 20159 (D.C.Kan.), aff'd 455 F.2d 650, 1 ELR 20478 (10th Cir. 1971) (NEPA "nothing less than a mandate . . . to either follow the prescribed procedure in taking the relevant action or to show that it is not 'possible' . . ."); Calvert Cliffs' Coord. Comm. v. Atomic Energy Comm'n, 146 U.S.App.D.C. 33, 39, 449 F.2d 1109, 1115, 1 ELR 20346, 20349 (1971), cert. denied 404 U.S. 942 (1972) ("Thus the Section 102 duties are not inherently flexible. They must be complied with to the fullest extent, unless there is a clear conflict of *statutory* authority") (emphasis in original); Rochester v. Postal Serv., 541 F.2d 967, 6 ELR 20723 (2d Cir. 1976); Rhode Island Comm. on Energy v. General Serv. Administration, 397 F.Supp. 41, 5 ELR 20685 (D.C.R.I.

1975) (indicating that energy crisis offers no excuse for noncompliance with NEPA); Silva v. Romney, 342 F. Supp. 783, 2 ELR 20385 (D.C.Mass. 1972), aff'd 473 F.2d 287, 3 ELR 20082 (1st Cir. 1973).

18. Cohen v. Price Comm'n, 337 F. Supp. 1236, 2 ELR 20178 (S.D.N.Y. 1972).

19. Dry Color Mfr's Ass'n v. Dep't of Labor, 486 F.2d 98, 107–08, 3 ELR 20855, 20858–59 (3d Cir. 1973) (although indicating that NEPA process must be completed for a permanent standard which replaces a temporary standard within six months).

20. Alabama Gas Corp. v. Federal Power Comm'n, 476 F.2d 142, 3 ELR 20213 (5th Cir. 1973).

21. Natural Resources Defense Council, Inc. v. Tennessee Valley Authority, 367 F.Supp. 122, 3 ELR 20455 (E.D. Tenn.1973).

22. Gulf Oil Corp. v. Simon, 502 F.2d 1154 (Temp.Em.Ct.App.1974).

23. See Students Challenging Regulatory Agency Procedures v. United States (SCRAP II), 371 F.Supp. 1291, 1312, 4 ELR 20267, 20275–76 (D.C.

ing opinion today is that NEPA calls for "strict" compliance.[24] The Act is "not rubber, neither is it iron," [25] but it must be complied with.

An interesting question of NEPA coverage is whether the Environmental Protection Agency, or another agency claiming to help not hurt the environment, is exempt from the impact statement requirements of NEPA. The Act contains no exemption for EPA while the legislative history is "highly ambiguous." [26] By statute, an exemption applies to most of EPA's responsibilities under the 1972 water pollution amendments [27] and all of them under the Clean Air Act.[28] A court developed exception for EPA regulatory activities providing "the functional equivalent of an impact statement" [29] has been cautiously but consistently applied.[30] The question is close: EPA has a need for expedition, regularly engages in a NEPA-type balancing process, and would be vulnerable to industry attacks motivated by self-protection instead of environmental protection. On the other hand, EPA can benefit from NEPA if any agency can, has no special claim to sound decisions by reason of pure motives, and engages in some activities— the funding of sewage treatment works is only one example—that beg

---

D.C.1974) (three-judge court) (Flannery, J., dissenting), rev'd sub nom. Aberdeen & Rockfish R. R. v. SCRAP, 422 U.S. 289, 95 S.Ct. 2336, 45 L.Ed. 2d 191 (1975).

24. Calvert Cliffs' Coord. Comm. v. Atomic Energy Comm'n, 146 U.S.App. D.C. 33, 36, 449 F.2d 1109, 1112, 1 ELR 20346, 20347 (1971), cert. denied 404 U.S. 942 (1972) (*Calvert Cliffs'* dictum of strict compliance has been quoted repeatedly).

25. Natural Resources Defense Council, Inc. v. Morton, 148 U.S.App.D.C. 5, 15, 458 F.2d 827, 837, 2 ELR 20029, 20034 (1972).

26. Portland Cement Ass'n v. Ruckelshaus, 158 U.S.App.D.C. 308, 315 n. 31, 486 F.2d 375, 382 n. 31, 3 ELR 20642, 20644 n. 31 (1973); see Opinion of Comptroller General Elmer Staats on NEPA's application to EPA, 119 Cong.Rec. 31394–96 (1973); Anderson, The National Environmental Policy Act, in Environmental Law Institute, Federal Environmental Law 238, 256–67 (E. L. Dolgin & T. G. P. Guilbert eds. 1974).

27. 33 U.S.C.A. § 1371(c)(1).

28. 15 U.S.C.A. § 793(c)(1). Compare § 7.2 nn. 95–98 above.

29. Portland Cement Ass'n v. Ruckelshaus, 158 U.S.App.D.C. 308, 317, 486 F.2d 375, 384, 3 ELR 20642, 20646 (1973).

30. See, e. g., Environmental Defense Fund, Inc. v. Environmental Protection Agency, 160 U.S.App.D.C. 123, 133, 489 F.2d 1247, 1257, 4 ELR 20031, 20037 (1973) (no EIS required for a cancellation order affecting uses of DDT); Anaconda Co. v. Ruckelshaus, 482 F.2d 1301, 1305–06, 3 ELR 20714, 20720 (10th Cir. 1973) (dictum) (no EIS required for proposed sulfur oxide emission standards); Buckeye Power, Inc. v. Environmental Protection Agency, 481 F.2d 162, 174, 3 ELR 20634, 20637 (6th Cir. 1973) (no EIS required for approval of state implementation plan under the Clean Air Act) (following Appalachian Power Co. v. Environmental Protection Agency, 477 F.2d 495, 508, 3 ELR 20310, 20314 (4th Cir. 1973)); International Harvester Co. v. Ruckelshaus, 155 U.S.App.D.C. 411, 446 n. 130, 478 F.2d 615, 650 n. 130, 3 ELR 20133, 20149 n. 130 (1973) (no EIS required for Administrator's decision not to suspend auto emission standards); Getty Oil Co. v. Ruckelshaus, 467 F.2d 349, 359, 2 ELR 20583, 20686– 87 (3d Cir.), cert. denied 409 U.S. 1125 (1972) (no EIS required for EPA compliance order under the Clean Air Act).

for a NEPA analysis.[31] It is true, moreover, that functional equivalents easily may become sorry substitutes in light of the intense demands of NEPA.

An oft-litigated question of NEPA applicability concerns projects in various stages of planning and construction when the Act took effect on January 1, 1970. The issue is not so much one of retroactivity [32] as it is the application of changes in law to pending cases.[33] The rule is that NEPA applies "to the fullest extent possible" although options may be narrowed and procedures telescoped by prior events. The case law is a "tangled web," [34] and courts have developed several criteria for determining coverage of pending projects.[35] Many cases emphasize a balancing approach where applicability turns on a judgment about whether the project has gone so far as to render futile application of the NEPA procedures.[36] The pending project cases are analyzed better by simply asking whether what remains to be done would qualify independently under the Act as a "major federal action." If so, the NEPA reassessment should proceed even though alternatives to the partially constructed dam or unfinished stretch of highway may be circumscribed by preexisting realities.

31. EPA funding of treatment works is not exempted from NEPA under FWPCA § 511(c)(1), 33 U.S.C.A. § 1371(c)(1).

32. Note, Retroactive Application of the National Environmental Policy Act, 69 Mich.L.Rev. 732 (1972); Note, Retroactive Application of the National Environmental Policy Act, 39 Tenn.L.Rev. 735 (1972).

33. See, e. g., Hamm v. Rock Hill, 379 U.S. 306, 312, 85 S.Ct. 384, 389, 13 L.Ed.2d 300, 305 (1964); Vandenbark v. Owens-Illinois Glass Co., 311 U.S. 538, 541, 61 S.Ct. 347, 348–49, 85 L.Ed. 327, 329 (1940); United States v. Chambers, 291 U.S. 217, 222, 54 S.Ct. 434, 435, 78 L.Ed. 763, 765 (1934); United States v. Schooner Peggy, 5 U.S. (1 Cr.) 103, 2 L.Ed. 49 (1801).

34. Anderson, supra note 126, at 396.

35. Id. at 396–410.

36. Compare Arlington Coalition on Transp. v. Volpe, 458 F.2d 1323, 1331, 2 ELR 20162, 20164 (4th Cir. 1972) ("At some stage of progress, the costs of altering or abandoning the project could so definitely outweigh whatever benefits that might occur therefrom that it might no longer be 'possible' to change the project in accordance with Section 102") and Scherr v. Volpe, 466 F.2d 1027, 1034–35, 2 ELR 20453, 20456 (7th Cir. 1972) (following *Arlington Coalition*) and Swain v. Brinegar, 517 F.2d 766, 773–74, 5 ELR 20354, 20356 (7th Cir. 1974) (following *Scherr*) with Environmental Defense Fund, Inc. v. Tennessee Valley Authority (Tellico Dam), 468 F.2d 1164, 1177, 2 ELR 20726, 20731 (6th Cir. 1972) ("Although this formulation might compel the preparation of impact statements for projects that are so nearly complete that there is no reasonable prospect that the decision to proceed as planned would be reversed, there is no reason to adopt a lesser standard and thereby encourage bureaucratic evasion of responsibility") and Jones v. Lynn, 477 F.2d 885, 3 ELR 20358 (1st Cir. 1973). Factors that are considered include (1) the extent to which the community participated in early decision-making; (2) whether pre-NEPA judgments were sensitive to environmental factors; (3) the likelihood and substantiality of harm to the environment occasioned by the project; (4) costs to the state and public in the event of delay pending compliance. See Environmental Law Fund v. Volpe, 340 F.Supp. 1328, 1334–35, 2 ELR 20225, 20228, (N.D.Cal.1972). See also Comm. to Stop Route 7 v. Volpe, 346 F.Supp. 731, 738–39, 2 ELR 20446, 20448 (D.C.Conn.1972).

Experience with pending projects can make bad law; the EIS is prepared late in the game in a *pro forma* context by an agency whose commitment to the project is total. Obviously, because it is not "possible" to comply fully when evaluating projects caught by NEPA in midstream, partial compliance in pending cases should not dictate precedents of untimeliness, limited consideration of alternatives, and acceptable agency bias. Projects ongoing at the time of NEPA are special cases. Fortunately, with the passage of time the issue becomes less acute.

§ 7.7 The Recurring Issues: When

NEPA is a technology assessment statute;[1] its purpose is to require consideration of environmental factors before project momentum is irresistable, before options are closed, and before agency commitments are set in concrete. The statute speaks to timing in several particulars; importantly, an EIS must be included in "every recommendation or report on proposals" for legislation and other actions with environmental effects. A proposal is, by definition, a tentative plan or course of action offered for consideration. The proposal necessarily precedes the decision to go ahead. Requiring an EIS before the action and the authorization comports fully with NEPA's twin objectives of an improved environment and improved decisions affecting the environment.

a. *Proposals for Action*

Section 102(2)(C) also states that the EIS prepared in connection with "proposals" for action "shall accompany the proposals through the existing agency review process." This makes clear that the EIS included with every proposal must be evaluated by agency decision-makers concurrently with their review of the project offered for consideration. That the EIS must accompany the proposal through "existing" review processes is an indication that environmental considerations should be confronted in the normal course as the agency evaluates the action proposed. Presumably, most of the "existing agency review processes" occur after a project has reached the "proposal" stage.

The timing of EIS preparation is especially important because project momentum can narrow alternatives drastically: "It does little good to shut the barn doors after the horses have run away."[2] Or again: NEPA "does not authorize defendants to meet their responsibilities by locking the barn door after the horses are stolen."[3] Stolen horses and open barn doors is the language of technology assess-

---

1. § 1.3 above.

2. La Raza Unida v. Volpe, 337 F.Supp. 221, 231, 1 ELR 20642, 20645 (N.D. Cal.1971).

3. Lathan v. Volpe (II), 350 F.Supp. 262, 266, 2 ELR 20545, 20547 (W.D. Wash.1972), aff'd 506 F.2d 677, 4 ELR 20802 (9th Cir. 1974).

ment. Unfortunately, late EIS' are one of NEPA's continuing problems,[4] and not all of the procrastination is due to the pendency of projects when the law became effective. The late EIS can lead to costly delay and *pro forma* compliance. NEPA enforcement will be disruptive as long as statement preparation is treated as an afterthought.

The Supreme Court in *SCRAP II*[5] indicated that the timing of agency preparation of a final EIS is controlled by the emergence of a recommendation or report on a "proposal" for federal action. In the context of the case, this meant an EIS was not required until the appearance of an ICC report declining to hold unlawful selected rate increases proposed by railroads several months earlier. *SCRAP II* went out of its way to repudiate a line of cases reading a duty of early EIS preparation into the requirement that the statement "accompany the proposal through the existing agency review processes." [6]

SCRAP II can be read as sanctioning unnecessary delay in statement preparation; if an agency is said to make no recommendation on a "proposal" for action until actually passing on a matter submitted, it can find itself sitting back, "like an umpire," [7] blandly "calling balls and strikes" for adversaries appearing before it.[8] It should be recognized that a recommendation on "proposals" for action need not be confined to formal agency recommendations. "Proposals" can be made by the staff at early and tentative stages. Staff recommendations in support of an application for a license or permit, to mention

4. Anderson, The National Environmental Policy Act, in Environmental Law Institute, Federal Environmental Law 238, 327 (E. L. Dolgin & T. G. P. Guilbert eds. 1974) ("virtually unanimous opinion that early impact statement preparation is necessary has not kept late preparation from becoming one of the main shortcomings of the NEPA process today").

5. Aberdeen & Rockfish R. R. v. Students Challenging Regulatory Agency Procedures (SCRAP II), 422 U.S. 289, 95 S.Ct. 2336, 45 L.Ed.2d 191 (1975). The Council on Environmental Quality reads *SCRAP II* as requiring "no general change in agency NEPA procedures." Hearings on National Environmental Policy Act Oversight, Before the Subcomm. on Fisheries and Wildlife Conservation and the Environment of the House Comm. on Merchant Marine and Fisheries, H.R.Doc. No. 14, 94th Cong., 1st Sess. 247 (1975) (Memorandum to the Heads of Agencies from Russell W. Peterson, Chairman, CEQ).

6. 422 U.S. at 321 n. 20, 95 S.Ct. at 2356 n. 20, 45 L.Ed.2d 216 n. 20; see Harlem Valley Transp. Ass'n v. Stafford, 500 F.2d 328, 336, 4 ELR 20638, 20642 (2d Cir. 1974) ("the ICC ignores that we held in *Greene County I* that the literal language of NEPA requires that impact statements be prepared prior to hearings since the statements must accompany the proposal through the 'existing agency review processes,' of which a public hearing under the Federal Power Act is a part").

7. Calvert Cliffs' Coord. Comm. v. Atomic Energy Comm'n, 146 U.S.App. D.C. 33, 43, 449 F.2d 1109, 1119, 1 ELR 20346, 20350 (1971), cert. denied 404 U.S. 942 (1972).

8. Scenic Hudson Preservation Conf. v. Federal Power Comm'n (I), 354 F.2d 608, 620, 1 ELR 20292, 20297 (2d Cir. 1965), cert. denied 384 U.S. 941 (1966); see California v. Morton, 404 F.Supp. 26, 31, 6 ELR 20088, 20089 (C.D. Cal.1975) ("It was an appropriate compliance with [section 102] for the Secretary to time the completion of a final statement so as just to precede his final decision whether there should be a sale").

two prominent categories, can be viewed as "proposals" for action requiring the inclusion of "a detailed statement by the responsible official." [9] One test is whether a responsible official presents for decision a specific course of agency action that arguably will have an environmental impact.

SCRAP II suggests that while NEPA itself may not require the preparation of a final statement until a formal "proposal" appears, the CEQ guidelines on draft statements assure a consideration of environmental factors well before that.[10] Actually, a requirement of preproposal consultation is found in the Act. Obviously, an environmental impact statement does not spring into the picture unannounced when a "proposal" emerges. The statute says that "prior to" making the statement there must be consultation with federal agencies having expertise on any environmental impact involved. Informed consultation on effects requires that consultants be informed about the nature of the undertaking. Section 102(2)(C) also makes clear that comments of federal, state and local agencies must be secured prior to completion of the statement since they too "shall accompany the proposal through the existing agency review processes." Thus, while references to the "detailed statement" in Section 102(2)(C) of NEPA must be understood as referring to a final environmental impact statement,[11] there is ample authority in the statute for anticipating a consultative and review process prior to agency preparation of the final EIS.

As a practical matter, the timing of statement preparation is governed largely by the CEQ guidelines on draft and final EIS'. They call for a draft statement "as early as possible in the agency review process in order to permit agency decisionmakers and outside reviewers to give meaningful consideration to the environmental issues involved." [12] To assure that statements genuinely assess impacts and not merely rationalize decisions previously made, the guidelines urge that the drafts "should be prepared and circulated for comment prior to the first significant point of decision in the agency review process." [13] The statute makes clear, of course, that not only the draft but also the final EIS must be included in reports on proposals for action evaluated by the normal agency review process. The guidelines call for a period of not less than forty-five days for comment on the draft.[14] Final statements are then prepared, filed with CEQ and distributed to interested agencies and groups.[15]

9. See Greene County Planning Bd. v. Federal Power Comm'n (I), 455 F.2d 412, 422 n. 24, 2 ELR 20017, 20021 n. 24 (2d Cir.), cert. denied 404 U.S. 849 (1972).

10. See 422 U.S. at 321, 95 S.Ct. at 2356, 45 L.Ed.2d at 215–16.

11. 422 U.S. at 320, 95 S.Ct. at 2356, 45 L.Ed.2d at 215.

12. 40 CFR § 1500.7(a).

13. Ibid.

14. Id. § 1500.9(f).

15. Id. §§ 1500.10(b), 1500.11(a).

As a general rule, no administrative action subject to section 102 (2)(C) should be taken sooner than thirty days after a final EIS, or ninety days after a draft EIS, is made available to the Council and the public.[16]

Other language in the statute may affect the timing of statement preparation. A prerequisite of EIS preparation is that an action be "Federal" and this characterization may not occur until an action already is in the process of being implemented.[17] The presence or absence of significant effects also may present a question of timing.[18] The EIS' study of "alternatives to the proposed action" and its assessment of effects "which cannot be avoided should the proposal be implemented" presupposes completion of the statement before something happens. Plainly futuristic is the requirement that an EIS address "any irreversible or irretrievable commitments of resources which would be involved in the proposed action should it be implemented."[19] Quite clearly, an agency finding itself embarked on a course involving an irretrievable commitment of resources might conclude safely that it is engaging in an action or at least is considering proposals for action significantly affecting the environment.

The cases stress repeatedly the desirability of early preparation of the EIS, citing both agency regulations,[20] and the specific provisions [21] and general purposes [22] of the Act. An oft-quoted excerpt from *Calvert Cliffs* ties early NEPA compliance, if not EIS preparation, to the general section 102 directive that agencies comply "to the fullest extent possible":

> Compliance to the 'fullest' possible extent would seem to demand that environmental issues be considered at every important stage in the decision-making process concerning a particular action

---

16. Id. § 1500.11(b).

17. See text accompanying notes 47–64, infra.

18. § 7.6 above.

19. 42 U.S.C.A. § 4332(2)(C)(v).

20. See Daly v. Volpe, 350 F.Supp. 252, 256, 2 ELR 20443, 20444 (W.D. Wash.1971); cf. Natural Resources Defense Council, Inc. v. Callaway, 524 F.2d 79, 87–90, 5 ELR 20640, 20644–45 (2d Cir. 1975) (discussing EIS consideration of cumulative effects) (quoting CEQ Guideline, 40 CFR § 1500.6(a), emphasizing that consideration be given not only to the action that is the subject of the EIS but also to "related Federal actions and projects in the area, and further actions contemplated").

21. Lathan v. Volpe (I), 455 F.2d 1111, 1120–21, 1 ELR 20602, 20605–06 (9th Cir. 1971), modified 2 ELR 20090 (9th Cir. 1972).

22. Citizens for Clean Air v. Corps of Engineers, 349 F.Supp. 696, 708, 2 ELR 20650, 20655 (S.D.N.Y.1972):
> Where several federal permits or approvals are required for a project, NEPA requires a § 102 review at the point where the action is 'distinctive and comprehensive'. Once a project has reached a coherent stage of development it requires an environmental impact study. The comprehensive review contemplated by the Act can only be efficacious if undertaken as early as possible.

—at every stage where an overall balancing of environmental and non-environmental factors is appropriate and where alterations might be made in the proposed action to minimize environmental costs.[23]

At the same time, how early is soon enough is not at all clear since it depends on deciding when an agency recommendation on a "proposal" for action emerges. Perhaps for this reason courts accord agencies wide autonomy in deciding when and how to comply,[24] even after a proposal for action comes into being.[25]

One of the most important timing questions is to determine when a federal research and development or study program is sufficiently far along to give rise to a "recommendation or report on proposals for legislation and other major Federal actions significantly affecting the quality of the human environment." The timing argument is implicit at different points in the statute: a study program is not a proposal for action; if it is, the action does not significantly affect the quality of the environment; and if it involves a proposal for legislation, i. e., a budget request, then it too does not significantly affect the quality of the environment. The statement writer is in something of a dilemma with study programs: judgments about effects are tentative and hypothetical because implementation may never occur; yet at the same time the research effort may be a blueprint for action that might close the doors on alternatives. The leading case of Scientists' Institute for Public Information v. Atomic Energy Commission,[26] resolves the dilemma by requiring a statement for the Commission's breeder reactor research and development program while allowing flexibility in addressing hypothetical effects.[27] *SIPI* says: "Statements must be written late enough in the development process to contain meaningful information, but they must be written early enough so that whatever information is contained can practically serve as an input into the decision-making process."[28] Suggested tests on when a statement is due

---

23. Calvert Cliffs' Coord. Comm. v. Atomic Energy Comm'n, 146 U.S.App. D.C. 33, 42, 449 F.2d 1109, 1118, 1 ELR 20346, 20350 (1971), cert. denied. 404 U.S. 942 (1972).

24. Aberdeen & Rockfish R. R. v. Students Challenging Regulatory Agency Procedures (SCRAP II), 422 U.S. 289, 326, 95 S.Ct. 2336, 2358–59, 45 L.Ed. 2d 191, 219 (1975); Scientists' Inst. for Pub. Information v. Atomic Energy Comm'n (SIPI), 156 U.S.App.D.C. 395, 410, 481 F.2d 1079, 1094, 3 ELR 20525, 20532 (1973).

25. No East-West Highway Comm., Inc. v. Whitaker, 403 F.Supp. 260, 6 ELR 20053 (D.C.N.H.1975) (finding that although a plan to construct a highway existed, it lacked sufficient definition for the court to require an EIS).

26. 156 U.S.App.D.C. 395, 481 F.2d 1079, 3 ELR 20525 (1973).

27. 156 U.S.App.D.C. at 408, 481 F.2d at 1092, 3 ELR at 20531 (the EIS on the research program need not foresee impact "with the same degree of accuracy" as another agency would be required to forecast traffic congestion).

28. 156 U.S.App.D.C. at 410, 481 F.2d at 1094, 3 ELR at 20532.

are: (1) how likely is the technology to prove commercially feasible and when will that occur? (2) to what extent is information available on effects and alternatives? (3) whether "irreversible and irretrievable commitments of resources" are being made; and (4) the severity of the likely adverse effects if the technology under study proves technologically feasible.[29]

Judgments about when EIS' must be included in government studies involving application of a particular technology reflect the *SIPI* considerations of the imminency of implementation, predictability of effects, availability of information, and coherency of purpose. Under these criteria statements have been required for the Department of Interior's national coal leasing program, but not for its Northern Great Plains Resource Program [30] and not for its Southwest Power Study;[31] required for a city annexation proposal likely to lead to development,[32] but not for preliminary plans to locate defense facilities in the State of Hawaii;[33] required for a plan to transfer surplus land to a utility as a future power plant site,[34] but not for a proposal to build a federal office building somewhere in Jackson, Mississippi;[35] required for a 280-mile stretch of highway already being built,[36] but not for a tentative twenty-year highway construction plan,[37] and not for the Department of Transportation's Highway Needs Reports which are no more than a gleam in a planner's eye.[38]

There are policy reasons opposed to pushing back the EIS requirements to the formative stages of administrative decision-making. An agency should be free to brainstorm and speculate, and to in-

---

29. Id. The *SIPI* criteria have been repudiated specifically by the Supreme Court. See Sierra Club v. Kleppe, 427 U.S. 390, 404–05, 96 S.Ct. 2718, 2728–29, 49 L.Ed.2d 576, 587–88 (1976).

30. See Sierra Club v. Morton, 169 U.S.App.D.C. 20, 514 F.2d 856, 5 ELR 20463 (1975), rev'd 427 U.S. 390, 96 S.Ct. 2718, 49 L.Ed.2d 576 (1976).

31. Jicarilla Apache Tribe v. Morton, 471 F.2d 1275, 1278, 3 ELR 20045, 20046 (9th Cir. 1973).

32. Bozung v. Local Agency Formation Comm'n, 13 Cal.3d 263, 529 P.2d 1017, 118 Cal.Rptr. 249 (1975) (arising under the California Environmental Quality Act).

33. Life of the Land v. Secretary of Defense, 4 ELR 20295, 20296 (D.Ha. 1974) (plaintiffs conceded lack of necessity for a statement "for general plans of a preliminary nature").

34. Rhode Island Comm. on Energy v. General Serv. Administration, 397 F. Supp. 41, 61, 5 ELR 20685, 20694 (D.C.R.I.1975).

35. Crosley Bldg. Corp. v. Sampson, —— F.Supp. ——, 5 ELR 20711 (D.D.C. 1975) (submittal of lease prospectus by GSA to House and Senate Public Works Committees for their approval is not a proposal for legislation).

36. Conservation Soc'y of Southern Vermont v. Secretary of Transp. (I), 508 F.2d 927, 5 ELR 20068 (1974), vacated 423 U.S. 809 (1975).

37. Indian Lookout Alliance v. Volpe, 345 F.Supp. 1167, 3 ELR 20051 (S.D. Iowa 1972), aff'd 484 F.2d 11, 3 ELR 20739 (8th Cir. 1973).

38. Environmental Defense Fund, Inc. v. Volpe, Civ. No. 151–72 (D.D.C. 1972).

Sec. 7.7   THE RECURRING ISSUES: WHEN   773

vestigate,[39] and perhaps adjudicate,[40] before it chooses a course. But premature impact statements are not now, nor are they likely to become, a serious impediment to administraion of the Act. Acting first and thinking later is a more common failing. The courts will face continuing difficulties in identifying "proposals" for action and, before that, actions without benefit of proposals that trigger the EIS requirements.

As of this writing, prospects for early statements and their consequent use for technology assessment and other planning purposes are poor. In Kleppe v. Sierra Club [41] the Supreme Court reaffirmed its literal insistence in *SCRAP II* that an EIS need not be prepared until something clearly identifiable as a "proposal" for action emerges from the agency's deliberations. The Court comes very close to allowing an agency to dictate the timing of statement preparation by the simple expedient of withholding the "proposal" characterization from its plans for future development.[42] The Court also explicitly repudiates *SIPI's* four criteria for determining the timing of statement preparation, which means as a practical matter that the chief determinant of whether a "proposal" exists depends upon whether the agency says it is so. The decision in *Kleppe* also affords considerable discretion to the agency to define narrowly the scope of an intended action.[43] The combination of tardy preparation and limited focus forces the EIS into the role of project apologist and out of the mould of project planner.

The CEQ guidelines state that an agency "may at any time supplement or amend a draft or final environmental statement, particularly when substantial changes are made in the proposed action, or

39. California v. Morton, 404 F.Supp. 26, 31, 6 ELR 20088, 20089 (C.D. Cal.1975) (rejecting argument that an EIS is required before taking any step in the direction of final action; such a requirement would "unduly fetter early investigative stages of [the Department of Interior] aimed only at testing possible feasibility of the program").

40. Gifford-Hill & Co., Inc. v. Federal Trade Comm'n, 173 U.S.App.D.C. 135, 523 F.2d 730, 6 ELR 20019 (1975) (per curiam) (decision to investigate and adjudicate involves no irretrievable commitment of resources requiring an EIS). Compare note 43, infra.

41. 427 U.S. 390, 96 S.Ct. 2718, 49 L. Ed.2d 576 (1976).

42. 427 U.S. at 406, 96 S.Ct. at 2728–29, 49 L.Ed.2d at 586–87.

43. § 7.9 below. The Court insists that NEPA "does not require an agency to consider the possible environmental impacts of less imminent actions when preparing the impact statement of proposed actions." 427 U.S. at 410 n. 20, 96 S.Ct. at 2730 n. 20, 49 L.Ed.2d at 590 n. 20. This observation appears to confuse fundamentally the issue of statement timing, which is tied to the appearance of a recommendation on a "proposal," with that of statement scope, which is controlled by the particulars of subsections 102(2)(C)(i)–(v). Manifestly, the obligation to assess in the EIS "any irreversible and irretrievable commitments of resources" very well might require an agency to consider possible impacts of less imminent actions when preparing a statement on a proposed action.

significant new information becomes available concerning its environmental costs." [44] Supplements can prevent EIS's from rapidly becoming obsolete. At the same time the possibility of supplements can encourage putting off hard questions. The insistence that the statement should be a "self-contained instrument" [45] not subsequently justified by argument of counsel or in-court testimony indicates an unwillingness to accept the possibility of later supplementation as an excuse for partial compliance the first time around. It is also clear that a supplement is something that cannot simply be tacked onto the original. It must go through the ordinary review and commenting procedures.[46] A supplemental EIS should be prepared whenever new information or changed plans render the initial effort inadequate. A supplemental statement is, by definition, a late statement, subject to the difficulties discussed in this section. Supplements should be discouraged by a judicial insistence on an early statement and a definitive statement on the first attempt.

b. *Delayed Federal Involvement*

An issue that combines the questions of whether and when an EIS is required flows from the fact that section 102(2)(C) is limited to proposals for "Federal actions." Ongoing projects that assume their federal character late in life present special difficulties. The issue is one of timing:[47] the project has momentum; planning is advanced; design commitments narrowed; contracts are drawn, and construction may be underway. Reconsideration of these projects becomes less meaningful with the passage of time. Case law discloses that NEPA does not reach a private power company's condemnation program preparatory to applying for a federal license to construct a nuclear power plant; [48] a city's early planning and initial construction of a dam to be funded partly under the federal Disaster Relief Act of 1974; [49] the planning, design, and early construction of airport improvements ultimately to be funded in part under the federal

---

44. 40 CFR § 1500.11(b).

45. Id. at 1500.8(b).

46. Natural Resources Defense Council, Inc. v. Morton, 337 F.Supp. 170, 2 ELR 20071 (D.C.D.C.1972).

47. See No East-West Highway Comm., Inc. v. Whitaker, 403 F.Supp. 260, 277, 6 ELR 20053, 20060 (D.C.N.H.1975) ("While this factor [the danger of incremental construction undermining the effectiveness of a NEPA analysis] is one that is traditionally considered in determining whether the time is 'ripe' for an EIS to be prepared, it is also highly relevant in determining whether a partnership exists between the state and the FHWA").

48. Gage v. Atomic Energy Comm'n, 156 U.S.App.D.C. 231, 479 F.2d 1214, 3 ELR 20479 (1973).

49. Homeowners Emergency Life Protection Comm. v. Lynn, 388 F.Supp. 971, 5 ELR 20195 (C.D.Cal.1974), rev'd on other grounds per curiam 541 F.2d 814, 6 ELR 20659 (9th Cir. 1976).

Sec. 7.7   THE RECURRING ISSUES: WHEN   775

Airport and Airway Development Act of 1970;[50] and state highway planning and improvements prior to a firm federal involvement.[51]

Alert to the temptations of NEPA avoidance, courts are inclined to mark the action "Federal" as soon as a discrete federal go-ahead can be identified.[52] As indicated above, the Act itself calls for an impact statement to be included in "proposals" for action which clearly anticipates a look before the leap is taken. Where an action is irrevocably underway, albeit at the initiative of nonfederal parties, the preference ought to be to find a "Federal" involvement at an early stage. Otherwise, a project that ultimately is paid for by federal dollars may escape a federal environmental analysis. Determining the "Federal" presence requires an analysis not only of formal indicia (contracts, memoranda of understanding, or firm commitments of federal funds) but also informal ones (federal recommendations, active participation in project planning, understandings of future support). As soon as federal influence over the action is detectable, the NEPA obligations should attach.[53]

Determining when a project ripens into a "Federal" action today is a difficult task. Courts recognize the early warning value of NEPA may be lost as a result of nonfederal momentum. The analysis is clouded by ticklish questions of the power to enjoin, pending preparation of an EIS by the federal agency, nonfederal entities who, after all, may be doing nothing more than spending private money to develop private lands on a project that probably, but may not ulti-

50. Boston v. Volpe, 464 F.2d 254, 2 ELR 20501 (1st Cir. 1972) (distinguishing discrete stages of federal-aid highway planning from single up or down vote on airport funding); cf. Friends of the Earth v. Coleman, 513 F.2d 295, 5 ELR 20429 (9th Cir. 1975).

51. Bradford Township v. Illinois State Toll Highway Authority, 463 F.2d 537, 2 ELR 20322 (7th Cir. 1972), cert. denied 409 U.S. 1047; Northeast Welfare Rights Organization v. Volpe, 1 ELR 20186, 20187 (E.D.Wash.1970) (proposed freeway connector was not federal because "at this time" the project is proceeding "without federal financial participation"); Highland Park v. Train, 374 F.Supp. 758, 772, 4 ELR 20677, 20683 (N.D.Ill. 1974), aff'd 519 F.2d 681, 5 ELR 20408 (7th Cir. 1975); Hill v. Coleman, 399 F.Supp. 194, 6 ELR 20001 (D.C.Del. 1975) (not a federal project because location approval had not been granted; excellent discussion of four stages of federal approvals for reimbursement of highway construction expenses—program approval, location approval, design approval, and plans specifications and estimates [P.S. & E.] approval).

52. E. g., La Raza Unida v. Volpe, 488 F.2d 559, 4 ELR 20090 (9th Cir. 1973), cert. denied 417 U.S. 968 (1974) (state highway had received location approval from Federal Highway Administration but state had not yet requested funds); Lathan v. Volpe (I), 455 F.2d 1111, 1 ELR 20602 (9th Cir. 1971); Steubing v. Brinegar, 511 F.2d 489, 492, 5 ELR 20183, 20185 (2d Cir. 1975) ("In those circumstances subsequent decisions by [federal highway officials] approving final plans and committing federal funds for construction of the bridge, constituted major federal actions requiring preparation of an EIS") (footnotes omitted); cf. No East-West Highway Comm., Inc. v. Whitaker, 403 F.Supp. 260, 6 ELR 20053 (D.N.H.1975) (finding a federal plan but not yet requiring preparation of an EIS).

53. See note 52, supra.

mately, win some federal support.[54] The temptation for evasion is high since many factors affecting the federal-nonfederal relationship are artificially controllable.[55]

The basic problem is that federal agencies must have time to decide in order to make NEPA work. The court in Silva v. Romney [56] made an unusual recommendation urging agencies to adopt *status quo* regulations to guide the government, aid applicants and the general public where potential major federal actions are involved. Only administrative legislation, in the view of the court, could define fully "circumstances where developers should be allowed to do certain things on a project, pending completion and review of an impact statement, as when the preparatory work is environmentally neutral or the adverse impact is virtually non-existent." [57] Status quo regulations "could prevent the irony which might occur where a partially built project which went ahead with little concern for the environment could not be completed because federal funds were denied to avoid subsidizing environmental harm, the twin results being no housing and an impaired environment." [58] If regulations do not appear, of course, judges must continue to make ad hoc anticipatory judgments about federal involvement and enforce NEPA late in the game. This will lead to costly delays for procedural compliance and partial or incomplete relief.[59]

The law at its manipulative worst is demonstrated by cases involving attempts to de-federalize an action explicitly for purposes of avoiding NEPA. It is clear that at some unspecified point an action becomes irrevocably federal, even if a state offers to return all federal funds and proceed on its own. "[W]hile this marriage between the federal and state defendants seems to have been an un-

---

54. The courts have developed a "partnership" theory to ascertain whether nonfederal aspects of a project can be enjoined pending compliance. Compare Proetta v. Dent, 484 F.2d 1146, 3 ELR 20781 (2d Cir. 1973) (denying injunction against a non-recipient of the loan) with Silva v. Romney, 473 F.2d 287, 3 ELR 20082 (1st Cir. 1973) (granting injunction against the developer expected to benefit by federal assistance).

55. Compare Ely v. Velde, 451 F.2d 1130, 1139, 1 ELR 20612, 20615 (4th Cir. 1971) with Silva v. Romney, 473 F.2d 287, 289–90, 3 ELR 20082, 20084 (1st Cir. 1973).

56. 473 F.2d 287, 3 ELR 20082 (1st Cir. 1973).

57. 473 F.2d at 291, 3 ELR at 20084; see 10 CFR pt. 51 (containing Nuclear Regulatory Commission status quo regulations on the construction of nuclear power plants). See also Scientists' Inst. for Pub. Information v. Atomic Energy Comm'n, 156 U.S. App.D.C. 395, 401 n. 19, 581 F.2d 1079, 1085 n. 19, 3 ELR 20525, 20526 n. 19 (1973) (EIS on breeder reactor demonstration plant prepared prior to application for construction permit at request of President).

58. 473 F.2d at 291, 3 ELR at 20084.

59. E. g., Friends of the Earth v. Coleman, 513 F.2d 295, 5 ELR 20429 (9th Cir. 1975) (enjoining federally but not locally funded aspects of airport development project; there was said to be a "substantial functional complementarity" between the federal and locally funded projects but not a "functional interdependence" between them).

happy one," said the Fifth Circuit in the San Antonio freeway case, "it has produced an already huge concrete offspring whose existence it is impossible for us to ignore." [60] The courts are not inclined to accept mere "bookkeeping" shifts as a justification for NEPA avoidance—that is, where federal funding is diverted or made available to another project.[61] But some cases have rewarded manipulative artistry, both in undoing a project admittedly federal [62] and preventing the federal characterization from attaching initially.[63] A strong presumption of once federal, always federal [64] would limit this gamemanship; the federal agency could escape from its NEPA obligations only by showing that it is entirely divorced from the project. Requiring an EIS in close cases is not objectionable on the ground that implementation of its recommendations is dependent upon cooperation by others.

§ 7.8 The Recurring Issues: Who

Section 102(2)(C) [1] of NEPA says that recommendations on proposals for action must include "a detailed statement by the responsible official." The extent to which "the responsible official" can delegate authority to write the statement or to collect data used in the statement is a subject of continuing controversy. In 1975 Congress dealt with the issue indecisively with the first major amendment [2] to the National Environmental Policy Act. This section addresses the delegation issue and the separate question of who writes the statement when several agencies are involved in implementation.

---

60. Named Individual Members of the San Antonio Conservation Soc'y v. Texas Highway Dep't (I), 446 F.2d 1013, 1027, 1 ELR 20379, 20388 (5th Cir. 1971), cert. denied 406 U.S. 933 (1972). Of course Congress can divorce even parties irrevocably wedded for NEPA purposes. See Named Individual Members of the San Antonio Conservation Soc'y v. Texas Highway Dep't (II), 496 F.2d 1017, 4 ELR 20643 (5th Cir. 1974), cert. denied 420 U.S. 926.

61. See Named Individual Members of the San Antonio Conservation Soc'y v. Texas Highway Dep't, supra note 60; Sierra Club v. Volpe, 351 F.Supp. 1002 (N.D.Cal.1972).

62. See Ely v. Velde, 363 F.Supp. 277, 3 ELR 20764 (E.D.Va.1973) (finding plaintiffs failed to prove an impermissible bookkeeping maneuver).

63. James River & Kanawa Canal Parks, Inc. v. Richmond Metropolitan Authority, 359 F.Supp. 611, 3 ELR 20556 (E.D.Va.1973) (state-funded city expressway exempted from reach of NEPA despite admission by state highway commissioner that federal funding was diverted from the project to avoid environmental constraints).

64. But see Friends of the Earth v. Coleman, 513 F.2d 295, 300, 5 ELR 20428, 20430 (9th Cir. 1975) ("Considerations of the actual degree of federal involvement are consistent with the . . . rejection of the notion that once the federal government has participated in a development, it is necessarily forever federal").

1. 42 U.S.C.A. § 4332(2)(C).

2. Pub.L. No. 94-83, 89 Stat. 424, adding 42 U.S.C.A. § 4332(D).

a. *Delegation*

Before turning to the specifics of congressional attempts to resolve the controversy, some background is in order. NEPA, as conceived originally, clearly anticipates that the thought process going into the EIS be an in-house effort. After all, a basic purpose of the Act is to improve agency decision-making by forcing consideration of different points of view. Good faith consideration is hardly shown by farming out responsibility for rationalizing effects and alternatives. The offense is compounded if the party selected to participate in EIS preparation is interested; advocates are poorly suited to look skeptically at their own problems. At the same time, NEPA encourages widespread consultation prior to agency action. If an interest in the result disqualifies information sources, the store of available knowledge suffers an appreciable decline.

The leading case of Greene County Planning Board v. Federal Power Comm'n [3] required the Commission to prepare its own EIS on a proposal prior to an adjudicatory hearing. The Commission would abdicate "a significant part of its responsibility," the court said, if it tied its deliberations to the applicant's statement which will be "based upon self-serving assumptions." [4] The *Greene County* delegation issue, which arises mostly in the highway cases, has divided the courts three ways: (1) those allowing a virtually complete delegation and requiring only a *pro forma* ratification by federal officials; (2) those inquiring into the circumstances to determine the extent of federal involvement in the actual preparation of the statement; and (3) those insisting upon a strict enforcement of *Greene County* and clear responsibility for physical preparation by federal officials.

Cases allowing delegation of responsibility for preparing the statement with little or no control [5] are clearly wrong; "a detailed statement by the responsible [federal] official" is what the statute requires and the obligation to consider alternatives, measure effects, and propose mitigation seems a nonassignable one. Recognizing this,

---

3. 455 F.2d 412, 2 ELR 20017 (2d Cir. 1972), cert. denied 409 U.S. 849; see Comment, Delegation of the Drafting of Environmental Impact Statements: Greene County Planning Board v. Federal Power Commission, 2 ELR 10153 (1972); Note, Environmental Impact Statements—A Duty of Independent Investigation by Federal Agencies, 44 Colo.L.Rev. 161 (1972); Comment, The Preparation of Environmental Impact Statements by State Highway Commissions, 58 Iowa L.Rev. 1268 (1973).

4. 455 F.2d at 420, 2 ELR at 20020.

5. E. g., Pizitz, Inc. v. Volpe, 467 F.2d 208, 2 ELR 20371 (5th Cir. 1972), modified on this point on rehearing 467 F.2d 208, 2 ELR 20635; Citizens Environmental Council v. Volpe, 364 F.Supp. 286, 3 ELR 20077 (D.Kan. 1973), aff'd 484 F.2d 870, 4 ELR 20009 (10th Cir.), cert. denied 416 U.S. 936 (1974); Iowa Citizens for Environmental Quality, Inc. v. Volpe, 3 ELR 20013 (S.D.Ia.1972), aff'd 487 F.2d 849, 4 ELR 20057 (8th Cir. 1973) (the Circuit Court opinion requires significant and active federal participation and oversight).

Sec. 7.8　　THE RECURRING ISSUES: WHO

most of the cases ask whether there has been "significant," "active," [6] and "extensive" [7] involvement by federal officials in the process of statement preparation. The courts inquire into whether federal officials wrote, edited, or reviewed the report, made field inspections or recommendations contributing to it, met and consulted with the actual authors, or analyzed and passed upon the findings in it. A determination of significant involvement suffices to defeat charges that federal officials rubber-stamped somebody else's work or abdicated their responsibilities.

Federal responsibility for preparing the statement is not relinquished by assigning significant responsibilities for data gathering and even production of the finished product to outside, independent consultants. The question is whether the assignee serves the interest of NEPA or the cause of project fulfillment. The Second Circuit [8] has distinguished *Greene County* as a case where the evil sought to be avoided "is the preparation of the EIS by a party, usually a state agency, with an individual 'axe to grind', i. e., an interest in seeing the project accepted and completed in a specific manner as proposed. Authorship by such a biased party might prevent the fair and impartial evaluation of a project envisioned by NEPA. Here no problem of self-interest on the part of the author exists. As the Navy's

---

6. Life of the Land v. Brinegar, 485 F.2d 460, 468, 3 ELR 20811, 20814 (9th Cir. 1973) (sustaining initial preparation of the EIS by private consulting firm with a financial stake in the outcome); see Rankin v. Coleman, 394 F.Supp. 647, 656, 5 ELR 10626, 20629 (E.D.N.C.1975) (must "independently weigh costs and benefits").

7. Movement Against Destruction v. Volpe, 361 F.Supp. 1360, 1393, 3 ELR 20667, 20680 (D.C.Md.1973), aff'd per curiam 500 F.2d 29, 4 ELR 20278 (4th Cir. 1974); Finish Allatoona's Interstate Right, Inc. v. Volpe, 335 F.Supp. 933, 938, 3 ELR 20433, 20434 (M.D.Ga.1973), aff'd 484 F.2d 638, 3 ELR 20769 (5th Cir.); Ecology Center of Louisiana, Inc. v. Coleman, 515 F.2d 860, 5 ELR 20488 (5th Cir. 1975) (affirming summary judgment finding proper delegation on basis of affidavit stating federal agency, after independent review and analysis, adopted state prepared statement as its own); Iowa Citizens for Environmental Quality, Inc. v. Volpe, 487 F.2d 849, 4 ELR 20056 (8th Cir. 1973); Fayetteville Area Chamber of Commerce v. Volpe, 515 F.2d 1021, 1025, 5 ELR 20379, 20390 (4th Cir. 1975) ("Not only did the federal officials review with care from time to time the work on the preparation of the statement, the physical preparation of which was largely handled by the state authorities, the record also includes such activity by the federal officials as field inspections, erosion control recommendations, directions to the state to include appropriate consideration of the comments from the Council on Environmental Quality, joint meetings to determine the design concept, and progress meetings to review the draft statement"); Life of the Land v. Brinegar, 485 F.2d 460, 4 ELR 20295 (9th Cir. 1973); cf. Sierra Club v. Lynn, 502 F.2d 43, 59, 4 ELR 20844, 20850 (5th Cir. 1974), cert. denied 422 U.S. 1049 (1975) (making clear the applicant can provide the agency with data, information, reports, environmental studies and other assistance); Citizens Airport Comm. v. Volpe, 3 ELR 20021, 20023 (E.D.Va.1972) (upholding an environmental review under the Airport and Airway Development Act of 1970 based upon draft prepared by sponsoring body).

8. Natural Resources Defense Council, Inc. v. Callaway, 524 F.2d 79, 87, 5 ELR 20640, 20644 (2d Cir. 1975).

hiree, the independent consultant has no interest but the Navy's to serve and is fully responsible to the Navy for any shortcomings in the EIS. Therefore, we see no difference for NEPA purposes between this procedure [preparation of draft and final versions of the EIS by a consultant] and preparation of the EIS by Navy personnel. In both cases the preparers are guided exclusively by the interests of the Navy and the dictates of the NEPA process."

This green light on the use of consultants is subject to two caution signals. One is that independent consultants must be truly independent and not subtly biased.[9] The second is that the use of consultants might impede fulfillment of the legislative aim that environmental considerations be weighed along with the proposal throughout the agency review process. Shunting off environmental studies to outsiders can encourage the post-script or afterthought treatment NEPA seeks to avoid. It might make a difference, for example, if an agency uses contractors to fill in gaps of in-house expertise or if it routinely farms out EIS studies that could be handled internally by present personnel.

While statement preparation by a biased source is strongly discouraged,[10] there exists at the same time a legitimate need favoring the transmission of data to the agency by interested parties. Some sympathy is due the developer who is forbidden by *Greene County* from writing the agency's statement but potentially liable for counsel fees to those who sue to correct its inadequacies.[11] The best protection here is for the courts to give a hard look at the process to confirm that the EIS in actuality represents the judgments of the agency. The EIS is a document of the decision-maker and represents fully—not significantly, extensively or mostly—the thought process of the responsible official. One way to assure this is to require an applicant to pay for studies going into the EIS while divesting it of control over their content and form.[12] There is, unfortunately, often not a bright line between decision-makers and advocates, especially when the judge chooses to adopt without qualification proposed findings and conclusions.

---

9. See § 1.11 above (discussing the Federal Advisory Committee Act).

10. Greene County Planning Bd. v. Federal Power Comm'n (I), 455 F.2d 412, 2 ELR 20017 (2d Cir. 1972), cert. denied 409 U.S. 849.

11. Sierra Club v. Lynn, 364 F.Supp. 834, 847, 4 ELR 20110, 20116 (W.D. Tex.1973), rev'd 502 F.2d 43, 4 ELR 20844 (5th Cir. 1974), cert. denied 422 U.S. 1049 (1975); see Florida Audubon Soc'y v. Callaway, 4 ELR 20251, 20254 (N.D.Fla.1974) ("though the Corps did receive [the applicant's] data concerning alternative sites, it independently examined the data and reached its own conclusion . . .").

12. See Comment, The Independent Offices Appropriations Act of 1952: Who Should Pay for Preparing the Impact Statement, 3 ELR 10059 (1973); Comment, Who Should Pay for the Impact Statement: More on the Independent Offices Appropriations Act of 1952, 3 ELR 11086 (1973). On the advantages of "sanitizing" research contributions, see Rodgers, Siting Power Plants in Washington State, 47 Wash.L.Rev. 9 (1971).

Recently, the Second [13] and Seventh [14] Circuits opted for a strict enforcement of *Greene County* to still the perpetual arguments over whether there is "enough" [15] federal involvement to negate a finding of improper delegation. Both courts reaffirmed that delegation, however qualified, puts important powers in the hands of persons who may be limited in perspective, subject to political pressures, or otherwise incapable of dispassionate assessment. Administrative and policy considerations thus converged to support a *per se* rule requiring statement preparation by the federal agency. This eminently sensible disposition ran into one formidable barrier—congressional disapproval.

In 1975 Congress determined that the detailed statement required under section 102(2)(C) "for any major Federal action funded under a program of grants to States shall not be deemed to be legally insufficient solely by reason of having been prepared by a State agency or official. . . ." [16] This approval of the delegation of statement preparation is qualified; the state agency or official must have "statewide jurisdiction" and "the responsibility" for the action carried out by the program of grants. Delegation to state highway officials thus is permitted but not a delegation to local port authorities, mosquito and water districts or public power entities, and certainly not to a private corporation. More importantly, the responsible federal official must "[furnish] guidance and [participate] in" the preparation of the statement and must "independently" evaluate it prior to its approval and adoption. The Act makes clear that the limited delegation procedures "shall not relieve the Federal of-

---

13. Conservation Soc'y of Southern Vermont v. Secretary of Transp. (I), 508 F.2d 927, 930–34, 5 ELR 20068, 20069–71 (2d Cir. 1974), vacated 423 U.S. 809 (1975). Contra, Fayetteville Area Chamber of Commerce v. Volpe, 515 F.2d 1021, 1026, 5 ELR 20379, 20380–81 (4th Cir. 1975); Rankin v. Coleman, 394 F.Supp. 647, 654, 5 ELR 20626, 20629 (E.D.N.C.1975) (following *Fayetteville*).

14. Swain v. Brinegar, 517 F.2d 766, 5 ELR 20354 (7th Cir. 1975), rev'd en banc 542 F.2d 364 (1976).

15. 517 F.2d at 779, 5 ELR at 20359.

16. Pub.L. No. 94–83, 89 Stat. 424, adding 42 U.S.C.A. § 4332(D), which reads in part as follows:
    Any detailed statement required under subparagraph (C) after January 1, 1970, for any major Federal action funded under a program of grants to States shall not be deemed to be legally insufficient solely by reason of having been prepared by a State agency or official, if:
    (i) the State agency or official has statewide jurisdiction and has the responsibility for such action,
    (ii) the responsible Federal official furnishes guidance and participation in such preparation,
    (iii) the responsible Federal official independently evaluates such statement prior to its approval and adoption, and
    (iv) . . .
    The procedures in this subparagraph shall not relieve the Federal official of his responsibilities for the scope, objectivity, and content of the entire statement or of any other responsibility under this Act; and further, this subparagraph does not affect the legal sufficiency of statements prepared by State agencies with less than statewide jurisdiction;
    . . . .

ficial of his responsibilities for the scope, objectivity, and content of the entire statement or of any other responsibility under this Act. . . ." This means, presumably, that an inadequate statement prepared initially by state highway authorities must be redone by federal authorities to assure its acceptability.

In situations covered by the 1975 amendment, the consequence is this: Congress has disavowed the extremes in favor of a middle ground. The reformation offers no support for the cases [17] permitting a near complete abdication by federal officials of responsibility for preparing the statement. At the other end of the spectrum, Congress disavows a *per se* rule [18] permitting nothing short of full statement preparation by officials within the sponsoring agency. It calls for a factual inquiry into whether there has been the furnishing of guidance and supervision and the conducting of an independent scrutiny to permit the conclusion that the responsible federal official genuinely evaluated the environmental effects of the proposed action. That the task is a difficult one is suggested by the recent opinions of a divided panel of the Second Circuit [19] disagreeing over whether the federal supervision of statement preparation there involved met the requirements of the 1975 amendment.

In one category of cases, Congress has sanctioned an extreme delegation. Section 104(h) of the Housing and Community Development Act of 1974 [20] permits the Secretary of HUD, under certain circumstances, to "provide for the release of funds for particular projects to applicants who assume all of the responsibilities for environmental review, decision-making, and action pursuant to [NEPA] that would apply to the Secretary were he to undertake such projects as federal projects." An applicant assuming NEPA responsibilities must certify to the Secretary that it has "fully carried out its responsibilities" and, interestingly, must assume the status of the responsible federal officer and accept the jurisdiction of the federal courts for enforcement purposes.[21] Under the Community and Housing Development Act of 1974 an array of HUD categorical aid programs was replaced by the Community Development Block Grant Program, transferring from federal to state and local governments decision-making powers on where and how the funds would be spent. Congress' decision to delegate EIS responsibilities thus was prompted [22] by an absence of federal control over the project which has led

17. Note 5, supra.

18. See cases cited in notes 13, 14, supra.

19. Conservation Soc'y of Southern Vermont, Inc. v. Secretary of Transp. (II), 531 F.2d 637, 6 ELR 20207 (2d Cir. 1976).

20. Pub.L. No. 93–383, 88 Stat. 638, adding 42 U.S.C.A. § 5304(h); see 24 CFR pt. 58 (Environmental Review Procedures for the Community Development Block Grant Program).

21. 42 U.S.C.A. § 5304(h)(3)(D).

22. For the legislative history, see Senate Comm. on Banking, Housing,

the courts on many occasions to find no "federal action" triggering the NEPA requirements.[23] Permitting a stand-in for the responsible federal official, according to one view, is a poor substitute for compliance at the federal level, but it is not a bad substitute for no compliance at all.

Delegation is a sensitive topic and is supported by the notion that all wisdom does not reside within federal agencies undertaking major actions. Responsibility is a sensitive topic also. NEPA requires the decision-maker to evaluate effects and alternatives. Allowing somebody else, particularly an interested somebody else, to make these decisions for the responsible agency and record the rationale [24] jeopardizes the premise that "all agencies of the Federal Government" conform their charters to environmental values.

b. *The Multiple Agency Problem*

A second major issue of EIS drafting arises from the multifaceted project implicating the jurisdictions of several federal agencies. Construction of the trans-Alaska pipeline, for example, "required major federal actions involving the Department of the Interior, which issues permits to cross public lands, the Forest Service, which grants permits for locating terminal facilities on national forest lands, and the Corps of Engineers, which issues permits for crossing navigable streams, for taking gravel for streams, and for harbor work."[25] This relatively common situation of joint agency action can be treated in either one of three ways: [26] (1) each agency can comply separately; (2) the EIS can be jointly prepared; or (3) responsibility for compliance can be assigned to a lead agency.

The CEQ guidelines make allowance for "the possibility of joint preparation of a statement by all agencies concerned, or designation of a single 'lead agency' to assume supervisory responsibility for preparation of the statement." [27] CEQ is available to resolve disputes. Selection of the lead agency turns on "the time sequence in which the agencies become involved, the magnitude of their respective in-

and Urban Affairs, S.Rep. No. 383, 93d Cong., 2d Sess. (1974); House Comm. on Banking and Currency, H.R.Rep. No. 1114, 93d Cong., 2d Sess. (1974); Comm. of Conference, H.R. Rep. No. 1279, 93d Cong., 2d Sess. (1974). HUD's interpretation of its powers under the block grant program is found in Hearings on National Environmental Policy Act Oversight, Before the Subcomm. on Fisheries and Wildlife Conservation and the Environment of the House Comm. on Merchant Marine and Fisheries, H.R.Doc. No. 14, 94th Cong., 1st Sess. 109–12 (1975).

24. See Mowry v. Central Elec. Power Coop., 3 ELR 20843 (D.C.S.C.1973) (Rural Electrification Administration's conclusions on environmental effects rest entirely upon study by the applicant).

25. F. R. Anderson, NEPA in the Courts: A Legal Analysis of the National Environmental Policy Act 196 (1973).

26. Id. at 196–200.

27. 40 CFR § 1500.7(b).

23. § 7.6 above.

volvement, and their relative expertise with respect to the project's environmental effects." [28] This is consistent with the case law allowing statement preparation by the principal sponsoring agency and consultation by those peripherally involved.[29] The executive is given considerable discretion in parceling out responsibilities among different agencies.

Of the three ways of handling the multi-agency statement, it has been argued that separate compliance should be the preferred alternative since it is most likely to assure early and full satisfaction of NEPA responsibilities.[30] The distinct trend is to favor the lead agency approach. This promises efficiency and improved coordination among agencies. It can be abused if agency action with limited but decisive impact at the early stages is overlooked because the lead-agency acting later will comply eventually. The courts may step in to say there is more than one "responsible official." [31]

Who prepares the EIS within an agency and how it is to be prepared presents an intramural version of the lead agency problem. A similar tension exists between the desire for efficient treatment of environmental issues and the need to prevent an agency from shunting off NEPA matters onto a siding away from the mainstream of agency decision-making. Many courts interpreting NEPA express impatience with arguments that environmental issues should be left to a later day in another forum to be decided by somebody else. *Calvert Cliffs* insists that compliance to the "fullest extent possible" demands "that environmental issues be considered at every important stage in the decision-making process" where the decision can make a difference.[32] *SCRAP II*, on the other hand, assures the

28. Ibid; see Natural Resources Defense Council, Inc. v. Callaway, 524 F.2d 79, 86, 5 ELR 20640, 20643 (2d Cir. 1975) ("The dredging is being done for the benefit of the Navy, at the Navy's expense, and to fulfill a governmental responsibility entrusted to the Navy").

29. Upper Pecos Ass'n v. Stans, 452 F.2d 1233, 2 ELR 20085 (10th Cir. (1971), vacated 409 U.S. 1021 (1972), on remand 380 F.Supp. 191, 4 ELR 20037 (D.N.M.1973); Sierra Club v. Atomic Energy Comm'n, 4 ELR 20685 (D.D.C.1974); Hanly v. Mitchell (Hanly I), 460 F.2d 640, 645, 2 ELR 20216, 20218 (2d Cir. 1972), cert. denied 409 U.S. 990; Canal Authority of Florida v. Callaway, 4 ELR 20259, 20263 (M.D.Fla.1974) ("where the field involved is one in which more than one agency may have a subject matter interest on an environmental concern, generally speaking it is for the Executive Branch to say which one of them should be permitted to make the proposals for administrative action"), rev'd 489 F.2d 567, 4 ELR 20164 (5th Cir. 1974); Tierrasanta Community Council v. Richardson, 4 ELR 20309 (S.D.Cal.1973); Bozung v. Local Agency Formation Comm'n, 13 Cal.3d 263, 118 Cal.Rptr. 249, 529 P.2d 1017 (1975).

30. Anderson, The National Environmental Policy Act, in Environmental Law Institute, Federal Environmental Law 374–75 (E. L. Dolgin & G. P. Guilbert eds. 1974).

31. See Upper Pecos Ass'n v. Stans, 500 F.2d 17, 19, 4 ELR 20835, 20836 (10th Cir. 1974); Rhode Island Comm. on Energy v. General Serv. Administration, 397 F.Supp. 41, 60, 5 ELR 20685, 20691 (D.C.R.I.1975).

32. 146 U.S.App.D.C. at 42, 449 F.2d at 1118, 1 ELR at 20350.

executive wide autonomy in assigning compliance responsibilities.[33] The Supreme Court there focused on precisely the federal action taken—an ICC decision not to declare unlawful a small percentage rate increase (2.5) on its face applying equally to virgin and some recyclable commodities—and concluded that a thorough exploration of environmental effects of the underlying rate structure in a general rate proceeding was not required. The issues could be handled better, according to the Court, in a comprehensive rulemaking or perhaps even deferred to future proceedings involving challenges to rates on individual commodities.

NEPA requires "a detailed statement by the responsible official" in connection with a proposal for agency action. The "responsible official" is somewhere within the federal bureaucracy. Courts have a continuing interest in who he is, whether he is the right person for the job, and whether he has done the job.

§ 7.9 The Recurring Issues: What

Discussed above [1] are the general requirements of an adequate environmental impact statement and court enforcement of section 102 procedures. This section focuses more closely on the scope and content of a satisfactory impact statement. The subjects addressed are: (1) programmatic EIS'; (2) the segmentation problem; and (3) discussion of alternatives.

It is somewhat misleading to catalogue up and down votes on agency attempts at compliance without acknowledging the wide assortment of actions assessed—everything from the trans-Alaska pipeline to a new jail. Generalizations about adequacy should not be divorced from their context. The Supreme Court in *SCRAP II* made clear that determining what is required in a statement necessitates a careful definition of the "major federal action" being proposed.[2] Any analysis of the effects of an action, alternatives to it, and justifications for it turns on the initial understanding of the "action."

a. *Programmatic Impact Statements*

Understandably, the permissible scope and detail of a statement may differ depending on its function. The Act itself distinguishes between statements accompanying proposals for legislation and other major actions. Another important category of statements is the so-called programmatic or umbrella statement. They are comprehensive analyses of agency programs involving numerous actions

---

33. 422 U.S. at 326, 95 S.Ct. at 2357–59, 45 L.Ed.2d at 217–20.

1. §§ 7.3, 7.4 above.

2. Aberdeen & Rockfish R. R. v. Students Challenging Regulatory Agency Procedures (SCRAP II), 422 U.S. 289, 322, 95 S.Ct. 2336, 2357, 45 L.Ed.2d 191, 217, (1975); see Atchison, Topeka & Santa Fe Ry. v. Callaway, 382 F.Supp. 610, 5 ELR 20086 (D.C.D.C. 1974) (scope of the statement determined by purpose of the action).

with environmental effects. Examples include statements on the Upper Mississippi River Basin Study (Corps of Engineers), the Central Arizona Project (Bureau of Reclamation), Minimum Property Standards (HUD),[3] federal coal leasing (Bureau of Land Management),[4] contracts for stripmined coal (Tennessee Valley Authority),[5] the livestock grazing program (Bureau of Land Management),[6] the annual budget proposals for financing the National Wildlife Refuge System (National Park Service),[7] annual regulations on the sport hunting of migratory birds (Fish & Wildlife Service),[8] tanker subsidies (Maritime Administration),[9] the breeder reactor program (Atomic Energy Commission),[10] the Forest and Rangeland Renewable Resources Program (Forest Service)[11] and a series of overseas pest control endeavors (Agency for International Development).[12]

The CEQ guidelines encourage use of programmatic statements and explain how they are integrated with individual statements on specific actions: "In many cases broad program statements will be required in order to assess the environmental effects of a number of individual actions on a given geographical area (e. g., coal leases), or environmental impacts that are generic or common to a series of agency actions (e. g., maintenance or waste handling practices), or the overall impact of a large-scale program or chain of contemplated projects (e. g., major lengths of highway as opposed to small segments). Subsequent statements on major individual actions will be necessary where such actions have significant environmental impacts not adequately evaluated in the program statement." [13] The promise of umbrella statements is clear; they allow a comprehensive consideration, a broader look at alternatives and long-range effects,

---

3. The first three examples are cited or discussed in Anderson, The National Environmental Policy Act, in Environmental Law Institute, Federal Environmental Law 238, 335–38 (E. L. Dolgin & T. G. P. Guilbert eds. 1974).

4. Final Environmental Impact Statement on Proposed Federal Coal Leasing (undated).

5. See Natural Resources Defense Council, Inc. v. Tennessee Valley Authority, 367 F.Supp. 128, 3 ELR 20725 (E.D.Tenn.1973).

6. See Natural Resources Defense Council, Inc. v. Morton, 388 F.Supp. 829, 5 ELR 20327 (D.C.D.C.1974).

7. See Sierra Club v. Morton, 395 F. Supp. 1187, 5 ELR 20383 (D.C.D.C. 1975).

8. See Fund for Animals v. Frizzell, 174 U.S.App.D.C. 130, 530 F.2d 982, 6 ELR 20188 (1975) (per curiam).

9. See Environmental Defense Fund, Inc. v. Peterson, 4 ELR 20298 (D.C. D.C.1973) (by stipulation).

10. See Scientists' Inst. for Pub. Information v. Atomic Energy Comm'n (SIPI), 156 U.S.App.D.C. 395, 495 F. 2d 1079, 3 ELR 20525 (1973).

11. Final Environmental Statement on Forest & Rangeland Renewable Resources Program—1977 to 2020 (1973).

12. Environmental Defense Fund, Inc. v. Agency for Int'l Dev., 6 ELR 20120 (D.C.D.C.1975) (by stipulation).

13. 40 CFR § 1500.6(d).

an analysis of the forest not the trees.[14] They invite serious planning commitments. They permit a questioning or restatement of basic objectives and value judgments, assessments of progress and projections of future program directions, and a taking stock of what all this activity and expenditure has meant. They usually can be prepared at an earlier date and with more leisure and contemplation than individual statements under pressures of project momentum. They also permit a more realistic focus than individual project statements; at some point, for example, the Federal Highway Administration should discuss the progressive loss of productive farmland to road building but probably not in the context of assessing the impact of a small segment of highway that undoubtedly is going to be built.[15]

The risk of the umbrella statement is that it can serve to obscure the necessity for individualized statements as discrete parts of a project unfold. There is some evidence of programmatic essays being used to justify avoidance of individualized analyses.[16] The guidelines [17] point the way to a proper resolution: individual statements, building on the program EIS, should be required if later actions have significant impacts not adequately evaluated. Typically, individual action statements are required where localized effects not specifically addressed in the program statement are predictable (e. g., housing construction, waste disposal, and mining).

b. *Segmentation*

The issue of segmentation is related to the question of a properly drawn program statement. Impermissible segmentation, simply put, is the defining of a project too narrowly for purposes of environmental analyses. Typically, the segmentation issue raises no question about whether the Act applies; [18] there is an admitted proposal

14. Jones v. Lynn, 477 F.2d 885, 890–91, 3 ELR 20358, 20360 (1st Cir. 1973) ("one initial comprehensive study, which could be referred to and supplemented by less comprehensive individual studies for each parcel, would appear to reflect a better use of scarce resources . . . . It would not seem sensible to adopt the piecemeal approach which HUD seeks to adopt, whereby it will prepare a modified impact statement separately for each proposed construction akin to equating an appraisal of each tree to one of the forest").

15. See Iowa Citizens for Environmental Quality, Inc. v. Volpe, 487 F.2d 849, 852, 4 ELR 20056, 20058 (8th Cir. 1973).

16. Natural Resources Defense Council, Inc. v. Tennessee Valley Authority, 367 F.Supp. 128, 3 ELR 20725 (E.D.Tenn.1972) (accepting a programmatic statement in lieu of individual statements on TVA coal contracts); Port of Astoria v. Hodel, — F.Supp. —, —, 5 ELR 20657, 20659 (D.C.Or. 1975) (rejecting argument that Bonneville Power Administration's programmatic wholesale power EIS adequately assesses impact of direct sale to industrial customer; "This 'wholesale power' EIS deals primarily with the effect on energy consumption of varying wholesale price rates. It does not adequately consider the environmental effects of the sale of the industrial-grade power, nor could it have considered the recently signed Umatilla contract").

17. 40 CFR § 1500.6(d)(1).

18. § 7.7 above. This is not always true. Courts have no difficulty in interdicting segmentation into parts

for major federal action. Rather, the issue involves the scope of the EIS. Must it address anticipated effects and alternatives only in the narrow context of the precise proposal? Or must it inquire more deeply and range more widely, perhaps in the form of a programmatic statement, to assess related and spin-off proposals and longer range plans? The segmentation issue also is closely implicated in the question of timing of the preparation of an EIS;[19] elimination of segments from the scope of admittedly major federal actions permits a later preparation of statements for those segments, or perhaps dispenses with an EIS altogether if the segments never mature into a "proposal" for action. Courts weighing claims of impermissible segmentation must be sensitive as well to the question of remedies,[20] for the broader a project is defined for EIS purposes, the greater the potential reach of injunctive relief.

The rule against segmentation disallows excluding from consideration in the EIS segments of a project whose environmental fate is tied naturally to the proposed action. The language of the Act invites the segmentation inquiry. The EIS analysis must focus on the effects, and alternatives to, a "proposed action," which in turn requires an understanding of what the "action" is. Furthermore, the direction that the EIS address "any irreversible or irretrievable commitments of resources" involved in implementing the "proposed action" speaks directly to scope and content by calling for a discussion of how this action presages others.

In deciding whether a group of segments should be treated as a single project, courts look at "a multitude of factors, including the manner in which [the segments] were planned, their geographic locations, and the utility of each in the absence of the other."[21] The cases ask whether the excluded segment has "independent significance,"[22] whether there is a strong "nexus" between the two requiring concurrent EIS evaluation,[23] whether one part is a "mere com-

so minute as to avoid the "major federal action" characterization. See People of Enewetak v. Laird, 353 F. Supp. 811, 821, 3 ELR 20190, 20194 (1973); Natural Resources Defense Council, Inc. v. Grant, 341 F.Supp. 356, 367, 2 ELR 20185, 20188 (E.D. N.C.1972).

19. § 7.7 above.

20. § 7.10 below.

21. James River & Kanawha Canal Parks, Inc. v. Richmond Metropolitan Authority, 359 F.Supp. 611, 635, 3 ELR 20556, 20565 (E.D.Va.1973).

22. Appalachian Mtn. Club v. Brinegar, 394 F.Supp. 105, 115, 5 ELR 20311, 20314 (D.C.N.H.1975); see Indian Lookout Alliance v. Volpe, 484 F.2d 11, 19, 3 ELR 20739, 20742 (8th Cir. 1973) ("independent utility"); Movement Against Destruction v. Volpe, 361 F.Supp. 1360, 1384, 3 ELR 20667, 20672 (D.Md.1973), aff'd per curiam 500 F.2d 29, 4 ELR 20278 (4th Cir. 1974) (the relationship of several roads "may be so interrelated that no one road or part of a road can function as an efficient carrier of motor vehicles except in conjunction with the others").

23. Sierra Club v. Callaway (Wallisville-Trinity River), 499 F.2d 982, 990, 4 ELR 20731, 20735 (5th Cir. 1974); Farwell v. Brinegar, 3 ELR 20881, 20886 (W.D.Wis.1973) (finding an in-

ponent" or "increment" of the other,[24] whether the scope of the project addressed permits the evaluation of alternatives the Act requires.[25] The segmentation problem can be compounded when the excluded fragments are nonfederal in origin. A narrow statement of the rule, in a highway case where the issue commonly arises, is that "state and federal highway authorities may not avoid the requirements of federal law by splitting what is in essence a single, federal project into several segments and funding certain of those segments with state funds only." [26] The working premise, quite clearly, is that a suitable segment for funding or construction purposes might not be the appropriate piece to examine for purposes of environmental analyses. NEPA discourages the cramped look that segmentation represents.

In its grosser forms the rule against segmentation forbids a bifurcated treatment of a single stretch of highway arbitrarily chopped at the boundaries of a public park,[27] or of one stretch of road where the second segment is dictated by the first,[28] or of a single highway cut in half for purposes of analysis.[29] It has been extended to require planning of a more comprehensive nature in connection with discrete steps along the way. Impact statements thus have been required to discuss the Liquid Metal Fast Breeder Reactor program, not only the construction of a single demonstration plant; [30] a 280-mile anticipated superhighway, not only the 20 mile stretch under construction; [31] an entire urban renewal project, not only individual

sufficient "nexus" between the 21 mile highway project and the larger highway alleged).

24. Sierra Club v. Stamm, 507 F.2d 788, 793, 5 ELR 20209, 20211 (10th Cir. 1974); see Indian Lookout Alliance v. Volpe, 484 F.2d 11, 19, 3 ELR 20739, 20743 (8th Cir. 1973) ("the minimum length of state highway projects that are supported in part by federal funds must be extended to embrace projects of a nature and length that are supportable by logical termini at each end").

25. Comm. to Stop Route 7 v. Volpe, 346 F.Supp. 731, 740, 2 ELR 20446, 20449 (D.C.Conn.1972); Citizen for Balanced Environment & Transp., Inc. v. Volpe, 503 F.2d 601, 4 ELR 20798 (2d Cir. 1974) (per curiam); cf. Rhode Island Comm. on Energy v. General Serv. Administration, 397 F.Supp. 41, 5 ELR 20685 (D.C.R.I.1975) (must prepare EIS at a time when alternatives can be fairly evaluated).

26. James River & Kanawha Canal Parks, Inc. v. Richmond Metropolitan Authority, 359 F.Supp. 611, 634, 3 ELR 20556, 20565 (E.D.Va.1973).

27. Named Members of San Antonio Conservation Soc'y v. Texas Highway Dep't (I), 446 F.2d 1013, 1 ELR 20379 (5th Cir. 1971), cert. denied 406 U.S. 933 (1972).

28. Indian Lookout Alliance v. Volpe, 345 F.Supp. 1167, 3 ELR 20051 (S.D. Iowa 1972), aff'd 484 F.2d 11, 3 ELR 20739 (8th Cir. 1973).

29. Ecology Center of Louisiana, Inc. v. Coleman, 515 F.2d 860, 5 ELR 20488 (5th Cir. 1975) (finding factual issues over whether the two segments should be treated as a whole).

30. Scientists' Inst. for Pub. Information v. Atomic Energy Comm'n, (SIPI), 156 U.S.App.D.C. 395, 481 F.2d 1079, 3 ELR 20525 (1973).

31. Conservation Soc'y of Southern Vermont, Inc. v. Secretary of Transp. (I), 508 F.2d 927, 5 ELR 20068 (2d Cir. 1974), vacated and remanded 423 U.S. 809 (1975), on remand 531 F.2d

buildings within it;[32] the overall development of the upper Mississippi navigation system, not only a single dam and locks;[33] the cumulative impact of radioactive waste handling and disposal, not only the impact of wastes generated by a single nuclear power facility;[34] all likely proposals for ocean dumping at a specific site, not only the one recently approved.[35]

At the same time, courts are reluctant to permit the use of NEPA to compel comprehensive planning. The tests of independent significance or separate utility of the segmentation cases are not particularly difficult to satisfy. Thus, impact statements are sufficiently broad if they discuss a highway by-pass of a small community but not a major regional superhighway;[36] a 17 mile stretch of highway but not a canal project in the same vicinity;[37] the federally funded features of an airport expansion program but not a locally funded terminal and parking garage;[38] a single aqueduct and collection system but not the Central Utah Project or the Bonneville Unit consisting of a series of dams, reservoirs and aqueducts;[39] the New Melones Dam Project but not the more comprehensive Central Valley Project of which it is a

---

637, 6 ELR 20207 (2d Cir. 1976) (applying Aberdeen & Rockfish R. R. v. SCRAP (II), 422 U.S. 289, 95 S.Ct. 2336, 45 L.Ed.2d 191 (1975)).

32. Jones v. Lynn, 477 F.2d 885, 3 ELR 20358 (1st Cir. 1973).

33. Atchison, Topeka & Santa Fe Ry. v. Callaway, 382 F.Supp. 610, 5 ELR 20085 (D.C.D.C.1974).

34. Natural Resources Defense Council, Inc. v. Nuclear Regulatory Comm'n (Vermont Yankee), — U.S. App.D.C. —, 547 F.2d 633, 6 ELR 20615 (1976); Aeschliman v. Nuclear Regulatory Comm'n (Midland), — U.S.App.D.C. —, 547 F.2d 622, 6 ELR 20599 (1976); Natural Resources Defense Council, Inc. v. Nuclear Regulatory Comm'n (GESMO), 539 F.2d 824, 6 ELR 20513 (2d Cir. 1976).

35. Natural Resources Defense Council, Inc. v. Callaway, 524 F.2d 79, 5 ELR 20640 (2d Cir. 1975); see Prince George's County v. Holloway, 404 F. Supp. 1181, 6 ELR 20109 (D.C.D.C. 1975) (must consider other actions that might greatly increase the population at a site proposed for transfer of a Navy oceanographic program with civilian personnel); § 7.4 above (discussing the requirement that the EIS address cumulative effects).

36. Daly v. Volpe, 514 F.2d 1106, 5 ELR 20257 (9th Cir. 1975).

37. Friends of the Earth v. Coleman, 513 F.2d 295, 300, 5 ELR 20259, 20261 (9th Cir. 1975) ("While appellants may be correct that the presence of the highway excavations will most likely determine the path of the Peripheral Canal, if it is built, we do not find in this a sufficiently significant nexus to the highway excavations to warrant linking the two projects for EIS purposes").

38. Friends of the Earth v. Coleman, 518 F.2d 323, 329, 5 ELR 20428, 20429–30 (9th Cir. 1975) ("even though there may be substantial functional complementarity between the locally- and federally-funded projects, there is lacking the kind of functional interdependence between parts of the same project present in the highway construction cases").

39. Sierra Club v. Stamm, 507 F.2d 788, 791, 5 ELR 20209, 20210 (10th Cir. 1974) (treating as a question of fact the issue "as to whether the Strawberry System is a unit unto itself, and can stand on its own two feet, or, on the contrary, whether it is so intertwined with the rest of the Bonneville Unit and the Central Utah Project that it is but an increment of the larger plan").

Sec. 7.9   THE RECURRING ISSUES: WHAT   791

Southwest Energy Study;[41] the mostly completed Wallisville Dam Project but not the much larger Trinity River Project;[42] individual housing sites but not an entire scattered-site housing program;[43] the construction of the Teton Dam and Reservoir but not the second phase involving disposition of 100,000 acre feet of reservoir water;[44] the Meramec Park Lake Dam but not the entire comprehensive plan for flood control in the Meramec Basin.[45]

Specifying the proper scope of an EIS has emerged as one of the most difficult questions for the courts under NEPA. The form of the action may be important. Plaintiffs in *SIPI*[46] sought no injunctive relief and won a ruling compelling preparation of a programmatic EIS, whereas plaintiffs who seek to enjoin viable segments pending broader study are less likely to succeed.[47] Judicial intervention also is improbable where the facts suggest the agency plans to meet its NEPA commitments at a time and in a form that will allow full consideration of environmental values.[48] The Supreme Court decision in *Kleppe* affords the agencies broad discretion to trim the scope of their EIS', even by contradicting well defined ecological boundaries.[49]

Comprehensive planning is legitimately a part of NEPA, however, and it should not be sacrificed because agencies are too lazy or part;[40] several power plants individually but not a comprehensive

40. Environmental Defense Fund, Inc. v. Armstrong, 352 F.Supp. 50, 2 ELR 20735 (N.D.Cal.1972), supplemental opinion 356 F.Supp. 131, 139, 3 ELR 20294, 20297 (N.D.Cal.), aff'd 487 F.2d 814, 4 ELR 20001 (9th Cir. 1973), cert. denied 419 U.S. 1041 (1974) ("So long as each major federal action is undertaken individually and not as an indivisible, integral part of an integrated state-wide system, then the requirements of NEPA are determined on an individual major federal action basis").

41. Jicarilla Apache Tribe v. Morton, 471 F.2d 1275, 3 ELR 20045 (9th Cir. 1973).

42. Sierra Club v. Callaway, 499 F.2d 982, 990, 4 ELR 20731, 20735 (5th Cir. 1974) (the two projects "are not interdependent. The nexus between the projects is not such as to require an EIS evaluation of the Trinity Project as a condition precedent to an EIS evaluation of Wallisville. The Wallisville EIS should speak for itself. Wallisville is a separate viable entity. It should be examined on its own merits").

43. Nucleus of Chicago Homeowners Ass'n v. Lynn, 524 F.2d 225, 5 ELR 20698 (7th Cir. 1975), cert. denied 424 U.S. 967 (1976).

44. Trout Unlimited v. Morton, 509 F.2d 1276, 5 ELR 20151 (9th Cir. 1974).

45. Sierra Club v. Froehlke, 534 F.2d 1289, 6 ELR 20448 (8th Cir. 1976).

46. Scientists' Inst. for Pub. Information v. Atomic Energy Comm'n (SIPI), 156 U.S.App.D.C. 395, 481 F.2d 1079, 3 ELR 20525 (1973).

47. E. g., Sierra Club v. Stamm, 507 F.2d 788, 5 ELR 20209 (10th Cir. 1974).

48. E. g., Nucleus of Chicago Homeowners Ass'n v. Lynn, 524 F.2d 225, 5 ELR 20098 (7th Cir. 1975), cert. denied 424 U.S. 967 (1976).

49. Kleppe v. Sierra Club, 427 U.S. 390, 414, 96 S.Ct. 2718, 2732, 49 L.Ed.2d 576, 593 (1976) ("Even if environmental interrelationships could be shown conclusively to extend across basins and drainage areas, practical considerations of feasibility might well necessitate restricting the scope of comprehensive statements"). Compare § 7.7 n. 43 above.

result-oriented to develop a broader plan [50] or too myopic to understand the consequences of what they are doing. Rather than asking whether a particular segment has an "independent significance" [51] or whether it "can stand on its own two feet,"[52] the courts might better inquire into whether the projects and subjects sought to be joined reasonably should be considered as a whole for purposes of the analysis anticipated by NEPA. This should be determined by asking whether the commitment to implementation of certain projects is likely to lead to others and whether today's undertaking will restrict tomorrow's options. If so, the EIS should address those ramifications.

c. *Alternatives*

The requirement that the impact statement address "alternatives to the proposed action" [53] is crucial. A substantive evaluation of a project is utterly dependent upon an understanding of other possible courses of conduct. An adequate discussion of alternatives can bring out mitigation measures that can be made part of the project.[54] The first test of credibility in any environmental lawsuit is whether plaintiffs have a better idea of what should be done than does the challenged agency.

Natural Resources Defense Council, Inc. v. Morton [55] is recognized widely as laying down a rule of reason for the impact statement discussion of alternatives: "The requirement in NEPA of discussion as to reasonable alternatives does not require 'crystal ball' inquiry. Mere administrative difficulty does not interpose such flexibility into the requirement of NEPA as to undercut the duty of compliance 'to the fullest extent possible.' But if this requirement is not rubber, neither is it iron. The statute must be construed in the light of reason if it is not to demand what is, fairly speaking, not meaningfully possible, given the obvious, that the resources of energy and research —and time—available to meet the Nation's needs are not infinite." [56] And again: "There is reason for concluding that NEPA was not meant to require detailed discussion of the enviromental effects of

---

50. § 7.7 above.

51. Note 22, supra.

52. Sierra Club v. Stamm, 507 F.2d 788, 791, 5 ELR 20209, 20210 (10th Cir. 1974).

53. 42 U.S.C.A. § 4332(2)(C)(iii); see Jordan, Alternatives Under NEPA: Toward an Accommodation, 3 Ecology L.Q. 705 (1973).

54. See Sierra Club v. Froehlke (Wallisville-Trinity River), 359 F.Supp. 1289, 1343, 3 ELR 20248, 20268 (S.D. Tex.1973), rev'd on other grounds 499 F.2d 982, 4 ELR 20731 (5th Cir. 1974) ("The role that possible alternatives play in the environmental process is particularly critical because it is usually through this medium that mitigation measures may be discovered"); Environmental Defense Fund, Inc. v. Froehlke (Cache River), 473 F.2d 346, 351, 3 ELR 20001, 20003 (8th Cir. 1972).

55. 148 U.S.App.D.C. 5, 458 F.2d 827, 2 ELR 20029 (1972).

56. 148 U.S.App.D.C. at 15, 458 F.2d at 837, 2 ELR at 20034.

Sec. 7.9   THE RECURRING ISSUES: WHAT   793

'alternatives' put forward in comments when these effects cannot be readily ascertained and the alternatives are deemed only remote and speculative possibilities, in view of basic changes required in statutes and policies of other agencies—making them available, if at all, only after protracted debate and litigation not meaningfully compatible with the time-frame of the needs to which the underlying proposal is addressed." [57] In the context of the case, this meant that the EIS accompanying the Department of the Interior's proposal to lease 380,000 acres offshore for oil and gas development required a discussion of the alternatives of executive elimination of oil import quotas, increased onshore exploration and development, increased nuclear development, changes in FPC natural gas pricing and state prorationing, but not the development of oil shale and tar sands, desulfurization of coal, coal liquefaction and gasification, and geothermal resources.

NRDC v. Morton's rule of reason does not preclude a discussion of alternatives because implementation is dependent upon action by another agency or official; [58] or because they do not offer a complete solution to the problem; [59] or because they require radically new approaches to the agency mission; [60] or because they would take time to implement.[61] Courts stress the need for discussion of the alternatives of no action,[62] of projects drastically scaled down in size,[63] and of projects developed concurrently with mitigation measures designed to minimize adverse effects.[64] The EIS discussion of alternatives must make clear the reasons for the agency's choice,[65] address the

57. 148 U.S.App.D.C. at 15–16, 458 F.2d at 837–38, 2 ELR at 20034.

58. 148 U.S.App.D.C. at 12, 458 F.2d at 834, 2 ELR at 20032.

59. Montgomery v. Ellis, 364 F.Supp. 517, 526, 3 ELR 20845, 20847 (N.D.Ala.1973).

60. 148 U.S.App.D.C. at 13, 458 F.2d at 835, 2 ELR at 20033.

61. Cf. Carolina Environmental Study Group v. United States, 166 U.S.App.D.C. 416, 421, 510 F.2d 796, 801, 5 ELR 20181, 20182 (1975) (must consider alternatives "as they exist and are likely to exist"); Scientists' Inst. for Pub. Information v. Atomic Energy Comm'n (SIPI), 156 U.S.App.D.C. 395, 481 F.2d 1079, 3 ELR 20525 (1973).

62. E. g., Monroe County Conservation Council, Inc. v. Volpe, 472 F.2d 693, 3 ELR 20006 (2d Cir. 1972); Rankin v. Coleman, 394 F.Supp. 647, 658–59, 5 ELR 20626, 20630 (E.D.N.C.1975); Comm. to Stop Route 7 v. Volpe, 346 F.Supp. 731, 739, 2 ELR 20446, 20448 (D.C.Conn.1972); Environmental Defense Fund, Inc. v. Corps of Engineers (Gillham Dam), 325 F.Supp. 749, 761, 1 ELR 20130, 20142 (E.D.Ark.1971). See 40 CFR § 1500.8(4).

63. See Farwell v. Brinegar, 3 ELR 20881 (W.D.Wis.1973).

64. Simmans v. Grant, 370 F.Supp. 5, 18, 4 ELR 20197, 20202 (S.D.Tex.1974); Akers v. Resor, 3 ELR 20157, 20159 (W.D.Tenn.1972).

65. E. g., Rankin v. Coleman, 394 F.Supp. 647, 5 ELR 20226 (E.D.N.C.1975); Minnesota Pub. Interest Research Group v. Butz (II), 401 F.Supp. 1276, 6 ELR 20133 (D.Minn.1975), rev'd en banc 541 F.2d 1292, 6 ELR 20736 (8th Cir. 1976).

environmental effects of the alternatives,[66] compare them,[67] explain how future options may be narrowed by present decisions,[68] and respond to the recommendations of responsible critics.[69]

On the other hand, the EIS need not discuss, or need mention only briefly, remote and speculative alternatives, dependent upon major research breakthroughs or revolutionary legislative changes such as repeal of the antitrust laws;[70] those shown by the record to be unrealistic;[71] and those affecting only a miniscule part of the problem,[72] or with consequences indistinguishable from the action proposed.[73] A discussion of alternatives may be circumscribed by scientific realities[74] or impossibility of implementation,[75] and need not address options precisely as proposed by the plaintiff.[76]

The "detailed statement" requirement of section 102(2)(C) requires the production of information "sufficient to permit a reasoned choice of alternatives so far as environmental aspects are concerned."[77] It is not enough to make passing mention of possible alterna-

66. Davis v. Coleman, 521 F.2d 661, 681, 5 ELR 20633, 20640 (9th Cir. 1975) (finding no "discussion of the respective social, economic and environmental effects of those alternatives or their relative consistency with the urban planning" of the affected communities); Daly v. Volpe, 376 F. Supp. 987, 995, 4 ELR 20568, 20571 (W.D.Wash.1974), aff'd 514 F.2d 1106, 5 ELR 20257 (9th Cir. 1975) (finding alternatives adequately quantified).

67. Natural Resources Defense Council, Inc. v. Callaway, 524 F.2d 79, 92, 5 ELR 20640, 20648 (2d Cir. 1975).

68. See Sierra Club v. Morton (Sacramento Delta), 400 F.Supp. 610, 646 (N.D.Cal.1975).

69. Environmental Defense Fund, Inc. v. Froehlke (Cache River), 473 F.2d 346, 3 ELR 20001 (8th Cir. 1972).

70. Natural Resources Defense Council, Inc. v. Morton, 148 U.S.App.D.C. 5, 15, 458 F.2d 827, 837, 2 ELR 20029, 20034 (1972).

71. Life of the Land v. Brinegar, 485 F.2d 460, 471, 3 ELR 20811, 20815 (9th Cir. 1973); Environmental Defense Fund, Inc. v. Corps of Engineers (Tennessee-Tombigbee), 492 F.2d 1123, 1136, 4 ELR 20329, 20334 (5th Cir. 1974) ("The appropriateness of such a transportation scheme [involving various non-water alternatives] in the Tennessee-Tombigbee project area remains technically, economically and ecologically speculative").

72. Life of the Land v. Brinegar, 485 F.2d 460, 471, 3 ELR 20811, 20816 (9th Cir. 1973) (need not discuss alternatives that would have a "token effect").

73. Iowa Citizens for Environmental Quality, Inc. v. Volpe, 487 F.2d 849, 4 ELR 20056 (8th Cir. 1973); Citizens for Safe Power v. Nuclear Regulatory Comm'n, 173 U.S.App.D.C. 317, 524 F.2d 1291, 6 ELR 20095 (1975).

74. Cummington Preservation Comm. v. Federal Aviation Administration, 524 F.2d 241, 5 ELR 20696 (1st Cir. 1975).

75. Note 70, supra; Nucleus of Chicago Homeowners Ass'n v. Lynn, 524 F.2d 225, 5 ELR 20698 (7th Cir. 1975), cert. denied 424 U.S. 967 (1976).

76. Carolina Environmental Study Group v. United States, 166 U.S.App. D.C. 416, 421–22, 510 F.2d 796, 800–01, 5 ELR 20181, 20183 (1975); Sierra Club v. Lynn, 502 F.2d 43, 62, 4 ELR 20844, 20852 (5th Cir. 1974), cert. denied 421 U.S. 994 (1975).

77. Natural Resources Defense Council, Inc. v. Morton, 148 U.S.App.D.C. 5, 14, 458 F.2d 827, 836, 2 ELR 20029, 20033 (1972); see Sierra Club v. Froehlke (Meramec Park Dam), 534 F.2d 1289, 6 ELR 20448 (8th Cir. 1976).

Sec. 7.9   THE RECURRING ISSUES: WHAT   795

tives "in such a conclusory and uninformative manner that [the EIS] affords no basis for a comparison of the problems involved with the proposed project and the difficulties involved in the alternatives." [78] What is required is substance not superficiality. A greater depth and analysis may be required in discussing alternatives to projects that have been in the planning stages for many years; [79] or projects that are an "integral part of a coordinated plan to deal with a broad problem"; [80] or projects where other courses of conduct or mitigation measures are strongly indicated.[81] Conversely, less discussion and analysis may suffice for minor projects of limited scope and inflexible design. Thus, the longer range alternatives of rapid rail or bus transit need not be discussed in an EIS on a small segment of highway; [82] nor the alternatives of discouraging use of electric power and rate changes in an EIS on coal contracts; [83] nor the alternative of birth control in an EIS on a housing project.[84] At the same time, programmatic statements on transportation, energy and population policies would be remiss if they neglected to address rapid transit, inverted rates or birth control.

The consideration of alternatives under NEPA is enhanced greatly by section 102(2)(E),[85] which makes clear that all agencies of the federal government shall "study, develop and describe appropriate alternatives to recommended courses of action in any proposal which involves unresolved conflicts concerning alternative uses of available resources." An "unresolved conflict" occurs whenever an action can be achieved in one or more ways having different impacts on the environment.[86] It is clear that Section 102(2)(E) of NEPA requires

---

78. Monroe County Conservation Council v. Volpe, 472 F.2d 693, 697, 3 ELR 20006, 20007 (2d Cir. 1972).

79. Environmental Defense Fund, Inc. v. Froehlke (Cache River), 473 F.2d 346, 352, 3 ELR 20001, 20003 (8th Cir. 1972).

80. Natural Resources Defense Council, Inc. v. Morton, 148 U.S.App.D.C. 5, 13, 458 F.2d 827, 835, 2 ELR 20029, 20033 (1972).

81. Sierra Club v. Mason, 351 F.Supp. 419, 428, 2 ELR 20694, 20697 (D.C. Conn.1972).

82. Movement Against Destruction v. Volpe, 361 F.Supp. 1360, 1389, 3 ELR 20667, 20678 (D.Md.1973), aff'd per curiam 500 F.2d 29, 4 ELR 20278 (4th Cir. 1974).

83. Natural Resources Defense Council, Inc. v. Tennessee Valley Authority, 367 F.Supp. 128, 134, 3 ELR 20725, 20727 (E.D.Tenn.1973).

84. Cf. Nucleus of Chicago Homeowners Ass'n v. Lynn, 372 F.Supp. 147, 149, 4 ELR 20106, 20107 (N.D.Ill.1973), aff'd 524 F.2d 225, 5 ELR 20698 (7th Cir. 1975), cert. denied 424 U.S. 967 (1976) ("social and economic characteristics of the potential occupants of public housing as such are not decisive in determining whether an impact statement is required"); Sierra Club v. Lynn, 502 F.2d 43, 62, 4 ELR 20844, 20852 (5th Cir. 1974), cert. denied 422 U.S. 1049 (1975) (need not discuss alternative of eliminating federal development assistance program in an EIS discussing the environmental impact of a single development).

85. 42 U.S.C.A. § 4332(2)(E) (formerly 102(2)(D)).

86. Trinity Episcopal School Corp. v. Romney, 523 F.2d 88, 5 ELR 20497 (2d Cir. 1975).

federal decision-makers to weigh alternatives without regard to the need for preparing an impact statement under section 102(2)(C).[87] This distinction, often noted,[88] is probably of limited long-run significance under the Act.[89] The reason is that the threshold requirements of a "major Federal action" under section 102(2)(C) are set sufficiently low to cover virtually all agency actions of importance.[90] An alternatives study under section 102(2)(E) alone for minor action would cover much of the same ground that would be included in a normal EIS analysis.[91] Courts are likely to be tempted, therefore, to merge the duties required by the two provisions.[92]

---

87. Trinity Episcopal School Corp. v. Romney, supra note 86. Many courts have noted in dicta the differences between the references addressing alternatives in sections 102(2)(C)(iii) and 102(2)(E). See, e. g., Scenic Hudson Preservation Conference v. Federal Power Comm'n (II), 407 U.S. 926, 929 (1972) (Douglas, J., dissenting from denial of certiorari) (issues presented under both section 101(2)(C) and section 102(2)(E)); Environmental Defense Fund, Inc. v. Callaway (Truman Dam), 497 F.2d 1340, 1341, 4 ELR 20686, 20687 (8th Cir. 1974) (per curiam) (consideration of alternatives satisfied both EIS and section 102(2)(E) requirements); Environmental Defense Fund, Inc. v. Corps of Engineers (Tennessee-Tombigbee), 492 F.2d 1123, 1135, 4 ELR 20329, 20334 (5th Cir. 1974) (section 102(2)(E) supplemental and more extensive than § 102(2)(C)(iii) but EIS gave consideration to all appropriate alternatives); Environmental Defense Fund, Inc. v. Corps of Engineers (Gillham Dam), 470 F.2d 289, 296, 2 ELR 20740, 20743 (8th Cir. 1972), cert. denied 412 U.S. 931 (1973); Calvert Cliffs' Coord. Comm. v. Atomic Energy Comm'n, 146 U.S.App.D.C. 33, 38, 449 F.2d 1109, 1114, 1 ELR 20346, 20348 (1971), cert. denied 404 U.S. 942 (1972) (section 102(2)(E) exists beyond the EIS but with similar import); Maryland-Nat'l Capital Park & Planning Comm'n v. Schultz, 3 ELR 20702, 20703 (D.C.D.C.1973) (section 102(2)(E) overlaps section 102(2)(C)(iii); EIS complied with both); Conservation Council of North Carolina v. Froehlke, 340 F.Supp. 222, 227–28, 2 ELR 20155, 20157 (M.D.N.C. 1972), remanded 473 F.2d 664, 3 ELR 20132 (4th Cir. 1973); City of New York v. United States, 337 F.Supp. 150, 158, 2 ELR 20275, 20276 (E.D. N.Y.1972) (3 judge court); Nucleus of Chicago Homeowners Ass'n v Lynn, 524 F.2d 225, 232, 5 ELR 20698 (7th Cir. 1975), cert. denied 424 U.S. 967 (1976); Hanly v. Kleindienst (Hanly II), 471 F.2d 823, 834–35, 2 ELR 20717, 20723 (2d Cir. 1972), cert. denied 412 U.S. 908 (1973); Natural Resources Defense Council, Inc. v. Callaway, 524 F.2d 79, 93, 5 ELR 20640, 20647 (2d Cir. 1975) (describing the section 102(2)(E) duty as "independent of and of wider scope than the duty to file the EIS"); Illinois ex rel. Scott v. Butterfield, 396 F.Supp. 632, 641, 5 ELR 20587, 20591 (N.D.Ill.1975). But see Fayetteville Area Chamber of Commerce v. Volpe, 515 F.2d 1021, 1027, 2 ELR 20504, 20505 (4th Cir. 1975) (dictum) (combining standards under sections 102(2)(E) and 102(2)(C)(iii)).

88. See cases cited in note 87, supra.

89. One interesting situation where the distinction between the provisions might be significant is the Federal Water Pollution Control Act exemption of certain EPA actions from the impact statement requirements but arguably not from section 102(2)(E). See § 4.13 above.

90. § 7.6 above.

91. Note, Section 102(2)(D) of NEPA Requires Federal Decision-makers to Consider Alternative Means of Achieving Results Without Regard to the Need for an Environmental Impact Statement Under Section 102(2)(C), 64 Geo.L.J. 1153 (1976).

92. See Jordan, Alternatives Under NEPA: Toward an Accommodation, 3

Sec. 7.9   THE RECURRING ISSUES: WHAT   797

The important contribution of section 102(2)(E) is that it requires alternatives to be considered in depth. Section 102(2)(C) requires only a "detailed statement" on "alternatives to the proposed action" while section 102(2)(E) makes clear that the agencies must "study, develop and describe appropriate alternatives." A description calls for a detailed and comprehensible account of alternatives.[93] This only can enhance a reasoned choice among them and further an outsider's understanding of what that reasoning is. The requirement that agencies "develop" alternatives means they must elaborate upon them, carry them beyond the stage of a mere idea, and present them as mature proposals.[94] The "study" required by section 102(2)(E) goes beyond mere consideration to include feasibility studies, a cost-benefit analysis if appropriate, perhaps modeling, development of management plans and other research endeavors. The discussion of alternatives is the "linchpin" of the impact statement,[95] and section 102(2)(E) makes clear that agency consideration of alternatives must be sober, reasoned and thorough.

One issue of recurring significance is the extent to which an EIS can be sufficiently "detailed" or reasoned to the extent it delegates unresolved environmental problems for further study. While section 102(2)(E) suggests the agency must research alternatives, sections 102(2)(A) and (B) can be read as calling for research into both effects and alternatives.[96] Calls for further research create an obvious tension between the desire to get the project under way within a reasonable time and to avoid headlong commitments before proper investigation. The tension is reflected in the decisions; some courts accept study or research commitments in the EIS as being fully consistent with NEPA,[97] while others insist that the Act requires an-

Ecology L.Q. 705, 716 (1973). Compare F. R. Anderson, NEPA in the Courts 111 (1973) (considering the requirements to be wholly distinct).

93. Cf. Minnesota Pub. Interest Research Group v. Butz (II), 401 F.Supp. 1276, 1302, 6 ELR 20133, 20142 (D.C. Minn.1975), rev'd en banc 541 F.2d 1292, 6 ELR 20736 (8th Cir. 1976) (EIS must disclose clearly the policy that is being evaluated).

94. See Environmental Defense Fund, Inc. v. Corps of Engineers (Tennessee-Tombigbee), 492 F.2d 1123, 1136, 4 ELR 20329, 20334 (5th Cir. 1974) (permitting defendants to stop short of full development of transportation alternatives to waterway project because alternatives not shown to be appropriate or viable).

95. Monroe County Conservation Council v. Volpe, 472 F.2d 693, 697–98, 3 ELR 20006, 20008 (2d Cir. 1972).

96. § 7.5 above.

97. E. g., Warm Springs Dam Task Force v. Gribble, 378 F.Supp. 240, 4 ELR 20661 (N.D.Cal.), stay 417 U.S. 1301, aff'd per curiam 418 U.S. 910 (1974); Environmental Defense Fund, Inc. v. Corps of Engineers (Tennessee-Tombigbee), 348 F.Supp. 916, 938, 2 ELR 20536, 20545 (N.D.Miss.1972), aff'd 492 F.2d 1123, 4 ELR 20329 (5th Cir. 1974) (permitting dam project to proceed upon representations that Corps of Engineers would undertake an archeological survey and implement appropriate mitigation measures); Sierra Club v. Lynn, 502 F.

swers before action.[98] Several distinctions are likely to emerge; some questions are so central to the viability of a project—say, the safety of a dam—that adequate study is a prerequisite to action while peripheral issues suitably may be addressed over time. A commitment to future study may be taken more seriously if mechanisms exist to enforce the findings through mitigation, change of site, or otherwise. Short-term experiments or studies compatible with the time frame for preparing impact statements may be required under section 102(2)(C) whereas longer-term research is called for under other provisions of the Act not tied directly to specific agency actions.

§ 7.10 The Recurring Issues: Remedies

Precedents for just about every point of view can be invoked by courts fashioning equitable relief to correct NEPA violations. It is said, on the one hand, that violation of the statute is injury enough to justify an injunction [1] while, on the other, that traditional equitable grounds for relief still must be shown.[2] Authority can be found for

2d 43, 63, 4 ELR 20844, 20851 (5th Cir. 1974), cert. denied 422 U.S. 1049 (1975) (court sanctions a continuation of the project and a continuing study of effects); Sierra Club v. Morton, 510 F.2d 813, 828, 5 ELR 20249, 20255 (5th Cir. 1975) (court sanctions continuing study after sale of offshore oil leases; "where shortcomings in a major federal action can be corrected or minimized when and if they surface, the EIS upon which such action is authorized may meet NEPA's objectives with some less detail and analysis than would otherwise be required").

98. E. g., Brooks v. Volpe, 350 F.Supp. 269, 279, 2 ELR 20704, 20708 (W.D. Wash.1972) (the "detail" required in an EIS must flow from research) (court orders defendants to show cause why construction should not be enjoined pending compliance); Montgomery v. Ellis, 364 F.Supp. 517, 528, 3 ELR 20845, 20849 (N.D.Ala. 1973) ("NEPA requires each agency to undertake research needed adequately to expose environmental harms and, hence, to appraise available alternatives") (project enjoined pending preparation of an adequate EIS); Environmental Defense Fund, Inc. v. Hardin, 325 F.Supp. 1401, 1403 (D.D.C.1971) (interpreting section 102(2)(A) as making "the completion of an adequate research program a prerequisite to agency action . . . .

The Act envisions that program formulation will be directed by research results rather than that reseach programs will be designed to substantiate programs already decided upon") (dictum) (EIS found to be adequate); Natural Resources Defense Council, Inc. v. Callaway, 524 F.2d 79, 5 ELR 20640 (2d Cir. 1975) (inadequate discussion of alternatives in EIS; further ocean dumping prohibited pending compliance; dissent argues that a two-year monitoring program of the site would permit necessary corrective action); Rankin v. Coleman, 394 F.Supp. 647, 658, 5 ELR 20626, 20630 (E.D.N.C.1975) (highway project enjoined for inadequate EIS on effects and alternatives; alternatives must be "affirmatively studied").

1. E. g., Environmental Defense Fund, Inc. v. Froehlke (Truman Dam), 477 F.2d 1033, 3 ELR 20383 (8th Cir. 1973) (dictum); Lathan v. Volpe (I), 455 F.2d 1111, 1116, 1 ELR 20602, 20606 (9th Cir. 1971); Sierra Club v. Coleman, 405 F.Supp. 53, 6 ELR 20051 (D.C.D.C.1975); Atchison, Topeka & Santa Fe Ry. v. Callaway, 382 F.Supp. 610, 623, 5 ELR 20086, 20093 (D.C. D.C.1974).

2. Canal Authority of Florida v. Callaway, 489 F.2d 567, 578, 4 ELR 20164, 20170 (5th Cir. 1974) (NEPA does not alter traditional tests for a pre-

Sec. 7.10 THE RECURRING ISSUES: REMEDIES 799

the proposition that environmental quality and health are preferred values entitled to special judicial protection,[3] while none other than Chief Justice Burger has warned that courts should not be led to exercise equitable powers "loosely or casually whenever a claim of 'environmental damage' is asserted." [4] These mutually discordant themes reflect a recognition of new rights in environmental cases and enforcement of them by the time tested discretionary techniques of the chancellor.

As in nuisance cases, courts construing NEPA often suggest the relief afforded is a product of balancing equities or balancing hardship.[5] This certainly does not mean that injunctive relief is dependent upon plaintiff showing that the injury occasioned by going ahead with the project is greater on a cost-benefit basis than the loss occasioned by delay. Indeed, the cases reflect a determination that "[c]onsiderations of administrative difficulty, delay or economic cost will not suffice to strip [section 102] of its fundamental importance." [6] The remedy presumptively available in all cases is the injunction to maintain the *status quo;* the project is stopped in its tracks until studies are concluded, disclosures made, and consultation completed. Forcing the agencies to mark time until they comply is thought to be the best way to assure NEPA's purposes of eliminating environmental damage by accident or coincidence and allowing it only by design and after justification with consequences fully understood. Thus agencies have been enjoined from pursuing a wide range of activities pending compliance with NEPA—approving filings,[7] acquiring rights of way,[8]

liminary injunction); Ohio ex rel. Brown v. Callaway, 497 F.2d 1235, 1240, 4 ELR 20492, 20495 (6th Cir. 1974) (general principles of equity apply in NEPA cases).

3. Environmental Defense Fund, Inc. v. Ruckelshaus, 142 U.S.App.D.C. 74, 87, 439 F.2d 584, 597, 1 ELR 20059, 20063–64 (1971); cf. Stockslager v. Carroll Elec. Coop. Corp., 528 F.2d 949, 6 ELR 20388 (8th Cir. 1976) (NEPA is within the "expressly authorized" exception to 28 U.S.C.A. § 2283 prohibiting injunction against state proceedings).

4. Aberdeen & Rockfish R. R. v. SCRAP (I), 409 U.S. 1207, 1217–18, 93 S.Ct. 1, 6–7, 34 L.Ed.2d 21, 28–29 (1972) (Burger, C. J., sitting as Circuit Justice) (denying injunction pending appeal).

5. E. g., Environmental Defense Fund, Inc. v. Armstrong (New Melones Dam), 352 F.Supp. 50, 60, 2 ELR 20735, 20739 (N.D.Cal.1972); Minnesota Pub. Interest Research Group v. Butz (I), 358 F.Supp. 584, 625, 3 ELR 20457, 20474–76 (D.C.Minn.1973), aff'd 498 F.2d 1314, 4 ELR 20700 (8th Cir. 1974); Comm. for Green Foothills v. Froehlke, 3 ELR 20861, 20866 (N.D. Cal.1973).

6. Calvert Cliffs' Coord. Comm. v. Atomic Energy Comm'n, 146 U.S.App. D.C. 33, 39, 449 F.2d 1109, 1115, 1 ELR 20346, 20349 (1971); see Environmental Defense Fund, Inc. v. Froehlke (Truman Dam), 477 F.2d 1033, 1037, 3 ELR 20383, 20385 (8th Cir. 1973).

7. Scenic Rivers Ass'n v. Lynn, 520 F.2d 240, 5 ELR 20536 (10th Cir. 1975), rev'd 427 U.S. 390, 96 S.Ct. 2430, 49 L.Ed.2d 205 (1976).

8. Rankin v. Coleman, 394 F.Supp. 647, 5 ELR 20626 (E.D.N.C.1975).

transferring facilities and personnel,[9] authorizing increases in airport trafic,[10] issuing permits,[11] dumping dredge spoils,[12] and so on.

In context, the balancing of equities in NEPA cases means nothing more than that the courts will consider all the circumstances in fashioning appropriate relief.[13] Thus broad injunctions bringing work to a halt are more likely if the project is in its early stages not yet beyond the point of no return,[14] if alternatives are clearly viable,[15] if serious economic,[16] social,[17] or environmental [18] harm is threatened, if defendants have been unusually recalcitrant or stubborn,[19] or if the damage threatened is irreparable.[20] On the other hand, injunctions more narrowly drawn or no relief at all may be forthcoming if the alleged environmental harm is nonexistent or minimal,[21] if the

9. Prince George's County v. Holloway, 404 F.Supp. 1181, 6 ELR 20109 (D.D.C. 1975) (the decree also forbade the Navy from requiring civilian personnel to transfer involuntarily); Breckinridge v. Schlesinger, —— F.Supp. ——, 6 ELR 20111 (E.D.Ky.1975), rev'd 537 F.2d 864, 6 ELR 20597 (6th Cir. 1976); McDowell v Schlesinger, 404 F.Supp. 221, 6 ELR 20224 (W.D.Mo. 1975) (injunction modified for national security purposes to permit transfer of certain units).

10. Illinois ex rel. Scott v. Butterfield, 396 F.Supp. 632, 5 ELR 20587 (N.D. Ill.1975).

11. Sierra Club v. Morton (Sacramento Delta), 400 F.Supp. 610 (N.D.Cal. 1975).

12. Natural Resources Defense Council, Inc. v. Callaway, 524 F.2d 79, 5 ELR 20640 (2d Cir. 1975).

13. A good example of the range of remedial discretion is found in Conservation Soc'y of Southern Vermont v. Secretary of Transp. (I), 508 F.2d 927, 5 ELR 20068 (2d Cir. 1974), vacated 423 U.S. 809 (1975) (simultaneously affirming in companion cases the grant and denial of injunctive relief by the district courts).

14. Steubing v. Brinegar, 511 F.2d 489, 5 ELR 20183 (2d Cir. 1975).

15. Steubing v. Brinegar, supra note 14; Sierra Club v. Mason, 351 F.Supp. 419, 428, 2 ELR 20694, 20697 (D.C. Conn.1972) ("numerous techniques exist for substantially reducing the adverse environmental impact of dredging and dumping operations").

16. Atchison, Topeka & Santa Fe Ry. v. Callaway, 382 F.Supp. 610, 624, 5 ELR 20086, 20093 (D.C.D.C.1974).

17. Prince George's County v. Holloway, 404 F.Supp. 1181, 6 ELR 20109 (D.D.C.1975); Breckinridge v. Schlesinger, —— F.Supp. ——, 6 ELR 20111 (E.D.Ky.1975), rev'd 537 F.2d 864, 6 ELR 20597 (6th Cir. 1976).

18. E. g., Steubing v. Brinegar, 511 F.2d 489, 5 ELR 20183 (2d Cir. 1975).

19. Brooks v. Volpe, 350 F.Supp. 269, 283, 2 ELR 20704 20709 (W.D.Wash. 1972) (defendants "have stubbornly refused to comply with the letter and spirit of the law"); City of New York v. United States, 337 F.Supp. 150, 160, 2 ELR 20275, 20277 (E.D.N.Y.1972) ("to permit an agency to ignore its duties under NEPA with impunity because we have serious doubts that its ultimate decision will be affected by compliance would subvert the very purpose of the Act and encourage further administrative laxity in this area").

20. Lathan v. Volpe (I), 455 F.2d 1111, 1117, 1 ELR 20602, 20603 (9th Cir. 1971) (this is "one of those comparatively rare cases in which, unless the plaintiffs receive *now* whatever relief they are entitled to, there is danger that it will be of little value to them or to anyone else when finally obtained") (emphasis in original).

21. E. g., Public Interest Research Group of Michigan v. Brinegar, 517 F. 2d 917, 918, 5 ELR 20502 (6th Cir. 1975); Environmental Defense Fund, Inc. v. Froehlke (Truman Dam), 477 F.2d 1033, 1036, 3 ELR 20383, 20384

resources at stake are not environmentally unique,[22] if the EIS contains only "relatively minor defects,"[23] if project delay could result in safety hazards,[24] if sizeable costs would be incurred for little apparent reason,[25] if the project is in an advanced stage of completion,[26] if the outcome is virtually preordained,[27] or if maximum mitigation efforts have been undertaken.[28] Most cases involve a mix of considerations that are weighed in drafting a particular decree; compromises in result are common.

NEPA has twin objectives of protecting the environment and improving decision-making. This supports an argument that all further work on a project should cease pending reconsideration in light of the data adduced by NEPA processes.[29] Several NEPA injunctions reflecting this view have enjoined virtually all activity in connection with a project including a great deal not remotely threatening the integrity of the environment.[30] Many courts, on the other hand,

(8th Cir. 1973); Maddox v. Bradley, 345 F.Supp. 1255, 1259, 2 ELR 20404, 20405 (N.D.Tex.1972).

22. E. g., Conservation Soc'y of Southern Vermont v. Secretary of Transp. (I), 508 F.2d 927, 937, 5 ELR 20068, 20073 (2d Cir. 1974), vacated 423 U. S. 809 (1975).

23. Environmental Defense Fund, Inc. v. Armstrong (New Melones Dam), 356 F.Supp. 131, 134, 3 ELR 20294, 20295 (N.D.Cal.1973), aff'd 487 F.2d 814, 4 ELR 20001 (9th Cir.), cert. denied 419 U.S. 1041 (1974).

24. Comm. for Green Foothills v. Froehlke, 3 ELR 20861, 20867 (N.D.Cal.1973) (citing public health considerations as a reason for refusing to enjoin use of wetlands area as a landfill); Environmental Defense Fund, Inc. v. Armstrong (New Melones Dam), 356 F.Supp. at 134, 3 ELR at 20296 (N.D.Cal.1973) (increased flood hazard cited as reason for not interfering with construction of a dam); cf. Concerned About Trident v. Rumsfeld, —— U.S.App.D.C. ——, —— F.2d ——, 6 ELR 20787 (1976) (allowing construction of Trident submarine support site despite EIS deficiencies).

25. Environmental Defense Fund, Inc. v. Froehlke (Truman Dam), 477 F.2d 1033, 3 ELR 20383 (8th Cir. 1973).

26. Conservation Soc'y of Southern Vermont v. Secretary of Transp. (I), 508 F.2d 927, 936–37, 5 ELR 20068, 20073 (2d Cir. 1974), vacated 423 U. S. 809 (1975); Jones v. District of Columbia Redev. Land Agency, 162 U.S.App.D.C. 366, 499 F.2d 502, 4 ELR 20479 (1974).

27. Conservation Soc'y of Southern Vermont v. Secretary of Transp. (I), supra note 26.

28. Conservation Soc'y of Southern Vermont v. Secretary of Transp. (I), 508 F.2d at 937 n.55, 5 ELR at 20073 n.55; Comm. for Green Foothills v. Froehlke, 3 ELR 20861 (N.D.Cal.1973) (50 acre wildlife mitigation area pertinent in denying injunction against the use of marshland as a sanitary landfill); Sierra Club v. Lynn, 502 F.2d 43, 4 ELR 20844 (5th Cir. 1974), cert. denied 421 U.S. 994 (1975).

29. Jones v. District of Columbia Redev. Land Agency, 162 U.S.App.D.C. 366, 377, 499 F.2d 502, 513, 4 ELR 20479, 20483 (1974).

30. E. g., Montgomery v. Ellis, 364 F. Supp. 517, 535, 3 ELR 20845, 20853 (N.D.Ala.1973) (enjoined "from constructing, installing, or further authorizing or financing any stream modification or channelization of . . . Blue Eye Creek pursuant to the so-called Blue Creek Watershed Project . . . or otherwise"); Nelson v. Butz, 337 F.Supp. 819, 4 ELR 20840 (D.C.Minn.1974); Natural Resources Defense Council, Inc. v. Grant, 341 F.Supp. 356, 2 ELR 20185 (E.D. N.C.1972); Nolop v. Volpe, 333 F. Supp. 1364, 1 ELR 20617 (D.C.S.D. 1971).

fashion NEPA injunctions mostly to protect the environmental integrity of the site.[31] Typically, these decrees forbid the clearcutting of trees, removal of brush and ground cover, stripping away and destruction of topsoil, and "any other construction activity which would alter the natural environment of the project area."[32] They might permit certain planning activities,[33] the ordering and assembling of materials and work crews,[34] dam construction and building on land already cleared,[35] the completion of work under old contracts but not the entering into new contracts,[36] consummating new design contracts but not new construction contracts,[37] some road-surfacing, map making and reporting activities,[38] road and cemetery relocations and voluntary property acquisitions,[39] cleanup work involved in terminating the existing ditching contract and the removal of construction debris from the river,[40] or completion of a small part of the project.[41] Courts

31. E. g., Ohio ex rel. Brown v. Callaway, 497 F.2d 1235, 4 ELR 20492 (6th Cir. 1974), aff'g 364 F.Supp. 296, 3 ELR 20892 (S.D.Ohio 1973); Arkansas Community Organization for Reform Now v. Brinegar, 398 F.Supp. 685 (E.D.Ark.1975) (enjoining further construction and restricting future land purchases only on the eastern half of a highway project); Arlington Coalition on Transp. v. Volpe, 458 F.2d 1323, 2 ELR 20162 (4th Cir. 1972), cert. denied 409 U.S. 1000; Civic Improvement Comm. v. Volpe, 2 ELR 20170 (W.D.N.C.1972); Environmental Defense Fund, Inc. v. Froehlke (Cache River), 3 ELR 20519 (E.D.Ark.1973) (on remand); Romulus v. Wayne, 392 F.Supp. 578, 5 ELR 20302 (E.D.Mich.1975).

32. Ohio ex rel. Brown v. Callaway, 497 F.2d 1235, 1241, 4 ELR 20492, 20494 (6th Cir. 1974).

33. Environmental Defense Fund, Inc. v. Froehlke (Cache River), 3 ELR 20519 (E.D.Ark.1973) (on remand).

34. Environmental Defense Fund, Inc. v. Armstrong (New Melones Dam), 352 F.Supp. 50, 60–61, 2 ELR 20735, 20739 (N.D.Cal.1973).

35. Conservation Council of North Carolina v. Froehlke, 473 F.2d 644, 3 ELR 20132 (4th Cir. 1973).

36. Brooks v. Volpe, 350 F.Supp. 287, 290, 3 ELR 20211, 20213 (W.D.Wash. 1972); Environmental Defense Fund, Inc. v. Froehlke (Cache River), 473 F.2d 346, 3 ELR 20001 (8th Cir. 1972) (remanding for a determination whether to allow contracting despite a general injunction).

37. E. g., Smith v. Cookeville, 381 F. Supp. 100, 112, 5 ELR 20015, 20021 (M.D.Tenn.1974) (defendants allowed to finalize plans and receive bids subject to completion of final EIS).

38. Environmental Defense Fund, Inc. v. Tennessee Valley Authority (Tellico Dam), 339 F.Supp. 806, 2 ELR 20044 (E.D.Tenn.1972), aff'd 468 F.2d 1164, 2 ELR 20726 (6th Cir.).

39. Environmental Defense Fund, Inc. v. Froehlke (Truman Dam), 477 F.2d 1033, 1036, 3 ELR 20383, 20384 (8th Cir. 1973) (affirming injunction allowing defendants "to continue certain on-going construction activities, road relocations, cemetery relocations, voluntary property acquisitions, and design contracts" pending the filing of a final EIS).

40. Environmental Defense Fund, Inc. v. Froehlke (Cache River), 3 ELR 20519 (E.D.Ark.1973) (on remand).

41. Soc'y for Protection of New Hampshire Forests v. Brinegar, 381 F.Supp. 282, 5 ELR 20004 (D.C.N.H.1974) (enjoining federal and state participation in a highway project with the exception of "a single bridge across the Connecticut River"); cf. Arkansas Community Organization for Reform Now v. Brinegar, 398 F.Supp. 685 (E. D.Ark.1975) (enjoining construction and land purchases on eastern half of a highway project).

Sec. 7.10   THE RECURRING ISSUES: REMEDIES   803

are divided on whether to permit condemnation proceedings [42] or the destruction of properties already condemned pending compliance with NEPA.[43]

The difficulty of drawing lines between permissible and impermissible activities pending NEPA compliance reflects the perplexing factor of project momentum. Obviously, the assembling of work crews, letting of contracts, completion of planning or materials commitments, and continuation of condemnations all are practical reasons for ultimate approval even in the rare case where courts insist that work allowed despite NEPA violations will not be weighed in fashioning a permanent decree.[44] One can question the utility, if not the good faith, of an agency reconsidering one of its partially completed projects. A late statement and speedy implementation may allow a *fait accompli* and reduce available relief to a charade—nothing more than a momentary pause in the course of the project.[45] Stopping a project well along seems equally futile from the builder's view; offering a plaintiff meaningless relief is no less absurd because the defendant has to pay for it. While this problem will not be easily solved, it does point up the need for early statements and strong enforcement at an early date.[46]

The ultimate constraint upon those who proceed contrary to law is not the threat of a temporary halt but an order to undo what was done. This occurs in common law nuisance cases [47] and in many of the dredge and fill cases.[48] Dismantling a structure built in violation of NEPA, however, is said to be an extreme step only remotely

---

42. Compare Gage v. Commonwealth Edison Co., 356 F.Supp. 80, 3 ELR 20068 (N.D.Ill.1972) (allowing it) (on ground, however, that no federal action was involved) with Keith v. Volpe, 352 F.Supp. 1324, 2 ELR 20425 (C.D.Cal.1972), aff'd 506 F.2d 696, 4 ELR 20809 (9th Cir. 1974), cert. denied 420 U.S. 908 (1975) (disallowing it).

43. Compare Sansom Comm. v. Lynn 382 F.Supp. 1242, 1245, 5 ELR 20093, 20094 (E.D.Pa.1974) (concluding that agency inaction would pose "an imminent threat to the public safety and welfare") with Boston Waterfront Residents Ass'n, Inc. v. Romney, 343 F.Supp. 89, 91, 2 ELR 20359, 20360 (D.C.Mass.1972) (alternatives of preservation and rehabilitation "permanently foreclosed once [buildings] have been razed").

44. Environmental Defense Fund, Inc. v. Armstrong (New Melones Dam), 356 F.Supp. 131, 134, 3 ELR 20294, 20295 (N.D.Cal.1973), aff'd 487 F.2d 814, 4 ELR 20001 (9th Cir.), cert. denied 419 U.S. 1041 (1974); cf. Environmental Defense Fund, Inc. v. Froehlke (Truman Dam), 477 F.2d 1033, 1037, 3 ELR 20383, 20384–85 (8th Cir. 1973) (amount of money expended during period of limited injunction is not sufficient to affect balance of costs and benefits in determining whether project should continue after final EIS is prepared).

45. Romulus v. Wayne, 392 F.Supp. 578, 596, 5 ELR 20302, 20308 (E.D. Mich.1975) ("Unless [the project is] enjoined the Court, on ultimate review, may be faced with a *fait accompli* insofar as construction of the runway is concerned . . . .").

46. §§ 7.7, 7.9 above.

47. § 2.11 above.

48. §§ 4.5, 4.6 above.

possible or conceivable.[49] The *status quo* was maintained in one case by requiring the removal of waters allowed to intrude into the Rainbow Bridge National Monument,[50] but the order ultimately was reversed on other grounds.[51] Despite NEPA violations the courts also did not require the voiding of a grant of the Economic Development Administration for the construction of a roadway through the Santa Fe Forest although requiring the applicant to start over would have assured a new look at the project unencumbered by past indiscretions.[52] The Supreme Court's opinion in *SCRAP II*[53] also indicates NEPA violations can be corrected without a serious retracing of steps and repudiation of prior actions.

Courts ordering compliance with the Act may go into specifics on how an impact statement is prepared and what it must contain. Timetables may be established for preparing a statement, circulating it, the gathering of comments, and submitting it to CEQ.[54] Courts may order hearings,[55] the publication of detailed notice in lieu of hearings,[56] specific consultations, or the seeking out of certain information.[57] Agencies may be required to conduct research programs and report the results.[58] Other extensive reporting obligations also may be imposed;[59] requiring notice to plaintiffs of future proposed

---

49. Compare § 4.5 above (Rivers and Harbors Act).

50. Friends of the Earth v. Armstrong, 3 ELR 20235 (D.Ut.), vacated 485 F.2d 1, 3 ELR 20752 (10th Cir. 1973).

51. Friends of the Earth v. Armstrong, 485 F.2d 1, 3 ELR 20752 (10th Cir. 1973).

52. Upper Pecos Ass'n v. Stans (II), 500 F.2d 17, 4 ELR 20835 (10th Cir. 1974).

53. 422 U.S. 289, 321, 95 S.Ct. 2336, 2356, 45 L.Ed.2d 191, 216 (1975).

54. E. g., Environmental Defense Fund, Inc. v. Froehlke (Truman Dam), 348 F.Supp. 338, 346, 2 ELR 20620, 20623 (W.D.Mo.1972), 368 F.Supp. 231, 237, 4 ELR 20062, 20064 (W.D.Mo.1973) (approving a supplemental EIS), aff'd 497 F.2d 1340, 4 ELR 20686 (8th Cir. 1974); Jones v. District of Columbia Redev. Land Agency, 162 U.S.App. D.C. 366, 378, 499 F.2d 502, 514, 4 ELR 20479, 20484 (1974) (finding no abuse of discretion in district court's decision to allow agencies "to telescope their compliance").

55. E. g., Saunders v. Washington Metropolitan Area Transit Authority, 159 U.S.App.D.C. 55, 486 F.2d 1315, 4 ELR 20001 (1973); Rankin v. Coleman, 394 F.Supp. 647, 661, 5 ELR 20626, 20632 (E.D.N.C.1975); Keith v. Volpe, 352 F.Supp. 1324, 1340, 2 ELR 20425, 20431 (C.D.Cal.1972), aff'd 506 F.2d 696, 4 ELR 20809 (9th Cir. 1974), cert. denied 420 U.S. 908 (1975).

56. Hanly v. Kleindienst (Hanly II), 471 F.2d 823, 836, 3 ELR 20016, 20020 1972), cert. denied 412 U.S. 908 (1973); Daly v. Volpe, 350 F.Supp. 252, 261, 3 ELR 20032, 20033 (W.D. Wash.1972).

57. E. g., Sierra Club v. Froehlke (Wallisville-Trinity River), 359 F. Supp. 1289, 1383, 3 ELR 20248, 20285 (S.D.Tex.1973), rev'd on other grounds 499 F.2d 982, 4 ELR 20731 (5th Cir. 1974); Sierra Club v. Butz, 6 ELR 20369 (N.D.Cal.1975) (by stipulation).

58. E. g., Daly v. Volpe, 350 F.Supp. 252, 261, 3 ELR 20032, 20033 (W.D. Wash.1972); cf. Concerned Residents of Buck Hill Falls v. Grant, 388 F. Supp. 394, 5 ELR 20207 (M.D.Pa. 1975), rev'd 537 F.2d 29 (3d Cir. 1976) (research and planning on effects and mitigation inadequate).

59. E. g., Sierra Club v. Lynn, 502 F.2d 43, 66–67, 4 ELR 20844, 20851 (5th

Sec. 7.10 THE RECURRING ISSUES: REMEDIES 805

actions is a common provision.[60] One useful type of remedy sought as a matter of course by many plaintiffs is a court order requiring an agency to correct a defective EIS by addressing specific topics or alternatives, even to the point of conducting research to answer the questions raised. This technique puts disputed subjects sharply in focus and forces the agency to respond to claimed deficiencies both in the statement and in the underlying project. Examples of considerable significance for the ultimate substantive review of projects are orders requiring an agency to spell out precisely mitigation measures[61] and to recalculate cost-benefit assumptions using corrected hypotheses.[62] One court ordered the parties to use their "best efforts" to prepare jointly a plan on how a highway could be completed "with as little interference [as possible] with the patterns of life and society, and the total human environment."[63] They were obliged to consider better landscaping, soundproofing and pedestrian walkways.

Substantive changes brought about by NEPA, measured in terms of projects modified or abandoned, are not unimpressive.[64] It is the nature of the judicial process, however, that these changes are rarely ordered directly into being. They are usually the result of reconsideration, often prompted by judicial intervention stopping short of direct compulsion. Notwithstanding this, the substantive backbone of NEPA ultimately is dependent upon the courts' willingness to order agencies to change their plans or to abandon some pursuits. The increase of judicial activism witnessed during the formative years of

Cir. 1974), cert. denied 421 U.S. 994 (1975) (discussing district court order to file with the court semi-annual reports regarding a development on top of an aquifer, its effect, and environmental control measures being implemented) (court disapproves exercise of continuing jurisdiction after a finding for defendants); cf. United States v. Washington, 384 F.Supp. 312 (W.D.Wash.1974), aff'd 520 F.2d 676, 5 ELR 20552 (9th Cir.), cert. denied 423 U.S. 1086 (1975) (interpreting treaty provisions reserving fishing rights to Indian tribal fishermen and requiring various reports from state agencies).

60. E. g., Conservation Council of North Carolina v. Froehlke, 4 ELR 20529 (M.D.N.C.1974) (consent judgment); Environmental Defense Fund, Inc. v. Brinegar, 4 ELR 20534 (E.D.Pa. 1974).

61. E. g., Simmans v. Grant, 370 F. Supp. 5, 22, 4 ELR 20197, 20203 (S.D. Tex.1974); Civic Improvement Comm.

v. Volpe, 2 ELR 20170 (W.D.N.C.), aff'd per curiam 459 F.2d 957, 2 ELR 20249 (4th Cir. 1972).

62. E. g., Cape Henry Bird Club v. Laird, 359 F.Supp. 404, 422, 3 ELR 20571, 20577 (E.D.Va.), aff'd 484 F.2d 453, 3 ELR 20786 (4th Cir. 1973); Concerned Residents of Buck Hill Falls v. Grant, 388 F.Supp. 394, 5 ELR 20207 (M.D.Pa.1975), rev'd 537 F.2d 29 (3d Cir. 1976); Montgomery v. Ellis, 364 F.Supp. 517, 534, 3 ELR 20845, 20853 (N.D.Ala.1973); Sierra Club v. Froehlke (Wallisville-Trinity River), 359 F.Supp. 1289, 1383, 3 ELR 20248, 20285 (S.D.Tex.1973), rev'd 499 F.2d 982, 4 ELR 20731 (5th Cir. 1974).

63. Civic Improvement Comm. v. Volpe, 2 ELR 20171 (W.D.N.C.1972).

64. § 7.5 above; Council on Environmental Quality, Environmental Impact Statements: An Analysis of Six Years' Experience by Seventy Federal Agencies (1976).

NEPA suggests that this proposition is well on the way towards acceptance.[65]

Stipulated settlements or consent decrees in NEPA cases are common[66] and produce an interesting array of provisions: requirements for public hearings and Federal Register notice; identification of alternatives to be addressed in the EIS; obligations to prepare an economic viability analysis, conduct field investigations, implement mitigation measures, withhold assistance for the use of certain pesticides; develop with plaintiffs air pollution studies and noise standards; and convene a task force of identified individuals to reevaluate scientific data pertinent to proposed logging activities. These are important precedents. What agencies agree to do in the past, courts may order in the future.

Occasionally, hearings in court bring out obvious defects in the statement but suggest no clearly indicated corrective measures. The court may simply declare plaintiffs winners of a pyrric victory,[67] admonish the agency in dicta,[68] or perhaps order incorporation of the court exhibits in the EIS.[69] An impact statement inadequately addressing certain topics, it would appear, at least should be supplemented with the additional information and reconsidered as the Act requires.

A few common procedural practices occurring in NEPA litigation can be identified. It is settled, after some uncertainty, that only nominal bonds are required of citizens groups on the theory that oth-

---

65. E. g., Keith v. Volpe, 506 F.2d 696, 4 ELR 20809 (9th Cir. 1974), cert. denied 420 U.S. 908 (1975); Concerned Residents of Buck Hill Falls v. Grant, 388 F.Supp. 394, 5 ELR 20207 (E.D.Pa. 1975), rev'd 537 F.2d 29 (3d Cir. 1976); Montgomery v. Ellis, 364 F. Supp. 517, 3 ELR 20845 (N.D.Ala. 1973); Sierra Club v. Froehlke (Wallisville-Trinity River), 359 F.Supp. 1289, 3 ELR 20248 (S.D.Tex.1973), rev'd 499 F.2d 982, 4 ELR 20731 (5th Cir. 1974).

66. The examples in text are borrowed from the stipulated decrees in Environmental Defense Fund, Inc. v. Peterson, 4 ELR 20898 (D.C.D.C.1973) (tanker subsidy program); Conservation Council of North Carolina v. Froehlke, 4 ELR 20529 (M.D.N.C. 1974) (B. Everett Jordan Dam); Concerned Citizens of East Brunswick, Inc. v. New Jersey Turnpike Authority, 2 ELR 20109 (N.J.Super.Ct.1972); Citizens Comm. for the Columbia River v. Callaway, 494 F.2d 124, 4 ELR 20368 (9th Cir. 1974); Environmental Defense Fund, Inc. v. Agency for Int'l Dev., 6 ELR 20121 (D.C.D.C. 1975); Sierra Club v. Butz, 6 ELR 20128 (N.D.Cal.1975); see Davis, A NEPA Settlement: Conservation Council of North Carolina v. Froehlke, 5 ELR 50079 (1975); Huffman, The Opportunities for Environmentalists in the Settlement of NEPA Suits, 4 ELR 50001 (1974).

67. James v. Lynn, 374 F.Supp. 900, 4 ELR 20675 (D.C.Colo.1974).

68. E. g., Comm. for Nuclear Responsibility v. Seaborg, 149 U.S.App.D.C. 393, 463 F.2d 796, 798, 1 ELR 20532, 20533 (1971); Environmental Defense Fund, Inc. v. Froehlke (Gillham Dam), 368 F.Supp. 231, 240, 1 ELR 20130, 20134 (E.D.Ark.1971). See also Greene County Planning Bd. v. Federal Power Comm'n (II), 490 F.2d 256, 259, 4 ELR 20080, 20081 (2d Cir. 1973) (Mansfield, J., dissenting).

69. Environmental Defense Fund, Inc. v. Froehlke (Truman Dam), 368 F. Supp. 231, 4 ELR 20062 (W.D.Mo. 1973).

Sec. 7.10 THE RECURRING ISSUES: REMEDIES 807

erwise private enforcement would be undermined seriously.[70] The hearing on the merits often is advanced and consolidated with the hearing on an application for a preliminary injunction under Rule 65(a)(2), Federal Rules of Civil Procedure, for the reason that the proof on both issues is coextensive. Another common practice is for the district court to assume continuing jurisdiction over NEPA disputes. This makes possible supervision of compliance with court directives and ultimate substantive review of the project if and when a satisfactory EIS is prepared.[71] Occasionally, the trial court may withhold relief initially but retain jurisdiction on the theory that "[a] watchful judicial eye is, at times, more appropriate than an interfering judicial hand." [72] While some appellate courts encourage the exercise of continuing jurisdiction,[73] others are decidedly hostile, at least where continuing jurisdiction is asserted despite rendition of a judgment for defendants.[74] The reluctance of the courts to exercise jurisdiction in the absence of a concrete controversy is evidenced further by cases refusing to incorporate into a court order agency commitments made in the EIS, absent a showing of possible noncompliance.[75]

One especially sensitive question arising in NEPA litigation is the extent to which courts are empowered to enjoin private parties involved in a project whose status is arguably federal. The court's power is dependent, first, upon a determination that a "major Federal action" is involved.[76] Next, under Rule 65(d), Federal Rules of Civil Procedure, the decree may run not only against the federal agency and its officers but also against "those persons in active concert or participation with them who receive actual notice of the order by personal service or otherwise." Of course the private developer may be made a party. Case law emphasizes that one "in partnership" with the federal government properly may be enjoined.[77] As a gen-

70. E. g., Friends of the Earth v. Brinegar, 518 F.2d 322, 5 ELR 20223 (9th Cir. 1975) ($1000 bond for NEPA injunction against expansion of San Francisco International Airport); Natural Resources Defense Council, Inc. v. Morton, 337 F.Supp. 167, 168–69, 2 ELR 20089 (D.C.D.C.1971); Natural Resources Defense Council, Inc. v. Grant, 2 ELR 20555 (4th Cir. 1972).

71. E. g., Port of Astoria v. Hodel, —— F.Supp. ——, ——, 5 ELR 20657, 20660 (D.C.Or.1975).

72. No East-West Highway Comm., Inc. v. Whitaker, 403 F.Supp. 260, 281, 6 ELR 20053, 20060 (D.C.N.H. 1975); see Citizens for Mass Transit Against Freeways v. Brinegar, 357 F. Supp. 1269, 1282–83, 3 ELR 20747, 20751 (D.Ariz.1973).

73. Environmental Defense Fund, Inc. v. Froehlke (Cache River), 473 F.2d 346, 356, 3 ELR 20001, 20006 (8th Cir. 1972) (remanding with instructions to retain jurisdiction to rule on the sufficiency of a new EIS).

74. Sierra Club v. Lynn (San Antonio Ranch New Town), 502 F.2d 43, 66–67, 4 ELR 20844, 20854–55 (5th Cir. 1974), cert. denied 421 U.S. 944 (1975).

75. E. g., Sierra Club v. Mason, 365 F.Supp. 47, 50, 4 ELR 20186, 20187 (D.C.Conn.1973).

76. §§ 7.6, 7.7 above.

77. E. g., Silva v. Romney, 473 F.2d 287, 3 ELR 20082 (1st Cir. 1973).

eral rule, however, courts are reluctant to enjoin private activities licensed or sanctioned by the federal government because of NEPA noncompliance.[78]

The defense of laches in NEPA cases, as in nuisance cases,[79] is raised commonly [80] and sustained rarely.[81] The doctrine requires a showing of unreasonable delay by the plaintiffs and prejudice to the party against whom the claim is asserted.[82] Courts have tolerated delays of up to three years between the preparation of an impact statement and the initiation of a lawsuit.[83] The reasons vary: important public rights protected by NEPA should not be sacrificed by a litigant's lack of diligence; [84] the complexity and uncertainty of the law cuts against condemning plaintiffs for lack of diligence; [85] mere expenditures alone,[86] without a further showing that little is to be

78. E. g., Conservation Council of North Carolina v. Costanzo (II), 398 F.Supp. 653, 5 ELR 20666 (E.D.N.C. 1975), aff'd 528 F.2d 250, 6 ELR 20116 (4th Cir.) (requires an EIS in connection with Corps of Engineers issuance of a permit but refuses to invalidate the permit); Citizens for Clean Air v. Corps of Engineers, 349 F.Supp. 696, 2 ELR 20650 (S.D.N.Y.1972) (permittee a party) (same). Contra, Friends of Mammoth v. Bd. of Supervisors, 8 Cal.3d 247, 104 Cal.Rptr. 761, 502 P.2d 1049 (1972) (arising under state law); Montana Wilderness Ass'n v. Bd. of Health & Environmental Sciences, 6 ELR 20043 (Mont. Dist.Ct. Lewis & Clark County 1975) (arising under state law) (enjoining a private development pending compliance).

79. § 2.9 above.

80. Leading cases include Lathan v. Brinegar (II), 506 F.2d 677, 692, 4 ELR 20802, 20807 (9th Cir. 1974); Environmental Defense Fund, Inc. v. Tennessee Valley Authority (Tellico Dam), 468 F.2d 1164, 1182, 2 ELR 20726, 20734 (6th Cir. 1972); Arlington Coalition on Transp. v. Volpe, 458 F.2d 1323, 1329–30, 2 ELR 20162, 20163–64 (4th Cir. 1972); Minnesota Pub. Interest Research Group v. Butz (I), 358 F.Supp. 584, 619–20, 3 ELR 20457, 20469 (D.C.Minn.1973), aff'd 498 F.2d 1314, 4 ELR 20700 (8th Cir. 1974); Natural Resources Defense Council, Inc. v. Grant, 341 F.Supp. 356, 368, 2 ELR 20185, 20189–90 (E. D.N.C.1972).

81. See cases cited in note 80, supra. But see Lathan v. Volpe (I), 455 F.2d 1111, 1122, 1 ELR 20602, 20606 (9th Cir. 1971); Smith v. Schlesinger, 371 F.Supp. 559, 561, 4 ELR 20473, 20474 (C.D.Cal.1974).

82. Ecology Center of Louisiana, Inc. v. Coleman, 515 F.2d 860, 868, 5 ELR 20488, 20591 (5th Cir. 1975).

83. Beaucatcher Mtn. Defense Ass'n v. Coleman, —— F.Supp. ——, 6 ELR 20198 (W.D.N.C.1975); Davis v. Coleman, 521 F.2d 661, 5 ELR 20633 (9th Cir. 1975) (15 months' delay between negative declaration and the filing of suit).

84. Beaucatcher Mtn. Defense Ass'n v. Coleman, supra note 83; Davis v. Coleman, 521 F.2d at 677, 5 ELR at 20638 (alternative ground); City of New York v. United States, 337 F. Supp. 150, 160 (E.D.N.Y.1972) (three-judge court); Arlington Coalition on Transp. v. Volpe, 458 F.2d 1323, 1329, 2 ELR 20162, 20163 (4th Cir. 1972) ("we decline to invoke laches against appellants because of the public interest status accorded ecology preservation by the Congress") (footnote omitted).

85. Davis v. Coleman, 521 F.2d at 677, 5 ELR at 20638 (9th Cir. 1975) (plaintiff received copy of negative declaration; 15 months' delay in filing suit) ("an indispensable element of lack of diligence is knowledge, or reason to know, of the legal right, assertion of which is 'delayed' ").

86. Ecology Center of Louisiana, Inc. v. Coleman, 515 F.2d 860, 869, 5 ELR 20488, 20491–92 (5th Cir. 1975) ($1

gained by an injunction,[87] are insufficient to establish a showing of prejudice by the government; or the recalcitrance of the defendants contributed to plaintiffs' inability to acquire knowledge and act on it promptly to protect their rights.[88] Laches involves an appeal to the discretion of the chancellor, however, and even though a court may be reluctant to dismiss a plaintiff explicitly on the ground of laches, a lawsuit otherwise delayed may change the equities between the parties so as to lead to a denial of injunctive relief.[89]

§ 7.11 State Environmental Policy Acts

There are limits to federal authority, even in these days of pervasive nationalism. The arrival of state and local counterparts to the National Environmental Policy Act obviously extends the reach of the law to a myriad of activities falling short of NEPA's "major Federal action" threshold.[1] Equally important, however, is that the state and local environmental policy acts (SEPA's) can provide procedural protections and improve decision-making at all government levels—local, state, and federal. NEPA, after all, requires consultation with local decision-makers and disclosures to the interested public,[2] although the slighting of local interests more than occasionally inspires retaliation in the courts.[3] Thus, the new crop of SEPA's both extends the horizons of environmental law and gives greater depth to existing federal mandates.[4]

million in expenditures); Jones v. Lynn, 477 F.2d 885, 3 ELR 20358 (1st Cir. 1973) ($12 million expended); Arlington Coalition on Transp. v. Volpe, 458 F.2d 1323, 2 ELR 20162 (4th Cir. 1972) ($28.6 million expended); Environmental Defense Fund, Inc. v. Tennessee Valley Authority (Tellico Dam), 468 F.2d 1164, 1170, 2 ELR 20726, 20728 (6th Cir. 1972) ($29 million expended).

87. Clark v. Volpe, 342 F.Supp. 1324 (E.D.La.), aff'd 461 F.2d 1266, 2 ELR 20459 (5th Cir. 1972).

88. Minnesota Pub. Interest Group v. Butz (I), 358 F.Supp. 584, 619–20, 3 ELR 20457, 20460 (D.C.Minn.1973), aff'd 498 F.2d 1314, 4 ELR 20700 (8th Cir. 1974).

89. Steubing v. Brinegar, 511 F.2d 489, 496–97, 5 ELR 20183, 20186 (2d Cir. 1975).

1. § 7.6 above.

2. 42 U.S.C.A. § 4332(2)(C).

3. E. g., Citizens to Preserve Overton Park v. Volpe, 401 U.S. 402, 91 S.Ct. 814, 28 L.Ed.2d 136 (1971); Davis v. Coleman, 521 F.2d 661, 5 ELR 20633 (9th Cir. 1975); Hanly v. Mitchell (Hanly I), 460 F.2d 640, 2 ELR 20216 (2d Cir. 1972), cert. denied 409 U.S. 990; Scenic Hudson Preservation Conference v. Federal Power Comm'n (I), 354 F.2d 608 (2d Cir. 1965), cert. denied 384 U.S. 941 (1966); McLean Gardens Residents Ass'n v. Nat'l Capital Planning Comm'n, 390 F.Supp. 165, 2 ELR 20659 (D.D.C.), motion for stay of injunction and summary reversal denied 2 ELR 20662 (1972).

4. See generally R. Burchell & D. Listokin, The Environmental Impact Handbook 7–36 (1974); Council on Environmental Quality, Fifth Ann.Rep. 401–26 (1974); Council on Environmental Quality, Sixth Ann.Rep. 651–53 (1975); Yost, NEPA's Progeny: State Environmental Policy Acts, 3 ELR 50090 (1973); Tryzna, Environmental Impact Requirements in the States, 102 Monitor, vol. 3, no. 3, at 21 (1973).

As of January 1, 1976, environmental impact statement requirements had been adopted by 30 states and Puerto Rico.[5] Comprehensive legislation is found in 13 states and Puerto Rico,[6] and administrative equivalents in four others.[7] Special SEPA's, limited to identifiable actions or geographical areas, are effective in 14 states.[8] The legislative bodies of at least 15 other states have considered impact state-

5. A few states have adopted statutes which, while not requiring the preparation of impact statements, direct government agencies to consider the environmental impact of certain actions. See, e. g., Maine, 38 Me.Rev. Stat.Ann. §§ 481–87, as amended (development site location); New Hampshire, N.H.Rev.Stat.Ann. ch. 7, § 18–a et seq. (creating an environmental protection division within the state attorney general's office with responsibility to advise and counsel state agencies concerning environmental matters); New Mexico, Exec. Order No. 72–7 (1972); Vermont, 10 Vt.Stat. Ann. §§ 6001–89 (state and private activities that require changes in land use).

6. California, Environmental Quality Act of 1970, Cal.Pub.Res.Code §§ 21000–174; Connecticut, Conn.Gen. Stat.Ann. ch. 439, § 22a–1a et seq.; Indiana, Ind.Stat.Ann. §§ 35–5301 to –5308; Maryland, Maryland Environmental Policy Act, Ann.Code of Md.Nat.Res. §§ 1–301 to –305; Massachusetts, Ann.Laws Mass. ch. 30, §§ 61–62, as amended; Minnesota, Minnesota Environmental Policy Act of 1973, Minn.Stat.Ann. ch. 116D; Montana, Montana Environmental Policy Act of 1971, Rev.Code Mont. § 69–6501 et seq.; New York, N.Y. Environmental Conservation Laws § 8–0101 et seq.; North Carolina, North Carolina Environmental Policy Act of 1971, N.C.Gen.Stat. ch. 113A; South Dakota, South Dakota Environmental Policy Act, S.D.Comp.Laws ch. 11–1A; Virginia, Va.Code Ann. §§ 10–17.107– .112, 10–177–186; Washington, State Environmental Policy Act of 1971, Rev.Code Wash. ch. 43.21C; Wisconsin, Wisc.Stat.Ann. ch. 1, § 1.11 et seq.; Puerto Rico, Puerto Rico Environmental Policy Act, 12 Laws P.R. Ann. § 1121 et seq. The New Mexico Environmental Quality Act was repealed following the decision in Roswell v. Water Quality Comm'n, 84 N.M. 561, 505 P.2d 1237, 3 ELR 21081 (Ct.App.1972) (invalidating effluent discharge regulations for failure to prepare an impact statement). See N.M.Stat.Ann. § 12–20–1 et seq., repealed; Comment, The Rise and Demise of the New Mexico Environmental Quality Act, "Little NEPA", 14 Nat.Res.J. 401 (1974).

7. Michigan, Michigan Exec. Order No. 1974–4 (1975); New Jersey, New Jersey Exec. Order No. 53 (1973); Texas, Interagency Council for Natural Resources and the Environment, Policy for the Environment, Environment Tomorrow: The Texas Response (1973); Utah, Utah Exec. Order, Aug. 27, 1974.

8. Alabama, 8 Code Ala. §§ 312–20; Arizona, Game and Fish Comm'n Policy, Memorandum, Requirements for Environmental Impact Statements (June 9, 1971); Arkansas, Utility Facilities Environmental Protection Act, Ark.Stat.Ann. ch. 73, § 276 et seq.; Colorado, Colo.Rev.Stat. ch. 24, § 32–202 et seq.; Delaware Coastal Zone Act, 7 Del.Code Ann. § 7001 et seq., and Delaware Wetlands Law of 1973, 7 Del.Code Ann. § 6601 et seq.; Florida, Florida Electrical Power Plant Siting Act, Fla.Stat.Ann. § 95A–1241(e)(1); Hawaii, Hawaii Rev.Stat. ch. 334; Mississippi, Mississippi Coastal Wetlands Protection Act, Miss.Code Ann. § 49–27–1 et seq.; Nebraska, Nebraska Dep't of Roads, Department of Roads Action Plan (1973); Nevada, Utility Protection Act, 58 Nev.Rev. Stat. ch. 704; New Jersey Coastal Area Facility Review Act, N.J.S.A. § 13:19–1 et seq., and New Jersey Wetlands Act of 1970, N.J.S.A. § 13:19A–1 et seq.; Pennsylvania, Air Pollution Control Act, 35 Pa.Stat.Ann. § 4001, Clean Streams Act, 35 Pa.Stat.Ann. § 750.1, Solid Waste Management Act, 35 Pa.Stat.Ann. § 60001 et seq., and Surface Mining Conservation and Reclamation Act, 52 Pa.Stat.Ann. § 1396.1 et seq.; Rhode Island, Coastal Resource Management Council Act, Gen. Laws R.I. § 46–23–1 et seq. Compare § 2.17 above.

Sec. 7.11   STATE ENVIRONMENTAL POLICY ACTS

ment proposals.[9] An increasing number of county and municipal jurisdictions have adopted their own versions of the impact statement procedures.[10] This section addresses (1) the applicability of the SEPA's, then looks more closely at (2) who prepares them, (3) their content, (4) the procedures and institutions relied upon for enforcement, and (5) their substantive effect.

a. *Applicability*

Generally, the SEPA's adhere closely to the language of NEPA.[11] Several, in fact, incorporate virtually verbatim the federal provisions.[12] Many of the state statutes, however, deviate from the federal model and from one another in notable particulars. Perhaps the most important question of coverage is whether the enactment reaches the activities of local government authorities as well as those of the state.[13] The decision to include or exclude local government functionaries is an important measure of effectiveness for the obvious reason that local governments exercise primary authority over many environmentally significant activities, prominently including private land use and development.

A few of the state statutes are limited explicitly to actions by named state agencies or agencies involved in certain types of activity.[14] Others expressly require local agencies to prepare impact state-

---

9. Council on Environmental Quality, Fifth Ann.Rep. 402 (1974). SEPA legislation is currently receiving some consideration in Alaska, Georgia, Idaho, Illinois, Iowa, Kentucky, Louisiana, Maine, Missouri, North Dakota, Oregon, South Carolina, West Virginia, and Washington, D. C.; there is no current state activity in Kansas, Nebraska, Oklahoma, and Tennessee. R. Burchell & D. Listokin, supra note 4, at 8.

10. See, e. g., New York, N.Y., Exec. Order No. 87 (1973); Bowie, Md., Environmental Policy and Impact Statement Ordinance, May 3, 1971, and Ordinance 0-2-73, July 16, 1973. In California, several counties are utilizing the environmental impact report (EIR) requirements of the California Environmental Quality Act (CEQA) as a regulatory or land use planning mechanism. See Council on Environmental Quality, Fifth Ann.Rep. 407 (1974). The City of Irvine, an incorporated area located within the privately owned Irvine Ranch, has adopted the EIR process as a management device. Id. at 407–08; see R. Burchell & D. Listoken, supra note 4, at 14–36.

11. See Suggested State Environmental Policy Act, in Council of State Governments, 33 Suggested State Legislation 3–9 (1974).

12. See, e. g., Ind.Stat.Ann. § 35–5301 et seq.; Rev.Code Mont. § 69–6501 et seq.; Rev.Code Wash. ch. 43.21C; 12 Laws P.R.Ann. § 1121 et seq.

13. The Washington state law goes so far as to impose the impact statement requirement on the activities of public corporations. Rev.Code Wash. § 43.21C.030(2); see Minn.Stat.Ann. § 116D–04(1) (EIS required for any private action of more than local significance). Of course, as in the case of NEPA, essentially private activity requiring some form of official approval is more easily comprehended by the SEPA's. See Friends of Mammoth v. Bd. of Supervisors, 8 Cal.3d 247, 104 Cal.Rptr. 761, 502 P.2d 1049, 2 ELR 20673 (1972); § 7.6 above.

14. See, e. g., Arizona, Game and Fish Comm'n Memorandum, June 9, 1971 (proposed water development projects); Delaware, 7 Del.Code § 6601 et seq. (issuance of certain permits by the Department of Natural Re-

ments.[15] Still others call for impact statement preparation only on actions wholly or partially supported by state funds.[16] Most of the comprehensive SEPA's include a threshold reference to "state" action without specifying further whether local agencies are included.[17] Although there is room for interpretation, most of these generic references to "state" activities presumably will not be read as imposing duties on local officials.[18]

The SEPA's differ also as to what constitutes an "action" triggering the impact statement requirements. Some states limit the use of impact statements to proposals for legislation [19] or projects requiring the expenditure of state funds in a certain amount.[20] Others, follow-

sources and Environmental Control), and 7 Del.Code § 7701 et seq. (issuance of location permits by the State Coastal Zone Industrial Board); Georgia, Ga.Code Ann. ch. 95A–1, § 241(e)(1) (proposals by the State Tollway Authority); Nevada, 58 Nev. Rev.Stat. ch. 704 (issuance of power plant and ancillary facilities siting permits by the State Environmental Commission); Texas, Interagency Council for Natural Resources and the Environment, Policy for the Environment (1972) (actions by the 16 agency members of the Council).

15. See, e. g., Cal.Pub.Res.Code § 21063; Mass.Ann.Laws ch. 30, § 62, as amended; N. Y. Environmental Conservation Law § 8–0105(1); Rev. Code Wash. § 43.21C.030. The North Carolina Environmental Policy Act authorizes, but does not require, local governments to implement impact statement programs. N.C.Gen.Stat. ch. 113A, § 8. The Minnesota Environmental Policy Act requires the preparation of an impact statement for any major government action or for any private action "of more than local significance." Minn.Stat.Ann. § 116D.04(1). See Freeborn v. Bryson, 297 Minn. 218, 210 N.W.2d 290, 4 ELR 20215 (1973) (applying the Minnesota Environmental Rights Act to the condemnation of private marshland for a county highway project).

16. See, e. g., Cal.Pub.Res.Code § 21065 (b); Conn.Gen.Stat.Ann. ch. 439, § 22a–1c; N. Y. Environmental Conservation Law § 8–0105(2)(i); N.C.Gen. Stat. ch. 113A, § 4(2).

17. See, e. g., Ind.Stat.Ann. § 35–5303; Rev.Code Mont. § 69–6504(b)(3);

Wis.Stat.Ann. ch. 1, § 1.11(2)(c). The South Dakota Environmental Policy Act applies to "units of the state government." S.D.Comp.Laws ch. 11–1A, § 1(1). The Maryland Environmental Policy Act defines agencies as "units of the state government and any such bodies created by the State." Md. Ann.Code Nat.Res. § 1–301(d). The reference to "bodies created by the State" would seem to apply to entities such as special improvement districts which are created by state legislation and are generally recognized as possessing the attributes of a state agency. See, e. g., Hall v. Taft, 47 Cal.2d 177, 302 P.2d 574 (1956) (holding school district not subject to municipal building ordinance); Reclamation Dist. No. 1500 v. Superior Court, 171 Cal. 672, 154 P. 845 (1916) (holding district not required to pay compensation for flooding of municipal property under plenary power doctrine of state government).

18. Suggested State Environmental Policy Act, supra note 11, § 4(1), offers alternative definitions of "agency". For application to state action only, agencies are defined as "units of the state government, and any such bodies created by the State." For state and local applicability, the definition reads "any state agency . . . and any local agency, including any city, county, and other political subdivision of the State."

19. See, e. g., Ann.Code of Md.Nat.Res. § 1–301(c). Contra, S.D.Comp.Laws ch. 11–1A, § 3(4) (statement not required for proposals for legislation).

20. See, e. g., N.C.Gen.Stat. ch. 113A, § 4(2) (proposals requiring expendi-

ing NEPA, require impact statements to accompany "proposals for legislation and other major state action" without further clarification.[21] Several, including all those that impose obligations on local agencies, define "action" to include regulatory or licensing activities.[22] As a matter of judicial construction, the National Environmental Policy Act has been accorded a similar interpretation.[23] It is by this route that environmental legislation, state or federal, is applied to a wide range of essentially private activities.

The states with legislation resembling the federal NEPA, led by California, are moving towards a low threshold standard that would require an impact statement "whenever it can be fairly argued on the basis of substantial evidence that the project may have a significant environmental impact."[24] In the leading case of Friends of Mammoth v. Board of Supervisors of Mono County,[25] the California Supreme Court held that the California Environmental Quality Act (CEQA) required the preparation of an environmental impact report (EIR) in connection with the issuance of a building permit for a condominium to be located in an undeveloped rural area. Relying heavily on the federal NEPA cases and the Council on Environmental Quality guidelines,[26] the court concluded that the CEQA was to be "interpreted in such a manner as to afford the fullest possible protection to the environment within the reasonable scope of the statutory language. We also conclude that to achieve that maximum protection the Legislature necessarily intended to include within the operation of the act private activities for which a government permit or other entitlement for use is necessary."[27] Specifically rejected was the argument that the EIR requirement was limited to public works projects: "It is undisputed that the Legislature intended that environmental considerations play a significant role in governmental decision-making and that such an intent was not to be effectuated by vague and illusory assurances by state and local entities that the effect of a project on

---

ture of state funds); Va.Code Ann. § 10–17.107(b) (state construction projects, excluding highways, costing at least $100,000 to complete).

21. E. g., Ind.Stat.Ann. § 35–5303(2)(c); Rev.Code Mont. § 69–6504(b)(3); Wisc.Stat.Ann. ch. 1, § 1.11(2)(c).

22. See, e. g., Cal.Pub.Res.Code § 21065; Ann.Laws Mass. ch. 30, § 62, as amended; Michigan Exec.Order No.1974–4 (1974); Minn.Stat.Ann. § 116D.03; N.Y. Environmental Conservation Law § 8–0105(2)(i); S.D. Comp.Laws ch. 11–1A, § 2(1); Rev. Code Wash. § 43.21C.030; Utah Exec. Order, Aug. 27, 1974. Contra, Ind. Stat.Ann. § 35–5306 ("Nothing in this [Act] shall be construed to require an environmental impact statement for the issuance of a license or permit by any agency of the state").

23. § 7.6 above.

24. No Oil, Inc. v. Los Angeles, 13 Cal. 3d 68, 75, 82–86, 118 Cal.Rptr. 34, 38, 43–46, 529 P.2d 66, 70, 75–76, 5 ELR 20166, 20168, 20170 (1974).

25. 8 Cal.3d 247, 104 Cal.Rptr. 761, 502 P.2d 1049, 2 ELR 20673 (1972).

26. See § 7.2 above.

27. 8 Cal.3d at 259, 104 Cal.Rptr. at 768, 502 P.2d at 1056, 2 ELR at 20675.

the environment has been 'taken into consideration.' "[28] The courts of Massachusetts,[29] Washington,[30] and Wisconsin[31] have been equally receptive to broad readings of their respective SEPA's, as have administrators preparing impact statement guidelines in several other states.[32]

Already, the case law on SEPA applicability is falling into the broad categories of coverage familiar under NEPA. Thus, impact statement requirements apply to the construction of a county water supply and storage system,[33] the building of a state office building,[34] a city's extraction of subsurface water,[35] the improvement of a municipal avenue,[36] and an airport development project.[37] They also apply to official activity clearing the way for private actions with potential environmental effects, as by a city annexation,[38] an amendment to

---

28. 8 Cal.3d at 263, 104 Cal.Rptr. at 771, 502 P.2d at 1059, 2 ELR at 20676 (footnote omitted). The holding of *Friends of Mammoth* has been codified by the California legislature. See Cal.Pub.Res.Code § 21151. For background, see Seneker, The Legislative Response to Friends of Mammoth, 48 State (Cal.) Bar.J. 127 (1973); Comment, Aftermammoth: Friends of Mammoth and the California Environmental Quality Act, 3 Ecol.L.Q. 349 (1973); Comment, Friends of Mammoth and the California EQA, 121 U.Pa.L.Rev. 1404 (1973).

29. Secretary of Environmental Affairs v. Port Authority, —— Mass. ——, 323 N.E.2d 329, 5 ELR 20200 (1974).

30. See Eastlake Community Council v. Roanoke Associates, 82 Wash.2d 475, 513 P.2d 36, 3 ELR 20867 (1973) (renewal of conditional building permit); Loveless v. Yantis, 82 Wash.2d 754, 513 P.2d 1023 (1973) (approval of preliminary subdivision plat); Norway Hill Preservation & Protection Ass'n v. King County Council, 87 Wash.2d 267, 552 P.2d 674 (1976) (same); Juanita Bay Valley Community Ass'n v. Kirkland, 9 Wash.App. 59, 510 P.2d 1140 (1973); Merkel v. Brownsville, 8 Wash.App. 844, 509 P.2d 390 (1973).

31. Wisconsin's Environmental Decade, Inc. v. Pub. Serv. Comm'n, Civil No. 140–284 (Wis.Cir.Ct. June 17, 1975) (remanding for a hearing on whether an EIS required in connection with the approval of an electric power rate increase).

32. See, e. g., Massachusetts Executive Office of Environmental Affairs, Regulations to Create a Uniform System for the Preparation of Environmental Impact Reports § 2.4 (1973); Michigan Exec.Order No. 197 (1973); Michigan Exec. Order No. 1974–4 (1974); Montana Environmental Quality Council, Revised Guidelines for Environmental Impact Statement Required by the Montana Environmental Policy Act of 1971, § 5(a)(2)(1973); Wisconsin Exec. Order No. 69 (1973).

33. Environmental Defense Fund, Inc. v. Coastside County Water Dist., 27 Cal.App.3d 695, 104 Cal.Rptr. 197, 2 ELR 20593 (1972).

34. Orange v. Valenti, 37 Cal.App.3d 240, 112 Cal.Rptr. 379 (1974).

35. Inyo County v. Yorty, 32 Cal.App. 3d 795, 108 Cal.Rptr. 377, 3 ELR 20513 (1973).

36. Plan for Arcadia, Inc. v. Arcadia City Council, 42 Cal.App.3d 712, 117 Cal.Rptr. 96 (1974).

37. Secretary of Environmental Affairs v. Massachusetts Port Authority, —— Mass. ——, 323 N.E.2d 329, 5 ELR 20200 (1975).

38. Bozung v. Local Agency Formation Comm'n, 13 Cal.3d 263, 18 Cal.Rptr. 249, 529 P.2d 1017, 4 ELR 20338 (1974).

Sec. 7.11   STATE ENVIRONMENTAL POLICY ACTS

a zoning ordinance,[39] the issuance of a conditional use permit,[40] the renewal of a building permit,[41] the approval of a preliminary subdivision plat,[42] the sanction of a housing subdivision,[43] the issuance of test oil well drilling permits,[44] and the approval of an electric power rate increase.[45]

In addition to indicating whether state "action" is involved, the meaning of the "environment" is another threshold term addressed differently by the various SEPA's. Several state laws explicitly restrict the definition of "environment" to the physical or natural resources of the state.[46] New York defines "environment" to include demographic and community effects.[47] Maryland also specifically requires consideration of socio-economic effects.[48] Several other states refer to effects on the "human environment" without further elaboration.[49] Following the lead of the federal case law,[50] the "human environment" should be read as including social, aesthetic, and cultural effects.

---

39. People v. Kern County, 39 Cal.App. 3d 830, 115 Cal.Rptr. 67 (1974).

40. Concerned Citizens of Palm Desert, Inc. v. Riverside County Bd. of Supervisors, 38 Cal.App.3d 272, 113 Cal. Rptr. 338 (1974).

41. Eastlake Community Council v. Roanoke Associates, 82 Wash.2d 475, 513 P.2d 36, 3 ELR 20867 (1973).

42. Loveless v. Yantis, 82 Wash.2d 754, 513 P.2d 1023 (1973).

43. Montana Wilderness Ass'n v. Bd. of Health & Environmental Sciences, 6 ELR 20043 (Mont.Dist.Ct.1975), aff'd 559 P.2d 1157, 6 ELR 20695 (1976).

44. No Oil, Inc. v. Los Angeles, 13 Cal.3d 68, 118 Cal.Rptr. 34, 529 P.2d 66, 5 ELR 20166 (1974).

45. See Wisconsin's Environmental Decade, Inc. v. Pub. Serv. Comm'n, Civil No. 140–284 (Wis.Cir.Ct. June 17, 1975) (remanding for a hearing on whether an EIS required).

46. See, e. g., Cal.Pub.Res.Code § 21060.5; Conn.Gen.Stat.Ann. § 10–17.-107(a); Rev.Code Wash. § 41.41C.030. The Massachusetts act declares that "damage to the environment" includes but is not limited to:
   air pollution, water pollution, improper sewage disposal, pesticide pollution, excessive noise, improper operation of dumping grounds, impairment and eutrophication of rivers, streams, flood plains, lakes, ponds, or other surface or subsurface water resources, destruction of seashores, dunes, marine resources, underwater archeological resources, wetlands, open spaces, natural areas, parks, or historic districts or sites.
Ann.Laws Mass. ch. 30, § 61, as amended.

47. N.Y. Environmental Conservation Law § 8–0107(4) defines "environment" as:
   the physical conditions which will be affected by a proposed action, including land, air, water, minerals, flora, fauna, noise, objects of historic or aesthetic significance, existing patterns of population concentration, distribution, or growth, and existing community or neighborhood character.

48. Md.Ann.Code Nat.Res. § 1–301(6). See also Suggested State Environmental Policy Act, supra note 11, § 4(4).

49. See, e. g., Ind.Stat.Ann. § 35–5303 (2)(c); Michigan Exec. Order No. 1974–4 (1974); Rev.Code Mont. § 69–6504 (3); N.Y. Environmental Conservation Law § 8–0103(7); Wisc.Stat. Ann. ch. 1, § 1.11(2)(c).

50. § 7.6 above.

An important threshold question under the SEPA's involves the reach of the generally recognized proposition that officials engaged in merely ministerial duties are exempted from the general directives of a statute like the National Environmental Policy Act.[51] A few of the SEPA's specifically exempt the conduct of officials engaged in ministerial duties.[52] This doctrine is of particular significance in the law of many states where a general hostility to the delegation of authority to administrators supports a characterization of what they do as being purely ministerial and lacking discretion. The public policy functions of restricting excessively broad delegations, which include the prevention of administrative abuse,[53] would be thwarted by broad readings protecting state agencies from the SEPA requirements. The impact statement process itself is designed to bring rationality and control to administrative decision-making, and thus points the same way as the restrictive delegation doctrine. Nor does it help, except perhaps the conscience, to characterize agency decisions as being purely "ministerial" when clearly they are not and are subject to modifications for the better. Not to be overlooked either is the fact that the legislatures are among those served by the impact statement exercise.[54] Loose exemptions to the SEPA's cuts the lawmakers off from important sources of information.

b. *Responsibility for Preparation*

Coordination of joint federal-state efforts to prepare an EIS covering aspects of the same project presents some difficulty. New York deals with the problem with particularity to make sure that state concerns are addressed fully in both state-prepared and federally prepared impact statements.[55] The laws of several other states provide that the preparation of a federal statement extinguishes the need for a state statement on the same project.[56] This issue involves dele-

---

51. Ibid.

52. See, e. g., Cal.Pub.Res.Code § 21080; S.D.Comp.Laws ch. 11–1A, § 3(2); Suggested State Environmental Policy Act, supra note 11, § 4(2)(ii). See also Wildlife Ahve v. Chickering, 17 Cal.3d 768, 132 Cal.Rptr. 377, 553 P. 2d 537, 6 ELR 20748 (1976) (refusing to exempt Fish and Game Commission from CEQA); Plan for Arcadia, Inc. v. Arcadia City Council, 42 Cal.App.3d 712, 117 Cal.Rptr. 96 (1974) (holding approval of final building plan for shopping center is ministerial duty); Eastlake Community Council v. Roanoke Associates, 82 Wash.2d 475, 513 P.2d 36, 3 ELR 20867 (1973) (holding that the State Environmental Policy Act requires the preparation of an impact statement at any stage of an ongoing project significantly affecting the environment whenever the governmental agency engages in a discretionary nonduplicative action relating to the project); Loveless v. Yantis, 82 Wash.2d 754, 513 P.2d 1023 (1973) (same).

53. F. Cooper, State Administrative Law 73–91 (1965); L. Jaffee, Judicial Control of Administrative Action 73–77 (1965).

54. § 7.3 above.

55. See N.Y. Environmental Conservation Law § 8–0111.

56. See, e. g., Cal.Pub.Res.Code § 21083.5 (provided the substituted EIS is prepared in compliance with the CEQA); Conn.Gen.Stat.Ann. § 22a–1f (provided EIS complies with state law); Ind.Stat.Ann. § 35–5308 (unless proposal requires state legislation or

gation.[57] While there is nothing to prevent a legislative body from allowing the state's opinion to be controlled by federal thinkers on a particular subject, the resolution, absent specific legislative direction, should go the other way. That is, often both state and federal actions are required on the same project, and both state and federal decision-makers ought to engage independently in the consultation, consideration, and documentation requirements of their respective laws.[58] A separately prepared state EIS would provide a full record of the state or local position and a greater assurance that this position would be honored by federal decision-makers. A full-fledged state consideration also provides a reason for federal equity courts to stay their hands when asked to enjoin segments of a state-federal project.[59] Procedurally, a state-prepared EIS becomes part of the federal document as commentary developed under Section 102(2)(C) of NEPA.[60]

c. *Content*

The content requirements of the SEPA's parallel those of federal law,[61] except where specific legislative judgments are made to narrow the scope of the impact statements—for example, by limiting analysis to effects on physical and natural resources.[62] All state laws require a description of adverse effects and a discussion of alternatives. Many of them contain innovative directives that should assist the responsible agency in evaluating the overall desirability of the subject action. The approach is to require the agency to focus upon certain predictably sensitive topics. Thus, several of the SEPA's expressly

---

appropriations); S.D.Comp.Laws § 11–1A–11 (provided EIS complies with state law); Rev.Code Wash. § 43.21C.-150 (except thermal power plant site evaluations).

57. § 7.8 above.

58. Most of the SEPA's specifically provide that the state law is not to be construed as affecting any agency's statutory obligation to coordinate or consult with federal agencies. See, e. g., Ind.Stat.Ann. § 35–5305; Rev. Code Mont. § 79–6506(b); N.C.Gen. Stat. ch. 113A, § 7; Wisc.Stat.Ann. ch. 1, § 1.11(4)(b).

59. See, e. g., Friends of the Earth, Inc. v. Coleman, 513 F.2d 295, 5 ELR 20429 (9th Cir. 1974) (airport expansion project receiving 10% federal funding); Homeowners Emergency Life Protection Comm. v. Lynn, 388 F.Supp. 971, 5 ELR 20195 (C.D.Cal. 1974) (construction of a dam and reservoir); cf. Davis v. Coleman, 521 F.2d 661, 682, 5 ELR 20633, 20640 (9th Cir. 1975) (enjoining highway interchange construction project for failure to comply with impact statement requirements under NEPA and the CEQA). See also Boston v. Brinegar, 512 F.2d 319, 320, 5 ELR 20241, 20242 (1st Cir. 1975) (appeal dismissed as moot on grounds that federal EIS was prepared and action enjoined by state court pending completion of state impact statement).

60. 42 U.S.C.A. § 4332(2)(C). Federally prepared EIS' presumably would be treated similarly under state law. The concept of designating a lead agency to prepare a single EIS is awkward even where only federal agencies are involved. § 7.8 above. It raises more severe questions of administration where the delegation extends to agencies of another jurisdiction.

61. §§ 7.4, 7.9 above.

62. Note 46, supra.

call for discussion of the "no action" alternative,[63] a cost-benefit analysis,[64] an assessment of the action's economic impact,[65] or a discussion of beneficial environmental effects.[66] A consideration and description of mitigation measures is a common requirement,[67] which opens the way to judicial discovery of a substantive obligation to implement them.[68] Several states mandate consideration of the growth inducing impact of the action [69] or its effect on the consumption of energy,[70] both of which enhance the utility of the statements as land use planning tools. Minnesota anticipates use of the statements to uncover administrative difficulties in implementation by requiring a discussion of the "impact on state government of any Federal controls associated with the proposed action" [71] and consideration of the "multistate responsibilities associated with the proposed action." [72]

d. *Procedures and Implementing Institutions* [73]

The SEPA's do not work significant changes in existing agency procedures. Most states require that completed statements be filed

63. See, e. g., Md.Ann.Code Nat.Res. § 1–304(a)(3).

64. Conn.Gen.Stat.Ann. ch. 439, § 22a–1b(c); Wis.Stat.Ann. ch. 1, § 1.11(2)(c)(6); cf. Cal.Pub.Res.Code § 21001(g) (requiring consideration of "economic and technical factors and long-term benefits and costs in addition to short-term benefits and costs").

65. See, e. g., Minn.Stat.Ann. § 116D.04(1)(b); Rev.Code Mont. § 69–6504(b)(2). The Michigan law requires a discussion of the "economic gains and losses including the effect on employment, income levels, property taxes, and the cost of alternatives to the proposed action." Michigan Exec. Order No. 1974–4 (1974).

66. See, e. g., Md.Ann.Code Nat.Res. § 1–304(a)(1); Wisc.Stat.Ann. ch. 1, § 1.11(2)(c)(6). See also Texas Interagency Council for Natural Resources and the Environment, Policy for the Environment 2 (1972).

67. See, e. g., Cal.Pub.Res.Code § 21100(c); Md.Ann.Code Nat.Res. § 1–304(a)(2); Ann.Laws Mass. ch. 30, § 62; N.Y. Environmental Conservation Law § 8–0109(2)(f); N.C.Gen.Stat. ch. 113A, § 4; S.D.Comp.Laws ch. 11–1A, § 7(6); Va.Code Ann. § 10–17.108(3). See also Suggested State Environmental Policy Act, supra note 11, § 5(b). New York agencies are required to make explicit findings that the chosen alternative is "consistent with social, economic, and other essential consideration of state policy" and that it minimizes or avoids the adverse environmental effects revealed by the impact statement. N.Y. Environmental Conservation Law §§ 8–0109(1), (8).

68. § 7.5 above.

69. See, e. g., Cal.Pub.Res.Code § 21100(g); Montana Environmental Quality Council, Revised Guideline for Environmental Impact Statements Required by the Montana Environmental Policy Act of 1971, § 6(a)(9) (1973); N.Y. Environmental Conservation Law § 8–0109(2)(g); S.D.Comp.Laws ch. 11–1A, § 7(7); cf. Minn.Stat.Ann. § 116D.02. See also Suggested State Environmental Policy Act, supra note 11, § 5(7).

70. See, e. g., Cal.Pub.Res.Code § 21100(c); Montana Environmental Quality Council, Revised Guidelines for Environmental Impact Statements Required by the Montana Environmental Policy Act of 1971, § 6(a)(9) (1973); N.Y. Environmental Conservation Law § 8–0109(2)(h).

71. Minn.Stat.Ann. § 116D.04(1)(f).

72. Id. § 116D.04(1)(g).

73. Compare §§ 7.2, 7.3 above.

Sec. 7.11   STATE ENVIRONMENTAL POLICY ACTS

with a designated agency, and some provide for public notice of the event, whether by publication [74] or by posting a list of the completed statements in a designated government office.[75] Only New York imposes a sanction for noncompliance with the public notice requirements.[76] Most states also provide that the statements are to be available for public inspection, and some authorize the collection of reasonable charges by the agencies to cover costs.[77] Only a few of the SEPA's require the agencies to hold public hearings or solicit public comment.[78] In no case is an adjudicatory hearing prescribed. Normally, as at the federal level,[79] the impact statement is supposed to accompany the proposal for action throughout the agency's existing procedures and be considered in the ordinary course pursuant to that procedure.

State laws vary considerably in addressing oversight of the impact statement procedures. Most provide for some formal review by one of three authorities—a council of environmental protection or similar body,[80] the governor,[81] or the state courts.[82] All of the SEPA

---

74. See, e. g., N.Y. Environmental Conservation Law § 8–0109(b)(4); Wash. Rev.Code § 43.21C.080(d) (legal newspaper of general circulation in the affected area); Wis.Stat.Ann. ch. 1, § 1.11(d) (newspaper covering the affected area, or if action affects the entire state, official state newspaper). See also Massachusetts Executive Office of Environmental Affairs, Regulations to Create a Uniform System for the Preparation of Environmental Impact Reports § 7.3 (1973).

75. See, e. g., N.Y. Environmental Conservation Law §§ 8–0109(4)(6) (Office of the Commissioner of the Department of Environmental Conservation); S.D.Comp.Laws ch. 11–1A, § 9 (Office of the Secretary of the Department of Environmental Protection); Rev.Code Wash. § 43.21C.080(b) (Office of the Department of Ecology).

76. N.Y. Environmental Conservation Law § 8–0109(b)(6). But see Cal. Pub.Res.Code § 21161 ("Failure to file the notice required by this section shall not affect the validity of a project").

77. See, e. g., Cal.Pub.Res.Code § 21089; N.Y. Environmental Conservation Law § 8–0109(7).

78. See, e. g., Mass.Ann.Laws ch. 30, § 62; Minn.Stat.Ann. § 116D.04(a); 58 Nev.Rev.Stat. § 704.885; Wis.Stat. Ann. ch. 1, § 1.11(2)(d). Several states require that public comment on the impact statements be received, but do not mandate public hearings. See, e. g., Conn.Gen.Stat.Ann. ch. 439, § 22a–1d; S.D.Comp.Laws ch. 11–1A, § 8. California requires that agencies adopt procedures for wide public involvement. 14 Cal.Admin.Code ch. 3, Guidelines for Implementation of the California Environmental Quality Act of 1970 (Reg. 73, No. 40–12–15–73), as amended Order of the Secretary for Resources, Mar. 22, 1974. Michigan calls for "maximum use of public involvement procedures and public hearings." Michigan Exec.Order No.1973–9 (1973). North Carolina's regulations call for consultation with the public "if deemed appropriate." North Carolina Dep't of Administration, Implementation of the Environmental Policy Act of 1971, at 2 (1972); see N.Y. Environmental Conservation Law §§ 8–0109(4), (5), 8–0113 (hearing discretionary).

79. § 7.3 above.

80. See, e. g., Conn.Gen.Stat.Ann. ch. 439, § 22a–13 (State Planning Commission); Ann.Laws Mass. ch. 30, § 62, as amended; Minn.Stat.Ann. § 116D.-04(6) (Environmental Quality Council); Rev.Code Mont. § 69–6514(b) (Environmental Quality Council); 58 Nev.Rev.Stat. § 704.890 (Public Utility Commission); N.Y. Environmental Conservation Law § 8–0113 (Commissioner of the Department of Environmental Conservation).

---

81. See note 81 on page 820.
82. See note 82 on page 820.

states designate an agency with general oversight responsibilities, although its powers almost always are merely advisory.[83] A notable exception is the Minnesota Environmental Quality Council, which can direct an agency to prepare a statement upon receipt of a petition bearing at least 500 signatures and further evidence that a statement is needed.[84] The Council also is empowered to "reverse or modify the decisions or proposals [of an agency] where it finds, upon notice and hearing, that the action is inconsistent" with the policies and standards set forth in the act.[85] This unusual power to contradict another agency no doubt will be exercised gingerly within the institutional realities of Minnesota.[86] A more common veto power prescribed explicitly by legislation in a few states, and no doubt by custom in many others, is to require approval by the governor or his designate before an action can be initiated [87] or state funds in support of it disbursed.[88]

In most states the principal instrumentality of enforcement is the courts, and specific provisions for judicial review are not uncommon. Often a time limitation is imposed on the filing of suits challenging agency decisions.[89] The scope of review also is addressed in several statutes. One standard, comparable to the federal Administrative Procedure Act,[90] limits the courts to a determination of whether the agency's action is arbitrary or capricious or otherwise in violation of the laws of the state.[91] Other formulations, which invite a closer scrutiny, require only that the agency's decision be accorded "substantial weight" [92] or that it be "adequate." [93] The Massachusetts

---

81. See, e. g., Conn.Gen.Stat.Ann. ch. 439, § 22a–1e; Ga.Code Ann. § 95A–1241(e)(1); Hawaii Exec.Order, Aug. 23, 1971; Michigan Exec.Order No. 1973–9 (1973); N.C.Gen.Stat. ch. 113A, § 5; Va.Code Ann. § 10–17.110.

82. See, e. g., Cal.Pub.Res.Code § 21168; Minn.Stat.Ann. § 116D.04(9); 58 Nev.Rev.Stat. § 704.895; Wash.Rev.Code § 43.21C.080(2).

83. See, e. g., Cal.Pub.Res.Code § 21083; Md.Ann.Code Nat.Res. § 1–304(a)(b); Mass.Ann.Laws ch. 30, § 62, as amended; Wash.Rev.Code § 43.-21C.100.

84. Minn.Stat.Ann. § 116D.04(3).

85. Id. § 116D.04(2).

86. Compare § 7.2 above (discussing the Environmental Protection Agency's powers under Section 309 of the Clean Air Act).

87. See, e. g., Hawaii Exec.Order, Aug. 23, 1971; Michigan Exec.Order No. 1973–9 (1973).

88. See, e. g., Va.Code Ann. § 10–17.-110.

89. See, e. g., Cal.Pub.Res.Code § 21167; Mass.Ann.Laws ch. 30, § 62, as amended; 58 Nev.Rev.Stat. § 704.-895; Wash.Rev.Code § 43.21C.080(2).

90. § 1.5 above.

91. See, e. g., Cal.Pub.Res.Code §§ 21168, 21168.5; 58 Nev.Rev.Stat. § 704.895.

92. Wash.Rev.Code § 43.21C.090 (applying to the agency determination of whether an impact statement is required and the adequacy of a prepared statement); see Leschi Improvement Council v. State Highway Comm'n, 84 Wash.2d 271, 525 P.2d

93. See note 93 on page 821.

Sec. 7.11 STATE ENVIRONMENTAL POLICY ACTS

statute is silent on the standard of review but the state Supreme Court has held that an agency's threshold determination of applicability may be reviewed de novo because it involves fundamental issues of "health or life." [94]

Not to be overlooked on the subject of enforcement is the role the federal courts may play in interpreting state acts raised as pendent claims in suits brought under the National Environmental Policy Act. This will be especially true as to state laws paralleling NEPA. Federal courts, confident in their treatment of NEPA claims, can be expected to give generous readings to state provisions as the need arises.[95] While the state courts obviously have the last word, the example of the federal judiciary is likely to favor a receptive reading of the SEPA's.

e. *Substantive Consequences*

The jury is still out on the question of whether state courts will assume the power to curb agency actions adversely impacting the environment. Despite the rush to adopt and refine the SEPA's, the fact remains that implementation is taken seriously in only a handful of states.[96] With the forms of compliance only now being unlimbered, it is yet too early to talk unhesitatingly of substance.

The roots of future directions of the case law are in place, however. Most of the state statutes restate verbatim the vague substantive reminders of Section 101(b) of the National Environmental Policy Act.[97] A few states are a good deal more specific in their substantive aims.[98] In either case, enforceable standards may be found, particularly by state courts accustomed to probing the generalities of the nuisance [99] and public trust [1] doctrines. These standards include

---

774 (1974) (holding that the adequacy of an impact statement is a matter of law for determination by the court regardless of the agency's findings); Swift v. Island County, 87 Wash.2d 348, 552 P.2d 175, 6 ELR 20684 (1976) (reversing agency threshold determination on applicability under a clearly erroneous test); Comment, The 1974 Amendments to Washington's State Environmental Policy Act, 10 Gonzaga L.Rev. 707 (1975).

93. Conn.Gen.Stat.Ann. ch. 439, § 22a–18(c).

94. Secretary of Environmental Affairs v. Massachusetts Port Authority, — Mass. —, —, 323 N.E.2d 329, 340, 5 ELR 20200, 20204 (1974).

95. E. g., Davis v. Coleman, 521 F.2d 661, 5 ELR 20633 (9th Cir. 1975).

96. In California, approximately 6000 statements are being issued each year, and in Washington perhaps 200. See Council on Environmental Quality, Fifth Ann.Rep. 406 (1975). By comparison, only between 10 and 50 statements are prepared each year in the other states. Ibid.

97. Ind.Stat.Ann. §§ 35–5301, 35–5302; Minn.Stat.Ann. §§ 116D–01, 116D–02; Mont.Rev.Code §§ 69–6502, 69–6503; N.C.Gen.Stat. §§ 113A–2, 113A–3; Wash.Rev.Code §§ 43.21C.010, 43.-21C.020; see § 7.5 above.

98. See, e. g., Cal.Pub.Res.Code §§ 21000–01; N.Y.Environmental Conservation Law §§ 8–0101, 8–0102.

99. §§ 2.1–.11 above.

1. § 2.16 above.

the principles of best control technology, best management practices, and maximum mitigation.[2]

Several of the state statutes go considerably farther than the federal NEPA in pointing the way towards a result that affords maximum protection for the environment. Legislation that instructs agencies to prepare cost-benefit analyses [3] and identify mitigation measures [4] normally should not be read as approving agency actions that flout cost-benefit assumptions and ignore mitigation. Some states go further to require findings that all feasible mitigation measures will be utilized or that adverse environmental effects will be avoided or minimized.[5] If these findings are unsupported, the courts cannot accept them, which is another way of saying they cannot accept the project as designed.[6] Minnesota affirms that no state action significantly affecting the environment may be undertaken unless there are no other possible and prudent alternatives.[7] The courts must draw the line on agency actions straying beyond that mandate.

Like the federal decisions,[8] the state courts will approach the substantive content of the SEPA's with circumspection. One court in California has indicated in dicta that it "does *not* have the duty of passing on the validity of the conclusion expressed in the EIR, but only on the sufficiency of the report as an informative document." [9] Going the other way is dicta by Justice Robert Utter of the Washington Supreme Court indicating that evidence of avoidable adverse environmental effects could result in the invalidation of agency action as arbitrary and capricious.[10] Justice Utter happens to be right although the proposition is offered as a prediction, not yet a recorded happening.

§ 7.12 National Environmental Policy Act: Complementary Federal Law

NEPA has dominated the legal landscape so thoroughly in recent times that it is tempting to overlook a host of other statutes protecting environmental values in agency decision-making. Discussed

2. See § 7.5 above.

3. Note 64, supra.

4. Note 67, supra.

5. N.Y.Environmental Conservation Law §§ 8–0109(1), (8); S.D.Comp. Laws § 11.A–1A–10.

6. See § 7.5 n. 2 above.

7. Minn.Stat.Ann. § 116D.04(6) (economic considerations alone are an inadequate justification).

8. § 7.5 above.

9. Environmental Defense Fund, Inc. v. Coastside County Water District, 27 Cal.App.3d 695, 705, 104 Cal.Rptr. 197, 206, 2 ELR 20593, 20595 (1972) (emphasis in original).

10. Stempel v. Dep't of Water Resources, 82 Wash.2d 109, 114, 508 P.2d 166, 170, 3 ELR 20685, 20687 (1973); see Eastlake Community Council v. Roanoke Associates, 82 Wash.2d 475, 497 n. 6, 513 P.2d 36, 49 n. 6, 3 ELR 20867, 20872 n. 6 (1973).

Sec. 7.12 COMPLEMENTARY FEDERAL LAW

above [1] are the state environmental policy acts, which may supplement and reinforce claims litigated primarily under NEPA. Federal law also contains numerous mandates that, to a greater or lesser extent, augment and anticipate the obligations made manifest in the National Environmental Policy Act of 1969. NEPA claims commonly are joined with claims under other federal laws, and the cases are not always careful to distinguish the sources of the obligations imposed. Some of these NEPA complements are nineteenth century leftovers enjoying a contemporary revival; others are of recent vintage, fashioned with an understanding of the metes and bounds of NEPA. Some say hesitatingly and with heavy qualifiers what NEPA makes manifestly clear; others impose an agenda of obligations going substantially beyond the NEPA requirements. These laws take various forms: they may require precautions to resist certain hazards, as does the Noise Control Act; [2] or they may protect vulnerable species, as does the Endangered Species Act,[3] or fragile environments, as does the Department of Transportation Act [4] or the Wilderness Act.[5] Although these provisions may accomplish several ends, they may be grouped roughly under the categories of procedural and substantive supplements to NEPA.

a. *Procedural Protection*

Leading the list of the NEPA procedural enhancements is the two-step process calling for a corridor public hearing and design public hearing prior to the location and design approval, respectively, of a federally aided highway project.[6] The hearing requirements of the highway laws often have been litigated in the NEPA context,[7]

1. § 7.11.

2. 49 U.S.C.A. § 4903(a); § 5.2 above.

3. 16 U.S.C.A. § 1536.

4. 49 U.S.C.A. § 1653(f).

5. Pub.L. No. 88–577, 78 Stat. 890 (1964), as amended Pub.L. No. 93–622, 88 Stat. 2096 (1975), 16 U.S.C.A. §§ 1131–36.

6. 23 U.S.C.A. § 128; 23 CFR pt. 790; see Mashaw, The Legal Structure of Frustration: Alternative Strategies for Public Choice Concerning Federally Aided Highway Construction, 122 U.Pa.L.Rev. 1 (1973); Peterson & Kennan, The Federal-Aid Highway Program: Administrative Procedures and Judicial Interpretation, 2 ELR 5001 (1972); Comment, Federal-Aid Highway Legislation and the National Environmental Policy Act of 1969, 3 N.Y.U.Rev.L. & Soc.Change 11 (1973).

7. E. g., Lathan v. Brinegar (II), 506 F. 2d 677, 4 ELR 20802 (9th Cir. 1974) (en banc); Rankin v. Coleman, 394 F. 1975); I–291 Why? Ass'n v. Burns, 1975); 1–291 Why? Ass'n v. Burns, 372 F.Supp. 223, 4 ELR 20230 (D.C. Conn.1974), aff'd per curiam 517 F.2d 1077, 5 ELR 20430 (2d Cir. 1975); Keith v. Volpe, 352 F.Supp. 1324, 2 ELR 20632 (C.D.Cal.1972), aff'd 506 F.2d 696, 4 ELR 20809 (9th Cir. 1974), cert. denied 420 U.S. 908 (1975); Willamette Heights Neighborhood Ass'n v. Volpe, 334 F.Supp. 990, 2 ELR 20043 (D.C.Or.1971). But see Citizens Environmental Council v. Volpe, 484 F.2d 870 (10th Cir. 1973), cert. denied 416 U.S. 936 (1974) (hearings held before effective date of NEPA and no substantial change in plans); Swain v. Brinegar, 378 F.Supp. 753, 4 ELR 20836 (S.D.Ill.1974), rev'd on other grounds 517 F.2d 766, 5 ELR 20354 (7th Cir. 1975) (same); Centerview/ Glen Avalon Homeowners Ass'n v. Brinegar, 367 F.Supp. 633 (C.D.Cal. 1973) (applying laches); Ford v. Train, 364 F.Supp. 227, 4 ELR 20177 (D.C. Wis.1974), rev'd on other grounds 517

and afford plaintiffs a significant tool for attacking the propriety of a decision approving the location or design of a highway. NEPA itself probably does not require the holding of hearings,[8] although when they are otherwise available they are part of the "existing agency review processes"[9] through which proposals for action and accompanying impact statements must progress. Numerous other provisions of federal law prescribe hearings prior to major actions with potential environmental effects—for example, a legislative hearing before the Secretaries of Agriculture or Interior must precede the making of recommendations to the President on the suitability of any area for wilderness preservation,[10] and adjudicatory hearings at the Nuclear Regulatory Commission normally are concluded before the issuance of a construction or operating license for a nuclear power plant.[11]

Special provisions for notice or opportunity to comment may serve to supplement or supplant the hearing process. The public is entitled to Federal Register and newspaper notice of any proposed action to designate a wilderness area.[12] The Secretary of the Interior must be given written notice before any federal agency constructs a dam or authorizes a private party to do so and whenever any agency receives formal notification that its construction or licensing activities "may cause irreparable loss or destruction of significant scientific, prehistorical, historical or archeological data. . . ."[13] Limited provisions for comment are provided as an alternative procedure under the Coastal Zone Management Act in connection with the issuance of a federal license or permit to conduct activity impacting the coastal zone.[14] Sometimes comments or recommendations from identified sources are accorded a special status, as by a requirement that they be incorporated in recommendations to Congress[15] or implemented in fact.[16]

F.2d 766, 5 ELR 20354 (7th Cir. 1975) (same).

8. § 7.3 above.

9. 42 U.S.C.A. § 4332(2)(C).

10. 16 U.S.C.A. § 1132(d).

11. See 42 U.S.C.A. § 2239.

12. 16 U.S.C.A. § 1332(d).

13. Id. §§ 469a, 469a–1.

14. Id. § 1456(c); See id. § 470f (Advisory Council on Historic Preservation must be given a "reasonable opportunity" to comment on agency undertakings that may affect historic buildings and sites). See also id. §§ 1373, 1381(b) (Marine Mammal Protection Act of 1972) (consultation with the Marine Mammal Commission); id. § 1432 (Marine Protection, Research, and Sanctuaries Act of 1972) (consultation with the Secretaries of State, the Interior, and Transportation, the Administrator of EPA, and the responsible officials of affected states); 33 U.S.C.A. § 1412(a) (EPA permits for ocean dumping) (consultation with the Secretary of the Army); 46 U.S.C.A. § 391a(3) (Ports and Waterways Safety Act of 1972) (consultation with the Secretary of Transportation and the Administrator of EPA).

15. 16 U.S.C.A. § 662(b) (Fish and Wildlife Coordination Act); id. §§ 4601–17 (Federal Water Project Recreation Act).

16. E. g., 49 U.S.C.A. § 1712(f) (Airport and Airway Development Act)

Sec. 7.12   COMPLEMENTARY FEDERAL LAW   825

The reasoned administrative decision-making that is central to the National Environmental Policy Act is encouraged by a variety of other enactments. Thus, the Secretary of the Army must accord "a due regard" for wildlife conservation [17] in connection with river and harbor improvements. The Secretary of Transportation must "consider fully" environmental and economic factors in carrying out duties under the Ports and Waterways Safety Act of 1972.[18] The Administrator of the Energy Research and Development Administration must "analyze and consider" environmental and social consequences of programs initiated under the Federal Nonnuclear Energy Research and Development Act of 1974.[19] Any federal agency investigating a flood control, reclamation, or other water resource project must give "full consideration" to the opportunities for outdoor recreation and for fish and wildlife enhancement.[20] The Secretary of Transportation is obliged to "take into consideration" the relationship of each airport to the rest of the transportation system in formulating and revising the national airport system plan.[21] Any federal agency must "take into account" the effect of its undertakings "on any district, site, building, structure or object" listed in the National Register of Historic Places.[22] Economic, social, and environmental effects, including air, noise, and water pollution, must be "fully considered" in developing any proposed project on the federal-aid highway system.[23]

The obligation to weigh environmental and other values may be reinforced by directives to prepare reports or analyses or to make explicit findings. One of the more interesting features of the 1975 amendments to the Federal Insecticide, Fungicide, and Rodenticide Act is a requirement that an agricultural economy impact analysis be prepared by the Administrator of EPA and published in the Federal Register in connection with pesticide suspension or cancellation de-

("The recommendations of the Secretary of the Interior, the Secretary of Health, Education and Welfare, the Secretary of Agriculture, and the National Council on Environmental Quality, with regard to the preservation of environmental quality, shall, to the extent that the Secretary of Transportation determines to be feasible, be incorporated in the national airport system plan"); 33 U.S.C.A. § 1413(c) (Marine Protection, Research and Sanctuaries Act of 1972) (Corps of Engineers ocean dumping permits for dredged material) ("In any case in which the Administrator [of EPA] disagrees with the determination of the Secretary [of the Army] as to compliance with the criteria established . . . relating to the effects of dumping or with restrictions established . . . relating to critical areas, the determination of the Administrator shall prevail").

17. 33 U.S.C.A. § 540.

18. Id. § 1222(e).

19. 42 U.S.C.A. § 5904(a). The statute uses the past tense.

20. 16 U.S.C.A. § 4601–12 (Federal Water Project Recreation Act).

21. 49 U.S.C.A. § 1712(b) (Airport and Airway Development Act of 1970).

22. 16 U.S.C.A. § 470f.

23. 23 U.S.C.A. § 109(h) (Federal-Aid Highway Act of 1970).

cisions.[24] The Secretary of Transportation is forbidden from authorizing certain airport development projects having an "adverse effect" on environmental values unless he renders "a finding, in writing, following a full and complete review, which shall be a matter of public record, that no feasible or prudent alternative exists and that all possible steps have been taken to minimize such adverse effect."[25] If any one of a number of federal agencies recommends disapproval of a license to construct and operate a deepwater port, "it shall set forth in detail the manner in which the application does not comply with any law or regulation within its area of responsibility and shall notify the [Secretary of Transportation] how the application may be amended so as to bring it in compliance with the law or regulation involved."[26] The Administrator of EPA may not ban a fuel or fuel additive under the Clean Air Act "unless he finds, and publishes the finding, that in his judgment [the] prohibition will not cause the use of any other fuel or fuel additive which will produce emissions which will endanger the public health or welfare to the same or greater degree than the use of the fuel or fuel additive proposed to be prohibited."[27]

The obligation to consult other authorities, made explicit by NEPA, often is prescribed elsewhere. Recommendations elicited perhaps must be honored or discarded only upon a reasoned basis. Under the Fish and Wildlife Coordination Act, federal agencies proposing to approve the impounding or diversion of the waters of a stream must consult with the U. S. Fish and Wildlife Service with a view to preventing losses.[28] Reports and recommendations of the Service "shall be made an integral part of any report" prepared by the sponsoring agency for presentation to Congress,[29] a procedural requirement strongly suggesting that substantive protection and mitigation steps must be implemented concurrently with the project.[30] The "reason-

---

24. 7 U.S.C.A. § 136d(b)(2); see §§ 8.3, 8.7 below.

25. 49 U.S.C.A. § 1716(c)(4).

26. 33 U.S.C.A. § 1504(e).

27. 42 U.S.C.A. § 1857–6c(c)(2)(C); see § 3.18 above.

28. 16 U.S.C.A. § 662(a) states that consultation be:
with a view to the conservation of wildlife resources as well as providing for the development and improvement thereof in connection with such water-resource development.
In practice, the emphasis has not been upon protecting and augmenting the resource but rather limiting the losses, and this aim has been achieved poorly.

29. Id. § 662(b); see Akers v. Resor, 339 F.Supp. 1375, 2 ELR 20221 (W.D. Tenn.1972).

30. See Akers v. Resor, supra note 29; Environmental Defense Fund, Inc. v. Corps of Engineers (Cross-Florida Barge Canal), 324 F.Supp. 878, 1 ELR 20079 (D.C.D.C.1971); cf. Udall v. Federal Power Comm'n, 387 U.S. 428, 87 S.Ct. 1712, 18 L.Ed.2d 869 (1967). Compare Environmental Defense Fund, Inc. v. Corps of Engineers (Tennessee-Tombigbee), 492 F.2d 1123, 1138, 4 ELR 20329, 20336 (5th Cir. 1974); Environmental Defense Fund, Inc. v. Froehlke (Cache River), 473 F. 2d 346, 356, 3 ELR 20001, 20005 (8th Cir. 1972) (holding that the Fish and

able opportunity" to comment on agency undertakings affecting sites included in the National Register of Historic Places, accorded by law to the Advisory Council on Historic Preservation,[31] has evolved into a full-fledged consultation process where the advice is taken seriously and usually followed.[32] Courts considering claims under the National Historic Preservation Act in tandem with NEPA have made clear that while the Council lacks veto power over federal projects that threaten listed historic sites, the consultation process makes manifest the need for reasoned results.[33] EPA must consult with the Department of Agriculture and with a scientific advisory group before taking regulatory initiatives under the pesticide laws.[34] The Federal Aviation Administration must consult with EPA in connection with regulatory initiatives to control jet noise.[35] Any agency issuing a license or permit for the disposal of solid waste must consult with EPA to insure compliance with federal guidelines.[36] In developing the national airport system plan, the Secretary of Transportation must consult with several agencies, and to the extent it is "feasible," incorporate their recommendations in the plan.[37]

Sometimes, the courts have insisted upon procedural correctness from the agencies by reference to very general directives. The Federal Power Act says merely that an FPC licensed project "shall be such as in the judgment of the Commission will be best adapted to a comprehensive plan for improving or developing a waterway or waterways for the use or benefit of interstate or foreign commerce, for the improvement and utilization of waterpower development, and for other beneficial public uses, including recreational purposes."[38] In an opinion that in many respects is the harbinger of the close scrutiny doctrine of judicial review,[39] Judge Hays found in this general language an obligation to develop affirmatively a record, seek out opposing views, investigate alternatives, and make plans for

Wildlife Coordinating Act adds nothing to NEPA); Cape Henry Bird Club v. Laird, 359 F.Supp. 404, 417–18, 3 ELR 20571, 20576 (W.D.Va.), aff'd 484 F.2d 453, 3 ELR 20786 (4th Cir. 1973) (same); Environmental Defense Fund, Inc. v. Corps of Engineers (Gillham Dam), 325 F.Supp. 749, 754, 1 ELR 20130, 20134 (E.D.Ark.1971), aff'd 470 F.2d 289, 2 ELR 20740 (8th Cir. 1972) (same).

31. 16 U.S.C.A. § 470f.

32. Fowler, Protection of the Cultural Environment in Federal Law, in Environmental Law Institute, Federal Environmental Law 1466, 1481–505 (E.L. Dolgin & T. G. P. Guilbert eds. 1974).

33. Stop H–3 Ass'n v. Coleman, 533 F.2d 434, 6 ELR 20424 (9th Cir. 1976); Ely v. Velde (I), 451 F.2d 1130, 1 ELR 20612 (4th Cir. 1971); see Boston Waterfront Residents Ass'n v. Romney, 343 F.Supp. 89, 2 ELR 20359 (D.C. Mass.1972); Thompson v. Fugate, 347 F.Supp. 120, 2 ELR 20612 (E.D.Va. 1972) (finding no differences between obligations under NEPA and the Historic Preservation Act).

34. §§ 8.3, 8.7 below.

35. § 5.7 above.

36. 42 U.S.C.A. § 6004(a)(3).

37. 49 U.S.C.A. § 1712(f).

38. 16 U.S.C.A. § 803(a).

39. § 1.5 above.

mitigation.[40] Mid-nineteenth century treaties with the Northwest Indian tribes reserved "the right of taking fish, at all usual and accustomed grounds and stations . . . in common with all citizens of the territory."[41] Judge Boldt found in this general language support for the imposition of obligations on state agencies managing the resource to consult with affected Indian tribes, give adequate notice of regulatory actions, and share management responsibilities in other ways.[42]

b. *Substantive Obligations*

Substantive obligations to protect environmental values are scattered throughout the United States Code. Often, the mandate is generally phrased in terms reminiscent of section 101(b) of the National Environmental Policy Act.[43] Thus, the Fish and Wildlife Coordination Act declares that wildlife conservation shall receive "equal consideration" along with other features of water resource development programs.[44] A public trust obligation to conserve natural resources and protect historical objects can be found in the Park Service Organic Act.[45] The Noise Control Act of 1972 espouses a policy "to promote an environment for all Americans free from noise that jeopardizes their health or welfare."[46] Principles of nondegradation, maximum restoration, and public trust protection can be found in various provisions of the Wilderness Act.[47]

The substantive obligations of federal agencies to protect the environment often, but not always, are subject to discretionary qualifiers. Thus, under the Federal Water Project Recreation Act multiple-purpose water resource projects must be constructed and maintained for outdoor recreation and for fish and wildlife enhancement purposes "wherever [the] project can reasonably serve either or both

---

40. See Scenic Hudson Preservation Conference v. Federal Power Comm'n (I), 354 F.2d 608, 1 ELR 20292 (2d Cir. 1965).

41. E. g., Treaty of Medicine Creek, 10 Stat. 1132, 1133 (1854).

42. United States v. Washington, 384 F.Supp. 312 (W.D.Wash.1974), aff'd 520 F.2d 677, 5 ELR 20552 (9th Cir.), cert. denied 423 U.S. 1086 (1975). Claims seeking protection of the resource from actions resulting in environmental degradation are pending before the court. The author is an attorney of record in the case. See also Peele v. Morton, 396 F.Supp. 584, 5 ELR 20593 (E.D.N.C.1975) (construing a provision in the Cape Hatteras National Seashore Act, 16 U.S.C.A. § 459a–1, reserving to the villagers "the right to earn a livelihood by fishing").

43. § 7.5 above.

44. 16 U.S.C.A. § 661; see 43 U.S.C.A. § 422h (Small Reclamation Projects Act of 1956) (incorporating all requirements of the Fish and Wildlife Coordination Act).

45. 16 U.S.C.A. § 1, identifies a management purpose "to conserve the scenery and the natural and historic objects and the wildlife [in national parks, monuments and reservations] and to provide for the enjoyment of the same in such manner and by such means as will leave them unimpaired for the enjoyment of future generations"; see § 2.16 above.

46. 42 U.S.C.A. § 4901(b); see § 5.2 above.

47. 16 U.S.C.A. §§ 1131(a), (c), 1133(b), (c), (d).

of these purposes consistently with the provisions of this Act. . . . ."[48] Mining under the grandfather clause of the Wilderness Act can proceed within certain national forest lands only upon "restoration as near as practicable of the surface of the land disturbed" in the operations.[49] According to the Noise Control Act of 1972, all federal agencies, "to the fullest extent consistent with their authority under Federal laws administered by them," must "carry out the programs within their control in such a manner as to further" a policy of eliminating noise having health or welfare effects.[50] This very well may impose a judicially enforceable constraint on agency activities creating injurious noise excusable only by reference to a directly contradictory statutory mandate. Federal agency activities affecting the coastal zone shall be conducted and supported "in a manner which is, to the maximum extent practicable, consistent with approved state management programs."[51] This is an enforceable substantive obligation not greatly different from the NEPA directive to "use all practicable means" to achieve identifiable environmental objectives. The reference to an existing land use program, however, makes the search for standards that much easier.

One of the most important substantive provisions of federal environmental law, only now being discovered,[52] is Section 7 of the Endangered Species Act of 1973.[53] Section 7 requires all federal departments and agencies, among other things, to take steps "necessary to insure that actions authorized, funded, or carried out by them do not jeopardize the continued existence of [listed] endangered species and threatened species or result in the destruction or modification of habitat of such species which is determined by the Secretary, after consultation as appropriate with the affected states, to be critical." Despite being partly dependent on administrative action that may be withheld or long delayed, i. e., the listing of a species or the identification of certain habitat as "critical",[54] section 7 is a potent weap-

---

48. Id. § 460*l*–12.

49. Id. § 1133(d)(3). Compare Izaak Walton League v. St. Clair, 353 F. Supp. 698, 3 ELR 20196 (D.C.Minn. 1973), rev'd on other grounds 497 F.2d 849, 4 ELR 20556 (8th Cir. 1974) (holding that mining within the Boundary Waters Canoe Area in the Superior National Forest is prohibited by the Wilderness Act of 1964).

50. 42 U.S.C.A. § 4903(a). Compare § 5.2 above.

51. 16 U.S.C.A. § 1456(c)(1); see id. § 1456(c)(2) (applying same standard to federal agency development projects in the coastal zone).

52. The first cases interpreting section 7 include Hill v. Tennessee Valley Authority, 549 F.2d 1064 (6th Cir. 1977) (snail darter); National Wildlife Federation v. Coleman, 529 F.2d 359, 6 ELR 20344 (5th Cir. 1976) (sandhill crane); and Sierra Club v. Froehlke (Meramec Park Lake Dam), 534 F.2d 1289, 6 ELR 20448 (8th Cir. 1976) (Indiana brown bat); see Wood, Section 7 of the Endangered Species Act of 1973: A Significant Restriction for all Federal Activities, 5 ELR 50189 (1975).

53. 16 U.S.C.A. § 1536.

54. Courts asked to intervene to protect a species not yet listed or habitat not yet adjudged to be "critical"

on. While challengers of agency action may have the burden of coming forward with proof of a threat to a listed species or its habitat, it is arguable that the agency has the burden of justification.[55] Action may "jeopardize" the continued existence of a species by setting in motion a chain of events that reduce chances for survival.[56] It is unnecessary to show that all surviving members of the species are placed in jeopardy but only a biologically significant population. Habitat can be destroyed or modified not only by direct intrusion but by predictable indirect effects.[57] Action that "insure[s]" avoidance of the forbidden results includes project abandonment or modification,[58] which emphasizes the substantive import of the provision. The standard is not the familiar test of maximum mitigation[59] but a more demanding guarantee of nondegradation. While an assurance of safe passage in this world is to be accepted with skepticism, section 7 seems to require it. Finally, although both courts of appeals to consider the question have concluded that the Interior Department has no veto power over other agency action impacting an endangered species,[60] the correct reading very well may be otherwise. Certainly the Secretary of Interior has the last word on what habitat is "critical," and if he offers advice on actions necessary to "insure" protection of a species, the sponsoring agency would be hard put to defend a contrary conclusion.

Specific action and management decisions affecting the environment are circumscribed by a great variety of legislation, much of it sweepingly vague, but some of it embarrassingly specific. Noted for its vagueness, and perforce its unenforceability in the courts, is the Multiple-Use Sustained Yield Act, which contains such instructive directives as "that the national forests are established and shall be administered for outdoor recreation, range, timber, watershed, and wildlife and fish purposes."[61] Under the Taylor Grazing Act the

would be faced with questions of primary jurisdiction. See § 1.9 above.

55. But see National Wildlife Federation v. Coleman, 529 F.2d 359, 372, 6 ELR 20344, 20349–50 (5th Cir. 1976) (indicating that challengers have burden of persuasion); Sierra Club v. Froehlke (Meramec Park Lake Dam), 534 F.2d 1289, 1300, 6 ELR 20448, 20455 (8th Cir. 1976) (same).

56. See National Wildlife Federation v. Coleman, supra note 55.

57. See ibid.

58. See Hill v. Tennessee Valley Authority, 549 F.2d 1064 (6th Cir. 1977).

59. § 7.5 above.

60. National Wildlife Federation v. Coleman, 529 F.2d 359, 371, 6 ELR 20344, 20349 (5th Cir. 1976); Sierra Club v. Froehlke (Meramec Park Lake Dam), 534 F.2d 1289, 1303–04, 6 ELR 20448, 20454 (8th Cir. 1976).

61. 16 U.S.C.A. § 528; see id. § 531(a) (defining multiple use). The inutility of "multiple use" as a planning concept is often noted. E. g., Note, Managing Federal Lands: Replacing the Multiple-Use System, 82 Yale L.J. 787 (1973). An imaginative but unsuccessful attempt to discover judicially enforceable standards in the concept of multiple use is found in Sierra Club v. Hardin, 325 F.Supp. 99, 1 ELR 20161 (D.C.Alas.1971). See also Hamel, Applicability of NEPA to Forest Service Land Use Decisions, 11

Sec. 7.12 COMPLEMENTARY FEDERAL LAW

Secretary of the Interior must administer grazing districts so as "to regulate their occupancy and use, to preserve the land and its resources from destruction or unnecessary injury, to provide for the orderly use, improvement, and development of the range."[62] Grazing is permitted within national parks and monuments, with the exception of Yellowstone National Park, if the Secretary determines that such a use "is not detrimental to the primary purpose" for which the park or monument was created.[63] The Outer Continental Shelf Lands Act, which governs offshore oil development, must be administered by the Secretary "as he determines to be necessary and proper in order to provide for the prevention of waste and conservation of the natural resources of the Outer Continental Shelf."[64] The Secretary of Transportation's decision on licensing a deepwater port facility turns on whether the project "best serves the national interest," and the determination is characterized as "discretionary and nonreviewable."[65] The standards for the issuance of a license to construct and operate a nuclear power plant under the Atomic Energy Act are whether the facility would be "inimical" to the health and safety of the public, and whether there is "reasonable assurance that the health and safety of the public will not be endangered."[66] These and other vague charters carry the traits of other instances of broad legislative delegation—congressional abandonment of the field, limited reviewability in the courts, and administrative discretion virtually unconfined by substantive policy considerations.

Sometimes the Congress legislates with unmistakable clarity. A fifty foot limit prescribed by the Mineral Leasing Act of 1920 for rights-of-way necessary for construction of the trans-Alaska pipeline was the ground for judicial intervention, forcing congressional reconsideration of the project.[67] Recent injunctions against clearcutting were based on narrow language in the National Forest Organic Act of 1897 permitting the sale of "dead, matured or large growth of trees" in the national forests, provided the trees to be sold

---

Idaho L.Rev. 113 (1975); Siegel, Some Implications for Forest Resource Management, 4 Environmental Law. 115 (1973).

62. 43 U.S.C.A. § 315a.

63. 16 U.S.C.A. § 3.

64. 43 U.S.C.A. § 1334. Courts have found in this provision powers to enforce environmental protection measures. § 4.18 above.

65. 33 U.S.C.A. § 1503(d).

66. 42 U.S.C.A. § 2232; 10 CFR § 50.-35(c); see North Anna Environmental Coalition v. Nuclear Regulatory Comm'n, 174 U.S.App.D.C. 428, 533 F.2d 655 (1976) (rejecting argument that agency transgressed the limits of its discretion by approving a reactor on a site with risks of catastrophe above and beyond the norm; the plant is located on a fault presenting a small risk of movement). The author is an attorney of record in the North Anna case. Compare § 3.18 above (on the meaning of the fuel additive provisions of the Clean Air Act).

67. Wilderness Soc'y v. Morton, 156 U.S.App.D.C. 121, 479 F.2d 842, 3 ELR 20085 (1973) (en banc), cert. denied 411 U.S. 917.

were "marked and designated," and removed "under the supervision" of a person appointed by the Secretary of Agriculture.[68] The 160 acre and residency limitations on beneficiaries of the federal reclamation laws sharply confine administrative discretion in their administration.[69] A statutory assurance that the Boundary Waters Canoe Area be administered so as to protect its "primitive" character has been read as banning the commercial exploitation of virgin timber within the area protected.[70] The status of low-flow augmentation for water pollution control in multi-purpose planning is defined carefully by the Federal Water Pollution Control Act Amendments of 1972.[71] Inclusion of a river in the national wild and scenic rivers system restricts the uses to which it may be put although the New River litigation demonstrates that designation is a prerequisite to the curtailment of administrative authority.[72]

The most unmistakable illustrations of federal substantive environmental law are those incorporating the principles of best technology, cost-benefit justification, and maximum mitigation found generally in the National Environmental Policy Act and at common law.[73] The "best technology" standard is accepted widely as a measure of performance for newly constructed sources.[74] Regulations governing the transportation of hazardous materials must conform to "the best-known practicable means" for accomplishing the job.[75] Techniques and equipment used in commercial fishing must produce "the least practicable hazard"[76] to marine mammals caught incidentally. It "shall be the immediate goal that the incidental kill or incidental serious injury of marine mammals permitted in the course of commercial fishing operations be reduced to insig-

---

68. West Virginia Division of the Izaak Walton v. Butz, 522 F.2d 945, 5 ELR 20573 (4th Cir. 1975); Zieske v. Butz, 406 F.Supp. 258, 6 ELR 20129 (D.C.Alas.1975), further proceedings, 412 F.Supp. 1403 (D.Alas. 1976); cf. Miller v. Mallery, 410 F. Supp. 1283, 6 ELR 20499 (D.C.Or. 1976) (interpreting Bull Run Trespass Act). The 1897 Act was repealed by the National Forest Management Act of 1976, Pub.L. No. 94–588, § 13, 90 Stat. 2958.

69. E. g., United States v. Tulare Lake Canal Co., 535 F.2d 1093, 6 ELR 20487 (9th Cir. 1976); Annot. 27 A.L.R.Fed. 831 (1976); cf. 16 U.S.C.A. § 688dd(d)(1).

70. Minnesota Pub. Interest Research Group v. Butz (II), 401 F.Supp. 1276, 6 ELR 20133 (D.Minn.1975), rev'd en banc 541 F.2d 1292, 6 ELR 20736 (8th Cir. 1976).

71. § 4.10 above.

72. North Carolina v. Federal Power Comm'n, 174 U.S.App.D.C. 475, 533 F.2d 702, 6 ELR 20336 (1976). See also Tarlock & Tippy, The Wild & Scenic Rivers Act of 1968, 55 Cornell L.J. 707 (1970).

73. §§ 2.6, 7.4 above.

74. §§ 3.10, 4.12, 4.13 above.

75. 18 U.S.C.A. § 834(c).

76. 16 U.S.C.A. § 1371; see id. § 1381 (a) (establishing a research program to develop methods and gear "so as to reduce to the maximum extent practicable" the incidental take of marine mammals); id. § 1318(b) (regulations must restrict incidental catch "to the lowest practicable level").

Sec. 7.12   COMPLEMENTARY FEDERAL LAW   833

nificant levels approaching a zero mortality and serious injury rate." [77]

Cost-benefit provisions, which supply a standard enforceable in the courts,[78] are increasingly important not only in the context of traditional water development projects [79] but also with regard to other agency activities.[80] The maximum mitigation principle is more prominent yet. Perhaps best known are Sections 4(f) of the Department of Transportation Act of 1966 and 18(a) of the Federal-Aid Highway Act of 1968, construed in Citizens to Preserve Overton Park, Inc. v. Volpe,[81] which forbid the use of publicly owned land, such as parks and wildlife and waterfowl refuges, for highway purposes "unless (1) there is no feasible and prudent alternative to the use of such land, and (2) such program includes all possible planning to minimize harm" to the area protected.[82] This simply means that parks can be sacrificed to highways only if the project cannot be accomplished another way [83] and, then, only after a maximum effort ("all possible

---

77. Id. § 1371(a)(2). Judge Richey relied upon this language to conclude that the Act went beyond a standard of "best feasible technology" to require a result oriented test of no substantial disadvantage to porpoises incidentally caught by tuna fishermen. Comm. for Humane Legislation, Inc. v. Richardson, 414 F.Supp. 297, 6 ELR 20500 (D.C.D.C.1976), aff'd and modified in part — U.S.App. D.C. —, 540 F.2d 1141, 6 ELR 20661, cert. denied — U.S. — (1976); see Comment, Federal Courts and Congress Review Tuna-Porpoise Controversy, 6 ELR 10147 (1976). See also Coggins, Legal Protection for Marine Mammals: An Overview of Innovative Resource Conservation Legislation, 6 Environmental Law. 1 (1975).

78. The authorities debating the proposition are collected in § 7.5 n. 57 above.

79. 33 U.S.C.A. § 701a (Flood Control Act of 1936); 16 U.S.C.A. § 1003 (Watershed Protection Act).

80. E. g., 42 U.S.C.A. § 1857–6c(2)(B) (cost-benefit analysis must be undertaken in connection with regulatory restrictions on fuel or fuel additives).

81. 401 U.S. 402, 91 S.Ct. 814, 28 L.Ed. 2d 136 (1975); § 1.5 above.

82. 49 U.S.C.A. § 16543(f); 23 U.S.C.A. § 138.

83. Citizens to Preserve Overton Park v. Volpe, 401 U.S. 402, 412, 91 S.Ct. 814, 821, 28 L.Ed.2d 136, 150 (1971) ("For this exemption to apply the Secretary must find that as a matter of sound engineering it would not be feasible to build the highway along any other route"). These provisions giving parkland a special protected status often are raised in NEPA litigation. E. g., Coalition for Responsible Regional Div. v. Brinegar, 518 F.2d 522, 5 ELR 20432 (4th Cir. 1975); Brooks v. Coleman, 518 F.2d 17, 5 ELR 20444 (9th Cir. 1975); Public Interest Research Group of Michigan v. Brinegar, 517 F.2d 917, 5 ELR 20502 (6th Cir. 1975); Citizens Comm. for the Columbia R. v. Callaway, 494 F.2d 124, 4 ELR 20368 (9th Cir. 1974); Finish Allatoona's Interstate Right, Inc. v. Brinegar, 484 F.2d 638, 3 ELR 20771 (7th Cir. 1973); Monroe County Conservation Council, Inc. v. Volpe, 472 F.2d 693, 3 ELR 20006 (2d Cir. 1972); Fayetteville Area Chamber of Commerce v. Volpe, 463 F.2d 402, 2 ELR 20504 (4th Cir. 1972); D.C. Federation of Civic Ass'ns v. Volpe, 148 U.S.App.D.C. 207, 459 F.2d 1231, 2 ELR 20093 (1972), cert. denied 405 U.S. 1030; Arlington Coalition on Transp. v. Volpe, 458 F. 2d 1323, 2 ELR 20162 (4th Cir. 1972), cert. denied 409 U.S. 1000; Citizens to Preserve Foster Park v. Volpe, 446 F. 2d 991, 2 ELR 20560 (7th Cir. 1972); Named Individual Members of San Antonio Conservation Soc'y v. Texas Highway Dep't (I), 446 F.2d 1013, 1

planning") to mitigate. A similar formulation appears in the Airport and Airway Development Act, which forbids the approval of any project having an adverse environmental effect unless the Secretary finds, and presumably acts in accordance with the finding, "that no feasible and prudent alternative exists and that all possible steps have been taken to minimize [the] adverse effect." [84]

The lesson to be learned is that while NEPA is an important component of federal environmental law, the concepts it expresses are neither original nor exclusive. Commonly, NEPA gives the close scrutiny doctrine of judicial review a special intensity and focus insofar as environmental questions are concerned.[85] Quite often, NEPA claims are joined with others providing serious substantive limits on resource use decisions.

ELR 20379 (8th Cir. 1971), cert. denied 406 U.S. 933 (1972); Arkansas Community Organization for Reform Now v. Brinegar, 398 F.Supp. 685 (E.D.Ark.1975), aff'd per curiam 531 F.2d 864, 6 ELR 20511 (8th Cir. 1976) (also considering relocation provisions of federal law); Stop H–3 Ass'n v. Brinegar, 389 F.Supp. 1102 (D.C.Hawaii 1974), rev'd, 533 F.2d 434, 6 ELR 20424 (6th Cir. 1976); Citizens Environmental Council v. Volpe, 364 F.Supp. 286, 3 ELR 20077 (D.C.Kan.1973), aff'd 484 F.2d 870, 4 ELR 20009 (8th Cir.), cert. denied 416 U.S. 936 (1974); Movement Against Destruction v. Volpe, 361 F.Supp. 1360, 3 ELR 20667 (D.C.Md. 1973), aff'd per curiam 500 F.2d 29, 4 ELR 20278 (4th Cir. 1974); Citizens for Mass Transp. Against Freeways v. Brinegar, 357 F.Supp. 1269, 3 ELR 20747 (D.C.Ariz.1973); Lathan v. Volpe (II), 350 F.Supp. 262, 2 ELR 20545 (W.C.Wash.1972), aff'd 506 F.2d 677, 4 ELR 20802 (9th Cir. 1974); Thompson v. Fugate, 347 F.Supp. 120, 2 ELR 20612 (E.D.Va.1972); Comm. to Stop Route 7 v. Volpe, 346 F.Supp. 731, 2 ELR 20446 (D.C.Conn.1972); La Raza Unida v. Volpe, 337 F.Supp. 221, 1 ELR 20642 (N.D.Cal.1971), aff'd 488 F.2d 559, 4 ELR 20090 (9th Cir. 1973), cert. denied 417 U.S. 968 (1974); Harrisburg Coalition Against Ruining Environment v. Volpe, 330 F.Supp. 918, 1 ELR 20237 (M.D.Pa.1971); Pennsylvania Environmental Council, Inc. v. Bartlett, 315 F.Supp. 238, 2 ELR 20752 (M.D.Pa.1970), aff'd 454 F.2d 613, 1 ELR 20622 (3d Cir. 1971).

84. 49 U.S.C.A. § 1716(c)(4).

85. §§ 1.5, 7.3, 7.4 above.

Chapter VIII

PESTICIDES AND TOXIC SUBSTANCES

§ 8.1 Background

In recent years, conflicts over the use of pesticides have served as archetypical examples of contemporary environmental law, replete with scientific complexity, profound economic implications, and overlapping administrative authority. A pesticide is a substance used to cause the death of nonhuman organisms considered by man to be inimical to human interests.[1] A "pest" is virtually any form of plant or animal life declared by the Administrator of EPA to be "injurious to health or the environment."[2] The generic term pesticide often is subdivided further by reference to the intended target—that is, insecticides (insects), herbicides (plants), fungicides (fungi), nematocides (invertebrate animals such as hookworms), rodenticides (rodents), and miticides (mites).[3] By law,[4] a pesticide includes substances used to control plant growth short of destruction—defoliants which cause the leaves to drop from the plant,[5] dessicants which accelerate the drying of plant tissue,[6] and plant regulators which accelerate or retard the rate of growth or maturation.[7]

Pesticides for farm use were manufactured first in 1902.[8] But the industry did not experience widespread growth until the end of hostilities in World War II when it put to use knowledge acquired from wartime research on DDT and other compounds. Four leading chemical companies account for more than 50 percent of sales al-

---

1. 7 U.S.C.A. § 136(u) reads, in part: The term 'pesticide' means (1) any substance or mixture of substances intended for preventing, destroying, repelling, or mitigating any pest, and (2) any substance or mixture of substances intended for use as a plant regulator, defoliant, or dessicant . . . .

2. Id. § 136(t); id. § 136w(c)(1).

3. See Environmental Protection Agency, Production, Distribution, Use and Environmental Impact Potential of Selected Pesticides (1975).

4. Note 1, supra.

5. 7 U.S.C.A. § 136(f).

6. Id. § 136(g).

7. Id. § 136(v).

8. For general background with different perspectives, see National Agricultural Chemical Ass'n Speaker's Kit, Facts on Pesticides (undated); H. Wellford, Sowing the Wind (1972) (the Nader report on pesticides); R. L. Rudd, Pesticides and the Living Landscape (1964) (an informative effort by an entomologist); F. Graham, Since Silent Spring (1970). The well known classic is R. Carson, Silent Spring (1962). The less well known rebuttal is J. Whitten, That We May Live (1966). A highly authoritative source is Dep't of HEW, Report of the Secretary's Commission on Pesticides and Their Relationship to Environmental Health (1969) [hereinafter cited as the Mrak Commission Report].

though pesticides are a small part of their diversified output.[9] Pesticide manufacturers number at least fifty while more than 2500 other companies, many of them small businesses, formulate the chemicals into brand name products and market them to farmers, public health agencies, foresters and homeowners. The retail value of the products sold rose from $440 million in 1964 to $12 billion in 1969.[10] In 1976, U. S. farmers used pesticides on 70 percent of the acreage planted, up from 50 percent only five years earlier.[11]

The taking of life and the saving of life by the application of pesticides, in the opinion of a respected academic panel, coincidentally has created the world's foremost pollution problem.[12] The reasons are many and complex but the predominant fact is that large quantities of chemical compounds that are toxic, mobile, and persistent are released deliberately into the environment each year. In 1970 nearly a billion pounds (5 pounds per person) of some 900 registered pesticides (more than 50 percent for farm use) were applied in the United States. They were aimed primarily at about 2000 pest species of plants and animals but many of the other 200,000 species present in the environment "were either directly or indirectly affected by these widespread pesticides applications." [13]

It is acknowledged that pesticides, particularly the chlorinated hydrocarbon insecticides (DDT, dieldrin, toxaphene, chlordane, TDE, aldrin, and heptachlor), have caused "measurable damage" to non-target bird, fish, and beneficial insect populations. The prime reasons are the chemicals' "persistence, movement through the ecosystem, and characteristics for biological concentration in the food chain." [14] The effects of trace amounts of pesticides on human health are largely unknown. According to the highly influential 1969 Mrak Commission Report, "The field of pesticide toxicology exemplifies the absurdity of a situation in which 200 million Americans are undergoing lifelong exposure, yet our knowledge of what is happening to them is at best fragmentary and for the most part indirect and inferential. While there is little ground for foreboding of disaster, there is even less for complacency." [15]

9. J. Backman, The Economics of the Chemical Industry (1970).

10. Mrak Commission Report, supra note 8, at 46. Data on production, use, and distribution is "inadequate." Environmental Protection Agency, Production, Distribution, Use and Environment Impact of Selected Pesticides 4 (1975).

11. See Wall St. J., June 14, 1976, at 24, col. 1.

12. Report of the Study of Critical Environmental Problems: Man's Impact on the Global Environment 158–59 (1970).

13. Office of Science and Technology, Ecological Effects of Pesticides on Non-Target Species 177 (1971).

14. Id. at 182.

15. Mrak Commission Report, supra note 8, at 37. The Mrak Commssion Report recommendations, which urge changes in the federal regulation of pesticides, are scrutinized in Rodgers, The Persistent Problem of the Persistent Pesticides: A Lesson in En-

Economic benefits of pesticide use, like the environmental effects, are not well known. Obviously, pesticides are "the tools of choice because, based on the information available to farmers, they are more effective and convenient and, especially, more profitable than other alternatives." [16] It is common in the older literature to find statements estimating pest losses to approach 10 percent of crops and stored commodities.[17] But research is limited, and has been involved primarily "with an attempt to measure in aggregate the effects on farm sales associated with varying levels of pesticide use." [18] Determining economic advantages in the aggregate and even on an individual user level is extremely complex; for example, a cost sensitive decision to use an agricultural pesticide can go awry because of immunities developed by the target species, pest resurgence (due to incidental destruction of predators of the target species), or secondary pest outbreaks (due to elimination of predators of a heretofore innocuous species).[19] Needless to say, a full cost-benefit appraisal of the use of pesticides in the American economy would be even more complex, and it has not been undertaken.[20]

Pesticides are strongly driven by the imperatives of technology. Bringing a new chemical from the laboratory to the farm involves time (five years), capital ($4.5 million), patience (one compound in 5000 tested emerges as a marketable product), and specialized manpower.[21] Traditionally, testing for safety or environmental side effects involves more time, money, and uncertainty.[22] These substantial economic commitments, no less than an investment in a major industrial plant, affect research and regulatory decisions. Research may be forced into a short-term posture in defense of existing products.[23]

vironmental Law, 70 Colum.L.Rev. 567 (1970).

16. Environmental Protection Agency, Farmer's Pesticide Use Decisions and Attitudes on Alternate Crop Protection Methods 6 (1974).

17. Mrak Commission Report, supra note 8, at 56. Another common estimate not subject to substantiation is that as much as 50 percent of pesticides used are wasted or wholly counter-productive. President's Science Advisory Comm., Restoring the Quality of Our Environment 291 (1965).

18. Mrak Commission Report, supra note 8, at 56.

19. See Van den Bosch, Insecticides and the Law, 22 Hastings L.J. 615, 616–18 (1971).

20. Mrak Commission Report, supra note 8, at 57.

21. Von Rumker, Guest & Upholt, The Search for Safer, More Selective, and Less Persistent Pesticides, 20 BioScience 1004 (1970). Julius Johnson of Dow Chemical Co. estimates that one new pesticide emerges from each ten thousand tested and that the lapse of time from discovery to marketing ranges from eight to ten years at a cost of $10 million or more. Speech, "Safety in the Development of Herbicides," presented to the California Weed Conference, Jan. 19, 1971.

22. Kolata, Chemical Carcinogens: Industry Adopts Controversial "Quick" Tests, 192 Science 1215 (1976) (reporting on new procedures facilitating premarket testing).

23. Ernst & Ernst, Trade Ass'n Dep't, Pesticide Industry Profile Study 18 (1971) (reporting that an industry-wide survey for 1970 indicated that 23 percent of research and development expenditures were devoted to

Regulation also practically is confined when the option of a product ban is made less palatable by the considerable economic and social disruption it might entail. Shutting down the plant always has been a disfavored alternative,[24] and a product ban is the equivalent of a shutdown.

Installing technological controls on a polluting factory usually offers a satisfactory middle ground between a remedy ordering mere changes in operations and a complete shutdown of the facility.[25] The application of polluting pesticides, for all practical purposes, admits of no middle ground: if regulation is prescribed, the product either is sharply restricted or banned or its use is controlled. These two options—product ban and operational controls—are featured prominently in the law of pesticides. In recent years, partial bans have been implemented against some of the chlorinated hydrocarbon compounds, of which DDT is best known.[26] For many years, careful use has been a regulatory byword. This is implemented mostly through labeling statutes but it also appears in an infinite variety of forms—in pamphlets, handbooks, warning signs to field workers, speeches and sales literature. "Accidents do not result from use of pesticides," according to this philosophy, "only from misuse." [27]

Alternatives to the use of pesticides are many but only occasionally are put in issue in legal forums.[28] A substitute product is one possibility. Conventional environmental wisdom holds that narrow spectrum pesticides, specific in effect, are much preferred to broader spectrum poisons which take a toll among nontarget species.[29] At the

"Regulatory Maintenance of Existing Products"); Hearings on Federal Pesticide Control Act of 1971, Before the House Comm. on Agriculture, H.R.Doc. No. A, 92d Cong., 1st Sess. 404 (1971) ("The biggest thing that has happened to us very lately is that we have had to spend, I would guess, about 50 or 60 percent of our research money in defense of our current products, to try to keep them registered and satisfy all the questions that are being asked about these") (testimony presented on behalf of Hercules, Inc.).

24. See §§ 2.6, 2.11 above.

25. See ibid.

26. See § 8.7 below.

27. Speech by James R. Mills, Director of Public Relations, National Agricultural Chemicals Ass'n, Canner/Packer, before the National Canners Ass'n, March, 1971, at 4. It has been suggested that the strategy for controlling the user is simultaneously a strategy for protecting the product. See also Stearns Elec. Paste Co. v. Environmental Protection Agency, 361 F.2d 293, 310–11, 2 ELR 20368, 20374 (7th Cir. 1972); W. Rodgers, Corporate Country ch. 5 (1973).

28. Application of the National Environmental Policy Act to government pesticide programs of course requires consideration of alternatives. E. g., Environmental Defense Fund, Inc. v. Agency for Int'l Dev., 6 ELR 20121 (D.C.D.C.1975) (requiring consideration of reasonable alternatives to AID's pest management program, including possible termination and limiting assistance to non pesticide activities) (by stipulation). Compare Wyoming v. Hathaway, 525 F.2d 66, 6 ELR 20169 (10th Cir. 1975) (exempting Environmental Protection Agency pesticide regulatory decisions from the National Environment Policy Act).

29. The incidental catch of nontarget species is a recurring problem of fisheries management. See, e. g., Comm.

same time, the considerable investment involved in bringing a pesticide to the marketplace favors a product with a wide market appeal and a broad spectrum effect—DDT, again, is a good example. Thus, ecological wisdom and economic wisdom are polls apart, albeit not for the first time. Yet new products do replace the old, often but not always to the advantage of the environment: "malathion, carbaryl, and related materials are now used for the control of many insects where it is essential that crops or livestock are not treated with persistent materials." [30] For gypsy moth control, DDT has been replaced by sevin (carbaryl). Unfortunately, sevin has proven to be notoriously toxic to honeybees, giving rise again to further scientific and legal conflict.

Cultural control techniques offer alternatives to chemical usage. Rotation of crops is an efficient way to curtail weeds and insects. Another cultural practice that has been "very effective" is the development of insect or disease-resistant plant varieties although this is a "tedious" process typically directed at a single type of pest.[31] Biological control techniques, usually involving the use of parasitic or predacious insects, have been used successfully in the United States on many occasions. The use of chemosterilants to control insect populations is a widely mentioned idea not yet applied seriously on a commercial basis. The most realistic option to a heavy chemical diet is called integrated pest management, which is an interdisciplinary approach combining selected uses of pesticides, natural enemies, insect pathogens, and other methods.[32] Unfortunately, although biological and other controls are urged strongly as preferable alternatives to chemical usage, established commercial patterns have not been breached effectively. As with the recycling and reuse of solid waste,[33] acceptance of the ideas must precede the changes.

Many important legal confrontations in recent years have involved pesticides and related toxic substances: devastation of the Michigan farm economy by the fire retardant polybrominated byphenyl (PBB) that was accidentally mixed into livestock feeds;[34] hospitalization of thirty persons, injury to many others, and poisoning

---

for Humane Legislation, Inc. v. Richardson, 414 F.Supp. 297, 6 ELR 20500 (D.C.D.C.1976), aff'd and modified in part —— U.S.App.D.C. ——, 540 F.2d 1141.

30. Mrak Commission Report, supra note 8, at 59.

31. Id. at 60.

32. Russell Train, EPA Administrator, Speech on Herbicides, Energy and the Environment, Before the Weed Science Soc'y of America, Feb. 4, 1975. See also CEQ, Integrated Pest Management (1973); R. L. Rudd, supra note 8, at 36–41.

33. § 6.1 above.

34. Carter, Michigan's PBB Incident: Chemical Mix-Up Leads to Disaster, 192 Science 240, 243 (1976) ("[A]t last tally, the losses included 29,800 cattle, 5,920 hogs, 1,470 sheep, and about 1.5 million chickens. In addition, at least 865 tons of feed, 17,990 pounds of cheese, 2,630 pounds of butter, 34,000 pounds of dry milk products, and nearly 5 million eggs have been destroyed").

of shellfish 64 miles away by Kepone produced in Hopewell, Virginia;[35] contamination of virtually every species of fish in the Hudson River by polychlorinated byphenyls (PCB's) escaping from two industrial plants;[36] implication of a widely used herbicide, 2,4,5–T, as a cause of fetal defects in test animals;[37] conflicts over the fire ant in the South,[38] the gypsy moth in the East,[39] and the tussock moth in the West.[40]

Experiences with DDT represent a classic scientific and legal test case on pesticides specifically and environmental law generally. The compound is, at once, an extraordinary lifesaver and a worldwide pollutant.[41] It has been estimated that one billion pounds of DDT are circulating through the world's air and water supply. Traces of the chemical have been found in penguins in the Antarctic, and tuna in the mid-Pacific; residues have been detected in the body tissues of people throughout the world. While DDT's qualities of persistence, mobility, and toxicity pose an acute threat to certain forms of wildlife, it also is a possible carcinogen (cancer-causing agent) for man. On the other hand, millions benefitted from the use of DDT. It became deeply embedded in the economic and social fabric of society. It saved lives, provided jobs, and aided the producing sector. Small wonder that the legal system has struggled for a decade to unravel this technological dilemma, with the issue quite alive if not still in doubt.[42] Whether or

35. Wash.Post, Dec. 21, 1975, at E6, col. 1.

36. Wall St.J., Apr. 14, 1976, at 1, col. 4; see In re General Elec. Co., 6 ELR 30007 (1976) (N.Y. Dep't of Environmental Conservation) (Interim Opinion of Hearing Officer) (holding that General Electric's discharges of PCB's into the upper Hudson River violate the New York Environmental Conservation Law).

37. For details, see T. Whiteside, The Withering Rain: America's Herbicidal Folly (1971).

38. Environmental Defense Fund, Inc. v. Hardin (mirex), 325 F.Supp. 1401, 1 ELR 20207 (D.C.D.C.1971).

39. Graham, The War Against the Dreaded Gypsies, Audubon Magazine, May 1972, at 46; Ehrlich & Holdren, The Gypsy Moth Backlash, Saturday Review, Oct. 2, 1971, at 71; Hinckley, The Gypsy Moth, 14 Environment 41 (1972); Godwin, Gypsy Moth, U.S. Forest Service, Forest Pest Leaflet 41 (Apr. 1972); Anderson, To Everything There Is a Season (unpublished paper prepared for course in environmental law, Georgetown U.Law Center, Dec. 1972); see Murphy v. Benson, 164 F.Supp. 120 (E.D.N.Y. 1958), aff'd 270 F.2d 419 (2d Cir.), cert. denied 362 U.S. 929 (1960) (Douglas, J. dissenting) (upholding DDT spraying program to stop the spread of the gypsy moth as within the police power of the state).

40. See Recent Developments, 4 ELR 10039–40 (1974).

41. Authorities are collected in Rodgers, supra note 15, at 575–78. See Man's Impact on the Global Environment, supra note 12, at 126–36.

42. An early decision is Yannacone v. Dennison, 55 Misc.2d 468, 285 N.Y.S. 2d 476 (1967) (denying injunctive relief against the continued use of DDT for mosquito control in Suffolk County, New York). Many observers, including this author, mark the hearings on DDT before the Wisconsin Dep't of Natural Resources as a major landmark of modern environmental law. In Re Izaak Walton League, Inc., Dkt. No. 3–DR (Wis. Dep't Natural Resources, May 21, 1970). See H. Henkin, M. Merta, & J. Staples, The

not the right answers have emerged, we have learned something about the process.

§ 8.2 Common Law

Not surprisingly, the widespread application of toxic substances in the form of chemical pesticides has spawned a considerable body of case law. Litigation for the most part is confined to seeking compensation for injury to crops, persons, or other living things (typically honeybees) caused by drifting pesticides.[1] Usually [2] plaintiffs shun a nuisance theory, which is better suited to governing a continuing relationship between the parties,[3] in favor of a theory more readily associated with an isolated tortious event—negligence, trespass, and strict liability.

Thus, liability on a negligence theory has been imposed for a pilot's failure to curtail the spray while making a turn over plaintiff's land,[4] for spraying during high winds [5] or breezes,[6] for failure to give notice that spraying would be done on a particular day,[7] for spraying despite a warning that plaintiff's crop was immature,[8] and for releasing a pesticide so close to plaintiff's property as to fall with-

Environment, the Establishment, and the Law (1971); V. J. Yannacone, Jr., B. S. Cohen, & S. G. Davison, 2 Environmental Rights & Remedies ch. 8 (1972); Wurster, DDT Goes to Trial in Madison, 19 Bio-Science 809 (1969). The culmination of Federal administrative action against DDT is reported in Environmental Defense Fund, Inc. v. Environmental Protection Agency (DDT III), 160 U.S.App. D.C. 123, 489 F.2d 1247, 4 ELR 20031 (1973).

1. E. g., Annot., 37 A.L.R.3d 833 (1971); Rohrman, Pesticide Laws and Legal Implications of Pesticide Uses (pts. 1 & 2), 23 Food, Drug & Cos.L.J. 142, 172 (1968); Rohrman, The Law of Pesticides: Present and Future, 17 J. Pub.L. 351 (1968); Van den Bosch, Insecticides and the Law, 22 Hastings L.J. 615 (1971); Hunt, Regulation of Pesticide Use: Common Law Liability and Administrative Policy in Implementing the Federal Insecticide, Fungicide and Rodenticide Act (unpublished paper submitted for a course in environmental law, Georgetown U. Law Center, Fall 1974); Note, Crop Dusting: Legal Problems in New Industry, 6 Stan.L.Rev. 69 (1953); Note, Liability for Chemical Damage From Aerial Crop Dusting, 43 Minn.L.Rev. 531 (1959); Comment, Crop Dusting—Scope of Liability and a Need for Reform in Texas Law, 40 Tex.Rev. 527 (1962); Note, Regulation and Liability in the Application of Pesticides, 49 Iowa L.Rev. 135 (1963); Comment, Liability in Crop Dusting: A Survey, 42 Miss.L.J. 104 (1971).

2. But not always. See Texas v. Pankey, 441 F.2d 236, 239 (10th Cir. 1971) (holding that residue of pesticides used in one state that allegedly polluted interstate stream forming source of water supply for municipalities in another state constitutes violation of federal common law of nuisance).

3. §§ 2.1–.12 above.

4. Hammon Ranch Corp. v. Dodson, 199 Ark. 846, 136 S.W.2d 484 (1940).

5. Burns v. Vaughn, 216 Ark. 128, 224 S.W.2d 365 (1949); W. B. Bynum Cooperage Co. v. Coulter, 219 Ark. 818, 244 S.W.2d 955 (1952).

6. Miles v. A. Arena & Co., 23 Cal. App.2d 680, 685, 73 P.2d 1260, 1263 (1939).

7. Brown v. Sioux City, 242 Iowa 1196, 1201, 49 N.W.2d 853, 855 (1951).

8. Parks v. Atwood Crop Dusters, 118 Cal.App.2d 368, 257 P.2d 653 (1953).

in reach of his cattle.[9] Some courts, while professing reliance on a negligence theory, are satisfied with virtually no proof of fault.[10] Others explicitly embrace strict liability for trespass [11] or for abnormally dangerous activities,[12] as appropriate, for injurious invasions by pesticides.

As elsewhere, negligence per se is established easily by showing a violation of registration, labeling, or other provisions of the law,[13] although conformity with labeling requirements will not necessarily be a complete defense.[14] One author points out [15] that the breadth of labeling obligations under federal law make per se violations highly probable, even for courts determined to require proof of negligence. A typical label: "Avoid contamination of food and feed." [16] Another: "Do not allow this material to drift onto neighboring crops or noncrop areas . . . ." [17] And another: "Do not contaminate feed or foodstuffs. Keep all unprotected persons out of the operating area in vicinity where there may be danger of drift." [18]

Negligence also can be proven by showing a departure from standards laid down by state statutes and regulations, and probably also by reference to insect control handbooks distributed by many extension services as a guide to pesticide usage. The former [19] contain many explicit standards of conduct—prohibitions against aerial or daytime applications of certain pesticides, and protection of vulnerable areas (populated areas, bodies of water, grape vineyards). State

9. Underhill v. Motes, 158 Kan. 173, 146 P.2d 374 (1944).

10. E. g., Kennedy v. Clayton, 216 Ark. 851, 227 S.W.2d 934 (1950); Kentucky Aerospray, Inc. v. Mays, 251 S.W.2d 460, 462 (Ky.1952).

11. Cross v. Harris, 230 Or. 398, 370 P.2d 703 (1962); Loe v. Lenhardt, 227 Or. 242, 362 P.2d 312 (1961); Schronk v. Gilliam, 380 S.W.2d 743 (Tex.Civ. App.1964); see § 2.13 above.

12. E. g., Luthringer v. Moore, 31 Cal. 2d 489, 190 P.2d 1 (1948); Gotreaux v. Gary, 232 La. 373, 94 So.2d 293 (1957); Young v. Darter, 363 P.2d 829 (Okla.1961); Jones v. Morgan, 96 So.2d 109 (La.Ct.App.1957); Romero v. Chris Crusta Flying Service, Inc., 140 So.2d 734 (La.Ct.App.1962); see § 2.14 above.

13. Gonzalez v. Virginia-Carolina Chem. Co., 239 F.Supp. 567 (E.D.S.C. 1965); Perzinski v. Chevron Chem. Co., 503 F.2d 654 (7th Cir. 1974); see 7 U.S.C.A. § 136j(a)(2)(P) (making it unlawful to test a pesticide on human beings who are not "fully informed" of the consequences and who "freely volunteer" to participate).

14. Griffin v. Planters Chem. Corp., 302 F.Supp. 937 (E.D.S.C.1969); Rumsey v. Freeway Manos Minimax, 423 S.W.2d 387 (Tex.Civ.App.1968); Hubbard-Hall Chem. Co. v. Silverman, 340 F.2d 402 (1st Cir. 1965).

15. Hunt, supra note 1, at 24–26; see 7 U.S.C.A. § 136j(a)(2)(G) (making unlawful the "use of any registered pesticide in a manner inconsistent with its labeling").

16. Diazinon 4E, EPA Reg. No. 100–463 AA.

17. Mono Copper Lime 10–90 Dust, EPA Reg. No. 279–1054.

18. Guthion 50% Wettable Powder, EPA Reg. No. 3125–193.

19. See generally Environmental Protection Agency, Digest of State Pesticide Use and Application Laws (1973).

Sec. 8.2 COMMON LAW 843

law also may contain a variety of other provisions helpful in satisfying tort claims—registration of all aerial applicators, financial responsibility laws (requiring posting of a bond or proof of insurance), and provisions for reporting damage. The insect control handbooks lack the force of law but may establish the customary way of doing business, deviations from which are negligence.[20] The handbooks often are quite specific in prescribing the pesticide and the amount, manner, and time of application for controlling a given pest.[21]

The most likely viable defense in pesticide damage cases is an absence of cause in fact between the defendant's conduct and the resultant injury.[22] This is to be expected in contemporary technological conflicts where injuries may be long delayed and subtly inflicted by mechanisms not well known. The defenses of contributory negligence or assumption of risk usually are given short shrift,[23] and properly so. Indeed, given the fact that negligence often is only a technical requirement,[24] the courts ought to take the next step by

20. Cf. The T. J. Hooper, 60 F.2d 737 (2d Cir. 1932) (holding the evidence did not establish a custom); Ellis v. Louisville & Nashville R.R., 251 S.W. 2d 577 (Ky.App.1952) (same) (negligence alleged was failure to provide worker with a respirator to prevent him from breathing silica dust).

21. Sometimes the handbooks understate the case. Note this advice about the use of TEPP, a deadly organophosphate compound (a single drop can be lethal):

Mild poisoning in people and severe symptoms and death in cattle have resulted from exposure to static clouds of TEPP dust. When TEPP dust is applied in very still, hot weather, note should be taken of the position and movement of the dust cloud. If, even at a point distant from the area of application, the TEPP dust cloud tends to settle over homes or pastures in more than usual concentration, the people should be urged to remove themselves and their cattle to an uncontaminated area until the cloud has dissipated.

Washington State University Cooperative Extension Service, 1969 Washington State Chemical Insect Control Handbook, at 6 (recent revisions of the handbook have eliminated this language, presumably not because the advice is unsound).

Instructions may run to the beekeeper as well as the pesticide applicator:

Confine the bees when hazardous materials are applied. Beehives can be covered with plastic sheeting that will confine the bees and exclude pesticide sprays, dusts or fumes. Since heat builds up rapidly under plastic exposed to the sun, confinement can only last for a few hours after dawn on warm days. This may be long enough to protect the bees from some materials.

U. S. Department of Agriculture, Beekeeping in the United States 101 (rev. ed. 1971) (Agriculture Handbook No. 335). It is doubtful that a beekeeper failing to confine his bees would be barred by contributory negligence. See note 23, infra.

22. E. g., Wall v. Trogdon, 249 N.C. 747, 107 S.E.2d 757 (1959); Hodges v. Fuller Brush Co., 104 R.I. 85, 242 A.2d 307 (1918); Council v. Duprel, 250 Miss. 269, 165 So.2d 134 (1964). The cause in fact defense, however, typically is unavailable in the two most common pesticide poison categories—poisoning of children, usually in the home, and of applicators. See 40 Fed.Reg. 28242, 28258 (1975).

23. E. g., Hubbard-Hall Chem. Co. v. Silverman, 340 F.2d 402 (1st Cir. 1965); Sanders v. Beckwith, 79 Ariz. 67, 283 P.2d 235 (1955).

24. Cases cited in note 10, supra.

explicitly imposing strict liability. The question should be answered, after all, "by reference to such factors as who is better able to insure against the risk, allocate the costs, reduce or warn against the dangers. Justice Blackburn [in Rylands v. Fletcher] had the right idea when he suggested that operating a technology that gets out of hand usually is reason enough for imposing liability." [25]

Although pesticide suits most often are filed against the applicator, or the person who has hired him,[26] there is no doctrinal barrier to a suit by a user or bystander against the manufacturer under a strict products liability theory pursuant to Section 402A, Restatement (Second) of Torts.[27] Some suits against the manufacturer have succeeded, usually for inadequate testing [28] or improper warning.[29] Failures of testing and warning are fully in the mainstream of modern products liability case law.[30] In the future, pesticide products damaging nontarget species are more likely to be condemned as "defective" products "unreasonably dangerous to the user or consumer." [31] This liability would be consistent with the desire to develop specific pesticides to replace broad spectrum poisons such as DDT.

Interesting questions of tort law are raised by the issue of whether the government is liable for using pesticides and registering them for use by others. One case invoked the discretionary function exception to the Federal Tort Claims Act [32] to protect the United States from a damage claim arising out of the aerial application by public employees of the herbicide 2, 4–D.[33] The result is indefensible; no policy making deserving of immunity is involved in the selection and use of a pesticide.[34] Similarly important is the question whether government negligence in registering a compound might result in lia-

25. § 2.14 above.

26. Loe v. Lenhardt, 227 Or. 242, 362 P.2d 312 (1961) (stating generally accepted rule that an employer remains liable for the negligence of an independent contractor engaged in an inherently dangerous activity such as crop dusting).

27. See D. W. Noel & J. J. Phillips, Cases and Materials on Products Liability 173–95 (1976).

28. Chapman Chem. Co. v. Taylor, 215 Ark. 630, 222 S.W.2d 820 (1949).

29. E. g., Gonzales v. Virginia-Carolina Chem. Co., 239 F.Supp. 567 (E.D.S.C. 1965); Griffin v. Planters Chem. Corp., 302 F.Supp. 937 (E.D.S.C.1969); Wise v. Hays, 58 Wash.2d 106, 361 P.2d 171 (1961); Golden Gate Hop Ranch, Inc. v. Velsicol Chem. Corp., 66 Wash.2d 469, 403 P.2d 351 (1965);

see Van den Bosch, supra note 1, at 616 (discussing possible manufacturers liability for the agricultural phenomena of target pest resurgence and secondary pest outbreaks; both problems are caused by a pesticide's effectiveness against nontarget predators and parasites).

30. E. g., Borel v. Fibreboard Paper Prods. Corp., 493 F.2d 1076, 4 ELR 20133 (5th Cir. 1973); Hall v. E. I. DuPont de Nemours & Co., 345 F. Supp. 353 (E.D.N.Y.1972).

31. Restatement, Second, Torts § 402A (1965).

32. § 1.8 above.

33. Harris v. United States, 205 F.2d 765 (10th Cir. 1953).

34. See § 1.8 above.

bility for damages from its use. An affirmative answer is suggested by precedents under the drug laws.[35] To mention but one possibility, federal law presently requires that any pesticide containing a substance highly toxic to man bear on its label "a statement of practical treatment (first aid or otherwise) in case of poisoning by the pesticide." [36] The continued registration of some compounds—for example, paraquat—for which there is no known antidote may offend these provisions and thus be potential grist for a successful tort claim.

Government liability for losses occasioned by pesticide usage takes an unusual form in the dairy [37] and beekeeping indemnity [38] programs administered by the Department of Agriculture. Both are legislative efforts to protect innocent persons who suffer losses as a result of somebody else's use of pesticides—government seizures of contaminated milk in one case, the direct loss of honeybees in the other.[39] Both are strongly criticized for indirectly subsidizing manufacturers and applicators who should learn to pay for their own mistakes.[40] Both are emulated by other proposals to substitute government for private liability, the best known examples being the abortive attempt to enact a cyclamates indemnification program in the wake of a ban on the artificial sweetener imposed by the Food and Drug Administration [41] and the successful inclusion of an indem-

35. Griffin v. United States, 351 F. Supp. 10 (E.D.Pa.1972), aff'd 500 F.2d 1059 (3d Cir. 1974).

36. 7 U.S.C.A. § 1365(q)(2)(D)(iii).

37. Id. § 450(j).

38. Id. §§ 135(b), (n), (t).

39. See Polner, Federal Regulatory Indemnification (unpublished paper completed as an independent research project, Georgetown U. Law Center, Spring 1973).

40. Rep. Silvio Conte had this to say about the beekeepers indemnity program:
> This morning, as I was driving in to Capitol Hill, I heard a popular song on the radio, called Rip-Off. It occurred to me that this could be the theme song for this ridiculous giveaway program operated by the Department of Agriculture.
>
> . . .
>
> One apiary owner claims to have lost a minimum of 12,937 hives from pesticide activity each year for the past 5 years. That evidence would seem to indicate that someone's being pretty careless with pesticides—if that was indeed the cause of this massacre. If so, I cannot understand why the Agriculture Stabilization and Conservation Service is planning no action against these careless pesticide applicators.
>
> . . .
>
> In my mind, then, there still has been no adequate justification presented for this ludicrous bonanza for enterprising beekeepers.
>
> . . .
>
> I, for one, am tired of being stung. We need to protect live bees, by going after careless pesticide applicators. We need to improve the guidelines and procedures under which claims are awarded, instead of doling out payments for corpses. Our program should be designed to promote and expand our beekeeping operators, rather than merely awarding funeral benefits.

118 Cong.Rec. 23361 (1972).

41. H.R. 13366, 92d Cong., 2d Sess. (1972). A bill passed the House by a seven vote margin but the proposal died in the Senate Judiciary Committee. Cong.Q., Dec. 16, 1972, at 3147.

nification provision in the Federal Environmental Pesticide Control Act of 1972.[42] Needless to say, paying for honeybee losses with public money does not appear to encourage the development and use of pesticides that are safe for honeybees.[43]

§ 8.3 Federal Environmental Pesticide Control Act: Background and Summary

The evolution of federal pesticides legislation can be described under four headings: (1) early enactments; (2) the Federal Environmental Pesticide Control Act of 1972; (3) the 1975 amendments, which modify the 1972 FEPCA only in a few respects; and (4) miscellaneous provisions of federal law.

a. *Early Enactments*

Federal regulation of pesticides began with the Insecticide Act of 1910,[1] which essentially was a labeling measure covering all insecticides and fungicides. The Act forbade the manufacture or shipment of any adulterated or misbranded product.[2] Adulteration was defined as a deviation from product standards—specific requirements for Paris green and lead arsenate,[3] general standards for the others.[4] A misbranded product, as defined in the Act, contained false or misleading information on the package or label or omitted required statements as to product ingredients.[5] The Department of Agriculture was empowered to examine specimens,[6] but no provision was made for registration or other government approval of products. The

---

42. 7 U.S.C.A. § 136m; see § 8.3 below. Compare §§ 8.9 (for further discussion), 8.10 (mentioning the indemnity study provisions of the Toxic Substances Control Act) below.

43. Under the beekeeper indemnity program the Department of Agriculture has made the following total yearly payments for the period from 1967 through 1975:
    1967 $1,758,022
    1968 $1,629,435
    1969 $1,660,347
    1970 $1,651,752
    1971 $3,243,852
    1972 $2,145,552
    1973 $1,589,122
    1974 $2,917,155
    1975 $2,063,575
Dep't of Agriculture, Agriculture Stabilization and Conservation Service, Beekeeper Indemnity Program, Payments by States and by Year of Loss, March 1, 1976.

1. Act of Apr. 26, 1910, ch. 191, 36 Stat. 331, repealed 61 Stat. 163, 172 (1947).

2. Id. §§ 1, 2.

3. Id. § 7.

4. Id. § 7, read in part as follows:
    In the case of insecticides or fungicides, other than Paris green and lead arsenate [an article shall be deemed to be adulterated]: First, if its strength or purity fall below the professed standard or quality under which it is sold; second, if any substance has been substituted wholly or in part for the article; third, if any valuable constituent of the article has been wholly or in part abstracted; fourth, if it is intended for use on vegetation and shall contain any substance or substances which although preventing, destroying, repelling, or mitigating insects shall be injurious to such vegetation when used.

5. Id. § 8.

6. Id. § 4.

Sec. 8.3 ENVIRONMENTAL PESTICIDE CONTROL ACT

remedies under the Act were limited to criminal penalties and civil actions initiated by the government to condemn adulterated or misbranded products.[7]

In 1947 the Insecticide Act was repealed and replaced by the comprehensive Federal Insecticide, Fungicide, and Rodenticide Act (FIFRA),[8] which remained intact through a generation of sweeping technological change until the arrival of the Federal Environmental Pesticide Control Act of 1972 (FEPCA).[9] The 1947 FIFRA provided that an "economic poison," otherwise defined as a chemical pesticide, must be registered before being marketed in interstate commerce.[10] Elaborate provisions for suspending or cancelling a registration were included.[11] Criminal penalties were prescribed for violations[12] as were provisions authorizing the United States to go to court to seize and dispose of products that were adulterated, misbranded, or unregistered.[13] Like its 1910 predecessor, the principal thrust of the 1947 FIFRA was to protect consumers from ineffective products.

Labeling was the credo of control of the 1947 FIFRA, and remains so today. Labeling was defined broadly to include all written, printed or graphic matter on the product or any of its containers, wrappers, or even in literature accompanying the product or referenced on it.[14] The contents of mandatory labeling were greatly expanded over the 1910 Act; misbranding resulted if, among other deficiencies, the labeling lacked directions for use, warning, or caution statements and an ingredient statement, all prominently placed and sufficiently conspicuous "as to render it likely to be read and understood by the ordinary individual under customary conditions of purchase and use."[15] Significantly, the concept of labeling in FIFRA went somewhat further than mere disclosure by defining "misbranded" to include certain products remaining unacceptably dangerous despite labeling disclosures. First, a product was misbranded if the labeling accompanying it did not contain directions for use which "if complied with were adequate for the protection of the public."[16] Second, a product was misbranded if it did not contain a warning or caution statement which "if complied with [was] adequate to prevent injury to living man and other vertebrate animals, vegetation, and useful invertebrate animals."[17] Third, misbranding resulted if "when

---

7. Id. §§ 2, 11.

8. Ch. 125, 61 Stat. 163 (1947), as amended Federal Environmental Pesticide Control Act of 1972, Pub.L. No. 92–516, 86 Stat. 973, 7 U.S.C.A. § 135 et seq.

9. Note 8, supra.

10. Section 4(a), 61 Stat. 167 (1947).

11. Section 2(c), 61 Stat. 163.

12. Section 8, 61 Stat. 170.

13. Section 9, 61 Stat. 170.

14. Section 2(x), 61 Stat. 164.

15. Sections 2(z)(2)(c), (d), (e), (f), 61 Stat. 165.

16. Section (z)(2)(c), 61 Stat. 165.

17. Section (z)(2)(d), 61 Stat. 165.

used as directed or in accordance with commonly recognized practice [the pesticide] shall be injurious to living man or other vertebrate animals, or vegetation, except weeds, to which [the product] is applied, or to the person" applying it.[18]

In 1954, federal pesticide regulation was expanded further by the Miller amendment to the Food, Drug, and Cosmetic Act authorizing the Administrator of the Food and Drug Administration, now the Environmental Protection Agency, to establish tolerance limits for residues of pesticides on raw agricultural commodities and processed food.[19] The manufacturer is required to include detailed data in a petition for a pesticide tolerance—i. e., reports on the amount, frequency and time of application of the pesticide, safety reports, the results of tests on residue remaining on food crops, and suggestions for practical methods for removing a residue that may exceed the proposed tolerance.[20] The Administrator then sets tolerances at a level "to the extent necessary to protect the public health." [21] Food products containing residues in excess of tolerance levels are adulterated and subject to seizure under other provisions of the Act.[22]

Amendments in 1959 brought several new types of pesticides, including defoliants, under the coverage of FIFRA.[23] In 1964, protest registrations were eliminated. (The process had permitted marketing prior to registration in certain situations).[24] Amendments also provided the first administrative authority to deny registration applications covering adulterated or misbranded products. Additional changes were made in the procedures for suspending sales of previously registered pesticides found to be unsafe.[25]

Perhaps the most important legal development of the 1960's was not the enactment of new laws but a recognition of a lack of enforcement of the old ones. By the end of the decade an important House subcommittee investigation of the Pesticides Regulation Division of the Department of Agriculture (USDA) found [26] that pesticide prod-

---

18. Section (z)(2)(g), 61 Stat. 165; see Environmental Defense Fund, Inc. v. Dep't of Health, Educ., & Welfare, 138 U.S.App.D.C. 381, 385 n. 9, 428 F. 2d 1083, 1087 n. 9, 1 ELR 20045, 20047 n. 9 (1970); Environmental Defense Fund, Inc. v. Hardin (DDT I), 138 U.S.App.D.C. 391, 393 n. 2, 428 F.2d 1093, 1095 n. 2, 1 ELR 20050 n. 2 (1970).

19. 1953 Reorganization Plan No. 1, § 5, 18 Fed.Reg. 2053, 67 Stat. 631 (1954). A partial transfer of functions was accomplished by 1970 Reorganization Plan No. 3, § 2(a)(4), 35 Fed.Reg. 15623, 84 Stat. 2087 (1970); see § 8.8 below (tolerances).

20. 40 CFR § 180.7.

21. 21 U.S.C.A. § 346a(b).

22. Id. § 334.

23. Pub.L. No. 86–139, § 2, 73 Stat. 286 (1959), amending 7 U.S.C.A. § 135.

24. Pub.L. No. 88–305, § 2, 78 Stat. 190 (1964); see 100 Cong.Rec. 2948–49 (1964) (remarks of Rep. Sullivan).

25. Pub.L. No. 88–305, § 2, 78 Stat. 190 (1964), amending 7 U.S.C.A. § 135b(c); see Stearns Elec. Paste Co. v. Environmental Protection Agency, 461 F.2d 293, 303, 2 ELR 20368, 20371 (7th Cir. 1972).

26. House Comm. on Government Operations, Deficiencies in Administra-

Sec. 8.3 ENVIRONMENTAL PESTICIDE CONTROL ACT   849

ucts had been approved for use without compliance with interdepartmental procedures for resolving safety questions; that they had been approved for uses practically certain to result in the illegal adulteration of food; that some labels approved for registration failed to inform users of possible hazards and provide accurate directions; that actions to cancel registered products were long delayed; that, despite completion of uncontested cancellation proceedings, hazardous products lingered in marketing channels for years; and that conflicts of interest had clouded some administrative decisions. These disclosures contributed in no small way to a government reorganization plan in 1970 that stripped USDA of its authority over the regulation of chemical pesticides and transferred that authority to the newly established Environmental Protection Agency. The rivalry between the two agencies has not abated in the intervening years. Increased congressional interest and public awareness, symbolized by the DDT controversy in the late 1960's, set the stage for major amendments in 1972.

b. *Federal Environmental Pesticide Control Act of 1972*

Unlike most recent national environmental legislation, the 1972 FEPCA, amending FIFRA,[27] was not unabashedly the product of the deliberations of congressional committees strongly committed to environmental values. The House Committee on Agriculture and the Senate Committee on Agriculture and Forestry generally were hostile to environmentalists, as the hearings [28] and reports [29] clearly indicate.

tion of the Federal Insecticide, Fungicide, and Rodenticide Act, H.R.Rep. No. 637, 91st Cong., 1st Sess. (1969); see Hearings on Deficiencies in Administration of Federal Insecticide, Fungicide and Rodenticide Act, Before a Subcomm. of the House Comm. on Gov't Operations, 91st Cong., 1st Sess. (1969).

27. An internal EPA memorandum describing the amendments earned recognition as the Memo of the Month, Wash. Monthly, Jan. 1974 at 46:

Due to the uncertainty which exists as to the name of the current law governing pesticide regulation, and to the currency of the acronym FEPCA, the Office of Pesticide Programs issues the following statement as definitive.

The Federal Environmental Pesticide Control Act, or FEPCA, was a legislative mechanism used to amend the 1947 FIFRA. The law under which pesticides are regulated by the Federal Government is correctly known as the Federal Insecticide, Fungicide and Rodenticide Act. When the effective dates contained in Sec. 4 of P.L. 92-516 have passed, FEPCA will pass out of existence, leaving only "FIFRA as amended," or "FIFRA of 1972."

The Office of Pesticide Programs realizes that many individuals, including some representatives of the Environmental Protection Agency, have mistakenly used "FEPCA" where "FIFRA as amended" was intended. It is our hope that this statement will clarify the situation, and lead to a uniform usage.

28. See, e. g., Hearings on the Federal Environmental Pesticide Control Act, Before the Subcomm. of Agricultural Research and General Legislation of the Senate Comm. on Agriculture and Forestry, 92d Cong., 1st Sess. 608–71 (1971); Hearings on the Federal Pesticide Control Act of 1971, Before the House Comm. on Agriculture, H.R.Doc. No. A, 92d Cong., 1st Sess., 1, 3 (1971) (opening remarks of Rep. Poage, Chairman).

29. See, Comm. of Conference, Federal Environmental Pesticide Control Act of 1972, H.R.Rep. No. 1540, 92d Cong., 2d Sess. (1972); Senate Comm. on Agriculture and Forestry, Federal

Intervention in the legislative process by the Senate Commerce Committee [30] produced several changes favored by environmental groups but the final product was a "severely compromised" [31] measure. The statute's mixed origins and sometimes contradictory aims compound the usual problems of interpretation.

At the heart of FEPCA, whose essentials are still firmly in place, are the registration provisions borrowed with substantial modifications from prior law. Registration with the Environmental Protection Agency is a precondition of sale.[32] The Act goes into some detail concerning registration procedures,[33] the criteria for approval,[34] and the consequences of disapproval.[35] A registered pesticide may be classified for general use, restricted use, or both.[36] A restricted use pesticide, which is high in personal or environmental risk, can be applied only under the supervision of a certified applicator or subject to other restrictions.[37] The classification also must be reflected in the packaging and labeling of the pesticide.[38] The registration requirements are not all encompassing. There are minor exemptions for pesticides transferred between registered establishments and those "of a character which is unnecessary to be subject" to the Act,[39] and potentially major ones for pesticides used under experimental use permits [40] or used by state or federal agencies after the Administrator determines that emergency conditions exist.[41] Under certain circumstances, a state may register a pesticide "to meet special local needs" [42] even though criteria for federal registration are not met.

The historical desire to protect consumers from ineffective products and misleading claims is strongly evident in the 1972 FEPCA. The criteria for approval of a registration call for findings that the product composition warrants the claims made for it and that the labeling and related material submitted for approval conform to the requirements of the Act.[43] Also carried over from the 1947 FIFRA,

Environmental Pesticide Control Act of 1972, S.Rep. No. 838, 92d Cong., 2d Sess. (1972); House Comm. on Agriculture, Federal Environmental Pesticide Control Act of 1971, H.R. Rep. No. 511, 92d Cong., 1st Sess. (1971).

30. Senate Comm. on Commerce, Federal Environmental Pesticide Control Act of 1972, S.Rep. No. 970, 92d Cong., 2d Sess. (1972).

31. Butler, Federal Pesticide Law, in Environmental Law Institute, Federal Environmental Law 1232, 1234 (E. L. Dolgin & T. G. P. Guilbert eds. 1974). The legislative history is chronicled fully in id. at 1234–35 n. 5.

32. 7 U.S.C.A. § 136a(a); see § 8.4 below.

33. 7 U.S.C.A. § 136a(c).

34. Id. § 136a(c)(5).

35. Id. § 136a(c)(6).

36. Id. § 136a(d); see § 8.5 below.

37. 7 U.S.C.A. § 136a(d)(1)(C)(i).

38. Id. § 136(a)(2)(B).

39. Id. § 136w(b)(2); see § 8.6 below.

40. 7 U.S.C.A. § 136c.

41. Id. § 136p.

42. Id. § 136v(c).

43. Id. §§ 136a(c)(5)(A), (B).

Sec. 8.3 ENVIRONMENTAL PESTICIDE CONTROL ACT 851

with some modifications, are the broad definitions of label and labeling,[44] and the definitions of adulterated [45] and misbranded [46] products. The concept of adulteration obviously is aimed at maintaining the strength and purity of a product, while that of misbranding seeks to assure accurate and useful information on the labels and containers. A product can be misbranded if the labels and other protections are not "adequate to protect health and the environment." [47] An interesting question, raised first by the 1947 FIFRA and discussed below,[48] is the extent to which certain high risk products remain misbranded despite accurate descriptions on the labels and in the directions for use and warning statements.

The registration provisions in the 1972 amendments are complemented by cancellation provisions anticipating an adjudicatory hearing.[49] An immediate suspension of a registration is authorized if the Administrator determines that the action "is necessary to prevent an imminent hazard during the time required for cancellation or change in classification proceedings." [50] Elaborate procedures are called for in the cancellation or suspension proceedings,[51] including the possibility of a referral of "the relevant questions of scientific fact" to an advisory committee convened by the National Academy of Sciences.[52] Although some improvement was made on the tortuous mechanism of the 1947 FIFRA by the 1972 amendments, Congress changed course again in 1975, erecting more procedural obstacles along the cancellation-suspension path.

FEPCA of 1972 strengthened the enforcement mechanism not inconsiderably. Procedurally, establishments producing pesticides must register with the Administrator.[53] The Administrator is given the power to prescribe regulations requiring the maintenance of records in a form compatible with effective enforcement,[54] to call for the production of records,[55] to inspect establishments,[56] to issue warning notices [57] and orders to stop selling or using a product,[58] to seize (among other things) adulterated, misbranded, or unregistered pesticides,[59] to initiate civil penalty proceedings,[60] and to delegate to the

44. Id. § 136(p).

45. Id. § 136(c).

46. Id. § 136(q).

47. Id. § 136(q)(1)(G).

48. § 8.5 below.

49. 7 U.S.C.A. §§ 136d(a), (d); see § 8.7 below.

50. 7 U.S.C.A. § 136(c)(1).

51. Id. §§ 136d(b), (c), (d).

52. Id. § 136d(d); see § 1.12 above (discussing The National Academy of Sciences).

53. 7 U.S.C.A. § 136e; see § 8.9 below.

54. 7 U.S.C.A. § 136f(a).

55. Id. § 136f(b).

56. Id. § 136g(a).

57. Id. § 136g(c)(3).

58. Id. § 136k(a).

59. Id. § 136k(b).

60. Id. § 136*l*.

states authority to cooperate in the enforcement of the Act.[61] Made unlawful under the Act are a wide range of activities, the most important of which are the selling or receiving of an adulterated, misbranded, or unregistered pesticide.[62] A number of individual activities are forbidden for the first time. These include using a registered pesticide in a manner inconsistent with its labeling [63] and using a pesticide contrary to the provisions of an experimental use permit.[64] It also is unlawful to falsify knowingly part of any application for registration or for an experimental use permit [65] and to use pesticides in tests on human beings unless they are fully informed and freely volunteer.[66]

The remaining miscellaneous provisions of the 1972 FEPCA include both the routine and the unusual. Among the routine are judicial review provisions,[67] and powers granted to the Administrator to conduct and support research and cooperate with other agencies in establishing a national plan for monitoring pesticides.[68] A section on effective dates is included, unfortunately not without ambiguities.[69] The Administrator is given powers to intercept imports of pesticides that are adulterated, misbranded, or "otherwise injurious to health or the environment," [70] but pesticides intended for export are virtually exempt.[71] More unusual are the indemnity provisions for the benefit of persons caught unwittingly with quantities of banned pesticides [72] and the powers to prescribe regulations for the disposal of pesticide containers and banned pesticides.[73] This latter authority gives EPA a foothold on the subject of land disposal of hazardous substances, which until 1976 remained largely beyond the reach of federal law.[74]

The Administrator is given other powers of debatable consequence. After notice and opportunity for hearing, he may "declare a pest any form of plant or animal life", other than man and microorganisms that live on or in man or other living animals, which "is injurious to health or the environment." [75] Apart from wondering what might have happened if Congress had neglected to exempt man from this power to condemn virtually every species on the planet, a question arises as to the consequences of being declared "a pest." The

---

61. Id. § 136v(a).

62. Id. § 136j(a)(1)(E).

63. Id. § 136j(a)(2)(G).

64. Id. § 136j(a)(2)(H).

65. Id. § 136j(a)(2)(M).

66. Id. § 136j(a)(2)(P).

67. Id. § 136n.

68. Id. § 136r(b).

69. Section 4, 86 Stat. 998 (1972); see 1 EPA, Collection of Legal Opinions December 1970–December 1973, at 431–32 (1974).

70. 7 U.S.C.A. § 136o(c).

71. Id. § 136o(a).

72. Id. § 136m; § 8.9 below.

73. 7 U.S.C.A. § 136q.

74. § 6.10 above.

75. 7 U.S.C.A. § 136w(c)(1).

most obvious result is that this declaration opens the way for the registration of pesticides having as a purpose "preventing, destroying, repelling or mitigating any pest." [76] The Administrator has published a wholesale declaration that just about every living thing that is "deleterious" to man or the environment is a pest.[77] This very well may amount to an abuse of discretion because the legislation clearly anticipates an administrative judgment that something is a pest before clearing the way for registration of substances to destroy it.

Also after notice and opportunity for hearing, the Administrator may identify "any pesticide which contains any substance or substances in quantities highly toxic to man." [78] The consequences of such a declaration are various. It might be collaterally significant in a suspension or cancellation proceeding. Any pesticide containing a substance "highly toxic to man" automatically is misbranded unless the label bears the skull and crossbones, the word "poison" prominently displayed in red, and "a statement of practical treatment (first aid or otherwise) in case of poisoning by the pesticide." [79] In cases of a pesticide having no known antidote and thus being incapable of escaping the misbranding provisions, an administrative judgment that the product is "highly toxic to man" would amount to a de facto decision to cancel or suspend the registration.

c. *The 1975 Amendments*

Authorizations for appropriations under the 1972 amendments to FIFRA terminated on June 30, 1975.[80] After intensive hearings,[81] Congress eventually enacted a two-year extension of FIFRA that includes several amendments.

Not adopted were provisions urged by environmental groups, such as the elimination of the indemnity section for unused pesticides banned by EPA and a clarification that the burden of proving the safety of a pesticide in suspension and cancellation proceedings remains on the proponent of continued use. Congress also rejected several proposals backed by agribusiness interests that would have given USDA a veto over EPA's pesticide decisions.[82] The struggle between EPA

76. Id. § 136(u)(1).

77. 40 CFR § 162.14.

78. 7 U.S.C.A. § 136w(c)(2).

79. Id. § 136q(2)(D).

80. Section 27, 86 Stat. 998 (1972).

81. In order to have sufficient time to deliberate, Congress passed two interim funding extensions for FIFRA. Senate Comm. on Agriculture and Forestry, Extension of the Federal Insecticide, Fungicide, and Rodenticide Act, S.Rep. No. 452, 94th Cong., 1st Sess. 5 (1975).

82. During the House Committee on Agriculture's mark-up, the Committee's original bill was substituted by a bill offered by Congressmen Poage and Wampler which required the concurrence of the Secretary of USDA on decisions made by EPA regarding pesticide registrations and classifications as well as proposed and final regulations. House Comm. on Agriculture, Federal Insecticide, Fungicide, and Rodenticide Act, As Amended, H.R.Rep. No. 497, 94th Cong., 1st

and USDA over pesticides is a longstanding one,[83] resembling that between EPA and the Federal Aviation Administration over jet noise,[84] except that as to noise EPA has sought to enhance its authority and as to pesticides to defend it. Ultimately, Congress kept intact the structure of FEPCA, including EPA's registration powers, while opting to impose additional procedural constraints on the agency's decision-making and to make several other technical changes in the Act. The procedural techniques chosen, familiar to any student of the National Environmental Policy Act [85] and the hard look doctrine of judicial review,[86] were additional documentation, consultation, and reasoned decision-making.

One aspect of the decision-making process touched by these requirements for more study and consultation is concerned with registration suspensions and cancellations, discussed below.[87] A second involves the promulgation of regulations. Section 21(a) of the 1972 FEPCA had obliged the Administrator of EPA to solicit the views of the Secretary of Agriculture before publishing regulations.[88] Despite this invitation to get together, the relationship between the two agencies has remained adversarial rather than cooperative. The 1975 amendments enforce a shotgun wedding: at least 60 days prior to signing a proposed regulation and 30 days prior to signing a final regulation the Administrator must provide the Secretary with a copy.[89] Timely comments by the Secretary, together with the responses of the Administrator, must be published in the Federal Register along with the text of the regulations. Also brought into the consulting process is a scientific advisory committee appointed by the Administrator from among nominees of the National Institutes of Health and the National Science Foundation.[90] The committee must be given an opportunity to review and comment "as to the impact on health and the environment of the action" proposed in notices of intent to cancel or change a classification or in proposed or final regulations.[91] The comments of the scientific advisory committee, together with the responses of the Administrator, are published in the Federal Register

---

Sess. 33 (1975) [hereinafter cited as 1975 House Report]. The Poage-Wampler bill subsequently was modified by an amendment offered by Congressman Vigorito to require the consultation procedure set forth in sections 1 and 2 of the amendments as enacted. Id. at 34.

83. Lack of cooperation between USDA and HEW was one of the reasons that prompted the 1970 reorganization, shifting much of USDA's regulatory power over pesticides to the newly established EPA. Since reorganization, USDA and EPA often have appeared as adversaries in adjudicatory proceedings.

84. § 5.7 above.

85. §§ 7.1–7.10 above.

86. § 1.5 above.

87. § 8.7 below.

88. 86 Stat. 996.

89. 7 U.S.C.A. § 136w(a)(1).

90. Id. § 136w(d).

91. Ibid.

Sec. 8.3   ENVIRONMENTAL PESTICIDE CONTROL ACT

as are the comments of USDA. The purposes of the scientific advisory committee process is to strengthen the technical input on issues that are closely contested within the scientific community and to provide an alternative to the procedure, not often used, for referring scientific facts to the National Academy of Sciences.[92] Administration of the pesticide laws often has relied upon the use of advisory committees.[93] They are awkward procedurally, and can be abused,[94] but they also can strengthen EPA's substantive decision-making.

A third consultative process, this one political, involves advance notice from EPA to the congressional agricultural committees of proposed and final regulations at the time notice is given to USDA.[95] This is an increasingly common technique used by congressional committees to stay close to the action, and there is nothing inherently wrong with it. The ostensible purpose is said to be a desire to make sure EPA acts consistently with the intent of Congress,[96] although the actual effect may be to enforce the intent of the committees. The obvious risk is that political intervention may skew the better judgments of EPA, and the legislation does nothing to undermine this possibility since it does not require publication of congressional comments on pending rules. Still, it is difficult to oppose this consultative arrangement without making an untenable argument for less congressional oversight. The basic problem from the perspective of the environmental constituency is that the pesticides program administered by EPA is in the hands of congressional committees decidedly hostile to it.

One of the most important changes made by the 1975 amendments is to require EPA approval of state plans permitting self-certification of private applicators, notably farmers.[97] The effect is to undermine seriously the classification system, distinguishing between general and restricted use pesticides, and cast doubt on the "careful use" premises of FIFRA. An indirect consequence might be to encourage EPA to seek more cancellations and suspensions of high risk pesticides.[98]

The 1975 amendments change FIFRA in several other respects. First, the Act's implementation deadlines are extended one year.[99]

92. 1975 House Report, supra note 82, at 11; see Hearings on H.R. 8841, Before the Subcomm. on Agricultural Research and General Legislation of the Senate Comm. on Agriculture and Forestry, 94th Cong., 1st Sess. 116–17 (1975) (testimony of Russell Train, Administrator, Environmental Protection Agency) [hereinafter cited as 1975 Senate Agriculture Hearings].

93. See § 1.11 above.

94. Ibid.

95. 7 U.S.C.A. § 136w(a)(3).

96. 1975 House Report, supra note 82, at 8.

97. 7 U.S.C.A. § 136b(a)(1); see § 8.5 below.

98. 1975 Senate Agriculture Hearings, supra note 92, at 95 (testimony of Russell Train, Administrator, Environmental Protection Agency).

99. Federal Insecticide, Fungicide, and Rodenticide Act, Extension § 4, 89 Stat. 752 (1975).

Second, the statutory definition of "pesticide" is modified to exclude certain products that come within the purview of the Federal Food, Drug, and Cosmetic Act.[1] Third, EPA's authority to issue experimental use permits to agricultural research facilities for educational or research purposes is clarified.[2] Fourth, in determining whether an emergency exists necessitating the use of a prohibited pesticide by a federal agency, EPA formally is required to consult with USDA and the governor of any concerned state.[3] Fifth, it is made clear that the cost sharing responsibilities of later applicants who attempt "piggyback" rides on an earlier registrant's data apply only to applications submitted on or after the date of enactment of FEPCA, October 21, 1972.[4]

d. *Miscellaneous Provisions of Federal Law*

Numerous other federal statutes contribute to the regulatory mosaic covering pesticides. The Clean Air Amendments of 1970 and Federal Water Pollution Control Act Amendments of 1972, particularly insofar as they address toxic discharges,[5] are potentially relevant. The Food, Drug, and Cosmetic Act contains tolerance provisions that govern pesticide residues in the food supply.[6] The Occupational Safety and Health Act gives the Occupational Safety and Health Administration (OSHA) a jurisdictional claim as regards farmworker field reentry standards that prevent hasty reentry by workers into fields recently sprayed, although prospects for their ultimate enforcement appear dim.[7] OSHA has undisputed authority over in-plant safety standards protecting workers from pesticide and other chemical residues.[8] The Poison Prevention Packaging Act,[9] now administered by

1. 7 U.S.C.A. § 136(v). The provision was prompted by testimony presented by the Animal Health Institute regarding confusion and prolonged delays encountered in attempts to register certain substances within the dual jurisdiction of EPA and FDA. Hearings on the Federal Insecticide, Fungicide, and Rodenticide Act Extension, Before the House Comm. on Agriculture, H.R.Doc. No. O, 94th Cong., 1st Sess., 444 (1975) (statement of Robert E. Boyles, Chairman, Pesticide Task Force, Animal Health Institute).

2. 7 U.S.C.A. § 136c(g); see § 8.6 below.

3. 7 U.S.C.A. § 136p; see § 8.6 below.

4. 7 U.S.C.A. § 136a(c)(1)(D).

5. §§ 3.11, 4.15 above; see 41 Fed.Reg. 48088 (1976) (interim effluent limitations and guidelines for pesticides manufacturing point source category).

6. § 8.8 below.

7. See Organized Migrants in Community Action v. Brennan, 172 U.S. App.D.C. 147, 520 F.2d 1161, 5 ELR 20681 (1975) (EPA's issuance of field reentry standards ousts Secretary of Labor of jurisdiction); Florida Peach Growers Ass'n v. Dep't of Labor, 489 F.2d 120, 4 ELR 20170 (5th Cir. 1974) (vacating an amended emergency temporary standard on ground that substantial evidence did not support finding of a grave danger).

8. The cases accumulating on OSHA's in-plant regulatory powers include Soc'y of the Plastics Indus., Inc. v. Occupational Safety & Health Administration, 509 F.2d 1301, 5 ELR 20157 (2d Cir. 1975), cert. denied 421 U.S. 992 (vinyl chloride); Synthetic Organic Chem. Mfrs. Ass'n v. Brennan, 506 F.2d 385 (3d Cir. 1974), cert.

9. See note 9 on page 857.

the Consumer Product Safety Commission, provides authority to regulate the packaging of pesticide products that pose a distinct and well documented [10] hazard to children in the home. The 1972 FEPCA gives EPA authority on the same topic,[11] thus requiring an eventual accommodation between the two agencies. No doubt numerous other examples of legislative fragmentation of the pesticide picture exist. More important, and less easily answered, is whether this legislative and administrative army has subdued the health and environmental hazards that prompted its enlistment.

§ 8.4 Registration: Generally

As of January 1975, approximately 29,000 pesticide products made up of some 1800 chemicals were registered with the Environmental Protection Agency.[1] Thousands of other applications are pending, including some 17,000 intrastate pesticides not previously required to be registered.[2] Of the products now registered, the largest number are insecticides (49%), followed by herbicides (17%), disinfectants (17%), fungicides (14%) and rodenticides (3%).[3]

The basic regulatory premise of the Federal Environmental Pesticide Control Act (FEPCA) is found in section (3)(a), which forbids the distribution and sale to any person of a pesticide not registered with the Administrator.[4] The Administrator is obliged to register a

denied 420 U.S. 973 (1975) (14 carcinogenic substances); Synthetic Organic Chem. Mfrs. Ass'n v. Brennan, 503 F.2d 1155 (1975) (ethyleneimine); Industrial Union Dep't, AFL-CIO v. Hodgson, 162 U.S.App.D.C. 331, 499 F.2d 467, 4 ELR 20415 (1974) (asbestos); Dry Color Mfrs. Ass'n, Inc. v. Dep't of Labor, 486 F.2d 98, 3 ELR 20855 (3d Cir. 1973) (carcinogenic substances).

9. 84 Stat. 1970, 15 U.S.C.A. §§ 1471–73 (1971).

10. See 40 Fed.Reg. 28241, 28259–60 (1975) (discussing problem and collecting authorities).

11. 7 U.S.C.A. § 136w(c)(3).

1. Comptroller General of the United States, Report to the Congress on the Federal Pesticide Registration Program: Is It Protecting the Public and the Environment Adequately From Pesticide Hazards? 1 (1975) [hereinafter cited as 1975 GAO Report]. This is the third in an informative series of General Accounting Office reports on the pesticides program. By year's end, the number of registered pesticide products had risen to 32,000. Letter to Mr. William Sierks and author, from Charles E. Colledge, Office of Pesticide Programs, EPA, Dec. 19, 1975.

2. 1975 GAO Report, supra note 1, at 67:

The FECPA registration program workload of about 46,000 pesticides is composed of about 29,000 currently registered pesticides that must be reregistered and 17,000 intrastate pesticides that were not previously required to be registered by EPA.

. . .

In addition to the 46,000 FEPCA registrations, EPA's projected workload during the 2-year period includes 13,000 anticipated new pesticide registrations and 14,000 amended registrations (applications for changes, such as changes in product formulations, uses, or labeling).

3. Id. at 1.

4. 7 U.S.C.A. § 136a(a). Id. § 136a (b) exempts transfers pursuant to an

pesticide if, taking into account restrictions he may impose upon its use, he determines it satisfies four criteria: (1) "its composition is such as to warrant the proposed claims for it;" (2) "its labeling and other material required to be submitted comply with the requirements of this Act"; (3) "it will perform its intended function without unreasonable adverse effects on the environment"; and (4) "when used in accordance with widespread and commonly recognized practice it will not generally cause unreasonable adverse effects on the environment." [5]

The first two criteria, dealing with composition and labeling, fulfill the historic functions of federal pesticide law by protecting consumers from ineffective products and misleading claims.[6] The latter two criteria impart a substantive test of safety and thus set the threshold standards of acceptability.

The phrase "unreasonable adverse effects on the environment" is defined in the Act to mean "any unreasonable risk to man or the environment, taking into account the economic, social, and environmental costs and benefits of the use of any pesticide." [7] Environment is defined broadly to include "water, air, land, and all plants and man and other animals living therein, and the interrelationships which exist among these." [8] The "unreasonable adverse effects" clause originated with the Senate Commerce Committee and was aimed at tightening the criteria for registration; "substantial adverse effects" had appeared in the House bill.[9] The Commerce Committee explains: "[T]he bill on its face would require the EPA to make a full weighing of competing interests in making its determinations. Thus, it is intended that any adverse effect ought not to be tolerated unless there are overriding benefits from the use of a pesticide." [10] The Report uses the language of cost-benefit analysis: "[T]he necessary balancing of risk versus benefit [should be undertaken] in determining whether a pesticide should be registered." [11] Given the prevalence of incommensurables, however, and the consequent lack of mathematical certainty, the test for registration boils down to whether a reasonable man, with knowledge of the risks and benefits, would register the product for use. Judicial review of this adminis-

experimental use permit and some transfers among establishments of a producer for packaging or formulation prior to sale. See § 8.6 below.

5. 7 U.S.C.A. §§ 136a(c)(5)(A)–(D).

6. § 8.5 below.

7. 7 U.S.C.A. § 136(bb).

8. Id. § 136(j).

9. House Comm. on Agriculture, Federal Environmental Pesticide Control Act of 1971, H.R.Rep. No. 511, 92d Cong., 1st Sess. 49 (1971) [hereinafter cited as House Report].

10. Senate Comm. on Commerce, Federal Environmental Pesticide Control Act of 1972, S.Rep. No. 970, 92d Cong., 2d Sess. 11 (1972) [hereinafter cited as Commerce Committee Report].

11. Id. at 10.

Sec. 8.4　REGISTRATION: GENERALLY　859

trative determination of course is circumscribed by familiar standards.[12]

The Act makes clear that the Administrator "shall not make any lack of essentiality a criterion for denying registration of any pesticide."[13] The provision was inspired by objections of the House Committee on Agriculture to the executive practice over the years of restricting persistent pesticides to "essential uses" only.[14] The Senate Commerce Committee was concerned that rejection of the "doctrine of essentiality" could be read as precluding consideration of less hazardous substitutes in the balancing judgment on registration.[15] While the Committee did not succeed in striking the repudiation of essentiality as a criteria for registration, it was instrumental in adding an explanatory sentence: "Where two pesticides meet the requirements of this paragraph, one should not be registered in preference to the other."[16] Thus, dismissal of "the lack of essentiality" criterion should be read as allowing registration even though another pesticide, equally safe and effective, is available to do the job.[17] It does not bar the Administrator, in evaluating risks and benefits, from taking into account the fact that less risky alternatives are available.[18]

The differences between the third and fourth criteria are not entirely clear. Criterion three requires a determination that a pesticide "will perform its intended function without unreasonable adverse effects on the environment." The preferred reading of this provision is that a product qualifies for registration if it works (i. e., kills insects which is the "intended function") without taking an unreasonable toll on nontarget species (by misuse, inevitably even with careful use, or by accident). Criterion three also can be read as meaning that a product qualifies for registration if it works without unreasonable effects if not misused; that is, the "intended function" is that it be applied in the theoretical circumstance where labels and instructions for use always are read and heeded. If criterion three does not reach the situation of normal, sloppy use, criterion four certainly does. This states that a pesticide qualifies for registration if when "used in accordance with widespread and commonly recognized prac-

12.　§ 1.5 above.

13.　7 U.S.C.A. § 136a(c)(5).

14.　House Report, supra note 9, at 14. In 1969, the prestigious Mrak Commission Report recommended restricting use of DDT and DDD to those uses "essential to the preservation of human health or welfare . . . ." Dep't of HEW, Report of the Secretary's Commission on Pesticides and Their Relationship to Environmental Health 8 (1969). The "essential use" limitations were recommended first by the President's Science Advisory Committee, Use of Pesticides (1963).

15.　Commerce Committee Report, supra note 10, at 11.

16.　7 U.S.C.A. § 135a(c)(5).

17.　Commerce Committee Report, supra note 10, at 11.

18.　See House Report, supra note 9, at 14 (explaining as superfluous the deletion of a registration requirement that "alternative means of control" be considered).

tice it will not generally cause unreasonable adverse effects on the environment." This should be read as meaning that a pesticide does not qualify for registration if it causes unreasonable effects if "used in accordance with widespread and commonly recognized practice" that may or may not be sanctioned by the labeling.[19] A practice is "recognized" not by receiving some form of official sanction but because it occurs with predictable regularity.[20] It may be a "widespread and commonly recognized practice" to use excessive amounts or apply a product in prohibited areas but not to use it for suicide or homicide.

The important proposition established by criteria three and four is that they set a substantive standard of safety for man and the environment as a prerequisite to registration. This point was much in doubt under the 1947 FIFRA.[21] In registering a pesticide, or re-registering one, the Administrator also must judge unreasonable effects without assuming artificially that all labels and warnings will be drafted with clarity, read, and heeded.

The statute goes into only limited details on the registration procedure and the data necessary to support a registration,[22] but the Administrator has filled in the specifics.[23] Basically, the Administrator must decide whether the pesticide satisfies the registration criteria and, if so, the classification it should be given (general or restricted use) and the labeling required.[24] Data submissions are supposed to meet these aims. Thus, an applicant must submit data on the product's efficacy, general and environmental chemistry, and

---

19. See Southern Nat'l Mfg. Co. v. Environmental Protection Agency, 470 F.2d 194, 3 ELR 20323 (8th Cir. 1972).

20. But see Stearns Elec. Paste Co. v. Environmental Protection Agency, 461 F.2d 293, 311, 2 ELR 20368, 20374 (7th Cir. 1972) (interpreting "commonly recognized practice" language in misbranding provisions of 1947 FIFRA) ("Perhaps the phrase indicates that whenever misuse occurs with sufficient frequency to be considered a common practice, a finding of misbranding is required. Such an interpretation, however, would attach no significance to the word 'recognized.' We believe a fair reading of the phrase relates to common practices which are 'recognized' in the sense that they are approved by widespread custom or practice. In this case there has been no finding that misuse of Stearns Paste is either a common practice or a commonly recognized practice . . . ") (footnote omitted). Compare Nor-Am Agricultural Prods., Inc. v. Hardin, 435 F.2d 1133, 1 ELR 20032 (7th Cir. 1970), rev'd on procedural grounds on rehearing en banc 435 F.2d 1151, 1164 (7th Cir.) (Pell, J., dissenting) ("The fact that misuse may result in damage does not in my opinion make a product imminently hazardous in the absence of an evidentiary showing that such misuse is frequent or was reasonably likely to occur"); see § 8.5 n. 30 below (collecting authorities on frequency of misuse).

21. See Stearns Elec. Paste Co. v. Environmental Protection Agency, supra note 20.

22. 7 U.S.C.A. § 136a(c).

23. 40 Fed.Reg. 28242, 41788 (1975), amending 40 CFR pt. 162.

24. § 8.5 below. A pre-condition of registration is the obtaining of a tolerance or exemption if use of the pesticide is expected to result in residues on food. 40 CFR § 162.7 (d)(v); see § 8.8 below.

Sec. 8.4 REGISTRATION: GENERALLY

hazards to man and to the environment including nontarget species. Over the years, data requirements for pesticides registration have become progressively more demanding—acute toxicity testing (single exposure that will result in mortality in 50 percent of the animals exposed) and subacute toxicity testing (usually over a period of 90 days) were first required in 1954, chronic feeding—oncogenicity testing (for tumors) in 1963, reproduction testing (to determine effects on reproduction capabilities) in 1963, teratogenicity testing (for birth defects) in 1970, and mutagenicity testing (for permanent genetic changes) in 1972.[25] For pesticides intended for outdoor application, data to evaluate effects on nontarget species "may be obtained from avian reproduction studies, aquatic invertebrate acute toxicity testing, aquatic organism life cycle studies, submitted field testing, and or field monitoring and observation, as specified in the Registration Guidelines." [26]

The registration process is decidedly a private affair. Public participation is not expected and does not occur. Federal Register notice of each application usually is required,[27] but the data supporting the registration (more accurately, that part of it not given trade secret protection) need not be made available to the public until 30 days after a pesticide is registered.[28] Environmental impact statements are not prepared in connection with registration decisions although respectable arguments can be made that they ought to be, at least in certain cases.[29] The GAO's evaluation of this private registration process discloses marked deficiencies—required studies are not submitted for many registered pesticides; often little or no information is included on long-term effects or synergistic effects of two or more active ingredients; inadequate testing of potentially hazardous inert ingredients is common; and information on environmental effects often is missing.[30]

Administratively, EPA has established criteria giving rise to a rebuttable presumption that a notice of intent to deny registration, or cancel an existing regulation, should issue.[31] The case law makes clear that the burden of proving safety is on the applicant and remains that way after registration through succeeding challenges raised in cancellation or reregistration proceedings.[32] Notwithstand-

25. 1975 GAO Report, supra note 1, at 7–8.

26. 40 CFR § 162.8(b)(4)(ii)(B).

27. 7 U.S.C.A. § 136a(c)(4).

28. Id. § 136a(c)(2).

29. Cf. Wyoming v. Hathaway, 525 F.2d 66, 73–74, 6 ELR 20169, 20172 (10th Cir. 1975) (Seth, J., dissenting) (contending that EIS should be required for EPA pesticide suspension or cancellation decisions because no functional equivalent is prepared).

30. 1975 GAO Report, supra note 1, ch. 2.

31. 40 CFR § 162.11.

32. Environmental Defense Fund, Inc. v. Environmental Protection Agency (heptachlor/chlordane), —— U.S.App. D.C. ——, ——, 548 F.2d 998, 1004, 7 ELR 20012, 20014 (1976); Environmental Defense Fund, Inc. v. Environ-

ing this, EPA certainly is not to be discouraged from invoking the rebuttable presumption technique to assist in sorting out the good from the bad. Rebuttable presumptions can arise if the data suggests certain types of high risks—for example, if a pesticide's ingredients or degradation products occur as a residue on the feed of a mammalian species representative of a species likely to be exposed "at levels equal to or greater than the acute oral LD 50 measured in mammalian test animals . . . ."[33] A rebuttable presumption of unacceptability can be overcome by, among other techniques, showing that the economic, social, and environmental benefits of use "outweigh the risk of use."[34]

An applicant refused registration has certain rights of notice, a reasoned disposition, and a hearing.[35] A successful registration is required to be cancelled automatically at the end of five years.[36] The purpose of the latter provision is to avoid the vesting of rights in perpetuity long associated with registrations under the 1947 FIFRA. Theoretically, renewed registrations must satisfy the same criteria as new ones. Practically, renewals are easier to come by; one reason is that better data is available. The GAO has found that sometimes renewals do not occur because "EPA has not renewed or canceled pesticide registrations as required, and, as a result, many pesticides whose registrations are over 5 years old are being marketed, although their registrations have not been renewed."[37] Not to be confused with the five-year renewal registrations is a reregistration which is a one-time process for bringing previously registered products into compliance.[38] EPA also recognizes an amended registration (to cover such subjects as changes in proposed labeling to add new uses)[39] and supplemental registrations (to permit the distributor of a registered product to market it under the distributor's brand name).[40]

One of the most lively controversies in the registration process involves allocating the costs of research necessary for product regis-

mental Protection Agency (aldrin/dieledrin II), 167 U.S.App.D.C. 71, 81, 510 F.2d 1292, 1302, 5 ELR 20243, 20246–47 (1975); Stearns Elec. Paste Co. v. Environmental Protection Agency, 461 F.2d 293, 304–05, 2 ELR 20368, 20371 (7th Cir. 1972).

33. 40 CFR § 162.11(a)(3)(i)(B)(1). LD 50 refers to the acute toxicity test where a single exposure results in mortality of 50 percent of the animals exposed.

34. Id. § 162.11(a)(5)(iii).

35. 7 U.S.C.A. § 136a(c)(6). Rights to participate in various hearings occasioned by registration denials, can-

cellations, and especially reclassifications are one of the murkier subjects of the pesticide law. See Butler, Federal Pesticide Law, in Environmental Law Institute, Federal Environmental Law 1232, 1249 (E. L. Dolgin & T. G. P. Guilbert eds. 1974).

36. 7 U.S.C.A. § 136d.

37. 1975 GAO Report, supra note 1, at 67.

38. 7 U.S.C.A. § 136(z).

39. 40 CFR § 162.6(b)(3).

40. Id. § 162.6(b)(4); 7 U.S.C.A. § 136a(c).

tration among two manufacturers seeking to register similar products. The 1972 FEPCA included a "piggy-back provision" providing that data prepared in support of one registration could not be considered in connection with a second unless the later applicant seeking the free ride agrees to pay the first registrant a fair share of expenses.[41] EPA has had enough difficulties in defining the costs and making allocations,[42] but there also was a question whether the provision applied to data or applications submitted prior to the enactment of the 1972 FEPCA. This ambiguity resulted in a great deal of controversy holding up the registration of several pesticides.[43] The 1975 amendments resolve the dispute by providing that EPA's authority to compel reasonable compensation applies only to data submitted on or after January 1, 1970 and used in connection with applications submitted on or after October 21, 1972.[44]

§ 8.5 Registration: Classification, Misbranding and Labeling

The Federal Environmental Pesticide Control Act of 1972 (FEPCA) introduced what has been described as "key new authorities" to overcome the widespread suspicion that labels often were not read and followed.[1] Originally, the administration proposed three classifications of registered pesticides (general use, restricted use, and use by permit only). Ultimately, a twofold classification scheme was adopted—general and restricted use. A third possibility, it must be remembered, is not to register a pesticide at all. This section addresses (1) the classification system and its relationship to (2) the labeling and misbranding provisions. Classification and labeling are complementary in many ways but they can clash to the extent labeling is viewed as a satisfactory alternative to more severe use restrictions.

a. *Classification*

The standards for classification, applied during the registration process, pose difficulties. The statute invites, in the first place, a classification by use not product. Thus a single product registered for several uses may be classified for both general and restricted use.[2] The hope (and it is little more than a prayer)[3] is that a prod-

---

41. Section 3(c)(1)(D), 86 Stat. 979 (1972).

42. Butler, supra note 35, at 1239–40.

43. Hearing on Extension of the Federal Insecticide, Fungicide, and Rodenticide Act, Before the Subcomm. on Agricultural Research and General Legislation of the Senate Comm. on Agriculture and Forestry, 94th Cong., 1st Sess. 105 (1975) (statement of John Quarles, Deputy Administrator, EPA); see Amchem Prod., Inc. v. GAF Corp., 391 F.Supp. 124 (N.D.Ga. 1975); Dow Chemical Co. v. Train, 423 F.Supp. 1359, 7 ELR 20262 (E.D. Mich.1976).

44. 7 U.S.C.A. § 136a(c)(1)(D).

1. Senate Comm. on Agriculture and Forestry, Federal Environmental Pesticide Control Act of 1972, S.Rep.No. 838, 92d Cong., 2d Sess. 21 (1972).

2. 7 U.S.C.A. § 136a(d)(1).

3. Id. § 136a(d)(1)(A) contains a proviso:

That the Administrator may require that [the pesticide's] packaging and

uct purchased for general use, i. e., as a herbicide on range land, is not put to a restricted use, i. e., to kill mice in the home. The criterion for a general use classification reads as follows: "If the Administrator determines that the pesticide, when applied in accordance with its directions for use, warnings and cautions and for the uses for which it is registered, or for one of more of such uses, or in accordance with a widespread and commonly recognized practice, will not generally cause unreasonable adverse effects on the environment, he will classify the pesticide, or the particular use or uses of the pesticide to which the determination applies, for general use." [4] This calls for both a hypothetical judgment about effects if the product is used as prescribed and a candid judgment about effects if the product is used "in accordance with a widespread and commonly recognized practice."

This language tracks the language of criterion four, governing registration,[5] and thus supports the inference that the third criterion for registration is the stiffest standard since it precludes any registration if the product causes unreasonable adverse effects—by misuse or accident, or inevitably even when used carefully.[6] Once adjudged suitable for general use, the only remaining constraints upon misuse are dependent upon the labeling and directions for use and whatever deterrence is found in the prohibition against using a product inconsistently with its labeling.[7]

The restricted use classification obviously is of greater significance than the general use category since it applies to higher risk products and uses. The criterion for classification is phrased awkwardly along the lines of the standard for general uses: "If the Administrator determines that the pesticide, when applied in accordance with its directions for use, warnings and cautions and for the uses for which it is registered, or for one or more of such uses, or in accordance with a widespread and commonly recognized practice, may generally cause without additional regulatory restrictions, unreasonable adverse effects on the environment, including injury to the applicator, he shall classify the pesticide, or the particular use or uses

---

labeling for restricted uses shall be clearly distinguishable from its packaging and labeling for general uses.

4. Id. § 136a(c)(5) reads in part:
The Administrator shall register a pesticide if he determines that, when considered with any restrictions imposed under subsection (d) of this section—

. . . .

(D) when used in accordance with widespread and commonly recognized practice it will not generally cause unreasonable adverse effects on the environment.

Although a product can be registered only after satisfying subsection (D), it does not automatically qualify for general use classification because the Administrator may deem it acceptable only in light of "restrictions imposed under subsection (d)" (the classification provisions).

5. Id. § 136a(c)(5)(D).

6. § 8.4 above.

7. 7 U.S.C.A. § 136j(2)(G).

Sec. 8.5 CLASSIFICATION, MISBRANDING & LABELING 865

to which the determination applies, for restricted use . . . .[8]" Like the determination on general use, this requires a hypothetical estimate about effects if the product is used as prescribed and a candid judgment about effects if the product is used "in accordance with a widespread and commonly recognized practice." If "additional regulatory restrictions" will not suffice to prevent unreasonable effects, the product or use cannot be registered. This is true under criterion three regardless of whether the unreasonable effects are caused by routine or occasional misuse, accident, or simply by the product's traits of mobility and toxicity.[9]

Two consequences follow if a pesticide or use falls within the restricted category. If the classification rests upon a determination "that the acute dermal or inhalation toxicity of the pesticide presents a hazard to the applicator or other persons," then the pesticide shall be applied for the restricted use "only by or under the direct supervision of a certified applicator."[10] If the classification rests upon a judgment that its use without additional regulatory restriction "may cause unreasonable adverse effects on the environment," then the pesticide shall be applied for the restricted use "only by or under the direct supervision of a certified applicator, or subject to such other restrictions as the Administrator may provide by regulation."[11] These provisions are drafted inartfully,[12] but a sensible distinction emerges. For acutely toxic pesticides posing a human health hazard, application "by or under the direct supervision of a certified applicator" is a *sine qua non*. The provision should not be read as precluding resort to supplementary restrictions. For pesticides hazardous for reasons other than acute toxicity to humans, application by an experienced hand is not necessarily required, although it is a preferred alternative, so long as other restrictions are imposed. The House Committee on Agriculture anticipated restrictions "which are suited to the degree of hazard and adverse environmental effect that could be caused by the misuse of the pesticide. For example, in some cases only the signing of a poison or pesticide register would be required while in other cases the purchaser or user might be required to certify that he has read the instructions and will apply it in accordance with such instructions. In other cases general seasonal licenses, permits, or other similar forms of approval may be required."[13]

Obviously, the viability of the restricted use classification is heavily dependent on who "a certified applicator" is and how strin-

---

8. Id. § 1.36a(d)(1)(C).

9. § 8.4 above.

10. 7 U.S.C.A. § 136a(d)(1)(C)(i).

11. Id. § 136a(d)(1)(C)(ii).

12. For example, the term "environment" is defined to include man. 7 U.S.C.A. § 136(j).

13. House Comm. on Agriculture, Federal Environmental Pesticide Control Act of 1971, H.R.Rep. No. 511, 92d Cong., 1st Sess. 15 (1971).

gent the qualifications are. Since a restricted use pesticide usually will be applied "only by or under the direct supervision of a certified applicator," a question first arises whether the "certified" person must be in the field or whether he can be back in the office answering the telephone while those under his "supervision" apply the pesticides. This is one of those questions upon which a lawyer's opinion means very little, but let it be said for the record that "direct supervision" ought to involve on-the-spot surveillance and control not lax oversight. The issue involves the application of toxic substances which requires more than armchair supervision.

FIFRA calls for the Administrator to prescribe standards for the certification of applicators. The standards "shall provide that to be certified, an individual must be determined to be competent with respect to the use and handling of the pesticide or class of pesticides covered by such individual's certification." [14] Provision is made for the states to certify the applicators of pesticides upon approval by EPA of a plan meeting limited federal standards of adequate funding, assurances of qualified personnel to administer the program, and the like.[15] A state submitting a plan is entitled to notice and hearing before it is rejected.[16] The mechanism is not meant to enforce strict federal supervision of the means by which applicators are certified.

The 1975 amendments go so far as to declare the federal certification standards satisfied by a state plan allowing a private applicator, i. e., a farmer, to certify his own competence.[17] Under this type of program, referred to as the "Minnesota Plan," pesticide dealers are licensed periodically and instructed in the proper use of the pesticides they are licensed to sell; when a buyer purchases a restricted pesticide for private use, the dealer reviews the label information with the buyer, and if satisfied that the buyer understands the instructions, gives him a form for signature which certifies that he understands the proper uses of the pesticides and that he will follow

---

14. 7 U.S.C.A. § 136b(a)(1).

15. Id. § 136b(a)(2); see 40 Fed.Reg. 11702–04 (1975), adding 40 CFR § 171.7.

16. 7 U.S.C.A. § 136b(b); see 40 Fed. Reg. 11704 (1975), adding 40 CFR § 171.8.

17. The proviso to 7 U.S.C.A. § 136b (a)(1) reads:
That the certification standard for a private applicator shall, under a state plan submitted for approval, be deemed fulfilled by his completing a certification form. The Administrator shall further assure that such form contains adequate information and affirmations to carry out the intent of this Act, and may include in the form an affirmation that the private applicator has completed a training program approved by the Administrator so long as the program does not require the private applicator to take, pursuant to a requirement established by the Administrator, any examination to establish competency in the use of the pesticide. The Administrator may require any pesticide dealer participating in a certification program to be licensed under a state licensing program approved by him.

Sec. 8.5 CLASSIFICATION, MISBRANDING & LABELING 867

the instructions accordingly.[18] EPA may require that the form include an affirmation that the applicator has completed an approved training program; however, EPA may not require the applicator to take or pass any test to establish his competency.[19]

This self-certification provision is intended to relieve farmers of the burden of attending extended pesticide training programs in the belief that they generally are familiar with proper pesticide practices and have a strong self-interest in applying pesticides safely.[20] Notwithstanding this faith in the good sense of rural America, the provision substantially undermines the efficacy of the classification scheme. Agricultural pesticide usage, most of which involves restricted pesticides, accounts for more than half of all pesticides consumed annually in the United States.[21] A successful self-certification program is dependent upon the combined good faith and good sense of all dealers and all farmers not to mention skills they may not have. Relying upon self-certification stretches the concept of pesticide applications "only by or under the direct supervision of a certified applicator" beyond the point of believability. Legislative abandonment of the concept of tightly controlled applications, in the long run, may lead to more registration denials and cancellations. That is exactly what the statute anticipates because it requires, after all, estimates about unreasonable adverse effects in light of "any restrictions imposed" under the classification provisions.[22]

The 1975 amendments also contain a half-hearted attempt to reduce farmers' reliance on chemical pesticides by providing that EPA require state certification plans for applicators to include provisions for notifying interested individuals of the availability upon request of information on integrated pest management techniques.[23] EPA, how-

---

18. House Comm. on Agriculture, Extension and Amendment of the Federal Insecticide, Fungicide, and Rodenticide Act, As Amended, H.R. Rep.No.497, 94th Cong., 1st Sess. 9–10 (1975) [hereinafter cited as 1975 House Report].

19. Note 17, supra.

20. 1975 House Report, supra note 18, at 9.

21. In 1971, use by farmers accounted for approximately 59 percent of the total consumption of pesticides in the United States. Dep't of Agriculture, Economic Research Service, Quantities of Pesticides Used by Farmers in 1971 (1974).

22. 7 U.S.C.A. § 136a(c)(5).

23. Id. § 136b(c) reads:
Standards prescribed by the Administrator for the certification of applicators of pesticides . . ., and State plans submitted to the Administrator . . . shall include provisions for making instructional materials concerning integrated pest management techniques available to individuals at their request [through the state extension services], but such plans may not require that any individual receive instruction concerning such techniques or be shown to be competent with respect to the use of such techniques. The Administrator and States implementing such plans shall provide that all interested individuals are notified of the availability of such instructional material.

ever, is prohibited expressly from requiring states to impose instruction and examination requirements on certified applicators with respect to the use of integrated pest management practices.[24] This treats information on integrated pest management somewhat like pornographic material—determined adults can seek it out but it by no means is an educational prerequisite.

b. *Labeling and Misbranding*

Apart from registration and classification, the last remaining legal line of defense against injury by pesticides is the labeling. Drawing upon the broad definitions of the 1947 FIFRA, the term "label" now includes the written, printed, or graphic material attached to the pesticide or any of its containers.[25] The term "labeling" includes all labels and any other written or graphic material accompanying the pesticide at any time, including material referenced on the label or in literature accompanying it.[26] Labeling clearly includes ingredient statements,[27] warnings and precautionary statements, directions for use, hazard signal words (such as "Danger" and "Poison", with the skull and crossbones), and statements of practical treatment.[28] Labeling might even include commercial advertising of a pesticide product, which would give EPA regulatory powers over false advertising under the misbranding provisions.[29]

A substantial body of authority suggests that labeling offers a porous line of defense against pesticide misuse.[30] It is dependent,

---

24. Ibid.

25. Id. § 136(p)(1).

26. Id. § 136(p)(2) reads:
 The term 'labeling' means all labels and all other written, printed, or graphic matter—
 (A) accompanying the pesticide or device at any time; or
 (B) to which reference is made on the label or in literature accompanying the pesticide or device, except to current official publications of the Environmental Protection Agency, the United States Departments of Agriculture and Interior, the Department of Health, Education and Welfare, State experiment stations, State agricultural colleges, and other similar Federal or State institutions authorized by law to conduct research in the field of pesticides.

27. See Id. § 136(n).

28. These various types of labeling are referred to in 40 CFR § 162.10 (labeling requirements); see 7 U.S. C.A. § 126(q) (the misbranding provisions spelling out the requirements of adequate labeling).

29. EPA Legal Opinion on Authority to Regulate Advertising of Pesticide Products, in EPA, Collection of Legal Opinions December 1970 to December 1973, at 439 (1974). The Federal Trade Commission clearly has power to forbid the false and deceptive advertising of pesticides. See In re Sterling Drug, Inc., FTC Dkt. No. 8899, Trade Reg.Rep. (CCH) ¶ 20,655 (1974) (consent order) (restraining the advertising of Lysol as false and misleading).

30. E. g., Dep't of HEW, Report of the Secretary's Commission on Pesticides and Their Relationship to Environmental Health 149 (1969) (Mrak Commission Report) ("all groups tend to disregard the labeled instruction for safe application and storage"); Rodgers, The Persistent Problem of the Persistent Pesticides: A Lesson in Environmental Law, 70 Colum.L.Rev. 567, 608 & n. 254 (citing studies indicating that most pesticide users

Sec. 8.5 CLASSIFICATION, MISBRANDING & LABELING

after all, upon a label being accurately written, read and comprehended by the reader, and obeyed. Each part of this system is breached repeatedly by human frailties, not excluding the regulatory people who pass on the adequacy of labeling.

FIFRA requires that each applicant for registration file with the Administrator "a complete copy of the labeling of the pesticide, a statement of all claims to be made for it, and any directions for its use . . . ."[31] Satisfactory labeling is a precondition of registration,[32] and the substantive standards of acceptability are found in the misbranding provisions:[33] the labeling cannot contain statements that are "false and misleading"; the information presented must be "prominently placed" on the label "with such conspicuousness . . . and in such terms as to render it likely to be read and understood by the ordinary individual under customary conditions of purchase and use." In addition to these standards of accuracy and comprehensibility, the labeling must conform to substantive standards of safety and environmental protection carried over from the 1947 FIFRA. First, the labeling, in order to escape the misbranding provisions and satisfy the requirements of product registration, must "contain directions for use which are necessary for effecting the purpose for which the product is intended and if complied with," together with classification restrictions, "are adequate to protect health and the environment."[34] EPA cannot register a pesticide that, regardless of labeling, will cause unreasonable adverse effects on the environment.[35] This provision requires that the labeling of a registered product always contain directions for use that are consistent with health and environmental protection. Similarly, the labeling must "contain a warning and caution statement which may be necessary and if complied with," together with classification restrictions, "are adequate to protect health and the environment."[36] As with the provision requiring directions for use, this should be read as requir-

either do not read pesticide labels or do not understand the labels when read); Comptroller General of the United States, Report to the Congress, The Federal Pesticide Registration Program: Is It Protecting the Public and the Environment Adequately From Pesticide Hazards? 27–28 (1975) (labels on 22 of 28 environmentally hazardous pesticides are either missing or contain inadequate precaution statements or lacked data in the files to determine whether precautions required).

31. 7 U.S.C.A. § 136a(c)(1)(C).

32. Id. § 136a(c)(5)(B) conditions registration approval upon a determination that the product's "labeling and other material required to be submitted comply with the requirements of this subchapter." The "requirements" are found in the misbranding provisions. See Continental Chemiste Corp. v. Ruckelshaus (lindane), 461 F.2d 331, 341, 2 ELR 20209, 20211 (7th Cir. 1972) (discussing the "substantive standards" of safety in the misbranding provisions of the 1947 FIFRA).

33. 7 U.S.C.A. § 136q.

34. Id. § 136q(1)(F).

35. § 8.4 above.

36. 7 U.S.C.A. § 136q(1)(G).

ing warning and caution statements that, in combination with other protections, are "adequate" to preserve health and environmental values.

This misbranding provision goes further to require the labeling to bear an ingredient statement, a disclosure of the use classification, and various information about the producer and product.[37] The label of any pesticide containing a substance in quantities "highly toxic to man" must bear the skull and crossbones, the word "poison" prominently in red on a background of distinctly contrasting color, and a "statement of a practical treatment (first aid or otherwise) in case of poisoning by the pesticide."[38] A highly toxic product with no known antidote, presumably, is by definition misbranded and disqualified from registration.

EPA has clarified a number of requirements for satisfactory labeling.[39] Virtually every pesticide product label should bear on the front panel the statement "Keep out of the reach of children." Pesticides of different toxicity categories must carry different signal words: "Danger", "Warning" or "Caution". Examples of statements considered false and misleading include: nonnumerical and comparative statements on safety such as "Contains all Natural Ingredients," "Among the Least Toxic Chemicals Known," and "Pollution Approved." All labeling and text should appear in the English language except that additional text in other languages may be required.[40] Environmental hazards, depending on the risk, are dealt with by standard precautionary statements: "This Pesticide is Toxic to Wildlife," "This Pesticide is Toxic to Fish," "Keep Out of Lakes, Ponds or Streams," "Do Not Contaminate Water by Cleaning of Equipment or Disposal of Wastes."

Data requirements imposed by EPA in the registration process are intended simultaneously to assist the classification decision and identify suitable restrictions and labeling requirements. Five criteria [41] are used to adjudge the adequacy of labeling to protect against unreasonable adverse effects on the environment: (1) whether the instructions can be followed easily; (2) whether limited noncompliance would result in minor or no adverse effects; (3) whether widespread and commonly recognized use practices would nullify label directions; (4) whether application anticipates the use of specialized apparatus or protective equipment not customarily available to the general public; (5) whether adverse effects, through bioaccumulation or otherwise, might result even if directions are followed. EPA

---

37. Id. §§ 136q(2)(A)–(C).

38. Id. § 136q(2)(D).

39. The requirements discussed are found in 40 CFR § 162.10 (labeling requirements).

40. See Hubbard-Hall Chem. Co. v. Silverman, 340 F.2d 402 (1st Cir. 1965) (jury could find negligence based on inadequate warning on a parathion product used by illiterate farmworkers).

41. 40 CFR § 162.11(c)(3).

explains:[42] "Use and accident history of a pesticide or of a similar pesticide will bear on the evaluation and application of these criteria to the classification decision of a particular pesticide. [These criteria] were selected as representing the factors that would determine the degree that an unskilled applicator would be expected to follow label directions for use and required safety procedures. They require a weighing of the complexity of use of a pesticide in accordance with label instructions, the likelihood that instructions commonly will be followed, and the adverse effects likely to result if the label instructions are not followed. Secondly, the applicant or registrant may submit data or arguments challenging the finding of the Agency that the criteria have been met or may be able to establish that the formulation, packaging or method of use of the product is such as to eliminate the hazardous routes of exposure. For example, a pesticide which meets the criteria for restricted use classification on the basis of dermal risk may be marketed as a granular formulation rather than as a liquid formulation and thereby reduce the hazards of dermal exposure. So too, if the formulation of the pesticide is extremely toxic while its dilution is not, the pesticide may be packaged as a 'closed system' to prevent hazardous exposure during mixing."

§ 8.6 Registration: Exceptions

The present version of FIFRA, like most environmental legislation, has a system of variances. FIFRA exceeds its contemporaries, however, in the open-endedness and uncertainty of its qualifiers. While policy reasons support these exceptions, Congress placed more than the usual burden of definition upon the administrative agency. The exceptions, roughly in order of their significance, include: (1) experimental uses; (2) emergency uses; (3) special local needs; and (4) miscellaneous exemptions.

a. *Experimental Uses*

Any person may seek from the Administrator an experimental use permit to apply a pesticide not yet registered.[1] The purpose of

---

42. 40 Fed.Reg. 28242, 28264 (1975) (comments and revisions).

1. 7 U.S.C.A. § 136(a) reads:
Any person may apply to the Administrator for an experimental use permit for a pesticide. The Administrator may issue an experimental use permit if he determines that the applicant needs such information in order to accumulate information necessary to register a pesticide under section 136a of this title. An application for an experimental use permit may be filed at the time of or before or after an application for registration is filed.
The 1975 amendments add subsection 136c(g) which provides that the Administrator may issue an experimental use permit to an agricultural research facility or an educational institution to allow the use of any pesticide for a period not to exceed one year. Pub.L.No.94–140, § 10, 89 Stat. 754, adding 7 U.S.C.A. § 136c(g). The purpose of the amendment is to clarify the Administrator's authority to issue experimental use permits for pesticides that have been suspended or cancelled. House

the provision, as the name suggests, is to permit field testing "to accumulate information necessary to register a pesticide . . . ."[2] Plot testing normally will follow laboratory or greenhouse screening to assess the pesticide's properties and the toxicity of a particular substance. Consistently with this research purpose, the Act makes clear that the issuance of an experimental use permit may be conditioned upon conducting studies and reporting results "to detect whether the use of the pesticide under the permit may cause unreasonable adverse effects on the environment."[3] Not at all clear is the duration of a permit, its scope, the extent of sales or use allowed under it, and the conditions of its use.[4]

Environmental Protection Agency forms[5] and regulations[6] shed some light on the mechanics and reach of the experimental use exception. An applicant must identify the states where the pesticide is to be used, along with the amount and acreage to be treated. The details of the proposed program must be disclosed, including the target pests and sites to be treated, use pattern, plot sizes, and number, dosage rates, methods, and timing of applications. The objectives of the program should be spelled out, including long-range testing plans and the data sought to be accumulated—that is, on performance, crop yields, phylotoxicity (toxicity to plants), and environmental residue. An explanation justifying the quantity of material requested must be submitted, and a suitable duration for the permit must be proposed. The regulations state that a permit "normally" will be effective for one year, although it may be renewed, extended, or amended.[7] Label-

Comm. on Agriculture, Extension and Amendment of the Federal Insecticide, Fungicide, and Rodenticide Act, As Amended, H.R.Rep.No.497, 94th Cong., 1st Sess. 11 (1975). The only express statutory limitations on the use of such a pesticide are that it may be used only by the agency or institution to which the permit is issued and only for bona fide experimentation purposes. 7 U.S.C.A. § 136c(a).

2. 7 U.S.C.A. § 136c(g).

3. Id. § 136c(d) reads:
When any experimental use permit is issued for a pesticide containing any chemical or combination of chemicals which has not been included in any previously registered pesticide, the Administrator may specify that studies be conducted to detect whether the use of the pesticide under the permit may cause unreasonable adverse effects on the environment. All results of such studies shall be reported to the Administrator before such pesticide may be registered under section 136a of this title.

4. If experimental use of the pesticide "may reasonably be expected to result in any residue on or in food or feed," the Administrator "may establish a temporary tolerance level for the residue of the pesticide before issuing the experimental use permit." 7 U.S.C.A. § 136c(b); see § 8.8 below.

5. Application for an Experimental Use Permit to Ship and Use a Pesticide for Experimental Purposes Only, WH–567 (undated); Temporary Permit Issued Under the Federal Insecticide, Fungicide, and Rodenticide Act for Shipment of an Economic Poison for Experimental Purposes Only, PR Form 9–229, May 1968.

6. 40 Fed.Reg. 18780 (1975), 40 CFR pt. 172.

7. 40 CFR § 172.5.

Sec. 8.6   REGISTRATION: EXCEPTIONS   873

ing that discloses the experimental purpose is required,[8] as is reporting at frequent intervals ("immediately" if adverse effects are detected from use or exposure, ordinarily on a three month basis, and within 180 days after expiration of the permit), although the detail required in reports is minimal.[9] Notice of receipt of an experimental use permit application appears in the Federal Register,[10] and a public hearing is possible if the Administrator determines there is "sufficient interest."[11] Environmental impact statements are not prepared although they might be required.[12] Refusals or revocations of a permit must be accompanied by written notice and the opportunity for a conference.[13] Noncompliance with a permit condition is a violation of the Act.[14]

The problem of supervising experimental uses is made more difficult by a provision authorizing the Administrator to delegate to the states the authority to issue experimental use permits.[15] The conditions for state plans regarding certification of applicators[16] are said to apply with "equal force" to the issuance of experimental use permits.[17] This cannot mean that the later enacted self-certification provisions apply to experimental users but it does mean that states can dispense experimental permits with limited federal oversight. Regulations proposed[18] to implement state permit issuance require that state programs be consistent generally with the federal program, that Federal Register notice be given of the state issuance of a permit, and that EPA be empowered to revoke a permit if its terms and conditions "are inadequate to avoid unreasonable adverse effects on the environment."[19] Despite attempts at uniformity of administration, it is safe to assume that different standards will creep into the day to day functioning of the various experimental use permits programs. While uniformity of administration is not indisputably a good thing, especially when Congress says so, it is difficult to discern why the same principles that demand federalization of the pesticide registration process do not apply equally to the data gathering prerequisites.

In fiscal year 1975, EPA issued 162 experimental use permits and denied 23;[20] for the first half of fiscal year 1976, 47 permits were is-

8. Id. § 172.6.

9. Id. § 172.8.

10. Id. § 172.11(a).

11. Id. § 172.11(b).

12. § 8.1 n. 28 above.

13. 40 CFR § 171.10.

14. 7 U.S.C.A. § 136j(a)(2)(H).

15. Id. § 136c(f).

16. § 8.5 above.

17. 7 U.S.C.A. § 136c(f).

18. 40 Fed.Reg. 40545 (1975), proposing 40 CFR pt. 172.

19. 40 CFR § 172.25(c)(ii) (proposed).

20. Letter to William Sierks and author from Charles K. Colledge, Chief, Information Coordination Section, Technical Services Division, Office of Pesticide Programs, EPA, Dec. 19, 1975.

sued and 15 were denied.[21] The substantive weaknesses of the experimental use concept are apparent on the face of the legislation inasmuch as no meaningful limits on the time, scope, or manner of experimental uses are provided. Improperly administered, the program could permit commercial sales of unregistered pesticides and "grant the functional equivalent of registration itself." [22] There is some evidence that the experimental use exemption can be invoked to circumvent the strictures of the exemption for emergency uses,[23] prolong the use of banned pesticides,[24] support a vast usage over a five state area where the need for research is in doubt,[25] and otherwise skirt direct use controls.[26] The program, while mostly within the firm grasp of the administrative process, should be justified by research purposes and anticipated registration. The statutory criterion, after all, allows a permit only "in order to accumulate information necessary to register a pesticide." The research format must be laid out clearly and professionally conceived, the need established, the data accumulated, and the prospects for future registration must be high.

b. *Emergency Uses*

Section 18 of the Federal Environmental Pesticide Control Act of 1972 (FEPCA) makes an immodest allocation of authority to the EPA Administrator, permitting him, "at his discretion, [to] exempt any Federal or State agency from any provision of this Act if he determines that emergency conditions exist which require such exemption." [27] This broad power to dispense with registration, labeling, penalty, and other provisions has been narrowed somewhat by administrative action.[28] Thus, "emergency conditions" exist if a pest outbreak is about to occur, if no registered pesticide or alternative is available for control, and if the time remaining is insufficient to permit registration of a pesticide for control purposes.[29] Three types of ex-

21. Ibid.

22. Butler, Federal Pesticide Law, in Environmental Law Institute, Federal Environmental Law 1232, 1240 (E. L. Dolgin & T. G. P. Guilbert eds. 1974).

23. Recent Developments, 5 ELR 10164 (1975) (reporting that the Louisiana Department of Agriculture, having been denied a request to use DDT on emergency grounds, reapplied to EPA for authorization to pursue the same use under an experimental permit).

24. Ibid.

25. Comment, Coyote Control: Ford Heeds Rancher's Howls, 5 ELR 10156, 10157 (1975) (discussing M–44 cyanide injection device to destroy coyotes) ("devices" are instruments for trapping or controlling pests, 7 U.S.C.A. § 136(h), and are regulated in some respects under FIFRA).

26. Ibid.

27. 7 U.S.C.A. § 136p. The 1975 amendments require the Administrator, in making his determination about emergency conditions, to consult with the Secretary of Agriculture and the governor of a concerned state if they request it.

28. 38 Fed.Reg. 33303 (1973), 40 CFR pt. 166.

29. 40 CFR § 166.1 reads in part: An emergency will be deemed to exist when: (a) A pest outbreak

emptions are foreseen [30] though others may be approved: (1) a specific exemption, valid only for a specific pest outbreak extending, under no circumstances, longer than a year; (2) a quarantine or public health exemption, also not to exceed a year but subject to extensions, that excuses government programs aimed at preventing the introduction or spread of a foreign pest into or throughout the United States; and (3) a crisis exemption, not expected to involve treatment for more than fifteen days, that permits control action merely upon notice to the Administrator.[31]

Procedurally, the specific and quarantine exemptions require written requests setting forth the nature of the emergency and the type of action proposed.[32] A request for a specific exemption (but for some reason not a quarantine exemption) must contain a "statement of economic benefits and losses anticipated with and without the exemption and under reasonable alternatives." [33] An analysis of possible adverse effects on man and the environment is required for both exemptions, but a formal environmental impact statement need be submitted only if the agency has prepared one as standard practice.[34] Both specific and quarantine exemptions, if granted, require Federal Register notice after the fact,[35] follow-up reports on the action taken, and the outcome of monitoring if required.[36] Federal Register publication of an application for an exemption, as distinguished from a grant of one, is forthcoming only if the Administrator so desires,[37] which is poor sportsmanship to say the least. Presumably to head off avoidance of registration requirements by indefinite extensions of quarantine exemptions, EPA has made it clear that "where [a] pesticide is used under this exemption and recurrence of the pest can be reasonably expected, the Federal or State agency shall take prompt action to comply with the registration requirements of the act for the particular use." [38] The regulation clearly states that pesticides whose registrations have been suspended, as distinguished presumably from those that have been cancelled, may not be used under the quarantine exemption.[39]

has or is about to occur and no pesticide registered for the particular use, or alternative method of control, is available to eradicate or control the pest, (b) significant economic or health problems will occur without the use of the pesticide and (c) the time available from discovery or prediction of the pest outbreak is insufficient for a pesticide to be registered for the particlar use.

30. Id. § 166.2.

31. Id. § 166.8.

32. Id. §§ 163.3, 163.4.

33. Id. § 163.3(b).

34. Id. §§ 166.3(a)(7), 166.4(a)(5).

35. Id. § 166.10.

36. Id. §§ 166.5, 166.6.

37. Id. § 166.10.

38. Id. § 166.2(b).

39. Ibid.

The crisis exemption is destined for controversy because it involves a delegation of virtually all decision-making powers to the official who chooses to invoke it. To avail oneself of a crisis exemption, all that is involved is notice by telegram to the Administrator within 36 hours of an agency decision and a written report within ten days specifying the action taken, describing steps initiated to reduce possible adverse effects on man and the environment, and alleging that "there was no time to request one of the other exemptions."[40] The Administrator publishes in the Federal Register notice that a federal or state agency has availed itself of a crisis exemption,[41] and he may step in to permit further treatment after 15 days.[42] While this provision may be abused from time to time by officials whose constituents call for a "crisis," a procedure of this genre dealing with grave public health hazards properly seems to be within the Administrator's discretion.

During fiscal year 1975, EPA approved 19 emergency use applications and denied 20; for the first half of fiscal year 1976, it approved 20 and denied 1.[43] Uses at issue have involved controversial pesticides and applications—DDT by the Forest Service to combat tussock moths in the Pacific Northwest,[44] 2, 4–D by the Corps of Engineers to control water hyacinths in Texas,[45] strychnine and other substances by the Colorado Department of Agriculture to control predators,[46] and Tergitol Nonionic 15–S–9 by the U.S. Fish and Wildlife Service to destroy cholera infected coots in Back Bay, Virginia.[47] Given the open-ended nature of the emergency exemption, EPA has not done poorly in its implementation. The general standard for an emergency is acceptable.[48] The challenge administratively is to confine the exemption to circumstances truly emergent where threatened damages are grave, and alternatives are out of the question. An emergency will be found more readily where the damage threatened is unarguable and severe, where the use permitted is closely related to a use already registered, and where the circumstances do not suggest an attempt to avoid the otherwise applicable registration requirements.

c. *Special Local Needs*

Section 24(c) of FEPCA permits states to register pesticides for intrastate distribution and use "to meet special local needs."[49] This

---

40. Id. § 166.8.

41. Id. § 166.10.

42. Id. § 166.8(c).

43. Letter to William Sierks and author from Charles F. Colledge, Chief, Information Coordination Section, Technical Services Division, Office of Pesticide Programs, EPA, Dec. 19, 1975.

44. 39 Fed.Reg. 8377 (1974).

45. 40 Fed.Reg. 29123, 29124 (1975) (granted).

46. Id. at 7479 (denied).

47. Id. at 12540 (granted).

48. Note 29, supra.

49. 7 U.S.C.A. § 136v(c) reads:
A State may provide registration

provision has been characterized as "perhaps the single largest loophole in the Act" giving states the power "to avoid federal regulation by permitting blanket registrations for special local needs." [50] More optimistically, the loophole is only medium-sized, not much bigger or smaller than several others in the Act. To be sure, Congress neglected to define "special local needs," which raises the spectre that it means "any old uses the state wishes to approve." But the legislative history makes clear that the purpose of the subsection is to facilitate registrations for local or minor pest problems that nobody would bother to address with an expensive federal registration.[51] EPA's initial regulatory effort on the subject opts for a definition of "special local need" as one falling through the cracks of the regulatory scheme because there is no adequate EPA-registered product.[52]

In addition, state registration for "special local needs" is conditioned upon an EPA certification that the state "is capable of exercising adequate controls" in the registration process. Delay in publishing standards [53] governing certification had the practical effect of limiting the number of "special local needs" registrations to no more than eight by the end of 1975.[54] As the states meet the certification requirements, the number of registrations of course will increase. Even then, as section 24(c) clearly indicates, EPA has 90 days to veto any registered use, and it plans to exercise that authority on a number of grounds, including the obvious one that the state-registered product "will cause unreasonable adverse effects on the environ-

---

for pesticides formulated for distribution and use within that state to meet special local needs if that state is certified by the Administrator as capable of exercising adequate controls to assure that such registration shall be in accord with the purposes of this subchapter and if registration for such use has not previously been denied, disapproved, or canceled by the Administrator. Such registration shall be deemed registration under section 136a of this title for all purposes of this subchapter, but shall authorize distribution and use only within such state and shall not be effective for more than ninety days if disapproved by the Administrator within that period.

50. Butler, supra note 22, at 1245.

51. Senate Comm'n on Agriculture and Forestry, Pesticide Control, S. Rep.No.838, 92d Cong., 2d Sess. 30 (1972):
    The purpose of this subsection is to give a state the opportunity to meet expeditiously and with less cost and administrative burden on the registrant the problem of registering for local use a pesticide needed to treat a pest infestation which is a problem in such state but is not sufficiently widespread to warrant the expense and difficulties of federal registration.

52. 40 Fed.Reg. 40539, 40543 (1975), proposing 40 CFR § 162.152(k).

53. 40 Fed.Reg. 40530, 40542 (1975) (authorizes an interim certification procedure for a limited period prior to final adoption of the section 24(c) regulations); see id. at 57482 (approving requests for interim certification of New Mexico, California, and Washington).

54. Letter to William Sierks and author from Charles F. Colledge, Chief, Information Coordination Section, Technical Services Division, Office of Pesticide Program, EPA, Dec. 19, 1975.

ment." [55] Finally, from an environmental perspective the section 24(c) authority does not necessarily reverse the familiar premise of federal legislation that gives states the power to impose tougher pollution control standards but never looser ones.[56] Section 24(c) makes clear that registrations that have "been denied, disapproved or canceled by the Administrator" at the federal level cannot seek refuge in the several states. Registrations for "special local needs" exemptions thus are more likely to be on the rise as prospective candidates for federal registration rather than those on the retreat as refugees from cancellation proceedings.

With this much conceded, there is reason enough to be wary of the "special local needs" exemption and to assure its confinement to pest problems that are unique, local, and minor. Veterans of the pesticide wars recognize how easy it is to find another species of mite troubling a special variety of plants in a somewhat different climate. It is by no means impertinent to point out that the definition of "special local needs" will be undertaken largely "by state agricultural officials, those under the greatest political and economic pressures from pesticide users to certify special uses of pesticides." [57]

d. *Miscellaneous Exemptions*

Exempted from registration, but not misbranding, under the Act are pesticides that are transferred from one registered establishment to another operated by the same producer solely for the purpose of packaging [58] and pesticides that are transferred for purposes of disposal.[59] Pesticides intended for export are exempt both from the registration and misbranding requirements if they are prepared or packaged according to the directions of a foreign purchaser.[60]

Of greater potential significance is the authority of the Administrator to exempt from the requirements of the Act any pesticide which he determines "either (1) to be adequately regulated by another Federal agency, or (2) to be of a character which is unnecessary to be subject to this subchapter in order to carry out the purposes of this subchapter." [61] That EPA is more likely to hold dearly its regulatory powers than abandon them is perhaps best illustrated by its successful struggle with the Occupational Safety and Health Administration over authority as regards farmworkers' safety.[62] At the same time, EPA's

---

55. 40 Fed.Reg. 40538, 40543 (1975), proposing 40 CFR § 162.156(b)(ii).

56. E. g., ch. 3 (Clean Air Act); ch. 4 (Federal Water Pollution Control Act); ch. 5 (Noise Control Act) above.

57. Butler, supra note 22, at 1245.

58. 7 U.S.C.A. § 136a(b)(i).

59. 40 CFR § 162.5(b)(3).

60. Id. § 162.5(b)(4); See § 8.3 n. 71 above.

61. 7 U.S.C.A. § 136w(b).

62. Organized Migrants in Community Action, Inc. v. Brennan, 172 U.S.App. D.C. 147, 520 F.2d 1161, 5 ELR 2068 (1975) (plaintiffs preferred OSHA regulation); see Weisman, Pesticides, Farmworkers, and OSHA, 27 Res Ipsa Loquitur 41 (1975).

position on the regulation of pesticides advertising can best be described as one of impatient deference to the Federal Trade Commission.[63] Conflict among agencies are ever more common in this regulatory age. The most that can be said for this exemption is that EPA might advance when it should retreat and might retreat when it should advance. These encroachments often are resolved by interagency agreement [64] or by executive decision through the Office of Management and Budget.

The "unnecessary" regulation exemption is aimed at harmless products undeserving of the time and effort involved in regulating them. It makes as much sense to exempt the small stuff as it does to ignore it or defer it indefinitely, which is the customary manner of agency disposition.

§ 8.7 Cancellation; Suspension

The familiar criteria governing the registration [1] and classification [2] decisions apply also to cancellation. If "it appears to the Administrator that a pesticide or its labeling or other material required to be submitted does not comply with the provisions of this subchapter or, when used in accordance with widespread and commonly recognized practice, generally causes unreasonable adverse effects on the environment," the Administrator may issue a notice of intent to cancel the registration or change its classification or to hold a hearing to determine whether either of these steps should be taken.[3] The Administrator also is obliged to cancel automatically the registration of any pesticide at the end of a five-year period except that he may permit continued sale and use "if he determines that [it will not be] inconsistent with the purposes of this subchapter and will not have unreasonable adverse effects on the environment." [4] Thus the key determination on cancellation is whether continued use promises "unreasonable adverse effects on the environment." The standards for registration and cancellation should be coextensive in the sense that continued use should be sanctioned no more readily than initial use. Practically, the equation changes because a pesticide in use develops momentum and a constituency whose interests must be weighed in a cancellation proceeding just as it produces field data on effects that may confirm or dispel earlier hypothetical concerns.

63. Opinion on Authority to Regulate Advertising of Pesticide Products, in Environmental Protection Agency, Collection of Legal Opinions December 1970–December 1973, at 439 (1974).

64. Rodgers, The Persistent Problem of the Persistent Pesticides: A Lesson in Environmental Law, 70 Colum.L. Rev. 568, 570 (1970); cf. 40 Fed.Reg. 25078 (1975) (setting forth a memorandum of understanding on pesticide regulatory responsibilities of EPA and the Food and Drug Administration).

1. § 8.4 above.

2. § 8.5 above.

3. 7 U.S.C.A. § 136d(b).

4. Id. § 136d(a).

A second option open to the Administrator to deal with suspect pesticides is that of suspension. Consistently with earlier case law,[5] the 1972 FEPCA permits an immediate registration suspension "if the Administrator determines that action is necessary to prevent an imminent hazard during the time required for cancellation or change in classification proceedings. . . ."[6] The term "imminent hazard" means "a situation which exists when the continued use of a pesticide during the time required for cancellation proceeding would be likely to result in unreasonable adverse effects on the environment or will involve unreasonable hazard to the survival of a species declared endangered or threatened" pursuant to the Endangered Species Act of 1973.[7] The most important element of an "imminent hazard" is a "serious threat to public health."[8] A hazard may be "imminent" even though its impact may not be apparent for many years and even though the threat is to fish and wildlife and not directly to people.[9] Judge Leventhal cautions against any approach to the term "imminent hazard" that "restricts it to a concept of crisis. It is enough if there is substantial likelihood that serious harm will be experienced during the year or two required in any realistic projection of the administrative process."[10]

The most important consequence of a suspension order is that sales and use can be interdicted immediately rather than strung out over what has proven to be the considerable life span of a cancellation proceeding. Understandably, a registrant receiving a suspension notice is entitled to an expedited hearing. Normally, if no request for a hearing is made within five days of receipt of a notification, the suspension order issues and is not subject to judicial review.[11] If a hearing is requested, it must commence within five days unless delayed by an agreement between the agency and the registrant. The presiding officer "shall have ten days from the conclusion of the presentation of evidence to submit recommended findings and conclusions to the Administrator who shall then have seven days to render a final decision on the issue of suspension."[12] A finding of an "emergency" permits issuance of a suspension order in advance of notification to

5. Wellford v. Ruckelshaus (2,4,5–T I), 142 U.S.App.D.C. 88, 439 F.2d 598, 1 ELR 20065 (1971); Nor-Am Agricultural Prod., Inc. v. Hardin (mercury compounds), 435 F.2d 1133 (7th Cir. 1970), vacated and rev'd on other grounds 435 F.2d 1151 (7th Cir.) (en banc).

6. 7 U.S.C.A. § 136d(c)(1).

7. Id. § 136(*l*); see § 7.12 above (discussing section 7 of the Endangered Species Act).

8. Environmental Defense Fund, Inc. v. Ruckelshaus (DDT II), 142 U.S.App. D.C. 74, 87, 439 F.2d 584, 597, 1 ELR 20059, 20062 (1971).

9. Ibid.

10. Environmental Defense Fund, Inc. v. Environmental Protection Agency (aldrin-dieldrin I), 150 U.S.App.D.C. 348, 360, 465 F.2d 528, 540, 2 ELR 20228, 20234 (1972).

11. 7 U.S.C.A. § 136d(c)(2).

12. Ibid.

Sec. 8.7 CANCELLATION; SUSPENSION

the registrant.[13] The best illustration of the contrasts between a cancellation and suspension proceeding is the case of aldrin-dieldrin where the Administrator interrupted an extended cancellation proceeding with the issuance of a notice of intention to suspend.[14] A 15-day hearing was held within two months, which resulted in a final suspension order issued by the Administrator [15] and eventual affirmance by the U. S. Court of Appeals for the District of Columbia.[16]

Case law growing out of the Administrator's cancellation-suspension decisions have contributed significantly to the issues of timing [17] and scope [18] of judicial review. Refusals to cancel or suspend are final orders appealable to the appropriate court of appeals for the obvious reason that the staying of the administrative hand in either case can lead to serious and irreparable environmental damage.[19] Similarly, administrative inaction for an appreciable period of time in face of a request to cancel or suspend may be "tantamount" to a denial,[20] entitling a petitioner to an order requiring the agency to explain what it is up to. On the other hand, the issuance of an order of cancellation putting in motion the extensive hearing and consultation requirements of the Act is nonappealable for the equally obvious reason that "interlocutory judicial jousting" [21] should not be permitted to derail the administrative proceeding until it has run its course. Courts are divided over whether a suspension decision is reviewable immediately. The

---

13. Id. § 136d(c)(3) reads:
    Whenever the Administrator determines that an emergency exists that does not permit him to hold a hearing before suspending, he may issue a suspension order in advance of notification to the registrant. In that case, paragraph (a) shall apply except that (i) the order of suspension shall be in effect pending the expeditious completion of the remedies provided by that paragraph and the issuance of a final order on suspension, and (ii) no party other than the registrant and the Agency shall participate except that any person adversely affected may file briefs within the time allotted by the Agency's rules. Any person so filing briefs shall be considered a party to such proceedings for the purposes of [seeking judicial review].

14. The aldrin-dieldrin case history is discussed in Spector, Regulation of Pesticides by the Environmental Protection Agency, 5 Ecology L.Q. 229 (1976).

15. EPA, Opinion of the Administrator, on the Suspension of Aldrin-Dieldrin, 39 Fed.Reg. 37265 (1974).

16. Environmental Defense Fund, Inc. v. Environmental Protection Agency (aldrin-dieldrin II), 167 U.S.App.D.C. 71, 510 F.2d 1292, 5 ELR 20243 (1975).

17. § 1.9 above.

18. § 1.5 above.

19. See Environmental Defense Fund, Inc. v. Environmental Protection Agency (aldrin-dieldrin I), 150 U.S.App.D.C. 348, 465 F.2d 528, 2 ELR 20228 (1972) (refusal to suspend); Environmental Defense Fund, Inc. v. Ruckelshaus (DDT II), 142 U.S.App.D.C. 74, 439 F.2d 584, 1 ELR 20059 (1971) (same).

20. Environmental Defense Fund, Inc. v. Hardin (DDT I), 138 U.S.App.D.C. 391, 398, 428 F.2d 1093, 1100, 1 ELR 20050, 20053 (1970) (prolonged delay on a request to suspend; remand allows a further deferral if an adequate explanation is forthcoming).

21. Pax Co. v. United States (arsenic trioxide), 454 F.2d 93, 2 ELR 20087 (10th Cir. 1972); Dow Chem. Co. v. Ruckelshaus (2,4,5–T II), 477 F.2d 1317, 3 ELR 20343, 20347 (8th Cir. 1973).

hands-off school argues that expedited administrative autonomy is necessary to protect health and safety,[22] while the interventionist school insists that injury to business interests alone is enough to justify immediate judicial review.[23]

Judicial decisions on pesticides presage and confirm the close scrutiny doctrine of judicial review that has been given emphasis and direction by the National Environmental Policy Act.[24] It is clear that any substantial question of safety should trigger the issuance of cancellation notices, shifting the burden to the manufacturer in a formal proceeding to justify continued registration.[25] The adjudicatory hearing prescribed for pesticide decision-making has been praised as a device for bringing the public into the process and facilitating the judicial review that follows,[26] and condemned as the ultimate debasement of technical decision-making. The delicate assessment of risks and benefits is called a balancing analysis,[27] which is a concept in the mainstream of environmental law relating back to common law nuisance principles [28] and finding contemporary expression in the National Environmental Policy Act.[29] Most important, the courts have demanded attentive consideration and careful exposition [30] from the agencies, as they chaperone the administrative process. Thus, courts are prone to remand for a statement of reasons why a suspension of a suspect product is not forthcoming and what standards are applied in reaching a decision.[31] They may demand a further explanation of

22. Nor-Am Agricultural Prod., Inc. v. Hardin (mercury compounds), 435 F.2d 1151, 1 ELR 20032 (7th Cir. 1970) (en banc).

23. Environmental Defense Fund, Inc. v. Ruckelshaus (DDT II), 142 U.S. App.D.C. 74, 80, 439 F.2d 584, 590, 1 ELR 20059, 20061 (1971) (dictum) (criticizing *Nor-Am*).

24. §§ 7.1–.10 above.

25. Environmental Defense Fund, Inc. v. Environmental Protection Agency (heptachlor-chlordane), —— U.S.App. D.C. ——, ——, 548 F.2d 998, 1004, 7 ELR 20012, 20014 (1976); Environmental Defense Fund, Inc. v. Environmental Protection Agency (aldrin-dieldrin II), 167 U.S.App.D.C. 71, 76, 510 F.2d 1292, 1297, 5 ELR 20243, 20244 (1975); Environmental Defense Fund, Inc. v. Ruckelshaus (DDT II), 142 U.S.App.D.C. 74, 83 & n. 34, 439 F.2d 584, 593 & n. 34, 1 ELR 20059, 20062 & n. 34 (1972) (ordering issuance of cancellation notices on all uses of DDT); see Southern Nat'l Mfg. Co. v. Environmental Protection Agency (lindane), 470 F.2d 194, 197 (8th Cir. 1972); Stearns Elec. Paste Co. v. Environmental Protection Agency, 461 F.2d 293, 302–05, 2 ELR 20368, 20372 (7th Cir. 1972).

26. Environmental Defense Fund, Inc. v. Environmental Protection Agency (DDT II), 142 U.S.App.D.C. 74, 84, 439 F.2d 584, 594, 1 ELR 20059, 20062 (1971).

27. Ibid.

28. §§ 2.5, 2.11 above.

29. § 7.5 above.

30. Environmental Defense Fund, Inc. v. Environmental Protection Agency (aldrin-dieldrin I), 150 U.S.App.D.C. 348, 361, 465 F.2d 528, 541, 2 ELR 20228, 20235 (1972); cf. Stearns Elec. Paste Co. v. Environmental Protection Agency, 461 F.2d 293, 2 ELR 20368 (7th Cir. 1972).

31. Environmental Defense Fund, Inc. v. Ruckelshaus (DDT II), 142 U.S. App.D.C. 74, 439 F.2d 584, 1 ELR 20059 (1971).

Sec. 8.7   CANCELLATION; SUSPENSION

decisions that appear implausible, as where a hazardous product is approved for continued use on food crops,[32] or superficial, as with a single sentence dismissal of questions raised about carcinogenic effects.[33] While it is not clear that the Administrator must consider the benefits of a pesticide's usage at the preliminary stage of suspension, if he purports to do so, his decision "must be explained, not merely explainable, in terms of the ingredients announced . . . as comprising the Agency's policy and standards."[34] Under these ground rules a mere recitation of a pesticide's uses cannot be passed off as a weighing of benefits without a further explanation and analysis of alternatives.[35]

This close scrutiny of the Administrator's actions, however, stops short of dictating results. Judge Leventhal has written in explanation: "Environmental law marks out a domain where knowledge is hard to obtain and appraise, even in the administrative corridors; in the courtrooms, difficulties of understanding are multiplied. But there is a will in the courts to study and understand what the agency puts before us. And there is a will to respect the agency's choices if it has taken a hard look at its hard problems."[36] Once the Administrator has conformed to the niceties of procedural correctness and reasoned results, his basic judgments on cancellations and suspensions[37] survive rather easily under the substantial evidence test of judicial review applicable to adjudicatory proceedings.[38] It is clear that the Administrator has broad discretion to cancel or suspend or to enter compromise orders falling short of complete suspension—including, for

---

32. Wellford v. Ruckelshaus (2,4,5–T I), 142 U.S.App.D.C. 88, 92–93, 439 F.2d 598, 602–03, 1 ELR 20065, 20066–67 (1971).

33. Environmental Defense Fund, Inc. v. Environmental Protection Agency (aldrin-dieldrin I), 150 U.S.App.D.C. 348, 358, 465 F.2d 528, 538, 2 ELR 20228, 20233 (1972) ("when the matter involved is as sensitive and fright-laden as cancer, even a court scrupulous to the point of punctilio in deference to administrative latitude is beset with concern when the cross-reference is so abbreviated") (record remanded for other reasons but with directions to address the question of carcinogenicity).

34. Ibid.

35. 150 U.S.App.D.C. at 359, 465 F.2d at 539, 2 ELR at 20334.

36. 150 U.S.App.D.C. at 361, 465 F.2d at 541, 2 ELR at 20335.

37. Environmental Defense Fund, Inc. v. Environmental Protection Agency (DDT III), 160 U.S.App.D.C. 123, 489 F.2d 1247, 4 ELR 20031 (1973); Environmental Defense Fund, Inc. v. Environmental Protection Agency (heptachlor/chlordane), —— U.S.App.D.C. ——, 548 F.2d 998, 7 ELR 20012 (1976); Environmental Defense Fund, Inc. v. Environmental Protection Agency (aldrin-dieldrin II), 167 U.S.App.D.C. 71, 510 F.2d 1292, 3 ELR 20243 (1975); Southern Nat'l Mfg. Co. v. Environmental Protection Agency (lindane), 470 F.2d 194, 3 ELR 20323 (8th Cir. 1972).

38. See 7 U.S.C.A. § 136n(b) (review by courts of appeals). Slight differences between the standard of review under the 1947 FIFRA and the 1972 FEPCA are discussed in Environmental Defense Fund, Inc. v. Environmental Protection Agency (DDT III), 160 U.S.App.D.C. 123, 126–27, 489 F.2d 1247, 1250–51, 4 ELR 20031, 20033–34 (1973).

example, conditional suspensions to take effect only if certain volumes or limits are exceeded.[39]

His discretionary judgments are not overcome by arguments that the general evidence on damage was not linked up to a particular use at issue,[40] or that his conclusions were contested by reputable scientific authority, reached without establishing an acceptable threshold limit for the pesticide involved, based on the extrapolation to human beings of animal test results, departed from prior policy positions, strayed from the findings of the administrative law judge, were unsupported by evidence addressing each and every crop and geographical area, or without benefit of a risk-benefit analysis for each use contested.[41]

It often has been observed that the burden of proving safety remains on the registrant.[42] The screening standards established by EPA as a part of the registration requirements [43] apply equally to cancellation decisions. The mechanism used, explained above,[44] "is a rebuttable presumption against new or continued registration of a pesticide with high acute toxicity characteristics, immediate danger from inhalation, skin contact, or residues in human or animal food, or with any chronic toxicity characteristics, which primarily involve long-term danger from cancerous tumor formation or genetic mutation." [45] If the presumption against registration is overcome, toxicity characteristics become pertinent to the classification decision.[46] By drawing attention to, and concentrating the evidence on, the chemical characteristics of a pesticide that give rise to the presumption and whether a justification exists to rebut it, EPA regulations bring some focus to what is otherwise a very diffuse proceeding. One author suggests [47] that the decision on whether a presumption has been rebutted necessarily involves policy-making beyond technical metes and bounds and, thus, should be assigned explicitly to higher level employees.

The close scrutiny that the courts bring to bear on agency decisions affecting pesticide usage has been assured a greater intensity

---

39. Environmental Defense Fund, Inc. v. Environmental Protection Agency (aldrin-dieldrin I), 150 U.S.App.D.C. 348, 360, 465 F.2d 528, 540, 2 ELR 20228, 20234 (1972) (dictum).

40. Environmental Defense Fund, Inc. v. Environmental Protection Agency (DDT III), 160 U.S.App.D.C. 123, 130, 489 F.2d 1247, 1254, 4 ELR 20031, 20035 (1973).

41. Environmental Defense Fund, Inc. v. Environmental Protection Agency (aldrin-dieldrin II), 167 U.S.App.D.C. 71, 510 F.2d 1292, 5 ELR 20243 (1975).

42. E. g., Environmental Defense Fund, Inc. v. Environmental Protection Agency (heptachlor-chlordane), —— U.S.App.D.C. ——, ——, 548 F.2d 998, 1004, 7 ELR 20012, 20014 (1976); Environmental Defense Fund, Inc. v. Ruckelshaus (DDT II), 142 U.S.App.D.C. 74, 439 F.2d 584, 1 ELR 20059 (1972); Stearns Elec. Paste Co. v. Environmental Protection Agency, 461 F.2d 293, 304, 2 ELR 20368, 20372 (7th Cir. 1972).

43. 40 CFR § 162.11.

44. § 8.4.

45. Spector, note 14 supra, at 252–53 (footnote omitted).

46. 40 CFR § 162.11(c).

47. Spector, note 14 supra, at 256.

Sec. 8.7 CANCELLATION; SUSPENSION

by the 1975 amendments to FIFRA. The techniques chosen, in the tradition of the National Environmental Policy Act (NEPA),[48] are a stiffer mix of documentation, consultation, and reasoned decision-making. The core of EPA's substantive pesticide authority as regards both registration and cancellation is embodied in the definition of "unreasonable adverse environmental effects" which calls for a balancing of the "economic, social and environmental costs and benefits of the use of any pesticide."[49] This plainly anticipates an evaluation of economic effects, although Congress in 1975 thought the agency could do better. Moved by claims that EPA had slighted economic considerations and the food and fiber needs of the nation in its pesticide decisions,[50] Congress sought to rectify the balance by requiring the agency to prepare an "economic impact analysis" (EIA) to accompany its major pesticide regulatory initiatives. The idea obviously is borrowed from NEPA,[51] not without precedent by the way,[52] and seeks to compel straight economic thinking from an agency with an environmental bias just as the environmental impact statement under NEPA seeks to compel straight environmental thinking from agencies with a developmental bias. More closely reasoned results from the agencies appears to be an aim shared by diverse interest groups.

Procedurally, under the 1975 amendments EPA must prepare a draft EIA at least 60 days before issuing a notice of intent to suspend or cancel a pesticide registration.[53] The EIA must address the proposed action's impact on the "production and prices of agricultural commodities, retail food prices, and otherwise on the agricultural economy."[54] Not clear is whether the EIA should include a full-blown cost-benefit analysis and discuss projected losses to pesticide manufacturers, alternatives, and the costs of alternatives. The best bet is that comprehensiveness is required, in keeping with the spirit of the

---

48. §§ 7.1–.10 above. Compare § 7.3 above (discussing related aspects of the 1975 amendments).

49. 7 U.S.C.A. § 136(bb).

50. See House Comm. on Agriculture, Extension and Amendment of the Federal Insecticide, Fungicide, and Rodenticide Act, As Amended, H.R.Rep.No.497, 94th Cong., 1st Sess. 6 (1975) [hereinafter cited as House Report]; Senate Comm. on Agriculture and Forestry, Extension of the Federal Insecticide, Fungicide, and Rodenticide Act, S.Rep.No.452, 94th Cong., 1st Sess. 8 (1975) [hereinafter cited as Senate Report].

51. § 7.4 above. The legislative insistence upon an economic impact analysis also may be a reaction against the case law exempting EPA pesticide decision-making from the environmental impact statement requirement under NEPA. See, e. g., Environmental Defense Fund, Inc. v. Environmental Protection Agency (DDT III), 160 U.S.App.D.C. 123, 489 F.2d 1247, 3 ELR 40031 (1973); Wyoming v. Hathaway, 525 F.2d 66, 6 ELR 20169 (10th Cir. 1975).

52. There are many examples, including inflationary impact statements, energy impact statements, and economic impact statements. See, e. g., Independent Meat Packers Ass'n v. Butz, 526 F.2d 228 (8th Cir. 1975) (refusing to enforce inflationary impact statement requirements of Executive Order No. 11821).

53. 7 U.S.C.A. § 136d(b).

54. Ibid.

amendment and earlier interpretations of the Act.[55] Upon completing the analysis, EPA is required to submit the EIA to the U. S. Department of Agriculture for comment.[56] Comments are to be received within thirty days, or within another period agreed to by the agencies, and EPA must publish them together with its response in the Federal Register.[57] Publication of the EIA must precede the taking of final action in the suspension or cancellation process.[58] The process probably is intended to function like agencies with adjudicatory procedures under NEPA: a draft statement is prepared prior to the hearing and may be put in issue at the hearing; issuance of the final statement precedes the taking of final agency action.

Normally, the economic analysis referral to the Department of Agriculture is supplemented by a separate referral to a Scientific Advisory Panel routinely given an opportunity to review and comment "as to the impact on health and environment of the action" proposed in notices of intent to cancel or change a classification.[59] The purpose of the Scientific Advisory Panel referral is to strengthen the technical input on issues that inspire disagreement within the scientific community.[60] In the event that the Administrator determines that the suspension of a pesticide "is necessary to prevent an imminent hazard to human health," he may waive both the procedures for consulting with the Department of Agriculture and submitting the proposals to the Scientific Advisory Panel. Apparently, he cannot waive the requirement that he consider the economic impact of what he is doing.[61] These referral mechanisms obviously are cumbersome and reflect an opinion that adjudication may not be the best model for resolving complex technological disputes. There is a school of thought that holds that the purpose of the 1975 amendments was to cripple EPA, disabling the agency from moving effectively against polluting pesticides. Yet, the referrals that can waste time also can improve substance. It cannot be said that the procedural obligations to consult USDA and the Scientific Advisory Panel have compromised seriously EPA's ability to protect public health and the environment.

While the twin referrals prescribed by the 1975 amendments were inspired in part by dissatisfaction with existing procedures, the struc-

---

55. Apparently EPA does not concur in this conclusion. According to the agency's interim guidelines implementing the 1975 amendments, the content of the EIA is to be limited to an analysis of the impacts on pesticide users and consumers of the users' products. EPA, Interim Procedures & Guidelines for Health Risk & Economic Impact Assessments of Suspected Carcinogens, app. II (May 19, 1976). The impact on pesticide manufacturers is irrelevant to EPA's analysis. Ibid.

56. 7 U.S.C.A. § 136d(b).

57. Ibid.

58. Ibid.

59. Id. § 136w(d). For additional discussion of this advisory apparatus, see § 8.3 above.

60. See 1975 House Report, supra note 50, at 11; Senate Report, supra note 50, at 9.

61. 7 U.S.C.A. § 136d(b).

ture for adjudicatory hearings on notices to suspend, cancel or change a classification was left intact.[62] Generally, it envisages a familiar trial-type hearing with one exception. Upon request of any party or when the presiding administrative law judge deems it "necessary or desirable" any time before the hearing record is closed, the judge shall refer "to a Committee of the National Academy of Sciences [NAS] the relevant questions of scientific fact involved in the public hearing."[63] This process leaves open several questions: How is the committee selected? What happens if the report is delayed? Are the members subject to cross-examination? Are the working papers obtainable under other provisions of law?[64] It is clear, however, that the expert commentary provided by the NAS Committee must be weighed carefully by the decision-maker. The hard look doctrine of judicial review demands that departures from the advice of qualified experts be considered and deliberate, and that the reasons for the departure be explained painstakingly.[65] A similar treatment will be required of the commentary generated by the twin referrals to the Department of Agriculture and the Scientific Advisory Panel that normally precede the adjudicatory hearing.

Pesticide cancellation proceedings, perhaps more than any other type of environmental case, strain the utility of the adjudicatory model for resolving disputes. The 1975 amendments, by compelling the consideration of outside views, convey a doubt that the traditional trial-type model for cancellations is an adequate vehicle for resolving these issues. It deserves emphasis that the decision-making process on registration, which is decidedly nonadjudicatory, also leaves much to be desired. Discussion over the best model for resolving disputes of this type deserves the attention it will get in the years ahead.[66] Not to be overlooked is the tendency of participants in the process, who are interested solely in results, to aim their objections at the procedures they believe have served them poorly.

62. Id. § 136d(d).

63. Ibid.

64. See § 1.12 above (on the role of the National Academy of Sciences).

65. See Environmental Defense Fund, Inc. v. Environmental Protection Agency (aldrin-dieldrin II), 167 U.S. App.D.C. 71, 85, 510 F.2d 1292, 1306, 5 ELR 20243, 20249 (1975); cf. International Harvester Co. v. Ruckelshaus, 155 U.S.App.D.C. 411, 445, 478 F.2d 615, 649, 3 ELR 20133, 20144 (1973) (discussing referral mechanism to NAS committee under the Clean Air Act).

66. Spector, note 14 supra, at 252–63, citing among others L. Tribe, Channeling Technology Through Law (1973); Gelpe & Tarlock, The Uses of Scientific Information in Environmental Decision Making, 48 S.Cal.L. Rev. 371 (1974); Stewart, The Reformation of American Administrative Law, 88 Harv.L.Rev. 1667 (1975). See also National Academy of Sciences, Decision Making for Regulating Chemicals in the Environment (1975); Tribe, Technology Assessment and the Fourth Discontinuity: The Limits of Instrumental Rationality, 46 S.Cal.L. Rev. 617 (1973).

§ 8.8 Tolerances

The Food, Drug, and Cosmetic Act sets forth procedures under which tolerances are established for pesticide chemical residues in raw agricultural commodities and processed food.[1] A tolerance, not explicitly defined in the legislation, is a ceiling on residues adequate to protect public health with a margin of safety. It is expressed in terms of permissible quantity for a particular food product (e. g., 2.0 parts per million of the insecticide dimethoate on spinach)[2] and thus, is the food equivalent of an ambient air standard.[3]

Authority to establish tolerances, monitor the food supply, and take enforcement action is distributed uneasily among several government agencies. The Reorganization Plan establishing the Environmental Protection Agency transferred to the new agency functions "of establishing tolerances for pesticide chemicals," previously vested in the Secretary of Health, Education, and Welfare (HEW), together with authority "to monitor compliance with the tolerances and the effectiveness of surveillance and enforcement."[4] Remaining with HEW, acting through the Food and Drug Administration, is the power to enforce compliance with the tolerances promulgated by EPA.[5] This awkward allocation of authority recently has been the subject of a memorandum of understanding between the two agencies setting forth their working arrangements.[6] Under the agreement, EPA "is to furnish all FDA district offices and appropriate FDA headquarters with a list of pesticides and their approved uses, updating this compendium as changes occur. EPA and FDA will each notify the other of any incidents of pesticide misuse that may result in illegal residues in food or feed products. Each agency will investigate reports from the other agency which give probable cause to suspect a violation of [the Federal Insecticide, Fungicide, and Rodenticide Act or the Food, Drug, and Cosmetic Act] and, where appropriate, initiate regulatory action. Each agency will report to the other the results of investigations arising out of information received from the other agency. FDA and EPA will make available to each other the necessary documents to support regulatory action under their respective acts and upon request will make personnel available for testimony. Any information obtained during the course of an investigation which may involve a statutory violation within the other agency's jurisdiction will be provided to that agency".[7] There is further agreement to coordinate investigations, sample analysis, and enforcement actions.

1. 21 U.S.C.A. §§ 346, 346a, 348.

2. 40 Fed.Reg. 49575 (1975), amending 40 CFR § 180.204.

3. See §§ 3.1, 3.4 above.

4. Reorganization Plan No. 3 of 1970, § 2(4), 5 U.S.C.A. App. §§ 609, 610.

5. See United States v. Goodman, 486 F.2d 847, 3 ELR 20817 (7th Cir. 1973).

6. 40 Fed.Reg. 25078 (1975).

7. Recent Developments, 5 ELR 10136, 10137 (1975).

Sec. 8.8   TOLERANCES   889

EPA regulations make clear that obtaining a tolerance or exemption is a prerequisite to registration of a pesticide that reasonably may be expected to result in residues in food.[8] This is a proper conclusion,[9] although there is some legal support for the view that registration may be completed independently of the tolerance procedures.[10] A proceeding to establish a tolerance, like a registration proceeding, is a closeknit affair between the petitioner and the agency with little interference from outsiders.[11] A petition in support of a tolerance or exemption must contain the chemical identity and composition of the pesticide, amount, frequency and time of its application, reports on safety and residue tests, an identification of methods for removing residues in excess of a proposed tolerance, any proposed tolerances, and "reasonable grounds in support of the petition."[12] Provisions are made for certifying the usefulness of the pesticide for the purpose for which a tolerance is sought,[13] convening an advisory committee for the preparation of a report and recommendations on a tolerance petition,[14] and the holding of a hearing upon objection by "any person adversely affected" by a regulation establishing a tolerance or approving an exemption.[15] The formal procedures, apart from notice, are rarely invoked. No environmental impact statement is prepared in connection with the tolerance decision. Data submitted in support of a petition are closely held and confidential.[16] Time

---

8. 40 CFR § 162.7(d)(5).

9. See Environmental Defense Fund, Inc. v. Dep't of Health, Educ. & Welfare, 138 U.S.App.D.C. 381, 385, 428 F.2d 1083, 1087, 1 ELR 20045, 20047 (1970) ("the House and Senate Reports suggest that ordinarily Agriculture's decisions as to whether to register a pesticide under FIFRA for use on food crops should depend upon HEW's decision to grant a tolerance") (discussing legislative history of the 1954 Miller amendment to the Food, Drug, and Cosmetic Act). Environmental Defense Fund, Inc. v. Dep't of Health, Educ., & Welfare also states that "the Department of Agriculture should presumably deregister a pesticide for use on food crops if HEW revokes an existing tolerance." 138 U.S.App.D.C. at 385–86 n. 11, 428 F.2d at 1087–88 n. 11, 1 ELR at 20047 n. 11.

10. Cf. Environmental Defense Fund, Inc. v. Dep't of Health, Educ., & Welfare, supra note 9 (holding that the Departments of Agriculture and HEW must exercise an independent safety judgment on registration and tolerances, respectively; decision preceded the transfer of both functions to EPA); United States v. Goodman, 486 F.2d 847, 3 ELR 20817 (7th Cir. 1973) (holding that 21 U.S.C.A. § 346a does not make the establishment of tolerances mandatory).

11. 21 U.S.C.A. § 346a(d)(1)(A)–(G).

12. Id. § 346a(d)(1).

13. Id. § 346a(*l*).

14. Id. § 346a(d)(3).

15. Id. § 346a(d)(5).

16. Id. § 346a(f) reads:
All data submitted to the Administrator or to an advisory committee in support of a petition under this section shall be considered confidential by the Administrator and by such advisory committee until publication of a regulation . . . . Until such publication, such data shall not be revealed to any person other than those authorized by the Administrator or by an advisory committee in the carrying out of their official duties under this section.

limits are placed on the administrative decision,[17] which avoid the problem of indefinite delay but telescope the opportunity for adequate study.

The Administrator may exempt any pesticide chemical from the tolerance requirement if one "is not necessary to protect the public health." [18] Tolerances are to be established for "poisonous or deleterious pesticide chemicals" and for pesticide chemicals "which are not generally recognized, among experts qualified by scientific training and experience to evaluate the safety of pesticide chemicals, as safe for use, to the extent necessary to protect the public health." [19] Among the factors the Administrator must consider in establishing a tolerance are: the necessity for the production of an adequate, wholesome, and economical food supply; other ways in which the consumer may be affected by the same pesticide chemical or related substances; and the opinion submitted with a certification of usefulness.[20] The Administrator may establish a tolerance for any commodity "at zero level if the scientific data . . . does not justify the establishment of a greater tolerance." [21] Thus, pesticide food tolerances, like the ambient air standards,[22] are tied to public safety, except that food supply necessities are not to be disregarded. This presumably means that an incremental risk to human health in the form of a higher tolerance may be approved if a strong showing of necessity for use on an important food crop can be made.[23]

The tolerance setting procedures sound simple enough, but they are exceedingly difficult to implement. One author [24] observes: "EPA basically sets tolerances by accepting the petitioner's estimate of the amount of residue which will remain if a pesticide is applied to a given crop in a given manner, and then tries to determine, by evaluating data submitted by the petitioner, if this residue is safe. EPA does little of its own independent testing of the petitioner's chemistry and toxicology, and frequently does not even do a literature search for pertinent information. This creates a built-in bias toward granting the tolerance requested. Further, the agency judges the safety of the requested tolerances on the basis of estimated average daily intake, thereby leaving those with above average daily intake less well protected by the 'safety margins,' which are themselves usually speculative at best. The agency requires animal tests, but permits the petitioner to choose the two species of animals used; test animals chosen

---

17. Id. § 346a(d)(2), (1).

18. Id. § 346a(c).

19. Id. § 346a(b).

20. Ibid.

21. Ibid.

22. § 3.4 above.

23. See United States v. Goodman, 486 F.2d 847, 855, 3 ELR 20817, 20820–21 (7th Cir. 1973) (suggesting that the food supply factor is pertinent to an enforcement decision).

24. Butler, Federal Pesticide Law, in Environmental Law Institute, Federal Environmental Law 1232, 1276–77 (E. L. Dolgin & T. G. P. Guilbert eds. 1974) (footnotes omitted).

frequently are the two species the would-be registrant has found relatively resistant to the substance at issue. The use of relatively more sensitive species should be required, and the choice of species formalized for all pesticides. Further, where there is reason to believe that effects of a requested pesticide residue may be additive or synergistic with those of other residues for which tolerances have been approved, acceptance of the proposed additional food residue should not be, but is, judged in isolation without consideration of the total dietary pesticide burden." Add to this the pressures of deciding under tight time constraints (generally the Administrator must publish a final regulation within 90 days after the certification of usefulness [25]) and the extremely hypothetical nature of the judgment, and it must be recognized that setting pesticide tolerances is not confidently undertaken.

The debate over "zero" tolerances illustrates the difficulties involved. While the statute permits the establishment of a tolerance at "zero level" if the scientific data does not justify a "greater tolerance," [26] improved analytical technology now permits measurements at trace levels. EPA administratively has abandoned the practice of "zero tolerances" and replaced them with finite limits. There have been several consequences. One is a policy of "interim" tolerances to handle the flood of applications, some of which have remained outstanding and of questionable legal validity for years.[27] Another is the controversy surrounding the setting of tolerances for carcinogenic (cancer-causing), or potentially carcinogenic, pesticide residues. The well known Delaney amendment to the Food, Drug, and Cosmetic Act,[28] states unequivocally, with exceptions not here material, that no food additive "shall be deemed to be safe if it is found to induce cancer when ingested by man or animal, or if it is found, after tests which are appropriate for the evaluation of the safety of food additives, to induce cancer in man or animal." A similar per se prohibition applies to color additives.[29] While it is fairly well established as

---

25. 21 U.S.C.A. § 346a(d)(2).

26. Id. § 346a(b).

27. See Butler, supra note 24, at 1277. The statute, 21 U.S.C.A. § 346a(i), authorizes the Administrator to establish "temporary tolerances" for use in connection with an experimental permit authorizing application of an unregistered pesticide. See § 8.4 above. Unclear is the policy ground that would allow any contamination of food produced by a pesticide still in an experimental stage.

28. 21 U.S.C.A. § 348(c)(3)(A); see Rodgers, The Persistent Problem of the Persistent Pesticides: A Lesson in Environmental Law, 70 Colum.L. Rev. 567, 592–603 (1970). For background on the Delaney amendment, see generally Blank, The Delaney Clause: Technical Naivete and Scientific Advocacy in the Formulation of Public Health Policies, 62 Calif.L.Rev. 1084 (1974); Kleinfeld, Delaney Proviso—Its History and Prospects, 28 Food, Drug & Cosm.L.J. 556 (1973); Oser, Assessment of the Delaney Clause After 15 Years, 29 Food, Drug & Cosm.L.J. 201 (1974); Turner, Delaney Anticancer Clause: A Model Environmental Law, 24 Vand.L.Rev. 889 (1971).

29. 21 U.S.C.A. § 376(b)(5)(B); see Certified Color Mfr. Ass'n v.

a technical matter that the Delaney amendment is inapplicable to pesticide chemical residues,[30] it is not immediately clear from a policy perspective why cancer-causing food or color additives must be kept out of the food supply while cancer-causing pesticide residues, which can be described as uninvited additives, may be allowed in. The courts have been troubled by this situation and have made it very clear that they will scrutinize closely any administrative decision allowing residues of a carcinogenic pesticide to accumulate on food products.[31]

Equally challenging are the questions of surveillance and enforcement that follow the fixing of tolerances. EPA has several pesticide monitoring programs, including "the Human Monitoring Program whose function is to determine the level and significance of certain pesticides in humans. The major components of this program are the Community Studies Project, which examines long-term occupational exposure to pesticides, and the General Population Study, where exposure levels are identified."[32] The Food and Drug Administration (FDA) conducts "an annual Market Basket Survey, in which foods selected to represent the average total two-week diet for an adult, and the diet for the unusually high consumption of a 16 to 19 year old boy, are both purchased in grocery stores and analyzed for total content of a few selected pesticides."[33] FDA also conducts routine sampling and inspection and special investigations of suspected commodities. The Department of Agriculture has a surveillance program affecting meat and poultry, and the Interior Department monitors pesticide levels in fish and wildlife.[34] State health officials also maintain testing programs for commodities intended for intrastate shipment.

Section 402(a)(1) of the Food, Drug, and Cosmetic Act makes clear that food is deemed "adulterated" if it is a "raw agricultural commodity" and it bears or contains a pesticide chemical which is "unsafe" within the meaning of section 407.[35] Section 407, in turn, states that any pesticide not generally recognized as safe shall be deemed "unsafe" when added to a raw agricultural commodity unless—

> (1) a tolerance for such pesticide chemical in or on the raw agricultural commodity has been prescribed by the Administrator of the [Environmental Protection Agency] . . . and the

Mathews, (red dye no. 2), — U.S.App.D.C. —, 543 F.2d 284, 6 ELR 20629 (1976), cert. denied — U.S. —.

30. Environmental Defense Fund, Inc. v. Dep't of Health, Educ., & Welfare, 138 U.S.App.D.C. 381, 389–90, 428 F.2d 1083, 1091–92, 1 ELR 20045, 20049 (1970); Environmental Defense Fund, Inc. v. Ruckelshaus (DDT II), 142 U.S.App.D.C. 74, 86 n. 41, 439 F.2d 584, 596 n. 41, 1 ELR 20059, 20063 n. 41 (1971).

31. Cases cited in note 30, supra.

32. Butler, supra note 24, at 1275.

33. Id. at 1275–76.

34. Ibid.

35. 21 U.S.C.A. § 342(a)(2)(B).

quantity of such pesticide chemical in or on the raw agricultural commodity is within the limits of the tolerance so prescribed; or

(2) with respect to use in or on such raw agricultural commodity, the pesticide chemical has been exempted from the requirement of a tolerance by the Administrator . . . .[36]

The upshot of a tour through the relevant provisions is that a raw agricultural commodity is adulterated, and subject to seizure, if it contains quantities of a pesticide above the tolerance level. This is true even though EPA has established no tolerance level and granted no exemption, thus effectively imposing a "zero" tolerance for the pesticide at issue.[37] Moreover, one court has reasoned that a raw commodity adulterated before processing with an unsafe "pesticide chemical" also may be adulterated after processing with an unsafe "food additive."[38] The principal consequence of reading the definition of "food additive" as being broad enough to embrace the residue of a pesticide chemical remaining in food after processing is to limit the occasion when the government must prove actual damage, as distinguished from a deviation from the tolerance, to support an enforcement action.[39] It is unlawful to introduce adulterated food into interstate commerce,[40] and the remedies range from injunctions to criminal penalties to the seizure of the offending goods.[41]

§ 8.9. Enforcement

The Federal Insecticide, Fungicide, and Rodenticide Act (FIFRA) is relatively comprehensive in its enforcement potentiality. Each establishment producing pesticides subject to FIFRA must register with the Administrator.[1] Registration brings with it obligations to disclose information on amounts of production[2] and to maintain records that the Administrator deems necessary for effective enforcement.[3] Producers, dealers, and other sellers must allow EPA, state or local officers "at all reasonable times" to have access to their books and records showing the delivery and movement of pesticides.[4] Similarly, FIFRA authorizes EPA employees to enter an establishment "at

---

36. Id. § 346(a).

37. United States v. Goodman, 486 F.2d 847, 3 ELR 20817 (7th Cir. 1973) (court acknowledges that FDA has some discretion to withhold enforcement action as regards food with low level contamination); see United States v. Bodine Produce Co., 206 F.Supp. 201 (D.C.Ariz.1962) (lettuce containing excess amounts of DDT).

38. United States v. Ewing Bros., 502 F.2d 715, 4 ELR 20763 (7th Cir. 1974) (interpreting 21 U.S.C.A. § 342(a)(2)(C)).

39. United States v. Ewing Bros., supra note 38.

40. 21 U.S.C.A. § 331(a).

41. Id. §§ 332–34.

1. 7 U.S.C.A. § 136c(a). Compare §§ 3.19 (air pollution enforcement), 4.21 (water pollution enforcement) above.

2. 7 U.S.C.A. § 136c(c).

3. Id. § 136f(a).

4. Id. § 136f(b).

reasonable times" for purposes of inspecting and obtaining samples of pesticides, devices, or containers.[5] Before undertaking an inspection, the agency employee must present to the agent in charge of the establishment appropriate credentials, "and a written statement as to the reason for the inspection, including a statement as to whether a violation of law is suspected. If no violation is suspected, an alternative and sufficient reason shall be given in writing."[6] Warrants may be obtained authorizing the entry into premises, inspection, the reproduction of records and the seizure of any pesticide or device which is in violation of law.[7]

A lengthy list of unlawful acts includes both the expected and the unexpected. Predictably, it is an offense under FIFRA to distribute or sell any adulterated, misbranded, or unregistered pesticide.[8] It is unlawful to refuse to keep required records or to refuse to allow an EPA employee to take samples, to advertise a registered product without giving its classification, to use any pesticide contrary to terms of an experimental use permit, to violate a "stop sale, use, or removal" order, to violate a suspension or cancellation order, or to contravene the registration requirements of the Act.[9] Less predictably, it is unlawful for a person to deface or destroy any labeling required under the Act.[10] This is the pesticide version of the familiar anti-tampering provisions under the Clean Air Act.[11] It is unlawful for any person to use a registered pesticide in a manner inconsistent with its labeling.[12] This much ballyhooed first step to outlaw improper use in the 1972 FEPCA is of course altogether unenforceable. It is unlawful "to use any pesticide in tests on human beings unless such human beings (i) are fully informed of the nature and purposes of the test and of any physical and mental health consequences which are reasonably foreseeable therefrom, and (ii) freely volunteer to participate in the test."[13] This probably restates the common law on battery and consent,[14] which is not necessarily a bad thing, and leaves open the question of whether persons incarcerated in institutions can consent

---

5. Id. § 136g(a).

6. Ibid. The provision continues: Each . . . inspection shall be commenced and completed with reasonable promptness. If the officer or employee obtains any samples, prior to leaving the premises, he shall give to the [agent] in charge a receipt describing the samples obtained and, if requested, a portion of each such sample equal in volume or weight to the portion retained. If an analysis is made of such samples, a copy of the results of such analysis shall be furnished promptly to the [agent] in charge.

7. Id. § 136g(b).

8. Id. §§ 136j(a)(1)(A), (E).

9. Id. §§ 136j(a)(2)(B), (E), (H)–(L).

10. Id. § 136j(a)(2)(A).

11. § 3.15 above.

12. 7 U.S.C.A. § 136j(2)(G).

13. Id. § 136j(a)(2)(P).

14. E. g., Relf v. Weinberger, 372 F.Supp. 1196 (D.D.C.1974).

"freely." The misbranding provisions, discussed above,[15] are the key to the careful use assumptions of the contemporary law of pesticides. They forbid false and misleading labeling, require the disclosure of the product's registration number, call for directions for use and warning or caution statements adequate to protect health and the environment, require an ingredient statement and a statement of use classification together with information about the product and manufacturer. They also mandate a statement of treatment in case of poisoning by certain highly toxic pesticides.[16] The adulteration provisions, which have their origins in the Insecticide Act of 1910,[17] are designed to assure that the consumer gets what he pays for. Thus, a pesticide is adulterated if (1) "its strength or purity falls below the professed standard of quality as expressed on its labeling under which it is sold;" (2) "any substance has been substituted wholly or in part for the pesticide;" or (3) "any valuable constituent of the pesticide has been wholly or in part abstracted." [18] Many violations simultaneously give rise to misbranding and adulteration violations, as where a shoe spray with hexochlorophene was found to contain 26 times the amount of the active ingredient declared in the labeling.[19]

Penalties available for violations also include the obvious and the not-so-obvious. Whenever there is "reason to believe" on the basis of inspection or tests that a pesticide is in violation of the Act, the Administrator may issue a written or printed "stop, sale, use or removal" order which is intended to interdict further distribution of the product.[20] This is useful when directed at a specific pesticide known to be at a specific location; but the procedure generally has not been put to service in the more serious situation where a cancellation or suspension leaves large quantities of a pesticide lingering widely in commercial channels. Knowing violations are misdemeanors, which in the case of commercial applicators or dealers are punishable by imprisonment for up to one year and a fine of not more than $25,000, and in the case of private applicators (farmers) by imprisonment of up to 30 days and a $1000 fine.[21] An adulterated, misbranded, or unregistered pesticide, among other items, may be proceeded against in rem in the district court and may be disposed of by destruction or sale.[22] Court costs, storage fees, and other expenses are to be awarded against a person intervening unsuccessfully as claimant.[23] The statute specifically invites a form of dispensation that would obtain in any

15. § 8.5.

16. 7 U.S.C.A. § 136(q).

17. § 8.3 above.

18. 7 U.S.C.A. § 136(c).

19. In re U.S. Polychem. Corp., Environmental Protection Agency, Notices of Judgment Under FIFRA, June 1975, No. 1466 (May 3, 1974) (default order) (case prosecuted as a misbranding offense).

20. 7 U.S.C.A. § 136k(a).

21. Id. § 136l(b)(1), (2).

22. Id. § 136k(b)(c).

23. Id. § 135k(d).

event by stating that the Administrator is not required to institute proceedings to correct "minor violations" whenever he believes the public interest "will be adequately served by a suitable written notice of warning." [24] In fact, the Administrator routinely sends letters of warning pointing out minor violations as well as citations which are sent as precursors of possible criminal action.

An often discussed feature of FIFRA's enforcement apparatus is the indemnity provision allowing payments to persons suffering losses by reason of suspension or cancellation of a pesticide on grounds of "an imminent hazard." [25] The indemnity clause leaves open several questions: payments need not be made to persons who "had knowledge of facts which, in themselves, would have shown" the pesticide did not meet registration requirements, and who "continued thereafter to produce [the] pesticide without giving timely notice of the facts" to the Administrator.[26] The amount of an indemnity payment "shall be determined on the basis of the cost of the pesticide" owned by the person immediately before receiving the cancellation or suspension notice, "except that in no event shall an indemnity payment to any person exceed the fair market value of the pesticide owned" by him immediately before the receipt of a notice.[27] Most importantly, indemnification is not payable if nobody suffers losses. That may give the agency a distinct incentive to take no action against pesticides caught in channels by a cancellation or suspension notice. Thus, a provision that theoretically works in favor of greater expedition in banning dangerous pesticides (by removing from the equation the constraint imposed by potential economic disruption) can cut the opposite way (by deterring action incurring potential liabilities).

The most productive enforcement feature of FIFRA is the provision for civil penalties, which is comparable in many ways to the civil penalty scheme administered by the U. S. Coast Guard for oil pollution incidents.[28] The Act allows the imposition of a civil penalty of not more than $5000 for each offense committed by a person engaged in the business and a fine of not more than $1000 for each offense committed by a private applicator or other individual.[29] No civil penalty can be assessed unless the person charged is given an opportunity for a hearing in the county or city of his residence.[30] What has evolved is a decentralized operation where civil penalty assessments are handled by the ten EPA regional offices throughout the country. Whatever can be said of its effectiveness, the civil penalty program is ac-

24. Id. § 136g(c)(3).

25. Id. § 136m(a); see Hearings on the Federal Environmental Pesticide Control Act, Before the Subcomm. on the Environment of the Senate Comm. on Commerce, S.Doc.No.36, 94th Cong., 1st Sess. 31 (1975).

26. 7 U.S.C.A. § 136m(a).

27. Id. § 136m(b)(1).

28. § 4.17 above.

29. 7 U.S.C.A. §§ 136*l*(a)(1), (2).

30. Id. § 136*l*(a)(3).

Sec. 8.9 ENFORCEMENT 897

tively and visibly enforced.[31] Administrative action has filled in some of the details of the program. Thus, EPA has published rules of practice,[32] factors to be considered in assessing civil penalties,[33] and a civil penalty assessment schedule.[34] Decisions of the administrative law judges in contested penalty proceedings are producing precedents of importance. For example, it has been held at the administrative level that civil violations are strict liability offenses not dependent upon proof of culpability,[35] that an inconsistent pleading may be cured by amendment,[36] and that the administrative law judge is not bound by the agency's civil penalty assessment schedule.[37]

In many cases, the only seriously contested issue is the appropriate size of the penalty to be assessed. The statute makes clear that in determining the amount of a civil penalty the Administrator "shall consider the appropriateness of such penalty to the size of the business of the person charged, the effect on the person's ability to continue in business, and the gravity of the violation." [38] The gravity of the violation is a function both of the seriousness of the harm and of the misconduct.[39] It requires a determination as to "(1) the potential that the act committed has to injure man or the environment; (2) the severity of [the] potential injury; (3) the scale and type of use anticipated; (4) the identity of the persons exposed to a risk of injury; (5) the extent to which the applicable provisions of the Act were in fact violated; (6) the particular person's history of compliance and actual knowledge of the Act; and (7) evidence of good faith in the instant circumstance." [40] Thus, the proof ranges widely over such topics as compliance history, the possibly confusing nature of the communications between the agency and the violator, the temporary unavailability of the man in the business who understands the regulations,

---

31. Pursuant to 7 U.S.C.A. § 136n(d), the Administrator publishes on a regular basis Notices of Judgment under the Federal Insecticide, Fungicide, and Rodenticide Act. The Notices of Judgment report civil, criminal, and seizure cases taken against firms or individuals charged with FIFRA violations. The synopses include the name of the product and firm, the nature of the violation alleged, and the disposition of the action. The February 1976 publication reports on cases numbered 1651–700.

32. 39 Fed.Reg. 27656 (1974), adding 40 CFR pt. 168.

33. Id. at 27712.

34. Ibid.

35. In re Johnson Chem. Co., Environmental Protection Agency Notices of Judgment Under FIFRA, June 1975, No. 1475 (Oct. 8, 1974).

36. In re Southern Mill Creek Prods., Inc., Environmental Protection Agency, Notices of Judgment Under FIFRA, June 1975, No. 1479 (Mar. 6, 1974).

37. In re Pen-Kote Paint Co., Environmental Protection Agency, Notices of Judgment Under FIFRA, Feb. 1975, No. 1406 (Sept. 25, 1973).

38. 7 U.S.C.A. § 136l(a)(3).

39. See In re Johnson Chem. Co., supra note 35.

40. 39 Fed.Reg. 27711, 27712 (1974) (Application of Civil Penalty Schedule).

and the general condition and reputation of the enterprise. A stiffer penalty is likely to be forthcoming where there is a demonstration over the years of "carelessness, negligence, inadequate controls, and disregard for requirements of the Act." [41] A lighter sanction is in order where the trier of fact is moved by the following factors: "[R]espondent's violation was not intentional; respondent promptly applied for registration after the non-registration violation was brought to its attention and the product was subsequently registered; respondent is primarily in the paint business and the product in question is the only pesticide in which it deals; lack of history of previous violations; and the honest and forthright manner in which respondent's president and only witness testified".[42]

As expected, most of the civil penalty proceedings have involved classic instances of adulteration, misbranding, or nonregistration. It is certainly important to single out instances of inadequate warning and caution statements, nonregistration, labeling claims differing from those represented in connection with the registration, false and misleading claims of safety, inclusion of active ingredients not identified on the label or of active ingredients above the limits specified on the labeling. Proceedings arising out of misuse, however, are less common. This is understandable given the substantive gaps in the law,[43] impressive problems of proof, and doubtful deterrent value of a successful judgment. The recognition that misuse is something to be abhorred, not penalized, puts in better perspective the labeling control assumptions of federal pesticide law.[44]

§ 8.10 Toxic Substances

A major milestone in the regulation of environmental hazards was achieved with enactment of the Toxic Substances Control Act of 1976,[1] after several years consideration by the Congress.[2] The prin-

---

41. In re Beaulieu Chem. Co., Environmental Protection Agency, Notices of Judgment Under FIFRA, June 1975, Nos. 1500, 991, 1003 (July 24, 1974).

42. In re Pen-Kote Paint Co., supra note 37, at 888, 895.

43. It is important to note that 7 U.S.C.A. § 136j(a)(2)(G) only forbids use of a registered pesticide in a manner inconsistent with its labeling. It is not an offense to use an unregistered pesticide. This has proven to be a problem with respect to predator control efforts in the West. See Master, Little Bo-Peep, Where Are You When We Need You? A Look at the Issue of Predacide Use in the West (unpublished paper prepared for a course in environmental law, Georgetown U. Law Center, Spring 1976).

44. See § 8.3 above.

1. Pub.L. 94–469, 90 Stat. 2003 (1976), 15 U.S.C.A. § 2601 et seq.

2. See, e. g., Comm. of Conference, Toxic Substances Control Act of 1976, S.Rep.No.1302, 94th Cong., 2d Sess. (1976) [hereinafter cited as Senate Conference Report]; Comm. of Conference, Toxic Substances Control Act, H.R.Rep.No.1679, 94th Cong., 2d Sess. (1976); Comm. on Commerce Toxic Substances Control Act, S.Rep. No.698, 94th Cong., 2d Sess. (1976) [hereinafter cited as Senate Report]; Hearings on Toxic Substances Con-

cipal impulse for the legislation was the technological revolution in the chemical industry that has outflanked thoroughly the traditional legal regimes such as the pesticide laws. The Senate Commerce Committee noted with concern the development of "a vast new array of chemicals. In fact, it is estimated that there are presently 2 million recognized chemical compounds in existence with nearly 250,000 new compounds produced each year. While most of these compounds will never be commercialized, the Environmental Protection Agency estimates that approximately 1,000 new chemicals each year will find their way into the marketplace and subsequently into the environment through use and disposal."[3] Congress acted against the background of chemical pollution controversies that have become commonplace in these days (PCB's, vinyl chloride, fluorocarbons), and with the understanding that controlling toxic chemicals is a priority health requirement of the nation. The Senate Commerce Committee report recites estimates of the National Cancer Institute that 60 to 90 percent of human cancers occurring are attributable to environmental contaminants.[4]

If problem chemicals are to be intercepted before the damage is done, a preclearance regulatory system is necessary. Ideally, the safety decision should be made before commercial momentum develops. At the same time, linking the economic success of a product to an express bureaucratic approval is a prospect discouraging to some. The compromise reflected in the Toxic Substances Control Act is rejection of a rigid preclearance regulatory scheme, familiar in the pesticide and drug laws, in favor of a system of notice and selective interdiction.

a. *New Chemical Substances*

The scope of the Act is tied to a definition of "chemical substance" which is defined broadly as "any organic or inorganic substance of a particular molecular identity" including "any combination of such substances occurring in whole or in part as a result of chemical reaction or occurring in nature."[5] The Administrator of EPA is obliged to compile and keep current a list of each chemical substance which is manufactured or processed in the United States.[6] Subject to certain exemptions and time requirements,[7] under section

trol Act, Before the Subcomm. on Consumer Protection and Finance of the House Comm. on Interstate and Foreign Commerce, 94th Cong., 1st Sess. (1975); Hearings on the Toxic Substances Control Act of 1971 and Amendment, Before the Subcomm. on the Environment of the Senate Comm. on Commerce, S.Doc. 92–50, 92d Cong., 1st Sess. (1971).

3. Senate Report, supra note 2, at 3.

4. Id. at 4.

5. 15 U.S.C.A. § 2602(2). The definition includes also "any element or uncombined radical" and excludes a number of substances, such as drugs and pesticides, regulated under other laws.

6. Id. § 2607(b).

7. Id. § 2604(h).

5 no person may manufacture a "new chemical substance" or manufacture or process any chemical substance for "a significant new use" unless a notice of intention is filed with the Administrator at least 90 days earlier.[8] The notice must include a variety of information, including all known data on health and environmental effects.[9] The 90-day notice period may be extended for additional 90-day periods "for good cause" explained in the Federal Register.[10]

Obviously, the notice requirements "are intended to provide the Administrator with an opportunity to review and evalute information"[11] to determine if manufacture or use should be limited or delayed because data "is insufficient to permit a reasoned evaluation of the health and environmental effects" or because anticipated uses "may present an unreasonable risk of injury to health or the environment."[12] Upon making these findings the Administrator is authorized to issue a proposed order "to prohibit or limit the manufacture, processing, distribution in commerce, use, or disposal of such substance"[13] although formal objections from a manufacturer or processor[14] may compel the Administrator to go to court for injunctive relief.[15] An injunction pending development of adequate information should issue automatically, without regard to traditional equitable considerations, upon a judicial finding that the information available is insufficient to permit a reasoned evaluation of health and environmental effects or that anticipated uses will present an unreasonable risk of injury to health or the environment.[16] In the event of a finding that commercial activity as regards a new substance or use will present "an unreasonable risk of injury to health or the environment" before a restrictive rule may be published under section 6, the Administrator may issue a restrictive rule effective upon publication in the Federal Register.[17] A flat prohibition against manufacture also can be ordered although objections can send this issue to the district court.[18] In theory at least, the Administrator has a full

---

8. Id. § 2604(a).

9. Id. §§ 2604(a), (b), (d), 2607(b).

10. Id. § 2604(c).

11. Senate Conference Report, supra note 2, at 65.

12. 15 U.S.C.A. § 2604(e)(1)(A).

13. Ibid.

14. Id. § 2604(e)(1)(C).

15. Id. §§ 2604(e)(2)(A), (B).

16. Senate Conference Report, supra note 2, at 69:

The conferees do not intend that the Administrator be required to make any showing other than that which is required for the court to make the two findings described above. Application of any other standard by the court would frustrate the purposes of this section that suspect chemicals be adequately tested to determine their health and environmental effects before commercial manufacture or processing begins.

17. 15 U.S.C.A. § 2604(f)(2).

18. See id. § 2604(f)(3).

range of powers to stop commercial development of a chemical substance in its tracks.

The most likely outcome of the notification procedure for a new chemical substance or use is administrative inaction during the notification period. The Act is quite clear that a no action decision must be explained by a Federal Register publication before expiration of the notification period [19] although a failure to publish does not work to interrupt the manufacture or processing of the chemical substance. Unquestionably, noncompliance is enforceable by citizen suit.[20]

b. *Existing Chemical Substances*

The central regulatory assumptions of the Toxic Substances Control Act are found in section 6,[21] which anticipates a series of sophisticated rulemakings leading to the regulation of chemical substances. The unspoken premise of section 6 is that the data necessary to decide is available, with or without resort to interim regulations under section 5 pending the development of information. If the Administrator finds that there is a "reasonable basis" for concluding that manufacture, processing, distribution, use or disposal of a chemical substance "presents or will present an unreasonable risk of injury to health or the environment," he may apply any one or more of a number of restrictions "to the extent necessary to protect adequately against such risk using the least burdensome requirements."[22] Encouraging the "least burdensome" controls can be read as eschewing the margin of safety written into various "best technology" pollution control standards[23] although it resists automatic assumption of the adequacy of labeling found in the pesticide laws.[24] The regulatory requirements anticipated by section 6 include the expected roster of manufacturing and use controls—outright prohibitions against manufacture, processing or distribution of the product,[25] bans against manufacture for a particular use, limitation on amounts that may be manufactured for a particular use, restrictions on labeling, monitoring and testing, commercial use, disposal, warnings, manufacturing quality controls and the like.[26]

In the case of polychlorinated byphenyls, the archetypical chemical villian that stimulated passage of the Act, specific regulatory steps are called for: within six months the promulgation of rules prescrib-

---

19. Id. § 2604(g).

20. Senate Conference Report, supra note 2, at 71.

21. 15 U.S.C.A. § 2605.

22. Id. § 2605(a).

23. See §§ 2.6, 3.10, 4.11–.13 above.

24. § 8.5 above.

25. The conferees did not anticipate the use of section 6 to impose a total prohibition on the manufacture or distribution of a new substance. See Senate Conference Report, supra note 2, at 70. That requires resort to the procedures of 15 U.S.C.A. § 2604(f), which include a probable trip to court.

26. See 15 U.S.C.A §§ 2605(a)(1)–(7), (b).

ing methods for disposal, warnings and instructions for use; and within a year a flat prohibition against manufacture, process and use "in any manner other than in a totally enclosed manner." [27] The definition of a "totally enclosed manner" leaves some room for escape since it means any manner "which will ensure that any exposure of human beings or the environment to a polychlorinated byphenyl will be insignificant as determined by the Administrator by rule." [28] The total enclosure is breached also by an assignment of discretion to the Administrator to waive the requirement upon a finding that manufacture or use "will not present an unreasonable risk of injury to health or the environment." [29]

In making a judgment about the unreasonableness of the risk posed by a chemical substance under section 6(c),[30] the Administrator is directed to consider and publish a statement with respect to—

(A) the effects of such substance or mixture on health and the magnitude of the exposure of human beings to such substance or mixture,

(B) the effects of such substance or mixture on the environment and the magnitude of the exposure of the environment to such substance or mixture,

(C) the benefits of such substance or mixture for various uses and the availability of substitutes for such uses, and

(D) the reasonably ascertainable economic consequences of the rule, after consideration of the effect on the national economy, small business, technological innovation, the environment and public health.

The Administrator also is instructed to refrain from addressing risks within reach of other federal laws administered by him unless he exercises a discretion meant to be unreviewable [31] by finding that promulgation of a rule under the Toxic Substances Control Act is "in the public interest." [32]

This openended standard of acceptability does not differ greatly from that governing the registration of chemical pesticides.[33] The

---

27. Id. § 2605(e)(2)(A).

28. Id. § 2605(e)(2)(C).

29. Id. § 2605(e)(2)(B).

30. Id. § 2605(c).

31. See Senate Conference Report, supra note 2, at 76.

32. 15 U.S.C.A. § 2605(c). The problem of coordinating actions under various federal laws is especially acute with regard to toxic substances. Compare §§ 3.11, 4.15, 6.10 above. Elsewhere the Toxic Substances Control Act prescribes specifics, including the preparation of reports by the Administrator, for dealing with issues of overlapping statutory authority. See 15 U.S.C.A. § 2608.

33. § 8.4 above. The criteria for registering a chemical pesticide include a judgment about whether the product and use "will perform its intended function without unreasonable adverse effects on the environ-

loose alignment of costs and benefits suggests a balancing approach although without any presumed mathematical certainty. The test amounts to a standard of whether a reasonable man, with knowledge of risks, benefits and other consequences, would prescribe regulatory restrictions and, if so, what the "least burdensome" protection would be. Given the breadth of the discretion assigned to the Administrator, litigation is likely to focus not on the statutory parameters but on the form and persuasiveness of the justification for regulation.[34] Procedurally, section 6 borrows from the teachings of the close scrutiny doctrine of judicial review [35] by prescribing findings and hearings requirements that include possible cross-examination by interested parties.[36] One of the more interesting features of a toxic substances rulemaking is a grant of authority to the EPA Administrator to provide "compensation for reasonable attorneys' fees, expert witness fees, and other costs of participating in a rulemaking proceeding" to any person who represents an interest "which would substantially contribute to a fair determination of the issues to be resolved" and who meets certain tests of poverty or marginal economic interest.[37] Financial assistance for groups of limited means in administrative proceedings is one of the keys to the realization of the nobler aims of citizen suits.[38]

The routine rulemaking provisions of section 6 are supplemented by an extraordinary authority of section 7 authorizing the Administrator to seek judicial relief against an "imminently hazardous chemical substance or mixture."[39] An action may go forward without regard to the pendency of another administrative or judicial proceeding.[40] The relief authorized may include a seizure order and a mandatory directive requiring notification of purchasers or the general public of the risk, recall, or replacement or repurchase of the substance.[41] The extraordinary nature of the remedy is emphasized by the definition of "imminently hazardous chemical substance or mixture" which is a substance "which presents an imminent and unreasonable risk of serious or widespread injury to health or the environment. Such a risk to health or the environment shall be considered imminent if it is shown that the manufacture, processing, distribution in commerce, use, or disposal of the chemical substance or mixture, or that any combination of such activities, is likely to result

ment." 7 U.S.C.A. § 136a(c)(5)(C). The "environment" is defined broadly in both the pesticides and toxic substances legislation. Compare 7 U.S.C.A. § 136(j) with 15 U.S.C.A. § 2602(5).

34. See § 1.5 above.

35. See ibid.

36. 15 U.S.C.A. § 2605(c)(1)–(3).

37. Id. § 2605(c)(4).

38. § 1.13 above.

39. 15 U.S.C.A. § 2606(a)(1)(A).

40. Id. § 2606(a)(1).

41. Id. § 2606(b).

in such injury to health or the environment before a final rule under section 6 can protect against such risk."[42]

The testing and data collection needs met for new chemicals by the notification provisions of section 5 are satisfied for existing chemicals by separate testing requirements of section 4.[43] Upon certain findings that a substance presents unreasonable or unknown risks,[44] the Administrator is obliged by rule to require the development of data on health and environmental effects.[45] The testing and data requirements are imposed upon manufacturers and processors [46] and may address a wide range of effects, chemical characteristics, testing methodologies, and time periods.[47] Provision is made for third party testing by disinterested persons although the Act stops short of encouraging this commendable practice.[48] A formal system of exemptions is prescribed to avoid the submission of duplicate data and to provide for equitable reimbursement to persons previously submitting data.[49] A notice of the receipt of test data pursuant to a rule must be published in the Federal Register within fifteen days of its receipt.[50] It is clear that data adduced in response to section 4 rulemakings falls within the statutory definition of a "health and safety study." This is a term of art meaning "any study of any effect of a

42. Id. § 2606(f).

43. Id. § 2603.

44. Id. § 2603(a); see Senate Conference Report, supra note 2, at 61:
In the first situation, the conferees intend to focus the Administrator's attention on those chemical substances and mixtures about which there is a basis for concern, but about which there is inadequate information to reasonably predict or determine their effects on health or the environment. The Administrator need not show that the substance or mixture does or will present a risk.
The second situation reflects the conferees' recognition that there are certain situations in which testing should be conducted even though there is an absence of information indicating that the substance or mixture *per se* may be hazardous.

45. 15 U.S.C.A. § 2603(a). The term "standards for the development of test data" means, according to id. § 2602 (12), a prescription of:
(A) . . .
(i) health and environmental effects, and
(ii) information relating to toxicity, persistence, and other characteristics which affect health and the environment, for which test data for a chemical substance or mixture are to be developed and any analysis that is to be performed on such data, and
(B) To the extent necessary to assure that data respecting such effects and characteristics are reliable and adequate—
(i) the manner in which such data are to be developed,
(ii) the specification of any test protocol or methodology to be employed in the development of such data, and
(iii) such other requirements as are necessary to provide such assurance.

46. Id. § 2603(b)(3)(B).

47. Id. § 2603(b)(1), (2).

48. Id. § 2603(b)(3)(A).

49. Id. § 2603(c).

50. Id. § 2603(d).

Sec. 8.10　　　　　　TOXIC SUBSTANCES　　　　　　　905

chemical substance or mixture on health or the environment or on both, including underlying data and epidemiological studies, studies of occupational exposure to a chemical substance or mixture, toxicological, clinical, and ecological studies of a chemical substance or mixture, and any test performed pursuant to the Act."[51] Section 8(d) of the Act requires the promulgation of rules directing manufacturers, processors, or distributors to submit to the agency copies of all health and safety studies known to, or reasonably ascertainable by, them.[52] Similarly, section 14(b) exempts health and safety studies from trade secret protection against public disclosure under the Freedom of Information Act.[53]

Consistently with recently established tradition,[54] the Act establishes an interagency advisory committee "to make recommendations to the Administrator respecting the chemical substances and mixtures to which the Administrator should give priority consideration for the promulgation of a rule" on testing requirements.[55] Committee recommendations are to be based on a number of factors relevant to the risks involved,[56] and are to take the form of a list of substances and mixtures, no more than 50 of which may be designated for administrative action within a year. The list and designations are transmitted by the committee to the Administrator and are published in the Federal Register, together with the reasons for inclusion of a substance.[57] With respect to each designated substance or mixture, the Administrator is obliged to initiate a testing requirement rulemaking within a year or to explain in the Federal Register his reasons for not doing so.[58]

Obviously, the collection of test data under section 4 does not proceed oblivious of regulatory responsibilities under sections 5, 6 and 7. In one particular situation of gravity, section 4 mandates action by the Administrator upon receipt of test data or other information indicating "a reasonable basis to conclude that a chemical substance or mixture presents or will present a significant risk of serious or widespread harm to human beings from cancer, gene mutations, or birth defects. . . ."[59] Under these circumstances the Administrator, within 180 days subject to a 90-day extension, either must initiate appropriate action under sections 5, 6 or 7, or publish in the

---

51.　Id. § 2602(6).

52.　Id. § 2607(d).

53.　Id. § 2613(b).

54.　§ 1.11 above.

55.　15 U.S.C.A. § 2603(e)(1)(A).

56.　See ibid, stating among other requirements that the committee "shall give priority attention to those chemical substances and mixtures which are known to cause or contribute to or which are suspected of causing or contributing to cancer, gene mutations, or birth defects."

57.　Id. § 2603(e)(1)(B).

58.　Ibid.

59.　Id. § 2603(f).

Federal Register a finding that the risk is not unreasonable.[60] The mandatory nature of the obligation makes it subject to citizen suit enforcement.[61]

c. *Miscellaneous Requirements*

In addition to prescribing a full agenda of regulatory authority to cope with existing and new chemical substances, the Toxic Substances Control Act contains a miscellany of provisions not unfamiliar to mature legal regimes in technological fields. Section 10[62] gives the Administrator authority to conduct research, development and monitoring in pursuit of the objectives of the Act. The Administrator is directed to set up an interagency committee to establish a system for collecting and using submitted data,[63] to design and coordinate a system for retrieving toxicological data,[64] to undertake development of screening techniques for toxic effects of chemical substances,[65] and to aim research towards developing techniques and instruments for detecting and monitoring chemical substances.[66] The Administrator is directed to conduct a study of indemnification of those hit by regulation,[67] and a continuing evaluation of the potential effects on employment of regulatory moves under sections 4, 5 and 6.[68]

Reporting and enforcement provisions are closely linked and far reaching. Section 8[69] grants to the Administrator rulemaking powers on maintenance of records and reporting. Records must be kept on adverse effects of chemical substances.[70] Provisions are included for the reporting of health and safety studies[71] and giving notice to the Administrator of health and safety information of consequence. Indeed, section 8(c) prescribes an obligation that ought to be accepted without question in all regulatory systems of high risk activity: "Any person who manufactures, processes, or distributes in commerce a chemical substance or mixture and who obtains information which reasonably supports the conclusion that [the] substance or mixture presents a substantial risk of injury to health or the environment shall immediately inform the Administrator of [the] information unless [the] person has actual knowledge that the Administrator has been adequately informed of [the] information."[72] Unfortunately, this reporting obligation can succumb to rationaliza-

60. Ibid.
61. Id. § 2619.
62. Id. § 2609.
63. Id. § 2609(b)(1).
64. Id. § 2609(b)(2).
65. Id. § 2609(c).
66. Id. § 2609(d); see id. § 2626.
67. Id. § 2624.
68. Id. § 2623(a).
69. Id. § 2607(a).
70. Id. § 2607(c).
71. Id. § 2607(d).
72. Id. § 2607(e).

tions that the risk isn't all that "substantial" or the threat of it not "reasonably" justified.

The penalty and enforcement provisions conform to established patterns.[73] The Act prohibits noncompliance with rules and requirements established under sections 4, 5 and 6.[74] Use of a chemical substance "for commerial purposes" is forbidden if the actor knows or has reason to know of prohibitions against its manufacture.[75] Also forbidden are failures to establish or maintain records or submit required reports and notices.[76] A violation is punishable as a civil penalty "in an amount not to exceed $25,000 for each such violation."[77] Each day of a continuing violation is a separate offense.[78] A civil penalty may be assessed only after an adjudicatory hearing before the Administrator,[79] a procedure quite like that governing violations of the pesticide laws.[80] In determining the amount of a civil penalty, the Administrator is obliged to take into account "the nature, circumstances, extent, and gravity of the violation or violations and, with respect to the violator, ability to pay, effect on ability to continue to do business, any history of prior . . . violations, the degree of culpability, and . . . other matters as justice may require."[81] Petitions for review may be filed in the courts of appeals within thirty days of the entry of an order imposing a penalty.[82]

The federal district courts are given jurisdiction over seizure actions and actions to enjoin violations of the Act.[83] The Act contains a conventional citizens suit provision,[84] which will be invoked often because of an incentive in the form of counsel and expert witness fees and the relatively large number of mandatory obligations imposed by the law. Review of EPA rulemakings is available in the courts of appeals,[85] subject to a number of conditions, including a highly unusual provision allowing another discretionary award of counsel and expert witness fees.[86] Yet another potentially important section lays down procedures for citizen rulemaking petitions, subject to judicial review in the district courts.[87]

As with other federal environmental legislation, the Toxic Substances Control Act contains a carefully crafted preemption section

---

73. §§ 3.19, 4.21, 8.9 above.

74. 15 U.S.C.A. § 2614(1).

75. Id. § 2614(2).

76. Id. § 2614(3).

77. Id. § 2615(a)(1).

78. Ibid.

79. Id. § 2615(a)(2)(A).

80. § 8.9 above.

81. 15 U.S.C.A. § 2615(a)(2)(B).

82. Id. § 2615(a)(3).

83. Id. § 2616.

84. Id. § 2619; see § 1.13 above.

85. Id. § 2618.

86. Id. § 2618(d).

87. Id. § 2620.

attempting to reconcile state and local autonomy with the demands of interstate trade in chemical substances.[88] A broad override requires the Administrator to waive compliance "with any provision of this Act upon a request and determination by the President that the requested waiver is necessary in the interest of national defense." [89] A now familiar statutory protection for whistle blowers forbids retaliatory action by employers against employees who aid proceedings under the Act.[90] A modest grant program is established to assist states in developing programs for combatting risks from chemical substances unlikely to be reached under the Act.[91] The legislation also requires an annual report which should prove to be a useful first source for those desiring to compare the sweeping legislative promise with the administrative returns. The annual report is supposed to include: [92]

> (1) a list of the testing required under section 4 during the year for which the report is made and an estimate of the costs incurred during [the] year by the persons required to perform [the] tests;

> (2) the number of notices received during [the] year under section 5, the number of . . . notices received during [the] year under [the] section for chemical substances subject to a section 4 rule, and a summary of any action taken during [the] year under section 5(g);

> (3) a list of rules issued during [the] year under section 6;

> (4) a list, with a brief statement of the issues, of completed or pending judicial actions under this Act and administrative actions under section 16 during [the] year;

> (5) a summary of major problems encountered in administration of this Act; and

> (6) such recommendations for additional legislation as the Administrator deems necessary to carry out the purposes of this Act.

88. Id. § 2617.
89. Id. § 2621.
90. Id. § 2622.
91. Id. § 2627.
92. Id. § 2629.

TABLE OF CASES

References are to Pages

Aaron v. Los Angeles, 577, 579, 583
Abbott Laboratories v. Gardner, 18, 46
Aberdeen & Rockfish R.R. v. SCRAP, 651, 732, 765
Aberdeen & Rockfish R.R. v. SCRAP (I), 799
Aberdeen & Rockfish R.R. v. SCRAP (II), 652, 718, 768, 771, 785, 790
Activated Sludge, Inc. v. Sanitary Dist. of Chicago, 148
Adams Constr. Co. v. Bentley, 146
Aeschliman v. Nuclear Regulatory Comm'n, 691, 790
Aircraft Owners & Pilots Ass'n v. Port Authority, 595, 596
Air Pollution Variance Bd. of Colorado v. Western Alfalfa Corp., 337, 339
Air Transport Ass'n v. Crotti, 596
Air Transport Ass'n v. Inglewood, 594
Akers v. Resor, 720, 729, 731, 749, 793, 826
Alabama Gas Corp. v. Federal Power Comm'n, 764
Alameda Conservation Ass'n v. California, 396
Aldridge v. Saxey, 560
Aldworth v. Lynn, 128
Alevizos v. Metropolitan Airports Comm'n, 578, 579, 582, 583
Alexander Bros., Inc., State v., 141
Allatoona's Interstate Right, Inc. v. Volpe, 779
Allegheny Airlines, Inc. v. Cedarhurst, 594
Allegheny-Ludlum Steel Corp., United States v., 22, 233
Alliston v. Shell Petroleum Corp., 371
Allview, Inc. v. Howard County, 688
Allway Taxi, Inc. v. City of New York, 572
Allyn v. United States, 224
Alonso v. Hills, 119
Altman, People v., 594
Alyeska Pipeline Serv. Co. v. Wilderness Soc'y, 85, 86
Amalgamated Meat Cutters v. Connolly, 179
Ambrosini v. Alisal Sanitary Dist., 115
Amchem Prod., Inc. v. GAF Corp., 863
American Airlines, Inc. v. Audubon Park, 594
American Airlines, Inc. v. Hempstead, 594
American Beef Packer, United States v., 538
American Can Co. v. Oregon Liquor Control Comm'n, 516, 688
American Capital Land Corp., United States v., 404
American Cyanamid Co. v. Sparto, 165

American Cyanamid Co., United States v., 389, 392
American Fed'n of Gov't Employees v. Acree, 42
American Frozen Food Inst. v. Train, 469
American Horse Protection Ass'n v. Frizzell, 757
American Horse Protection Ass'n v. Kleppe, 757
American Iron & Steel Inst. v. EPA, 455, 465, 468, 469
American Meat Inst. v. EPA, 455, 456, 464, 469
American Paper Inst. v. Train, 454, 469
American Petroleum Inst. v. EPA, 469
American Petroleum Inst. v. Train, 454
American Smelting & Refining Co. v. Godfrey, 114, 121
American Smelting & Refining Co. v. Occupational Safety & Health Review Comm'n, 618
Amherst v. Niagara Frontier Port Authority, 577
Amoco Oil Co. v. EPA, 332, 336
Anaconda Co. v. Ruckelshaus, 48, 234, 265, 708, 765
Anaconda Wire & Cable Co., United States v., 396
Anaheim Union Water Co. v. Fuller, 166
Anderson v. Souza, 562
Anglo-American & Overseas Corp. v. United States, 39
Anstee v. Monroe Light & Fuel Co., 371
Anthony Wilkinson Live Stock Co. v. McIlquam, 105
Appalachian Elec. Power Co., United States v., 391, 401
Appalachian Mtn. Club v. Brinegar, 732, 733, 735, 738, 788
Appalachian Power v. EPA, 20, 21, 233, 234, 261, 264, 765
Appalachian Power Co. v. Train, 532
Arizona v. California, 149
Arizona Copper Co. v. Gillespie, 149
Arizona Mines Supply Co., State v., 340, 350
Arizona Pub. Serv. Co. v. Federal Power Comm'n, 738, 755
Arizona Pub. Serv. Co. v. Fri, 265
Arizona Pub. Serv. Co., State v., 44, 45, 106
Arizona Pub. Serv. Co., State ex rel. Norvell v., 137
Arkansas Community Organization for Reform Now v. Brinegar, 802, 834
Arlington Coalition on Transp. v. Volpe, 766, 802, 808, 809, 833
Armco Steel Corp., United States v., 373, 405
Arminius Chem. Co. v. Landrum, 148
Arneil v. Schnitzer, 626
Arvidson v. Reynolds Metals Co., 156

TABLE OF CASES
References are to Pages

Asbury Park, United States v., 392, 410, 411, 699
Asheville Constr. Co. v. Southern R.R., 155
Ash Grove Cement Co. v. FTC, 56
Ashland Oil & Transp. Co., United States v., 403, 500, 502, 503
Ashmore, State v., 178
Askew v. American Waterways Operators, Inc., 163, 517
Aspin v. Department of Defense, 57
Associated Contractors Stone Co. v. Pewee Valley Sanitarium & Hospital, 123
Associated Home Builders v. Walnut Creek, 188
Associated Indus. of Massachusetts v. Fredette, 350
Association for the Protection of the Adirondacks v. MacDonald, 183, 743
Association of Data Processing Service Organizations v. Camp, 23
Association of Northwest Steelheaders v. Corps of Engineers, 33
Atchison, Topeka & Santa Fe Ry. v. Callaway, 785, 790, 798, 800
Atkinson v. Dallas, 138, 577
Atkinson v. Herington Cattle Co., 165, 370
Atlanta Coop. News Project v. Postal Service, 95
Atlanta Processing Co. v. Brown, 106
Atlantic Richfield Co. v. Evans, 516
Audubon Soc'y of Rhode Island v. Hayes, 49
Augustine v. Hinne, 371
Automobile Mfrs. Ass'n, United States v., 288
Avery v. United States, 578
Aviation Consumer Action Project v. Washburn, 68, 70
Awad v. McColgan, 110

Babcock, People ex rel. Director of Conservation, v., 183
Bach v. Sarich, 167
Baggett v. Montgomery, 601
Bakersfield v. Miller, 136
Ballard Oil Co., United States v., 393
Ballentine v. Nester, 349
Baltimore & Carolina Line, Inc., United States v., 504
Baltimore & Potomac R.R. v. Fifth Baptist Church, 129
Baltzeger v. Carolina Midland Ry., 103
Banks v. Fayette County Bd. of Airport Zoning Appeals, 600
Barnes & Tucker Co., Commonwealth v., 106, 135, 182, 383, 549
Barracuda Tanker Corp., In re, 519
Bar Realty Corp., State ex rel. v. Locker, 549
Barrier v. Troutman, 577
Barroll v. United States, 35
Bartel v. Ridgefield Lumber Co., 109, 129
Bartholomae Corp. v. United States, 34
Bartie v. United States, 35

Bartlett v. Zoning Comm'n, 204
BASF Wyandotte Corp., State ex rel. Brown v., 547
Bates v. Quality Ready Mix Co., 145, 559, 562
Bath, Inc. v. Pollution Control Bd., 625
Batten v. United States, 578, 580
Bauerle v. Board of County Road Commissioners, 167
Bayou Des Familles Dev. Corp., United States v., 404
Bayside Timber Co. v. Board of Supervisors of San Mateo County, 179, 384, 613
Beane v. H. K. Porter, Inc., 561
Beatty, Inc., United States v., 500
Beaucatcher Mtn. Defense Ass'n v. Coleman, 26, 808
Beaulieu Chem. Co., In re, 898
Beecher v. Dull, 155, 562
Bellamy v. United States, 578
Belle Harbor Realty Corp. v. Kerr, 195
Belle Terre v. Boraas, 190
Belmar Drive-In Theatre Co. v. Illinois State Toll Highway Comm'n, 112
Bemmerly v. Lake County, 118
Bennett v. Long Island R.R., 581
Benton v. Kernan, 135, 563
Berg v. Reaction Motors Div., Theokol Chem. Corp., 147
Berkeley, United States v., 626
Berkson v. Morton, 758
Berman v. Parker, 114, 190
Berry v. Shell Petroleum Co., 371
Bethlehem Steel Corp. v. EPA, 419
Bethlehem Steel Corp. v. Train, 540
Beven, Donald E. v. State Wash. Dept. of Ecology Pollution Control Hearing Bd. No. 148, p. 169
Bianchini v. Humble Pipe Line Co., 160
Bicknell v. Boston, 123, 410
Biderman v. Morton, 188, 760, 763
Bigan, United States v., 390
Bigelow v. Virginia, 95
Biggs v. Griffith, 103
Big Rivers Elec. Corp. v. EPA, 254, 259
Billings v. Camp, 759
Birmingham Water Works Co. v. Martini, 146
Bishop Processing Co. v. Davis, 214
Bishop Processing Co. v. Gardner, 214
Bishop Processing Co., United States v., 214
Black Jack, United States v., 192
Bleiler v. Wellesley, 81
Bloss v. Canastota, 623, 625
Board of Commissioners v. Department of Pub. Health, 623
Board of Commissioners v. Elm Grove Mining Co., 114
Board of Commissioners of Lake County v. Mentor Lagoons, Inc., 138
Board of County Commissioners v. Thompson, 626, 675
Board of Education v. Palmer, 583
Board of Health v. Crew, 548

TABLE OF CASES
References are to Pages

Board of Health v. New York Central R.R., 340
Board of Purification of Waters v. East Providence, 547
Board of Supervisors v. Rowe, 188
Bodine Produce Co., United States v., 893
Bohan v. Post Jervis Gas Light Co., 130
Bohley v. Crofoot, 623
Bohn v. Albertson, 176
Bohnsack v. McDonald, 140
Bollinger v. Henry, 167
Bonelli v. Arizona, 173
Boomer v. Atlantic Cement Co., 108, 117, 120, 126, 143
Boone v. Kingsbury, 176, 179
Boone v. Tillatoba Creek Drainage Dist., 736
Boone Landfill, Inc. v. Boone County, 675
Borel v. Fibreboard Paper Prods. Corp., 844
Bortz Coal Co. v. Air Pollution Comm'n, 135, 340, 349, 350
Bortz Coal Co. v. Department of Environmental Resources, 339, 349
Bostick v. Smoot Sand & Gravel Corp., 113
Boston v. Brinegar, 817
Boston v. Volpe, 612, 775
Boston Edison Co. v. Great Lakes Dredge & Dock Co., 34
Boston Waterfront Residents Ass'n, Inc. v. Romney, 803, 827
Botton v. State, 167
Bouquet v. Hackensack, 105
Bove v. Donner-Hanna Coke Corp., 123, 140
Bowie Inn, Inc. v. Bowie, 678
Bowker v. Morton, 29
Bowling Green, State v., 36, 173, 174, 176
Boyd, United States v., 500
Boynton v. Lakeport Municipal Sewer Dist., 480
Bozung v. Local Agency Formation Comm'n, 189, 772, 784, 814
Bradford Township v. Illinois State Toll Highway Authority, 775
Brainard v. West Hartford, 623
Brandes v. Mitterling, 561, 577
Brecciaroli v. Commissioner of Environmental Protection, 204
Breckinridge v. Schlesinger, 732, 754, 800
Brede v. Minnesota Crushed Stone Co., 119
Bresett v. Ogdensburg, 624
Brockway v. Department of Air Force, 59
Brookhaven v. American Rendering, Inc., 137
Brooks v. Coleman, 833
Brooks v. Volpe, 732, 737, 798, 800, 802
Brotherhood Blocks Ass'n of Sunset Park v. Secretary of Housing & Urban Dev., 756
Brown v. EPA, 321, 323, 324, 342
Brown v. Sioux City, 841
Brown, State v., 623
Brown, State ex rel. v. BASF Wyandotte Corp., 547
Bruskland v. Oak Theatre, 139

Bryant v. Lefever, 136, 144
Buck v. Bell, 98
Buckeye Power, Inc. v. EPA, 48, 234, 261, 765
Buckeye Power, Inc. v. EPA (I), 240, 245, 266, 267
Buckeye Power, Inc. v. EPA (II), 45
Bucks County Bd. of Commissioners v. Interstate Energy Co., 718, 731, 745, 749
Bucks County Bd. of Commissioners v. Public Utilities Comm'n, 180
Buffalo v. Savage, 123
Bulloch v. United States, 34
Buntin, United States v., 538
Burbank v. Lockheed Air Terminal, 594
Bureau of Mines v. George's Creek Coal & Land Co., 203
Burke v. Hollinger, 561
Burke v. Smith, 107
Burns v. Vaughn, 841
Burr v. Adam Eidemiller, Inc., 371
Bushey & Sons, Inc., Ira S., United States v., 152
Bynum Cooperage Co., B. W. v. Coulter, 841
Byram River v. Port Chester, 152
Byron, People v., 604

Cady v. Morton, 750, 762
Caeppert v. United States, 370
California v. Byers, 504
California v. Morton, 514, 768, 773
California Dep't of Fish & Game v. S.S. Bournemouth, 518
California Fish Co., People v., 178
California Orange Co. v. Riverside Portland Cement Co., 145, 147
Calvert Cliffs' Coordinating Comm'n v. Atomic Energy Comm'n, 218, 475, 529, 697, 699, 712, 715, 716, 718, 721, 726, 727, 729, 737, 739, 741, 744, 762, 764, 765, 768, 771, 796, 799
Camp v. Warrington, 577
Campbell v. Seamen, 121, 133
Canal Authority of Florida v. Callaway, 731, 784, 798
Candlestick Properties, Inc. v. San Francisco Bay Conservation & Dev. Comm'n, 204, 205
Cannon, United States v., 401
Cape Henry Bird Club v. Laird, 716, 721, 731, 746, 747, 805, 827
Cappture Realty Corp. v. Board of Adjustment, 194
Capurro v. Galaxy Chem. Co., 102, 106, 146
Carolina Action v. Simon, 763
Carolina Environmental Study Group v. United States, 793, 794
Carter v. Harper, 188
Cartwright Van Lines, Inc. v. United States, 761
Case Co., J. I., v. Borak, 84, 104, 142, 152, 701
Causby, United States v., 575
Center for Auto Safety v. Tieman, 68
Center for Nat'l Policy Review on Race and Urban Issues v. Weinberger, 56, 57

TABLE OF CASES
References are to Pages

Centerview/Glen Avalon Homeowners Ass'n v. Brinegar, 823
Certain Parcels of Land, United States v., 582
Certain Property in the Borough of Manhattan, United States v., 182
Certified Color Mfrs. Ass'n v. Matthews, 16, 891
Chain O'Lakes Protective Ass'n v. Moses, 176
Chambers, United States v., 766
Chapman Chem. Co. v. Taylor, 844
Charles River Park A, Inc. v. Department of Housing & Urban Dev., 59
Cheek v. Floyd County, 582
Chelsea Neighborhood Ass'ns v. Postal Serv., 735, 737
Chemehuevi Tribe v. Federal Power Comm'n, 199
Chemical Leaman Tank Lines, Inc. v. United States, 29, 652, 736
Cheskov v. Port of Seattle, 128
Chicago v. Commonwealth Edison Co., 136, 224
Chicago v. General Motors Corp., 45, 162
Chicago Dep't of Environmental Control Appeal Bd. v. United States Steel Corp., 350
Chillisquaque Creek Watershed Ass'n v. Sanitary Water Bd., 549
Choctaw, O. & G. R. R. v. Drew, 139
Chongris v. Corrigan, 601
Christiansen & Sons, Inc., H. v. Duluth, 397
Christie v. Davey, 560
Chrysler Corp. v. Department of Transp., 338
Chrysler Corp. v. Tofany, 572, 609
Citizens Against the Destruction of NAPA v. Lynn, 721
Citizens Airport Comm. v. Brinegar, 612
Citizens Airport Comm. v. Volpe, 614, 615, 779
Citizens Ass'n of Georgetown v. Washington, 86, 286, 320
Citizens Ass'n of Georgetown, Inc. v. Zoning Comm'n, 188
Citizens Comm. for the Columbia River v. Callaway, 806, 833
Citizens Environmental Council v. Volpe, 712, 778, 823, 834
Citizens for Balanced Environment & Transp., Inc. v. Volpe, 789
Citizens for Clean Air, Inc. v. Corps of Engineers, 25, 320, 770, 808
Citizens for Food & Progress, Inc. v. Musgrove, 26
Citizens for Mass Transit Against Freeways v. Brinegar, 807, 834
Citizens for Reid State Park v. Laird, 724, 750, 760
Citizens for Safe Power v. Nuclear Regulatory Comm'n, 794
Citizens Organized to Defend the Environment v. Volpe, 752, 759, 763
Citizens to Preserve Foster Park v. Volpe, 833
Citizens to Preserve Overton Park, Inc. v. Volpe, 17–21, 32, 52, 186, 264, 598, 716, 737, 741, 809, 833
Citizens Util. Co. v. Pollution Control Bd., 346, 542, 543

Civic Improvement Comm. v. Volpe, 615, 802, 805
Clarke v. Volpe, 809
Clayton v. Mayfield, 623
Cleveland Elec. Illuminating Co. v. Scapell, 177
Clinton Community Hospital Corp. v. Southern Maryland Medical Center, 29
Clifton Iron Co. v. Dye, 130
Coalition for Responsible Regional Div. v. Brinegar, 833
Coates v. United States, 34
Cogswell v. New York, N. H. & N. R. R., 138
Cohen v. Price Comm'n, 764
Colgate Palmolive Co., United States v., 392
Collens v. New Canaan Water Co., 167
Collier v. Ernst, 560
Colligan v. Activities Club of New York, 29
Collins v. Wayne Iron Works, 562
Colorado Pub. Interest Research Group, Inc. v. Train, 369
Colorado River Water Conservation Dist. v. Rocky Mountain Power Co., 169
Colorado Spring v. Bender, 168
Columbia River Fishermen's Protective Union v. St. Helens, 106
Columbus, State v., 578
Commerce Oil Ref. Corp. v. Miner, 114, 140
Commissioner of Pub. Health v. Board of Health, 623, 625
Committee for Consideration of Jones Fall Sewage System v. Train, 82, 151
Committee for Green Foothills v. Froehlke, 627, 799, 801
Committee for Humane Legislation, Inc. v. Richardson, 833, 838
Committee for Nuclear Responsibility, Inc. v. Seaborg, 18, 719, 721, 730, 737, 806
Comm. for Nuclear Responsibility, Inc. v. Schlesinger, 703
Committee for the Consideration of the Jones Falls Sewage System v. Train, 543
Committee to Stop Route 7 v. Volpe, 766, 789, 793, 834
Concerned About Trident v. Rumsfeld, 801
Concerned Citizens of East Brunswick, Inc., v. New Jersey Turnpike Authority, 615, 806
Concerned Citizens of Palm Desert, Inc. v. Riverside County Bd. of Supervisors, 189, 815
Concerned Residents of Buck Hill Falls v. Grant, 747, 755, 804–806
Confederation de la Raza Unida v. Morgan Hill, 194
Connecticut Action Now v. Roberts Plating Co., 396
Connecticut Bank & Trust Co. v. Mularcik, 560
Conservation Council of North Carolina v. Costanzo, 25
Conservation Council of North Carolina v. Costanzo (II), 28, 729, 757, 759, 762, 808

TABLE OF CASES

References are to Pages

Conservation Council of North Carolina v. Froehlke, 708, 741, 796, 802, 805, 806
Conservation Council of North Carolina v. Froehlke (I), 716, 724
Conservation Foundation v. Department of Interior, 54
Conservation Soc'y of Southern Vermont v. Brinegar (I), 734
Conservation Soc'y of Southern Vermont, Inc. v. Secretary of Transp. (I), 78, 84, 706, 708, 720, 722, 740, 741, 772, 781, 789, 800, 801
Conservation Soc'y of Southern Vermont, Inc. v. Secretary of Transp. (II), 781
Consolidated Coal Co., United States v., 391
Consolidated Edison Co., In re, 530
Consolidation Coal Co., United States v., 389, 395, 404
Construction Industry Ass'n of Sonoma County v. Petaluma, 90, 190, 191, 282
Consumers' Light and Power Co. v. Holland, 134
Consumers Union v. Department of Health, Education & Welfare, 68
Continental Chemiste Corp. v. Ruckelshaus, 869
Continental Oil Co. v. Federal Power Comm'n, 60
Cook v. Priester, 594
Cook County v. Lloyd A. Fry Roofing Co., 117
Cook Indus., Inc. v. Carlson, 135, 149
Corporation of the Presiding Bishop of the Church of Latter Day Saints v. Ashton, 559
Council v. Duprel, 843
Country Club Bank v. Smith, 755, 759, 763
County Commissioners v. Miles, 194
Coupland v. Morton, 760
CPC Int'l, Inc. v. Train, 454, 479
CPC Int'l Inc. v. Train (II), 469
Crandall v. Biergans, 102, 624
Crawford v. Magnolia Petroleum Co., 134
Crawford County Levee & Drainage Dist. No. 1, In re, 178
Cresskill v. Dumont, 188
Crofoot Lumber, Inc. v. Ford, 157
Cronin v. J. B. E. Olson Corp., 302
Crosley Bldg. Corp. v. Sampson, 29, 772
Cross v. Harris, 842
Croton-on-Hudson v. Westchester, 675
Crow v. Brown, 192
Crowther v. Seaborg, 31
Crushed Stone Co. v. Moore, 119
Cullum v. Topps-Stillman's, Inc., 126
Cumberland Torpedo Co. v. Gaines, 115
Cummington Preservation Comm. v. Federal Aviation Administration, 727, 734, 794
Cunard White Star, Ltd., People v., 351
Cuneo v. Schlesinger, 56
Curry v. Farmers Livestock Market, 135
Curry Coal Co. v. M. C. Arnoni Co., 623, 626
Cutler v. Civil Aeronautics Bd., 63

Daigle v. Continental Oil Co., 130
Dailey v. Lawton, 192
Dairyland Power Coop., State v., 41, 43, 44, 137–139
Dale v. Bryant, 130, 624
Dalehite v. United States, 34
Daly v. Volpe, 734, 740, 746, 770, 790, 794, 804
Darling Co., L. A. v. Water Resources Comm'n, 548
Dauberman v. Grant, 560
Davis v. Coleman, 26, 729, 732, 735, 748, 750, 751, 755, 794, 808, 809, 817, 821
Davis v. Georgia-Pacific Corp., 157, 158
Davis v. Ichord, 46
Davis v. Kansas City, 623, 624
Davis v. Morton, 750, 762
Davoust v. Mitchell, 559
Dawson v. Laubersweiler, 131
Daytona Beach v. Tona-Rama, Inc., 171
Dayton Power & Light Co. v. EPA, 263
D. C. Federation of Civic Ass'ns v. Volpe, 21, 833
Deaconess Hospital v. State Highway Comm'n, 581
DeAlbert v. Novah, 561
DeBlois v. Bowers, 123
DeLange v. United States, 39
Delaware Citizens for Clean Air, Inc. v. Stauffer Chem. Co., 84, 242
Delaware River Port Authority v. Tiemann, 26
Demarest v. Hardham, 130
Dennison v. State, 582
Denver & Rio Grande R. R. v. Peterson, 458
Department of Environmental Protection v. Jersey Central Power & Light Co., 173, 528
Department of Environmental Resources v. Pennsylvania Power Co., 267
Department of Game v. Federal Power Comm'n, 24
Department of Game v. Puyallup Tribe, 181
Department of Health v. Concrete Specialties, Inc., 340
Department of Health v. Passaic Valley Sewerage Comm'n, 542, 549
Department of Health v. Roselle, 350
Department of Pub. Works v. Adco Advertisers, 203
Department of Water Resources v. A. H. Smith Sand & Gravel Co., 549, 550
Derby v. Water Resources Comm'n, 542, 549, 550
DeRham v. Diamond, 367, 549
Detrex Chem. Indus., United States v., 540
Detroit Edison Co. v. EPA, 243
Dexter Corp., United States v., 389, 393
Dexter, State v., 203
Diamond v. Bruleen Minerals, Ltd., 350
Diamond v. General Motors Corp., 162
Diamond v. Mobil Oil Co., 548, 549
Diamond Match Co. v. Savercool, 176
Diamond Motors, Inc., State v., 183
Diamond, United States v., 391, 404
Diapulse Corp. v. Food & Drug Administration, 41

TABLE OF CASES
References are to Pages

Dietz v. King, 176
Director of Conservation, People ex rel. v. Babcock, 183
District of Columbia v. Train, 313, 323, 324, 342
Ditlow v. Brinegar, 57, 58
DiVosta Rentals, Inc. v. Lee, 710
Dixon v. New York Trap Rock Corp., 145
Doe v. Bolton, 96
Dolphin Gardens, Inc. v. United States, 35
Donnelly & Sons, Inc., John v. Outdoor Advertising Bd., 203
Dooley v. Town Plan & Zoning Comm'n, 204
Dorsett v. Nunis, 560
Douglas County, United States v., 418
Dow Chem. Co. v. Ruckelshaus, 47
Dow Chem. Co. v. Ruckelshaus (2, 4, 5–T II), 881
Dow Chem. Co. v. Train, 863
Dry Color Mfr's Ass'n v. Department of Labor, 757, 764, 857
Dugan v. Rank, 30, 31, 33, 37
Duke City Lumber Co. v. Butz, 29, 760
Duncan Coal Co., W. G. v. Jones, 134
DuPont de Nemours & Co., E. I. v. Dodson, 140
DuPont de Nemours & Co., E. I. v. Train, 454, 455, 458, 464, 465, 468, 469, 571
Duquesne Light Co. v. EPA, 233, 234
Duquesne Light Co. v. EPA (I), 264, 267
Duquesne Light Co. v. EPA (II), 261
Durnford v. Ruckelshaus, 753, 759
Dutton v. Mendocino County, 600
Dworkin v. Lakeview, 103
Dyecraftsmen, Inc. v. EPA, 460
Eastlake Community Council v. Roanoke Associates, 189, 814–816, 822
East St. John Shingle Co. v. Portland, 132
Eau Claire v. Department of Natural Resources, 173
Ebur v. Alloy Metal Wire Co., 124
Echo Park Residents Comm. v. Romney, 760
Ecology Action v. Atomic Energy Comm'n, 47
Ecology Center of Louisiana, Inc. v. Coleman, 41, 718, 779, 789, 808
Economy Light & Power Co. v. United States, 391, 401
Edgeboro, Inc. v. East Brunswick, 675
Edwards v. Allouez Mining Co., 132
Eisenstadt v. Baird, 94
Elizabeth Bd. of Education, State v., 582
Eller v. Koehler, 561
Ellis v. Blanchard, 131, 139
Ellis v. Louisville & Nashville R.R., 843
Ellison v. Rayonier, Inc., 45
Elmo Div. of Drive-X Co. v. Dixon, 42
El Paso v. American Smelting & Refining Co., 149
Ely v. Velde, 730, 733, 757, 762, 763, 776, 777, 827
Emeryville, People ex rel. San Francisco Bay Conservation & Dev. Comm'n, v., 176
Enewetak, People of v. Laird, 788
Ensign v. Walls, 560

Environmental Defense Fund, Inc. v. Agency for Int'l Dev., 786, 806, 838
Environmental Defense Fund, Inc. v. Armstrong, 727, 746, 747, 791, 799, 801–803
Environmental Defense Fund, Inc. v. Brinegar, 805
Environmental Defense Fund, Inc. v. California Air Resources Bd., 349
Environmental Defense Fund, Inc. v. Callaway, 796
Environmental Defense Fund, Inc. v. Coastside County Water Dist., 814, 822
Environmental Defense Fund, Inc. v. Corps of Engineers, 21, 31, 708, 716, 717, 720–722, 724, 726–728, 732–734, 736, 737, 739–741, 744, 747, 793, 794, 796, 797, 826, 827
Environmental Defense Fund, Inc. v. Department of Health, Education & Welfare, 848, 889, 892
Environmental Defense Fund, Inc. v. Department of Transp., 720
Environmental Defense Fund, Inc. v. East Bay Municipal Util. Dist. No. 1, 182
Environmental Defense Fund, Inc. v. Environmental Protection Agency, 21, 25, 115, 765, 841, 861, 880–885, 887
Environmental Defense Fund, Inc. v. Froehlke, 31, 715, 726, 727, 730, 731, 739, 746–748, 792, 794, 795, 798–804, 806, 807, 826
Environmental Defense Fund, Inc. v. Hardin, 15, 46, 720–722, 798, 840, 848, 881
Environmental Defense Fund, Inc. v. Hoerner Waldorf, 701
Environmental Defense Fund, Inc. v. Mathews, 653, 700
Environmental Defense Fund, Inc. v. Montrose Chem. Corp., 2, 481
Environmental Defense Fund, Inc. v. Peterson, 512, 786, 806
Environmental Defense Fund, Inc. v. Ruckelshaus, 16, 17, 47, 115, 277, 799, 880–882, 884, 892
Environmental Defense Fund, Inc. v. Tennessee Valley Authority, 706, 708, 715, 731, 735, 741, 746, 747, 766, 802, 808, 809
Environmental Defense Fund, Inc. v. United States Agency for International Development, 762
Environmental Defense Fund, Inc. v. Volpe, 715, 772
Environmental Hearings on the Proposed Sports Complex in the Hackensack Meadowlands, In re, 177, 181
Environmental Law Fund v. Volpe, 706, 766
EPA v. Brown, 345
EPA v. California ex rel. State Water Resources Control Bd., 544, 640
EPA v. Maryland, 345
EPA v. Mink, 53, 55, 61, 62
Environmental Review of the Maritime Administration Tanker Constr. Program, In re, 511
Erickson v. Queen Valley Ranch Co., 183

TABLE OF CASES

References are to Pages

Escondido v. Desert Outdoor Advertising Co., 137, 203
Eskind v. Vero Beach, 203
Essex Chem. Corp. v. Ruckelshaus, 269, 271, 272, 338
Esso Standard Oil Co., United States v., 397, 645
Ethridge v. Lavonia, 626
Ethyl Corp. v. EPA, 53, 54, 75, 115, 333, 334, 710
Eubanks, State v., 349
Euclid, Village of v. Ambler Realty Co., 129, 189
Eureka Pipeline Co., United States v., 500, 503, 504
Evans v. Moffat, 129
Evansville v. Rhinehart, 145, 146
Everett v. Paschall, 116, 754
Ewing Bros., United States v., 893
Executive Jet Aviation, Inc. v. Cleveland, 518
Exxon Corp. v. Federal Trade Comm'n, 57
Eyde v. State, 176
Fagliarone v. North Bergen, 36
Fairfax County Bd. of Supervisors v. Carper, 193
Fairfax County Bd. of Supervisors v. McLucas, 596
Fairview Farms, Inc. v. Reynolds Metals Co., 147, 156, 157
Fargason v. Economy Furniture, Inc., 118
Farmington v. Scott, 136
Farwell v. Brinegar, 788, 793
Fayetteville Area Chamber of Commerce v. Volpe, 779, 781, 796, 833
Federal Aviation Administration v. Robertson, 63
Ferguson v. Keene, 576, 580
Finish Allatoona's Interstate Right, Inc. v. Brinegar, 833
Finley v. Teeter Stone, Inc., 370
First Iowa Hydro-Elec. Coop. v. Federal Power Comm'n, 367
First Nat'l Bank v. Watson, 759, 763
Firth v. Scherzberg, 122
Fitzgerald v. Pan American World Airways, 142
531.13 Acres of Land, United States v., 548
Fixico, United States v., 145
Flanigan v. Springfield, 128
Fletcher v. Bealey, 2, 114, 126
Fletcher v. Rylands, 158
Flint Ridge Dev. Co. v. Scenic Rivers Ass'n, 197, 700, 718, 763, 764
Florida Audubon Soc'y v. Callaway, 740, 780
Florida Peach Growers Ass'n v. Department of Labor, 856
Florida Power & Light Co., United States v., 389, 528
Florida, United States v., 513
Flowers v. Northampton Bucks County Municipal Authority, 114
FMC Corp. v. Train, 466, 468, 469
Folmar v. Elliott Coal Mining Co., 123, 155, 156
Fontainebleau Hotel Corp. v. Forty-Five Twenty-Five, Inc., 114
Food Chem. News, Inc. v. Davis, 67–69

Ford v. Train, 823
Ford Motor Co., United States v., 309
Forestier v. Johnson, 176
Fort Smith v. Western Hide & Fur Co., 103
Fort Story—Its Future? v. Schlesinger, 26, 757
Frankel v. Securities & Exch. Comm'n, 57
Fredericktown v. Osborne, 559
Freeborn v. Bryson, 173, 176, 186, 812
Freeman Coal Mining Co. v. Interior Bd. of Mining Operations Appeals, 335
Frey v. Queen City Paper Co., 128
Friends of Mammoth v. Board of Supervisors of Mono County, 189, 197, 808, 811, 813
Friends of the Earth v. Armstrong, 33, 804
Friends of the Earth v. Brinegar, 807
Friends of the Earth v. Carey, 44, 77–80
Friends of the Earth v. Coleman, 775–777, 790
Friends of the Earth, Inc. v. Butz, 761
Friends of the Earth, Inc. v. Coleman, 612, 613, 817
Fritz v. E. I. DuPont de Nemours & Co., 160, 161
Fry Roofing Co., Lloyd A. v. Department of Health Air Pollution Variance Bd., 349
Fry Roofing Co., Lloyd A., State v., 339
Fund for Animals v. Frizzell, 718, 786
Furrer v. Talent Irrigation Dist., 168
GAF Corp., United States v., 372, 373
Gage v. Atomic Energy Comm'n, 42, 700, 774
Gage v. Commonwealth Edison Co., 31, 803
Galaxy Chem. Co., State v., 102
Game & Fish Comm'n v. Farmer's Irrigation Co., 165
Gates v. Schlesinger, 70
Geer v. Connecticut, 173
Gelfand v. O'Haver, 138
Gelsumino v. E. W. Bliss Co., 124
General Elec. Co., In re, 418, 486, 547, 840
General Motors Corp., United States v., 163
George v. Beavark, Inc., 391
George Campbell Painting Co. v. Reid, 337
Georgia v. Tennessee Copper Co., 111, 122, 125, 149, 151, 518
Gerrard Co., S.A. v. Fricker, 115
Getman v. N. L. R. B., 63
Getty Oil Co. v. Ruckelshaus, 48, 265, 266, 342, 765
Gewirtz v. Long Beach, 171, 742
Gibbons v. Hoffman, 105
Gifford-Hill & Co. v. Federal Trade Comm'n, 29, 761, 763, 773
Gilbough v. West Side Amusement Co., 560
Gion v. Santa Cruz, 171
Girsh, Appeal of, 192
Glace v. Pilot Mountain, 626
Glen Alden Corp., Commonwealth v., 137
Godard v. Babson-Dow Mfg. Co., 149, 150, 561
Goldblatt v. Hempstead, 203
Golden v. Planning Bd. of the Town of Ramapo, 191, 194, 204, 205, 282

Golden Gate Hop Ranch, Inc. v. Velsicol Chem. Corp., 844
Gomez v. Florida State Employment Serv., 85
Gonzalez v. Virginia-Carolina Chem. Co., 842, 844
Goodman, United States v., 888, 889, 893
Goose Hollow Foothills League v. Romney, 733, 756, 762
Gorman v. Sabo, 146, 147, 560, 563
Gotreaux v. Gary, 842
Gould v. Greylock Reservation Comm'n, 172, 178, 180, 182
Grain Processing Corp. v. EPA, 468
Grain Processing Corp. v. Train, 454, 455, 469
Grand Jury Proceedings, United States Steel-Clairton Works, In re, 348
Granite State Packing Co., United States v., 392
Granite Steel Co. v. EPA, 234, 265
Grant v. Baltimore, 203
Gravelle, United States v., 162
Greater Boston Television Corp. v. FCC, 20, 22, 264
Greater Westchester Homeowners' Ass'n v. City of Los Angeles, 134, 563, 577, 579, 581
Green v. Castle Concrete Co., 114, 139
Green v. General Petroleum Corp., 162, 522
Green v. Smith, 122
Green v. T. A. Shoemaker & Co., 155
Greene County Planning Bd. v. Federal Power Comm'n, 47, 778, 806
Greene County Planning Bd. v. Federal Power Comm'n (I), 20, 705, 708, 728, 738, 769, 780
Greer v. Lennox, 626
Griffin v. Northridge, 147
Griffin v. Planters Chem. Corp., 842, 844
Griffin v. United States, 36, 845
Griggs v. Allegheny County, 576
Griswold v. Connecticut, 92, 94
Groover v. Hightower, 155
Grosse Isle v. Dunbar & Sullivan Dredging Co., 174, 181
Groton v. Laird, 734, 750, 753, 759
Grzelka v. Chevrolet Motor Car Co., 126, 561
Gulf Oil Corp. v. Morton, 513, 514
Gulf Oil Corp. v. Simon, 764
Guthrie v. Alabama By-Products Co., 397
Guttinger v. Calaveros Cement Co., 119
Haber v. Paramount Ice Corp., 130
Hackensack Meadowlands Dev. Comm'n v. Municipal Sanitary Landfill Authority, 516, 667
Hadacheck v. Sebastian, 133, 205
Hageman v. Wayne Township Bd. of Trustees, 601
Haines, Commonwealth v., 625
Hakkila v. Old Colony Broken Stone Co., 155
Hall v. Budde, 123
Hall v. DeWeld Mica Corp., 155
Hall v. E. I. DuPont de Nemours & Co., 162, 844
Hall v. Taft, 812
Hamlin v. Matarazzo, 188

Hamm v. Rock Hill, 766
Hammon Ranch Corp. v. Dodson, 841
Hampton v. North Carolina Pulp Co., 147
Hancock v. Train, 352, 353, 544, 640
Hanly v. Kleindienst, 443, 718
Hanly v. Kleindienst (II), 18, 708, 716, 721, 724, 751–755, 796, 804
Hanly v. Mitchell, 784
Hanly v. Mitchell (I), 1, 25, 750, 752, 754, 755, 809
Hannum v. Gruber, 124, 126
Hanover v. Morristown, 138, 578–580, 595
Hansen v. Independent School Dist. No. 1, p. 122
Harbor Towing Corp., In re, 519
Hardy Salt Co. v. Southern Pacific Transp. Co., 106
Hark v. Mountain Fork Lumber Co., 118
Harlem Valley Transp. Ass'n v. Stafford, 26, 41, 47, 720, 768
Harmar Coal Co., Commonwealth v., 549
Harrell's Candy Kitchen v. Sarasota-Manatee Airport Authority, 601
Harris v. Skirving, 623
Harris v. United States, 35, 844
Harrisburg Coalition Against Ruining Environment v. Volpe, 834
Harrison v. Indiana Auto Shredders Co., 121, 131, 559–562, 624, 680
Harrisonville v. W. S. Dickey Clay Mfg. Co., 123, 128, 145
Hartung v. County of Milwaukee, 103
Hassell v. San Francisco, 579
Hathaway v. Worcester City Hospital, 97
Hauck v. Tide Water Pipe Line Co., 371
Hawaii, County of v. Sotomura, 172
Hayes, State v., 349
Hay, State ex rel. Thorton, v., 171
Healey v. Citizens' Gas & Elec. Co., 108
Heck v. Beryllium Corp., 104, 141
Helms v. Diamond, 183
Hendry v. United States, 36
Hennessey v. Carmony, 119
Henthorner v. Oklahoma City, 578
Herbert v. Smyth, 563
Hercules, Inc., United States v., 389, 395, 396
Herring v. H. W. Walker Co., 126
Herzog v. Grosso, 146
Hewlett v. Hempstead, 625, 675
Hickory v. Chadderton, 601
Hidalgo County Water Improvement Dist. v. Cameron County Water Control & Improvement Dist., 149
Higginbotham v. Barrett, 26
Highland Park v. Train, 78, 775
Hi Hat Elkhorn Coal Co. v. Inland Steel Co., 147
Hill v. Coleman, 775
Hill v. Tennessee Valley Authority, 829, 830
Hillsdale v. Hillsdale Iron & Metal Co., 675
Hinderlider v. LaPlata & Cherry Creek Ditch Co., 153
Hiram Clarke Civic Club, Inc. v. Lynn, 705, 751, 759

TABLE OF CASES

References are to Pages

Hodges v. Fuller Brush Co., 843
Hodges v. Pine Product Co., 165
Hoffman Sons Inc., George E. v. Pollution Control Bd., 350
Holland, United States v., 401, 403–405
Holt State Bank, United States v., 401
Homeowners Emergency Life Protection Comm. v. Lynn, 703, 774, 817
Hoogasian, People ex rel. v. Sears, Roebuck & Co., 114
Hooks v. International Speedways, Inc., 560
Hooper v. United States, 35
Houston Compressed Steel Corp. v. State, 44, 349, 351
Howard v. Robinette, 563
Hubbard-Hall Chem. Co. v. Silverman, 141, 842, 843, 870
Hudson County Water Co. v. McCarter, 667
Hughes v. Alexandria Scrap Corp., 683
Hughes v. Ranger Fuel Corp., Div. of Pittston Co., 396
Hughes Aircraft Co. v. Schlesinger, 60
Hulbert v. California Portland Cement Co., 118, 119
Huntington, State v., 139, 625
Hutcherson v. Alexander, 117
Hutchinson v. Valdosta, 547
Hyde v. Somerset Air Serv., 577
Idaho v. Oregon, 154
Idaho Gold Dredging Co. v. Payette Lumber Co., 127
Illinois v. Milwaukee, 150–154
Illinois v. Rosing, 77
Illinois Central R.R. v. Illinois, 174, 175, 180, 742
Illinois ex rel. Scott v. Butterfield, 41, 42, 576, 612, 700, 758, 796, 800
Independent Meat Packers Ass'n v. Butz, 885
Indiana & Michigan Elec. Co. v. EPA, 234, 261, 262, 266, 267
Indianapolis Water Co. v. American Strawboard Co., 165
Indian Lookout Alliance v. Volpe, 733, 772, 788, 789
Indian Towing Co. v. United States, 38
Industrial Union Dep't, AFL–CIO v. Hodgson, 857
Ingham v. Eastern Air Lines, Inc., 38
In re ——— (see name of party)
Interlake Steel Corp., United States v., 393
International Acceptance Corp., In re, 548
International Harvester Co. v. Ruckelshaus, 20, 21, 74, 125, 234, 269, 296, 298, 300, 571, 718, 737, 765, 887
International Paper Co. v. Federal Power Commission, 53
International Paper Co. v. State Highway Dep't, 176, 181
International Shoe Co. v. Heatwole, 105
International Steel Corp., People v., 340
Inyo County v. Yorty, 814
Iowa Citizens for Environmental Quality, Inc. v. Volpe, 726, 727, 731, 733, 734, 778, 779, 787, 794
Irby v. Panama Ice Co., 561
Ironstone Corp. v. Zoning Hearing Bd., 559, 572

Isley v. Little, 115
I–291 Why? Ass'n v. Burns, 615, 721, 725, 730, 733, 740, 823
Izaak Walton League v. St. Clair, 15, 42, 829
Izaak Walton League v. Schlesinger, 529
Izaak Walton League, Inc., In re, 840
Jackson Municipal Airport Authority v. Evans, 601
Jackson, State v., 176
Jacksonville v. Schumann, 578, 579
Jacobs v. Seattle, 626
James v. Lynn, 735, 806
James River and Kanawha Canal Parks, Inc. v. Richmond Metropolitan Authority, 391, 397, 777, 788, 789
Jaycox v. United States, 393
Jedneak v. Minnesota General Elec. Co., 140
Jersey Central Power & Light Co., State v., 162, 525, 528
Jewell, Inc., J. D. v. Hancock, 139
Jezowski v. Reno, 623
Jicarilla Apache Tribe v. Morton, 716, 718, 720, 740, 749, 772, 791
Johnson v. Greenville, 578
Johnson v. Morton, 26
Johnson v. Mount Ogden Enterprises, Inc., 559
Johnson v. State, 35
Johnson Chem. Co., In re, 897
Johnson, State v., 204
Jones v. District of Columbia Redev. Land Agency, 717, 726, 801, 804
Jones v. Lynn, 735, 763, 766, 787, 790, 809
Jones v. Morgan, 842
Joseph Co., David J. v. Ashland, 680
Jost v. Dairyland Power Coop., 112, 119
Juanita Bay Valley Community Ass'n v. Kirkland, 189, 814
Julis v. Cedar Rapids, 753, 759
Juneau, State v., 550
Just v. Marinette County, 175, 177, 204, 206
Kalur v. Resor, 31, 398, 757, 762
Kankakee v. New York Central R.R., 349
Kansas v. Colorado, 151, 518
Kasala v. Kalispell Pee Wee Baseball League, 559
Kavanewsky v. Zoning Bd. of Appeals, 193
Keith v. California Highway Commission, 719
Keith v. Volpe, 739, 803, 804, 806, 823
Kellerhals v. Kallenberger, 123
Kennebec Log Driving Co., United States v., 389, 395
Kennebunk, Kennebunkport and Wells Water Dist. v. Maine Turnpike Authority, 165
Kennecott Copper Corp. v. EPA, 22, 224, 226, 229, 264
Kennecott Copper Corp. v. Train, 75, 259
Kennecott Copper Corp., United States v., 500, 503, 504
Kennedy v. Clayton, 842
Kennedy v. Mendoza-Martinez, 504
Kennedy v. Moog, 138
Kennedy Park Homes Ass'n v. Lackawanna, 192

TABLE OF CASES
References are to Pages

Kent v. Hamilton Township, 36
Kentland-Elkhorn Coal Corp., United States v., 390, 391, 404
Kentucky Aerospray, Inc. v. Mays, 842
Kentucky ex rel. Hancock v. Train, 416
Kentucky West Virginia Gas Co. v. Lafferty, 146, 147, 561
Kern County, People v., 189, 815
Kerpelman v. Board of Pub. Works, 177
Kings County Economic Community Dev. Ass'n v. Hardin, 763
Kinsley, State v., 549
Kirk v. United States, 577
Kisner v. Butz, 751
Kissinger v. Los Angeles, 600
Kitchen v. Federal Communications Comm'n, 700
Kit-Mar Builders, Inc., Appeal of, 192
Kleppe v. Sierra Club, 773, 791
Koczwara, Commonwealth v., 394
Kohr v. Weber, 562
Kosanke Sand Corp., United States v., 379, 594, 763
Koseris v. J. R. Simplot Co., 118, 123, 130
Kosich v. Poultrymen's Serv. Corp., 122, 139
Kramer v. Sweet, 561
Krocker v. Westmoreland Planing Mill Co., 561
Kuntz v. Werner Flying Serv., 140
Kurtz, In re, 623
Kutner v. Delaware Tool Steel Corp., 113
Kozesnik v. Montgomery, 140
Laird v. Nelms, 38, 552, 580
Lake Developing Enterprises v. Kojetinsky, 135
Lakeland Property Owners Ass'n v. Northfield, 148
Lambert v. California, 394
Land v. Dollar, 30
Lansco, Inc. v. Department of Environmental Protection, 163, 522
La Raza Unida v. Volpe, 767, 775, 834
Larsen Baking Co. v. State, 480
Larson v. Domestic Foreign Commerce Corp., 30
Lassiter v. Norfolk & Carolina R.R., 145
Lathan v. Brinegar (II), 718, 731, 741, 808, 823
Lathan v. Volpe (I), 718, 762, 770, 775, 798, 800, 808
Lathan v. Volpe (II), 721, 731, 735, 767, 834
Lauritzen v. Chesapeake Bay Bridge & Tunnel Dist., 397
Lawson v. Price, 155
Leavell v. United States, 578
Le Boeuf Bros. Towing Co., United States v., 504
Ledbetter Bros., Inc. v. Holcomb, 145
Lee v. Resor, 49
Lee v. Stewart, 155
Leet v. Montgomery County, 681
Lemler v. Nevada Cement Co., 146
Lenari v. Kingston, 623
LeRoy Fibre Co. v. Chicago, Minn. & St. Paul R.R., 134

Leschi Improvement Council v. State Highway Comm'n, 820
Leslie Salt Co. v. Froehlke, 401, 403
Lewis, United States v., 390, 391, 395, 404
Life of the Land v. Brinegar, 599, 612, 613, 734, 736, 749, 779, 794
Life of the Land v. Secretary of Defense, 772
Lindsay, United States v., 151
Lindsey v. Normet, 196
Livezey v. Bel Air, 165
Locker, State ex rel. Bar Realty Corp. v., 549
Loe v. Lenhardt, 155, 842, 844
Loma Portal Civic Club v. American Airlines, Inc., 577, 594
Lombardo v. Handler, 53, 67, 69, 75
Lombardy v. Peter Kiewit Son's Co., 581, 582
Long Beach v. Mansell, 180
Longstrean v. Owen-McCaffrey's Sons, 397
Los Angeles, People v., 139
Louisiana, United States v., 513
Louisville & Nashville Terminal Co. v. Lellyett, 109, 146
Loveless v. Yantis, 189, 814–816
Love Petroleum Co. v. Jones, 145
Luthringer v. Moore, 842
Lynn Open Air Theatre v. Sea Crest Cadillac-Pontiac, Inc., 112
McCarthy v. Bunker Hill & Sullivan Mining Co., 356
McCarty v. Macy & Co., 130
McCarty v. Natural Carbonic Gas Co., 122
McCaw v. Harrison, 116
McCoy v. Weinberger, 60
McDonald v. City of New York, 624
McDowell v. Schlesinger, 732, 733, 754, 800
McElwain v. Georgia-Pacific Corp., 157, 158
MacGibbon v. Board of Appeals (III), 204
Machin v. Zuckert, 54
McKart v. United States, 40
McKee v. Akron, 146, 577
Mack, People v., 106, 148
McLane v. Northwest Natural Gas Co., 159
McLean Garden Residents Ass'n v. National Capital Planning Comm'n, 763, 809
McNabb v. United States, 718
McQuail v. Shell Oil Co., 115
McQueary v. Laird, 32
Maddox v. Bradley, 753, 801
Madison v. Ducktown Sulfur, Copper & Iron Co., 118
Mahaska Bottling Co., United States v., 538
Maher v. New Orleans, 204
Mahlstadt v. Indianola, 623
Maier v. Publicker Commercial Alcohol Co., 390
Maine v. M/V Tamano, 518
Maine, United States v., 513
Maitland v. Twin City Aviation Corp., 141, 577
Malone v. Bowdoin, 30

TABLE OF CASES

References are to Pages

Manius River Preservation Comm. v. Administrator, 460, 541
Mann v. Willey, 166
Marathon Battery Co., United States v., 404
Marion County v. Mid-Williamette Valley Air Pollution Authority, 349
Marks v. Whitney, 175, 177
Marsh Wood Prods. Co. v. Babcock & Wilcox Co., 124
Mar-Tee Contractors, Inc., United States v., 504
Martin v. Herzog, 419
Martin v. Port of Seattle, 578, 579
Martin v. Reynolds Metals Co., 156
Martin v. United States, 36
Martin Bldg. Co. v. Imperial Laundry Co., 149, 150
Martinez v. Arkansas Fuel Oil Corp., 371
Maryland v. Amerada Hess Corp., 518, 519
Maryland v. EPA, 323, 324, 342
Maryland v. Train, 411, 495
Maryland Dep't of Natural Resources v. Amerada Hess Corp., 174, 176
Maryland-Nat'l Capital Park & Planning Comm'n v. Postal Serv., 16, 733, 734, 736, 739, 749, 752, 753, 757
Maryland-Nat'l Capital Park & Planning Comm'n v. Schultz, 796
Massachusetts v. United States Veterans Administration, 78
Massachusetts Air Pollution & Noise Abatement Comm. v. Brinegar, 26, 48, 758
Mathewson v. State Throughway Authority, 582
Maynard v. United States, 577
Mayor and City Council of Baltimore v. Price, 680
Mayor & Council of Rockville v. Brookeville Turnpike Constr. Co., 188
Mead Data Control, Inc. v. Department of Air Force, 53
Meadowland Regional Dev. Agency v. Hackensack Meadowlands Dev. Comm'n, 194
Meeks v. Wood, 560
Menzer v. Elkhart Lake, 176
Mercer v. Brown, 625
Meriwether Sand & Gravel Co. v. State, 119
Merkel v. Brownsville, 814
Messer v. Dickinson, 139
Metropolitan Coalition for Clean Air v. District of Columbia, 410
Metropolitan Housing Corp. v. Arlington Heights, 192
Metropolitan Washington Coalition for Clean Air v. Department of Economic Dev., 760, 763
Metropolitan Washington Coalition for Clean Air v. District of Columbia, 77, 79–81
Miami v. Coral Gables, 340
Michelian, United States v., 405, 625, 626, 646
Michie v. Great Lakes Steel, 136
Michigan State Highway Comm'n v. Vanderkloot, 183
Middlestadt v. Waupaca Starch & Potato Co., 165
Middleton Iron & Steel Co. v. Evatt, 680

Midland Elec. Coal Co. v. Knox County, 203
Mile Road Corp. v. Boston, 624
Miles v. A. Arena & Co., 841
Miller v. Mallery, 832
Miller v. Schoene, 204
Millett v. Minnesota Crushed Stone Co., 145, 146
Mills, Inc., J. M., v. Murphy, 184, 204
Milo Community Hospital v. Weinberger, 700
Milwaukee v. State, 176, 180
Minnesota v. Callaway, 408
Minnesota v. Hoffman, 408
Minnesota Environmental Control Citizens Ass'n v. Atomic Energy Comm'n, 31
Minnesota Pub. Research Group v. Butz, 3
Minnesota Pub. Interest Research Group v. Butz (I), 750, 751, 754, 757, 762, 799, 808, 809
Minnesota Pub. Interest Research Group v. Butz (II), 732, 735, 793, 797, 832
Miranda, State ex rel. Reynolds v., 169
Missouri v. Illinois, 151, 153, 423, 518
Mitchell v. Hines, 624, 627
Mizokami v. United States, 39
Mobil Oil Corp. v. Huntington, 523
Mobil Oil Corp., United States v., 504
Mock v. United States, 576
Molokai Homesteaders Coop. Ass'n v. Morton, 760
Monroe Carp Pond Co. v. River Raisin Paper Co., 118
Monroe County Conservation Council, Inc. v. Volpe, 726, 762, 793, 795, 797, 833
Montana Wilderness Ass'n v. Board of Health & Environmental Sciences, 189, 808, 815
Montgomery v. Ellis, 731, 732, 735, 736, 746, 747, 793, 798, 801, 805, 806
Montgomery County v. Richardson, 757
Montgomery Environmental Coalition v. Fri, 26, 78, 81, 419
Montgomery Environmental Coalition v. Washington Suburban Sanitary Comm'n, 79
Montrose Chem. Corp. v. Train, 54
Moore v. Central Oklahoma Master Conservancy Dist., 549
Moore v. Coleman, 559
Moore-McCormack Lines, Inc. v. I. T. O. Corp., 54
Morash & Sons, Inc. v. Commonwealth, 31
Moretti, Inc., Joseph G., United States v., 395, 404
Moretti, Inc. (I), United States v., 44, 45
Moretti, Inc. (II), Joseph G., United States v., 405
Morgan v. Automobile Mfrs. Ass'n, 288
Morrell, United States v., 35
Morris County Land Improvement Co. v. Parsippany-Troy Hills, 204
Morrisville v. Delaware River Basin Comm'n, 761
Morse v. County of San Luis Obispo, 601
Morshead v. Regional Water Quality Control Bd., 543
Motors Ins. Corp. v. Aviation Specialties, Inc., 36
Mount Pleasant v. Van Tassell, 103

TABLE OF CASES
References are to Pages

Movement Against Destruction v. Volpe, 320, 779, 788, 795, 834
Mowry v. Central Elec. Power Coop., 759, 783
Mueller v. Fruen, 155
Mulchanock v. Whitehall Cement Mfg. Co., 155
Multidist. Vehicle Air Pollution, In re, 56, 288
Municipal Authority v. Bloomsberg Coop. Canners, Inc., 480
Municipal Sanitary Landfill Authority v. Hackensack Meadowlands Dev. Comm'n, 668
Murphy v. Benson, 840
Mutual Chem. Co. v. Mayor and City Council of Baltimore, 600
Myer v. Kemper Ice Co., 560
Myer v. Minard, 560
Myers v. Bethlehem Shipbuilding Corp., 265
Myers v. Hagertown, 623
Nader v. Baroody, 67, 68
Nader v. Butterfield, 612, 753
Nader v. Dunlop, 70
Nader v. Nuclear Regulatory Comm'n, 42, 457
Nader v. Ray, 42
Nair v. Thaw, 561
Nally & Gibson v. Mulholland, 148
Named Individual Members of the San Antonio Conservation Soc'y v. Texas Highway Dep't, 777
Named Individual Members of the San Antonio Conservation Soc'y v. Texas Highway Dep't (I), 777, 789, 833
Named Individual Members of the San Antonio Conservation Soc'y v. Texas Highway Dep't (II), 777
National Asphalt Pavement Ass'n v. Train, 271, 272, 286
National Ass'n of Gov't Employees v. Rumsfeld, 752
National Aviation v. Hayward, 595
National City Lines, United States v., 289
National Forest Preservation Group v. Butz, 711, 731, 758
National Gettysburg Battlefield Tower, Inc., Commonwealth v., 114, 183
National Helium Corp. v. Morton, 29
National Helium Corp. v. Morton (I), 764
National Helium Corp. v. Morton (II), 716, 731, 742
National Independent Coal Operators Ass'n v. Morton, 503
N. L. R. B. v. Hearst Publications, Inc., 20, 751
N. L. R. B. v. Marcus Trucking Co., 17
N. L. R. B. v. Sears, Roebuck & Co., 53
National Land & Inv. Co. v. Kohn, 193
National Parks & Conservation Ass'n v. Kleppe, 60
National Parks & Conservation Ass'n v. Morton, 59
National Petroleum Refiners Ass'n v. Federal Trade Comm'n, 657
National R. R. Passenger Corp. v. National Ass'n of R. R. Passengers, 78
National Renderers Ass'n v. EPA, 469

National Wildlife Federation v. Coleman, 78, 82, 557, 829, 830
Natural Resources Defense Council, Inc. v. Callaway, 77, 80, 82, 403, 406, 494, 720, 728, 731, 732, 735, 770, 779, 784, 790, 794, 796, 798, 800
Natural Resources Defense Council, Inc. v. EPA, 22, 26, 58, 87, 88, 235, 236, 238–242, 245, 248, 249, 251–255, 257, 259, 261, 262, 264, 311, 327, 337, 458
Natural Resources Defense Council, Inc. v. Fri, 82, 84, 86, 484
Natural Resources Defense Council, Inc. v. Grant, 390, 397, 405, 726, 727, 735–737, 739, 751, 752, 788, 801, 807, 808
Natural Resources Defense Council, Inc. v. Morton, 379, 514, 700, 728, 730, 733, 734, 736–738, 748, 762, 765, 774, 786, 792–795, 807
Natural Resources Defense Council, Inc. v. Nuclear Regulatory Comm'n, 46, 691, 790
Natural Resources Defense Council, Inc. v. Ruckelshaus, 297, 655
Natural Resources Defense Council, Inc. v. Securities & Exch. Comm'n, 26, 700, 725
Natural Resources Defense Council, Inc. v. Stamm, 739
Natural Resources Defense Council, Inc. v. Tennessee Valley Authority, 41, 734, 764, 786, 787, 795
Natural Resources Defense Council, Inc. v. Train, 41, 77–79, 82, 84, 225, 376, 432, 434, 453, 456, 458, 463, 473, 483, 485, 486
Nebraska v. Wyoming, 148, 151
Nebraska Press Ass'n v. Stuart, 58
Neches Canal Co. v. Miller & Vidor Lumber Co., 150, 397
Nedtweg v. Wallace, 181
Neher v. United States, 578
Nelson v. Butz, 733, 735, 736, 801
Nelson v. C. & C. Plywood Corp., 370, 371
Neptune City v. Avon-by-the-Sea, 174, 176, 181, 676
Nestle v. City of Santa Monica, 31, 36, 576, 579, 580, 583
Neustadt, United States v., 38
New Hampshire v. Atomic Energy Comm'n, 524, 529
New Haven, United States v., 138
New Jersey v. City of New York, 148, 149
New Jersey Barging Corp., In re, 518
New Jersey Dep't of Health v. Jersey City, 539, 542
New Jersey Sports & Exposition Authority v. McCrane, 48, 177, 179
New Mexico Citizens for Clean Air & Water v. Train, 286
New Mexico State Game Comm'n v. Udall, 32
New Penn Mines, Inc., People v., 137
Newton v. Grundy Center, 165
New Windsor v. Rowan, 14
New York v. New Jersey, 518
New York City, Interim Ocean Disposal Permit No. NY 009, In re, 411

TABLE OF CASES

References are to Pages

New York, City of v. Train, 31, 82
New York, City of v. United States, 288, 738, 756, 796, 800, 808
New York, Interim Ocean Disposal Permit No. NY 009, In re City of, 495
Nicholson v. Connecticut Half-Way House, Inc., 116
Nitram Chem. v. Parker, 146
No East-West Highway Comm., Inc. v. Whitaker, 771, 774, 775, 807
Noel v. United Aircraft Corp., 124, 149
Nolan v. Fitzpatrick, 40
Nolan v. New Britain, 165
Nolop v. Volpe, 801
No Oil, Inc. v. Los Angeles, 755, 813, 815
Nor-Am Agricultural Prods., Inc. v. Hardin, 47, 860, 880, 882
Norfolk & W. Ry. v. Allen, 128
Norvell, State ex rel. v. Arizona Pub. Serv. Co., 137
North American Coal Corp. v. Air Pollution Comm'n, 339
North Anna Environmental Coalition v. Nuclear Regulatory Comm'n, 51, 120, 831
North Carolina v. Federal Power Comm'n, 832
Northcutt v. State Road Dep't, 582
North Dakota v. Minnesota, 518
Northeast Welfare Rights Organization v. Volpe, 775
Northern Indiana Pub. Serv. Co. v. Vesey, 128, 146, 147
Northern States Power Co. v. Minnesota, 517, 528
North Georgia Petroleum Co. v. Lewis, 371
Northpoint Irrigation Co. v. Utah & Salt Lake Canal Co., 165
North Shore Sanitary Dist. v. Pollution Control Bd., 548
North Shore Sanitary Dist., People ex rel. Scott v., 668
North Suburban Sanitary Sewer Dist. v. Water Pollution Control Comm'n, 549
Northwestern Laundry v. Des Moines, 340
Northwest Home Owners Ass'n, Inc. v. Detroit, 624, 625
Norway Hill Preservation & Protection Ass'n v. King County Council, 814
Nucleus of Chicago Homeowners Ass'n v. Lynn, 733, 751, 752, 754, 755, 791, 794–796
Oak Haven Trailer Court, Inc. v. Western Wayne County Conservation Ass'n, 131
Oakwood at Madison, Inc. v. Madison, 192, 194
Obrecht v. National Gypsum Co., 174, 177, 180
O'Brien v. Brinegar, 763
O'Brien v. Greenburgh, 623, 624, 675
O'Connor v. Aluminum Ore Co., 145
O'Connor v. Rockford, 625
Ogo Associates v. Torrance, 195
Ohio v. Wyandotte Chem. Corp., 44, 151, 152
Ohio ex rel. Brown v. Callaway, 79, 450, 799, 802
Ohio River Sand Co. v. Commonwealth, 43
Oklahoma v. Guy F. Atkinson Co., 746

Oklahoma City v. West, 128
Oklahoma ex rel. Phillips v. Guy F. Atkinson Co., 401
Oljato Chapter of the Navajo Tribe v. Train, 83, 87, 88, 275
Olson v. Arctic Enterprises, Inc., 123
Olympia Oyster Co. v. Rayonier, Inc., 141, 418
Opinion of the Justices, 288, 594
Oppen v. Aetna Ins. Co., 106, 518, 519
Orange v. Heim, 180
Orange v. Valenti, 814
Organized Migrants in Community Action, Inc. v. Brennan, 856, 878
Oriental Blvd. Co. v. Heller, 349
Oronoco v. Rochester, 625, 668
Osborn v. Akron, 626
Osborn v. Whittier, 626
Owens-Corning Fiberglass Corp., State v., 351
Oxford v. Spears, 146
Ozark Poultry Prods., Inc. v. Garman, 106
Paepcke v. Public Bldg. Comm'n, 106, 177, 179, 181, 742
Page v. Niagara Chem. Div., 105, 108, 147
Palisades Citizens Ass'n, Inc. v. Civil Aeronautics Bd., 593, 700
Pana v. Crowe, 183
Pan American Petroleum Co. v. Byars, 154, 371
Parachutes, Inc. v. Lakewood, 577
Parker v. United States, 15
Parkersberg Builders Material Co. v. Barrack, 113, 130
Parks v. Atwood Crop Dusters, 841
Parks, Commonwealth v., 136
Pascagoula Veneer Co., State v., 350
Patrick v. Smith, 560
Patterson v. Peabody Coal Co., 140
Pax Co. v. United States, 47, 881
Payne v. Johnson, 562
Payne v. Kassab, 177, 180
Peacock v. County of Sacramento, 601
Peele v. Morton, 828
Pelletier v. Transit-Mix Concrete Corp., 561–563
Pen-Kote Paint Co., In re, 897, 898
Penn Central Transp. Co. v. City of New York, 204
Penn-Dixie Cement Corp. v. Kingsport, 340
Pennsylvania v. Dallas Corp., 539
Pennsylvania v. EPA, 316, 323, 324
Pennsylvania v. Morton, 762
Pennsylvania Coal Co. v. Mahon, 203, 205
Pennsylvania Coal Co. v. Sanderson, 118
Pennsylvania Environmental Council, Inc. v. Bartlett, 834
Pennsylvania Indus. Chem. Corp., United States v., 389, 393, 395
Pennsylvania Power Co., Commonwealth v., 351
Pennsylvania R.R. v. Sagamore Coal Co., 165
People v. ——— (see opposing party)
People for Environmental Progress v. Leisz, 26

TABLE OF CASES
References are to Pages

Peoples Gas Light & Coke Co. v. Buckles, 370
Perma Paving Co., United States v., 404
Permenter, United States v., 396, 405
Perrin's Appeal, 131
Perzinski v. Chevron Chem. Co., 842
Peterson, People v., 123
Petkas v. Staats, 60
Pettengill v. Turo, 147
Petterson v. Froehlke, 612
Phelps v. Winch, 561
Phelps Dodge Corp., United States v., 537
Philadelphia v. New Jersey, 516
Philadelphia, City of, Interim Ocean Disposal Permit No. PA 010, In re, 411
Philadelphia, Interim Ocean Disposal Permit No. PA 010, In re City of, 492
Phillips v. Sun Oil Co., 371
Phoenix v. Johnson, 128
Piedmont Cotton Mills, Inc. v. General Warehouse No. Two, Inc., 148
Piercefield v. Remington Arms Co., 580
Pigorsh v. Fahner, 172
Pigott v. United States, 36
Pike v. Bruce Church, Inc., 667
Pitts v. Camp, 18
Pittsburgh Coal Co. v. Sanitary Water Bd., 548, 549
Pizitz, Inc. v. Volpe, 778
Plan for Arcadia, Inc. v. Anita Associates, 81, 286
Plan for Arcadia, Inc. v. Arcadia City Council, 814, 816
Planned Parenthood of Central Missouri v. Danforth, 96
Plymouth Village Fire Dist. v. Water Pollution Comm'n, 548
Plywood Mfgs., People v., 340
Poe v. Ullman, 46
Porter County Chapter of Izaak Walton League, Inc. v. Atomic Energy Comm'n, 55, 62
Portland Cement Ass'n v. Ruckelshaus, 21, 119, 124, 234, 269, 271, 272, 338, 339, 466, 468, 569, 765
Portland Cement Ass'n v. Ruckelshaus (I), 22, 340
Portland Cement Ass'n v. Train (II), 655
Portland Pipe Line Corp. v. Environmental Improvement Comm'n, 523
Port of Astoria v. Hodel, 29, 48, 762, 787, 807
Port of New York Authority v. Eastern Airlines, Inc., 594, 595
Port of New York Authority v. United States, 754
Potomac River Ass'n v. Lundeberg Maryland Seamanship School, Inc., 45, 48, 174
Potomac Sand & Gravel Co. v. Governor, 203, 548
Potomac Sand & Gravel Co. v. Mandel, 408
Pottock v. Continental Can Co., 138, 139
Powell v. Superior Portland Cement, Inc., 118
Powell v. United States, 35
Price v. Dickson, 146

Price v. Osborne, 155
Prince George's County v. Holloway, 733, 735, 736, 748, 754, 790, 800
Proctor & Gamble, Inc. v. Chicago, 516, 547
PROD, Inc. v. Train, 82, 85, 86
Proetta v. Dent, 776
Protokowicz v. Lesofski, 563
Providence Journal Co. v. Shea, 548
Prudential Trust Co. v. Laramie, 188
Public Interest Research Group of Michigan v. Brinegar, 800, 833
Public Serv. Comm'n, State v., 175, 179
Puente de Reynosa v. McAllen, 397
Pumpelly v. Green Bay Co., 205
Pye v. Department of Transp. of Georgia, 701
Quinn v. American Spiral Spring & Mfg. Co., 562
Rabbitt v. Department of the Air Force, 59
Railroad Comm'n v. Manziel, 371
Rancho Santa Margarita v. Vail, 168
Randall v. Milwaukee, 582
Rankin v. Coleman, 731–733, 779, 781, 793, 798, 799, 804, 823
Ratzlaff v. Franz Foods, 150, 168
Rauh & Sons Fertilizer Co., E. v. Shreffler, 115
Ravndal v. Northfolk Placers, 170
Ray v. Mason County Drain Comm'n, 177, 186
Rayborn v. Smiley, 141
Rayonier, Inc. v. United States, 38
Reclamation Dist. No. 1500 v. Superior Court, 812
Red Star Towing & Transp. Co. v. Department of Transp., 397
Reedley, People v., 141
Regenstein v. Anderson, 756
Reinhart v. Lancaster Area Refuse Authority, 371
Relf v. Weinberger, 894
Renegotiation Bd. v. Grumman Aircraft Engineering Corp., 53, 54
Renken v. Harvey Aluminum, Inc., 123, 126, 158
Reno v. Fields, 623
Republic Steel Corp., United States v., 142, 392, 395, 397, 504
Reserve Mining Co. v. EPA, 335, 351, 486, 536, 538, 547
Reserve Mining Co. v. Minnesota Pollution Control Agency, 417
Reserve Mining Co. v. United States, 111, 115, 141, 152
Reserve Mining Co., United States v., 6, 114, 621
Rey v. United States, 39
Reynolds Metals Co. v. Lampert, 157
Reynolds, State ex rel. v. Miranda, 169
Rhode Island Comm. on Energy v. General Serv. Admin., 29, 51, 710, 732, 733, 755, 762, 764, 772, 784, 789
Rhodia, Inc. v. Harris County, 550
Riblet v. Spokane-Portland Cement Co., 146
Ricci v. Chicago Mercantile Exch., 42

TABLE OF CASES

Richards v. Washington Terminal Co., 108, 129, 137, 140, 581, 602
Richardson v. Murphy, 115
Richmond County v. Williams, 582
Rindge v. Sargent, 155
Ringlieb v. Parsippany-Troy Hills, 668
Riter v. Keokuk Electro-Metals Co., 118, 130
Riverside v. Ruckelshaus, 78, 82, 235, 311
Roark v. Caldwell, 601
Robbins v. Department of Public Works, 178
Roberts v. State, 349
Robertson v. Cincinnati, N. O. & Tex. Pac. Ry., 128, 144
Robertson v. Department of Defense, 61
Robinson v. Boulder, 543
Robinson Brick Co. v. Luthi, 140
Robles v. EPA, 63
Rochester v. Postal Serv., 764
Rockenback v. Apostle, 131
Rodgers v. FTC, 47
Rodo Land, Inc. v. Board of County Commissioners, 187
Roe v. Wade, 49, 96
Rogers v. Elliott, 560
Rogers v. Park & Planning Comm'n, 177
Rohm & Haas Co., United States v., 44, 390, 398
Romani, People v., 559, 561
Romero v. Chris Crusta Flying Service, Inc., 842
Romulus v. Wayne, 614, 731, 732, 738, 802, 803
Rosado v. Wyman, 42
Rose v. Department of the Air Force, 63
Roswell v. New Mexico Water Quality Control Comm'n, 548
Roswell v. Water Quality Comm'n, 810
Roy v. Chevrolet Motor Car Co., 131
Rucker v. Willis, 25, 406, 753, 759, 763
Rumsey v. Freeway Manos Minimax, 842
Rusch v. Phillips Petroleum Co., 165
Ryan v. Emmetsburg, 128, 156
Rykar Indust. Corp. v. Gill, 184
Rylands v. Fletcher, 158–162, 844
St. Joe Minerals Corp. v. EPA, 261
St. Paul v. Haugbro, 340
St. Regis Paper Co. v. State, 350, 548
St. Regis Paper Co., United States v., 396
Sakler v. Huls, 560, 563
Salasnek Fisheries, Inc. v. Cashner, 183
Sampson v. Schultz, 615
Sam Warren & Sons Stone Co. v. Grueser, 122
Sanders v. Beckwith, 843
Sanders v. Roselawn Memorial Garden, 559
Sandusky Portland Cement Co. v. Dixon Pure Ice Co., 165, 525, 527
San Francisco Bay Conservation & Dev. Comm'n, People ex rel. v. Emeryville, 176
San Francisco Tomorrow v. Romney, 756

San Juan County v. Russell, 32
Sansom Comm. v. Lynn, 753, 803
Santa Barbara v. Hickel, 514
Santa Barbara v. Modern Neon Sign Co., 203
Saunders v. Washington Metropolitan Area Transit Authority, 718, 804
Save America's Vital Environment, Inc. v. Butz, 49
Save Our Invaluable Land, Inc. v. Needham, 450
Save Our Ten Acres v. Kreger, 751, 754
Save the Dolphins v. Department of Commerce, 60
Scallet v. Stock, 139
Scanwell Labs, Inc. v. Shaffer, 32
Scattering Fork Drainage Dist. v. Ogilvie, 182, 183
Scenic Hudson Preservation Conference v. Callaway, 399
Scenic Hudson Preservation Conference v. Federal Power Comm'n, 828
Scenic Hudson Preservation Conference v. Federal Power Comm'n (I), 21, 24, 89, 768, 809
Scenic Hudson Preservation Conference v. Federal Power Comm'n (II), 721, 796
Scenic Rivers Ass'n v. Lynn, 762, 799
Schapiro & Co., M. A., v. Securities & Exch. Comm'n, 63
Schatz v. Abbott Laboratories, Inc., 147, 148
Scherr v. Volpe, 736, 751, 766
Schlafly v. Volpe, 33
Schlotfelt v. Vinton Farmers' Supply Co., 119, 130, 561, 563
Schofield v. Material Transit, Inc., 44
Schooner, United States v., 766
Schronk v. Gilliam, 842
Schubert v. United States, 578
Schumpert v. Moore, 155
Schwab v. Burgese, 577
Schwartz v. IRS, 53
Scientists Institute for Public Information v. AEC, 13, 25, 708, 715, 771, 736, 776, 786, 789, 791, 793
Scott, People ex rel. v. North Shore Sanitary Dist., 668
Seaboard Coast Line R.R. v. United States, 36
Seadade Indus. Inc. v. Florida Power & Light Co., 183, 529
Seagraves v. Portland City Temple, 577, 580
Seaman, State v., 404, 405
Sears, Roebuck & Co. v. General Serv. Administration, 63
Sears, Roebuck & Co., People ex rel. Hoogasian, v., 114
Seaway Co. v. Attorney General, 171
Secretary of Environmental Affairs v. Massachusetts Port Authority, 601, 612, 814, 821
Selby Smelting & Lead Co., People v., 122
Severt v. Beckley Coals, Inc., 559

TABLE OF CASES
References are to Pages

Sexton Cove Estates, Inc., United States v., 391, 404, 405
Shahmoon Indust., Inc. v. Department of Health, 350
Shaw v. Salt Lake County, 130
Shearing v. Rochester, 128, 145
Sheppard Envelope Co. v. Arcade Malleable Iron Co., 155
Sherry v. Algonquin Gas Transmission Co., 46
Shevin, State ex rel. v. Tampa Elec. Co., 139
Shipp v. Louisville & Jefferson County Air Bd., 601
Shoffner v. Sutherland, 165
Shumaker v. New York & Pennsylvania Co., 138
Sibson v. State, 184, 204
Sickman v. United States, 34
Sierra Club v. AEC, 784
Sierra Club v. Butz, 804, 806
Sierra Club v. Callaway, 729, 788, 791
Sierra Club v. Coleman, 758, 798
Sierra Club v. Department of Interior, 176, 383, 742
Sierra Club v. Drain, 274, 286
Sierra Club v. EPA, 279, 285, 286, 328
Sierra Club v. Froehlke, 25, 710, 716, 720, 729, 731, 732, 736, 737, 740, 741, 746, 747, 749, 791, 792, 794, 804-806, 829, 830
Sierra Club v. Hardin, 14, 42, 830
Sierra Club v. Hickel, 32
Sierra Club v. Kleppe, 772
Sierra Club v. Laird, 758
Sierra Club v. Leslie Salt Co., 395
Sierra Club v. Leslie Salt Co. (I), 397
Sierra Club v. Los Angeles, 612
Sierra Club v. Lynn, 86, 371, 717, 779, 780, 794, 795, 797, 801, 804, 807
Sierra Club v. Mason, 26, 406, 725, 795, 800, 807
Sierra Club v. Morton, 24-28, 54, 83, 106, 397, 514, 706, 710, 715, 734, 736, 746, 758, 772, 786, 794, 798, 800
Sierra Club v. Ruckelshaus, 82, 281
Sierra Club v. Sanitary Water Bd., 548, 549
Sierra Club v. Stamm, 746, 792
Sierra Club v. Volpe, 777
Sigety v. State Bd. of Health, 548
Silva v. Lynn, 716, 730, 737, 739, 741, 751, 755
Silva v. Romney, 612, 708, 762, 764, 776, 807
Simmans v. Grant, 708, 719, 720, 726, 731, 735, 736, 749, 758, 793, 805
Simmons v. Paterson, 108
Sioux Valley Empire Elec. Ass'n, Inc. v. Butz, 31
Sitkin's Junk Co., Commonwealth v., 680
Sittner v. Seattle, 340
Skil Corp., United States v., 503, 504
Skinner v. Oklahoma, 98
Smith v. Ann Arbor, 122, 624, 625
Smith v. Cookeville, 752, 753, 802
Smith v. County of Santa Barbara, 601
Smith v. Pittston Co., 119
Smith v. Schlesinger, 808
Smith v. Skagit County, 187, 188
Smith v. Staso Milling Co., 115, 559, 560
Smith v. Western Wayne County Conservation Ass'n, 559-561
Smoke Rise, Inc. v. Washington Suburban Sanitary Comm'n, 77
Sneed v. Riverside County, 600
Snohomish County, State v., 195
Soap & Detergent Ass'n v. Chicago, 516, 547
Soap Corp. v. Reynolds, 103
Society for Animal Rights, Inc. v. Schlesinger, 720, 752
Society for Protection of New Hampshire Forests v. Brinegar, 802
Society of Plastics Indus., Inc. v. City of New York, 678
Society of Plastics Indus., Inc. v. Occupational Safety & Health Administration, 125, 677, 856
Soucie v. David, 49, 53
Soukoup v. Republic Steel Corp., 139
Southern Alameda Spanish Speaking Organization (SASSO) v. Union City, 193
Southern Burlington County NAACP v. Mt. Laurel, 192, 193
Southern Cal. Ass'n of Governments v. Kleppe, 514
Southern Idaho Fish & Game Ass'n v. Picabo Livestock Co., 171
Southern Illinois Asphalt Co. v. Environmental Protection Agency, 349, 752
Southern Mill Creek Prods., Inc., In re, 897
Southern Nat'l Mfg. Co. v. EPA, 860, 882, 883
Southern Pac. Terminal Co. v. Interstate Commerce Comm'n, 49
South Terminal Corp. v. EPA, 22, 228, 257, 260, 311, 313, 317, 323, 324
Spannaus, State ex rel. v. United States Steel Corp., 41, 44
Spano v. Perini, 162
Spaulding v. Cameron, 144, 145
Spillway Marina, Inc. v. United States, 35
Springer v. Joseph Schlitz Brewing Co., 168, 478
Spring Valley Dev., In re, 197, 199
Spur Indus., Inc. v. Del E. Webb Dev. Co., 111, 125, 144, 621
Squaw Island Freight Terminal Co. v. Buffalo, 138, 140
Stagg v. Municipal Court, 595
Standard Oil Co., United States v., 357, 388, 393, 395
State v. ——— **(see opposing party)**
State Air Pollution Control Bd. v. Train, 345
State Dep't of Fish & Game v. S.S. Bournemouth, 518
State Highway Comm'n v. Colonial Inn, Inc., 582
State Highway Dep't v. Touchberry, 582
State Thruway Authority v. Ashley Motor Court, Inc., 203
State Water Control Bd. v. Train, 471
State Water Pollution Control Bd. v. Salt Lake City, 548

TABLE OF CASES
References are to Pages

Stearns Elec. Paste Co. v. EPA, 838, 848, 860, 862, 882, 884
Steele v. Queen City Broadcasting Co., 132
Steel Hill Dev., Inc. v. Sanbornton, 194, 195, 197, 204, 205
Steifer v. Kansas City, 623
Steinmetz v. Kelley, 134
Stempel v. Dep't of Water Resources, 548, 822
Stephens v. Bacon Park Commissioners, 115
Stephenson v. County of Monroe, 172, 174, 175, 178, 626
Sterling Drug, Inc., In re, 868
Sterling Drug, Inc. v. FTC, 59
Steubing v. Brinegar, 775, 800, 809
Stevens v. Rockport Granite Co., 123, 561, 562
Stock v. State, 548, 549
Stockslager v. Carroll Elec. Coop. Corp., 799
Stodder v. Rosen Talking Machine Co., 562
Stoeco Homes, Inc., United States v., 152, 390, 391, 395, 404
Stone v. Maitland, 188
Stop H-3 Ass'n v. Brinegar, 827, 834
Storey v. Central Hide & Rendering Co., 118
Storm v. City of New York, 624
Stratford Theatre, Inc. v. Town of Stratford, 148
Stratton v. Mt. Herman Boys' School, 167
Stream Pollution Control Bd. v. United States Steel Corp., 81, 152
Stretch v. Weinberger, 63
Strobel v. Kerr Salt Co., 167
Strong v. Winn-Dixie Stores, Inc., 115
Students Challenging Regulatory Agency Procedures v. United States (SCRAP I), 754
Students Challenging Regulatory Agency Procedures v. United States (SCRAP II), 732, 756, 764
Students Challenging Regulatory Agency Procedures (SCRAP I), United States v., 27, 651
Suffolk Gold Co. v. San Miguel Consol. Mining Co., 170
Sullivan v. Jones & Laughlin Steel Co., 119
Sundowner, Inc. v. King, 107
Sunset Cove, Inc., United States v., 390, 391, 395
Superior Constr. Co. v. Elno, 145
Superior Pub. Rights, Inc. v. Department Natural Resources, 175
Suspension of 1975 Motor Vehicle Exhaust Emission Standards, In re Application for, 295
Susquehanna Fertilizer Co. v. Malone, 108
Swain v. Brinegar, 762, 766, 781, 823
Swetland v. Curtiss Airports Corp., 138, 561, 577
Swift v. Island County, 821
Symons, People v., 582
Synthetic Organic Chem. Mfrs. Ass'n v. Brennan, 856, 857
Tampa Elec. Co., State ex rel. Shevin v., 139
Tanner v. Armco Steel Corp., 701
Tanners' Council of America, Inc. v. Train, 464, 465

Tate v. Short, 681
Tatje, People v., 350
T/B NMS No. 40, United States v., 396
Teagen v. Bergenfield, 676
Texas v. EPA, 9, 21, 237, 264, 310, 313, 324
Texas v. Pankey, 151, 841
Texas & N. O. R.R. v. Brotherhood of Ry. & S.S. Clerks, 142
Texas & Pac. Ry. v. Rigsby, 142
Texas Comm. on Natural Resources v. United States, 758, 762
Texas Co. v. Giddings, 371
Texas Eastern Transmission Corp. v. Wildlife Preserves, Inc., 123, 176–178, 181
Texas Oyster Growers Ass'n v. Odom, 177
Thermal Ecology Must Be Preserved v. Atomic Energy Comm'n, 46
Thomas v. Clear Lake, 165
Thomas v. United States, 35
Thompson v. Atlanta, 577
Thompson v. Chicago, 81, 83
Thompson v. Enz, 167
Thompson v. Fugate, 827, 834
Thomsen v. State, 582
Thornburg v. Port of Portland, 576–579
Thornton, State ex rel. v. Hay, 171
Thrasher v. Atlanta, 146
3276.21 Acres of Land, United States v., 576
Tidewater Oil Co. v. Jackson, 371
Tiede v. Schneidt, 165
Tierrasanta Community Council v. Richardson, 730, 735, 756, 784
T. I. M. E., Inc. v. United States, 45
Tipping v. St. Helen's Smelting Co., 130
Tobacco Inst. v. Federal Trade Comm'n, 60
Toilet Goods Ass'n v. Gardner, 48
Toro Dev. Co., Commonwealth v., 548
Tortorella v. H. Traiser & Co., 139
Towaliga Falls Power Co. v. Sims, 145
Townsend v. Norfolk Ry. & Light Co., 139
Train v. City of New York, 435, 436, 438
Train v. Colorado Public Interest Research Group, Inc., 82, 369
Train v. District of Columbia, 345
Train v. Natural Resources Defense Council, Inc., 233, 238, 254, 257, 261, 264, 347
Transcontinental Gas Pipe Line Corp. v. Gault, 139, 559
Transcontinental Gas Pipeline Corp. v. Hackensack Meadowlands Dev. Comm'n, 753, 760
Trempealeau Drainage Dist. Merwin v. Houghton, 175
Trinity Episcopal School Corp. v. Romney, 724, 736, 795, 796
Trout Unlimited v. Morton, 708, 734, 736, 746, 791
Tuebner v. California St. R.R., 138
Tulare Lake Canal Co., United States v., 832

Turner v. Big Lake Oil Co., 159
Turner v. Del Morte, 204
Turnpike Realty Co. v. Dedham, 204
247.37 Acres of Land, United States v., 757
2,606.84 Acres of Land in Tarrant County, Texas, United States v., 746
Udall v. Federal Power Comm'n, 21, 826
Underhill v. Motes, 842
Underwood, United States v., 404
Union Elec. Co. v. EPA, 234, 260, 261, 264, 266, 345
Union Mechling v. United States, 759
Union of Concerned Scientists v. Atomic Energy Comm'n, 457
Union Oil Co. v. California, 340
Union Oil Co. v. Morton, 513, 514
Union Oil Co. v. Oppen, 147, 162, 518, 519, 522
United Air Lines, Inc. v. Wiener, 35
United Farmworkers of Florida Housing Project, Inc. v. Delray Beach, 192
United States v. ——— (see opposing party)
United States Polychem Corp., In re, 895
United States Smelting Co. v. Sisam, 145, 146
United States Steel Corp. v. Gary Air Pollution Control Bd., 350
United States Steel Corp., Commonwealth v., 103
United States Steel Corp., State ex rel. Spannaus v., 41, 44
United States Steel Corp., United States v., 138, 152, 389, 392, 393, 504
United Verde Copper Co. v. Ralston, 147
Upper Pecos Ass'n v. Stans, 784
Upper Pecos Ass'n v. Stans (II), 804
Upper Pecos Ass'n v. United States, 756
Upper Saddle River v. Goess Environment Serv. Corp., 668
Ure, United States v., 35
Urie v. Franconia Paper Corp., 137, 140, 416
Utah Int'l, Inc. v. EPA, 263
Utica v. Water Pollution Control Bd., 548
Valley View v. Rockside Hideaway Sanitary Landfill, Inc., 625, 668
Vandenbark v. Owens-Illinois Glass Co., 766
Vanderslice v. Shawn, 122
Vann v. Bowie Sewerage Co., 145
Vaughn v. Rosen, 53, 56
Vautier v. Atlantic Refining Co., 147
Venuto v. Owens-Corning Fiberglas Corp., 141
VEPCO v. Nuclear Regulatory Comm'n, 89, 343, 540, 727
Vermont v. New York, 154
Vermont Woolen Corp. v. Wackerman, 548
Verrazzano Trading Corp. v. United States, 52
Vile v. Pennsylvania R.R., 126
Virginia Elec. & Power Co., In re, 5, 51, 89, 343, 540, 727
Virginians for Dulles v. Volpe, 32, 577, 579, 592, 611
Virginia State Water Quality Bd. v. Train, 541

Virginia Water Bd. v. Supervisors, 543
Volunteers of America, People v., 583
Vosburg v. Putney, 113
Vowinckel v. N. Clark & Sons, 111, 123, 132, 559, 561
Walker v. Birmingham, 265
Walker v. Delaware Trust Co., 131
Wall v. Trogdon, 843
Walla Walla v. Conkey, 100
Walsh v. Spadaccia, 188
Ward v. Ackroyd, 31
Waring v. Peterson, 601
Warm Springs Dam Task Force v. Gribble, 703, 734, 746, 797
Warner-Quinlan Co. v. United States, 390
Warner Valley Stock Co. v. Lynch, 168
Warren Co. v. Dickson, 560
Warth v. Seldin, 27, 28, 77
Waschak v. Moffat, 118
Washington v. General Motors Corp., 153, 154, 288
Washington v. Udall, 32, 33
Washington Coca Cola Bottling Co. v. Montgomery County, 688
Washington Research Project, Inc. v. Department of Health, Education & Welfare, 60
Washington, United States v., 4, 49, 149, 196, 805, 828
Waterford v. Water Pollution Control Bd., 21, 418
Waterford Processing & Reclaiming Co. v. Township of Waterford, 625, 668
Watson v. Great Lakes Pipe Line Co., 371
Waukegan v. Pollution Control Bd., 349
Wayne County Dep't of Health v. Chrysler Corp., 351
W. B. Enterprises, Inc., United States v., 504
Weaver v. Yoder, 119
Weaver & Sons, A. P. v. Sanitary Water Bd., 548
Webb v. Rye, 126
Weeks-Thorn Paper Co. v. Glenside Woolen Mills, 165
Weisberg v. Department of Justice, 56
Weiszmann v. District Engineer, 391, 395, 396, 404, 405
Wellford v. Hardin, 58
Wellford v. Ruckelshaus, 880, 883
Weltner v. Producers Pipeline Co., 81, 520
Wante v. Commonwealth Fuel Co., 119
Western Alfalfa v. Air Pollution Variance Bd., 339, 340
Western Pac. R.R., United States v., 40
West Muncie Strawboard Co. v. Slack, 165
West Penn Power Co. v. Train, 265, 266
West Point v. Meadows, 626
Westville v. Whitney Home Bldrs., 165
West Virginia Div. of the Izaak Walton League v. Butz, 832
Westwood Forest Estates v. South Nyack, 195
Whalen v. Union Bag & Paper Co., 112, 120, 241
Wheat v. Freeman Coal Mining Corp., 147
White v. Bernhart, 116
White v. Long, 138
White Fuel Corp., United States v., 389, 393, 394

TABLE OF CASES

References are to Pages

Whitehead v. Jessup, 105
White Lake Improvement Ass'n v. Whitehall, 45, 548
Wilbour v. Gallagher, 408
Wilderness Soc'y v. Morton, 48, 86, 87, 762, 831
Wildlife Alive v. Chickering, 816
Williamette Heights Neighborhood Ass'n v. Volpe, 823
Williams v. Blue Bird Laundry Co., 134, 139
Williams Co., J. B., United States v., 54
Williamson v. Lee Optical Co., 191
Willoughby Hill v. Corrigan, 601
Wilmont Homes v. Weiler, 149
Wilmore v. Chaino Mines, Inc., 165
Wilson v. Lynn, 750
Wilson v. Portland, 624
Wisconsin v. Butz, 753
Wisconsin v. Callaway, 406, 725
Wisconsin v. Illinois, 148, 149
Wisconsin's Environmental Decade, Inc. v. Public Serv. Comm'n, 814, 815
Wisconsin Student Ass'n v. Regents of the University of Wisconsin, 104
Wise v. Hays, 844
W. N. C. Pallet & Forest Prods. Co., State v., 350

Woodruff v. North Bloomfield Gravel Mining Co., 118
Wright v. Best, 170
Wuillamey v. Werblin, 286, 320, 330
Wyandotte Transp. Co. v. United States, 104, 142, 150, 395
Wylie Bros. Constr. Co. v. Albuquerque-Bernalillo County Air Quality Control Bd., 349, 350
Wyoming v. Hathaway, 838, 861, 885
Wyoming Outdoor Coord. Council v. Butz, 751, 757, 762
Yannacone v. Dennison, 840
Yara Engineering Corp. v. Newark, 600
Yates v. Missouri Pac. R.R., 115
Ybarra v. Los Altos Hills, 194
Yick Wo v. Hopkins, 193
York v. Stallings, 132, 563
Young v. Darter, 842
Young v. Public Bldg. Comm'n, 172
Zabel v. Tabb, 699, 407, 475
Zahn v. International Paper Co., 117
Zengerle v. Board of County Commissioners, 624
Zieske v. Butz, 832
Zlotnick v. Redevelopment Land Agency, 29

INDEX

References are to Pages

ABNORMALLY DANGEROUS ACTIVITIES
Liability for, 158

ADMINISTRATIVE PROCEDURE
See also Judicial Review; National Environmental Policy Act
Citizen intervention, 88
Delegation doctrine, 179
Preclusion of judicial review, 18
Waiver of sovereign immunity, 31

ADMINISTRATIVE PROCEDURE ACT
See Administrative Procedure; Judicial Review; Sovereign Immunity

ADVISORY COMMITTEES
California Solid Waste Resource Recovery Program, 672
Clean Air Act,
  Automobile emissions, 289, 300
  Legislative studies, 217
Coordinating Research Council, 4
Federal Advisory Committee Act,
  Advisory committee, defined, 67
  Disclosure of information, relationship with Freedom of Information Act, 69
  Exemptions,
    Ad hoc groups, 68
    Private contractors, 69
    Subgroups, 67
  Procedure, 66
  Sanctions, 71
Federal Insecticide, Fungicide, and Rodenticide Act,
  Cancellation, 851, 886
  Pesticide tolerances, 889
  Regulations, 854
  Suspension, 851, 886
Federal Water Pollution Control Act,
  Generally, 355
  National Commission on Water Quality, 363
National Academy of Sciences,
  Clean Air Act, 300–301
  Contracts with federal agencies, 73

ADVISORY COMMITTEES—Cont'd
National Academy of Sciences—Cont'd
  Federal Insecticide, Fungicide, and Rodenticide Act, 851
  Federal Water Pollution Control Act, 422
  Legislative studies, 74
  Pesticide cancellation, 851
  Pesticide suspension, 851
  Solid waste recycling, 648
  Suspension of mobile source emission standards, 300–301
  Technology assessment, 12
  Use of reports in litigation, 74
  Water quality criteria, 422
National Commission on Materials Policy, 634
National Commission On Water Quality, 363
Occupational Safety and Health Act, noise regulation, 618
Solid Waste Disposal Act, 634
Toxic Substances Control Act, priority substances, 905

AIR POLLUTION
Atmospheric areas, defined, 211
Clean Air Act,
  See also Citizen Suits; Judicial Review
  Advisory committees, 217–218
  Air pollutant, defined, 222
  Air pollution control agency, defined, 215
  Air quality control region,
    Defined, 211
    Designation, 222
  Air quality criteria,
    Defined, 212
    Public health, defined, 223
    Public welfare, defined, 223, 226
  Air quality maintenance plan,
    Air quality maintenance area, defined, 235
    Defined, 236
    State implementation plan, 235

AIR POLLUTION—Cont'd
Clean Air Act—Cont'd
  Ambient air quality standards,
    See also Prevention of Significant Deterioration
    Adequate margin of safety, 226, 260
    Attainment,
      Noninterference, 253
      Primary, 242, 261
      Secondary, 261
    Burden of proof, 226
    Criteria pollutants,
      Identification, 224
      Listed, 225, 228
    Defined, 212
    Kennecott statements, 230
    Primary, defined, 225
    Procedure, 222
    Public welfare,
      Defined, 223, 226
      Economic values, 227
    Secondary, defined, 226
    Standards, 229
  Annual reports, 220
  Bubble concept, 273
  Citizen suits, 217
  Control techniques documents, 212, 223
  Cost-benefit analysis,
    Fuel additives, 331, 334
    Suspension of automobile emission standards, 297
    Transportation control plans, 323
  Criteria documents, 223
  Disclosure of trade secrets,
    Fuel additives, 331
    Mobile sources, 248–249
    State implementation plans, 248–249
  Economic and technological defenses,
    Administrative order, 345
    Contempt proceedings, 267
    Enforcement proceedings, 266
    Getty Oil dilemma, 266
    Mobile source compliance, 296
    State enforcement proceedings, 351
  Economic and technological feasibility,
    Adoption of state implementation plan, 260, 262
    Appellate review, 263
    Approval of state implementation plans, 261
    Collateral injunctive relief, 265
    Emission control strategy, 260
    Hazardous pollutants, 277

AIR POLLUTION—Cont'd
Clean Air Act—Cont'd
  Economic and technological feasibility—Cont'd
    Mobile source emission standards, 295, 300
    New source performance standards, 270
    Promulgation of ambient air quality standards, 260
    Variances, 264
  Emission limitations, see State implementation plan
  Emission standards,
    See also Hazardous pollutants; New source performance standards, this topic
    Administrative variances, 347
    Defined, 213
    Opacity, 338
  Enforcement,
    Administrative orders,
      Content, 344
      Economic and technological defenses, 345
      Variance, 345
    Assembly line testing, mobile sources, 297, 302
    Averaging, 298
    Baseline measurements, mobile sources, 297
    Compliance schedule, 344
    Conference,
      Generally, 213, 216
      Procedures, 340
    Contempt, 267
    Criminal, 342
    Defined, 336
    Delegation to states, 337
    Economic and technological defenses, 266–267, 296, 345, 351
    Emergency powers, 340
    Federal assumption of delegated authority, 341
    Hearings, 344
    Injunction, 342
    Measuring compliance, 297
    Misrepresentation, 343
    Mobile sources, 307–309
    Motor vehicle inspection, 303
    New source performance standards, 274
    Notice, 343
    On site inspection, 337
    Opacity, 338
    Recall, mobile sources, 307
    Record keeping, 337

INDEX

References are to Pages

AIR POLLUTION—Cont'd
Clean Air Act—Cont'd
  Enforcement—Cont'd
    Ringelmann chart, 339
    Sampling, 298, 337
  Existing source,
    Hazardous pollutants, 277
    Noncriteria pollutants, 275
  Federal facilities,
    Presidential exemption, 352
    State permits, 352
  Fuel additives,
    Lead, 331
    Preregistration testing, 331
    Prohibition, standards, 331
    Protection of emission control devices, 332
    Registration, 290, 330–331
  Hazardous pollutants,
    Defined, 276
    Designated substances, 277
    Economic and technological feasibility, 277
    Exemption, 276
    Existing sources,
      Generally, 277
      Waiver, 278
    Pesticides, 856
    Preconstruction review,
      Generally, 276
      Modification, defined, 278
    Procedure, 276
    Standards,
      Asbestos, 278
      Beryllium, 278
      Mercury, 279
  Indirect sources,
    See also Air quality maintenance areas; Prevention of significant deterioration, this topic
    Associated parking facility, defined, 329
    Citizen suits, 330
    Defined, 325
    Preconstruction review,
      Applicability, 327, 329
      Conditional approval, 328
      Procedure, 328
      Standards, 328
    State implementation plans, transportation controls, 327
  Inspection and Maintenance Program, defined, 315
  Interstate compacts, 215

AIR POLLUTION—Cont'd
Clean Air Act—Cont'd
  Legislative history, 209–214
  Mobile sources,
    See also Transportation control plans, this topic
    Antitampering,
      Applicability, 304
      Nonoriginal equipment, 305
    Antitrust,
      Mass transportation, 289
      Smog conspiracy, 288
    Assembly line monitoring, 277, 302
    Barth Report, 292
    Certificate of conformity,
      Conditions, 307
      Defined, 306
    Compliance, economic and technological feasibility, 296
    Control strategies, interrelationships, 287
    Defined, 221
    Emission standards,
      Baseline, 297
      Evolution, 291–299
      Technological feasibility, 295, 300
    Fuel additives, 291
    In use vehicles,
      Inspection, 303
      Owner maintenance, 303
    Legislative history, 289–292
    Light duty vehicles, defined, 296
    Low Emission Vehicle Certification Board, 219
    Motor vehicle, defined, 295
    New motor vehicle, defined, 295
    New motor vehicle engine, defined, 295
    Nonconforming vehicles,
      Enforcement actions, 309
      Sanctions, 309
    Recall criteria, 308
    Suspension,
      Generally, 296–299
      Criteria, 299
      Procedure, 298
    Useful life, defined, 295
    Warranty,
      Design, 302
      Inspection, 304
      Owner maintenance, 302, 303
      Performance, 293, 303
      Production, 302
  National ambient air quality standards, see Ambient air quality standards, this topic

AIR POLLUTION—Cont'd
Clean Air Act—Cont'd
  National Environmental Policy Act, exemption from, 272
  New source performance standards,
    Achievable, defined, 271
    Adequacy of data base, 272
    Adequately demonstrated, defined, 270
    Bubble concept, 273
    Citizen suit, 274
    Cost-benefit analysis, 270
    Economic and technological feasibility, 270
    Enforcement, 274
    Environmental impacts, 271
    Judicial review, 275
    Modification, defined, 273
    New source, defined, 267
    New source categories, 268
    Preconstruction review, 274
    Reconstruction, defined, 273
    Standard of performance, defined, 268
    Stationary source, defined, 267
  Particulates, defined, 231
  Preemption, 216
  Prevention of significant deterioration,
    Best available technology, 284, 286
    Citizen suit, 286
    Classification,
      Generally, 283
      Adoption, 284
      Reclassification, 285
    Criteria pollutants, 285
    Indirect sources, 326
    Land use regulations, 285
    Legislative history, 280
    Mobile sources, 326
    Preconstruction review, 284
    Relationship to ambient air quality standards, 280
    Significant, defined, 283
    Standards, 284
    State implementation plan, 280
  Protection of public health, 334
  State implementation plan,
      See also air quality maintenance plan; Indirect sources, Prevention of significant deterioration; Transportation control plans, this topic
    Adequate assurances, 253

AIR POLLUTION—Cont'd
Clean Air Act—Cont'd
  State implementation plan—Cont'd
    Adoption, economic and technological feasibility, 260, 262
      Air quality model, 237
    Approval,
      Generally, 234
      Economic and technological feasibility, 261
    Attainment of ambient air quality standards, 242
    Contents, 231, 248–249
    Defined, 230
    Disclosure of trade secrets, 248–249
    Dispersion enhancement, 253, 255–256
    Emission limitations,
      Compliance schedule, defined, 255
      Continuous emission reduction systems, 258
      Control strategy,
        Defined, 255
        Economic and technological feasibility, 260
      Defined, 254
      Emission standard, defined, 254
      Intermittent controls, 255
      Land use controls, 255
      Timetable for compliance, defined, 255
    Extensions,
      Generally, 244, 313
      Regional limitation, 247
      Significant risk, 247
    Guidelines for air quality maintenance planning and analysis, 235
    Hearings, 233
    Intergovernmental cooperation, 252
    Monitoring, 248–249
    Noninterference with ambient air quality standards attainment, 253
    Operational control
      Generally, 256–258
      Sufficiency, 257
    Postponement, 239–240
    Preconstruction review,
      Scope, 250
      Tradeoff policy, 251, 253
    Priority classification, 236
    Revisions,
      Attainment of ambient air quality standards, 242

INDEX

References are to Pages

AIR POLLUTION—Cont'd
Clean Air Act—Cont'd
  State implementation plan—Cont'd
    Revisions—Cont'd
      Availability, 243
      Energy Supply and Environmental Coordination Act, 244
        Generally, 233–240
      Hearings, 254
    Right of entry, 249
    Scope, 230
    Source control, 256–258
    Suspension,
      Generally, 245
      Compliance date extension, 246
      Temporary, 246
    Variance,
      Administrative orders, 345
      Economic and technological feasibility, 264
      Generally, 238
  Stationary source,
    Defined, 221, 267
    Installation, defined, 221
  Technological feasibility, see Economic and technological feasibility, this topic
  Transportation control plans,
    See also Indirect sources, this topic
    Bicycle lanes, 321
    Bus and carpool priority, 317
    Carpooling, 318, 664
    Control priorities, 314
    Control strategies, 314–322
    Defined, 310
    Employer transit incentive, 318
    Energy conservation plan, 663
    Extension, 313
    Gasoline rationing, 320
    History, 311
    In use vehicle inspection-maintenance, 315
    Land use regulation, 311
    Management of parking supply, 319
    Necessity, 313
    Reducing total vehicle miles of travel, 317–322
    Retrofit, 316
    Selected vehicle use prohibitions, 322
    Service station vapor controls, 317
    Transit improvement, 318
    Transportation controls, defined, 310
    Vehicle free zones, 321
  309 review, 219, 709–714
  Tradeoff policy, 251

AIR POLLUTION—Cont'd
Clean Air Act—Cont'd
  Voluntary certification, 290
  Dispersion enhancement, 6, 255–256
  Energy Reorganization Act, 215
  Energy Supply and Environmental Coordination Act,
    Continuous emission reduction systems, 258
    Management of parking supply, 319
    State implementation plans,
      Generally, 244
      Suspensions, 245
  Mobile sources, systems analysis, 8
  Operational controls,
    Intermittent controls, 255
    Tall stacks, 253, 255–256
  Smog conspiracy, 288
  Source control, 256
  State laws,
    Criminal, 350
    Economic and technological defenses, 351
    Strict liability, 350
  Tall stacks, see Operational controls

AIRPORT AND AIRWAY DEVELOPMENT ACT
See Land Development Controls

BEST TECHNOLOGY
Clean Air Act,
  New source performance standards, 267–271
  Prevention of significant deterioration,
    Design of equipment standard, 284
    Generally, 281
    Stationary source, 255–58
Defined, 124
Energy Policy and Conservation Act,
  Automobile fuel economy standards, 655–656
Federal law, generally, 832–33
Federal Water Pollution Control Act,
  Existing industrial sources, 464
  Municipal treatment works, 445–448, 470–472
  New industrial sources, 467–468
  No discharge, 467, 471
  Nonpoint source controls, 431, 433
  Pretreatment standards, 479
  Thermal pollution, 533
National Environmental Policy Act, 742, 747, 832

934 INDEX

BEST TECHNOLOGY—Cont'd
Noise Control Act,
    Motor vehicle emission standards, 607–608
    Railroad emission standards, 609
Nuisance,
    Generally, 122–126, 180, 267
    Noise, 609
    Solid waste, 624–625
Occupational Safety and Health Act, noise regulation, 618
Operational controls,
    Aircraft noise,
        Generally, 562, 575, 591–597
        Concorde, 592
    Automobile pollution, 310, 317–322
    Federal Water Pollution Control Act, low-flow augmentation, 448
    Nuisance,
        Generally, 122, 149
        Noise, 562
        Solid waste, 624–625
    Occupational noise, 616
    Oil pollution,
        Deepwater ports, 512
        Load-on-top, 256, 509
        Tanker regulation, 509–512
    Pesticides, 838
    Solid wastes,
        Beverage containers, 685
        Sanitary landfills, 675–677
Source controls, contrasted with operational controls, 256–258

BURDEN OF PROOF
Clean Air Act,
    Ambient air quality standards, 226
    Regulation of fuel additives, 334
Endangered Species Act, 830
Federal Insecticide, Fungicide, and Rodenticide Act, pesticide safety, 853
Federal Water Pollution Control Act,
    Thermal pollution, 533
    Toxic pollutants, compatability with treatment works, 481
    Water quality standards, 359
Freedom of Information Act, nondisclosure, 50
National Environmental Policy Act,
    Impact statement adequacy, 736
    Prediction capabilities, 723
Nuisance, 126, 141
Ocean dumping, 492, 496
Public trust, 177, 185
Trespass, 155–156

CITIZEN SUITS
Administrative proceedings, 88
Clean Air Act,
    Generally, 217
    Indirect sources, 330
    New source performance standards, 274
    Prevention of significant deterioration, 286
    Section 309, 709
Courts of appeals, 87
Energy Policy and Conservation Act, 660
Enforceable duties, defined, 80
Federal Water Pollution Control Act, water quality standards, 419
Jurisdiction, 76
Michigan Environmental Protection Act, 185
National Environmental Policy Act,
    Bonds, 806
    Consent decrees, 806
    Settlements, 806
Noise Control Act, motor vehicle emission standards, 610
Oil spill liability, 520
Preemption by government action, 78–79
Procedure,
    Direct appellate review, 87
    Intervention, 78
    Notice, 77
Remedies,
    Equitable, 84
    Litigation costs, 50, 85
    Measure, 86
    Monetary damages, 84
    Qui tam, Rivers and Harbors Act, 396
Solid Waste Disposal Act,
    Generally, 635
    Hazardous wastes, 696
    Open dumps, 638
Standing, 76
State constitution and statutory provisions, 184–186
Toxic Substances Control Act,
    Litigation expenses, 903
    Premarket notification, 901
    Reasonable risk, 906

CLEAN AIR ACT
See Air Pollution

COASTAL ZONE MANAGEMENT ACT
See Dredge and Fill; Land Development Controls

COST–BENEFIT ANALYSIS
Clean Air Act,
    Ambient air quality standards, 227
    Fuel additives, 331, 334

INDEX

References are to Pages

COST–BENEFIT ANALYSIS—Cont'd
Clean Air Act—Cont'd
  New source performance standards, 270
  Suspension of mobile source emission standards, 299
  Transportation control plans, 323
Energy Policy and Conservation Act,
  Automobile fuel economy standards, 655–656
  Energy efficiency improvement targets, 660
  Energy efficiency standards, 660
Federal Insecticide, Fungicide, and Rodenticide Act,
  Exemptions, 875
  Pesticide cancellation, 882
  Pesticide registration, 858, 875
  Pesticide suspension, 885
Federal law, generally, 833
Federal Water Pollution Control Act,
  Dredge and fill disposal, 406
  Existing industrial sources, 464
  Low-flow augmentation, 450
  Municipal treatment works, 442
  New industrial sources, 467–468
  NPDES proceedings, 456, 458–459
  Regional plans, 433
  Toxic pollutants, 483
  Water quality related effluent limitations, 423
  Water quality standards, 418
Federal water projects, 450
Importance, 7
National Environmental Policy Act, 721, 724, 728, 745
Noise Control Act,
  Aircraft emission standards, 584, 591
  Motor vehicle emission standards, 607–608
  Nontransportation source emission standards, 569–570
Occupational Safety and Health Act, noise regulation, 618
Ocean dumping, 491, 493, 495–497
Pesticides, generally, 840
State environmental policy acts, 817–818, 822
Toxic Substances Control Act, existing substances, 903

DREDGE AND FILL
See also Ocean Dumping
Coastal Zone Management Act, 408–409
Corps of Engineers regulations,
  Applicability to federal projects, 407
  Navigable waters, 403

DREDGE AND FILL—Cont'd
Discharge, defined, 400
Disposal site selection,
  Criteria, 407
  Economic and technological feasibility, 406
  Permit procedure, 405
  Preparation of environmental impact statement, 406
  Prohibited areas, 406
Dredged material, defined, 400
Fill material, defined, 400
Navigable waters, defined, 401–403
Rivers and Harbors Act, 399–404, 645

ENDANGERED SPECIES ACT
See National Environmental Policy Act, Complementary federal laws

ENERGY POLICY AND CONSERVATION ACT
See Solid Waste

ECOLOGY
Defined, 1

ENVIRONMENTAL LAW
Defined, 1
Interdisciplinary demands, 5–9
Legal context, 14

EXTERNALITIES
Defined, 6

FEDERAL ENVIRONMENTAL PESTICIDE CONTROL ACT
See Pesticides

FEDERAL FACILITIES
Air pollution, 352
Solid waste, 636, 639
Water pollution, 544

FEDERAL INSECTICIDE, FUNGICIDE, AND RODENTICIDE ACT
See Pesticides

FEDERAL TORT CLAIMS ACT
See Sovereign Immunity

FEDERAL WATER POLLUTION CONTROL ACT
See Water Pollution

FOOD, DRUG, AND COSMETIC ACT
See Pesticides

FREEDOM OF INFORMATION ACT
See also Advisory Committees
Agency, defined, 53
Discovery, 49

INDEX

References are to Pages

FREEDOM OF INFORMATION ACT—Cont'd
Exemptions,
  Confidential data, 58–60
  Intra-agency memoranda,
    Generally, 52
    National Environmental Policy Act, 706, 724
  Investigatory files, 56
  Medical files, 62
  National security, 61
  Personal privacy, 62
  Specific statutory exemptions, 63
  Trade secrets,
    Generally, 58–60
    Clean Air Act,
      Air pollution emissions, 248–249
      Fuel additives, 331
    Federal Water Pollution Control Act, ocean dumping, 492
    Toxic Substances Control Act, 905
Nondisclosure, burden of proof, 50
Procedures, 50

GROUNDWATER
Aquifer, defined, 370
Defined, 369
Federal reserved rights doctrine, 372
Federal Water Pollution Control Act,
  Construction grant program, 373
  Disposal of wastewater treatment sludge, 373
  Federal authority, 372
  National Pollutant Discharge Elimination System, 369–372
Safe Drinking Water Act,
  Designated acquifer, 374
  State programs, 374
Underground injection, defined, 374

JUDICIAL REVIEW
See also National Environmental Policy Act; Public Trust
Administrative Procedure Act,
  Arbitrary and capricious standard of review, 743
  Preclusion of judicial review, 18
  Substantial inquiry, 740
Burden of proof, see Burden of Proof
Citizen suits, see Citizen Suits
Clean Air Act,
  Appellate review,
    Economic and technological defenses, 263
    Venue, 263
  State implementation plans, economic and technological factors, 263

JUDICIAL REVIEW—Cont'd
Close scrutiny,
  Burden of proof, 22
  Clean Air Act,
    Ambient air quality standards, 230
    Economic and technological feasibility, 263–264
    Enforcement proceedings, 349
    Fuel additives, 332–333
    Kennecott statements, 229–230
    New source performance standards, 269, 272, 275
    Transportation control plans, 323
  Decision-making under NEPA, 730
  Doctrine, 16, 185
  Federal Insecticide, Fungicide, and Rodenticide Act, pesticide cancellation, 875
  Federal Water Pollution Control Act,
    Effluent standards, 468
    Pretreatment standards, 479
    Siting of sewage treatment plant, 549
    State enforcement, 547
    Toxic pollutant standards, 485
  Land development controls, 192, 196
  National Environmental Policy Act,
    Procedural requirements, 614, 717, 728, 731, 737, 741, 749
    Procedural-substantive dichotomy, 717, 739
    Rule of reason, 682
    Substantive obligations,
      Good faith test, 739–740
      Substantial inquiry, 740, 743–749
  Noise Control Act, nontransportation source emission standards, 570
  Oil lease, suspension, 514
  Procedural compliance, 20
  Reasoned decision-making, 21
  State air pollution laws, 349
Exhaustion of administrative remedies,
  Generally, 40–42
  Michigan Environmental Protection Act, 185
Federal Water Pollution Control Act, appellate jurisdiction, 454
Finality, 46
Hard look, see Close scrutiny, this topic
Mootness, 48–49
National Environmental Policy Act, applicability, 751
Primary jurisdiction,
  Generally, 40, 43
  Michigan Environmental Protection Act, 185
Ripeness, 46

INDEX

References are to Pages

JUDICIAL REVIEW—Cont'd
Sovereign immunity, see Sovereign Immunity
Standards of review,
   See also Close scrutiny, this topic
   Administrative Procedure Act, 17–21, 743–745
Standing, see Standing
State environmental impact statement requirements, 820–821
Substantial inquiry, see Close scrutiny
Toxic Substances Control Act, 907

LAND DEVELOPMENT CONTROLS
   See also National Environmental Policy Act, State environmental policy acts; Public Trust; Taking
Agriculture, water pollution, 384
Airport and Airway Development Act, 598, 614
Airports, nuisance, 575
Areas of critical state concern, 202
Clean Air Act,
   Air quality maintenance plan, 326
   Emission limitations, 255
   Indirect sources, 325–329
   Preconstruction review,
      Hazardous, pollutants, 276
      Indirect sources, 325
      New source performance standards, 274
      Prevention of significant deterioration, 284
   Prevention of significant deterioration, 285
   Transportation control plans, 311
Coastal Zone Management Act,
   Dredge and fill, 408
   Federal consistency, 409
   State plans, 200, 408
Construction, water pollution, 380
Exclusionary zoning, see Zoning, this topic
Federal Aid Highway Act, 602–603
Federal Water Pollution Control Act,
   Nonpoint source controls,
      Agricultural lands, 385
      Construction activities, 380
      Flood plain development, 386
      Mining, 388
      Sewer moratoria, 192, 474, 542
      Silviculture, 383
Florida Environmental Land and Water Management Act, 201–02
Growth controls,
   Environmental justifications, 193
   Moratoria, 194, 205

LAND DEVELOPMENT CONTROLS—Cont'd
Growth controls—Cont'd
   Recreational development, 195
   Regulation of nuisance, 189
   State Environmental Policy Acts, 189
   Zoning, see Zoning, this topic
Maine Site Location Act, 199
Mining, water pollution, 388
Noise,
   Federal lands, 604
   HUD assistance guidelines, 600, 603
   State laws, 565, 568
   State environmental policy acts, 601
   Zoning, 600
Phased growth controls, 191
Recreational development, 197
Rivers and Harbors Act, landfill regulation, 645
Sewer moratoria, 192, 474, 542
Silviculture, water pollution, 383
Siting,
   Industrial facilities, 199–201
   Oil terminal facilities, 199
   One-stop, 199–200
   Power plants, 199
Solid waste, landfill site selection, 668, 674–675
Vermont Land Use and Development Act, 197
Washington State Thermal Power Plant Siting Act, 199
Zoning,
   See also Nuisance
   Exclusionary,
      See also National Environmental Policy Act
      Generally, 187–192
      Defined, 191
      Population control, distinguished, 90
      Standard of review, 192
   Generally, 187–191
   Landfills, 675
   Noise, 600
   Nonconforming use, 136
   Regulation of nuisance, 129–130, 205
   Relevance of environmental factors, 188
   Spot zoning, defined, 188
   Standard of review, 191

MARINE PROTECTION, RESEARCH, AND SANCTUARIES ACT
See Ocean Dumping

MICHIGAN ENVIRONMENTAL PROTECTION ACT
   See also Public Trust
   Generally, 184–185

INDEX

References are to Pages

NATIONAL ACADEMY OF SCIENCES
See Advisory Committees

NATIONAL ENVIRONMENTAL POLICY ACT
See also Public Trust
Alternatives,
  Description, defined, 797
  Section 102(2)(E), 724, 795
  Study, defined, 797
Applicability,
  Air pollution, indirect source control, 328
  Dredge and fill operations, 406
  Ocean dumping, 494, 498
  Offshore oil leasing, 514
  Pesticide registration, 861
  Radioactive waste disposal, 691
  Water pollution,
    Effluent standards, 470
    Municipal treatment works, 443
    Nonpoint source control, 379
    NPDES proceedings, 475
    Thermal pollution, 529
Complementary federal laws,
  Procedure,
    Consideration, 826
    Consultation, 826
    General policy directives, 827
    Preparation of reports, 825
    Public hearings, 767, 770, 823–824
    Public notice, 824
    Reasoned decision-making, 825
    Requisite findings, 826
    Solicitation of comments, 824
  Substantive obligations,
    Airport and Airway Development Act, 834
    Atomic Energy Act, 831
    Best technology, 832
    Boundary Waters Canoe Area, 832
    Clean Air Act, 832
    Coastal Zone Management Act, 829
    Cost-benefit analysis, 833
    Deepwater Port Act, 831
    Department of Transportation Act, 833
    Endangered Species Act, 829
    Federal-Aid Highway Act, 833
    Federal Water Pollution Control Act, 832
    Federal Water Project Recreation Act, 828
    Fish and Wildlife Coordination Act, 826, 828
    Hazardous Materials Transportation Act, 832
    Marine Mammal Protection Act, 832

NATIONAL ENVIRONMENTAL POLICY ACT—Cont'd
Complementary federal laws—Cont'd
  Substantive obligations—Cont'd
    Mineral Leasing Act, 831
    Multiple Use-Sustained Yield Act, 830
    National Forest Organic Act, 831
    National Historic Preservation Act, 827
    Noise Control Act, 828–829
    Park Service Organic Act, 828, 829
    Reclamation Act, 832
    Wilderness Act, 828–829
Congress,
  Applicability,
    Proposals for legislation, 714
    Requests for appropriations, 715
  Enforcement, 714
  Legislative modification, 715
Consistency of federal programs, 699, 712
Consultation, agency veto, 729
Continuing responsibility of federal agencies, 698
Council on Environmental Quality,
  Advisory opinions, 707
  Annual report, 702
  Coordination of federal action, 702, 707, 783
  Guidelines for preparation of environmental impact statements,
    Conformity of agency regulations, 706
    Early notice system, 706
    Public disclosure, 706
    Public hearings, 707
    Use in litigation, 705, 708
  Legislative program, 703
  Review of federal programs, 702, 705, 707
  Special reports, 704
Environmental impact statement,
  Actions exempted from EIS requirement, 795
  Adequate statements, 733
  Agency comments, 729
  Content,
    Adverse impacts, social, 188
    Alternatives,
      Concurrent research, 797
      Environmental impact, 793
      In depth analysis, 797
      Long range, 725–728, 793
      No action, 793
      Reason for agency preference, 793
      Reasoned choice, 794
      Rule of reason, 792
      Scope of discussion, 792

INDEX

References are to Pages

NATIONAL ENVIRONMENTAL POLICY ACT—Cont'd
Environmental impact statement—Cont'd
  Content—Cont'd
    Detailed statement, 794
    Reasonable layman standard, 727
  Cost-benefit analysis, 721, 724, 728, 745
  Detailed statement, 725–728, 794
  Economic and technological considerations, 728
  Expert consultation, 729
  Full disclosure, 725–728
  Inadequate statements, 731, 735
  Inclusion of background data, 727
  Method of preparation, 769
  Necessity of preparation,
    See also Timing, this topic
    Actions not requiring statement, 758
    Actions requiring statement, 756
    Exemptions,
      Conflicting statutory mandate, 699, 706, 712, 764
      Environmental Protection Agency, 271, 765
      Environmentally protective actions, 765
      Functional equivalent, 271
      Substantial compliance, 271, 764
    Federal action,
      Actions not sufficiently federal, 763
      Actions sufficiently federal, 762
      Degree of federal involvement, 761, 789
      Nondiscretionary action, 763
    Human environment, defined, 754
    Indicia of necessity, 752
    Major action, defined, 752
    Negative determination,
      Procedure, 755
      Standard of review, 751, 755
    Ongoing actions, 766
    Significant environmental effects, defined, 752
    Standard of review, 751, 755
  Opposing expert opinion, 730
  Programmatic EIS,
    Criteria for need, 786
    Defined, 785
    Subsequent individual statements, 773, 786–787
  Reasoned decision-making, 730
  Responsibility for preparation,
    Delegation to nonfederal authorities,
      Degree of delegation, 778

NATIONAL ENVIRONMENTAL POLICY ACT—Cont'd
Environmental impact statement—Cont'd
  Responsibility for preparation—C't'd
    Delegation to nonfederal authorities—Cont'd
      Extent of federal involvement, 779, 781
      Independent consultant, 779
      Interested party, 778
      Partial delegation, 779
      State agency with statewide jurisdiction, 781
      Total delegation, 782
    Multiple agency actions,
      CEQ coordination, 783
      Independent preparation, 784
      Joint preparation, 783
      Lead agency, 783
  Segmentation,
    Agency discretion, 791
    Defined, 787
    Effect on remedy, 788
    Impermissible segmentation, 789
    Independent significance, 788, 790, 792
    Irreversible or irretrievable commitments, 788
    Nonfederal segments, 789
    Permissible segmentation, 790
  Self-sufficiency, 728
  Timing,
    See also Programmatic EIS, this topic; Segmentation
    Agency discretion, 773
    Agency recommendation, 768
    Defederalization, 776
    Delayed federal involvement, 770, 774
    Draft EIS, 769
    Existing agency procedures, 767, 770
    Prestatement consultation, 769
    Project momentum, 767, 770, 772, 774
    Proposals for action, defined, 767–768, 770, 773
    Research and development programs, 771
    Status quo regulations, 776
    Supplemental EIS, 773
Environmental Protection Agency,
  309 comments,
    Applicability, 219, 709, 714
    Comment classifications, 711
    Procedure, 711
    Referral to CEQ, 710–711
    Use in litigation, 710

NATIONAL ENVIRONMENTAL POLICY ACT—Cont'd
Expansion of agency jurisdiction, 700
Guidelines for preparation of impact statements,
    Generally, 705–708
  Use in litigation, 705, 708
National policy, 697, 701
Noise,
  Aircraft emission standards, 586, 593
  Airports,
    Airport and Airway Development Act, 614
    Alternatives, 614
    Construction grants program, 611
    Injunction of nonfederal activities, 613
    Reasonable layman standard, 614
    Responsibility for preparation, 613
    Timing, 612
  Highways, 615
Office of Management and Budget, 705, 714
Preservation of existing obligations, 701
Private right to healthful environment, 701
Procedure,
  Cooperation with CEQ, 725
  Direct statutory conflict, 718
  Disclosure of information, 724
  Environmental research, 722
  Expert consultation, 720
  Follow up assessment, 723
  Interdisciplinary analysis, 719
  Long-range consequences, 722
  Mandatory compliance, 718
  Mitigation, 722, 724, 748
  Monitoring, 723
  Public hearings, 718, 721
  Public notice, 718
  Quantification of environmental costs, 721, 723
  Supplemental EIS, 725, 728
  Solicitation of comments, 720
  State of the art, 722–723, 748
  Worldwide consequences, 722
Remedy,
  Consent decrees, 806
  Defenses, 808
  Enjoining nonfederal activities, 775–776
  Injunction,
    Grounds for denial of relief, 800
    Grounds for relief,
      Balancing of equities, 799
      Violation of statute, 798

NATIONAL ENVIRONMENTAL POLICY ACT—Cont'd
Remedy—Cont'd
  Injunction—Cont'd
    Procedural defects, 804
    Project momentum, 799, 801, 803
    Restoration, 803
    Scope of relief,
      Generally, 800–802
      Nonfederal parties, 807
      Substantive modification, 805
  Monetary damage, 142
  Procedure,
    Bonds, 806
    Consolidated hearings, 807
    Continuing jurisdiction, 805, 807
Research obligations, 797
State environmental policy acts,
  Applicability,
    Actions requiring statements, 814
    Incidental government action, 813
    Limited actions, 811
    Local agencies, 811
    Nondiscretionary action, 816
    State action, defined, 812
  Comprehensive SEPA's, 810
  Content,
    Cost-benefit analysis, 818
    Mitigation, 818
    No action, 818
    Socio-economic impacts, 815
  Environment, defined, 815
  Judicial review,
    Pendent federal jurisdiction, 821
    Scope of review, 820
  Land use control, 189, 201
  Oversight authorities, 819
  Procedure,
    Hearings, 819
    Public notice, 818
    Solicitation of comments, 819
  Responsibility for preparation, state-federal action, 816
  Special SEPA's, 810
  Substantive obligations,
    Cost-benefit analysis, 822
    Maximum mitigation, 822
Substantive obligations,
  Adequate margin of safety, 743
  Best technology, 742, 747
  Cost-benefit analysis, 724, 744–745
    Generally, 717, 724
  Land use accommodation, 743

INDEX

References are to Pages

NATIONAL ENVIRONMENTAL POLICY ACT—Cont'd
Substantive obligations—Cont'd
  Maximum mitigation,
    Generally, 724, 744, 747–749
    Concurrent implementation, 749
    State of the art, 748
  Nondegradation, 748
Supplement to existing authority, 699, 706, 712

NEGLIGENCE
Hazardous waste, 692
Pesticides,
  Customary use, insect control handbooks, 843
  Defenses,
    Assumption of the risk, 843
    Cause in fact, 843
    Contributory negligence, 843
  Federal indemnity programs, 845
  Governmental liability, 844.
  Per se,
    Use contrary to label, 842
    Violation of statute, 842
  Products liability, 844
  Strict liability, 842, 844

NOISE POLLUTION
See also National Environmental Policy Act; Nuisance; Taking
Airport and Airway Development Act, airport environments, 598
Airports, see Land Development Controls
Community noise equivalent level, defined, 596–597
Defined, 551
Effective perceived noise level, defined, 590
Federal Aviation Act, see Noise Control Act, Aircraft, this topic
Impact, 552
Impulsive sound, defined, 567
Indirect sources, defined, 558
Local law,
  Aircraft,
    Land use regulation, 596
    Operational controls, 595, 597
  Nontransportation sources,
    Ambient standards, 574
    Land use regulation, 573
    Noise sensitive areas, 574
    Nuisance, 574
    Performance standards, 573
Measuring methodology,
  Generally, 551
  A-scale, 552

NOISE POLLUTION—Cont'd
Motorcycles, 605
National Environmental Policy Act, EPA oversight, 557
Noise Control Act,
  Aircraft,
    Airport noise report, 586
    Certificate of convenience and necessity, 593
    Curfew, 592, 595
    Economic and technological feasibility, 584
    Emission standards, 584
    EPA consultation, 586
    Exemptions, EPA approval, 585
    Existing sources,
      Economic and technological feasibility, 591
      Fleet noise level, 590
      Retrofit, 589
    Keep 'em high, 591
    New sources,
      Applicability, 588
      Criteria levels, 588
      Exemptions, 588
      Minimum noise floor, 588
      Test methodology, 587, 590, 596–597
      Type certification, 587
    Operational controls, 591–597
    Operations specifications, 592
    Preemption, 594–597
    Preparation of environmental impact statement, 586
    Procedure, 586
    Sonic boom, 591
    Type certification,
      Compliance as condition of issuance, 585, 587
      Defined, 584
Control techniques documents, 554
Criteria documents, 554
Enforcement, 556
Environmental noise, defined, 572
EPA oversight, 557
Major source, identification, 555
Motor vehicle emission standards,
  Best available technology, 607, 608
  Economic and technological feasibility, 607
  Enforcement, 609, 611
  Exemptions, 608
  Motor carriers, 610
  Preemption, 607, 609
  Railroads, 607
National policy, 585

NOISE POLLUTION—Cont'd
Noise sensitive areas, 574, 604
  Nontransportation sources,
    Emission standards,
      Consistency with federal laws, 569
      Criteria, 569
      Defined, 551
      Discretionary regulation, 569
      Economic and technological feasibility, 569, 570
      Enforcement, 571
      Major noise sources, 568, 570
      Mandatory regulation, 568
      Performance standards, 570
      Preemption, 571–572
      Procedure, 570
      Product warranty, 571
    Labeling, 568
  Sanctions, 556
  Standards,
    Adoption procedure, 555
    Exemptions, 556
    Federal programs, consistency with, 556
  Substantive obligations, 829
Occupational,
  Occupational Safety and Health Act,
    Economic and technological feasibility, 618
    Noise study, 617
    Proposed regulations, 617
    Source control, 618
  Operational or source controls, 616–618
  Walsh-Healy Public Contracts Act, 616
Pure tones, defined, 567
Single event noise exposure level, defined, 597
Snowmobiles, 606
State law,
  Motor vehicles,
    Emission standards, 605
    Enforcement, 606, 609, 611
    Mufflers, 604
  Nontransportation sources,
    Ambient standards, 564
    Economic and technological feasibility, 567
    Land use restrictions, 565
    Model community noise ordinance, 565
    Noise disturbance, defined, 566
    Property-line noise source,
      Generally, 565
      Defined, 566

NOISE POLLUTION—Cont'd
State law—Cont'd
  Nontransportation sources—Cont'd
    Public nuisance, 565, 567
    Source regulation, 564
  Transportation sources, defined, 551
  Trucks, 610

NOISE POLLUTION CONTROL ACT
See Noise Pollution

NONDEGRADATION
Clean Air Act, 208, 236, 280–286
Endangered Species Act, 830
Federal reserved rights doctrine, 340
Federal Water Pollution Control Act, 208, 360, 417, 467, 471, 500
National Environmental Policy Act, 743
Noise Control Act, 585
Public trust, 181, 186
Riparian rights, 164
Rivers and Harbors Act, 359

NUISANCE
  See also Strict Liability; Taking
Abnormally dangerous activities,
  Generally, 161–163
  Common usage, defined, 161
Aircraft, 575, 579
Balancing,
  Extent of harm,
    Generally, 113–114
    Permanence of injury, 115
    Social, 116
    Threat of future injury, 114
  Utility of defendant's conduct, 119
Burden of proof, 126, 141
Coming to the nuisance, 132
Defenses,
  Avoidable consequences rule, 148
  Cause in fact, 136
  Contributory negligence, 134
  Estoppel, 134–135
  Laches, 135
  Prescriptive rights, 135
Effect of statute,
  Implied remedies, 142
  Preemption,
    Generally, 137
    Land use and technological regulations, distinguished, 139
  Violation of standards, 141
  Zoning, nonconforming use, 136
Federal common law,
  Availability, 151
  Interstate air pollution, 253
  Preemption, 153

INDEX

References are to Pages

NUISANCE—Cont'd
Federal common law—Cont'd
  Scope, 152
  Source, 150
In fact, defined, 129
Land use regulation, 189
Legalized nuisance,
  Landfills, 625
  Noise, 576, 581
Legislation, impact on nuisance law, 136–142, 560
Liability,
  Abnormally dangerous activities, 108
  Balancing of interests, 110, 117
  Extent of harm,
    Generally, 109
    Effect of zoning, 129
    Hypersensitive plaintiff, 112
    Objective standard, 112
    Priority of use, 132
National Environmental Policy Act, indicators of decision compared, 733
Noise,
  Airport operator liability, 576, 580
  Defenses, 563
  Nontransportation sources,
    Balancing, 560
    Best technology, 560
    Character of neighborhood, 561
    Defenses, 563
    Economic and technological feasibility, 563
    Effect of statute, 560
    Motive, 560
    Priority of use, 561
    Remedy,
      Damages, 562
      Injunction, 561
  Public nuisance 574, 604
  Railroads, 581
Per se, defined, 129, 136
Permanent and temporary distinguished, 127–128
Private, defined, 107
Protected interests, 108
Public,
  See also Public Trust
  Criminal, 103
  Defined, 102
  Different injury requirement, 104
  Distinguished from private nuisance, 102
  Scope, 106
  Standing, 106, 582
  Statutory,
    Landfills, 626, 666
    Noise, 565, 567, 574, 604

NUISANCE—Cont'd
Reciprocal nature of pollution, 143–144
Remedy,
    Generally, 180, 267
  Best technology,
    Defined, 124
    Research and development, 126
    State of the art, 122
  Effect of statute, 140
  Land use accommodation,
    As supplement to zoning, 130
    Generally, 125, 144
    Shutdown, 128
  Measure of damages, 144–145
  Monetary damages,
    Generally, 127, 144
    Property,
      Permanent, 144
      Temporary, 145
    Proximate cause limitations, 147
    Special damages,
      Economic loss, 146
      Emotional injury, 146
      Health, 146
  Operational controls,
    Generally, 122, 149
    Noise, 562, 575, 591–97
    Solid waste, 624–625
  Permanent and temporary injury,
    Availability of controls, 127
    Distinguished, 127
  Research and development, 150
  Use of special masters, 149
  Utility of defendant's conduct, 120
Social, distinguished from technological nuisance, 116
Solid waste,
  Balancing, 623
  Best technology, 624
  Defenses, 626
  Legalized nuisance, 625
  Operational controls, 625
  Priority of use, 624
  Public nuisance, 626
  Remedies, 625–626
Statutory regulation, taking, 133
Substantial harm, 107
Trespass, distinguished, 154

OCEAN DUMPING
Coast Guard, 498
Dredged material,
  Defined, 489
  Economic and technological feasibility, 491
  EPA veto, 491
  Procedure, 490
  Waiver, 491

OCEAN DUMPING—Cont'd
Dumping, defined, 489
Exemptions, 489
Marine sanctuary, defined, 489
Material, defined, 489
Nondredged material,
   Criteria, 493
   Economic and technological feasibility, 493, 495, 497
Ocean water, defined, 489
Permit,
   Generally, 489
   Contents, 495
   Emergency, 494
   Interim, 494
   Research, 495
   Special, 494
Preemption, 497
Preparation of environmental impact statement, 494, 497
Procedure, 492
Prohibited activity, 489
Regulated activities, 489
Sanctions, 498
Site designation, 496
Variance, 494

OIL POLLUTION
Cleanup, strict liability for costs, 512, 514, 521–523
Coast Guard, 507
Federal Water Pollution Control Act,
   Discharge, defined, 500
   Duty to notify, 501, 503
   Enforcement,
      Criteria for discretionary sanctions, 502
      Elements of offense, 502
      Procedure, 502
   Exemptions, 501
   Hazardous substances, defined, 506
   Liability for cleanup costs,
      Exemptions, 505, 510
      Willful misconduct, 506
   Mandatory sanctions, 501
   National Contingency Plan, 505
   No discharge, 500
   Oil, defined, 500
   Sheen test, 499
   Use immunity, 504
Load-on-top, 256, 509
Offshore drilling,
   Lease conditions, 514
   Outer continental shelf, defined, 513
   Outer Continental Shelf Lands Act, 413–414
   Strict liability, 514

OIL POLLUTION—Cont'd
Offshore drilling—Cont'd
   Submerged Lands Act, 513
   U.S. Geological Survey, 513
Oil Pollution Act of 1924, 500, 507
Private compensation,
   Deepwater port liability fund, 521
   Federal admiralty jurisdiction, 518
      Choice of law, 519
      Limited liability, 519
      Preemption, 519
      Strict liability, 519, 521
   International law,
      Convention on Civil Liability for Oil Pollution Damage, 523
      Convention on the Establishment of an International Fund for Oil Pollution Damage, 523
      CRISTAL, 524
      Preemption of national law, 523
      Strict liability, 523
      TOVALOP, 524
   State law,
      Liability funds, 522
      Strict liability, 522
      Vicarious liability, 523
Trans-Alaska pipeline liability fund, 521
Tanker regulation,
   Convention for the Prevention of Pollution by Ships, 515
   Convention for the Prevention of Pollution of the Sea by Oil, 515
   Deepwater Port Act,
      Deepwater port, defined, 512
      Operational controls, 512
      Permit, criteria, 512
      Strict liability, 512, 521
   International Governmental Maritime Consultative Organization, 515, 523
   Merchant Marine Act, 511
   Ports and Waterways Safety Act,
      Operational controls, 256, 509
      Technological controls, 509
      Traffic control, 509
   Preemption of state law, 516
   State law, burden on interstate commerce, 516
   Washington Tanker Act, 516

PESTICIDES
See also Negligence
Alternatives,
   Biological control, 839
   Cultural control, 839

INDEX

References are to Pages

PESTICIDES—Cont'd
Alternatives—Cont'd
  Integrated pest management, 839
  Narrow spectrum pesticides, 838
Cost-benefit analysis, 840, 858, 875, 885
DDT, 840
Defined, 835, 856
Defoliant, defined, 835
Dessicant, defined, 835
Economic significance, 835, 837
Federal Insecticide, Fungicide, and Rodenticide Act,
  Adulteration, defined, 850
  Cancellation,
    See also Suspension, this topic
    Adjudicatory hearing, 887
    Consultation, 886
    Cost-benefit analysis, 885
    Criteria, 879
    Economic impact analysis, 885
    Imminent hazard, 886
    Procedure, generally, 851
    Scientific referral, 886
    Use momentum, 879
  Classification,
    Certified applicator,
      Defined, 850, 865
      Self-certification, 855, 866
      State plans, 866–867
    Change of, 879
    General use,
      Criteria, 864
      Defined, 850
      Labeling, 850
    Restricted use,
      Criteria, 864
      Defined, 850
    Supervised use, defined, 865
    Use, defined, 863
  Consultation procedures, 854
  Disposal of containers and banned pesticides, 852
  Economic poison, defined, 847
  Efficacy, defined, 850
  Enforcement,
    Adulteration, 895
    Delegation to states, 851
    Imports, 852
    Indemnity, 896
    Inspection, 893
    Letter of warning, 895
    Misbranding, 895
    Misuse, 894, 898
    Prohibited activities, 852, 894
    Record keeping, 851, 893

PESTICIDES—Cont'd
Federal Insecticide, Fungicide, and Rodenticide Act—Cont'd
  Enforcement—Cont'd
    Sanctions,
      Civil penalty, 851, 896
      Court costs, 895
      Criminal, 895
      Criteria for assessing fines, 897
    Seizure, 851, 894–895
    Stop orders, 851, 895
    Strict liability, 897
  Exemptions,
    Adequate federal regulation, 878
    Emergency use,
      Cost-benefit analysis, 875
      Crisis exemption, 875–876
      Defined, 850, 856
      Emergency condition, defined, 874
      Preparation of EIS, 875
      Procedure, 875
      Quarantine exemption, 875
      Specific exemption, 875
    Experimental use,
      Defined, 850, 856
      Delegation to states, 873
      Permissible purposes, 871, 874
      Permit conditions, 872
      Preparation of EIS, 873
      Procedure, 872–873
      Public hearings, 873
    Exports, 852, 878
    Insignificant pesticide, 850, 879
    Special local needs,
      Criteria, 877
      Defined, 850, 877
      Procedure, 877
    Transfer between registered establishments, 850, 878
  Identification of highly toxic pesticides, 853
  Labeling,
    See also Misbranding, this topic
    Adequacy, 870
    Criteria, 869
    Data submissions, 870
    Defined, 847, 868
    Directions for use, 869
    Highly toxic substances, 870
    Ingredient statement, 870
    Procedure, 869
    Warnings, 869
  Legislative history, 846–848
  Misbranding,
    Defined, 847, 850
    Highly toxic pesticides, 853
    Per se, 853, 870, 895

INDEX
References are to Pages

PESTICIDES—Cont'd
Federal Insecticide, Fungicide, and Rodenticide Act—Cont'd
  Misuse, 859, 864, 868, 894
  Pest,
    Defined, 835
      Administrative declaration, 852
  Protest registration, 848
  Registration,
      See also Cancellation; Classification; Exemptions; Suspension
    Adequacy of label, 850, 858
    Amended registration, 862
    As condition for distribution, 857
    Balancing, 858
    Burden of proof, 861
    Cost-benefit analysis, 858
    Criteria, 850, 858–860
    Data submission,
      Cost sharing, 856, 862
      Requirements, 860, 870
    Disclosure of data, 861
    Efficacy, 850, 858
    Establishment of residue tolerance limitation, 856, 889
    Lack of essentiality, 859
    Mandatory five year termination, 862
    Nontarget species, 859, 861
    Performance of intended function, 859
    Preparation of EIS, 861
    Procedure, 861–862
    Public notice, 861
    Rebuttable presumption against registration, 861
    Renewal, 862
    Reregistration, 862
    Supplemental registration, 862
    Test methodology, 861
    Unreasonable environmental effects, 858
    Widespread and commonly recognized practice, defined, 860
  Registration of production facilities, 851
  Residue tolerances, see Food, Drug, and Cosmetic Act
  Suspension,
      See also Cancellation
    Generally, 879
    Emergency procedure, 880
    Expedited hearing, 880
    Imminent hazard, defined, 880
    Procedure, 851

PESTICIDES—Cont'd
Food, Drug and Cosmetic Act,
  Residue tolerance limitation,
    Adulterated, defined, 892
    As condition of registration, 856, 889
    Carcinogenic residue, 891
    Criteria, 848, 890
    Data submission, 848, 891
    Defined, 848, 888
    Enforcement procedures, 888
    Estimated average daily intake, 891
    Exemptions, 890
    Fragmentation of authority, 888
    Interim tolerance, 891
    Procedure, 889
    Seizure, 893
    Surveillance, 892
    Test methodology, 891
    Unsafe food additive, defined, 893
    Zero tolerance, 890–891
Fungicide, defined, 835
Herbicide, defined, 835
Impact, 836, 839
Insecticide, defined, 835
Integrated pest management, defined, 839
MDS, 888
Miticide, defined, 835
Nematocide, defined, 835
Occupational Safety and Health Act, 856
Operational controls, 838
Pest, defined, 835
Plant regulator, defined, 835
Poison Prevention Packaging Act, 856
Premarket safety research, 837
Product ban, 838
Rodenticide, defined, 835

POLLUTION
Defined, 2
Naturally induced, 4

POPULATION CONTROL
Abortion, 95
Comstock laws, 92
Contraception, 94
Defined, 90
Family planning, 93
Foreign aid, 91
National Environmental Policy Act, discussion in impact statement, 795
Sterilization,
  Involuntary, 98
  Voluntary, 97
Technology control, distinguished, 90

INDEX

References are to Pages

PREEMPTION
Clean Air Act, 216
Distinction between source and operational regulation, noise pollution, 571–572
Energy Policy and Conservation Act,
  Auto fuel economy standard, 657
  Consumer products standards, 660
Federal common law of nuisance, 153
Noise Control Act,
  Aircraft, 594–597
  Motor vehicle emission standards, 607, 609
  Nontransportation source emission standards, 571–572
  Railroad noise regulations, 607
  Railroad noise standards, 608
Ocean dumping, 497
Oil pollution, private compensation, 519
Oil tanker regulation, 516
Toxic Substances Control Act, 907

PRIOR APPROPRIATION
See Water Law

PUBLIC TRUST
  See also Judicial Review, Close Scrutiny
Burden of proof, 177, 185
Change of use,
  Legislative findings, 178
  Presumption of continuation of use, 178
Context of application, 175–177
Delegation of authority, limitation of, 179
Michigan Environmental Protection Act, 184
Oil pollution damage, 522
Park Service Organic Act, 828
Procedure,
  Compared with NEPA, 177–178
  Requirements, 177
  Statutory modifications, 184
Public nuisance, compared, 173
Scope of application,
  Generally, 172
  Public uses, 174
  State constitutional modification, 182
Standing, 177
Statutory enlargement, 173
Substantive obligations,
  Generally, 175
  Maximum mitigation, 180
  Nondegradation, 181, 186
  State constitutional provisions, 183
  Statutory modification, 185
  Unreasonable interference, 180
  Use allocation, 181

PUBLIC TRUST—Cont'd
Use in litigation, 175

RECREATIONAL DEVELOPMENT
See Land Development Controls

RESOURCE CONSERVATION AND RECOVERY ACT
See Solid Waste

RETROFIT
Clean Air Act, automobiles, 316
Energy Policy and Conservation Act, automobile fuel economy, 657
Noise Control Act, aircraft, 589

RIPARIAN RIGHTS
See Water Law

RIVERS AND HARBORS ACT
See Dredge and Fill; Water Pollution

SAFE DRINKING WATER ACT
See Groundwater

SOLID WASTE
  See also Dredge and Fill; Nuisance
Automobile hulks,
  Abandonment,
    Abandoned vehicle, defined, 682
    Bounty payments, 681
    Criminal penalties, 680
    Due process limitations, 681
    Impoundment, 681
    Presumption of abandonment, 682
    Revolving fund, 683
    Strict liability for disposal costs, 680
    Vehicle registration, 680
  Impact, 679
  Recycling,
    Economic and technological feasibility, 679
    Environmental tradeoffs, 680
    Resource Recovery Act, 679
Bailing, defined, 674
Bulk consumer goods,
  Collection, 684
  Impact, 683
  Recycling, economic and technological feasibility, 684
  Segregated disposal, 684
Defined, 619, 628
Energy Policy and Conservation Act,
  Automobile fuel economy,
    Defined, 655
    Exemptions, 655
    Labeling, 656
    Modification, 656
    Preemption, 657

INDEX

References are to Pages

SOLID WASTE—Cont'd
Energy Policy and Conservation Act
—Cont'd
  Automobile fuel economy—Cont'd
    Reasonable selected technology, defined, 655
    Report, 654
    Research and development, 657
    Retrofit, 657
    Sanctions, 657
    Standards, 654
    Test methodology, 655
  Consumer products,
    Covered product, defined, 658
    Economic and technological feasibility, 659
    Energy efficiency standards, 659
    Improvement target, 659
    Labeling, 658, 660
    Preemption, 660
    Reports, 659, 660
    Sanctions, 660
    Test methodology, 658
  Federal energy conservation programs,
    Building renovation, 663
    Procurement practices, 663
    Public education, 664
  Federal Trade Commission, 652
  Industrial energy conservation,
    Annual reports, 661
    Economic and technological feasibility, 661
    Priority ranking, 661
    Voluntary energy efficiency improvement targets, 661
  Recycled oil, 652
    Substitute equivalency, 652
  State energy conservation plan,
    Content, 662
    Eligibility for federal funding, 662
    Emergency standby plans, 663
    Energy conservation feasibility report, 662
    Federal assistance, 663
Federal tax policies,
  Depletion allowance, 649
  Investment credit, pollution control facilities, 650
  Municipal bonds, 650
  Virgin materials capital gains, 649
Federal Water Pollution Control Act, 645
Freight rate regulation,
  Federal Maritime Commission, 650
  Interstate Commerce Commission, 651

SOLID WASTE—Cont'd
Hazardous waste,
  See also Solid Waste Disposal Act, this topic
  Defined, 689, 693
  Impact, 690
  Incidental federal legislation, 691
  Pesticides, 852
  State law,
    Comprehensive hazardous waste management programs, 692
    Designated landfill, 693
    Haulers permits, 692
    Negligence, 692
    Processing and disposal regulation, 693
    Strict liability, 692
  State of the art, 689
Impact, 620, 645–646
Import prohibitions, burden on commerce, 667
Local law,
  Collection and disposal, 673
  Landfill,
    Health code regulations, 676
    Operational controls, 675–677
    Site selection, 674
  Nonreturnable beverage containers, 677
  Receptacle regulations, 676
  Source separation, 676, 678
National Materials Policy Act, 634
Nonreturnable beverage containers,
  Anti-litter laws, 685
  Federal guidelines, 688
  Impact, 685
  Litter assessment tax, 672, 686
  Mandatory deposit, 687
  Premarket clearance, 672, 686
  Prohibition, 686
  Recycling, 685
Nuisance related theories, 626
Postconsumer waste, defined, 647
Procurement policies, affecting, 646
Recycled material,
  Defined, 647
  Federal procurement, 648
Recycling,
  Automobile hulks, 679–680
  Beverage containers, 684–685
  Bulk consumer goods, 684
  Oil, 652
  Paper, 647
Resource Conservation and Recovery Act, 635
Resource recovery,
  Chemical conversion, 622

INDEX

SOLID WASTE—Cont'd
Resource recovery—Cont'd
  Composting, 621
  Defined, 619
  Economic and technological feasibility, 622, 626
  Energy recovery, 622
  Heat recovery, 622
  Materials recovery, 622
  Pyrolysis, 622
  Recycling, 619, 647, 652, 679–680, 684–685
  Reuse, 619
Resource Recovery Act, 629
Rivers and Harbors Act, 645–646
Sanitary landfill, defined, 625, 640
Shredding, defined, 674
Solid Waste Disposal Act,
  Annual reports, 633
  Demonstration grants,
    Consistency with state plan, 630
    Procedure, 628, 630
  Disposal and collection, 643
  Economic and technological feasibility,
    Disposal and collection, 643
    Federal facilities, 643
    Source separation, 644
  Federal facilities,
    Applicability of guidelines, 638, 642
    Economic and technological feasibility, 643
    Impact, 638
    Presidential exemption, 640, 642
    Sovereign immunity, waiver of, 639
  Federal procurement
    Contractor's warranty, 649
    Department of Defense, 648
    General Services Administration, 647
    Paper specifications, 647
    Recycled material, 648
  Grants, 628–632
  Guidelines,
    Applicability, 638, 640, 643
    Disposal and collection, 640–643
    Federal procurement, 646–649
    Nonreturnable beverage containers, 688
    Solid waste management, 638–640
    Source separation, 643–646
  Hazardous wastes,
    Criteria for designation, 694
    Defined, 694
    Enforcement, delegation to states, 695
    Permit regulations, 695
    Studies, 632

SOLID WASTE—Cont'd
Solid Waste Disposal Act—Cont'd
  Legislative history, 627–635
  Management system, defined, 664, 677
  National Commission on Materials Policy, 634
  Open dumps,
    Indentification, 638
    Prohibition, 635
  Recovered resources, defined, 629
  Resource conservation, defined, 629
  Resource recovery facility, defined, 643
  Resource recovery system, defined, 629
  Sanitary landfill, defined, 640
  Solid waste, defined, 628
  Solid waste disposal, defined, 628
  Solid waste management, defined, 619, 638
  Solid waste survey, 628–629
  Source separation, defined, 644
  State plans,
    Generally, 629, 635–637
    Adoption, 636
    Implementation, 637
  Studies, hazardous wastes, 632
  Variance, 666
  Volume reduction plant, defined, 665
State law,
  Fragmentation of authority, 664
  Freight rates, 673
  Landfill regulation, 665
  Nonreturnable beverage containers, 672, 685–687
  Preemption of local control, 667
  Public nuisance, 665
  Residential and commercial waste,
    California Solid Waste Management and Resource Recovery Act, 670
    Disposal charges, 666
    Enforcement, 666, 669
    Interstate importation, 667
    Operational controls, 665
  Resource recovery,
    Declarations of policy, 671
    Necessity of federal assistance, 673
    Statewide solid waste and resource recovery plans, 671
  Sanitary landfill criteria, 666
  Solid waste management plans, 669
  Variances, 666
Tax policies, affecting, 649
Transfer station, defined, 674

INDEX

SOLID WASTE—Cont'd
Water pollution,
  Dredge and fill, 646
  Leachate, 641, 645
  Runoff, 645

SOLID WASTE DISPOSAL ACT
See Solid Waste

SOVEREIGN IMMUNITY
Aircraft noise, taking, 575
Clean Air Act, federal facilities, 352
Committed to agency discretion, 32
Exceptions, 30
Federal Tort Claims Act,
  Discretionary function, 36
  Misrepresentation, 38
  Negligent or wrongful act, 37
  Pesticide application, 844
  Strict liability, 38
Federal Water Pollution Control Act,
  federal facilities, 544
Money damages, see Federal Tort Claims Act
Noise pollution, 575, 577, 580
Solid waste, landfill operators, 626
Solid Waste Disposal Act,
  Federal facilities, 636, 639
  Landfills, 626
Waiver,
  Administrative Procedure Act, 31
  Federal Tort Claims Act, 36

STANDING
Citizen suits, 76
Injury in fact,
  Denial of information, 25
  Users, 24, 26, 28
Nuisance, money damages, 106
Public nuisance,
    Generally, 105
  Noise, 582
Public trust, 177
Zone of interest, 29

STATE ENVIRONMENTAL POLICY ACTS
See National Environmental Policy Act

STRICT LIABILITY
Abandoned vehicle disposal costs, 680
Abnormally dangerous activities, 159
Deepwater Port Act, 512, 521
Federal Insecticide, Fungicide, and Rodenticide Act, 897
Federal Water Pollution Control Act, 539
Hazardous wastes, 692

STRICT LIABILITY—Cont'd
Nuisance, compared, 160
Oil pollution,
  Cleanup, 512, 514, 519, 521–523
  Offshore drilling, 514
Price-Anderson Act, 163
Rivers and Harbors Act, 393

TAKING
Balancing of interests, 205
Basic theories, 203–207
Diminution of value, 205–206
Inverse condemnation,
  Aircraft noise,
    Direct overflight rule, 578
    Injunction against public operator, 577
    Trespass, 578
  Balancing, 577
  Damages, 576–577
  Elements, 575–576
  Landfills, 675
  Physical appropriation rule, 582
  Public highways, 582
  Relationship to nuisance, 576
Land use regulation, moratoria, 205
Nuisance theory, priority of use, 133
Offshore oil, lease suspension, 514
Public trust, protection of, 176, 206
Regulation of nuisance, 205

TECHNOLOGY ASSESSMENT
  See also Best Technology; Cost-Benefit Analysis; Test Methodologies
Abnormally dangerous activities, 161
Adequate margin of safety,
  Clean Air Act, ambient air quality standards, 226, 260
  Federal Insecticide, Fungicide, and Rodenticide Act, pesticide safety, 853
  Federal Water Pollution Control Act,
    Toxic pollutants, 484
    Water quality criteria, 422
  National Environmental Policy Act, 743
Air Quality Act, 212
Clean Air Act,
  Adoption of state implementation plans, 260, 262
  Appellate review, 263
  Approval of state implementation plans, 261
  Automobile emissions, 289, 295
  Control techniques documents, 212, 223
  Emission control strategy, 260
  Hazardous pollutants, 277

INDEX

TECHNOLOGY ASSESSMENT—Cont'd
Clean Air Act—Cont'd
  Mobile sources, warranty testing procedures, 303
  New source performance standards, 267, 270–272
  Prevention of significant deterioration, 284, 286
  Promulgation of ambient air quality standards, 260
  Variances, 264
Defined, 11
Energy Policy and Conservation Act,
  Automobile fuel economy standards, 655–656
  Energy efficiency improvement targets, 660
  Energy efficiency standards, 660
Federal Water Pollution Control Act,
  Existing industrial sources, 464
  Low-flow augmentation, 450
  Municipal treatment works, 442, 445–448
  New industrial sources, 467–468
  NPDES permit proceedings, 456, 458–459
  Planning, 424–434
  Pretreatment standards, 479
  Regional plans, 433
  Research and development studies, 362–364
  Toxic pollutants, 483–485
  Water quality related effluent limitations, 423
  Water quality standards, 418, 422
Input-output analysis, defined, 7
Legislation, 13
Modeling,
  Clean Air Act, 237
  Defined, 8
National Academy of Sciences, generally, 12
National Environmental Policy Act, research and development programs, 771
Noise Control Act,
  Aircraft emission standards, 584, 591
  Control techniques document, 554
  Motor vehicle emission standards, 607–608
  Nontransportation source emission standards, 569–670
Occupational Safety and Health Act, noise regulation, 618
Ocean dumping, 491, 493, 495–497
Office of Technology Assessment, 11

TECHNOLOGY ASSESSMENT—Cont'd
Public trust, 180
Quality of life, defined, 9
Scope, 14
Solid Waste Disposal Act,
  Federal facilities, 643
  Source separation, 644
Systems analysis,
  Defined, 8
  National Environmental Policy Act, 717, 719
Total energy concept, defined, 7
Toxic Substances Control Act, 898, 906

TEST METHODOLOGY
Aircraft noise, 597, 599
Automobile fuel economy standards, 655
Clean Air Act,
  Fuel additives, 331
  Mobile source certificate of conformity, 305
  Opacity, 338
  Ringelmann chart, 339
Federal Water Pollution Control Act,
  Averaging, 462
  Composite samples, 461
  Grab sample, 462
  Sheen test, 499
Food, Drug, and Cosmetic Act, pesticide residue tolerance limitations, 891
Highway noise standards, 603
Noise pollution,
  Aircraft emission standards, 587
  Generally, 551–553
Pesticide registration, 861

THERMAL POLLUTION
Atomic Energy Act, 529
Blowdown, defined, 527
Closed cycle, 526
Control techniques, 526
Defined, 524
Federal Water Pollution Control Act,
  Best technology, 533
  Mixing zone, defined, 531
  Necessity, 533
  Point source effluent limitation, 531
  Variance, 532
  Water quality criteria, 530
Impact, 525
Mitigation processes, 526
National Environmental Policy Act, 529
Nuclear Regulatory Commission, 529
Once through, 526
Riparian rights, 527
Rivers and Harbors Act, 528

INDEX

References are to Pages

TOXIC SUBSTANCES
Asbestos, hazardous emission standards, 278
Beryllium, hazardous emission standards, 278
Clean Air Act, emission standards, 276–279
Federal Insecticide, Fungicide, and Rodenticide Act, declaration of toxic pesticide, 853
Federal Water Pollution Control Act, toxic pollutants, 481, 506
Impact, 899
Mercury, hazardous emission standards, 279
Solid Waste Disposal Act, hazardous wastes, 689–696
Toxic Substance Control Act,
  Annual reports, 908
  Chemical substance,
    Defined, 899
    Listing, 899
  Citizen suits, 901, 903, 906
  Civil penalty, 907
  Existing chemical substance,
    Data submission, 904
    Defined, 901
    Imminent hazard, defined, 903
    PCB, 901
    Priority substances, 905
    Regulation,
      Cost-benefit analysis, 903
      Criteria, 902
      Procedure 903
  Health and safety study, defined, 904
  Mandatory reporting of violations, 906
  New chemical substance,
    Adequacy of data, 900
    Defined, 899
    Interim restrictions, 900
    Premarket notification, 899
    Significant new use defined, 900
    Submission of data, 900
  Preemption, 907
  Prohibited activities, 907
  Research and development programs, 906
  Seizure, 907

TOXIC SUBSTANCES CONTROL ACT
See Toxic Substances

TRESPASS
Burden of proof, 155–156
Direct and immediate impact, 156–157
Noise, aircraft, 575
Nuisance, distinguished, 154

TRESPASS—Cont'd
Physical invasion, 156
Remedy,
  Equitable, 156, 158
  Monetary damages, 157

VARIANCES
Clean Air Act, administrative enforcement orders, 345
Federal Insecticide, Fungicide, and Rodenticide Act, 871
Federal, Water Pollution Control Act, 457–459, 532
Ocean dumping, 494
Solid Waste Disposal Act, 666

WATER LAW
Federal reserved rights doctrine, groundwater, 370
Navigable waters,
  Basin, defined, 430
  Dredge and fill, 401–403
  Federal Water Pollution Control Act, 461
  Mean high tide line, defined, 391
  Mean higher high water, defined, 401
  Rivers and Harbors Act, 390–392
  Territorial seas, defined, 402
  Tributaries, 392
Prior appropriation,
  Appropriation, defined, 169
  Beneficial use, 168
  Defined, 168
  Pollution abatement, 170
Riparian rights,
  Grounds for relief, 167
  Lake, defined, 163
  Natural flow doctrine, 164
  Nuisance, compared, 163–169
  Reasonable use, 164
  Riparian land, defined, 164
  Riparian proprietor, defined, 163
  Thermal pollution, 527
  Watercourse, defined, 163

WATER POLLUTION
See also Dredge and Fill; Groundwater; Ocean Dumping; Oil Pollution; Thermal Pollution
Effluent standards,
  Averaging, 462
  Defined, 356
Federal multipurpose water projects, 448–450
Federal reserved rights doctrine, groundwater, 390
Federal Water Pollution Control Act,
  Annual reports, 378

INDEX

WATER POLLUTION—Cont'd
Federal Water Pollution Control Act—Cont'd
  Construction grant program, see Municipal treatment works, this topic
  Criteria documents, 363, 422
  Discharge of pollutant, defined, 377
  Economic and technological feasibility,
    Existing industrial sources, 464
    Low-flow augmentation, 450
    Municipal treatment works, 442, 448
    New industrial sources, 467–468
    NPDES proceedings, 456, 458–459
    Regional plans, 433
    Toxic pollutants, 483, 485
    Water quality related effluent limitations, 423
    Water quality standards, 418
  Effluent limitations,
    See also National pollutant discharge elimination system; Water quality standards, this topic
    Defined, 451
    Water quality related,
      Alternative effluent control strategies, 423
      Defined, 422
      Economic and technological feasibility, 423
      Enforcement, 424
  Effluent limited segment, defined, 430
  Effluent standards, see Municipal treatment works; National pollutant discharge elimination system; Standards of performance; Thermal pollution; Toxic pollutants, this topic
  Enforcement,
    Abatement conference, 535
    Administrative order, 540
    Choice of remedy, 537
    Civil fines, 537, 539–540
    Consent decrees, 537, 539
    Construction grants, 541
    Continuing violations, 540
    Criminal penalty, 537
    Defenses,
      Contingency of federal funding, 471, 541
      Economic and technological feasibility, 539, 549
      Generally, 547–549
    Delegation to states, 535
    Emergency authority, 536

WATER POLLUTION—Cont'd
Federal Water Pollution Control Act—Cont'd
  Enforcement—Cont'd
    Federal contracts, 541
    Federal facilities, sovereign immunity, 544
    Federally assumed enforcement, 536
    Injunction, 538
    Methodologies, 462
    Municipal treatment works, sewer moratoria, 542
    Record keeping, 534
    Strict liability, 539
  Industrial sources, see Standards of performance, this topic
  Legislative history, 355–359
  Low-flow augmentation,
    EPA approval, 449
    Federal multipurpose water projects, 448
    Prohibition as substitute for source control, 449
  Municipal treatment works,
    Best practicable technology,
      Consideration of alternatives, 446
      Control options, 446
        Generally, 445–446, 470–472
      Land treatment, 446
      Recycling, 446
    Combined sewer overflows, 472
    Construction grant program,
      Annual report, 439
      Annual survey, 439
      Areawide plans, 436
      Consistency with plans, 437, 476
      Construction, defined, 437
      Construction grants, 438, 440, 445
      Facility design, 440, 443, 445
      Facility plans,
        Alternatives, 441, 443
        Cost effectiveness, 442
        Defined, 441
        Infiltration-inflow documentation, 442
        Preparation of environmental impact statement, 443
      Federal approval,
        As federal contract, 438
        Conditions, 436, 439
      Federal share, 437
      Grant categories, 440–441
      Hearings, 441
      Needs formula, 438
      Procedure, 440–445
      State priority list, 440

WATER POLLUTION—Cont'd
Federal Water Pollution Control Act—Cont'd
Municipal treatment works—Cont'd
Construction grant program—Cont'd
Step 1 study plan, 441
Use of consultants, 444
Economic and techological feasibility, 442, 448
Incompatible industrial pollutants, 478
Infiltration, defined, 442
Inflow, defined, 442
Lack of federal funding as defense for noncompliance, 471, 541
1983 best practicable technology, 445, 470
1977 secondary treatment, 445
No discharge, 471
Pretreatment, see Pretreatment, this topic
Reclamation, defined, 446
Recycling, defined, 446
Reuse, defined, 447
Secondary treatment,
Defined, 445, 472
Defined as best practicable technology, 472
Sewage collection system, defined, 438, 439
Sewer hookup ban, 192, 474, 542
Sludge disposal methods, 475
Storm sewer, defined, 473
Storm sewer runoff, 473
Treatment works, defined, 439
User charges, 437, 480
National Commission on Water Quality, 363
National policy, 361
National pollutant discharge elimination system,
Adjudicatory hearing, 459
Administrative variance, 458
Applicability, 461
Economic and technological feasibility, 456, 458–459
Exemptions, 369–372, 398
Existing sources, 459
Groundwater,
Generally, 369
Incidental to control of surface waters, 371
Guidelines, 456
Noncategory industrial sources, 459
Nonpoint sources, 369

WATER POLLUTION—Cont'd
Federal Water Pollution Control Act—Cont'd
National pollutant discharge elimination system—Cont'd
Opinions of the EPA general counsel, 460
Permit,
Applicability, 461
Contents, 462
Procedure, 459
Pretreatment, 480
Refuse Act Permit Program, 398
Schedule of compliance, 451
Sludge disposal, 413
State water pollution permit programs, 452
Uniformity of conditions, 453
Variance, 458
Water quality standards, 421
Weil injection disposal, 372
Navigable waters, defined, 461
New source performance standard, see Standards of performance, this topic
No discharge, 419, 467, 471, 500
Nondegradation, 208, 417
Nonpoint source control,
Areawide waste treatment management plans, 378
Best management practices, 431, 433
Landfills, 645
State waste treatment management plan, 279
State water quality management plan, 430
State water quality reports, 378
Swimmable-fishable water, 377
Water quality standards implementation plan, 429
Planning,
Areawide plans, see Regional plans, this topic
Areawide waste treatment management plan, 378
Basin plans,
Basin, defined, 430
Incorporation with state plans, 427
Priorities, 427
Water Resources Act, 427
Facility plans, see Municipal treatment works, this topic
Federal multipurpose projects, 448–450
Interrelationships, 425

INDEX

References are to Pages

WATER POLLUTION—Cont'd
Federal Water Pollution Control Act—Cont'd
  Planning—Cont'd
    Programs, 426
    Regional plans,
      Compliance, 433, 437
      Contents, 433
      Designated management agency, 432
      Economic and technological feasibility, 423
      Federal grants, 434
      Scope, 432
    State plans,
      Annual reports, 428
      Continuing planning process, defined, 429
      Incorporation of basin plans, 427
      Nonpoint sources, 379
      Waste load allocation, 420, 430
      Water quality limited segment, identification, 420
      Water quality management plan, 430
      Water quality standards and implementation plans, 428
  Point sources,
    Defined, 375
    Exclusions, 376
  Pollutant, defined, 369, 372
  Pollution, defined, 368
  Pretreatment,
    Allocation of costs, 479
    Best practicable technology, 479
    Compliance schedule, 480
    Enforcement, 481
    Incompatible pollutants, 478
    Major contributing industry, 478
    Permit, 480
    User charges, 478
  Research and development, 362–364
  Schedule of compliance, defined, 451
  Sewer moratoria, as a land development measure, 192, 474, 542
  Sludge disposal,
    See also Ocean Dumping
    As condition of construction grant, 413
    As condition of NPDES permit, 413
    Incineration, 410
    Land treatment,
      Generally, 411
      Industrial wastes, 412

WATER POLLUTION—Cont'd
Federal Water Pollution Control Act—Cont'd
  Sludge disposal—Cont'd
    Ocean dumping, 410
    Sludge, defined, 409
  Standards of performance,
    Applicability of NEPA, 470
    Categories and classes of point sources, 453
    Defined, 467
    Existing industrial sources,
      Applicability, 462
      Best available technology, defined, 464
      Best practicable technology, defined, 464
      Economic and technological feasibility, 464
      Guidelines, 463
    New industrial sources,
      Best available demonstrated control technology, defined, 468
      Categories of industrial sources, 453
      Economic and technological feasibility, 467
      Modifications, 467
      New source, defined, 466
      No discharge, 467
    New source performance standards, see New industrial sources, this topic
    Pretreatment, see Pretreatment, this topic
  State certification of compliance, 367
  Studies,
    Generally, 362–365
    In place pollutants, 365
    In-stream enhancement, 364
  Swimmable-fishable water, 377
  Toxic pollutants,
    Category of sources, 484
    Defined, 482
    Economic and technological feasibility, 483, 485
    Margin of safety, 484
    Pesticides, 856
    Procedure, 482, 485, 487
    Settlement agreement, 486
  Uniform effluent limitations, EPA authority, 454
  Water quality standards,
    As condition in NPDES permit, 421
    As effluent limitation, 419, 422–424
    Burden of proof, 359
    Citizen suits, 419

WATER POLLUTION—Cont'd
Federal Water Pollution Control Act—Cont'd
  Water quality standards—Cont'd
    Criteria,
      Defined, 415
      Descriptive, 415
      Quantitative, 415
    Criteria document, 422
    Defined, 356, 360, 415
    Designated use,
      Classes, 415
      Defined, 415
    Economic and technological feasibility, 418
    Enforcement, 419
    Federal approval, 416, 424
    Nondegradation, 417
    Overly stringent, 424
    Procedure, 416
    State water quality management plan, 430
    Thermal pollution, 530
    Toxic pollutants, 486
    Waste load allocation, 420
    Water Quality Act, 356, 416
    Water quality limited segments, defined, 366, 420
    Water quality segments, defined, 429
    Water quality standards and implementation plan, 428
  Water quality surveillance system, 362
Hazardous substances, defined, 506
Infiltration, defined, 442
Inflow, defined, 442
In-place pollutants, defined, 365
In-stream enhancement techniques, defined, 364
Leachate, defined, 621
Low-flow augmentation, defined, 448
Navigable waters, see Water Law, this index
Nonpoint source,
  See also Federal Water Pollution Control Act; Rivers and Harbors Act, this topic
  Agricultural activities, 384
  Construction activities, 380
  Defined, 375

WATER POLLUTION—Cont'd
Nonpoint source—Cont'd
  Flood plain development, 386
  National Environmental Policy Act, 379
  Silvicultural activities, 383
  Sludge disposal,
    Land treatment, 411–412
    State laws, 414
  State environmental policy acts, 386
  Surface mining, 381
Point Source, defined, 375
Refuse Act, see Rivers and Harbors Act, this topic
Rivers and Harbors Act,
  See also Dredge and Fill, this index
  Defenses,
    Generally, 393–394
    Reliance upon official conduct, 394
  Effluent limitations, 357
  Landfill regulation, 645–646
  Municipal discharge, 393
  Navigable waters,
    Defined, 390, 401
    Mean high tide line, 391
    Tributaries, 392
  No discharge, 359
  Nonpoint sources, 377, 397–398
  Refuse, defined, 389
  Refuse Act Permit Program, 357, 398–400
  Remedies,
    Civil fines, 396
    Private, 396
    Qui tam, 396
    Restoration, 404
  Sewage, refuse in suspension, 392
  Strict liability, 393
  Thermal pollution, 528
Salt water intrusion, defined, 375
Secondary treatment, defined, 445
State laws,
  Civil fines, 545
  Liability for cleanup costs, 545
  Sludge disposal, 414
User charges, defined, 480
Water quality standards, 415–424

ZONING
See Land Development Controls, this index